THE GREAT CONVERSATION

THE GREAT CONVERSATION

A Historical Introduction to Philosophy

Fifth Edition

NORMAN MELCHERT

Professor Emeritus, Lehigh University

New York   Oxford
OXFORD UNIVERSITY PRESS
2007

Oxford University Press, Inc., publishes works that further Oxford University's objective of excellence in research, scholarship, and education.

Oxford   New York
Auckland   Cape Town   Dar es Salaam   Hong Kong   Karachi
Kuala Lumpur   Madrid   Melbourne   Mexico City   Nairobi
New Delhi   Shanghai   Taipei   Toronto

With offices in
Argentina   Austria   Brazil   Chile   Czech Republic   France
Greece   Guatemala   Hungary   Italy   Japan   Poland
Portugal   Singapore   South Korea   Switzerland   Thailand
Turkey   Ukraine   Vietnam

Published by Oxford University Press, Inc.
198 Madison Avenue, New York, New York 10016
http://www.oup.com

Oxford is a registered trademark of Oxford University Press

Library of Congress Cataloging-in-Publication Data

Melchert, Norman.
   The great conversation : a historical introduction to philosophy / by Norman Melchert.
      —5th ed.
         p. cm.
   Includes bibliographical references and indexes.
   ISBN-13: 978-0-19-530682-8

   1. Philosophy—Textbooks.   I. Title.

BD21.M43 2006b
190—dc22
                                                2006048339

9 8 7 6 5 4 3 2

Printed in the United States of America on acid-free paper

For Lance

CONTENTS

A WORD
TO INSTRUCTORS

The fourth edition of *The Great Conversation* brought the story up to recent times with a chapter featuring Derrida, Rorty, Quine, and Dennett. This fifth edition fills another gap with a chapter titled "Simone de Beauvoir: Existentialist, Feminist." There seems to be a de Beauvoir revival lately, with numerous articles and several books being published, including translations of some formerly untranslated works. She is subject to certain criticisms, but on all sides she is recognized as a major figure in feminist thought and an engaging thinker along existentialist lines.

Added in this edition are brief profiles of Avicenna, Averroës, Maimonides, the Buddha, and Rousseau. I have tried to reduce redundancy, cut back on some quotations, and simplify explanations where I could. There are more diagrams and illustrations. References are included to Web pages where background material can be accessed. The basic study questions have been moved from the ends of chapters to locations within the chapters, where I hope they will be of more direct use to students. I have resisted the temptation to dumb the book down. Some say that we live in an age in which

being entertained is confused with learning how to think. My aim is to teach students how to think by apprenticing them to a succession of the best thinkers humanity has produced. I hope to draw students into the conversation by presenting the dramatic story of philosophy in a lively and engaging way.

The book retains the distinctive features of earlier editions, representing major philosophers through extensive quotations set in a fairly rich cultural and intellectual context. It still contains the four complete works: *Euthyphro, Apology, Crito,* and *Meditations.* It remains available both in a single hardback edition and in two paperback volumes, so it can be used economically in either a whole-year or a single-semester course. Athough the entire book contains too much material for a single semester, it provides a rich menu of choices for instructors of such courses who do not wish to restrict themselves to the earlier or later periods.

I continue to try to keep my own views out of the book as much as possible, realizing all the while that no one can do this perfectly. My aim is to show the great philosophers not only coming up with intriguing ideas, but also reacting to and criticizing each other. So we see how Aristotle builds on and criticizes Plato, how Kant responds to Hume, why Wittgenstein thought most of previous philosophy was meaningless, and so on. This critique internal to the story is highlighted by the large number of cross-references and footnotes that continue to make the conversation metaphor more than just a flight of fancy.

In this era, when even the educated have such a thin sense of history, teaching philosophy in this conversational, cumulative, back-and-forward-looking way can be a service not just to philosophical understanding, but also to the culture as a whole.

A WORD
TO STUDENTS

We all have opinions—we can't help it. Having opinions is as natural to us as breathing. Opinions, moreover, are a dime a dozen. They're floating all around us and they're so different from each other. One person believes this, another that. You believe in God, your buddy doesn't. John thinks there's nothing wrong with keeping a found wallet, you are horrified. Some of us say, "Everybody's got their own values"; others are sure that *some* things are just plain wrong—wrong for everybody. Some delay gratification for the sake of long-term goals; others indulge in whatever pleasures happen to be at hand. What kind of world do we live in? Jane studies science to find out, Jack turns to the occult. Is death the end for us?—Some say yes, some say no.

What's a person to do?

Study Philosophy!

You don't want simply to be at the mercy of accident in your opinions—for your views to be de-

cided by irrelevant matters such as whom you happen to know or where you were brought up. You want to believe for *good reasons*. That's the right question, isn't it? Which of these many opinions has the best reasons behind it? You want to live your life as wisely as possible.

Fortunately, we have a long tradition of really smart people who have been thinking about issues such as these, and we can go to them for help. They're called "philosophers"—lovers of wisdom—and they have been trying to straighten out all these issues. They are in the business of asking which opinions or views or beliefs there is good reason to accept.

Unfortunately, these philosophers don't all agree either. So you might ask, If these really smart philosophers can't agree on what wisdom says, why should I pay them any attention? The answer is—because it's the best shot you've got. If you seriously want to improve your opinions, there's nothing better you can do than engage in a "conversation" with the best minds our history has produced.

One of my own teachers, a short, white-haired, elderly gentleman with a thick German accent, used to say, "Whether you will philosophize or won't philosophize, you *must* philosophize." By this, he meant that we can't help making decisions about these crucial matters. We make them either well or badly, concious of what we are doing or just stumbling along. As Kierkegaard would say, we express such decisions in the way we live, whether or not we have ever given them a moment's thought. In a sense, then, you are already a philosopher, already engaged in the business philosophers have committed themselves to. So you shouldn't have any problem in making a connection with what they write.

Does it help to think about such matters? You might as well ask whether it helps to think about the recipe before you start to cook. Socrates says that "the unexamined life is not worth living." And that's what philosophy is: an examination of opinions—and also of our lives, shaped by these opinions. In thinking philosophically, we try to sort our opinions into two baskets: the good-views basket and the trash.

We want to think about these matters as clearly and rationally as we can. *Thinking* is a kind of craft. Like any other craft, we can do it well or poorly, with shoddy workmanship or with care, and we improve with practice. It is common for people who want to learn a craft—cabinetmaking, for example—to apprentice themselves for a time to a master, doing what the master does until the time comes when they are skillful enough to set up shop on their own. You can think of reading this book as a kind of apprenticeship in thinking, with Socrates, Plato, Kant, and the rest as the masters. By thinking along with them, noting their insights and arguments, following their examinations of each other's opinions, you should improve that all-important skill of your own.

This Book

This book is organized historically because that's how philosophy has developed. It's not just a recital of this following that, however. It is also intensively *interactive* because that's what philosophy has been. I have taken the metaphor of a conversation seri-

ously. These folks are all talking to each other, arguing with each other, trying to convince each other—and that makes the story of philosophy a dramatic one. Aristotle learns a lot from his teacher, Plato, but argues that Plato makes one big mistake—and that colors everything else he says. Aquinas appreciates what Aristotle has done but claims that Aristotle neglects a basic feature of reality—and that makes all the difference. In the seventeenth century, Descartes looks back on his predecessors with despair, noting that virtually no agreement has been reached on any topic; he resolves to wipe the slate clean and make a new start. Beginning with an analysis of what it is to believe anything at all, C. S. Peirce argues that what Descartes wants to do is impossible. And so it goes.

This conversational and interactive aspect of philosophy is emphasized by a large number of cross-references provided in footnotes. Your understanding of an issue will be substantially enriched if you follow up on these. In order to appreciate the line one thinker is pushing, it is important to see what he is arguing against, where he thinks that others have made mistakes. No philosopher simply makes pronouncements in the dark. There is always something that bugs each thinker, something she thinks is terribly wrong, something that needs correction. This irritant may be something current in the culture, or it may be what other philosophers have been saying. Using the cross-references to understand that background will help you to make sense of what is going on—and why. The index of names and terms at the back of this book will also help you.

Philosophers are noted for introducing novel terms, or using familiar words in novel ways. They are not alone in this, of course; poets and scientists do the same. There is no reason to expect that our everyday language will be suited, just as it is, to express the truth of things, so you will have some vocabulary to master. Unusual terms are explained as they are introduced. In addition, you will find a glossary of key words at the back of this book, which you can use to refresh your memory about the meanings of these words. In the text, the first appearance of each glossary item is set in **boldface** type.

The Issues

The search for wisdom—that is, philosophy—ranges far and wide. Who can say ahead of time what might be relevant to that search? Still, there are certain central problems that especially concern philosophers. In your study of this text, you can expect to find extensive discussions of these four issues in particular:

1. *Metaphysics,* the theory of reality. In our own day, Willard Quine has said that the basic question of metaphysics is very simple: *What is there?* The metaphysical question, of course, is not like, "Are there echidnas in Australia?" but "What kinds of things are there fundamentally?" Is the world through and through made of material stuff, or are there souls as well as bodies? Is there a God? If so, of what sort? Is the world-order itself God? Are there universal features to reality, or is everything just the particular thing that it is? Does everything happen necessarily, given what has happened before, or are fresh starts possible?

2. *Epistemology,* the theory of knowledge. We want to think not only about what there is, but also about *how we know* what there is—or, maybe, whether we can know anything at all! So we reflectively ask, What is it to know something anyway? How does that differ from just believing it? Are there different kinds of knowledge? How is knowing something related to its being true? What is truth? How far can our knowledge reach? Are there things that are just unknowable?

3. *Ethics,* the theory of right and wrong, good and bad. It is obvious enough that we aren't just knowers and believers. We are doers. The question then arises of what wisdom might say about how best to live our lives. Does the fact that something gives us pleasure make it the right thing to do? Do we need to think about how our actions affect others? If so, in what way? Are there really goods and bads, or does thinking so make it so? Do we have duties?

If so, where do they come from? What is virtue and vice? What is justice? Is justice important?

4. *Human nature*—Socrates took as his motto a slogan that was inscribed in the temple of Apollo in Delphi: Know Thyself. But that has proved none too easy to do. What are we, anyway? Are we simply bits of matter caught up in the universal mechanism of the world, or do we have minds that escape this deterministic machine? What is it to have a mind? Is mind separate from body? How is it related to the brain? Do we have a free will? How important to my self-identity is my relationship to others? To what degree can I be responsible for the creation of myself?

Running through these issues is a fifth one that perhaps deserves special mention. It centers on the idea of *relativism.* The question is whether there is a way to get beyond the prejudices and assumptions peculiar to ourselves or our culture—or whether that's all there is. Are there *just* opinions, with no one opinion ultimately any better than any other? Are all views relative to time and place, to culture and position? Is there no *truth*—or, anyway, no truth that we can know to be true?

This problem, which entered the great conversation early, with the Sophists of ancient Greece, has persisted to this day. Most of the Western philosophical tradition can be thought of as a series of attempts to kill such skepticism and relativism, but this phoenix will not die. Our own age has the distinction, perhaps, of being the first age ever in which the basic assumptions of most people, certainly of most educated people, are relativistic, so this theme will have a particular poignancy for us. We will want to understand how we came to this point and what it means to be here. We will also want to ask ourselves how adequate this relativistic outlook is.

What we are is what we have become, and what we have become has been shaped by our history. In this book, we look at that history, hoping to understand ourselves better and, thereby, gain some wisdom for living our lives.

ACKNOWLEDGMENTS

I want to thank the readers of the fourth edition who provided me with many good ideas for improvement. I am particularly grateful to William Springer, University of Texas, El Paso; Edward Langerak, St. Olaf College; James E. Taylor, Westmont College; John Clark, Loyola University; Bill E. Lawson, Michigan State University; Jerald Wallulis, University of South Carolina; and Mark Smillie, Carroll College. Their suggestions have made this a better book.

Special thanks are extended to Jolyon Troscianko for his charming cartoons.

Comments relating to this new edition may be sent to me at norm.mel@comcast.net.

I was aware that the reading of all good books is indeed like a conversation with the noblest men of past centuries who were the authors of
them, nay a carefully studied conversation, in which they reveal to us
none but the best of their thoughts.

—*René Descartes*

In truth, there is no divorce between philosophy and life.

—*Simone de Beauvoir*

We—mankind—are a conversation.

—*Martin Heidegger*

1

BEFORE PHILOSOPHY

Myth in Hesiod and Homer

Everywhere and at all times, we humans have wondered at our own existence and at our place in the scheme of things. We have asked, in curiosity and amazement, "What's it all about?" "How are we to understand this life of ours?" "How is it best lived?" "Does it end at death?" "This world we find ourselves in—where does it come from?" "What is it, anyway?" "How is it related to us?"

These are some of the many philosophical questions we ask. Every culture offers answers, though not every culture has developed what we know as philosophy. Early answers to such questions universally take the form of stories, usually stories involving the gods—gigantic powers of a personal nature, engaged in tremendous feats of creation, frequently struggling with one another and intervening in human life for good or ill.

We call these stories *myths*. They are told and retold, elaborated and embroidered; they are taught to children as the plain facts and attain an authority by their age, by repetition, and by the apparent fact (within a given culture) that virtually everyone accepts them. They shape a tradition, and traditions shape lives.

Philosophy, literally "love of wisdom," begins when certain individuals start to ask, "Why should we believe these stories?" "How do we know they are true?"—and when they attempt to supply answers that have more going for them than antiquity and the plausibility that comes from common acceptance. Philosophers try to give us good reasons for believing one thing or another about these matters—or perhaps good reasons for thinking we can't answer such questions at all. They look at myth with a critical eye, sometimes appreciating what myths try to do, sometimes attacking myths' claims to literal truth. So there is a tension between these stories and philosophy, a tension that occasionally breaks into open conflict.

This conflict is epitomized in the execution of Socrates by his fellow Athenians in 399 B.C. Socrates was accused of not believing in the city's gods and, not coincidentally, of corrupting the young people of Athens. Socrates is a philosopher. One might almost say he is the patron saint of philosophy, reminding us in age after age of what it means to love wisdom—in the way philosophers do.

We want to understand who Socrates is, what

happened to him and why. We will also trace the story of the quest for wisdom after Socrates—in Plato and Aristotle, Augustine and Aquinas, Descartes and Hume and Kant—through our intellectual history down to the twentieth century. Myth is not dead in our day of "New Age" movements, of cults and gurus, prophets and mystics, and astrological forecasts. The conflict continues, and it is important that we understand it, for we do want to be wise.

To understand the character of this conflict, we need a sense for the nature of myth. In principle we could look at any of the great mythological traditions, in Babylon or Egypt, India or Rome. Such traditions all have a great deal in common, despite their dramatic differences of detail. But because it was the Greeks of the sixth and fifth centuries B.C. who first began to ask the questions that led to philosophical thinking, it will pay us to look at certain Greek myths. Our aim is neither a comprehensive survey nor mere acquaintance with some of these stories. We will be trying to understand something of Greek religion and culture, of the intellectual and spiritual life of the people who told these stories. As a result, we should be able to grasp why some of Socrates' contemporaries reacted to him as they did. With that in mind, we take a brief look at two of the great Greek poets: Hesiod and Homer.

Hesiod: War among the Gods

The poet we know as Hesiod probably composed his poem *Theogony* toward the end of the eighth century B.C. He was clearly drawing on much older traditions and seems to be synthesizing stories that have different origins and are not always consistent. The term *theogony* means "origin or birth of the gods," and the stories contained in the poem concern the beginnings of all things. He includes an immense amount of detail in this relatively short work. In this chapter, we look only at certain central events, as Hesiod relates them to us.

First, however, note that Hesiod claims to have written these lines under divine inspiration. (Sug-

gestion: Read quotations aloud, especially poetry; you will find that they become more meaningful.)

> The Muses once taught Hesiod to sing
> Sweet songs, while he was shepherding his lambs
> On holy Helicon; the goddesses
> Olympian, daughters of Zeus who holds
> The aegis,* first addressed these words to me:
> "You rustic shepherds, shame: bellies you are,
> Not men! We know enough to make up lies
> Which are convincing, but we also have
> The skill, when we've a mind, to speak the truth."
>
> So spoke the fresh-voiced daughters of great Zeus
> And plucked and gave a staff to me, a shoot
> Of blooming laurel, wonderful to see,
> And breathed a sacred voice into my mouth
> With which to celebrate the things to come
> And things which were before.
>
> —*Theogony,* 21–35 [1]

The Muses, according to the tradition Hesiod is drawing on, are nine daughters born to Zeus and Memory. In this passage, Hesiod is telling us that the stories he narrates are not vulgar shepherds' lies but are backed by the authority of the chief god and embody the remembrance of events long past. They thus represent the *truth,* Hesiod says, and are worthy of belief.

What have the Muses revealed?

> And sending out
> Unearthly music, first they celebrate
> The august race of first-born gods, whom Earth
> Bore to broad Heaven, then their progeny,
> Givers of good things. Next they sing of Zeus
> The father of gods and men, how high he is
> Above the other gods, how great in strength.
>
> —*Theogony,* 42–48

Note that the gods are themselves *born;* their origin, like our own, is explicitly sexual. Their ancestors are Earth (Gaea, or Gaia) and Heaven (Ouranos).†

---

*The *aegis* is a symbol of authority. Just so, we today may say that an event is presented "under the aegis" of an authoritative sponsor.

†Some people nowadays speak of the Gaea hypothesis and urge us to think of Earth as a living organism. Here we have a self-conscious attempt to revive an ancient way of thinking about the

Note also that the gods are characterized as "givers of good things." For this, of course, they deserve our reverence and our gratitude. While there are many gods, they are not all equal in power and status. Zeus is king, the "father of gods and men."

There is confusion in the Greek stories about the very first things (no wonder), and there are contradictions among them. According to Hesiod, first of all there is *chaos,* apparently a formless mass of stuff, dark and without differentiation. Out of this chaos, Earth appears. (Don't ask how.) Earth then gives birth to starry Heaven,

> to be
> An equal to herself, to cover her
> All over, and to be a resting-place,
> Always secure, for all the blessed gods.
> —*Theogony,* 27–30

After lying with Heaven, Earth bears the first race of gods, the Titans, together with the Cyclops—three giants with but one round eye in the middle of each giant's forehead. Three other sons, "mighty and violent," are born to the pair, each with a hundred arms and fifty heads:

> And these most awful sons of Earth and Heaven
> Were hated by their father from the first.
> As soon as each was born, Ouranos hid
> The child in a secret hiding-place in Earth*
> And would not let it come to see the light,
> And he enjoyed this wickedness.
> —*Theogony,* 155–160

Earth, distressed and pained with this crowd hidden within her, forms a great sickle of hardest metal and urges her children to use it on their father for his shameful deeds. The boldest of the Titans, Kronos, takes the sickle and plots vengeance with his mother.

> Great Heaven came, and with him brought the
>   night.
> Longing for love, he lay around the Earth,

———————
planet we inhabit. Ideas of the Earth-mother and Mother Nature are also echoes of such early myths.
*This dank and gloomy place below the surface of the earth and sea is known as Tartarus.

> Spreading out fully. But the hidden boy
> Stretched forth his left hand; in his right he took
> The great long jagged sickle; eagerly
> He harvested his father's genitals
> And threw them off behind.
> —*Theogony,* 176–182

Where Heaven's bloody drops fall on land, the Furies spring up—monstrous goddesses who hunt down and punish wrongdoers.* Where they fall on the sea, the beautiful goddess of love and desire, Aphrodite, appears.

Hesiod tells of many other gods and goddesses, some obscure and some identifiable with features of the earth, natural forces, human passions, or moral enforcement. Most relevant to our story, however, is Hesiod's version of a characteristic theme in Greek thought, a theme repeated again and again in the great classical tragedies and also echoed in later philosophy: Violating the rule of justice—even in the service of justice—brings consequences. The Titans exact vengeance from their father for his wickedness, and they are overthrown in turn. The myths tell us: Wickedness does not pay.

Kronos, now ruler among the Titans, has children by Rhea, among them Hera, Hades, and Poseidon. Learning of a prophecy that he will be dethroned by one of these children, Kronos seizes the newborns and swallows them![†] When Rhea bears yet another son, however, she hides him away in a cave on Crete and gives Kronos a stone wrapped in swaddling clothes to swallow. The hidden son, of course, is Zeus.

When grown to full strength, Zeus disguises himself as a cupbearer and persuades Kronos to drink a potion. This causes Kronos to vomit up his brothers and sisters—together with the stone. (The stone, Hesiod tells us, is set up at Delphi, northwest of Athens, to mark the center of the earth.)

———————
*In contemporary literature, you can find these Furies represented in Jean-Paul Sartre's play *The Flies.*
[†]"Kronos" is closely related to the Greek word for time, "chronos." What might it mean that Kronos devours his children? And that they overthrow his rule to establish cities—communities of justice—that outlive their citizens?

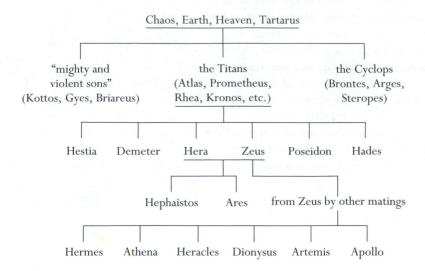

Genealogy of the Principal Greek Gods

Together with his brothers and their allies, Zeus makes war on the Titans. The war drags on for ten years until Zeus frees the Cyclops from their imprisonment in Tartarus. The Cyclops give Zeus a lightning bolt, supply Poseidon with a trident, and provide Hades with a helmet that makes him invisible. With these aids, the gods overthrow Kronos and the Titans and hurl them down into Tartarus. The three victorious brothers divide up the territory: Zeus rules the sky (he is called "cloud-gatherer" and "storm-bringer"); Poseidon governs the sea; and Hades reigns in Tartarus. Earth is shared by all three.

Thus, the gods set up a relatively stable order in the universe, an order both natural and moral. Although, as we will see, the gods quarrel among themselves and are not above lies, adultery, and favoritism, each of them guards something important and dear to humans. They also see to it that wickedness is punished and virtue is rewarded, just as was the case among themselves.

1. Why are philosophers dissatisfied with mythological accounts of reality?
2. What is the topic of Hesiod's *Theogony*?

3. Tell the story of how Zeus came to be king of the gods.
4. What moral runs through these early myths?

Homer: Heroes, Gods, and Excellence

Xenophanes, a philosopher we will meet later,* tells us that "from the beginning all have learnt in accordance with Homer."[2] As we have seen, poets were thought to write by divine inspiration, and for centuries people listened to or read the works of Homer, much as they read the Bible or the Koran today. He, above all others, was the great teacher of the Greeks. To discover what was truly excellent in battle, governance, counsel, sport, the home, and human life in general, the Greeks looked to Homer's tales. These dramatic stories offered a picture of the world and people's place in it that molded the Greek mind and character. Philosophy begins against the Homeric background, so we need to understand something of Homer.

---

*See "Xenophanes: The Gods as Fictions," in Chapter 2.

It is important to note that Homer simply takes for granted the tradition set down in Hesiod's *Theogony*. It is true that there are other strains in Greek culture, older and more primitive than Hesiod and Homer: religions of fertility and the earth, cults of ecstatic communion with gods, and purification rites that cleanse adherents from sin or pollution and promise immortality. These cults never entirely disappear; some of them are partially incorporated into Olympian religion, as the cult of Dionysus seems to have been. When the classical period ends in the fourth century B.C., they reawaken and grow enormously in influence.

At the beginning of our story, however, the high religion of Homer's gods and heroes dominate Greek life. This is the culture of conquerors who swept down in several waves from north and east into the Aegean area. Their sky-god tradition of Zeus, Athena, and Apollo celebrates clarity and order, mastery over chaos, intellect and beauty: fertile soil, one must think, for philosophy.

Homer's two great poems, of course, are *The Iliad* and *The Odyssey*. Here, we focus on *The Iliad,* a long poem about a brief period during the nine-year-long Trojan war.* This war came about when Paris, a son of Priam, king of Troy, seduced Helen and stole her away from her home in Achaea, in southern Greece (see Map 1). Helen was the most beautiful of women and was wife to Menelaus, king of Sparta. Agamemnon, the brother of Menelaus, was king of Argos, north of Sparta. He became commander in chief of the Greek forces that sailed across the Aegean to recover Helen, to avenge the wrong against his brother, and—not just incidentally—to gain honor, glory, and plunder. Among these forces was Achilles, the greatest warrior of them all, together with his formidable band of soldiers.

---

*The date of the war is uncertain; scholarly estimates tend to put it near the end of the thirteenth century B.C. The poems took form in song and were passed along in an oral tradition from generation to generation. They were written down some time in the eighth century B.C. Tradition ascribes them to a blind bard known as Homer, but the poems we now have may be the work of more than one poet.

Here is how *The Iliad* begins.

> Rage—Goddess, sing the rage of Peleus' son Achilles,
> murderous, doomed, that cost the Achaeans countless losses,
> hurling down to the House of Death so many sturdy souls,
> great fighters' souls, but made their bodies carrion,
> feasts for the dogs and birds,
> and the will of Zeus was moving toward its end.
> Begin, Muse, when the two first broke and clashed,
> Agamemnon lord of men and brilliant Achilles.
> What god drove them to fight with such a fury?
> Apollo the son of Zeus and Leto. Incensed at the king
> he swept a fatal plague through the army—men were dying
> and all because Agamemnon had spurned Apollo's priest.
>
> —*The Iliad*, Book 1, 1–12 [3]

The poet begins by announcing his theme: rage, specifically the excessive, irrational anger of Achilles—anger beyond all bounds that brings death and destruction to so many Greeks and almost costs them the war. So we might expect that the poem has a *moral* aspect. Moreover, in the sixth line we read that what happened was in accord with the will of Zeus, who sees to it that flagrant violations of good order do not go unpunished. In these first lines we also learn of Apollo, the son of Zeus, who has sent a plague on the Greek army because Agamemnon offended him. We can see, then, that Homer's world is one of kings and heroes, majestic but flawed, engaged in gargantuan projects against a background of gods who cannot safely be ignored.

The story Homer tells goes roughly like this. In a raid on a Trojan ally, the Greeks capture a beautiful girl who happens to be the daughter of a priest of Apollo. The army awards her to Agamemnon as part of his spoils. The priest comes to plead for her return, offering ransom, but he is rudely rebuffed. Agamemnon will not give back the girl. The priest appeals to Apollo, who, angered by the treatment his priest is receiving, sends a plague to Agamemnon's troops.

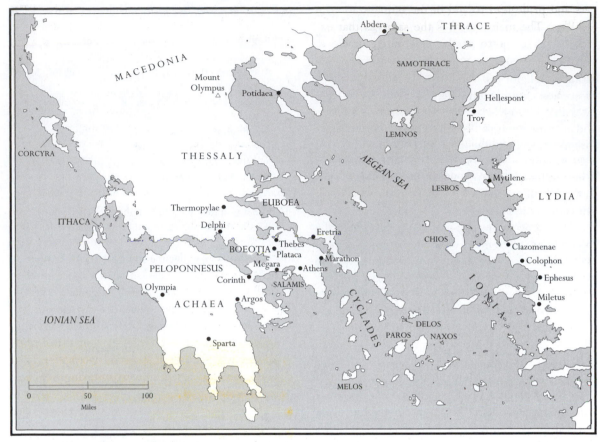

MAP I   The Greek Mainland

The soldiers, wanting to know what is causing the plague, appeal to their seer, Calchas, who explains the situation and advises that the girl be returned. Agamemnon is furious. To be without his prize while the other warriors keep theirs goes against the honor due him as commander. He finally agrees to give up the girl but demands Achilles' prize, an exceptionally lovely woman, in exchange. The two heroes quarrel bitterly. Enraged, Achilles returns to his tent and refuses to fight any more.

Because Achilles is the greatest of the great among Greek warriors, his anger has serious consequences. The war goes badly for the Greeks. The Trojans fight their way to the beach and begin to burn the ships. Patroclus, Achilles' dearest friend, pleads with him to relent, but he will not. If Achilles won't have pity on his comrades, Patroclus says, then at least let him take Achilles' armor and fight

in his place. To this Achilles agrees, and the tactic has some success. The Trojans are driven back toward the city, but in the fighting Patroclus is killed by Hector, another son of Priam and the greatest of the Trojan warriors.

Achilles' rage now turns on Hector and the Trojans. He rejoins the war to wreak havoc among them. After slaughtering many, he comes face to face with Hector. Achilles kills him and drags his body back to camp behind his chariot—a very, very bad thing to do. As the poem ends, King Priam goes alone by night into the Greek camp to plead with Achilles for the body of his son. He and Achilles weep together, for Hector and for Patroclus, and Achilles gives up the body.

This summary emphasizes the human side of the story. From that point of view, *The Iliad* can be thought of as the story both of the tragedy that excess and pride lead to and of the humanization of Achilles. The main moral is the same as that expressed by a motto at the celebrated oracle at Delphi: "Nothing too much."* *Moderation* is what Achilles lacked, and his lack led to disaster. At the same time, the poem celebrates the "heroic virtues": *strength, courage, physical prowess,* and the kind of *wisdom* that consists in the ability to devise clever plans to achieve one's ends. For Homer and his audience, these characteristics, together with moderation, make up the model of human excellence. These are the virtues ancient Greeks teach their children.

Throughout the story there is also the counterpoint of the gods, who look on, are appealed to, take sides, and interfere. For instance, when Achilles is sulking about Agamemnon having taken his woman, he prays to his mother, the goddess Thetis. (Achilles has a mortal father.) He asks her to go to Zeus and beg him to give victory to—the Trojans! She does so, saying,

> "And now the lord of men Agamemnon has
>   disgraced him,
> seizes and keeps his prize, tears her away himself.
>   But you—
> exalt him, Olympian Zeus: your urgings rule the
>   world!
> Come, grant the Trojans victory after victory
> till the Achaean armies pay my dear son back,
> building higher the honor he deserves!"
>   —*The Iliad,* Book 1, 604–609

Zeus frets that his wife Hera will be upset—she favors the Greeks—but he promises, saying,

> "I will see to this. I will bring it all to pass.
> Look, I will bow my head if that will satisfy you.
> That, I remind you, that among the immortal gods
> is the strongest, truest sign that I can give."
>   —*The Iliad,* Book 1, 625–628

Although there are numerous gods, one is supreme. If Zeus grants an appeal by bowing his head, that will be done. (Recall the sixth line of the poem.) Homeric religion, while certainly not a monotheism, is not exactly a true polytheism either. The powers that govern the world, though many, seem to be under the rule of one.* That rule gives a kind of order to the universe: Homer's world is not a chaos. There are even suggestions in Homer that Zeus himself, though the most powerful of the gods, is under the domination of Fate. Some things simply *will be,* and even Zeus cannot alter them.

Moreover, this order is basically a just order, though it may not be designed altogether with human beings in mind. Zeus is the power who sees to it that certain customs are enforced: that oaths are kept, that suppliants are granted mercy, and that the rules governing guest and host are observed—the rules that Paris violated so grossly when he stole Helen away from her husband, Menelaus. Homer suggests that the Greeks eventually win the war because Zeus punishes the violation of these customs. On the other hand, the Greeks are punished with great losses before their eventual victory because Agamemnon had acted unjustly in taking Achilles' prize of war.

The Homeric idea of justice is not exactly the same as ours. We must see it in relation to the ambition of both mortals and gods in Homer's world. What they all covet is honor and glory. Agamemnon is angry not primarily because his woman was taken back to her father but because his honor has been offended. Booty is valued not for its own sake so much as for the honor it conveys—the better the loot, the greater the honor. Achilles is overcome by rage because Agamemnon has humiliated him, thus depriving him of the honor due him. That is why Thetis begs Zeus to let the Trojans prevail until the Greeks restore to Achilles "the honor he deserves."

What is just in this social world is that each person receive the honor that is due, given that person's status and position. Nestor, wise counselor of the Greeks, tries to make peace between Agamemnon and Achilles by appealing to precisely this principle.

---

*This was one of several mottoes that had appeared mysteriously on the temple walls. No one could explain how they got there, and it was assumed that Apollo himself must have written them.

*We shall see philosophers wrestling with this problem of "the one and the many." In what sense, exactly, is this world *one* world?

"Don't seize the girl, Agamemnon, powerful as
   you are—
leave her, just as the sons of Achaea gave her,
his prize from the very first.
And you, Achilles, never hope to fight it out
with your king, pitting force against his force:
no one can match the honors dealt a king,
   you know,
a sceptered king to whom Zeus gives glory.
Strong as you are—a goddess was your mother—
he has more power because he rules more men."
               —*The Iliad,* Book 1, 321–329

Nestor tries to reconcile them by pointing out what is just, what each man's honor requires. Unfortunately, neither one heeds his good advice.

The gods are also interested in honor. It has often been remarked that Homer's gods reflect the society that they allegedly govern; they are powerful, jealous of their prerogatives, quarrel among themselves, and are not above a certain deceitfulness, although some sorts of evil are simply beneath their dignity. The chief difference between human beings and the gods is that human beings are bound for death and the gods are not. Greeks often refer to the gods simply as "the immortals." Immortality makes possible a kind of happiness or blessedness among the gods that is impossible for human beings.

As immortals, the gods are interested in the affairs of mortals, but only insofar as they are entertained or their honor is touched. They are spectators of the human comedy—or tragedy; they watch human affairs the way we watch the soaps. There is a famous section in *The Iliad* where Zeus decides to sit out the battle about to rage on the plain below and simply observe. He says,

"These mortals do concern me, dying as they are.
Still, here I stay on Olympus throned aloft,
here in my steep mountain cleft, to feast my eyes
and delight my heart."
               —*The Iliad,* Book 20, 26–29

The gods both deserve and demand honor. We have already seen what can happen if it is not accorded. Apollo sent the plague because Agamemnon refused the ransom offered by Apollo's priest. When humans dishonor the gods or do not respect their prerogatives, they are guilty of arrogance, or

hubris. In this state, human beings in effect think of themselves as gods, forgetting their finitude, their limitations, their mortality. Hubris is punished by the gods, as hero after hero discovers to his dismay.

The gulf between Homeric gods and mortals—even those heroes like Achilles who have one divine parent—is clear and impassable. In closing this brief survey of Greek myths, I want to emphasize two aspects of this gulf. First, those whose thoughts were shaped by Homer neither believed in nor aspired to any immortality worth prizing. True, there is a kind of shadowy existence after death, but the typical attitude toward it is expressed by Achilles when he is visited in the underworld by Odysseus.

"No winning words about death to *me,* shining
   Odysseus!
By god, I'd rather slave on earth for another
   man—
some dirt-poor tenant farmer who scrapes to keep
   alive—
than rule down here over all the breathless dead."
            —*The Odyssey,* Book 11, 554–558[4]

For these conquerors who glory in the strength of their bodies, it seems impossible to suppose that there could be anything after death to compare. They know they are destined to die, believe that death is the end of any life worth living, and take the attitude expressed by Hector when faced with Achilles:

"And now death, grim death is looming up
   beside me,
no longer far away. No way to escape it now. This,
this was their pleasure after all, sealed long ago—
Zeus and the son of Zeus, the distant deadly
   Archer—
though often before now they rushed to my
   defense.
So now I meet my doom. Well let me die—
but not without struggle, not without glory, no,
in some great clash of arms that even men to come
will hear of down the years!"
            —*The Iliad,* Book 22, 354–362

Again, even at the end, the quest for honor is paramount.

The second aspect is a corollary to the first. It is best expressed by Pindar, a poet of the sixth century B.C., but the thought is thoroughly Homeric:

> Seek not to become Zeus.
> For mortals a mortal lot is best.
> Mortal minds must seek what is fitting
> at the hands of the gods,
> knowing what lies at our feet
> and to what portion we are born.
> Strive not, my soul, for an immortal life,
> but use to the full the resources
> that are at thy command.[5]

Mortal thoughts for mortals. Human beings are not divine, not gods, not immortal. Let them strive for excellence, to "use to the full the resources" at their command (and no other people, perhaps, have surpassed the Greeks in this). Let it be, however, an excellence appropriate to the "portion" allotted to humans. The deification of rulers, in Persian or Roman fashion, was not for the Greeks. They never blurred the line by worshipping living men (although dead heroes, like saints, may occasionally receive sacrifice and prayer). Here too, in its estimate of the status human beings have in the world, the Homeric tradition praises moderation.

---

1. Describe the main characters in Homer's poem *The Iliad*—for example, Agamemnon, Achilles, Apollo, Zeus, and Hector.
2. Retell the main outline of the story.
3. What is the theme of the poem, as expressed in the first lines?

4. How are honor and justice related in Homer's view of things?
5. What virtues are said to constitute human excellence?
6. Describe the relationship between humans and gods. In what ways are they similar, and how do they differ?
7. What is hubris, and what is its opposite?
8. Do Homer's heroes long for immortality? Explain.

For Further Thought

Gather examples of mythological thinking that are current today. What questions would a philosopher want to ask about them?

Notes

1. Hesiod, *Theogony,* trans. Dorothea Wender, in *Hesiod and Theognis* (New York: Penguin Books, 1973). All quotations are taken from this translation; numbers are line numbers.
2. Kathleen Freeman, *Ancilla to the Pre-Socratic Philosophers* (Cambridge, MA: Harvard University Press, 1948), 22.
3. Homer, *The Iliad,* trans. Robert Fagles (New York: Penguin Books, 1990). All quotations are taken from this translation; references are to book and line numbers.
4. Homer, *The Odyssey,* trans. Robert Fagles (New York: Penguin Books, 1996). References are to book and line numbers.
5. Pindar, *Isthmia and Pythis III,* trans. W. K. C. Guthrie, in *The Greeks and Their Gods* (Boston: Beacon Press, 1950), 113–114.

2

PHILOSOPHY BEFORE SOCRATES

Although we can think of Hesiod and Homer as opening our conversation, this starting point is somewhat artificial, as there are other voices to be heard. Not only are there other traditions in Greece, but the Greek city-states are not the only source of this conversation. Even if philosophical thought truly begins there, we need also to pay attention to the Hebrew tradition that was taking shape while Homeric bards were singing of Troy. Because that tradition, together with its Christian successor, did not by itself lead to philosophy, despite making significant contributions to the conversation, we will consider it later (see Chapter 9).

We turn now to the first recognizably philosophical voices: those of the nature philosophers or protoscientists of Ionia (see Map 1). It is seldom entirely clear why thinkers raised in a certain tradition become dissatisfied enough to try to establish a new one. The reason is even more obscure here because we have a scarcity of information regarding these thinkers. Although most of them wrote books, these writings are almost entirely lost, some surviving in small fragments, others known only by references to them and quotations or paraphrases by later writers.

As a group, these thinkers are usually known as the "pre-Socratics." This name testifies to the pivotal importance put on Socrates by his successors.*

For whatever reason, a tradition grew up in which questions about the nature of the world took center stage, a tradition that was not content with stories about the gods. For thinkers trying to *reason* their way to a view about reality, the Homeric tales, to say nothing of Hesiod's divine genealogy, must have seemed impossibly crude. Still, the questions addressed by these myths were real questions: What is the true nature of reality? What is its origin? What is our place in it? How are we related to the powers that govern it? What is the best way to live? Philosophy is born when thinkers attempt to answer these questions more rationally than myth does.

In early philosophical thought, certain issues take center stage. There is the problem of *the one*

---

*In this chapter, we look only at selected pre-Socratic thinkers. A more extensive and very readable treatment of others — including Anaximenes, Empedocles, and Anaxagoras — can be found in Merrill Ring, *Beginning with the Pre-Socratics* (Boston: McGraw-Hill, 1999).

and the many: If reality is in some sense one, what accounts for the many different individual things (and kinds of things) that we experience? Greek myth tends to answer this question in animistic or personal terms by referring either to birth or to spontaneous emergence. For instance, we find Hesiod simply asserting that "Chaos was first of all, but next appeared / Broad bosomed Earth" (*Theogony,* 116, 117). How, why, when, and by what means did it appear? On these questions the tradition is silent.

Then there is the problem of *reality and appearance.* True, things appear to change; they appear to be "out there," independent of us. But we all know that things are not always what they seem. Might reality in fact be very different from the way it appears in our experience? How could we know?

Of course, there is also the question about *human reality:* Who are we, and how are we related to the rest of what there is? These questions perplex our first philosophers. We shall see them struggling to frame ever-more satisfactory answers to them.

Thales: The One as Water

Thales (c. 625–547 B.C.) of Miletus, a Greek seaport on the shore of Asia Minor (see Map 1), seems to have been one of those dissatisfied with the traditional stories. Aristotle calls him the founder of philosophy. We know very little about Thales, and part of what we do know is arguably legendary. So, our consideration here is brief and somewhat speculative. He is said to have held (1) that the cause and element of all things is water, and (2) that all things are filled with gods. What could these two rather obscure sayings mean?

Concerning the first, it is striking that Thales supposes there is some *one* thing that is both the origin and the underlying nature of all things. It is surely not obvious that wine and bread and stones and wind are really the same stuff despite all their differences. It is equally striking that Thales chooses one of the things that occur naturally in the world of our experience to play that role. Notice that neither Zeus nor Kronos (Zeus' father, according to Hesiod) nor

Rhea (the Earth-goddess mother who bore him) plays this role but water. Here we are clearly in a different thought-world from that of Homer. Thales' motto seems to be this: *Account for what you can see and touch in terms of things you can see and touch.* This idea is a radical departure from anything prior to it.

Why do you think Thales chooses water to play the role of the primeval stuff? Aristotle speculates that Thales must have noticed that water is essential for the nourishment of all things and that without moisture, seeds will not develop into plants. We might add that Thales must have noticed that water is the only naturally occurring substance that can be seen to vary from solid to liquid to gas. The fact that the wet blue sea, the white crystalline snow, and the damp and muggy air seem to be the very same thing despite their differences could well have suggested that water might take even more forms.

At first glance, the saying that all things are full of gods seems to go in a quite different direction. If we think a moment, however, we can see that it is quite consistent with the saying about water. What is the essential characteristic of the gods, according to the Greeks? Their immortality. To say that all things are full of gods, then, is to say in effect that *in* them—not, note well, outside them or in addition to them—is a principle that is immortal. But this suggests that the things of experience do not need explanations from outside themselves as to why they exist. Moreover, tradition appeals to the gods as a principle of action. Why did lightning strike just there? Because Zeus was angry with *that man.* But to say that all things are themselves full of gods may well mean that we do not have to appeal beyond them to explain why events happen. Things have the principles of their behavior within themselves.

Both sayings, then, point thought in a direction quite different from the tradition of Homer and Hesiod. They suggest that if we want to understand this world, then we should look to this world, not to another. Thales seems to have been the first to have tried to answer the question, Why do things happen as they do? in terms that are not immediately personal. In framing his answer this way, Thales is not only the first philosopher, but the first scientist as well. It is almost impossible to overestimate the significance of this shift for the story of Western culture.

---

1. In what way are the two sayings attributed to Thales consistent?
2. Contrast the view suggested by Thales' sayings with that of Homer.

Anaximander: The One as the Boundless

Let's grant that Thales produced a significant shift in Western thought. What next? Although he may have done so, we have no evidence that Thales addresses the question of *how* water accounts for everything else. If everything is water, why does it seem as though so many things are *not* water, that water is just one kind of thing among many? Thales leaves us with a puzzle for which he offers no solution.

There is something else unsatisfactory about his suggestion: Even though water has those unusual properties of appearing in several different states, water itself is not unusual. It is, after all, just one of the many things that need to be explained. If we demand explanations of dirt and bone and gold, why should we not demand an explanation for water as well?

Ancient Greeks would have found a third puzzling feature in Thales' idea. They tended to think in terms of opposites: wet and dry, hot and cold. These pairs are opposites because they cancel each other out. Where you have the wet, you can't have the dry, and so on. Water is wet, yet the dry also exists. If the origin of things had been water, how could the dry have ever come into existence? It seems impossible.

Although again we are speculating, it is reasonable to suppose that problems such as these led to the next stage in our story. We can imagine Anaximander, a younger fellow citizen from Miletus born about 612 B.C., asking himself—or perhaps asking Thales—these questions. How does water produce the many things of our experience? What makes water so special? So the conversation develops.

Like Thales, Anaximander wants an account of origins that does not appeal to the gods of Homer and Hesiod, but as we'll see, he does not reject the divine altogether. We can reconstruct Anaximander's reasoning thus:

1. Given any state of things *X*, it had a beginning.
2. To explain its beginning, we must suppose a prior state of things *W*.
3. But *W* also must have had a beginning.
4. So we must suppose a still prior state *V*.
5. Can this go on forever? No.
6. So there must be something that itself has no beginning.
7. We can call this "the infinite" or "the Boundless."

It is from this, then, that all things come.

We are ready now to appreciate a passage of Aristotle's, in which he looks back and reports the views of Anaximander.

> Everything either is a beginning or has a beginning. But there is no beginning of the infinite; for if there were one, it would limit it. Moreover, since it is a beginning, it is unbegotten and indestructible. . . . Hence, as we say, there is no source of this, but this appears to be the source of all the rest, and "encompasses all things" and "steers all things," as those assert who do not recognize other causes besides the infinite. . . . And this, they say, is the divine; for it is "deathless" and "imperishable" as Anaximander puts it, and most of the physicists agree with him. (DK 12 A 15, *IEGP,* 24)[1]

Only the Boundless, then, can be a beginning for all other things. It *is* a beginning, as Aristotle puts it; it does not *have* a beginning. Because it is infinite, moreover, it has not only no beginning but also no end—otherwise it would have a limit and not be infinite.

It should be no surprise that the infinite is called "divine." Recall the main characteristic of the Greek gods: They are immortal; they cannot die. As Anaximander points out, this is precisely the key feature of the Boundless.

Here we have the first appearance of a form of reasoning that we will meet again when later thinkers try to justify belief in a god (or God) conceived in a much richer way than Anaximander is committed to.* Yet even here some of the key features of later thought are already present. The Boundless "encompasses all things" and "steers all things." Those familiar with the New Testament will be reminded of Paul's statement that in God "we live and move and have our being" (Acts 17:28).[2]

We should note that Aristotle remarks almost casually that those who use this language "do not recognize other causes besides the infinite." Here he hints at what he considers a defect in the view of Anaximander: It is too abstract to account in detail for the nature and behavior of the many species and individuals we actually find in the world. What we need is not one big cause but many little causes.[†] But that is getting ahead of our story.

We have seen how Anaximander deals with one of the puzzles bequeathed to him by Thales. It is not water but the Boundless that is the source and element of all things. What about the other problem? By what process does the Boundless produce the many individual things of our experience?

Here we have to note that the Boundless is thought of as indefinite in character, neither clearly this nor that. If it had a clear nature of its own, it would already exclude everything else; it would be, for instance, water but not fire, so it would have limits and not be infinite. Therefore, it must contain all things, but in a "chaotic" mixture.[‡] The hot, the cold, the dry, and the wet are all present in the Boundless, but without clear differentiation.

How, then, does the process of differentiation from the Boundless work? If Anaximander could show how these basic four elements (hot, cold, dry, and wet) separate out from the chaos, his basic problem would be solved. The *one* would generate *many* things. The question of how particular things are formed could be solved along similar lines. Note that at this early stage of thought, no clear distinction is made between heat as a property of a thing and the thing that is hot. There is just "the hot" and "the cold," what we might think of as hot stuff and

cold stuff. In fact, these stuffs are virtually indistinguishable from earth (the cold), air (the dry), fire (the hot), and water (the wet). The universe as we experience it seems to be composed of various mixtures of these elemental stuffs.*

To solve his problem, Anaximander uses an analogy: Fill a circular pan with water; add some bits of limestone, granite, and lead (what you need is a variety of different weights); and then swirl the water around. You will find that the heavier bits move toward the middle and the lighter bits to the outside. Like goes to like; what starts as a jumble, a chaos, begins to take on some order. Anaximander is apparently familiar with this simple experiment and makes use of it to explain the origin of the many.

If the Boundless were swirling in a *vortex motion,* like the water in the pan, then what was originally indistinguishable in it would become separated out according to its nature. You might ask: Why should we think that the Boundless engages in such a swirling, vortex motion? Anaximander would simply ask you to look up. Every day we see the heavenly bodies swirl around the earth: the sun, the moon, and even the stars. Did you ever lie on your back in a very dark, open spot (a golf course is a good place) for a long time and look at the stars? You can see them move, although it takes a long while to become conscious of their movement.[†]

Furthermore, it seems clear that the motions we observe around us exemplify the vortex principle that like goes to like. What is the lightest of the elements? Anyone who has stared at a camp fire for a few moments will have no doubt about the answer. The sticks stay put, but the fire leaps up, away from the cold earth toward the sky—toward the immensely hot, fiery sun and the other bright but less hot heavenly bodies.

According to the geography accepted at the time, moreover, the habitable earth was surrounded

---

*For examples, see Thomas Aquinas' proofs of the existence of God (Chapter 11).
[†]See pp. 169–171.
[‡]Remember that Hesiod tells us that "Chaos was first of all."

---

*Much of Greek medicine was based on these same principles. A feverish person, for instance, has too much of the hot, a person with the sniffles too much of the wet, and so on. What is required is to reach a balance among the opposite elements.
[†]Copernicus, of course, turns this natural view inside out. The stars only *appear* to move; in actuality, Copernicus suggests, it is *we* who are moving. See pp. 312–313.

by an ocean of water, which was surrounded in turn by the air. Thus, we have an ordered, sorted world: earth (cold and heavy) in the middle, water next (wet and not quite so heavy), then air, and in an outermost ring the fiery element—all in a continuous vortex motion that both produces and sustains the order. This explanation seems plausible and fits the observable data. What more could one ask?

Anaximander has other interesting ideas, too.[3] He explains why we do not see a blaze of fiery light covering the sky but bright spots: The blaze is mostly hidden by an opaque covering. He calculates (inaccurately) the orbits of the sun and the moon. He offers an explanation of why the earth stays where it does (it rides on air—what we might call the Frisbee principle). He gives us a non-Zeusian explanation of thunder and lightning (caused by the wind compressed in clouds). He suggests that humans originated inside other animals (fish, in particular). We needn't stop to discuss most of these points, but we need to give some attention to one more principle.

Anaximander tells us that existing things "make reparation to one another for their injustice according to the ordinance of time" (DK 12 B 1, *IEGP*, 34). Several questions arise here. What existing things? No doubt it is the opposites of hot and cold, wet and dry that Anaximander has in mind, but why does he speak of injustice? How can the hot and cold do each other injustice, and how can they "make reparation" to each other?

There can be little doubt of the answer. He presupposes a principle of balance in nature that must ultimately be served, however much one or the other element seems to have gotten the upper hand. The hot summer is hot at the expense of the cold; it requires a cold winter to right the balance. A too dry winter, we still tend to think, will have to be paid for by a too wet spring. Thus, each season encroaches on the "rights" due to the others and does them an injustice, but reparation is made in turn when each gets its due—and more. This keeps the cycle going.

Notice two points in particular. First, this view is, in its own way, an extension of the Homeric view that requires a certain moderation in human behavior. Too much of anything—too much anger, too much pride—brings down the wrath of the gods.

Anaximander imagines a cosmic principle of moderation at work in the elements of the world. It is as if he were saying to Homer, "You are right, but your view is too limited; the principle applies not only within the human world but also in the universe at large."

The second point, however, is equally important. This principle is not imposed on reality from without; it is not applied by the gods. Anaximander conceives it as immanent in the world process itself. Thus, he says, does the world work. In this he is faithful to the spirit of Thales, and in this both of them depart from the tradition of Homer, the first and foremost teacher of the Greeks. Anaximander's explanations are framed impersonally. It is true that the Boundless "steers all things," but the Homeric gods who intervene at will in the world have vanished. To explain particular facts in the world, no will, no purpose, no intention is needed. The gods turn out to be superfluous.

You can easily see that a cultural crisis is on the way. If the Homeric tradition is still alive and flourishing in the religious, artistic, political, and social life of Greek cities, what will happen when this new way of thinking begins to take hold? Our next thinker begins to draw some conclusions.

1. What puzzling features of Thales' view seem to have stimulated Anaximander to revise it?
2. State Anaximander's argument for the Boundless.
3. How, according to Anaximander, does the Boundless produce the many distinct things of our experience?
4. What evidence do we have in our own experience for a vortex motion?
5. How is the injustice that Anaximander attributes to existing things related to the Homeric virtue of moderation?
6. What sort of crisis is brewing?

Xenophanes: The Gods as Fictions

From what we know about Anaximander, it seems that his criticism of the mythological tradition was implicit rather than explicit. He was intent on solving his problems about the nature and origins of the world. Although his results were at odds with tradition, we have no record that he took explicit notice of this. Not so with Xenophanes. A native of Colophon, about forty miles north of Miletus (see Map 1), he was, like Thales and Anaximander, an Ionian Greek living on the eastern shores of the Aegean Sea. We are told that he fled in 546 B.C., when Colophon was taken by the Persians, and that he lived at least part of his life thereafter in Sicily. Xenophanes was a poet and apparently lived a long life of more than ninety-two years.

Xenophanes is important to our story because he seems to have been the first to state clearly the religious implications of the new nature philosophy. He explicitly criticizes the traditional conception of the gods on two grounds. First, the way Hesiod and Homer picture the gods is unworthy of our admiration or reverence:

> Homer and Hesiod have attributed to the gods all those things which in men are a matter for reproach and censure: stealing, adultery, and mutual deception. (DK Z1 B11, *IEGP,* 55)*

What he says is true, of course. It has often been remarked that Homer's gods are morally no better (and in some ways may be worse) than the band of ruthless warrior barons on whom they are so clearly modeled. They are magnificent in their own fashion, but flawed, like a large and brilliant diamond containing a vein of impurities. What is significant about Xenophanes' statement is that he not only notices this but clearly expresses his disapproval.†

He thinks it is *shameful* to portray the gods as though they are no better than human beings whom good men regard with disgust. That Homer, to whom all Greeks of the time look for guidance in life, should give us this view of the divine seems intolerable to Xenophanes. This moral critique is further developed by Plato.* For both of them, such criticism is the negative side of a more exalted idea of the divine.

This kind of criticism makes sense only on the basis of a certain assumption: that Homer is not simply mirroring the truth for us but is inventing stories. Several sayings of Xenophanes make this assumption clear.

> The Ethiopians make their gods snub-nosed and black; the Thracians make theirs gray-eyed and red-haired. (DK 21 B 16, *IEGP,* 52)

> And if oxen and horses and lions had hands, and could draw with their hands and do what man can do, horses would draw the gods in the shape of horses, and oxen in the shape of oxen, each giving the gods bodies similar to their own. (DK 21 B 15, *IEGP,* 52)

Here we have the first recorded version of the saying that god does not make man in his own image but that we make the gods in our image. This, Xenophanes tells us, is what Homer and Hesiod have done. Atheists and agnostics have often made this point since Xenophanes' time. Was Xenophanes, then, a disbeliever in the divine? No, not at all. No more than Anaximander, who says the infinite sees all and steers all. Xenophanes tells us there is

> one god, greatest among gods and men, in no way similar to mortals either in body or mind. (DK 21 B 23, *IEGP,* 53)

Several points in this brief statement stand out. There is only one god.† Xenophanes takes pains to

---

*When the Greeks talk about "men," they may not have been thinking about women. Women were not citizens, for example, in ancient Athens. It does not follow, of course, that what the Greeks say about "men" has no relevance for women of today. Here is a useful way to think about this. Aristotle formulated the Greek understanding of "man" in terms of *rational animal,* a concept that can apply to human beings generally. What the Greeks say about "man" may well apply to women, too, although one should be on guard lest they sneak masculinity too much into this generic "man." Their mistake (and not theirs alone!) was to have underestimated the rationality and humanity of women.

I will occasionally use the term "man" in this generic sense, but I will often paraphrase it with "human being" or some other substitute. Rather than the awkward "he or she," I will sometimes use "he" and sometimes "she," as seems appropriate.
†For a contrary evaluation, see Nietzsche, p. 535.

*See *Euthyphro* 6a, for instance. This criticism is expanded in Plato's *Republic,* Book II, where Plato explicitly forbids the telling of Homeric and Hesiodic tales of the gods to children in his ideal state.
†It may seem that Xenophanes allows the existence of other gods in the very phrase he uses to praise this one god. Scholars disagree about the purity of his monotheism. In the context of other things he says, however, it seems best to understand this reference to "gods" as a reference to "what tradition takes to be gods."

PYTHAGORAS

A figure about whom there are as many legends as facts, Pythagoras (b. 570 B.C.) lived most of his adult life in Croton in southern Italy (see Map 2 on page 25). He combined mathematics and religion in a way strange to us and was active in setting up a pattern for an ideal community. The Pythagorean influence on Plato is substantial.

Pythagoras and his followers first developed geometry as an abstract discipline, rather than as a tool for practical applications. It was probably Pythagoras himself who discovered the "Pythagorean theorem" (the square of the hypotenuse of a triangle is equal to the sum of the squares on the other two sides), as well as the principle that the interior angles of a triangle are equal to two right angles.

He also discovered the mathematical ratios of musical intervals: the octave, the fifth, and the fourth. Because mathematics informs these intervals, the Pythagoreans held, somewhat obscurely, that *all things are numbers*. They also believed that the sun, the moon, and other heavenly bodies make a noise as they whirl about, much as a piece of wood whirled on a string produces noise. They believed that these sounds produce a cosmic harmony, the "music of the spheres."

Pythagoras believed that the soul is a distinct and immortal entity, "entombed" for a while in the body. After death, the soul migrates into other bodies, sometimes the bodies of animals. To avoid both murder and cannibalism, the Pythagoreans were vegetarians. Xenophanes tells the story, probably apocryphal, that Pythagoras saw a puppy being beaten and cried out, "Do not beat it; I recognize the voice of a friend."

Mathematics was valued not just for itself but as a means to purify the soul, to disengage it from bodily concerns. In mathematical pursuits the soul lives a life akin to that of the gods.

It is said that Pythagoras was the first to call himself a philosopher, a *lover* of wisdom. No one, he said, is wise except the god. Compare Socrates (*Apology* 23a).

---

stress how radically different this god is from anything in the Homeric tradition. It is "in no way similar to mortals." This point is brought out in some positive characterizations he gives of this dissimilar god.

> He sees all over, thinks all over, hears all over. (DK 21 B 24, *IEGP,* 53)
>
> He remains always in the same place, without moving; nor is it fitting that he should come and go, first to one place and then to another. (DK 21 B 26, *IEGP,* 53)
>
> But without toil, he sets all things in motion by the thought of his mind. (DK 21 B 25, *IEGP,* 53)

This god is very different from human beings indeed. We see with our eyes, think with our brain, and hear with our ears. We seldom remain in the same place for more than a short time; indeed, if we are strict enough about what constitutes the "same place," we might come to agree with Heraclitus, who argues that we and all things are constantly moving from one place to another.* Furthermore, if we want to set anything besides ourselves in motion, just thinking about it or wishing for it isn't enough. In all these ways we are different from the one god.

Yet there is a similarity after all, and Xenophanes' "in no way similar" must be qualified. The one god sees and hears and thinks; so do we. He does not do it in the way we do it; the way the god does it is indeed "in no way similar." But god is intelligent, and so are we.

Here is a good place to comment on an assumption that seems to have been common among the Greeks. Where there is order, there is intelligence. Order, whether in our lives or in the world of nature, is not self-explanatory; only intelligence can

---

*See pp. 19–20.

explain order. This assumption doesn't seem to be explicitly argued for. It lies in the background as something almost too obvious to comment on. We can find experiences to give it some support, and perhaps these are common enough to make it *seem* self-evident—but it is not. For example, consider the state of papers on your desk or tools in your workshop. If you are like me, you find that these things, if left to their own devices, degenerate slowly into a state of chaos. Soon it is impossible to find what you want when you need it and it becomes impossible to work. What you need to do then is *deliberately* and with some *intelligent plan in mind* impose order on the chaos. Order is the result of intelligent action, it seems. It doesn't just happen.

Whether this assumption is correct is an interesting question, one about which modern physics and evolutionary biology have had interesting things to say.* Modern mathematicians tell us that however chaotic the jumble of books and papers on your desk, there exists some mathematical function according to which they are in perfect order. But for these ancient Greeks, the existence of order always presupposes an ordering intelligence. We find this assumption at work in the idea of god that Anaximander and Xenophanes have given us.

Consider now a saying that shows how closely Xenophanes' critique of the traditional gods relates to the developing nature philosophy:

> She whom men call "Iris," too, is in reality a cloud, purple, red, and green to the sight. (DK 21 B 32, *IEGP*, 52)

In *The Iliad,* Iris is a minor goddess, a messenger for the other gods. For instance, after Hector has killed Patroclus, Iris is sent to Achilles to bid him arm in time to rescue Patroclus' body (Book 18, 192–210). She seems to have been identified with the rainbow, which many cultures have taken as a sign or message from the gods. (Compare its significance to Noah, for example, after the flood in Genesis 9:12–17.)

Xenophanes tells us that rainbows are simply natural phenomena that occur in natural circumstances and have natural explanations. A rainbow, he thinks, is just a peculiar sort of cloud. This idea suggests a theory of how gods are invented. Natural phenomena, especially those that are unusual, particularly striking, or important to us, are personified and given lives that go beyond what is observable. Like the theory that the gods are invented, this theory has often been held. It may not be stretching things too far to regard Xenophanes as its originator.

It is clear that there is a kind of natural unity between nature philosophy and criticism of Homer's gods. They go together and mutually reinforce one another. Together they are more powerful than either could be alone. We will see that they come to pose a serious threat to the integrity of Greek cultural life.

There is one last theme in Xenophanes that we should address. Poets in classical times typically appealed to the Muses for inspiration and seemed often to think that what they spoke or wrote was not their own—that it was literally in-spired, breathed into them, by these goddesses. Remember Hesiod's claim that he was taught to sing the truth by the Muses. Similarly, Homer begins *The Iliad* by inviting the goddess to sing through him the rage of Achilles.* No doubt this is more than a literary conceit; many writers have experiences of inspiration when they seem to be no more than a mouthpiece for powers greater and truer than themselves. Hesiod and Homer may well have had such experiences. Whether such experiences guarantee the *truth* of what the writer says in such ecstatic states is, of course, another question. Listen to Xenophanes:

> The gods have not revealed all things from the beginning to mortals; but, by seeking, men find out, in time, what is better. (DK 21 B 18, *IEGP*, 56)

> No man knows the truth, nor will there be a man who has knowledge about the gods and what I say about everything. For even if he were to hit by

---

*See p. 321 for an example. Here Descartes claims that a chaos of randomly distributed elements, if subject to the laws of physics, would by itself produce an order like that we find in the world. For more recent views, see the fascinating book by James Gleick, *Chaos: Making a New Science* (New York: Penguin Books, 1987). The dispute over "intelligent design" shows that this is still a live issue.

---

*Look again at these claims to divine inspiration on pp. 2 and 5.

chance upon the whole truth, he himself would not be aware of having done so, but each forms his own opinion. (DK 21 B 38, *IEGP,* 56)

Let these things, then, be taken as like the truth. (DK 21 B 35, *IEGP,* 56)

This is a very rich set of statements. Let us consider them in six points.

1. Xenophanes is deliberately, explicitly, denying our poets' claims of inspiration. The gods have *not* revealed to us in this way "from the beginning" what is true, Xenophanes says. If we were to ask him why he is so sure about this, he would no doubt remind us of the unworthy picture of deity painted by the poets and of the natural explanations that can be given for phenomena they ascribe to the gods. Xenophanes' point is that a poet's claim of divine revelation is no guarantee of her poem's truth.

2. How, then, is it appropriate to form our beliefs? By "seeking," Xenophanes tells us. This idea is extremely vague. How, exactly, are we to seek? No doubt he has in mind the methods of the Ionian nature philosophers, but we don't have a very good idea of just what they were, so we don't get much help at this point.

Still, his remarks are not entirely without content. He envisages a process of moving toward the truth. If we want the truth, we should face not the past but the future. It is no good looking back to the tradition, to Homer and Hesiod, as though they had already said the last words. We must look to ourselves and to the results of our seeking. He is confident, perhaps because he values the results of the nature philosophers, that "in time"—not all at once—we will discover "what is better." We may not succeed in finding the truth, but our opinions will be "better," or more "like the truth."*

3. It may be that we know some truth already. Perhaps there is even someone who knows "the whole truth." But even if he did, that person could not know for certain that it is the truth. To use a distinction Plato later makes much of, the person

would not be able to distinguish his knowledge of the truth from mere opinion.* (Plato, as we'll see, does not agree.) There is, Xenophanes means to tell us, no such thing as *certainty* for limited human beings such as ourselves. Here is a theme that later skeptics take up.†

4. It does not follow from this somewhat skeptical conclusion that all beliefs are equally good. Xenophanes is very clear that although we may not ever be certain we have reached the truth, some beliefs are better or more "like the truth" than others. Unfortunately, he does not tell us how we are to tell which are more truthlike. Again we have a problem that many later thinkers take up.

5. Here we have a new direction for thought. Until now, thought has basically been directed outward—to the gods, to the world of human beings, to nature. Xenophanes directs thought back upon itself. His questioning questions itself. How much can we know? How can we know it? Can we reach the truth? Can we reach certainty about the truth? These are the central questions that define the branch of philosophy called **epistemology,** the theory of knowledge. It seems correct to say that Xenophanes is its father.

6. If we ask, then, whether there is anyone who can know the truth *and* know that he knows it, what is the answer? Yes. The one god does, the one who "sees all over, thinks all over, hears all over." In this answer, Xenophanes carries forward that strain of Homeric tradition emphasizing the gulf between humans and gods. The most important truth about humans is that they are not gods.‡ Xenophanes' remarks about human knowledge seem designed to drive that point home once and for all.

---

1. What are Xenophanes' criticisms of the Homeric gods?

---

*In recent philosophy these themes have been taken up by the *fallibilists.* See C. S. Peirce (p. 574).

*See pp. 118–120.

†See, for instance, the discussions by Sextus Empiricus (pp. 209–214) and Montaigne (pp. 309–312). Similar themes are found in Descartes' first *Meditation.*

‡Compare the poem of Pindar, part of which is quoted on p. 9.

2. What is his conception of the one god?
3. Can we know the truth about things, according to Xenophanes? If so, how?
4. Relate his sayings about knowing the truth to the idea of hubris and to claims made by Hesiod and Homer.

Heraclitus: Oneness in the *Logos*

Heraclitus is said to have been at his peak (probably corresponding to middle age) shortly before 500 B.C. A native of Ephesus (see Map 1), he was, like the others we have considered, an Ionian Greek living on the shores of Asia Minor. We know that he wrote a book, of which about one hundred fragments remain. He had a reputation for writing in riddles and was often referred to in Roman times as "Heraclitus the obscure." His favored style seems to have been the epigram, the short, pithy saying that condenses a lot of thought into a few words. Despite his reputation, most modern interpreters find that the fragments reveal a powerful and unified view of the world and man's place in it. Furthermore, Heraclitus is clearly an important influence on subsequent thinkers such as Plato and the Stoics.

One characteristic feature of his thought is that reality is a flux.

> All things come into being through opposition, and all are in flux, like a river. (DK 22 A 1, *IEGP*, 89)

There are two parts to this saying, one about opposition and one about flux. Let's begin with the latter and discuss the part about opposition later.

Plato ascribes to Heraclitus the view that "you cannot step twice into the same river." If you know anything at all about Heraclitus, it is probably in connection with this famous saying. What Heraclitus actually says, however, is slightly different.

> Upon those who step into the same rivers flow other and yet other waters. (DK 22 B 12, *IEGP*, 91)

You can, he says, step several times into the same river. Yet it is not the same, for the waters into which you step the second time are different waters. So, you both can and cannot.

This oneness of things that are different—even sometimes opposite—is a theme Heraclitus plays in many variations:

> The path traced by the pen is straight and crooked. (DK 22 B 59, *IEGP*, 93)

> Sea water is very pure and very impure; drinkable and healthful for fishes, but undrinkable and destructive to men. (DK 22 B 61, *IEGP*, 93)

> The way up and the way down are the same. (DK 22 B 60, *IEGP*, 94)

The road from Canterbury to Dover is the road from Dover to Canterbury. They are "the same," just as it is the same water that is healthful and destructive, the same movement of the pen that is crooked (when you consider the individual letters) but also straight (when you consider the line written).

Consider the river. It is the same river, although the water that makes it up is continually changing. A river is not identical with the water that makes it up but is a kind of structure or pattern that makes a unity of ever-changing elements. It is a *one* that holds together the *many*. So it is, Heraclitus tells us, with "all things." All things are in flux, like the river: ever-changing, yet preserving an identity through the changes. The river is for that reason a fit symbol for reality.

Another appropriate symbol for this flux is fire.

> This world-order, the same for all, no god made or any man, but it always was and is and will be an ever-lasting fire, kindling by measure and going out by measure. (DK 22 B 30, *IEGP*, 90)

Is Heraclitus here expressing disagreement with Thales? Is he telling us Thales is wrong in thinking that water is the source of all things—that it isn't water, but fire? Not exactly.

Remember that at this early stage of thought the very language in which thoughts can be expressed is itself being formed. This means that thought is somewhat crude, as we observed earlier. Thinkers have not yet made a distinction between "hot-stuff" and "fire that is hot." Heraclitus is reaching for abstractions that he hasn't quite got and cannot quite express. What he wants to talk about is the "world-order." This is, we would say, not itself a thing but an abstract pattern or structure in which the things of the world are displayed. Heraclitus, though, hasn't quite got that degree of abstraction, so he uses the most ethereal, least solid thing he is acquainted with to represent this world-order: fire.

We can be certain, moreover, that Heraclitus does not have ordinary cooking fires primarily in mind. Recall the view of Anaximander that the outermost sphere of the universe, in which the sun and stars are located, is a ring of fire. If you have ever been to Greece on a particularly clear day, especially on or near the sea, you can see even through our polluted atmosphere that not only the sun but also the entire sky shines. The heavens are luminous, radiant. It is not too much to say the sky blazes. In this luminous *aether,* as it was called, the gods are supposed to live. Olympus is said to be their home because its peak is immersed in this fiery element. Notice the epithet Heraclitus gives to fire: He calls it "ever-lasting." What, for the Greeks, deserves this accolade? Only, of course, the divine.

It is, then, the world-order itself that is immortal, divine. Heraclitus represents it as fire, the most ethereal and least substantial of the elements. No god made *that,* of course, for the world-order is itself eternal and divine.

This divine fire is both the substance of the world and its pattern. In its former aspect it is ever "kindling by measure and going out by measure." This thought is also expressed in the following fragments:

> The changes of fire: first sea, and of sea half is earth, half fiery thunderbolt. . . . (DK 22 B 31, *IEGP,* 91)

> All things are an exchange for fire, and fire for all things; as goods are for gold, and gold for goods. (DK 22 B 90, *IEGP,* 91)

The sea, we learn, is a mixture, half earth and half fire. All things are in continuous exchange. Earth is washed into the sea and becomes moist; sea becomes air, which merges with the fiery heavens, from which rains fall and merge again with earth. If Heraclitus were able to use the distinction between things and patterns, he might say that *as substance* fire has no priority over other things. It is just one of the four elements taking part with the others in the constant cycles of change. But *as pattern,* as world-order, it does have priority, for this pattern

is eternal and divine. He does not, of course, say this; he can't. If he were able to, he might be less obscure to his successors.

We need now to go back to the first part of our original fragment, where Heraclitus says that "all things come into being through opposition." What can this mean? Compare the following statements:

> War is the father and king of all. . . . (DK 22 B 53, *IEGP,* 93)

> It is necessary to understand that war is universal and justice is strife, and that all things take place in accordance with strife and necessity. (DK 22 B 80, *IEGP,* 93)

Strife, opposition, war. Why are these elevated into universal principles? To see what Heraclitus is saying, think about some examples. A lyre will produce music, but only if there is a tension on the strings. The arms of the lyre pull in one direction, the strings in the opposite. Without this opposition, there is no music. Consider the river. What is it that makes a river a river? It is the force of the flowing water struggling with the opposing forces of the containing banks. Without the opposition between the banks and the water, there would be no river. Think of a sculpture. It is the result of the efforts of the artist and the chisel fighting the resistance of the stone.

Here's another example, showing two of Heraclitus' themes: A bicycle wheel is *one* thing, though it is composed of *many* parts: hub, spokes, and rim. What makes these many items into one wheel? The tension that truing the wheel puts on the spokes, so that the hub and rim are pulling in opposite directions.

Now, if we think not about physical phenomena but about society, we see that the same is true. What is justice, Heraclitus asks, but the result of the conflict between the desires of the wealthy and the desires of the poor? Were either to get the upper hand absolutely, there would be no justice. Tension, opposition, and conflict, he tells us, are *necessary.* Without them the universe could not persist. If we look carefully at each of these examples, we see that each consists of a unity of diverse elements. The lyre, the river, the statue, the bicycle wheel, and justice are each a one composed in some sense of many. In every "one," "many" strive.

In *The Iliad,* Achilles laments the death of Patroclus, saying,

"If only strife could die from the lives of gods and men."

—*The Iliad,* Book 18, 126

To this cry, Heraclitus responds,

He did not see that he was praying for the destruction of the whole; for if his prayers were heard, all things would pass away. (DK 22 A 22, *IEGP,* 93)

Strife, then, is necessary. It produces not chaos but the opposite; in fact, the divine world-order is the guarantee that a balance of forces is maintained. The result is this:

To god all things are beautiful and good and just; but men suppose some things to be just and others unjust. (DK 22 B 102, *IEGP,* 92)

Again we see the Homeric contrast between gods and mortals, and again the contrast is to the disadvantage of mortals. God, the divine fire, the world-order, sees things as they are; and they are good. Strife is not opposed to the good; strife is its necessary presupposition. Mortals, such as Achilles, only "suppose," and what they suppose is false.

It is not characteristic of men to be intelligent; but it is characteristic of god. (DK 22 B 78, *IEGP,* 98)

We are now ready to consider the most explicit version of Heraclitus' solution to the problem of the one and the many. To do that, I must introduce a term that I will usually leave untranslated. It is a term that has numerous meanings in Greek and has had a long and important history, stretching from Heraclitus to the Sophists, to Plato and Aristotle, into the writings of the New Testament and the Christian church fathers, and beyond. The term is *logos.**

Logos is derived from a verb meaning "to speak" and refers first of all to the word or words that a speaker says. As in English, however, a term is easily stretched beyond its simple, literal meaning. As we can ask for the latest word about the economy,

the Greek can ask for the *logos* about the economy, meaning something like "message" or "discourse." This meaning easily slides into the *thought* expressed in a discourse. Because such thought is typically backed up by reasons or has a rationale behind it, *logos* also comes to mean "rationale" or "argument." Arguments are composed of conclusions and the reasons offered for those conclusions. So, an argument has a typical pattern or structure to it, which is the job of *logic* to display. (Our term "logic" is derived from the Greek *logos.*) *Logos,* then, can also mean a structure or pattern, particularly if the pattern is a rational one.

You can see that *logos* is a very rich term, containing layers of related meanings: word, message, discourse, thought, rationale, argument, pattern, structure. When the word is used in Greek, it reverberates with all these associations. We have no precise equivalent in English, and for that reason I usually do not translate it.

As we have seen, Heraclitus claims that all things are in a process of continual change and that part of what makes them the things they are is a tension between opposite forces. This world of changes is not a chaos but is structured by a world-order that is divine in nature; in itself, therefore, it is good and beautiful. Unfortunately,

the many do not understand such things.* (DK 22 B 17, *IEGP,* 94)

Though the *logos* is as I have said, men always fail to comprehend it, both before they hear it and when they hear it for the first time. For though all things come into being in accordance with this *logos,* they seem like men without experience. (DK 22 B 1, *IEGP,* 94)

Now Heraclitus tells us that there is a *logos* by which "all things come into being." What else is this but the structure or pattern of the world-order that we have met before? But now the conception is deepened. The *logos* is not just accidentally what it is. There is a logic to it that can be seen to be reasonable and right. It is not understood, however, by

---

*Postmodern critics of the Western philosophical tradition often call it "logocentric," meaning that it privileges rationality and assumes that words—especially spoken discourse—can adequately mirror reality. See Jacques Derrida, pp. 705–707.

*His term "the many" usually applies to all the individual things of which the world is composed; here, of course, it means "most people."

"the many." As Socrates does later, Heraclitus contrasts the few who are wise, who listen to the *logos,* with the many who are foolish.

Why is it that the many do not understand the *logos?* Is it so strange and distant that only a few people ever have a chance to become acquainted with it? Not at all.

> Though they are in daily contact with the *logos* they are at variance with it, and what they meet appears alien to them. (DK 22 B 73, *IEGP,* 94)

> To those who are awake the world-order is one, common to all; but the sleeping turn aside each into a world of his own. (DK 22 B 89, *IEGP,* 95)

> We ought to follow what is common to all; but though the *logos* is common to all, the many live as though their thought were private to themselves. (DK 22 B 2, *IEGP,* 95)

All people are "in daily contact" with this *logos.* It is all about us, present in everything that happens. You can't do or say anything without being immersed in it. Yet we ignore it. We are like sleepers who live in private dreams rather than in awareness of this rational pattern of things that "is common to all." We each manufacture a little world of our own, no doubt distorted by our own interests, fears, and anxieties, which we take for reality.

In so doing, we miss the *logos* and become foolish rather than wise. What is it, after all, to be wise?

> Wisdom is one thing: to understand the thought which steers all things through all things. (DK 22 B 41, *IEGP,* 88)

> The one and only wisdom is willing and unwilling to be called Zeus. (DK 22 B 32, *IEGP,* 88)

To be wise is to understand the nature and structure of the world. To be wise is to see that all is and must be ever-changing, that strife and opposition are necessary and not evil, and that if appreciated apart from our narrowly construed interests, they are good and beautiful. To be wise is to grasp the *logos,* the "thought which steers all things."* To be wise is to participate in the perspective of Zeus.

Why is this wisdom both "willing and unwilling" to be called by the name of Zeus? We can assume it is willing because Zeus is the common name for the highest of the gods, for the divine; to have such wisdom makes one a participant in the divine. Acting according to the *logos* is manifesting in one's life the very principles that govern the universe. However, such wisdom refuses the name of Zeus as Homer pictures him: immoral, unworthy, and no better than one of the many who do not understand the *logos.* Heraclitus, we see, agrees with the criticisms of traditional religion offered by Xenophanes.

Hesitant to reinforce these traditional pictures of deity, Heraclitus tells us,

> Thunderbolt steers all things. (DK 22 B 64, *IEGP,* 89)

As we have just seen, there is a "thought" (a *logos*) that steers all things. Now we are told it is "thunderbolt." Thus we are brought back to the idea that a divine fire both *is* the world-order and manifests itself *in* that world-order. Reluctant to use the name of Zeus, Heraclitus chooses the most dramatic form of fire familiar to early humans: lightning, the weapon Zeus supposedly uses to enforce his will. This "fire" is also the *logos,* the pattern or structure providing the unity of the world. This is what makes one world out of the many things.

Perhaps people are not to be too much blamed, however, for their lack of wisdom. For

> Nature loves to hide. (DK 22 B 123, *IEGP,* 96)

and

> The lord whose oracle is at Delphi neither speaks out nor conceals, but gives a sign. (DK 22 B 93, *IEGP,* 96)

Even though the *logos* is common to all, even though all our experience testifies to it, discerning this *logos* is difficult. It is rather like a riddle; the answer may be implicit, but it is still hard to make out. Solving the problem is like interpreting the ambiguous pronouncements of the famous oracle at Delphi, located north and west of Athens (see Map 1). People could go there and ask the oracle a question, as Croesus, king of the Lydians (see Map 1), once did. He wanted to know whether to go to war against the Persians. He was told that if he

---

*Compare Anaximander, p. 12. Heraclitus here identifies that which "steers all things" as a thought. This theme is later developed by the Stoics. See pp. 206–208.

went to war a mighty empire would fall. Encouraged by this reply, he set forth, only to find the oracle's pronouncement validated by his own defeat.

How, then, is the riddle to be unraveled? How can we become wise, learning the secrets of the *logos*? This is a question, remember, that we have asked before. Xenophanes has told us that by "seeking" we can improve our opinions, but that is pretty uninformative.* Does Heraclitus advance our understanding any? To some degree he does. Two fragments that seem to be in some tension with each other address this issue:

> Those things of which there is sight, hearing, understanding, I esteem most. (DK 22 B 55, *IEGP,* 96)

> Eyes and ears are bad witnesses to men if they have souls that do not understand their language. (DK 22 B 107, *IEGP,* 96)

We can come to understand the world-order, then, not by listening to poets, seers, or self-proclaimed wise men but by using our eyes and ears. Yet we must be careful, for the senses can deceive us, can be "bad witnesses." They must be used critically, and not everyone "understands their language." These few remarks do not, of course, take us very far. Later philosophers will fill in this picture.

Finally, Heraclitus draws from his view of the *logos* some significant conclusions for the way humans should live:

> It is not good for men to get all they wish. (DK 22 B 110, *IEGP,* 97)

> If happiness consisted in bodily pleasures we ought to call oxen happy who find vetch to eat. (DK 22 B 4, *IEGP,* 101)

> It is hard to fight against impulse; for what it wants it buys at the expense of the soul. (DK 22 B 85, *IEGP,* 101)

> Moderation is the greatest virtue, and wisdom is to speak the truth and to act according to nature, giving heed to it. (DK 22 B 112, *IEGP,* 101)

Why is it not good for men to get all they wish? If they did so, they would destroy the necessary tensions that make possible the very existence of both themselves and the things they want. They would overstep the bounds set by the *logos,* which allows the world to exist at all—a "many" unified by the "one." We must limit our desires, not for prudish or puritanical reasons, but because opposition is the very life of the world-order. Suppose I have a taste for sweets and indulge that taste without limit. I soon find myself ill or, if I persist, dead. Suppose, instead, you want at any cost to be thin like the supermodels. We know what sad consequences such unlimited desires bring. Similarly, Achilles indulges his impulse to anger with disastrous results. Of course, such impulses are "hard to fight against." Why? Because indulging them at all strengthens them, and we cannot help indulging them to some degree. Indulging an impulse seems to diminish the resources of the soul to impose limits on that impulse. Such indulgence is bought "at the expense of the soul."*

That is why wisdom is difficult and why it is missed by the many. They, like cattle, seek to maximize their bodily pleasures. In doing so, they are "at variance" with the *logos,* which requires of every force that it be limited. That is why "moderation is the greatest virtue"—and why it is so rare.

Note that Heraclitus ties his ethics intimately to his vision of the nature of things. The *logos* without is to be reflected in the *logos* within. Wisdom is "to speak the truth and to act according to nature." To speak the truth is to let one's words (one's *logos*) be responsive to the *logos* that is the world-order. To speak falsely is to be at variance with that *logos*. All one's actions should reflect that balance, the moderation nature displays to all who understand its ways. In the plea for moderation, Heraclitus reflects the main moral tradition of the Greeks since Homer, but he sets it in a larger context and justifies it in terms of the very nature of the universe itself and its divine *logos*.

In his exaltation of the few over the many, Heraclitus also reflects Homeric values.

> One man is worth ten thousand to me, if only he be best. (DK 22 B 49, *IEGP,* 104)

---

*See p. 18.

*For a more recent semi-Heraclitean view of the need to be hard on oneself, see Nietzsche, p. 556.

For the best men choose one thing above all the rest: everlasting fame among mortal men. But the many have glutted themselves like cattle. (DK 22 B 29, *IEGP,* 104)

The Homeric heroes seek their "everlasting fame" on the field of battle. Heraclitus, we feel, would seek it on the field of virtue.

In Heraclitus, then, we have a solution to the problem of the one and the many. We do live in one world, a *uni*-verse, despite the multitude of apparently different and often conflicting things we find in it. It is made one by the *logos,* the rational, divine, firelike pattern according to which things behave. Conflict does not destroy the unity of the world; unless it goes to extremes, such tension is a necessary condition of its very existence. And if we see and hear and think rightly, we can line up our own lives according to this same *logos,* live in a self-disciplined and moderate way, and participate in the divine wisdom.

---

1. What does Heraclitus mean when he says that all things are "in flux"? Give your own examples.
2. In what sense is the "world-order" fire? Why was it not made by any god?
3. Explain the saying "War is the father and king of all."
4. What is the *logos?*
5. How is it that we "fail to comprehend" the *logos?*
6. What is wisdom? Why is it "willing and unwilling" to be called Zeus?
7. Why is it not good for us to get all we wish? Why is it "hard to fight against impulse"? Why should we fight against it anyway?
8. Sum up Heraclitus' solution to the problem of the one and the many.

Parmenides: Only the One

Parmenides introduces the strangest thought so far. His view is hard for us to grasp. Once we see what he is saying, moreover, we find it hard to take seriously. So we need to make a special effort to understand. It helps to keep in mind that Parmenides is not an isolated figure independent of any context; he is a participant in the great conversation and constantly

has in mind the views of his predecessors and contemporaries, some of whom are familiar to us.

What makes the argument of Parmenides so alien to us is its conclusion; most people simply cannot believe it. The conclusion is that there is no "many"; only "the one" exists. We find this hard to believe because our experience is so obviously manifold. There is the desk, and here is the chair. They are two; the chair is not the desk and the desk is not the chair. So, at least, it seems. If Parmenides is to convince us otherwise, he has his work cut out for him. He is well aware of this situation and addresses the problem explicitly.

Parmenides was not an Ionian, as were Thales, Anaximander, Xenophanes, and Heraclitus. This fact is significant because, in a sense, geographical location is not intellectually neutral. Different places develop different traditions. Parmenides lived at the opposite edge of Greek civilization in what is now the southern part of Italy, where there were numerous Greek colonies. He came from a city called Elea (see Map 2), which, according to tradition, was well governed in part through Parmenides' efforts. Plato tells us that Parmenides once visited Athens in his old age and conversed with the young Socrates. If this is so, Parmenides must have been born about 515 B.C. and lived until at least the year 450 B.C.

Parmenides wrote a book, in verse, of which substantial parts have come down to us. In the prologue, he claims to have been driven by horse and chariot into the heavens and escorted into the presence of a goddess who spoke to him, saying,

Welcome, youth, who come attended by immortal charioteers and mares which bear you on your journey to our dwelling. For it is no evil fate that has set you to travel on this road, far from the beaten paths of men, but right and justice. It is meet that you learn all things—both the unshakable heart of well-rounded truth and the opinions of mortals in which there is no true belief. (DK 28 B 1, *IEGP,* 108–109)

Such language might seem to be a throwback to the kinds of claims made by Hesiod.* Parmenides is

---

*Look again at Hesiod's description of his inspiration by the Muses, p. 2.

MAP 2   Southern Italy and Sicily

telling us that the content of his poem has been revealed to him by divine powers. Is this philosophy? In fact, it is. The content of the revelation is an **argument,** and the goddess admonishes him to

> judge by reasoning the much-contested argument that I have spoken. (DK 28 B 7, *IEGP,* 111)

The claim that this argument was revealed to him by a goddess may reflect the fact that the argument came to him in an ecstatic or inspired state. Or it may just be a sign of how different from ordinary mortal thought the "well-rounded truth" really is. In either case, the claim that the poem is a revelation is inessential. We are invited to *judge* it, not just to accept it; we are to judge it "by reasoning." This is the key feature of philosophy.*

Note that the goddess reveals to him two ways: the truth and the "opinions of mortals," which deal not with truth but with **appearance.** His poem is in fact set up in two parts, "The Way of Truth" and "The Way of Opinion." Because it is the former that has been influential, we'll concentrate on it.

What, then, is this argument that yields such strange conclusions? It begins with something Parmenides thought impossible to deny.

> Thinking and the thought that it is are the same; for you will not find thought apart from what is, in relation to which it is uttered. (DK 28 B 8, *IEGP,* 110)

When you *think,* the content of your thinking is a *thought.* And every thought has the form: It *is* so and so. If you think, "This desk is brown," you are thinking what *is,* namely, the desk and its color. If you think "This desk is not brown," once more you are

---

*Socrates insists that when a statement is made, we must "examine" it. See pp. 63–66.

thinking of what *is,* namely the desk. Suppose you say, "But I am thinking that it is *not brown;* so I am thinking of what is *not.*" Parmenides will reply that "not brown" is just an unclear way of expressing the real thought, which is that the desk *is,* let us say, gray. If you are thinking of the desk, you are thinking of *it* with whatever color it has. Suppose you say, "But I am thinking of a unicorn, and there aren't any unicorns; so am I not thinking of what is not?" No, Parmenides might say, for what is a unicorn? A horse with a single horn, and horses and horns both *are.** So once again we do not "find thought apart from what is." To think at all, he tells us, is to think that something *is.*

> For thought and being are the same. (DK 28 B 3, *IEGP,* 110)

They are "the same" in much the same way that for Heraclitus the way up and the way down are the same. If you have the one, you also have the other. The concept of "being" is just the concept of "what is," as opposed to "what is not." Whenever you think, you are thinking of what is. Thinking and being, then, are inseparable.

This is Parmenides' starting point. It seems rather abstract and without much content. How can the substantial conclusions we hinted at be derived from such premises? The way to do it is to derive a corollary of this point.

> It is necessary to speak and to think what is; for being is, but nothing is not. (DK 28 B 6, *IEGP,* 111)

You cannot think "nothing." Why not? Because nothing *is not,* and to think is (as we have seen) to think of what *is.* If you could think of nothing, it would (by the first premise) be *something.* But that is contradictory. Nothing cannot be something! Nothing "is not."

That still does not seem very exciting. Yet from this point remarkable conclusions follow (or seem

to follow; whether the argument is a sound one we will examine later).* In particular, all our beliefs about *the many* must be false. You believe, for example, that this book you are reading is one thing and the hand you are touching it with is another, so you believe that there are *many* things. If Parmenides' argument is correct, however, that belief is false. In reality there is no distinction between them. Parmenides describes ordinary mortals who do not grasp that fact in this way:

> Helplessness guides the wandering thought in their breasts; they are carried along deaf and blind alike, dazed, beasts without judgment, convinced that to be and not to be are the same and not the same, and that the road of all things is a backward-turning one. (DK 28 B 6, *IEGP,* 111)

This is harsh! The language he uses makes it clear that he has in mind not only common folks but also philosophers—Heraclitus in particular. It is Heraclitus who insists more rigorously than anyone else that "to be and not to be are the same" (to be straight, for instance, and not straight).† Whatever is, Heraclitus tells us, is only temporary; all is involved in the universal flux, coming into being and passing out of being. In that sense, "the road of all things" is indeed "a backward-turning one." You may be reminded of the phrase common in funeral services: "Ashes to ashes, dust to dust."

Parmenides tells us, however, that to think in this way is to be blind, deaf, helpless, dazed—no better than a beast. Things cannot be so. To say that something "comes into being" is to imply that it formerly *was not.* But this is something that you can neither imply, nor say, nor even think sensibly, for it involves the notion of "not-being." And we have already seen that not-being cannot be thought. It is inconceivable, for "thought and being are the same." So we are confused when we speak of something coming into being. We do not know what we are saying.

The same argument holds for passing away. The fundamental idea involved in passing away is that

---

*Actually, it is not entirely clear how Parmenides deals with thoughts that are apparently about nonexistent things. This is a puzzle that is not cleared up until the twentieth century by Bertrand Russell. See the brief treatment of his celebrated Theory of Definite Descriptions on p. 595.

---

*See the critique by Democritus on pp. 31–32.

†See the remark on p. 19 about the path traced by the pen.

something leaves the realm of being (of what is) and moves into the realm of not-being (of what is not). My dog dies and *is no more*—or so it seems. But Parmenides argues that this is really inconceivable. Passing away would involve the notion of what is not, but *what is not* cannot be thought. If it cannot be thought, it cannot be. There is no "realm of not being." There couldn't be.

Parmenides summarizes the argument:

> How could what is perish? How could it have come to be? For if it came into being, it is not; nor is it if ever it is going to be. Thus coming into being is extinguished, and destruction unknown. (DK 28 B 8, *IEGP,* 113)

But if there can be no coming into being and passing away, then there can be no Heraclitean flux. Indeed, the common experience that things do have beginnings and endings must be an illusion. Change is impossible!

> For never shall this prevail: that things that are not, are. But hold back your thought from this way of inquiry, nor let habit born of long experience force you to ply an aimless eye and droning ear along this road; but judge by reasoning the much-contested argument that I have spoken. (DK 28 B 7, *IEGP,* 111)

We have already examined the last part of this passage, but it is important to see what contrasts with the "reasoning" that Parmenides commends. We are urged not to let our thought be formed by "habit born of long experience." Parmenides acknowledges that experience is contrary to the conclusions he is urging upon us. Of course the senses tell us that things change, that they begin and end, but Parmenides says not to rely on sensory experience. You must rely on reasoning alone. You must *go wherever the argument takes you,* even if it contradicts common sense and the persuasive evidence of the senses.*

In urging us to follow reason alone, Parmenides stands at the beginning of one of the major traditions

in Western philosophy. Although we shouldn't take such "isms" too seriously, it is useful to give that tradition a name. It is called **rationalism.** Parmenides is rightly considered the first rationalist philosopher.

Notice the contrast to the Ionian nature philosophers. They all try to explain the nature of the things we observe; they start by assuming that the world is composed of many different things changing in many different ways, and it never occurs to them to question this assumption. Heraclitus, remember, says that he esteems most the things we can see and hear and understand.* Parmenides resolutely rejects this reliance on the senses.

He has not finished, however, deriving surprising conclusions from his principles. If we grant his premises, he tells us, we must also acknowledge that what exists

> is now, all at once, one and continuous. (DK 28 B 8, *IEGP,* 113)

> Nor is it divisible, since it is all alike; nor is there any more or less of it in one place which might prevent it from holding together, but all is full of what is. (DK 28 B 8, *IEGP,* 114)

What is must exist "all at once." This means that time itself must be unreal, an illusion. Why? Because the present can only be identified as the present by distinguishing it from the past (which is *no longer*) and from the future (which is *not yet*), and this shows that the notions of past and future both involve the unthinkable notion of "what is not." So "what is" must exist all at once in a continuous present. This thought is later exploited by St. Augustine in his notion of God.[†]

Moreover, *what is* must be indivisible; it cannot have parts. Why? Well, what could separate one thing from another? Only *what is not,* and what is not *cannot be.* You might be inclined to object at this

---

*We will see this theme repeated by Socrates; if it is true that as a young man Socrates conversed with Parmenides (as Plato tells us), it is likely that he learned this principle from him. For an example, see *Crito* 46b, p. 105.

---

*In the seventeenth and eighteenth centuries, such reliance on sensory data is called *empiricism* and is starkly contrasted to rationalism. For an example, see pp. 401–402.

†For Augustine, however, it is only God who enjoys this atemporal kind of eternity; time has a certain reality for Augustine—created and dependent, but not ultimate. See pp. 242–243.

point and say that one thing can be separated from another by some third thing. But the question repeats itself: What separates the first thing from the third? There can't be an infinite number of things between any two things, so at some point you will have to say that the only difference between them is that the one just *is not* the other. But, if Parmenides is right, that's impossible. So all is "full of what is."

It follows, of course, that there cannot be a vortex motion, as Anaximander thought, scattering stuff of different kinds to different places, because there cannot be things of different kinds. It is "all alike." There is not "any more or less of it in one place which might prevent it from holding together."* Why not? Because if there were "less" in some place, this could only be because it is mixed with some nonbeing. Because there is no nonbeing, there cannot be a "many." The problem of the one and the many should never have come up!

It also follows that being must be uncreated and imperishable, without beginning or end. If *what there is* had come into being, it must have come from not being—but this is impossible. To perish, it would have to pass away into nothingness—but nothingness is not. So being can neither begin nor end. "For never shall this prevail: that things that are not, are."

We can characterize *what is* in the following terms. It is one, eternal, indivisible, and unchanging. If experience tells you otherwise, Parmenides says, so much the worse for experience.

If you think about it for just a moment, you can see that Parmenides has thrust to the fore one of the basic philosophical problems. It is called the problem of *appearance and reality.* Parmenides readily admits that the world *appears* to us to be many and to change continuously and that the things in it seem to move about. What he argues is that it is not so *in reality.* In reality, he holds, there is just the one. Any convictions we have to the contrary are just

"the opinions of mortals in which there is no true belief."

We are all familiar with things not really being what they appear to be. Sticks in water appear to be bent when they are not. Roads sometimes appear to be wet when there is no water on them, and so on. The distinction is one we can readily understand. What is radical and disturbing about Parmenides' position is that everything our senses acquaint us with is allocated to the appearance side of the dichotomy. Nowhere do we sense what really is. Can this be right? This problem puzzles many a successor to Parmenides—or at least *appears* to do so!

Because these views are so strange, so alien to the usual ways of thinking, it is worth noting the response of Parmenides' contemporaries and successors. Do they dismiss him as "that crazy Eleatic" who denies multiplicity and change? Do they think of him as a fool and charlatan? No, they take him very seriously. Plato, for example, always treats Parmenides with respect. Why? Because he, more successfully than anyone else up to his time, does what they are all trying to do: to follow reason wherever it leads. If his conclusions are uncongenial, that means only that his arguments must be examined carefully for any errors. Parmenides provides for the first time a coherent, connected argument—something you can really wrestle with. Succeeding philosophers have to come to terms with Parmenides in one way or another. Even though few accept his positive views, his influence is great, and his impact is still felt today.

---

1. What does Parmenides mean when he says that "thought and being are the same"?
2. What is the argument that there are not, in reality, *many* things?
3. If Parmenides is right, why must Heraclitus be wrong about all things being in flux?
4. Doesn't the testimony of our senses prove that there are many things? Why does Parmenides maintain that it does not?
5. How must reality (as opposed to appearance) be characterized?
6. In what sense is Parmenides a rationalist?

---

*Anaximenes, a nature philosopher we are not considering, holds that air, when compressed, becomes cloud, then water, then earth and stone. When more rarefied, it becomes fire. Parmenides argues that such an explanation for the many kinds of things we seem to experience is impossible, because such compression and rarefaction implicitly involve nonbeing.

Zeno: The Paradoxes of Common Sense

In response to Parmenides' strange argument, you may be tempted to slice an apple in two just to prove that there really are many things, or wiggle your ears to show change actually happens. Of course, that won't do, because Parmenides has arguments to show that all this is merely appearance, not reality. Still, his conclusion is so at odds with common sense that we feel there must be something wrong with it.

One of Parmenides' pupils, Zeno by name, claims to have arguments showing that there is something even more wrong with common sense (and the natural science developing out of it) than simple falsity: It generates logical contradictions. It is bad enough if a view conflicts with deeply held convictions, but it is even worse if those convictions turn out to be contradictory in themselves. So, Zeno holds, his arguments not only counter those who abuse his teacher, but also "pay them back with interest" (Plato, *Parmenides,* 128d).

Some of Zeno's arguments concern the many, but his most famous arguments concern change —in particular, the sort of change that we call "motion." Common sense assumes that motion is something real. The question is, however, Can we understand in a consistent way what common sense assumes? Let us look at three of Zeno's arguments.

1. Suppose Achilles were to enter a race with a tortoise. Being honorable and generous, the great runner would offer the tortoise a head start. The tortoise would lumber laboriously along, and after a suitable interval Achilles would spring from the starting blocks. But surprise! He would be unable, despite his utmost efforts, to catch the tortoise. Why?

Consider this: when Achilles begins to run, the tortoise is already at some point down the race course, call it A. In order to catch him, Achilles must first reach that point. That seems obvious. By the time Achilles has reached A, however, the tortoise has moved on to some further point, B.

That also seems obvious. So Achilles needs to race to point B. He does so. Of course, by the time Achilles has attained B, the tortoise is at C. Another effort, this time to get to C, and again the tortoise is beyond him —at D. You can see that no matter how long the race goes on, Achilles will not catch the tortoise. So much for all that training!

This looks like a perfectly fair deduction from commonsense principles. So common sense holds both that one runner can catch another (because we see it done) *and* that one runner cannot catch another (as the argument shows). This is self-contradictory.

2. Consider an arrow in flight. Common sense holds that the arrow moves. Where does it move? Once this question is asked, it looks as though there are just two possibilities. Either the arrow moves in the space where it is, or it moves in some space where it is not —but neither is possible.

It obviously cannot move in a space it does not occupy, because it simply isn't there. Nor can it move in the space it occupies at any given moment, because at that moment it takes up the whole of that space, and there is no place left for it to move into. So the arrow cannot move at all. Once again, this seems a commonsense deduction; however, once again it is at odds with common sense itself, because nothing is more common than believing you can shoot an arrow at a target.

3. You no doubt believe that you can move from where you are now sitting to the door of the room. If you get a sudden yen for a pizza, you might just do it. Before you could get to the door, however, there is something else you would have to do first. You would have to get to the midpoint between where you are now and the door. That seems obvious —but consider: Before you could get to that point, there is something else you would have to do first. You would have to get to the midpoint between *that* point and where you are sitting. You can see how it goes. If you always have to get to one point before getting to a second, you will not even be able to get out of your chair!

Once again we see common sense in conflict with itself. If our common belief in motion contains self-contradictions, it cannot possibly be true; therefore, it cannot describe reality. You can see why Zeno thought these arguments paid back Parmenides' opponents "with interest."

Let us pause a moment to reflect on what kind of argument Zeno is using here. Logicians call it a *reductio ad absurdum* argument, or a reduction to absurdity. It has a form like this. (Let's take the arrow case as an example.)

Assume the truth of a proposition.

1. The arrow can move.

Deduce consequences from that assumption.

2. a. It must move either where it is or where it is not.

   b. It can do neither.

Draw the conclusion.

3. The arrow cannot move.

Display the contradiction.

4. The arrow can move (by 1), and the arrow cannot move (by 3).

Draw the final conclusion.

5. Motion is impossible because assuming it yields a contradiction—in 4—and no contradiction can possibly be true.

Reductio arguments are **valid** arguments.* They are very powerful arguments. That is why Zeno's arguments are so disturbing, and that is why articles trying to resolve the paradoxes still appear today in philosophical and scientific journals.

These are serious paradoxes. Their importance for our story is that they present examples of rigorous argument that opponents had to imitate to refute—another push toward rationalism. They also force a reconsideration of the basic notions of space, time, and motion—a process still going on in contemporary physics.

---

1. State Zeno's arguments against motion, and explain how they support Parmenides.
2. What is the pattern of a reductio ad absurdum argument?

---

*See the discussion of validity in the discussion of Aristotle's logic, Chapter 7, and the definition in the Glossary.

Atomism: The One and the Many Reconciled

Anaximander and other nature philosophers proceed on the assumption that the world is pretty much as it seems. We learn of it, as Heraclitus tells us, by sight, hearing, and understanding. We need only to set forth the elements of which it is made, its principles of organization, and why it changes. This might be difficult to do because the world is complex and human minds are limited, but there doesn't seem to be a shadow of suspicion that sight and hearing on the one hand (the senses) and understanding (reasoning) on the other hand might come into conflict. Yet that is precisely the outcome of Parmenidean logic. The world as revealed by our senses *cannot* be reality, and the force of that "cannot" is the force of reason itself. Parmenides has *proved* it. These arguments of Parmenides shake Ionian nature philosophy to its core.

Clearly, it is difficult simply to acquiesce in these results. It is not easy to say that our sensory convictions about the manyness of things, their changeableness, and their motion are all illusory. Several notable thinkers attempt to reconcile the arguments of Parmenides and his pupil Zeno with the testimony of the senses. Empedocles and Anaxagoras, in particular, struggle with these problems, but it is generally agreed that neither of them really resolves the issue. It is not until we come to the atomists that we find, in principle, a satisfactory solution.

Two figures are important in developing atomist thought: Leucippus and Democritus. About the former we know very little; two ancient authorities doubt even that he existed. Others, however, attribute to Leucippus the key idea that allows the Parmenidean argument to be met. About Democritus we know much more. He lived in Abdera, a city of Thrace in northern Greece (see Map 1), during the middle of the fifth century B.C. He wrote voluminously, perhaps as many as fifty-two books, of which well over two hundred fragments are preserved. He is also thoroughly discussed by later philosophers such as Aristotle, so we have a fairly complete notion of his teachings.

We need not try to sort out the separate contributions of Leucippus and Democritus. (We can't do so with certainty in any case.) They seem together to have developed the view known as **atomism,** to which we now turn.

The Key: An Ambiguity

In a work titled *Of Generation and Corruption* (concerned with coming into being and passing away), Aristotle summarizes the Parmenidean arguments against these kinds of changes and then says,

> Leucippus, however, thought he had arguments which, while consistent with sense perception, would not destroy coming into being or passing away or the multiplicity of existing things. These he conceded to be appearances, while to those who upheld the "one" he conceded that there can be no motion without a void, that the void is not-being, and that not-being is no part of being; for what is, in the strict sense, is completely full. But there is not one such being but infinitely many, and they are invisible owing to the smallness of their bulk. They move in the void (for void exists) and, by coming together and separating, effect coming into being and passing away. (DK 67 A 7, *IEGP,* 196)

Notice that Aristotle does not say simply that Leucippus disagrees with Parmenides. To disagree with an opinion is easy—too easy. What is needed is a *reason* to disagree. Aristotle says that Leucippus has, or thinks he has, *arguments*. These arguments concede some things to the *monists* (the believers in the "one"), but they show that these concessions are not as damaging to common sense as the monists had thought. The acceptable parts of the monistic argument can be reconciled with sense perception, with beginning and ending, and with multiplicity. What are these arguments?

Surprisingly, a follower of Parmenides, Melissus, gives us a hint toward an adequate solution:

> If there were a many, they would have to be such as the one is. (DK 30 B 8, *IEGP,* 148)

Melissus does not accept that there is a many. He just tells us that *if* there were a many, each thing would have to have the characteristics Parmenides ascribes to the one. Each would have to be all-alike, indivisible, full, and eternal. What Leucippus does is to accept this principle and to say there are many such "ones." There are, in fact, an infinite number of them. Democritus was to call them "atoms."

From all we have seen so far, however, this is mere assertion; we need an argument. It goes like this. We must grant to Parmenides that being and not-being are opposites, and of course not-being *is not.* It doesn't follow from these concessions, though, that there is no such thing as empty space. Space can be empty in precisely this sense: It contains no *things* or *bodies.* Nonetheless, space may have *being.* Empty space, which Democritus calls "the void," is *not* the same as not-being. It only seems so if you do not distinguish *being* from *body.* Being a body or a thing may be just one *way* of being something. There may be others. Moreover, *what-does-not-contain-any-body* need not be the same as *what-is-not-at-all.*

Once that distinction is recognized, we can see that Parmenides' argument confuses the two. He argues that there can be only a "one" because if there were "many" they would have to be separated by *what is not;* and what is not *is not.* So there cannot be a many; what is must be all full and continuous. The atomists argue that there is an ambiguity here. Some of what is *can* be separated from other parts of what is—by the void. So there *can* be a many. The void does not lack being altogether. It only lacks the kind of being characteristic of *things.* Democritus also calls the void "no-thing"—not, note carefully, "nothing" (nothing at all), which he acknowledges *is not.* No-thing (the void) is a kind of being in which no body exists. He puts the point this way:

> No-thing exists just as much as thing. (DK 68 B 156, *IEGP,* 197)

A diagram may help to make this clear.

Parmenides

Being	Not-being
is	is not

Democritus

	Being	
Thing	No-thing	Not-being
(Body)	(Void)	is not
	is	

We noted earlier the struggle to develop a language adequate to describe reality. Language begins, as the language of children does, tied to the concrete. Only with great difficulty does it develop enough abstraction—enough distance, as it were, from concrete things—to allow for the necessary distinctions. The language of Parmenides simply lacks the concepts necessary to make these crucial distinctions. Leucippus and Democritus are in effect forging new linguistic tools for doing the job of describing the world. This is a real breakthrough: It makes possible a theory that does not deny the evidence of the senses and yet is rational (that is, does not lead to contradictions).

The World

Reality, then, consists of atoms and the void. Atoms are so tiny that they are mostly, perhaps entirely, invisible to us. Each of them is indivisible (the word "atom" comes from roots that mean "not cuttable").* Because they are indivisible, they are also indestructible; they exist eternally. Atoms are in constant motion, banging into each other and bouncing off, or maybe just vibrating like motes of dust in a stream of sunlight. Such motion is made possible by the existence of the void; the void provides a place into which a body can move. Their motion, moreover, is not something that must be imparted to them from outside. It is their nature to move.

These atoms are not all alike, although internally each is homogeneous, as Melissus argues it must be. Atoms differ from each other in three ways: in shape (including size), in arrangement, and in position. Aristotle gives us examples from the alphabet to illustrate these ways. *A* differs from *N* in shape, *AN* differs from *NA* in arrangement, and *Z*

---

*What we call "atoms" nowadays are not, as we well know, indivisible. We also know, since Einstein, that matter and energy are convertible. Nonetheless, physicists are still searching for the ultimate building blocks of nature. Perhaps they are what scientists call "quarks." Whether that is so or not, however, the ancient atomists' assumption that there are such building blocks and that they are very tiny indeed is alive and well in the twenty-first century.

differs from *N* in position. As the atoms move about, some of them hook into others, perhaps of the same kind, perhaps different. If enough get hitched together, they form bodies that are visible to us. In fact, such compounds or composites are what make up the world of our experience. Teacups and sparrow feathers differ from each other in the kinds of atoms that make them up and in the way the atoms are arranged. Light bodies differ from heavy bodies, for example, because the hooking together is looser and there is more void in them. Soft bodies differ from hard ones because the connections between the atoms are more flexible.

The atomists can explain coming into being and passing away as well. A thing comes into being when the atoms that make it up get hooked together in the appropriate ways. It passes away again when its parts disperse or fall apart.

These principles are obviously compatible with much of the older nature philosophy, and the atomists adopt or adapt a good bit of that tradition. The structure of the universe, for instance, is explained by a vortex motion or whirl that separates out the various kinds of compounds. Like tends to go to like, just as pebbles on a seashore tend to line up in rows according to their size. In this way, we get a picture of the world that is, in its broad features, not very different from that of Anaximander. There is, however, one crucial and very important difference.

Anaximander said that the Boundless "encompasses all things" and "steers all things." Xenophanes claims that the one god "sets all things in motion by the thought of his mind." Heraclitus identifies the principle of unity holding together the many changing things of the world as a divine *logos,* or thought. In contrast, Democritus' principles leave no room for this kind of intelligent direction to things. Remember: What exist are atoms and the void. Democritus boldly draws the conclusions from this premise. If we ask why the atoms combine to form a world or why they form some particular thing in this world, the only answer is that they *just do.* The only reason that can be given is that these atoms happened to be the sort, and to be in the vicinity of other atoms of a sort, to produce the kind of thing they did produce. There is no further reason, no intention or purpose behind it.*

> Nothing occurs at random, but everything occurs for a reason and by necessity. (DK 67 B 2, *IEGP*, 212)

By this, Democritus means that events don't just happen, but neither do they occur in order to reach some goal or because they were planned or designed to happen that way. If we are asked why so and so occurred, the proper answer will cite previously existing material causes. In one sense, this is the final destination of pre-Socratic speculation about nature. It begins by casting out the Homeric gods. It ends by casting out altogether intelligence and purpose from the governance of the world. Everything happens according to laws of motion that govern the wholly mechanical interactions of the atoms. In these happenings, mind has no place.

This account has—or seems to have—serious consequences for our view of human life. We normally think that we are pretty much in control of our lives, that we can make decisions to do one thing or another, go this way or that. It's up to us. If everything occurs "by necessity," however, as Democritus says, then each of these decisions is itself determined by mechanical laws that reach back to movements of atoms that long preceded our birth. It begins to look as if we are merely cogs in the gigantic machine of the world, no more really in control of our actions than the clouds are in control of (can choose) when it is going to rain. Supposing Democritus (or his modern followers) are right, what happens to our conviction that we have a free will? Democritus does not solve this problem, but he is the first to set out the parameters of the problem with some clarity.†

---

*Compare the nonpurposive character of evolutionary accounts of the origin of species with creationist accounts.

†Concerning free will, see the discussions by Epicurus (p. 201), the Stoics (pp. 206–207), Augustine (pp. 248–251), Descartes (*Meditation IV*), Hume (pp. 412–415), Kant (pp. 444–447), Hegel (pp. 479–480), Nietzsche (pp. 551–552), and de Beauvoir (pp. 686, 691).

The Soul

If mind or intelligence cannot function as an explanation of the world-order, it is nonetheless obvious that it plays a role in human life. Democritus owes us an explanation of human intelligence that is compatible with his basic principles. His speculations are interesting and suggestive, though still quite crude. This problem is one we cannot claim to have solved completely even in our own day.

Atomistic accounts of soul and mind must, of course, be compatible with a general materialist view of reality: What exist are atoms and the void. According to Democritus, the soul is composed of exceedingly fine and spherical atoms; in this way, soul interpenetrates the whole of the body. Democritus holds that

> spherical atoms move because it is their nature never to be still, and that as they move they draw the whole body along with them, and set it in motion. (DK 68 A 104, *IEGP*, 222)

Soul-atoms are in this sense akin to fire-atoms, which are also small, spherical, and capable of penetrating solid bodies and (as Heraclitus has observed) are strikingly good examples of spontaneous motion. The soul or principle of life is, like everything else, *material*.

Living things, of course, have certain capacities that nonliving things do not: They experience sensations (tastes, smells, sights, sounds, pains). Some, at least, are capable of thought, and humans seem to have a capacity to know. Can Democritus explain these capacities using his principles regarding atoms and the void?

Think first about sensations. There doesn't seem to be too much difficulty in explaining tastes. Sweet and sour, salt and bitter are just the results of differently shaped atoms in contact with the tongue. The sweet, Democritus says, consists of atoms that are "round and of a good size," the sour of "bulky, jagged, and many-angled" atoms, and so on (DK 68 A 129, *IEGP*, 200). These speculations are not grounded in anything like modern experimental method, but the kind of explanation is surely familiar to those who know something of modern chemistry.

Smells are explained along analogous lines, and sounds, too, are not difficult; Democritus explains them in terms of air being "broken up into bodies of like shape . . . rolled along with the fragments of the voice."[4] Vision is the sense most difficult to explain in terms of an atomistic view. Unlike touch, taste, and even hearing, it is a "distance receptor." With sight, it is as though we were able to reach out to the surfaces of things at some distance from us without any material means of doing so. In this respect, the eye seems quite different from the hand or the tongue.

Democritus, however, holds that sight is not really different. Like the other senses, it works by contact with its objects, only in this case the contact is more indirect than usual. The bodies made up of combined atoms are constantly giving off "images" of themselves, he tells us. These images are themselves material, composed of exceptionally fine atoms. These "effluences" strike the eye and stamp their shape in the soft and moist matter of the eye, whereupon it is registered in the smooth and round atoms of soul present throughout the body.

This kind of explanation is regarded by most of his Greek successors as very strange. Aristotle even calls it a great absurdity. It may not strike us as absurd. Indeed, it seems somewhere near the truth.

It does have a paradoxical consequence, though, which Democritus recognizes and is willing to accept. It means that our senses *do not give us direct and certain knowledge of the world*. If you think a moment, you will see that this is indeed an implication of his view. Our experience of vision is a product, in the mathematical sense. It is the outcome of a complex set of interactions between the object seen, the intervening medium, and our sensory apparatus. Exactly what our experience is when we look at a distant mountain is not a simple function of the characteristics of the mountain. That experience depends also on whether the air is clear or foggy, clean or polluted. It depends on whether it is dawn, dusk, or noon. Moreover, what we experience depends on what kinds and proportions of rods and cones we have in our eyes, on complex sending mechanisms in the optic nerve, and the condition of the visual center in the brain.

Democritus cannot express his point in these contemporary terms, of course. Nonetheless, this is exactly his point. Similar explanations also apply to the other senses. It was recognized in ancient times that honey, for example, can taste sweet to a healthy person and bitter to a sick one. Clearly, the difference depends on the state of the receptor organs. What is the character of the honey itself? Is it both sweet and bitter? That seems impossible. Democritus draws the conclusion that it is neither. Sweetness and bitterness, hot and cold, red and blue exist only in us, not in nature.

> Sweet exists by convention, bitter by convention, color by convention; but in reality atoms and the void alone exist. (DK 68 B 9, *IEGP*, 202)

To say that something exists by **convention** is to say that its existence depends upon us.* In nature alone, it is not to be found. If our sense experience is conventional in this sense, then we cannot rely on it to tell us what the world is really like. In a way, Parmenides was right after all!†

> It is necessary to realize that by this principle man is cut off from the real. (DK 68 B 6, *IEGP*, 203)

We are "cut off from the real" because whatever impact the real has on us is in part a product of our own condition. This is true not only of the sick person but also of the well one. The sweetness of the honey to the well person depends on sensory receptors just as much as the bitterness to the sick one. Neither has a direct and unmediated avenue to what honey really is.

Later philosophers exploit these considerations in skeptical directions, doubting that we can have any reliable knowledge of the world at all. For Democritus, however, they do not lead to utter skepticism:

> There are two forms of knowledge: one legitimate, one bastard. To the bastard sort belong all the following: sight, hearing, smell, taste, touch. The legitimate is quite distinct from this. When the bastard form cannot see more minutely, nor hear

---

*For a fuller discussion of the distinction between nature and convention, see "*Physis* and *Nomos*" in Chapter 3.
†See pp. 25–27.

nor smell nor taste nor perceive through the touch, then another, finer form must be employed. (DK 68 B 11, *IEGP*, 203–204)

He seems to be telling us that the senses can take us only so far, because they have a "bastard" parentage (that is, they are the products of both the objects perceived and the perceiving organs). But there is "another, finer" and "legitimate" form of knowledge available to the soul. This knowledge is no doubt based on reasoning. Its product is the knowledge that what really exist are atoms and the void. At this point, we would like reasoning itself to be explained in terms of the atomistic view, as the senses have been explained. No such explanation is offered. This is not surprising; indeed, many think that a satisfactory account of reasoning on these materialistic principles is only now, after the invention of the computer, beginning to be constructed—but that, of course, is reaching far ahead of our story.*

How to Live

Democritus wrote extensively on the question of the best life for a human being, but only fragments remain. Many of them are memorable, however, and I simply list without comment a number of his most lively aphorisms.

- Disease occurs in a household, or in a life, just as it does in a body. (DK 68 B 288, *IEGP*, 221)

- Medicine cures the diseases of the body; wisdom, on the other hand, relieves the soul of its sufferings. (DK 68 B 31, *IEGP*, 222)

- The needy animal knows how much it needs; but the needy man does not. (DK 68 B 198, *IEGP*, 223)

- It is hard to fight with desire; but to overcome it is the mark of a rational man. (DK 68 B 236, *IEGP*, 225)

- Moderation increases enjoyment, and makes pleasure even greater. (DK 68 B 211, *IEGP*, 223)

- It is childish, not manly, to have immoderate desires. (DK 68 B 70, *IEGP*, 225)

- The good things of life are produced by learning with hard work; the bad are reaped of their own accord, without hard work. (DK 68 B 182, *IEGP*, 226)

- The brave man is he who overcomes not only his enemies but his pleasures. There are some men who are masters of cities but slaves to women. (DK 68 B 214, *IEGP*, 228)

- In cattle excellence is displayed in strength of body; but in men it lies in strength of character. (DK 68 B 57, *IEGP*, 230)

- I would rather discover a single cause than become king of the Persians. (DK 68 B 118, *IEGP*, 229)

Many of the themes expressed here should be familiar by now. We will see them worked out more systematically in later Greek philosophy, particularly by Plato and Aristotle.

1. State as clearly as you can the argument by which the atomists defeat Parmenides and reconcile the one and the many.
2. How would atomists explain the difference between, say, chalk and cheese? How do they explain coming into being and passing away again?
3. On atomistic principles, what happens to the notion of a cosmic intelligence?
4. What is the atomist's account of soul?
5. What does it mean to say that sweet and bitter exist "by convention"?
6. Why does Democritus say that our senses cut us off from the real? Why are we not absolutely cut off?
7. What problem does atomism pose for the idea that we have a free will?

For Further Thought

1. Twentieth-century philosopher of science Karl Popper quotes Xenophanes approvingly and asserts that the development of thought we can trace in the pre-Socratics exemplifies perfectly the basic structure of scientific thinking. He calls it the "rational critical" method and says it works through a

---

*But take a look at "The Matter of Minds" in Chapter 26, pp. 736–742.

sequence of bold conjectures and incisive refutations. Can you identify such moves in the thinking of the philosophers we have studied so far? (See Popper's *Conjectures and Refutations: The Growth of Scientific Knowledge* [New York: Harper and Row, 1968]).

2. What sort of defense could you mount against the attacks on common sense put forth by rationalists such as Parmenides and Zeno? Is there something you could do to show that the world of our sense experience is, after all, the real world?

3. Here is an argument to prove that a ham sandwich is better than perfect happiness: (1) A ham sandwich is better than nothing; (2) nothing is better than perfect happiness; therefore (3) a ham sandwich is better than perfect happiness. Will untangling this fallacy throw light on the atomists' critique of Parmenides?

4. If you know something about the physiology of the central nervous system, try to determine whether modern accounts of that system also "cut us off from the real."

Notes

1. Quotations from the pre-Socratic philosophers are in the translation by John Manley Robinson, *An Introduction to Early Greek Philosophy* (Boston: Houghton Mifflin, 1968). They are cited by the standard Diels/Kranz number, followed by *IEGP* and the page number in Robinson.

2. Biblical quotations in this text are taken from the Revised Standard Version, 1946/1971, National Council of Churches.

3. If you would like to pursue these details, the books by Robinson (see Note 1) and Ring (cited in a footnote at the beginning of this chapter) are excellent sources. A more extensive treatment with original Greek texts is found in G. S. Kirk and J. E. Raven, *The Presocratic Philosophers* (Cambridge, England: Cambridge University Press, 1957).

4. Quoted in G. S. Kirk and J. E. Raven, *The Presocratic Philosophers* (Cambridge: Cambridge University Press, 1960), 423.

3

THE SOPHISTS

Rhetoric and Relativism in Athens

When we think of "the glory that was Greece," we think inevitably of Athens (see Map 1). To this point, however, we have mentioned Athens scarcely at all. Greek culture, as we have seen, ranged from the southern parts of Italy and Sicily in the west to the Ionian settlements on the shores of Asia Minor and to Thrace in the north. Important contributions to the great conversation about the nature of the world and the place of human beings in it were made from all those areas. In the fifth and fourth centuries B.C., however, Greek culture came more and more to center in one city: Athens. The story of how this came about is a fascinating tale related for us by the Greek historian Herodotus and pieced together by modern writers from his history and many other sources. For our purposes, we need to understand several key elements of the rise of Athens. What kind of city was Athens in that time, what was it like to live in Athens, and how was it different from other cities?[1]

Although we have used the terms "Greece" and "Greek culture," there was at the beginning of the fifth century (around 500 B.C.) nothing like a uni-fied Greek state. People lived in or owed allegiance to a large number of city-states. A city-state (a *polis*) was an area—an island, perhaps, or an arable plain with natural boundaries of mountains and the sea—in which one city was dominant. The city was usually fortified and offered protection to the farmers, who sometimes lived within the walls and sometimes outside in smaller villages. The prominent city-states of that time were Thebes, Corinth, Argos, Sparta, and Athens, but there were many more. Among these city-states there were often rivalries, quarrels, shifting alliances, and wars.

Two things happened around the beginning of the fifth century that contributed to the preeminence of Athens among the city-states: the beginnings of democracy in government and the Persian wars.

Democracy

For nearly a century, ever since the reforms of Solon, the common people had had some voice in the government of Athens. According to the constitution of Solon, the powers of government were divided among several bodies. Among them were the Council, which was composed of "the best men" (aristocrats), and the Assembly, to which all free men belonged. Important decisions were made by the Council, but the Assembly could veto measures that were excessively unpopular. This structure was modified over the years, but it took on the character of an ideal; again and again reforms of various kinds were justified as being a return to the constitution of Solon.*

During a large part of the sixth century, Athens was ruled by "tyrants." This word did not originally have all the negative connotations it now has. It simply meant "boss" or "chief" and was applied to a ruler who was not a hereditary king but had seized power some other way. Some of the tyrants of Athens more or less respected Solon's constitution, but at least one tyrant was killed to restore the democracy.

In 508 B.C., a quarrel arose concerning citizenship for a large influx of immigrants to the city. The aristocrats, fearful for their power, tried to purge the citizenship rolls, but the Assembly passed a proposal to extend citizenship to many of the new residents. After a three-day siege of the Acropolis by the people, the aristocrats—who had been backed by a king of Sparta and his soldiers—capitulated. Citizenship was broadened, though not so far as to include women and slaves, and thereafter the citizens had control of major decisions. It was to be so for the next hundred years and, with a few exceptions, for some time after that.

The Persian Wars

The Greek colonies on the shores of Asia Minor were always in a precarious state. Their language and heritage bound them to the Greek mainland, but their geographical situation made them of natural interest to whatever power was dominant to the east. These Greek cities paid taxes to the rising Persian power, but in 499 B.C. they rebelled. Athens sent twenty ships to aid these Greeks, and in the fighting they burnt Sardis, one of the principal Persian cities. The rebellion was put down by Persia, and anxiety began to increase among mainland Greeks. The Persians now had reason to take revenge and, having reasserted their control over the Asian Greek cities, were free to concentrate on the mainland.*

In 490 B.C., the Persians came in force across the Aegean, conquered a coastal island, and landed at Marathon. In a famous battle on the plain twenty-six miles north and east of Athens, the Greeks under Miltiades, an Ionian general, defeated the Persians, killing 6,400 of them. The victory had an exhilarating effect on the democratic city of Athens, which had supplied most of the soldiers for the battle.

It was clear to the Athenians, however, that the Persians were not about to be stopped by the loss of one battle, no matter how decisive at the time. Herodotus represents the Persian monarch Xerxes, who had recently succeeded his father Darius, as saying:

> I will bridge the Hellespont [see Map 1] and march an army through Europe into Greece, and punish the Athenians for the outrage they committed upon my father and upon us. As you saw, Darius himself was making his preparations for war against these men; but death prevented him from carrying out his purpose. I therefore on his behalf, and for the benefit of all my subjects, will not rest until I have taken Athens and burnt it to the ground, in revenge for the injury which the Athenians without provocation once did to me and my father [the burning of Sardis]. . . . If we crush the Athenians and their neighbours in the Peloponnese, we shall so extend the empire of Persia that its boundaries will be God's own sky, so that the sun will not look down upon any land beyond the boundaries of what is ours. (*Histories* 7.8)[2]

There was much debate in Athens about how to meet the danger. One party favored land-based defenses, citing the former victory at Marathon. The other party, led by Themistocles, favored building

---

*For democracy in Athens, see http://en.wikipedia.org/wiki/Athenian_democracy.

*For Persian Wars, see http://lilt.ilstu.edu/drjclassics/lectures/history/PersianWars/persianwars.shtm.

up the navy and a defense by sea. After much infighting, the Athenians decided on a large increase in fighting ships of the latest style — and just in time. In the year 480 B.C., Xerxes, lashing ships together to make a bridge, led an army of perhaps 200,000 men across the Hellespont (which separates Asia from Europe), brought Thrace under submission, and began to advance south toward Athens. Advice was sought, in time-honored fashion, from the Oracle at Delphi (see Map 1). The oracle was not favorable. A second plea brought this response:

> That the wooden wall only shall not fall, but help you and your children. (*Histories* 7.141)

How should this opaque answer be interpreted? Some believed that wooden walls on the hill of the Acropolis would withstand the aggressor. Themistocles argued that the "wooden wall" referred to the ships that had been built and that they must abandon Athens and try to defeat the Persians at sea. Most of the Athenians followed Themistocles, though some did not.

First, however, it was necessary to stop the advance of the Persian army. Many saw it as a threat against Greece as a whole, not just against Athens. A force led by Spartan soldiers under the Spartan king Leonidas met the Persians at Thermopylae, eighty miles northwest of Athens (see Map 1). Greatly outnumbered, the Greeks fought valiantly, inflicting many deaths, but were defeated. Leonidas was killed.

The Persians took Athens, overwhelmed the defenders on the Acropolis, and burned the temples. However, the main Athenian forces, in ships off the nearby island of Salamis, were still to be dealt with. On a day splendid in Greek history, Xerxes sat on a mountain above the bay of Salamis (see Map 1) and saw the Greeks tear apart his navy. Themistocles' strategy had worked. The next spring (479 B.C.), however, the Persians occupied Athens again. It took a great victory by the combined Athenian and Spartan armies at Plataea to expel the Persians for good.

These victories had several results. Athens, which had borne the brunt of the defense of Greece, became preeminent among the city-states. The city had displayed its courage and prowess for all to see and took the lead in forming a league for the future defense of the Greek lands. In time, the league turned into an Athenian empire. Other states paid tribute to Athens, which saw to their protection, and Athens became a great sea power.

Athens also became very wealthy. It was not only the tribute from the allies, although that was significant. With their control of the sea, Athenians engaged in trading far and wide. A large and wealthy merchant class grew up, and Athens became the center of Greek cultural life. Under Pericles, the most influential leader of the democratic city in the middle of the fifth century B.C., the city built the magnificent temples on the Acropolis. Pericles was influential in encouraging Greek art and sculpture, supported the new learning, and was a close associate of certain philosophers. A speech of his, commemorating fallen soldiers in the first year of the tragic war with Sparta, gives a sense of what it meant to Athenians to be living in Athens at that time. Only part of it, as represented for us by the historian Thucydides, is quoted here. (Suggestion: Read it aloud.)

> Let me say that our system of government does not copy the institutions of our neighbours. It is more a case of our being a model to others, than of our imitating anyone else. Our constitution is called a democracy because power is in the hands not of a minority but of the whole people. When it is a question of settling private disputes, everyone is equal before the law; when it is a question of putting one person before another in positions of public responsibility, what counts is not membership of a particular class, but the actual ability which the man possesses. No one, so long as he has it in him to be of service to the state, is kept in political obscurity because of poverty. And, just as our political life is free and open, so is our day-to-day life in our relations with each other. We do not get into a state with our next-door neighbour if he enjoys himself in his own way, nor do we give him the kind of black looks which, though they do no real harm, still do hurt people's feelings. We are free and tolerant in our private lives; but in public affairs we keep to the law. This is because it commands our deep respect.
>
> We give our obedience to those whom we put in positions of authority, and we obey the laws

themselves, especially those which are for the protection of the oppressed, and those unwritten laws which it is an acknowledged shame to break.

And here is another point. When our work is over, we are in a position to enjoy all kinds of recreation for our spirits. There are various kinds of contests and sacrifices regularly throughout the year; in our own homes we find a beauty and a good taste which delight us every day and which drive away our cares. Then the greatness of our city brings it about that all the good things from all over the world flow in to us, so that to us it seems just as natural to enjoy foreign goods as our own local products.

Then there is a great difference between us and our opponents in our attitude towards military security. Here are some examples: Our city is open to the world, and we have no periodical deportations in order to prevent people observing or finding out secrets which might be of military advantage to the enemy. This is because we rely, not on secret weapons, but on our own real courage and loyalty. . . .

Our love of what is beautiful does not lead to extravagance; our love of the things of the mind does not make us soft. We regard wealth as something to be properly used, rather than as something to boast about. As for poverty, no one need be ashamed to admit it: the real shame is in not taking practical measures to escape from it. Here each individual is interested not only in his own affairs but in the affairs of the state as well. . . . We do not say that a man who takes no interest in politics is a man who minds his own business; we say that he has no business here at all. . . .

Again, in questions of general good feeling there is a great contrast between us and most other people. We make friends by doing good to others, not by receiving good from them. . . . We are unique in this. When we do kindnesses to others, we do not do them out of any calculations of profit or loss: we do them without afterthought, relying on our free liberality. Taking everything together then, I declare that our city is an education to Greece, and I declare that in my opinion each single one of our citizens, in all the manifold aspects of life, is able to show himself the rightful lord and owner of his own person, and do this, moreover, with exceptional grace and exceptional versatility. . . . Mighty indeed are the marks and monuments of our empire which we have left.

Future ages will wonder at us, as the present age wonders at us now. We do not need the praises of a Homer, or of anyone else whose words may delight us for the moment, but whose estimation of facts will fall short of what is really true. For our adventurous spirit has forced an entry into every sea and into every land; and everywhere we have left behind us everlasting memorials of good done to our friends or suffering inflicted on our enemies.[3]

Such was the spirit of the Golden Age of classical Athens: proud, confident, serenely convinced that the city was "an education to Greece"—and not without reason. Twenty-five hundred years later, we still are moved by their tragedies, laugh at their comedies, admire their sculpture, are awed by their architecture, revere their democracy, and study their philosophers.

1. How did Athens come to preeminence among Greek cities?
2. For what qualities does Pericles praise Athens?

The Sophists

The social situation in fifth-century B.C. Athens called for innovations in education. The "best men" in the old sense no longer commanded a natural leadership. What counted was actual ability, as Pericles said, so men sought to develop their abilities. Aristocratic education centering on Homer was no longer entirely adequate. Most citizens received an elementary education that made them literate and gave them basic skills. If a father wanted his son to succeed in democratic Athens, however, more was needed.

To supply this need, there arose a class of teachers offering what we can call higher education. Many of these teachers were itinerant, moving from city to city as the call for their services waxed and waned. They were professionals who charged for their instruction. The best of them became quite wealthy, because there was a substantial demand for their services. We can get a sense of what they claimed to provide for their students and of the eagerness with which they were sought out from the beginning of Plato's dialogue *Protagoras*. As we'll see, Protagoras was one of the greatest of these teachers.* Socrates is the speaker.

> Last night, just before daybreak, Hippocrates, the son of Apollodorus and brother of Phason, began knocking very loudly on the door with his stick, and when someone opened it he came straight in in a great hurry, calling out loudly, "Socrates, are you awake or asleep?" I recognized his voice and said, "It's Hippocrates; no bad news, I hope?" "Nothing but good news," he said. "Splendid," I said; "what is it, then? What brings you here so early?" He came and stood beside me; "Protagoras has come," he said. "He came the day before yesterday," I said; "have you only just heard?" "Yes, indeed," he said; "yesterday evening. . . . Late as it was, I immediately got up to come and tell you, but then I realized that it was far too late at night; but as soon as I had had a sleep and got rid of my tiredness, I got up straight away and came over here, as you see."
>
> I knew him to be a spirited and excitable character, so I said, "What's all this to you? Protagoras hasn't done you any wrong, has he?"
>
> He laughed. "By heavens, he has, Socrates. He is the only man who is wise, but he doesn't make me wise too."
>
> "Oh yes, he will," I said; "If you give him money and use a little persuasion, he'll make you wise as well."
>
> "I wish to God," he said, "that that was all there was to it. I'd use every penny of my own, and of my friends too. But it's just that that I've come to you about now, so that you can put in a word for me with him. First of all, I'm too young, and then I've never seen Protagoras." (*Protagoras* 310a–e)[4]

Note the eagerness expressed by Hippocrates— and for education, too! What could this education be that excited such desire? What did the **Sophists,** as these teachers were called, offer?

While they wait for day to dawn, Socrates tries in his questioning fashion to see whether Hippocrates really knows what he is getting into. Not surprisingly, it turns out that he doesn't. Undaunted, they set off and go to the home where Protagoras is staying. After some difficulty (the servant at the door is sick of Sophists and slams the door in their faces), they meet Protagoras, who is in the company of a number of other young men and fellow Sophists. Socrates makes his request:

> Hippocrates here is anxious to become your pupil; so he says that he would be glad to know what benefit he will derive from associating with you. (*Protagoras* 318a)

Protagoras answers,

> Young man, . . . if you associate with me, this is the benefit you will gain: the very day you become my pupil you will go home a better man, and the same the next day; and every day you will continue to make progress. (*Protagoras* 318a)

Socrates, of course, is not satisfied with this answer. If Hippocrates were to associate with a famous painter, then each day his painting might improve. If he studied with a flutist, his flute playing would get better. But in what respect, exactly, will associating with Protagoras make Hippocrates "a better man"?

> You have put a good question, Socrates, and I like answering people who do that. . . . What I teach is the proper management of one's own affairs, how best to run one's household, and the management of public affairs, how to make the most effective contribution to the affairs of the city both by word and action. (*Protagoras* 318d–319a)

Here we have the key to the excitement of Hippocrates and to the demand for this instruction from the rising middle class of Athens. The Sophists claim to be able to teach the things that foster success, both personal and political, in this democratic city. Many of them also teach specialized subjects such as astronomy, geometry, arithmetic, and music. Nearly all are committed to the new learning developed by the nature philosophers. They are self-consciously "modern," believing they represent progress and enlightenment as opposed to ignorance and superstition.

---

*Protagoras was paid in the following way. Before the instruction he and his pupil would go to the temple; there the student would vow to pay, when the course was finished, whatever he then thought Protagoras' instruction was worth. It is said that when he died, Protagoras was wealthier than five Phidiases. (Phidias was the most famous sculptor in Athens.)

However, it is their claim to teach "excellence" or "virtue" (the Greek word *arete* can be translated either way) both in mastering one's own affairs and in providing leadership in the city that makes them popular.* The excellences they claim to teach are the skills, abilities, and traits of character that make one competent, successful, admired, and perhaps even wealthy.

The term "sophist" has rather negative connotations for us. A *sophism,* for instance, is a fallacious argument that looks good but isn't, and *sophistry* is verbally pulling the wool over someone's eyes. The term did not always have such connotations. "Sophist" comes from the Greek *sophos,* meaning wise. The term was applied in the fifth century to many earlier wise men, including Homer and Hesiod. Undoubtedly, the best of the Sophists, such as Protagoras, were neither charlatans nor fools. In connection with their teaching the young, they also made important contributions to the great conversation. They were philosophers who had to be taken seriously; for this reason, they are of interest to us.

Rhetoric

All of the Sophists taught **rhetoric,** the principles and practice of persuasive speaking. Some of the Sophists, Gorgias for example, claimed to teach nothing but that. Clearly, in democratic Athens this art would be very valuable. Suppose, for instance, that you are brought into court by a neighbor. If you hem and haw, utter only irrelevancies, and cannot present the evidence on your side in a coherent and persuasive way, you are likely to lose whether you are guilty or not. Or suppose you feel strongly about some issue that affects the welfare of the city; only if you can stand up in the Assembly of citizens

and speak persuasively will you have any influence. You must be able to present your case, marshal your arguments, and appeal to the feelings of the audience. This is the art the Sophists developed and taught.

In one of his dialogues, Plato represents Gorgias as claiming to teach

> the ability to use the spoken word to persuade the jurors in the courts, the members of the Council, the citizens attending the Assembly—in short, to win over any and every form of public meeting. (*Gorgias* 452e) [5]

> A rhetorician is capable of speaking effectively against all comers, whatever the issue, and can consequently be more persuasive in front of crowds about—to cut a long story short—anything he likes. (*Gorgias* 457b)

We need to understand what rhetoric means to the Sophists because its philosophical consequences are deep. The central idea is that by using the principles of persuasive speaking, one can make a case for any position at all. It follows that if there are, as we often say these days, two sides to every issue, someone skilled in rhetoric should be able to present a persuasive argument for each side. In fact, this idea was embodied in one of the main teaching tools of the Sophists.

A student was encouraged to construct and present arguments on both sides of some controversial issue. He was not judged to be proficient until he could present a case as persuasive on one side as on the other. This method, presumably, was designed to equip a student for any eventuality; one never knew on what side of some future issue one's interests would lie.

A humorous story about Protagoras and one of his students illustrates this method. Protagoras agreed to teach a young man how to conduct cases in the courts. Because the young man was poor, it was agreed that he would not have to pay his teacher until he won his first case. Some time elapsed after the course of instruction was over, and the student did not enter into any cases. Finally Protagoras himself brought the student to court, prosecuting him for payment. The student argued thus: If I win this case, I shall not have to pay Protagoras, according to

---

*The Greek *arete* (ahr-e-tay) can apply to horses and knives, to flutists and cobblers, as well as to human beings as such. It has to do with the excellence of something when it does well what it is supposed to do. So it goes beyond the sphere of morality but includes it. Though usually translated "virtue," this English word is really too narrow. I will often use the broader term "excellence," and especially "human excellence," when what is in question is not someone's excellence as a teacher or sailor but as a human being.

the judgment of the court; if I lose this case, I will not yet have won my first case, and so I will not have to pay Protagoras according to the terms of our agreement; since I will either win or lose, I shall not have to pay the sum. Protagoras, not to be outdone by his student, argued as follows: If he loses this case, then by the judgment of the court he must pay me; if he wins it, he will have won his first case and therefore will have to pay me; so, in either case, he will have to pay me.

The story is probably apocryphal, and the arguments may be "sophistical" in the bad sense, but it is not easy to see what has gone wrong. The example is not far from the flavor of much of the Sophists' teaching.

The philosophical interest of this technique can be seen if we recall certain meanings of the term *logos,* which connotes speech, thought, argument, and discourse. What the Sophists were training their students to do was to present opposite *logoi.* There was the *logos* (what could be said) on one side, and there was the *logos* on the other. The presumption was that for every side of every issue a persuasive *logos* could be developed. Some Sophists seem to have written works consisting of just such opposed *logoi,* presumably as examples and practice pieces for their students.

In this connection, we must note a phrase that became notorious later on. It seems to have expressed a boast made by Protagoras and some of the other Sophists. They claimed to teach others *how to make the weaker argument into the stronger.* Suppose you are in court with what looks like a very weak case. The principles of rhetoric, if cleverly applied, could turn your argument into the stronger one— in the sense that it would be victorious.

Such a technique has profoundly skeptical implications. Think back to Heraclitus.* He believes, or perhaps simply takes for granted, that there is one *logos* uniting the many changing things of the world into one world-order. This *logos* is "common to all." Although many deviate from the *logos,* it is there and available to everyone. The wise are those who "listen to the *logos*" and order their own lives in

accord with the pattern of the world-order. Think of Parmenides, who acknowledges that there is such a thing as the way of opinion but holds that it is quite distinct from the way of truth, in which "thought and being are the same."*

The practice of the Sophists seems to show that thought and being are *not* the same. Thought and being fall apart; there is no necessary correlation at all. No matter what the reality is, thought can represent it or misrepresent it with equal ease. If a *logos* that will carry conviction can be constructed on any side of any issue, how is one to tell when one is in accord with Heraclitus' *logos* and when one is not? How is one to discriminate the truth from mere opinion?

The Sophists' answer is that one cannot. All we have—and all we ever can have—are opinions. Parmenides writes of two ways, the way of truth and the way of opinion. The former represents the way things *are,* whereas the latter sets forth the way things *appear.* The practice of rhetoric raises doubts about our ability to discern reality. It suggests that human beings are confined to appearances; truth is beyond us. For human beings, things are as they seem to be. No more can be said.

So the Sophists agree with Democritus that we are "cut off from the real" by the conventional nature of our sense experience.† But unlike Democritus, they hold that there is no other avenue to the truth. Democritus thinks that intelligence or mind can penetrate where the senses fail us; he holds that reasoning can reveal what the eyes and ears cannot— that reality is composed of atoms and the void. However, if the Sophists are right in their conviction that an equally persuasive *logos* can be constructed on every side of every issue, then the appeal to reasoning cannot be sustained. For one can reason equally well for and against atoms and the void—or, indeed, anything else!

As you can see, the Sophists tend to be skeptical about their predecessors' claims to reveal the truth, skeptical of human ability to come to know truth at all. You should be able to see how this

---

*See especially p. 22.

*See pp. 25–26.
†See p. 34.

skepticism is intimately related to the way they conceive and teach rhetoric. If rhetoric can make a convincing case for absolutely anything, then what can one know?

Such skepticism does not reduce them to silence, however. A person can still talk intelligibly about how things seem, even if not about how they really are. No doubt many of the theories of the nature philosophers are understood in just this way; they are plausible stories that represent the way the world seems to be. These stories represent probabilities at best, not the truth; but probabilities are the most that human beings can hope to attain. Without trying to penetrate to the core of reality, the Sophists are content with appearances. Without insisting on certainty, they are content with plausibility. Without knowledge, they are content with opinion.*

The skeptical attitude is displayed in a statement by Protagoras concerning the gods. He is reported to have said:

> Concerning the gods I am not in a position to know either that they are or that they are not, or what they are like in appearance; for there are many things that are preventing knowledge, the obscurity of the matter and the brevity of human life. (DK 80 B 4, *IEGP,* 269)[6]

This statement seems to have been the basis for an accusation that Protagoras was an atheist. We know that he was at one time banished from Athens and that certain of his books were burned; it is likely that such statements were among those that aroused the anger of the citizens. (We will see a parallel in the case of Socrates.) Protagoras does not, however, deny the existence of the gods. He says that in light of the difficulty of the question and because of the brevity of human life, we are prevented from knowing about the gods. His view is not that of the atheist, then, but that of the agnostic. The only reasonable thing to do, he says, is to suspend judgment on this issue. This is the view of the skeptic.

1. What do the Sophists claim to teach? How do they understand *arete?*
2. What is rhetoric? How was it taught?
3. How does the concept of a *logos* come into Sophist teaching?

Relativism

The Sophists' point of view is best summed up in a famous saying by Protagoras. It is the first sentence of a book titled *On Truth.* Unfortunately, it is the only part of the book that has come down to us.

> Of all things the measure is man: of existing things, that they exist; of non-existing things, that they do not exist. (DK 80 B 1, *IEGP,* 245)

A "measure" is a standard or criterion to appeal to when deciding what to believe. Protagoras' statement that man is the measure of all things means that there is no criterion, standard, or mark by which to judge, except ourselves. We cannot jump outside our skins to see how things look independently of how they appear to us. *As they appear to us, so are they.*

Clearly, he means, in the first instance at least, that things are as they appear to the individual. A common example is the wind. Suppose to one person the wind feels cold and to another it feels warm. Can we ask whether the wind is cold or warm in itself—apart from how it seems? How could that be settled? Protagoras draws the conclusion that this question has no answer. If the wind seems cold to the first one, then to that person it *is* cold; and if it seems warm to the second, then it *is* warm—to that person. About the warmth or coldness of the wind, no more than this can be said. The first person cannot correct the second, and the second cannot correct the first. Each is the final judge of how the wind seems. Since it is not possible to get beyond such seemings, each individual is the final judge of how things *are* (to that individual, of course).

This doctrine is the heart of a viewpoint known as **relativism.** Here is the first appearance of one of the focal points of this book. From this point on,

---

*For a contemporary version of this viewpoint, see the discussion of Richard Rorty's views, pp. 714–716.

we see the major figures in our tradition struggling with the problems raised by relativism and the skepticism about our knowledge that attends it. Most of them oppose it. Some are willing to make certain concessions to it. But it has never been banished for long, and in one way or another it reappears throughout our history to pose its disturbing questions. In our own century, many have adopted some form of it. It is the merit of the Sophists that they set out the question in the clearest of terms and force us to come to grips with it.

We have now its essence. We need yet to understand what recommends it and what its implications are.

One implication that must have been obvious is that well-meaning citizens, not clearly prejudiced by self-interest, could disagree about the course the city should take. Another is that a well-wrought and persuasively delivered speech on any side of an issue could in fact convince a court or assembly of citizens. If you put these two observations together, it is not hard to draw the conclusion that the *best logos* about an issue is simply the one that does the best job of convincing. How can one judge which of two opposing *logoi* is the best, if not in terms of success? (An independent "logic," in terms of which one might judge that a certain persuasive device was "fallacious," had not yet been developed.) However, if there is no way to tell which *logos* is best except by observing which one *seems* best, then knowledge cannot be distinguished from opinion.* The best opinion is simply that which is generally accepted. But that means it may differ from culture to culture, from time to time, and even from individual to individual. There is no truth independent of what seems to be true. What seems true to one person or at one time may not seem true to another person or at another time. The best *logos* (what passes for truth) is relative to the individual, the culture, or the time. These observations and arguments were surely among those that motivated the Sophists to adopt their relativism.

There was another factor. Greeks in general, and Athenians in particular, had expanded their horizons. They continued to distinguish, as Greeks always had done, between themselves and "barbarians," whom they took to be inferior to themselves. But the more they traveled and became acquainted with the customs and characters of other nations, the harder it became to dismiss them as stupid and uncivilized. This exposure to non-Greek ways of doing things exerted a pressure on thought. These ways came to be seen not as inferior but as just different. There is a famous example given by the historian Herodotus, who was himself a great traveler and observer.

> Everyone without exception believes his own native customs, and the religion he was brought up in, to be the best. . . . There is abundant evidence that this is the universal feeling about the ancient customs of one's country. One might recall, in particular, an anecdote of Darius. When he was king of Persia, he summoned the Greeks who happened to be present at his court, and asked them what they would take to eat the dead bodies of their fathers. They replied that they would not do it for any money in the world. Later, in the presence of the Greeks, and through an interpreter, so they could understand what was said, he asked some Indians, of the tribe called Callatiae, who do in fact eat their parents' dead bodies, what they would take to burn them. They uttered a cry of horror and forbade him to mention such a dreadful thing. One can see by this what custom can do, and Pindar, in my opinion, was right when he called it "king of all."[7]

Physis and *Nomos*

The Sophists developed this notion that custom was "king of all" in terms of a distinction between *physis* and *nomos*. The word **physis** is the term for what the nature philosophers were studying. It is usually translated as "nature" and means the characteristics of the world, or things in general, independent of what human beings impose on it. As you can see, it is the word from which our "physics" is derived.

Nomos is the word for custom or convention, for those things that are as they are because human

---

*See "Knowledge and Opinion" in Chapter 6 to see how Plato struggles against this view.

beings have decided they should be so. In America cars are driven on the right side of the road, in England on the left. Neither practice is "natural," or by *physis*. This is a clear example of convention. We drive on one side in America and on the other side in England simply because we have agreed to. In the case Herodotus refers to, it is not so clear that an explicit decision is responsible for how the Greeks and the Indians care for their dead. These are practices that probably go back into prehistory. Still, it is clear enough that neither practice is "by nature." Herodotus assigns the difference to custom, which is certainly *nomos,* for it is possible that, difficult as it might be, Greeks and Indians alike might take thought and change their practices. The mark of what is true by *physis* is that it is not up to us to decide, nor can we change the pattern if we want to. If by agreement we can change the order of certain things (for example, which side of the road to drive on), then these things exist by *nomos,* not by *physis.*

There is an important corollary. Let us talk in terms of "the way things are." The way things are may be due to *physis* or to *nomos.* If they are due to *physis,* then we cannot go against them. For instance, it is part of the way things are that taking an ounce of strychnine will, unless immediate remedies are taken, cause one to die. It is not possible to swallow an ounce of strychnine, take no remedy, and continue to live. The connection between taking strychnine and death is a matter of *physis.* It does not depend on our decisions.

It is also part of the way things are that poisoning another human being is punished in some way. Yet it is possible (and it has happened) that someone might poison another and not receive punishment. Perhaps the killer is never discovered, or perhaps his lawyer is particularly skilled in rhetoric. If the way things are can be evaded, provided one is lucky or clever enough, then those connections are established by *nomos* and not by *physis.* It is for this reason that in cases of *nomos* we are likely to talk in terms of what a person "ought" to do: what is "right" or "appropriate," or "good" to do. It is neither right nor appropriate to follow the laws of nature. With respect to them, we have no choice. But conventions, customs, or laws that exist by *nomos* have a "normative" character to them. They state what we

should do but may fail to do. It is possible to go against them. We should not, in England, drive on the right, but we can. Murderers should be punished, but they sometimes are not.

The distinction is an important one, and the credit for making it clearly must go to the Sophists. But how, you might ask, did they use it?

The question about the gods can be put clearly using this terminology. Do the gods exist by *physis* or by *nomos?* To answer that they exist by nature is to claim that their existence is quite independent of whatever humans believe about them. To say that the gods exist only by *nomos* amounts to saying that they are dependent on our belief; they have no reality independent of what we happen to believe about them. It is clear that the skeptical and relativistic nature of Sophist thought favors the latter alternative. Certain Sophists may have said that if it seems to you the gods exist, then they do exist— for you. But the agnosticism of Protagoras is probably more representative.

The distinction between *nomos* and *physis* is also applied to the virtues and, in particular, to justice. If a settled community like a city-state is to survive, then it is necessary that a certain degree of justice should prevail. Agreements must be kept, deceptions must be exceptions, and each individual must be able to count on others to keep up their end of things. So much is clear.* But is justice, which demands these things, something good by nature? Or is it merely a convention, foisted on individuals perhaps against their own best interest? Is justice a matter of *physis,* or is it entirely *nomos?* This question is important. It is extensively debated by the Sophists and, as we will see, by Plato and his successors.

It is clear what answer the Sophists must give to this question. They can look back to the institution of democracy, which is obviously a change made by human beings. They can see the process of laws being debated and set down. They observe decisions

---

*Justice in this context is clearly something more than the justice of Homeric heroes giving one another the honor due to each (see pp. 7–8). What is needed in settled city-states is more extensive than what is needed by warrior bands. Some notion of fair play or evenhandedness seems to be involved. The nature of justice is a perennial problem, and we will return to it.

being made and sometimes reversed again. Clearly, forms of government, laws, and customs are matters of *nomos.* They are made by and can be altered by human decisions.

From the Sophists' point of view, if you want to know what is right or just, consult the laws. Is it just to keep agreements made? Then the laws will say so. How much tax is owed? The laws will tell you. For matters not covered explicitly by law, you must look to the customs of the people. Where else can one look? Just as there is no sense in asking whether the wind in itself is either cold or warm (apart from the way it seems to those who feel it), so is there no sense in asking whether a given law is really just. If it seems just to the people of Athens, say, then it is just (for the Athenians).

For clarity's sake, let's call this sense of justice conventional justice. Conventional justice is defined as whatever the conventions (the *nomoi*) of a given society lay down as just.

We can contrast with this the idea of natural justice. Heraclitus, for instance, holds that

all human laws are nourished by the one divine law. For it governs as far as it will, and is sufficient for all things, and outlasts them. (DK 22 B 114, *IEGP*, 103)

His idea is that human laws do not have their justification in themselves. They are "nourished," or get their sustenance, from a "divine law." This divine law, of course, is "common to all," the one *logos,* which is the same as the world-order. So human laws are not self-sufficient, in Heraclitus' view. Because people are often "at variance" with the *logos,* furthermore, we can infer that human law, too, may diverge from the *logos.* It makes sense for Heraclitus to contrast conventional justice with real or natural justice. He believes not only that there is a court of appeal from a possibly unjust human law, but also that human beings can know what divine law requires.

An example of such an appeal is found in Sophocles' play *Antigone.* Following a civil war, Creon, king of Thebes, proclaims that the body of Polyneices, leader of the opposition, remain unburied. This was, in Greek tradition, a very bad thing; only if one's body was buried could the spirit depart for

Hades. Polyneices' sister, Antigone, defies the decree and covers the body with dirt. Before the king she acknowledges that she knew of the king's order and defends her action in these words.

It was not Zeus who published this decree,
Nor have the Powers who rule among the dead
Imposed such laws as this upon mankind;
Nor could I think that a decree of yours—
A man—could override the laws of Heaven
Unwritten and unchanging. Not of today
Or yesterday is their authority;
They are eternal; no man saw their birth.
Was I to stand before the gods' tribunal
For disobeying them, because I feared
A man?[8]

Both Heraclitus and Antigone suggest that beyond conventional justice there is another justice. If the laws established by convention violate these higher laws, it may be permissible to violate the conventions.* For the Sophists, however, no such appeal is possible. One might not like a law and therefore work to change it, but there is no appeal to another kind of law to justify its violation. Their skepticism about any reality beyond appearances and their consequent relativism rule out any such appeal.

A certain conservatism seems to be a consequence of this way of looking at justice. Protagoras, for instance, in promising to make Hippocrates a "better man," one able to succeed in Athenian society, would scarcely teach him that Athens is profoundly mistaken in her ideas of justice. He certainly would not turn him into a rebel and malcontent, or even into a reformer. That is no way to attain the admiration of one's fellow citizens; that is the way to earn their hostility and hatred. So it is likely that the Sophists taught their students to adapt to whatever society they found.

Some of the Sophists, though, draw different conclusions. They agree with Heraclitus that there is a natural justice, but they disagree completely about its content. Natural justice, they hold, is not

---

*Note that we have here a justification for civil disobedience. A more recent example is Martin Luther King, Jr.'s, 1963 "Letter from Birmingham Jail."

the "nourisher" of conventional justice, but its enemy. A Sophist named Antiphon writes,

> Life and death are the concern of nature, and living
> creatures live by what is advantageous to them and
> die from what is not advantageous; and the advan-
> tages which accrue from law are chains upon na-
> ture, whereas those which accrue from nature are
> free. (DK 87 B 44, *IEGP,* 251)

Antiphon is telling us that if we only observe, we
can see that a *natural* law governs the affairs of
men and other living creatures: the law of self-
preservation. Like all laws, it carries a punishment
for those who violate it: death. Unlike conventional
laws, this punishment necessarily follows the violation of the law. That is what makes it a natural law
rather than a matter of convention. All creatures,
he says, follow this law by seeking what is "advantageous" to themselves.

In contrast to *this* natural law, the restraints
conventional justice places on human behavior are
"chains upon nature." Antiphon goes as far as to
claim that

> most of the things which are just by law [in the
> conventional sense] are hostile to nature. (DK 87
> B 44, *IEGP,* 251)

It is natural, then, and therefore right or just (in
the sense of *physis*) to pursue what is advantageous.
Some of the time your advantage may coincide with
the laws of the city. But because there is a tension
between conventional law and your advantage, and
because seeking your advantage is in accord with a
natural law, Antiphon gives us this remarkable
piece of advice:

> A man will be just, then, in a way most advanta-
> geous to himself if, in the presence of witnesses, he
> holds the laws of the city in high esteem, and in the
> absence of witnesses, when he is alone, those of
> nature. For the laws of men are adventitious, but
> those of nature are necessary; and the laws of men
> are fixed by agreement, not by nature, whereas the
> laws of nature are natural and not fixed by agree-
> ment. He who breaks the rules, therefore, and es-
> capes detection by those who have agreed to them,
> incurs no shame or penalty; if detected he does.
> (DK 87 B 44, *IEGP,* 250−251)

If you incur no "shame or penalty" by breaking the
conventional laws (that is, if you are not caught),
then you have not brought any disadvantage upon
yourself by doing so. Furthermore, the law of self-
preservation takes precedence over the conventional laws because it is "necessary" and "natural."
Only *its* prescriptions cannot be evaded. Antiphon
drives the point home:

> If some benefit accrued to those who subscribed to
> the laws, while loss accrued to those who did not
> subscribe to them but opposed them, then obedi-
> ence to the laws would not be without profit. But
> as things stand, it seems that legal justice is not
> strong enough to benefit those who subscribe to
> laws of this sort. For in the first place it permits the
> injured party to suffer injury and the man who
> inflicts it to inflict injury, and it does not prevent
> the injured party from suffering injury nor the man
> who does the injury from doing it. And if the case
> comes to trial, the injured party has no more of an
> advantage than the one who has done the injury;
> for he must convince his judges that he has been in-
> jured, and must be able, by his plea, to exact jus-
> tice. And it is open to the one who has done the in-
> jury to deny it; for he can defend himself against
> the accusation, and he has the same opportunity to
> persuade his judges that his accuser has. For the
> victory goes to the best speaker. (DK 87 B 44,
> *IEGP,* 252−253)

"For the victory goes to the best speaker": We come
around again to rhetoric. No matter which of the
sophistic views of justice you take, rhetoric is of supreme importance. Whether you say that conventional justice is the only justice there is or hold that
there is a natural justice of self-preservation, it is
more important to *appear* just than to *be* just. According to the former view, appearances are all
anyone can know; according to the latter, the way
you appear to others determines whether you obtain what is most advantageous to yourself.

The Sophists produced a theory of the origins of
conventional justice as well. It is not clear how
widespread it was; there was no unified sophistic
doctrine. But it is of great interest and was picked
up in the nineteenth century by Friedrich Nietzsche, who made it a key point in his attempt at a

"revaluation of values."* It is represented for us in Plato's *Gorgias,* where it is presented by Callicles.

In my opinion it's the weaklings who constitute the majority of the human race who make the rules. In making these rules, they look after themselves and their own interest, and that's also the criterion they use when they dispense praise and criticism. They try to cow the stronger ones—which is to say, the ones who are capable of increasing their share of things—and to stop them getting an increased share, by saying that to do so is wrong and contemptible and by defining injustice in precisely those terms, as the attempt to have more than others. In my opinion, it's because they're second-rate that they're happy for things to be distributed equally. Anyway, that's why convention states that the attempt to have a larger share than most people is immoral and contemptible; that's why people call it doing wrong. But I think we only have to look at nature to find evidence that it is *right* for better to have a greater share than worse, more capable than less capable. The evidence for this is widespread. Other creatures show, as do human communities and nations, that right has been determined as follows: the superior person shall dominate the inferior person and have more than him. By what right, for instance, did Xerxes make war on Greece or his father on Sythia, not to mention countless further cases of the same kind of behaviour? These people act, surely, in conformity with the natural essence of right and, yes, I'd even go so far as to say that they act in conformity with natural *law,* even though they presumably contravene our man-made laws.

What do we do with the best and strongest among us? We capture them young, like lions, mould them, and turn them into slaves by chanting spells and incantations over them which insist that they have to be equal to others and that equality is admirable and right. But I'm sure that if a man is born in whom nature is strong enough, he'll shake off all these limitations, shatter them to pieces, and win his freedom; he'll trample all our regulations, charms, spells, and unnatural laws into the dust; this slave will rise up and reveal himself as our master; and then natural right will blaze forth. (*Gorgias* 483b–484a)

Callicles' basic idea is that we are by nature equipped with certain passions and desires. It is natural to try to satisfy these. Although the weak may try to fetter those who are strong by imposing a guilty conscience on them, the strong do nothing contrary to nature if they exert all their power and cleverness to satisfy whatever desires they have. Such behavior may be conventionally frowned upon, but it is not, in itself, unjust.

Note how dramatically this contrasts with the ethics of the Greek tradition. Compare it, for instance, to Heraclitus, who holds that it is not good for men to get all they wish, that "moderation is the greatest virtue."*

Callicles holds that enjoyment consists not in moderating one's desires but in satisfying them to the fullest extent. The really happy man is the one who is strong enough to do this without fear of retaliation. Here we have the very opposite of the "nothing too much" doctrine at Delphi—a negation of the tradition of self-restraint.

The views of the Sophists are bold and innovative, a response to the changing social and political situation, particularly in democratic Athens. But they are more than just reflections of a particular society at a given time. They constitute a serious critique of the beliefs of their predecessors and a challenge to those who come after them. These views force us to face the question: Why shouldn't we be Sophists too?

1. Explain Protagoras' saying "Man is the measure of all things."
2. What in the Sophists' teaching tends toward relativism?
3. Contrast *physis* with *nomos.*
4. Contrast conventional justice with natural justice. What two different concepts of natural justice can be distinguished?
5. How could the *physis/nomos* distinction be turned toward an antisocial direction?
6. Would a Sophist say that is more important to be just or to appear just? Why?

*See Chapter 20, especially pp. 546–552.

*See p. 23.

Athens and Sparta at War

In the context of the sophistic movement, we are philosophically prepared to understand Socrates and his disciple, Plato. But to understand why Socrates was brought to trial, we need to know something of the war. It was called the Peloponnesian War by Thucydides, who lived through it and wrote its history in a fascinating book by that title.* The Peloponnesus is the large peninsula at the southern tip of mainland Greece, connected by the narrow Isthmus of Corinth to Greece proper. It was named for a largely mythical ancestor, Pelops, supposedly the grandson of Zeus and the grandfather of Agamemnon and Menelaus of Trojan War fame. In the fifth century B.C., the dominant power on the peninsula was the city-state of Sparta (see Map 1).

Sparta was quite unlike Athens. The Spartans had taken an important role in the defeat of the Persians, but thereafter, unlike Athens, they had followed a more cautious and defensive policy. Sparta was primarily a land power; Athens ruled the seas. Although the Spartans had allies, mostly in the Peloponnesus, Athens had created an empire dominating most of the north of Greece and most of the islands in the Aegean. Sparta was not democratic. Rule in Sparta was in the hands of a relatively small portion of the population, in effect a warrior class. Their way of life was austere and, as we say, spartan—devoted not to wealth and enjoyment but to rigorous training and self-discipline. They were supported by a large slave population called Helots and by other subject peoples in the area who paid tribute.

Perhaps it was inevitable that two such formidable powers in close proximity and so different would clash. They cooperated well enough in repelling the Persian invasion, but when that danger was past, their interests diverged. Thucydides tells us,

> It was by a common effort that the foreign invasion was repelled; but not long afterwards the Hellenes [the Greeks' name for themselves] . . . split into two divisions, one group following Athens and the other Sparta. These were clearly the two most powerful states, one being supreme on land, the other on the sea. For a short time the war-time alliance held together, but it was not long before quarrels took place and Athens and Sparta, each with her own allies, were at war with each other. . . . So from the end of the Persian War till the beginning of the Peloponnesian War, though there were some intervals of peace, on the whole these two Powers were either fighting with each other or putting down revolts among their allies. They were consequently in a high state of military preparedness and had gained their military experience in the hard school of danger. . . .
>
> What made war inevitable was the growth of Athenian power and the fear which this caused in Sparta. (*HPW* 1.18, 23)[9]

War may indeed have been inevitable, but its coming was tragic. In the end, it led to the defeat of Athens and to the weakening of Greece in general. It meant the beginning of the end of the Golden Age of Greece.

The war itself was long and drawn out, lasting from 431 to 404 B.C., with an interval of seven years of relative peace in the middle. It was immensely costly to both sides, both in terms of men lost and wealth squandered. We will not go into the details of the war; they can be found in Thucydides or any of a number of modern histories.* But war does things to a people, especially a long and inconclusive war fought with increasing desperation. And we need to have a sense for the temper of the times.

The war intensified the internal struggles within the city-states. Athens had been democratic for eighty years by the time the war started; nevertheless, tension between the descendants of the old aristocracy and the *demos,* or common people, still remained. These divisions were even more intense in other city-states, for Athens encouraged the development of democracy in her allies and appealed to the people (as opposed to the aristocrats) in cities she hoped to bring into her empire. These moves were resisted by the aristocratic or oligarchical parties in these states, who were often supported by Sparta. Thucydides records the events in Corcyra

---

*For Peloponnesian War, see http://en.wikipedia.org/wiki/Peloponnesian_War.

*See suggestions in Note 1, at the close of this chapter.

(see Map 1) after the victory of the democratic side over the oligarchs.

> They seized upon all their enemies whom they could find and put them to death. They then dealt with those whom they had persuaded to go on board the ships, killing them as they landed. Next they went to the temple of Hera and persuaded about fifty of the suppliants there to submit to a trial. They condemned every one of them to death. Seeing what was happening, most of the other suppliants, who had refused to be tried, killed each other there in the temple; some hanged themselves on the trees, and others found various other means of committing suicide. During the seven days that Eurymedon [an Athenian naval commander] stayed there with his sixty ships, the Corcyreans continued to massacre those of their own citizens whom they considered to be their enemies. Their victims were accused of conspiring to overthrow the democracy, but in fact men were often killed on grounds of personal hatred or else by their debtors because of the money they owed. There was death in every shape and form. And, as usually happens in such situations, people went to every extreme and beyond it. There were fathers who killed their sons; men were dragged from the temples or butchered on the very altars; some were actually walled up in the temple of Dionysus and died there. . . .
>
> Later, of course, practically the whole of the Hellenic world was convulsed, with rival parties in every state—democratic leaders trying to bring in the Athenians, and oligarchs trying to bring in the Spartans. (*HPW* 3.81–3.83)

We can see here the disintegration of the traditional Greek ideal of moderation; people "went to every extreme and beyond it." Moreover, the arguments of the more extreme Sophists found a parallel in concrete political undertakings. Naked self-interest came more and more to play the major role in decisions no longer even cloaked in terms of justice. Perhaps worst of all, Thucydides says, the very meaning of the words for right and virtue changed. When that happens, confusion reigns while moral thought and criticism become impossible.

The people of the island of Melos off the coast of the Peloponnesus (see Map 1), who were originally colonists from Sparta, had remained neutral in the war. Athens sent an expedition to the island seeking their alliance. Thucydides reconstructs a discussion between the ruling oligarchs of the island and the Athenian commanders. There are doubts about the authenticity of the dialogue, but it seems to represent the spirit of the times. We can think of each side as attempting to present the most persuasive *logos*.

> Athenians: Then we on our side will use no fine phrases saying, for example, that we have a right to our empire because we defeated the Persians, or that we have come against you now because of the injuries you have done us—a great mass of words that nobody would believe. And we ask you on your side not to imagine that you will influence us by saying that you, though a colony of Sparta have not joined Sparta in the war, or that you have never done us any harm. Instead we recommend that you should try to get what it is possible for you to get, taking into consideration what we both really do think; since you know as well as we do that, when these matters are discussed by practical people, the standard of justice depends on the equality of power to compel and that in fact the strong do what they have the power to do and the weak accept what they have to accept. (*HPW* 5.89)

The Melians argue that conquering them will not in fact be in the interest of Athens. In other words, they argue as "practical people." They do not have much success, however, and at last appeal to the gods, who will protect them because they "are standing for what is right against what is wrong" (*HPW* 5.104). To this the Athenians reply,

> So far as the favor of the gods is concerned, we think we have as much right to that as you have. Our aims and our actions are perfectly consistent with the beliefs men hold about the gods and with the principles which govern their own conduct. Our opinion of the gods and our knowledge of men lead us to conclude that it is a general and necessary law of nature to rule whatever one can. This is not a law that we made ourselves, nor were we the first to act upon it when it was made. We found it already in existence, and we shall leave it to exist for ever among those who come after us. We are merely acting in accordance with it, and we know that you or anybody else with the same power as ours would be acting in precisely the same way. (*HPW* 5.105)

The Athenian general who is represented as making this speech might have gone to school under Antiphon! He even frames the character of the law of self-interest in the same terms; it is "necessary" and not man-made. In effect, he claims this is a law of *physis,* not just a matter of *nomos.* For that reason, so the argument goes, the Athenians are perfectly justified in conquering Melos if they have the power to do so.

The Melians, not wise in these matters of power politics, refuse to surrender. After a siege, the Athenians

> put to death all the men of military age whom they took, and sold the women and children as slaves. Melos itself they took over for themselves, sending out later a colony of 500 men. (*HPW* 5.116)

Such hardness was common on all sides.

After the death of Pericles in the early years of the war, Athens had no natural leader. Leadership tended to flow to those who could speak persuasively before the Assembly. These leaders were called "demagogues," those who could lead (*agoge*) the *demos.* Policy was inconstant and sometimes reversed, depending on who was the most persuasive speaker of the day. Dissatisfaction with democracy began to grow, especially in quarters traditionally allied with the "best people." When Athens was finally defeated in 404, treachery on the part of these enemies of democracy was suspected but could not be proved.

According to the terms of the peace treaty imposed on Athens, she had to receive returning exiles (most of whom were antidemocratic), agree to have the same friends and enemies as Sparta, and accept provisional government by a Council that came to be known as the Thirty. A new constitution was promised, but naturally the Thirty were in no hurry to form a new government. Supported by a cohort of Spartan men-at-arms, they carried out a purge of "wrongdoers," executing criminals and those who had opposed surrender. But their rule soon involved the persecution of any dissidents, as well as people they just didn't like, and the expropriation of their property to support the new system. They claimed, of course, to be enforcing virtue. In classic fashion, they tried to involve as many

Athenian citizens as possible in their adventures to prevent them from making accusations later. Socrates, as we learn, was one of five persons summoned to arrest a certain Leon of Salamis. (He refused.) The rule of the Thirty became, in short, a reign of terror. Ever after, Athenians could not hear the words "the Thirty" without a shudder.

This rule lasted less than a year. Exiles, joined by democratic forces within the city, attacked and defeated the forces backing the Thirty. Their leader Critias was killed in the fighting, the others were exiled, and democracy was restored. Though a bloodbath was resisted, bad feelings on all sides continued for many years.

Because of the war and its aftermath, Athenians lost confidence in their ability to control their own destiny. The satisfaction in their superiority expressed so well by Pericles disintegrated. Men seemed torn by forces beyond their ability to control in a world that was not well ordered, whether by the gods or by something like the Heraclitean *logos.* The world and human affairs seemed chaotic, beyond managing.

The Greeks had always believed, of course, that humans were not complete masters of their own fate. This belief was expressed in the ideas that the gods intervene in human affairs for their own ends and that none of us can escape our fate. We find such ideas in the works of Homer and in the tragedies of Aeschylus and Sophocles. But in the time of the war, these notions were tinged with a new sense of bitterness and despair. The third of the great Greek tragedians, Euripides, expresses the new mood.

Hippolytus, in the play by that name, is devoted to Artemis (the Roman Diana), goddess of the woodlands, of the hunt, and of chastity. Phaedra, his father's second wife, falls passionately in love with him under the influence of Aphrodite (Venus). She is literally sick with love—sick, she says, to death. Her nurse first admonishes her in classic fashion.

> I have learned much
> from my long life. The mixing bowl of friendship,
> the love of one for the other, must be tempered.
> Love must not touch the marrow of the soul.
> Our affections must be breakable chains that we

can cast them off or tighten them. . . .
The ways of life that are most fanatical
trip us up more, they say, than bring us joy.
They're enemies to health. So I praise less
the extreme than temperance in everything.
The wise will bear me out.

—*Hippolytus* 251–266 [10]

Temperance, moderation in all things, is her message. It is not wise to let one's passions get such a hold that they are beyond control. It is the old message that comes down through the philosophers from Homer. Her words suggest that Phaedra should give up her passion.

But upon learning the object of Phaedra's love and her inability or unwillingness to give it up, the nurse changes her mind:

In this world second thoughts, it seems, are best.
Your case is not so extraordinary,
beyond thought or reason. The Goddess in her anger
has smitten you, and you are in love. What wonder
is this? . . .
            The tide of love,
at its full surge, is not withstandable. . . .
He who has read the writings of the ancients
and has lived much in books, he knows
that Zeus once loved the lovely Semele. . . .
        Yet all these dwell in heaven.
They are content, I am sure, to be subdued
by the stroke of love. . . .
We should not in the conduct of our lives
be too exacting.

—*Hippolytus* 436–468

Here we have the nurse as rhetorician, constructing a plausible *logos* to suit the one who hears her. She even appeals to the example of the gods; if they give in to their passions, she says, why should you think it wrong for you to do the same? Phaedra, hanging on to her virtue as best she can despite her acknowledged love, gives this reply:*

This is the deadly thing which devastates
well-ordered cities and the homes of men —
that's it, this art of oversubtle words.
It's not the words ringing in the ear
that one should speak, but those that have the power
to save their hearer's honorable name.

—*Hippolytus* 486–489

The nurse responds:

This is high moralizing! What you want
is not fine words, but the man!

—*Hippolytus* 490–491

To Phaedra's protests that this is "wicked, wicked!" and her refusal to listen to such "shameful" words, the nurse admits,

O, they are shameful! But they are better than
your noble-sounding moral sentiments.
"The deed" is better if it saves your life:
than your "good name" in which you die exulting.

—*Hippolytus* 500–503

Here again we have the morality of certain Sophists. What is important is that you save your life. Considerations of honor and morality must be held strictly in second place. It is quite the opposite of the Homeric morality; Achilles, for instance, and Hector too, are quite ready to die for honor and glory; death is, by comparison, unimportant.

As the play develops, the nurse tells Hippolytus of Phaedra's love for him. He rejects it and vows to tell his father, Theseus, who is out of the city at the time. When Phaedra learns of this, she kills herself and leaves a note (to save her good name) accusing Hippolytus of rape. Theseus returns, reads the note, and curses his son. The consequence is Hippolytus' death in a chariot accident; only then does Theseus learn of his son's innocence.

The play is framed at beginning and end by speeches of the two goddesses, Aphrodite and Artemis, respectively. Aphrodite vows to take vengeance on Hippolytus because he despises her and worships only chastity. This she does, using Phaedra as her tool. Artemis at the end vows to avenge Hippolytus by destroying some favorite of Aphrodite's. (Some vengeance!) The impression left by

---

*Is it necessary to point out that we have here a critique of the practice of rhetoric?

the play is that humans are mere pawns in the hands of greater powers—powers that are in opposition to each other, that make no sense, and have no rhyme or reason in some higher unity of purpose. Led this way or that by passions we cannot control, we are bound for destruction.

The chorus laments near the end:

> The care of God for us is a great thing,
> if a man believe it at heart:
> it plucks the burden of sorrow from him.
> So I have a secret hope
> of someone, a God, who is wise and plans;
> but my hopes grow dim when I see
> the deeds of men and their destinies.
> For fortune is ever veering, and the currents of
>   life are shifting
> shifting, wandering forever.
>   —*Hippolytus* 1102–1110

We have the hope, the chorus says, that our lives are more than "sound and fury, signifying nothing."* We would like to believe that there is a wise plan to our lives, but if we look about us at the world— and, the Sophists would say, what else can we do?— we find no such reason to hope. Men's fortunes are "ever veering, and the currents of life are shifting, shifting, wandering forever."

So things must have looked in the last decades of the fifth century B.C. in Athens.

Aristophanes and Reaction

Although the Sophists were obviously popular in some circles, they were hated and feared in others. They were a phenomenon that both depended on and fostered the kind of democracy Athens practiced: direct democracy where decisions were made by whichever citizens were present in the Assembly on a given day. Political power rested directly with the people in this system, but the masses, of course, tended to be at the mercy of those who possessed the rhetorical skills to sway them in the direction of their own interests: the demagogues.

The old families who could look back to the "good old days" when the "best people" made the decisions were never happy in this state of affairs. As we have seen, they tried, when they could, to reverse the situation—not always with better results!

Among those who were unhappy were certain intellectuals, including a writer of comedies named Aristophanes. One of his plays, *The Clouds,** is a satire on the new education provided by the Sophists and on the sophistic movement in general. It is worth a look not only because it gives us another point of view on the Sophists but also because he makes Socrates a principal character in the play. In fact, Socrates is presented in *The Clouds* as the leading Sophist, who runs a school called the "Thinkery" to which students come to learn—provided they pay. When we first see Socrates, he is hanging in the air, suspended in a basket.

> You see,
> only by being suspended aloft, by dangling
> my mind in the heavens and mingling my rare
>   thought
> with the ethereal air, could I ever achieve strict
> scientific accuracy in my survey of the vast
>   empyrean.
> Had I pursued my inquiries from down there
>   on the ground,
> my data would be worthless. The earth, you
>   see, pulls down
> the delicate essence of thought to its own gross
>   level.
>   —*Clouds,* p. 33[11]

This is, of course, attractive nonsense. As we'll see, Socrates neither had a Thinkery, charged for instruction, nor was interested in speculations about the heavens and earth. Most important, although he did share the Sophists' interest in human affairs, Socrates was one of their most severe critics. Aristophanes' picture of Socrates is satire painted with a broad brush.

Socrates' students are represented as engaging in scientific studies to determine, for example, how far a flea can jump and out of which end does a gnat

---

*Shakespeare's *Macbeth,* act V, scene 5.

*First performed in Athens in 423 B.C., the eighth year of the war.

tootle. But that is not the main interest of the play. Strepsiades, a man from the country who has married an extravagant city wife and has a son who loves horse racing, is worried about the debts they have piled up. In particular, several of his son's debts are coming due and he hasn't the money to pay them. So he decides to send his son to the Thinkery to learn the new sophistic logic, which can make the weaker argument into the stronger. He thinks that by getting his son to learn these rhetorical tricks he may be able to avoid paying back the money.

Strepsiades is at first unable to persuade his son to go. So he becomes a student himself. He does not prove an apt pupil, however, and Socrates eventually kicks him out, but not before he has learned a thing or two. When he meets his son, Pheidippides, he again tries to force him to go to the school.

PHEIDIPPIDES: But Father,
what's the matter with you? Are you out of your head?
Almighty Zeus, you must be mad!
STREPSIADES: "Almighty Zeus!"
What musty rubbish! Imagine, a boy your age still believing in Zeus!
P: What's so damn funny?
S: It tickles me when the heads of toddlers like you are still stuffed with such outdated notions. Now then,
listen to me and I'll tell you a secret or two that might make an intelligent man of you yet. But remember. You mustn't breathe a word of this.
P: A word of what?
S: Didn't you just swear by Zeus?
P: I did.
S: Now learn what Education can do for you: Pheidippides, there is no Zeus.
P: There is no Zeus?
S: No Zeus. Convection-Principle's in power now. Zeus has been banished.

—*Clouds*, pp. 75–76

The "convection principle" is our old friend the vortex motion or cosmic whirl, by means of which the nature philosophers explain the structure of the world. In the form given this principle by the

atomists, as we have seen, there is no need for—indeed, no room for—any intelligent purpose at all. Everything is caused to happen necessarily, in a completely mechanical fashion. Zeus has indeed been "banished."

Aristophanes, far from conceding that this is progress, deplores the new thought. The old methods of education are farcically confronted with the new by means of two characters, dressed in the masks of fighting cocks, called the just *logos* and the unjust *logos*. (In this translation, they are called "Philosophy" and "Sophistry," respectively.) After some preliminary sparring and insult trading, the just *logos* speaks first.

PHILOSOPHY: Gentlemen,
I propose to speak of the Old Education, as it flourished once
beneath my tutelage, when Homespun Honesty, Plainspeaking, and Truth
were still honored and practiced, and throughout the schools of Athens
the regime of the three D's—DISCIPLINE, DECORUM, and DUTY—
enjoyed unchallenged supremacy.
Our curriculum was Music and Gymnastics, enforced by that rigorous discipline summed up in the old adage:
BOYS SHOULD BE SEEN BUT NOT HEARD. . . .
SOPHISTRY: Ugh, what musty, antiquated rubbish. . . .
P: Nonetheless, these were the precepts on which I bred a generation of heroes, the men who fought at Marathon. . . .
No, young man, by your courage I challenge you. Turn your back upon his blandishments of vice,
the rotten law courts and the cheap, corrupting softness of the baths.
Choose instead the Old, the Philosophical Education. Follow me
and from my lips acquire the virtues of a man:—
A sense of shame, that decency and innocence of mind that shrinks from doing wrong. To feel the true man's blaze of anger when his honor is provoked.

Deference toward one's elders; respect for
one's father and mother.

—*Clouds,* pp. 86—89

This speech is applauded roundly by the chorus,
who say that the unjust *logos* will have to produce
"some crushing *tour de force,* some master stroke"
to counter these persuasive comments. The unjust
logos is not at a loss.

SOPHISTRY: Now then, I freely admit
   that among men of learning I am—somewhat
   pejoratively—dubbed
   the Sophistic, or Immoral Logic. And why?
   Because I first
   devised a Method for the Subversion of
   Established Social Beliefs
   and the Undermining of Morality. Moreover,
   this little invention of mine,
   this knack of taking what might appear to be
   the worse argument
   and nonetheless winning my case, has, I might
   add, proved to be
   an *extremely* lucrative source of income. . . .
      —Young man,
   I advise you to ponder this life of Virtue with
   scrupulous care,
   all that it implies, and all the pleasures of which
   its daily practice
   must inevitably deprive you. Specifically,
   I might mention these:
   Sex. Gambling. Gluttony. Guzzling. Carousing.
   Etcet.
   And what on earth's the point of living, if you
   leach your life
   of all its little joys?
      Very well then, consider your natural needs.
   Suppose, as a scholar of Virtue, you commit
      some minor peccadillo,
   a little adultery, say, or seduction, and suddenly
   find yourself
   caught in the act. What happens? You're ruined,
   you can't defend yourself
   (since, of course, you haven't been taught). But
   follow me, my boy,
   and obey your nature to the full; romp, play,
   and laugh

without a scruple in the world. Then if caught
in flagrante,
   you simply inform the poor cuckold that you're
   utterly innocent
   and refer him to Zeus as your moral sanction.
   After all, didn't he,
   a great and powerful god, succumb to the love
   of women?
   Then how in the world can you, a man, an
   ordinary mortal,
   be expected to surpass the greatest of gods in
   moral self-control?
   Clearly, you can't be.

—*Clouds,* pp. 91—94

To his father's satisfaction, Pheidippides is persuaded to study with the Sophists. But the climax
comes when the son turns what he has learned, not
on the creditors, but on his father. After a quarrel,
he begins to beat his father with a stick. This is not
bad enough; he claims to be able to *prove* that he is
right to do so!

PHEIDIPPIDES: Now then, answer my question:
   did you lick me when I was a little boy?
STREPSIADES: Of course I licked you.
   For your own damn good. Because I loved you.
P: Then *ipso facto,*
   since you yourself admit that loving and lick-
   ings are
   synonymous, it's only fair that I—for your own
   damn good,
   you understand—whip you in return.
      In any case by what right do you whip me
   but claim exemption for yourself?
      What do you think I am? A slave?
   Wasn't I born as free a man as you?
      Well?
S: But . . .
P: But what?
   Spare the Rod and Spoil the Child?
   Is that your argument?
      If so,
   then I can be sententious too. *Old Men Are Boys
   Writ Big,*
   as the saying goes.

A fortiori then, old men logically deserve to
be beaten more, since at their age they have
clearly less
excuse for the mischief that they do.

S: But it's unnatural! It's . . . *illegal!*
Honor your father and mother.
    That's the law.
    Everywhere.

P: The *law?*
And who made the law?
    An ordinary man. A man like you or me.
A man who lobbied for his bill until he
persuaded the people to make it law.
    By the same token, then, what prevents me
now
from proposing new legislation granting sons
the power to
inflict corporal punishment upon wayward
fathers? . . .
    However, if you're still unconvinced,
look to Nature for a sanction. Observe the
roosters,
for instance, and what do you see?
    A society
whose pecking order envisages a permanent
state of open
warfare between fathers and sons. And how do
roosters
differ from men, except for the trifling fact that
human
society is based upon law and rooster society
isn't?

                                    —*Clouds,* pp. 122–124

Strepsiades is forced by the "persuasive power" of
this rhetoric to admit defeat: "The kids," he says,
"have proved their point: naughty fathers should be
flogged." But when Pheidippides adds that since
"misery loves company" he has decided to flog his
mother, too, and can prove "by Sokratic logic" the
propriety of doing so, that's the last straw. Strepsiades cries out:

By god, if you prove *that,*
then for all I care, you heel,
you can take your stinking Logics
and your Thinkery as well

with Sokrates inside it
and damn well go to hell!

                                    —*Clouds,* p. 126

Disillusioned by the promise of sophistry, Strepsiades admits he was wrong to try to cheat his son's
creditors. Convinced that the new education is, as
the just *logos* has put it, the "corrupter and destroyer"
of the youth, he ends the play by burning down the
Thinkery. The moral is drawn, as it typically is, by
the chorus—in this case a chorus of Clouds representing the goddesses of the new thought:

This is what we are,
the insubstantial Clouds men build their hopes
    upon,
shining tempters formed of air, symbols of
    desire; and so we act, beckoning, alluring
    foolish men
through their dishonest dreams of gain to over-
    whelming
ruin. There, schooled by suffering, they learn
    at last
to fear the gods.

                                    —*Clouds,* p. 127

The Clouds is surely not a fair and dispassionate
appraisal of the sophistic movement. It is partisan
in the extreme, a caricature by a traditionalist
deeply antagonistic to the changes Athenian society
was going through. And yet it poses some serious
questions. Is there a way to distinguish between *logoi* independently of their persuasiveness? If not, is
argument just a contest that the most persuasive
must win? And if Strepsiades can think of no logical
rejoinder to his son's sophisms, what is the outcome? Are arson and violence the only answer? But
if that is so, in what sense is that answer superior to
the rhetoric that it opposes? Isn't it just employing
another tool of force, less subtle than the verbal
manipulations of the rhetorician?
    What is put in question by the Sophists and Ar-
istophanes' response to them is this: Is there any
technique by which people can discuss and come to
agree on matters important to them that does not
reduce to a power struggle in the end? It is the
intellectual parallel to the question that lurked in

the Melian debate. Is there something that can be identified as being reasonable, as opposed to being merely persuasive? Can human beings, by discussing matters together, come to know the truth? Or is it always just a question of who wins?

This is the question that interests Socrates.

---

1. Sketch the argument between Phaedra and the Nurse in Euripides' *Hippolytus.*
2. What philosophical question is posed by Aristophanes' play *The Clouds*?

For Further Thought

1. Sophist/relativist views about the good or the true are often expressed by the question "Who's to say?" Is that a good question? If not, why not?

2. What do you think? Is it more important to *be* just or to *appear* just? Why?

Notes

1. *The Pelican History of Greece* by A. R. Burn (New York: Penguin Books, 1984) is a lively treatment of these matters. A standard source is J. B. Bury, *A History of Greece* (London: Macmillan and Co., 1951). The Greek historians Herodotus, Thucydides, and Xenophon are also quite readable.
2. Quotations from Herodotus, *The Histories* (New York: Penguin Books, 1972), are cited in the text by title, book number, and section number.
3. Thucydides, *History of the Peloponnesian War,* trans. Rex Warner (New York: Penguin Books, 1954), 2.35–41.
4. Quotations from Plato's *Protagoras,* trans, C. C. W. Taylor (Oxford: Oxford University Press, 1996), are cited in the text by title and section numbers.
5. Quotations from Plato's *Gorgias,* trans. Robin Waterfield (Oxford: Oxford University Press, 1994), are cited in the text by title and section number.
6. Quotations from John Manley Robinson's *An Introduction to Early Greek Philosophy* (Boston: Houghton Mifflin Co., 1968) are cited in the text using the standard Diels/Kranz numbers, followed by the page number in *IEGP.*
7. Herodotus, *The Histories* (Penguin Books, 1972), bk. 3, sec. 38.
8. Sophocles, *Antigone,* trans. H. D. F. Kitto, in *Sophocles: Three Tragedies* (London: Oxford University Press, 1962), ll. 440–450.
9. Quotations from Thucydides, *History of the Peloponnesian War,* trans. Rex Warner (New York: Penguin Books, 1954), are cited in the text using the abbreviation *HPW.* References are to book and section numbers.
10. Quotations from Euripides' *Hippolytus,* trans. David Grene, in *Euripides I,* ed. David Grene and Richmond Lattimore (Chicago: University of Chicago Press, 1965), are cited in the text by title and line numbers.
11. Quotations from Aristophanes' *Clouds,* trans. William Arrowsmith (New York: New American Library, 1962), are cited in the text by title and page numbers.

4

SOCRATES

To Know Oneself

Some philosophers are important just for what they say or write. Others are important also for what they are—for their personality and character. No better example of the latter exists than Socrates.

Socrates wrote nothing, save some poetry written while he was waiting to be executed; he is said to have written a hymn to Apollo and to have put the fables of Aesop into verse. But those have not survived. His impact on those who knew him, however, was extraordinary, and his influence down to the present day has few parallels.

The fact that he wrote nothing poses a problem, of course. We have to look to other writers for our knowledge of him. Aristophanes is one source, but such farce must be taken with more than one grain of salt. Another source is Xenophon, who tells numerous stories involving Socrates but is philosophically rather unsophisticated.* Aristotle, too,

discusses him. But our main source is Plato, a younger companion of Socrates and a devoted admirer.

Plato didn't, however, write a biography, nor did he write a scholarly analysis of his master's thought. He has left us a large number of dialogues, or conversations, in most of which Socrates is a participant, often the central figure. These might be very reliable, if Plato had carried with him a tape recorder and then transcribed the conversations, but of course he couldn't have. These dialogues were all written after Socrates' death, many of them long after. And there can be no doubt that in the later dialogues Plato is putting ideas of his own into the mouth of Socrates. We should not think there is anything dishonest about this practice. The ancient world would have accepted it as perfectly in order; Plato surely believed that his own ideas were a natural development from those of Socrates and that in this way he was honoring his master. But it does pose a problem if we want to discuss the historical Socrates rather than Plato's Socrates.

No definitive solution to this problem may ever be found. One scholar has acknowledged that "in

---

* *Note:* This is not Xenophanes, the pre-Socratic philosopher discussed in Chapter 2.

the end we must all have to some extent our own Socrates."[1] Still, some things are reasonably certain.

The dialogues of Plato can pretty well be sorted into three periods, as follows.

1. The early dialogues, such as *Euthyphro, Crito,* and the *Apology,* are thought to represent quite accurately Socrates' own views and ways of proceeding. They seem to have been written soon after his death. In these dialogues, Socrates questions various individuals about the nature of piety, courage, justice, or virtue/excellence (*arete*).* The outcome of the conversation is usually negative in just this sense: No agreed-upon solution is reached. The participant, who at the dialogue's beginning claims to know the answer, is forced to admit ignorance. You might ask, Is there any point to such conversations? Well, the participants do learn something—that is, how little they really know. In this way the ground is cleared of at least some intellectual rubbish.

2. In the middle dialogues, such as *Meno, Phaedo, Symposium,* and the monumental *Republic,* Socrates is still the main protagonist. Here, however, we find positive doctrines aplenty, supported by many arguments. Here Plato is working out his own solutions to the problems that the Sophists posed and trying to go beyond the negative outcomes of Socratic questioning. What Plato is doing here will be the main subject of Chapter 6.

3. The late dialogues contain further developments and explore difficulties discovered in the doctrines of the middle period. Here Socrates begins to play a lesser role; in the very late *Laws,* he disappears altogether.

In this chapter and the next, we discuss Socrates primarily as he appears in the early works of Plato, and we read in their entirety three short dialogues. Before reading those, however, we need to learn something about Socrates' character and person.

Character

Socrates was born in 470 or 469 B.C. His father was a stonemason and perhaps a minor sculptor. It is thought that Socrates pursued this same trade as a young man. He was married to Xanthippe, a woman with a reputation for shrewishness, and had three sons, apparently rather late in life.

Of some importance is the fact that his mother was a midwife. Socrates calls himself a "midwife" in the realm of thought. It is interesting to note that one of the duties of a Greek midwife in classical times was to determine whether the child was a bastard (presumably by way of resemblance to the purported father). A midwife does not give birth herself, of course. In a similar way, Socrates makes no claim to be able to give birth to true ideas but says he can help deliver the ideas of others and determine their truth. He does this by "examining" them, trying to discover their "resemblance" or consistency with other ideas expressed in the conversation. The question is always this: Do the answers to Socrates' questions fit together with the original claim that what was said is true? (Compare: Does the baby the midwife delivers accord with the claim that so and so is the father?) As we read the three dialogues, we will see numerous examples of his "midwifery."*

No one ever claimed that Socrates was good looking, except in a joke. In a charming work designed to let us see "great and good men" in their "lighter moods," Xenophon reports on an impromptu "beauty contest" held at a banquet. The contestants are Critobulus, a good-looking young man, and Socrates. Socrates is challenged to prove that he is the more handsome.

SOCRATES: Do you think beauty exists in man alone, or in anything else?

---

*The meaning of this important word is discussed in Chapter 3, on p. 42.

*You might like to look at the actual words in which Socrates claims this role of midwife for himself. See Chapter 5, p. 102.

CRITOBULUS: I believe it is found in horse and ox and many inanimate things. For instance, I recognize a beautiful shield, sword or spear.

s: And how can all these things be beautiful when they bear no resemblance to each other?

c: Why, if they are well made for the purposes for which we acquire them, or well adapted by nature to our needs, then in each case I call them beautiful.

s: Well then, what do we need eyes for?

c: To see with of course.

s: In that case my eyes are at once proved to be more beautiful than yours, because yours look only straight ahead, whereas mine project so that they can see sideways as well.

c: Are you claiming that a crab has the most beautiful eyes of any animal?

s: Certainly, since from the point of view of strength also its eyes are best constructed by nature.

c: All right, but which of our noses is the more beautiful?

s: Mine, I should say, if the gods gave us noses to smell with, for your nostrils point to earth, but mine are spread out widely to receive odours from every quarter.

c: But how can a snub nose be more beautiful than a straight one?

s: Because it does not get in the way but allows the eyes to see what they will, whereas a high bridge walls them off as if to spite them.

c: As for the mouth, I give in, for if mouths are made for biting you could take a much larger bite than I.

s: And with my thick lips don't you think I could give a softer kiss?[2]

After this exchange, the banqueters take a secret ballot to determine who is the more handsome. Critobulus gets every vote, so Socrates exclaims that he must have bribed the judges! It must have been nearly impossible to resist caricaturing this odd-looking man who shuffled about Athens barefoot and peered sideways at you out of his bulging eyes when you spoke to him. Aristophanes was not the only writer of comedies to succumb to the temptation.

"I do not even have any knowledge of what virtue itself is."

—SOCRATES

We see several things about Socrates in this little excerpt: (1) It was not for his physical attractiveness that Socrates was sought after as a companion; he was acknowledged on all sides to be extraordinarily ugly, though it seems to have been an interesting kind of ugliness; (2) we see something of Socrates' humor; here it is light and directed at himself, but it could also be sharp and biting; (3) we have our first glimpse of the typical Socratic method, which proceeds by question and answer, not by long speeches; and (4) we see that Socrates here identifies the good or the beautiful in terms of usefulness or advantage, and this is typical of his views on these questions of value.

He served in the army several times with courage and distinction. In Plato's *Symposium*, the story of an all-night banquet and drinking party, Alcibiades, a brilliant young man we shall hear more of, gives the following testimony:

> Now, the first thing to point out is that there was no one better than him in the whole army at enduring hardship: it wasn't just me he showed up. Once, when we were cut off (as happens during a campaign), we had to do without food and no one else could cope at all. At the same time, when there *were* plenty of provisions, he was better than the rest of us at making the most of them, and especially when it came to drinking: he was reluctant to drink, but when pushed he proved more than a match for everyone. And the most remarkable thing of all is that no one has ever seen Socrates drunk. . . .
>
> Once—and this was the most astonishing thing he did—the cold was so terribly bitter that everyone was either staying inside or, if they did venture out, they wore an incredible amount of clothing, put shoes on, and then wrapped pieces of felt and sheepskin around their feet. Socrates, however, went out in this weather wearing only the outdoor cloak he'd usually worn earlier in the campaign as well, and without anything on his feet; but he still made his way through the ice more easily than the rest of us with our covered feet. . . .
>
> One morning, a puzzling problem occurred to him and he stayed standing where he was thinking about it. Even when it proved intractable, he didn't give up: he just stood there exploring it. By the time it was midday, people were beginning to notice him and were telling one another in amazement that Socrates had been standing there from early in the morning deep in thought. Eventually, after their evening meal, some men from the Ionian contingent took their pallets outside—it was summer at the time—so that they could simultaneously sleep outside where it was cool and watch out for whether he'd stand there all night as well. In fact, he stood there until after sunrise the following morning, and then he greeted the sun with a prayer and went on his way. (*Symposium* 219e–220d) [3]

Alcibiades goes on to tell how Socrates saved his life and in a retreat showed himself to be the coolest man around, so that

> anyone could tell, even from a distance, that here was a man who would resist an attack with considerable determination. And that's why he and

Laches got out of there safely, because the enemy generally don't take on someone who can remain calm during combat. (*Symposium* 221b)e

He sums up his view by saying that

> there's no human being, from times past or present, who can match him. . . .
>
> The first time a person lets himself listen to one of Socrates' arguments, it sounds really ridiculous. . . . He talks of pack-asses, metal-workers, shoemakers, tanners; he seems to go on and on using the same arguments to make the same points, with the result that ignoramuses and fools are bound to find his arguments ridiculous. But if you could see them opened up, if you can get through to what's under the surface, what you'll find inside is that his arguments are the only ones in the world which make sense. And that's not all: under the surface, his arguments abound with divinity and effigies of goodness. They turn out to be extremely far-reaching, or rather they cover absolutely everything which needs to be taken into consideration on the path to true goodness. (*Symposium* 221c–222a)

It is somewhat ironic to hear Alcibiades talking of "true goodness" here. He was for a time a close associate of Socrates but in later life became notorious for lechery and lust for power. He was suspected of being responsible for the mutilation of statues of Hermes (often set by the gates or doors of Athenian houses) and was put on trial while he was away on a military mission. Eventually he deserted and offered his services as a general to the Spartans! The common opinion was that Alcibiades was handsome and brilliant but also treacherous and despicable. Nonetheless, there is no reason to doubt the testimony to Socrates that Plato here puts into his mouth.

The party is invaded by a bunch of revelers; everyone drinks a great deal, many leave, and some fall asleep. Near morning, only three persons are still awake: Agathon the host, Aristophanes (yes, the comic playwright), and Socrates. They are still drinking and arguing, now about whether one and the same person could write both tragedies and comedies.

> They were coming round to his point of view, but they were too sleepy to follow the argument very

well; Aristophanes fell asleep first and Agathon joined him after daybreak.

Now that he'd put them to sleep, . . . Socrates went to the Lyceum for a wash, spent the day as he would any other, and then went home to sleep in the evening. (*Symposium* 223d)

He "spent the day as he would any other." How was that? Socrates' days seem to have been devoted mainly to conversations in the public places of Athens. He was not independently wealthy, as you might suspect. Xenophon tells us that

he schooled his body and soul by following a system which . . . would make it easy to meet his expenses. For he was so frugal that it is hardly possible to imagine a man doing so little work as not to earn enough to satisfy the needs of Socrates. (*Memorabilia* 1.3.5)[4]

He was temperate in his desires and possessed remarkable self-control with regard not only to food and drink but also to sex. He apparently refrained from the physical relationship that was a fairly common feature of friendships between older men and their young protégés in ancient Athens.* Although he used the language of "love" freely, he held that the proper aim of such friendships was to make the "beloved" more virtuous, self-controlled, and just. No doubt he believed that the young could not learn self-control from someone who did not display it. By common consent the judgment of Alcibiades was correct: Socrates was unique.

Is Socrates a Sophist?

In *The Clouds,* Aristophanes presents Socrates as a Sophist. There are undeniable similarities between Socrates and the Sophists, but there are also important differences. We need to explore this a bit.

Socrates clearly moves in the same circles as the Sophists; he converses with them eagerly and often, and his interests are similar. His subject matter is human affairs, in particular *arete*—excellence or virtue. As we have seen, the Sophists set themselves up as teachers of such excellence. Socrates does not. He cannot do so, he might insist, because he does not rightly know what it is, and no one can teach what he doesn't understand. Nonetheless, he explores this very area, trying to clarify what human excellence consists in, whether it is one thing or many (for example, courage, moderation, wisdom, justice), and whether it is the kind of thing that can be taught at all.

We have noted that many of the Sophists also teach specialized subjects, including geometry, astronomy, and nature philosophy in general. Socrates apparently was interested in nature philosophy as a youth but gave it up because it could not answer the questions that really intrigue him, such as, Why are we here? and What is the best kind of life? Human life is what fascinates him. So he and the Sophists share a community of interest.

Young men associate themselves with Socrates, too, sometimes for considerable periods of time, and consider him their teacher. He does not, as we noted in connection with Aristophanes' "Thinkery," have a school. And he does not consider himself a teacher. In fact, we will hear his claim that he has never taught anyone anything. (This takes some explaining, which we will do later.) So he is unlike the Sophists in that regard, for they do consider that they have something to teach and are proud to teach it to others.

Socrates is unlike the Sophists in another regard. He takes no pay from those who associate themselves with him. This is, of course, perfectly consistent with his claim that he has nothing to teach. Xenophon adds that Socrates "marvelled that anyone should make money by the profession of virtue, and should not reflect that his highest reward would be the gain of a good friend" (*Memorabilia* 1.2.7).

Like the Sophists, Socrates is interested in the arts of communication and argument, in techniques of persuasion. But it is at just this point that we find the deepest difference between them, the difference that perhaps allows us to deny that Socrates is a Sophist at all. For the Sophists, these arts (rhetoric) are like strategies and tactics in battle. The whole point is to enable their practitioner to win. Argument and persuasion are thought of as a kind of strife or contest where, as Antiphon put it, "victory

---

*See, for example, the complaint of Alcibiades in *Symposium* 217a–219d.

goes to the best speaker." No concern for *truth* underlies the instruction of the Sophists; the aim is *victory*. This is wholly consistent with their denial that truth is available to human beings, with their skepticism and relativism. If all you can get are opinions anyway, then you might as well try to make things appear to others as they appear to you. That is what serves your self-interest. And rhetoric, as they conceive and teach it, is designed to do just that.*

For Socrates, on the other hand, the arts of communication, argument, and persuasion have a different goal. His practice of them is designed not to win a victory over his opponent but to advance toward the truth. He is convinced that there is a truth about human affairs and that we are capable of advancing toward it, of shaping our opinions so that they are more "like truth," to use that old phrase of Xenophanes.† Socrates could never agree that if a man *thinks* a certain action is just, then it *is* just—not even "for him." So he is neither a relativist nor a skeptic. Justice, Socrates believes, is something quite independent of our opinions about it. And what it is needs investigation.

Socrates' way of proceeding coheres well with this conviction about truth. He usually refrains from piling up fine phrases in lengthy speeches that might simply overwhelm his listeners; he does not want them to agree with his conclusions for reasons they do not themselves fully understand and agree to. So he asks questions. He is very insistent that his listeners answer in a sincere way, that they say what they truly believe. Each person is to speak for himself. In the dialogue *Meno,* for instance, Socrates professes not to know what virtue is. Meno expresses surprise, for surely, he says, Socrates listened to Gorgias when he was in town. Yes, Socrates admits, but he does not altogether remember what Gorgias said; perhaps Meno remembers and agrees with him. When Meno admits that he does, Socrates says,

> Then let's leave him out of it; he's not here, after all. But in the name of the gods, Meno, please do tell me in your own words what you think excellence is. (*Meno* 71d) [5]

So Meno is put on the spot and has to speak for himself. Again and again Socrates admonishes his hearers not to give their assent to a proposition unless they really agree.

The course of Socrates' conversations generally goes like this. Someone, often Socrates himself, asks a question: "What is piety?" or "Can human excellence be taught?" In response to the question, an answer is put forward, usually by someone other than Socrates. Socrates in turn proposes they "examine" whether they agree or disagree with this proposition. The examination proceeds by further questioning, which leads the person questioned to realize that the first answer is not adequate. A second answer that seems to escape the difficulties of the first is put forward, and the pattern repeats itself. A good example is found in *Euthyphro,* to which we'll turn shortly. In the early, more authentically Socratic dialogues, we are usually left at the end with an inconsistent set of beliefs; it is clear that we cannot accept the whole set, but neither Socrates nor his partner knows which way to go. Thus the participant is brought to admit that he doesn't understand the topic at all—although he thought he did when the conversation began.

This technique of proposal–questions–difficulties–new proposal–questions is a technique that

---

*See the Antiphon quote on p. 48.
†Look again at the fragment from Xenophanes on pp. 17–18.

Plato calls **dialectic.** Socrates thinks of it as a way, the very best way, of improving our opinions and perhaps even coming to knowledge of the truth. What is the connection between dialectic and truth? The connection is this: So long as people sincerely say what they believe and are open to revising this on the basis of good reasons, people can *together* identify inadequate answers to important questions. There really can be no doubt that certain answers won't do. But if you can be sure that some opinions aren't right, what remains unrefuted may well be in the vicinity of the truth. It is important, however, to note that even in the best case this sort of examination cannot *guarantee* the truth of what is left standing at the end. Socrates apparently knows this; that's why he so often confesses his ignorance.

This dialectical procedure, then, is better at detecting error than identifying truth, and for it to do even that certain conditions must be met. Each participant must say what he or she really believes, and no one must be determined to hang on to a belief "no matter what." In other words, the aim must be, not victory over the other speaker, but progress toward the truth. Dialectic is the somewhat paradoxically cooperative enterprise in which each *assists* the others by *raising objections* to what the others say.

We should reflect a moment on how odd this seems. We usually think we are being helped when people agree with us, support us in our convictions, and defend us against attacks. Socrates, however, thinks the best help we can get—what we really need—is given by questions that make us think again, questions that make us uncomfortable and inclined to be defensive. Again like Xenophanes, Socrates does not think that truth is evident or obvious; he does not agree that if something is widely accepted, this is a good reason to believe it. We sometimes even get the impression that if everybody believes it, it *must* be suspect! It is by "seeking" that we approach the truth, and that's neither easy nor comfortable. Socrates' technique for seeking the truth is this dialectic of question and answer.

That this is a cooperative enterprise and not merely a competition to see who wins is displayed in the fact that communication is not one way. Socrates does not deliver sermons; he does not lecture, at least not in the early dialogues. Also, anyone can ask the questions. In Plato's dialogues, it is usually Socrates who asks, but not always. Sometimes he gives his partner a choice of either asking or answering questions.

As you can imagine, this rather antagonistic procedure was not always understood or appreciated by Socrates' compatriots. It was certainly one of the factors that generated hostility toward him. In fact, you had to be a certain kind of person to enjoy talking with Socrates and to benefit from a conversation with him, as a passage from the *Gorgias* makes clear. Here the topic is rhetoric, or the art of persuasion. At issue is whether persuasion can lead to knowledge of truth or whether it is restricted to opinion. Socrates says to Gorgias, who teaches rhetoric,

> If you're the same kind of person as I am, I'd be glad to continue questioning you; otherwise, let's forget it. What kind of person am I? I'm happy to have a mistaken idea of mine proved wrong, and I'm happy to prove someone else's mistaken ideas wrong, I'm certainly not *less* happy if I'm proved wrong than if I've proved someone else wrong, because, as I see it, I've got the best of it: there's nothing worse than the state which I've been saved from, so that's better for me than saving someone else. You see, there's nothing worse for a person, in my opinion, than holding mistaken views about the matters we're discussing at the moment. (*Gorgias* 458a) [6]

This is a crucial passage for understanding Socrates' technique. He is in effect telling us that he will converse only with those who have a certain *character.* Progress in coming to understand the truth is as much a matter of character as intelligence. If you care more for your reputation, for wealth, for winning, or for convincing others that your opinion is the right one, Socrates will leave you alone. Or, if you insist on talking with him, you are bound to leave feeling humiliated rather than enlightened; for your goals will not have been reached. In order to make progess, he says, you must be such a person as he himself claims to be. What sort of person is that? You must be just as happy to be shown wrong as to show someone else to be wrong. No—you must be even *happier,* for if you are weaned from a false opinion, you have escaped a great evil.

It is worth expanding on this point a bit. To profit from a conversation with Socrates, you must (1) be open and honest about what you really do believe; and (2) not be so wedded to any one of your beliefs that you consider an attack on it as an attack on yourself. In other words, you must have a certain objectivity with respect to your own opinions. You must be able to say, "Yes, that is indeed an opinion of mine, but I shall be glad to exchange it for another if there is good reason to do so." This outlook skirts two dangers: wishy-washiness and **dogmatism.** People with these Socratic virtues are not wishy-washy, because they really do have opinions. But neither are they dogmatic, because they are eager to improve their opinions. We might ask to what extent people must have this attitude if they are to be able to learn at all.

This attitude does, in any case, seem to characterize Socrates. At this point, the character and aims of Socrates stand as a polar opposite to those of the Sophists. There could never have been a day on which Socrates taught his students "how to make the weaker argument into the stronger." To take that as one's aim is to show that one cares not for the truth but only for victory. To teach the techniques that provide victory is to betray one's character, to show that one is looking for the same thing oneself: fame, wealth, and the satisfaction of one's desires. That is why the Sophists taught for pay and grew wealthy. That is why Socrates refused pay and remained poor. And that is why the portrait Aristophanes gives us in *The Clouds* is only a caricature—not the real Socrates.

What Socrates "Knows"

Socrates' most characteristic claim concerns his ignorance. In his conversations, he claims not to know what human excellence, courage, or piety is. He begs to be instructed. Of course, it is usually the instructors who get instructed, who learn that they don't know after all. How shall we understand Socrates' claim not to know?

In part, surely, he is being ironic, especially in begging his partner in the conversation to instruct him. It is a role that Socrates is playing, the role of

ignorant inquirer. But there is more to it than that. With respect to those large questions about the nature of human excellence, it is fairly clear that Socrates never does get an answer that fully satisfies him. In the sense of "know" which implies you can't be wrong, Socrates does not claim to know these things. Only "the god," he says in the *Apology,* is truly wise. Even on points he might be quite confident about, he must allow that the next conversation could contain questions or objections that raise new difficulties—difficulties he cannot overcome. In this respect, his confession of ignorance is quite sincere.

Nonetheless, there are things that are *as good as known* for Socrates, things he is so confident about that he is even willing to die for them. When we read his defense before the jury, we will see him affirm a number of things—remarkable things—with the greatest confidence. He will say, for instance, that a good man cannot be harmed—something, I wager, that you probably don't believe. This combination of ignorance and conviction seems paradoxical. How can we understand it?

As Socrates continues to examine his convictions and the beliefs of others, discarding what was clearly indefensible, certain affirmations survive all the scrutiny and rude questions. These are claims that neither Socrates nor any of his conversational partners have been able to undermine; these claims have stood fast. You can imagine that as the years go by and his convictions come under attack from every conceivable quarter, those few principles that withstand every assault must come to look more and more "like the truth," to recall that phrase from Xenophanes, so much like the truth that it becomes almost inconceivable that they should be upset in the future. These convictions Socrates is willing to bet on, even with his life.

Before we examine some of the early dialogues, it will be useful to identify several of them.[*]

---

[*]Because in this section I make use of material from several of the middle dialogues, I cannot claim with certainty to be representing the historical Socrates. In line with the earlier remark that each of us must to some degree construct our own Socrates, you might think of the picture painted here as Melchert's Socrates.

We Ought to Search for Truth

In his conversation with Meno, Socrates says that

> there's one proposition that I'd defend to the
> death, if I could, by argument and by action: that
> as long as we think we should search for what we
> don't know we'll be better people — less faint-
> hearted and less lazy — than if we were to think
> that we had no chance of discovering what we
> don't know and that there's no point in even
> searching for it. (*Meno* 86b–c)

This remark occurs in the context of an argument we will examine later* that the soul is directly acquainted with truth before it enters a human body. This argument has the practical consequence that we may hope to recover the knowledge we had before birth. Socrates says that although he is not certain about every detail of this argument, he is sure that we will be better persons if we do not give up hope of attaining the truth.

Again we can see the Sophists lurking in the background; for it is they who claim that knowledge of truth is not possible for human beings, each of us being the final "measure," or judge, of what seems so to us. Socrates believes that this doctrine (relativism) will make us worse persons, faint-hearted and lazy. After all, if we can dismiss any criticism by saying, "Well, it's true for *me*," then our present beliefs are absolutely secure; so why should we undertake the difficult and dangerous task of examining them? The Sophist point of view seems to Socrates like a prescription for intellectual idleness and cowardice. And he is certain that to be idle and cowardly is to be a worse person rather than a better one. So one thing that "stands fast" for Socrates is that we ought to search for the truth and not despair of finding it.

Human Excellence Is Knowledge

Socrates seems to have held that human excellence consists in knowledge. No doubt this strikes us as slightly odd; it seems overintellectualized, somehow. Knowledge, we are apt to think, may be one facet of being an excellent human being, but how could it be the whole of it?

The oddness is dissipated somewhat when we note what sort of knowledge Socrates has in mind. He is constantly referring us to the craftsmen — to "metal-workers, shoe-makers, tanners," as Alcibiades said — and to such professions as horse training, doctoring, and piloting a ship. In each case, what distinguishes the expert from a mere novice is the possession of knowledge. Such knowledge is not just having abstract intellectual propositions in your head, however; it is knowledge of *what* to do and *how* to do it. The Greek word here is *techne,* from which our word "technology" comes. This *techne* is a kind of applied knowledge. What distinguishes the competent doctor, horse trainer, or metal-worker, then, is that they possess a *techne*. The amateur or novice does not.

Socrates claims that human excellence is a *techne* in exactly this same sense. What does the doctor know? She knows the human body and what makes for its health — its physical excellence. What does the horse trainer know? He knows horses — their nature and how they can be made to respond so that they will turn into excellent beasts. In a quite parallel fashion, the expert in human excellence (or virtue) — if there is one — would have to know human nature, how it functions, and wherein its excellence consists.*

Just as the shoemaker must understand both his materials (leather, nails, thread) and the use to which shoes are put — the point of having shoes — so those who wish to live well must understand themselves and what the point of living is. And just as one who has mastered the craft of shoemaking will turn out fine shoes, Socrates thinks, so one who has mastered the craft of living will live well. In the *Gorgias,* for instance, Socrates argues in this way:

s: Now, isn't a person who's come to understand building a builder?
g: Yes.
s: While a person who's come to understand music is a musician. Yes?

---

*See pp. 101–102.

*See Aristotle's development of just this point, pp. 187–188.

G: Yes.

s: And a person who's come to understand medicine is a doctor, and so on and so forth. By the same token, anyone who has come to understand a given subject is described in accordance with the particular character his branch of knowledge confers. Do you agree?

G: Yes.

s: So doesn't it follow that someone who has come to understand morality is moral?

G: Definitely. No doubt about it.

—*Gorgias* 460b

Knowledge in this *techne* sense, Socrates holds, is both a necessary condition for human excellence (without it you cannot be a good person) and a sufficient condition (when it is present, so are all the excellent qualities of human life).

In the *Meno* we find another argument with the same conclusion. Socrates gets agreement that human excellence must be something beneficial. But, he argues, things that are generally beneficial need not always be so. For instance, whether wealth, health, and strength are an advantage to the possessor depends on whether they are used wisely or foolishly. And the same goes for what people generally call virtues.

s: Now, among these qualities, take those that you think aren't knowledge—those that are different from knowledge—and let me ask you whether they're sometimes harmful and sometimes beneficial. Take courage, for instance, when it isn't wisdom but is something like recklessness. Isn't it the case that unintelligent recklessness harms people, while intelligent boldness does them good?

M: Yes.

s: And does the same go for self-control and cleverness? Are intelligent learning and training beneficial, while unintelligent learning and training are harmful?

M: Most definitely.

s: In short, then, mental endeavour and persistence always end in happiness when they are guided by knowledge, but in the opposite if they are guided by ignorance.

—*Meno* 88b–c

The conclusion that human excellence consists in knowledge faces a difficulty. If it is knowledge, then it should be teachable. Recall Socrates' conversation with Protagoras. He points out that if a father wanted his son to be a painter, he would send him to someone who knew painting. If he wanted him to learn the flute, he would send him to someone who was an expert in flute playing. But where are the teachers of human excellence? Socrates could not allow that the Sophists were such. And he disclaims any knowledge of what such excellence consists in, so he can't teach it. But if there are no teachers, perhaps it isn't knowledge after all.

Socrates is able to resist this conclusion by a device that we'll examine soon.* For now, it is enough to note that this is one thing that "stands fast" for him: that human excellence is wisdom or knowledge.†

All Wrongdoing Is Due to Ignorance

This thesis is a corollary to the claim that virtue is knowledge. If to know the right is to do the right, then failing to do the right must be due to not knowing it. Not to know something is to be ignorant of it. So whoever acts wrongly does so out of ignorance. If we knew better, we would do better.

Socrates holds, in fact, that we always act out of a belief that what we are doing is good. At the least, we think that it will produce good in the long run. We never, Socrates thinks, intend to do what we *know* is wrong or bad or evil or wicked. So if we do things that are wrong, it must be that we are not well-informed. We believe to be good what is in fact evil—but that is to believe something false, and to believe the false is to be ignorant of the true. Here we have a strong argument for the importance of moral education for the young. They can

---

*See pp. 101–102.

†There is a kind of paradox here, as you may already suspect. Socrates claims (1) that human excellence is knowledge, (2) that he lacks this knowledge, and yet (3) that he is a good man. It seems impossible to assert all three consistently; to assert any two seems to require the denial of the third. Socrates, however, has a way out. In Chapter 5, we address this Socratic paradox. See p. 99.

be brought up to be excellent human beings if only they come to learn what is in fact good and right and true.

For a comparison, let us look again to Euripides' *Hippolytus,* where Phaedra (who is, you remember, in love with her stepson) struggles with her passion.

> We know the good, we apprehend it clearly.
> But we can't bring it to achievement. Some
> are betrayed by their own laziness, and others
> value some other pleasure above virtue.[7]

Here Phaedra expresses an opinion opposed to that of Socrates: We do sometimes "know the good," she says, and yet fail to do it. One can imagine Euripides and Socrates debating this point over a glass of wine. Perhaps Euripides even writes this play as he does and puts these words into Phaedra's mouth as part of an ongoing argument. Socrates does not agree; he believes it is not possible to apprehend the good clearly and not do it. Neither laziness nor pleasure can stand in the way. For human excellence *is* knowledge.

This view is connected intimately to Socrates' practice. He is not a preacher exhorting his fellow men to live up to what they know to be good. He is an inquirer trying to discover exactly what human excellence is. All people, he assumes, do the best they know. If people can be brought to understand what human excellence consists in, an excellent life will follow.

This view has seemed mistaken to many people. Not only Euripides disagrees. Among others, so do Aristotle, Saint Paul, and Augustine.*

The Most Important Thing of All Is to Care for Your Soul

There is a final cluster of things Socrates seems to "know." They all hang together and are represented in the dialogues we'll be reading, so I'll just mention several of them briefly here.

Among the striking and unusual propositions that Socrates thinks have survived all the examination are these:

- It is better to suffer injustice than to commit injustice.
- A good person cannot be harmed in either life or death.

These have to do with the soul. The most important part of a human being, Socrates believes, is not the body but the soul; from convictions in the soul flow all those actions that reveal what a person really is. Indeed, Socrates even seems to identify himself with his soul.* For that reason, the most important task any person has is to care for the soul. And to that end nothing is more crucial than self-knowledge. Just as the shoemaker cannot make good shoes unless he understands his material, you cannot construct a good life unless you know yourself.

In the *Apology,* Socrates says that for a human being "the unexamined life is not worth living." In particular, we need to know what we *do* know and what we *do not* know so that we can act wisely, and not foolishly. For foolishness is behavior based on false opinions. As you can see, this concern with the soul animates Socrates' practice; it is in pursuit of such self-knowledge that he questions his contemporaries—both for their sake and for his. One of the two mottoes at the Delphic Oracle might be the motto for Socrates' own life and practice: "Know Thyself."

---

1. Describe briefly the character of Socrates, as we know it from the testimony of his friends.
2. In what ways is Socrates like the Sophists?
3. In what ways is he different?
4. How does Socrates proceed in his "examination" of his fellow citizens?
5. What is the connection between dialectic and truth?
6. What kind of person do you have to be to profit from a conversation with Socrates?
7. A number of things seem to have "stood fast" for Socrates in the course of all his examinations, things that in some sense we can say he "knows." What are they?

---

*See pp. 186, 224, and 246–251.

*See the jest Socrates makes just before he drinks the hemlock in *Phaedo* 115c, p. 114.

For Further Thought

Here are several convictions Socrates thinks have withstood all the criticisms to which they have been exposed:

- That the most important thing in life is to care for the well-being of the soul
- That a good person cannot be harmed by a worse person
- That it is better to suffer injustice than to commit it

Choose one to consider. If you agree, try to say why. If you disagree, try to come up with a critique that might get Socrates to change his mind.

Notes

1. W. K. C. Guthrie, *Socrates* (Cambridge: Cambridge University Press, 1971), 4.

2. Xenophon, *Symposium V,* trans. W. K. C. Guthrie, in *Socrates,* 67–68.

3. Quotations from Plato's *Symposium,* trans. Robin Waterfield (Oxford: Oxford University Press, 1994), are cited in the text by title and section number.

4. Quotations from Xenophon, *Memorabilia,* in *Xenophon: Memorabilia and Oeconomicus,* ed. E. C. Marchant (London: Heinemann, 1923), are cited in the text by title and book and section number.

5. Quotations from Plato's *Meno,* trans. Robin Waterfield in *Meno and Other Dialogues* (Oxford: Oxford University Press, 2005), are cited in the text by title and section number.

6. Quotations from Plato's *Gorgias,* trans. Robin Waterfield (Oxford: Oxford University Press, 1994), are cited by title and section number.

7. Euripides, *Hippolytus,* trans. David Grene, in *Euripides I,* ed. David Grene and Richmond Lattimore (Chicago: University of Chicago Press, 1965), ll. 380–384.

5

THE TRIAL AND DEATH OF SOCRATES

We are now ready to read several of Plato's early dialogues. In each of them Socrates is the major figure. They must have been written soon after Socrates' death. Because many people witnessed the trial and would have known of his conduct while awaiting execution, scholars think they present as accurate a picture of the historical Socrates as we can find. We'll read *Euthyphro, Apology,* and *Crito* in their entirety, and a selection from *Phaedo.*

This chapter is partitioned into two parts for each dialogue. The text of the dialogue is printed first; this is followed by a section of commentary and questions. Here is a suggestion for you. Begin by giving each dialogue in turn a quick reading (they are all quite short). Don't try to understand everything the first time through; just get a feel for it. It would be ideal to read them aloud with a friend, each taking a part. After you have done the quick read-through, go to the commentary and questions that follow. Using these as a guide, reread each dialogue section by section, trying this time to understand everything and answering the questions as you go along. A good plan is to write out brief answers. You will be amazed at how rich these brief works are.

References are to page numbers in a standard Greek text of Plato.[1] These numbers are printed in the margins and are divided into sections *a* through *e.*

EUTHYPHRO
Translator's Introduction

Euthyphro is surprised to meet Socrates near the king-archon's court, for Socrates is not the kind of man to have business with courts of justice. Socrates explains that he is under in- *dictment by one Meletus for corrupting the young and for not believing in the gods in whom the city believes. After a brief discussion of this, Socrates inquires about Euthyphro's business at court and is told that he is prosecuting his own father for the murder of a laborer who is himself a murderer. His family and friends believe his course of action to be impious, but Euthyphro explains that in this they are mistaken and reveal their ignorance of the nature of piety. This naturally leads Socrates to ask, What is piety? and the rest of the dialogue is devoted to a search for a definition of piety, illustrating the Socratic search for universal definitions of ethical terms, to which a number of early Platonic dialogues are devoted. As usual, no definition is found that satisfies Socrates.*

The Greek term hosion *means, in the first instance, the knowledge of the proper ritual in prayer and sacrifice, and of course its performance (as Euthyphro himself defines it in 14b). But obviously Euthyphro uses it in the much wider sense of pious conduct generally (e.g., his own) and in that sense the word is practically equivalent to righteousness (the justice of the Republic), the transition being by way of conduct pleasing to the gods.*

Besides being an excellent example of the early, so-called Socratic dialogues, Euthyphro *contains several passages with important philosophical implications. These include those in which Socrates speaks of the one Form, presented by all the actions that we call pious (5d), as well as the one in which we are told that the gods love what is pious because it is pious, it is not pious because the gods love it (10d). Another passage clarifies the difference between genus and species (11e). The implications are discussed in the notes on those passages.*

The Dialogue

2   EUTHYPHRO:[1] What's new, Socrates, to make you leave your usual haunts in the Lyceum and spend your time here by the king-archon's court? Surely you are not prosecuting anyone before the king-archon as I am?

SOCRATES: The Athenians do not call this a prosecution but an indictment, Euthyphro.

b   E: What is this you say? Someone must have indicted you, for you are not going to tell me that you have indicted someone else.

s: No indeed.

E: But someone else has indicted you?

---

[1] We know nothing about Euthyphro except what we can gather from this dialogue. He is obviously a professional priest who considers himself an expert on ritual and on piety generally, and, it seems, is generally so considered. One Euthyphro is mentioned in Plato's *Cratylus* (396d) who is given to *enthousiasmos,* inspiration or possession, but we cannot be sure that it is the same person.

s: Quite so.

E: Who is he?

s: I do not really know him myself, Euthyphro. He is apparently young and unknown. They call him Meletus, I believe. He belongs to the Pitthean deme, if you know anyone from that deme called Meletus, with long hair, not much of a beard, and a rather aquiline nose.

E: I don't know him, Socrates. What charge does he bring against you?

c   s: What charge? A not ignoble one I think, for it is no small thing for a young man to have knowledge of such an important subject. He says he knows how our young men are corrupted and who corrupts them. He is likely to be wise, and when he sees my ignorance corrupting his contemporaries, he proceeds

d   to accuse me to the city as to their mother. I think he is the only one of our public men to start out the right way, for it is right to care first that the young should be as good as possible, just as a good farmer is likely to take care of the young plants first, and of the others later. So, too, Meletus first gets rid of us who

3   corrupt the young shoots, as he says, and then afterwards he will obviously take care of the older ones and become a source of great blessings for the city, as seems likely to happen to one who started out this way.

E: I could wish this were true, Socrates, but I fear the opposite may happen. He seems to me to start out by harming the very heart of the city by attempting to wrong you. Tell me, what does he say you do to corrupt the young?

b   s: Strange things, to hear him tell, for he says that I am a maker of gods, and on the ground that I create new gods while not believing in the old gods, he has indicted me for their sake, as he puts it.

E: I understand, Socrates. This is because you say that the divine sign keeps coming to you.[2] So he has written this indictment against you as one who makes innovations in religious matters, and he comes to court to slander you,

---

[2] In Plato, Socrates always speaks of his divine sign or voice as intervening to prevent him from doing or saying something (e.g., *Apology* 31d), but never positively. The popular view was that it enabled him to foretell the future, and Euthyphro here represents that view. Note, however, that Socrates dissociates himself from "you prophets" (3e).

c knowing that such things are easily misrepresented to the crowd. The same is true in my case. Whenever I speak of divine matters in the assembly and foretell the future, they laugh me down as if I were crazy; and yet I have foretold nothing that did not happen. Nevertheless, they envy all of us who do this. One need not worry about them, but meet them head-on.

s: My dear Euthyphro, to be laughed at does not matter perhaps, for the Athenians do not mind anyone they think clever, as long as he does not teach his own wisdom, but if they think that he makes others to be like himself they get

d angry, whether through envy, as you say, or for some other reason.

e: I have certainly no desire to test their feelings towards me in this matter.

s: Perhaps you seem to make yourself but rarely available, and not to be willing to teach your own wisdom, but I'm afraid that my liking for people makes them think that I pour out to anybody anything I have to say, not only without charging a fee but even glad to reward anyone who is willing to listen. If then they

e were intending to laugh at me, as you say they laugh at you, there would be nothing unpleasant in their spending their time in court laughing and jesting, but if they are going to be serious, the outcome is not clear except to you prophets.

e: Perhaps it will come to nothing, Socrates, and you will fight your case as you think best, as I think I will mine.

s: What is your case, Euthyphro? Are you the defendant or the prosecutor?

e: The prosecutor.

s: Whom do you prosecute?

4 e: One whom I am thought crazy to prosecute.

s: Are you pursuing someone who will easily escape you?

e: Far from it, for he is quite old.

s: Who is it?

e: My father.

s: My dear sir! Your own father?

e: Certainly.

s: What is the charge? What is the case about?

e: Murder, Socrates.

s: Good heavens! Certainly, Euthyphro, most

b men would not know how they could do this and be right. It is not the part of anyone to

do this, but of one who is far advanced in wisdom.

e: Yes, by Zeus, Socrates, that is so.

s: Is then the man your father killed one of your relatives? Or is that obvious, for you would not prosecute your father for the murder of a stranger.

e: It is ridiculous, Socrates, for you to think that it makes any difference whether the victim is a stranger or a relative. One should only watch

c whether the killer acted justly or not; if he acted justly, let him go, but if not, one should prosecute, even if the killer shares your hearth and table. The pollution is the same if you knowingly keep company with such a man and do not cleanse yourself and him by bringing him to justice. The victim was a dependent of mine, and when we were farming in Naxos he was a servant of ours. He killed one of our household slaves in drunken anger, so my father bound him hand and foot and threw him in a ditch, then sent a man here to enquire from the priest what should be done. During

d that time he gave no thought or care to the bound man, as being a killer, and it was no matter if he died, which he did. Hunger and cold and his bonds caused his death before the messenger came back from the seer. Both my father and my other relatives are angry that I am prosecuting my father for murder on behalf of a murderer when he hadn't even killed him, they say, and even if he had, the dead man does not deserve a thought, since he was

e a killer. For, they say, it is impious for a son to prosecute his father for murder. But their ideas of the divine attitude to piety and impiety are wrong, Socrates.

s: Whereas, by Zeus, Euthyphro, you think that your knowledge of the divine, and of piety and impiety, is so accurate that, when those things happened as you say, you have no fear of having acted impiously in bringing your father to trial?

e: I should be of no use, Socrates, and Euthyphro

5 would not be superior to the majority of men, if I did not have accurate knowledge of all such things.

s: It is indeed most important, my admirable Euthyphro, that I should become your pupil, and as regards this indictment challenge Meletus about these very things and say to him: that in the past too I considered knowledge about the divine to be most important, and that now that he says I am guilty of improvising and innovating about the gods I have become your pupil. I

b

would say to him: "If, Meletus, you agree that Euthyphro is wise in these matters, consider me, too, to have the right beliefs and do not bring me to trial. If you do not think so, then prosecute that teacher of mine, not me, for corrupting the older men, me and his own father, by teaching me and by exhorting and punishing him." If he is not convinced, and does not discharge me or indict you instead of me, I shall repeat the same challenge in court.

E: Yes, by Zeus, Socrates, and, if he should try to

c

indict me, I think I would find his weak spots and the talk in court would be about him rather than about me.

S: It is because I realize this that I am eager to become your pupil, my dear friend. I know that other people as well as this Meletus do not even seem to notice you, whereas he sees me so sharply and clearly that he indicts me for ungodliness. So tell me now, by Zeus, what you just now maintained you clearly

d

knew: what kind of thing do you say that godliness and ungodliness are, both as regards murder and other things; or is the pious not the same and alike in every action, and the impious the opposite of all that is pious and like itself, and everything that is to be impious presents us with one form[3] or appearance in so far as it is impious?

E: Most certainly, Socrates.

S: Tell me then, what is the pious, and what the impious, do you say?

E: I say that the pious is to do what I am doing now, to prosecute the wrongdoer, be it about

murder or temple robbery or anything else,

e

whether the wrongdoer is your father or your mother or anyone else; not to prosecute is impious. And observe, Socrates, that I can quote the law as a great proof that this is so. I have already said to others that such actions are right, not to favour the ungodly, whoever they are. These people themselves believe that Zeus is the best and most just of the gods,

6

yet they agree that he bound his father because he unjustly swallowed his sons, and that he in turn castrated his father for similar reasons. But they are angry with me because I am prosecuting my father for his wrongdoing. They contradict themselves in what they say about the gods and about me.

S: Indeed, Euthyphro, this is the reason why I am a defendant in the case, because I find it hard to accept things like that being said about the gods, and it is likely to be the reason why I shall be told I do wrong. Now, however, if you, who have full knowledge of such things,

b

share their opinions, then we must agree with them too, it would seem. For what are we to say, we who agree that we ourselves have no knowledge of them? Tell me, by the god of friendship, do you really believe these things are true?

E: Yes, Socrates, and so are even more surprising things, of which the majority has no knowledge.

S: And do you believe that there really is war among the gods, and terrible enmities and battles, and other such things as are told by

c

the poets, and other sacred stories such as are embroidered by good writers and by representations of which the robe of the goddess is adorned when it is carried up to the Acropolis? Are we to say these things are true, Euthyphro?

E: Not only these, Socrates, but, as I was saying just now, I will, if you wish, relate many other things about the gods which I know will amaze you.

S: I should not be surprised, but you will tell me these at leisure some other time. For now, try to tell me more clearly what I was asking just

d

now, for, my friend, you did not teach me adequately when I asked you what the pious was, but you told me that what you are doing now, prosecuting your father for murder, is pious.

---

[3] This is the kind of passage that makes it easier for us to follow the transition from Socrates' universal definitions to the Platonic theory of separately existent eternal universal Forms. The words *eidos* and *idea,* the technical terms for the Platonic Forms, commonly mean physical stature or bodily appearance. As we apply a common epithet, in this case pious, to different actions or things, these must have a common characteristic, present a common appearance or form, to justify the use of the same term, but in the early dialogues, as here, it seems to be thought of as immanent in the particulars and without separate existence. The same is true of 6d where the word "form" is also used.

E: And I told the truth, Socrates.

S: Perhaps. You agree, however, that there are many other pious actions.

E: There are.

S: Bear in mind then that I did not bid you tell me one or two of the many pious actions but that form itself that makes all pious actions pious, for you agreed that all impious actions are impious and all pious actions pious through one form, or don't you remember?

E: I do.

S: Tell me then what this form itself is, so that I may look upon it, and using it as a model, say that any action of yours or another's that is of that kind is pious, and if it is not that it is not.

E: If that is how you want it, Socrates, that is how I will tell you.

S: That is what I want.

7 E: Well then, what is dear to the gods is pious, what is not is impious.

S: Splendid, Euthyphro! You have now answered in the way I wanted. Whether your answer is true I do not know yet, but you will obviously show me that what you say is true.

E: Certainly.

S: Come then, let us examine what we mean. An action or a man dear to the gods is pious, but an action or a man hated by the gods is impious. They are not the same, but quite opposite, the pious and the impious. Is that not so?

E: It is indeed.

S: And that seems to be a good statement?

b E: I think so, Socrates.

S: We have also stated that the gods are in a state of discord, that they are at odds with each other, Euthyphro, and that they are at enmity with each other. Has that, too, been said?

E: It has.

S: What are the subjects of difference that cause hatred and anger? Let us look at it this way. If you and I were to differ about numbers as to which is the greater, would this difference make us enemies and angry with each other, or would we proceed to count and soon re-

c solve our difference about this?

E: We would certainly do so.

S: Again, if we differed about the larger and the smaller, we would turn to measurement and soon cease to differ.

E: That is so.

S: And about the heavier and the lighter, we would resort to weighing and be reconciled.

E: Of course.

S: What subject of difference would make us angry and hostile to each other if we were un-

d able to come to a decision? Perhaps you do not have an answer ready, but examine as I tell you whether these subjects are the just and the unjust, the beautiful and the ugly, the good and the bad. Are these not the subjects of difference about which, when we are unable to come to a satisfactory decision, you and I and other men become hostile to each other whenever we do?

E: That is the difference, Socrates, about those subjects.

S: What about the gods, Euthyphro? If indeed they have differences, will it not be about these same subjects?

E: It certainly must be so.

e S: Then according to your argument, my good Euthyphro, different gods consider different things to be just, beautiful, ugly, good, and bad, for they would not be at odds with one another unless they differed about these subjects, would they?

E: You are right.

S: And they like what each of them considers beautiful, good, and just, and hate the opposites of these?

E: Certainly.

S: But you say that the same things are considered

8 just by some gods and unjust by others, and as they dispute about these things they are at odds and at war with each other. Is that not so?

E: It is.

S: The same things then are loved by the gods and hated by the gods, and would be both god-loved and god-hated.

E: It seems likely.

S: And the same things would be both pious and impious, according to this argument?

E: I'm afraid so.

S: So you did not answer my question, you surprising man. I did not ask you what same thing is both pious and impious, and it appears that

b what is loved by the gods is also hated by them. So it is in no way surprising if your present action, namely punishing your father, may be pleasing to Zeus but displeasing to Kronos and Ouranos, pleasing to Hephaestus but displeasing to Hera, and so with any other gods who differ from each other on this subject.

E: I think, Socrates, that on this subject no gods would differ from one another, that whoever has killed anyone unjustly should pay the penalty.

c S: Well now, Euthyphro, have you ever heard any man maintaining that one who has killed or done anything else unjustly should not pay the penalty?

E: They never cease to dispute on this subject, both elsewhere and in the courts, for when they have committed many wrongs they do and say anything to avoid the penalty.

S: Do they agree they have done wrong, Euthyphro, and in spite of so agreeing do they nevertheless say they should not be punished?

E: No, they do not agree on that point.

S: So they do not say or do anything. For they do not venture to say this, or dispute that they must not pay the penalty if they have done

d wrong, but I think they deny doing wrong. Is that not so?

E: That is true.

S: Then they do not dispute that the wrongdoer must be punished, but they may disagree as to who the wrongdoer is, what he did and when.

E: You are right.

S: Do not the gods have the same experience, if indeed they are at odds with each other about the just and the unjust, as your argument maintains? Some assert that they wrong one another, while others deny it, but no one

e among gods or men ventures to say that the wrongdoer must not be punished.

E: Yes, that is true, Socrates, as to the main point.

S: And those who disagree, whether men or gods, dispute about each action, if indeed the gods disagree. Some say it is done justly, others unjustly. Is that not so?

E: Yes, indeed.

9 S: Come, now, my dear Euthyphro, tell me, too, that I may become wiser, what proof you have that all the gods consider that man to have been killed unjustly who became a murderer while in your service, was bound by the master of his victim, and died in his bonds before the one who bound him found out from the seers what was to be done with him, and that

it is right for a son to denounce and to prosecute his father on behalf of such a man. Come, try to show me a clear sign that all the gods

b definitely believe this action to be right. If you can give me adequate proof of this, I shall never cease to extol your wisdom.

E: This is perhaps no light task, Socrates, though I could show you very clearly.

S: I understand that you think me more dull-witted than the jury, as you will obviously show them that these actions were unjust and that all the gods hate such actions.

E: I will show it to them clearly, Socrates, if only they will listen to me.

c S: They will listen if they think you show them well. But this thought came to me as you were speaking, and I am examining it, saying to myself: "If Euthyphro shows me conclusively that all the gods consider such a death unjust, to what greater extent have I learned from him the nature of piety and impiety? This action would then, it seems, be hated by the gods, but the pious and the impious were not thereby now defined, for what is hated by the gods has also been shown to be loved by them." So I will not insist on this point; let us assume, if you wish, that all the gods consider this unjust and that they all hate it. How-

d ever, is this the correction we are making in our discussion, that what all the gods hate is impious, and what they all love is pious, and that what some gods love and others hate is neither or both? Is that how you now wish us to define piety and impiety?

E: What prevents us from doing so, Socrates?

S: For my part nothing, Euthyphro, but you look whether on your part this proposal will enable you to teach me most easily what you promised.

e E: I would certainly say that the pious is what all the gods love, and the opposite, what all the gods hate, is the impious.

S: Then let us again examine whether that is a sound statement, or do we let it pass, and if one of us, or someone else, merely says that something is so, do we accept that it is so? Or should we examine what the speaker means?

E: We must examine it, but I certainly think that this is now a fine statement.

10 S: We shall soon know better whether it is. Consider this: Is the pious loved by the gods be-

cause it is pious, or is it pious because it is loved by the gods?

E: I don't know what you mean, Socrates.*

. . . .

11 S: I'm afraid, Euthyphro, that when you were asked what piety is, you did not wish to make its nature clear to me, but you told me an affect or quality of it, that the pious has the quality of being loved by all the gods, but you

b have not yet told me what the pious is. Now, if you will, do not hide things from me but tell me again from the beginning what piety is, whether loved by the gods or having some other quality—we shall not quarrel about that—but be keen to tell me what the pious and the impious are.

E: But Socrates, I have no way of telling you what I have in mind, for whatever proposition we put forward goes around and refuses to stay put where we establish it.

S: Your statements, Euthyphro, seem to belong

c to my ancestor, Daedalus. If I were stating them and putting them forward, you would perhaps be making fun of me and say that because of my kinship with him my conclusions in discussion run away and will not stay where one puts them. As these propositions are yours, however, we need some other jest, for they will not stay put for you, as you say yourself.

E: I think the same jest will do for our discussion, Socrates, for I am not the one who makes them go round and not remain in the

d same place; it is you who are the Daedalus; for as far as I am concerned they would remain as they were.

S: It looks as if I was cleverer than Daedalus in using my skill, my friend, in so far as he could only cause to move the things he made himself, but I can make other people's move as well as my own. And the smartest part of my skill is that I am clever without wanting to be, for I would rather have your statements to me

e remain unmoved than possess the wealth of Tantalus as well as the cleverness of Daedalus.

---

*From 10a to 11a, there appears a complex and rather confusing argument. I omit it here and supply a paraphrase in the commentary section that follows the dialogue.—N.M.

But enough of this. Since I think you are making unnecessary difficulties, I am as eager as you are to find a way to teach me about piety, and do not give up before you do. See whether you think all that is pious is of necessity just.

E: I think so.

S: And is then all that is just pious? Or is all that

12 is pious just, but not all that is just pious, but some of it is and some is not?

E: I do not follow what you are saying, Socrates.

S: Yet you are younger than I by as much as you are wiser. As I say, you are making difficulties because of your wealth of wisdom. Pull yourself together, my dear sir, what I am saying is not difficult to grasp. I am saying the opposite of what the poet said who wrote:

> You do not wish to name Zeus, who had done it, and who made all things grow, for

b where there is fear there is also shame.

I disagree with the poet. Shall I tell you why?

E: Please do.

S: I do not think that "where there is fear there is also shame," for I think that many people who fear disease and poverty and many other such things feel fear, but are not ashamed of the things they fear. Do you not think so?

E: I do indeed.

S: But where there is shame there is also fear. For is there anyone who, in feeling shame and em-

c barrassment at anything, does not also at the same time fear and dread a reputation for wickedness?

E: He is certainly afraid.

S: It is then not right to say "where there is fear there is also shame," but that where there is shame there is also fear, for fear covers a larger area than shame. Shame is a part of fear just as odd is a part of number, with the result that it is not true that where there is number there is also oddness, but that where there is oddness there is also number. Do you follow me now?

E: Surely.

S: This is the kind of thing I was asking before,

d whether where there is piety there is also justice, but where there is justice there is not always piety, for the pious is a part of justice. Shall we say that, or do you think otherwise?

E: No, but like that, for what you say appears to be right.

s: See what comes next: if the pious is a part of the just, we must, it seems, find out what part of the just it is. Now if you asked me something of what we mentioned just now, such as what part of number is the even, and what number that is, I would say it is the number that is divisible into two equal, not unequal, parts. Or do you not think so?

e: I do.

e s: Try in this way to tell me what part of the just the pious is, in order to tell Meletus not to wrong us any more and not to indict me for ungodliness, since I have learned from you sufficiently what is godly and pious and what is not.

e: I think, Socrates, that the godly and pious is the part of the just that is concerned with the care of the gods, while that concerned with the care of men is the remaining part of justice.

s: You seem to me to put that very well, but I

13 still need a bit of information. I do not know yet what you mean by care, for you do not mean the care of the gods in the same sense as the care of other things, as, for example, we say, don't we, that not everyone knows how to care for horses, but the horse breeder does.

e: Yes, I do mean it that way.

s: So horse breeding is the care of horses.

e: Yes.

s: Nor does everyone know how to care for dogs, but the hunter does.

e: That is so.

s: So hunting is the care of dogs.

b e: Yes.

s: And cattle raising is the care of cattle.

e: Quite so.

s: While piety and godliness is the care of the gods, Euthyphro. Is that what you mean?

e: It is.

s: Now care in each case has the same effect; it aims at the good and the benefit of the object cared for, as you can see that horses cared for by horse breeders are benefited and become better. Or do you not think so?

e: I do.

s: So dogs are benefited by dog breeding, cattle

c by cattle raising, and so with all the others. Or do you think that care aims to harm the object of its care?

e: By Zeus, no.

s: It aims to benefit the object of its care?

e: Of course.

s: Is piety then, which is the care of the gods, also to benefit the gods and make them better? Would you agree that when you do something pious you make some of the gods better?

e: By Zeus, no.

s: Nor do I think that this is what you mean— far from it—but that is why I asked you what you meant by the care of gods, because I did

d not believe you meant this kind of care.

e: Quite right, Socrates, that is not the kind of care I mean.

s: Very well, but what kind of care of the gods would piety be?

e: The kind of care, Socrates, that slaves take of their masters.

s: I understand. It is likely to be a kind of service of the gods.

e: Quite so.

s: Could you tell me to the achievement of what goal service to doctors tends? Is it not, do you think, to achieving health?

e: I think so.

e s: What about service to shipbuilders? To what achievement is it directed?

e: Clearly, Socrates, to the building of a ship.

s: And service to housebuilders to the building of a house?

e: Yes.

s: Tell me then, my good sir, to the achievement of what aim does service to the gods tend? You obviously know since you say that you, of all men, have the best knowledge of the divine.

e: And I am telling the truth, Socrates.

s: Tell me then, by Zeus, what is that excellent aim that the gods achieve, using us as their servants?

e: Many fine things, Socrates.

14 s: So do generals, my friend. Nevertheless you could easily tell me their main concern, which is to achieve victory in war, is it not?

e: Of course.

s: The farmers too, I think, achieve many fine things, but the main point of their efforts is to produce food from the earth.

e: Quite so.

s: Well then, how would you sum up the many fine things that the gods achieve?

e: I told you a short while ago, Socrates, that it

b is a considerable task to acquire any precise

knowledge of these things, but, to put it simply, I say that if a man knows how to say and do what is pleasing to the gods at prayer and sacrifice, those are pious actions such as preserve both private houses and public affairs of state. The opposite of these pleasing actions are impious and overturn and destroy everything.

c s: You could tell me in far fewer words, if you were willing, the sum of what I asked, Euthyphro, but you are not keen to teach me, that is clear. You were on the point of doing so, but you turned away. If you had given that answer, I should now have acquired from you sufficient knowledge of the nature of piety. As it is, the lover of inquiry must follow his beloved wherever it may lead him. Once more then, what do you say that piety and the pious are? Are they a knowledge of how to sacrifice and pray?

E: They are.

s: To sacrifice is to make a gift to the gods, whereas to pray is to beg from the gods?

E: Definitely, Socrates.

d s: It would follow from this statement that piety would be a knowledge of how to give to, and beg from, the gods.

E: You understood what I said very well, Socrates.

s: That is because I am so desirous of your wisdom, and I concentrate my mind on it, so that no word of yours may fall to the ground. But tell me, what is this service to the gods? You say it is to beg from them and to give to them?

E: I do.

s: And to beg correctly would be to ask from them things that we need?

E: What else?

e s: And to give correctly is to give them what they need from us, for it would not be skillful to bring gifts to anyone that are in no way needed.

E: True, Socrates.

s: Piety would then be a sort of trading skill between gods and men?

E: Trading yes, if you prefer to call it that.

s: I prefer nothing, unless it is true. But tell me, what benefit do the gods derive from the gifts they receive from us? What they give us is obvious to all. There is for us no good that we

15 do not receive from them, but how are they benefited by what they receive from us? Or do we have such an advantage over them in the

trade that we receive all our blessings from them and they receive nothing from us?

E: Do you suppose, Socrates, that the gods are benefited by what they receive from us?

s: What could those gifts from us to the gods be, Euthyphro?

E: What else, do you think, than honour, reverence, and what I mentioned just now, gratitude?

b s: The pious is then, Euthyphro, pleasing to the gods, but not beneficial or dear to them?

E: I think it is of all things most dear to them.

s: So the pious is once again what is dear to the gods.

E: Most certainly.

s: When you say this, will you be surprised if your arguments seem to move about instead of staying put? And will you accuse me of being Daedalus who makes them move, though you are yourself much more skillful than Daedalus and make them go round in a circle? Or do you not realize that our argument has moved around and come again to the same place? You surely remember that earlier the pious and the

c god-beloved were shown not to be the same but different from each other. Or do you not remember?

E: I do.

s: Do you then not realize now that you are saying that what is dear to the gods is the pious? Is this not the same as the god-beloved? Or is it not?

E: It certainly is.

s: Either we were wrong when we agreed before, or, if we were right then, we are wrong now.

E: That seems to be so.

s: So we must investigate again from the beginning what piety is, as I shall not willingly give up before I learn this. Do not think me un-

d worthy, but concentrate your attention and tell the truth. For you know it, if any man does, and I must not let you go, like Proteus, before you tell me. If you had no clear knowledge of piety and impiety you would never have ventured to prosecute your old father for murder on behalf of a servant. For fear of the gods you would have been afraid to take the risk lest you should not be acting rightly, and would have been ashamed before men, but now I know well that you believe you have e   clear knowledge of piety and impiety. So tell me, my good Euthyphro, and do not hide what you think it is.

E: Some other time, Socrates, for I am in a hurry now, and it is time for me to go.

S: What a thing to do, my friend! By going you have cast me down from a great hope I had, that I would learn from you the nature of the

16   pious and the impious and so escape Meletus' indictment by showing him that I had acquired wisdom in divine matters from Euthyphro, and my ignorance would no longer cause me to be careless and inventive about such things, and that I would be better for the rest of my life.

Commentary and Questions

Read 2a–5a   Note that Euthyphro is surprised to find Socrates at court. His surprise indicates that Socrates is neither the sort who brings suit against his fellow citizens nor the sort one would expect to be prosecuted.

Q1.   Why does Socrates say that Meletus is likely to be wise? (2c)

Q2.   What sort of character does Socrates ascribe to Meletus here? Is Socrates sincere in his praise of Meletus?

Q3.   There seem to be two charges against Socrates. Can you identify them? (2c, 3b)

It is well known that Socrates claims to have a "divine sign" that comes to him from time to time. We hear of it again in the *Apology*. That the gods should speak to mortals in signs does not strike the ancient Greeks as a strange notion. Usually the gods speak through oracles, prophets, or seers. When Agamemnon wants to know why his troops are being wasted with plague, he calls on Calchas, who is described as

the clearest by far of all the seers
who scan the flight of birds. He knew all things that are,
all things that are past and all that are to come.
—*The Iliad,* Book 1, 80–82

When Oedipus seeks the cause for his city's distress, he calls the blind seer Tiresias. So the idea that the gods make their will known to mortals is a familiar one.

Euthyphro claims this ability for himself, saying that he "foretells the future." He assumes (mistakenly) that Socrates too claims this ability, and he concludes that it is out of envy for this talent that Meletus and the others are pressing charges. Moreover, Socrates' "sign" from the gods, Euthyphro thinks, would also explain the accusation that Socrates is introducing "new gods."

Does Socrates believe in the "old gods"? There can be little doubt that his view of the Olympians is much the same as that of Xenophanes or Heraclitus: The stories of Homer cannot be taken literally. (See *Euthyphro* 6a.) Yet he always speaks reverently of "god" or "the god" or "the gods" (these three terms being used pretty much interchangeably). And he feels free to use traditional language in speaking about the divine, so he writes that last hymn to Apollo and would probably have agreed with Heraclitus that the divine is "willing and unwilling to be called Zeus."*

Moreover, Xenophon tells us that Socrates behaves in accord with the advice given by the Priestess at Delphi when asked about sacrifice and ritual matters: "Follow the custom of the State: that is the way to act piously." Xenophon goes on to tell us,

And again, when he prayed he asked simply for good gifts, "for the gods know best what things are good." Though his sacrifices were humble, according to his means, he thought himself not a whit inferior to those who made frequent and magnificent sacrifices out of great possessions. . . . No, the greater the piety of the giver, the greater (he thought) was the delight of the gods in the gift.[2]

There seems every reason to suppose that Socrates is pious in the conventional sense. Still, he would not have held back his beliefs if asked directly about the gods; as he says in 3d, his "liking for people" makes it seem that he pours out to anybody what he has to say. And traditionalists might well take exception to some of that.

_____
*See p. 22.

What of the "sign"? Was that an introduction of new gods? There is no reason to believe that Socrates ever thought of it as such. It seems to be analogous to what we would call the voice of conscience, though clearly it was much more vivid to him than to most of us. It never, he tells us, advises him positively to do something; it only prevents him, and it is clearly not anything like Euthyphro's future-telling. (Note that in 3e he separates himself from "you prophets.") But he clearly thinks of the sign as a voice of the divine, however that is best conceived.

Q4.   Why is Euthyphro in court?

Q5.   What does Euthyphro claim to know?

Read 5a–6e   We now know what the topic of this conversation is to be. Socrates says he is "eager" to be Euthyphro's pupil.

Q6.   Why does Socrates say he wants Euthyphro to instruct him? Do you think he really expects to be helped?

Q7.   Do you think this is going to be a serious inquiry? Or is Socrates just having some sport with Euthyphro?

Notice in 5d the three requirements that must be met to satisfy Socrates. He wants to know what the "pious" or the "holy" or the "godly" is (all these words may translate the Greek term).

1. A satisfactory answer will pick out some feature that is the same in every pious action.

2. This feature will not be shared by any impious action.

3. It will be that feature (or the lack of it) that *makes* an action pious (or impious).

What Socrates is searching for, we can say, is a *definition* of piety or holiness.* He wants to know what it is so that it can be recognized when it appears. It is like wanting to know what a crow is: We want to know what features all crows have that are not shared by eagles and hedgehogs, the possession of which ensure that this thing we see before us is indeed a crow.

Would a knowledge of what piety is be useful if one were on the brink of being brought to trial for impiety? A Sophist might not think so at all. At that point, the typical Sophist would construct a dazzling rhetorical display that would emotionally engage the jury on his side. But Socrates, as always, wants to know the truth. He wants to know the truth even more than he wants to be acquitted. We can think of this as one aspect of his persistent search to know himself. Who is he? Has he been guilty of impiety? Only an understanding of what piety truly is will tell.

Q8.   What does Euthyphro say piety is?

Q9.   What does Socrates focus on as the likely reason he is on trial?

Q10.   What is Socrates' objection to the definition Euthyphro has proposed?

Note particularly the term "form" in 6d–e. It clearly does not mean "shape," except perhaps in a most abstract sense. The form of something is whatever makes it the kind of thing it is. The form may sometimes be shape, as the "form" of a square is to be an area bounded by equal straight lines and right angles, but it need not be. When we ask in this sense for the "form" of an elephant, we are asking for more than an outline drawing, and for more than even a photograph can supply. What we want is what the biologist can give us; we are asking what an elephant is. Notice that the biologist can do this not only for elephants but also for mammals—and no one can draw the geometrical shape of a mammal. (True, you can draw a picture of *this* mammal or *that* mammal, but not a picture of a mammal *as such*. Yet it can be given a definition.) In the same way, it is perfectly in order to ask for the "form" of abstract qualities such as justice, courage, or piety.

Read 7a–9b   Here we have Euthyphro's second attempt at answering Socrates' question.

Q11.   What is Euthyphro's second answer?

Q12.   Why does Socrates exclaim, "Splendid!"?

---

*There are a number of different kinds of definition. For a critique of Socrates' kind, see Wittgenstein's notion of "family resemblances" in Chapter 23.

Q13.   What is the difference between answering "in the way" he wanted and giving a "true" answer?

Note Socrates' characteristic invitation in 7a: "Let us examine what we mean." How does this examination proceed? He reminds Euthyphro of something he admitted earlier—that there is "war among the gods" (6b)—and wonders whether that is *consistent* with the definition Euthyphro now proposes; do the two fit together, or do they clash?

Q14.   How does Socrates derive the conclusion (8a) that "the same things then are loved by the gods and hated by the gods"? Is this a correct deduction from the statements Euthyphro previously agreed to?

Q15.   What further conclusion follows? Why is that disturbing?

In 8b, Socrates drives the disturbing consequence home by applying it to Euthyphro's own case. Socrates is never one to leave things up in the air, unconnected to practical life. If this is a good understanding of piety, then it ought to illumine the matter at hand. But of course, Euthyphro cannot admit that his own prosecution is loved by some of the gods and hated by others—that it is both pious and impious. He protests that *none* of the gods would disagree that "whoever has killed anyone unjustly should pay the penalty."

Now, this is sneaky. Can you see why? It is a move that might slide past a lesser antagonist, but Socrates picks it up immediately.

Q16.   What do people dispute about concerning wrongs and penalties? And what not?

So Socrates drives Euthyphro back to the issue: In light of the admission that the gods quarrel, what reason is there to think that prosecuting his father is an instance of what the gods love and thus an example of piety?

Q17.   Do you believe that Socrates has put Euthyphro in an untenable position here?

Read 9c–11d   Socrates takes the lead here and proposes a modification to the earlier definition.

Euthyphro embraces the suggestion with enthusiasm in 9e. Be sure you are clear about the new definition. Write it down.

Again we get the invitation to examine this new attempt. In 9e, Socrates backs it up with this question: "Or do we let it pass, and if one of us, or someone else, merely says that something is so, do we accept that it is so?" Are there reasons why this should not be accepted? The mere fact that someone—anyone—says it is so does not make it so. Do you agree with Socrates here?

In 10a, we get an important question, one that reverberates through later Christian theology and has a bearing on whether there can be an **ethics** independent of what God or the gods approve. Is a secular ethics possible? Suppose we agree that in normal circumstances it is wrong to lie (allowing that a lie may be justified, for example, if it is the only way to save a life). And suppose, for the sake of the argument, we also agree that God or the gods hate lying (in those normal circumstances). What is it, we still might ask, that *makes* lying wrong? Is it the fact that it is hated by the divine power(s)? Or is there something about lying itself that makes it wrong—and that is why the gods hate it? To ask these questions is a way of asking for the "form" of wrongness. (Look again at the three requirements for a satisfactory definition in 5d and on page 81; it is the third requirement that is at issue.)

Suppose we agree, Socrates says, that what all the gods love is pious and what they all hate is impious; the question remains whether it is this love and hate that explains the piety of the pious. Suppose it is. Then a behavior is pious or holy *simply because* that behavior pleases the gods. It follows that if the gods loved lying, stealing, or adultery, that would make it right to lie, steal, or sleep with your neighbor's spouse. In this case, ethics is tied intrinsically to religion.

The alternative is that there is something about these actions that makes them wrong—and that is why the gods hate them. If this alternative is correct, then a secular ethics is possible. If we could identify what it is about lying that makes it wrong, we would have a reason not to lie whether we believe in the gods or not. Those who think that God's command (or love) is what *makes* lying wrong will be likely to say, if they lose faith in God, that "everything is permitted."* But on the alternative to divine command theory, this radical consequence does not follow. The question Socrates raises is an important one.

Assuming that the alternatives are clear, which one should we prefer? There is no doubt about Socrates' answer: the pious is pious *not* because the gods love it; rather, the gods love what is pious because of what it is. In the omitted section (10a—11a), Socrates piles up analogies to explain this. Let's try to simplify. Suppose that Henry, a gardener, loves his roses. The roses are loved, then, because Henry loves them. But he doesn't love them because they are loved by him! That would be absurd. He loves them because of something in the roses, something that makes them worthy of his love—their fragrance, perhaps, or their beauty.

In the same way, Socrates argues, if the gods love piety in humans, it must be because there is something lovable about it. Socrates wants to understand what it is. That is why he complains in 11a that Euthyphro has not answered his question. He says that Euthyphro has told him only "an affect or quality" of the pious—namely, that it is loved by the gods. But, he claims, Euthyphro has not yet made its "nature" or "form" clear. To be told only that the pious is what all the gods love is to learn only about how it is regarded by them. Euthyphro has spoken only of something quite external; he has not revealed a single thing about what it really is!

Q18.   Is this a good argument? Suppose, in response to the question, "Why do the gods love the pious?" one were to reply, "They just do!" Is Socrates assuming that there must be a reason? Is he assuming what he needs to prove? Think about this.

Socrates probably calls Daedalus (in 11c) his "ancestor" because Daedalus was the mythical "patron saint" of stonemasons and sculptors. He

was reputed to be such a cunning artisan that his sculptures took life and ran away.

Q19.   Why is Socrates reminded of Daedalus here?

Read 11e–end   Again Socrates makes a suggestion, this time that piety and justice are related somehow. It seems a promising line to investigate, but some clarifications are needed. Are they identical? Or is one a part of the other? And if the latter, which is part of which?

Q20.   What answer do the two settle on? Why?

Q21.   In what way are the fear/shame and odd/number distinctions analogous?

Q22.   What are the two kinds of "care" that are distinguished? (13a–c and 13d–e)

Q23.   Which one is the relevant one? Why?

In 14c we reach a crucial turning point in the dialogue. Note that Socrates here says they were on the verge of solving the problem, but Euthyphro "turned away." If only he had answered a certain question, Socrates says, he "should now have acquired . . . sufficient knowledge of the nature of piety." But Euthyphro didn't answer it.

Apparently Socrates feels that they were on the right track. Let us review. Piety is part of justice. It is that part consisting in care of the gods. The kind of care at issue is the kind that slaves offer their masters. Such service on the part of slaves is always directed to some fine end (for example, health, ships, houses). The question arises, to what fine end is service to the gods devoted? To put it another way, what is the point of piety? What is it *for?* What is "that excellent aim that the gods achieve, using us as their servants?" Remember that for Socrates the good is always something useful or advantageous. He is here asking—on the tacit assumption that piety is something good—what the advantage is that piety produces. We can identify the good things produced by service to doctors. What good things are produced by service to the gods? If one could answer this question, the nature of piety might finally be clarified. It would be service to the gods for the sake of *X*. All we need to know is what *X* is.

---

*This formula, "Everything is permitted," is that of Ivan Karamazov, the atheist in Dostoyevsky's novel, *The Brothers Karamazov*. The servant of the family, Smerdyakov, is persuaded that this is so, and on these grounds he murders the brothers' father.

Unfortunately, all Euthyphro can say with regard to X is that it is "many fine things." When pressed harder, he in effect changes the subject, although he probably doesn't realize he is doing so. He says in 14b that "to put it simply," piety is knowing "how to say and do what is pleasing to the gods at prayer and sacrifice." This certainly does not answer the question of what aim the gods achieve through our service!

Let us, however, briefly consider Euthyphro's statement. First, it does go some way toward answering the question of what we should do to be pious. Euthyphro's answer is in fact the traditional answer common to most religions: pray and offer sacrifice. That answer would have been the standard one in Athens, and it is a little surprising that it comes out so late in the dialogue. It corresponds to the advice of the Delphic Oracle to "follow the custom of the state."

Second, Euthyphro's statement mentions some advantages to being pious in this way: preserving "both private houses and public affairs of state." But this is puzzling. Why does Socrates not accept this as an answer to the question about the nature of X, for the sake of which we ought to be pious in just this way?

No answer is given in the dialogue; perhaps it must just remain puzzling. But here is a suggestion. Socrates, at the end of the Peloponnesian War, may simply be unable to believe this is true. No doubt Athens had offered many prayers and had made all the required sacrifices during the war. Athens had prayed for victory, just as Sparta must have prayed for victory. Yet Athens not only lost, she did irreparable damage to herself; such piety, it seemed, did *not* preserve private houses and public affairs. If the promised advantages do not materialize, Socrates would conclude, this kind of piety is not after all a good thing. Perhaps the exasperation evident in 14c expresses Socrates' view that by this time in history it is all too clear piety can't be that. It can't be a kind of "trading skill" between gods and mortals. And on the assumption that piety is a good thing, it must be something quite different from Euthyphro's version of it. So the nature of X remains unclarified.

Well, this is rather speculative but not, I think, implausible. As we'll see, Jesus and the Christians have an answer about the nature of X. We find it clearly, for instance, in St. Augustine.* It is an answer that Socrates is close to but does not quite grasp. It demands that we rethink the nature of God and the relations of man to God altogether. But that is a story for later.

Socrates, regretfully, feels it is necessary to follow his "teacher," and once more takes up his questioning in 14c. There is a fairly simple argument running through these exchanges, but it is not easy to pick it out. Let me try to identify the steps; check the text to see that I am getting it right.

1. Piety is prayer and sacrifice. (This is Euthyphro's latest definition, now up for examination.)

2. Prayer and sacrifice are begging from the gods and giving to the gods.

3. The giving must, to be "skillful," be giving what they need.

4. To give what they need would be to benefit them.

---

*See p. 254.

5. But we cannot benefit the gods.

6. If our giving does not benefit the gods, the only alternative is that this giving "pleases" them.

7. But that is just to say that they like it, it is dear to them—it is what they love.

8. And that returns us to the earlier definition: that piety is what all the gods love. (And we already know that this is not satisfactory. So we are going in a circle.)

The crux of the argument is, no doubt, Premise 5. It is expressed by Euthyphro in a surprised question in 15a and accepted by Socrates. Why can't we benefit the gods? No reasons are given here, but they are not hard to find. The gods, recall, are the immortals; as such they are also the happy ones. To think of them as having needs that mere mortals could supply would have seemed to many Greeks—especially to those who had the "high" view of "the god" characteristic of Xenophanes, Heraclitus, and Socrates—as impious in the extreme. We receive all our benefits from them. To think that we could benefit them would be arrogance and hubris of the first rank.

Q24. Do you agree with this view? What do you think of this argument? Has the discussion really come full circle?

Q25. What characteristic of Socrates do you think Plato means to impress upon us in Socrates' next-to-last speech?

Q26. Has Euthyphro learned anything in the course of this discussion?

Q27. Have you? If so, what?

APOLOGY
Translator's Introduction

The Apology [1] *professes to be a record of the actual speech that Socrates delivered in his own defence at the trial. This makes the question of its historicity more acute than in the dialogues in which the conversations themselves are mostly fictional and the question of historicity is concerned only with how far the theories that Socrates is represented as expressing were those of the historical Socrates. Here, however, we are dealing with a speech that Socrates made as a matter of history. How far is Plato's account accurate? We should always remember that the ancients did not expect historical accuracy in the way we do. On the other hand, Plato makes it clear that he was present at the trial (34a, 38b). Moreover, if, as is generally believed, the* Apology *was written not long after the event, many Athenians would remember the actual speech, and it would be a poor way to vindicate the Master, which is the obvious intent, to put a completely different speech into his mouth. Some liberties could no doubt be allowed, but the main arguments and the general tone of the defence must surely be faithful to the original. The beauty of language and style is certainly Plato's, but the serene spiritual and moral beauty of character belongs to Socrates. It is a powerful combination.*

Athenian juries were very large, in this case 501, and they combined the duties of jury and judge as we know them by both convicting and sentencing. Obviously, it would have been virtually impossible for so large a body to discuss various penalties and decide on one. The problem was resolved rather neatly, however, by having the prosecutor, after conviction, assess the penalty he thought appropriate, followed by a counter-assessment by the defendant. The jury would then decide between the two. This procedure generally made for moderation on both sides.

Thus the Apology *is in three parts. The first and major part is the main speech (17a–35a), followed by the counter-assessment (35a–38c), and finally, last words to the jury (38c–42a), both to those who voted for the death sentence and those who voted for acquittal.*

---

[1] The word *apology* is a transliteration, not a translation, of the Greek *apologia,* which means defense. There is certainly nothing apologetic about the speech.

The Dialogue

17 I do not know, men of Athens, how my accusers affected you; as for me, I was almost carried away in spite of myself, so persuasively did they speak. And yet, hardly anything of what they said is true. Of the many lies they told, one in particular surprised me, namely that you should be careful not to be deceived by an accomplished speaker like

b me. That they were not ashamed to be immediately proved wrong by the facts, when I show myself not to be an accomplished speaker at all, that I thought was most shameless on their part—unless indeed they call an accomplished speaker the man who speaks the truth. If they mean that, I would agree that I am an orator, but not after their manner, for indeed, as I say, practically nothing they said was true. From me you will hear the

c whole truth, though not, by Zeus, gentlemen, expressed in embroidered and stylized phrases like theirs, but things spoken at random and expressed in the first words that come to mind, for I put my trust in the justice of what I say, and let none of you expect anything else. It would not be fitting at my age, as it might be for a young man, to toy with words when I appear before you.

One thing I do ask and beg of you gentlemen: if you hear me making my defence in the same kind of language as I am accustomed to use in the market place by the bankers' tables,[2] where many of you have heard me, and elsewhere, do not be surprised or create a disturbance on that account.

d The position is this: this is my first appearance in a law-court, at the age of seventy; I am therefore simply a stranger to the manner of speaking here. Just as if I were really a stranger, you would certainly excuse me if I spoke in that dialect and

18 manner in which I had been brought up, so too my present request seems a just one, for you to pay no attention to my manner of speech—be it better or worse—but to concentrate your attention on whether what I say is just or not, for the excellence of a judge lies in this, as that of a speaker lies in telling the truth.

It is right for me, gentlemen, to defend myself first against the first lying accusations made against me and my first accusers, and then against the later

accusations and the later accusers. There have

b been many who have accused me to you for many years now, and none of their accusations are true. These I fear much more than I fear Anytus and his friends, though they too are formidable. These earlier ones, however, are more so, gentlemen; they got hold of most of you from childhood, persuaded you and accused me quite falsely, saying that there is a man called Socrates, a wise man, a student of all things in the sky and below

c the earth, who makes the worse argument the stronger. Those who spread that rumour, gentlemen, are my dangerous accusers, for their hearers believe that those who study these things do not even believe in the gods. Moreover, these accusers are numerous, and have been at it a long time; also, they spoke to you at an age when you would most readily believe them, some of you being children and adolescents, and they won their case by default, as there was no defence.

What is most absurd in all this is that one can-

d not even know or mention their names unless one of them is a writer of comedies.[3] Those who maliciously and slanderously persuaded you—who also, when persuaded themselves then persuaded others—all those are most difficult to deal with: one cannot bring one of them into court or refute him; one must simply fight with shadows, as it were, in making one's defence, and cross-examine when no one answers. I want you to realize too that my accusers are of two kinds: those who have accused me recently, and the old ones I mention; and to think that I must first defend myself against the latter, for you have also heard their accusations

e first, and to a much greater extent than the more recent.

Very well then. I must surely defend myself and

19 attempt to uproot from your minds in so short a time the slander that has resided there so long. I wish this may happen, if it is in any way better for you and me, and that my defence may be successful, but I think this is very difficult and I am fully aware of how difficult it is. Even so, let the matter proceed as the god may wish, but I must obey the law and make my defence.

Let us then take up the case from its beginning.

---

[2] The bankers or money-changers had their counters in the market place. It seems that this was a favourite place for gossip.

[3] This refers in particular to Aristophanes, whose comedy, *The Clouds,* produced in 423 B.C., ridiculed the (imaginary) school of Socrates.

b What is the accusation from which arose the slander in which Meletus trusted when he wrote out the charge against me? What did they say when they slandered me? I must, as if they were my actual prosecutors, read the affidavit they would have sworn. It goes something like this: Socrates is guilty of wrongdoing in that he busies himself studying things in the sky and below the earth; he makes the worse into the stronger argument, and he teaches these same things to others. You have seen **c** this yourselves in the comedy of Aristophanes, a Socrates swinging about there, saying he was walking on air and talking a lot of other nonsense about things of which I know nothing at all. I do not speak in contempt of such knowledge, if someone is wise in these things——lest Meletus bring more cases against me——but, gentlemen, I have no part in it, and on this point I call upon the majority of you as witnesses. I think it right that all those of you who have heard me conversing, and many of **d** you have, should tell each other if anyone of you have ever heard me discussing such subjects to any extent at all. From this you will learn that the other things said about me by the majority are of the same kind.

Not one of them is true. And if you have heard from anyone that I undertake to teach people and **e** charge a fee for it, that is not true either. Yet I think it a fine thing to be able to teach people as Gorgias of Leontini does, and Prodicus of Ceos, and Hippias of Elis.[4] Each of these men can go to any city and persuade the young, who can keep company with anyone of their own fellow-citizens **20** they want without paying, to leave the company of these, to join with themselves, pay them a fee, and be grateful to them besides. Indeed, I learned that there is another wise man from Paros who is visiting us, for I met a man who has spent more money on Sophists than everybody else put together, Callias, the son of Hipponicus. So I asked him—— he has two sons——"Callias," I said, "if your sons

were colts or calves, we could find and engage a supervisor for them who would make them excel **b** in their proper qualities, some horse breeder or farmer. Now since they are men, whom do you have in mind to supervise them? Who is an expert in this kind of excellence, the human and social kind? I think you must have given thought to this since you have sons. Is there such a person," I asked, "or is there not?" "Certainly there is," he said. "Who is he?" I asked, "What is his name, where is he from? and what is his fee?" "His name, Socrates, is Evenus, he comes from Paros, **c** and his fee is five minas." I thought Evenus a happy man, if he really possesses this art, and teaches for so moderate a fee. Certainly I would pride and preen myself if I had this knowledge, but I do not have it, gentlemen.

One of you might perhaps interrupt me and say: "But Socrates, what is your occupation? From where have these slanders come? For surely if you did not busy yourself with something out of the common, all these rumours and talk would not have arisen unless you did something other than most people. Tell us what it is, that we may not **d** speak inadvisedly about you." Anyone who says that seems to be right, and I will try to show you what has caused this reputation and slander. Listen then. Perhaps some of you will think I am jesting, but be sure that all that I shall say is true. What has caused my reputation is none other than a certain kind of wisdom. What kind of wisdom? Human wisdom, perhaps. It may be that I really possess this, while those whom I mentioned just now are **e** wise with a wisdom more than human; else I cannot explain it, for I certainly do not possess it, and whoever says I do is lying and speaks to slander me. Do not create a disturbance, gentlemen, even if you think I am boasting, for the story I shall tell does not originate with me, but I will refer you to a trustworthy source. I shall call upon the god at Delphi as witness to the existence and nature of my wis- **21** dom, if it be such. You know Chairephon. He was my friend from youth, and the friend of most of you, as he shared your exile and your return. You surely know the kind of man he was, how impulsive in any course of action. He went to Delphi at one time and ventured to ask the oracle——as I say, gentlemen, do not create a disturbance——he asked if any man was wiser than I, and the Pythian replied that no one was wiser. Chairephon is dead, but his brother will testify to you about this.

---

[4] These were all well-known Sophists. Gorgias, after whom Plato named one of his dialogues, was a celebrated rhetorician and teacher of rhetoric. He came to Athens in 427 B.C., and his rhetorical tricks took the city by storm. Two dialogues, the authenticity of which has been doubted, are named after Hippias, whose knowledge was encyclopedic. Prodicus was known for his insistence on the precise meaning of words. Both he and Hippias are characters in the *Protagoras* (named after another famous Sophist).

b   Consider that I tell you this because I would inform you about the origin of the slander. When I heard of this reply I asked myself: "Whatever does the god mean? What is his riddle? I am very conscious that I am not wise at all; what then does he mean by saying that I am the wisest? For surely he does not lie; it is not legitimate for him to do so." For a long time I was at a loss as to his meaning; then I very reluctantly turned to some such investigation as this: I went to one of those reputed **c** wise, thinking that there, if anywhere, I could refute the oracle and say to it: "This man is wiser than I, but you said I was." Then, when I examined this man—there is no need for me to tell you his name, he was one of our public men—my experience was something like this: I thought that he appeared wise to many people and especially to himself, but he was not. I then tried to show him **d** that he thought himself wise, but that he was not. As a result he came to dislike me, and so did many of the bystanders. So I withdrew and thought to myself: "I am wiser than this man; it is likely that neither of us knows anything worthwhile, but he thinks he knows something when he does not, whereas when I do not know, neither do I think I know; so I am likely to be wiser than he to this small extent, that I do not think I know what I do not know." After this I approached another man, **e** one of those thought to be wiser than he, and I thought the same thing, and so I came to be disliked both by him and by many others.

After that I proceeded systematically. I realized, to my sorrow and alarm, that I was getting unpopular, but I thought that I must attach the greatest importance to the god's oracle, so I must go to all those who had any reputation for knowledge to examine its meaning. And by the dog,[5] gentlemen **22** of the jury—for I must tell you the truth—I experienced something like this: in my investigation in the service of the god I found that those who had the highest reputation were nearly the most deficient, while those who were thought to be inferior were more knowledgeable. I must give you an account of my journeyings as if they were labours I had undertaken to prove the oracle irrefutable. After the politicians, I went to the poets, the writers

b   of tragedies and dithyrambs and the others, intending in their case to catch myself being more ignorant than they. So I took up those poems with which they seemed to have taken most trouble and asked them what they meant, in order that I might at the same time learn something from them. I am ashamed to tell you the truth, gentlemen, but I must. Almost all the bystanders might have explained the poems better than their authors could. **c** I soon realized that poets do not compose their poems with knowledge, but by some inborn talent and by inspiration, like seers and prophets who also say many fine things without any understanding of what they say. The poets seemed to me to have had a similar experience. At the same time I saw that, because of their poetry, they thought themselves very wise men in other respects, which they were not. So there again I withdrew, thinking that I had the same advantage over them as I had over the politicians.

Finally I went to the craftsmen, for I was conscious of knowing practically nothing, and I knew **d** that I would find that they had knowledge of many fine things. In this I was not mistaken; they knew things I did not know, and to that extent they were wiser than I. But, gentlemen of the jury, the good craftsmen seemed to me to have the same fault as the poets: each of them, because of his success at his craft, thought himself very wise in other most important pursuits, and this error of **e** theirs overshadowed the wisdom they had, so that I asked myself, on behalf of the oracle, whether I should prefer to be as I am, with neither their wisdom nor their ignorance, or to have both. The answer I gave myself and the oracle was that it was to my advantage to be as I am.

As a result of this investigation, gentlemen of **23** the jury, I acquired much unpopularity, of a kind that is hard to deal with and is a heavy burden; many slanders came from these people and a reputation for wisdom, for in each case the bystanders thought that I myself possessed the wisdom that I proved that my interlocutor did not have. What is probable, gentlemen, is that in fact the god is wise and that his oracular response meant that human wisdom is worth little or nothing, and that when **b** he says this man, Socrates, he is using my name as an example, as if he said: "This man among you, mortals, is wisest who, like Socrates, understands that his wisdom is worthless." So even now I continue this investigation as the god bade me—and I

---

[5] A curious oath, occasionally used by Socrates, it appears in a longer form in the *Gorgias* (482b) as "by the dog, the god of the Egyptians."

go around seeking out anyone, citizen or stranger, whom I think wise. Then if I do not think he is, I come to the assistance of the god and show him that he is not wise. Because of this occupation, I do not have the leisure to engage in public affairs to any extent, nor indeed to look after my own, but I live in great poverty because of my service to the god.

c   Furthermore, the young men who follow me around of their own free will, those who have most leisure, the sons of the very rich, take pleasure in hearing people questioned; they themselves often imitate me and try to question others. I think they find an abundance of men who believe they have some knowledge but know little or nothing. The result is that those whom they question are angry,

d   not with themselves but with me. They say: "That man Socrates is a pestilential fellow who corrupts the young." If one asks them what he does and what he teaches to corrupt them, they are silent, as they do not know, but, so as not to appear at a loss, they mention those accusations that are available against all philosophers, about "things in the sky and things below the earth," about "not believing in the gods" and "making the worse the stronger argument;" they would not want to tell the truth, I'm sure, that they have been proved to lay claim to knowledge when they know nothing. These people are ambitious, violent and numer-

e   ous; they are continually and convincingly talking about me; they have been filling your ears for a long time with vehement slanders against me. From them Meletus attacked me, and Anytus and Lycon, Meletus being vexed on behalf of the poets, Anytus on behalf of the craftsmen and the politicians, Lycon on behalf of the orators, so that, as

24 I started out by saying, I should be surprised if I could rid you of so much slander in so short a time. That, gentlemen of the jury, is the truth for you. I have hidden or disguised nothing. I know well enough that this very conduct makes me unpopular, and this is proof that what I say is true, that such is the slander against me, and that such

b   are its causes. If you look into this either now or later, this is what you will find.

Let this suffice as a defence against the charges of my earlier accusers. After this I shall try to defend myself against Meletus, that good and patriotic man, as he says he is, and my later accusers. As these are a different lot of accusers, let us again take up their sworn deposition. It goes something like this: Socrates is guilty of corrupting the young

and of not believing in the gods in whom the city believes, but in other new divinities. Such is their

c   charge. Let us examine it point by point.

He says that I am guilty of corrupting the young, but I say that Meletus is guilty of dealing frivolously with serious matters, of irresponsibly bringing people into court, and of professing to be seriously concerned with things about none of which he has ever cared, and I shall try to prove that this is so. Come here and tell me, Meletus.

d   Surely you consider it of the greatest importance that our young men be as good as possible?[6] —Indeed I do.

Come then, tell the jury who improves them. You obviously know, in view of your concern. You say you have discovered the one who corrupts them, namely me, and you bring me here and accuse me to the jury. Come, inform the jury and tell them who it is. You see, Meletus, that you are silent and know not what to say. Does this not seem shameful to you and a sufficient proof of what I say, that you have not been concerned with any of this? Tell me, my good sir, who improves

e   our young men?   —The laws.

That is not what I am asking, but what person who has knowledge of the laws to begin with? —These jurymen, Socrates.

How do you mean, Meletus? Are these able to educate the young and improve them? —Certainly.

All of them, or some but not others?   —All of them.

Very good, by Hera. You mention a great

25 abundance of benefactors. But what about the audience? Do they improve the young or not? —They do, too.

What about the members of Council?   —The Councillors, also.

But, Meletus, what about the assembly? Do members of the assembly corrupt the young, or do they all improve them?   —They improve them.

All the Athenians, it seems, make the young into fine good men, except me, and I alone corrupt them. Is that what you mean?   —That is most definitely what I mean.

---

[6] Socrates here drops into his usual method of discussion by question and answer. This, no doubt, is what Plato had in mind, at least in part, when he made him ask the indulgence of the jury if he spoke "in his usual manner."

b   You condemn me to a great misfortune. Tell me: does this also apply to horses do you think? That all men improve them and one individual corrupts them? Or is quite the contrary true, one individual is able to improve them, or very few, namely the horse breeders, whereas the majority, if they have horses and use them, corrupt them? Is that not the case, Meletus, both with horses and all other animals? Of course it is, whether you and Anytus say so or not. It would be a very happy state of affairs if only one person corrupted our youth, while the others improved them.

c   You have made it sufficiently obvious, Meletus, that you have never had any concern for our youth; you show your indifference clearly; that you have given no thought to the subjects about which you bring me to trial.

And by Zeus, Meletus, tell us also whether it is better for a man to live among good or wicked fellow-citizens. Answer, my good man, for I am not asking a difficult question. Do not the wicked do some harm to those who are ever closest to them, whereas good people benefit them?   —Certainly.

d   And does the man exist who would rather be harmed than benefited by his associates? Answer, my good sir, for the law orders you to answer. Is there any man who wants to be harmed?   —Of course not.

Come now, do you accuse me here of corrupting the young and making them worse deliberately or unwillingly?   —Deliberately.

What follows, Meletus? Are you so much wiser at your age than I am at mine that you understand that wicked people always do some harm to their

e   closest neighbours while good people do them good, but I have reached such a pitch of ignorance that I do not realize this, namely that if I make one of my associates wicked I run the risk of being harmed by him so that I do such a great evil deliberately, as you say? I do not believe you, Meletus, and I do not think anyone else will. Either I do not

26   corrupt the young or, if I do, it is unwillingly, and you are lying in either case. Now if I corrupt them unwillingly, the law does not require you to bring people to court for such unwilling wrongdoings, but to get hold of them privately, to instruct them and exhort them; for clearly, if I learn better, I shall cease to do what I am doing unwillingly. You, however, have avoided my company and were unwilling to instruct me, but you bring me here, where

the law requires one to bring those who are in need of punishment, not of instruction.

And so, gentlemen of the jury, what I said is clearly true: Meletus has never been at all concerned with these matters. Nonetheless tell us,

b   Meletus, how you say that I corrupt the young; or is it obvious from your deposition that it is by teaching them not to believe in the gods in whom the city believes but in other new divinities? Is this not what you say I teach and so corrupt them? —That is most certainly what I do say.

Then by those very gods about whom we are

c   talking, Meletus, make this clearer to me and to the jury: I cannot be sure whether you mean that I teach the belief that there are some gods— and therefore I myself believe that there are gods and am not altogether an atheist, nor am I guilty of that—not, however, the gods in whom the city believes, but others, and that this is the charge against me, that they are others. Or whether you mean that I do not believe in gods at all, and that this is what I teach to others.   —This is what I mean, that you do not believe in gods at all.

d   You are a strange fellow, Meletus. Why do you say this? Do I not believe, as other men do, that the sun and the moon are gods?   —No, by Zeus, jurymen, for he says that the sun is stone, and the moon earth.

My dear Meletus, do you think you are prosecuting Anaxagoras? Are you so contemptuous of the jury and think them so ignorant of letters as not to know that the books of Anaxagoras[7] of Clazomenae are full of those theories, and further, that the young men learn from me what they can buy

e   from time to time for a drachma, at most, in the bookshops, and ridicule Socrates if he pretends that these theories are his own, especially as they are so absurd? Is that, by Zeus, what you think of me, Meletus, that I do not believe that there are any gods?   —That is what I say, that you do not believe in the gods at all.

You cannot be believed, Meletus, even, I think, by yourself. The man appears to me, gentlemen

---

[7] Anaxagoras of Clazomenae, born about the beginning of the fifth century B.C., came to Athens as a young man and spent his time in the pursuit of natural philosophy. He claimed that the universe was directed by Nous (Mind), and that matter was indestructible but always combining in various ways. He left Athens after being prosecuted for impiety.

27 of the jury, highly insolent and uncontrolled. He seems to have made this deposition out of insolence, violence and youthful zeal. He is like one who composed a riddle and is trying it out: "Will the wise Socrates realize that I am jesting and contradicting myself, or shall I deceive him and others?" I think he contradicts himself in the affidavit, as if he said: "Socrates is guilty of not believing in gods but believing in gods," and surely that is the part of a jester!

b Examine with me, gentlemen, how he appears to contradict himself, and you, Meletus, answer us. Remember, gentlemen, what I asked you when I began, not to create a disturbance if I proceed in my usual manner.

Does any man, Meletus, believe in human affairs who does not believe in human beings? Make him answer, and not again and again create a disturbance. Does any man who does not believe in horses believe in equine affairs? Or in flute music but not in flute-players? No, my good sir, no man could. If you are not willing to answer, I will tell c you and the jury. Answer the next question, however. Does any man believe in divine activities who does not believe in divinities? —No one.

Thank you for answering, if reluctantly, when the jury made you. Now you say that I believe in divine activities and teach about them, whether new or old, but at any rate divine activities according to what you say, and to this you have sworn in your deposition. But if I believe in divine activities I must quite inevitably believe in divine beings. Is that not so? It is indeed. I shall assume that you d agree, as you do not answer. Do we not believe divine beings to be either gods or the children of gods? Yes or no?   —Of course.

Then since I do believe in divine beings, as you admit, if divine beings are gods, this is what I mean when I say you speak in riddles and in jest, as you state that I do not believe in gods and then again that I do, since I believe in divine beings. If on the other hand the divine beings are children of the gods, bastard children of the gods by nymphs or some other mothers, as they are said to be, what man would believe children of the gods to exist, but not gods? That would be just as absurd as e to believe the young of horses and asses, namely mules, to exist, but not to believe in the existence of horses and asses. You must have made this deposition, Meletus, either to test us or because you

were at a loss to find any true wrongdoing of what to accuse me. There is no way in which you could persuade anyone of even small intelligence that it is not the part of one and the same man to be- 28 lieve in the activities of divine beings and gods, and then again the part of one and the same man not to believe in the existence of divinities and gods and heroes.

I do not think, gentlemen of the jury, that it requires a prolonged defence to prove that I am not guilty of the charges in Meletus' deposition, but this is sufficient. On the other hand, you know that what I said earlier is true, that I am very unpopular with many people. This will be my undoing, if I am undone, not Meletus or Anytus but b the slanders and envy of many people. This has destroyed many other good men and will, I think, continue to do so. There is no danger that it will stop at me.

Someone might say: "Are you not ashamed, Socrates, to have followed the kind of occupation that has led to your being now in danger of death?" However, I should be right to reply to him: "You are wrong, sir, if you think that a man who is any good at all should take into account the risk of life or death; he should look to this only in his actions, whether what he does is right or wrong, whether c he is acting like a good or a bad man." According to your view, all the heroes who died at Troy were inferior people, especially the son of Thetis who was so contemptuous of danger compared with disgrace.[8] When he was eager to kill Hector, his goddess mother warned him, as I believe, in some such words as these: "My child, if you avenge the death of your comrade, Patroclus, and you kill Hector, you will die yourself, for your death is to follow immediately after Hector's." Hearing this, he despised death and danger and was much more afraid to live a coward who did not avenge his d friends. "Let me die at once," he said, "when once I have given the wrongdoer his deserts, rather than remain here, a laughingstock by the curved ships, a burden upon the earth." Do you think he gave thought to death and danger?

This is the truth of the matter, gentlemen of the jury: wherever a man has taken a position that

---

[8] The scene between Thetis and Achilles is from *The Iliad* (18, 94ff.).

he believes to be best, or has been placed by his commander, there he must I think remain and face danger, without a thought for death or anything

e else, rather than disgrace. It would have been a dreadful way to behave, gentlemen of the jury, if, at Potidaea, Amphipolis and Delium, I had, at the risk of death, like anyone else, remained at my post where those you had elected to command had ordered me, and then, when the god ordered me, as I thought and believed, to live the life of a philosopher, to examine myself and others, I had aban-

29 doned my post for fear of death or anything else. That would have been a dreadful thing, and then I might truly have justly been brought here for not believing that there are gods, disobeying the oracle, fearing death, and thinking I was wise when I was not. To fear death, gentlemen, is no other than to think oneself wise when one is not, to think one knows what one does not know. No one knows whether death may not be the greatest of all blessings for a man, yet men fear it as if they knew that it is the greatest of evils. And surely it is

b the most blameworthy ignorance to believe that one knows what one does not know. It is perhaps on this point and in this respect, gentlemen, that I differ from the majority of men, and if I were to claim that I am wiser than anyone in anything, it would be in this, that, as I have no adequate knowledge of things in the underworld, so I do not think I have. I do know, however, that it is wicked and shameful to do wrong, to disobey one's superior, be he god or man. I shall never fear or avoid things of which I do not know, whether they may not be good rather than things that I know

c to be bad. Even if you acquitted me now and did not believe Anytus, who said to you that either I should not have been brought here in the first place, or that now I am here, you cannot avoid executing me, for if I should be acquitted, your sons would practise the teachings of Socrates and all be thoroughly corrupted; if you said to me in this regard: "Socrates, we do not believe Anytus now; we acquit you, but only on condition that you spend no more time on this investigation and do not practise philosophy, and if you are caught

d doing so you will die," if, as I say, you were to acquit me on those terms, I would say to you: "Gentlemen of the jury, I am grateful and I am your friend, but I will obey the god rather than you, and as long as I draw breath and am able, I shall not cease to practise philosophy, to exhort

you and in my usual way to point out to any one of you whom I happen to meet: Good Sir, you are an Athenian, a citizen of the greatest city with the greatest reputation for both wisdom and power;

e are you not ashamed of your eagerness to possess as much wealth, reputation and honours as possible, while you do not care for nor give thought to wisdom or truth, or the best possible state of your soul?" Then, if one of you disputes this and says he does care, I shall not let him go at once or leave him, but I shall question him, examine him and test him, and if I do not think he has attained the goodness that he says he has, I shall reproach him because he attaches little importance to the

30 most important things and greater importance to inferior things, I shall treat in this way anyone I happen to meet, young and old, citizen and stranger, and more so the citizens because you are more kindred to me. Be sure that this is what the god orders me to do, and I think there is no greater blessing for the city than my service to the god. For I go around doing nothing but persuading both young and old among you not to care for

b your body or your wealth in preference to or as strongly as for the best possible state of your soul as I say to you: "Wealth does not bring about excellence, but excellence brings about wealth and all other public and private blessings for men."

Now if by saying this I corrupt the young, this advice must be harmful, but if anyone says that I give different advice, he is talking nonsense. On this point I would say to you, gentlemen of the jury: "Whether you believe Anytus or not, whether you acquit me or not, do so on the understanding

c that this is my course of action, even if I am to face death many times." Do not create a disturbance, gentlemen, but abide by my request not to cry out at what I say but to listen, for I think it will be to your advantage to listen, and I am about to say other things at which you will perhaps cry out. By no means do this. Be sure that if you kill the sort of man I say I am, you will not harm me more than yourselves. Neither Meletus nor Anytus can harm me in any way; he could not harm me, for I do not

d think it is permitted that a better man be harmed by a worse; certainly he might kill me, or perhaps banish or disfranchise me, which he and maybe others think to be great harm, but I do not think so. I think he is doing himself much greater harm doing what he is doing now, attempting to have a man executed unjustly. Indeed, gentlemen of the jury, I am far from making a defence now on my own behalf, as might be thought, but on yours, to prevent you from wrongdoing by mistreating the god's gift to you by condemning me; for if you kill me you will not easily find another like me. I was attached to this city by the god—though it seems a ridiculous thing to say—as upon a great and noble horse which was somewhat sluggish because of its size and needed to be stirred up by a kind of gadfly. It is to fulfill some such function that I believe the god has placed me in the city. I never cease to rouse each and every one of you, to persuade and reproach you all day long and everywhere I find myself in your company.

Another such man will not easily come to be among you, gentlemen, and if you believe me you will spare me. You might easily be annoyed with me as people are when they are aroused from a doze, and strike out at me; if convinced by Anytus you could easily kill me, and then you could sleep on for the rest of your days, unless the god, in his care for you, sent you someone else. That I am the kind of person to be a gift of the god to the city you might realize from the fact that it does not seem like human nature for me to have neglected all my own affairs and to have tolerated this neglect now for so many years while I was always concerned with you, approaching each one of you like a father or an elder brother to persuade you to care for virtue. Now if I profited from this by charging a fee for my advice, there would be some sense to it, but you can see for yourselves that, for all their shameless accusations, my accusers have not been able in their impudence to bring forward a witness to say that I have ever received a fee or ever asked for one. I, on the other hand, have a convincing witness that I speak for truth, my poverty.

It may seem strange that while I go around and give this advice privately and interfere in private affairs, I do not venture to go to the assembly and there advise the city. You have heard me give the reason for this in many places. I have a divine sign from the god which Meletus has ridiculed in his deposition. This began when I was a child. It is a voice, and whenever it speaks it turns me away from something I am about to do, but it never encourages me to do anything. This is what has prevented me from taking part in public affairs, and I think it was quite right to prevent me. Be sure, gentlemen of the jury, that if I had long ago attempted to take part in politics, I should have died long ago, and benefited neither you nor myself. Do not be angry with me for speaking the truth; no man will survive who genuinely opposes you or any other crowd and prevents the occurrence of many unjust and illegal happenings in the city. A man who really fights for justice must lead a private, not a public, life if he is to survive for even a short time.

I shall give you great proofs of this, not words but what you esteem, deeds. Listen to what happened to me, that you may know that I will not yield to any man contrary to what is right, for fear of death, even if I should die at once for not yielding. The things I shall tell you are commonplace and smack of the lawcourts, but they are true. I have never held any other office in the city, but I served as a member of the Council, and our tribe Antiochis was presiding at the time when you wanted to try as a body the ten generals who had failed to pick up the survivors of the naval battle.[9] This was illegal, as you all recognized later. I was the only member of the presiding committee to oppose your doing something contrary to the laws, and I voted against it. The orators were ready to prosecute me and take me away, and your shouts were egging them on, but I thought I should run any risk on the side of law and justice rather than join you, for fear of prison or death, when you were engaged in an unjust course.

This happened when the city was still a democracy. When the oligarchy was established, the Thirty[10] summoned me to the Hall, along with four others, and ordered us to bring Leon from Salamis, that he might be executed. They gave many such orders to many people, in order to implicate as many as possible in their guilt. Then I showed again, not in words but in action, that, if it were not rather vulgar to say so, death is something

---

[9] This was the battle of Arginusae (south of Lesbos) in 406 B.C., the last Athenian victory of the war. A violent storm prevented the Athenian generals from rescuing their survivors. For this they were tried in Athens and sentenced to death by the assembly. They were tried in a body, and it is this to which Socrates objected in the Council's presiding committee which prepared the business of the assembly. He obstinately persisted in his opposition, in which he stood alone, and was overruled by the majority. Six generals who were in Athens were executed.

[10] This was the harsh oligarchy that was set up after the final defeat of Athens in 404 B.C. and that ruled Athens for some nine months in 404–3 before the democracy was restored.

I couldn't care less about, but that my whole concern is not to do anything unjust or impious. That government, powerful as it was, did not frighten me into any wrongdoing. When we left the Hall, the other four went to Salamis and brought in Leon, but I went home. I might have been put to death for this, had not the government fallen

e shortly afterwards. There are many who will witness to these events.

Do you think I would have survived all these years if I were engaged in public affairs and, acting as a good man must, came to the help of justice and considered this the most important thing? Far from it, gentlemen of the jury, nor would any other

33 man. Throughout my life, in any public activity I may have engaged in, I am the same man as I am in private life. I have never come to an agreement with anyone to act unjustly, neither with anyone else nor with any one of those who they slanderously say are my pupils. I have never been anyone's teacher. If anyone, young or old, desires to listen to me when I am talking and dealing with my own concerns, I have never begrudged this to anyone, but I do not converse when I receive a fee and not

b when I do not. I am equally ready to question the rich and the poor if anyone is willing to answer my questions and listen to what I say. And I cannot justly be held responsible for the good or bad conduct of these people, as I never promised to teach them anything and have not done so. If anyone says that he has learned anything from me, or that he heard anything privately that the others did not hear, be assured that he is not telling the truth.

Why then do some people enjoy spending con-

c siderable time in my company? You have heard why, gentlemen of the jury, I have told you the whole truth. They enjoy hearing those being questioned who think they are wise, but are not. And this is not unpleasant. To do this has, as I say, been enjoined upon me by the god, by means of oracles and dreams, and in every other way that a divine manifestation has ever ordered a man to do anything. This is true, gentlemen, and can easily be established.

d If I corrupt some young men and have corrupted others, then surely some of them who have grown older and realized that I gave them bad advice when they were young should now themselves come up here to accuse me and avenge themselves. If they are unwilling to do so themselves, then some of their kindred, their fathers or

brothers or other relations should recall it now if their family had been harmed by me. I see many of these present here, first Crito, my contempo-

e rary and fellow demesman, the father of Critoboulos here; next Lysanias of Sphettus, the father of Aeschines here; also Antiphon the Cephisian, the father of Epigenes; and others whose brothers spent their time in this way; Nicostratus, the son of Theozotides, brother of Theodotus, and Theodotus has died so he could not influence him;

34 Paralios here, son of Demodocus, whose brother was Theages; there is Adeimantus, son of Ariston, brother of Plato here; Acantidorus, brother of Apollodorus here.

I could mention many others, some one of whom surely Meletus should have brought in as witness in his own speech. If he forgot to do so, then let him do it now; I will yield time if he has anything of the kind to say. You will find quite the contrary, gentlemen. These men are all ready to come to the help of the corruptor, the man who

b has harmed their kindred, as Meletus and Anytus say. Now those who were corrupted might well have reason to help me, but the uncorrupted, their kindred who are older men, have no reason to help me except the right and proper one, that they know that Meletus is lying and that I am telling the truth.

Very well, gentlemen of the jury. This, and maybe other similar things, is what I have to say in my defence. Perhaps one of you might be angry as he recalls that when he himself stood trial on a less

c dangerous charge, he begged and implored the jury with many tears, that he brought his children and many of his friends and family into court to arouse as much pity as he could, but that I do none of these things, even though I may seem to be running the ultimate risk. Thinking of this, he might

d feel resentful toward me and, angry about this, cast his vote in anger. If there is such a one among you—I do not deem there is, but if there is—I think it would be right to say in reply: My good sir, I too have a household and, in Homer's phrase, I am not born "from oak or rock" but from men, so that I have a family, indeed three sons, gentlemen of the jury, of whom one is an adolescent while two are children. Nevertheless, I will not beg you to acquit me by bringing them here. Why do I do none of these things? Not through arrogance,

e gentlemen, nor through lack of respect for you. Whether I am brave in the face of death is another matter, but with regard to my reputation and yours and that of the whole city, it does not seem right to me to do these things, especially at my age and with my reputation. For it is generally believed, whether it be true or false, that in certain respects Socrates is superior to the majority of men. Now if those of you who are considered superior, be it in wisdom or courage or whatever other virtue makes them so, are seen behaving like that, it would be a disgrace. Yet I have often seen them do this sort of thing when standing trial, men who are thought to be somebody, doing amazing things as if they thought it a terrible thing to die, and as if they were to be immortal if you did not execute them. I think these men bring shame upon the city so that a stranger, too, would assume that those who are outstanding in virtue among the Athenians, whom they themselves select from themselves to fill offices of state and receive other honours, are in no way better than women. You should not act like that, gentlemen of the jury, those of you who have any reputation at all, and if we do, you should not allow it. You should make it very clear that you will more readily convict a man who performs these pitiful dramatics in court and so makes the city a laughing-stock, than a man who keeps quiet.

Quite apart from the question of reputation, gentlemen, I do not think it right to supplicate the jury and to be acquitted because of this, but to teach and persuade them. It is not the purpose of a juryman's office to give justice as a favour to whoever seems good to him, but to judge according to law, and this he has sworn to do. We should not accustom you to perjure yourselves, nor should you make a habit of it. This is irreverent conduct for either of us.

Do not deem it right for me, gentlemen of the jury, that I should act towards you in a way that I do not consider to be good or just or pious, especially, by Zeus, as I am being prosecuted by Meletus here for impiety; clearly, if I convinced you by my supplication to do violence to your oath of office, I would be teaching you not to believe that there are gods, and my defence would convict me of not believing in them. This is far from being the case, gentlemen, for I do believe in them as none of my accusers do. I leave it to you and the god to judge me in the way that will be best for me and for you.

[The jury now gives its verdict of guilty, and Meletus asks for the penalty of death.]

There are many other reasons for my not being angry with you for convicting me, gentlemen of the jury, and what happened was not unexpected. I am much more surprised at the number of votes cast on each side, for I did not think the decision would be by so few votes but by a great many. As it is, a switch of only thirty votes would have acquitted me. I think myself that I have been cleared on Meletus' charges, and not only this, but it is clear to all that, if Anytus and Lycon had not joined him in accusing me, he would have been fined a thousand drachmas for not receiving a fifth of the votes.

He assesses the penalty at death. So be it. What counter-assessment should I propose to you, gentlemen of the jury? Clearly it should be a penalty I deserve, and what do I deserve to suffer or to pay because I have deliberately not led a quiet life but have neglected what occupies most people: wealth, household affairs, the position of general or public orator or the other offices, the political clubs and factions that exist in the city? I thought myself too honest to survive if I occupied myself with those things. I did not follow that path that would have made me of no use either to you or to myself, but I went to each of you privately and conferred upon him what I say is the greatest benefit, by trying to persuade him not to care for any of his belongings before caring that he himself should be as good and as wise as possible, not to care for the city's possessions more than for the city itself, and to care for other things in the same way. What do I deserve for being such a man? Some good, gentlemen of the jury, if I must truly make an assessment according to my deserts, and something suitable. What is suitable for a poor benefactor who needs leisure to exhort you? Nothing is more suitable, gentlemen, than for such a man to be fed in the Prytaneum,[11] much more suitable for him than for any of you who has won a victory at Olympia with a pair or a team of horses. The Olympian victor makes you think yourself happy; I make you be happy. Besides, he does not need food, but I do. So if I must make a just assessment of what I deserve, I assess it at this: free meals in the Prytaneum.

---

[11] The Prytaneum was the magistrates' hall or town hall of Athens in which public entertainments were given, particularly to Olympian victors on their return home.

When I say this you may think, as when I spoke of appeals to pity and entreaties, that I speak arrogantly, but that is not the case, gentlemen of the jury; rather it is like this: I am convinced that I never willingly wrong anyone, but I am not convincing you of this, for we have talked together but a short time. If it were the law with us, as it is elsewhere, that a trial for life should not last one but many days, you would be convinced, but now it is not easy to dispel great slanders in a short time. Since I am convinced that I wrong no one, I am not likely to wrong myself, to say that I deserve some evil and to make some such assessment against myself. What should I fear? That I should suffer the penalty Meletus has assessed against me, of which I say I do not know whether it is good or bad? Am I then to choose in preference to this something that I know very well to be an evil and assess the penalty at that? Imprisonment? Why should I live in prison, always subjected to the ruling magistrates? A fine, and imprisonment until I pay it? That would be the same thing for me, as I have no money. Exile? for perhaps you might accept that assessment.

I should have to be inordinately fond of life, gentlemen of the jury, to be so unreasonable as to suppose that other men will easily tolerate my company and conversation when you, my fellow citizens, have been unable to endure them, but found them a burden and resented them so that you are now seeking to get rid of them. Far from it, gentlemen. It would be a fine life at my age to be driven out of one city after another, for I know very well that wherever I go the young men will listen to my talk as they do here. If I drive them away, they will themselves persuade their elders to drive me out; if I do not drive them away, their fathers and relations will drive me out on their behalf.

Perhaps someone might say: But Socrates, if you leave us will you not be able to live quietly, without talking? Now this is the most difficult point on which to convince some of you. If I say that it is impossible for me to keep quiet because that means disobeying the god, you will not believe me and will think I am being ironical. On the other hand, if I say that it is the greatest good for a man to discuss virtue every day and those other things about which you hear me conversing and testing myself and others, for the unexamined life is not worth living for man, you will believe me even less.

What I say is true, gentlemen, but it is not easy to convince you. At the same time, I am not accustomed to think that I deserve any penalty. If I had money, I would assess the penalty at the amount I could pay, for that would not hurt me, but I have none, unless you are willing to set the penalty at the amount I can pay, and perhaps I could pay you one mina of silver.[12] So that is my assessment.

Plato here, gentlemen of the jury, and Crito and Critoboulus and Apollodorus bid me put the penalty at thirty minae, and they will stand surety for the money. Well then, that is my assessment, and they will be sufficient guarantee of payment.

[The jury now votes again and sentences Socrates to death.]

It is for the sake of a short time, gentlemen of the jury, that you will acquire the reputation and the guilt, in the eyes of those who want to denigrate the city, of having killed Socrates, a wise man, for they who want to revile you will say that I am wise even if I am not. If you had waited but a little while, this would have happened of its own accord. You see my age, that I am already advanced in years and close to death. I am saying this not to all of you but to those who condemned me to death, and to these same jurors I say: Perhaps you think that I was convicted for lack of such words as might have convinced you, if I thought I should say or do all I could to avoid my sentence. Far from it. I was convicted because I lacked not words but boldness and shamelessness and the willingness to say to you what you would most gladly have heard from me, lamentations and tears and my saying and doing many things that I say are unworthy of me but that you are accustomed to hear from others. I did not think then that the danger I ran should make me do anything mean, nor do I now regret the nature of my defence. I would much rather die after this kind of defence than live after making the other kind. Neither I nor any other man should, on trial or in war, contrive to avoid death at any cost. Indeed it is often obvious in battle that one could escape death by throwing

---

[12] One mina was 100 drachmas, equivalent to, say, twenty-five dollars, though in purchasing power probably five times greater. In any case, a ridiculously small sum under the circumstances.

away one's weapons and turning to supplicate one's pursuers, and there are many ways to avoid death in every kind of danger if one will venture to do or say anything to avoid it. It is not difficult to avoid death, gentlemen of the jury, it is much more difficult to avoid wickedness, for it runs faster than death. Slow and elderly as I am, I have been caught by the slower pursuer, whereas my accusers, being clever and sharp, have been caught by the quicker, wickedness. I leave you now, condemned to death by you, but they are condemned by truth to wickedness and injustice. So I maintain my assessment, and they maintain theirs. This perhaps had to happen, and I think it is as it should be.

Now I want to prophesy to those who convicted me, for I am at the point when men prophesy most, when they are about to die. I say gentlemen, to those who voted to kill me, that vengeance will come upon you immediately after my death, a vengeance much harder to bear than that which you took in killing me. You did this in the belief that you would avoid giving an account of your life, but I maintain that quite the opposite will happen to you. There will be more people to test you, whom I now held back, but you did not notice it. They will be more difficult to deal with as they will be younger and you will resent them more. You are wrong if you believe that by killing people you will prevent anyone from reproaching you for not living in the right way. To escape such tests is neither possible nor good, but it is best and easiest not to discredit others but to prepare oneself to be as good as possible. With this prophecy to you who convicted me, I part from you.

I should be glad to discuss what has happened with those who voted for my acquittal during the time that the officers of the court are busy and I do not yet have to depart to my death. So, gentlemen, stay with me awhile, for nothing prevents us from talking to each other while it is allowed. To you, as being my friends, I want to show the meaning of what has occurred. A surprising thing has happened to me, judges—you I would rightly call judges. At all previous times my usual mantic sign frequently opposed me, even in small matters, when I was about to do something wrong, but now that, as you can see for yourselves, I was faced with what one might think, and what is generally thought to be, the worst of evils, my divine sign has not opposed me, either when I left home

at dawn, or when I came into court, or at any time that I was about to say something during my speech. Yet in other talks it often held me back in the middle of my speaking, but now it has opposed no word or deed of mine. What do I think is the reason for this? I will tell you. What has happened to me may well be a good thing, and those of us who believe death to be an evil are certainly mistaken. I have convincing proof of this, for it is impossible that my customary sign did not oppose me if I was not about to do what was right.

Let us reflect in this way, too, that there is good hope that death is a blessing, for it is one of two things: either the dead are nothing and have no perception of anything, or it is, as we are told, a change and a relocating for the soul from here to another place. If it is complete lack of perception, like a dreamless sleep, then death would be a great advantage. For I think that if one had to pick out that night during which a man slept soundly and did not dream, put beside it the other nights and days of his life, and then see how many days and nights had been better and more pleasant than that night, not only a private person but the great king would find them easy to count compared with the other days and nights. If death is like this I say it is an advantage, for all eternity would then seem to be no more than a single night. If, on the other hand, death is a change from here to another place, and what we are told is true and all who have died are there, what greater blessing could there be, gentlemen of the jury? If anyone arriving in Hades will have escaped from those who call themselves judges here, and will find those true judges who are said to sit in judgement there, Minos and Radamanthus and Aeacus and Triptolemus and the other demi-gods who have been upright in their own life, would that be a poor kind of change? Again, what would one of you give to keep company with Orpheus and Musaeus, Hesiod and Homer? I am willing to die many times if that is true. It would be a wonderful way for me to spend my time whenever I met Palamedes and Ajax, the son of Telamon, and any other of the men of old who died through an unjust conviction, to compare my experience with theirs. I think it would be pleasant. Most important, I could spend my time testing and examining people there, as I do here, as to who among them is wise, and who thinks he is, but is not.

What would one not give, gentlemen of the jury, for the opportunity to examine the man who led the great expedition against Troy, or Odys-

c   seus, or Sisyphus, and innumerable other men and women one could mention. It would be an extraordinary happiness to talk with them, to keep company with them and examine them. In any case, they would certainly not put one to death for doing so. They are happier there than we are here in other respects, and for the rest of time they are deathless, if indeed what we are told is true.

You too must be of good hope as regards death, gentlemen of the jury, and keep this one truth in mind, that a good man cannot be harmed either

d   in life or in death, and that his affairs are not neglected by the gods. What has happened to me now has not happened of itself, but it is clear to me that it was better for me to die now and to escape from trouble. That is why my divine sign did not oppose me at any point. So I am certainly not angry with those who convicted me, or with my accusers. Of course that was not their purpose when they accused and convicted me, but they

e   thought they were hurting me, and for this they deserve blame. This much I ask from them: when my sons grow up, avenge yourselves by causing them the same kind of grief that I caused you, if you think they care for money or anything else more than they care for virtue, or if they think they are somebody when they are nobody. Reproach them as I reproach you, that they do not care for the right things and think they are worthy

42   when they are not worthy of anything. If you do this, I shall have been justly treated by you, and my sons also.

Now the hour to part has come. I go to die, you go to live. Which of us goes to the better lot is known to no one, except the god.

Commentary and Questions

As we delve into the character of Socrates as Plato portrays it in this dialogue, we should be struck by his single-mindedness. If it should turn out that death is a "change from here to another place," how would Socrates spend his time there? He would continue precisely the activities that had occupied him in this life; he would "examine" all the famous heroes to see which of them is wise. And why does he think such examination is so important, a "ser-

vice to the god"? No doubt because it undermines hubris, that arrogance of thinking one possesses "a wisdom more than human."

Read 17a–18a   In this short introductory section, Socrates draws a contrast between himself and his accusers, characterizes the kind of man he is, and reminds the jury of its duty.

Q1.   What is the function of Socrates' contrast between *persuasion* and *truth?* List the terms in which each is described.

Q2.   What kind of man does Socrates say that he is?

Q3.   What is his challenge to the jury?

Read 18b–19a Socrates makes a distinction between two sets of accusers.

Q4.   Identify the earlier accusers and the later accusers. How do they differ?

Q5.   Why is it going to be very difficult for Socrates to defend himself against the earlier accusers?

Read 19b–24b   Here we have Socrates' defense against the "earlier accusers." He tries to show how his "unpopularity" arises from his practice of questioning. He describes the origins of this occupation of his and discusses the sort of wisdom to which he lays claim.

Q6.   What are the three points made against him in the older accusations?

Q7.   What does Socrates say about each of these accusations?

Q8.   How does Socrates distinguish himself from the Sophists here?

We have mentioned the Oracle at Delphi before. One could go there and, after appropriate sacrifices, pose a question. The "Pythian" (21a) was a priestess of Apollo who would, in the name of the god, reply to the questions posed. We have noted that it was characteristic of the Oracle to reply in a riddle, so it is not perverse for Socrates to wonder what the answer to Chairephon's question means. What sort of wisdom is this in which no one can surpass him? He devises his questioning technique to clarify the meaning of the answer.

Note that several times during his speech Socrates asks the jury not to create a disturbance (20e, 27b, 30c). We can imagine that he is interrupted at those points by hoots, hissing, catcalls, or their ancient Greek equivalents.

Q9.   Which three classes of people did Socrates question? What, in each case, was the result?

Q10.   What conclusion does Socrates draw from his investigations?

Here we can address that paradox noted earlier (page 68) arising out of Socrates' simultaneous profession of ignorance, his identification of virtue with knowledge, and the claim (obvious at many points in the *Apology*) that he is both a wise and a good man. In light of his confessed ignorance and the identification of knowledge with virtue, it seems he should conclude that he *isn't* virtuous. But it is the distinction drawn in 22e–23b between a wisdom appropriate for "the god" on the one hand and "human wisdom" on the other that resolves this paradox. The god, Socrates assumes, actually knows the forms of piety, justice, *arete,* and the other excellences proper to a human being. Humans, by contrast, do not; and this is proved, Socrates thinks, by the god's declaration that there is no man wiser than he—who knows that he doesn't know!

Because humans do not know what makes for virtue and a good life, the best they can do is subject themselves to constant dialectical examination. This searching critique will tend to rid us of false opinions and will also cure us of the hubris of thinking that we have a wisdom appropriate only to the god. The outcome of such examination, acknowledging our ignorance, Socrates calls "human wisdom," which by comparison with divine wisdom is "worth little or nothing." Still, it is the sort of wisdom, Socrates believes, that is appropriate to creatures like us. And that is why "the unexamined life is not worth living" for a human being (38a). And that is why there is "no greater blessing for the city" than Socrates' never-ending examination of its citizens (30a). Such self-examination is the way for us to become as wise and good as it is possible for human beings to be.

Read 24b–28a   At this point, Socrates begins to address the "later accusers." He does so in his usual question-and-answer fashion. Apparently, three persons submitted the charge to the court: Meletus, Anytus, and Lycon. Meletus seems to have been the primary sponsor of the charge, seconded by the other two. So Socrates calls Meletus forward and questions him. As in the *Euthyphro,* two charges are mentioned. Be sure you are clear about what they are.

In 24c Socrates tells the jury his purpose in cross-examining Meletus. He wants to demonstrate that Meletus is someone who ought not to be taken seriously, that he has not thought through the meaning of the charge, and that he doesn't even care about these matters.[*] In short, Socrates is about to demonstrate before the jury—before their very eyes!—not only what sort of man Meletus is, and that he is not wise, but also what sort of man Socrates is. It is the truth, remember, that Socrates is after; if the jury is going to decide whether Socrates is impious and a corrupter of youth, they should have the very best evidence about what sort of man they are judging. Socrates is going to oblige them by giving them a personal demonstration.

He begins by taking up the charge of corrupting the youth. If Meletus claims that Socrates corrupts the youth, he must understand what corrupting is. To understand what it is to corrupt, one must also understand what it is to improve the youth. And so Socrates asks him, "Who improves them?"

Q11.   Does Meletus have a ready answer? What conclusion does Socrates draw from this? (24d)

When Meletus does answer, Socrates' questions provoke him to say that all the other citizens improve the youth and only Socrates corrupts them!

Q12.   How does Socrates use the analogy of the horse breeders to cast doubt on Meletus' concern for these matters?

---

[*]Compare *Apology* 24c, 25c, 26a,b with *Euthyphro* 2c–d, 3a.

Starting in 25c, Socrates presents Meletus with a dilemma. The form of a dilemma is this: Two alternatives are presented between which it seems necessary to choose, but each alternative has consequences that are unwelcome, usually for different reasons. The two alternatives are called the "horns" of a dilemma, and there are three ways to deal with them. One can grasp one of the horns (that is, embrace that alternative with its consequences); one can grasp the other horn; or one can (sometimes, but not always) "go between the horns" by finding a third alternative that has not been considered.

Q13.   What are the horns of the dilemma that Socrates presents to Meletus?

Q14.   How does Meletus respond?

Q15.   How does Socrates refute this response?

Q16.   Supposing that this refutation is correct and that one cannot "pass through" the horns, what is the consequence of embracing the other horn? How does Socrates use the distinction between punishment and instruction?

Again Socrates drives home the conclusion that Meletus has "never been at all concerned with these matters." If he had been, he surely would have thought these things through. As it is, he cannot be taken seriously.

At 26b, the topic switches to the other charge. As the examination proceeds, we can see Meletus becoming angrier and angrier, less and less willing to cooperate in what he clearly sees is his own destruction. No doubt this is an example — produced right there for the jury to see — of the typical response to Socrates' questioning. We might think Socrates is not being prudent here in angering Meletus and his supporters in the jury. But again, it is for Socrates a matter of the truth; this is the kind of man he is. And the jury should see it if they are going to judge truly.

Q17.   Socrates claims that Meletus contradicts himself. In what way?

Q18.   What "divine activities" must the jury have understood him to be referring to? (27d–e)

Q19.   What does Socrates claim will be his undoing, if he is undone?

Read 28b–35d   Socrates is now finished with Meletus, satisfied that he has shown him to be thoughtless and unreliable. Notice that at this point he claims to have proved that he is "not guilty" of the charges Meletus has brought against him. No doubt Socrates believes that one cannot be rightly convicted on charges that are as vague and undefined as these have proved to be. Do you think this suffices for a defense?

Socrates then turns to more general matters relevant to his defense. He first imagines someone saying that the very fact that he is on trial for his life is shameful. How could he have behaved in such a manner as to bring himself to this?

Q20.   On what principle does Socrates base his response? Do you agree with this principle? (Compare the speech of the nurse in *Hippolytus* on page 53.)

Q21.   To whom does Socrates compare himself? Do you think the comparison is apt? How do you think this would have struck an Athenian jury?

Q22.   Socrates refers to his military service; in what respects does he say his life as a philosopher is like that?

Q23.   Why does he say that to fear death is to think oneself wise when one is not? Do you agree with this? If not, why not?

In 29c–d Socrates imagines that the jury might offer him a "deal," sparing his life if only he ceased practicing philosophy. Xenophon tells us that during the reign of the Thirty, Critias and another man, Charicles, demanded that Socrates cease conversing with the young. If this story is accurate, it may be that Socrates has this demand in mind. Or it may be that there had been talk of such a "deal" before the trial.

Q24.   What does Socrates say his response would be? (Compare Acts 5:29 in the Bible.)

Q25.   Why does he say that "there is no greater blessing for the city" than his service to the god? What are "the most important things"? Do you agree?

In the section that begins in 30b, Socrates makes some quite astonishing claims:

- If they kill him, they will harm themselves more than they harm him.

- A better man cannot be harmed by a worse man.

- He is defending himself not for his own sake but for theirs.

All these claims seem to turn the usual ways of thinking about such matters completely upside down. Indeed, to our natural common sense, they seem incredible. Surely they must have seemed so to the jury as well. We usually think, don't we, that others can harm us. So we are on our guard. Socrates tells us, however, that this natural conviction of ours is false. It's not that we cannot be harmed at all, however. Indeed, we can be harmed—but only if we do it to ourselves! How can we harm ourselves? By making ourselves into worse persons than we otherwise would be. We harm ourselves by acting unjustly. That is why Socrates says that if his fellow citizens kill him they will harm themselves more than they will harm him. They will be doing injustice, thereby corrupting their souls; and the most important thing is care for the soul.

Q26.   Socrates claims throughout to be concerned for the souls of the jury members. Show how this is consistent with his daily practice in the streets of Athens.

Q27.   What use does Socrates make of the image of the "gadfly"?

Socrates feels a need to explain why, if he is so wise, he has not entered politics. There are two reasons, one being the nature of his "wisdom." He focuses here on the other reason: his "sign" prevented

it. If it had not, he says, there is little doubt that he would "have died long ago" and could not have been a "blessing to the city" for all these years.

He cites two incidents as evidence of this, one occurring when the city was democratic, one under the rule of the Thirty. He is trying to convince the jury that he is truly apolitical because he was capable of resisting both sorts of government. In both cases, he resisted alone because the others were doing something contrary to law, and in both cases he was in some danger. Why should he feel the need to establish his political neutrality? Surely because there was a political aspect to the trial—not explicit, but in the background.

In 33a, he gets to what many people feel is the heart of the matter. Let us ask: Why was Socrates brought to trial at all? There was his reputation as a Sophist, of course—all those accusations of the "earlier accusers." There was the general hostility that his questioning generated. There was his "divine sign." But it is doubtful that these alone would have sufficed to bring him to court. What probably tipped the balance was the despicable political career of some who had at one time been closely associated with him, in particular Critias, leader of the Thirty, and Alcibiades, the brilliant and dashing young traitor. This kind of "guilt by association" is very common and very hard to defend against. If these men had spent so much time with Socrates, why hadn't they turned out better? Socrates must be responsible for their crimes! This could not be mentioned in the official charge because it would have violated the amnesty proclaimed by the democracy after the Thirty were overthrown. But it is hard not to believe that it is lurking in the background.

How does Socrates defend himself against this charge? He makes another remarkable claim. He has *never,* he says, "been anyone's teacher." For that reason, he cannot "be held responsible for the good or bad conduct of these people, as I never promised to teach them anything and have not done so." This requires some explaining.

In the *Meno,* where the topic is whether virtue can be taught, Socrates invites Meno to join in a search for the nature of virtue. Meno asks,

And how will you search for something, Socrates, when you don't know what it is at all? I mean, which of the things you don't know will you take in advance and search for, when you don't know what it is? Or even if you come right up against it, how will you know that it's the unknown thing you're looking for? (*Meno* 80d) [3]

In response to this puzzle, Socrates calls over a slave boy who has never studied geometry. He draws a square on the ground and divides it equally by bisecting the sides vertically and horizontally. (Draw such a square yourself.) He then asks the boy to construct another square with an area twice the original area. This is a nice problem. Clearly, if the original area is four, we want a square with an area of eight. But how can we get it? (Before you go on, think a minute and see if you can solve it.)

Socrates proceeds by asking the boy questions. The first, rather natural suggestion is to double the length of the sides. But on reflection, the boy can see (as you can, too) that this gives a square of sixteen. Wanting something between four and sixteen, the boy tries making the sides of the new square one and one-half times the original. But this gives a square of nine, not eight. Finally, at a suggestion from Socrates, the boy sees that taking the diagonal of the original square as one side of a new square solves the problem. (Do you agree that this solves the problem? How can you be sure?)*

What is the relevance of this to Meno's puzzle? And what does it have to do with Socrates' claim never to have been anyone's teacher? The crucial point is that the boy can just "see" that the first two solutions are wrong. And when the correct solution is presented, he "recognizes" it as correct. But he has never been taught geometry! Moreover, his certainty about the correct solution does not now rest on the authority of Socrates. For one thing, Socrates doesn't *tell* him that this is a correct solution. For another, even if he did, why should the boy believe him? No, the boy sees the truth for himself. So Socrates doesn't teach him this truth!

---

*A fuller explanation with a diagram of the square can be found on p. 120.

This leaves us with another puzzle. How could the boy have recognized the true solution as the true one? Consider this analogy. You are walking down the street and see someone approaching. At first she is too far away to identify, but as she gets nearer you say, "Why, that's Joan!" Now, what must be the case for you to "recognize" Joan truly? There can be no doubt: You must already have been acquainted with Joan in some way. That alone is the condition under which recognition is possible.

Socrates thinks the slave boy's case must be similar. He must already have been acquainted with this truth; otherwise, it is not possible to explain how he recognizes it when it is present before him. But when? Clearly not in this life. Socrates draws what seems to be the only possible conclusion: that he was acquainted with this truth before birth and that it was always within him. (This is taken as evidence that the soul exists before the body, but that is not our present concern.) Coming to know is just recognizing what, in some implicit sense, one has within oneself all along. What Socrates does is ask the right questions or present the appropriate stimuli. But he doesn't "implant" knowledge; he doesn't teach.

In the dialogue *Theatetus,* Plato represents Socrates as using a striking image:

> I am so far like the midwife that I cannot myself give birth to wisdom, and the common reproach is true, that, though I question others, I can myself bring nothing to light because there is no wisdom in me. . . . Those who frequent my company at first appear, some of them, quite unintelligent, but, as we go further with our discussions, all who are favored by heaven make progress at a rate that seems surprising to others as well as to themselves, although it is clear that they have never learned anything from me. The many admirable truths they bring to birth have been discovered by themselves from within. But the delivery is heaven's work and mine. (*Theatetus* 150c–d) [4]

Here, then, is the background for the claim that Socrates has never taught anyone anything. His role is not that of teacher or imparter of knowledge and wisdom but that of "midwife" (recall that this was his mother's profession), assisting at the birth of ideas which are within the "learner" all along and identifying those that are "illegitimate." This is why he says—though he could not have explained all this to the jury—that he cannot be held responsible for the behavior of men like Critias and Alcibiades.

Q28.   What additional arguments does Socrates use in 33d—34b?

Q29.   Why does he refuse to use the traditional "appeal to pity"? See particularly 35c.

Read 35e—38b   The verdict has been given, and now, according to custom, both the prosecution and the defense may propose appropriate penalties. Meletus, of course, asks for death.

Q30.   What penalty does Socrates first suggest? Why?

Along the way, Socrates says something most interesting. "The Olympian victor makes you think yourself happy; I make you be happy." What could this mean? Compare health. Is it possible to feel healthy, think yourself healthy, while actually being unhealthy? Of course. A beginning cancer hurts not at all; in that condition, one can feel perfectly all right. No one, however, would say that a person in whom a cancer is growing is healthy. In the same way Socrates suggests that feeling happy is not the same thing as actually being happy. Think of a city the night after its major league team brings back the championship. People are dancing in the streets, hugging each other, laughing and celebrating. They are feeling happy. Are these happy people? Not necessarily. When the euphoria wears off, they may well return to pretty miserable lives. Happiness, Socrates suggests, is a condition or state of the soul,

not a matter of how you feel.* This condition, he claims, his questioning about virtue can produce.

Q31.   Why does Socrates resist exile as a penalty?

Q32.   What does he say is "the greatest good" for a man? Why?

Q33.   What penalty does he finally offer?

Read 38c—end   After being sentenced to death, Socrates addresses first those who voted to condemn him and then his friends. To both he declares himself satisfied. He has presented himself for what he is; he has not betrayed himself by saying only what they wanted to hear in order to avoid death.

Q34.   What does Socrates say is more difficult to avoid than death? And who has not avoided it?

Q35.   What does he "prophesy"?

Q36.   What "surprising thing" does he point out to his friends? What does he take it to mean?

Q37.   What two possibilities does Socrates consider death may hold? Are there any he misses?

Q38.   What is the "one truth" that Socrates wishes his friends to keep in mind? How does he try to comfort them?

---

*If Socrates is right, our contemporary, endless fascination with how we feel about things—especially how we feel about ourselves—is a mistake we could have learned to detect long ago, from him.

CRITO
Translator's Introduction

About the time of Socrates' trial, a state galley had set out on an annual religious mission to Belos and while it was away no execution was allowed to take place. So it was that Socrates was kept in prison for a month after the trial. The ship has now arrived at Cape Sunium in Attica and is thus expected at the Piraeus momentarily. So Socrates' old and faithful friend,

Crito, makes one last effort to persuade him to escape into exile, and all arrangements for this plan have been made. It is this conversation between the two old friends that Plato professes to report in this dialogue. It is, as Crito plainly tells him, his last chance, but Socrates will not take it, and he gives his reasons for his refusal. Whether this conversation took place at this particular time is not important, for there is every reason to believe that Socrates' friends tried to plan his escape, and that he refused. Plato more than hints that the authorities would not have minded much, as long as he left the country.

The Dialogue

43   SOCRATES: Why have you come so early, Crito? Or is it not still early?

CRITO: It certainly is.

S: How early?

C: Early dawn.

S: I am surprised that the warder was willing to listen to you.

C: He is quite friendly to me by now, Socrates. I have been here often and I have given him something.

S: Have you just come, or have you been here for some time?

C: A fair time.

b   S: Then why did you not wake me right away but sit there in silence?

C: By Zeus no, Socrates. I would not myself want to be in distress and awake so long. I have been surprised to see you so peacefully asleep. It was on purpose that I did not wake you, so that you should spend your time most agreeably. Often in the past throughout my life, I have considered the way you live happy, and especially so now that you bear your present misfortune so easily and lightly.

S: It would not be fitting at my age to resent the fact that I must die now.

c   C: Other men of your age are caught in such misfortunes, but their age does not prevent them resenting their fate.

S: That is so. Why have you come so early?

C: I bring bad news, Socrates, not for you, apparently, but for me and all your friends the news is bad and hard to bear. Indeed, I would count it among the hardest.

d   S: What is it? Or has the ship arrived from Delos, at the arrival of which I must die?

C: It has not arrived yet, but it will, I believe, arrive today, according to a message brought by

some men from Sunium, where they left it. This makes it obvious that it will come today, and that your life must end tomorrow.

S: May it be for the best. If it so please the gods, so be it. However, I do not think it will arrive today.

C: What indication have you of this?

44   S: I will tell you. I must die the day after the ship arrives.

C: That is what those in authority say.

S: Then I do not think it will arrive on this coming day, but on the next. I take to witness of this a dream I had a little earlier during this night. It looks as if it was the right time for you not to wake me.

C: What was your dream?

S: I thought that a beautiful and comely woman dressed in white approached me. She called me and said: "Socrates, may you arrive at fer-

b   tile Phthia[1] on the third day."

C: A strange dream, Socrates.

S: But it seems clear enough to me, Crito.

C: Too clear it seems, my dear Socrates, but listen to me even now and be saved. If you die, it will not be a single misfortune for me. Not only will I be deprived of a friend, the like of whom I shall never find again, but many people who do not know you or me very well will think that I could have saved you if I were willing to spend money, but that I did not care

c   to do so. Surely there can be no worse reputation than to be thought to value money more highly than one's friends, for the majority will not believe that you yourself were not willing to leave prison while we were eager for you to do so.

S: My good Crito, why should we care so much for what the majority think? The most reasonable people, to whom one should pay more attention, will believe that things were done as they were done.

---

[1] A quotation from the ninth book of *The Iliad* (363). Achilles has rejected all the presents of Agamemnon for him to return to the battle, and threatens to go home. He says his ships will sail in the morning, and with good weather he might arrive on the third day "in fertile Phthia" (which is his home). The dream means, obviously, that on the third day Socrates' soul, after death, will find its home. As always, counting the first member of a series, the third day is the day after tomorrow.

d c: You see, Socrates, that one must also pay attention to the opinion of the majority. Your present situation makes clear that the majority can inflict not the least but pretty well the greatest evils if one is slandered among them.

s: Would that the majority could inflict the greatest evils, for they would then be capable of the greatest good, and that would be fine, but now they cannot do either. They cannot make a man either wise or foolish, but they inflict things haphazardly.

e c: That may be so. But tell me this, Socrates, are you anticipating that I and your other friends would have trouble with the informers if you escape from here, as having stolen you away, and that we should be compelled to lose all our property or pay

45 heavy fines and suffer other punishment besides? If you have any such fear, forget it. We would be justified in running this risk to save you, and worse, if necessary. Do follow my advice, and do not act differently.

s: I do have these things in mind, Crito, and also many others.

c: Have no such fear. It is not much money that some people require to save you and get you out of here. Further, do you not see that those informers are cheap, and that not much money would be needed to deal with them? My money is available and is, I think, sufficient. If, because of your affection for me,

b you feel you should not spend any of mine, there are those strangers here ready to spend money. One of them, Simmias the Theban, has brought enough for this very purpose. Cebes, too, and a good many others. So, as I say, do not let this fear make you hesitate to save yourself, nor let what you said in court trouble you, that you would not know what to do with yourself if you left Athens, for you

c would be welcomed in many places to which you might go. If you want to go to Thessaly, I have friends there who will greatly appreciate you and keep you safe, so that no one in Thessaly will harm you.

Besides, Socrates, I do not think that what you are doing is right, to give up your life when you can save it, and to hasten your fate as your enemies would hasten it, and indeed have hastened it in their wish to destroy you. Moreover, I think you are betraying your sons

d by going away and leaving them, when you could bring them up and educate them. You thus show no concern for what their fate may be. They will probably have the usual fate of orphans. Either one should not have children, or one should share with them to the end the toil of upbringing and education. You seem to me to choose the easiest path, whereas one should choose the path a good and courageous man would choose, particularly when one claims throughout one's life to care for virtue.

e I feel ashamed on your behalf and on behalf of us, your friends, lest all that has happened to you be thought due to cowardice on our part: the fact that your trial came to court when it need not have done so, the handling of the trial itself, and now this absurd ending which will be thought to have got beyond our

46 control through some cowardice and unmanliness on our part, since we did not save you, or you save yourself, when it was possible and could be done if we had been of the slightest use. Consider, Socrates, whether this is not only evil, but shameful, both for you and for us. Take counsel with yourself, or rather the time for counsel is past and the decision should have been taken, and there is no further opportunity, for this whole business must be ended tonight. If we delay now, then it will no longer be possible, it will be too late. Let me persuade you on every count, Socrates, and do not act otherwise.

s: My dear Crito, your eagerness is worth much

b if it should have some right aim; if not, then the greater your keenness the more difficult it is to deal with. We must therefore examine whether we should act in this way or not, as not only now but at all times I am the kind of man who listens only to the argument that on reflection seems best to me. I cannot, now that this fate has come upon me, discard the arguments I used; they seem to me much the same. I value and respect the same principles

c as before, and if we have no better arguments to bring up at this moment, be sure that I shall not agree with you, not even if the power of the majority were to frighten us with more bogeys, as if we were children, with threats of incarcerations and executions and confiscation of property. How should we examine this matter most reasonably? Would it be by taking

d

up first your argument about the opinions of men, whether it is sound in every case that one should pay attention to some opinions, but not to others? Or was that well-spoken before the necessity to die came upon me, but now it is clear that this was said in vain for the sake of argument, that it was in truth play and nonsense? I am eager to examine together with you, Crito, whether this argument will appear in any way different to me in my present circumstances, or whether it remains the same, whether we are to abandon it or be-

e

lieve it. It was said on every occasion by those who thought they were speaking sensibly, as I have just now been speaking, that one should greatly value some people's opinions, but not others. Does that seem to you a sound statement?

You, as far as a human being can tell, are exempt from the likelihood of dying tomorrow, so the present misfortune is not likely

47

to lead you astray. Consider then, do you not think it a sound statement that one must not value all the opinions of men, but some and not others, nor the opinions of all men, but those of some and not of others? What do you say? Is this not well said?

c: It is.

s: One should value the good opinions, and not the bad ones?

c: Yes.

s: The good opinions are those of wise men, the bad ones those of foolish men?

c: Of course.

s: Come then, what of statements such as this:

b

Should a man professionally engaged in physical training pay attention to the praise and blame and opinion of any man, or to those of one man only, namely a doctor or trainer?

c: To those of one only.

s: He should therefore fear the blame and welcome the praise of that one man, and not those of the many?

c: Obviously.

s: He must then act and exercise, eat and drink in the way the one, the trainer and the one who knows, thinks right, not all the others?

c: That is so.

c

s: Very well. And if he disobeys the one, disregards his opinion and his praises while valuing

those of the many who have no knowledge, will he not suffer harm?

c: Of course.

s: What is that harm, where does it tend, and what part of the man who disobeys does it affect?

c: Obviously the harm is to his body, which it ruins.

s: Well said. So with other matters, not to enumerate them all, and certainly with actions just and unjust, shameful and beautiful, good and bad, about which we are now deliberat-

d

ing, should we follow the opinion of the many and fear it; or that of the one, if there is one who has knowledge of these things and before whom we feel fear and shame more than before all the others. If we do not follow his directions, we shall harm and corrupt that part of ourselves that is improved by just actions and destroyed by unjust actions. Or is there nothing in this?

c: I think there certainly is, Socrates.

s: Come now, if we ruin that which is improved by health and corrupted by disease by not following the opinions of those who know, is life

e

worth living for us when that is ruined? And that is the body, is it not?

c: Yes.

s: And is life worth living with a body that is corrupted and in bad condition?

c: In no way.

s: And is life worth living for us with that part of us corrupted that unjust action harms and just action benefits? Or do we think that part of us, whatever it is, that is concerned with

48

justice and injustice, is inferior to the body?

c: Not at all.

s: It is more valuable?

c: Much more.

s: We should not then think so much of what the majority will say about us, but what he will say who understands justice and injustice, the one, that is, and the truth itself. So that, in the first place, you were wrong to believe that we should care for the opinion of the many about what is just, beautiful, good, and their opposites. "But," someone might say "the many are able to put us to death."

b

c: That too is obvious, Socrates, and someone might well say so.

s: And, my admirable friend, that argument that we have gone through remains, I think, as before. Examine the following statement in turn as to whether it stays the same or not, that the most important thing is not life, but the good life.

c: It stays the same.

s: And that the good life, the beautiful life, and the just life are the same; does that still hold, or not?

c: It does hold.

c

s: As we have agreed so far, we must examine next whether it is right for me to try to get out of here when the Athenians have not acquitted me. If it is seen to be right, we will try to do so; if it is not, we will abandon the idea. As for those questions you raise about money, reputation, the upbringing of children, Crito, those considerations in truth belong to those people who easily put men to death and would bring them to life again if they could, without thinking; I mean the majority of men. For us, however, since our argument leads to this, the only valid consideration, as we were saying just now, is whether we should be acting rightly in giving

d

money and gratitude to those who will lead me out of here, and ourselves helping with the escape, or whether in truth we shall do wrong in doing all this. If it appears that we shall be acting unjustly, then we have no need at all to take into account whether we shall have to die if we stay here and keep quiet, or suffer in another way, rather than do wrong.

c: I think you put that beautifully, Socrates, but see what we should do.

e

s: Let us examine the question together, my dear friend, and if you can make any objection while I am speaking, make it and I will listen to you, but if you have no objection to make, my dear Crito, then stop now from saying the same thing so often, that I must leave here against the will of the Athenians. I think it important to persuade you before I act, and not to act against your wishes. See whether the

49

start of our enquiry is adequately stated, and try to answer what I ask you in the way you think best.

c: I shall try.

s: Do we say that one must never in any way do wrong willingly, or must one do wrong in one way and not in another? Is to do wrong never good or admirable, as we have agreed in the past, or have all these former agreements been washed out during the last few days? Have we

b

at our age failed to notice for some time that in our serious discussions we were no different from children? Above all, is the truth such as we used to say it was, whether the majority agree or not, and whether we must still suffer worse things than we do now, or will be treated more gently, that nonetheless, wrongdoing is in every way harmful and shameful to the wrongdoer? Do we say so or not?

c: We do.

s: So one must never do wrong.

c: Certainly not.

s: Nor must one, when wronged, inflict wrong in return, as the majority believe, since one must never do wrong.

c

c: That seems to be the case.

s: Come now, should one injure anyone or not, Crito?

c: One must never do so.

s: Well then, if one is oneself injured, is it right, as the majority say, to inflict an injury in return, or is it not?

c: It is never right.

s: Injuring people is no different from wrongdoing.

c: That is true.

s: One should never do wrong in return, nor injure any man, whatever injury one has suffered at his hands. And Crito, see that you do

d

not agree to this, contrary to your belief. For I know that only a few people hold this view or will hold it, and there is no common ground between those who hold this view and those who do not, but they inevitably despise each other's views. So then consider very carefully whether we have this view in common, and whether you agree, and let this be the basis of our deliberation, that neither to do wrong or to return a wrong is ever right, not even to injure in return for an injury received. Or do you disagree and do not share this view as a basis for discussion? I have held it for a long

e

time and still hold it now, but if you think otherwise, tell me now. If, however, you stick to our former opinion, then listen to the next point.

c: I stick to it and agree with you. So say on.

s: Then I state the next point, or rather I ask you: when one has come to an agreement that is just with someone, should one fulfill it or cheat on it?

c: One should fulfill it.

s: See what follows from this: if we leave here **50** without the city's permission, are we injuring people whom we should least injure? And are we sticking to a just agreement, or not?

c: I cannot answer your question, Socrates. I do not know.

s: Look at it this way. If, as we were planning to run away from here, or whatever one should call it, the laws and the state came and confronted us and asked: "Tell me, Socrates, what are you intending to do? Do you not **b** by this action you are attempting intend to destroy us, the laws, and indeed the whole city, as far as you are concerned? Or do you think it possible for a city not to be destroyed if the verdicts of its courts have no force but are nullified and set at naught by private individuals?" What shall we answer to this and other such arguments? For many things could be said, especially by an orator on behalf of this law we are destroying, which orders that **c** the judgments of the courts shall be carried out. Shall we say in answer, "The city wronged me, and its decision was not right." Shall we say that, or what?

c: Yes, by Zeus, Socrates, that is our answer.

s: Then what if the laws said: "Was that the agreement between us, Socrates, or was it to respect the judgments that the city came to?" And if we wondered at their words, they would perhaps add: "Socrates, do not wonder at what we say but answer, since you are ac-**d** customed to proceed by question and answer. Come now, what accusation do you bring against us and the city, that you should try to destroy us? Did we not, first, bring you to birth, and was it not through us that your father married your mother and begat you? Tell us, do you find anything to criticize in those of us who are concerned with marriage?" And I would say that I do not criticize them. "Or in those of us concerned with the nurture of babies and the education that you too re-

ceived? Were those assigned to that subject not right to instruct your father to educate **e** you in the arts and in physical culture?" And I would say that they were right. "Very well," they would continue, "and after you were born and nurtured and educated, could you, in the first place, deny that you are our off-spring and servant, both you and your fore-fathers? If that is so, do you think that we are on an equal footing as regards the right, and that whatever we do to you it is right for you to do to us? You were not on an equal footing with your father as regards the right, nor with **51** your master if you had one, so as to retaliate for anything they did to you, to revile them if they reviled you, to beat them if they beat you, and so with many other things. Do you think you have this right to retaliation against your country and its laws? That if we under-take to destroy you and think it right to do so, you can undertake to destroy us, as far as you can, in return? And will you say that you are right to do so, you who truly care for vir-tue? Is your wisdom such as not to realize that your country is to be honoured more than your mother, your father and all your ances-tors, that it is more to be revered and more sacred, and that it counts for more among the **b** gods and sensible men, that you must worship it, yield to it and placate its anger more than your father's? You must either persuade it or obey its orders, and endure in silence what-ever it instructs you to endure, whether blows or bonds, and if it leads you into war to be wounded or killed, you must obey. To do so is right, and one must not give way or retreat or leave one's post, but both in war and in courts and everywhere else, one must obey **c** the commands of one's city and country, or persuade it as to the nature of justice. It is im-pious to bring violence to bear against your mother or father, it is much more so to use it against your country." What shall we say in reply, Crito, that the laws speak the truth, or not?

c: I think they do.

s: "Reflect now, Socrates," the laws might say "that if what we say is true, you are not treat-ing us rightly by planning to do what you are planning. We have given you birth, nurtured you, educated you, we have given you and all

d   other citizens a share of all the good things we could. Even so, by giving every Athenian the opportunity, after he has reached manhood and observed the affairs of the city and us the laws, we proclaim that if we do not please him, he can take his possessions and go wherever he pleases. Not one of our laws raises any obstacle or forbids him, if he is not satisfied with us or the city, if one of you wants to go and live in a colony or wants to go anywhere else, and keep his property. We say, however,

e   that whoever of you remains, when he sees how we conduct our trials and manage the city in other ways, has in fact come to an agreement with us to obey our instructions. We say that the one who disobeys does wrong in three ways, first because in us he disobeys his parents, also those who brought him up, and because, in spite of his agreement, he neither obeys us nor, if we do something wrong,

52   does he try to persuade us to be better. Yet we only propose things, we do not issue savage commands to do whatever we order; we give two alternatives, either to persuade us or to do what we say. He does neither. We do say that you too, Socrates, are open to those charges if you do what you have in mind; you would be among, not the least, but the most guilty of the Athenians." And if I should say "Why so?" they might well be right to upbraid me and say that I am among the Athenians who most definitely came to that agreement with them. They

b   might well say: "Socrates, we have convincing proofs that we and the city were congenial to you. You would not have dwelt here most consistently of all the Athenians if the city had not been exceedingly pleasing to you. You have never left the city, even to see a festival, nor for any other reason except military service; you have never gone to stay in any other city, as people do; you have had no desire to

c   know another city or other laws; we and our city satisfied you.

"So decisively did you choose us and agree to be a citizen under us. Also, you have had children in this city, thus showing that it was congenial to you. Then at your trial you could have assessed your penalty at exile if you wished, and you are now attempting to do against the city's wishes what you could then

have done with her consent. Then you prided yourself that you did not resent death, but you chose, as you said, death in preference to ex-

d   ile. Now, however, those words do not make you ashamed, and you pay no heed to us, the laws, as you plan to destroy us, and you act like the meanest type of slave by trying to run away, contrary to your undertakings and your agreement to live as a citizen under us. First then, answer us on this very point, whether we speak the truth when we say that you agreed, not only in words but by your deeds, to live in accordance with us." What are we to say to that, Crito? Must we not agree?

c: We must, Socrates.

s: "Surely," they might say, "you are breaking the undertakings and agreements that you made with us without compulsion or deceit,

e   and under no pressure of time for deliberation. You have had seventy years during which you could have gone away if you did not like us, and if you thought our agreements unjust.

53   You did not choose to go to Sparta or to Crete, which you are always saying are well governed, nor to any other city, Greek or foreign. You have been away from Athens less than the lame or the blind or other handicapped people. It is clear that the city has been outstandingly more congenial to you than to other Athenians, and so have we, the laws, for what city can please without laws? Will you then not now stick to our agreements? You will, Socrates, if we can persuade you, and not make yourself a laughingstock by leaving the city.

"For consider what good you will do yourself or your friends by breaking our agreements and committing such a wrong? It is pretty obvious that your friends will themselves be in danger of exile, disfranchisement

b   and loss of property. As for yourself, if you go to one of the nearby cities—Thebes or Megara, both are well governed—you will arrive as an enemy to their government; all who care for their city will look on you with suspicion, as a destroyer of the laws. You will also strengthen the conviction of the jury that

c   they passed the right sentence on you, for anyone who destroys the laws could easily be thought to corrupt the young and the ignorant. Or will you avoid cities that are well

d governed and men who are civilized? If you do this, will your life be worth living? Will you have social intercourse with them and not be ashamed to talk to them? And what will you say? The same as you did here, that virtue and justice are man's most precious possession, along with lawful behaviour and the laws? Do you not think that Socrates would appear to be an unseemly kind of person? One must think so. Or will you leave those places and go to Crito's friends in Thessaly? There you will find the greatest license and disorder, and they may enjoy hearing from you how absurdly you escaped from prison in some disguise, in a leather jerkin or some other things in which escapees wrap themselves, thus altering your appearance. Will there be no one to say that

e you, likely to live but a short time more, were so greedy for life that you transgressed the most important laws? Possibly, Socrates,if you do not annoy anyone, but if you do, many disgraceful things will be said about you.

"You will spend your time ingratiating yourself with all men, and be at their beck and call. What will you do in Thessaly but feast, as if you had gone to a banquet in Thessaly? As for those conversations of yours about justice and the rest of virtue, where will they be? You

54 say you want to live for the sake of your children, that you may bring them up and educate them. How so? Will you bring them up and educate them by taking them to Thessaly and making strangers of them, that they may enjoy that too? Or not so, but they will be better brought up and educated here, while you are alive, though absent? Yes, your friends will look after them. Will they look after them if you go and live in Thessaly, but not if you go away to the underworld? If those who profess themselves your friends are any good at all,

b one must assume that they will.

"Be persuaded by us who have brought you up, Socrates. Do not value either your children or your life or anything else more than goodness, in order that when you arrive in Hades you may have all this as your defence before the rulers there. If you do this deed, you will not think it better or more just or more pious here, nor will any one of your friends, nor will it be better for you when you

c arrive yonder. As it is, you depart, if you depart, after being wronged not by us, the laws, but by men; but if you depart after shamefully returning wrong for wrong and injury for injury, after breaking your agreement and contract with us, after injuring those you should injure least—yourself, your friends, your country and us—we shall be angry with you while you are still alive, and our brothers, the laws of the underworld, will not receive you kindly, knowing that you tried to destroy us as far as you could. Do not let Crito persuade

d you, rather than us, to do what he says."

Crito, my dear friend, be assured that these are the words I seem to hear, as the Corybants seem to hear the music of their flutes, and the echo of these words resounds in me, and makes it impossible for me to hear anything else. As far as my present beliefs go, if you speak in opposition to them, you will speak in vain. However, if you think you can accomplish anything, speak.

c: I have nothing to say, Socrates.

s: Let it be then, Crito, and let us act in this way, since this is the way the god is leading us.

Commentary and Questions[5]

Read 43a–44b   Plato opens the dialogue with a scene designed to emphasize yet again how different Socrates is from most men. The time is approaching for his execution, yet he sleeps peacefully—as though he had not a care in the world. His dream confirms what he had concluded at the end of the trial: Death is not an evil to be feared but is more like the soul coming home again after many hardships.

Read 44b–46a   Crito loses no time in trying to persuade Socrates to escape. He piles reason upon reason.

Q1.   List at least seven reasons Crito urges upon Socrates for making his escape.

Most of these reasons are prudential in nature, not moral. The one that does appeal to "what is right" seems to come right out of the Sophist's playbook: What is right, Crito says, is to preserve one's own life whenever one can.* Several of the reasons appeal to "what people will think" or "how things will look" if Socrates does not take this opportunity. This leads Socrates to ask why one should pay any attention at all to what the majority of people say.

Q2. What does Crito say in response to this question, and what is Socrates' reply?

Q3. What does Socrates indicate as "the greatest good"?

Read 46b–49a Characteristically, Socrates says they must "examine" whether to act in this way.

Q4. What kind of man does Socrates here say that he is?

Socrates reminds Crito that he has always maintained that one should pay attention only to the opinions of some people, the "most reasonable" people. He then invites Crito to reexamine this conviction in the light of his present situation—his facing imminent death. Does it "stand fast" even now? Perhaps it will now appear unserious, nothing more than "play and nonsense," and Socrates will want to change his mind.

The examination is conducted, as so often, in terms of an analogy; Socrates draws a comparison between the health of the body and the health of the soul. He points out that you don't listen to just anybody when it comes to matters of bodily health. The same must also be true when it is a matter of the soul's well-being. You want to listen to those who are wise, not to the opinions of the many. So what most people might think if Socrates escapes or does not escape is, strictly speaking, irrelevant. It should be set aside. Reluctantly perhaps, Crito agrees.

Socrates adds that life is really not worth living when the body is corrupted by disease and ruined; the important thing is "not life, but the good life." The same must then be true of the soul.

Q5. What corrupts and ruins the soul, according to Socrates? What benefits it?

---

*See the quotations from Antiphon, p. 48.

Q6. Which, body or soul, is most valuable? Why do you think he says that?

Q7. Socrates says that three kinds of life are "the same": The good life, the beautiful life, and the just life. Think about the lives you are familiar with. Do you agree? Is it really the just people whose lives are beautiful and good?

They agree, then, that the right thing to do is the only thing they should have in mind when making the decision. The question is simply this: Is it just or unjust to escape? Will escaping bring benefit or harm to the soul?

Read 49a–50a The next principle Socrates brings up for reexamination is this: that one should never willingly do wrong. Why not? Because doing wrong is "harmful and shameful to the wrongdoer." Again we see Socrates emphasizing that we harm ourselves by harming our souls, and we harm our souls by doing wrong, which makes us into worse people than we otherwise would be.

Q8. What corollary to this "never do wrong" principle does Socrates draw out in 49b–d?

Q9. Socrates says this is not something the majority of people believe. Do you believe it?

Note that injuring is not the same as inflicting harm. Remember, Socrates was a soldier, and a good one. He even cited his military experience with pride in his defense before the jury. But soldiers inflict damage on other soldiers, perhaps even kill them. Moreover, Athens is about to execute Socrates, but he says nothing to suggest that capital punishment is wrongdoing or injury. It may, then, be justifiable—in war or according to law—to inflict harm. Still, we must never injure each other. Injury is *unjust* harming of another.

What is wrong, Socrates says, is doing injustice in return for an injustice done to you. Wrong done to you never justifies your doing wrong. The reason is simply that doing injustice is *always* wrong, always a corruption of the soul. When you consider how to act, according to Socrates, you should never think about revenge, or paying back, or getting even. All these motivations look to the past, to what has happened to you, and you should look only to actions that will promote excellence—in your soul and in others. That is the way to care for your soul, and Crito says that he agrees.

Socrates says they should examine next whether one should always keep agreements made, providing they are just agreements (49e). Crito agrees immediately, so we come to the major part of the argument.

Read 50a–54d   In this section, we have a dramatic piece of rhetoric. Plato gives us a dialogue within the dialogue in the form of an imaginary "examination" of Socrates by the laws of Athens. It is rhetoric all right; but, like Parmenides' poem, it contains an argument. Socrates will look to this argument, this *logos,* in making his decision. Remember that Socrates says he is the kind of man who listens only to the best *logos.* So it is the argument that we must try to discern.

Socrates indicates the conclusion of the argument right off: that escaping will constitute an attempt to injure the laws, and indeed the whole city, insofar as it is in Socrates' power to do so. It is this proposition that the laws have to prove. If they can do so, it will follow immediately that Socrates must not escape, because an escape attempt will amount to doing injury. It will also be no good for Socrates to reply, "Well, the laws injured me by convicting me unjustly!" because we have already agreed that one must not return injury for injury.

How will escaping injure the laws of Athens? This part of the argument begins with the laws claiming that they are to be honored more than mother, father, or all one's ancestors.

Q10.   What reasons are offered by the laws for this claim?

Q11.   What alternatives does Athens offer its citizens if they do not agree with or like the laws?

Q12.   Could Socrates have left Athens at any time if he was not pleased with the laws?

Q13.   What conclusion follows from the fact that Socrates stayed?

So the situation is this: In virtue of his long residence in Athens, Socrates has agreed to be a citizen under the laws, to accept their benefits and "live in accordance" with them. This agreement was made without any compulsion and in full knowledge of what was involved. There can be no doubt that it is a just agreement. Further, Socrates and Crito have already agreed that just agreements must be kept. But it is not yet clear how breaking this agreement will injure the laws and the city of Athens.

A clue is found in 54b, where the laws say that Socrates was wronged not by them, but by men. No legal order can exist without application and enforcement, courts and punishments, and part of voluntarily accepting citizenship is agreeing to abide by decisions of the legally constituted courts. There can be no doubt that the court that convicted Socrates was a legal court. It should also be noted that Socrates does not criticize the Athenian law against impiety on which he was tried. If the jury made a mistake and decided the case unjustly, that cannot be laid at the door of the laws. Such things can always happen. So the laws did Socrates no injustice. (Though even if they had, that would not, on Socrates' principles, justify his doing wrong in return.)

The situation then is this: To escape would be tantamount to an attack on the authority of this court to decide as it did. If *this* court lacks authority over its citizens, what court has such authority? To attack the authority of the courts is to attempt, insofar as it is possible for one man, to destroy the legal system, and the city, as a whole. "Or do you think it is possible for a city not to be destroyed if the verdicts of its courts have no force but are nullified and set at naught by private individuals?" (50b)

The argument is complex, and it may be useful to set it out in skeleton form.

1. One must never do wrong.
    a. Because to do wrong is "in every way harmful and shameful to the wrongdoer." (49b)
    b. Because doing wrong harms the part of ourselves that is "more valuable." (48a)

2. One must never return wrong for wrong done. (This follows directly from 1.)

3. To injure others (treat them unjustly) is to do wrong.

4. One must never injure others. (This follows from 1 and 3.)

5. To violate a just agreement is to do injury.

6. To escape would be to violate a just agreement with the laws. (Here we have the argument presented in the dialogue between Socrates and the laws.)

7. To escape would be an injury to the laws. (This follows from 5 and 6.)

8. To escape would be wrong. (This follows from 3 and 7.)

9. Socrates must not escape. (This follows from 1 and 8.)

This *logos* is one that Socrates finds convincing, and Crito has nothing to say against it. So it is the one Socrates will be content to live—and die—by. Once again, it is better to *suffer* injustice than to *do* it, even if that means losing one's life to avoid committing an unjust act.

There remains the task of countering the considerations Crito has put forward in favor of escape. In 53a–54a, the laws address these arguments point by point.

Q14. Go back to your list in Q1, and state the rebuttal offered by the laws. Who is more persuasive—Crito or the laws?

Read 54d–e *Corybants* are priests of Earth and the fertility goddess Cybele, who express their devotion in ecstatic dances, oblivious to what is going on around them. The dialogue ends with Plato once again emphasizing the very real piety of Socrates. He quietly accepts the verdict of the *logos* as guidance from the god. The voice of reason, as far as it can be discerned, is the voice of the divine.*

---

*Remember that human reason, for Socrates, is not the same as divine wisdom. We are not gods. That is why continual examination of ourselves is in order; and that is why his "voice" is significant; it supplies something human *logoi* could not. Compare what Heraclitus says about wisdom, the *logos,* and the divine, p. 22.

PHAEDO (DEATH SCENE)

Translator's Introduction

In the Phaedo, *a number of Socrates' friends have come to visit him in prison on the last day of his life, as he will drink the hemlock at sundown. The main topic of their conversation is the nature of the soul and the arguments for its immortality. This takes up most of the dialogue. Then Socrates tells a rather elaborate myth on the shape of the earth in a hollow of which we live, and of which we know nothing of the splendours of its surface, the purer air and brighter heavens. The myth then deals with the dwelling places of various kinds of souls after death. The following passage immediately follows the conclusion of the myth.*

The Dialogue (Selection)

No sensible man would insist that these things are as I have described them, but I think it **114d** is fitting for a man to risk the belief—for the risk is a noble one—that this, or something like this, is true about our souls and their dwelling places, since the soul is evidently immortal, and a man should repeat this to himself as if it were an incantation, which is why I have been prolonging my tale. That is the reason why a man should be of good cheer about his own soul, if during life he has ignored the pleasures e of the body and its ornamentation as of no concern to him and doing him more harm than good, but has seriously concerned himself with the pleasures of learning, and adorned his soul not with alien but with its own ornaments, namely moderation, righteousness, courage,

115 freedom, and truth, and in that state awaits his journey to the underworld.

Now you, Simmias, Cebes, and the rest of you, Socrates continued, will each take that journey at some other time but my fated day calls me now, as a tragic character might say, and it is about time for me to have my bath, for I think it better to have it before I drink the poison and save the women the trouble of washing the corpse.

When Socrates had said this Crito spoke:

b Very well, Socrates, what are your instructions to me and the others about your children or anything else? What can we do that would please you most?   —Nothing new, Crito, said Socrates, but what I am always saying, that you will please me and mine and yourselves, by taking good care of your own selves in whatever you do, even if you do not agree with me now, but if you neglect your own selves, and are un-

c willing to live following the tracks, as it were, of what we have said now and on previous occasions, you will achieve nothing even if you strongly agree with me at this moment.

We shall be eager to follow your advice, said Crito, but how shall we bury you?

In any way you like, said Socrates, if you can catch me and I do not escape you. And laughing quietly, looking at us, he said: I do not convince Crito that I am this Socrates talking to you here

d and ordering all I say, but he thinks that I am the thing which he will soon be looking at as a corpse, and so he asks how he shall bury me. I have been saying for some time and at some length that after I have drunk the poison I shall no longer be with you but will leave you to go and enjoy some good fortunes of the blessed, but it seems that I have said all this to him in vain in an attempt to reassure you and myself too. Give a pledge to Crito on my behalf, he said, the opposite pledge to that he gave to the jury. He pledged that I would stay, you must

e pledge that I will not stay after I die, but that I shall go away, so that Crito will bear it more easily when he sees my body being burned or

buried and will not be angry on my behalf, as if I were suffering terribly, and so that he should not say at the funeral that he is laying out, or carrying out, or burying Socrates. For know you well, my dear Crito, that to express oneself badly is not only faulty as far as the language goes, but does some harm to the soul. You must be of good cheer, and say you are burying my body, and bury it in any way you like and think

116 most customary.

After saying this he got up and went to another room to take his bath, and Crito followed him and he told us to wait for him. So we stayed, talking among ourselves, questioning what had been said, and then again talking of the great misfortune that had befallen us. We all felt as if we had lost a father and would be

b orphaned for the rest of our lives. When he had washed, his children were brought to him— two of his sons were small and one was older— and the women of his household came to him. He spoke to them before Crito and gave them what instructions he wanted. Then he sent the women and children away, and he himself joined us. It was now close to sunset, for he had stayed inside for some time. He came and sat down after his bath and conversed for a short

c while, when the officer of the Eleven came and stood by him and said: "I shall not reproach you as I do the others, Socrates. They are angry with me and curse me when, obeying the orders of my superiors, I tell them to drink the poison. During the time you have been here I have come to know you in other ways as the noblest, the gentlest, and the best man who has ever come here. So now too I know that you will not make trouble for me; you know who is responsible and you will direct your anger against them. You know what message I bring. Fare you well, and try to endure what you must as easily as possible." The officer was

d weeping as he turned away and went out. Socrates looked up at him and said: "Fare you well also, we shall do as you bid us." And turning to us he said: How pleasant the man is! During the whole time I have been here he has come in and conversed with me from time to time, a most agreeable man. And how genuinely he now weeps for me. Come, Crito, let us obey him. Let someone bring the poison if it is ready; if not, let the man prepare it.

e   But Socrates, said Crito, I think the sun still shines upon the hills and has not yet set. I know that others drink the poison quite a long time after they have received the order, eating and drinking quite a bit, and some of them enjoy intimacy with their loved ones. Do not hurry; there is still some time.

117   It is natural, Crito, for them to do so, said Socrates, for they think they derive some benefit from doing this, but it is not fitting for me. I do not expect any benefit from drinking the poison a little later, except to become ridiculous in my own eyes for clinging to life, and be sparing of it when there is none left. So do as I ask and do not refuse me.

Hearing this, Crito nodded to the slave who was standing near him; the slave went out and after a time came back with the man who was to administer the poison, carrying it made ready in a cup. When Socrates saw him he said: Well, my good man, you are an expert in this, what must one do?   —"Just drink it and walk
b   around until your legs feel heavy, and then lie down and it will act of itself." And he offered the cup to Socrates who took it quite cheerfully, . . . without a tremor or any change of feature or colour, but looking at the man from under his eyebrows as was his wont, asked: "What do you say about pouring a libation from this drink? Is it allowed?"   —"We only mix as much as we believe will suffice," said the man.

c   I understand, Socrates said, but one is allowed, indeed one must, utter a prayer to the gods that the journey from here to yonder may be fortunate. This is my prayer and may it be so.

And while he was saying this, he was holding the cup, and then drained it calmly and easily. Most of us had been able to hold back our tears reasonably well up till then, but when we saw him drinking it and after he drank it, we could hold them back no longer; my own tears came in floods against my will. So I covered my face. I was weeping for myself—not for him, but for my misfortune in being deprived of such a com-
d   rade. Even before me, Crito was unable to restrain his tears and got up. Apollodorus had not ceased from weeping before, and at this moment his noisy tears and anger made everybody present break down, except Socrates. "What is this," he said, "you strange fellows. It is mainly for this reason that I sent the women away, to

e   avoid such unseemliness, for I am told one should die in good omened silence. So keep quiet and control yourselves."

His words made us ashamed, and we checked our tears. He walked around, and when he said his legs were heavy he lay on his back as he had been told to do, and the man who had given him the poison touched his body, and after a
118   while tested his feet and legs, pressed hard upon his foot and asked him if he felt this, and Socrates said no. Then he pressed his calves, and made his way up his body and showed us that it was cold and stiff. He felt it himself and said that when the cold reached his heart he would be gone. As his belly was getting cold Socrates uncovered his head— he had covered it—and said—these were his last words— "Crito, we owe a cock to Asclepius;[1] make this offering to him and do not forget."   —"It shall be done," said Crito, "tell us if there is anything else," but there was no answer. Shortly afterwards Socrates made a movement; the man uncovered him and his eyes were fixed. Seeing this Crito closed his mouth and his eyes.

Such was the end of our comrade, . . . , a man who, we would say, was of all those we have known the best, and also the wisest and the most upright.

Commentary and Questions

Read 114d–115e   About fifteen people were present for this last conversation. Plato, it is said, was absent because he was ill. By this point, they have agreed that the soul is immortal and that the souls of the just and pious, especially if they have devoted themselves to wisdom, dwell after death in a beautiful place.

Q1.   What are said to be the "ornaments" of the soul?

Q2.   What harm, do you think, can it do the soul to "express oneself badly"?

---

[1] A cock was sacrificed to Asclepius by the sick people who slept in his temples, hoping for a cure. Socrates obviously means that death is a cure for the ills of life.

Read 116—end   Socrates seems to have kept his calm and courage to the end—and his humor. There is a little joke about burial at 115c. Xenophon, too, records this:

> A man named Apollodorus, who was there with him, a very ardent disciple of Socrates, but otherwise simple, exclaimed, "But Socrates, what I find it hardest to bear is that I see you being put to death unjustly!" The other, stroking Apollodorus' head, is said to have replied, "My beloved Apollodorus, was it your preference to see me put to death justly?" and smiled as he asked the question.[6]

The simple majesty of the final tribute is, perhaps, unmatched anywhere.

For Further Thought

1. Socrates believes that acts of injustice cannot be wrong simply because the gods disapprove of them. There must be something about such acts themselves, he claims, that makes them wrong. If you agree, try to say what that is. If you disagree, argue for that conclusion.

2. Imagine that you are a member of the Athenian jury hearing the case of Socrates. How would you vote? Why?

3. Should Socrates have accepted Crito's offer of escape? Construct a *logos* that supports your answer.

Notes

1. The dialogues and translator's introductions in this chapter are from Plato, *The Trial and Death of Socrates,* 2d ed., trans. G. M. A. Grube (Indianapolis: Hackett, 1975).

2. Xenophon, *Memorabilia,* trans. E. C. Marchant, in *Xenophon IV,* ed. E. C. Marchant and O. J. Todd (Cambridge, MA: Harvard University Press, 1979), bk. 1, 3, 2–3.

3. Plato, *Meno,* trans. Robin Waterfield, in *Meno and Other Dialogues* (Oxford: Oxford University Press, 2005).

4. Plato, *Theatetus,* in *The Collected Dialogues of Plato,* ed. E. Hamilton and H. Cairns (Princeton: Princeton University Press, 1961).

5. I am indebted to R. E. Allen's interpretation of the *Crito* in his *Socrates and Legal Obligation* (Minneapolis: University of Minnesota Press, 1980).

6. Xenophon, *Apology 28,* trans. O. J. Todd, in *Xenophon IV,* ed. E. C. Marchant and O. J. Todd (Cambridge, MA: Harvard University Press, 1979).

6

PLATO

Knowing the Real and the Good

When Socrates died in 399 B.C., his friend and admirer Plato was just thirty years old. He lived fifty-two more years. That long life was devoted to the creation of a philosophy that would justify and vindicate his master, "the best, and also the wisest" man he had ever known (*Phaedo* 118). It is a philosophy whose influence has been incalculable in the West. Together with that of his own pupil Aristotle, it forms one of the two foundation stones for nearly all that is to follow; even those who want to disagree first have to pay attention. In a rather loose sense, everyone who thinks about philosophy at all is either a Platonist or an Aristotelian. Not without cause did Alfred North Whitehead write in 1929 that "the safest general characterization of the European philosophical tradition is that it consists of a series of footnotes to Plato."[1]

In Raphael's remarkable painting *The School of Athens* (see the cover of this book), all the sight lines draw the eye toward the two central figures. Plato is the one on the left, pointing upward. Aristotle is on the right with a hand stretched out horizontally. We will not be ready to appreciate the symbolism

of these gestures until we know something of both, but that these two occupy center stage is entirely appropriate.

Plato apparently left Athens after Socrates' death and traveled quite widely. About 387 B.C., he settled again in his home town and established a school near a grove called "Academus," from which comes our word "academy." There he inquired, taught, and wrote the dialogues.

Let us briefly review the situation leading up to Socrates' death. These are extremely troubled times. An ugly, drawn-out war with Sparta ends in humiliation, accompanied by internal strife between democrats and oligarchs, culminating in the tyranny of the Thirty, civil war, and their overthrow. The Sophists, meanwhile, have been teaching doctrines that seem to undermine all the traditions and cast doubt on everything people hold sacred. And the intellectual situation in general, though it will look active and fruitful from a future vantage point, surely looks chaotic and unsettled from close up. It is a war of ideas no one has definitely won. You have Parmenides' One versus Heraclitus' flux, Democritus' atomism versus the skepticism of the Sophists, and the controversy over *physis* and *nomos*. Some urge conformity to the laws of the city; others hold that such human justice is inferior to the pursuit of self-interest, which can rightly override such "mere" conventions.

In this maelstrom appears Socrates—ugly to look at, fascinating in character, incredibly honest, doggedly persistent, passionately committed to a search for the truth, and convinced that *none* of his contemporaries know what they are talking about. Plato is not the only one entranced. But clearly Plato has genius of his own, and he takes the Socratic task on his own shoulders. Animating Socrates' practice, as we have seen, is the conviction that there is a truth about the matters he investigates; but Socrates seldom feels he has found it. Plato sets for himself the goal—nothing less!—of refuting skepticism and relativism. He intends to *demonstrate,* contrary to the Sophists, that there is a truth about reality and that it can be known. And he intends to show, contrary to Democritus, that this reality is not indifferent to moral and religious values.

His basic goal, and in this he is typically Greek, is to establish the pattern for a good state.* If you were to ask him, "Plato, exactly what do you mean by 'a good state'?" he would have a ready answer. He would say that a good state is one in which a good person can live a good life. And if you pressed him about what kind of person was a good person, he would acknowledge that here was a hard question, one needing examination. But he would at least be ready with an example. And by now you know who the example would be. It follows that Athens as it existed in 399 B.C. was not, despite its virtues, a good state, for it had executed Socrates.

To reach this goal of setting forth the pattern of a good state, Plato has to show that there is such a thing as goodness—and not just by convention. It couldn't be that if Athens *thought* it was a good thing to execute Socrates then it *was* a good thing to execute Socrates. Plato knew in his heart that was wrong. But now he has to *show* it was wrong. Mere assertion was never enough for Socrates, and it

won't do for Plato, either. He will construct a *logos,* a true *logos,* a *dialectic,* to show us the goodness that exists in *physis,* not just in the opinions of people or the conventions of society. And he will show us how we can come to know what this goodness is and become truly wise. These, at least, are his ambitions.

Knowledge and Opinion

We sometimes make the following contrast: Do you only believe that, or do you know it? This contrast between mere belief, or opinion, and knowledge is important for Plato. Indeed, he uses it to derive surprising conclusions—conclusions that make up the heart and center of his philosophy. It is on this distinction that his critique of the sophistic relativism and skepticism turns.

The Sophists argue, you will recall, that if someone thinks the wind is cold, then it is cold—for that person.* And they generalize this claim. "Of *all* things, the measure is man," asserts Protagoras. In effect, all we can have are opinions or beliefs. If a certain belief is satisfactory to a certain person, then no more can be said. We are each the final authority of what seems right to us. We are restricted to appearance; knowledge of reality is beyond our powers. This is the heart of their skepticism and relativism.

Plato tries to meet this challenge in three steps. First, he has to clarify the distinction between opinion and knowledge. Second, he has to show that we do have knowledge. Third, he needs to explain the nature of the objects that we can be said to know. As we will see, Plato's *epistemology* (his theory of knowledge) and his **metaphysics** (his theory of reality) are perfectly knit together in his unique solution to these problems.

Making the Distinction

What is the difference between knowing something and just believing it? The key seems to be this: You can believe falsely, but you can't know falsely.

---

*His *Republic* is an attempt to define an ideal state. The *Laws,* perhaps his last work, is a long and detailed discussion trying to frame a realistic constitution for a state that might actually exist.

*See p. 44.

Suppose that at a certain time, call it T1, you claim to know that John is Kate's husband. Later, at T2, you find out that John is really unmarried and has never been anyone's husband. What will you then say about yourself at T1? Will you say, "Well, I used to know (at T1) that John was married, but now I know he is not"? This would be saying, "I did know (falsely) that John was married, but now I know (truly) that he is not." Or will you say, "Well, I *thought* I knew (at T1) that John was married, but I *didn't* know it at all"? Surely you will say the latter. If we become convinced that something we claim to know is false, we retract that claim. We do not claim to know things we believe are false. We can put this in the form of a principle: Knowledge involves truth.

Believing or having opinions is quite the opposite. If at T1 you *believe* that John is married to Kate and you later find out he isn't, you won't retract the claim that you did believe that at T1. You will simply say, "Yes, I did believe that; but now I believe (or know) it isn't so." It is quite possible to believe something false; it happens all the time. Believing does not necessarily involve truth.

We can, of course, believe truly. But even so, belief and knowledge are not the same thing. In the *Meno,* Plato has Socrates say,

> As long as they stay put, true beliefs too constitute a thing of beauty and do nothing but good. The problem is that they tend not to stay for long; they escape from the human soul and this reduces their value, unless they're anchored by working out the reason. . . When true beliefs are anchored, they become pieces of knowledge and they become stable. That's why knowledge is more valuable than true belief, and the difference between the two is that knowledge has been anchored. (*Meno* 98a) [2]

In the *Republic,* Plato compares people who have only true opinions to blind people who yet follow the right road (*R* 506c). [3] Imagine a blind woman who wanders along, turning this way and that. It just happens that each of her turnings corresponds to a bend in the road, but her correct turnings are merely an accident. She might equally well go straight over the cliff at the next bend. By contrast, we who can see the road, have a reason why we turn as we do; we can see that the road bends here

to avoid the precipice. We know that we must turn left here precisely because we can give an account of why we turn as we do. Our belief that we must turn left here is "anchored" by our "reason" that there is a cliff dead ahead.

We can connect this contrast between true belief and knowledge with the practice of Socrates. It is his habit, as we have seen, to examine others about their beliefs. And we can now say that surviving such examination is a necessary condition for any belief to count as knowledge. It is only a negative condition, however, because such survival doesn't guarantee truth; perhaps we simply have not yet come across the devastating counterexample. But Plato wants more than survival. In addition to surviving criticism, he wants to supply positive reasons for holding on to a belief. What he hopes to supply is a *logos* that gives *the reason why.*

We have here a second and a third point of distinction between knowledge and belief (even true belief). Not only does knowledge invariably involve truth, but it also "stays put." And it endures in this way because it involves the reason why.

And this leads to a final difference. In the *Timaeus,* Plato tells us that

> the one is implanted in us by instruction, the other by persuasion; . . . the one cannot be overcome by persuasion, but the other can. (*Timaeus* 51e) [4]

The instruction in question will be an explanation of the reason why. But what is persuasion? Can there be any doubt that Plato has in mind here all the tricks and techniques of rhetoric? If you truly know something, he is saying, you will understand why it is so. And that understanding will protect you from clever fellows (advertisers, politicians, public relations experts) who use their art to "make the weaker argument appear the stronger." Opinion or mere belief, by contrast, is at the mercy of every persuasive talker that comes along. If you believe something but don't clearly understand the reason why it is so, your belief will easily be "overcome" by persuasion. Compare yourself, for instance, to the blind woman at the bend of the road just before the cliff. She might easily be persuaded to go straight ahead; no one could persuade you to do so.

As you can see, Plato draws a sharp and clear line between opinion and knowledge. We can summarize the distinction in a table.

Opinion	Knowledge
is changeable	endures or stays put
may be true or false	is always true
is not backed up by reasons	is backed up by reasons
is the result of persuasion	is the result of instruction

So far even Sophists need not quarrel; they could agree that such a distinction can be made. But they would claim that it cannot be *applied* because all we ever have are opinions. We can perhaps understand what it would be like to have knowledge, but it doesn't follow that we actually have any. So Plato has to move to his second task; he has to demonstrate that we can in fact know certain things.

We Do Know Certain Truths

Plato's clearest examples are the truths of mathematics and geometry. Think back to the slave boy and the problem of doubling the area of a square.* The correct solution is to take the diagonal of the original square as a side of the square to be con-

structed. That solution can be seen to be correct because an "account" or explanation can be given: the reason why. Now look at the following diagram.

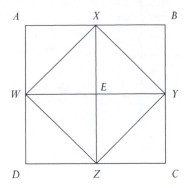

The reason why the square *WXYZ* is double the original square *WEZD* is that it is made up of four equal triangles, each of which is the same size as one-half the original. Because four halves make two wholes, we have a square twice the size of *WEZD*. This *logos* gives the reason why this is the correct solution. Once you (or the slave boy) understand this rationale, it will not be easier to persuade you otherwise than to persuade you to go straight over the cliff edge. What we have here, then, is an opinion that is true, will stay put, is backed up by reason, and is the result of instruction. In other words, we have not just opinion—we have knowledge.

This example (and innumerable others of the same kind can be constructed) is absolutely convincing to Plato. There can be no doubt, he thinks, that this solution is not just a matter of how it seems to one person or another. About these matters cultures do not differ.* There is no sense in which man is the "measure" of this truth. It is not conventional or up to us to decide; we *recognize* it. Relativism, at least as a general theory, is mistaken. Skepticism is wrong. We do have knowledge of the truth.

But two important questions are still unsettled. First, what exactly do we have knowledge about

---

---

*Compare Socrates on what the gods do not quarrel about (*Euthyphro* 7 b,c).

"So the philosopher, who consorts with what is divine and ordered, himself becomes godlike and ordered as far as a man can see. . . ."

—PLATO

when we know that this is the correct solution to the problem? Socrates probably drew the squares in the sand. Are we to suppose that he drew so accurately that the square made on the diagonal was really twice the area of the original? Not likely. The truth the slave boy came to know, then, is not a truth about that sand drawing. What is it about, then? Here is a puzzle. And Plato's solution to this puzzle is the key to understanding his whole philosophy.

The second question is whether this kind of knowledge can be extended to values and morality. Can we know that deception is unjust with the same certainty as that a square on the diagonal is twice the size of an original square? We address the first of these questions now and come back to the second later.

1. What are Plato's goals? What does he aim to do?
2. Distinguish knowledge from opinion.

The Objects of Knowledge

Plato would say that Socrates' sand drawing is not the object of the slave boy's knowledge. Let's make sure we see Plato's point here. "I agree," you might say, "that Socrates' sand drawing is not exact. But we can do much better than sand drawings nowadays. Surely we can draw, or construct, a square exactly double the size of a given square!" Ah, but can we? Suppose the area of the original square is 4; then we want a square that is 8 — not, note well, 7.999999999. And not 8.000000001 either.

There are two interesting points here. One is that we could not draw or make such a square, except perhaps by accident. Our instruments are not precise enough for that. The second is that even if we had such a square before us, we could not know that it was such a square, for all our measurements are valid only within a certain range of error. The slave boy's knowledge (and yours), it seems, cannot be derived from the drawing you see before you; and neither is it about that drawing. Yet it is true, and it does constitute knowledge. Plato puts the point in this way:

> Do sight and hearing afford mankind any truth, or aren't even the poets always harping on such themes, telling us that we neither hear nor see anything accurately? And yet if those of all the bodily senses are neither accurate nor clear, the others will hardly be so; because they are, surely, all inferior to those. Don't you think so?
>
> Certainly.
>
> So when does the soul attain the truth? Because plainly, whenever it sets about examining anything in company with the body, it is completely taken in by it.
>
> That's true.
>
> So isn't it in reasoning, if anywhere at all, that any realities become manifest to it?
>
> Yes. (*Phaedo*, 65b–c) [5]

The senses (sight, hearing, and the rest) never get it right, Plato tells us; they are not "clear" or "accurate." We grasp the truth only through a *logos* that "works out the reason."

Here Plato agrees with Parmenides, who admonishes us not to trust our senses but to follow reasoning alone.* In this sense, Plato too is a rationalist. You should be able to see, from the example we have considered, why he thinks this is the only way to proceed. (There is a role for the senses in the formulation of opinion about the world of experience, as we'll see, but they cannot give us *knowledge*.)

You should also be able to see that Plato agrees with Heraclitus about the world revealed to us through the senses.† Consider the drawing of the square again. Suppose we did get it just right; the area is exactly 8. But of course we drew it with a pencil, pen, or laser—with some physical material. What is to prevent it, once drawn correctly, from turning incorrect in the very next moment? Suppose a molecule of ink or a particle of light gets displaced? It might bounce in and out of correctness from nanosecond to nanosecond. It seems like a continual flux. And that is just what Heraclitus thinks it is. But our solution doesn't bounce in and out of truth that way. It "stays put." Once again, the truth we know cannot be about the world disclosed to our senses. Nothing in that world "stays put."

Interestingly, Plato holds that both Parmenides and Heraclitus are correct. They aren't in fact contradicting each other, even though one holds that reality is unchangeable and the other that reality is continually changing. Both are correct because each is talking about a different reality. The one is revealed to us through the senses, the other through reasoning. You are familiar with the reality of Heraclitus; it is just the everyday world we see, hear, smell, taste, and touch. The other world is not so ordinary, and we must say more about it.

We need to go back to the question, what is our truth about the square *true of*? If it is not about any square you could see or touch, what then? Plato's answer is that it is a truth about the Square Itself. This is an object that can be apprehended only by the intellect, by thinking and reasoning. Still, it is an object, a reality; why should we suppose that the senses are our only avenue to what there is? It is, moreover, a public object, for you and I (and indeed anyone) can know the same truths about it. In fact, it is more public than sense objects. The square I see as red you may see as green, but everyone agrees that a square may be doubled by taking its diagonal as the base of another square.

Here is another feature of the Square Itself. It is not some particular square or other. It is not, for instance, one with an area of 4 rather than 6 or 10 or 19⅜. The doubling principle works for *any* square. So if our truth is a truth about the Square Itself, this must be a very unusual object! It must be an object that in some sense is *shared* by all the particular squares that ever have or ever will exist.

Here we are reminded of what Socrates is looking for. Remember that when Socrates questions Euthyphro, he isn't satisfied when presented with an *example* of piety. What he wants is something common to all pious actions, present in no impious actions, and which accounts for the fact that the pious actions are pious. He wants, he says, the "form" of piety.* Plato takes up the term **Form** and uses it as the general term for the objects of knowledge. In our example, what we know is something about the Form of the Square. We may use the terms "Form of the Square" and "the Square Itself" interchangeably. What we can know, then, are Forms (the Square Itself, the Triangle Itself) and how they are related to each other.

About the world of the senses, Plato tells us, no knowledge in the strict sense is possible. Here there are only opinions. Because the Square Itself does not fluctuate like visible and tangible squares, it can qualify as an object of knowledge.

Up to this point we have traced Plato's reasoning about the Forms on the basis of the assumption that we do have some knowledge. Let us recapitulate the major steps.

---

*You might like to review briefly what Parmenides says; see p. 27.

†See p. 19.

---

*See *Euthyphro* 6d–e.

- Knowledge is enduring, true, rational belief based on instruction.
- We do have knowledge.
- This knowledge cannot be about the world revealed through the senses.
- It must be about another world, one that endures.
- This is the world of Forms.

Let us call this the Epistemological Argument for the Forms. Epistemology, you may recall, is the fancy term for the theory of knowledge—what knowledge is and what it is about.* And Plato has here concluded from a theory of what knowledge is that its objects must be realities quite different from those presented by the senses. These are realities that, like Parmenides' One, are eternal and unchanging, each one forever exactly what it is.

This very statement, however, reveals that Parmenides was not wholly right. For there is not just One Form—or the Form of the One—but many. There is the Square Itself, the Triangle Itself, the Equal Itself, and indeed, as we shall see, the Just Itself, the Good Itself, and the Form of the Beautiful as well. The reality that is eternal is not a blank One but a most intricately related, immensely complex pattern of Forms. This pattern is reflected partly in our mathematical knowledge. It is what mathematics is about.

This Epistemological Argument is one leg supporting the theory of Forms, but it is not the only one. Before we consider further the nature of Forms and their function in Plato's thought, let us look briefly at two more reasons why Plato believes in their reality.

In a late dialogue where Socrates is no longer the central figure, Plato has Parmenides say:

> I imagine your ground for believing in a single form in each case is this. When it seems to you that a number of things are large, there seems, I suppose, to be a certain single character which is the same when you look at them all; hence you think that largeness is a single thing. (*Parmenides* 132a)

Socrates agrees. What we might call the Metaphysical Argument* for the Forms goes like this. Consider two things that are alike. Perhaps they are both large or white or just. Think of two large elephants, Huey and Gertrude. They have a certain "character" in common. Each is large. Now, what they have in common (largeness) cannot be the same as either one; largeness is not the same as Huey and it is not the same as Gertrude. Nor is it identical with the two of them together, since their cousin Rumble is also large. What they share, then, must be a reality distinct from them. Let us call it the Large Itself. Alternatively, we could call it the Form of the Large.

This argument starts not from the nature of knowledge and its difference from opinion, but from the nature of *things*. That is why we can call it a "metaphysical" argument. A similarity among things indicates that they have something in common. What they have in common cannot be just another thing of the same sort as they are. Gertrude, for example, is not something that other pairs of things could share in the way they can share largeness; each of two other things can be large, but it is nonsense to suppose that each can be Gertrude. What Gertrude and Huey have in common must be something of another sort altogether. It is, Plato holds, a Form.

Finally, let us look at a Semantic Argument for the Forms. Semantics is a discipline that deals with words, in particular with the meanings of words and how words are related to what they are about. In the *Republic* we read that

> any given plurality of things which have a single name constitutes a specific type [Form]. (*R* 596a)

The interesting phrase here is "have a single name." What Plato has in mind here is the fact that we have names of several different kinds. "Gertrude" is a name, and it stands for a certain elephant—for Gertrude, in fact. But "elephant" also seems to be a name, yet it functions quite differently from "Gertrude." A proper name like "Gertrude" names or picks out or stands for one particular thing in the world. But we give the name "elephant" to Gertrude and Huey and Rumble and all the other elephants there ever have been or ever will be. Why? Because, Plato suggests, we are assuming that one Form is common to them all. Just as the name "Gertrude" names some particular elephant, the name "elephant" names the Form Elephant—what all elephants have in common. Whenever we give the same name to a plurality of things, Plato tells us, it is legitimate to assume that we are naming a Form.

This line of reflection offers an answer to a somewhat puzzling question: how do *general* words get their meaning? What we call "proper names" seem to get their meaning by standing for or naming some object. "Socrates" is meaningful (not just a noise) because it stands for Socrates, and "Gertrude" gets its meaning by naming Gertrude. Plato's theory tells us that general terms such as "man" or "elephant" get their meaning in the same basic way. They too stand for something; they too are names. But they are the names of Forms, not of particular things that our senses could allow us to meet.

What we have in Plato's philosophy is a single answer to three problems that any philosophy striving for completeness must address. Let us summarize.

- *Problem One.* Assuming that we do have some knowledge, what is our knowledge about? What are the objects of knowledge? Plato's answer is that what we know are the Forms of things.

- *Problem Two.* The particular things that we are acquainted with can be grouped into kinds on the basis of what they have in common. How are we to explain these common features? Plato tells us that what they have in common is a Form.

- *Problem Three.* Some of our words apply not to particular things but to all things of a certain kind. How are we to understand the meaning of these general words? Plato's theory is that these general terms are themselves names, and that what they name is not a particular sensible thing but a Form.

The Reality of the Forms

We have, then, a number of lines of investigation— epistemological, metaphysical, and semantic—all of which seem to point in the same direction: In addition to the world of sense so familiar to us, there is another world, the world of Forms. The Forms are not anything we can smell, taste, touch, or see, but that is not to say they are unreal or imaginary. To suppose that they must be unreal if our senses do not make contact with them is just a prejudice; we could call it the Bias Toward the Senses. But Plato believes he has already exposed this as a mere bias.*

Consider again the problem of doubling the size of a square. In the *Republic* Socrates imagines that he is questioning someone who only has opinion but thinks it is knowledge:

> "But can you tell us please, whether someone with knowledge knows something or nothing?" You'd better answer my questions for him.
>
> My answer will be that he knows something. . . .
> Something real or something unreal?
> Real. How could something unreal be known?
> (*R* 476e)

You can't know what *isn't,* Plato tells us, for the simple reason that in that case there isn't anything there to know. You can only know what *is.*[†] In other words, if you do know something, there must be something in reality for you to know. In the case of doubling the square, what you know concerns a set of Forms and their relations to each other. So there must be Forms; they cannot be merely unreal and imaginary.

There is a further and more radical conclusion. The Forms are not only real; they are more real than anything you can see or hear or touch. What is Plato's argument for this surprising conclusion?

---

*Here again Plato agrees with Parmenides. For Parmenides' critique of the senses, see pp. 26–27.

†This is a narrower version of the Parmenidean principle that thought and being always go together (see p. 26). Plato accepts that *thought* might diverge from being, but the thought that meets the tests of *knowledge* will not. That is why we value it.

Recall the distinction between knowledge and opinion.* If we reflect a little, however, we can see that we ought to have a threefold division rather than a twofold one; in addition to Knowledge and Opinion, there is Invincible Ignorance. As Plato says, "Something completely real is completely accessible to knowledge, and something utterly unreal is entirely inaccessible to knowledge" (*R* 477a). About the unreal we are ignorant—not just ignorant for the time being or in such a way that we might learn, but *invincibly* ignorant. We then have three capacities to correlate with their objects.

Knowledge	Opinion	Invincible Ignorance
—of what is—	—?—	—of what is not—

What corresponds to opinion in the same way as reality and nothingness correspond to knowledge and ignorance? Opinion, Plato suggests, stands midway between knowledge and ignorance. It is more than ignorance but less than knowledge. Because it is a capacity of ours, there must be objects that answer to it; when we have an opinion, it is always an opinion *about something*. The natural solution is to find something midway between *what is* on the one hand and *what is not* on the other hand. Can we find something of which it is accurate to say that it both *is* and *is not*?

Consider someone who doesn't acknowledge the reality of the Forms, but does think there are beautiful, moral, and just things in this visible world.

> What we'll say to him is, "My friend, is there one beautiful thing . . . which won't turn out to be ugly? Is there one moral deed which won't turn out to be immoral? Is there one just act which won't turn out to be unjust?
>
> . . . And there are doubles galore—but they turn out to be halves just as much as doubles, don't they?
>
> . . . And do things which are large, small, light, and heavy deserve these attributes any more than they deserve the opposite attributes?" (*R* 479a, b)

There do exist things that both are and are not, Plato tells us. What things? None other than those items embedded in the Heraclitean flux, the visible world of our experience. For nothing in this sensible world of ours is unqualifiedly beautiful. There are beautiful things, to be sure, but they are beautiful for a time, or beautiful in these circumstances but not in those. Even the beauty of Helen of Troy faded with age. It would be true to say that Helen both was and was not beautiful. Gertrude the elephant is large, but not in comparison to Mount Everest. In comparison to Mount Everest, Gertrude is small, even tiny. So Gertrude is both large and not large. And this kind of reflection applies to absolutely everything in the sensory world.* How these things are regarded depends on the perspective taken, the aspect considered, the comparisons in mind. Moreover, all of them come into being and pass away again. None just *is*. Each of them can *appear* now this way, now that.

So we can now fill in the question mark in the foregoing chart: Opinion is about

—the world of experience—

Notice that we have reached the conclusion that Plato wants us to reach. The Forms are more real than anything you can experience by means of your senses. Unlike sensible things, they are unchangeably what they are—forever. Even if every square thing ceased to exist, the Square Itself would remain. In comparison to the Forms, Helen and Gertrude—and just and pious actions, too—are only partly real. They surely have some reality; they are not nothing. But they are less real than the Forms, for they do not endure. For that reason we can have no knowledge of them; about them the best we can hope for is opinion. They don't "stay put" long enough to be known. As Plato charmingly puts it, these things "mill around somewhere between unreality and perfect reality" (*R* 479d).

Plato thinks that in a sense there are two worlds. There is the world of the Forms, which can be known, but only by reasoning, by the intellect.

---

*Review the table on p. 120.

*Compare Heraclitus, p. 19.

This is the most real world. And there is the world of the many particular, ever-changing things that make up the flux of our lives. These can be sensed; about them we may have opinions, but they cannot be known. This world is real, but less real than the world of the Forms.

It is clear that Plato needs to go on. No one could be satisfied to stop at this point. Even if we grant that he is right to this point (and let us grant it provisionally), we now must insist on an answer to a further question: How are the two worlds related? With this question we arrive at the most interesting part of Plato's answer to sophistic skepticism and relativism.

---

1. In what way does Plato agree with Parmenides? With Heraclitus?
2. Be sure you can sketch the three lines of argument for the reality of the Forms: epistemological, metaphysical, and semantic.
3. If the objects of knowledge are the Forms, what are the objects of opinion?
4. Why does Plato think the Form of Bicycle is *more real* than the bicycle I ride to work?

The World and the Forms

If Plato is right, reality is not at all what it seems to be. What we usually take as reality is only partly real; reality itself is quite different. For convenience' sake, let us use the term "the world" to refer to this flux of things about us that appear to our senses: rivers, trees, desks, elephants, men and women, runnings, promisings, sleepings, customs, laws, and so on. This corresponds closely enough to the usual use of that term; however, the world must now be understood as less than the whole of reality, and none of it entirely real. We can then put Plato's point in this way: In addition to the world, there are also the Forms, and they are what is truly real. This much, he would add, we already know. For we have given an account (a *logos*) of the reason why we must believe in the reality of the Forms.

How Forms Are Related to the World

We must now examine the relationship between the two realities. Let us begin by thinking about shadows. We could equally well consider photographs, mirror images, and reflections in a pool of water. A shadow is in a certain sense less real than the thing that casts it. It is less real because it doesn't have any independent existence; its shape depends wholly on the thing that it is a shadow of (and of course the light source). Think about the shadow shapes you can make on a wall by positioning your hands in various ways in front of a strong lamp. Shaping your hands one way produces the shape of a rabbit; another way, an owl. What the shadow is depends on the shape of your hands. The shape of your hands does *not,* note well, depend on the shape of the shadow. If you put your hands in your pockets, your hands and their shape still exist, but the shadows vanish. This is the sense in which shadows are less real; your hands have an independent existence, but the shadows do not.

Both shadows and hands are parts of the world. So there are different degrees of reality *within* the world, too. Could we use the relationship between shadows and hands to illuminate the relationship between world and Forms? This is in fact what Plato does in a famous diagram called the Divided Line. Plato here calls the world "the visible" and the Forms "the intelligible," according to how we are acquainted with them.

> Well, picture them as a line cut into two unequal sections and, following the same proportions, subdivide both the section of the visible realm and that of the intelligible realm. Now you can compare the sections in terms of clarity and unclarity. The first section in the visible realm consists of likenesses, by which I mean a number of things: shadows, reflections . . . and so on.
>
> And you should count the other section of the visible realm as consisting of the things whose likenesses are found in the first section: all the flora and fauna there are in the world, and every kind of artefact, too. (*R* 509e–510a)

Let us draw Plato's line, labeling as much of it as he has so far explained.

It is important for the symbolism that the lengths of the various sections are *not equal*. These lengths are related to each other by a certain ratio or proportion: As *B* is related to *A,* and *D* to *C,* so is (*C* + *D*) related to (*A* + *B*). Plato intends this proportionality between the line segments to represent the fact that the intelligible world of the Forms is related to the entire visible world in exactly the same way as things within the visible world are related to their likenesses. (Note that the actual length of the sections is irrelevant; we could draw the line with *D* being the longest just as well. All that counts is how they are related to each other.)

Let's construct a more realistic example than shadows of arbitrarily shaped hands. Imagine that we live at the bottom of a canyon. Our society has a very strong taboo against looking up, which has been handed down by our earliest ancestors from generation to generation. We do not look up to the rim of the canyon and the sky beyond. The sun shines down into the canyon during the middle part of each day, and we can see the shadows of the canyon walls move across the canyon floor from west to east. Eagles live high up in the canyon wall, but they never come down to the canyon floor, preferring to forage for their food in the richly supplied plains above. We have never seen an eagle, nor are we likely to.

We do see the shadows of eagles as they glide from one wall of the canyon to the other. Sometimes the eagles perch directly on the edge of the canyon wall and cast shadows of a very different shape, of many different shapes, in fact; sometimes they perch facing west, sometimes north, and so on. We do not know that these are eagle shadows, of course, for we are not acquainted with eagles. All we know are the shadows.

Could we have any reliable beliefs about eagles? We could. If we collected all the shadow shapes that we had seen, we could get a pretty good idea of what an eagle looks like and at least some idea of its behaviors. We might even get a kind of science of eagles on this basis; from certain shadows we might be able to make predictions about the shapes of others, and these predictions might often turn out to be true. The concept "eagle" would be merely a construct for us, of course; it would be equivalent to "that (whatever it is) which accounts for shadows of this sort." We would think of eagles as the things that explain such shadows, the things making the shadow-patterns intelligible. But we would never have any direct contact with eagles.

One day, an eagle is injured in a fight and comes fluttering helplessly down to the canyon floor. This has never happened before. We catch the injured bird and nurse it back to health. While we have it in our care, we examine it carefully. We come to realize that this is the creature responsible for the shadows we have been observing with interest all these generations. We already know a good bit about it, but now our concept of "eagle" is no longer just a construct. Now we have the *thing* in our sight, and we can see just what features of an eagle account for that shadow science we have constructed. We can say that this creature explains the shadows we were familiar with; it makes it intelligible that our experience of those shadows was what it was; now we understand why those shadows had just the shapes they did have and no others.

We can also say that this great bird is what produces these shadows; we now see that the shadows are caused by creatures like this; birds of this kind are responsible for the existence of those shadows. So we are attributing two kinds of relations between eagles themselves and their shadows, which we'll call the relations of *Making Intelligible* and of *Producing*.

Remember now that our example has been framed entirely within the sphere of the world, what Plato calls "the visible." So we have been discussing what falls only within the *A* and *B* portions of the Divided Line. Now we need to apply the relations between *A* and *B* to the relations between $(A + B)$ and $(C + D)$. In other words, we need now to talk about the relationship between the world and the Forms, between "the visible" and "the intelligible."

Let us return to our example. While we have the eagle in our care, we examine it carefully, take measurements and X rays (imagine that although we know nothing of astronomy because we never look up, our science is otherwise quite advanced), do behavioral testing, and come to understand the bird quite thoroughly. What do we learn? We learn a lot, of course, about this particular eagle (we have named him "Charlie"), but we are also learning about the *kind* of creature that produces and makes intelligible the shadows we have long observed. So we are learning about eagles in general. It is true that if we generalize from this one case only, we may make some mistakes. Charlie may in some respects not be a typical eagle, but we can ignore this complication for the moment.

If we are learning about eagles, not just about Charlie, then we could put it this way: We are getting acquainted with what makes an eagle an eagle (as opposed to an owl or an egret). This is very much like, we might reflect, coming to understand what makes pious actions pious. Socrates says that he wants to know not just which actions are pious, you remember, but what it is that *makes* them pious rather than impious. He wants to understand the Form of the Pious. So we can say that we are coming to know the Form of the Eagle. This Form is what explains or makes intelligible the fact that this particular bird is an eagle. We might go as far as to say that it is what makes Charlie an eagle; his having this Form rather than some other produces Charlie-as-eagle—is responsible for the fact that Charlie is an eagle.

It may be that Charlie is not a perfect eagle. And further acquaintance with eagles would doubtless

improve our understanding of what makes an eagle an eagle, of those characteristics that constitute "eaglehood." If we were to improve our understanding of the Eagle Itself, we might well reach the same conclusion we reached about squares: that no visible eagle is a perfect example of the type or Form. Still, any particular eagle must have the defining characteristics of the species; it must, Plato says, *participate* in the Form Eagle, or it wouldn't be an eagle at all.

What is this "participation" in a Form? We can now say that it is strictly analogous to the relationship between eagle shadows and actual eagles. Actual eagles participate in the Form Eagle in this sense: The Form makes the actual eagle intelligible and accounts for its existence as an eagle. So again there are two kinds of relationships, this time between the Form Eagle and particular eagles: the relationships of Making Intelligible and of Producing. The relationship on the Divided Line between $(A + B)$ and $(C + D)$ is indeed analogous to the relationship between *A* and *B*.

We should remind ourselves, too, that Forms have a kind of independence actual eagles lack. Should an ecological tragedy kill all the eagles in the world, the Form Eagle would not be affected. We might never again see an eagle, but we could perfectly well still think about eagles; we could, for instance, regret their passing and recall what magnificent birds they were.* The intelligible has this kind of superiority to the visible: It endures. And this, Plato would conclude, is a sign that the Form (the object of thought) is more real than those things (the objects of sight) that participate in it. In Forms we have the proper objects of knowledge, which must itself endure.

Lower and Higher Forms

Let us return to the Divided Line. We need to note that the section of the Line representing the Forms is itself divided. There are, it seems, two kinds of Forms, just as there are two kinds of things in the

---

*Those of you familiar with *Star Trek IV: The Voyage Home* may recall that Kirk and Spock in the twenty-third century could still think about humpback whales, long after they became extinct.

visible world (likenesses and things). We need to understand why Plato thinks so and why he thinks this distinction is important.

He takes an example from mathematics to explain the leftward portion of the intelligible section of the line.

> I'm sure you're aware that practitioners of geometry, arithmetic, and so on take for granted things like numerical oddness and evenness, the geometrical figures, the three kinds of angle, and any other things of that sort which are relevant to a given subject. They act as if they know about these things, treat them as basic, and don't feel any further need to explain them either to themselves or to anyone else, on the grounds that there is nothing unclear about them. They make them the starting points for their investigations. (R 510c, d)

The important idea here is "taking for granted." When we thought about doubling the square, we took the ideas of Square, Triangle, Double, and Equal for granted. Operating in the leftward reaches of the right "half" of the divided line, we used these Forms as "starting points" for thinking about the square Socrates drew in the sand.

Actually, the movements go like this: Beginning with the sand square, we hypothetically posit Forms to account for it. That is, we move rightward on the line from the visible to the intelligible. Then, taking these Forms for granted, we produce an explanation of the visible phenomenon. Explanation moves leftward. But we can now see that the Forms we posit as hypotheses—the Square, the Triangle, etc.—themselves need to be explained. And so we need to move rightward again, this time into the highest section of the line. Think about the Square again. The Square is *explained and produced* by Forms like Plane, Line, Straight, Angle, and Equal. (A square is a plane figure bounded by four equal straight lines joined by right angles.) In this kind of reasoning, reasoning that explains a Form, there is no reliance on sensory input. In moving to section *D* we move from Forms to more basic Forms in a purely intelligible fashion.

So the Forms in *D* make intelligible the Forms in *C*. Again, explanation goes right to left. But there must come a point where this pattern of explanation cannot be used anymore, where making intelligible can't operate by appealing to something still more basic. When you get to the end of the Divided Line, whatever is there will serve as the explanation for everything to the left of it. But that must be intelligible in itself.

Plato calls the construction of lower Forms "science." The scientist examines the actual things in the visible world (Charlie or the sand square) and posits explanations of them in terms of hypothetical Forms. Things that explain shadows are now treated by the scientist just as the shadows were—as likenesses of something still more real, to be explained by appeal to Forms. A Form loses its merely hypothetical character when it is explained in terms of higher Forms. We then understand why that Form must be as it is. And this purely conceptual process of moving from Forms to Forms, and eventually to the highest Form—the First Principle—Plato calls "dialectic."* (see R 511b, c)

Dialectic, then, is a purely intellectual discipline, no longer relying on the world of sense at all. It is a search for the ultimate presuppositions of all our hypothetical explanations and proceeds solely through awareness of Forms. If by such dialectical reasoning we should come to an ultimate presupposition, we will, Plato assures us, have discovered "the starting point for everything" (R 511b).

We obviously need to explore what Plato has to say about this Starting Point. But first let us amplify our understanding of the Divided Line (see the following chart) by adding some further characterizations. Notice the difference in labels given to the sections of the line on the second and third levels down. The second level characterizes reality in terms of what it is. These labels are *metaphysical* in nature. The third level (written in capital letters) characterizes reality in terms of how it is apprehended, so these labels have an *epistemological* flavor to them. (The first level is also epistemological, but less fine-grained than the third.) Here we see how intimately Plato's theory of knowledge is related to his theory of reality. We add two directional indicators to show that things get more

---

*Note that the term "dialectic" is used in a narrower sense here than that discussed in connection with Socratic question-and-answer method. For a comparison, see pp. 64–65.

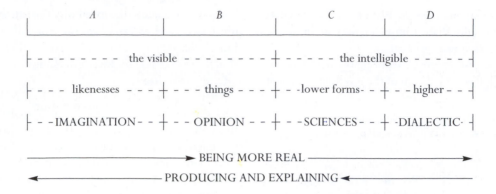

real as you progress along the line from *A* to *D,* and that items to the right are responsible for the existence of items to the left and provide explanations for them.

The sciences, we can now say, are only stages on the way to true and final understanding. They are not yet "that place which, once reached, is traveller's rest and journey's end" (*R* 532e). The sciences do grasp reality to some extent; but because they do not themselves lead us to the Starting Point, Plato thinks scientists still live in a kind of dream world. "There's no chance of their having a conscious glimpse of reality as long as they refuse to disturb the things they take for granted and remain incapable of explaining them" (*R* 533c).

It is for dialectic to give this reasoned account of first things. Its

> quest for certainty causes it to uproot the things it takes for granted in the course of its journey, which takes it towards an actual starting-point. When the mind's eye is literally buried deep in mud, far from home, dialectic gently extracts it and guides it upwards. (*R* 533c–d)

Let us note that dialectic, in leading us to the Starting Point, is supposed to give us certainty. This is very important to Plato; indeed, the quest for certainty is a crucial theme in most of Western philosophy. Why should Plato suppose that acquaintance with the Starting Point will be accompanied by certainty, by "traveller's rest and journey's end"? Because it is no longer hypothetical. The truth of the Starting Point need no longer be supported by principles beyond itself. It does not cry out for explanation; it does not beckon us on beyond itself. Its truth is evident. To see it—with "the mind's eye"—is to understand. Here we need no longer anxiously ask, "But is this really true?" Here we know we are not just dreaming. Here the soul can "rest."*

The Form of the Good

The examples we have considered recently—doubling the square, Charlie, and the Forms they participate in—are examples from mathematics and the world of natural science. But we should not forget that there are other Forms as well: Piety, Morality, Beauty, and the Good. We'll soon explore the dialectic showing that the Form of Morality participates in the Form of the Good and say at least something about Beauty. But if we want to illuminate Plato's Starting Point, it is to the Form of the Good that we shall have to look directly.

Let us begin by asking why Plato should think of Goodness Itself as that Form to which dialectic will lead us in our search for the ultimate presupposition. As we consider this, we should remember that in moving higher and higher on the Divided Line we are always gaining clearer, less questionable explanations of why something is the way it is.

---

*Compare Heraclitus on how the many who do not recognize the *logos* live as though they were asleep, lost in a dream-world of their own making. See pp. 21–22.

In the dialogue *Phaedo,* Plato relates a conversation that Socrates had with his friends on the day of his death. At one point Socrates says,

> When I was young . . . I was remarkably keen on the kind of wisdom known as natural science; it seemed to me splendid to know the reasons for each thing, why each thing comes to be, why it perishes, and why it exists. (*Phaedo* 96a)

He relates that he was unable to make much progress toward discovering those causes and became discouraged until hearing one day someone read from a book of Anaxagoras.* Socrates heard that Mind directs and is the cause of everything.

> Now this was a reason that pleased me; it seemed to me, somehow, to be a good thing that intelligence should be the reason for everything. And I thought that, if that's the case, then intelligence in ordering all things must order them and place each individual thing in the best way possible; so if anyone wanted to find out the reason why each thing comes to be or perishes or exists, this is what he must find out about it: how is it best for that thing to exist, or to act or be acted upon in any way? (*Phaedo* 97c–d)

Socrates procured the books of Anaxagoras and read them eagerly. But he was disappointed. For when it came down to cases, Anaxagoras cited as causes the standard elements of Greek nature philosophy—air and water and such.

> In fact, he seemed to me to be in exactly the position of someone who said that all Socrates' actions were performed with his intelligence, and who then tried to give the reasons for each of my actions by saying, first, that the reason why I'm now sitting here is that my body consists of bones and sinews, and the bones are hard and separated from each other by joints, whereas the sinews, which can be tightened and relaxed, surround the bones, together with the flesh and the skin that holds them together; so that when the bones are turned in their sockets, the sinews by stretching and tensing enable me somehow to bend my limbs at this mo-

ment, and that's the reason why I'm sitting here bent this way. (*Phaedo* 98c–d)

Are these facts about his body the true explanation of why Socrates is sitting there in prison? It does not seem to Socrates to even be the right kind of explanation. These considerations do not even mention

> the true reasons: that Athenians judged it better to condemn me, and therefore I in my turn have judged it better to sit here, and thought it more just to stay behind and submit to such penalty as they may ordain. . . . Fancy being unable to distinguish two different things: the reason proper, and that without which the reason could never be a reason! (*Phaedo* 98e–99b)

Why is Socrates sitting in prison? The true explanation is that the Athenians decided it was better to condemn him and that Socrates has decided that not escaping was for the best. The behaviors of the various bodily parts are not irrelevant, but they are not the "true reason." They are just conditions necessary for that real reason to have its effect. We do not get a satisfactory explanation until we reach one that mentions what is *good,* or *better,* or *best.*

This suggests that explanations in which we can "rest" must be framed in terms of what is good. Because explanations proceed by citing Forms, the ultimate explanation of everything must be in terms of the Form of the Good. The Form of the Good, then, must play the part of the Starting Point. In the final analysis, to understand why anything is as it is, we must see that it is so because it participates in this Form, because it is good for it to be so.

That is why Plato thinks the Form of the Good is the Starting Point. But what is it? To call this Starting Point the Form of the Good is not very illuminating. It doesn't tell us any more than Socrates knows about the pious at the beginning of his examination of Euthyphro. Socrates knows that he is looking for the Form of the Pious, but he also knows that he doesn't know what that is. In just this sense, we might now ask Plato, "What is this Form which plays such a crucial role? Explain it to us."

---

*A pre-Socratic nature philosopher. You may recall that Socrates mentions him in the speech at his trial: *Apology* 26d.

At this point, Plato disappoints us; he tells us plainly that he cannot give such an explanation.* He says that "our knowledge of goodness is inadequate" (R 505a). When he is pressed to discuss it, he says, "I'm afraid it'll be more than I can manage" (R 506d). But he does agree to describe "something which seems to me to be the child of goodness and to bear a very strong resemblance to it" (R 506e).

Consider sight, Plato suggests. What makes sight possible? Well, the eyes, for one thing. But eyes alone see nothing; there must also be the various colored objects to be seen. Even this is not enough, for eyes do not see colors in the dark. To eyes and objects we must add light. Where does light come from? From the sun. It is the sun, then, that is

the child of goodness I was talking about. . . . It is a counterpart to its father, goodness. As goodness stands in the intelligible realm to intelligence and the things we know, so in the visible realm the sun stands to sight and the things we see. . . .

What I'm saying is that it's goodness which gives the things we know their truth and makes it possible for people to have knowledge. It is responsible for knowledge and truth, and you should think of it as being within the intelligible realm, but you shouldn't identify it with knowledge and truth, otherwise you'll be wrong: for all their value, it is even more valuable. (R 508b–509a)

Knowledge, truth, and beauty are all good things. For Plato this means that they participate in the Form of the Good. This Form alone makes it intelligible that there should be such good things. You might ask in wonderment, why is there such a thing as knowledge at all? What accounts for that? If Plato is right here, you will not find a satisfactory answer to your question until you discover why it is for the best that knowledge should exist; and discovering that is equivalent to seeing its participation in the Form of Goodness Itself.

However, although knowledge is a good thing, Plato cautions us that it must not be thought of as

identical with Goodness. It is no more identical with Goodness than Charlie is identical with the Form Eagle. That Form explains Charlie, but, as we saw, it has an existence quite independent of Charlie. The Form of the Good surpasses all the other Forms as well as the visible world in beauty and honor. If we think again about the Divided Line, we can now say that the Form of the Good is at the point farthest to the right of that Line, at the very end of section D. It makes intelligible everything to the left of it.

This ultimate Form not only makes everything else intelligible, it also is responsible for the very existence of everything else.

I think you'll agree that the ability to be seen is not the only gift the sun gives to the things we see. It is also the source of their generation, growth, and nourishment. . . .

And it isn't only the known-ness of the things we know which is conferred upon them by goodness, but also their reality and their being, although goodness isn't actually the state of being, but surpasses being in majesty and might. (R 509b)

Just as the sun is responsible for the world of sight, is actually its cause, so the Form of the Good is the cause of the reality of everything else; it both *produces* and *makes intelligible* everything that is. To emphasize the uniqueness of this Form, Plato goes so far as to say that it "surpasses being." Since we usually understand what is beyond being to be nothing at all, this is a dark saying. And Plato does not do much to make it clear.*

Let us pause and see what Plato claims to have accomplished. He has proved, he believes, that we do have knowledge; so, wholesale skepticism is a mistake. This knowledge is not dependent on what

_____

*This reticence on Plato's part contrasts dramatically with the confidence many have since displayed in giving us their accounts of what is good. These accounts, of course, do not all agree with one another.

_____

*It is as if the Form of the Good were not the point farthest to the right on the Divided Line but were pushed right off the end. Plato seems to be saying that this Form is strictly incomparable to everything else, both other Forms and the world. Yet it is responsible for them all. Later Christian thinkers took this as an "anticipation" of the Judeo–Christian concepts of God and creation. See, for instance, St. Augustine, pp. 238–241. For a different understanding of the idea of "beyond being," see Martin Heidegger, pp. 681–682.

individuals or cultures happen to think; so, relativism is a mistake. Moreover, knowledge must have objects that endure; so, this knowledge must be of realities other than those in the world. So, there are Forms, whose being is eternal and unchanging. Knowledge of these Forms enables us to understand not only them and their relations to each other but also the things in the world, which owe their being and characteristics to participation in these Forms. And supreme among the Forms is that of Goodness. Therefore, atomism is a mistake.

But how does it follow that atomism is a mistake? Recall the central claim of the atomists: What exists is made up of atoms and the void. Nothing else. Plato, however, thinks he has proved that there are Forms, indeed, that these are the most real things of all. And Forms are radically different from atoms because each atom is a tiny particular thing and a Form can be shared by many particulars.

Moreover, Democritus holds that events happen necessarily, mechanically, according to how the atoms happen to combine and fall apart again. No purpose, no goal, no direction toward the best can be discerned in the world.* But Plato believes he has shown us that a complete explanation must be like the one given by Socrates in prison; it will have to explain why what happens is for the best and so will involve the Form of the Good. Science, pursued to its basic presuppositions, reveals a world with a moral and religious dimension.

It follows that reality is not, as Democritus thinks, indifferent to values; a kind of piety toward reality is quite in order. Democritus would overthrow the traditional religion altogether. Plato is no happier than his philosophical predecessors with the Homeric picture of the gods; belief in such gods is insupportable. Yet religious attitudes can be preserved. We shall soon see how Plato's metaphysical viewpoint—that values are realities, too—affects what he says about practical matters such as morality and the good state. But first we need to conclude this part of our consideration with his most famous story, the Myth of the Cave.

---

† See pp. 32–33.

1. Draw Plato's Divided Line and explain what each of its parts represents. (Close the book, then try to draw and label it.)
2. What two relationships exist between a Form and some visible thing that "participates" in it?
3. What is the distinction Plato draws between "science" and "dialectic," and how does this relate to the distinction between hypotheses and first principles?
4. What is the argument that purports to show that the Starting Point—the rightmost point on the Divided Line—is the Form of the Good?
5. How do Plato's arguments up to this point help him achieve his aims?

The Love of Wisdom

There is a progress in the soul that corresponds to the degrees of reality in things. This idea is indicated in the various sections of the Divided Line. Contemplating the images of worldly things is analogous to the use of *imagination;* indeed, mental images are quite like shadows and mirror images in their dependence on things. About things and events in the world we can have probable beliefs or *opinions.* When we reason about them we are hypothesizing Forms; here is the domain of *science.* Finally, we reach *understanding* through the process of dialectic, which takes us upward to the highest Forms on which all the others depend.

We can think of this progress as progress toward wisdom.

What Wisdom Is

A wise person would understand everything in the light of the Forms, particularly the Form of the Good. To produce such wise individuals is the aim of education. The progress toward wisdom is illustrated for us in a dramatic myth told in the seventh book of the *Republic.* As you read it, keep the Divided Line and the analogy of the sun in mind.

"Imagine people living in a cavernous cell down under the ground; at the far end of the cave, a long way off, there's an entrance open to the outside world. They've been there since childhood, with their legs and necks tied up in a way which keeps them in one place and allows them to look only straight ahead, but not to turn their heads. There's firelight burning a long way further up the cave behind them, and up the slope between the fire and the prisoners there's a road, beside which you should imagine a low wall has been built—like the partition which conjurors place between themselves and their audience and above which they show their tricks."

"All right," he said.

"Imagine also that there are people on the other side of this wall who are carrying all sorts of artefacts, human statuettes, and animal models carved in stone and wood and all kinds of materials stick out over the wall; and as you'd expect, some of the people talk as they carry these objects along, while others are silent."

"This is a strange picture you're painting," he said, "with strange prisoners."

"They're no different from us," I said. "I mean, in the first place, do you think they'd see anything of themselves and one another except the shadows cast by the fire on to the cave wall directly opposite them?"

"Of course not," he said. "They're forced to spend their lives without moving their heads."

"And what about the objects which were being carried along? Won't they only see their shadows as well?"

"Naturally."

"Now, suppose they were able to talk to one another: don't you think they'd assume that their words applied to what they saw passing by in front of them?"

"They couldn't think otherwise."

"And what if sound echoed off the prison wall opposite them? When any of the passers-by spoke, don't you think they'd be bound to assume that the sound came from a passing shadow?"

"I'm absolutely certain of it," he said.

"All in all, then," I said, "the shadows of artefacts would constitute the only reality people in this situation would recognize."

"That's absolutely inevitable," he agreed.

"What do you think would happen, then," I asked, "if they were set free from their bonds and cured of their inanity? What would it be like if they found that happening to them? Imagine that one of them has been set free and is suddenly made to stand up, to turn his head and walk, and to look towards the firelight. It hurts him to do all this and he's too dazzled to be capable of making out the objects whose shadows he'd formerly been looking at. And suppose someone tells him that what he's been seeing all this time has no substance, and that he's now closer to reality and is seeing more accurately, because of the greater reality of the things in front of his eyes—what do you imagine his reaction would be? And what do you think he'd say if he were shown any of the passing objects and had to respond to being asked what it was? Don't you think he'd be bewildered, and would think that there was more reality in what he'd been seeing before than in what he was being shown now?"

"Far more," he said.

"And if he were forced to look at the actual firelight, don't you think it would hurt his eyes? Don't you think he'd turn away and run back to the things he could make out, and would take the truth of the matter to be that these things are clearer than what he was being shown?"

"Yes," he agreed.

"And imagine him being dragged forcibly away from there up the rough, steep slope," I went on, "without being released until he's been pulled out into the sunlight. Wouldn't this treatment cause him pain and distress? And once he's reached the sunlight, he wouldn't be able to see a single one of the things which are currently taken to be real, would he, because his eyes would be overwhelmed by the sun's beams?"

"No, he wouldn't," he answered, "not straight away."

"He wouldn't be able to see things up on the surface of the earth, I suppose, until he'd got used to his situation. At first, it would be shadows that he could most easily make out, then he'd move on to the reflections of people and so on in water, and later he'd be able to see the actual things themselves. Next he'd feast his eyes on the heavenly bodies and the heavens themselves, which would be easier at night: he'd look at the light of the stars and the moon, rather than at the sun and sunlight during the daytime."

"Of course."

"And at last, I imagine, he'd be able to discern and feast his eyes on the sun—not the displaced image of the sun in water or elsewhere, but the sun on its own, in its proper place."

"Yes, he'd inevitably come to that," he said.

"After that, he'd start to think about the sun and he'd deduce that it is the source of the seasons and the yearly cycle, that the whole of the visible realm is its domain, and that in a sense everything which he and his peers used to see is its responsibility."

"Yes, that would obviously be the next point he'd come to," he agreed.

"Now, if he recalled the cell where he'd originally lived and what passed for knowledge there and his former fellow prisoners, don't you think he'd feel happy about his own altered circumstances, and sorry for them?"

"Definitely."

"Suppose that the prisoners used to assign prestige and credit to one another, in the sense that they rewarded speed at recognizing the shadows as they passed, and the ability to remember which ones normally come earlier and later and at the same time as which other ones, and expertise at using this as a basis for guessing which ones would arrive next. Do you think our former prisoner would covet these honours and would envy the people who had status and power there, or would he much prefer, as Homer describes it, 'being a slave labouring for someone else—someone without property', and would put up with anything at all, in fact, rather than share their beliefs and their life?"

"Yes, I think he'd go through anything rather than live that way," he said.

"Here's something else I'd like your opinion about," I said. "If he went back underground and sat down again in the same spot, wouldn't the sudden transition from the sunlight mean that his eyes would be overwhelmed by darkness?"

"Certainly."

"Now, the process of adjustment would be quite long this time, and suppose that before his eyes had settled down and while he wasn't seeing well, he had once again to compete against those same old prisoners at identifying those shadows. Wouldn't he make a fool of himself? Wouldn't they say that he'd come back from his upward journey with his eyes ruined, and that it wasn't even worth trying to go up there? And wouldn't they—if they could—grab hold of anyone who tried to set them free and take them up there, and kill him?"

"They certainly would," he said. (*R* 514a–517a)

Any such myth is subject to multiple interpretations. But let us see if we can, in light of what we know of Plato so far, identify the various stages of the ascent to wisdom. The people fettered in the cave, seeing only the shadows of things, are like those who gain their understanding of things from the poets, from Homer and Hesiod. Or, in our day, they are like those who get their impressions of the world by paying attention to the media—to movies, to the soaps, to television news programs. They see only images of reality—reflections, interpretations.

Those who climb up to the wall, on which are carried various items casting the shadows, are like those who can look directly on things in the visible world. The fire, I think, represents the physical sun, lighting up these perceptible realities so they can be apprehended. Looking on them directly reveals how fuzzy and indistinct the shadows of them on the wall actually were.

But to really understand these things it is necessary to climb higher, out of the cave altogether. This move is like the transition on the Divided Line between the visible world and the intelligible world; it is the transition from things to Forms. The sun outside the cave represents the Form of the Good, just as it does in the Analogy of the Sun. First our adventurer can only see the lower Forms, reflections of the "Sun." But gradually, through dialectic, he can come to see the Form of the Good itself.

And what would happen if someone like that, who had come to understand things to that extent, who saw things as they really were and understood their participation in Goodness—what would happen if that person were to return to the cave? Can there be any doubt that Plato is thinking of Socrates here?

To love wisdom is to be motivated to leave the Cave. At each stage, Plato emphasizes how difficult, even painful, the struggle for enlightenment is. It is much easier, much more comfortable, to remain a

The Divided Line

| A | B | C | D |

prisoner in relative darkness and occupy oneself with what are, in reality, only shadows.

The myth gives us an interesting picture of education. Education, Plato says, is not

> capable of doing what some people promise. They claim to introduce knowledge into a mind which doesn't have it, as if they were introducing sight into eyes which are blind. . . .
>
> An implication of what we're saying at the moment, however, ... is that the capacity for knowledge is present in everyone's mind. If you can imagine an eye that can turn from darkness to brightness only if the body as a whole turns, then our organ of understanding is like that. Its orientation has to be accompanied by turning the mind as a whole away from the world of becoming, until it becomes capable of bearing the sight of real being and reality at its most bright, which we're saying is goodness. . . .
>
> That's what education should be, . . . the art of orientation. Educators should devise the simplest and most effective methods of turning minds around. It shouldn't be the art of implanting sight in the organ, but should proceed on the understanding that the organ already has the capacity,

but is improperly aligned and isn't facing the right way. (*R* 518b–d)

We should be reminded here of Socrates and the slave boy. The capacity to understand is already there. All Socrates needs to do is point the boy in the right direction, and that he does with his questions. Education is not stuffing the mind with facts, Plato tells us, but turning the soul to face reality, trusting that the student will recognize the truth when confronted by it. Recall Socrates' claim that he has never *taught* anyone anything.* Here is a whole philosophy of education in a nutshell.

This "turning minds around" is not easy to do, however. The prisoners in the cave are not happy to be told that they suffer from an illusion. Wisdom can be resisted. If we can resist this turning of the soul and be comfortable in the cave, focused on the pleasures of feasting, drinking, and so on, what motivation is there to engage in a struggle that Plato insists is both difficult and dangerous? We need now to talk not just of what wisdom is, but of the *love* of wisdom.

Love and Wisdom

The theme of Plato's dialogue *Symposium,* from which Alcibiades' tribute to the character of Socrates was taken,† is love. After dinner each guest is obliged to make a speech in praise of love. When Socrates' turn comes, he protests that he cannot make such a flattering speech as the others have made, but he can, if they like, tell the truth about love.‡ They urge him to do so.

Socrates claims to have learned about love from a wise woman named Diotima, who instructed him by the same question-and-answer method he

now uses on others.* I'll abbreviate the speech in which Socrates relates her instruction, keeping the question-and-answer mode. This very rich discussion of love is found in *Symposium* 198a–212b.

Q: Is love the love of something or not?
A: Of something.
Q: Does love long for what it loves?
A: Certainly.
Q: Is this something that love has, or something love lacks?
A: It must be what love lacks, for no one longs for what he or she has.
Q: What does love love?
A: Beauty.
Q: Then love must lack beauty?
A: Apparently so.
Q: Is love ugly, then?
A: Not necessarily. For just as opinion is a middle term between ignorance and knowledge, so love may be between beauty and ugliness.
Q: Is love a god?
A: No. For the gods lack nothing in the way of beauty or happiness. For that reason, the gods do not love beauty or happiness either. Nor do the gods love wisdom, for they are wise and do not lack it.
Q: What is love, then?
A: Midway between mortals and the gods, love is a spirit that connects the earthly and the heavenly. [Think of the world and the Forms.]
Q: What is the origin of love?
A: Love is the child of Need and Resourcefulness (the son of Craft). It is a combination of longing for what one does not have and ingenuity in seeking it.
Q: But what, more exactly, is it that love seeks?
A: Love seeks the beautiful. And the good.
Q: To what end?

---

*See *Apology* 33b and Chapter 5, pp. 101–102.

†Review pp. 62–63.

‡This should remind you of the contrast Socrates draws between rhetoric and his own plain speaking at the very beginning of the *Apology.* About love, it must be noted that the Greeks had distinct words for several different kinds of love; in this their language was more discriminating than ours. The kind of love Socrates is here discussing is *eros,* from which our term "erotic" is drawn.

---

*Although women are not prominent among the ancient philosophers whose works have been preserved, there are hints here and there that they played a larger role in the pursuit of wisdom than is superficially apparent. See Kathleen Wider, "Women Philosophers in the Ancient Greek World: Donning the Mantle," *Hypatia* 1, no. 1 (Spring 1986).

A: To make them its own.

Q: And what will the lover gain by making the beautiful and the good his own?

A: Happiness.

Q: Does everyone seek happiness?

A: Of course.

Q: Then is everyone always in love?

A: Yes and no. We tend to give the name of love to only one sort of love. Actually, love "includes every kind of longing for happiness and the good." So those who long for the good in every field—business, athletics, philosophy—are also lovers.

Q: For how long does a lover want to possess that good that he or she longs for?

A: Certainly not for a limited time only. To think so would be equivalent to wanting to be happy for only a short time. So the lover must want the good to be his or hers forever.

Q: How could a mortal attain this?

A: By becoming immortal.

Q: So a mortal creature does all it can "to put on immortality"?

A: Evidently.

Q: Could this be why lovers are interested not just in beauty but in procreation by means of such beauty?

A: Yes. It is by breeding another individual as like itself as possible that mortal creatures like animals and humans attain as much of immortality as is possible for them. Such a creature cannot, like the gods, remain the same throughout eternity; it can only leave behind new life to fill the vacancy that is left in its species by its death.

Q: Is there any other way to approach immortality?

A: Yes, by attaining the "endless fame" that heroes and great benefactors of humankind attain. Think, for example, of Achilles and Homer and Solon.

Q: So some lovers beget children and raise a family, and others "bear things of the spirit . . . wisdom and all her sister virtues," especially those relevant to "the ordering of society, . . . justice and moderation"?

A: Yes. And the latter will be especially concerned to share these goods with friends and, with them, to educate each other in wisdom.

Q: Is there a natural progression of love?

A: Yes.

At this point, we need to hear Plato's words themselves. Diotima is speaking as if someone were to be initiated into a cult devoted to love.

> Well then, she began, the candidate for this initiation cannot, if his efforts are to be rewarded, begin too early to devote himself to the beauties of the body. First of all, if his preceptor instructs him as he should, he will fall in love with the beauty of one individual body, so that his passion may give life to noble discourse. Next he must consider how nearly related the beauty of any one body is to the beauty of any other, when he will see that if he is to devote himself to loveliness of form it will be absurd to deny that the beauty of each and every body is the same. Having reached this point, he must set himself to be the lover of every lovely body, and bring his passion for the one into due proportion by deeming it of little or of no importance.
>
> Next he must grasp that the beauties of the body are as nothing to the beauties of the soul, so that wherever he meets with spiritual loveliness, even in the husk of an unlovely body, he will find it beautiful enough to fall in love with and to cherish—and beautiful enough to quicken in his heart a longing for such discourse as tends toward the building of a noble nature. And from this he will be led to contemplate the beauty of laws and institutions. And when he discovers how nearly every kind of beauty is akin to every other he will conclude that the beauty of the body is not, after all, of so great moment.
>
> And next, his attention should be diverted from institutions to the sciences, so that he may know the beauty of every kind of knowledge. . . . And, turning his eyes toward the open sea of beauty, he will find in such contemplation the seed of the most fruitful discourse and the loftiest thought, and reap a golden harvest of philosophy, until, confirmed and strengthened, he will come upon one single form of knowledge, the knowledge of the beauty I am about to speak of.

And here, she said, you must follow me as closely as you can.

Whoever has been initiated so far in the mysteries of Love and has viewed all these aspects of the beautiful in due succession, is at last drawing near the final revelation. And now, Socrates, there bursts upon him that wondrous vision which is the very soul of the beauty he has toiled so long for. It is an everlasting loveliness which neither comes nor goes, which neither flowers nor fades, for such beauty is the same on every hand, the same then as now, here as there, this way as that way, the same to every worshiper as it is to every other.

Nor will his vision of the beautiful take the form of a face, or of hands, or of anything that is of the flesh. It will be neither words nor knowledge, nor a something that exists in something else, such as a living creature, or the earth, or the heavens, or anything that is—but subsisting of itself and by itself in an eternal oneness, while every lovely thing partakes of it in such sort that however much the parts may wax and wane, it will be neither more nor less, but still the same inviolable whole. (*Symposium* 210a–211b)

These are the steps, Plato tells us, that a resourceful lover takes. It is important to recognize that he sees these as making up a natural progression; there is nothing arbitrary about this series. In discussing these stages, let us remember that one can love in ways other than sexual. A lover, then, is someone who lacks that which will make him or her happy. What will make the lover happy is to possess the beautiful and the good—forever. For that the lover yearns. It is the lover's resourcefulness, propelled by longing, that moves the lover up the ladder of love. At each rung the lover is only partially satisfied and is therefore powerfully motivated to discover whether there might be something still more satisfying.

Being in the world, the lover naturally begins in the world. His or her first object is some beautiful body. But he or she will soon discover that the beauty in this body is not unique to that individual. It is shared by every beautiful body. What shall the lover do then? Although Plato does not say so explicitly, we might conjecture that at this point it is easy for the lover to go wrong by trying to possess each of these bodies in the same way as he or she longed to possess the first one—like Don Juan. We might think of it like this. Don Juan (with 1,003 conquests in Spain alone) has moved beyond the first stage of devotion to just one lovely body. He now tries to devote to each the same love that he devoted to the one. This is bound to be unsatisfying; if a single one does not satisfy, there is no reason to think that many ones will satisfy.

How does Plato describe the correct step at this point? The lover of "every lovely body" must "bring his passion for the one into due proportion by deeming it of little or of no importance." Rather than trying to multiply the same passion many times, the discovery of beauty in many bodies must occasion what we might call a "sublimation" of the original passion. It must be transferred to a more appropriate kind of object. Indeed, it is at this point that the lover first becomes dimly aware of the Form of Beauty.* The resourcefulness of love makes it clear that only this sort of object is going to satisfy; only this sort of object endures.

The lover, moreover, discovers that a beautiful soul is even more lovely than a beautiful body, finding it so much more satisfying that he or she will "fall in love with" and "cherish" a beautiful soul even though it is found "in the husk of an unlovely body." (Could Plato here be thinking of the physical ugliness of Socrates?) The lover will then come to love *all* beautiful souls.

The next step is to "contemplate the beauty of laws and institutions." Presumably the transition from lovely individual souls to a pleasing social order is a small one. What explains, accounts for, the existence of lovely souls? They must have been well brought up. And that can happen only in a moderate, harmonious, and just social order. The beauty

---

*Recall the doctrine of learning by recollection (p. 102). The beautiful individual is the "occasion" for recollecting what the soul previously knew, Beauty Itself. Only by a prior acquaintance with this Form can the lover recognize the beloved as beautiful.

of a good state comes into view, and we move one more step away from the original passion for an individual beautiful body; when this stage is reached, the lover "concludes that beauty of the body is not, after all, of so great moment."

Once in the sphere of "spiritual loveliness," the lover comes to long for knowledge. Why? It is not difficult to see why if you keep the Divided Line in mind. What is it that makes intelligible and produces good social institutions? Surely they must be founded, not on opinion, but on knowledge. Plato speaks movingly here of "the beauty of every kind of knowledge," and supposes that the lover—not yet satisfied—will explore all the sciences. Here the lover will find an "open sea of beauty," in contemplation of which he or she will be able to bring forth "the most fruitful discourse and the loftiest thought, and reap a golden harvest of philosophy."

But even this is not the last stage. And we must note that Diotima cautions Socrates at this point to "follow . . . as closely as you can." The final stage, then, must be difficult to grasp. Indeed, those who have not attained it might well be unable to appreciate it fully. It is, in fact, a kind of mystical vision of the Form of Beauty Itself.* Note the rapturously emotional language Plato uses here. There can be little doubt that he is describing an experience that he himself had, one to which he ascribes a supreme value.

It is called a "wondrous vision," an "everlasting loveliness which neither comes nor goes, which neither flowers nor fades." Like all the Forms, the Form of Beauty is eternal. The object of this vision is not any individual thing; it is not a face, not hands, not "anything that is of the flesh." Nor is it "words" or "knowledge." It is nothing human or worldly. But it subsists "of itself and by itself in an eternal oneness, while every lovely thing partakes of it." The religious character of

---

*The language Plato uses to describe this experience is remarkably similar to the language of Christian mystics describing the "beatific vision" of God.

the vision is indicated by the term "worshiper," which Plato applies to the lover who attains this "final revelation."

A diagram may make the stages of love more vivid.

The Ladder of Love

Note that the steps of the ladder are related to each other in precisely the same way as the sections of the Divided Line or the ascent from the Cave. Climbing the ladder gets the lover more and more reality, and the higher rungs explain the lower.

We began this discussion of love in order to find an answer to a question. Why, we wondered, would anyone be motivated to leave the Cave and make the difficult ascent to the sunlight, leaving behind the easy pleasures of worldly life? We now have Plato's answer. It is because we are all lovers.* We all want to be happy, to possess the beautiful and the good, forever. This is what we lack and long for. And to the extent of our resourcefulness, we will come to see that this passion cannot be satisfied by the possession of one beautiful body or even of many. We will be drawn out of the Cave toward the sun, toward the beautiful and the good in themselves, by the very nature of love. Plato is convinced that within each of us there is motivation that, if followed, will lead us beyond shadows to the Forms. The educator does not need to implant that in us; it is already there. All the educator needs to do is point us in the right direction.

In Plato's discussion of the love of wisdom we have an example of dialectic at work—the very dialectic that occupies the fourth section on the Divided Line. We see Plato exploring the nature of *eros,* teasing out of the Form of Love its intimate connections with the Forms of Knowledge and Beauty. In one sense we all know beauty when we see it; the wolf whistle of the construction worker when the attractive woman passes by is proof of that. But if we truly understand *eros,* Plato tells us, we will see that its combination of need and resource must lead us beyond its immediate objects to the highest levels of intellectual activity and spirituality.

Wisdom, which for Plato is equivalent to seeing everything in the light of the Forms, particularly in the light of the highest Forms of Beauty and Goodness, is something we all need, lack, and want. Wisdom alone will satisfy. Only wisdom, where the soul actually participates in the eternality of the Forms, will in the end bring us as close to immortality as mortals can possibly get.

But this conclusion is not yet quite accurate. As stated, it assumes the Homeric picture of human beings as mortal through and through. This is not

---

*Actually, this is not quite Plato's view. He thinks there are distinctly different sorts of people, and only some of them are lovers of wisdom. But I take here the more democratic view and give you all the benefit of the doubt!

Plato's considered view, and we need now to inquire into his theory of the soul.

1. Relate the Myth of the Cave.
2. What does an educator do for those he or she "teaches"?
3. What is love (*eros*)?
4. Sketch the "ladder" of love.

The Soul

Plato thought about his central problems throughout a long life. And it is apparent, particularly in his doctrine of the soul, that his thought developed complexities unimagined early on. Scholars dispute whether this development involves some inconsistency, whether his later thought is in conflict with the earlier. Some say yes, some say no. There is no doubt that there is at least a tension between the earlier and the later views of the soul. In this introductory treatment I will ignore these problems, presenting a picture of the soul that will be oversimplified and less than complete but true in essentials to Plato's views on the subject.[6]

The Immortality of the Soul

At the end of his defense before the jury, Socrates concludes that "there is good hope that death is a blessing." He thinks one of two things must be true: Either death is a dreamless sleep, or we survive the death of the body and can converse with those who died before. But he does not try to decide between them.*

Plato offers arguments to demonstrate that the latter is the true possibility—that the soul is immortal. We find such an argument in the story of Socrates and the slave boy.† According to Socrates,

---

*See *Apology* 40a–41c.
†In *Meno* 82b–86b.

the boy is able to recognize the truth when it is before him because he is remembering or recollecting what he was earlier acquainted with. But if that is so, then he—or rather his soul—must have existed before he was born, and in such a state that he was familiar with the Forms. Similarly, in judging two numbers to be equal we are using a concept that we could not have gained from experience, for no two worldly things are ever exactly equal. Plato concludes that

> it must, surely, have been before we began to see and hear and use the other senses that we got knowledge of the equal itself, of what it is, if we were going to refer the equals from our sense-perceptions to it, supposing that all things are doing their best to be like it, but are inferior to it. (*Phaedo* 75b)

If we had knowledge of the Equal "before we began to see and hear and use the other senses," then we must have been acquainted with this Form before our birth.

We may have doubts about the adequacy of this argument for the preexistence of the soul; if we could give another explanation of how we come to know the truth or of how we develop ideal concepts such as "equal," it might be seriously undermined. But even if it were a sound argument, it would not yet prove that the soul is immortal. For even if our souls do antedate the beginnings of our bodies, it is still possible that they dissipate when our bodies do (or some time after). In that case, the soul would still be mortal.

Plato considers this possibility, but he has other arguments. Recall Socrates in his prison cell. Why is he there? As we have seen, it is not because his body has made certain movements rather than others—or at least this is a very superficial explanation. Socrates is still in prison because he has thought the matter through (with Crito) and as a result has decided not to escape.

Now Plato contrasts two kinds of things: those that move only when something else moves them and those that move themselves. To which class does the body belong? It must, Plato argues, belong to the first class; for a corpse is a body, but it doesn't

move itself. The difference between living and nonliving bodies is that the former possess a principle of activity and motion within themselves. Such a principle of energy, capable of self-motion is exactly what we call a soul.

> Any body that has an external source of motion is soulless, but a body deriving its motion from a source within itself is animate or besouled. (*Phaedrus* 245e)

So a soul is essentially a self-mover, a source of activity and motion. It is because Socrates is "besouled," capable of moving himself, that he remains in prison. No explanation that does not involve Socrates' soul can be adequate. Therefore, his remaining in prison cannot be explained by talking only about his body, for the body is moved only by something other than itself.

It is precisely because the body is not a self-mover that it can die. The body must be moved either by a soul or by some other body. But if the soul is a self-mover, if it is inherently a source of energy and life, if it does not depend on something outside itself to galvanize it into action—then the soul cannot die.

> All soul is immortal, for that which is ever in motion is immortal. But that which while imparting motion is itself moved by something else can cease to be in motion, and therefore can cease to live; it is only that which moves itself that never intermits its motion, inasmuch as it cannot abandon its own nature; moreover this self-mover is the source and first principle of motion for all other things that are moved. (*Phaedrus* 245c)

The argument seems to be that life—a principle of self-motion—is the very essence of the soul. Because nothing can "abandon its own nature," the soul cannot die.

If the soul is a source of energy distinct from the body, if it survives the body's decay, and if the soul is the essential self, then Socrates was right in not being dismayed at death. But Plato goes further. It must be the task of those who love wisdom to maximize this separation of soul from body even in this life. As we have seen, it is not through the body that we can come to know the reality of the Forms. The body confuses and distracts us. Only the intellect can lead us through the sciences, via dialectic, to our goal: the Beautiful and the Good. And intellect is a capacity of the soul.

It follows that those who seek to be wise should aim at

> ==the parting of the soul from the body as far as possible, and the habituating of it to assemble and gather itself together, away from every part of the body, alone by itself, and to live, so far as it can, both in the present and in the hereafter, released from the body, as from fetters.== (*Phaedo* 67c–d)

==Pursuing philosophy, loving wisdom, means wanting to free the soul, to release it from its bondage to the body.== But if the separation of the soul from the body is death, it follows that

> those who practise philosophy aright are cultivating dying, and for them, least of all men, does being dead hold any terror. (*Phaedo* 67e)

If we understand by "the world" what we indicated previously, then it is accurate to say that Plato's philosophy contains a drive toward otherworldliness. Raphael was thus right to paint Plato pointing upward. Our true home is not in this world but in another. The love of wisdom, as he understands it, propels us out and away from the visible, the changeable, the bodily—out and away from the world. The most extreme expression of this drive is the assertion that the philosopher cultivates dying. It is true that one who has climbed out of the Cave into the sunlight of the Forms may return to the darkness below, but only for the purpose of encouraging others to turn their souls, too, toward the eternal realities.

Yet this is not a philosophy of pure escape from the world. The otherworldly tendency is balanced by an emphasis on the practical, this-worldly usefulness of acquaintance with the Forms. In order to see this practical side of Plato at work, we must talk about the internal structure of the soul.

The Structure of the Soul

When a subject is both difficult and important, Plato often constructs an analogy or a myth. The analogy of the sun presented the Form of the Good. The struggle toward wisdom is the subject of the Myth of the Cave. And to help us comprehend the soul, Plato tells the Myth of the Charioteer.*

> As to soul's immortality then we have said enough, but as to its nature there is this that must be said. What manner of thing it is would be a long tale to tell, and most assuredly a god alone could tell it, but what it resembles, that a man might tell in briefer compass. Let this therefore be our manner of discourse. Let it be likened to the union of powers in a team of winged steeds and their winged charioteer. Now all the gods' steeds and all their charioteers are good, and of good stock, but with other beings it is not wholly so. With us men, in the first place, it is a pair of steeds that the charioteer controls; moreover, one of them is noble and good, and of good stock, while the other has the opposite character, and his stock is opposite. Hence the task of our charioteer is difficult and troublesome. (*Phaedrus* 246a–b)

> Now of the steeds, so we declare, one is good and the other is not, but we have not described the excellence of the one nor the badness of the other, and that is what must now be done. He that is on the more honorable side is upright and clean-limbed, carrying his neck high, with something of a hooked nose; in color he is white, with black eyes; a lover of glory, but with temperance and modesty; one that consorts with genuine renown, and needs no whip, being driven by the word of command alone. The other is crooked of frame, a massive jumble of a creature, with thick short neck, snub nose, black skin, and gray eyes; hot-blooded, consorting with wantonness and vainglory; shaggy of ear, deaf, and hard to control with whip and goad. (*Phaedrus* 253d–e)

==We are presented with a picture of the soul in three parts, two of which contribute to the motion of the whole and one whose function is to guide the ensemble.== The soul is not only internally complex, however; it is beset by internal conflict. The two horses are of very different sorts and struggle against each other to determine the direction the

---

*The image Plato uses here may well have been suggested by chariot racing in the Olympic games.

soul is to go. For this reason, "the task of our charioteer is difficult and troublesome."

In the *Republic*, Plato tells a story to illustrate one type of possible conflict in the soul.

> Leontius the son of Aglaeon was coming up from the Piraeus, outside the North Wall but close to it, when he saw some corpses with the public executioner standing near by. On the one hand, he experienced the desire to see them, but at the same time he felt disgust and averted his gaze. For a while, he struggled and kept his hands over his eyes, but finally he was overcome by the desire; he opened his eyes wide, ran up to the corpses, and said, "There you are, you wretches! What a lovely sight! I hope you feel satisfied!"
>
>   Now what it suggests . . . is that it's possible for anger to be at odds with the desires, as if they were different things. (R 439e—440a)

This story also gives us a clue to further identification of the two horses in the Myth of the Charioteer. The black, unruly, and hot-blooded steed is desire, or appetite. Leontius *wants* to look at the corpses. Though he struggles against it, he is finally "overcome by the desire."

This desire is opposed by what Plato calls the "spirited" part of the soul, which corresponds to the white horse. When we call someone "animated" (in the sense this has in ordinary speech), we are calling attention to the predominance of "spirit" in that person. Children "are full of spirit from birth," Plato tells us. Spirit puts sparkle in the eyes and joy in the heart. Spirit makes us angry at injustice; it drives the athlete to victory and the soldier to battle. It is, Plato tells us, "an auxiliary of the rational part, unless it is corrupted by bad upbringing" (R 440e—441a).

The two horses, then, represent desire and spirit. What of the charioteer? Remember that the function of the charioteer is to guide the soul. What else could perform this guiding function, from Plato's point of view, but the rational part of the soul? Think of a desperately thirsty man in the desert. He sees a pool of water and approaches it with all the eagerness that deprivation can create. But when he reaches the pool, he sees a sign: "Danger: Do not drink. Polluted." He experiences

conflict within. His *desire* urges him to drink. But *reason* tells him that such signs usually indicate the truth, that polluted water will make him very ill and may kill him, and that if he drinks he will probably be worse off than if he doesn't. He decides not to drink. In this case, it is the rational part of him that opposes his desire. His reason guides him away from the water and tries to enlist the help of spirit to make that decision effective.

Desire, spirit, and reason, then, make up the soul. Desire *motivates,* spirit *animates,* and reason *guides*. In the gods, these parts are in perfect harmony. The charioteer in a god's soul has no difficulty in guiding the chariot. In humans, though, there is often conflict, and the job of the rational charioteer is hard.*

Plato supposes that any one of these parts may be dominant in a given person. This allows for a rough division of people into three sorts, according to what people take pleasure in:

> We found that one part is the intellectual part of a person, another is the passionate [spirited] part, and the third has so many manifestations that we couldn't give it a single label which applied to it and it alone, so we named it after its most prevalent and powerful aspect: we called it the desirous part, because of the intensity of our desires for food, drink, sex, and so on, and we also referred to it as the mercenary part, because desires of this kind invariably need money for their fulfilment. . . .
>
>   Now, sometimes this intellectual part is the motivating aspect of one's mind; sometimes—as circumstances dictate—it's one of the other two. . . .
>
>   Which is why we're also claiming that there are three basic human types—the philosophical, the competitive, and the avaricious. (R 580d—581c)

Plato uses the idea of three kinds of human beings in his plan for an ideal state, as we'll see. But first we need to examine his views on how the various parts of the soul *should* be related. This will allow us to see the practical use to which Plato thinks the Forms can be put.

---

*Recall the saying by Democritus, the atomist: "It is hard to fight with desire; but to overcome it is the mark of a rational man." See p. 35.

1. What argument is offered for the soul's immortality?
2. Why does Plato consider philosophy as "training for dying"?
3. What are the parts of the soul? What are their functions?

Morality

Plato believes that he has met the challenge of skepticism. We do have knowledge; knowing how to double the square is only one example of innumerable other things we either know or can come to know. Relativism is also a mistake, he thinks; for the objects of such knowledge are public and available to all. It is by introducing the Forms that he has solved these problems. They are the public, enduring objects about which we can learn through reasoning and instruction. They are the realities that make intelligible all else and give even the fluctuating things of the world such stability as they do have.

We might not be satisfied yet, however. We might say, "That's all very well in the sphere of geometry and the like, but what about ethics and politics? Is there knowledge here, too?" And we might remind Plato of Socrates reminding Euthyphro that even the gods dispute with each other—not about numbers, lengths, and weights, but about "the just and the unjust, the beautiful and the ugly, the good and the bad" (*Euthyphro* 7d). If we are to meet the challenge of skepticism and relativism, we must do it in this sphere, too. Can we *know,* for instance, that justice is good rather than bad? Are there public objects in this sphere, too, about which rational persons can come to agreement? Or, in this aspect of human life, is custom "king of all"?* Is it true here, as the Sophists argue, that *nomos* rules entirely, that morality, for example, is merely conventional? Unless this challenge can be met, Plato

has not succeeded. Skepticism and relativism, ruled out of the theoretical sphere, will reappear with renewed vigor in our practical life. And Plato will neither be able to prove that Athens was wrong to have executed Socrates nor be convincing about the structure of a good state.

Plato makes the problem of morality one of the main themes in the *Republic.* He is asking the Socratic question: What is morality? For Plato, this is equivalent to asking about the Form of Morality. The particular question is this: Is the Form of the Moral related to the Form of the Good? And if so, how? To put it in more familiar terms, is morality something good or not?* Remembering that for Socrates the good is always some sort of *advantage,* we can ask: Will I be *better off* being moral than being immoral? Again Plato takes us up the Divided Line, this time with a dialectic designed to show us that the answer is yes, that being moral is indeed something good—and good by nature, not by convention.

As we have seen, Antiphon argues that conventional morality, which forbids deception, stealing, and breaking contracts, may not be in the interest of the individual. When it is not to his advantage, he says, there is nothing wrong with violating the conventional rules, following the law of self-preservation, and being (in the conventional sense) immoral. If you can deceive someone and get away with it when it is to your advantage, that is what you should do.

Plato always tries to present his opponents' views in a strong way, and in the *Republic* we find Thrasymachus, another Sophist, arguing the case. Because, he claims, the rules of morality are purely conventional and are made by those with the power to make them, it will seldom be to the advantage of an individual to be moral.† Thrasymachus addresses Socrates:

> You're so far off understanding right and wrong,
> and morality and immorality, that you don't even

---

*Quoted by Herodotus from Pindar, after he tells the story of the Greeks and Indians before Darius (p. 45). Review the *nomos/physis* controversy that follows.

---

*This is Nietzsche's question, too. But unlike Plato, he answers no. See pp. 557–563.

†This principle is sometimes humorously called "The Golden Rule: He who has the gold, makes the rule." Another version of it is the principle that might makes right.

realize that morality and right are actually good for someone else—they are the advantage of the stronger party, the ruler—and bad for the underling at the receiving end of the orders. . . .

In any and every situation, a moral person is worse off than an immoral one. Suppose, for instance, that they're doing some business together, which involves one of them entering into association with the other: by the time the association is dissolved, you'll never find the moral person up on the immoral one—he'll be worse off. Or again, in civic matters, if there's a tax on property, then a moral person pays more tax than an immoral one even when they're both equally well off; and if there's a hand-out, then the one gets nothing, while the other makes a lot. And when each of them holds political office, even if a moral person loses out financially in no other way, his personal affairs deteriorate through neglect, while his morality stops him making any profit from public funds, and moreover his family and friends fall out with him over his refusal to help them out in unfair ways; in all these respects, however, an immoral person's experience is the opposite. . . .

So you see, Socrates, immorality—if practised on a large enough scale—has more power, licence, and authority than morality. And as I said at the beginning, morality is really the advantage of the stronger party, while immorality is profitable and advantageous to oneself. (*R* 343c–344c)

From Thrasymachus' point of view, being moral is "sheer simplicity," whereas being immoral is "sound judgment" (*R* 348c–d). When the question is, "How anyone can live his life in the most rewarding manner?" (*R* 344e), Thrasymachus answers: Be immoral!

Now Plato accepts this as the right question, but he thinks Thrasymachus gives the wrong answer. Which life is the most worthwhile? Which kind of life is advantageous to the one who lives it? That is indeed the question. But how shall we answer it?

Here is a clue. As we saw in our discussion of love, everyone desires to be happy. No one doubts that what makes you truly happy (enduringly happy) is good. So it looks like happiness is one thing that everyone admits is good by nature (*physis*); it isn't just by convention (*nomos*) that we agree

on that. This suggests a strategy that could counter the argument of Thrasymachus. If Plato could show that being moral is in your long-term interest because it is the only way to be truly happy, Thrasymachus would be defeated.

But is the moral person the happy person? That question is posed in a radical way by another participant in the dialogue of the *Republic,* Glaucon, who tells the following story. It is about an ancestor of Gyges.

He was a shepherd in the service of the Lydian ruler of the time, when a heavy rainstorm occurred and an earthquake cracked open the land to a certain extent, and a chasm appeared in the region where he was pasturing his flocks. He was fascinated by the sight, and went down into the chasm and saw there, as the story goes, among other artefacts, a bronze horse, which was hollow and had windows set in it; he stopped and looked in through the windows and saw a corpse inside, which seemed to be that of a giant. The corpse was naked, but had a golden ring on one finger; he took the ring off the finger and left. Now, the shepherds used to meet once a month to keep the king informed about his flocks, and our protagonist came to the meeting wearing the ring. He was sitting down among the others, and happened to twist the ring's bezel in the direction of his body, towards the inner part of his hand. When he did this, he became invisible to his neighbours, and to his astonishment they talked about him as if he'd left. While he was fiddling about with the ring again, he turned the bezel outwards, and became visible. He thought about this and experimented to see if it was the ring which had this power; in this way he eventually found that turning the bezel inwards made him invisible, and turning it outwards made him visible. As soon as he realized this, he arranged to be one of the delegates to the king; once he was inside the palace, he seduced the king's wife and with her help assaulted and killed the king, and so took possession of the throne. (*R* 359d–360b)*

Would you want a ring like this? How would you use it? You are invited to imagine a situation in

---

*This ring is obviously an ancestor to the One Ring that plays a central role in Tolkien's *The Lord of the Rings.*

which you could avoid any nasty consequences for behaving unjustly; all you have to do is use the ring. You could behave as badly as you like while invisible and no one could pin it on you. You would never be caught or punished. If you took a fancy to something, you could just take it. If you wanted to do something, nothing would prevent you. In a situation like this, what would be the best thing to do? What use of the ring would bring the greatest advantage?

On the one hand, if being moral is worthwhile only because of its consequences, then removing the consequences would diminish the worth of being a moral person; you might as well be unjust and satisfy your desires. On the other hand, if being moral is the true good, good in itself, then it would be better to refrain from unjust actions; it would be more advantageous not to steal, kill, or commit adultery, even if you could get away with it. Your life would be better being moral, even though you would have to do without some of the things that would please you.

Glaucon challenges Socrates to prove that being a moral person is something good in itself, not good just because it usually brings good consequences in its wake. He imagines two extreme cases:

> Our immoral person must be a true expert. . . . [He] must get away with any crimes he undertakes in the proper fashion, if he is to be outstandingly immoral; getting caught must be taken to be a sign of incompetence, since the acme of immorality is to give an impression of morality while actually being immoral. So we must attribute consummate immorality to our consummate criminal, and . . . . we should have him equipped with a colossal reputation for morality even though he is a colossal criminal. He should be capable of correcting any mistakes he makes. He must have the ability to argue plausibly, in case any of his crimes are ever found out, and to use force wherever necessary, by making use of his courage and strength and by drawing on his fund of friends and his financial resources.
>
> Now that we've come up with this sketch of an immoral person, we must conceive of a moral person to stand beside him—someone who is straightforward and principled, and who . . .

wants genuine goodness rather than merely an aura of goodness. So we must deprive him of any such aura, since if others think him moral, this reputation will gain him privileges and rewards, and it will become unclear whether it is morality or the rewards and privileges which might be motivating him to be what he is. We should strip him of everything except morality, then, and our portrait should be of someone in the opposite situation to the one we imagined before. I mean, even though he does no wrong at all, he must have a colossal reputation for immorality, so that his morality can be tested by seeing whether or not he is impervious to a bad reputation and its consequences; he must unswervingly follow his path until he dies—a saint with a lifelong reputation as a sinner. When they can both go no further in morality and immorality respectively, we can decide which of them is the happier. (R 361a–d)

Perhaps the just man languishes in prison, dirty, cold, and half-starved; all he has is justice. The unjust man, meanwhile, revels in luxuries and the admiration of all. The challenge is to show that the one who does right is, despite all, the happier of the two—the one who has the best life. If Plato can demonstrate this, he will have shown that morality, not immorality, participates in the Form of the Good. It is this bit of dialectic we now want to understand.

We should note at this point, however, that we have so far been discussing whether being moral has the advantage over being immoral without being very clear about the nature of morality. We have assumed we know what it is we are talking about; as Socrates makes clear, however, this is often an unwarranted assumption. So we now have to address this Socratic question directly: What is it to be moral? Only if we are clear about that can we hope to answer the question whether it is something good, even apart from its consequences.

To answer this question, Plato draws on his description of the soul. As we have seen, there are three parts to the soul: reason, spirit, and appetite. Each has a characteristic function. In accord with its function, each has a peculiar excellence. Just as the function of a knife is to cut, the best knife is the one that cuts smoothly and easily; so the excellence of anything is the best performance of its function. What are the functions of the various parts of the soul?

The function of appetite or desire is to motivate a person. It is, if you like, the engine that supplies the energy driving the whole mechanism. If you never *wanted* anything, it is doubtful that you would ever *do* anything. Your heart might beat and your lungs take in air, but there would be no actions on your part. So appetite is performing its function and doing it well when it motivates you strongly to achievement.

Spirit's function is to animate life, so that it is more than the dull drudgery of satisfying wants. Without spirit, life would perhaps go on, but it wouldn't be enjoyable; it might not even be worth living. Spirit is "doing its thing" if it puts sparkle into your life, determination into your actions, and courage into your heart. It supplies the pride and satisfaction that accompany the judgment that you have done well, and it is the source of indignation and anger when you judge that something has been done badly.

It is the task of the rational part of the soul to pursue wisdom and to make judgments backed by reasons. It performs this task with excellence when it judges in accord with knowledge. The rational part of the soul, then, works out by reasoning the best course of action. Its function is to guide or rule the other two parts. Desire, one could say, is blind; reason gives it sight. Spirit may be capricious; reason gives it sense.

Just as the body is in excellent shape when each of its parts is performing its function properly—heart, lungs, digestive system, muscles, nerves, and so on—so the whole soul is excellent when desire, spirit, and reason are all functioning well. The excellent human being is one who is strongly motivated, emotionally vivacious, and rational. Such a person, Plato believes, will also be happy.

For what is the source of unhappiness? Isn't it precisely a lack of harmony among the various parts of the soul? Desire wants what reason says it may not have. Spirit rejoices at what reason advises against. These are cases in which the parts of the soul are not content to perform their proper function. One wants to usurp the function of another.

When, for example, you want what reason says is not good for you, it may be that your desire is so great that it overrides the advice given. In that case, desire takes over the guiding function that properly belongs to reason. But then you will do something unwise; and if it is unwise, you will suffer for it. And that is no way to be happy.

On the assumption that we all want to be happy and that being happy is what is good, the good life for human beings must be one in which each part of the soul performs its functions excellently—where reason makes the decisions, supported by spirit, and desire is channeled in appropriate directions. The good and happy person is the one who is internally harmonious. Though we do not all realize it, this internal harmony is what we all most want; for that is the only way to be happy.

Do you remember what Socrates said at his trial—that "the Olympian victor makes you think yourself happy; I make you happy" (*Apology* 36e)? We said then that Socrates thinks happiness is not *feeling* happy, but *being* happy, and that *being* happy is a condition of the soul. We now know more clearly what that condition is: harmony among the parts of the soul.

But what does this have to do with morality? We can answer this question if we think again of an unharmonious soul. Suppose that desire, for instance, overrides reason. It wrongs reason, displacing it from its rightful place as a guide. It is not too much to say that it does reason an *injustice*. So there is a kind of justice and injustice in the individual soul, having to do with the way its parts relate to each other. Let us then speak of *justice in the soul*. In a just soul desire, spirit, and reason all do their thing without overreaching their proper bounds.

Given what we have just said about happiness, it is clear that justice in the soul correlates with happiness and injustice (internal conflict) with unhappiness. Insofar as we are internally just we will be happy. Now happiness, we said, is something good by nature; everyone naturally desires to be happy. It follows that justice in the soul is also something good by nature. If we were wise, we would seek our happiness by trying to keep our souls harmonious, by promoting justice in the soul.

What Thrasymachus claims, of course, is not that injustice in the soul is a good thing but that our lives will be better if we are unjust in the community. He no doubt thinks that you can be internally happy and externally immoral. What Plato needs to demonstrate is that this combination won't work, that there is a strict correlation between *justice in the soul* and *morality in the community*. Will the internally just person also be externally just? Will a just soul naturally express itself by keeping promises, refraining from stealing and deception, respecting the rights of others? That's the question. To put it another way, Will the person who behaves immorally in the community find it impossible to be just (and therefore happy) within herself?

Near the end of the *Republic* Plato has Socrates construct an imaginary model of the mind to address this question.

"Make a model, then, of a creature with a single—if varied and many-headed—form, arrayed all around with the heads of both wild and tame animals, and possessing the ability to change over to a different set of heads and to generate all these new bits from its own body."

"That would take some skilful modelling," he remarked, "but since words are a more plastic material than wax and so on, you may consider the model constructed."

"A lion and a man are the next two models to make, then. The first of the models, however, is to be by far the largest, and the second the second largest."

"That's an easier job," he said. "It's done."

"Now join the three of them together until they become one, as it were."

"All right," he said.

"And for the final coat, give them the external appearance of a single entity. Make them look like a person, so that anyone incapable of seeing what's inside, who can see only the external husk, will see a single creature, a human being."

"It's done," he said.

"Now, we'd better respond to the idea that this person gains from doing wrong, and loses from doing right, by pointing out to its proponent that this is tantamount to saying that we're rewarded if we indulge and strengthen the many-sided beast and the lion with all its aspects, but starve and weaken the man, until he's subject to the whims of the others, and can't promote familiarity and compatibility between the other two, but lets them bite each other, fight, and try to eat each other."

"Yes, that's undoubtedly what a supporter of immorality would have to say," he agreed.

"So the alternative position, that morality is profitable, is equivalent to saying that our words and behaviour should be designed to maximize the control the inner man has within us, and should enable him to secure the help of the leonine quality and then tend to the many-headed beast as a farmer tends to his crops—by nurturing and cultivating its tame aspects, and by stopping the wild ones growing. Then he can ensure that they're all compatible with one another, and with himself, and can look after them all equally, without favouritism."

"Yes, that's exactly what a supporter of morality has to say," he agreed. (*R* 588b–589b)

Plato uses this image to show the *identity* of the harmonious, internally just person and the moral person who does what is right. To do wrong to others is to allow the beast within to rule, to allow it to overwhelm the man within (who represents reason). But that means that the internal parts of the soul are no longer doing their own thing, but struggling for dominance. Harmony, and therefore happiness, is destroyed and the good is lost.*

The internally just person, on the other hand, fostering the excellent functioning of each part of the soul in inner harmony, allows the man within to master the beast and tame the lion. The various parts are "compatible with one another." The external result of this inner harmony is a moral life, for the beast will not wildly demand what reason says it is not proper to want.

Can there be any profit in the immoral acquisition of money, if this entails the enslavement of the best part of oneself to the worst part?. . . .

[And] do you think the reason for the traditional condemnation of licentiousness is the same—

---

*Compare this to Heraclitus' aphorism on p. 23, where he says that what impulse wants it buys "at the expense of the soul." Giving in to impulse is—in terms of Plato's image—feeding the beast. The beast grows strong at the expense of the lion and the man.

because it allows that fiend, that huge and many-faceted creature, greater freedom than it should have?. . .

And aren't obstinacy and bad temper considered bad because they distend and invigorate our leonine . . . side to a disproportionate extent?. . .

Whereas a spoilt, soft way of life is considered bad because it makes this part of us so slack and loose that it's incapable of facing hardship? (R 589da—590b)

You can go through a list of the vices and show, Plato believes, that in each case they result from feeding the monster or from letting the lion run amok. The moral virtues, on the other hand, are exactly the opposite.

Here, then, is Plato's answer to Thrasymachus, and to the challenge posed by Glaucon. The immoral man does not have the advantage after all. If we reason carefully about it, Plato says, we can see that it is more profitable to be moral because immorality entangles one's soul in disharmony. And disharmony in the soul is unhappiness. And a life of unhappiness is not the good life.

Justice in the soul, then, is correlated with a moral life. When each part of the soul is justly "doing its thing"—reason making the decisions, supported by the lion of the spirit and a domesticated appetite—a person's external actions will be morally acceptable actions. As we have seen, justice in the soul is happiness, and happiness is a natural good—good by *physis,* not just by *nomos.* So an attempt to understand the Form of Morality takes us necessarily to the Form of the Good. It is best to be moral, even though we suffer for it. And Plato can think he has given us a *logos* that supports Socrates' claim that it is worse to *do* injustice than to *suffer* it. Socrates believed this with full conviction; Plato thinks we can know it is true. The advantage lies with the moral person.

The argument is complex, but the heart of it is straightforward. Let us set down the key notions in this bit of dialectic.

1. Moral actions flow from a soul in harmony.
2. A harmonious soul is a happy soul.
3. Happiness is a natural good.

4. So morality is itself a natural good. (This follows from 1, 2, and 3.)
5. So acting morally is not good simply for its consequences, but is something good in itself. (The Form of the Moral participates in the Form of the Good.)

Plato claims that by such dialectical reasoning we can have knowledge in the sphere of practice as well as in the theoretical sphere. Such dialectic, he believes, has defeated the skepticism and relativism of the Sophists and vindicated the practice of his master, who went around "doing nothing but persuading both young and old among you not to care for your body or your wealth in preference to or as strongly as for the best possible state of your soul" (*Apology* 30b).

---

1. What question does the Ring of Gyges story pose?
2. What is happiness? Unhappiness?
3. What is the psychology of the just person? Of the unjust person?
4. How is justice in the soul related to moral behavior in the community? Relate this to the image of the man, the lion, and the monster.

The State

We will not discuss Plato's views of the ideal state in any detail, but we must note several political implications of doctrines we have already canvassed. Like his views on the soul, his views on an ideal community developed throughout his lifetime, and his later thought manifests some deep changes in attitude and outlook. We will simplify by focusing on several famous doctrines of the middle-period *Republic.*

Plato sees a parallel between the internal structure of a soul and the structure of a community. Just as the parts of the soul have distinctive functions, individual men and women differ in their capacities and abilities. They can be grouped into three classes: (1) Some will be best fitted to be laborers, carpenters, plumbers, stonemasons, merchants, or farmers; these can be thought of as the *productive* part of the community; they correspond to the part of the soul called "appetite." (2) Others, who are adventurous, strong, brave, and in love with danger, will be suited to serve in the army and navy; these form the *protective* part of the state, and they correspond to spirit in the soul. (3) Some, a very few, who are intelligent, rational, self-controlled, and in love with wisdom, will be suited to make decisions for the community; these are the *governing* part; and obviously their parallel in the soul is reason.

Up to this point, we have more or less been taking for granted that the search for wisdom is open to everyone. But this is not in fact Plato's view. Like Socrates, he contrasts the few who know with the many who do not. A basic principle for Plato's ideal state is that there are, and always will be, only a few who are fit to rule. Obviously, Plato is consciously and explicitly rejecting the foundations of Athenian democracy as it existed in his day, where judges were selected by lot rather than by ability and where laws could be passed by a majority of the citizens who happened to show up in the Assembly on any given day. It is *not* the case, Plato urges, that everyone is equally fit to govern. Where democracy is the rule, rhetoric and persuasion carry the day, not reason and wisdom.

He is not, of course, in favor of tyranny or despotism, either; we can think of these as forms of government where the strong rule—that is, whoever has the power to seize the reins. Nor does he favor oligarchy, or rule by the wealthy. Who, then, are these "few" who are fit to be rulers? Consider again the harmonious, internally just soul. In such a soul, reason rules. So in the state,

> Unless communities have philosophers as kings, . . . or the people who are currently called kings and rulers practise philosophy with enough integrity . . . there can be no end to political troubles, . . . or even to human troubles in general, I'd say. (R 473c–d)

The philosopher kings will be those who love wisdom and are possessed of the ability to pursue it, those who have the ability to *know*. Because, as we have seen, knowledge is always knowledge of the Forms, philosopher kings will be those who have attained such knowledge, especially knowledge of the Forms of Justice and Morality and the Form of the Good. For how can one rule wisely unless one knows what is good for the community and what is right?

This is supported by an analogy, some form of which Plato uses again and again:

> Imagine the following situation on a fleet of ships, or on a single ship. The owner has the edge over everyone else on board by virtue of his size and strength, but he's rather deaf and short-sighted, and his knowledge of naval matters is just as limited. The sailors are wrangling with one another because each of them thinks that he ought to be the captain, despite the fact that he's never learnt how, and can't name his teacher or specify the period of his apprenticeship. In any case, they all maintain that it isn't something that can be taught, and are ready to butcher anyone who says it is. They're for ever crowding closely around the owner, pleading with him and stopping at nothing to get him to entrust the rudder to them. Sometimes, if their pleas are unsuccessful, but others get the job, they kill those others or throw them off the ship, subdue their worthy owner by drugging him or getting him drunk or something, take control of the ship, help themselves to its cargo, and have the kind of drunken and indulgent voyage you'd expect from people like that. And that's not all: they think highly of anyone who contributes towards their gaining power by showing skill at winning over or subduing the owner, and describe him as an accomplished seaman, a true captain, a naval expert; but they criticize anyone different as useless. They completely fail to understand that any genuine sea-captain has to study the yearly cycle, the seasons, the heavens, the stars and winds, and everything relevant to the job, if he's to be properly equipped to hold a position of authority in a ship. . . . When this is what's happening on board ships, don't you think that the crew of ships in this state would think of any true captain as nothing but a windbag with his head in the clouds, of no use to them at all?
>
> . . . I'm sure you don't need an analysis of the analogy to see that it's a metaphor for the attitude

of society towards true philosophers. (*R* 488a–489a)

It is indeed a fairly transparent analogy, the details of which do not need much comment. But we need to make explicit something that Plato takes for granted here. The analogy assumes that there is a body of knowledge available to the statesman similar to that utilized by the navigator. It assumes that this can be taught and learned and that it involves some theory that can be applied by the skilled practitioner. Clearly, the knowledge of statecraft involves acquaintance with the Forms.

In a similar way, Plato compares the statesman to a doctor (*Gorgias* 463a–465e). We would never entrust the health of our bodies to just anybody. We rely on those who have been trained in that craft by skilled teachers. Furthermore, just as not everyone is by nature qualified to be a doctor, not everyone is fit to rule. Because the education necessary to reach the higher level of the Forms is rigorous and demanding, only a few will be able to do it. And for that reason, government in the best state will be by the few: the few who are wise.

A large part of the *Republic* is devoted to a description of the social and educational arrangements that will make it possible to produce philosophers who are kings and kings who are philosophers. Though these discussions are interesting, we omit them here. We still need, however, to ask about the many. If only the few will ever make it to wisdom, what are the many to do? If they cannot *know* the good, how can they be depended on to *do* the good? And if they do not do the good, won't the state fall apart in anarchy and chaos?

The state can be saved from this fate by the principle that, for purposes of action, right opinion is as effective as knowledge. If you merely believe that the cliff is directly ahead and as a result turn left, you will avoid falling over just as surely as if you knew that it was. The problem then, is to assure that the large majority has correct beliefs. They may not be able to follow the complicated dialectical reasoning demonstrating the goodness of morality, but they should be firmly persuaded that it pays to be moral.

Such right opinion is inculcated in the young by education, which is directed by the guardians or rulers, who know what is best. There are detailed discussions in the *Republic* about what sort of stories the young should be told and what sort of music should be allowed. Consider music. It is clear that the young cannot be allowed to listen to whatever kind of music they desire; for there is music that feeds the many-headed beast within and encourages passions that will destroy the harmony of a good state. (You might ask yourself what Plato would say about the popular music of today.) Music and stories should both encourage the belief—which Plato thinks can be demonstrated dialectically to the few—that the best and happiest life is a life of moderation and rational self-control, a moral life.

There is in Plato's state, then, a distinct difference between the few and the many. The latter are brought up on a carefully censored educational regime; it would not be unfair to call the diet offered to the many propaganda, for it is persuasive rather than rational. The few, of course, are those who know what is best, for they have attained knowledge of the Forms. They arrange the education of the others so that they will attain as much goodness as they are capable of.

With respect to knowledge, Plato is both an optimist and a pessimist: an optimist about the few, a pessimist about the many. It is worth noting that Plato is in effect jettisoning one of the basic principles of his master, Socrates: that "the unexamined life is not worth living for a man" (*Apology* 38a). Plato seems to have concluded that for most people this sets the standard too high. They will do best not under Socratic "examination," but conditioned by censorship, propaganda, indoctrination, and persuasion under the guidance of those for whom such dialectical examination leads to a knowledge of the Forms.

Those who find these antidemocratic consequences disturbing have reason to go back to their presuppositions. We will find subsequent philosophers raising serious questions both about the Forms and about Plato's view that some—but not all—of us are capable of knowing them.

1. Who should rule in the state? And why?
2. Explain the analogy of the navigator.
3. How will "the many" be "educated" in Plato's ideal republic?

Problems with the Forms

Plato offers a complete vision of reality, including an account of how knowledge is possible, an ethics that guides our practical lives, and a picture of an ideal community. As we have seen, all these aspects of reality involve the Forms. The Forms are the most real of all the things there are. They serve as the stable and enduring objects of our knowledge. The Forms of Goodness, Morality, and Beauty function as guides to our goals, our behaviors, and our creative drives. And knowledge of them is the foundation for a good state.

But are there such realities? It is not only the political consequences that lead people to raise this question. It is raised in Plato's own school, and serious objections are explored—and not satisfactorily answered—by Plato himself in a late dialogue, the *Parmenides*. Here the leading character is made out to be Parmenides himself, the champion of the One, from whom Plato undoubtedly derives his inspiration in devising the doctrine of the eternal and unchanging Forms.

Parmenides examines the young Socrates:

I imagine your ground for believing in a single form in each case is this. When it seems to you that a number of things are large, there seems, I suppose, to be a certain single character which is the same when you look at them all; hence you think that largeness is a single thing.

True, he replied.

But now take largeness itself and the other things which are large. Suppose you look at all these in the same way in your mind's eye, will not yet another unity make its appearance—a largeness by virtue of which they all appear large?

So it would seem.

If so, a second form of largeness will present itself, over and above largeness itself and the things

that share in it, and again, covering all these, yet another, which will make all of them large. So each of your forms will no longer be one, but an indefinite many. (*Parmenides* 131e–132b)

The argument begins with a statement we used before when the Forms were introduced.[*] But then an unacceptable conclusion is derived. Let us see if we can follow the argument.

Think again about Gertrude and Huey, the two elephants. Both are large. Let the small letters g and h represent Gertrude and Huey. Let the capital letter L represent the property they share of being large.[†] Then we have

$$Lg \quad Lh$$

According to Plato's view of the Forms, this common feature means that Gertrude and Huey "participate" in a Form—the Large. Let's represent this Form by F. So we add the following to our diagram:

It is the Form F that *makes* the two elephants large and makes it intelligible that they are just what they are—that is, large.

Now Plato also regularly thinks of the Forms as *possessing* the very character that they engender in the particulars. Or, to put it the other way around, he says that individual things "copy" or "imitate" the Form. When writing about the Form of Beauty, for example, Plato says that it is in itself beautiful, that it exemplifies "the very soul of the beauty he has toiled for so long," that it possesses "an everlasting loveliness."[‡] Particular individuals are beautiful

---

[*] See p. 123.

[†] We here use a convention of modern logicians, for whom small letters symbolize individuals and large letters represent properties or features. The property symbols are written to the left of the individual symbols.

[‡] See p. 139.

just to the extent that they actually have that Beauty which belongs in preeminent fashion to the Form.

If that is right, then Largeness must itself be large. So we have to add this feature to our representation:

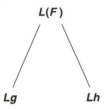

But now a problem stares us in the face: Now the Form and the two elephants all have something in common—Largeness. And according to the very principle Plato uses to generate the *F* in the first place, there will now have to be a *second F* to explain what the first *F* shares with the individuals! And that, of course, will also be Large. So we will have to put down:

And now you can probably see how this is going to go. There will have to be a third *F,* a fourth, a fifth, and so on and on and on. We will no longer have just one Largeness, but two, three, four. . . . As Plato acknowledges through the character of Parmenides, each Form "will no longer be one, but an indefinite many." We are on the escalator of an *infinite regress.*

Moreover, at any stage of the regress what is real is supposed to depend on there already being a level above it, which explains the features at that stage. So this is what philosophers call a *vicious* infinite regress. For any stage to exist, there must actually be an infinite number of stages in reality, on which its existence depends. We thought we were explaining something about Gertrude and Huey. But this explanation now dissipates itself in the requirement for a never-ending series of explanations—and all of exactly the same sort. This is bad news for Plato's theory of Forms.

Still further, this argument can be applied to any characteristic whatever. It is traditionally formulated in terms of the Form of Man. Heraclitus and Socrates are both men; so there must be a Form of Man to explain this similarity. If that Form is itself a man, you have a third man. In this guise the argument has a name. It is called the **Third Man** argument. It could as well be called the Third, Fourth, Fifth, Sixth. . . . Man Argument.

The Forms are posited to explain the fact of knowledge, the meaning of general terms, and the common features of individuals.* But the Third Man Argument shows that—on principles accepted by Plato himself, at least in his middle period—the Forms do *not* explain what they are supposed to explain.

Like all such paradoxes derived from a set of premises, this indicates that something is wrong. But it does not itself tell us *what* is wrong. Some solution to the problem is needed. As we will see, Aristotle offers a solution.

Explain the threat posed to Plato's philosophy by the Third Man argument.

For Further Thought

1. How persuaded are you by Plato's arguments for the reality of intelligible Forms? If you are not convinced, try to formulate your objections to these arguments in such a way that Plato would have to pay attention.

2. Consider someone you know whom you regard as an exceptionally good person. How much does this person resemble Plato's portrait of the just person? How is he or she different?

3. Would you characterize Plato's views about a good state as elitist, or just realist? Justify your answer with a bit of dialectical reasoning.

*Review pp. 122–124.

Notes

1. A. N. Whitehead, *Process and Reality* (1929; reprint, New York: Harper Torchbooks, 1960), part II, p. 63.
2. Plato, *Meno,* trans. Robin Waterfield, in *Meno and Other Dialogues* (Oxford: Oxford University Press, 2005).
3. Quotations from Plato's *Republic,* trans. Robin Waterfield (Oxford: Oxford University Press, 1993), are cited in the text using the abbreviation *R.* References are to section numbers.
4. Quotations from Plato's *Timaeus, Parmenides, Symposium,* and *Phaedrus,* in *The Collected Dialogues of Plato,* ed. E. Hamilton and H. Cairns (Princeton: Princeton University Press, 1961), are cited in the text by title and section numbers.
5. Quotations from Plato's *Phaedo,* trans. David Gallop (Oxford: Oxford University Press, 1993), are cited in the text by title and section numbers.
6. A discussion of these problems may be found in W. K. C. Guthrie, "Plato's Views on the Nature of the Soul," in *Plato II: A Collection of Critical Essays,* ed. Gregory Vlastos (Notre Dame, IN: University of Notre Dame Press, 1978), 230–243.

7

ARISTOTLE

The Reality of the World

The year was 384 B.C. Socrates had been dead for fifteen years; Plato had begun his Academy three years earlier. In northern Thrace, not far from the border of what Athenians called civilization, a child was born to a physician in the royal court of Macedonia. This child, named Aristotle, was destined to become the second father of Western philosophy.

At the age of eighteen he went to Athens, where bright young men from all over desired to study, and enrolled in the Academy. He stayed there for twenty years, as student, researcher, and teacher, until the death of Plato in 347 B.C. He then spent some time traveling around the Greek islands, pursuing research in what we would call marine biology. For a short time he went back to Macedonia, where he had a position at court as a tutor to the young Alexander, later known as "The Great," who was shortly to complete his father's ambition of conquering and unifying the known world.

By 335, Aristotle was back in Athens, where he founded a school of his own, the Lyceum. He re-

mained there until 323, when he was apparently forced to flee — lest, he said, the Athenians "should sin twice against philosophy."[1] He died the following year at the age of sixty-three.

Aristotle and Plato

Let us begin by drawing some comparisons between Aristotle and his teacher, Plato.[2] First, Plato was born into an aristocratic family with a long history of participation in the political life of the city. Aristotle's father was a doctor. These backgrounds can serve as symbols of their different interests and outlook. The influence of Plato on Aristotle's thought is marked; still, Aristotle is a quite different person with distinct concerns, and his philosophy in some respects takes quite a different turn. That Aristotle's hand is stretched out horizontally in Raphael's painting symbolizes perfectly the contrast with Plato. Here are some comparisons.

Otherworldliness

As we see, there is a strong drive toward other-worldliness in Plato.* One feels in Plato a profound dissatisfaction with the familiar world of sense, which is to him no more than a pale shadow of reality. The real is quite different—unchanging, eternal, and unperceivable. The aim of philosophy, the love of wisdom, is to grasp by intellect this otherworldly reality, the Forms, and ultimately to be so caught up in contemplating the True, the Good, and the Beautiful as to escape the Heraclitean flux altogether. To philosophize is to die away from sense and desire.

Aristotle, by contrast, does not seem to suffer the same discontents. While he develops a profound view of the divine and its relation to the world, he does not seem driven to denigrate life in this world as something to be fled from. Life in this world, if not perfect, is as good as one could reasonably expect. The snails and octopuses he studies so avidly, dissects, classifies, and writes about are nothing if not real things. And philosophy is not an escape from them, but a way of comprehending them.

The Objects of Knowledge

Plato is a combination of rationalist and mystic. He is committed to the idea that reality is ultimately rational. The Forms are perfectly definite realities, hanging together in perfectly rational ways, just as geometrical forms make up a perfectly systematic whole. Mathematics, in fact, seems to embody the ideal of knowledge, and reasoning is the way to discover truth. Yet it seems that even reason is not ultimately sufficient. Eventually, when you get far enough up the hierarchy of the Forms, you just have to "see" the truth (with "the mind's eye"). Thus Diotima in the *Symposium* is supposed to have spoken about the "vision" of Beauty when the lover comes to "see the heavenly beauty face to face."†

It is perhaps for this reason that Plato—unable to describe what must be seen—offers us in crucial

places his memorable myths and analogies. These fit with the idea that teaching is "turning the soul toward reality." The myths point us in a direction where we might be able to see for ourselves what language is inadequate to describe.

Aristotle, much more down to earth, is convinced that language is quite capable of expressing the truth of things. This truth concerns the sensible world, and our knowledge of it begins with actually seeing, touching, and hearing the things of the world. The senses, although not sufficient in themselves to lead us to knowledge, are the only reliable avenues along which to pursue knowledge. We must be careful, of course, and mistakes are easy to make. But we can come to both know and adequately express this knowledge of the changing world about us.

Human Nature

Plato is sure that the real person is the soul, not the body. Souls inhabit bodies for a time but are neither bound to nor dependent on them for their existence. The body is nothing more than a temporary and ultimately unreal prison. Our souls possess knowledge of the Forms before we are born, and with determination, intelligence, and virtue, we can enjoy a blessed communion with the Forms after death.

Aristotle's view of human beings is more complicated. There is some question whether the things he says about this topic can all be harmonized into one account. But the main theme is simple. Man is a "rational animal." The person is not identical with a soul-thing distinct from the body; a person is an animal of a certain special sort. As such, a person has a soul of a certain, very special sort. But the soul is not a thing; it is simply the "form" of the particular sort of body that a man has. Human beings are not "tandem" creatures composed of a "stoker" and a "captain." A person is one unified creature. What we get in Aristotle is a (basically) this-worldly account of the soul.*

---

*See pp. 141–143.

†*Symposium* 211e; see the discussion on pp. 138–140.

*There is a complication here that should be noted. See the discussion of *nous,* later in this chapter.

Relativism and Skepticism

Plato is preoccupied, one might even say obsessed, with the problem of refuting Protagorean relativism and skepticism. This is terribly important to him; it matters enormously. We can sense in his writing the passionate concern to prove these doctrines wrong. Its urgency is the motivational source behind his introduction of the Forms to serve as the unchanging, public objects of knowledge.

Plato is convinced that it was sophistic relativism and skepticism that had really killed Socrates, not the particular members of that jury. It is the views they had come to hold—that every opinion is as true as every other, that what seems good to someone *is* good (for that person), that if it seems right for Athens to condemn Socrates, then it is right. Plato knows in his heart that this is not right. So there must be standards that are more than conventional, standards that are not just *nomos* but have a reality in *physis*. Hence the Forms, the dialectic about morality, the subordination of everything else to the Form of the Good, and his outline of an ideal state. In a sense, this is Plato's *one* problem; it almost seems as if everything else in Plato gets its sense from that one center.

To that problem Aristotle seems almost oblivious, as though it were not on his horizon at all. The explanation may be partly that he believes Plato has succeeded in refuting the skeptics, so it doesn't have to be done again. But there is probably more to it. As a biologist, he knows that not every opinion about crayfish, for example, is equally good, so he isn't overwhelmed by the arguments of the skeptics. So he pursues his research and writes up his results, which, he believes, do constitute knowledge of the sensory world. The only problem, philosophically speaking, is to analyze the processes by which we attain such knowledge and to set out the basic features of the realities disclosed.

Ethics

Plato wants and thinks we can get the same kind of certainty in rules of behavior that we have in mathematics. Dialectic, reasoning about the Forms, can

"It is those who act rightly who get the rewards and the good things in life."

—Aristotle

lead us to moral truths. And the ultimate vision of the Form of the Good will provide a single standard for deciding practical questions. Apprehension of the latter seems to promise, in a flash of insight, the solution for all questions of value—but only for the few specially qualified individuals able to make the tortuous journey out of the Cave.

Characteristically, Aristotle is less inclined to make such grandiose claims. We ought not, he advises, to ask for more certainty in a given subject matter than the subject matter allows. In matters of practical decision, we are not likely to get the same certainty we can get in mathematics. He proceeds, therefore, in a more cautious and specific way, discussing particular virtues and the conditions under which it is and isn't reasonable to hold people responsible for the exercise of these virtues. There is no suggestion that ethical knowledge is something restricted to a small coterie of specially trained experts. The ordinary citizen, he holds, is quite able to make good decisions and to live a good life.* Appeal to the Form of the Good is in any case useless in these matters.

The Greek poet Archilochus had written in the seventh century,

> The fox knoweth many things, the hedgehog one great thing.[3]

Two quite different intellectual styles are exemplified by Plato and Aristotle. Plato is a man with one big problem, one passion, one concern; everything he touches is transformed by that concern. Aristotle has many smaller problems. These are not unrelated to each other, and there is a pattern in his treatment of them all. But he is interested in each for its own sake, not just in terms of how they relate to some grand scheme. Plato is a hedgehog. Aristotle is a fox.

It is quite possible to overdraw this contrast, however. There is a very important respect in which Aristotle is a "Platonist" from beginning to end. He agrees with his teacher without qualification that knowledge—to be knowledge—must be certain and enduring. And for that to be so, knowledge must be of objects that are themselves free from the ravages of time and change. For both Plato and Aristotle, knowledge is knowledge of forms.† But they understand the forms differently—and thereon hangs the tale to come.

Logic and Knowledge

The Sophists' claim to teach their pupils "to make the weaker argument appear the stronger" has been satirized by Aristophanes, scorned by Socrates, and repudiated by Plato. But until Aristotle does his work in logic, no one gives a good answer to the question,

Just what makes an argument weaker or stronger anyway? An answer to this question is absolutely essential for appraising the success of either the Sophists or those who criticize them. Unless you have clear criteria for discriminating weak from strong arguments, bad arguments from good, the whole dispute remains in the air. Are there standards by which we can divide arguments into good ones and bad ones? Aristotle answers this question.

He does not, of course, answer it once and for all—though for two thousand years many people will think he very nearly has. Since the revolution in logic of the last hundred years, we can now say that Aristotle's contribution is not the last word. But it is the first word, and his achievement remains a part of the much expanded science of logic today.

It is undoubtedly due in part to Aristotle's ability to produce criteria distinguishing sound arguments from unsound ones that he can take the sophistic challenge as lightly as he does. To Aristotle, the Sophists can be dismissed as the perpetrators of "sophisms," of bad arguments dressed up to look good. They are not such a threat as they seem, because their arguments can now be *shown* to be bad ones.

But it is not mainly as an unmasker of fraudulent reasoning that Aristotle values logic.* Aristotle thinks of logic as a *tool* to be used in every intellectual endeavor, allowing the construction of valid "accounts" and the criticism of invalid ones. As his universal intellectual tool, logic is of such importance that we need to understand at least the rudiments of Aristotle's treatment of the subject.

It will be useful, however, to work toward the logic from more general considerations. Why should we care about logic? What can it do for us? We need to think again about *wisdom*.

Aristotle begins the work we know as *Metaphysics* with these memorable words:

> All men by nature desire to have knowledge. An indication of this is the delight that we take in the

---

*Here it must be remembered that in Athens there were many slaves and that women were not citizens.

†Note that "form" is here uncapitalized. I will use the capitalized version, Form, only when referring to Plato's independent, eternal reality. For Aristotle's forms, an uncapitalized version of the word will do.

---

*Aristotle does not himself use the term "logic," which is of a later origin. What we now call "logic" is termed by his successors the "organon," or "instrument" for attaining knowledge.

senses; quite apart from the use that we make of them, we take delight in them for their own sake, and more than of any other this is true of the sense of sight. . . . The reason for this is that, more than any other sense, it enables us to get to know things, and it reveals a number of differences between things. (*M* 1.1)[4]

This delight is characteristic even of the lower animals, Aristotle tells us, though their capacities for knowledge are more limited than ours. They are curious and take delight in the senses and in such knowledge as they are capable of. Some of the lower animals, though not all, seem to have *memory,* so that the deliverances of their senses are not immediately lost. Memory produces *experience,* in the sense that one can learn from experience. (We have learned that taking aspirin relieves a headache; we do not totally understand why.) Some of the animals are quite good at learning from experience. Humans, however, are best of all at this; in humans, *universal judgments* can be framed in *language* on the basis of this experience. We not only see numerous black crows and remember them but also form the judgment that all crows are black and use this statement together with others to build up a knowledge of that species of bird.

We regard those among us as wisest, Aristotle says, who know not only that crows are black but also why they are so. Those who are wise, then, have knowledge of the *causes* of things, which allows them to use various arts for practical purposes (as the doctor is able to cure the sick because she knows the causes of their diseases). Knowing the causes, moreover, allows the wise person to teach others how and why things are the way they are.

Wisdom, then, either is or at least involves knowledge. And knowledge involves both *statements* (*that* something is so) and *reasons* (statements *why* something is so). Furthermore, for the possession of such statements to qualify as wisdom, they must be true. As Plato has pointed out, falsehoods cannot constitute knowledge.

It is Aristotle's intention to clarify all this, to sort it out, put it in order, and show how it works. So he has to do several things. He has to (1) explain the nature of *statements*—how, for instance, they are put together out of simpler units called *terms;*

(2) explain how statements can be *related* to each other so that some can give "the reason why" for others; and (3) give an account of what makes statements *true* or *false*. These tasks make up the logic.

Terms and Statements

When Aristotle discusses terms, the basic elements that combine to form statements, he is also discussing the world. In his view, the terms we use can be classified according to the kinds of things they pick out. He insists that things in the world can *be* in a number of different ways.* Correlated with the different kinds of things there are—or different ways things can be—are different kinds of terms. These kinds, called **categories,** are set out this way:

> Every uncombined term indicates substance or quantity or quality or relationship to something or place or time or posture or state or the doing of something or the undergoing of something. (*C* 4)

Aristotle gives some examples:

- Substance—man or horse
- Quantity—two feet long, three feet long
- Quality—white or literate
- Relationship—double, half, or greater
- Place—in the Lyceum, in the marketplace
- Time—yesterday or last year
- Posture—reclining at table, sitting down
- State—having shoes on, being in armor
- Doing something—cutting, burning
- Undergoing something—being cut, being burnt

He does not insist that this is a complete and correct list. But you can see that categories are very general concepts, expressing the various *ways* in which being is manifested. Such distinctions exist and must be observed.

None of these terms is used on its own in any statement, but it is through their combination with one

---

*One of the mistakes made by Parmenides and others, he claims, is failing to recognize that being comes in kinds.

another that a statement comes into being. For every statement is held to be either true or false, whereas no uncombined term—such as "man," "white," "runs," or "conquers"—is either of these. (*C* 4)

Neither "black" nor "crow" is true or false. But "That crow is black" must be one or the other. Terms combine to make statements. For example, we might combine terms from the preceding list to make statements such as these:

- A man is in the Lyceum.
- A white horse was in the marketplace yesterday.
- That man reclining at a table was burning rubbish last year.

Terms can be combined in a wide variety of ways, but there are, Aristotle believes, certain standard and basic forms of combination to which all other combinations can be reduced. This means there is a limited number of basic forms that statements can take.

The clue to discovering these basic forms is noting that every statement is either true or false. Not every *sentence* we utter, of course, is either true or false. "Close the door, please," is neither. It may be appropriate or inappropriate, wise or foolish, but it isn't the right kind of thing to be true or false. It is not, Aristotle would say, a *statement.* Aristotle's own example is a prayer; it is, he says, "a sentence, but it is neither true nor false" (*I* 4).

Statements (the kinds of things that can be true or false) say something. And they say something *about* something. We can then analyze statements in two parts: there is the part indicating what we are talking about, and there is the part indicating what we are saying about it. Call the first part the *subject* and the second part the *predicate.* Every statement, Aristotle believes, displays (or can be reformulated to display) a pattern in which some term plays the role of subject and another term the role of predicate. It will be convenient to abbreviate these parts as *S* and *P*, respectively.

Not every term, however, can play both roles. And this fact is of very great importance for Aristotle, for it allows him to draw the most fundamen-

tal distinction on which his whole view of reality is based.

> What is most properly, primarily, and most strictly spoken of as a substance is what is neither asserted of nor present in a subject—a particular man, for instance, or a particular horse. (*C* 5)

Look back to the list of terms on page 160. There is one kind of term that stands out from the rest: **substance.** Although there are several kinds of substance (as we shall see), the kind that is "properly, primarily, and most strictly" called substance is distinguishable by the kind of role the term for it can play in statements—or rather, the kind of role it *cannot* play. Terms designating such substances can play the role only of subject, never of predicate. They can take only the *S* role in statements, not the *P* role.

Consider the term "Socrates." This term indicates one particular man, namely Socrates himself. And it cannot take the *P* place in a statement; we can say things about Socrates—that he is wise, or snub-nosed—but we cannot use the term "Socrates" to say something about a subject. We cannot, for example, say "Snub-nosed is Socrates," except as a fancy and poetic expression for "Socrates is snub-nosed." In both of these expressions, "Socrates" is in the *S* place and "is snub-nosed" in the *P* position. In both, "is snub-nosed" is used to say something about Socrates. It is not *spatial* position in the sentence that counts, then, but what we could call *logical* position. In a similar way, it is clear that Socrates cannot be "present in" a subject, in the way the color blue can be present in the water of the Aegean Sea or knowledge of Spanish can be present in those who know the language.

Things *are,* Aristotle holds, in all these different ways. Some things have being as qualities, some as relations, some as places, and so on. But among all these, there is one *basic* way in which a thing can be: being an individual substance, a thing, such as Socrates. All the other ways of being are parasitic on this. They are all characteristics of these basic substances; our terms for them express things we can say *about* these primary substances. For example, we can say that Socrates is five feet tall (Quantity), that he is ugly (Quality), that he is twice as heavy as Crito

(Relationship), that he is in prison (Place), and so on. But that about which we say all these things, of which they all are (or may be) true, is some particular individual. And that Aristotle calls *primary substance.*

> The reason why primary substances are said to be more fully substances than anything else is that they are subjects to everything else and that all other things are either asserted of them or are present in them. (*C* 5)

It is clear that Aristotle will reject the Platonic Forms. We shall explore what he says about the Forms more fully later, but here he says that those things which are "more fully substances than anything else" are particular, individual entities such as this man, this horse, this tree, this snail. These are not shadows of more real things, as Plato held; they are the most real things there are. Everything else is real only in relation to them.

For now, however, we want to concentrate not on this metaphysical line of reasoning, but on the logical. Let us review. The wise person is the one who knows—both what is and why it is. Such knowledge is expressed in statements. Statements are composed of terms put together in certain definite ways. All of them either are already or can be reformulated to be subject–predicate statements, in which something is said about something. And the ultimate subjects of statements are primary substances.

Before we leave this topic, we need to note a complication. We can say, "Socrates is a *man.*" This conforms to our *S–P* pattern. But we can also say, "*Man* is an animal." This seems puzzling. How could "man" play the role of both *P* (in the first statement) and *S* (in the second)? If primary substances (individual things) are the ultimate subjects of predication, shouldn't we rule out "Man is an animal" as improper? Yet it is a very common kind of thing to say; indeed, biology is chock full of such statements!

Aristotle solves this problem by distinguishing two senses of "substance."

> But people speak, too, of secondary substances, to which, as species, belong what are spoken of as the primary substances, and to which, as genera, the species themselves belong. For instance, a particu-

lar man belongs to the species "man," and the genus to which the species belongs is "animal." So it is these things, like "man" and "animal," that are spoken of as secondary substances. (*C* 5)

Individual humans, he notes, belong to a *species:* the species man. And each man, each human, is a kind of animal. So "animal" is a *genus,* under which there are many species: humans, lions, whales, and so on. In a sense, then, species and genera are substances, too. They are substances by virtue of expressing the essential nature of primary substances (the individual people, lions, whales). A genus or species, Aristotle holds, has no reality apart from the particular things that make it up, but we can think of it as a derivative kind of substance about which we can say lots of interesting things. Terms for secondary substances, then, can also play the *S* role in a statement.

---

1. What is logic *for?*
2. What is a "category"? Give some examples.
3. What makes a statement different from a term?
4. What two roles can terms play in statements?
5. What distinguishes primary substance from all the other categories?
6. What kind of thing is *most real* for Aristotle? Contrast with Plato.

Truth

So far Aristotle has been dealing with issues of *meaning.* We turn now to what he has to say about *truth.* In one of the most elegant formulations in all philosophy, using only words any four-year-old can understand, Aristotle defines truth.

> To say that what is is not, or that what is not is, is false and to say that what is is, or that what is not is not, is true. (*M* 4.7)

Note that truth pertains to what we say. Grass is green. To say of it that it is green is to say something true about it. To say that it is not green—red or blue, perhaps—is to say something false. Contrariwise, the snail in my garden is not a mathematician.

If I say that it is not a mathematician, I speak truthfully, whereas if I say that it is a mathematician, I speak falsely. Truth represents things as they are. Falsehood says of them that they are other than they are. This view of truth is not the only possible one.* We should, therefore, have a name for it. Let us call it the **correspondence** theory of truth, because it holds that a statement is true just when it "corresponds" to the reality it is about. We can also call it the classical view of truth.

Reasons Why: The Syllogism

We can now say that the wise person is able to make true statements about whatever subject she discusses. But she is able to do more than that; she is able to "give an account" of *why* what she says is true. In Aristotle's terminology, she is able to specify the *causes* of things.

With this we come to logic proper, the study of *reason-giving*. In giving the cause why a certain statement is true, the wise person offers other statements. Will these constitute good reasons for what she claims to know or not? If she is truly wise, they presumably will; but to discover whether someone is wise, we may have to decide (1) whether what she says is true and (2) whether the reasons she offers for what she says actually support her claim. Giving a reason is giving an *argument:* offering premises for a conclusion. Perhaps it will be only a weak argument, perhaps a strong one. How can we tell? Aristotle is committed to the view that we cannot determine the strength of an argument on the basis of how far it convinces us, or even most people. To Aristotle, the Sophist's reliance on persuasiveness as the key to goodness in argument must seem like Euthyphro's third answer to Socrates' questions about piety—that it gives at best a property of good arguments, not the essence of the matter. Aristotle

is trying to find what it is about an argument that explains why people should—or should not—be convinced.

Remember that for Aristotle all statements have an *S–P* form; they all say something about something. Such statements may either affirm that something is the case ("Grass is green") or deny it ("My snail is not a mathematician"). Call the former affirmative statements and the latter negative statements.

Moreover, *S–P* statements may either be about *all* of the subject ("All whales are mammals") or only about *some* of the subject ("Some dogs are vicious"). The former statements can be called *universal,* because they predicate something of each and every item talked about; each and every whale, for instance, is said to be a mammal. The latter statements can be called *particular;* our example does not say something about each and every dog, only about this or that dog or some collection of dogs. These distinctions give us a fourfold classification of statements. It will be useful to draw a chart, with some examples of each.

	Affirmative	Negative
Universal	All men are mortal. (All *S* is *P*)	No men are mortal. (No *S* is *P*)
Particular	Some men are mortal. (Some *S* is *P*)	Some men are not mortal. (Some *S* is not *P*)

There are some interesting logical relationships among these statement forms. For example, a universal affirmative statement is the *contradictory* of a particular negative statement. To say that these are contradictories is to say that if either of them is true, the other must be false; and if either is false, the other must be true. (Look at the following chart and check whether this is so.) Universal negatives and particular affirmatives are likewise contradictories.

---

*For other views of truth, see Hegel's claim that the truth is not to be found in isolated statements, but is only the *whole* of a completed system of knowledge ("Reason and Reality: The Theory of Idealism," in Chapter 17), and the pragmatist view that truth consists of all that a community of investigators would agree upon if they inquired sufficiently long (Chapter 21, p. 584).

The two statements at the top of the Square of Opposition (universal affirmative and negative) cannot be true together, but they can both be false. Analogously, the two statements at the bottom (particular affirmative and negative) can be true together, but they cannot both be false. For ease of reference each of the statement forms is assigned a letter: *A, E, I,* or *O.*

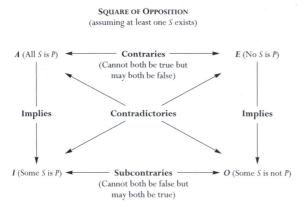

SQUARE OF OPPOSITION
(assuming at least one *S* exists)

A (All *S* is *P*) ←——— **Contraries** ———→ *E* (No *S* is *P*)
(Cannot both be true but
may both be false)

Implies   **Contradictories**   **Implies**

I (Some *S* is *P*) ←——— **Subcontraries** ———→ *O* (Some *S* is not *P*)
(Cannot both be false but
may both be true)

Inferences in this square are called "immediate" inferences because they go from one statement directly or immediately to another. There are also "mediate" inferences, and to these we must now turn. Such inferences constitute arguments in which reasons are given to support a conclusion. Again, an example is useful. Suppose that someone claiming to be wise asserts, "All men are mortal." Remembering that wisdom includes not only knowing truths but also knowing their causes or reasons, we ask her why this is so. In response, she says, "Because animals are mortal, and all men are animals." She has given us an argument.

All animals are mortal.

All men are animals.

Therefore: All men are mortal.

Aristotle calls this kind of argument a **syllogism.** Every syllogism is made up of three statements. In the three statements are three terms (here the terms are "man," "animal," and "mortal"), two terms in each statement. Two of the statements function as reasons for the third. These are the *premises,* and what is to be proved is the *conclusion.*

Consider the terms that occur in the conclusion; each of these occurs also in just one of the premises. And the third term, which Aristotle calls the middle term, occurs once in each of the premises. It is the middle term that links the two terms in the conclusion. The fact that the middle term is related to each of the others in a certain specific way is supposed to be the *cause* or the *reason why* the conclusion is true.

One of Aristotle's greatest achievements is the realization that what makes a syllogism good or bad not only has nothing to do with its persuasiveness, but it also has nothing to do with its subject matter. Its goodness or badness as a piece of reason-giving is completely independent of what it is about. It is not because it is about men and animals rather than gods and spirits that it either is or is not successful. Its success is wholly a matter of its form.* In evaluating a syllogism, we might as well use letters of the alphabet in place of meaningful terms. In fact, this is exactly what Aristotle does. How good an argument is, then, depends only on how terms are related to each other, not on what they are about.

We can represent the relevant structure or form of this example in the following way, using *S* for the subject of the conclusion, *P* for its predicate, and *M* for the middle term that is supposed to link these together.

All *M* is *P.*

All *S* is *M.*

Therefore: All *S* is *P.*

Remember, all that matters is how the terms are related to each other. What the terms mean doesn't matter. This suggests that if our original argument was a good one, any other argument that has this same form will also be a good one. What counts is form, not content.

But what is it for *any* argument to be good? Let us remind ourselves of the point and purpose of giving arguments in the first place. The point is to answer *why.* Any good argument, then, must satisfy

---

*Form is here contrasted with content, or subject matter; it is not the Platonic contrast between the ultimate reality and the world of the senses.

two conditions: (1) The reasons offered (the premises) must be *true;* and (2) the *relation* between the premises and the conclusion must be such that if the premises are true, the conclusion can't possibly be false.* When an argument satisfies the second condition (if the premises are true, the conclusion *must* be true) it is *valid*. (Note that an argument may have that part of logical goodness we call validity even though its premises are false.) A poor argument fails to satisfy at least one of these conditions: Either (1) the premises are *not true,* or (2) the relation between premises and conclusion is not such as to *guarantee* the truth of the conclusion when the premises are true. Poor arguments give poor reasons, then, either in the sense that you shouldn't even believe the reasons (because they aren't true) or in the sense that although the reasons are true they do not provide a *reason why* the conclusion is true.

Now we can ask, is the syllogism above a good argument? It should be obvious that it is. (Not all syllogisms are so obviously either bad or good; Aristotle uses obviously good ones like this as axioms to prove the goodness of less obvious ones.) If it is not obvious, it can easily be made so. Remembering that correctness is a matter of *form,* not content, let us take the terms as names for shapes. Then we can represent the argument in the following way:

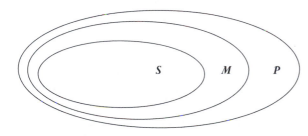

Simply by looking at these shapes, we can now see that if all of *S* is included in *M,* and all of *M* is included in *P,* then all of *S* must be included in *P.* It couldn't be any other way. But that is exactly what a good argument is supposed to do: to show you that, given the truth of the premises, the conclusion must also be true. It gives you a reason why the conclusion is true. So this argument form is a valid one. Since our original argument (1) is an instance of this valid form and (2) has true premises, it is a good argument.

Let us consider another syllogism:

No sparrows are mammals.

No mammals are plants.

Therefore: No sparrows are plants.

Each of these statements is true. But is this a *valid* argument? Do the reasons offered *make true* the conclusion? No. It has this form:

No *S* is *M.*

No *M* is *P.*

Therefore: No *S* is *P.*

If that is a correct argument form, then any other argument having that form must be correct. This suggests a method of testing for goodness in arguments. Try to find another argument that has the same form as this one but that has true premises and a false conclusion. If you can, you have shown that these reasons do *not* guarantee the truth of the conclusion. The middle term is not doing its job of linking the subject and the predicate of the conclusion. So the argument is not a good one. Can we find such an argument? Easy.

No Toyotas are Ferraris.

No Ferraris are inexpensive.

Therefore: No Toyotas are inexpensive.

You can see (check to be sure you do) that this argument has the same form as the argument about sparrows. But here, although the premises are both true, the conclusion is false. In a valid argument, however, the conclusion *must* be true if the premises are true. So this argument is not valid. The reasons offered do not give us the *reason why* the conclusion is true (since it *isn't* true). Since it is form that accounts for goodness in arguments, then if this argument is no good, neither is the one about sparrows—even though the conclusion in that example happens to be true. That is the problem; it just

---

*Note that we are talking about *deductive* arguments here. There are also *inductive* arguments, in which the tie between the premises and the conclusion is a looser one; the premises in an inductive argument give some reason to believe the conclusion, but they fall short of guaranteeing its truth.

happens to be true; it is not true *because* the premises are true. So the argument doesn't do the job that arguments are supposed to do. It doesn't give the *reason why*. It is an *invalid* argument.

On the basis of fairly simple examples such as these, Aristotle develops a complex system of logic. He tries to set out all the correct and all the incorrect forms of reasoning.* The result is a powerful tool both for testing arguments and for constructing arguments that tell us the cause or reason why things are as they are. In its latter use, logic is called *demonstration*. What can be demonstrated, we can know.

Knowing First Principles

Can everything knowable be demonstrated? Can we give reasons for everything? Aristotle's answer is no:

> For it is altogether impossible for there to be proofs of everything; if there were, one would go on to infinity, so that even so one would end up without a proof. (*M* 4.4)

Giving a proof for a statement, as we have seen, means constructing a syllogism; that means finding premises from which the statement logically follows. But we can ask whether there is also a proof for these premises. (Why should we believe *them?*) If so, other syllogisms can be constructed with these premises as their conclusions. But then, what about the premises of these syllogisms? This kind of questioning, like the child's "why?" can go on indefinitely. And so we will continue to be unsatisfied about the truth of the statement we were originally seeking reasons to believe. But this means, as Aristotle says, that "it is impossible for there to be proofs for everything."

The chain of demonstrations must come to an end if we are to have knowledge. But where can it end? Socrates has an answer to this question.† If, as

he thinks, our souls existed before we were born and had lived in the presence of the truth, then we might be able to "recollect" the truth when we were reminded of it. This recollection would not be demonstrative, needing argument and premises and such; it would be an immediate recognition of the truth. But Aristotle cannot use this Socratic solution. As we'll discover, he can see no reason to believe that our souls existed before we were born, nor does he think there are independently existing Forms we could have been acquainted with.

So Aristotle is faced with this problem: Since not everything can be known by demonstration, how do we come to know that which cannot be demonstrated? If we are to avoid an infinite regression, there must be starting points for our proofs.

> The starting point of demonstration is an immediate premise, which means that there is no other premise prior to it. (*PA* 1.2)

We can call these immediate premises *first principles*. If we are to have knowledge by demonstration, our knowledge of these starting points must not be inferior to what we prove from them. In fact, Aristotle says, they must be even better known. About them we must have the most certainty of all.

> Since we know and believe through the first, or ultimate, principles, we know them better and believe in them more, since it is only through them that we know what is posterior to them. . . . This is because true, absolute knowledge cannot be shaken. (*PA* 1.2)

This means that we must be more certain about what makes something an animal than about what makes something a monkey; in geometry, we must know the definition of line with greater clarity than that of isosceles triangle.

But how are such principles to be known? We can't just start from nothing and—by a leap—get to knowledge. In this respect Socrates was right.

> All instruction and all learning through discussion proceed from what is known already. (*PA* 1.1)

This seems paradoxical. It is as though we were required to know *something* prior to our coming to know *anything*. But this is impossible.

---

*Aristotle is mistaken in thinking that syllogisms of this sort exhaust the forms of correct reasoning; we now know that there are many more correct forms. He also neglects, or gives an inadequate picture of, so-called inductive reasoning. But his achievement is impressive nonetheless.

†Discussed on pp. 101–102.

The key to resolving the paradox, Aristotle holds, is not the preexistence of the soul but the recognition that things may be "known" in several senses. What Aristotle does is to show how knowledge of these first principles *develops*. This is a characteristically Aristotelian tactic. Instead of saying that we either know or we don't know, Aristotle shows us how knowledge develops from implicit to more and more explicit forms. What is presupposed is not full-blown, explicit, and certain knowledge (such as Socrates supposed the soul had in its preexistence), but a series of stages, beginning in a *capacity* of a certain sort. Though it is incredible to think that we are born knowing how to double a square (and just can't remember it), it makes good sense to think we are born with capacities of various kinds. One relevant capacity, moreover, human knowers share with other animals. Knowing begins in perceiving.

Aristotle agrees with Plato that perceiving something is not the same as knowing it. The object of perception is always an individual thing, but knowledge is of the universal; perception can be mistaken, but knowledge cannot. But these facts don't lead Aristotle, as they lead Plato, to disparage the senses, to cut them off from reality, and to install knowledge in another realm altogether. Perception is not knowledge, but it is where knowledge begins. (It is surely of crucial importance to note here that when Plato thinks of knowledge, his first thought is of mathematics; when Aristotle thinks of knowledge, his first thought is of biology.)

We noted earlier that some animals have memory in addition to their faculties of sense perception. Thus they can retain traces of what they perceive in their encounters with the environment. These traces build up into what Aristotle calls "experience." And experience is the source of a *universal,* a sense of the unity of the many things encountered. Aristotle compares it to a rout ending in battle: individual men are fleeing, each in his own way (many perceptions are pouring into the soul); one turns and stands (memory), then another (solidifying the memory), and another (experience), until finally a battle line is formed (One is made out of Many).

As soon as one individual percept "has come to a halt" in the soul, this is the first beginning of the presence there of a universal. . . . Then other "halts" occur among these (proximate) universals, until the indivisible genera or (ultimate) universals are established. E.g., a particular species of animal leads to the genus "animal," and so on. Clearly it must be by induction that we acquire knowledge of the primary premises, because this is also the way in which sense-perception provides us with universals.[5]

How do we come to know the first principles, from which demonstrations may then proceed? By **induction,** Aristotle tells us. Imagine the biologist observing creatures in a tidal pool. At first, she can distinguish only a few kinds, those very different from each other. As she keeps watching very closely, new differences (as well as new similarities) become apparent. She begins to group these creatures according to their similarities, bringing the Many under a variety of Ones. Then all these Ones are united under further universal principles, until finally all are classified under the One heading of "animals." "Is this like the one I saw a moment ago? Yes. So there is that kind; and that is different from this kind. Still, they are alike in a certain respect, so they may be species of the same genus. . . ." Eventually, the biologist comes to group the creatures according to characteristics they do and do not share with each other. Her perception provides her with "universals" under which she groups or organizes the various kinds of things that she has been observing.

These universals provide something like definitions of the natural kinds of things that exist. The wider one's experience of a certain field, the more firmly these inductive definitions are grounded. The first principles of any field are arrived at in this way. Thus we can come to know what a plant is, what an animal is, what a living being is. And these definitions can serve as the starting points, the ultimate principles of any science.

Not everything, as we have seen, can be known by demonstration. What cannot be demonstrated must be grasped some other way. That way is induction from sense perceptions. But what is there in us that is capable of such a grasp? It is clearly not the senses, nor memory, nor even experience. On the other hand, it is not our reasoning ability, for the capacity in question has nothing to do with proof. Aristotle uses a term for this capacity of ours that has no very adequate English counterpart: **nous**. It is sometimes translated as "mind" and sometimes as "intuition"; the English term "mind" seems too broad and "intuition" too vague. *Nous* is the name for that ability we have to grasp first principles by abstracting what is essential from many particular instances present to our senses.*

1. What is truth?
2. What is an argument? A syllogism? A middle term?
3. What is required in a good argument?
4. What is a first principle? Why are first principles needed? How are they known?
5. Do Aristotle's reflections on first principles do anything to resolve the puzzle about the slave boy and the preexistence of the soul? Explain.

The World

Aristotle discusses his predecessors often and in detail.† He believes that something can be learned from all of them and that by showing where they go wrong we can avoid their mistakes and take a better path. Such a dialectical examination of the older philosophers does not amount to knowledge, for it is neither demonstration of a truth nor insight into first principles. But it clears the ground for both and is therefore of considerable importance.

His fundamental conviction about the work of his predecessors is that they go wrong by not *observing* closely enough. With the possible exception of Socrates and certain of the Sophists who were interested in other things, they had all been searching for explanations that would make the world intelligible. But these explanations either are excessively general (Thales' water, Anaximander's Boundless, and the rather different *logos* of Heraclitus), or seem to conclude that there is no intelligibility in the world at all (Parmenides condemns the world to the status of mere appearance, and Plato believes only the Forms are completely intelligible). Even Democritus, who was from a theoretical point of view superior to all but Plato, misses the intelligibility in the observable world and tries to find it in the unobservable atoms.

Aristotle, drawing on his own careful observations, is convinced that the things that make up the world have principles of intelligibility *within* them.* In order to explain their nature, their existence, and the changes they regularly undergo, it is necessary only to pay close attention to *them*. The world as it offers itself to our perception is not an unintelligible, chaotic flux from which we must flee to find knowledge. It is made up of things—the primary substances—that are ordered; the principles of their order are internal to them, and these principles, through perception, can be known.

Nature

What Aristotle calls "nature" is narrower than what we have been calling "the world." Within the world there are two classes of things: *artifacts,* which are things made for various purposes by people (and by some animals), and "nature-facts." There are beds, and there are boulders. These two classes differ in important respects. The basic science concerned with the world (what Aristotle calls "physics") deals with boulders, but only in a derivative sense with

---

*Do we really have such a faculty? Can we get certainty about premises from which the rest of our knowledge can be logically derived? Modern philosophy from the seventeenth century on will be preoccupied with these questions. What if we can't? Are we thrown back again into that sophistic skepticism and relativism from which both Plato and Aristotle thought they had delivered us? See, for example, Montaigne, who thinks we are ("Skeptical Thoughts Revived," in Chapter 12) and Descartes, who is certain we are not (*Meditations*).

†In, for example, *Physics* I and *Metaphysics* I: The book you are now reading is itself an example of the Aristotelian conviction expressed in the next sentence.

---

*In this regard, Aristotle is carrying on the tradition begun by Thales but improving on it by making explanations more specific and detailed. See the discussion of Thales' remark, "All things are full of gods," p. 11.

beds. Aristotle draws the distinction in the following way:

> Of the things that exist, some exist by nature, others through other causes. Those that exist by nature include animals and their parts, plants, and simple bodies like earth, fire, air, and water—for of these and suchlike things we do say that they exist by nature. All these obviously differ from things that have not come together by nature; for each of them has in itself a source of movement and rest. This movement is in some cases movement from place to place, in others it takes the forms of growth and decay, in still others of qualitative change. But a bed or a garment or any other such kind of thing has no natural impulse for change—at least, not insofar as it belongs to its own peculiar category and is the product of art. (*PH* 2.1)

Of course, beds and garments change, too. But they change not because they are beds and garments but because they are made of natural things such as wood and wool. It is by virtue of being wood that the bedstead develops cracks and splinters, not by virtue of being a bedstead. The sword rusts not because it is a sword but because it is made of iron.

Nature, then, is distinguished from art and the products of art because it "has in itself a source of movement and rest." We should note that Aristotle understands "movement" here in a broad sense: there is (1) movement from place to place, also called local motion; (2) growth and decay; and (3) change in qualities. (We usually call only the first of these "movement.") Natural things, then, change in these ways because of what they are. An artifact like a bed may move from place to place, but only if someone moves it; it does not grow or decay; and any change in its qualities is due either to some external activity (I paint my bed red) or to a property of the natural substance it is made of (the wood in the bedstead fades from dark to light brown). By contrast, a beaver moves about from place to place on its own, is born, matures, becomes wiser with age, and dies because this is the *nature* of beavers.

Nature, then, is the locus of change. Aristotle is convinced that if we only observe closely enough, we can understand the principles governing these changes. Nature is composed of primary substances that are the *subjects* of change. They change in two ways: (1) they come into being and pass away again; (2) while in existence, they vary in quality, quantity, relation, place, and so on. About natural substances we can have knowledge. And because Aristotle agrees with his teacher Plato that knowledge is always knowledge of the real, it follows that nature is as real as anything could be!

The Four "Becauses"

The wise person, as we have seen, knows not only what things are but also why. Aristotle sees that all his predecessors are asking why things are the way they are and giving these answers: because of water, because of the Boundless, because of opposition and the *logos,* because of atoms and the void, because of the Forms. What none of them sees is that this is not one question but four distinct questions.

> Some people regard the nature and substance of things that exist by nature as being in each case the proximate element inherent in the thing, this being itself unshaped; thus, the nature of a bed, for instance, would be wood, and that of a statue bronze. Antiphon produces as evidence of this the fact that if you were to bury a bed, and the moisture that got into it as it rotted gained enough force to throw up a shoot, it would be wood and not a bed that came into being. For his view is that its arrangement according to the rules of an art, is an accidental attribute, whereas its substance is what remains permanently, and undergoes all these changes. (*PH* 2.1)

People who think this way identify the substance of a thing—its nature—with the element or elements it is made of. Thales, for instance, thinks that the nature of all things is water; everything else is nonessential, just accidental ways in which the underlying substance happens, for a time, to be arranged. The underlying substratum, however, is eternal; that is the real stuff!

Those who think this way are taking the why-question in one very specific sense. They answer, "Because it is made of such and such stuff." Aristotle does not want to deny that this is one very proper answer to the why-question. Why is this statue what it is? Because it is made of bronze. The answer points to the *matter* from which it is made. Let us call this kind of answer to the why-question the *material cause*. Material causes, then, are one type of **causation.**

But citing a material cause does not give a complete answer to the why-question. That should be obvious enough; lots of bronze is not formed into statues. Consider some wood that has not been made into a bed. We could call such wood a "potential bed," but it is not yet a *bed*. It is the same, he says,

> with things that come together by nature; what is potentially flesh or bone does not yet have its own nature until it acquires the form that accords with the formula, by means of which we define flesh and bone; nor can it be said at this stage to exist by nature. So in another way, nature is the shape and form of things that have a principle of movement in themselves—the form being only theoretically separable from the object in question. (*PH* 2.1)

Bone is what accords with "the formula" for bone—the definition that sets out the essential characteristics of bone. The elements of which bone is composed are not yet themselves bone; they are at best potential bone and may be formed into bone. In the case of bronze, there is no statue until it takes the shape of a statue. So here is another reason why a thing is the thing it is: It satisfies the requirements for being that sort of thing.

Aristotle here uses the term "form" both for the shape of something simple like a statue and for the definition of more complex things like bone. This is in accord with the usage for the term that comes down from Socrates and Plato. However, Aristotle adds this qualification: "the form being only theoretically separable from the object in question." He means that we can consider just the form of some substance independently of the material stuff that makes it up; but we must not suppose on that account that the form really is separable from the thing. Aristotle's forms are not Plato's Forms. The form of a thing is not an independent object, but just its-having-the-characteristics-that-make-it-the-thing-that-it-is.

So we can answer the why-question in a second way by citing the form. Why is this bit of stuff bone? Because it has the characteristics mentioned

in the definition of bone. Aristotle calls this the *formal cause.*

But there must be something else, particularly in cases where a substance such as a mouse or a man comes into being. There is the material stuff out of which mice and men are made, and each has its proper form. But what explains the fact of their *coming to be?*

> Thus, the answer to the question "why?" is to be given by referring to the matter, to the essence, and to the proximate mover. In cases of coming-to-be it is mostly in this last way that people examine the causes; they ask what comes to be after what, what was the immediate thing that acted or was acted upon, and so on in order. (*PH* 2.7)

Here is a third answer to the why-question. This answer names whatever triggered the beginning of the thing in question, what Aristotle calls the "proximate mover." This sense of cause comes closest to our modern understanding of causes. For Aristotle, though, such causes are always themselves substances ("man generates man"), whereas for us causes tend to be conditions, events, or happenings. This cause is often called the *efficient cause.*

There is one more sense in which the why-question can be asked. We might be interested in the "what for" of something, particularly in the case of artifacts. Suppose we ask, "Why are there houses?" One answer is that cement and bricks and lumber and wallboard exist. Without them (or something analogous to them) there wouldn't be any houses. This answer cites the material cause.

Another answer is that there are things which satisfy the definition for a house, an answer naming the formal cause. A third answer cites the fact that there are house builders—the efficient cause. But even if we had all these answers, we would not be satisfied. What we want to know is why there are houses in the sense of what purpose they serve, what ends they satisfy.

Why are there houses? To provide shelter from the elements for human beings. If it were not for this purpose they serve, there would be no such things; the materials for houses might exist, but they would not have come together in the sort of form that makes a house a house. When we answer the why-question in this way, Aristotle says we are giving the *final cause.**

> It is clear, then, that there are causes, and that they are as many in number as we say; for they correspond to the different ways in which we can answer the question "why?" The ultimate answer to that question can be reduced to saying what the thing is . . . or to saying what the first mover was . . . or to naming the purpose . . . or, in the case of things that come into being, to naming the matter. . . . Since there are these four causes, it is the business of the natural scientist to know about them all, and he will give his answer to the question "why?" in the manner of a natural scientist if he refers what he is being asked about to them all—to the matter, the form, the mover, and the purpose. (*PH* 2.7)

Is There Purpose in Nature?

The most controversial of the four "becauses" is the last. We say there is a purpose for artifacts (houses, for example), but only because human beings have purposes. We need, want, desire shelter; so we form an intention that shelters should exist. We think, plan, and draw up a blueprint, then gather the materials together and assemble a house. But the crucial thing here is the intention—without that, no houses. To say that there are final causes in nature seems like imputing intentions to nature. We might be able to answer the question, What is a

sheep dog for? because sheep dogs serve our purposes. But does it even make sense to ask what *dogs* are for?[6] In a humorous sketch Bill Cosby asks, "Why is there air?" He answers: to have something to blow up basketballs with. But that is obviously a joke.

Yet Aristotle holds seriously that the question about final causes applies to nature-facts just as much as to artifacts. There may be some things that are accidental by-products (two-headed calves and such), and they may not have a purpose. Such accidents, he says, occur merely from "necessity." But accidents apart, he thinks nature-facts are inherently purposive.

Aristotle does not think that there are *intentions* resident in all things; intentions are formed after deliberation, and only rational animals can deliberate. But that does not mean that nature in general is devoid of *purposes,* for the concept of purpose is broader than that of intention.

> Of things that come to be, some serve a purpose, others do not; of those that do, some come to be in accordance with an intention, others do not, although in both cases they serve a purpose. Plainly, then, even apart from things that happen according to necessity, or to what is usual, there are some things that can have a purpose. Things that serve a purpose include everything that might have been done intentionally, and everything that proceeds from nature. When such things come to be accidentally, we say that they are as they are by chance. (*PH* 2.5)

But why couldn't everything in nature happen by chance, without purpose, according to sheer necessity? This is what Democritus thinks the world is like—the accidental product of the necessary hooking up of atoms.* Why is that a mistake?

Aristotle has two arguments. (1) He draws on his close observations of nature to conclude that

> all natural objects either always or usually come into being in a given way, and that is not the case with anything that comes to be by chance. (*PH* 2.8)

Chance or accident makes sense only against a background of regularity, of what happens "either always

---

*Compare Socrates' answer to the question about why he is in prison, p. 131.

*See pp. 32–33.

or usually." Roses come from roses and not from grains of wheat; therefore, a rose coming from a rose is no accident. But since everything must occur either by chance or for a purpose, it must happen for some purpose. (2) Art (meaning something like the art of the physician or house builder) either completes nature or "imitates nature." But there is purpose in art, so there must be purpose in nature as well.*

Teleology

The idea that natural substances are *for* something is called **teleology,** from the Greek word *telos,* meaning end or goal. We can get a better feel for this by thinking about a concrete example. Consider a frog. Let it be a common leopard frog such as children like to catch by the lake in the summertime. We can consider the frog from two points of view: (1) at a given time we can examine a kind of cross section of its history, and (2) we can follow its development through time.

At the moment when he is caught by little Johnny, the frog has certain characteristics. Johnny might list them as spottedness, four-leggedness, and hoppiness. A biologist would give us a better list amounting to a definition of what a frog is. This "what-it-is" the frog shares with all other frogs; it is what makes it a frog rather than a toad or a salamander. This is what Aristotle calls its form.

But of course it is one particular frog, the one Johnny caught this morning. It is not "frog in general," or "all the frog there is." What makes it the particular individual that it is? Surely it is the matter composing it; this frog is different from the one Sally caught, because even though they share the same form, each is made up of different bits of matter.

So in a cross section it is possible to distinguish form from matter. But now let us look at the history of the frog. Each and every frog develops from a fertilized egg into a tadpole and then into an adult frog. At each of these temporal stages, moreover, one can distinguish form and matter. The egg is mat-

ter that satisfies the definition for eggs; the tadpole has the form for tadpoles; the frog satisfies the formula for frogs. These stages are related in a regular, orderly way. As Aristotle puts it, this development is something that happens "always or usually." There is a determinate pattern in this history. And it is always the same.

In the egg, Aristotle will say, there is a potentiality to become a frog. It won't become a toad. It has, so to speak, a direction programmed into it. There is a goal or end *in* the egg, which is what determines the direction of development. The term for this indwelling of the goal is **entelechy.** The goal, or *telos,* is present in the egg. The goal (being a frog) is not present in actuality, of course — otherwise, the egg would not be an egg but already a frog. The egg has *actually* the form for an egg, but the form frog is there *potentially.* If it were not, Aristotle would say, the egg might turn into anything! (Note that the final cause toward which the egg and tadpole develop is itself a form; the goal is to actualize the form of a frog.)

This indwelling of the end, entelechy, is what Aristotle means by the purpose that is in natural things. Such things have purpose in the sense that there is a standard direction of development for them; they move toward an end. Natural things, particularly living things, look in two directions. They look back to earlier forms (which contained the later forms potentially) and forward to still later forms (which they contain potentially). Earlier forms of a substance are already potentially what they will actually become only later. The tadpole is the potentiality of there being an actual frog. The frog is the actuality the tadpole tends toward.

Science, Aristotle says, can grasp not only the nature of static and eternal things, such as Plato's

---

*Are these sound arguments? A key move in the development of modern science is their rejection. See p. 315.

Forms, but also the natural laws of development. These laws are universals, too. Knowledge is always of the universal, of forms; in this Plato was right. But the forms are not outside the natural world; they are within it, guiding and making intelligible the changes that natural substances undergo either always or usually. The concepts of the four causes, plus actuality and potentiality, are the tools by which science can succeed in its task of understanding the natural world.

Once again we see a philosopher forging linguistic tools to make intelligible what seemed unintelligible to earlier thinkers. Parmenides, working only with concepts of being and not being, argued that change was impossible.* Aristotle uses the concepts of potentiality and actuality to discern universal laws governing orderly and intelligible change. Philosophy is argument and reason-giving. But it is also creation and invention, requiring the imagination to envision new conceptual possibilities.

---

1. How do nature-facts differ from artifacts? In what ways are they similar?
2. Explain each of the four causes.
3. How are Aristotle's forms both like and unlike Plato's Forms?
4. Describe how Aristotle uses the concepts of form/matter and actuality/potentiality to gain an understanding of the natural world, for example, of a frog.

First Philosophy

It is from a feeling of wonder that men start now, and did start in the earliest times, to practice philosophy. (*M* 1.2)

Practicing philosophy, Aristotle makes clear, is not the basic activity of human beings. They must first see to the necessities of life, and only when these are reasonably secure will they have the leisure to pursue wisdom. The wise person, as we have seen,

wishes to know, wishes to know everything, and wishes to know the causes in every case. So far does human wonder go.

There need not be any practical payoff to such knowledge. Indeed, Aristotle is quite convinced that there will not be. There are, of course, practical sciences such as medicine, which do have practical consequences. But the most uniquely human pursuit of knowledge is characterized by a delight in knowing "for its own sake." In a certain sense, Aristotle says, this pursuit is "more than human, since human nature is in many respects enslaved" (*M* 1.2). So much of our activity is devoted to the necessities of just staying alive that we are enslaved to the needs of our own nature. The knowledge that does nothing more than satisfy wonder, in contrast, is more than human because it would be free from this bondage. It is akin to the knowledge god would have. In our quest for such "divine" knowledge, we would have as our main concern those things that are "first" or "primary" or independent of everything else. We could call such a search "first philosophy."

Familiar as we are with the world of nature, we wonder now whether that is all there is.

If there is no other substance apart from those that have come together by nature, natural science will be the first science. But if there is a substance that is immovable, the science that studies it is prior to natural science and is the first philosophy. . . . It is the business of this science to study being qua being, and to find out what it is and what are its attributes qua being. (*M* 6.1)

Biology, we might say, studies *being qua* (as) *living being;* or to put it another way, the biologist is interested in *what there is* just insofar as it is *alive.* There are in fact a variety of sciences, theoretical and practical, each of which cuts out a certain area of what there is—of being—for study. Each such science brings its subject matter together under some unifying first principles. And this question must inevitably arise: Is there some still higher unity to what there is? Is being *one*? Is it unified by some principles that are true of it throughout?

If so, this too must be an area of knowledge, and the wise person's wonder will not be satisfied until it is canvassed and understood. This science would

*See p. 27.

be concerned with the characteristics or attributes of being in an unqualified sense: of being qua being. If there is such a science, it is "first" in the sense that it would examine the principles taken for granted by all the special sciences. It would ask about the ultimate causes of all things. If, says Aristotle, natural substances are the only ones there are, then natural science will be this first science or philosophy. But if there are other substances—ones not subject to change—then the science that studies those will be first philosophy.* So first philosophy, also called *metaphysics,* looks for the ultimate principles and causes of all things. What are they?

Not Plato's Forms

As we have seen, Plato gives an answer to this very question. The ultimate realities are the Forms, he says, and ultimately the Form of the Good. But Aristotle criticizes this answer severely. Not only are the Forms subject to the Third Man problem, they present many other difficulties.† Let us briefly explore some of them.

1. The things of this world are supposed to derive their reality from their "participation" in the Forms. But nowhere does Plato explain just what this "participation" amounts to. Without such an account, however, all we have are "empty phrases" and "poetic metaphors" (*M* 1.9).

2. The Forms are themselves supposed to be substantial realities—indeed, the most real of all the things there are. Aristotle's comment is this:

> In seeking to find the causes of the things that are around us, they have introduced another lot of objects equal in number to them. It is as if someone who wanted to count thought that he would not

be able to do so while the objects in question were relatively few, and then proceeded to do so when he had made them more numerous. (*M* 1.9)

To say that the Form Human is the cause of humans is simply to multiply the entities needing explanation. If it is difficult to explain the existence and nature of human beings, it is certainly no easier to explain the existence and nature of humans-plus-the-Form-Human.

3. The Forms are supposed to be what many individuals of the same kind have in common. Yet they are also supposed to be individual realities in their own right. But, says Aristotle, these requirements conflict. If the Forms are indeed individual substances, it makes no sense to think of them being shared out among other individual substances.* If, on the other hand, they are universal in character (nonindividual), there is no sense in thinking of them as things that exist separately from particulars. Being-a-man, Aristotle holds, is realized not in a substantial Form independently of all men, but precisely and only in *each individual man.* Because the "friends of the Forms" are unable to explain how such substances are both individual and universal,

> they make them the same in form as perishable things (since we know them), talking of "the man himself" and "the horse itself," just adding the word "self" to the names of sensible objects. (*M* 7.16)

But this is completely useless as an explanation.

4. Finally, there is no way to understand how the Forms, eternally unchanging, account for changes. They are supposed to be the first principles and causes of whatever happens in the world. But

> one is most of all bewildered to know what contribution the forms make either to the sensible things that are eternal or to those that come into being and perish; for they are not the cause of their movement or of any change in them. (*M* 1.9)

By "the sensible things that are eternal," Aristotle means the things in the natural world whose movement is (as he thought) regular and everlasting: the

---

*Aristotle seems to be assuming here that the cause that accounts for the entire world of changing substances cannot itself just be a changing substance; if it were, it would itself need accounting for. So it must be—if it exists—something unchanging. If nature is defined as the sphere of those things that change because of a source of movement or change within them, an ultimate, unchanging cause of natural things would be beyond nature.
†Review the Third Man argument on pp. 153–154.

---

*Review the discussion of substance on pp. 161–162.

sun, moon, and the fixed stars. How can eternally stable Forms explain change either in these things or in the even more unstable items on earth?

The outcome of Aristotle's critical appraisal of his master's metaphysics is a thoroughgoing rejection of the Forms. The fundamental things that exist have to be things that are *individual* and can exist *independently* of other things. Plato's Forms do not satisfy either requirement. The Forms are supposed to be the common features of things that are individual, but such features, Aristotle believes, have no independent being; they depend for such being as they have on individual substances (of which they are the qualities, relations, and so on). The sensible things of nature, humans and beavers, surely exist; but being mortal and having a broad, flat tail are qualities existing only as modifications of these. Whether anything beyond these individual entities exists is still an open question. But if it does, it too will be substantial, individual, and capable of independent existence. It will not be a "common feature" of individual things.*

What of Mathematics?

The most convincing arguments for the Forms seem to be mathematical in nature. Socrates is not talking about his sand figure, so Plato concludes that Socrates is talking about the Square Itself, the Triangle Itself, and the Equal. Aristotle wishes to avoid drawing this conclusion. So how does he deal with mathematics?

The natural scientist, in studying changeable things, deals with subjects like the shape of the moon and the sphericity of the earth.

> Such attributes as these are studied by mathematicians as well as by natural scientists, but not by virtue of their being limits of natural bodies. The mathematician is not interested in them as attributes of whatever they are attributes of, and so he separates them. For these attributes can be conceptually separated from movement, without this sep-

aration making any difference or involving any false statement. (*PH* 2.2)

The crucial point is that we can "conceptually" separate attributes of things and consider them on their own, without supposing that they must be independent things. To use one of Aristotle's favorite examples, consider a snub nose. As a natural thing, a nose is a compound made up of form and matter; as such, it is of interest to the natural scientist but not to the mathematician. What makes it "snub," though, is its being curved in a certain way. And we can consider the curve alone, abstracting away from the matter in the nose. When we do this, we are taking up the mathematician's point of view. But the fact that we can adopt this viewpoint does not mean that Curvedness exists independently of noses. There need be no Form of the Curve to make mathematics intelligible.

There is no argument, Aristotle holds, from knowledge in mathematics to the reality of Platonic Forms independent of the world of nature. Mathematics is a science that, like natural science, has the world of nature as its only object. But it does not study it *as nature;* it studies only certain abstractions from natural things, without supposing that such abstractions are themselves things.

Substance and Form

When we considered Aristotle's categories, it was already apparent that certain terms were more basic than others.* These terms picked out substances and could play only the subject role in a statement. Now Aristotle reinforces this conclusion, looking more directly at things themselves.

> There are many ways in which the term "being" is used, corresponding to the distinctions we drew earlier, when we showed in how many ways terms are used. On the one hand, it indicates what a thing is and that it is this particular thing; on the other, it indicates a thing's quality or size, or whatever else is asserted of it in this way. Although "being" is used in all these ways, clearly the primary kind of

---

*We can think of these reflections as a critique of Plato's metaphysical argument for the Forms (see p. 123). In the following section, Aristotle examines the epistemological argument.

*See pp. 160–161.

being is what a thing is; for it is this alone that indicates substance. . . . All other things are said to be only insofar as they are quantities, qualities, affections, or something else of this kind belonging to what is in this primary sense. (*M* 7.1)

We can ask many different questions about any given thing: How old is it? How large is it? What color is it? What shape is it? Is it alive? Does it think? Answers to each of these questions tell us something about the thing in question, describing a way the thing *is,* saying something about its *being.* But one question, Aristotle argues, is basic, namely, What is it? We may learn that it is thirty years old, six feet tall, white, fat, and thinking of Philadelphia, but until we learn that it is a *man* all these answers hang in the air. Aristotle puts it this way: that answer gives us the "substance." And substance is *what is,* in the basic, fundamental, primary sense.

This is the first answer to the metaphysical question about being qua being. For something to be, in the primary sense, is for it to be a substance. Whatever exists is dependent on substance. But more must be said. What is it that makes a given object a substance?

If we think back to the discussion of nature, we recall that natural things are composed of matter and form (the latter being expressed in a formula or definition). Could it be the matter that makes an object a substance? No. Matter, considered apart from form, is merely potentially something. If you strip off all form, you are tempted to say that what is left is sheer, undifferentiated, characterless something. But even that would be wrong, because every "something" has some character or form that differentiates it from something else. This "prime matter" can't be anything at all, on its own. It cannot have an independent existence; it exists only *as formed.* So matter cannot be what accounts for, or what makes or causes, something to be a substance. For what accounts for something being a substance must be at least as substantial as the substances it produces.

What of the other alternative? Could it be form that makes a portion of being into a substance? In a series of complex arguments, Aristotle argues that this is in fact the case. But not just any form makes the substance *what it is.* The form responsible for

the substantiality of substances he calls the **essence** of the thing. *Essences* are expressed by definitions telling us *what things are.*

Johnny's frog may weigh five ounces, but weighing five ounces is not part of the essence of that frog. The proof is that if the frog eats well and gains weight, it does not cease to be a frog. What makes it a frog remains the same whether it weighs five, six, or seven ounces. The definition of frog allows a variation in many of the qualities and quantities Johnny's frog might have. But not in all. It could not cease to be amphibious and still be a frog. Amphibiousness is part of the essence of what it is to be a frog. All natural things (and artifacts, too), Aristotle holds, have an essence: a set of characteristics without which they would not be the things they are.

> Why, for instance, are these materials a house? Because of the presence of the essence of house. One might also ask, "Why is this, or the body containing this, a man?" So what one is really looking for is the cause—that is, the form—of the matter being whatever it is; and this in fact is the substance. (*M* 7.17)

We are, remember, looking for first principles and causes. We want to know what it is that makes a bit of matter what it is. We know that natural things are substances; they can exist independently and individually. But what makes this bunch of bricks a house, this mass of protoplasm a human? The answer is that each satisfies the definition of the essence of that thing. The presence of the essence house in the one case and the essence human in the other is the *cause* of each one being what it is.

So here we come to a second answer. Even more basic than substances composed of form and matter is the form itself. The cause of something could not be less real than the thing itself. So we find Aristotle asserting that this form—essence—is the very substance of substance itself.

In a way, this should be no surprise. Thinking back to the account Aristotle gives of natural substances, we can see how prominent form is. There are four causes, four explanations of why something is the particular substance it is. The material cause cannot be fundamental, as we have seen. But think about the other three: the form or essence of the thing; the final cause or goal, which is itself a form; and the efficient cause. Even this latter must involve a form, for it must be something actual, and actualities always embody form; as Aristotle likes to say, "man begets man." From all three points of view, then, form is the principal cause of the substantiality of things.

Aristotle gives us a simple example. Consider a syllable, *ba*. What makes this a syllable? There is the "matter" that makes it up: the elements *b* and *a*. But it is not the matter that makes these into the syllable *ba*, for these elements might also compose *ab*. So it must be the form. Moreover, the form cannot itself be an element, or we would need to explain how it is related to the *b* and the *a* (that is, we would have the Third Man problem). So the form must be something else.

> But this "something else," although it seems to be something, seems not to be an element; it seems in fact to be the cause of . . . that [the *b* and the *a*] being a syllable . . . ; in each case it is the thing's substance, since that is the ultimate cause of a thing's being. (*M* 7.17)

So form is the substance of things. But substance is what can exist independently and as an individual entity. This raises a very interesting possibility. Might there be substances that are not compounds of matter and form? Might there be substances that are *pure forms*?

All of nature is made up of material substances in which matter is made into something definite by the presence of form within it. But might there be something more fundamental than nature itself, in just the way that form is more basic than the compounds it forms? If there were any such substances, knowledge of them might be what the wise person seeks. Wisdom is knowing the being and causes of things. If there were substances of pure form, they would be less dependent and more basic than the things of nature, since even natural things depend on form for their substantiality. Knowledge of such "pure" substances would therefore be the knowledge most worth having, the most divine knowledge; it would satisfy our wonder in the highest degree. We need now to explore this possibility.

Pure Actualities

One thing is clear. If there are such purely formal substances, without any matter, they would be pure *actualities* as well. They couldn't involve any "might be's," for the principle of potentiality is matter and they would have no matter. Nor could such substances admit of any change, for every change is a movement from something potential to something actual (for example, from tadpole into frog). But then it would be *eternal* as well.

A second thing is also clear. These would be the *best* things. Why? Think again about natural things, for example, the frog that Johnny caught. When is that frog at its very best? Surely when it is most froggy—hopping around, catching flies, doing all the things frogs most typically do. It is not at its best when it has a broken leg, nor when it is feeling listless, nor when it is a mere tadpole. In Aristotle's terms, the frog is best when the form that makes it a frog (the essence) is most fully actualized in the matter—when it most fully is *what it is*. If there are substances lacking matter and potency altogether, substances that are fully actual, then they must be the best substances. For they cannot fail to display all the perfection of their form.

But are there any such substances—perfect, immaterial, and eternal—pure actualities without the possibility of change? If so, what are they like?

God

In the world of nature, the best things would be those that come closest to these ideals. Aristotle believes these are the heavenly bodies that move eternally in great circles. They change their positions constantly, but in a perfectly regular way, without beginning or ending.[*] But even such eternal motion is not self-explanatory.

---

[*]His reasons for thinking so are complex, involving a theory of the nature of time; we will not discuss that theory here. It can be found in *Physics* IV, 10–14. His theory was combined with the astronomy of the second-century Alexandrian, Ptolemy, and was to dominate scientific thinking until the beginnings of modern science in the sixteenth century. For a fuller discussion of this Aristotelian / Ptolemaic theory of the universe, see "The World God Made for Us," in Chapter 12.

There is something that is always being moved in an incessant movement, and this movement is circular . . . : and so the first heaven will be eternal. There must, then, be something that moves it. But since that which is moved, as well as moving things, is intermediate, there must be something that moves things without being moved; this will be something eternal, it will be a substance, and it will be an actuality. (*M* 12.7)

Think about baseball. A bat may impart movement to a ball, but only if put into movement by a batter. The bat is what Aristotle calls an "intermediate" mover; it moves the ball and is moved by the batter. The batter himself is moved to swing the bat by his desire to make a hit. Aristotle would put it this way: Making a hit is the final cause (the goal) that moves him to swing as he does. So the batter himself is only an "intermediate" mover. He moves as he does for the sake of making a hit. The goal of making a hit in turn exists for the sake of winning the game, which has as *its* goal the league championship. In the world of baseball, the ultimate final cause putting the whole season in motion is the goal of winning the World Series. Each batter is striving to embody the form: Member of a Team That Wins the World Series.

Let's return to the world of nature, containing the eternal movements of the heavenly bodies. Is there any final or ultimate mover here? There must be, Aristotle argues; otherwise we could not account for the movement of anything at all. Not all movers can be "intermediate" movers. If they were, that series would go on to infinity, but there cannot be any actually existing collection of infinitely many things. There must, then, be "something that moves things without being moved."*

Moreover, we can know certain facts about it. It must itself be eternal because it must account for the eternal movement of the heavenly bodies and so cannot be less extensive than they. It must be a substance, for what other substances depend on cannot be less basic than they. And, of course, it must be

fully actual; otherwise, its being what it is would cry out for further explanation—for a mover for it.

What kind of cause could this *unmoved mover* be? Let's review the four causes. It clearly couldn't be a material cause, since that is purely potential. It couldn't be an efficient cause, for the eternal movement of the heavens does not need a temporal trigger. It is not the formal cause of a compound of form and matter because it contains no matter. It could only be a *final cause*. This conclusion is driven home by an analogy.

> Now, the object of desire and the object of thought move things in this way: they move things without being moved. (*M* 12.7)

Our baseball example already indicated this. What sets the whole baseball world in motion is a goal, namely, winning the World Series. Within the world of baseball, there is no further purpose. It moves the players, managers, umpires, and owners, but without being moved itself.* It is "the object of desire and thought," and functions that way as a final cause. It is what they all "love."

> The final cause then moves things because it is loved, whereas all other things move because they are themselves moved. . . . The first mover, then, must exist; and insofar as he exists of necessity, his existence must be good; and thus he must be a first principle. . . .
>
>   It is upon a principle of this kind, then, that the heavens and nature depend. (*M* 12.7)

The ultimate cause of all things is a final cause; it is what all other things love. Their love for it puts them in motion, just as the sheer existence of a bicycle stimulates a boy or girl into activity, delivering papers, mowing lawns, and saving to buy it. As the object of desire and love, this first mover must be something good. Can we say anything more about the nature of this unmoved mover?

> Its life is like the best that we can enjoy—and we can enjoy it for only a short time. It is always in

---

* This is a form of argument that looks back to Anaximander (see p. 12) and forward to Saint Thomas Aquinas (see his first and second arguments for the existence of God, pp. 276–278).

* You may object that there are further goals: fame, money, and so on. And you are right. But that just shows that the "world" of baseball is not a self-contained world; it is not *the* world, but has a place in a wider setting.

this state (which we cannot be), since its actuality is also pleasure. . . . If, then, God is always in the good state which we are sometimes in, that is something to wonder at; and if he is in a better state than we are ever in, that is to be wondered at even more. This is in fact the case, however. Life belongs to him, too; for life is the actuality of mind, and God is that actuality; and his independent actuality is the best life and eternal life. We assert, then, that God is an eternal and most excellent living being, so that continuous and eternal life and duration belong to him. For that is what God is. (*M* 12.7)

There must be such an actuality, Aristotle argues, to explain the existence and nature of changing things. As the final cause and the object of the "desire" in all things, it must be the best. What is the best we know? The life of the mind.* So God must enjoy this life in the highest degree.

God, then, is an eternally existing, living being who lives a life of perfect thought. But this raises a further problem. What does God think about? Aristotle's answer to this question is reasonable, but puzzling, too.

Plainly, it thinks of what is most divine and most valuable, and plainly it does not change; for change would be for the worse. . . . The mind, then, must think of itself if it is the best of things, and its thought will be thought about thought. (*M* 12.9)

It would not be appropriate for the best thought to be about ordinary things, Aristotle argues. It must have only the best and most valuable object. But that is itself! So God will think only of himself. He will not, in Aristotle's view, have any concern or thought for the world. He will engage eternally in a contemplation of his own life—which is a life of contemplation. His relation to the world is not that of *creator* (the world being everlasting needs no efficient cause), but of *ideal,* inspiring each thing in the world to be its very best in imitation of the divine perfection. God is not the origin of the world, but its goal. Yet he is and must be an actually existing, individual substance, devoid of matter, and the best in every way.

----

*This is discussed in more detail later in this chapter. See "The Highest Good."

God, then, is to *the* world as winning the World Series is to the "world" of baseball. He functions as the unifying principle of reality, that cause to which all other final causes must ultimately be referred. There is no multitude of ultimate principles, no polytheism. The world is one world. As Aristotle puts it,

The world does not wish to be governed badly. As Homer says: "To have many kings is not good; let there be one." (*M* 12.10)

----

1. What is "first" philosophy? Is there another name for it?
2. List four criticisms of Plato's doctrine that the Forms are the most real of all things.
3. How does Aristotle's understanding of mathematics tend to undermine Plato's epistemological argument for the Forms?
4. In what way is substance the primary category of being?
5. What is an essence?
6. In what ways is form the most basic thing in substances?
7. What is God like? What kind of cause is God?

The Soul

Plato holds that the essence of a person is found in the soul, an entity distinct from the body. Souls exist before their "imprisonment" in a body and survive the death of the body. The wise person tries to dissociate himself as much as possible from the obscure and harmful influences of the body. The practice of philosophy, the love of wisdom, is a kind of purification making a soul fit for blessedness after death.

Aristotle argues against the otherworldliness implicit in such views. One of the causes of such otherworldliness, Aristotle holds, is a too narrow focus.

Till now, those who have discussed and inquired about the soul seem to have considered only the human soul; but we must take care not to forget the question of whether one single definition can be given of soul in the way that it can of animal, or whether there is a different one in each case—for horse, dog, man, and god, for instance. (*PS* 1.1)

The term "soul" is the English translation of the Greek *psyche*. And that is the general word applied to life. So, things with *psyche*—ensouled things—are living things. But not only humans are alive. Aristotle is raising the question whether soul or life or *psyche* is something shared in common among all living things. If you think only about the life characteristic of humans, you might well think of soul as something quite other than nature; but if you pay attention to the broader context, you may find that you have to give a very different account of soul. Again we see Aristotle the biologist at work, trying to organize and classify all living things, humans being just one species among many.

Levels of Soul

There is "one definition of soul in the same way that there is one definition of shape" (*PS* 2.3). Just as there are plane figures and solid figures, and among the latter there are spheres and cubes, so souls come in a variety of kinds. Aristotle adds,

> In the case both of shapes and of things that have souls the one thing is potentially present in what follows it; the triangle is potentially present in the quadrilateral, for instance, and the nutritive soul in the sensitive. We must, then, inquire, species by species, what is the soul of each living thing—what is the soul of a plant, for instance, or what is that of a man or a beast. (*PS* 2.3)

The general definition of soul involves life: "that which distinguishes what has a soul from what has not is life" (*PS* 2.2). But the point here is that souls may differ from each other as triangles differ from rectangles; the latter are constructed on the basis of triangles, which are more fundamental (every rectangle is composed of two triangles). Similarly, there are more primitive souls (or forms of life) and more complex forms built upon them. Aristotle distinguishes three general levels of soul: that of plants, that of beasts, and that of humans.

The most fundamental of these forms is that of the plants,

> for clearly they have within themselves a faculty and principle such that through it they can grow or decay in opposite directions. For they do not just grow upwards without growing downwards; they grow in both directions alike, and indeed in every direction . . . for as long as they can receive nourishment. This nutritive faculty can be separated from the other faculties, but the other faculties cannot exist apart from it in mortal creatures. This is clear in the case of plants, since they have none of the other faculties of the soul. (*PS* 2.2)

Nutritive soul, the capacity to take in nourishment and convert it to life, is basic to living things and is found in plants and animals alike. Plants, however, do not share the higher levels of soul. They live and reproduce and so have a kind of soul, but without the capacities of movement, sensation, and thought.

We should pause a moment to consider reproduction. Why do plants (as well as animals) reproduce? We know that for Aristotle the answer is incomplete if it makes no mention of the final cause. What is the final cause for reproduction?

> The most natural function of any living being that is complete, is not deformed, and is not born spontaneously is to produce another being like itself . . . so that it may share, as far as it can, in eternity and divinity; that is what they all desire, and it is the purpose of all their natural activities. (*PS* 2.4)

This is an application of the principle uncovered in first philosophy. There is an unmoved mover, existing eternally in perfect independence and actuality—the final cause of whatever else exists. So the fact that plants and animals reproduce can be explained by their "desire" to share, as far as possible, the eternity and divinity that caps off the universe. Each thing imitates God in the way possible for it. God's eternal existence is responsible for the fact that the mature pine tree drops its cones and new plants of that very same species grow up, for the reproduction of beings like themselves is as close as mortal beings can come to a kind of eternity.*

---

*Compare Plato's discussion of love, pp. 137–141.

More complex forms of soul are built upon the nutritive soul and are never found in nature without it. The next level can be called the level of sensitive soul; it belongs to the animals.

> Plants possess only the nutritive faculty, but other beings possess both it and the sensitive faculty; and if they possess the sensitive faculty, they must also possess the appetitive; for appetite consists of desire, anger, and will. All animals possess at least one sense, that of touch; anything that has a sense is acquainted with pleasure and pain, with what is pleasant and what is painful; and anything that is acquainted with these has desire, since desire is an appetite for the pleasant. (*PS* 2.3)

Animals, then, have sensations and desires in addition to the faculties of nutrition and reproduction. Some animals, though not all, also have the capacity for locomotion.

Finally, there is soul that has the capacity to think, which we can call the rational faculty. Among naturally existing species, it seems to be characteristic only of human beings. Whether there is something unique and special about this kind of soul we'll consider in due course.

In general, then, there are three kinds or levels of soul: nutritive, sensitive, and rational. They correspond to three great classes of living things: plants, animals, and human beings. They are related in such a way that higher kinds of soul incorporate the lower, but the lower can exist without the higher.

Soul and Body

We need now to ask how souls are related to bodies. Can we give the same sort of answer for each of the kinds of soul? Plato, concentrating on human beings, holds that souls are completely distinct entities, capable of existence on their own. That is not so plausible in the case of plant and animal souls. What does Aristotle say?

Actually, Aristotle gives two answers, and that fact has been the cause of much subsequent debate. There is a general answer and an answer that pertains specifically to the rational form of soul. Let's look first at the general answer. The scene is set by a remark about the proper way to talk about soul.

> It is probably better to say not that the soul feels pity or learns or thinks, but that man does these things with his soul; for we should not suppose that the movement is actually in the soul, but that in some cases it penetrates as far as the soul, in others it starts from it; sensation, for instance, starts from the particular objects, whereas recollection starts from the soul and proceeds to the movements or their residues in the sense organs. (*PS* 1.4)

This view of soul is one that firmly embeds soul in the body and makes us unitary beings. It is not the case that certain operations can be assigned to the soul and certain others to the body. It is not the soul that feels or learns or thinks while the body eats and walks; it is the *person* that does all these things. It would be no more sensible, Aristotle holds, to say that the soul is angry than that the soul weaves or builds. Souls do none of these things; human beings do them all. Sensation is not something the soul accomplishes; it cannot occur at all without a body, sense organs, and objects to which those sense organs are sensitive. Recollection has its effects in bodily movements (remembering an appointment makes you run to catch the bus). A person is *one being* with *one essence*.

But what exactly is a soul, and how is it related to a body? We must remind ourselves of the results of Aristotle's investigations of being qua being. The basic things that exist are substances, and in natural substances there is a material substratum that is actualized—made into the substance it is—by a form.

> The soul, then, must be a substance inasmuch as it is the form of a natural body that potentially possesses life; and such substance is in fact realization, so that the soul is the realization of a body of this kind. (*PS* 2.1)

Suppose you have before you a living being (whether plant, animal, or human makes no difference just now). Subtract from it—in thought—its life. What you have left is a body that *could* be alive, but isn't—a body that is potentially alive. In one sense it is just a body, like a stone or a stove. But in another sense it isn't, for stones and stoves are not even potentially alive; they are not organized in the right way to be alive. Walt Disney can make stoves talk, perhaps, but only in cartoons. There are no talking stoves in reality, precisely because a stove is not the sort of body that is potentially alive.* The body from which we have in thought abstracted life, however, is such a body. It cannot now engage in nutrition or sensation or thought, but it could. It is a kind of "substratum" that could support life— *matter* that could have the *form* of a living thing.

Remember that "form" does not stand for shape (except in very simple cases) but for the essence, the definition, the satisfaction of which makes a thing the substance it is. Remember also that form is the principle of actualization or realization; it is what makes a bit of matter into an actual thing. And remember that form is itself substance: the very substance of substances.

Now you can understand Aristotle's view of soul as "the form of a natural body that potentially possesses life" and as the "realization of a body of this kind." Restore—in thought—life to that body from which you earlier abstracted it. Now it is capable of performing all the activities that are appropriate to that kind of being; it feeds itself and perhaps sees, desires, and thinks. And its being capable of those activities is the *same* as its having certain essential characteristics. Having those characteristics is having a form of a certain kind; having that form is having a soul.

> We have, then, said in general what the soul is: it is a formal substance. That means that it is the essence of a body of a particular kind. (*PS* 2.1)

Aristotle offers us several examples. Suppose that an axe were a natural body. Then its "formal substance" would be "being an axe." And that would be its soul. But axes are not alive, any more than stones or stoves. They don't actually have souls because the soul is the principle of life in living things. The analogy should show you, though, what *kind* of thing a soul is—a form for a *primary substance*. Similarly, Aristotle says, "If the eye were an animal, its soul would be sight; for sight is the formal substance of

the eye" (*PS* 2.1). From these examples it should be clear that the soul, so conceived, is not a separable entity; for neither "being an axe" nor sight have any existence independent of actual axes and eyes.

It should be no surprise, then, to hear Aristotle say rather offhandedly,

> We do not, therefore, have to inquire whether the soul and body are one, just as we do not have to inquire whether the wax and its shape, or in general the matter of any given thing and that of which it is the matter, are one. (*PS* 2.1)

This problem, which so occupies Plato and for which he constructs so many proofs, is simply one that we do not have to inquire into! The answer is *obvious,* as obvious as the answer to the question whether the shape of a wax seal can exist independently of the wax.

Aristotle gives a brief indication of how this view works in practice. Consider anger. Some people define anger as a disposition to strike out or retaliate in response to some perceived wrong. Its definition therefore involves beliefs, desires, and emotions—all mental states of one sort or another. Others say that anger is just a bodily state involving heightened blood pressure, tensing of muscles, the flow of adrenaline, and so on. Nothing mental needs to be brought into its explanation. What would Aristotle say? He contrasts the viewpoint of the natural scientist with that of the "logician," by which he means one who seeks the definition of such states.

> The natural scientist and the logician would define all these affections in different ways; if they were asked what anger is, the one would say that it was a desire to hurt someone in return, or something like that, the other that it was a boiling of the blood and the heat around the heart. Of these, one is describing the matter, the other the form and the definition; for the latter is indeed the definition of the thing, but it must be in matter of a particular kind if the thing is going to exist. (*PS* 1.1)

If Aristotle is right, psychology and physiology in fact study the same thing. The former studies the form, and the latter the matter. From one point of view anger is a mental state, from the other a physical state. There need be no quarrel between the psychologist and the physiologist. Certain kinds of

---

*From Aristotle's point of view, the reincarnationist idea that a human soul might enter into the body of a lower animal is absurd. Cows and dogs do not have the right sorts of bodies (including brains) to support human souls.

physical bodies have capacities for certain kinds of activities, and the exercise of those activities is their actuality and form; it is their life—their soul.*

Think of the body of Frankenstein's monster before it was jolted into life. What the tragic doctor provided for the body was a soul. But what is that? He didn't plug a new thing into that body; he just actualized certain potentialities the body already had. The doctor made it able to walk and eat, to see and talk, to think. Having a soul is just being able to do those kinds of things.

This, then, is Aristotle's general account of the relation of soul and body. Souls are the forms (the essential characteristics) of certain kinds of bodies, and as such they do not exist independently of bodies. This means, of course, that a soul cannot survive the death of the body to which it gives form any more than sight can survive the destruction of the eyes.

This general account, however, stands in tension with his account of the rational soul, or perhaps just a part of the rational soul, to which we now turn.

Nous

For the most part, Aristotle's account of the soul is thoroughly "naturalistic." Soul is just how naturally existing, living bodies of a certain kind function; it is not an additional part separable from such bodies. In this regard, things with souls are thoroughly embedded in the world of nature. But can this naturalistic form-of-the-body account can be the *complete* story about soul? Or could it be that a part of some souls—of rational souls—has an independent existence after all?

Sensation is passive, simply registering the characteristics of the environment, but thinking seems to be more active; otherwise mirrors and calm pools would be thinking about what they reflect. Consider, for example, using induction to grasp the first principles of natural kinds.† We aren't simply absorbing what comes in through the senses (as cream cheese might absorb the odor of garlic left

nearby), but are actively observing, noting, classifying things. Thinking is *doing* something. Aristotle's word for this active capacity of ours is *nous*. And the question is whether *nous* (translated below as "mind") can be adequately understood as nothing more than one aspect of the human form.

> There is the mind that is such as we have just described by virtue of the fact that it becomes everything; then, there is another mind, which is what it is by virtue of the fact that it makes everything; it is a sort of condition like light. For in a way light makes what are potentially colors become colors in actuality. This second mind is separable, incapable of being acted upon, mixed with nothing, and in essence an actuality. (*PS* 3.5)

Here Aristotle distinguishes between two aspects of *nous* itself. There is the side of *nous* that "becomes everything." What he means by this is that the mind can adapt to receive the form of just about anything; it is flexible, malleable, open to being written upon. But there is also the side of *nous* that "makes everything." Mind lights things up, makes them stand out clearly. Here is an example that may help. Think of daydreaming. Your eyes are open, and there is in your consciousness a kind of registration of everything in your visual field, but you aren't paying it any heed. Your mind is "elsewhere," and you don't *know* what is before you. Suddenly, however, your attention shifts and what has been present all along is noted. Actively paying attention makes what was just potentially knowable into something actually known—just as light makes colors visible, although the colors were there all along before they were lighted up.

According to Aristotle's principles, only an actuality can turn something that is potentially *X* into something actually *X*. So active *nous* must be an actual power to produce knowledge from the mere registrations of passive *nous*. In fact Aristotle concludes that the active and passive powers of *nous* are distinct and separable. Sometimes he goes so far as to speak not just of two powers, but of two minds.

The second mind, he says, is "mixed with nothing" and "separable" from the first. To say it is mixed with nothing must mean that it is a pure form unmixed with matter. If you think a moment, you

---

*This paragraph has a very contemporary ring to it. It expresses a view called "functionalism," the dominant theory of mind in recent cognitive science. See pp. 738–739.

†Review the discussion of induction on p. 167.

should be able to see that it must be a pure form if it can actualize *everything;* if it were mixed with matter, it would be some definite thing and would lack the required plasticity. The eye, for instance, is a definite material organ. As such, its sensitivity is strictly limited; it can detect light and colors, but not sounds or tastes. The ear is tuned to sounds alone and the tongue restricted to tastes. If *nous* is not limited in this way, it seems that it cannot be material. If it is not material, it cannot be a part of the body. And if it is not part of the body, it must be a separable entity.

There is another reason Aristotle believes that active *nous* must be an actuality separate from the body. He cannot find any "organ" or bodily location for this activity. Sight is located in the eyes, hearing in the ears, and so on. But where could the faculty of knowing be? Reflecting on his general view of the soul, Aristotle writes,

> Clearly, then, the soul is not separable from the body; or, if it is divisible into parts, some of the parts are not separable, for in some cases the realization is just the realization of the parts. However, there is nothing to prevent some parts being separated, insofar as they are not realizations of any body. (*PS* 2.1)

Sight is the "realization" of the eye. But what part of the body could have as its function something as infinitely complex as thinking and knowing? The seat of sensation and emotions, Aristotle thinks, is the heart. When we are afraid or excited we can feel our heart beating fast. The brain he considers an organ for cooling the body. (This is wrong, but not implausible; one of the best ways to keep warm on a cold day is to wear a hat.) Without a knowledge of the microstructure of the brain, it must have seemed to him that there is nothing available in the body to serve as the organ of thought, so the active part of *nous* must be separable from the body.

It is not only separable, Aristotle holds; it is

> immortal and eternal; we do not remember this because, although this mind is incapable of being acted upon, the other kind of mind, which is capable of being acted upon, is perishable. But without this kind of mind nothing thinks. (*PS* 3.5)

Why should active *nous* be eternal? Because it is not material; it is not the form of a material substance (i.e., of part of the body). It is rather one of those substantial forms that can exist separately. Lacking matter, it also lacks potentiality for change and is fully and everlastingly what it is. If *nous* is eternal and immortal, it must, like the soul of Socrates and Plato, have existed prior to our birth. But, Aristotle insists, we do not *remember* anything we know before birth—because there is nothing there to remember. Active *nous,* remember, is like the light. It lights up what the senses receive, making actual what is so far only a potentiality for knowledge. But it is not itself knowledge; it only produces knowledge from material delivered by the senses.* And before birth there were no senses or sense organs to produce this material. Aristotle cannot accept the Socratic and Platonic doctrine of recollection as an explanation of knowing.

For similar reasons, it does not seem that *nous* can be anything like personal immortality, in which an individual human being survives death and remembers his life. Active *nous,* in fact, seems impersonal.

A number of questions arise, but Aristotle does not give us answers. Is *nous* numerically the same thing in all individuals, or is there a distinct *nous* for each person? What is the relation between *nous* and God, to which it bears some striking resemblances? How, if *nous* is independent and separable, does it come to be associated with human souls at all?

These questions give rise to a long debate, partly about what Aristotle means, partly about what truth there is to all this. In the Middle Ages, for instance, Jewish, Muslim, and Christian thinkers, trying to incorporate Aristotle into a broader theological con-

---

* Immanuel Kant's view of the relation between concepts and percepts is very similar to this account of *nous.* Like *nous,* concepts alone cannot give us any knowledge; they structure, or interpret, or "light up" the deliverances of the senses; knowledge is a product of the interplay of "spontaneous" conceptualization and "receptive" sensation. (See pp. 439–440.) It is also interesting to compare this discussion of *nous* with Heidegger's view of the "clearing" in which things become present. See "Modes of Disclosure," in Chapter 24.

text, wrestle determinedly with these problems. But for our purposes it is enough to register his conviction that there is something about human beings, and particularly about them as knowers, that cannot be accounted for in purely naturalistic terms. There is a part of the soul that is, after all, otherworldly.

———————————————

1. What is Aristole's objection to Plato's account of the soul?
2. Characterize the three levels of soul.
3. Why do living things reproduce? (Compare Plato on love.)
4. How is a soul related to a body? Be sure you understand the concepts of "substratum," "realization," and "formal substance."
5. Why does Aristotle think there is something (*nous*) about human souls that is eternal?

The Good Life

Because Aristotle's views of knowledge, reality, and human nature are so different from Plato's, we might expect his views of the good for human beings to differ as well. So they do. They do not disagree much over specific goods; both, for instance, defend the traditional virtues of moderation, justice, and courage. Moreover, Aristotle is as insistent as Plato that adherence to such virtues can be rationally justified. And the general form of justification is the same; both strive to show that the virtuous person is the happy person. So there is a large measure of agreement. But the whole approach to ethics is quite different, for in repudiating the Forms, Aristotle denies the claim of Socrates and Plato that knowledge—in the strict, scientific sense—is possible in this sphere. He makes this quite explicit in the following paragraphs:

> Our treatment will be adequate if we make it as precise as the subject matter allows. The same degree of accuracy should not be demanded in all inquiries any more than in all the products of craftsmen. Virtue and justice—the subject matter of politics—admit of plenty of differences and uncertainty. . . .

> Then, since our discussion is about, and proceeds from, matters of this sort, we must be content with indicating the truth in broad, general outline. . . . The educated man looks for as much precision in each subject as the nature of the subject allows. (*NE* 1.3)

When he talks about knowledge of the natural world, Aristotle always insists that it is knowledge of its universal and unchanging aspects. Aristotle never repudiates Plato's principle that knowledge in the strict sense (science) must be certain; and to be certain, its objects must be eternal and unchanging. We can know the essences of natural things and their laws of development because these patterns never change. Members of a species may vary within limits, and each individual is born, changes, and dies. But the universal and unchanging character of the species persists.*

Theoretical knowledge like this, when disciplined by demonstration and insight into first principles, is different from what we can expect in the realm of ethics. The subject matter in ethics is practical—choice, character, and action. Ethics is a practical art; it is better not to call it a science. It is more like navigation than astronomy. It aims at wisdom about what to do and how to live. We always act in some particular situation or other, so ethics must pay attention to particulars as well as universals. Therefore, we "must be content with indicating the truth in broad, general outline" and look only "for as much precision . . . as the nature of the subject allows."

There are two consequences of looking at ethics this way. First, we should not be surprised if those who are ignorant of science sometimes make better decisions than those who are more knowledgeable. What counts here is experience of particulars, not just knowledge of what is universally true. Second, we ought not to expect young people to be very good at these matters, for "they are inexperienced in the practical side of living" and tend to be "ruled

———————————————

* Aristotle has no theory of the evolution of species. There were hints of such a view in at least one of the pre-Socratic philosophers (Empedocles), but Aristotle explicitly repudiates it.

by their emotions" (*NE* 1.3). There may be child prodigies in music and mathematics, but there are no child prodigies in ethics.

This focus on the practical and particular is the reason why Aristotle rejects Plato's Form of the Good as the apex of wisdom. If Plato were right here, not only should there be a science of the good, it should be one unified science. But, Aristotle says, there is no single science of the good. What we find instead is a multitude of goods; there is a good of medicine, a good of generalship, a good pertaining to politics, and so on. Each has its own end (health, victory, and well-being, for example) and must be judged in terms of the good it aims at.

Worse yet, even if there were a single unique Form of the Good, knowledge of it would be useless. Aristotle tells us that in all the arts and sciences

> people aim at some good and try to find where they fall short; yet they leave aside knowing this Idea [Form]! It would be unreasonable for all crafts-men to be unaware of it, if it is so useful, and not even try to find it. It is hard to see how a weaver or builder will benefit in his art, by knowing this Idea [Form] of the good.* (*NE* 1.6)

It is not, then, by a theoretical knowledge of the highest realities that we should try to address our practical problems of choice and action. Yet we must try to be as rational as possible. We can think of Aristotle as making the attempt to apply reason to the somewhat recalcitrant facts of human nature, in order to shape it into the best that it can be. The aim of ethics is not, after all, purely "theoretical." It should have a practical payoff.

> We are not studying in order to know what virtue is, but to become good, for otherwise there would be no profit in it. (*NE* 2.2)

What is it, then, to "become good," and how can we do so?

---

*The term *Eidos,* which we have been translating as "Form," is sometimes also rendered "Idea." This is all right, but we must remember that such Platonic "Ideas" are not subjectively located in our minds.

Happiness

Aristotle begins his main treatise on ethics, the *Nicomachean Ethics,* with these words:

> Every skill and every inquiry, and similarly, every action and choice of action, is thought to have some good as its object. This is why the good has rightly been defined as the object of all endeavor. (*NE* 1.1)

Whenever we do something, we have some end in view. If we exercise, our end is health; if we study, our end is knowledge or a profession; if we earn money, our end is security. And we consider that end to be good; no one strives for what he or she considers bad.*

> Now, if there is some object of activities that we want for its own sake (and others only because of that), and if it is not true that everything is chosen for something else—in which case there will be an infinite regress, that will nullify all our striving—it is plain that this must be the good, the highest good. Would not knowing it have a great influence on our way of living? Would we not be better at doing what we should, like archers with a target to aim at? (*NE* 1.2)

We often do one thing for the sake of another. But this cannot go on forever, or there will be no point to anything we do. What we want to find is some end that we want, but not for the sake of anything else: something we prize "for its own sake." That would be the highest good, since there is nothing else we want that *for.* If we can identify something like that and keep it clearly before our eyes, as an archer looks at the target while shooting, we will be more likely to attain what is truly good.

Is there anything like that?

---

*This is true in general. Both Socrates and Plato, however, hold it is universally true. For that reason, they hold that if we know what is good, we will do what is good. But Aristotle believes there are exceptions when people can act contrary to what they themselves consider to be their best judgment. See the view expressed in Euripides' *Hippolytus,* quoted on p. 69. Saint Paul and Augustine both agree with Aristotle that such inner conflict is possible. See pp. 224 and 246–251.

What is the highest good in all matters of action? As to the name, there is almost complete agreement; for uneducated and educated alike call it happiness, and make happiness identical with the good life and successful living. They disagree, however, about the meaning of happiness. (*NE* 1.4)

Aristotle's term for happiness is **eudaemonia.** Whether "happiness" is the best English translation for this term is unclear. A better alternative might be "well-being," and some speak of human "flourishing." In any case, it is clear that *eudaemonia* is not merely a matter of *feeling* happy; Aristotle, as much as Socrates, wants to distinguish being happy from just feeling happy.* In this book, we will follow the major tradition, however, and speak of what all of us desire as happiness.

Everyone wants to be happy. And the question, "Why do you want to be happy—for what?" seems to be senseless. This is the end, the final goal. Money we want for security, but happiness for its own sake. Yet, for us as well as for Aristotle, there is something unsatisfying about this answer, something hollow. For we immediately want to ask: "What is happiness, anyway?"

Many people, Aristotle notes, think that happiness is pleasure; in fact, they live as though that were so. But that cannot be correct. For the good of every creature must be appropriate to that creature's nature; it couldn't be right that the good life for human beings was the same as "the kind of life lived by cattle" (*NE* 1.4). It is true that "amusements" are pleasant, and that they are chosen for their own sake. Within limits, there is nothing wrong with that. But

> it would be absurd if the end were amusement and if trouble and hardship throughout life would be all for the sake of amusing oneself. . . . It would be stupid and childish to work hard and sweat just for childish amusement. (*NE* 10.6)†

Other people think that happiness is a matter of fame and honor. Again, there is something to be said for that; it is more characteristically human than mere pleasure. Aristotle does not want to deny that honor is something we can seek for its own sake; still

> it seems to be more superficial than what we are looking for, since it rests in the man who gives the honor rather than in him who receives it, whereas our thought is that the good is something proper to the person, and cannot be taken away from him. (*NE* 1.5)

Here Aristotle is surely drawing on the tradition of Socrates, who believes that "the many" could neither bestow the greatest blessings nor inflict the greatest harms.* The highest good, happiness, must be something "proper to the person" that "cannot be taken away." The problem with honor and fame—or popularity—is that you are not in control of them; whether they are bestowed or withdrawn depends on others. If what you most want is to be popular, you are saying to others: "Here, take my happiness; I put it into your hands." This seems unsatisfactory to Aristotle.

How, then, shall we discover what happiness is?

> We might achieve this by ascertaining the specific function of man. In the case of flute players, sculptors, and all craftsmen—indeed all who have some function and activity—"good" and "excellent" reside in their function. Now, the same will be true of man, if he has a peculiar function to himself. Do builders and cobblers have functions and activities, but man not, being by nature idle? Or, just as the eye, hand, foot, and every part of the body has a function, similarly, is one to attribute a function to man over and above these? In that case, what will it be? (*NE* 1.7)

The eye is defined by its function. It is a thing for seeing with; an eye is a good one if it performs that function well—gives clear and accurate images. A woman is a flutist by virtue of performing a certain function: playing the flute. A good flutist is one who plays the flute with excellence, and that is in

---

*See Socrates making this distinction in his trial speech, *Apology* 36e, and p. 103.

†Contemporary American culture sometimes makes one think that we are making this Aristotelian mistake on a massive scale.

---

*See *Apology* 30d, *Crito* 44d.

fact what each flutist aims at. Again we see that the good of a thing is relative to its proper function. Moreover—and this will be important—the flutist is *happy* when she plays with excellence.

This suggests to Aristotle that if human beings had a function—not as flutists or cobblers, but just in virtue of being human—we might be able to identify the good appropriate to them. He thinks we can discover such a function.

> The function of man is activity of soul in accordance with reason, or at least not without reason. (*NE* 1.7)

Let's examine this statement. Aristotle is claiming that there is something in human beings analogous to the function of a flutist or cobbler: "activity of soul in accordance with reason."* What does that mean? And why does he pick on that, exactly?

If we are interested in the function of a human being, we must focus on what makes a human being human: the soul. As we have seen, soul is the realization of a certain kind of body; it is its life and the source of its actuality as an individual substance. It is the *essence* of a living thing. A dog is being a dog when it is doing essentially doglike things. And humans are being human when they are acting in essentially human ways. Now what is peculiarly characteristic of humans? We already know Aristotle's answer to that: Humans are different from plants and the other animals because they have the *rational* level of soul. So the function of a human being is living according to reason, or at least, Aristotle adds, "not without reason." This addition is not insignificant. It means that although an excellent human life is a rational one, it is not limited to purely intellectual pursuits. There are excellences (virtues) that pertain to the physical and social aspects of our lives as well. The latter he calls the *moral virtues.*

Furthermore, although the function of the cobbler is simply to make shoes, the best cobbler is the one who makes excellent shoes. As Aristotle says,

---

*In one important respect, Aristotle is Plato's faithful pupil. Look again at the functions of the soul for Plato (pp. 143–144). Which one is dominant?

"Function comes first, and superiority in excellence is superadded." If that is so, then

> the good for man proves to be activity of soul in conformity with excellence; and if there is more than one excellence, it will be the best and most complete of these. (*NE* 1.7)

Doing what is characteristic of humans to do, living in accord with reason, and in the most excellent kind of way, is the good for humans. And if that is the human being's good, then it also constitutes human happiness. I used to have a big black Newfoundland dog named Shadow, a wonderful dog. When was Shadow happiest? When he was doing the things that Newfoundlands characteristically do—running along between the canal and the river, retrieving sticks thrown far out into the water. He loved that, he was *good* at it, and you could see it made him happy. It is the same with human beings, except that humans have capacities that my dog didn't have.

> It seems as though everything that people look for in connection with happiness resides in our definition. Some think it to be excellence or virtue; others wisdom; others special skill; whereas still others think it all these, or some of these together with pleasure, or at least not without pleasure. Others incorporate external goods as well. (*NE* 1.8)

Happiness is not possible without excellence or virtue (*arete*), any more than a flutist is happy over a poor performance. It surely includes wisdom, for excellent use of one's rational powers is part of being an excellent human being. Special skills are almost certainly included, for there are many necessary and useful things to be done in a human life, from house building to poetry writing. And it will include pleasure, not because pleasure is itself the good—we have seen it cannot be that—but because the life of those who live rationally with excellence is in itself pleasant.

> The things thought pleasant by the vast majority of people are always in conflict with one another, because it is not by nature that they are pleasant; but those who love goodness take pleasure in what is by nature pleasant. This is the characteristic of actions in conformity with virtue, so that they are in themselves pleasant to those who love goodness. Their life has no extra need of pleasure as a kind of wrapper; it contains pleasure in itself. (*NE* 1.8)

Does a happy life "incorporate external goods as well," as some say? Aristotle's answer is, yes—at least in a moderate degree.

> It is impossible (or at least not easy) to do fine acts without a supply of "goods." Many acts are done through friends, or by means of wealth and political power, which are all, as it were, instruments. When people are without some of these, that ruins their blessed condition—for example, noble birth, fine children, or beauty. The man who is quite hideous to look at or ignoble or a hermit or childless cannot be entirely happy. Perhaps this is even more so if a man has really vicious children or friends or if they are good but have died. So, as we have said, happiness does seem to require this external bounty. (*NE* 1.8)

A certain amount of good fortune is a necessary condition for happiness. One would not expect the Elephant Man, for example, to be entirely happy, nor a person whose children have become thoroughly wicked. This means, of course, that your happiness is not entirely in your own control. To be self-sufficient in happiness may be a kind of ideal, but in this world it is not likely to be entirely realized.

One point needs special emphasis. The happy life, which is one and the same with the good life, is a life of *activity*. Happiness is not something that happens to you. Even though it may require a foundation in moderate good fortune, winning the lottery will not guarantee happiness. Happiness is not something the world owes you or can give you. It is not passive. It is not rest. Think about the following analogy:

> At the Olympic games, it is not the handsomest and strongest who are crowned, but actual competitors, some of whom are the winners. Similarly, it is those who act rightly who get the rewards and the good things in life. (*NE* 1.8)

Happiness is an *activity* of soul in accord with excellence.

And finally, Aristotle adds, "in a complete life." Just as one swallow does not make a summer, so "a short time does not make a man blessed or happy" (*NE* 1.7). There is a certain unavoidable fragility to human happiness.

> There are many changes and all kinds of chances throughout a lifetime, and it is possible for a man who is really flourishing to meet with great disaster in old age, like Priam of Troy. No one gives the name happy to a man who meets with misfortune like that and dies miserably. (*NE* 1.9)

---

1. Why does Aristotle say that ethics cannot be an exact science?
2. Give two criticisms of the Form of the Good as a basis for ethics.
3. Why does Aristotle think happiness is the highest good?
4. Why cannot pleasure be the essence of happiness? Why not honor or fame?
5. How does the idea of function help in determining the nature of happiness?
6. What is the function of human beings? What is their good?
7. How does pleasure come into the good life?

Virtue or Excellence (*Arete*)

The good for human beings, then, is happiness, and happiness is the full development and exercise of our human capacities "in conformity with excellence." But what kind of thing is this excellence? How is it attained? Is there just one excellence which is appropriate to human beings, or are there many? We often speak of the "virtues" in the plural—courage, moderation, justice, temperance, and so on; are these independent of one another, or can you be an excellent human being only if you have them all? These are the questions we now address. (I shall speak in terms of "virtues" for the time being and postpone the question about their unity.)

1. In considering what kind of thing a virtue is, Aristotle notes that it is for our virtues and vices that we are praised and blamed. A virtue, then, cannot be a simple emotion or feeling, for two reasons: (1) we are blamed not for being angry, but for giving in to our anger, for nursing our anger, or for being unreasonably angry, and those things are in our control; and (2) we feel fear and anger without choosing to, but the virtues "are a sort of choice, or at least not possible without choice" (*NE* 2.5). Nor can the virtues be capacities we have by nature; again, we are called good or bad not because we are *capable* of feeling angry or *capable* of reasoning, but because of the ways we use these capacities.

But if the virtues are not emotions or capacities, what can they be? Aristotle's answer is that they are *dispositions* or *habits*. To be courageous is to be disposed to do brave things. To be temperate is to have a tendency toward moderation in one's pleasures. These dispositions have intimate connections with choice and action. People who never do the brave thing when they have the opportunity are not brave, no matter how brave they happen to feel. And the person who just happens to do a brave thing, in a quite accidental way, is not brave either. The brave person acts bravely whenever the occasion calls for it; and the more the person is truly possessed of that virtue, the more easily and naturally courageous actions come. There is no need to engage in fierce internal struggles to screw up the courage to act rightly.

So this is the answer to the first question. To have a virtue of a certain kind is to have developed a habit of choosing and behaving in ways appropriate to that virtue.

2. How are the virtues attained? They are not innate in us, though we have a natural capacity for them. They are, Aristotle tells us, learned. And they are learned as all habits are learned, by practice.

> Where doing or making is dependent on knowing how, we acquire the know-how by actually doing. For example, people become builders by actually building, and the same applies to lyre players. In the same way, we become just by doing just acts; and similarly with "temperate" and "brave." (*NE* 2.1)

This leads, moreover, to a kind of "virtuous circle."

> We become moderate through abstaining from pleasure, and when we are moderate we are best able to abstain. The same is true of bravery. Through being trained to despise and accept danger, we become brave; we shall be best able to accept danger once we are brave. (*NE* 2.2)

So we learn these excellences by practicing behavior that eventually becomes habitual in us. And if they can be learned, they can be taught. Socrates seems forever unsure whether human excellence is something that can be taught.* Aristotle is certain that it can be and tells us how.

> The point is that moral virtue is concerned with pleasures and pains. We do bad actions because of the pleasure going with them, and abstain from good actions because they are hard and painful. Therefore, there should be some direction from a very early age, as Plato says, with a view to taking pleasure in, and being pained by, the right things. (*NE* 2.3)

A child can be taught virtue—moderation, courage, generosity, and justice—by associating pleasures with them and pains with their violation—by rewarding and punishing. A child needs to be taught to find pleasure in virtuous behavior and shame in vice. If we can teach a person to build well or to play the lyre well in this way, we can also teach the more specifically human excellences. Why should we teach these virtues to our children? Aristotle has a clear answer: If they find pleasure in the most excellent exercise of their human nature, they

---

*See *Meno* and Chapter 5, pp. 68 and 102.

will be happier people. Such happy people are also the virtuous and good, for the good person is the one who takes pleasure in the right things.

3. Our third question is whether virtue is one or many. Can a person be partly good and partly bad, or is goodness all or nothing? Plato and Socrates are both convinced that goodness is one. For Plato, knowledge of the Form of the Good is the only secure foundation for virtue; and that Form is *one*. Whoever grasped it fully would be good through and through. We might expect Aristotle to be more pluralistic. In fact, he says that Socrates and Plato are in one sense right and in one sense wrong. There are indeed many virtues, and they can perhaps even exist in some independence of each other. Often, a brave man is not particularly moderate in choosing his pleasures; James Bond would be an example. But in their perfection, Aristotle holds, you can't have one virtue without having them all. What will the brave man without moderation do, for example, when he is pulled in one direction by his bravery and in another by some tempting pleasure? Won't his lack of moderation hamper the exercise of his courage?

The unity of human excellence in its perfection is a function of the exercise of reason. If you follow reason, you will not be able to develop only one of these virtues to the exclusion of others. This use of reason Aristotle calls *practical sense* or *practical wisdom*. "Once the single virtue, practical sense, is present, all the virtues will be present" (*NE* 6.13).

To this "single virtue," which provides the foundation and unity of all the rest, we now turn.

The Role of Reason

Happiness is living the life of an excellent human being; you can't be an excellent human being unless you use your rational powers. But how, exactly, does Aristotle think that rationality helps in living an excellent life?

> Let us consider this first: it is in the nature of things for the virtues to be destroyed by excess and deficiency, as we see in the case of health and strength—a good example, for we must use clear

cases when discussing abstruse matters. Excessive or insufficient training destroys strength, just as too much or too little food and drink ruins health. The right amount, however, brings health and preserves it. So this applies to moderation, bravery, and the other virtues. The man who runs away from everything in fear, and faces up to nothing, becomes a coward; the man who is absolutely fearless, and will walk into anything, becomes rash. It is the same with the man who gets enjoyment from all the pleasures, abstaining from none: he is immoderate; whereas he who avoids all pleasures, like a boor, is a man of no sensitivity. Moderation and bravery are destroyed by excess and deficiency, but are kept flourishing by the mean. (*NE* 2.2)

We can think of an emotion or an action tendency as laid out on a line, the extremes of which are labeled "too much" and "too little." Somewhere between these extremes is a point that is "just right." This point Aristotle calls "the mean." It is at this "just right" point that human excellence or virtue flourishes. To possess a virtue, then, is to have a habit that keeps impulse and emotion from leading action astray.

But where on such a line does the mean lie? Aristotle is very clear that it does not necessarily lie in the geometrical middle. The amount of training right for a beginner is not the right amount for a world-class runner. Aristotle distinguishes the mean relative to *the thing* from the mean relative to *us* and gives an example. Think about a trainer considering how much food to give her athletes. She may know that ten pounds is too much and two pounds too little. Does it follow that she should give them six (the mathematical mean)? Of course not. She has to consider each of the athletes and give *each one* an amount that is not too much and not too little *for him*.

So it is with the virtues.

> In feeling fear, confidence, desire, anger, pity, and in general pleasure and pain, one can feel too much or too little; and both extremes are wrong. The mean and good is feeling at the right time, about the right things, in relation to the right people, and for the right reason; and the mean and the good are the task of virtue. (*NE* 2.6)

Think about bravery, or courage, surely one of the virtues. Aristotle's analysis says that bravery lies on a mean between extremes of fear and confidence. If we feel too much fear and too little confidence, we are paralyzed and cannot act rightly; we are cowards. If we feel too little fear and are overconfident, we act foolishly, recklessly. At each extreme, then, there is a vice, and the virtue lies in a mean between these extremes. But it doesn't lie exactly in the middle. What is courageous in any given circumstance depends on the facts.

Consider this example. I am walking down a dark and lonely street, and I feel a pointed object pressed into my back and hear the words, "Your money or your life." What would be the brave thing for me to do? Turn and try to disarm the thug? Try to outrun him? No. In my case, either action would be foolhardy, rash, stupid. There would be no taint of cowardice in me if I meekly handed over my wallet. Compare that with the case of a Green Beret or a Navy Seal in a similar situation, someone superbly trained in hand-to-hand combat. If such a person meekly handed over the wallet, one might suspect a sudden attack of cowardice. If he instead turned to disarm the attacker, that would not be rash or reckless. The trained combatant and I differ in relevant ways, so what is courageous for one of us may not be for the other. One can construct equally plausible examples of relativity to the time, to the things involved, and to reasons.

X: the mean for me
Y: the mean for a Navy Seal

Or let's think about being angry; again it is a matter of degree. You can have too much anger (like Achilles) or too little (simply being a doormat for everyone to walk over). Each of these is a vice, wrathfulness at the one extreme and subservience at the other. The virtue (which, in this case, may not have a clear name) lies at the mean between these extremes. But it is the mean *relative to us* in our *particular situation*. Aristotle doesn't intend to say that we should always get only moderately angry. About certain things, in relation to a given person, and for some specific reason, it might be the right thing to be very angry indeed. But in relation to other times, occasions, persons, and reasons, that degree of anger may be altogether inappropriate. We should always seek the mean, but what that is depends on the situation in which we find ourselves. All of the virtues, Aristotle says, can be given this sort of analysis.

Notice that this is not a doctrine of *relativism* in the Sophist's sense. It is clearly not the case that if Jones thinks in certain circumstances that it's right to get angry to a certain degree, then it *is* (therefore) right—not even for Jones. Jones can be mistaken in his judgment. True, there is a certain relativity involved in judgments about the right; and without careful thought, this might be confusing. But it is an *objective* relativity; what is right depends on objective facts—on actual facts about the situation in which Jones finds himself. It is those facts that determine where the mean lies, not what Jones thinks or feels about them.

Finding the mean in the situation is the practical role of *reason* in ethics. The virtuous or excellent person is the one who is good at rationally discovering the mean relative to us with regard to our emotions, our dispositions or habits, and our actions. How much, for instance, shall we give to charity? About these things we deliberate and choose. Because these are matters of degree and because the right degree depends on our appreciation of subtle differences in situations, being truly virtuous is difficult. As Aristotle says,

> going wrong happens in many ways . . . , whereas doing right happens in one way only. That is why one is easy, the other difficult: missing the target is easy, but hitting it is hard. (*NE* 2.6)

This is why it is a hard job to be good. It is hard to get to the mean in each thing. It is the expert, not just anybody, who finds the center of the circle. In the same way, having a fit of temper is easy for anyone; so is giving money and spending it. But this is not so when it comes to questions of "for whom?" "how much?" "when?" "why?" and "how?"

This is why goodness is rare, and is praiseworthy and fine. (*NE* 2.9)

If you are good at using your reason to find the mean, you have *practical wisdom*. (The Greek word is *phronesis*.) Because virtue or excellence lies in the mean, and the mean is determined by reasoning, we can now also say that virtue is "disposition *accompanied* by right reason. Right reason, in connection with such matters is practical sense" (*NE* 6.13).

Aristotle does not give us a formula or an algorithm to use in making choices. He apparently thinks that no such formula is possible in practical matters pertaining to particular situations of choice. If a formula were possible, ethics could be a science rather than an art.* Nonetheless, there is a kind of standard for judging whether the right thing is being done. That standard is the virtuous and good person. The right thing to do in any situation is what the good person would do. In judging which are the best pleasures, for example, Aristotle's view is that

> the thing is as it appears to the good man. If this is true, as it seems to be and excellence and the good man, as good man, are the measure of each thing, then pleasures, too, will be the pleasures of the good man, and pleasant will apply to the things that please him. (*NE* 10.5)

Protagoras holds that "man is the measure of all things." We have seen how this leads to a kind of relativism; if Jones thinks something is good, then it is good—to Jones. Aristotle disagrees and argues in this way: We do not take the sick man's word about whether the pudding is sweet, nor the word of someone who is color blind about the color of a tie; in the same way, not everyone is adept at judging the goodness of things. Protagorean relativism is a mistake because it is not everyone, but only the good person, who is the "measure of each thing." In every situation, virtuous and good actions are defined by the mean. The mean is discovered by "right reason" or practical wisdom. So the "mea-

sure" of virtue and goodness will be the person who judges according to practical wisdom.

You might still want to ask, but how do we recognize these practically wise persons? To this question Aristotle has no very clear answer.* Again, there is no formula for recognizing such persons. But that need not mean we cannot in general tell who they are. They tend to be those persons, we might suggest, to whom you would turn for advice.

Responsibility

The virtues, as we have seen, are dispositions to choose and behave in certain ways, according to right reason or practical wisdom. If we have these dispositions, we are called good; if we lack them, we are called bad. It is for our virtues and vices that we are praised and blamed. But there are situations in which someone does a bad thing yet is not blamed. The presence of certain conditions can make praise and blame inappropriate. Let's call these "excusing conditions."

Aristotle is the first to canvass excusing conditions systematically, and so to define when persons should not be held responsible for their actions. This is an important topic in its own right, useful "for those who are laying down laws about rewards and punishments" (*NE* 3.1). It has, moreover, been discussed in a variety of ways by subsequent philosophers. So we must look briefly at the way Aristotle begins this conversation.

> Praise and blame are accorded to voluntary acts; but involuntary acts are accorded pardon, and at times pity. (*NE* 3.1)

Aristotle assumes that in the normal course of events most of our actions are voluntary. Occasionally, however, we do something involuntarily, and then we are pardoned or pitied. What conditions qualify an action as involuntary? He identifies two excusing conditions: compulsion and ignorance. Let us briefly discuss each.

---

*We will see that some later writers on ethics, the utilitarians, for example, try to supply such a formula (p. 516). Kant also tries to find a single principle from which the right thing to do can be derived. See p. 454.

*Compare Augustine, who does have a clear answer to this question, pp. 253–254.

When someone acts under compulsion we mean, says Aristotle, that

> the principle of action is external, and that the doer . . . contributes nothing of his own—as when the wind carries one off somewhere, or other human beings who have power over one do this. (*NE* 3.1)

Now, having your ship driven somewhere by a storm or being tied up and carried somewhere are particularly clear cases. If something bad should happen as a result of either of these, no one would blame you for it, for "the principle of action is external."

There are more debatable cases; for example, to save his ship a captain in a storm throws his cargo overboard. Here the action is one that we would normally blame a captain for. But it is not something a captain would ordinarily do; we might say that the storm forced him to do it. Yet we can't say that he contributed "nothing of his own." He did make the decision; in that respect, the action was voluntary. Still, because this is what "all people of sense" would do in those circumstances, the captain is pardoned. Aristotle concludes that though such actions are voluntary if considered as particular acts, they are involuntary when considered in context—for no one would ordinarily choose them. And that is the ground on which we excuse the captain from blame.

Again Aristotle insists that we not try to find a precise formula for deciding such cases. He stresses how difficult such decisions may be.

> There are times when it is hard to decide what should be chosen at what price, and what endured in return for what reward. Perhaps it is still harder to stick to the decision.
>
> It is not easy to say if one course should be chosen rather than another, since there is great variation in particular circumstances. (*NE* 3.1)

This does not mean, of course, that anything goes. The application of practical wisdom to such situations helps us discriminate whether something was done by compulsion.

Let us consider the second condition. What sort of ignorance excuses us from responsibility? It is not, Aristotle says, ignorance of what is right. Those who do not know what is right are not ignorant, but wicked! We do not excuse people for being wicked. (Here is the source of the adage that ignorance of the law is no excuse.)

If ignorance of the right does not excuse, neither does ignorance of what everybody ought to know. But

> ignorance in particular circumstances does— that is, ignorance of the sphere and scope of the action. . . . A man may be ignorant of *what* he is doing: e.g., when people say that it "slipped out in the course of a conversation"; or that they did not know these things were secret (like Aeschylus on the mysteries); or like the man with the catapult, who wanted "only to demonstrate it," but fired it instead. Someone, as Merope does, might think his son an enemy; or mistake a sharp spear for one with a button. . . . One might give a man something to drink, with a view to saving his life, and kill him instead. (*NE* 3.1)

It is ignorance about particular circumstances that makes an action involuntary and leads us to excuse the agent from responsibility. In such cases, a person can say: If I had only known, I would have done differently. The mark of whether that is true or not, Aristotle suggests, is regret. If someone does something bad through ignorance and later regrets doing it, that is a sign that she is not wicked. It shows that she would indeed have done otherwise if she had known. And in that case she can truly be said to have acted involuntarily and deserve pardon.

Again, there are difficult cases. What about the person who acts in ignorance because he is drunk and is not in a condition to recognize the facts of the case? Here Aristotle suggests that it is not appropriate to excuse him, because he was responsible for getting himself into that state. The same is true for someone ignorant through carelessness; that person should have taken care. Here is, perhaps, a harder case.

But perhaps the man's character is such that he cannot take care. Well, people themselves are responsible for getting like that, through living disorderly lives: they are responsible for being unjust or profligate, the former through evildoing, the latter through spending their time drinking, and so on. Activity in a certain thing gives a man that character; this is clear from those who are practicing for any contest or action, since that is what they spend their time doing. Not knowing that dispositions are attained through actually doing things is the sign of a complete ignoramus. (*NE* 3.5)

No one, Aristotle suggests, can be that ignorant.

There is further discussion of such cases, but this provides the main outlines of his views on responsibility. We can see that Aristotle assumes people must normally be held responsible for what they do, that compulsion and ignorance may be excusing conditions, and that he is rather severe in his estimation of when these conditions may hold. Although Aristotle does not explicitly say so, it is a fair inference that he considers the acceptance of responsibility and the sparing use of excuses as a part of the good life. By our choices and actions we create the habits that become our character. And so we are ourselves very largely responsible for our own happiness or lack thereof.

The Highest Good

When Aristotle defines the good for human beings as "activity of soul in conformity with excellence," he adds that "if there is more than one excellence, it will be the best and most complete of these." We need now to examine what the "best and most complete" excellence is.

The best activity of soul must be the one that activates whatever is best in us. And what is that? Think back to Aristotle's discussion of the human soul. It incorporates the levels of nutrition and reproduction, sensation, and reason. At the very peak is *nous,* or mind: the nonpassive, purely active source of knowledge and wisdom. Can there be any doubt that this, which contains no potentiality at all, is the best, the most divine part of us?

But if that is so, the activity that is best is the activity of *nous.* And such activity should be not only the highest good but also the greatest happiness for a human being. This is just what Aristotle claims.

> This is the best activity . . . and also the most continuous. We are better able to contemplate continuously than to *do* anything. (*NE* 10.7)

The activity of *nous*—discovering and keeping in mind the first principles of things—Aristotle calls "contemplation." The life of contemplation is said to be the very best life partly because it is the exer-

cise of the "best" part of us and partly because we can engage in it "continuously." But this life is also the most pleasant and the most self-sufficient. For these reasons it is the happiest life.

> We think it essential that pleasure should be mixed in with happiness, and the most pleasant of activities in accordance with virtue is admittedly activity in accordance with wisdom. Philosophy has pleasures that are marvelous for their purity and permanence. Besides, it is likely that those who have knowledge have a more pleasant life than those who are seeking it. Sufficiency, as people call it, will be associated above all with contemplation. The wise man, the just, and all the rest of them need the necessities of life; further, once there is an adequate supply of these, the just man needs people with and towards whom he may perform just acts; and the same applies to the temperate man, the brave man, and so on. But the wise man is able to contemplate, even when he is on his own; and the more so, the wiser he is. It is better, perhaps, when he has people working with him; but still he is the most self-sufficient of all. (*NE* 10.7)

Aristotle dismisses honor as a candidate for the good, you will recall, on the grounds that it is too dependent on others. What is truly good, it seems, must be more "proper to the person, and cannot be taken away." The same point is here used to recommend the life of contemplation as the very best life, for it is more "self-sufficient" than any other, less dependent on other people. The other virtues need the presence of other people for their exercise, while the wise man can engage in contemplation "even when he is on his own." And to Aristotle this seems to recommend such a life as the very best.*

Aristotle should not be taken to deny that there are good human lives that are noncontemplative. Ordinary men and women, not devoting themselves to science and philosophy, can also be excellent human beings—and therefore happy. But only those fortunate enough to be able to devote them-

---

*Contemplation, for Aristotle, is not what is often called "meditation" these days. It is not an attempt to empty the mind, but an active life of study to uncover the wonder and the whys of things.

selves to intellectual pursuits will experience the pinnacle of human happiness—that self-sufficient happiness which is most like the happiness of God.

Note that an assumption betrays its presence here, as it does elsewhere in Greek philosophy. Morality is inferior to wisdom, we are told, because the moral person needs other people and material goods for the exercise of his or her virtue. It is almost as if morality itself would be better if it could be exercised independently of other people.

Suppose we ask why the moral person acts morally. From what Aristotle says, we suspect that it is not because other people need the individual's just acts or are benefited by them; it is merely that he or she has come to see that this is the best way to live. This is the ground for Aristotle's recommendation of contemplation as well; it is the best way for an individual to live. "Best" always means "most self-sufficient" for Aristotle. So the life of contemplation is praised because it is a life independent of fortune—to the extent that is possible for a human being. We see clearly that Aristotle's ethics (and classical Greek ethics in general) is an ethics of self-perfection, or self-realization. There is not much in it that recommends caring for others for *their* sakes.*

This attitude underlies the rational justification for being virtuous in both Plato and Aristotle. They try to show that we should be just and moderate because, to put it crudely, it *pays*. True, neither argues that the consequences of virtue will necessarily be pleasing. Glaucon's picture of the perfectly moral and perfectly immoral men had ruled out that sort of appeal. Happiness is not related to virtue as a paycheck is related to a week's work. The relation for both Plato and Aristotle is internal; the just and virtuous life is recommended because it is *in itself* the happiest life (though they also believe that *in general* its consequences will be good). Although Aristotle always thinks of the good of a person as essentially involving the good of some community, and especially as involving friends, it

remains true nonetheless that individuals are primarily interested in their own happiness. This may, we might grant, be a stimulus to achievement, but there is not much compassion in it.

Aristotle sums up his discussion of the contemplative life (the happiest of all) by *disagreeing* with Pindar's aphorism, "For mortals, a mortal lot is best." The contemplation of the wise person, he tells us, will

> be more than human. A man will not live like that by virtue of his humanness, but by virtue of some divine thing within him. His activity is as superior to the activity of the other virtues as this divine thing is to his composite character. Now if mind is divine in comparison with man, the life of the mind is divine in comparison with mere human life. We should not follow popular advice and, being human, have only human ambitions, or, being mortal, have only mortal thoughts. As far as possible, we should become immortal and do everything toward living by the best that is in us. (*NE* 10.7)

The activity of a truly wise human being, then, resembles the activity of God, the unmoved mover. Indeed, this is another case of God acting as a final cause, an ideal that draws all things, in this case the philosopher, to imitate its own self-sufficient activity as far as possible. Because the best and most pleasant activity for any living creature is what most fully realizes its nature, contemplation—the life of reason—is the most happy life possible for human beings.

---

1. What *kind* of a thing is a virtue? Can virtue be taught? How?
2. Is virtue just one? Or are there many virtues?
3. Explain Aristotle's doctrine of the mean.
4. Why is it "a hard job to be good"?
5. What is practical wisdom?
6. What is "the measure of all things," so far as goodness goes?
7. What conditions, according to Aristotle, excuse a person from responsibility? Explain each.
8. Does having a bad character excuse a person? Explain.
9. What is the very best life?

---

†Such compassion, or caring, under the names of "love" and "charity" (*agape,* not *eros*) comes into our story with the Christians. See pp. 224–225.

For Further Thought

1. In your view, does Aristotle's logic do anything to undercut the relativism spawned by the Sophists' teaching of rhetoric? Explain your answer.

2. Keeping in mind Aristotle's doctrine of how soul and body are related, try to construct an Aristotelian account of *fear*. (Hint: You will have to consider both mental and physical factors, and how they are related.)

3. Write a short paragraph giving an Aristotelian account of the virtue of moderation.

4. We read that young people attracted to gang life are seeking "respect." Write an Aristotelian critique of this motivation.

Notes

1. Quoted from Ps. Ammonius, *Aristotelis Vita,* in W. D. Ross, *Aristotle* (New York: Meridian Books, 1959), 14.

2. I am indebted here to Marjorie Grene's excellent little book, *A Portrait of Aristotle* (Chicago: University of Chicago Press, 1963), 38–65.

3. Quoted in J. M. Edmonds, *Elegy and Iambus with the Anacreontea II* (New York: G. P. Putnam's Sons, 1931), 175.

4. All quotations from Aristotle's works are from *The Philosophy of Aristotle,* ed. Renford Bambrough (New York: New American Library, 1963), unless noted otherwise. Within this text, references to specific works will be as follows (numerical references are to book and section numbers).
   C: Categories
   I: On Interpretation
   M: Metaphysics
   PA: Posterior Analytics
   PH: Physics
   PS: Psychology
   NE: Nicomachean Ethics

5. As quoted in Grene, *Portrait of Aristotle,* 105.

6. I owe this example to J. L. Ackrill, *Aristotle the Philosopher* (Oxford: Oxford University Press, 1981), 42.

8

EPICUREANS, STOICS, AND SKEPTICS
Happiness for the Many

It is customary to discuss the development of philosophy in the Hellenistic and Roman periods after Aristotle in terms of three schools, or movements of thought. We will follow this practice, but without any claim to do full justice to these developments. We will look at only a few central tenets of these schools and show how they try to solve problems facing people of those times, problems not adequately addressed by the great systematic achievements of Plato and Aristotle.

To understand the appeal of these philosophies, however, we need to look at more than just their intellectual predecessors. A brief discussion of the altered social and religious climate will be useful. The era of the city-state was fading. After the war between Athens and Sparta, the regions of Greece engaged in a long series of struggles to achieve dominance, and some, Thebes and Macedonia for instance, managed it for a time (see Map 1). But the struggles with shifting alliances and continual warfare wore down the belief that a city could be an arena for living a good life. People lost confidence in it, retreating into smaller units and leaving the politics of cities to be settled by rather crude military

types. (The Epicureans, as we'll see, are prominent among those who seek their happiness not as citizens but as members of a smaller voluntary community.) Under Philip of Macedon and his son Alexander, vast territories were conquered and unified politically.* And finally Rome established her dominance over the entire Mediterranean basin, bringing a kind of stability and enforced peace to the region. The Romans were good administrators and warriors and contributed much in the sphere of law but not much original philosophy.

With the loss of confidence in the cities went a loss of faith in the gods of the cities. In the era of empires, Athena seemed too restricted even for Athens. The Olympians had apparently failed, and their authority waned. It is true that the Romans took over the Greek pantheon and gave the old gods new names (Jove, Juno, Venus), but the vigor of the religion was gone. This didn't mean, however, that religion was dead or dying—far from it. The

---

*For Alexander, see http://en.wikipedia.org/wiki/Alexander _the_Great.

old religions of the earth (religions of fertility, ancestor worship, and ecstasy), suppressed for a time by the Homeric gods of the sky, had never disappeared. Now they flourished with new vigor. To this was added a flood of religious cults and ideas from the East, all seeming to promise what the new age demanded. There was a proliferation of initiations into sacred and secret mysteries, of mediators and saviors, of claims to esoteric knowledge comprising fantastic systems, and of rites that promised a merging of the worshiper's very being with the being of some divinity.

Politicians, of course, made use of religion for their own ends, accepting (and encouraging) the accolades of divinity people laid upon them. Alexander was proclaimed a god; his successors liked the status it gave them and continued the practice.

The world seemed hostile and society brutal. People had lost control and grasped desperately at almost any promise to reestablish it. Fortune and Chance themselves came to seem divine and were worshiped and feared. Astrology, never a force in the Golden Age of Greece, "fell upon the Hellenistic mind," Gilbert Murray says, "as a new disease falls upon some remote island people."[1] The stars were thought to be gods, the planets living beings (or controlled by living beings).* Their positions in the heavens were consulted as signs of things happening and to happen on earth. The heavens were thought to be populated by myriads of spirits, powers, principalities, demons, and gods, and one never knew when they would cause some fresh disaster to overtake one.

The tradition established by Thales and his successors, never widespread, was impotent to stop all this. Rational criticism had not completely disappeared, but it must have seemed to many thinkers that they were in a new dark age. People were anxious and afraid, their confidence broken.

---

*The philosophers were, perhaps, not altogether blameless in this. It was common to ascribe greater perfection to the heavenly bodies in their eternal course than to the changeable world we live in. And more than one philosopher spoke of them as divine. In Plato's later political thought, the supreme object of worship for the masses was to be the sun.

What could those who wished to carry on the enterprise of the nature philosophers, of Socrates, Plato, and Aristotle, do to stem the tide? Let us look first at Epicurus.

The Epicureans

It is not possible for one to rid himself of his fears about the most important things if he does not understand the nature of the universe but dreads some of the things he has learned in the myths. Therefore, it is not possible to gain unmixed happiness without natural science. (*PD* 12.143)[2]

This passage strikes the key notes in the philosophy of Epicurus (341–270 B.C.). The aim of life is happiness. Happiness depends above all on ridding oneself of fears. And the basis for the removal of fear is science. We want to examine what fears Epicurus thinks stand in the way of happiness, what he thinks happiness is, why an understanding of the universe will help, and what kind of science will give us this understanding.

According to Epicurus,

pleasure is the beginning and end of the blessed life. We recognize pleasure as the first and natural good; starting from pleasure we accept or reject; and we return to this as we judge every good thing, trusting this feeling of pleasure as our guide. (*LM* 129a)

The Greek word translated as pleasure is *hedone,* and the viewpoint expressed in the preceding passage is therefore called **hedonism.** As we have seen, Aristotle considers the view that pleasure is the good and rejects it.* He argues that something we share with the lower animals could not be the distinctively human good. But Epicurus is unmoved. Just look about you, he seems to be saying. Every living thing takes pleasure as a natural good; it is clearly one thing that is good not by convention but by *physis*. It is the ground of what we accept and reject, of what we pursue and avoid. And if we

---

*See p. 187.

want to judge the goodness of some course of action, we ask whether there is more pleasure than pain involved in pursuing it.

He does not claim that this is the way it should be but that this is how it is. Good and evil are measured by this standard of pleasure and pain. It is no use, Epicurus might say, to complain that this is unworthy of human beings; this is the way we are made—all of us. This fact levels things out and defeats the elitism of the philosophers. Perhaps only a few are capable of the tortuous dialectic that leads to the vision of the Form of the Good. Not many can live the life of divine contemplation that Aristotle recommends as the highest good. But a pleasant life is available to all.

It is in terms of pleasure and pain, then, that we must understand happiness.* The happy life is the pleasant life. And philosophy, Epicurus holds, is the study of what makes for happiness—nothing more, nothing less.

> Let no young man delay the study of philosophy, and let no old man become weary of it; for it is never too early nor too late to care for the well-being of the soul. The man who says that the season for this study has not yet come or is already past is like the man who says it is too early or too late for happiness. (*LM* 122)

But what, exactly, can philosophy do for us to make us happy? Note that contrary to Aristotle's view, the pursuit of philosophy is not in itself the recipe for the happy life. Philosophy is basically a tool for Epicurus. Though philosophical discussion with a group of friends is one of the great pleasures in life, Epicurus is not interested in philosophical speculation for its own sake. So only those parts of philosophy which serve the end of happiness are recommended. As he says,

> do not think that knowledge about the things above the earth, whether treated as part of a philosophical system or by itself, has any other purpose than peace of mind and confidence. This is also true of the other studies. (*LP* 85b)

There is a single-minded practicality about Epicurus' thought that brushes to one side all that does not serve the goal. So we should not expect much from him in the way of new developments in science, logic, or epistemology; indeed, his contributions in these areas are mostly secondhand, as we will see. But in ethics he has some originality and has had some influence.

The study of philosophy can do two things for us. It can free us from certain fears and anxieties that spoil our happiness, and it can provide directions for maximizing pleasure in life. Let us look at each of these in turn.

There are pains and displeasures that are natural and cannot always be avoided, such as illness and separation from loved ones because of death. About these, however, Epicurus says that the intense pains typically do not last very long, whereas those that last a long time are usually not very intense; one way or another, these pains may be endured (*PD* 4; *VS* 4). But there are other pains that are due to certain *beliefs* we hold, and for these there is a sure remedy: change these beliefs. In fact, that is not only the expedient thing to do, he tells us, but also the right thing to do because the beliefs that cause us distress are *false*. So we can rid ourselves of these pains by a true apprehension of *the way things are.**

What are these false beliefs that distress us? In the main, they fall into two categories: beliefs about the gods and beliefs about death. About the gods, people are misled by the "myths," as Epicurus calls them, which permeate the cults of popular religion. The heart of such myths is that the gods are always poking around in the universe to make things happen according to their whims and wishes, that they are interested in human affairs, and that they need to be appeased if things are not to go badly with us. Such beliefs fill us with dread, Epicurus believes, because we never know when some god or demon is going to crush us—perhaps for no

---

*This theme is taken up in the nineteenth century by the utilitarians. See Chapter 19.

*In the first century B.C. the Roman poet Lucretius wrote a long poem popularizing the views of Epicurus. Its title in Latin is *De Rerum Natura* ("on nature"). I borrow the phrase "the way things are" from Rolfe Humphries' version of that title in his very readable translation (Indiana University Press, 1969).

reason we can discern at all. So we anxiously inquire of the diviners, prophets, augurs, soothsayers, astrologers, and priests about what went wrong or whether this is a good time to do so and so and, if not, whether we can do something to make it a good time. (Usually, of course, we can, to the benefit of the "sage" in question.) Fear of the gods, then, is one of the most potent spoilers of contentment.

The other fear concerns death. It is the same anxiety that pulls Hamlet up short and prevents him from taking his own life:

> To die, to sleep;
> To sleep: perchance to dream: ay, there's the rub;
> For in that sleep of death what dreams may come
> When we have shuffled off this mortal coil,
> Must give us pause. [3]

Tradition was full of dreadful stories of the fates of the dead. Lucretius lists some of them: Tantalus, frozen in terror, fears the massive rock balanced above him; Tityos is food for the vultures; Sisyphus must forever roll his rock up the hill, only to see it crash down again; and so on (*WTA*, pp. 114–115). [4]

The good news Epicurus proclaims is that none of this is true. As Lucretius put it:

> Our terrors and our darknesses of mind
> Must be dispelled, not by the sunshine's rays,
> Not by those shining arrows of the light,
> But by insight into nature, and a scheme
> Of systematic contemplation.

> —*WTA*, p. 24

Now, of course, you want desperately to know what this "insight into nature" is that will dispel such terrors. It is nothing new; we are already familiar with it, but not exactly in this guise. What the Epicureans have in mind is the atomism of Leucippus and Democritus.* Why do they choose atomism as the philosophy that tells us "the way things are"? They never make that very clear. One suspects that Epicurus and Lucretius see atomism as particularly serviceable in the role of terror dispeller.

Let us remind ourselves of a few of the main points of atomism:

- Atoms and the void alone exist.
- The common things of the world, including living things, are temporary hookings together of atoms.
- The soul is material, made of very fine atoms, and is therefore mortal.
- Whatever happens is mechanistically determined to happen according to the laws by which atoms combine and fall apart again.

Epicurus accepts atomism as an account of the way things are, except for a slight but crucial modification to the fourth point. The universal determinism envisaged by Democritus is modified so that our free will to act can be salvaged.* After all, if we were not free, how could we follow the prescriptions for happiness Epicurus sets out? Although the atoms mostly follow strictly determined mechanistic paths, *sometimes,* he holds, they "swerve" unaccountably. Lucretius presents the argument:

> If cause forever follows after cause
> In infinite, undeviating sequence
> And a new motion always has to come
> Out of an old one, by fixed law; if atoms
> Do not, by swerving, cause new moves which break
> The laws of fate; if cause forever follows,
> In infinite sequence, cause—where would we get
> This free will that we have, wrested from fate,
> By which we go ahead, each one of us,
> Wherever our pleasures urge? Don't we also swerve
> At no fixed time or place, but as our purpose
> Directs us?

> —*WTA*, p. 59

With this alteration, the rest of atomist metaphysics is acceptable to Epicurus. This is the "insight into nature" that will dispel the terrors of religious myths. But exactly how will it do this?

The gods, Epicurus maintains, surely exist. But like everything else, they too are composed of atoms and the void. Nonetheless, they seem to be immortal, being composed of exceedingly fine atoms

---

*You may find it helpful to review that philosophy, looking especially at pp. 32–35.

*Look again at p. 33 to see what problem atomism poses for free will.

and dwelling between the worlds, unaffected by the grosser impingements of worldly things. (Epicurus thinks there must be many worlds because space is infinite, and our world is clearly limited.) Moreover, we must acknowledge that they dwell in unchangeable blessedness. It follows that they have no concern with the world, nor with human affairs:

> That which is blessed and immortal is not troubled itself, nor does it cause trouble to another. As a result, it is not affected by anger or favor, for these belong to weakness. (*PD* 1)

To be concerned about human affairs, Epicurus thinks, would be an imperfection in the gods. How could they be blessed if they had to worry about what Jones is going to do tomorrow? To poke around in the world, changing this and adjusting that, would mean the gods' immortality would be in jeopardy, for they could not help but be affected by their interventions; and such bumps and bruises are what shake the atoms loose and lead to disintegration.

There is no reason, then, to fear the gods. They have no interest in us and do not intervene directly. The heavenly bodies, moreover, are not demons or divinities that rule our destinies. Sun and moon, planets and stars are composed of atoms and the void just like everything else. Their behavior can be explained in exactly the same kinds of ways we explain familiar phenomena on earth. So it is inappropriate—ignorant—to look to the heavens for signs and portents, to go to astrologers for predictions, and try to read the riddle of the future in the stars. After summarizing some of the traditional stories of the gods, Lucretius says:

> All this, all this is wonderfully told,
> A marvel of tradition, and yet far
> From the real truth. Reject it—for the gods
> Must, by their nature, take delight in peace,
> Forever calm, serene, forever far
> From our affairs, beyond all pain, beyond
> All danger, in their own resources strong,
> Having no need of us at all, above
> Wrath or propitiation.
>
> —*WTA,* p. 70

So much, then, for fear of the gods. What of death? Remember that if atomism is correct, soul and body dissipate together in the event we call death. So there is no future life to look forward to. In what is probably Epicurus' best known saying, he draws the moral.

> Accustom yourself to the belief that death is of no concern to us, since all good and evil lie in sensation and sensation ends with death. . . . Death, the most dreaded of evils, is therefore of no concern to us; for while we exist death is not present, and when death is present we no longer exist. It is therefore nothing either to the living or to the dead since it is not present to the living, and the dead no longer are. (*LM* 124b–125)

Good and evil, of course, are pleasure and pain. These are the sources of happiness and unhappiness. Fear of death is predicated on the assumption that we will experience these sensations after death and perhaps be wretchedly unhappy. But that makes no sense at all, for when we are, death is not, and when death is, we are not. What, then, is there to fear? Death "is of no concern to us." Epicurus adds that it is also foolish to quake in *anticipation* of death. For what isn't painful when it is present should cause no pain when it is anticipated.

Such "insight into nature" can remove at least certain virulent strains of unhappiness from our lives. This is the negative benefit philosophy can confer, but it is not yet enough for happiness. We need also to know how to *live well.* And here too Epicurus gives guidance. The key point is clearly put in the following passage:

> For the very reason that pleasure is the chief and the natural good, we do not choose every pleasure, but there are times when we pass by pleasures if they are outweighed by the hardships that follow; and many pains we think better than pleasures when a greater pleasure will come to us once we have undergone the long-continued pains. . . . By measuring and by looking at advantages and disadvantages, it is proper to decide all these things; for under certain circumstances we treat the good as evil, and again, the evil as good. (*LM* 129b–130a)

The terms "Epicurean" or "hedonist" nowadays suggest someone who is a glutton for pleasures of every kind and indulges to excess in the satisfaction of every desire. This is a complete distortion of the philosophy of Epicurus; in his view, there is no better way to secure for yourself a life of misery than such sensual indulgence. If what you want is pleasure—the most pleasure—then you must be prudent in your pursuit of it.

> When we say that pleasure is the end, we do not mean the pleasure of the profligate or that which depends on physical enjoyment . . . but by pleasure we mean the state wherein the body is free from pain and the mind from anxiety. Neither continual drinking and dancing, nor sexual love, nor the enjoyment of fish and whatever else the luxurious table offers brings about the pleasant life; rather it is produced by the reason which is sober, which examines the motive for every choice and rejection, and which drives away all those opinions through which the greatest tumult lays hold of the mind. (*LM* 131b–132a)

To implement these general principles, we must make a distinction between different sorts of desire.

> You must consider that of the desires some are natural, some are vain, and of those that are natural, some are necessary, others only natural. Of the necessary desires, some are necessary for happiness, some for the ease of the body, some for life itself. (*LM* 127b)

The classification of desires, then, looks like this:

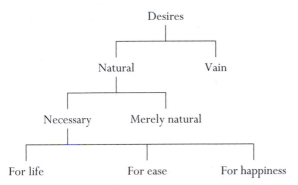

Let us fill in each of these categories with some plausible examples:

- Vain desires: luxuries of all kinds, designer clothing, being thin, keeping up with the Joneses
- Merely natural desires: sexual desire (natural but not necessary)

- Necessary for life: food, drink, shelter
- Necessary for ease: a bed
- Necessary for happiness: friendship

What philosophy can do for us is to make clear that not all desires are on a par and that satisfying some of them will cost more than it is worth. That is surely the case, Epicurus believes, with vain desires. It is likely to be the case with the merely natural desires; at least it is clear that following every sexual passion is a sure prescription for unhappiness. The point is that if we want to be happy, the crucial step is to control and limit our desires—if possible to those which are necessary. Epicurus recommends the simple life, as the following sayings make clear:

> Natural wealth is limited and easily obtained; the wealth defined by vain fancies is always beyond reach. (*PD* 15.144)

> Nothing satisfies him to whom what is enough is little. (*VS* 68)

> To be accustomed to simple and plain living is conducive to health and makes a man ready for the necessary tasks of life. It also makes us more ready for the enjoyment of luxury if at intervals we chance to meet with it, and it renders us fearless against fortune. (*LM* 131a)

So this hedonist, who finds pleasure to be the only natural good, values the old Greek virtue of moderation after all. Now, however, it is recommended on the grounds that it will give us the pleasantest life possible. What of the other virtues, of justice, for instance? Justice is not something good in itself, Epicurus argues, thus taking the view that Glaucon and Adeimantus urge against Socrates (*PD* 31–38).* Justice arises when people make a "compact" together not to injure one another, and it is reasonable to be just as long as that compact pays off—in increased pleasure, of course. Justice, then, is wholly a matter of *nomos* for the Epicureans. It is true that justice and the other virtues are praised, but only as means to a happy life for the individual (the "honesty is the best policy" syndrome).

We must say a word about friendship. The virtue of friendship is held in the highest esteem

---

*See *Republic* Book II and pp. 146–147.

among the Epicureans. They are famous for it. Epicurus established in Athens a "Garden" in which his followers lived, sharing work, study, and conversation. In this Garden and in similar communities across the ancient world, men—including at least some women and slaves—cultivated this virtue. Friendship, they believed, is the key to the highest blessings this life holds. As Epicurus says,

> Friendship dances through the world bidding us all to waken to the recognition of happiness. (*VS* 52)

This blessing, Epicurus assumes, is open to all people—or at least to all who pursue their pleasures with prudence and moderation. So, he assures us, happiness is not restricted to the few. The many, too, may participate.

---

1. Why does Epicurus fasten on pleasure as the good?
2. For what kinds of pain is there a remedy? What is it?
3. What, according to the Epicureans, are the false beliefs about the gods, and how do these false beliefs distress us?
4. What false beliefs about death distress us, according to the Epicureans?
5. How is atomism "corrected"?
6. How does the wise person sort out and deal with desires?
7. What is the Epicurean view of moderation? Of justice? Of friendship?

The Stoics

Our treatment of the Stoic philosophers will be even more incomplete than that of the Epicureans because the Stoics work harder at developing all the major fields of philosophy. They make original contributions to logic, set forth a detailed theory of knowledge, and spend considerable effort on theories of the nature of the universe, elaborated over a period of five centuries by a succession of good minds. Although in many respects the Stoics are consciously opposed to the main principles of the Epicureans, the two schools share one belief: that philosophy is to serve the aim of promoting the best

and happiest life a human being could live. We'll concentrate on the Stoics' views in this area, discussing their other philosophical contributions only to clarify their views about ethics.

The founder of **Stoicism** was Zeno from Citium, a city in Cyprus.* Like several other important figures in this tradition, he was not a native Greek, though he came to Athens as a young man (in about 320 B.C.), studied there, and taught there until his death, about 260 B.C. The fact that Stoic teachers came from areas that Plato and Aristotle would have regarded as barbarian is a sign that times had changed for philosophy. Stoic doctrines from the first had a universality about them that reached beyond the parochial concerns of any city or nation; in this way, they were both a reflection of the enlarged political situation and an influence on it. Socrates had thought of himself as a citizen of Athens. The Stoics considered themselves citizens of the world.

The universality of Stoicism is shown in another way. It appealed to members of all social classes. Among its leading figures was a freed slave, Epictetus (c. A.D. 51–135) and the Roman Emperor Marcus Aurelius (A.D. 121–180).

Let us begin with some reflections on happiness. Stoic ideas of happiness owe much to Socrates, Plato, and Aristotle, all of whom argue that what makes for a truly good life cannot depend on anything outside ourselves.† Stoics carry this ideal of self-sufficiency to the extreme by claiming that absolutely nothing that happens to the wise can disturb their calm happiness. This may seem a startling suggestion.‡

How can this be? Epictetus puts his finger on the crux of the matter:

---

*Note that this is not the Zeno of the paradoxes, the associate of Parmenides.

†Socrates holds that a good person cannot be harmed (*Apology* 41c–d) and Plato argues that happiness is a condition of the harmonious soul. Aristotle claims that "the good is something proper to the person and cannot be taken away from him" (see p. 187).

‡Compare Aristotle, p. 189. As you study Stoicism, ask yourself: Is this an improvement on Aristotle, who holds that there is nonetheless some element of fortune in our happiness?

What upsets people is not things themselves but their judgments about the things. For example, death is nothing dreadful (or else it would have appeared dreadful to Socrates), but instead the judgment about death that it is dreadful—*that* is what is dreadful. So when we are upset or distressed, let us never blame someone else but rather ourselves, that is, our own judgments. (*E* 5)[5]

What makes you unhappy? Suppose you learn that someone you trusted has been spreading untrue stories about you—vicious, nasty stories. This gossip is affecting your friendships. People are beginning to avoid you, act cool toward you. Would this make you unhappy? Most of us would probably say yes.

But, the Stoic urges, think more carefully. It can't really be these events as so far described that make you unhappy. What if you didn't care about such things? What if they meant nothing to you, if you thought this sort of thing was simply beneath your notice? Then they wouldn't make you unhappy.

This kind of thought experiment, the Stoic believes, proves that what happens to you can never *make* you unhappy. What makes you unhappy is "the judgment" you make on what happens to you: That this is important, terrible, and distressing. But if that is so, then your happiness and unhappiness are not beyond your control. Nothing can make you unhappy unless you allow it to do so. Your happiness is entirely up to you.

To understand this in depth, we need to appreciate a crucial distinction:

Some things are up to us and some are not up to us. Our opinions are up to us, and our impulses, desires, aversions—in short, whatever is our own doing. Our bodies are not up to us, nor are our possessions, our reputations, or our public offices, or, that is, whatever is not our own doing. The things that are up to us are by nature free, unhindered, and unimpeded; the things that are not up to us are weak, enslaved, hindered, not our own. So remember, if you think that things naturally enslaved are free or that things not your own are your own, you will be thwarted, miserable, and upset, and will blame both gods and men. But if you think that only what is yours is yours, and that what is not your own is, just as it is, not your own, then

no one will ever coerce you, no one will hinder you, you will blame no one, you will not accuse anyone, you will not do a single thing unwillingly, you will have no enemies, and no one will harm you, because you will not be harmed at all. (*E* 1)[6]

This distinction between what is and what is not within our power makes possible the remarkable claims of the Stoic. When are we happy? When we get what we desire. Suppose now that we set our heart on the things that are beyond our power—a beautiful body, a fine estate, fame, being chairman of the board. Reflection will surely convince you that these things are at best only partly in our power; circumstances must cooperate if they are to be ours. If these are what we really want, disappointment is sure to follow. If we don't get them, we will be unhappy. If we do get them, we will be anxious lest we lose them. And neither disappointment nor anxiety is part of a happy life.

What, then, is within our control? "Your way of dealing with appearances" (*E* 6), Epictetus answers. What appears in the world is not in our control, but how we deal with it is. How we view appearances, our opinions about them, whether we desire or fear them—all this is within our power. This is our proper business, the area of our concern. Of all that lies beyond this sphere, we should be prepared to say, "You are nothing in relation to me" (*E* 1).

What this means in practice can be gathered from several examples.

When you call the slave boy, keep in mind that he is capable of not paying attention, and even if he does pay attention he is capable of not doing any of the things that you want him to. But he is not in such a good position that your being upset or not depends on him. (*E* 12)

A person's master is someone who has power over what he wants or does not want, either to obtain it or take it away. Whoever wants to be free, therefore, let him not want or avoid anything that is up to others. Otherwise he will necessarily be a slave. (*E* 14)

It is possible to learn the will of nature from the things in which we do not differ from each other. For example, when someone else's little slave boy breaks his cup we are ready to say, "It's one of those things that just happen." Certainly, then, when your own cup is broken you should be just the way you were when the other person's was broken. Transfer the same idea to larger matters. Someone else's child is dead, or his wife. There is no one who would not say, "It's the lot of a human being." But when one's own dies, immediately it is, "Alas! Poor me!" But we should have remembered how we feel when we hear of the same thing about others. (*E* 26)

Suppose now that we have, by dint of determination and long practice (for this is what it would take), gotten to the point where we always make the distinction. We never set our hearts on the things that are not in our power to control. It seems we have gotten ourselves into a serious difficulty. Having enough food to eat (to take just one example) is not something entirely within our control. People who live in lands stricken by famine are evidence enough for that. Are we not to desire food? And if not, how are we to live? At this point, it seems as though the Stoics are condemned by their principles to starve virtuously, but perhaps contentedly, to death. Is there a way they can solve this problem?

The key to the solution is found in the positive advice the Stoic gives: *to keep our wills in harmony with nature* (*E* 4, 6, 13, 30; and *M* 2.9). But to understand this, we have to explore what the Stoics mean by "nature." We need not go into the details of their nature philosophy, but the central idea is crucial.

Whatever exists, according to the Stoics, is material or corporeal. Our only certainties come from sense experience, and sense experience always reveals the material. But like Heraclitus, they hold that the material world is ordered by a rational principle, a *logos*.* That is what makes the world a world rather than a chaos. This principle, which (like Heraclitus) they sometimes call the fiery element, is not just a passive pattern in things; it is the ordering of the world by and for a reason.† As the ordering principle of the world, it is appropriately called divine.

Thus God, for the Stoics, is not like the gods of the Epicureans, separate from the world and un-

concerned with it. Nor is the Stoic God like the unmoved mover of Aristotle, independent and self-sufficient, related to the world only as an ideal that the world tries to emulate. Neither of these divinities could be known through the senses. The Stoics conceive of God (whom, again like Heraclitus, they are willing to call Zeus) as *immanent* in the world.* Whatever material being you come across has a divine element within it. So the Stoics are committed to a version of pantheism (God is all and all is God), though the term "God" emphasizes the *ordering* and the term "nature" the *ordered* aspects of things. Marcus Aurelius expresses these views:

> Universal Nature's impulse was to create an orderly world. It follows, then, that everything now happening must follow a logical sequence; if it were not so, the prime purpose towards which the impulses of the World-Reason are directed would be an irrational one. Remembrance of this will help you to face many things more calmly. (*M* 7.75)

Everything "must follow a logical sequence." It is apparent that the Stoics are believers in Destiny or Fate. Whatever happens happens of necessity. But this is not a cause for despair, since Destiny is the same as Divine Providence. Whatever happens is determined by the divine reason, and so it must happen for the best.† As Epictetus says,

> Just as a target is not set up to be missed, in the same way nothing bad by nature happens in the world. (*E* 27)

Although "whatever will be, will be," it does not follow that we can simply drift. Your attitude toward what happens makes an enormous difference, for on that your happiness or unhappiness depends.

> Do not seek to have events happen as you want them to, but instead want them to happen as they do happen, and your life will go well. (*E* 8)

If we are to be happy, then, we must keep our wills in harmony with nature. And we now can see that this is identical with keeping our wills in harmony with both reason and God, for nature is the sphere of events governed by the benevolent pur-

---

*See pp. 21–22.
†See p. 21.

*See p. 22.
†Compare Heraclitus again, p. 21.

pose of a rational deity. The Stoics sometimes speak of the soul as a *microcosm* (a little world) and compare it to the macrocosm of the universe. Our task, they hold, is to use our reason to order the microcosm in a way that mirrors the ordering of the macrocosm. This is possible because the reason within us is merely an aspect of the divine reason that orders the world as a whole. God is not only immanent in the macrocosm but is also present within each of us.

Now we can see how the Stoics address the problem raised earlier. Everything in nature contains its own ordering principle in harmony with the great order of the whole. In living things there is a natural tendency toward certain ends—self-preservation in particular, together with all that serves that end. This is part of the Divine Providence and is not to be despised. This is why animals seek food and shelter; and this is why they naturally seek to preserve their species. Denying these *natural* tendencies would certainly not keep one's will in harmony with nature!

So the Stoics eat when hungry, drink when thirsty, and do what is necessary to preserve themselves from the weather. It is in accordance with nature so to do. But, and this point is crucial, they pursue these natural goals with equanimity, not being disturbed if their quest for them is frustrated. In regard to what is natural to a living being, the Stoics distinguish what is *preferred,* what is *shunned,* and what is *indifferent.* We humans "prefer" not only food and shelter, but also skills, knowledge, health, reputation, and wealth. We "shun" their opposites, and we find many things "indifferent"; about them we simply don't care. The natural tendencies in human beings determine what falls in one class or another.

So there is nothing wrong with pursuing what is preferred. Where people go wrong, however, is in attributing some *absolute value* to all these things. And the mark of this wrong turn is their reaction when they do not get what they want: distress, despair, resentment, and general unhappiness. The wise person, by contrast, "uses such things without requiring them."[7] This attitude makes possible the equanimity of the Stoics, in which nothing that happens can destroy their calm. There is only one thing

to which the Stoic attaches absolute value: that his will should be in harmony with nature. In comparison with that, even the things "preferred" seem only indifferent.

This means that the only true good is virtue: a life in harmony with nature, reason, and God. Stoics and Epicureans carry on a running battle over just this point. The Epicureans, of course, hold that the only good is pleasure, and everything else (including virtue) is good only in relation to that. Stoics typically respond in a most extreme fashion, denying not only that pleasure is the one true good, but also that it is even in the realm of the "preferred." Pleasure, according to the Stoics, is *never* to be pursued; it is not an appropriate end at all.

The Epicureans argue, as we have seen, that pleasure is the only natural good, the root of all our choosing. The Stoics reply that this is far from so. Our natural tendencies are for the acquisition of certain *things,* such as food, which is necessary for self-preservation. They do not deny that eating when hungry is pleasurable, but the pleasure is an *accompaniment* to the eating, not the end sought. Pleasure on its own won't keep you alive! People go wrong exactly here, in seeking the by-product instead of the end—a sure recipe, the Stoics think, for disaster. A virtuous person will in fact lead a pleasant life. But if she makes the pleasant life her object, she will miss both virtue *and* the pleasure that accompanies it!

There are two corollaries to the view that only virtue is the good. First, the only thing that counts in estimating the goodness of an action is the intention of the agent. You can see why this must be so. An action is an attempt to change the world in some way; whether the action succeeds depends upon the cooperation of the world; the world is not entirely in the control of the agent; and so the goodness or badness of the *person* or the *action* cannot depend on the action's outcome. But this means that a judgment on the agent must be a judgment on the agent's intention. Cleanthes gives the example of two slaves sent out to find someone. The one slave searches diligently but fails to find him. The other loafs about and runs into him by accident. Which is the better man? (*SES* 264). The Stoic has no doubt about the answer and takes it to show that results are to be considered indifferent. What counts is the state of your will; that is in your control, and that is what is absolutely good or bad. So the entire concentration of life must be put into the effort to set your will in harmony with nature. The outcome must be nothing to you.

This leads us to the second corollary. The important thing is to do one's duty. The notion of "duty" has not played a large role to this point. We hardly find it in Socrates or Plato, nor in Aristotle, nor Epicurus. These philosophers are asking: What is the best life for a human being to live? They never imagine that it might be a duty or an obligation to lead such a life. It is just a question of what the prudent or wise person would do. Why, we might wonder, does the notion of duty suddenly come to prominence in Stoic thought?

It has a natural home here because of the connection between the divine, rational principle that providentially guides the course of the world and the notion of *law*. It is law that shows us our duties. The principles governing the world are not only descriptions of how the world inevitably *does* go; they express how things, according to their natures, *should* go. So they take on for us the aspect of law reflected in civil law: they prescribe to us our duties and obligations. This notion of **natural law** (a concept we owe largely to the Stoics) is obviously a development of Heraclitean ideas about the *logos*. If we behave in certain ways, consequences—determined by the ordering principles of the world—necessarily follow. For example, if you smoke cigarettes for a while, you will become addicted. Since addictions are bad—they hand control of your life over to something "not your own"—understanding the order of the world is also understanding that you have a duty not to smoke.

The Stoics devote considerable attention to duties, distinguishing several classes of duties and examining particular cases. We need not explore the details, but we should note the one duty that is clear and always overriding: the duty to harmonize our intentions with the law of nature. This is the duty to be virtuous or to perfect ourselves. The microcosm of our soul *ought* to be in harmony with the order without. It is our first and most important task to see that it is. And this means that we must

concern ourselves above all with the things in our power—with our beliefs, attitudes, and desires. Everything else must be, as Epictetus says, nothing to us in comparison. We began the discussion of Stoic thought by considering happiness. But now we can see that if we devote ourselves to virtue, to doing our duty, our happiness will take care of itself.[*]

As you can see, Stoics believe that whatever city or nation we belong to, we are first of all citizens of the world. All men are brothers, for all are "children" of the same God. The consideration we owe to our neighbors is not different from that we owe to strangers. All of us, Greeks, Romans, and barbarians, are part of the same world and partake of the same divine reason. Marcus Aurelius says,

> If the power of thought is universal among mankind, so likewise is the possession of reason, making us rational creatures. It follows, therefore, that this reason speaks no less universally to us all with its "thou shalt" or "thou shalt not." So then there is a world-law; which in turn means that we are all fellow-citizens and share a common citizenship, and that the world is a single city. (*M* 4.4)

Finally, let us note one more point of contrast with the Epicureans. Stoics are much more tolerant of popular beliefs than are the Epicureans (*SES* 343–380). Stoics tend to tolerate the polytheism that permeates the times, think there is some truth in astrology, and even accept the legitimacy of divination (foretelling the future by interpreting signs). Though there is just one God, everything partakes of his nature. It is therefore easy to view the gods of popular religion as symbols of the sacredness of one aspect of nature or another. Since the entire cosmos is a harmony, why shouldn't the stars reflect what is happening and is to happen on earth? And since everything is necessarily connected with everything else, it seems not unreasonable that a diviner could "read" the signs and predict what is to come.

---

[*] Compare this thought with what Jesus says in the Sermon on the Mount: "Seek first the Kingdom of God and his righteousness, and all these things will be added to you as well" (Matthew 6:33).

This tolerance is bolstered by the development of a system of allegorical interpretation, by which tales of the gods (in Homer and Hesiod, for example) are accepted as symbolic representations of truths that can be supported in a more scientific way. No doubt this tolerance on the part of the Stoics helps the spread of their doctrine, but it also makes Stoicism susceptible to corruption by what tough-minded Epicurean atomists would call sheer superstition.

Let Gilbert Murray have the last word.

> The glory of the Stoics is to have built up a religion of extraordinary nobleness; the glory of the Epicureans is to have upheld an ideal of sanity and humanity stark upright amid a reeling world, and, like the old Spartans, never to have yielded one inch of ground to the common foe.[8]

---

1. On what distinction does Stoicism rest? Explain how making this distinction is the key, for the Stoic, to both happiness and freedom.
2. How are God and nature related? What of evil?
3. What does it mean to keep one's will in line with nature?
4. Why doesn't a Stoic starve to death?
5. What is virtue, according to the Stoics?
6. Explain the Stoic critique of Epicurean philosophy.
7. Why does the Stoic believe intention is more important than results in evaluating the worth of a person?
8. What is it about the Stoic view of nature that makes duty an important notion?

The Skeptics

What has skepticism to do with happiness? We are apt to suppose that someone who doesn't know, or at least thinks he doesn't know, must on that account be *unhappy*. Aristotle, who holds that all men by nature desire to know, would surely think so. Moreover, we are almost all brought up as believers in something or other. Belief is as natural to us as breathing. What sense could it make to suspend all our beliefs, to get rid of that habit? And how could that make us happy? These are the perplexing

questions we must now address. The ancient skeptics give some surprising answers.

Again we shall simplify, this time by focusing on the most radical group of skeptics, who call themselves by the name of a shadowy fourth-century figure Pyrrho, about whom little is known. From what we do know, it seems that Pyrrho is not interested in speculative or scientific philosophy, but only in the practical question of how best to live. But it is not sheer disinterest; it is what we might call principled disinterest. His pupil Timon is reported to have said that the nature of things is "indeterminable," meaning that we cannot determine that things are more like this than they are like that.[9] But why not? Let us review a little of the story we have been telling.

From the time of Parmenides it is maintained that a distinction must be drawn between things as they appear to us and things as they are in themselves. The core insight is that things may not appear as they really are. The realm of appearance is generally agreed to be the world of the senses, which sometimes deceives us about reality: The straight oar in water looks bent; square towers in the distance look round; honey tastes bitter to a sick person; and so on. So the question forces itself upon thinkers: Is there some way to tell what things are really like? The usual answer is given in terms of intelligence or reason, and we have seen some of the results. Parmenides, following what he takes to be the best argument, asserts that reality is the One. Democritus holds that it is atoms and the void. For Plato, the independent world of eternally unchanging Forms constitutes the really real. And for Aristotle, reality is made up of individual substances that are composites of matter and form.

It is partly this diversity of answers that motivates the Pyrrhonists, who like to gather these and even more examples of disagreement among the philosophers. But sheer disagreement does not prove that nothing can be known about reality; some one of these views may well be correct and the others mistaken; or perhaps none of them are correct, but some future development of them might be. And we might come to know that. To support the claim that the nature of things is "indeterminable," we must say more.

The later Pyrrhonists systematize the arguments in favor of skeptical conclusions in a number of types or *modes* of reasoning. Our best source for these is a Greek physician, Sextus Empiricus, who lived in the second century A.D. Let us survey several of these modes.

The first mode stresses that the sense organs of animals differ from species to species. His arguments are rather primitive, since not much was known about the details of animal sense organs until recent times. But we can think of the registration of the world in the many-faceted eye of a fly, in the echolocation of a bat, and in what the frog's eye tells the frog's brain.[10] Cats and owls see much better in the dark than we do, and the olfactory world of the dog must be immensely rich compared to ours. In terms like these, we can understand what Sextus says:

> But if the same things appear different owing to the variety in animals, we shall, indeed, be able to state our own impressions of the real object, but as to its essential nature we shall suspend judgment. For we cannot ourselves judge between our own impressions and those of the other animals, since we ourselves are involved in the dispute and are, therefore, rather in need of a judge than competent to pass judgment ourselves. . . . If, then, owing to the variety in animals their sense-impressions differ, and it is impossible to judge between them, we must necessarily suspend judgment regarding the external underlying objects.[11] (*OP* 1.59–61)

Here we have some of the key notions of skepticism. Because the nature of the "external underlying objects" appears differently to creatures with different sense organs, we cannot confidently judge that these objects are as they appear to us. If they appear one way to us and another way to the bat or fly or frog, it would be arbitrary to pick one of those ways rather than another and say that is how it really is. The result is that we must "suspend judgment."

The second mode concerns differences among human beings. These are particularly notable, Sextus tells us, with respect to objects of choice. He quotes poets and dramatists who exclaim about the variations in human preferences, and adds,

> Seeing, then, that choice and avoidance depend on pleasure and displeasure, while pleasure and

displeasure depend on sensation and sense-impression, whenever some men choose the very things which are avoided by others, it is logical for us to conclude that they are also differently affected by the same things, since otherwise they would all alike have chosen or avoided the same things. But if the same objects affect men differently owing to the differences in the men, then, on this ground also, we shall reasonably be led to suspension of judgment. For while we are, no doubt, able to state what each of the underlying objects appears to be, relatively to each difference, we are incapable of explaining what it is in reality. For we shall have to believe either all men or some. But if we believe all, we shall be attempting the impossible and accepting contradictories; and if some, let us be told whose opinions we are to endorse. (*OP* 1.87–88)

The message is the same; we must suspend judgment. What does that mean? It means that we do not say either yes or no; we do not affirm or deny any proposition about the real nature of the underlying objects. We do not say, as the Stoics do, that they are part of the divine nature, nor do we deny that. We do not say, as the atomists do, that reality is composed of atoms and the void, but neither do we deny it. We do not say, as the Platonists do, that the things of sense are shadows of the eternal Forms, but neither do we deny it.

Note carefully that we *can* state what the object *appears* to be. We just refrain from making any further judgments. In terms of the appearance/reality distinction, the skeptic restricts himself to appearance. He is forced to this by the considerations in the "modes," of which we have examined only two. Some of the others concern the differences among our own organs of sense, the dependence of appearances on differing circumstances, and the differences in customs and laws.

There are also modes of a more formal character, standard ways of criticizing the arguments of the philosophers. A skeptic considers someone who affirms what is not evident *dogmatic;* and any claim about how things *really* are, independently of their appearance to our senses, is a claim about the non-evident. To be dogmatic, in this sense, is to claim to know something for which you have no evidence. So all the other schools of philosophy, with their theories about the reality beyond the appearances, are classified as dogmatic by the skeptics.

One of these more formal modes is based on an "infinite regress" argument and another on the charge of "circular reasoning." An infinite regress is generated when a claim *A* is supported by another claim *B* and *B* itself needs to be supported. If it is supported by *C,* the skeptic will ask how *C* is to be supported, and so on. Circular reasoning occurs when *A* is supported by *B, B* by *C,* and *C* by *A.* The argument goes in a circle.

Here is an example of Sextus making use of these modes. Suppose one of the "dogmatic" philosophers (a Platonist, perhaps, or a Stoic) has made some claim about the real nature of an object.

> The matter proposed is either a sense-object or a thought-object, but whichever it is, it is an object of controversy; for some say that only sensibles are true, others only intelligibles, others that some sensibles and some intelligible objects are true. Will they then assert that the controversy can or cannot be decided? If they say it cannot, we have it granted that we must suspend judgement. . . . But if they say that it can be decided, we ask by what is it to be decided? For example, in the case of the sense-object . . . is it to be decided by a sense-object or a thought-object? For if they say by a sense-object, since we are inquiring about sensibles that object itself also will require another to confirm it; and if that too is to be a sense-object, it likewise will require another for its confirmation, and so on ad infinitum. And if the sense-object shall have to be decided by a thought-object, then, since thought-objects also are controverted, this being an object of thought will need examination and confirmation. Whence then will it gain confirmation? If from an intelligible object, it will suffer a similar regress ad infinitum; and if from a sensible object, since an intelligible was adduced to establish the sensible and a sensible to establish the intelligible, the Mode of circular reasoning is brought in. (*OP* 1.170–72)

The key question here is, "By what is it to be decided?" To use Protagoras' term, what is the "measure" we are to judge by? These modes attempt to show that the question cannot be satisfactorily answered, for the answer either will itself be subject to that very same question (infinite regress) or will

assume what is to be proved (circular reasoning). The moral is the same: We must suspend judgment.

All of the various modes circle around a central point, which we must now explore more explicitly. It can be called the problem of the **criterion.** Claims to knowledge and truth are a dime a dozen; the Hellenistic world, as we have seen, is filled with them (just as ours is)—religious, popular, and philosophical. The problem we face is how to decide among them. By what mark or standard or criterion are we to decide where truth and knowledge really lie? This problem faces thoughtful people in an insistent way, and numerous attempts are made to solve it. The skeptics argue, however, that this is an insoluble problem: *No* satisfactory criterion is to be found. In a chapter called "Does a Criterion of Truth Really Exist?" Sextus Empiricus writes,

> Of those, then, who have treated of the criterion some have declared that a criterion exists—the Stoics, for example, and certain others—while by some its existence is denied, as by . . . Xenophanes of Colophon, who say—"Over all things opinion bears sway";* while we have adopted suspension of judgement as to whether it does or does not exist. This dispute, then, they will declare to be either capable or incapable of decision; and if they shall say it is incapable of decision they will be granting on the spot the propriety of suspension of judgement, while if they say it admits of decision, let them tell us whereby it is to be decided, since we have no accepted criterion, and do not even know, but are still inquiring, whether any criterion exists. Besides, in order to decide the dispute which has arisen about the criterion, we must possess an accepted criterion by which we shall be able to judge the dispute; and in order to possess an accepted criterion, the dispute about the criterion must first be decided. And when the argument thus reduces itself to a form of circular reasoning, the discovery of the criterion becomes impracticable, since we do not allow them to adopt a criterion by assumption, while if they offer to judge the criterion by a criterion we force them to a regress ad infinitum. And furthermore, since demonstration requires a demonstrated criterion, while the criterion requires an approved demonstration, they are forced into circular reasoning. (*OP* 2.18–20)

*See pp. 17, 18.

Let us note several points in this passage. First, any claim that some principle is a criterion for truth itself needs to be supported. We shall need a criterion to decide whether that support is successful. And any attempt to provide such a criterion will either be forced into the infinite regress of criteria by which to decide criteria by which to decide . . . or it will be circular, begging the question in favor of some assumed criterion. We can represent the argument by a flow chart. (See the accompanying figure.)

No matter which alternatives we choose, the result is the same. And if we suspend judgment about a criterion, it follows that judgment is sus-

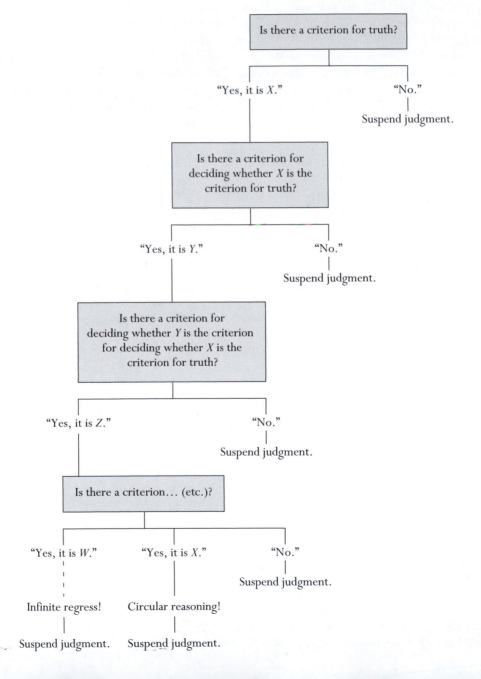

pended about each and every claim to knowledge; for each claim to know depends on there being a criterion by which it is singled out as true knowledge. So if we cannot solve the problem of the criterion, we must suspend judgment generally.

Second, note that Sextus does *not* claim there is no criterion of truth; about that very question—is there or is there not a criterion?—the Pyrrhonian skeptic suspends judgment. There is a kind of skeptic who claims that nothing can be known. This kind is subject to a devastating counter: He can be asked how he knows *that*. But Sextus is careful not to make any such claim. He does not know whether anything can be known or not. If he is pushed back a step and asked whether he knows that he does not know, he will presumably confess that he doesn't. His attitude throughout is one of *noncommitment* to any knowledge claims that concern how things really are.

The argument about the criterion seems like a very powerful argument indeed. It sweeps the board clean.*

But this surely leads to a pressing question: How then can we live? If we make no judgments about the world we are in, won't we be paralyzed? To eat bread rather than a stone seems to depend on a judgment that bread will nourish you and a stone will not. *Can* we suspend judgments like that?

Here we must remember that skeptics do not deny appearances. Skeptics claim that we can live, and live well, by restricting ourselves to how things seem. Though there may not be a criterion to distinguish reality from appearance, there is a criterion for life and action. Sextus tells us that this practical criterion

> denotes the standard of action by conforming to which in the conduct of life we perform some actions and abstain from others. . . . The criterion, then, of the Skeptic School is, we say, the appearance, giving this name to what is virtually the sense-presentation. For since this lies in feeling and involuntary affection, it is not open to question. . . .
>
> Adhering, then, to appearances we live in accordance with the normal rules of life, undogmati-

cally, seeing that we cannot remain wholly inactive. (*OP* 1.21–23)

Sextus was a physician, a member of a school of medicine that followed similar principles. These doctors were unwilling to speculate about the "real" nature of diseases, about underlying causes and unobservable entities—either physical or demonic—posited to explain illness. They wished to restrict themselves to what they observed, to appearances. If they observed that certain symptoms responded to certain medicines, they noted and remembered this. If they observed that diet positively affected the outcome of a certain disease, they had a rule to prescribe that diet for that disease. It was, we might say, empirical medicine rather than speculative. If medicine can be done in this way, then why can't life be lived according to the same principles?*

So if we are skeptics, we eat what experience has shown to be connected with health and behave in ways correlated with positive outcomes. We do not pronounce things to be truly good or truly bad, for about such claims we suspend judgment. But it is beyond question that bread *appears* to nourish us and scarcely less so that obedience to the law *appears* to be profitable. We do not worry about absolutes, either of truth or of goodness, for they are unattainable. But we follow appearances. In the matter of behavior, we conform to the customs of the land in which we live, for these customs express what appears to our fellow citizens to be good. We live "in accordance with the normal rules of life," but "undogmatically," not claiming that this is somehow the absolutely best or right thing to do.

As you can see, the relativism against which Plato struggles and which Aristotle thinks he has overcome is reborn. It is not reborn as a doctrine claiming to be the truth about matters, for no such claims are made. But since things may appear differently to different people or cultures, a *practical relativism* is the result. We might also note that

---

*Compare Montaigne, p. 311.

*One might question, of course, how successfully medicine can be done on such a restricted empirical base. Modern medicine does not restrict itself to what is observable but makes use of the theoretical constructions of modern science. Does the same hold for principles of living?

skepticism tends to be a profoundly conservative view, for it will nearly always be the case that adaptation to customs and laws—whatever they may be—will appear to be the best way to live. Plato struggles to delineate the outlines of an ideal state, because he is convinced that there is an absolute goodness in reality that states might (and typically do) miss. And the Stoics think they have a criterion for correcting customs and laws in the appeal to the law of nature. But a skeptic has no such fulcrum on which to work the lever of reform. Skeptics are not great revolutionaries, religiously, politically, or morally.

On what grounds, then, could the skeptic recommend his views? There are two. One, which we have looked at in some detail, amounts to the argument that there really is no alternative. Every nonskeptical view founders in one way or another on the problem of the criterion. But the second ground is a more positive one and brings us back to the connection between skepticism and happiness. As long as we seek certainty about the true nature of things, we will be in doubt; if we are in doubt, we will be perturbed; as long as we are perturbed, we won't be happy. So the key to quietude and happiness is to give up the search for certainty. We must cease to be dogmatists and become skeptics.

> For the man who opines that anything is by nature good or bad is for ever being disquieted; when he is without the things which he deems good he believes himself to be tormented by things naturally bad and he pursues after the things which are, as he thinks, good; which when he has obtained he keeps falling into still more perturbations because of his irrational and immoderate elation, and in his dread of a change of fortune he uses every endeavor to avoid losing the things which he deems good. On the other hand, the man who determines nothing as to what is naturally good or bad neither shuns nor pursues anything eagerly; and in consequence, he is unperturbed.
>
> The Skeptic, in fact, had the same experience which is said to have befallen the painter Apelles. Once, they say, when he was painting a horse and wished to represent in the painting the horse's foam, he was so unsuccessful that he gave up the attempt and flung at the picture the sponge on which he used to wipe the paints off his brush, and the

mark of the sponge produced the effect of a horse's foam. So, too, the Skeptics were in hopes of gaining quietude by means of a decision regarding the disparity of the objects of sense and of thought, and being unable to effect this they suspended judgment; and they found that quietude, as if by chance, followed upon their suspense, even as a shadow follows its substance. (*OP* 1.27–29)

This quietude, or tranquillity of soul, is what the skeptic means by happiness. Or, if happiness is more than this, it is at least a necessary condition for happiness; without it no one can be happy. Though no one can escape trouble entirely, most people are doubly troubled, once by the pain or suffering and once by two further beliefs: that this is something bad or evil they are undergoing, and that either they do not (in some absolute sense) deserve it, or—worse yet—that they do. The skeptic at least does not suffer these further agonies. So the skeptics recommend their attitude, the suspension of judgment about all claims to truth, on the grounds that doing so provides a basis on which a happy life can be built.

These may seem rather minimal claims and their kind of happiness rather a pale one. It seems to be a retreat of some magnitude from the "high" view of happiness expressed, for instance, by Aristotle: activity of soul in accord with excellence. But perhaps the times did not realistically allow for more—for most people. Furthermore, the problem of the criterion still remains; unless this can be solved, maybe no more can reasonably be expected. This is a very real problem with which numerous future philosophers struggle.*

1. What should we conclude from an examination of (a) differences in sense organs among animals; and (b) differences in taste among humans?
2. About what kind of thing does the skeptic "suspend judgment"? What does that term mean?
3. What is it to be "dogmatic"?
4. How does the skeptic use infinite regress and circular reasoning arguments?

---

*See for example Augustine (pp. 233–234) and particularly René Descartes (*Meditation III*) and Hegel (pp. 466–467).

5. What is the problem of the criterion? (Study the flow chart carefully.)

6. By what practical criterion does the skeptic live?

7. Why does the skeptic recommend suspending judgment as a key to happiness?

For Further Thought

1. Evaluate Epicurus' reasons for thinking that pleasure is the good for human beings in the light of (a) Aristotle's reasons for thinking that this could not possibly be correct and (b) the Stoic critique of this claim. Who do you think has the best of the argument here? Why?

2. Apply the problem of the criterion (with its considerations of infinite regress and circular reasoning) to Aristotle's theory of knowledge in terms of deduction, induction, and first principles. Can Aristotle survive such a critique? If you think he can, try to say how. If not, why not?

3. If you consider the popular culture of our day, would you say it is Platonistic, Aristotelian, Epicurean, Stoic, or Skeptical? Or is it just in large measure unwise?

Notes

1. Gilbert Murray, *Five Stages of Greek Religion* (New York: Doubleday, Anchor Books, 1955), 139. I am indebted to this source for numerous points in this section.

2. All quotations from Epicurus' works are from *Letters, Principal Doctrines, and Vatican Sayings,* trans. Russel M. Geer (Indianapolis: Library of Liberal Arts, 1964). Within this text, references to specific works will be as follows: *PD, Principal Doctrines; LM, Letter to Menoeceus; IP, Letter to Pythocles;* and *VS, Vatican Sayings.*

3. William Shakespeare, *Hamlet,* act 3, scene 1, lines 64–68.

4. Quotations from Lucretius, *The Way Things Are,* trans. Rolfe Humphries (Bloomington: Indiana University Press, 1969), are cited in the text using the abbreviation *WTA.* References are to page numbers of this edition.

5. Quotations from *The Handbook of Epictetus,* trans. Nicholas P. White (Indianapolis: Hackett, 1983), are cited in the text using the abbreviation *E.*

6. See also Marcus Aurelius, *Meditations,* trans. Maxwell Staniforth (New York: Penguin Books, 1964), 6.41. Quotations from this work are hereafter cited in the text using the abbreviation *M.*

7. Attributed to Chrysippus by Eduard Zeller in *Stoics, Epicureans, and Skeptics* (New York: Russell and Russell, 1962), 284–285. Subsequent quotations from this work are cited in the text using the abbreviation *SES.*

8. Murray, *Five Stages of Greek Religion,* 125.

9. Charlotte L. Stough, *Greek Scepticism* (Berkeley: University of California Press, 1969), 17.

10. There is a well-known study of interest in this connection: "What the Frog's Eye Tells the Frog's Brain," by J. Y. Lettvin, H. R. Maturana, W. S. McCulloch, and W. H. Pitts, *Proceedings of the Institute of Radio Engineers* 47 (1959): 1940–1951.

11. Quotations from Sextus Empiricus, *Outlines of Pyrrhonism* (Cambridge, MA: Harvard University Press, 1955), are cited in the text using the abbreviation *OP.*

THE CHRISTIANS

Sin, Salvation, and Love

Although Augustine in the late fourth and early fifth centuries would come to consider Christianity the one true philosophy, Judeo–Chistian thought is different from that of the Greek tradition we have been examining. Question and answer, proposal and critique, dialectical argument, and the reliance on human experience and rationality mark the Greek philosophers from Thales to Sextus Empiricus. They do not all agree about the success of this way of searching for the truth. Aristotle is confident, the skeptics pessimistic. But they do all agree that there is no alternative to using our wits to unravel the mystery of our existence.

Suppose we provisionally take this to be the peculiar conviction of the philosopher.* Then we could well say that what we find in early Christianity and the Hebrew tradition out of which it grew is not philosophy, but prophecy. The mode of procedure is not discussion, but proclamation. The typical form is not "let us examine" but "Thus says the Lord!" The appropriate response is not questioning but acceptance and, perhaps, repentance. From the very beginning, this tradition emphasizes righteousness, human deviation from it, and what it means to live before God.

Nonetheless, it is important for the story of Western philosophy to understand the essentials of this tradition. For in becoming the major religious tradition of the West, Christianity has had an enormous influence on the way men have philosophized ever since. For more than a thousand years, Christianity provided a framework in which nearly all serious intellectual work was done; ever since, its influence has never been lacking. In ethics particularly, the Christian ideal has been absorbed by many secular thinkers, while others have felt the need to attack it—thus indirectly manifesting its importance.* Let us try to capture some-

---

*Provisional because Augustine and other Christian philosophers will modify this conviction in an important way. See pp. 237 and 259–260.

*The two major ethical theories of modern times, utilitarianism and the duty-theory of Immanuel Kant, both develop Christian themes in a more or less secular way. See "Reason and Morality," in Chapter 16. See also Chapter 19. Nietzsche attacks the Christhing of the spirit, as well as the beliefs, of this tradition.

Background

Jesus, whom the Christians call "Christ" or "Messiah" (meaning "the anointed one"), was a Jew, as were all of his first followers; Christianity is a modification of the Jewish heritage. So if we want to understand the Christians, it is necessary to sketch something of the history in terms of which they understood themselves. Their history is the history of the Hebrew people. Let us outline, then, certain central convictions that grow out of that history and that the Christians take for granted.

Of the very first importance is the conviction that there is *one God.* We may be able to trace some development of this concept—from a kind of tribal deity, to a God superior to the gods of their neighbors, to one having the exclusive claim to worship—but by the time of the great prophets from the eighth to the sixth centuries B.C., it was already clear to the Hebrews that all other "gods" were mere pretenders, "idols" that it was sinful to reverence.*

> Thus says the Lord, the King of Israel
> and his Redeemer, the Lord of hosts:
> "I am the first and I am the last;
> besides me there is no god. . . .
>
> "To whom will you liken me and make me equal,
> and compare me, that we may be alike?
> Those who lavish gold from the purse,
> and weigh out silver in the scales,
> hire a goldsmith, and he makes it into a god;
> then they fall down and worship!
> They lift it upon their shoulders, they carry it,
> they set it in its place, and it stands there;
> it cannot move from its place.
> If one cries to it, it does not answer
> or save him from his trouble."
>
> —Isa. 44:6, 46:5–7[1]

The one true god differs from idols in all these respects. He is not made by men; he cannot be seen or touched or carried; he is not restricted to any one place; and when you cry to him, he does help. He is, moreover, "the first and the last," meaning that he has no beginning and no ending. He is eternal. He alone is worthy of worship and reverence.

God is the creator of the entire visible universe. The world is not eternal, as Aristotle thinks; nor is it God or an aspect of God, as the Stoics believed. God precedes and transcends the world, which is, however, wholly dependent on his power. The first words in the Hebrew scriptures are

> In the beginning God created the heavens and the earth. (Gen. 1:1)

Moreover, God is entirely good, righteous, just, and holy. And this goodness is transmitted to the creation; on each of the "days" of creation, after God made light, the heavens, dry land, vegetation, animals, and human beings, we read that "God saw that it was good." Finding the world to be good, the Hebrews have a positive attitude toward it; the world is not something to flee or escape from; it is not just a shadowy image of true reality; and the body is not—as it is for Plato—a prison in which we are alienated from our true home. It is in this world that we have a home; it is here that God has put us; it is here that our tasks and purposes are to be accomplished and our happiness achieved. The shadowy existence in the underworld after death is not anything to desire.*

But this task and happiness are complicated by the fact of sin. In the well-known story of the first man and woman, we read that human beings have succumbed to the temptation to "be like God, knowing good and evil" (Gen. 3:5). Not content with their status, unhappy in obedience, wanting to play God themselves, humans have made themselves corrupt and find themselves outside the

---

tian ideal as self-deceptively grounded in weakness and resentment. See Chapter 20.
*Compare Xenophanes, pp. 15–16, who is writing at about this same time.

*See for instance Psalms 39:3 and 88:3–5, 10–12. Compare also Homer's Achilles on p. 8. Belief in a "resurrection of the body" grew among Jews in the several centuries before Jesus, however. In Jesus' time, one party, the Sadducees, held out against the belief. See Mark 12:18–27.

Garden. Of the first pair of brothers, one murders the other. And so it has been ever since.

The story that occupies the rest of the Hebrew scriptures concerns a series of attempts to remedy this situation. It is the story of how God, sometimes directly and sometimes through representatives, acts to reestablish his rule in a community of righteousness and justice. It is often understood in terms of the concept of the "Kingdom of God." This story expresses the self-understanding of Jews and Christians alike. We sketch it briefly.

One tactic to clean up the unrighteousness of men would be to destroy them and start again. Something close to this is found in the story of Noah.

> The Lord saw that the wickedness of man was great in the earth, and that every imagination of the thoughts of his heart was only evil continually. And the Lord was sorry that he had made man on the earth, and it grieved him to his heart. So the Lord said, "I will blot out man whom I have created from the face of the ground, man and beast and creeping things and birds of the air, for I am sorry that I have made them." But Noah found favor in the eyes of the Lord. (Gen. 6 : 5 – 8)

The outcome is a great flood, from which only Noah and his family are saved, together with a pair of each kind of animal. But not many generations pass before wickedness again becomes widespread, and people become arrogant enough to think they can build a tower that reaches to heaven. This presumption is punished by the confusing of their languages, so that they cannot understand each other and cooperate in finishing that venture.

A crux comes when God calls a certain man, Abram (later called Abraham), to leave his home, his culture, his nation, and to venture out to a new land.

> Now the Lord said to Abram, "Go from your country and your kindred and your father's house to the land that I will show you. And I will make of you a great nation, and I will bless you, and make your name great, so that you will be a blessing." (Gen. 12 : 1–2)

It is in terms of this promise and burden that the Hebrew people identify themselves. They trace their heritage back to Abraham and believe that they have a special role to play in the history of the world: It is their privilege—and responsibility—to be agents for the reestablishment of God's kingdom on earth. They consider that they have entered into a covenant with God, the terms of which are to reverence him, obeying him only, establishing justice among themselves, and so be a blessing to the rest of corrupt mankind—who can learn from them the blessings of righteousness.

A second crux is the Exodus. After some generations, the children of Abraham, faced with famine in Palestine, move to Egypt. Eventually they are enslaved there and spend "four hundred years" suffering the considerable oppression of slaves. Against all odds, they leave Egypt under the guidance of Moses and establish themselves again in the land promised to Abraham. This remarkable occurrence, which leaves an indelible mark on the national character, is the sign and seal of their mission.

Corresponding to this deliverance from bondage and their establishment as a nation is the giving of the Law ("Torah"). It is the Law that marks the Hebrews as distinct and unique. It defines them as a people. What has distinguished the Jews to this day is the continuous possession of that Law, which begins with these words,

> "I am the Lord your God, who brought you out of the land of Egypt, out of the house of bondage. "You shall have no other gods before me."
> —Exo. 20 : 2–3

The Law goes on to forbid misusing God's name, killing, adultery, theft, false witness, and covetousness and to require keeping a Sabbath day holy and honoring one's parents. These statutes are well known as the Ten Commandments. But the Law also states in great detail how life is to be lived by the people of God, specifying dietary and health rules, principles of reparation for wrongs done, and regulations for religious observances.

The life of the Hebrew people in that continually troubled area of the Middle East is precarious. They achieve some years of security and prosperity in the time of David and Solomon.* But thereafter

---

*This apex of the nation's power corresponds roughly to the time of the Trojan War.

it is a struggle to keep the community together. Surrounded by hostile nations, dominated for a time by the powerful Assyrians, exiled to Babylon, conquered by Alexander's armies, and finally made a province of the Roman Empire, they fight tenaciously for their heritage. They are constantly falling away from the Abrahamic covenant and the Law, if we are to judge by the succession of prophets who unsparingly condemn their waywardness and call them back again to God. Still, despite the people's "hardness of heart," as the prophets call it, there is truth in the boast of Josephus, the first-century A.D. Jewish historian:

> Throughout our history we have kept the same laws, to which we are eternally faithful.[2]

During the period of foreign domination there grows up an expectation that God will send someone who will act decisively to establish God's kingdom of righteousness among men. This agent of God is sometimes conceived in terms of a political liberator who will expel the oppressors and restore the ancient kingdom of David; sometimes he is conceived in more cosmic and apocalyptic terms, as one who will institute a general judgment and destruction of all the wicked, together with the rescue of the faithful few. This hoped-for figure is given a variety of titles: Son of David, Son of Man, Messiah.

Together with the insistent hope that God will not fail in his promise to create a holy people, a righteous kingdom, these expectations provide a rich context for understanding the life of Jesus. Jesus is called by all of these titles and often calls himself "Son of Man." Christians will look back particularly to Isaiah's prophecy about a "Suffering Servant" who will create the kingdom not by might, but by bearing the burdens of the people.

> He was despised and rejected by men;
> a man of sorrows and acquainted with grief;
> and as one from whom men hide their faces
> he was despised, and we esteemed him not.
> Surely he has borne our griefs
> and carried our sorrows;
> yet we esteemed him stricken,
> smitten by God, and afflicted.
> But he was wounded for our transgressions,
> he was bruised for our iniquities;

> upon him was the chastisement that made us whole;
> and with his stripes we are healed.
> All we like sheep have gone astray;
> we have turned every one to his own way;
> and the Lord has laid on him the iniquity of us all.
> —Isa. 53:3–6

These words, familiar to all who are acquainted with Handel's *Messiah,* are applied to the life, and particularly to the death, of Jesus. We must now turn to Jesus himself to see what leads so many to think of him in these terms.

---

1. How do prophets differ from philosophers?
2. What are the characteristics of God, according to the Judeo–Christian tradition?
3. What is the significance of God's call to Abraham? Of the Exodus?

Jesus

In the earliest Gospel* Mark introduces Jesus, after his baptism by John, with these words:

> Now after John was arrested, Jesus came into Galilee, preaching the gospel of God, and saying, "The time is fulfilled, and the kingdom of God is at hand; repent and believe in the gospel." (Mark 1:14–15)

That which the prophets foretold and apocalyptic seers envisioned is now "at hand." The "kingdom of God" is about to be established, and Jesus sees himself as the one to whom that task falls.

That the kingdom is indeed at hand is manifest in the healing miracles of Jesus. According to the gospel writers, Jesus cures leprosy, gives sight to

---

*The word "gospel" means "good news." The four accounts we have of the life of Jesus (Matthew, Mark, Luke, and John) are called Gospels because they present the good news that God has fulfilled his promises to Abraham in the life and death of Jesus. It should be noted that each of these accounts is written from a Christian perspective by one who believes that Jesus is Lord, Savior, and the expected Messiah. We have no hostile or even neutral accounts of his life.

the blind and hearing to the deaf, casts out demons, and even brings the dead back to life. These miracles are signs of God's presence and power and stimuli to repentance and faith.

The attitude and behavior of Jesus bears out his sense of a new beginning. He is absolutely without any class consciousness, associating with poor and rich, learned and ignorant, righteous and sinner alike. A common complaint among those who carefully observe the Law is that he associates with outcasts and undesirables. He does not do so, of course, to sanction their sin, but to lead them to righteousness, as the following parable illustrates.

> Now the tax collectors and sinners were all drawing near to hear him. And the Pharisees and the scribes murmured, saying, "This man receives sinners and eats with them."
>
> So he told them this parable: "What man of you, having a hundred sheep, if he lost one of them, does not leave the ninety-nine in the wilderness, and go after the one which is lost, until he finds it? And when he has found it, he lays it on his shoulders, rejoicing. And when he comes home, he calls together his friends and his neighbors, saying to them, "Rejoice with me, for I have found my sheep which was lost." Just so, I tell you, there will be more joy in heaven over one sinner who repents than over ninety-nine righteous persons who need no repentance." (Luke 15:1–7)

Absolute indifference to wealth and worldly goods is characteristic of both his life and his teaching. Of himself he says,

> "Foxes have holes, and birds of the air have nests; but the Son of man has nowhere to lay his head." (Luke 9:58)

And he emphasizes again and again that attachment to riches will keep one out of the kingdom.* A wealthy man asks him what he must do to inherit eternal life. Jesus replies that he must keep the commandments. The man says he has done so all his life. Then,

> Jesus looking upon him loved him, and said to him, "You lack one thing; go, sell what you have, and

give to the poor, and you will have treasure in heaven; and come, follow me." At that saying his countenance fell, and he went away sorrowful; for he had great possessions.
>
> And Jesus looked around and said to his disciples, "How hard it will be for those who have riches to enter the kingdom of God!" (Mark 10:21–23)

There are many sayings to the same effect. To be part of the kingdom of God requires absolute singleness of mind; care for possessions distracts one from that intensity.

> And he said to him, "Take heed, and beware of all covetousness; for a man's life does not consist in the abundance of his possessions." (Luke 12:15)

No one can serve two masters; for either he will hate the one and love the other, or he will be devoted to the one and despise the other. You cannot serve God and mammon [riches].

> "Therefore I tell you, do not be anxious about your life, what you shall eat or what you shall drink, nor about your body, what you shall put on. Is not life more than food, and the body more than clothing? Look at the birds of the air: they neither sow nor reap nor gather into barns, and yet your heavenly Father feeds them. Are you not of more value than they? And which of you by being anxious can add one cubit to his span of life? And why are you anxious about clothing? Consider the lilies of the field, how they grow; they neither toil nor spin; yet I tell you, even Solomon in all his glory was not arrayed like one of these. But if God so clothes the grass of the field, which today is alive and tomorrow is thrown into the oven, will he not much more clothe you, O men of little faith? Therefore do not be anxious, saying, 'What shall we eat?' or 'What shall we drink?' or 'What shall we wear?' For the Gentiles seek all these things; and your heavenly Father knows that you need them all. But seek first his kingdom and his righteousness, and all these things shall be yours as well." (Matt. 6:24–33)

What is this righteousness that is to take such an absolutely preeminent place in our aims? When a lawyer asks him what to do to inherit eternal life, Jesus answers,

> "What is written in the law? How do you read?" And he answered, "You shall love the Lord your

---

*Compare Socrates' voluntary poverty and the way he describes his divine mission in *Apology* 29d–30b.

God with all your heart, and with all your soul, and with all your strength, and with all your mind; and your neighbor as yourself." And he said to him, "You have answered right; do this, and you will live." (Luke 10:26–28)

The key to the righteousness of the kingdom is *love*. But "love," as we have noted, is a word with many meanings.* What does it mean here? With reference to God, it clearly means a kind of undivided and absolute devotion; it is the appropriate response to the creator who provides for us and also for the birds of the air and the lilies of the fields. This devotion to God has a corollary: that we love our "neighbors" as ourselves. No better explanation of this requirement can be given than the one Jesus gives to the lawyer who asks, "Who is my neighbor?"

> "A man was going down from Jerusalem to Jericho, and he fell among robbers, who stripped him and beat him, and departed, leaving him half dead. Now by chance a priest was going down that road; and when he saw him he passed by on the other side. So likewise a Levite, when he came to the place and saw him, passed by on the other side. But a Samaritan, as he journeyed, came to where he was; and when he saw him, he had compassion, and went to him and bound up his wounds, pouring on oil and wine; then he set him on his own beast and brought him to an inn, and took care of him. And the next day he took out two denarii and gave them to the innkeeper, saying, 'Take care of him; and whatever more you spend, I will repay you when I come back.' Which of these three, do you think, proved neighbor to the man who fell among the robbers?" He said, "The one who showed mercy on him." And Jesus said to him, "Go and do likewise." (Luke 10:30–37)†

Several things in this famous parable of the good Samaritan are worth comment. First, note that Jesus does not exactly answer the question he is asked, "Who is my neighbor?" Rather, he answers the question, "What is it to *act* as a neighbor?" The lawyer's reaction to the story shows that he knows enough about *how to be a neighbor* that putting off action until he has clarified the concept of *what a neighbor is* just constitutes rationalization and evasion of responsibility.* So the closing line directs the lawyer's attention to himself: Do likewise—see that *you* act as a neighbor. This redirecting of attention from externals to the condition of one's own heart is quite characteristic of Jesus.

Second, note that the key word here is "compassion." Jesus is explaining how he understands the second part of the Law. To love your neighbor as yourself is to have compassion, to "feel with" your fellow human being, and to act in accord with that feeling. Just as we feel our own desires, anxieties, cares, pains, and joys, so are we to "feel with" the desires, anxieties, cares, pains and joys of others. And as we act to fulfill the intentions that grow out of these self-directed passions, so, like the Samaritan, must we act to satisfy the needs of others.

> "And as you wish that men would do to you, do so to them." (Luke 6:31)

Love, understood in this way, strikes a new note in our story. It is a conception quite foreign to the Greek philosophers. For them the basic human problem focuses on the control of the passions; by and large, they ascribe the locus of control to reason. Plato sees it as a struggle to subjugate the beast within, Aristotle as a matter of channeling the passions by means of virtuous habits; the Stoics come close to recommending the elimination of feelings altogether.† For all of them, the goal is finding the best possible way to live. And though it is true that the Platonic wise man will return to the cave to try

---

*See the discussion of love in Plato's *Symposium* (pp. 137–141). The word the New Testament writers use for love is *agape*. It is interesting to compare the *eros* that Socrates extols with the *agape* that, Jesus holds, is the key to the kingdom of God.
†Note the three types and their response to the injured man. The priest represents the religious leadership; Levites were lay assistants to the priests; and Samaritans were foreigners who were despised by the Jews.

---

*Compare Augustine on the priority of will over intellect, p. 261.
†The Stoics, for example, oppose pity. In considering what behavior is appropriate when someone is weeping, Epictetus advises us not to be overcome; we should remember that his weeping has its source not in what has happened but in the view he takes of it. We may, perhaps, go as far as to moan with him, but Epictetus says, "Be careful not to moan inwardly" (*The Handbook of Epictetus* 16).

to enlighten those still in bondage, none of them would say that the best way to live necessarily involves an equal concern for others—feeling for them just as we feel for ourselves. What Jesus recommends is not the control or extinction of passion, but its *extension;* it is in universal compassion that we will find the kingdom of God. Nor do the Greek philosophers recommend the universality of concern we find in Jesus, though the Stoics perhaps come closest in thinking of all men as brothers. But not even a Stoic would say this:

> "Love your enemies, do good to those who hate you, bless those who curse you, pray for those who abuse you." (Luke 6:27)

> "If you love those who love you, what credit is that to you? For even sinners love those who love them." (Luke 6:32)

We do seem to have something genuinely new here.

A corollary to this love is a new virtue: humility.* Humility is conspicuously lacking from the Greek lists of virtues, but it is nearly the very essence of perfection according to Jesus. For humility is the opposite of pride, and pride is the very root of sin. It is pride—wanting to be like God—that leads to the sin of Adam. And it is pride that sets human beings against each other; the proud man, glorying in his superiority, cannot consider his neighbor equal in importance to himself and so cannot love as Jesus requires.

Pride, particularly pride in one's righteousness or goodness, is the attitude most at variance with the kingdom of God.

> He also told this parable to some who trusted in themselves that they were righteous and despised others: "Two men went up into the temple to pray, one a Pharisee and the other a tax collector. The Pharisee stood and prayed thus with himself, 'God, I thank thee that I am not like other men, extortioners, unjust, adulterers, or even like this tax collector. I fast twice a week, I give tithes of

all that I get.' But the tax collector, standing far off, would not even lift up his eyes to heaven, but beat his breast, saying, 'God, be merciful to me a sinner!' I tell you, this man went down to his house justified rather than the other; for every one who exalts himself will be humbled, but he who humbles himself will be exalted." (Luke 18:9–14)*

Jesus issues scorching denunciations of those—usually the wealthy and powerful—who consider themselves righteous but do not act as neighbors should act. Like Socrates, he thereby incurs hostility among those in a position to do him harm. Unlike Socrates, of course, he does not do so by asking questions. Like the prophets of old, Jesus thunders out condemnation; and it is not a claim to know that he tries to undermine, but pretensions to righteousness.† Here are two samples.

> "Woe to you, scribes and Pharisees, hypocrites! for you tithe mint and dill and cummin, and have neglected the weightier matters of the law, justice and mercy and faith; these you ought to have done, without neglecting the others. You blind guides, straining out a gnat and swallowing a camel!" (Matt. 23:23–24)

> "Woe to you, scribes and Pharisees, hypocrites! for you are like whitewashed tombs, which outwardly appear beautiful, but within they are full of dead men's bones and all uncleanness. So you also outwardly appear righteous to men, but within you are full of hypocrisy and iniquity." (Matt. 23:27–28)

His antagonism to mere outward observance leads him to deepen and internalize the Law. About the Law he speaks with authority, contrasting the *words* of the Law, which can be kept simply by be-

---

*Edward Langerak suggests that the humility in question is spiritual humility, that Socrates had exhibited intellectual humility, and that Kant combined them in claiming we could not know the motivational roots of our actions. See p. 457.

*The Pharisees claimed that they observed all the details of the Law. Tax collectors, working for the Roman occupiers, were generally despised; and it is true that many of them were corrupt. A "tithe" is one-tenth of one's income, which is what the Law required to be given for religious and charitable purposes.
†This difference, while significant, may be diminished by the observation that for Socrates virtue is knowledge. So one who claims to know what piety is, for example, would also—in Socrates' eyes—be claiming to be pious.

having in certain ways, with the *spirit* of the Law, which requires an attitude of love. For example,

> "You have heard that it was said to the men of old, 'You shall not kill; and whoever kills shall be liable to judgment.' But I say to you that every one who is angry with his brother shall be liable to judgment." (Matt. 5:21–22)

> "You have heard that it was said, 'You shall not commit adultery.' But I say to you that every one who looks at a woman lustfully has already committed adultery with her in his heart." (Matt. 5:27–28)

> "You have heard that it was said, 'An eye for an eye and a tooth for a tooth.' But I say to you, Do not resist one who is evil. But if any one strikes you on the right cheek, turn to him the other also." (Matt. 5:38–39)

This attitude toward the Law, which the Jews hold so dear, brings him into severe conflict with the authorities. He seems to them to take the Law lightly; on several occasions, for example, they clash with him on the details of Sabbath observance. He is, moreover, popular among the common people and must seem to be undermining the authority of the Jewish leaders. They determine to put him to death.

Because of Roman law, they cannot execute Jesus themselves. So after a trial in the religious court in which he is convicted for blasphemy (putting himself in the place of God), the Jewish leaders bring him before the Roman governor, Pilate. Here he is accused of treason, of setting himself up as King of the Jews (a charge of blasphemy would not have impressed this cosmopolitan Roman). Pilate reluctantly accedes to their demands, and Jesus is crucified.

Each of the four Gospels ends with an account of the discovery, on the third day after Jesus' death, of an empty tomb and of numerous appearances of Jesus to his disciples. His followers come to believe that he has risen from the dead. And this is taken by them as a sign that he is indeed God's anointed, the suffering servant who takes upon himself in his death the sins of the world, thereby bringing in the kingdom of God in an unexpectedly spiritual way. Their response is to set about making disciples of all nations.

1. How, according to Jesus, are we to love God? Our neighbor?
2. Do the Christians present new virtues?
3. Christians accept as a fact that Jesus rose from the dead. What do they think that means for us?

The Meaning of Jesus

We have noted that all the Gospels are written by believers; they are shot through and through with the significance his followers attribute to Jesus after their experience of his resurrection. But it will be useful to discuss more explicitly some of the categories in terms of which his life and death are interpreted. For this purpose, we will look particularly at the Gospel of John and at some letters written by the greatest of the early missionaries, Paul.

John begins his Gospel with a majestic prologue.

> In the beginning was the Word, and the Word was with God, and the Word was God. He was in the beginning with God; all things were made through him, and without him was not anything made that was made. In him was life, and the life was the light of men. The light shines in the darkness, and the darkness has not overcome it. . . .
> The true light that enlightens every man was coming into the world. He was in the world, and the world was made through him, yet the world knew him not. He came to his own home, and his own people received him not. But to all who received him, who believed in his name, he gave power to become children of God; who were born not of blood nor of the will of the flesh nor of the will of man, but of God.
> And the Word became flesh and dwelt among us, full of grace and truth; we have beheld his glory, glory as of the only Son from the Father. . . .
> And from his fullness have we all received, grace upon grace. For the law was given through Moses; grace and truth came through Jesus Christ. No one has ever seen God; the only Son, who is in the bosom of the Father, he has made him known. (John 1:1–18)

Notice the exalted conception of Jesus we have here. He is identified with the Word—the *logos,* the wisdom through which all things are made. This *logos* was "in the beginning" with God (a phrase meant to recall the first line of Genesis). Though this Word exists beyond the world, it comes into the world through Jesus, and in him makes known the grace and truth of God, enlightening all and bringing those who are willing into the family of God.

These remarkable claims are elaborated in a number of discourses that John attributes to Jesus. Jesus says, "He who has seen me has seen the Father" (John 14:9). He says, "I and the Father are one" (John 10:30). He calls himself "the light of the world"(John 8:12), "the bread of life" (John 6:48), and "the good shepherd" who "lays down his life for the sheep" (John 10:11).

If Jesus is the manifestation of God in the world, what do we learn of God from him?

> For God so loved the world that he gave his only Son, that whoever believes in him should not perish but have eternal life. For God sent the Son into the world, not to condemn the world, but that the world might be saved through him. (John 3:16–17)

The God Jesus reveals is not Aristotle's unmoved mover, thinking true thoughts about himself. Nor is he akin to the gods of the Epicureans who live in blessedness, unconcerned with human beings. The message is that God is Love, that he cares for us, and will save us from our sinfulness through his Son Jesus, who took our sin upon himself in his death. The life and death of the Christ manifest the extremity of that Love and serve, in turn, as a model for life in the kingdom of God.

What is required is a "new birth," not of flesh and the will of man, but "of God."[*] And this new life—this is the gospel—is now available by trust in Jesus, the Christ.

Paul was a Jew, very strict about the observance of the Law, who was at first vigorously opposed to the new "sect" of Christians. While engaged in persecuting them, he saw a vision of Jesus and was converted, after which he devoted his life to spreading the gospel. He traveled extensively, establishing churches all over Asia Minor and Greece. He visited Athens and argued there with both the Jews and the philosophers, appalled by the "idolatry" he found there and preaching the one creator God and Jesus who rose from the dead.[*]

Paul comes to believe it is hopeless to try to attain the righteousness of the kingdom of God by observing the Law; no doubt this reflects in part his own zealous efforts before his conversion. All men, Paul holds, are inextricably caught in the web of sinfulness and cannot by their own (sinful) efforts "justify" themselves before the righteous judge. But what we cannot do for ourselves God has graciously done for us through Jesus.

> For no human being will be justified in his sight by works of the law, since through the law comes knowledge of sin.
> But now the righteousness of God has been manifested apart from the law, although the law and the prophets bear witness to it, the righteousness of God through faith in Jesus Christ for all who believe. (Rom. 3:20–22)

> There is therefore now no condemnation for those who are in Christ Jesus. For the law of the Spirit of life in Christ Jesus has set me free from the law of sin and death. (Rom. 8:1–2)

Having been freed from the burden of the Law and no longer needing to prove ourselves righteous, says Paul, allows us to participate in the Spirit of Christ, loving our neighbors and serving their needs. It really is Jesus, then, who has brought in the kingdom of God. Moreover, just as God raised Jesus from the dead, so will all who believe in him be raised to a blessed life with him.

Our consideration of Christian teaching can be brought to a close with these words from another author.

> We know that we have passed out of death into life, because we love the brethren. He who does not love remains in death. Any one who hates his brother is a murderer, and you know that no murderer has eternal life abiding in him. By this we

---

[*]See Jesus' conversation with the Jewish leader Nicodemus in John 3:1–15.

[*]See Acts 17:16–34.

know love, that he laid down his life for us; and we ought to lay down our lives for the brethren. But if anyone has the world's goods and sees his brother in need, yet closes his heart against him, how does God's love abide in him? Little children, let us not love in word or speech but in deed and in truth. (1 John 3 : 14–18)

1. What does it mean when John calls Jesus "the *logos*"? Relate this to Heraclitean and Stoic views.
2. How, according to Paul, can we be "justified" before God, the judge?
3. *Why* should we love our neighbors as ourselves?

For Further Thought

You should now have a fairly clear understanding of how Plato, Aristotle, Epicurus, and the Stoics envision the good life. Choose one of these philosophies, and work out a comparison (both similarities and differences) between it and the Christian view of the good life.

Notes

1. Biblical quotations in this text are taken from the Revised Standard Version.
2. Josephus, *Against Apion* 200 : 20; quoted in C. K. Barrett, ed., *The New Testament Background: Selected Documents* (London: S.P.C.K., 1956), 202.

10

AUGUSTINE
God and the Soul

Augustine is not only a fascinating figure personally but also something of a turning point historically. He lived (A.D. 354–430) in the days of what we call "late antiquity," just as it began to merge into the medieval period. He brings together nearly four centuries of debate and consolidation concerning Christian doctrine. And he melds that with what he takes to be the best in the heritage of the Greek philosophers—the tradition stemming from Plato. Both of these traditions are given a unique stamp by Augustine's penchant for introspection, his passionate search for happiness, and the impress of his undeniably powerful mind. He would himself say that if he had contributed anything of value, it was due entirely to the grace of God. This would not be merely an expression of modesty, such as it tends to be today; Augustine believes it to be the literal truth. Whether we agree with that or not, we can fairly say that no one else did as much to shape the intellectual course of the next thousand years.

The views of some philosophers can be discussed independently of their lives, but Augustine's thought is so entangled with his life experiences that we need to understand something of that life.[1] There is no better introduction to his early years than his own *Confessions,* in which he reflects—before God but also before us all—on his youthful waywardness. By the time he wrote this reflective look at his life (in 397), he was forty-three years old, had been a Christian for eleven years, a priest for eight years, and a bishop for two. We cannot hope here to imitate the richness of these meditations but will try just to get a feel for how he saw his life from the point of view he had reached.

Augustine was born in northern Africa, which had been Roman for many generations but was always precariously perched between the sea and the barbarian interior. Christianity had taken root there but, despite its legitimization by the emperor Constantine in 325, was still in competition with the old pagan beliefs and ways. Augustine was the child of a Christian mother, Monica, and a pagan father who converted to Christianity before he died. Monica was the stronger influence, convinced all her life that her son would be "saved." But it was Patricius, his father, who resolutely determined that Augustine should be educated; he studied literature and rhetoric and, for a while, the law. His education was intense but narrow, concentrating on the masters of Latin style and consisting of enormous amounts of memorization of, for example, Virgil's *Aeneid*. He read very little philosophy.

Meanwhile, he lived the life of pleasure. The bishop he became, looking back on those days, puts it this way:

> I cared for nothing but to love and be loved. But my love went beyond the affection of one mind for another, beyond the arc of the bright beam of friendship. Bodily desire, like a morass, and adolescent sex welling up within me exuded mists which clouded over and obscured my heart, so that I could not distinguish the clear light of true love from the murk of lust. Love and lust together seethed within me. In my tender youth they swept me away over the precipice of my body's appetites and plunged me in the whirlpool of sin. (*C* 2.2)[2]

It is not just sex, however, on which the bishop focuses in "the whirlpool of sin." He is almost more perplexed over a single act that comes to represent for him the puzzling nature of human wickedness. He, together with some companions, had shaken down an enormous quantity of pears from a neighbor's tree and had stolen them away. And why did they steal the pears? Did they need them? No. Did they eat them? No. They threw them to the pigs.

Why, then, did they steal the pears? This is what puzzles Augustine. In a judicial inquiry, he notes, no one is satisfied until the motive has been produced: a desire of gaining some good or of avoiding some evil. But what was the good gained here? What evil was avoided? He concludes: "our real pleasure consisted in doing something that was forbidden" (*C* 2.4). But why was that a pleasure? Augustine's reflective answer is that the act was, in a perverse sort of way, an imitation of God; it was an attempt to exercise a liberty that belongs to God alone: that of being unconstrained by anything outside himself (*C* 1.6). No one, Augustine felt, was going to make rules for *him* to live by. We come, then, even in this simple prank by a sixteen-year-old, to Augustine's analysis of the root of the human predicament: pride.

He also notes that he surely would not have stolen the pears on his own.

> It was not the takings that attracted me but the raid itself, and yet to do it by myself would have been no fun and I should not have done it. This was friendship of a most unfriendly sort, bewitching my mind in an inexplicable way. For the sake of a laugh, a little sport, I was glad to do harm and anxious to damage another; and that without a thought of profit for myself or retaliation for injuries received! And all because we are ashamed to hold back when others say "Come on! Let's do it!" (*C* 2.9)

This power of the group to incite to evil deeds is expressed also in the following passage, in which Augustine sets out a very common experience of the young.

> I was so blind to the truth that among my companions I was ashamed to be less dissolute than they were. For I heard them bragging of their depravity, and the greater the sin the more they gloried in it, so that I took pleasure in the same vices not only for the enjoyment of what I did, but also for the applause I won.
>
> Nothing deserves to be despised more than vice; yet I gave in more and more to vice simply in order not to be despised. If I had not sinned enough to rival other sinners, I used to pretend that I had done things I had not done at all, because I was afraid that innocence would be taken for cowardice and chastity for weakness. (*C* 2.3)

It is clear that the Christian bishop at age forty-three does not take lightly the peccadilloes of his youth. It is not prudishness that accounts for this, however; it is a considered judgment that pursuing such desires is a sure way to miss true happiness. But the young Augustine had a long way to go before he would see things this way.

He took a mistress, to whom he was apparently faithful for many years. They had a son. Augustine completed his education and became a teacher of rhetoric and literature, first in the provincial north African town of Thagaste, then in Carthage, the great city of Roman Africa. He was an able teacher and earned a reputation, for which he was most eager.

But he was eager for something else as well. At nineteen, he read a (now lost) work by Cicero, the great orator, which contains an exhortation to study philosophy. Augustine was carried away:

> The only thing that pleased me in Cicero's book was his advice not simply to admire one or another of the schools of philosophy, but to love wisdom itself, whatever it might be, and to search for it, pursue it, hold it, and embrace it firmly. (C 4.4)

The young Augustine embraced this love of wisdom with a "blaze of enthusiasm." But where to look? He knew very little of classical philosophy, which is what Cicero surely had in mind. In Augustine's circle in late fourth-century Africa, it was Christ who was portrayed as "the wisdom of God"; so Augustine turned to the Bible. But he was greatly disappointed. Not only did it seem to lack the polish of the best Roman poets, its conceptions seemed crude and naive to him. In Genesis, after Adam and Eve had disobeyed God, we read that they "heard the sound of the Lord God walking in the cool of the day." What a way to think of God!

Moreover, Christianity seemed unable to solve a great puzzle, which was to perplex Augustine sincerely for many years. The Christian God was proclaimed to be both almighty and perfectly good. But if this is so, where does evil come from? If the answer is the devil, the question can be repeated: Where does the devil come from? If from God, then God is the source of evil. And if God is almighty, where else could the devil come from? But God is good; so how could he be the source of evil?

It may be useful to set the problem out in a more formal way.

1. If God is omnipotent (all powerful), omniscient (all knowing), and perfectly good, then there can be no evil, because
   a. being all-powerful, he *could do* something about any existing evil,
   b. being all-knowing, he *would know* about any existing evil, and
   c. being perfectly good, he *would want to eliminate* any existing evil.
2. But there is evil.

3. Therefore God is either
   a. not all-powerful (He *can't* do anything about the evil), or
   b. not all-knowing (He could do something if only he *knew* about it), or
   c. not perfectly good (He does know and could do something, but He *doesn't care*) — or
   d. some combination of a, b, and c.

Augustine could not see that the Christians had any satisfactory answer to this puzzle, traditionally called "The Problem of Evil." You should be able to see that it is quite a formidable problem. The argument looks valid; that is, if its premises are true, it looks as though the conclusion will have to be true. So that leads us to ask whether the premises are true. Obviously, there are two main possibilities here. We could argue that Premise 1 is false; or we could argue that Premise 2 is false. Roughly speaking, Augustine tries out each of these possibilities.

The first possibility was represented for him by a popular movement in his day, which has similarities to New Age thinking today. It was called "Manicheanism." Augustine was a "hearer" (more than an outsider, but less than a full member) among the Manichees for nine years.

Manicheanism was a sect founded by the Babylonian Mani in the third century. Mani was martyred (some say crucified) by the religious establishment in A.D. 277, and that fact helped spread the sect widely. Mani synthesized themes from the Persian religion of Zoroastrianism and Christianity. Manicheanism is often thought of as one of the many "heresies" prevalent during the first centuries of the Christian era, as the Church tried to sort out an orthodox view of revealed truth.

The doctrines of the sect are enormously complex, involving facets of astrology and half-digested bits of natural science, as well as borrowings from traditional religions. But the key beliefs are simple and provide a solution of sorts to the problem of evil. The reason there is evil in the world, say the Manichees, is that there is *no omnipotent good power*. Rather, there are two equal and opposed powers, one good and one evil. It has always been this way, they say, and will always be so. So you can see that the Manichees deny the antecedent in the first premise.

This opposition, moreover, is not just "out there" in the world. It is resident within each of us, since we are ourselves a battleground between good and evil. That may not sound very profound; but the Manichees explain this dichotomy in a particular way. The good part of ourselves is the soul (composed of the light), and the bad part is the body (composed of the dark earth). A human being is literally part divine and part demonic.

> I have known my soul and the body that lies upon it, That they have been enemies since the creation of the worlds. (*MP,* p. 49)³

In fact, the entire earth is the province of the evil power, since evil resides in matter as such. We are, however, essentially *souls;* and as souls we experience ourselves to be under the domination of a foreign power—matter, the body, the world.

These equivalences between good, God, and the soul on the one hand and evil and matter on the other also affect their interpretation of the Christian scriptures. God could not be the *creator* of the physical world, for obvious reasons. Nor could the Word literally become flesh, as the Gospel of John states. Nor could Christ die or suffer any other sort of evil. The Old Testament, with its God of wrath and vengeance, is very largely dismissed as a product of the evil power, and they suggest that the parts of the New Testament that speak of judgment and punishment by God are inauthentic additions by "Judaizing" editors. In their eyes, God remains unsullied by any contact with matter, and Christ only *appeared* to be born, to suffer and die.

The "gospel" of the Manichees is their proclamation of the essentially noncorruptible nature of the soul, which they identify with the true person. We can be saved from the domination of the evil power—matter—if we come to *know who we are.*

> A man called down into the world saying: Blessed is he that shall know his soul. (*MP,* p. 47)

The man was Mani, and this was the heart of his message.

Manicheanism, then, claims to solve the *theoretical* problem of evil by the postulation of the two

powers—denying the infinite perfection of God—and the *practical* problem of evil by the doctrine that the soul is essentially good, untouched by the evil of the body. If only you can come to identify yourself with your soul, you will experience "salvation" from the evil. Augustine apparently felt that this solution freed him from his theoretical perplexities and allowed him to think of himself as "essentially good"—something he needed to be able to do. This, then, was the first "wisdom" that he embraced in his enthusiasm for the truth.

He noticed, however, that some of the doctrines were obscure and that others seemed to conflict with the best astronomical knowledge of the day. When one of the Manichean "Elect," a certain Faustus, came to Carthage, Augustine determined to inquire about these things. On examination it became obvious that Faustus was not wise.* So Augustine was disappointed a second time; neither Christianity nor Manicheanism seemed to offer the wisdom he was seeking.

Moreover, he found Manichean views unhelpful in a practical sense. Their key to salvation lay in knowledge, in a recognition of the true nature of the self as good. But this didn't seem to be of any help in actually changing one's life. It was too passive. (It may have been his experience as a Manichee that led to his later view that the root of sin lies not in the intellect but in the *will.*) The bishop he became reflects on his experience:

> I still thought that it is not we who sin but some other nature that sins within us. It flattered my pride to think that I incurred no guilt and, when I did wrong, not to confess it so that you [God] might bring healing to a soul that had sinned against you. (Psalm 41:4) I preferred to excuse myself and blame this unknown thing which was in me but was not part of me. The truth, of course, was that it was all my own self, and my own impiety had divided me against myself. My sin was all the more incurable because I did not think myself a sinner. (C 5.10)

These notions of pride, guilt, and a divided self we need to examine in more detail. But because of

---

*Compare Socrates asking questions in Athens: *Apology* 21b–22c.

"I was in love with beauty of a lower order and it was dragging me down."

—St. Augustine

these intellectual and spiritual dissatisfactions, Augustine began to drift away from the Manichees.

He began to read the philosophers and found himself attracted to skepticism. He left Africa and went to Rome, where again he taught rhetoric and literature. He was recommended to the more attractive post of Professor of Rhetoric in Milan, where he was joined by his widowed mother; with her, he attended Christian services conducted by the Bishop of Milan, Ambrose. Ambrose was an immensely learned man, far more learned in the traditions of the Greek church fathers and Greek philosophy than Augustine (whose Greek skills were always imperfect). Ambrose was also an accomplished orator. At first, Augustine went simply to hear him speak, but he soon found himself listening to the content as well as the style. And he began to discover the possibility of a Christianity that was not naive and crude but that could bear comparison with the best thought of the day.

What made the Christianity of Ambrose a revelation to Augustine, who had, in a sense, been familiar with Christianity since his childhood? There seem to have been three things. (1) There was the idea of God and the soul as *immaterial* realities. Augustine had found great difficulty in thinking of either as other than some sort of *body,* even if very ethereal bodies. (Recall that the Manichees thought of God and the soul as light.) But if God is a body, God cannot be everywhere present (and this idea fits with the Manichean dualism of two equal and opposite realities). If God is an immaterial spirit, however, then he is not excluded by the material world and he can be omnipresent. (2) Ambrose was not afraid to plunder the Greek philosophical tradition for help in making Christianity intelligible. The category of immaterial reality was drawn from philosophy, particularly from that of Plato and his successors. (Remember the Forms, especially the Form of the Good.)* (3) Finally, there was the possibility of giving allegorical interpretations to Scripture, particularly to the Old Testament. Taken allegorically rather than literally, many passages ceased to offend and took on the aspect of conveying deep spiritual truths.†

Augustine began to study the Bible seriously for the first time and to read philosophy. The Bible spoke of the Wisdom of God, and philosophers loved wisdom. Could Christianity contain the truth the philosophers were seeking? He began to suspect so. He grew more sure of it, then became virtually certain.

Yet he hesitated. What would happen if he became a Christian? In Augustine's view, this was a serious matter. His life would have to change drastically, for he was still preoccupied with worldly things: his career, his reputation, and sex. His mistress had returned to Africa, and marriage with an heiress was being arranged. Would he have to give all this up? Augustine was never one for half-measures, and it seemed to him that he would. But could he? He procrastinated. The bishop he had be-

---

*See pp. 130–133.

†The Stoics had adopted a similar strategy with respect to the works of the pagan poets, as you may recall. See p. 209.

come expresses the agony of that time in the following way:

> I was held fast, not in fetters clamped upon me by another, but by my own will, which had the strength of iron chains. The enemy held my will in his power and from it he had made a chain and shackled me. For my will was perverse and lust had grown from it, and when I gave in to lust habit was born, and when I did not resist the habit it became a necessity. These were the links which together formed what I have called my chain, and it held me fast in the duress of servitude. But the new will which had come to life in me and made me wish to serve you freely and enjoy you, my God, who are our only certain joy, was not yet strong enough to overcome the old, hardened as it was by the passage of time. So these two wills within me, one old, one new, one the servant of the flesh, the other of the spirit, were in conflict and between them they tore my soul apart. (*C* 8.5)

The *perversity of the will,* which leads to *lust,* which leads to *habit,* which becomes a virtual *necessity,* forms a chain that will play a crucial role in Augustine's analysis of what is wrong with human beings and how it can be cured.

In a dramatic experience, which Augustine relates in the *Confessions,* the chain of necessity was broken. After hearing from a traveler the stories of several others who had renounced the world and devoted themselves to God, Augustine rushed into a garden in a tumult. "My inner self," he says, "was a house divided against itself." "I was my own contestant. . . ."

> I felt that I was still the captive of my sins, and in my misery I kept crying, "How long shall I go on saying 'tomorrow, tomorrow'? Why not now? Why not make an end of my ugly sins at this moment?"
>
> I was asking myself these questions, weeping all the while with the most bitter sorrow in my heart, when all at once I heard the sing-song voice of a child in a nearby house. Whether it was the voice of a boy or a girl I cannot say, but again and again it repeated the refrain "Take it and read, take it and read." At this I looked up, thinking hard whether there was any kind of game in which children used

to chant words like these, but I could not remember ever hearing them before. I stemmed my flood of tears and stood up, telling myself that this could only be a divine command to open my book of Scripture and read the first passage on which my eyes should fall. . . .

> So I hurried back to the place where Alypius was sitting, for when I stood up to move away I had put down the book containing Paul's Epistles. I seized it and opened it, and in silence I read the first passage on which my eyes fell: Not in reveling and drunkenness, not in lust and wantonness, not in quarrels and rivalries. Rather, arm yourselves with the Lord Jesus Christ; spend no more thought on nature and nature's appetites. (Romans 13:13, 14) I had no wish to read more and no need to do so. For in an instant, as I came to the end of the sentence, it was as though the light of confidence flooded into my heart and all the darkness of doubt was dispelled. (*C* 8.12)

Augustine had found the wisdom he had been searching for.

He gave up his career and his prospects for marriage. He retired for some months with some friends and his mother to a retreat where he studied and wrote. On Easter Day in 387, he was baptized by Ambrose, thus making his break with "the world" public. Not long thereafter, his mother having died, he returned to Africa, was made a priest (somewhat against his will), and in 391 was ordained bishop of Hippo, a city on the Mediterranean coast of Africa.

Thereafter he was engaged in practical affairs of the church: in serving as a judge (one of the tasks of a bishop in those days), in controversies to define and defend the faith, and in much writing. There are, of course, the sermons. But there are also letters and pamphlets and book after book in which Augustine explores the meaning of the faith he had adopted. In these the theme is—again and again— to try to *understand* what he has *believed.* For Augustine, faith must come first; understanding may follow (though on some difficult topics, such as the Trinity, even understanding will be only partial). This order of things may seem strange to some of us. We may think that unless we understand first, we will not know what it is that we are believing. But it is a reflection of Augustine's conviction that will is more fundamental than intellect and that only if the will is first directed by faith to the right end will the intellect be able to do its job rightly.*

With this point we are ready to leave the life of Augustine and focus on his philosophy. It is characteristic of Augustine's thought that we cannot do so without at the same time discussing his theology, or doctrine of God. For wisdom, Augustine is convinced, is *one*. And that means that philosophy and theology, understanding and faith, science and religion are inextricably bound together. What the lover of wisdom wants is the truth. And the truth is God. And God is most fully known by faith in Christ. We will not do full justice to this unity, but in selecting out certain themes that are of particular philosophical interest, we will try to keep in mind the whole context in which they play their part for Augustine. Part of Augustine's legacy is just this unity of thought. It sets the intellectual tone for a thousand years. Eventually, as we see, thinkers begin to take it apart again; the consequence is our largely secular modern world.

---

1. Explain what Augustine thinks we should learn from the adventure of the pears.
2. What advice of Cicero's shaped Augustine's life?
3. What problem made Augustine dissatisfied with Christianity?
4. How did the Manichees explain evil? Where is evil located? Where is good located?
5. For what reasons did Augustine become dissatisfied with the Manichees?
6. Describe the links in the chain leading to the bondage of the will.
7. What, according to Augustine, is the relation between belief and understanding?

---

*Think about Socrates. We said that in order to benefit from a conversation with Socrates, you had to be a person of a certain *character*. The arrogant, the proud, the self-satisfied would only be humiliated. (See pp. 65–66.) Augustine agrees that character is more fundamental than intellect. But whereas Socrates thinks of virtue or character as a matter of knowledge, for Augustine it is a matter of faith, or commitment.

Wisdom, Happiness, and God

Augustine simply takes for granted that philosophy, the pursuit of wisdom, has just one aim: happiness. This was the common assumption in late antiquity, shared by the Epicureans, the Stoics, and the Skeptics. Augustine was never greatly interested in nature philosophy and eventually turned away from it as resolutely as Socrates had done.* It could not make one happy.

What does interest Augustine intensely is the soul—his own soul first of all, then what that could teach him about the souls of all. For happiness and unhappiness are clearly conditions of the soul. How does Augustine understand happiness? That soul is happy which possesses what it most desires, *provided* that it most desires what wisdom approves. And what does wisdom recommend? Shortly after his conversion he wrote some "soliloquies" in the form of dialogues between his soul and his reason:

AUGUSTINE: Behold, I have prayed to God.
REASON: What, then, do you desire to know?
A: Those things for which I have prayed.
R: Sum them up, briefly.
A: I desire to know God and the soul.
R: And nothing more?
A: Nothing whatever. (*SO* 2.7)

Note that he has already prayed to God, yet what he wants to know is God. If this sounds paradoxical, remember that Augustine thinks that belief must precede understanding, not follow it. To believe is to give one's assent to the testimony of others, to some authority. It is an act of the will. To understand is to grasp the matter in such a way that one sees the truth for oneself. Again and again Augustine quotes the Greek version of the prophet Isaiah: "Unless you believe, you shall not understand." The will must be open to the truth, or the intellect cannot do its proper work. He believes in God, yearns for him, hopes in him, but he does not yet understand what he believes. And so he addresses God in faith, but with a prayer that he

---

*See *Apology* 19c–d and p. 131.

may understand and know both *that* God is and *what* God is. God and the soul make a pair for Augustine, because it is only God that can supply the happiness his soul longs for. And nothing else matters.

But we are getting ahead of our story. Philosophically speaking, we do not yet understand what justifies bringing God into it at all. To be sure, Augustine has gone through a dramatic conversion experience and believes that in turning his will to God he has found the solution to the problem of happiness.* But what makes Augustine a philosopher is the fact that he is not satisfied simply to bask in the blessings of faith. He needs to *understand* what he has done, why it has produced the happiness that it has, and what justifies the turn to God. He never doubts that this can be understood. So we must go back to a stage of thought that is logically prior—though experientially subsequent—and ask whether the soul in pursuit of wisdom needs to take account of God at all.

The soul wants happiness. And for that reason it wants wisdom—the knowledge of what makes for happiness.

> Just as it is agreed that we all wish to be happy, so it is agreed that we all wish to be wise, since no one without wisdom is happy. No man is happy except through the highest good, which is to be found and included in that truth which we call wisdom. (*FCW* 2.9.102–103)

All humans desire to be happy. So all want to know what that "highest good" is which will provide such blessedness. The Epicureans think it is pleasure, the Stoics think it is virtue, and the skeptics think the best we can do is suspend judgment.

Can we do any better? Augustine thinks we can. Two things are evident: You cannot be happy unless you have what you desire; yet having what you desire does not guarantee happiness, for you must desire the right things. Certain things, if they are desired and attained, will produce misery rather than happiness. Augustine knows this from bitter experience.

Moreover, the appropriate objects of desire must be things that cannot be taken away from us against our will, and they must be enduring.* If they could be taken away from us, we could not be secure in the enjoyment of them; and if they could fade or disappear on their own, we would fear their prospective loss even if we had them. What makes for happiness must *last*. These are among the truths that wisdom teaches.

But again we need to backtrack a bit. For, as we have seen, some philosophers—the skeptics—doubt whether any such truths can be known. Augustine himself had been attracted to skepticism for a time. He feels the strength of this objection. And he sees that unless it is met, nothing else can stand firm. So we must take another logical step backward.

Can the skeptical objections be met? Augustine believes they can be met, and decisively so. He admits that we can be deceived by the senses and that we can make purely intellectual mistakes. But there are three things we know with absolute certainty:

> The certainty that I exist, that I know it, and that I am glad of it, is independent of any imaginary and deceptive fantasies.
>
> In respect of these truths I have no fear of the arguments of the Academics.† They say, "Suppose you are mistaken?" I reply, "If I am mistaken, I exist." A non-existent being cannot be mistaken; therefore I must exist, if I am mistaken. Then since my being mistaken proves that I exist, how can I be mistaken in thinking that I exist, seeing that my mistake establishes my existence? Since therefore I must exist in order to be mistaken, then even if I am mistaken, there can be no doubt that I am not mistaken in my knowledge that I exist. It follows that I am not mistaken in knowing that I know. For just as I know that I exist, I also know that I know. And when I am glad of those two facts, I can add the fact of that gladness to the things I know, as a fact of equal worth. For I am not mistaken about the fact of my gladness, since I am not mistaken about the things which I love. Even if they were

---

*Compare Plato on the "turning" of the soul in the Myth of the Cave, pp. 136–137.

*This is by now a familiar point. See, for instance, p. 187.
†The Academics were members of the Academy after Plato who turned to skepticism.

illusory, it would still be a fact that I love the illusions. (*CG* 11.27)

Skepticism, then, which doubts whether we can have knowledge at all, is an error. Knowledge and certainty are possible. Truth is available to us, at least to this small extent. And notice what this truth is about: his own existence, his thought, and his feelings. In short, the first thing we know for certain concerns ourselves and, in particular, the soul.*

The next question, obviously, is whether we can know *more* than this. In the spirit of the Platonic philosophers, Augustine turns to mathematics. He offers a number of examples, but the nicest one concerns a circle, from the center of which two radii are drawn to the circumference. Let the points at which the radii meet the circle be as close together as you like; it will still be the case that these two lines meet only at that point which is the center. You cannot draw it to look this way (Try!), but it is true nonetheless.† Furthermore, we know that between any two such lines, no matter how close together they are, innumerable other lines can be drawn. Moreover, between any two such lines, no matter how close together, another circle can be inscribed! This is true, and we know it to be true (*SO* 20.35). And this truth is not something private to any one of us. It is knowledge common to all.

> Whatever I may experience with my bodily senses, such as this air and earth and whatever corporeal matter they contain, I cannot know how long it will endure. But seven and three are ten, not only now, but forever. There has never been a time when seven and three were not ten, nor will there ever be a time when they are not ten. Therefore, I have said that the truth of number is incorruptible and common to all who think. (*FCW* 2.7.82–83)

Augustine concludes that mathematical truth exists and we can know it.

Perhaps, however, we grant that there is mathematical truth but doubt that there is such a thing

as practical truth—truth about what we should desire to be happy, about the highest good. But, Augustine asks,

> Will you deny that the incorrupt is better than the corrupt, the eternal better than the temporal, the inviolable better than the violable? (*FCW* 2.10.114)

Here is a truth that seems as secure to Augustine as the truths of mathematics. How could, for example, the beauty of a flower that lasts for a day be as good as an equivalent beauty that lasts for two days? And how could that be as good as the same beauty lasting forever? But this, notice, is a truth about what is "better," and so it has direct practical implications. Whatever is the highest good, whatever will actually fulfill the desire for happiness must be the best of all possible things —incorruptible, eternal, inviolable. Otherwise, even if we possessed it, it could be taken away from us without our consent. To settle for less than such a good is to resign ourselves to unhappiness.

But if this is *true,* then this truth is itself eternal—as unchanging a truth as seven plus three makes ten. And it is a truth common to all. These truths are not private possessions. I can know them, and you can know them; but their existence does not depend on either me or you. We do not *decide* their truth; we *acknowledge* it.

These truths are clearly superior to us and to the powers of our minds. This is shown in two ways. We do not make judgments *about* them, as we judge about sensible things or even ourselves; we make judgments *according to* them. For example, we say of an apple not only that it is ripe, but that it is *too* ripe, or that it *ought to be* riper. And we often say that a person has not done what he ought to have done. We do make judgments about apples and persons, but always according to certain principles. These principles we do not in turn judge about. Moreover, truth (unlike ourselves) is unchanging.

> When a man says that the eternal is more powerful than the temporal, and that seven plus three are ten, he does not say that it ought to be so; he knows it is this way, and does not correct it as an examiner would, but he rejoices as if he has made a discovery.
>
> If truth were equal to our minds, it would be subject to change. Our minds sometimes see

---

*At the beginning of modern philosophy in the seventeenth century, this theme will be picked up by René Descartes. See *Meditation II.*

†Compare discussion of Socrates' and drawings on pp. 121–122.

more and sometimes less, and because of this we acknowledge that they are mutable. Truth, remaining in itself, does not gain anything when we see it, or lose anything when we do not see it. It is whole and uncorrupted. With its light, truth gives joy to the men who turn to it, and punishes with blindness those who turn away from it. (*FCW* 2.12.134–35)

Let us review. We want to be happy, and in order to find happiness we desire to be wise. Wisdom will tell us what the highest good is. Possession of this good will make us happy. Such a good must be eternal, available to all, and superior to ourselves. But we have now found something with precisely those characteristics: truth itself.*

> We possess in the truth, therefore, what we all may enjoy, equally and in common; in it are no defects or limitations. For truth receives all its lovers without arousing their envy. It is open to all, yet it is always chaste. No one says to the other, "Get back! Let me approach too! Hands off! Let me also embrace it!" All men cling to the truth and touch it. The food of truth can never be stolen. (*FCW* 2.14.145)

Truth is something we cannot lose against our will. And since it is superior to our minds, it is a candidate for being the highest good and the source of our happiness.

Now we have reached the point where we can *understand* (not just believe) why God must be brought into the picture. Think back to what Augustine claims to know: he exists, he lives, and he knows and feels. These facts are ordered in a kind of hierarchy. The latter facts presuppose the former; you cannot live unless you exist, and you cannot know and feel unless you are alive. Moreover, this is a hierarchy of value, for it is better to be alive than just to exist, and it is better to know and feel than just to live. These are the reasons we judge plants superior to rocks, animals to plants, and ourselves to all. At the top of this hierarchy is our own rational nature, by which we judge the rest and guide our own behavior. This is best of all among the things of experience. But what if there were

something superior even to this? Would it not be right to acknowledge that as *God,* particularly if it were shown to be eternal and immutable?

But this is just what Augustine claims already to have shown! Truth itself exists. It is immutable and eternal. And it is superior to our reason. By definition, God is "that to whom no one is superior" (*FCW* 2.6.54).* So we can now say that, on the assumption that there is nothing superior to the truth, the truth itself is God. If there should exist something superior to the truth, then that is God. On either hypothesis, God exists! As Augustine puts it in a dialogue with a friend,

> You granted . . . that if I showed you something higher than our minds, you would admit, assuming that nothing existed which was still higher, that God exists. I accepted your condition and said that it was enough to show this. For if there is something more excellent than truth, this is God. If there is not, then truth itself is God. Whether or not truth is God, you cannot deny that God exists, and this was the question with which we agreed to deal. (*FCW* 2.15. 153–154)

Again let's set out the structure of the argument:

1. God is (by definition) that to whom there is nothing superior.

2. Truth exists and is superior to us.

3. If nothing is superior to truth, then God = truth and God exists.

4. If there is something superior even to truth, then God is that thing, and God exists.

5. Either 3 or 4.

6. So God exists.

To this demonstration his friend, Evodius, exclaims,

> I can scarcely find words for the unbelievable joy that fills me. I accept these arguments, crying out that they are most certain. And my inner voice shouts, for truth itself to hear, that I cling to this: not only does good exist, but indeed the highest good— and this is the source of happiness. (*FCW* 2.15.156)

---

*The common, public nature of truth is stressed also by Plato. See p. 120.

---

*This idea is the root from which a much more sophisticated and complex proof will be drawn by Anselm of Canterbury. See Chapter 11.

Since his experience in the garden Augustine has believed this, and now he also understands it in a way that satisfies his reason. But one's reason is not unaffected by one's will and desires; without a will to truth, even the best rational demonstration may fail to convince. As we'll see, in a certain sense Augustine holds that *will* is basic.

---

1. How are wisdom and happiness related?
2. What is Augustine's argument against the Skeptics?
3. What shows that truth is superior to ourselves?
4. What is Augustine's argument for the existence of God?
5. What is the essence of God?

The Interior Teacher

Augustine struggles with the same epistemological problem that puzzles Socrates: What accounts for the fact that we can recognize the truth when we stumble upon it? Socrates solves the problem, you will recall, by positing the preexistence of the soul in a life where it dwelt in intimate contact with the truth. Though Augustine toys with this idea, it is fundamentally inconsistent with Christian doctrine, and in his mature thought he rejects it. But then he needs another solution.

He draws this solution from both Platonic and biblical sources, between which he sees a remarkable congruence. In his letter to the Church in Rome, Saint Paul had written, concerning all people,

> For what can be known about God is plain to them, because God has shown it to them. Ever since the creation of the world his invisible nature, namely, his eternal power and deity, has been clearly perceived in the things that have been made. (Rom. 1 : 19–20)

And in Saint John's Gospel we read that the *logos* is "the light that enlightens every man."* If these things are so, then no one is entirely lacking the truth.

In the Platonists Augustine recognizes a view of the divine with remarkable affinities to the view presented in the Bible: God as one, eternal, immaterial, and immutable. Think back, for instance, to the way Plato describes the Form of the Good; it is the source of both the *being* and the *intelligibility* of all else. Remember, too, that Plato makes extensive use of the image of *light*. The Good is compared to the sun; just as the visible sun lights up and makes perceptible the things around us, so the Good illuminates the truth and makes it visible to the eye of the soul. Moreover, Plato insists that only those who participate in the Form of the Good will be wise, and only those with this wisdom can be truly virtuous and good.

Augustine notes the speculation of some that Plato may have read these things in the works of the Hebrew prophets. His own view is that this is possible, but not likely. Nor is it a necessary explanation, if the words of Paul and John are taken seriously—if *all* are "enlightened" by the Word. Augustine himself is most of all impressed with the following fact:

> that when the angel gave Moses the message from God, and Moses asked the name of him who gave the command to go and free the Hebrew people from Egypt, he received this reply, "I am HE WHO IS, and you will say to the sons of Israel, 'HE WHO IS has sent me to you.'" This implies that in comparison with him who really is, because he is unchangeable, the things created changeable have no real existence. This truth Plato vigorously maintained and diligently taught. (CG 8.11)

The most profound truth about God, Augustine holds, is expressed in this phrase: "He Who Is." If we want to say most fundamentally *what* God is, we must say that he is *being*.* Moreover, what truly is must be both eternal and immutable. Of nothing but God is this true. Only God *is* in an eternal perfection that admits no change—a doctrine that he finds both in the Platonists and in the Scriptures.

---

*Review the important beginning of this work. p. 223.

*To use Aristotle's terminology, this is to understand the "essence" of God. For *essence,* see p. 176.

Scripture writers and philosophers alike then have been "enlightened" by the *logos* of God.

Like Ambrose, Augustine gives an allegorical interpretation to the command that the fleeing Hebrews should take with them the gold and silver of the Egyptians, whose slaves they had so long been. There is "gold" in the writings of the pagan thinkers, and Christians may plunder their insights with a good conscience without feeling a sense of betrayal to God. For God is the author of truth wherever it is found (*OCD* 2.40).

There are, from Augustine's point of view, definite limits to the truths found in pagan writings. We do not find there that "the Word became flesh and dwelt among us," and that "grace and truth came through Jesus Christ." Though they may have truth, they do not have the whole truth. In particular, they do not have the truth concerning the way of salvation; for though wisdom may have led them to see that blessedness lies in participating in the Goodness of God, they are without a clear notion either of *sin* (which separates us from God) or of the *grace* of Christ (which makes possible the return to God).

In deciding what may be taken from the writings of the pagans, Augustine's rule always is this: Is it congruent with the Scriptures? And in the light of this rule, we can see that there is much in those writings that must be criticized and rejected—in particular, the continuing toleration for the worship of many gods and the vices that typically accompany such worship.

Let us now go back to the problem concerning recognition of the truth. Consider the proposition that the unchangeable is better than the changeable. How do we learn that this is so? Note that we do not learn it by being *told* it is so. First, we can be told false things as well as true; and second, we cannot, in any case, learn anything at all by means of mere *signs*. The second reason is the deeper one and needs to be explored. Words are signs, Augustine tells us. Since they are signs, they stand for, or represent, some reality. Some words signify other signs, such as the word "noun," but other words represent realities that are not themselves signs—"horse," for instance.

Knowledge is not knowledge of the signs that express it, but of the realities expressed by those signs. Suppose we read, "And their sarabelle were not altered" (an example Augustine takes from Daniel 3:27). Do we understand that? Probably not, because although we hear the word "sarabelle," we don't know what it stands for. Suppose we are told that sarabelle are head coverings. Then we do understand—provided we know what heads and coverings are. But we must be *acquainted* with the realities in question if we are to know whether something is true. In this case, an image of heads and coverings must be stored in the memory. We consult this memory to understand the words.

We do not, then, learn just by attending to signs or words. Words are merely reminders of something we are already acquainted with. How, then, do we learn that the unchangeable is superior to the changeable? Augustine draws on the common heritage of Plato and the Bible to say that

> it is not a speaker who utters sounds exteriorly whom we consult, but it is truth that presides within, over the mind itself; though it may have been words that prompted us to make such consultation. And He who is consulted, He who is said to dwell in the inner man, He it is who teaches—Christ—that is, the unchangeable Power of God and everlasting Wisdom. (*T* 11.38)

Like Plato, Augustine compares the inner light, which he takes to be Christ, to the light of the sun.

> Thus, as of the sensible sun, we may predicate three things: namely, that it is, that it shines, that it makes objects visible; even so may we predicate three things of that most mysterious God whom you long to know: viz., that He is, that He is apprehended, that He causes other things to be apprehended. (*SO* 8.15)

Suppose there were something truly good, the possession of which would make you truly happy. (Never mind for a moment what it might be.) Someone says, "It would be better if that thing were to persist unchangeably forever than that it should last only a few days." You consider: "Is that true?" Where do you look for the answer? Not to the words; they express a thought, but they cannot certify it as true. Not to the speaker, for how do you know the speaker can be trusted? Where then can you look? You consider the content of the remark—*what is said* in the utterance—as it reverberates in your mind. And if it is true, its truth is lighted up by the Interior Teacher, that Wisdom of God that lights up the truth in our souls.

Sensible objects may exist, but we can see them only in the light of the sun. In the same way, the truth may exist without being grasped unless it is illuminated for us by "the true light that enlightens every man" (John 1:9). As we have seen, Augustine argues that these truths do exist independently of us. These truths either are God himself or are, as Augustine often holds, resident in the mind of God. (For Augustine, Plato's Forms have the status of Ideas in God's mind.) But our minds are finite and limited. What can make eternal truths available to us? Only an "illumination" of them by that light which is God's Wisdom itself. Augustine's view is that these truths of wisdom are lighted up for everyone, but not everyone comes to understand and accept them. Only as much is available to us as our will is open to: The truth will escape one whose will is bad. Once more, we see how basic the will is.

Augustine's view of learning the truth is different from that of Socrates. But in one respect there is a striking similarity: Both hold that no one ever teaches another person anything. Socrates claims to be just a midwife, helping the hearers of his questions bring forth truths they already know and can recall. For Augustine, we learn by confronting realities directly, realities illuminated by the Interior Teacher, the Word of God, the Eternal Wisdom: Christ himself.

> Teachers do not claim, do they, that their own thoughts are perceived and grasped by the pupils, but rather the branches of learning that they think they transmit by speaking? For who would be so absurdly curious as to send his child to school to learn what the teacher thinks? But when they have explained, by means of words, all those subjects which they profess to teach, and even the science of virtue and of wisdom, then those who are called pupils consider within themselves whether what has been said is true. This they do by gazing attentively at that interior truth, so far as they

are able. Then it is that they learn; and when within themselves they find that what has been said is true, they give praise, not realizing that they are praising not so much teachers as persons taught—provided that the teachers also know what they are saying. (*T* 14.45)

---

1. How does Augustine justify his use of pagan philosophical writings?
2. Compare Augustine's view of learning with that of Socrates.

God and the World

Augustine has come to believe in the God of the Christians. Here, he is convinced, is wisdom and the path to happiness. But he needs also to understand what he has come to believe. He has discovered a rational proof that God exists. Could reason, employed in support of faith and enlightened by the divine light, also understand how this world is related to God?.

Here too Augustine draws from the wisdom of the philosophers, especially from the Platonists. For as Augustine reads them, they express in a perfectly rational way, without relying on the authority of revelation, ideas that mesh remarkably well with the Scriptures. His borrowings are not uncritical, but they are extensive. For this reason, it will be useful to take a detour to the views of Plotinus (A.D. 204–270), the main source for Neoplatonism. This tradition, within which Augustine himself must be counted a distinguished figure, lasted well into the eighteenth century.

The Great Chain of Being

The views of Plotinus are a blend of mystical insight and rational elaboration, the latter largely dependent on Plato. Mystical experience, which Plotinus is clearly familiar with, has certain characteristics that reappear in all ages and cultures. It is an experience of a particularly powerful and persuasive sort in which the focus is an absolute unity. The multiplicity of things disappears; one is no longer able even to distinguish oneself from other objects. Mystics talk of this experience in terms of identity of the self with "the All," with "the One," or with "God." It is accompanied by an absolutely untroubled bliss.

Plotinus knows such experience firsthand, so he is certain that there is another, better reality than the one we ordinarily experience. When he tries to express this reality, he speaks in terms of **the One.** About this One, Plotinus holds, we can literally say nothing; for to predicate any properties of it would be to imply some multiplicity in it, some division. It is "ineffable." We cannot even say that it *is.* It resides in a majesty *beyond being.** Plotinus allows that it can be given names, but none of these are to be understood literally; they are at best hints that point in a certain direction. Some of these names are "Unity," "the Transcendent," "the Absolute," "the Good," and "the Source."†

Like Plato's Form of the Good, the One is the source of whatever else exists. But at this point, we must ask: why should anything else exist? The One is absolutely self-sufficient; it needs nothing. But this is precisely the key. To make it clear, Plotinus uses a pair of analogies.

> Picture a spring that has no further origin, that pours itself into all rivers without becoming exhausted of what it yields, and remains what it is, undisturbed. The streams that issue from it, before flowing away each in its own direction, mingle together for a time, but each knows already where it will take its flood. Or think of the life that circulates in a great tree. The originating principle of this life remains at rest and does not spread through the tree because it has, as it were, its seat in the root. The principle gives to the plant all its life in its multiplicity but remains itself at rest. Not a plurality, it is the source of plurality. (*EP*, p. 173)⁴

The One is like the spring that, being itself full and lacking nothing, gives of itself without ever diminishing itself; or like the originating principle of life in a great tree that remains at rest in the root, though the whole tree pulses with life. Plotinus

thinks of all reality as an *emanation* from the One. To use another analogy, it is like the light that streams from the candle, while the light of the flame remains undiminished.

Note that this is the old problem of the one and the many: whence this plurality of beings, this multiplicity all about us? The answer is, they originate in the One.* If we ask why there are so *many,* the answer is that there must be as many as possible, for the One is ungrudging in its giving.

> Every nature must produce its next, for each thing must unfold, seedlike, from indivisible principle into a visible effect. Principle continues unaltered in its proper place; what unfolds from it is the product of the inexpressible power that resides in it. It must not stay this power and, as though jealous, limit its effects. It must proceed continuously until all things, to the very last, have within the limits of possibility come forth. All is the result of this immense power giving its gifts to the universe, unable to let any part remain without its share. (*EP*, p. 68)

Just as there are all possible degrees of brightness in the emanation of light from a candle, until it vanishes at last in the darkness, so there will be found all degrees of being, intelligibility, and life in the world. Reality is partitioned in graded steps, which are, however, infinitely close to each other. No degree can be lacking; every possible level of being is represented, from the complete self-sufficiency of the One to vanishingly small realities near absolute nothingness. In the world as we see it, being and nothingness are mixed in all degrees.

We get the picture of a **Great Chain of Being,** an image that is to be enormously influential for centuries.† It certainly has an impact on the

---

*Compare Plato on the Form of the Good, p. 132.

†Compare the terminology in the *Star Wars* movies.

---

*See the earlier discussion of this same problem by Heraclitus (pp. 21–22), Parmenides (p. 28), and Plato (p. 126ff.). At the very beginning of the process of emanation, Plotinus holds, the One produces an image of itself in which it knows itself. He calls this reflective image "Intelligence." Intelligence in turn produces "Soul," the principle of life. Augustine reads this as a pagan version of the Christian Trinity: the One = the Father, the Creator; the Intelligence = the Word, Wisdom, the Christ; and the Soul = the Holy Spirit.

†For a fascinating study of the history of this idea, see Arthur Lovejoy, *The Great Chain of Being: A Study of the History of an Idea* (Cambridge, MA: Harvard University Press, 1936).

thought of Augustine. How does he make use of these ideas in trying to understand what he has come to believe about God and the world?

First we must note that there is one aspect of Plotinus' thought that Augustine, as a Christian, cannot accept. For a Christian believes the world was *created,* and creation is a notion wholly distinct from emanation. Creation is a free act, voluntarily chosen; there is no necessity in it. Emanation, by contrast, is a necessary and continuous process. In the emanation picture, moreover, the *substance* of the world is not distinct from its source; the one flows indiscernibly into the other. Everything partakes of divinity. But in a creation scenario, there is discontinuity, not continuity; what is created does *not* have the same substance as the creator has. Augustine agrees with Plotinus that the world is not a self-sufficient reality, that it depends for both its being and character on a more fundamental reality. But the nature of that dependence is altogether different.

But how are we to understand the creation of the world? It could not be like the creation of buildings by stonemasons or of sculptures by artists. For in these cases people merely give new shape and form to realities that are already in existence. The creation of the world must account for those very realities. That is exactly what we discover in Genesis 1:3, where we read, "God said, 'Let there be light,' and there was light."

> You did not work as a human craftsman does, making one thing out of something else as his mind directs. . . . Nor did you have in your hand any matter from which you could make heaven and earth, for where could you have obtained matter which you had not yet created, in order to use it as material for making something else? Does anything exist by any other cause than that you exist?
>
> It must therefore be that you spoke and they were made. (Ps. 33:9) In your Word alone you created them. (C 11.5)

Other than God himself, there is nothing but what he has made—again a rejection of Manicheanism, according to which the powers of light and darkness, good and evil, are equally eternal and uncreated. God "spoke" and the heavens and the earth *were.* Remember that in this context "your Word"

represents not a spoken word but the *logos,* the Wisdom of God, the second person of the Trinity, who is "with God" and "is God," as John's Gospel tells us. It is through this rational, intelligent, and ultimately loving Word that God makes all things. And he makes them *ex nihilo,* or *out of nothing.* The world, then, is entirely, without any exception, dependent upon God.

Because the world is created through Wisdom (compare Plotinus' Intelligence, Plato's Forms), the world is a rational and well-ordered whole. Here again the philosophers confirm the biblical tradition. In the Genesis story we read that God looked at what he had made and "saw that it was good." How could it be otherwise, since God himself is good. For Augustine, as for Plotinus and Plato, there is a direct correlation between being and goodness. The more being something has (which means, of course, the more self-sufficient and eternal it is), the better it is. God, being completely self-sufficient and eternal, is completely good. The created world is less good than God. But still it is *good.* From the premise that the world is less good than God, one cannot conclude that it is therefore *bad.*

Here again Augustine parts company from the Manicheans. The source of evil is not to be found in body or matter, for these are creations of God and so are good. Not everything created is equally good, of course. As we have already seen, life is better than mere existence, and intellect better than mere life. In fact, Augustine follows Plotinus here and urges that there is a continuous gradation of goodness in things. The Great Chain of Being reaches from the most insignificant bits of inanimate matter through primitive life forms, to rational creatures like ourselves, and beyond to the angels. That this is a chain of *being* the following examples may make clear.

A dog does not have language, but you do. So, compared to you, there is something lacking in the dog. You have an ability, the power to utter truths and falsehoods, which the dog just does not have. So there is *more to you* than there is to the dog; you have more of being, and the dog has less.

Or suppose I am standing before you in class, an eraser in my hand. Suddenly, I wheel about and hurl the eraser at the chalkboard! You are surprised—

The Great Chain of Being

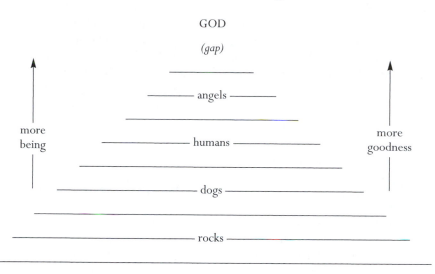

GOD

(gap)

more
being

more
goodness

angels

humans

dogs

rocks

N - O - T - H - I - N - G - N - E - S - S

no doubt startled. You can't imagine why I have done this. But you don't think any the less of me or my character because of it. Then I say, "Imagine now, imagine that instead of an eraser in my hand it had been a kitten. . . ." The situation is altogether different, and my character has taken a precipitous drop in your estimation. Why? Because a kitten is higher on the Chain of Being than an eraser? Perhaps you, too, believe in the great chain.

The second example makes clear that the chain is not only a chain of being, but a hierarchy of value. So value and being correlate: the more being, the more goodness. And the great ladder reaches from sheer nothingness at the bottom (no being, no value) to God at the top (supreme being, supreme value). Even the lowest degree of existence, however, has its correlative degree of goodness. Nothing God has made is to be despised.

Perhaps one more word of explanation is needed. We are likely to think that the distinction between existence and nonexistence is *absolute* and, therefore, that Augustine's idea of *degrees* of being is suspect. But Augustine thinks he can have both. There is indeed an absolute distinction between even the merest speck of being and nothing at all; however, among those things that are, he believes

it is obvious that some have more of being than others.

Evil

As you should be able to see, this picture of things brings Augustine right back to the problem of evil. It was to solve this problem that he had embraced the dualism of the Manichees in the first place. But now, if God is good and the material world is good, he is faced again with the question, Where does evil come from?

The problem can usefully be divided into two parts, which we can call the problems of *natural* evil and *moral* evil. Moral evil is evil that depends in some way on the free choices of rational agents. We will postpone consideration of moral evil until we have a better understanding of Augustine's views on human nature. But we can now address the problem of natural evil. The heart of Augustine's solution can be simply stated: Natural evil does not exist! You can see that Augustine now proposes to solve the problem as we stated it on page 228 by denying the *second* premise. This allows him to continue to assert the first premise and to deny the conclusion.

Augustine does not wish to deny that we experience some things as evil. But he does want to deny that evil is a *reality,* that it *is.* If you were to make a list of all the things there *are*—solar systems, chairs, lobsters, volcanoes, enchiladas—evil would appear nowhere on that list. Nor would anything on the list be evil—insofar as it *is.* Being, remember, is goodness. Insofar as something *is,* then, it is *good.* What we call evil is just a *lack* of the being that something should have. Evil is the *privation of good.*

> For as, in the bodies of animate beings, to be affected by diseases and wounds is the same thing as to be deprived of health, . . . so also of minds, whatever defects there are are privations of natural good qualities, and the healing of these defects is not their transference elsewhere, but that the defects which did exist in the mind will have no place to exist, inasmuch as there will be no room for them in that healthiness. (*AE* 2.10–25)

There is a kind of primitive magic that "cures" by moving the disease or wound out of the body and into, for example, a tree. From Augustine's point of view, this is to misconceive the nature of the problem altogether. For a disease or wound is not a "thing," having some reality of its own, nor is healing "removing" that thing. Disease is just the privation of healthiness, and healing is restoring the body to that condition of health (of being and goodness) in which there will be nothing lacking, leaving "no room" for the defect.

Augustine is again making use of Plotinus here. For if we equate goodness and being, we must also equate evil and nothingness. And, as Parmenides already taught us, nothing *is not.* So ignorance is not a reality, but just the lack of knowledge; it is knowledge that is the reality and, therefore, good. Nor is weakness a reality, but simply the absence of strength; strength—that good thing—is the reality.

Since all created things are arranged in degrees of reality, they all participate to some degree in nothingness. Does this mean that they are all evil to some degree? True, they do not have the full degree of being and goodness that belongs only to God, but we ought not to call them "evil" on that score. It is irrational to complain that created things are

not as good as God; to do so is tantamount to wishing that only God should exist and that there should be no created world at all! Created being is necessarily finite, inevitably limited. There is always much that any created thing *is not.* If it were not so, it would itself be God! For what makes the world distinct from God is precisely its admixture of nonbeing. The very *being* of created things, remember, is good to some degree; and isn't it better that the created world exist rather than not? It adds to the sum total of being and goodness in reality.

If, by contrast, you complain not that some created thing could have been perfectly good, but that it could have been better than it is, your complaint is equally irrational. For there is already in existence something better than that; and to wish the thing you complain about to be better is to wish it not to be what it is, but to be that other thing (see *FCW* 2.5).

The conclusion is that evil can exist only where there is good. To put it another way, evil depends on good. Whatever is, insofar as it is, is good; and if there is evil in it, the reason is only that it—like all things less than God—has some part in nothingness as well as being. But no aspect of its nature can be evil per se.

Time

It is not only the goodness of the world that Augustine is concerned to understand. He is also puzzled by its temporality. Creation is the realm of change and impermanence. Yet God is eternal, unchangeable. How comes the one from the other? There is an additional sting in the problem of time for Augustine because the Manichees target time as an irrational element in the orthodox notion of creation. They ask the Christians what they take to be an unanswerable question: What was God doing before he made the world? The supposition is that God must have chosen to create the world at some particular time. But why at that time rather than some other? There seems to be no answer to this question, no reason why God should suddenly, after ages of noncreation, decide to make the world; but without an answer, there seems to be something irrational about believing in creation (as opposed to belief in the *eternal* conflict of light and darkness).

Apparently there was a snappy answer in circulation.

> My answer to those who ask "What was God doing before he made heaven and earth?" is not "He was preparing Hell for people who pry into mysteries." This frivolous retort has been made before now, so we are told, in order to evade the point of the question. But it is one thing to make fun of the questioner and another to find the answer. So I shall refrain from giving this reply. (*C* 11.12)

Augustine's answer is, rather, a long and famous meditation on the nature of time and eternity. In it he establishes his view of God and God's relation to the created world. Let us see if we can follow his reasoning.

The first point is that God's eternity is not to be understood as everlastingness. God is not eternal in that he outlasts all other things; he is eternal in that he is not located in time at all. Those who imagine that God was idle through countless ages before engaging in the work of creation should think again.

> How could those countless ages have elapsed when you, the Creator, in whom all ages have their origin, had not yet created them? What time could there have been that was not created by you? How could time elapse if it never was?
>
> You are the Maker of all time. If, then, there was any time before you made heaven and earth, how can anyone say that you were idle? You must have made that time, for time could not elapse before you made it.
>
> But if there was no time before heaven and earth were created, how can anyone ask what you were doing "then"? If there was no time, there was no "then."
>
> Furthermore, although you are before time, it is not in time that you precede it. If this were so, you would not be before all time. It is in eternity, which is supreme over time because it is a never-ending present, that you are at once before all past time and after all future time. . . . You made all time; you are before all time; and the "time," if such we may call it, when there was no time was not time at all. (*C* 11.13)

So time was created along with the world. That is the way to answer the Manichees: Deny that God exists in time, and the question they asked simply cannot arise. God did not create the world at a given time, since before the creation, time itself did not exist.

Here we again see Augustine drawing on the resources of his philosophical tradition to understand a biblical concept. There may be a problem here. In the seventeenth century, Blaise Pascal would draw a sharp contrast between the God of revelation and the God of the philosophers.* It is for Pascal the difference between a God you can and a God you cannot worship. And many scholars subsequently have held that there is little biblical reason to understand God's eternity in this atemporal way. We must, I think, admit that this radically atemporal eternity is the eternity of mathematical truth, Plato's Forms, and the One of Plotinus. But Augustine sees no conflict at all between the Bible and the philosophers on this score. Again and again, he points out, the Scriptures proclaim the unchanging nature of God, and for Augustine, God's eternity is just that "never-ending present," that being "at once," he here describes. God, then, is outside of time, and time itself is a creation.

What, then, is time? It is something we are all intimately familiar with. But in a much-quoted sentence, Augustine says,

> I know well enough what it is, provided that nobody asks me; but if I am asked what it is and try to explain, I am baffled. (*C* 11.14)

It is clear enough that there are three divisions to time: the past, the present, and the future. And yet these are profoundly puzzling. Think, for instance, of the past. The obvious thing about the past is that *it is no more*. There is a correlative fact about the future: *it is not yet*. Neither past nor future ex-

---

*When he died there was discovered sewn into the lining of his jacket a piece of paper recording an experience he had on the night of November 23, 1654. Part of it read, "FIRE—God of Abraham, God of Isaac, God of Jacob, not of the philosophers and scholars."

ists. The only aspect of time that has any existence, then, must be the present.

Consider, though, what we call a "long time." It seems evident that only what exists can be long. What does not exist cannot be either long or short, any more than it can be white or sweet or smell of roses. When, then, is time "long"? Not in the past, for the past does not exist; nor in the future, for a similar reason. But this leaves only one alternative. A long time must exist in the present.

Let us, Augustine says, "see if our human wits can tell us whether present time can be long" (*C* 11.15). What would you call a long time? A century? Can that exist in the present? Suppose we are in the first year of the century; then ninety-nine years are still in the future—and these *are not yet*. Perhaps only a year, then, can be in the present. But suppose it is April. Three months have passed, and eight are yet to come; so most of the year either *is no more* or *is not yet*. Most of the year does not exist, and what does not exist cannot be long. Shall we count only the present month, then, as the present? But suppose today is the twenty-third day; most of the month is in the past and exists no more, while some of it is yet to come.

This thought experiment can be repeated, as you can readily see, for hours, minutes, seconds, until this conclusion is forced upon us:

> The only time that can be called present is an instant, if we can conceive of such, that cannot be divided even into the most minute fractions, and a point of time as small as this passes so rapidly from the future to the past that its duration is without length. For if its duration were prolonged, it could be divided into past and future. When it is present it has no duration. (*C* 11.15)

The present is just that knife edge where *what is not yet* becomes *what is no longer,* where the future turns into the past. The present itself "has no duration." So the present could not possibly be long. Where, then, does the time we call "long" exist? It cannot exist in the past or in the future, as we have seen. But now we see that it cannot exist in the present either. You can see why Augustine is baffled.

Nonetheless, with prayers to God for help, Augustine presses on. It is evident that we are aware of different periods of time; and we can compare them in length to each other. How do we do this? We can see only what exists; that much is certain. So we cannot see the past or the future. We may predict the future on the basis of what we are aware of in the present, and we can make inferences about past facts. But since only the present exists, it is only the present we can be aware of. How, then, are we aware of times that do not exist? Augustine again looks into his soul.

> When we describe the past correctly, it is not past facts which are drawn out of our memories but only words based on our memory-pictures of those facts, because when they happened they left an impression on our minds, by means of sense-perception. My own childhood, which no longer exists, is in past time, which also no longer exists. But when I remember those days and describe them, it is in the present that I picture them to myself, because their picture is still present in my memory. (*C* 11.18)

Augustine concludes that though there are three times, they are not—strictly speaking—past, present, and future. If we speak accurately, we should speak of a *present of things past* (the memory), a *present of things present* (direct awareness), and a *present of things future* (which he calls expectation). Where do these times exist? The answer is clear: in the mind; nowhere else.

> It is in my own mind, then, that I measure time. I must not allow my mind to insist that time is something objective. . . . I say that I measure time in my mind. For everything which happens leaves an impression on it, and this impression remains after the thing itself has ceased to be. It is the impression that I measure, since it is still present, not the thing itself, which makes the impression as it passes and then moves into the past. When I measure time it is this impression that I measure. . . .
>
> It can only be that the mind, which regulates this process, performs three functions, those of expectation, attention, and memory. The future, which it expects, passes through the present, to which it attends, into the past, which it remembers. (*C* 11.27–28)

This clinches the argument. Time has no meaning apart from the mind, so it must have come into being along with creation. Our minds—vacillating and changeable—are not eternal. Minds are a part of creation. In possessing these powers of expectation, attention, and memory, our minds are the locale where time realizes itself. Our minds are in this respect a faint image of the mind of God, which also sees past, present, and future. But God does not see them fragmentarily, as we do. We cannot see it all; we must be selective. But to God, who lives in that "never-ending present," all time is known "at once."

> If there were a mind endowed with such great power of knowing and foreknowing that all the past and all the future were known to it as clearly as I know a familiar psalm, that mind would be wonderful beyond belief. We should hold back from it in awe at the thought that nothing in all the history of the past and nothing in all the ages yet to come was hidden from it. It would know all this as surely as, when I sing the psalm, I know what I have already sung and what I have still to sing, how far I am from the beginning and how far from the end. But it is unthinkable that you, Creator of the universe, Creator of souls and bodies, should know all the past and all the future merely in this way. Your knowledge is far more wonderful, far more mysterious than this. It is not like the knowledge of a man who sings words well known to him or listens to another singing a familiar psalm. While he does this his feelings vary and his senses are divided, because he is partly anticipating words still to come and partly remembering words already sung. It is far otherwise with you, for you are eternally without change, the truly eternal Creator of minds. In the Beginning you knew heaven and earth, and there was no change in your knowledge. In just the same way, in the Beginning you created heaven and earth, and there was no change in your action. Some understand this and some do not; let all alike praise you. (C 11.31; see also CG 11.21)

Time is indeed puzzling, and Augustine expresses the perplexities as well as anyone ever has. But his reflections on creation and time are not just an attempt to solve a theoretically interesting problem. The problem is urgent for Augustine because it concerns the relation between God and the Soul, the two foci of wisdom that bear on human happiness. Augustine's meditations on time reaffirm the sharp line of distinction between creation—even including its highest part, the mind—and God who created it. We are not divine or parts of the divine.* We, together with the whole temporal order, are absolutely dependent upon God for our very being. Still, our relation to time is part of the image of God within us. Unlike God, we are in time; yet, like God to some degree, we are above it. God sees all time in a single moment. We cannot do that, but we do measure time and are aware of past, present, and future.

You should be able to see a correlation between being more like God in relation to time and our place on the Great Chain of Being. A stone, we think, has no temporal horizon at all, a honey bee is somewhat more open to past, present, and future, and a dog still more so, but less than we. (Wittgenstein once remarked that a dog can expect his master, but can he expect him *next week?*) Moreover, our relation to time, and particularly to our future, is the foundation for our free will, our responsibility, and our hope of happiness.

Time is significant not only for individuals but also for the human race. As a Christian, Augustine looks back to a sacred history (beginning with Adam, moving through Noah, Abraham, Moses, and the prophets to Christ) and looks forward to the culmination of God's kingdom in the future return of Christ as judge. To varying degrees, pagan thought diminishes the significance of time, often swallowing up the uniqueness of events in doctrines of circular eternal recurrence. The Socratic doctrine of reminiscence also fits this pattern: If learning is just recollecting what we have eternally known, then the moment of learning is not really very significant. It brings nothing new into being.† But for the Christians the course of events in history is tremendously significant; it occurs just once, and human decisions made in those never-recurring moments have a tremendous—an infinite—weight. For it is in time

---

*Here Augustine agrees with Homer (see p. 9) and disagrees with both the Manichees and more respectable philosophies such as Stoicism (see p. 206).

†This point of contrast between paganism and Christianity is focused on most insistently by Søren Kierkegaard in the nineteenth century. See pp. 499–500.

that our eternal destiny is settled. It is not surprising to find Augustine ending these meditations on time with expressions of awe and praise.

---

1. What are the characteristics of mystical experience?
2. What does Plotinus mean by "emanation"?
3. What is the Great Chain of Being? How are being and goodness related?
4. Explain what is meant by "creation *ex nihilo.*"
5. How does Augustine solve the problem of natural evil?
6. In what sense is God eternal, according to Augustine?
7. What is puzzling about past, present, and future?
8. How does Augustine resolve the puzzles about time?

Human Nature and Its Corruption

What is man? He is certainly a creature of God, but that does not yet distinguish him from any other creature. The Platonistic tradition on which Augustine draws so heavily is unequivocal: a person is an immaterial soul, who may for a time inhabit a body. If we look to the biblical story of creation, however, we get a view that seems to contradict this tradition, for we are told that God "formed man of dust from the ground, and breathed into his nostrils the breath of life" (Gen. 2:7). It seems obvious that human beings are here conceived as material beings—living bodies. Perhaps it is possible to understand the "breath of life" as the creation of an immaterial soul, but this seems strained.

Augustine's thought about human nature is thus pulled in two directions, and we can see an uneasy tension in his efforts to reconcile these traditions. In trying to remain true to the biblical tradition, he emphasizes that a human being is a unitary being: one thing. God did not create a soul when he took up the dust of the earth; he created *man.* But Augustine also believes in the soul and accepts Platonic arguments about its immateriality and its distinctness from the body. But if man is one thing, how can he be composed of two things? Aristotle solves this problem by considering the soul to be the form of a certain kind of living body; in the thirteenth century Thomas Aquinas will adapt this solution in his Christian Aristotelianism. But Augustine, drawing on the Platonic tradition, cannot take this line. And the result is an uneasy compromise. Man is one being, created by God, but he is composed of both body and soul, each a distinct created being.

How, then, are soul and body related to each other? Augustine tries to answer this question in the very definition of a soul.

> But if you want a definition of the soul, and so ask me—what is the soul? I have a ready answer. It seems to me to be a special substance, endowed with reason, adapted to rule the body. (*GS* 13)

So a soul is, by its very nature, suited to "rule the body" by virtue of possessing reason. One thing is clear, then. The soul and its powers are superior to the body. This fact is crucial to Augustine's view of the human predicament—of what stands in the way of our happiness and how we may after all attain it.

We are created by God and so, by nature, are something good. Yet on all sides we find ourselves involved in evil. We are created in the image of God's justice, yet we act unjustly. We are created for happiness, but we find ourselves miserable. Why? The biblical answer is that we have sinned. This seems precisely the right answer to Augustine. But, again, he wants to understand what that means. Augustine's analysis of sin and the way to blessedness draws heavily on his own experience. But to understand that experience he needs to come to terms with freedom and responsibility, with God's grace and foreknowledge, and above all with the nature of the will. These are perhaps the most original and penetrating parts of Augustine's philosophy.

Augustine takes the biblical story of the first human pair's sin quite literally. Adam and Eve—created good, happy, and dwelling in the Garden with all of their needs satisfied—are tempted by the serpent to disobey the commandment of God. And so they do. As punishment, they are made subject to death, driven out of the Garden, and forced into a struggle for survival. Their descendants inherit this status. They cannot "begin again" and take the position that Adam and Eve enjoyed before their sin. This status, into which they are simply born, is original sin. Its characteristics are ignorance (i.e., lack of wisdom) and what Augustine calls "concupiscence," or wrong desire. If Augustine is right, we are in trouble from the very start of our lives. Look, he says, at infants.

> It can hardly be right for a child, even at that age, to cry for everything, including things which would harm him; to work himself into a tantrum against people older than himself and not required to obey him; and to try his best to strike and hurt others who know better than he does, including his own parents, when they do not give in to him and refuse to pander to whims which would only do him harm. This shows that, if babies are innocent, it is not for lack of will to do harm, but for lack of strength.
>
> I have myself seen jealousy in a baby and know what it means. He was not old enough to talk, but whenever he saw his foster-brother at the breast, he would grow pale with envy. . . . it surely cannot be called innocence, when the milk flows in such abundance from its source, to object to a rival desperately in need and depending for his life on this one form of nourishment. (C 1.7)

Innocence and guilt, it should be noticed, are to be found not in outward actions but in desires, in such things as jealousy and the "will to do harm." It is this condition of the heart, much more than the actions that flow from it, that is the essence of *sin*. We may call babies "innocent," but this is a very shallow judgment. They are innocent only in their lack of ability to do what they very much want to do. As Augustine allows, babies tend to grow out of crying and throwing tantrums. But this does not mean that their desires change; it may only mean that their concupiscence takes on more sophisticated and socially acceptable forms.

We need to understand the elements of sin more clearly. And we have to face the problem of how it could have originated in a world that was created good. What, then, is sin? It clearly has something to do with the motivation for action. So we need to understand motivation better. Whatever we do, Augustine says, is done from a desire for something. These desires Augustine calls

"loves." We seek to delight in possessing the object of our love. If we think that wealth will make us happy, we love riches. We are sure that if only we can possess riches, we will delight in them, so we are moved by this love to acquire wealth.

Remember that reality is ordered in a Great Chain of Being, reaching from God to the merest speck of existence. This order is at the same time an order of value, for a thing's degree of being is an index to its degree of goodness. Clearly, things of higher value should be loved more and things of less value loved less. If our loves were rightly ordered, they would match the order of value in things themselves. In other words, there is an appropriate ordering of loves that matches perfectly the ordering of goodness in things. And this means that God, who is perfect being and goodness, should be loved most of all, and all the rest of creation in appropriate degrees corresponding to their goodness. In fact, the injunction of Jesus to love God absolutely, "with all your heart, and with all your soul, and with all your strength, and with all your mind," corresponds to the absolute value to be found in God. The rule to love our neighbors as ourselves also fits this ordering rule, for each of us has the same degree of value. Those who are perfectly virtuous—that is, righteous—have their loves rightly ordered. They love all things appropriately, in accord with their worthiness to be loved.

Sin, we can now say, is disordered love. It is loving things inappropriately, loving more what is of lower value and loving less what is of higher or highest value. Since we are motivated to act by our loves, these sinful desires produce wicked acts: murder, theft, adultery, deception, and so on. For example, Jones loves money and is willing to kill her aged aunt to get it. What this means is that she loves money (which is less valuable) more than she loves the person who has it (who is more valuable). Her desires are not ordered correctly, and the result is wickedness.

We have not yet plumbed the depths of sin, however. Two errors must be avoided. First, we may think that sin is just a *mistake*. We might think that vice and wickedness is simply not being aware of the true ordering of value in the world. This is akin to the view of Socrates, who holds that virtue is knowledge and vice ignorance.* The person who acts wrongly, according to this view, simply doesn't *know* what is right. Augustine agrees that there is a kind of ignorance involved in sin. But it is not *simple* ignorance, for he holds that the light of Wisdom has "enlightened every man," and the rules of righteousness are written in the human heart. So if we are ignorant, we are *willingly* ignorant. We don't *want* to see the truth. We obscure it and then complain that it is too obscure to make out. Sin, then, is not just ignorance. Socrates and Plato are on that score too optimistic; if the problem with human beings is not simple ignorance, there is no reason to hope that simple education will solve the problem. What is needed is not education alone, but *conversion*. And that concerns the *will*.

The second error is to suppose that sin might be something that just *happens* to us. Our environment and developmental history might just have produced certain loves in us rather than others. Our wickedness may be just bad luck—the luck of a bad upbringing, for example—and for luck no one is to blame. A key aspect of the notion of sin, however, is that we are to blame for it. For our sins we are punished, and justly so. Therefore something must be missing in this analysis.

We need to bring in the aspect of *will*. Augustine does this by offering an analysis of four basic emotions: desire, joy, fear, and grief.

> The important factor in those emotions is the character of a man's will. If the will is wrongly directed, the emotions will be wrong; if the will is right, the emotions will be not only blameless, but praiseworthy. The will is engaged in all of them; in fact they are all essentially acts of will. (*CG* 14.6)

To desire something is not just to have a tendency to acquire it. To desire is to *consent* to that tendency, to acquiesce in it, to give in to it, to say yes to it—in short, to *will* it. In a similar way, to fear something is not just to be disposed to avoid something, perhaps with a feeling of panic added. To be afraid is to "disagree" that something should happen, and that disagreement is an act of will. What are joy and grief? They, too, are acts of will,

joy being consent in the attainment of something desired and grief disagreement in the possession of something feared. In general, Augustine says that

> as a man's will is attracted or repelled in accordance with the varied character of different objects which are pursued or shunned, so it changes and turns into feelings of various kinds. (*CG* 14.6)

We noticed at various points the prominence that Augustine gives to the concept of will. Here we see why. It is the character of the human will that accounts for emotions and actions alike. We may be motivated by our loves, but in the last analysis, these loves come down to will. And for what we will we are responsible. The will is *free*.

Sin, then, for which we are properly held responsible, is a matter of the will having gone wrong. As Augustine puts it,

> When an evil choice happens in any being, then what happens is dependent on the will of that being; the failure is voluntary, not necessary, and the punishment that follows is just. (*CG* 12.8)

Note an important feature of this account of sin. Its root is not located in the body or anywhere in the material world. Its root is in the soul—precisely in that superior part of the human being which mirrors most clearly the image of God. The soul, which by means of reason is "fit to rule the body," consents instead to be the body's slave, preferring what is less good to what is better.

Again, of course, Augustine is rejecting the Manichean view of evil. If we really do manage to observe the injunction to know ourselves, what we will find is not the pure, unsullied soul that is part of God. What we will find is a rebel who has gone radically wrong by consenting to a disordered love life. The miser loves gold, but there is nothing wrong with gold. What is wrong is that the miser consents to loving gold (which is worth less) more than justice (which is worth more). The lustful person loves beautiful bodies, but there is nothing wrong with beautiful bodies. What is wrong is that the love of sensual pleasures is preferred to the love of self-control "by which we are made fit for spiritual realities far more beautiful, with a loveliness which cannot fade" (*CG* 12.8).

---

*See pp. 67–69.

But now we must face the question, How can this happen in a world created by a good God? Here we discover the second part of Augustine's solution to the problem of evil. The first part, you will remember, consisted in arguing that natural evil is not a reality but simply the privation of goodness. Whatever exists is good, simply in virtue of its *being*. The question now is whether this principle can be used in the sphere of moral evil, where it looks as though the bad will is itself a positive reality. Augustine is confident that it can.

The first thing to be established is that the will is itself a good thing. This is easily done, not only from the principle that all created things are good, but also from the reflection that without free will no one can live rightly. To live rightly is to choose to live rightly; no one can choose rightly without a free will; and since living rightly is acknowledged to be a good, the necessary condition for that good must itself be good (*FCW* 18.188–190).

There are, Augustine tells us, three classes of goods. There are great goods, such as justice, the mere possession of which guarantees a righteous life. There are lesser goods, such as wealth and physical beauty, which, though good, are not essential to the highest goods of happiness and a virtuous life. And then there are intermediate goods. Of these intermediate goods we can say that their possession does not guarantee either virtue or happiness, yet without them no one can be virtuous or happy. Such an intermediate good is free will. Whether it leads to happiness depends on what we do with it; and that is up to us.

Augustine thinks it obvious that the human race has made bad use of its free will; we have turned from the true and lasting good to lesser goods and have sought our happiness where it is not to be found. How are we to understand that?

> The will . . . commits sin when it turns away from immutable and common goods, towards its private good, either something external to itself or lower than itself. It turns to its own private good when it desires to be its own master; it turns to external goods when it busies itself with the private affairs of others or with whatever is none of its concern; it turns to goods lower than itself when it loves the pleasures of the body. Thus a man becomes proud,

meddlesome, and lustful; he is caught up in another life which, when compared to the higher one, is death. (*FCW* 19.199–200)

The result of such "turning away" from the higher goods and "turning toward" the lower is *pride, meddlesomeness,* and *lust*. When we value most highly the goods we can all have in common— such as justice, love, and truth—peace reigns in our community. When our loves are fastened on lower goods—such as money, power, and fine possessions—the result is discord and strife; for if you have something of this sort, I do not have it—and often enough, I want it. Proud, meddlesome, and greedy individuals will never be at peace with one another.

Pride, however, is more than the result of sin. It is the very root of sin itself.* Why did the first couple disobey God's command? Augustine emphasizes that it was not because the command was difficult to obey; in fact, nothing was easier. They simply had to refrain from eating the fruit of one of the many bountiful trees in the Garden. In no way did they *need* to eat that piece of fruit. Why, then, did they disobey? The words of the serpent that tempted them suggest the answer. He said, "God knows that when you eat of it your eyes will be opened, and you will be like God, knowing good and evil" (Gen. 3:5). This is the key. They wanted to be "like God." It is only because their wills had already "turned away" from a determination to be obedient to the truth that the temptation had any power over them.

> It was in secret that the first human beings began to be evil; and the result was that they slipped into open disobedience. For they would not have arrived at the evil act if an evil will had not preceded it. Now, could anything but pride have been the start of the evil will? For "pride is the start of every kind of sin." (Ecclesiasticus 10:13) And what is

---

*Note that in attacking pride Augustine is not recommending obsequiousness, or slavishness, or a groveling, fawning, or cringing attitude. There is a proper self-respect that each of us both needs and deserves. We are all creatures of God with a place on the Chain of Being; so each of us has an intrinsic value, and it is as bad to deny that as to claim more than is our due. Compare Augustine's pride to the Greek hubris, the sort of arrogance that puts oneself in the place of God. (See p. 8.)

pride except a longing for a perverse kind of exaltation? For it is a perverse kind of exaltation to abandon the basis on which the mind should be firmly fixed, and to become, as it were, based on oneself, and so remain. This happens when a man is too pleased with himself: and a man is self-complacent when he deserts that changeless Good in which, rather than in himself, he ought to have found his satisfaction. . . .

We can see then that the Devil would not have entrapped man by the obvious and open sin of doing what God had forbidden, had not man already started to please himself. That is why he was delighted also with the statement, "You will be like gods." In fact they would have been better able to be like gods if they had in obedience adhered to the supreme and real ground of their being, if they had not in pride made themselves their own ground. . . . By aiming at more, a man is diminished, when he elects to be self-sufficient and defects from the one who is really sufficient for him.

This then is the original evil: man regards himself as his own light, and turns away from that light which would make man himself a light if he would set his heart on it. (CG 14.13)

Pride, then, is the cause of man's fall. Not content to live by the light God supplies, we aim to be our own light. Trying to lift ourselves above the place proper to us in the Chain of Being, we seek to become "like God," to be "self-sufficient," to make ourselves the "ground" of our own being. But in trying to rise above our place, we fall. For in this attempt at self-sufficiency we are catapulted at once into anxiety and concern for our own well-being, which we ourselves now have to guarantee. Not content with the true goods that are available to all, we find ourselves engaged in ruthless competition with others for the lower goods. Our loves settle upon the things of this world, and greed, lust, and covetousness reign among our desires. No longer are our wills ordered according to the worthiness of goods to be desired, the order implicit in the created world. As though we were God, we create our own order. But our order is in fact disorder, both within our souls and among one another.

The sin of pride shows itself also in the fact that the first couple, when confronted with their disobedience, make excuses:

The woman said, "The serpent led me astray, and I ate," and the man said, "The woman whom you gave me as a companion, she gave me fruit from the tree, and I ate." There is not a whisper anywhere here of a plea for pardon, nor of any entreaty for healing. (CG 14.14)

One of the manifestations of sin is a refusal to admit that it is sin. Neither of the first humans would admit to sin; each tried to pin it on someone else.

The root of sin, then, is pride—setting ourselves up as the highest good when the highest good is rather something we should acknowledge as above us. Pride is the sixteen-year-old Augustine posing as the arbiter of right and wrong when stealing and trashing his neighbor's pears—ashamed to be less dissolute than his companions. Pride is the will turning away from God and to itself, resulting in a set of disordered loves.

Suppose we ask, what causes that? Why does that happen? God, after all, created us good. We have free will, to be sure, but why do we use our freedom in that way?

If you try to find the efficient cause of this evil choice, there is none to be found. For nothing causes an evil will, since it is the evil will itself which causes the evil act; and that means that the evil choice is the efficient cause of an evil act, whereas there is no efficient cause of an evil choice. . . . It is not a matter of efficiency, but of deficiency; the evil will itself is not effective but defective. For to defect from him who is the Supreme Existence, to something of less reality, this is to begin to have an evil will. To try to discover the causes of such defection deficient, not efficient causes—is like trying to see darkness or to hear silence. . . .

No one therefore must try to get to know from me what I know that I do not know. (CG 12.6–7)

We can understand Augustine's argument in this way. Suppose that there were an answer to the question, Why do we sin? Suppose that we could find something that is the cause of the will's turning away from the highest good. Then that something would—since it has being—be something good. But something good cannot cause something evil. So there cannot be such a cause in being.

Yet we must remember that created wills, living in time and subject to change, are a mixture of being and nonbeing. If the will, like God's will, were unmixed with nothingness, then it could not fall. So there is a "cause" for sin in the sense that the incomplete being of the will is a *necessary condition* for sin. This is what Augustine calls a "deficient" cause and compares to darkness or silence. Darkness is not a reality on its own; it is just the absence of light. Similarly, silence is the nonexistence of sound. A deficient cause is the absence of the fullness of being that would make sin impossible. The presence of such a deficient cause does not guarantee that the will turns away from God; it just makes that turning possible. So if we ask, then, what does cause the turning away of the evil will, the answer, literally, is *nothing.* The act is voluntary. For Augustine, this means that it cannot have an efficient cause. If it had an efficient cause it would occur necessarily and not be subject to just punishment.* Clearly Augustine is again relying on the Neoplatonic idea of the Chain of Being to solve this problem.

He has not yet solved it completely, however. Recall his doctrine of God. God exists "all at once" in a timeless eternity and "sees all things in a single moment." But that means that God knew—or foreknew—even before man was created that man would sin. So it was true that Adam was going to sin even before he chose to sin. And if that is so, did he really have any choice? Could he have refrained from sinning, even if he had wanted to? Doesn't God's foreknowledge take away man's free will?

Clearly Augustine needs to affirm both; free will is necessary for responsibility, and God's foreknowledge is a necessary consequence of his perfection. Can Augustine have it both ways? "It does not follow," he says,

> that there is nothing in our will because God foreknew what was going to be in our will; for if he foreknew this, it was not nothing that he foreknew. Further, if, in foreknowing what would be in our will, he foreknew something, and not nonentity,

it follows immediately that there is something in our will, even if God foreknows it. Hence we are in no way compelled either to preserve God's prescience by abolishing our free will, or to safeguard our free will by denying (blasphemously) the divine foreknowledge. We embrace both truths, and acknowledge them in faith and sincerity, the one for a right belief, the other for a right life. . . . The fact that God foreknew that a man would sin does not make a man sin; on the contrary, it cannot be doubted that it is the man himself who sins just because he whose prescience cannot be mistaken has foreseen that the man himself would sin. A man does not sin unless he wills to sin; and if he had not willed to sin, then God would have foreseen that refusal. (*CG* 5.10)

If God foresees that I am going to freely will something, then I will undoubtedly will that thing freely. But it would be a crazy mistake, Augustine thinks, to conclude that this somehow robs me of my free will. How could it not be my will if what God infallibly foresees is that I am going to exercise my will? So Augustine does not see that there is any conflict between God's omniscience and individual freedom.

Augustine's analysis of the human predicament, then, reveals us to be in a pretty sorry state. We are proud, determined to be masters of our own destiny, turned away from the highest goods and anxiously devoted to the lower; our desires are not ordered by the order of value in things. Furthermore, we are continually engaged in turning away from the source of our being. And we cannot escape responsibility for this descent into evil, with all its consequences, both personal and social.

Is there any way out of this desperate plight?

---

*Here we meet for the first time a theme that will puzzle philosophers down to the present day: Does responsibility require exemption from the causal order of the world? Augustine thought the answer was an obvious yes. For other views, see David Hume ("Rescuing Human Freedom," in Chapter 15) and Immanuel Kant (pp. 458–460).

1. How, for Augustine, are soul and body related?
2. What is "original" sin? We often say babies are "innocent." What does Augustine think?
3. What is "sin"? How is the will involved in it?
4. If the will is a good thing, why does it go bad?
5. In what way is pride the root of sin?
6. How does Augustine reconcile free will with God's foreknowledge?

Human Nature and Its Restoration

The result of sin is a diminution in the very being of human beings; they become smaller—more ignorant, weaker, and less in control of themselves.* Their very will is divided. With one part of the mind they continue to acknowledge the truth of God and the righteousness of his law (since they cannot entirely put out the light that enlightens everyone); but with another part they love what is of lesser value. This was Augustine's own experience before his conversion. He often quotes a passage from Saint Paul to the same effect.

> I do not understand my own actions. For I do not do what I want, but I do the very thing I hate. . . . I can will what is right, but I cannot do it. For I do not do the good I want, but the evil I do not want is what I do. Now if I do what I do not want, it is no longer I that do it, but sin which dwells within me. (Rom. 7:15, 18–20)

Augustine is convinced that this condition is so desperate that none of us can rescue ourselves from it.†

> For by the evil use of free choice man has destroyed both himself and it. For as one who kills himself, certainly by being alive kills himself, but by killing himself ceases to live, and can have no power to restore himself to life after the killing; so when sin was committed by free choice, sin became victor and free choice was lost. (AE 9.30)

Here, however, is the point where the distinctive "gospel" of Christianity comes into its own. What we cannot do for ourselves, God has done for us through his Son Jesus, the Mediator, who took upon himself the sins of the world. All that is required is to trust, by faith, that God has forgiven and received us, despite our turning away, and we will be healed.

This may seem simple enough. But once again there are problems in trying to understand it. We cannot save ourselves from our disordered loves, precisely because our loves are disordered. It would be as impossible as trying to lift ourselves off the ground by wrapping our arms around our own chests and lifting. The restoration of human nature —its re-creation—is no more possible for us than its original creation. So God has to do it. And he has in fact done it in Christ. All we need is to accept it by faith.

But is faith something we can do? This itself seems like an act of will. If our wills are divided against themselves, how can we wholeheartedly will to have faith? If we do not love God absolutely, what love that is actually present in us could lead us to do so?

This problem faces Augustine starkly because of the influence of a British monk, Pelagius. As Pelagius is usually understood, he emphasizes both the responsibility of individuals for their lives and the justice of God. Each of us is responsible for keeping the law of God; and if we *ought* to keep the law, it must follow that we *can* keep it.* Otherwise, it would be unjust of God to punish us for not doing so. Therefore, he argues, perfection must be possible for us, since it is demanded of us. The implication is that each individual comes into the world as fresh and innocent as Adam, and each has the same opportunity to earn, or merit, the reward of eternal life. Whether a person is saved or not, then, is entirely up to the will of the individual.

You can see that this starting point is at direct odds with that of Augustine. It contradicts both his inability before his conversion to make the decision he knew he ought to make and the flaws in his continuing desire-structure that a scrupulous examination finds even after his conversion. It seems to be a moralism that makes the work of Christ inessential. And it is in conflict with many passages in the Scriptures. But it does dramatically pose the problem of what individuals can and cannot do to re-

---

*Recall the correlation of knowledge and strength with being, p. 242.

†See again Augustine's theory of the "chain" that sin forms, by which the soul becomes enslaved and loses its ability to do even what it truly wants to do (p. 231).

---

*This principle, that "ought" implies "can," will be used in the eighteenth century by Immanuel Kant as one of the cornerstones of his moral philosophy. See pp. 456–458.

store themselves to the sort of creature they were made to be.

Augustine spent the last decade of his life struggling against Pelagian views. He wrote treatise after treatise trying to clarify the situation and work out a satisfactory answer. Two things were never in doubt for him: Our wills are free, and our salvation is a gift of God's grace. That there is a tension between these ideas is undeniable. But he thinks they can be reconciled. Let us see how.

First it is important to realize that we can never free ourselves from dependence upon God. Remembrance of this will be the surest way to guard against pride, which is, as we have seen, the root of sin. "What have you that you did not receive? If then you received it, why do you boast as if it were not a gift?" (1 Cor. 4:7). Augustine applies this principle of Paul's to the free will: That in itself is a gift, one of God's creations. Whenever we will anything, we are but exercising a power we owe to God.

But that is not enough, for the question concerns merit. If I use my will to turn to God in faith, is that something I do on my own, for which God owes me a reward? The very idea is repugnant to Augustine, for it would let pride back in at the very place where it should be most firmly excluded. It is precisely that turning back to God for which we owe God himself the greatest thanks. For what gift can compare with that? But, then, is it something we have done? Or did God do it in us?

Augustine wrestles with this puzzle again and again. Perhaps his most developed thought on the matter is that *faith* (the turning of our loves back to God) is something in our power. But whether it will be exercised or not depends on whether there are certain "inducements or invitations" present in us or our environment. We do not, after all, choose to take a candy bar unless there is a candy bar presented for us to choose. These inducements are not in our power but are a gift of God. Apparently God makes an offer that some cannot refuse, which is too good to turn down; though when they accept it, they are making use of their own free will. But the grace offered is so great that it overwhelms any pride in its acceptance. We do not

boast about possessing a candy bar when it has been offered to us. The appropriate response is gratitude (*SL* 52–60).

There is a section in the *Confessions* where Augustine is searching his soul for evidence of continuing sins and temptations. He sets forth his struggles to get his loves in order with respect to sex, food, pleasures of eye and ear, curiosity, the opinions of others, speech, and self-complacency. And in this section there is a phrase that is repeated again and again:

> Give me the grace to do as you command, and command me to do what you will! (*C* 10.29, 31, 37)

This phrase perfectly expresses that paradoxical combination of reliance on God's grace and determination to will the right that Augustine discovers when he tries to *understand* what he has come to *believe* in becoming a Christian. Our salvation—happiness, blessedness—is up to us. Yet it is wholly a product of God's grace; we have nothing that we have not received.

Let us say a bit more about the life in which Augustine claims to have found both wisdom and happiness. What is it like to live as a Christian? As we have seen, Augustine's theory of motivation holds that we are moved by our various "loves." Our loves are expressions of the will as we desire a variety of presumed goods. Since it is the interior life that really counts, the quality of our lives will be determined by the nature of our loves.

As we have seen, things in the world are ordered in value according to the degree of being they possess (the Great Chain of Being principle). And the degree of value a thing possesses determines its worthiness to be loved. Happiness and virtue (which coincide as surely for Augustine as they do for Plato or the Stoics) consist in "ordered love," where our loves are apportioned according to the worth of their objects.

> He lives in justice and sanctity who is an unprejudiced assessor of the intrinsic value of things. He is a man who has an ordinate love: he neither loves what should not be loved nor fails to love what should be loved; he neither loves more what should be loved less, loves equally what should

be loved less or more, nor loves less or more what should be loved equally. (*OCD* 1.27)

But we can now add two further distinctions.

Here is the first one. Some things are to be *used*, whereas others are to be *enjoyed*. And some may be both used and enjoyed.

> To enjoy something is to cling to it with love for its own sake. To use something, however, is to employ it in obtaining that which you love, provided that it is worthy of love. For an illicit use should be called rather a waste or an abuse. (*OCD* 1.4)

What is appropriately loved *for its own sake*? For Augustine there can be just one answer: only God alone. In loving the eternal truth, wisdom, and goodness of God we find blessedness. Here alone we can *rest*, content at last; for there exists no higher good to be enjoyed than the creator and restorer of our human nature. As Augustine says in a famous phrase,

> You made us for yourself and our hearts find no peace until they rest in you. (*C* 1.1)*

The enjoyment we seek is a never-ending delight in the object of our love, which nothing but the highest and eternal good will provide. All other things are to be used in the service of that end so that we may find the blessedness of that enjoyment. Even other humans, though we are to love them as we love ourselves, are not to be loved *for their own sake*. To do so would be a kind of idolatry, an attempt to find our end, our "rest" in them rather than in the source of all good. Delight in friends and neighbors or in our own talents and excellences must be a delight that always turns to gratitude by being referred to the One who provides it all.

We can see now that Augustinian Christianity is totally different from that "trading skill" piety Socrates rejects in the *Euthyphro* (see 13a–15b and p. 84). Like much religious practice in our day, Euthyphro seeks to "use" the gods to attain what he desires. And he "turns away" from the question that Socrates says is the crucial one: What is that good *X* the gods accomplish through our service to them? Augustine absolutely rejects the notion that we can "use" what is highest for our own ends or "trade" our sacrifice and prayer for some blessings from on high. Whatever good we now have is a gift from God; we have nothing to trade with! God is to be sought not for the sake of some worldly advantage, but for his own sake alone. We don't treat God as a means to some further end. In God we "rest." God is to be *enjoyed*. And you can see that Augustine has an answer to Socrates' question. The good in question is the transformation of our desire-structure so that our ordered loves enjoy and use each thing appropriately. The point of piety is not to get what we want from God, but to allow God to change us so that we don't want the same things any more.

The second distinction corresponds to that between enjoyment and use. Augustine divides love into two kinds: charity and cupidity.

> I call "charity" the motion of the soul toward the enjoyment of God for his own sake, and the enjoyment of one's self and of one's neighbor for the sake of God; but "cupidity" is a motion of the soul toward the enjoyment of one's self, one's neighbor, or any corporeal thing for the sake of something other than God. (*OCD* 3.10)

From cupidity comes both *vice* (by which Augustine means whatever corrupts one's own soul) and *crime* (which harms someone else). We try to enjoy what should only be used and destroy both ourselves and others. Greed, avarice, lust, and gluttony are all forms of cupidity. Cupidity is disordered love.

Charity, by contrast, is ordered love, directed toward enjoying God and all other things only in God. If charity is the motivation for one's life, all will be well. "Love, and do what you will," Augustine tells us.[5] You can do whatever you want, provided that your motivation is charity. Charity will motivate us to behave appropriately to all things (i.e., in accord with their actual value). From charity will flow all the virtues: temperance, prudence, fortitude, and justice.*

---

*Compare Plato on "traveller's rest and journey's end," p. 130.

*Compare Aristotle on the unity of the virtues, p. 191. There is much similarity between his view and that of Augustine. But there is one great difference: For Augustine, charity (the source of the virtues) is a result of God's grace, not something we have in our control.

We must never assume, however, that what motivates us is pure charity. Augustine's own self-examination revealed the cupidity that remained in his life even as a Christian bishop. The Christian may be "on the way" toward the blessedness of truly ordered loves but cannot expect to find it entire until the resurrection of the dead.

---

1. Why, according to Augustine, can we not save ourselves?
2. What problem did Pelagius pose to Augustine?
3. What is virtue? How is it related to grace?
4. What can we properly enjoy? What can we properly use?
5. Contrast Augustine's notion of piety with the piety described in *Euthyphro* 13a–15b.
6. What are the two kinds of love?

Augustine on Relativism

As we have seen, Augustine argues against skepticism. And everything we have seen so far should lead us to conclude that he is completely opposed to relativism as well. No believer in God could accept Protagoras' saying that *man* is the measure of all things. There is indeed a "measure," a standard by which to judge. But it could not be any created thing, much less a human being whose valuations are determined by a set of disordered loves.* Moreover, if the doctrine of relativism is that (1) Jones can judge some particular action to be right, (2) Smith can judge that very same action to be wrong, and (3) both Jones and Smith are correct, then Augustine is certainly not a relativist.

---

*Again, a comparison with Aristotle is instructive. Aristotle also disagrees with Protagoras; for him the "measure" is the good man (see p. 193), not just *any* man. Augustine might not disagree with this in principle, but he would ask, Where is this good man to be found? Among men, he would say, there is but one without sin—the Christ, the incarnation of the Wisdom of God, the *logos*. He can be the "measure." Aristotle's "good man" might have many virtues, but from Augustine's point of view, he is puffed up with pride—which undermines them all.

Nonetheless, there is a sense in which Augustine can admit a good deal of what the relativist wishes to urge. Part of what makes relativism plausible are the differences in customs among the nations.* Another part of its plausibility is the conviction (which most people share) that it is usually wrong to lie, or steal, but not always. Augustine does justice to both these intuitions by recognizing that particular actions are always done out of particular *motivations* and in particular *circumstances,* which must both be taken into account when judging the goodness or badness, the rightness or wrongness of someone's act. Remember Augustine's rule: Love and do what you will. One crucial fact in the evaluation of all actions concerns the way they are motivated: Is the motivation charity or cupidity, a sound will or an evil will? A second crucial fact is an appraisal of what the circumstances require.

Augustine's view on these issues comes up in a rather curious context. He is considering what to make of the fact that certain of the "patriarchs" whose stories are recorded in the Old Testament had more than one wife or had children by concubines. Did they act sinfully in behaving that way? Is the same behavior acceptable today? His answer to both questions is no. The principle is this: One and the same *kind* of action may be quite differently motivated. And that can make all the difference.

> The just men of antiquity imagined and foretold the Heavenly Kingdom in terms of an earthly kingdom. The necessity for a sufficient number of children was responsible for the blameless custom by which one man had several wives at the same time. And thus it was not virtuous for one wife to have several husbands, for one woman is not more fruitful by this means, and it is rather a whorish evil to seek either wealth or children by common intercourse. With reference to customs of this kind, whatever the holy men of those days did without libidinousness, even though they did things that may not now be done in that way, is not blamed by the Scriptures. (*OCD* 3.12)
>
> For if because of the times a man could then use many wives chastely, a man may nevertheless use

---

*Recall the example of the Greeks before Darius cited by Herodotus (see p. 45) and the judgment that custom is king over all.

one wife libidinously. I commend more a man who uses the fecundity of many wives for a disinterested purpose than a man enjoying the flesh of one wife for itself. In the first instance a utility congruous with the circumstances of the time is sought; in the second a cupidity implicated in temporal delights is satiated. (*OCD* 3.27)

In ancient times it was allowable for men to have many wives, but now it is not allowable. Why? Because the circumstances then required numerous children to be produced swiftly; but that "utility" is not present now. What counts is not whether a man has one wife or many, but the state of his "loves": whether the motivation is *cupidity,* the desire to "enjoy the flesh" for its "temporal delights," or *charity.** So neither is polygamy to be condemned absolutely, nor is monogamy to be universally praised. It all depends on what constitutes "a utility congruous with the circumstances of the time" and on the motivation.

It is clear that this principle gives Augustine great flexibility in one respect (with regard to outward behavior), while it rigorously constrains his judgment in another. An Augustinian will be very tolerant about any matter that is clearly nothing but *nomos* or convention, such as fashion. You can't imagine Augustine getting excited about the length or color of someone's hair. Whether more significant actions are judged good or bad depends partly on the motivation and partly on what is useful in the circumstances. Without a full knowledge of both motivation and circumstances, we should be very cautious about pronouncing judgment. As we shall see in the next section, there is even one sense in which such judgment is reserved to God.

In pointing to these two factors, Augustine makes a significant contribution to the debate about relativism. While allowing considerable relativity to moral judgments, Augustine is saved from a complete relativism by (1) the Neoplatonic conviction that reality itself is ordered in value, corresponding to the degrees of being, and (2) the thesis about

motivation. It is not merely by a conventional agreement that eternal things are of more value than temporal things. Nor is it just *nomos* to praise charity and condemn lust, greed, and hatred. Here we reach values that cannot be relativized. The command of Jesus to love God without reserve and our neighbors as ourselves is *absolute.* Augustine goes as far as to say, "Scripture teaches nothing but charity, nor condemns anything except cupidity, and in this way shapes the minds of men"* (*OCD* 3.10).

Similar considerations apply to justice. Some men, he says,

> misled by the variety of innumerable customs, thought that there was no such thing as absolute justice but that every people regarded its own way of life as just. . . . They have not understood, to cite only one instance, that "what you do not wish to have done to yourself, do not do to another"* cannot be varied on account of any diversity of peoples. When this idea is applied to the love of God, all vices perish; when it is applied to the love of one's neighbor, all crimes disappear. For no one wishes his own dwelling corrupted, so that he should not therefore wish to see God's dwelling, which he is himself, corrupted. And since no one wishes to be harmed by another, he should not harm others. (*OCD* 3.14)

In effect, then, Augustine makes two moves: (1) he breaks up the question about whether values are relative by saying that some are and some are not; and (2) he locates those that are not in the realm of motivation. Augustine is certainly not a relativist, but neither is he a simple absolutist. The subtlety of his analyses of the interior life serve him in good stead in advancing the conversation at this point.

---

1. How can one and the same behavior be sometimes right and sometimes wrong?
2. Contrast Augustine's view of relativism with that of Protagoras.

---

*Review the discussion of use and enjoyment, p. 254.

*Luke 6 : 31 and Matt. 7 : 12. See p. 221.

The Two Cities

There is an old joke that there are just two kinds of people in the world: those who think that there are just two kinds of people and those who don't. Augustine is emphatically a member of the first group and in this displays his primary allegiance to the Christian heritage. The two kinds are the saved and the damned, those destined for eternal blessedness in heaven and those to be punished for their sins in hell.

But, as you might expect, Augustine's view is more sophisticated and subtle than that bare statement suggests. It is set forth in a book of more than a thousand pages that presents us with an entire philosophy of history. Augustine's intense interest in time and temporal progression is never merely speculative or introspective. In *The City of God* he brings together all he has learned in the forty and more years since first dedicating himself to the search for wisdom. Here he provides a unified interpretation of human history from creation to the end of the world.

The occasion for writing this magnum opus was the sack of Rome by a Gothic army under the leadership of Alaric in August of A.D. 410. The late Roman empire had been harried by barbarians from the north and east for some time, but for a barbarian army to take Rome, the "eternal city," was a profound shock to every Roman citizen, Christian and pagan alike. People asked: "How could this happen?" Jerome, who had translated the Bible into Latin, wrote, "If Rome can perish, what can be safe?"[6]

Augustine's answer distinguishes "two cities," an earthly city and a heavenly city. The goal of each city is the same: peace. Members of the earthly city seek peace (harmony and order) in this life: such a peace is a necessary condition for happiness, the ultimate end of all men. For this reason states and empires are established, the noblest of them all (in Augustine's view) being the Roman empire. It is noblest in this respect: It succeeded in guaranteeing the earthly peace of its citizens better and for a longer time than any other state ever had.

Yet see to what a pass it had come! Why? To answer this question Augustine reaches back into his theory of motivation and applies its insights to Roman history. (Note again how everything is traced back to the soul and its relations with the highest good; God and the soul really do determine everything of interest in Augustine's world.) What motivated the founders of Rome and all its greatest statesmen? Like Homer's heroes, they wanted *glory*.[*]

> They were passionately devoted to glory; it was for this that they desired to live, for this they did not hesitate to die. This unbounded passion for glory, above all else, checked their other appetites. They felt it shameful for their country to be enslaved, but glorious for her to have dominion and empire; and so they set their hearts first on making her free, and then on making her sovereign. (*CG* 5.12)

The best among the Romans directed this quest for glory into the "right path"; it "checked their other appetites," and they were exemplars of virtue, "good men in their way," as Augustine puts it (*CG* 5.12). Those virtues (personal moderation and devotion to the good of their country) led to Rome's greatness. The passion for glory can yield magnificent results, and Augustine is ready to acknowledge them in full:

> By such immaculate conduct they laboured towards honours, power and glory, by what they took to be the true way. And they were honoured in almost all nations; they imposed their laws on many peoples; and today they enjoy renown in the history and literature of nearly all races. (*CG* 5.15)

And, Augustine adds (quoting from Matt. 6 : 2), "they have received their reward."

The passion for glory, however, is a peculiarly unstable motivation; it can lead as easily to vice and crime as to virtue. Since the glory sought is the praise and honor of others, what happens when the others honor wealth and domination more than moderation and justice? The result is obvious. In fact, the earthly city is always a mix of virtue and

*See pp. 7–8.

vice—precisely because it is an *earthly* city. The aim of its citizens is to *enjoy* what they should only *use*: earthly peace, possessions, and bodily well-being. Since these are exclusive goods (if I possess an estate, you necessarily do not possess it), any earthly city is bound to generate envy and conflict and to tend toward its own destruction.*

In fact, this is the essence of the difference between the two cities. The one seeks its ultimate good here in this world, where nothing is stable and goods are competitively achieved. The other realizes that the only eternal good is found in God, which all can have in common. The difference is precisely that difference between disordered and ordered love we explored earlier.

> We see then that the two cities were created by two kinds of love: the earthly city was created by self-love reaching the point of contempt for God, the Heavenly City by the love of God carried as far as contempt of self. In fact, the earthly city glories in itself, the Heavenly City glories in the Lord. The former looks for glory from men, the latter finds its highest glory in God, the witness of a good conscience. The earthly lifts up its head in its own glory, the Heavenly City says to its God: "My glory; you lift up my head." In the former, the lust for domination lords it over its princes as over the nations it subjugates; in the other both those put in authority and those subject to them serve one another in love, the rulers by their counsel, the subjects by obedience. The one city loves its own strength shown in its powerful leaders; the other says to its God, "I will love you, my Lord, my strength." (*CG* 14.28)

Pursuing earthly goods for their own sake is self-destructive, for it leads to competition, conflict, and disaster. And that is Augustine's explanation for Rome's fall. Rome was not, as some Christians held, particularly wicked; in fact, its empire

was a magnificent achievement, characterized by the real, though flawed, provision of peace and order for its citizens. But it reaped the inevitable consequence of earthly cities that set their loves on earthly glory.

Members of the heavenly city realize that here in this world they have no continuing home; they look for the fulfillment of their hopes in the life to come. Here they have a taste of blessedness, and through God's grace a beginning of true virtue can begin to grow on the ground of charity. But the culmination of these hopes lies beyond.

Nonetheless, citizens of the heavenly city duly appreciate the relative peace provided by the earthly city and contribute to it as they can. While on earth they consider themselves as resident aliens and follow the laws and customs of the society they are dwelling in, to the extent that doing so is consistent with their true citizenship. They *use* the arrangements of their society, but they do not settle down to *enjoy* them. In this world there are no lasting goods, and only what lasts can be enjoyed forever.

> However, it would be incorrect to say that the goods which [the earthly] city desires are not goods, since even that city is better, in its own human way, by their possession. . . . These things are goods and undoubtedly they are gifts of God. (*CG* 15.4)

So, with respect to laws that establish "a kind of compromise between human wills about the things relevant to mortal life," there is "a harmony" between members of the two cities. It is only when the earthly city tries to impose laws at variance with the laws of God that citizens of the heavenly city must dissent (*CG* 19.17).

There are, then, two kinds of people. They are distinguished by their loves. But this very fact—that it is motivation that makes the difference—removes the possibility that anyone can with certainty sort people into one class or the other. We might think Augustine would be tempted to equate membership in the Church with citizenship in the heavenly city, but he does not. The Church is, collectively, the custodian of the truth about God; individuals are another matter. We can tell who is

---

*It is the hope of Karl Marx and the communists that such envy and conflict can be overcome in *this* world; the key, they believe, is overcoming private property, so that the ground of envy is undercut. See Chapter 18. Augustine would have considered this naive.

on the church rolls, but we cannot tell for certain who is a member of the City of God. Only God can judge that.

Among the professed enemies of the City of God, Augustine tells us,

> are hidden future citizens; and when confronted with them she must not think it a fruitless task to bear with their hostility until she finds them confessing the faith. In the same way, while the City of God is on pilgrimage in this world, she has in her midst some who are united with her in participation in the sacraments, but who will not join with her in the eternal destiny of the saints. . . .
>
> In truth, these two cities are interwoven and intermixed in this era, and await separation at the last judgment. (*CG* 1.35)

This epistemological obscurity concerning the saints (for us, though not for God) is a direct consequence of the fact that it is motivation, desire, and the order of a person's loves that make the difference. Behavior is always ambiguous; once more it is the will that tells.

We shall not pursue the details of Augustine's interpretation of history in these terms. It is enough to say that *The City of God* understands human history as *meaningful*. It is not, as a distinguished historian once said, "just one damn thing after another." It has a narrative unity; there is plan and purpose in it; and the story found in the Christian Scriptures provides the key.*

Augustine believes that we can get a perspective on history only if we see it from the viewpoint of eternity—through God's eyes, so to speak. But just that viewpoint has been communicated by God himself through his prophets who prepared the way for the Christ; through the life, teachings, death, and resurrection of Jesus; and finally through the Church, which preserves and extends this "gospel." History is about God's calling citizens of a heavenly city out of the sinful world. These will eventually enjoy blessedness in perfect peace with one another and rest in enjoyment of the one eternal good. For Augustine, all of history must be seen in relation to that end.

---

1. What distinguishes the two cities from one another?
2. Why are we unable to tell with certainty who belongs to each city?

Christians and Philosophers

Augustine melds two traditions, the classical and the Christian. Certainly, tensions show up at various points in Augustine's work, but the degree of success he achieves makes him a peculiarly important figure. He is a culmination of the conversation that precedes him and one of the most influential contributors to the conversation still to come.

He is convinced that truth is one and that important contributions to our understanding of it have been made by both philosophers and prophets. But there is never any doubt which tradition has priority when there is a conflict: Augustine is first, last, and always a Christian, convinced that the one and only wisdom is most fully revealed in the Christ. Ready to acknowledge that pagan thinkers have much to contribute, he uses only what he judges to be consistent with his Christian faith. The rest is subject to severe, sometimes savage criticism.

Augustine has put us in a good position to draw some broad contrasts between classical philosophy and Christianity. These are suggestive rather than exact but point out certain patterns that tend to recur.

Reason and Authority

Augustine is no despiser of reason. Not for him the *credo quia absurdum est* of some church fathers.* He

---

*Review the major "chapters" in this story by looking again at Chapter 9.

*"I believe because it is absurd." This formula is attributed to Tertullian, a Christian writer of the second century.

wants to understand what he believes. He thinks that to a very large extent this can be done and so he must use his reason.

Nevertheless, belief has the priority. It must have, for rational understanding could never by itself discover the truth about the Word becoming flesh or about the Trinity. These things must be believed on the authority of the prophets and apostles who bear testimony to them. This authority is founded on eyewitnesses and is handed on in the Church. The key that unlocks the mystery of life is *revealed*, not *discovered*. Thus at the heart of wisdom Augustine finds a place for authority. This authoritative witness must be believed, and belief is a matter of giving one's assent by an act of will. As Augustine never tires of saying, unless you believe, you will not understand.

The following example may make this relation of belief and understanding clearer to you. Imagine a young woman who has listened only to rock music. Now put her in a concert hall where Beethoven's violin concerto is being performed. She is not likely to get much out of it, but should she believe that there is something of great value going on in that hall? At that point she could accept that this is superb music only by relying on authority. But there is such authority—that of musicians, music critics, and music lovers over nearly two centuries. Augustine would say that it is reasonable for her to believe this on the basis of such authority. This belief not only is reasonable, but also may lead her to listen to the concerto again and again, until she eventually comes to the point where she understands for herself how magnificent it is.[7] Belief, Augustine holds, often properly precedes understanding.

Greek philosophy, by contrast, takes the opposite point of view: Unless I understand, the philosopher says, I will not believe. The extreme case is, of course, the skeptic, who, applying this exact principle, suspends judgment about virtually everything. But Xenophanes already set the pattern:[*]

The gods have not revealed all things from the beginning to mortals; but, by seeking, men find out, in time, what is better.[8]

Having shaken themselves loose from their own tradition, from Homeric authority, philosophers on the whole are convinced that there is no alternative to trying to achieve wisdom on our own. And part of this pattern is the value they put on human excellence in the search for truth, on self-sufficiency, and on pride in one's attainments.

Here we have one of the great watersheds in the quest for wisdom: Is wisdom something we can *achieve*, or is it something we must *receive*? Augustine is convinced that we must receive it because of the absolute distinction between God and humans (we are too limited to discover truth on our own), sin (we are too corrupted to do it), grace (God provides it for us), and gratitude and humility (the appropriate responses to the situation).

In a sermon, Augustine explores the divergence between one who says, "Let me understand that I may believe," and another who says, "Believe rather that you may understand." He acknowledges the deep divide between these two by his suggestion, "Let us go before a judge with this dispute, for neither of us is able to settle the issue on his own" (*SS* 43). Who does he suggest as a judge? There is no surprise here: It must be someone with authority to settle such disputes, and it must obviously be someone with more than merely human authority (or he would be a party to the dispute). So Augustine appeals to the *prophet*. And the prophet (Isaiah) says: "If you do not believe, you shall not understand."[*]

This problem of the choice between reliance on authority or reliance on our native wits comes up

---

[*]Review the discussion of the whole passage from which these words are taken, pp. 17–18.

[*]It is unfortunate for Augustine's appeal that the text of Isaiah 7:9 is unclear. Some translations render the last part as "you shall not continue" and others as "you shall not be established." However that may be, we should ask whether such an appeal is likely to win over the philosopher. You might try to answer this question by looking again at what the skeptic calls "the problem of the criterion." (See pp. 211–212.) Here again we may have a contrast between those William James calls the tough- and tender-minded.

again when we discuss Aquinas, Descartes, Hume, and Kant.

Intellect and Will

Greek philosophers tend to see human problems and their solution in terms of ignorance and knowledge. This is particularly clear in Socrates, for whom virtue or excellence *is* knowledge. But the pattern is very broad, reflected in the importance of education for Plato's guardians, of practical wisdom and contemplation for Aristotle, and of knowledge of reality (in their different theories) by Epicureans and Stoics. Roughly, the pattern takes this form: Inform the intellect and the rest of life will take care of itself.*

Augustine, expressing both the Christian tradition and his own experience, disagrees. Intellect may well be impotent—or worse—unless the will is straightened out. The basic features of human life are desire and love, which are matters of the will. What is needed is not (at first) education, but *conversion;* not inquiry, but *faith.*

Again we have a watershed, which correlates fairly well with the first one. From the point of view of the Christian, we cannot rely upon our reason alone; its use depends on the condition of the will, and the will is corrupted. Our predicament is, on the Christian view, a deep one; we are not in a position to help ourselves out of it, but—this is also crucial—help is available. From the point of view of the Greek philosophers, the human predicament may be serious, but well-intentioned intellectual work will lead us out of it. (Even the skeptics think happiness is attainable.) Reason can master desire.

There is a sense, then, in which Christian thinkers are more pessimistic about humanity than the Greek philosophers.

Augustine on Epicureans and Stoics

We can cap this contrast by noting Augustine's criticisms of several pagan philosophies that may be serious rivals to Christianity's claim to wisdom. Platonism is the one Augustine thinks nearest the truth, but the Platonists go wrong in allowing worship of powers greater than human beings but inferior to God. Augustine concedes that there are such powers (whether called angels, demons, or gods) but insists that devotion, prayer, and worship belong only to God. To think otherwise is the ultimate betrayal.

Augustine's interest in Epicurean and Stoic philosophers is sharpened because Saint Paul is alleged to have debated with them in Athens (see Acts 17:18). Moreover, between them they seem to cover neatly the this-worldly possibilities for happiness, the Epicureans seeking it in the pleasures of a material world and the Stoics in the virtues of the soul.

Recall that Epicurus and Lucretius hold that there is no sense in which we survive our physical death; the soul is as physical as the body and disperses when the body disintegrates. Augustine combines this view with their hedonism and concludes that they recommend nothing but the pursuit of bodily pleasures.* He ascribes to them the slogan, "Let us eat and drink, for tomorrow we shall die," which expresses a hedonist's determination to experience as much of bodily pleasure as possible before death extinguishes all sensation.

This doctrine, Augustine says, is "more fitting for swine than for men." Even worse, it is a doctrine that will inevitably lead to injustice and the oppression of the poor (*SS* 150). And the reason is by now a familiar one: They are trying to enjoy what should only be used and as a result are dominated by their disordered loves. But the key error is their neglect of life after death. Epicureanism in this life makes sense only if they are right about

---

*The contrast, put this baldly, is overdrawn. We have to remember that for Plato's view of education, the *love* of the good is a crucial factor, and this isn't just a matter of intellect. Still, there is something essentially right about it. Compare Descartes, p. 348.

---

*Is this justified? Compare Epicurus on pp. 202–203. Could it be that Augustine is (in part) responsible for the bad press the Epicureans have gotten?

consciousness ending in the grave, and of course Augustine is convinced that cannot be right.

The Stoics, who locate happiness in the virtues of the soul, are considered more worthy opponents. Augustine cannot help admiring their courage and steadfastness. But the crucial question is whether the Stoics have indeed found the key to blessedness. Augustine is convinced that they have not. The Stoics' aim is to live in harmony with nature.* Recall the advice of Epictetus: "Do not seek to have events happen as you want them to, but instead want them to happen as they do happen, and your life will go well." Augustine caustically asks,

> Now is this man happy, just because he is patient in his misery? Of course not! (*CG* 14.25)

It is real happiness that we are interested in, not just contentment with what the world happens to dish out; the Stoic version of happiness is just a makeshift second best. True happiness is delight in the possession of the highest good, to which only the Christian has the key.

But, Augustine suggests, what else could you expect? The Stoic, like the Epicurean, "puts his hope in himself" (*SS* 150). This is simply another display of pride, which is the root of human trouble in the first place. From Augustine's point of view, even the virtues of the pagans are but "splendid vices."

Thus Augustine, though a great admirer of pagan learning, is also one of its most severe critics. He brings to the fore a number of "choice points" in which the Christian tradition differs from non-Christian rational philosophy. These traditions differ in their conceptions of God and of God's relation to the world; they differ about appeal to authority, about the priority of will or intellect in human nature, about whether pride is a virtue or a vice; and they differ in their conceptions of love. The general pattern on these issues that Augustine sets will dominate Western philosophy for a thousand years (although many variants are explored). But the fundamental questions that Augustine thinks he has settled will all come up for inquiry again at the beginning of the modern period.

---

*This concept is discussed on pp. 206–208.

1. What tension exists between reason and authority? Between intellect and will?
2. What is Augustine's critique of the Epicureans? Of the Stoics?

For Further Thought

1. Compare Socrates' view that no one ever knowingly does wrong with Augustine's contrary conviction. Which do you think is nearer the truth? Why?

2. State as clearly as you can Augustine's charge that the philosophers are guilty of pride. Then try to defend philosophy against that charge. Which position do you think has the stronger arguments?

Notes

1. An excellent and readable biography is *Augustine of Hippo* by Peter Brown (London: Faber and Faber, 1967). A classic discussion of his philosophy is Etienne Gilson, *The Christian Philosophy of St. Augustine* (London: Victor Gollanz, 1961).
2. References to the works of Augustine are as follows:
   C: Confessions, trans. R. S. Pine-Coffin (Harmondsworth, Middlesex, England: Penguin Books, 1961).
   FCW: On Free Choice of the Will, trans. Benjamin G. Hackstaff (New York: Macmillan, 1964).
   CG: The City of God, trans. Henry Bettenson (Harmondsworth, Middlesex, England: Penguin Books, 1972).
   OCD: On Christian Doctrine, trans. D. W. Robertson, Jr. (New York: Macmillan, 1958).
   SO: The Soliloquies of St. Augustine, trans. Rose Elizabeth Cleveland (London: Williams and Norgate, 1910).
   T: The Teacher, and *GS, The Greatness of the Soul,* in *Ancient Christian Writers,* ed. Johannes Quasten and Joseph C. Plumpe (Westminster, MD: Newman Press, 1964).
   AE: Saint Augustine's Enchiridion, trans. Ernest Evans (London: S.P.C.K., 1953).
   SL: The Spirit and the Letter, trans. John Burnaby, vol. 8 of *The Library of Christian Classics* (London: SCM Press, 1955).

SS: Selected Sermons of St. Augustine, ed. Quincy
  Howe, Jr. (London: Victor Gollanz, 1967).

3. Quotations from a *Manichean Psalmbook* in Brown,
   Augustine of Hippo, are cited in the text using the abbreviation *MP.* References are to page numbers.

4. Quotations from *The Essential Plotinus,* ed. Elmer
   O'Brien (Indianapolis: Hackett, 1980), are cited in
   the text using the abbreviation *EP.* References are
   to page numbers.

5. Quoted in Gilson, *Christian Philosophy of St. Augustine,* 140.

6. Quoted in Brown, *Augustine of Hippo,* 289.

7. The example is adapted from Jerry P. King, *The Art
   of Mathematics* (New York: Plenum Press, 1992),
   138.

8. Quoted in John Manley Robinson, *An Introduction
   to Early Greek Philosophy* (Boston: Houghton Mifflin,
   1968), 56.

CHAPTER

11

ANSELM AND AQUINAS
Existence and Essence in God and the World

Augustine's influence in Western philosophy and theology was so great that when Peter Lombard, about A.D. 1150, collected notable sayings of the church fathers in the *Book of Sentences,* 90 percent of the quotations were from Augustine's writings.[1]

After the fall of Rome, intellectual work in the West was carried on largely within the Church. It was churchmen who preserved libraries, copied manuscripts, and wrote books. Over most of this work presided the Augustinian spirit, with its convictions that Wisdom is one, that Scripture and Reason are essentially in harmony, and that the interesting and important topics are God and the soul.

Later medieval philosophy, from the eleventh to the fifteenth centuries, is exceedingly rich and inventive. Notable contributions to the conversation are made not only by Christian thinkers such as Abelard, Roger Bacon, Duns Scotus, and William of Ockham, but also by Muslims—Avicenna (Ibn Sinā) and Averroës (Ibn Rushd), among others—and by Jews such as Solomon Ibn Gabirol

and Moses Maimonides. For the purposes of this selective introduction, however, we focus on two examples: a famous argument put forward by Anselm of Canterbury, and—at considerably more length—the Christian Aristotelianism of Thomas Aquinas. Anselm and Aquinas, both made saints of the Church after their deaths, exemplify some of the best, though by no means the only, philosophy of this period. The chapter closes by considering some doubts that were raised about the confident claim that reason and faith are harmonious, doubts that look forward to the birth of self-conscious modern philosophy.

Anselm: On That, Than Which No Greater Can Be Conceived

In about three pages, Anselm (A.D. 1033–1109) sets forth an argument concluding not only that God exists but also that he exists "so truly" that we cannot even *conceive* that he doesn't. This apparently simple, yet deeply perplexing argument is known to history as the **ontological argument.**[*]

Before formulating the argument, we should note something of the context Anselm is working in. Anselm was a priest and a bishop—the Archbishop of Canterbury, in fact. And from all accounts, his character and spirit were such as to merit his later sainthood. He is, moreover, steeped in the Augustinian tradition. The work in which the argument is found was first called *Faith Seeking Understanding*[†] (a concept that should by now be familiar). It is, in Augustinian fashion, a meditative work, the first chapter of which is a prayer. Here Anselm resolves to "enter the inner chamber of [his] mind" and "shut out all thoughts save that of God" (*Proslogium* 1).[2] As you can see, questions about God and the soul again predominate—the former to be known most clearly by a withdrawal into the recesses of the latter. God is not sought by exploring the *world*. Anselm appeals to the Interior Teacher in these words:

> Teach me to seek thee, and reveal thyself to me, when I seek thee, for I cannot seek thee, except thou teach me, nor find thee, except thou reveal thyself. (*Proslogium* 1)

He acknowledges that he cannot fully comprehend God, but he says,

> I long to understand in some degree thy truth, which my heart believes and loves. For I do not seek to understand that I may believe, but I believe in order to understand. (*Proslogium* 1)

In the preface, Anselm notes that he had written an earlier work (*Monologium*, or *Soliloquy*), in which he had tried to see how far—setting Scripture aside—argument and reason could substantiate the central doctrines of Christianity. The answer was, pretty far—but not, of course, all the way. His aim there was to explore the truth, while making as few assumptions as possible. Because the arguments of this work were pretty involved, he began to wonder

> whether there might be found a single argument which would require no other for its proof than itself alone; and alone would suffice to demonstrate that God truly exists. (*Proslogium* preface, p. 1)

This argument he believes he has found—or has been taught by the Interior Teacher.

The argument begins with a rather abstractly stated expression of the *idea* of God, a definition, if you like, of what we have in mind when we use the word "God." God, says Anselm, is *that, than which no greater can be conceived.*[*] Let us think about this a moment. Why does Anselm use this strangely convoluted phrase, *that, than which no greater can be conceived?* Why not just say, more simply, that God is the greatest being we can conceive? There are two reasons, I think: (1) Anselm doesn't want the idea of God to be limited by what *we* may be able to conceive, and (2) he doesn't want to suggest that a positive conception of God may be entirely comprehensible to us. The strange phrase has this feature: It pushes us out beyond everything familiar by forcing us to ask again and again, Can something greater than this be conceived?

Suppose you imagine or conceive a certain being. Have you done it? Now ask yourself the question, Can I conceive of something that is in some way "greater" than this? If you can, then it is not yet God that you have conceived. Think, for instance, of an oak tree. Now an oak tree has certain powers and abilities but also some very definite limitations. It is not very hard to think of something "greater" than that—something, perhaps, that can move, that can seek nourishment and flee danger, rather than

[*]The term "ontological" comes from the Greek word for *being.* The argument in question was given this name in the eighteenth century by one of its critics, Immanuel Kant, because (unlike the arguments of Aquinas) it does not begin from facts about the world, but goes straight from the idea of God to a conclusion about his being. Many thinkers find it important to distinguish two, or even more, distinct arguments because at least one form of the argument is pretty obviously invalid. Anselm himself does not do so, and we will interpret it as one argument. I will try to formulate this argument in its strongest form, while remaining fairly colloquial in manner. (Discussions of the soundness of this argument often bristle with technical-logical apparatus.)
[†]It was later titled *Proslogium*, or *A Discourse.* This is the title under which it is now known.

[*]Compare Augustine's formulation, p. 235.

having to suffer whatever occurs at the spot where it is rooted. It follows that God is not an oak tree.

Suppose we think of a creature that does not have these limitations, a wolf, perhaps. Again, it is not hard to think of something "greater" than a wolf—a creature, for instance, that can plan ahead, build a shelter, heat and cool it, preserve food for the hard winter months. Because we can conceive something greater than a wolf, God is not a wolf.

What if we think of a human being? Is a human being something than which no greater can be conceived? Hardly. For one thing, human beings are mortal. Surely any being that were not subject to death would be greater than a human. Of two human lives, each of which is well worth living and equally happy, we judge the longer one to be preferable. And humans have many other limitations besides mortality; we can surely conceive a being that knows more than any human knows, is more powerful than any human, is not so dependent on other things, and is not subject to the moral failures of human beings. So when we think of God, we are not thinking of a human being, but of something much greater.

Another line of thought that helps make this conception intelligible is to consider what sort of being would be worthy of worship. To worship something is to "bow the knee" before it, to feel insignificant in its presence, to love it intensely, to defer to it absolutely; to worship is to acknowledge the object worshipped as holy, and as wholly other. Suppose you think of something, and then you think of a second thing that is greater. Isn't your immediate reaction that the first thing is not something you could worship?

Until we reach the conception of *that, than which no greater can be conceived,* we have not yet thought of God. That is what we mean when we use the word "God." Although this conception is peculiarly abstract, it does seem to capture the crucial idea of God as the only being worthy of worship. Devotion to anything less would be idolatry.

Let us note one more thing about this conception of God before we move on to the argument that Anselm finds embedded in it. It is framed in terms of the Great Chain of Being.* This Augustinian notion is so much a part of Anselm's outlook that it is simply taken for granted. That the world is ordered by the degrees of being and value (greatness) in its various parts must seem to Anselm so obvious that it is beyond question. If you run up and down the chain, you find it easy to conceive of beings both lesser and greater; and your mind is inevitably carried to the idea of something that is not only actually greater than other existing things, but something than which you cannot even conceive a greater. And that, Anselm says, is what we mean by God.

But now the question arises: Is there a being answering to that conception? There really are oak trees and wolves and human beings. Is there a being than which nothing greater can be conceived?†

According to Psalm 14:1, "The fool says in his heart, 'There is no God.'" Let us consider this "fool." There are two ways he might think "There is no God." (1) He might just have these words in mind, without really understanding what they mean; in this case he is a fool only in a weak sense —he is ignorant of what he means by the words he is using. In this case we could easily explain to him what the words mean, and he would cease to be this kind of fool. (2) He might, however, understand what it is he is denying. This fool has the *idea* of God in mind, and presumably he understands the words "that, than which no greater can be conceived." It is this second way of saying or thinking these words that is of interest. Anselm's "discovery" is that such a fool necessarily convicts himself of error every time he thinks, "There is no God."

For suppose the fool were right. Then *that, than which no greater can be conceived* would exist only in his understanding and not in reality. It would exist in the same way, Anselm says, as a painting exists in

---

*Review this Neoplatonic notion on pp. 238–241.

†Anselm, of course, does not doubt that there is. But he wishes to understand what it is that he so firmly believes. Though Anselm is writing at the request of (and primarily for the enlightenment of) his Christian brothers, there can be little doubt that he thinks the proof he has discovered is valid quite independently of any Christian assumptions. It should convince *anyone* who thinks about God at all. It should convince *you.*

the mind of a painter who changes his mind before putting brush to canvas. The painter has the painting "in his understanding," as Anselm puts it; but it does not exist also in reality.

It is easy to see how this might be the case with the painting. But can it be the case that *that, than which no greater can be conceived* exists only in the understanding? Anselm invites us to consider that it does. But then, he says, it is not after all *that, than which no greater can be conceived.* For you can certainly conceive of something greater than *that.* You can think that it exists both in the understanding and in reality.

Such a being will be "greater" in the sense that it has more powers and is less dependent on other things; it occupies a higher place on the Great Chain of Being. So it couldn't be true that *that, than which no greater can be conceived* exists only in our minds. God must exist in reality.

In fact, Anselm adds, this being exists so truly "that it cannot be conceived not to exist" (*Proslogium* 3). Most beings—trees, wolves, and humans, for example—you can imagine as never having existed. If a huge comet had collided with the earth several billion years ago, none of them would have existed. Could *that, than which no greater can be conceived* be like these beings? Could it be the sort of thing that we can conceive as not existing? Again let us suppose that it were; then it would depend on the co-operation or goodwill of other things for its existence—or maybe on sheer good luck!

But then it wouldn't be *that, than which no greater can be conceived,* for we can surely conceive a greater being than that. We can conceive of a being that is not so dependent on other things. In fact, we can conceive of a being that we cannot even *conceive* as not existing.

> Hence, if that, than which nothing greater can be conceived, can be conceived not to exist, it is not that, than which nothing greater can be conceived. But this is an irreconcilable contradiction. (*Proslogium* 3)

You cannot even conceive that God does not exist. You can, of course, say the words, "There is no God"; but, Anselm says, you cannot clearly think what they mean without falling into contradiction. What is contradictory cannot possibly be true. So what the fool says is necessarily false. It follows not only that God does exist but also that it is impossible that he does not.

Here is an analogy. You can *say* that one plus one equals three, but you cannot *conceive* that it is true. If you understand what one is and what three is, and if you understand the concepts of addition and equality, then you cannot possibly believe or even understand that one plus one equals three. To try to do so would be like trying to believe that three both *is* three and also *is not* three (but two). But that is impossible, a contradiction. It is necessarily false that three both is and is not three. Just so, it is necessarily false that *that, than which no greater can be conceived* does not exist. To try to believe it is like trying to believe that *that, than which no greater can be conceived* both does exist (since it *is* that, than which no greater can be conceived) and does not exist. But you can't believe both. So, you must believe that it does exist. You cannot even conceive that God does not exist. That God should not exist is as impossible as that one plus one should equal three.

Why, then, does the fool (in the second sense) say in his heart, "There is no God"? Because he is a dim-witted fool who believes contradictions! The nonexistence of God is something that cannot be rationally thought.

It is little wonder that Anselm exclaims,

> I thank thee, gracious Lord, I thank thee; because what I formerly believed by thy bounty, I now so understand by thine illumination, that if I were unwilling to believe that thou dost exist, I should not be able not to understand this to be true. (*Proslogium* 4)

Even if Anselm *wanted* to disbelieve in God, he couldn't manage it. It would now be clear to him that the very sentence in which he expressed his disbelief is necessarily false.

Anselm's argument can be formulated in a variety of ways. Here is one way. See whether you can follow the steps, then see whether you can pick out a flaw in the argument. (Note that it is in form a reductio ad absurdum; look again at the discussion of this kind of argument in the section on Zeno, pp. 29–30).

1. God does not exist. (assumption)

2. By "God," I mean that, than which no greater can be conceived (NGC).

3. So NGC does not exist. (from 1 and 2)

4. So NGC has being only in my understanding, not also in reality. (from 2 and 3)

5. If NGC were to exist in reality, as well as in my understanding, it would be greater. (from the meaning of "greater")

6. But then, NGC is not NGC. (from 4 and 5)

7. So NGC cannot exist only in my understanding. (from 6)

8. So NGC must exist also in reality. (from 5 and 7)

9. So God exists. (from 2 and 8)

10. So God does not exist and God exists. (from 1 and 9)

11. So Premise 1 cannot be true. (by 1 through 10 and the principle of reductio ad absurdum)

12. So God exists. (from 11)

Note that this is an argument that moves from the *essence* of God to God's *existence*. That is, it moves from our grasp of *what* God is—the NGC—to the fact *that* God is. In a certain clear sense, the argument is a claim that the existence of God is *self-evident*. What that means is that it is enough to understand the conception of God to know that God must exist. Nothing else is required. God's essence *entails* God's existence. In this regard, if the argument is correct, knowing that God exists is like knowing that all bachelors are unmarried. Knowing what bachelors are (their essence) is sufficient for knowing that they are unmarried. That's entailed by the definition of "bachelor." You don't have to add anything else to get that conclusion. It's not like knowing (supposing this is true) that all bachelors are melancholy—a proposition for which evidence in addition to understanding the terms would be required. If Anselm is right, thinking clearly about

the implications of the NGC concept is enough to guarantee the conclusion that there is a God. Just as it is necessarily false that there are married bachelors, so it is necessarily false that there is no God.

Is Anselm's argument a sound one? Should we be convinced by it? Or is it a tissue of confusions and ambiguities? Discussion since the eleventh century has been intense, beginning with Gaunilo of Marmoutier, a monk who was Anselm's contemporary. Gaunilo, writing "in behalf of the fool," notes that he has all manner of things in his understanding that have no existence in themselves. For instance, he says, he has the concept of a lost island filled with riches and delicacies, an island more excellent than any other island. This island he can conceive, and in that sense it is in his understanding. If we follow the principle of Anselm's argument, however, the island would be still more excellent if it were in reality as well. So, the island must exist. Otherwise, any actually existing island would be more excellent than it, and it wouldn't be the island more excellent than any other. But that is absurd.

Anselm replies to this criticism by acknowledging that it would indeed be absurd to infer the actual existence of such an island from the mere conception of it. But what holds for islands doesn't necessarily hold for the singular case of *that, than which no greater can be conceived*. If the argument works, it works only in the one case of purest generality—only for that one being described by this odd phrase, which pushes us to the very limits of conceivability. Perfect islands do not exist *necessarily*. But God does.

The argument has had both defenders and critics down to the present day. It is not only the conclusion that attracts attention—though if the argument were sound, the conclusion might be of the greatest importance. But it is interesting also because it involves the very difficult notions of existence, conceivability, possibility, and necessity. And these are notions that run very deep in our conception of reality—whatever it might be like.

We will meet the argument again.*

---

*See Descartes (*Meditation V,* Chapter 13) and Kant ("The Ontological Argument," Chapter 16).

1. What phrase does Anselm use to designate God? Why?
2. In what two ways may "the fool" say in his or her heart, "There is no God"?
3. Study carefully the steps in Anselm's argument. Write down questions you have about its correctness.
4. What is Gaunilo's objection to the argument? How does Anselm reply?

Thomas Aquinas: Rethinking Aristotle

In A.D. 1225, Thomas Aquinas was born in a castle near Naples, the seventh son in a family belonging to the lower nobility. He was destined from an early age for a career in the Church, but not for the career he eventually chose. When he was five years old, his family sent him to Monte Cassino, one of the great and wealthy Benedictine monasteries, hoping that he would rise to become an abbot with a position of power and influence. After nine years of schooling with the Benedictines, he went to the newly founded university at Naples, where he became acquainted with the works of Aristotle. For centuries the only Aristotle available in the West had been the logical treatises, together with some commentaries on them. More works had been preserved by Arab scholars in the East, however, and the ethics, the metaphysics, the physics, and the treatises on the soul were now becoming available again.

In 1244, at the age of nineteen or twenty, Thomas committed himself to becoming a friar in the newly founded Dominican order, much to his family's surprise and against their wishes. Now friars were very different from settled, respectable, and often wealthy monks. Friars were itinerant preachers, going from town to town, begging for a living. They took literally Jesus' directions to his disciples in Mark 6 : 8, to take nothing with them except their walking sticks—"no bread, no bag, no money in their belts; but to wear sandals and not put on two tunics." Aquinas' family was so unhappy with this decision that the Dominicans decided, for safety's sake, to send him away from Italy to Paris. On the way north, however, his brothers kidnapped him and stole him away to a family castle, where he was kept for a year.

Nothing, however, would induce him to change his mind, not even the seductive wench his brothers sent to his room one night. According to the story, he drove her from the room with a burning brand snatched from the fire. After his family finally released him, he studied for some years in Cologne, Germany, with a man of vast learning and Aristotelian persuasions, Albert the Great. Aquinas was rotund, a large man of slow movements, unusually quiet and calm. His fellow students began to call him "the dumb ox." His undoubted brilliance occasionally showed through, however, and on one such occasion, Albert is reported to have said, "This dumb ox will fill the whole world with his bellowing."

Aquinas was made a priest and studied to become a Master in Theology. He lectured on the Bible for several years and began to write. Meanwhile, he participated fully in regular *disputations,* as they were called. These were debates that took a more or less standard form. A question was announced for discussion—for instance, Is truth primarily in the mind or in things? Conflicting opinions were stated, often citing some authority. These opinions would then be critically evaluated, arguments for each and against each being put forward. Finally, a judgment would be given by a master or a professor. Much of what Aquinas wrote is structured in a similar way. This form of presentation, which came to be known (later, with scorn) as "scholastic," had certain advantages. It made for comprehensiveness and careful attention to detail. It depended absolutely on the ability of writers and readers to distinguish good arguments from bad. But it required enormous patience, and in the hands of lesser intellectuals than Aquinas it often degenerated into pedantry.

Aquinas spent time not only in Paris, but also in several places in Italy—and all the time, he wrote, or rather, he dictated to a secretary, and often to more than one. It is said that like a grand master

AVICENNA (IBN SINĀ)

Born in Persia, Avicenna (980–1037) was an important figure in the Islamic tradition that preserved and kept Greek philosophy alive when it had virtually disappeared in the dark ages of the West. A physician who wrote widely on medicine, the sciences, and philosophy, he produced a systematic vision of reality deeply indebted to Aristotle, but bent in important respects by pressures from Neoplatonism and Islam.

The most basic of all our notions is that of *being,* which cannot be defined (otherwise it wouldn't be basic), but with which we are intimately familiar because we ourselves and the things of common experience all manifest it. None of these things, when considered for what they are in themselves, exist necessarily. The essence of a horse, for example, does not carry its *being* with it. Horses are possible, but if there is to be an actual horse, some *cause* must supply its being. This cause—or some cause of that cause—must be more than merely possible; it must exist necessarily. In the final analysis, there must be a being that has its necessity in itself, not bestowed by another. And that being is God (Allah).

Contrary to Aristotle, then, Avicenna holds that God must be the *efficient* cause of the universe and not just its final cause or goal. Drawing on Neoplatonic thought, he posits a complex series of emanations that govern the heavenly spheres, and finally events here on earth. The world is not, as Augustine

thought, created from nothing, but is eternally unrolling the necessary effects of its eternal and necessary cause. Things that are merely possible in themselves are therefore necessary in virtue of their causes, and everything that occurs (including human action) happens just as it must happen.

Avicenna imagines a "flying man" suspended in midair who, though unaware of his body or of anything impacting his senses, still knows that he exists. Since he does not need to know he even has a body to know his own existence, Avicenna concludes that he is essentially an incorporeal being— a soul.* Because the essence of one soul is indistinguishable from the essence of another (what makes me the particular individual I am is the body), I could not have existed prior to my birth. But will I survive my death? Yes, Avicenna answers. God will supply a principle of individuation when the body can no longer do it, although we do not know what that principle is.

He believes that truth is one, whether discovered by philosophers or announced by prophets. The prophet presents truth in an imaginative way, suited to those who are not able to engage in metaphysical contemplation. In its purity, however, truth is found in philosophical reflection.

—————

*This is a clear anticipation of Descartes' argument for the distinction of soul and body in *Meditation VI* (see pp. 351–356).

at chess who can play numerous games at once, Aquinas could keep four secretaries busy writing separate texts. His collected works are enormous and touch every philosophical and theological topic.

In December of 1273, while saying mass, Aquinas seems to have had a mystical vision. He wrote no more. When urged to return to his writing, he said that he could not, that everything he had written to that point now seemed "like straw." He died in 1274 at the age of 49. Although there

was continuing suspicion of Aquinas' reliance on Aristotle—that pagan thinker—and several of his theses were condemned by ecclesiastical authorities, on July 21, 1323, the pope declared Aquinas to be a saint. Because few miracles had been attributed to him, the pope is reputed to have said, "There are as many miracles as there are articles of the *Summa.*"*

—————

*The *Summa Theologica* (*Summary of Theology*) is the major work of Aquinas' maturity.

"As sacred doctrine is based on the light of faith, so is philosophy founded on the natural light of reason."
—THOMAS AQUINAS

Philosophy and Theology

Aquinas does not think of himself as a philosopher. When he talks about philosophers, he usually has in mind the ancients (Plato, Aristotle, and so on), but sometimes the more recent Muslim thinkers, such as Ibn Sinā and Ibn Rushd. Philosophers are lovers of wisdom, Aquinas thinks, who lack the fullness of wisdom as it is revealed in Christ. Yet he has great respect for these philosophers, especially for Aristotle, whom he sometimes quotes as simply "the philosopher." He writes about the same topics as they do, discusses them frequently, borrows arguments from them, and is happy to acknowledge his

debt to them. Yet he never uses them uncritically. Aquinas agrees with Augustine that (1) truth is one, (2) all men have been enlightened by the word or the wisdom of God, and (3) humans, in pride, have turned away from God and from the truth. He concludes that the light of reason in sinful minds may be obscured, but it has not been wiped out. And intellect on its own can do a great deal.

> The divine rights of grace do not abolish the human rights of natural reason. (*ST,* 2a—2ae. x.10; *PT,* p. 31)[3]

Revelation, then, builds on reason but does not destroy it. Aquinas is very careful to discriminate what natural human reason can do from what must be learned from Scripture. You can compare the situation, as Aquinas sees it, to a three-story house. On the bottom floor, reason and natural experience do their work without the need of any supernatural aid. On the second floor, we find things that are both revealed to us by God and demonstrable by reason. Among the truths that overlap in this way are the existence of God and the immortality of the human soul.

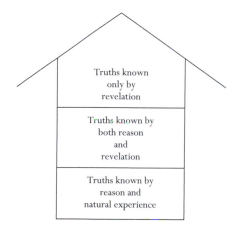

It is good, Aquinas thinks, that God has revealed such truths, even though reason can access them on its own,

> for otherwise they would have been arrived at only by a few, and after a long period, and then mixed with errors; more especially when we consider

that man's entire salvation, which is God, depends on such knowledge. (*ST,* 1a.i.1; *PT,* p. 32)

The third floor contains truths that are beyond the capacity of natural intellect to discover, such as the internal nature of God as triune—as Father, Son, and Holy Spirit—and the historical fact of God's becoming incarnate in Jesus of Nazareth.

Though Aquinas always writes as a theologian, we can set out his contributions to the philosophical conversation by focusing our attention on the first and second stories of this house. We do, however, need to keep in mind his view that human beings have a supernatural end. He says,

> The happiness of human beings is twofold. There is an imperfect happiness in this life of which Aristotle is speaking, consisting in the contemplation of immaterial substances to which wisdom disposes us, an imperfect contemplation such as is possible in this life, which does not know what such substances are. The other happiness is the perfect happiness of the next life, when we will see the very substance of God himself and the other immaterial substances. But what brings that happiness won't be any theoretical science, but the light of glory. (*DT,* question 6; *SPW,* p. 50)

Existence and Essence

Among the philosophers, it is Aristotle whom Aquinas thinks has the best arguments and the soundest overall vision. He wrote a number of careful commentaries on works by Aristotle, and when he speaks on his own behalf, Aquinas often sounds like a recording of Aristotle. As Augustine draws on the Platonists, Aquinas draws on the Aristotelians, including the Muslim commentators on Aristotle. But he also makes significant changes in Aristotle's outlook. Before we look at the ways Aquinas criticizes Aristotle, let's review some of the main features of Aristotelian metaphysics.*

We can remind ourselves of these features by considering an example. Think of a horse. According to the doctrine of Aquinas and Aristotle alike, a horse is a *substance*—that is, a complex item composed of form and matter. The *form* is what accounts for its being a horse rather than something else, and the *matter* is what makes it the particular horse it is. The form of the horse does not have any being outside of or beyond horses, as Plato had thought, but exists only in actual tangible, sensible horses. Its form as a horse is its *essence*—what it is, its defining characteristics. It is horses and the like—substances—that make up reality. This view is sometimes called **hylomorphism,** from the Greek words for matter (*hyle*) and form (*morphe*).

Such a substance does not, however, have only essential properties—its "horsiness," so to speak. A horse can be brown or black, fast or slow, daughter of Sparkplug or son of Trigger, in the barn or out at pasture, eating or sleeping. The medievals call these properties "accidents" or "incidental properties," to distinguish them from a horse's essential properties. Incidental properties are referred to by Aristotelian categories such as quantity, quality, relation, position, and so on. They are properties that can change without changing the essential nature of the horse they qualify. As a horse ages, it may grow grayer, thinner, and slower. If, by contrast, a horse should lose its essential properties, it would no longer be a horse Like essential properties, accidental properties have their being only in some substance. No such thing as *black* or *fast* exists on its own, though there are *fast black horses.*

We can address the question of why horses and other substances are the way they are in terms of Aristotle's four causes: (1) the *formal cause* or the formula that makes it the kind of thing it is; (2) the *material cause*—the stuff making it up; (3) its *efficient cause,* or the trigger that brought it into being at a given time; and (4) the *final cause,* the end or goal it is driving toward. In addition, we can explain change in substantial entities in terms of the principles of *potentiality* and *actuality.* Any change is a shift from potentially being so-and-so to actually being so-and-so.

Matter is the principle of potentiality in the horse, form the principle of actuality. For instance, the fertilized egg of a mare is not yet a horse, but, Ar-

---

*We do this briefly here. A more extended look back at pp. 173–179 might be helpful.

istotle would say, it is matter for becoming a horse. Actually, it is an egg (embodies the form of an egg), but potentially, it is a horse. That bit of matter has within it a *telos*—a dynamism that, if all goes normally, will result in its coming to embody the form of a horse in actuality.

Aquinas shares all these metaphysical principles with Aristotle. You then might ask, Why should we pay any separate attention to Aquinas? Why not be content with the metaphysics of the ancient philosopher? Here is the reason: Because Aquinas sees, or thinks he sees, that Aristotle misses something—something fundamental, far-reaching, and extremely important. Strange as it may seem at first, what Aristotle overlooks is *existence*.

Perhaps it would be better to say that Aristotle takes existence for granted. Remember that when he is pursuing what he calls "first" philosophy, he notes that form is prior to substances; it is form that makes a substance real. Form is what *actualizes,* what transforms a potentiality into some existing, substantial thing. For that reason he calls form the substance of substance itself. Form brings existence along with it.

When Aristotle asks about how a particular substance comes into being, his answer is in terms of efficient causation by a prior actuality, an earlier substance, itself made what it is by form. And when Aristotle asks about the final cause of everything, he answers in terms of the unmoved mover, a pure form who is not the creator of the world, but its *telos,* its goal, its ambition. Notice that we don't have to ask whether this god exists; that he is form without matter settles the question.

Individual things within the world—this or that horse, for instance—require an efficient cause for their beginning to be at a certain time; but as a whole, no efficient cause is required for the world. It has its being eternally. It's just there. Why? Because of form. Existence (actuality) and essence (form) simply make a package. It follows from this, and from the fact that whatever exists has some form or other, that there could be no further question about existence.

Aquinas, however, looking at the world through Christian eyes, argues that it is the essence of a horse to be an embodied animal.* That is, when you think of *what* a horse is, you are not thinking just of its form; horsiness is not a horse. Only a substantial union of form and matter is a horse.

> Note that what composes composite substances is material and its form (humans, for example, contain body and soul), and neither of these by itself can be the thing's essence. . . . For a thing's essence, we have said, is expressed by its definition, and unless the definition of a physical substance included not only its form but its material, definitions of natural objects wouldn't differ from those of mathematical objects. . . . Clearly then essence involves both material and form. (*BE,* 2; *SPW,* p. 93)

Now Aquinas notices that horses so considered might or might not exist.

> I can understand what humans or phoenixes are without knowing whether such things really exist; so clearly a thing's existence differs from its essence or whatness. (*BE,* 4; *SPW,* p. 104)

Even a phoenix, the mythical bird that rises again from the ashes of its own fiery destruction, must be conceived of as a union of form and matter. When we think of a phoenix, we are not imagining a disembodied form, but something substantial. It just so happens that it lacks something: existence. Existence, then, is not something to be taken for granted. Nor is it an automatic consequence of form. Existence, wherever we find it in the natural world, is *something added*.

The same is true of spiritual substances, beings that have no material stuff to be shaped by a form. If there are any such—and Aquinas is convinced that there are—these too are composite. Such substances are not composed of matter and form, of

---

* We should not be misled by this phrase, "through Christian eyes," as though existence were something only a believer could see. It may be that it took theistic presuppositions, whether Christian or Muslim, to bring the phenomenon to our attention (Aquinas finds something similar in Ibn Sīnā). If it is a real phenomenon, however, it is there no matter what our other convictions are. We find it in atheistic form in Jean-Paul Sartre's 1938 novel, *Nausea*. The difference is that Sartre's protagonist finds existence repulsive, whereas Aquinas finds it an occasion for praise and thanksgiving.

AVERROËS (IBN RUSHD)

A Spanish Arab living during the time of Islamic domination there, Averroës (1126–1198) wrote numerous influential commentaries on the works of Aristotle, whom he admired extravagantly. In fact, he was often later referred to simply as "the Commentator."

Averroës was famous for—and attacked because of—the doctrine of "double truth," the idea that truths from Koranic revelation could contradict what philosophical reason could demonstrate, and yet both be true. It is puzzling how this view came to be attributed to him, since he explicitly denies it. Like Avicenna before him, he holds that the Koran was revealed so that even the humblest could participate in the truth, though in its purity that truth is available only to the philosopher. The Koran has a surface meaning suited to ordinary intellects, but a deep meaning for those capable of understanding it. If there seems to be a conflict, it is by understanding the sacred text philosophically that it should be resolved.

He opposes the hierarchical emanation doctrines of Avicenna and the distinction between essence and existence. God (Allah) is directly responsible for all the celestial spheres and their correlated Intelligences, together with the sublunar things of earth. The universe, being the product of an eternal being, is itself eternal (as Aristotle held).

Averroës is usually understood as denying personal immortality. The human soul is, as Aristotle says, the form of a human body and its active intellect (*nous*) is indeed a substance; but what makes me an individual person (distinct from other humans) is not this form but the particular matter it "informs." As form, this Intelligence is identical in all humans. When my body dies, then, *nous* continues on, but not as *mine*. Thus there is a kind of immortality, but it is strictly impersonal.

Here, however, is one of the points at which Averroës was suspected of holding the double truth doctrine. He also wrote that those who deny personal immortality are wrong and should be put to death. The resolution of this apparent inconsistency is found in his acceptance of the revealed doctrine of the resurrection of the body. If the body is resurrected, or if God supplies a celestial body to take its place, individuality can be preserved in immortality.

---

course, but of pure form and existence. Even in this case, form does not suffice for existence. Even with angels or human souls, existence is something added.

What this means is that the entire world, including ourselves, is contingent; in no way is its existence necessary. It could just as well not ever have been. But this entails a radical revision of what an efficient cause must be. For Aristotle, an efficient cause is an already actualized potentiality (a substance), the motions of which actualize some second potentiality—which already is an actuality of some kind or other. Rain and soil and sun (actualities) stimulate an actual radish seed (potentially a radish plant) to bring forth the (actual) plant. But if both such a cause and such an effect might or might not exist, then a true efficient cause must bestow existence—from the ground up! Or at least there must be a *first* such efficient cause—otherwise nothing at all would exist.

> Now a thing's attributes are caused either from within its nature (like a human being's sense of the ridiculous) or by some extrinsic source (like light in the atmosphere by the sun). But the very existence of a thing can't be caused by its own form or whatness—I am talking of agent causality—because then something would be causing itself and bringing itself into existence, which is impossible. So everything in which existence and nature differ must get its existence from another. (*BE*, 4; *SPW*, p. 105)

Here Aquinas is clearly anticipating an argument for the existence of God. We turn to his five ways of proving God's existence in the next section, but for now we need to be certain that we understand the main point. Every finite substance, whether material or spiritual in nature, is composite. Material things are doubly composite, being a union of form and matter, this union joined to existence. Spiritual entities are simpler, not having a material component, but they are still a composite of form and existence. If there is to be anything at all, then, existence must be *added* to essence.

Aquinas begins his work *On Being and Essence* with a quote from Aristotle, to the effect that big mistakes grow from small beginnings. If Aristotle is mistaken here, at this fundamental metaphysical level, we can expect that error to have consequences throughout—and Aquinas thinks it does. Despite his undoubted respect for "the philosopher," Aquinas' philosophy turns out to be quite different from Aristotle's. For one thing, it radically changes the conception of God.

---

1. How does Aquinas understand the relationship between human reason and divine revelation?
2. What phenomenon does Aquinas think Aristotle has overlooked?
3. What is the double composition of material substances? In what way are purely intellectual substances simpler? Are they absolutely simple?
4. How does the recognition of a distinction between essence and existence necessitate a change in the notion of an efficient cause?
5. As Aristotle sees it, does the world need an efficient cause? How about Aquinas?

From Creation to God

Can we know, from the point of view of reason and experience, that God exists? And can we know anything about what God is, about his essence? We have seen that Anselm answered both questions at once with his conception of God as that, than which no greater can be conceived. If we understand what God is, he argued, we must know that God is. Aquinas is, of course, familiar with this famous argument, but he thinks it is not a good argument. Actually, he doesn't claim that the argument itself is

flawed, but he says that we, as human beings, are not in a position to use it.

> A self-evident proposition, though always self-evident in itself, is sometimes self-evident to us and sometimes not. For a proposition is self-evident when the predicate forms part of what the subject means: thus it is self-evident that human beings are animals, since being an animal is part of what being human means. . . . But if there are people to whom the meanings of subject and predicate are not evident, then the proposition, though self-evident in itself, will not be so to such people. . . .
>
> I maintain then that the proposition *God exists* is self-evident in itself, since its subject and predicate are identical: God, I shall argue later, is his own existence. But because what it is to be God is not evident to us the proposition is not self-evident to us. It needs to be made evident by things less evident in themselves but more evident to us, namely, God's effects. (*ST,* 1a.2.1; *SPW,* pp. 196–197)

Here, Aquinas is telling us that we cannot *start* where Anselm starts in his argument. Maybe we will end up in the same place, but we have to get there by another way. Why does Aquinas think that? Because he accepts the Aristotelian view of how humans acquire knowledge.* It may be appropriate for a Platonist such as Augustine or Anselm to think that we, being essentially souls, have direct insight into the essences of things (an immediate grasp of the Platonic Forms, if you will). For Aristotle and Aquinas, however, human beings are—as the quote shows—animals, and the knowledge animals have *begins* with sensation. Aquinas sometimes quotes Aristotle to the effect that our minds are like blank tablets until written on by our senses. What our physical senses disclose to us are material things in the world around us. We don't see God with our eyes or touch him with our fingers. Perhaps, as Aquinas suggests, material things can be shown to be effects of a first cause. But the argument about God's existence has to start with things "more evident to us" than Anselm's definition of the essence of God.

---

*Human knowledge is discussed in more detail in the subsequent section, "Humans: Their Knowledge."

Aquinas says that there are two kinds of arguments dealing with causes and effects. One begins from causes and shows why things are as they are. The other begins from effects and shows what must have been the case to bring these effects into existence. It is the latter kind of argument that we can use to prove the existence of God.

> Now any effect that is better known to us than its cause can demonstrate that its cause exists: for effects are dependent on their causes and can only occur if causes already exist. From effects evident to us, therefore, we can demonstrate something that is not self-evident to us, namely, that God exists. (*ST*, 1a.22; *SPW*, p. 198)

Now Aquinas holds that the existence of God can be proved in five ways. Like the proof of Anselm, these "five ways" have been subjected to exhaustive logical scrutiny, often in a forbidding forest of technical symbols. I present Aquinas' arguments in his own words and then add some interpretive remarks. In these remarks I try to present the argument in as strong and sympathetic a way as I can. You may be inclined to try to criticize these arguments, and that's fine, but it is important that you first understand them.

The Argument from Change

The first and most obvious way is based on change. For certainly some things are changing: this we plainly see. Now anything changing is being changed by something else. (This is so because what makes things changeable is unrealized potentiality, but what makes them cause change is their already realized state: causing change brings into being what was previously only able to be, and can only be done by something which already is. For example, the actual heat of fire causes wood, able to be hot, to become actually hot, and so causes change in the wood; now what is actually hot can't at the same time be potentially hot but only potentially cold, can't at the same time be actual and potential in the same respect but only in different respects; so that what is changing can't be the very thing that is causing the same change, can't be changing itself, but must be being changed by something else.) Again this something else, if itself changing, must be being changed by yet another thing; and this last by another. But this can't go on for ever, since then there would be no first cause of the change, and

as a result no subsequent causes. (Only when acted on by a first cause do intermediate causes produce a change; unless a hand moves the stick, the stick won't move anything else.) So we are forced eventually to come to a first cause of change not itself being changed by anything, and this is what everyone understands by *God*. (*ST*, 1a.3; *SPW*, p. 200)

Change is understood to be an alteration in something, by which it becomes *actually* what it was only *potentially* until then. If the sun heats the sidewalk so that you can't stand on it with bare feet, this is a change from being actually cool (but potentially hot) to being actually hot. The world is full of such changes.

The next point is that each of these changes is brought about by something that is, in the appropriate way, *actual*. The ball thrown by the pitcher has the potential of being over the fence, but it doesn't have the power to realize that potentiality by itself. It takes an actual batter swinging an actual bat and actually hitting the ball to get it actually over the fence. In the same way, the wood does not actualize its potentiality for being hot on its own; it takes something actually hot to make the wood hot, too. Because nothing can be both actual and potential in the same respect, the wood cannot be at the same time merely potentially hot and actually hot, so it cannot make itself hot.

So, Aquinas tells us, nothing can change itself. Everything that is changed must be changed by another thing. But here you can see a question: What accounts for this second thing that actually brings the change about? Well, there are two possibilities. Either it is actualized by some third thing, or it is not. If it is not, then it is what Aquinas calls a "first cause of change"; it changes the thing in question without itself being actualized by another. If, however, it is made to be a cause of change by another, then the question repeats itself about this third thing.

Now the question arises, Could this series of changes go on to infinity? Might it be that there is no first cause of change at all, nothing that is the source of change without itself being changed by some other thing? Could it be that *everything* is changed by something else, which thing in turn is itself changed by something else? This is a tricky question, but on this question the soundness of the proof probably rests.

Aquinas answers no. His reason is that if this were true there would be no first cause of change. But if there were no first, then there would not be any secondary changers either, since each of them causes change only insofar as it is itself actualized by some prior cause. And, of course, if there were no secondary changers, there would be no change at all. But that is obviously false. We do see home runs hit and camp fires started, so the series cannot go on to infinity. There must be a point where change originates. This must be something that is not merely potential, but is fully and entirely actual. Otherwise, it would need something outside itself to actualize its possibilities.

It is important to guard against a misinterpretation here. Aquinas is not thinking of a first thing in a temporal series. His argument is not that one change precedes another, a second precedes that, and so on to the beginning of the world in time. In fact, Aquinas does not think that reason can prove that the world had a beginning in time. If it were not revealed to us by God that the world had a beginning, we could just as well conclude that the world is eternal, without beginning or end—as Aristotle in fact believes. For the purposes of proving the existence of God, however, this does not matter. An eternal world would need a first cause of change just as much as a temporally limited world does.

We must think, then, not of a temporal series, but of a nested set of necessary conditions. A necessary condition for the actualization of something is the reality of something that is not merely potential. Unless there were already something actual no actualization of any potentiality could occur. The set of conditions cannot be infinite, so there must be some condition that is itself *sufficient* to account for the rest. There must be something, then, that exists on its own, without requiring something else to bring it into existence. This would be a completely actual first cause of change. And that, says Aquinas, is what "everyone understands by *God*."

The Argument from Efficient Causality

In the observable world causes are found ordered in series: we never observe, nor ever could, some-

thing causing itself, for this would mean it preceded itself, and this is not possible. But a series of causes can't go on for ever, for in any such series an earlier member causes an intermediate and the intermediate a last (whether the intermediate be one or many). Now eliminating a cause eliminates its effects, and unless there's a first cause there won't be a last or an intermediate. But if a series of causes goes on for ever it will have no first cause, and so no intermediate causes and no last effect, which is clearly false. So we are forced to postulate some first agent cause, to which everyone gives the name *God*. (*ST*, 1a. 3; *SPW* pp. 200–201)

An efficient (or agent) cause, you will recall, is the trigger that sets a process going. Examples are the spark that produces the explosion, the stroke of the key that generates an alphabet letter on the computer's screen, and the wind of the hurricane that blows down the fence. What we find in the world is that these efficient causes are ordered in series. We never find that something is the efficient cause of itself. The spark may cause the explosion, but it cannot be the cause of the spark. To be its own cause, it would have to preexist itself, and that is absurd. It cannot exist before it exists! The spark itself requires another efficient cause, perhaps a hammer striking a rock.

Another obvious fact is that if you take away the cause, you take away the effect: no hammer, no spark (or at least not this particular spark); no spark, no explosion (this particular explosion). What we find in the world, then, is that one cause depends on another for its existence. Again, this order need not be a temporal one, though it may be. Aquinas is not trying to prove that there was a temporally first event in the world's history. Even if the world is eternal, everything in it needs an efficient cause for its very existence. We can think of this as a hierarchically ordered set of dependencies, rather than a temporally ordered series of successive events.*

---

*If you want an example of a causal relation of the efficient sort that is not temporally ordered, think of the depression of the sofa cushion, which is simultaneous with your sitting on it. Your sitting is the efficient cause of the depression in the cushion, but they happen precisely together.

Again the question arises, Could this series of dependencies be infinite? Aquinas again says no. For if the series were infinite, there would be no cause that is "first." A "first" cause would be one on which the whole causal order depended, while it depended on nothing beyond itself. If there were no such cause, Aquinas says, there would be no intermediate causes and no ultimate effects. But there are causes and effects, so there must be a first cause. And that is what "everyone gives the name *God*."

One commentator gives a helpful analogy.[4] Suppose you are in your car, stopped at a red light, and are hit from behind. You want to know the cause of this unfortunate event. So you get out and see that the car that hit you had itself been stopped but was hit from behind. So you can't pin the collision on the driver of that car. As you look at the car behind that one, you notice that it, too, was hit from behind, and so on. Who caused your accident? Clearly, the driver of some car that hit a second car, but was not himself hit, caused each of the other cars to cause an accident, ending in yours. He produced the whole series of causes. He is the "first" cause.

Suppose, however, that it were an infinitely long pileup. Then *no one* would have started the chain. But if no one started it, it would not have happened. Since it did happen, we can conclude that someone did start it. He is the first efficient cause.

The Argument from Possibility and Necessity

Some of the things we come across can be but need not be, for we find them being generated and destroyed, thus sometimes in being and sometimes not. Now everything cannot be like this, for a thing that need not be was once not; and if everything need not be, once upon a time there was nothing. But if that were true there would be nothing even now, because something that does not exist can only begin to exist through something that already exists. If nothing was in being nothing could begin to be, and nothing would be in being now, which is clearly false. Not everything then is the sort that need not be; some things must be, and these may or may not owe this necessity to something else. But just as we proved that a series of agent causes can't go on for ever, so also a series of things which

must be and owe this to other things. So we are forced to postulate something which of itself must be, owing this to nothing outside itself, but being itself the cause that other things must be. (*ST*, 1a.3; *SPW*, p. 201)

This argument proceeds in two stages. To understand each stage, we must be clear about what Aquinas means by things that "need not be" and things that "must be." Both terms are applied to entities of various sorts, and he thinks we have examples of both sorts in our experience.

A thing that need not be can be generated (can come into being) and can be destroyed again (can pass away). The plants and animals of our experience are such beings. Mountains and rivers, too, are things that need not be. There was a time when the Rockies did not exist, and eventually erosion will wear them away. The mighty Mississippi, relatively stable though it has been for eons, will doubtless disappear some day, perhaps in the next ice age. Such beings, Aquinas would say, can suffer *essential* changes. By this he means that they can come to be what they are—and they can cease being that again. Fido is essentially a dog, but when Fido dies, he ceases to exist.

Given that account, we can consider the first stage of the argument. Aquinas argues that at one time, whatever need not be was not (did not exist). This is certainly true of Fido. He asks us to suppose that everything were like that. Then there would have been a time when Fido didn't exist, the Rockies didn't exist, the Mississippi didn't exist, and so on. There would have been a time when nothing existed. But if there ever had been such a time, there would be nothing now. Why? Because from nothing you get nothing. But as every waking moment proves to us, something does exist. So there could never have been a time when there was nothing at all. But that means that there must be things that don't just have possible being; there must be some things that have necessary being, things that *must* be.

This, then, is the first stage of the argument. Not everything can have merely possible being, or nothing at all would exist. Some beings simply must be.

In the second stage, Aquinas admits that some of these necessary beings may owe their necessity to another necessary being. But, using the same reasoning as he used for agent causation, he argues that this series of necessary dependencies could not go on forever. So there exists something that simply *must be* (period!)—something necessarily existing that doesn't owe its necessity to another, but is the cause of whatever is necessary in other beings. This being is in itself eternal and necessary in the most proper sense of the word. And this being, "all men speak of as *God*."

The Argument from Grades of Goodness in Things

Some things are found to be better, truer, more excellent than others. Such comparative terms describe varying degrees of approximation to a superlative; for example, things are hotter the nearer they approach what is hottest. So there is something which is the truest and best and most excellent of things, and hence the most fully in being; for Aristotle says that the truest things are the things most fully in being. Now *when many things possess a property in common, the one most fully possessing it causes it in the others: fire,* as Aristotle says, *the hottest of all things, causes all other things to be hot.* So there is something that causes in all other things their being, their goodness, and whatever other perfections they have. And this is what we call *God.* (*ST,* 1a.3; *SPW,* p. 201)

This proof begins with the observation that the things we experience do not all have the same value. Some are better than others, some truer, some more excellent. All of these comparative judgments, however, make sense only if we assume that in each case there is something which exemplifies those characteristics to a superlative degree.

Aquinas uses the example, which he borrows from Aristotle, of hot things, which are judged more or less hot as they more or less resemble the hotness of fire. (Again, *we* know there are many things hotter than ordinary fire, but that just means we have a longer scale by which to make such comparative judgments; perhaps we would judge heat in comparison with the temperature of atomic fusion in the sun, and cold in comparison with abso-

lute zero.) Something is better than another thing, then, to the extent that it more closely resembles the best. Something is truer if it is more like the truth, and so on.

But that is not the only point on which this argument rests. It is not just that the comparative degrees in such things are measured by the superlative; their very being depends on a superlative. As Aquinas says, fire is the cause of all hot things; and this must be actually existing fire. Again this is a *causal* proof. Aquinas is claiming that if there were not in existence a superlative degree of goodness, truth, and being, the existence of any lesser degree would be inexplicable. So there must be a maximum best, noblest, truest, and so on.

But since the lower degrees actually exist, the maximum must also really exist. This maximum is what explains the fact that we observe all these degrees of goodness in things: It is their cause. This maximum "best" of all things, Aquinas says, "we call *God.*"

The Argument from the Guidedness of Nature

Goal-directed behaviour is observed in all bodies in nature, even those lacking awareness; for we see their behaviour hardly ever varying and practically always turning out well, which shows they truly tend to goals and do not merely hit them by accident. But nothing lacking awareness can tend to a goal except it be directed by someone with awareness and understanding: arrows by archers, for example. So everything in nature is directed to its goal by someone with understanding, and this we call *God.* (*ST,* 1a.3; *SPW,* pp. 201–202)

This proof is often called "the argument from design." It is probably the one that turns up most often in popular "proofs" of the existence of God, and it has a famous history.* The key idea is that in-

---

*See particularly the discussion by David Hume ("Is It Reasonable to Believe in God?" in Chapter 15). Many people think that Darwinian modes of explanation also tend to undermine the argument. A recent version of the argument is presented in *Darwin's Black Box,* a book by biochemist Michael Behe. See, for instance, www.arn.org/behe/behehome.html and www.cs.colorado.edu/~lindsay/creation/behe.html.

telligent beings act purposefully, arranging means suitable to achieve ends they have in mind. We plant and harvest and store, for example, so that we will have food in the winter when we know there will be none to gather. We can look ahead to a situation that does not now exist and take steps to meet it satisfactorily.

This capacity is none too surprising in intelligent beings; perhaps it is even the main thing that constitutes intelligence. But when we look at the nonrational part of the world, we see the same thing. And this *is* surprising. We can hardly suppose that my Newfoundland dog, Shadow, grew a thick coat in the fall and shed it in the spring because he foresaw that otherwise he would be uncomfortable and perhaps even in danger of not surviving! Yet it is just as if he had planned that rationally.

We see the same apparently rational planning wherever we look. Rabbits are quick so that they can escape foxes. Foxes are cunning so that they can catch rabbits. Moths are camouflaged to escape predators. And so on. Everything happens as though it were planned to happen that way. But we cannot believe that dogs, rabbits, foxes, and moths are doing that planning. Someone else must be doing it for them.

Here is an analogy: People sometimes wonder whether computers are intelligent. Computers can certainly do some remarkable things: solve problems, rotate images in three dimensions on a screen, guide spacecraft. A standard reply is that though computers may look intelligent, the intelligence they display is not their own, but that of their designers and programmers. They have a "borrowed" intelligence.

Aquinas is claiming something similar for naturally existing beings. They do remarkable things, things that seem inexplicable in the absence of intelligence. We see their behavior "practically always turning out well." We cannot believe that they are themselves intelligent. So they must be directed to their goals "by someone with understanding."[*] This being, Aquinas says once more, "we call *God.*"

---

[*]Note the persistence of the Greek assumption that where there is order there is intelligence. See pp. 16–17.

Aquinas thinks, then, that by such reasoning from effects to causes we can prove the existence of God. In fact these five ways do not quite do that; they do not prove that there is one unique being who has all these traits: first cause of change, first efficient cause, a necessary being, a best being, and the intelligent designer of all the rest. But Aquinas thinks this is something reason can also prove. Such proofs provide a foundation on which Aquinas thinks all reasonable people should agree. If we think about the matter carefully, he contends, we should agree that atheism is irrational. This does not necessarily mean that the rational person will be a Christian, for some of the truths recognized in Christian faith cannot be rationally demonstrated. But the message of the Bible and the doctrines of the Church can rest on this foundation.

The Nature of God

Let us suppose we are convinced. We know *that* God exists. How much do we know about *what* God is? Here Aquinas is quite cautious. This is representative:

> In this life we cannot see God's substance but know him only from creatures: as their non-creaturely and transcendent cause. So this is where our words for God come from: from creatures. Such words, however, will not express the substance of God as he is in himself, in the way words like *human being* express the substance of what human beings are in themselves. (*ST,* 1a.13.1; *SPW,* p. 215)

There is no way our finite minds can adequately grasp what God is. Still, we are not entirely ignorant. We do know that God is the cause of all the features of the world we live in, and we know that God is the source of the very existence of anything at all. So what can we say about God on that basis?

The first and most important truth we know about God is that God *is.* If we ask, "Is what?" the most fundamental answer is that God is existence, being, itself. Like Augustine, Aquinas harks back to God's answer to Moses before the burning bush, when Moses asks who is sending him back into Egypt. God there says (Exodus 3:14), "I AM WHO I AM. . . . Say to the people of Israel, 'I AM has sent me to you.'" But Aquinas thinks philosophical reason also must reach this conclusion. (Here we have something on the second floor of our house!)

> God's existing doesn't differ from his substance. To be clear about this, note that when several causes producing different effects have also, besides those differing effects, one effect in common, then they must produce that common effect in virtue of some higher cause to which it properly belongs. For the effect properly belonging to a cause is determined by the cause's own proper nature and form; so that effects properly belonging to causes of diverse nature and form must differ, and any effect produced in common must properly belong not to any one of them but to a higher cause in virtue of which they act. . . . Now all created causes, distinguished by the effects that properly belong to each of them, have also one effect in common, namely existence: heat, for example, causes things to be—or exist as—hot, and builders cause there to be—or exist—houses. So they agree in causing things to exist, but differ in this: that heat causes heat and builders houses. So there must be some cause higher than all of them in virtue of which they all cause existence, a cause of which existence is the proper effect. And this cause is God. Now the proper effect of any cause issues from it by reproducing its nature. So existing must be God's substance or nature. (*DPG*, 7.2; *SPW*, pp. 205–206)

Because existence is (as we saw earlier) something added to essence, it cannot be just by virtue of their essence that fires or house builders produce their effects. True, their effects differ because of the kinds of things they are. But that they both bring into being something that actually exists cannot be ascribed to those kinds. That is something separate and requires a separate explanation. It must be that, in addition to being the kinds of things they are, they participate in being—which is not identical with either of them. This being, this existing, this energy or source of the existence of finite things cannot itself just be another finite thing. It is being itself. And that, Aquinas says, is the very substance of God. That's what God is—a great, unlimited, activity of existing. So Anselm is right after all: God's essence *is* his existence. But now we know that in a way appropriate to the kind of mind human

beings have: as the cause of effects we are aware of through our senses.

Note how different from Aristotle's conception of God this is. God thought of in this way is not a pure form existing in isolated splendor, contemplating its own contemplation. God is an efficient cause, an agent continually bringing into existence all the many things that do exist. This is a God who is involved in the creation, a God who might well (though this has not been proved) know the number of hairs on a man's head and be aware of the fall of every sparrow, a God who might love human beings with a love beyond all comparing. Whether we can go that far or not, this is clearly a God on whose creative activity we absolutely depend; if for one moment God turned away from the creation, everything would disappear back into nothingness. Existence, remember, is something added to essence. And now we know that it is added by God, whose very essence is existence.

As for what else we might know about God, Aquinas says two things. First, we can know a great deal about what God is not. Drawing on a long tradition of "negative theology," Aquinas says that God is not, for instance, finite, material, potential, a tree or star, bad, and so on. We can pile on negatives, and this is useful. But no list of negative terms, no matter how long, will tell us what God *is*.

The second truth about God derives from the way we know of God at all: as the cause of effects in creatures. In the world around us, we observe many good things; in their fullness, we could call them "perfections." Life is such a perfection, for example, or wisdom, or power. All of these derive their being from the source of all being. But we don't merely want to say, Aquinas reminds us, that God is the *cause* of life or wisdom or goodness.* We want to be ble to say that in some sense, this great act of existing is itself alive and wise and good. How can we do that?

We have to acknowledge that what we mean by these terms is not derived from a direct acquaintance with God. We learn what "wise" means by

---

*Note that an atheistic materialist might acknowledge a cause for life or wisdom; she would, however, point to matter or the evolutionary process as that cause. What she would want to deny is that the cause is itself alive or wise.

MAIMONIDES (MOSES BEN MAIMON)

Like Averroës, his contemporary, Maimonides (1135–1204), was born in Spain. At the age of thirty, however, he fled rather than be forcibly converted to Islam and spent the latter part of his life in more tolerant (at that time) Cairo. There he was physician to the vizier of Saladin, ruler of Egypt. He wrote extensively on medicine and Jewish law, but his most influential work is *Guide for the Perplexed.*

The *Guide* is addressed to those intellectuals who are in perplexity over apparent contradictions between Scripture and the best science and philosophy of the day. The latter he takes to be represented by Aristotle, especially as understood by his Muslim interpreters. He agrees with Avicenna that being and essence are separable, but holds that the celestial spheres and the Intelligences governing them are created by God ex nihilo, not emanations from the very substance of God himself. This allows him to deny that everything happens necessarily in this world, thus making room for free will, evil, and miracles.

As to whether the universe is eternal or not, he holds that this cannot be proved either way, but that on either assumption the existence of God can be demonstrated. We know God exists, but we know of his nature only what we can learn from his works. So the study of these works by way of natural science yields such knowledge as we can have of the divine nature. However, because all language is derived from our experience of the natural world, he holds that none of our words can apply literally to God, who infinitely exceeds his creation. We can, then, say what God is *not,* but never positively what God *is.* Thus Maimonides is one of the principal sources for the tradition of *negative theology.*

Maimonides believes that the highest perfection possible for a human being is to know God and to love him. Because we know God only through his works, the pursuit of science and metaphysics is, as Aristotle said, the best and happiest life. It also provides as much of immortality as is possible for us, since what will be preserved after death is the knowledge we have acquired. In the greatest human beings, however, this theoretical life can be combined with practical influence in the community, as is proved by the greatest of the prophets, Moses.

---

experience with human or animal wisdom in this finite creaturely world, but we are also familiar with extensions of a word's meaning. For instance, "healthy" is a term that belongs to people in its primary application, but because of cause and effect relations with other things, the term is extended. We call certain foods "healthy" because they contribute to health in humans. Or we call urine or blood healthy because they are a symptom or sign of health. Aquinas thinks something of the same sort is true of the words we use about God.

> So creatures having any perfection represent and resemble him . . . as effects partially resemble a cause of a higher kind though falling short of reproducing its form. . . . So the sort of words we are considering express God's substance, but do it imperfectly just as creatures represent him imperfectly.

So when we say *God is good* we mean neither *God causes goodness* nor *God is not bad,* but *What in creatures we call goodness pre-exists in a higher way in God.* Thus God is not good because he causes goodness; rather because he is good, goodness spreads through things. (*ST,* 1a.13.2; *SPW,* p. 218)

Because the words we use of God get their original meaning from our experience in this world, they cannot mean exactly the same thing when they are applied to God. For instance, Socrates is wise and Socrates exists, but Socrates' wisdom is not the same thing as his existence. So

> words expressing creaturely perfections express them as distinct from one another: *wise* for example, used of a human being expresses a perfection distinct from his nature, his powers, his existence, and so on; but when we use it of God we don't want to express anything distinct from his

substance, powers, and existence. So the word *wise* used of human beings somehow contains and delimits what is meant; when used of God, however, it doesn't, but leaves what it means uncontained and going beyond what the word can express. Clearly then the word *wise* isn't used in the same sense of God and man, and the same is true of all the other words. No word, then, is said of God and creatures univocally. (*ST,* 1a.13.5; *SPW,* p. 224)

A word is *univocal* when it is used with just one meaning. Aquinas denies that a word applied to both creatures and creator is used univocally. But it isn't used *equivocally,* either; that is, it's not the case that there is no connection between the meanings in the two cases, as there is between "bank" when used as a place to keep your money and "bank" as a place on which to stand while fishing. Rather,

> these words apply to God and creatures by analogy or proportion. . . .
> And this way of sharing a word lies somewhere between pure equivocation and straightforward univocalness. . . .
> Whenever words are used analogically of several things, it is because they are all related to some one thing; so that one thing must help define the others. . . . In the same way then all words used metaphorically of God apply first to creatures and then to God, since said of God they only express some likeness to creatures. Just as talking of a *smiling* meadow expresses a proportion: that flowers adorn a meadow like a smile on a man's face, so talking of God as a *lion* expresses this proportion: that God is powerful in his doings like lions in theirs. And so clearly we can't define what such words mean when used of God unless we refer to what they mean used of creatures. . . .
> But, as we have seen, such names don't simply express God's causality, but his substance, for calling God *good* or *wise* doesn't only mean that he causes wisdom or goodness, but that these perfections pre-exist in him in a more excellent way. (*ST,* 1a.13.5,6; *SPW,* pp. 224–227)

In this way Aquinas explains how we can talk intelligibly of God, while carefully preserving the ultimate mystery of God's being to creatures such as ourselves.

Humans: Their Souls

Aquinas takes for granted the basic concepts involved in the Great Chain of Being idea.[*] God, as perfect being and goodness, freely creates a hierarchy of creatures, from angels to stones, varying in being and goodness. But Aquinas elaborates the higher reaches of the chain much more than Augustine did.

Between God and the highest of creatures there is an unbridgeable gap. But there are many levels of created substances higher than human beings. These angelic beings are pure intelligences, spiritual beings defined by a form or essence, but lacking any material substratum.

Two things must be noted about angels: (1) Lacking any matter, they also lack what individuates material things. (Remember that what makes this frog distinct from that frog is not its form, but the fact that it is composed of different matter.) Still, an angel is not, like God, a simple existence whose essence just is its existence. Like all created beings, angels are composite; they are made up of a form or essence plus existence—which here, too, is something added. (2) This lack of material stuff in spiritual intelligences means that there cannot be more than one angel of a given kind. To put it another way, each angel is an entire species in itself, every one differing from every other in essence—differing not as this dog differs from that dog, but as dogs differ from horses.

Human beings exist on the border between such pure intelligences and the material world, sharing something with beings both above and below them on the chain. This participation in higher and lower levels of being is already summed up, Aquinas thinks, in Aristotle's formula for humans: They are *animals* (material beings) whose distinctive characteristic is *rationality* (or intelligence).

Aquinas agrees substantially with Aristotle about soul and body. Because soul is the principle of life in things, there are various levels of soul. Plants have a kind of soul, which enables them to nourish

---

[*]Review the development by Plotinus and Augustine of the idea of the Great Chain of Being, pp. 238–241.

themselves, grow, and reproduce. In addition to these powers, animals have sentient (sensitive) soul—that is, abilities to see and hear and so on, together with instincts and inclinations that draw them toward and move them away from things. Humans have rational soul, adding the abilities to abstract universals, think logically, and plan future actions in the light of goals. In all these ways, soul is the form of a body of a particular sort.

It is very important to Aquinas to insist that there are *not* three souls in a human being—vegetative, sensitive, and rational—as though we were composite beings made up of three substances.

> If we hold that the soul is united to the body as its substantial form, then the co-existence of several essentially different souls in the same body cannot be entertained. To begin with, an animal having several souls would not compose an essential unity, for nothing is simply one except by one form. Form gives being and unity. Were man alive by one form, namely by vegetable soul, and animal by another, namely by sensitive soul, and human by a third, namely by rational soul, he would not be one thing simply speaking. (*ST,* 1a.76.3; *PT,* pp. 204–205)

But a human being *is* one thing, and the rational soul incorporates and governs all the rest. This kind of holism means that features we in some way share with the lower animals—emotion and desire, for instance—are transformed into *human* emotion and desire. In us, emotion and desire involve conceptualizations impossible for a nonrational creature. We can, but a cat cannot, fear damage to our reputation or hope to meet someone we admire. In fact, everything in us, even our bodily state, is affected by our dominant form, the rational form of a human soul.

We could put this point another way. The human body is not, in a living human being, a substance. Some philosophers—Plato comes to mind—have thought so and have thought of a human being as a kind of dual creature: a body to which a substantial soul has for a time been conjoined. But Aquinas will have none of this. At death we are not left with one of the substances in a human being (the body), while

the other (the soul) departs. What we are left with is not, properly speaking, human at all, but an entity of a different kind: a corpse. We may call it human by extension or by analogy, but because the corpse has lost the form of a human being, it is no longer literally correct to call the corpse human. A human body is not a thing on its own, but *material* for a human being, made into one substance by the human soul, which is its form.

> So the human soul is the form of the human body. Further, if soul inhabited body like a sailor his ship, it wouldn't give body or its parts their specific nature; yet clearly it does since when it leaves the body the various parts lose the names they first had, or keep them in a different sense; for a dead man's eyes are eyes only in the sense that eyes in a picture or a statue are, and the same goes for the other parts of the body. Moreover, if soul inhabited body like a sailor his ship the union of body and soul would be accidental, and when death separated them it wouldn't be decomposition of a substance, which it clearly is.* (*PDS,* art. 1; *SPW,* p. 188)

Despite this insistence on the unity of a human being, however, Aquinas also agrees with Aristotle that a rational soul is not *just* the form of a human body, the way the soul of a lobster is just the form of life in a lobster. There is something substantial about a human soul after all, something akin to angelic intelligences.[†] He agrees, moreover, for essentially the same reason: Reasoning souls

> cannot share that special activity of theirs with any bodily organ, in the sense of having a bodily organ for thinking as an eye is the bodily organ for seeing. And so the life principle of a thing with understanding has to act on its own, with an activity peculiar to itself not shared with the body. And because activity flows from actuality, the understanding soul must possess an existence in and

---

*Descartes, in the seventeenth century, uses this same figure, also denying that the soul is like a sailor in a ship. But he has an even harder time than Aquinas in making it stick, since he thinks the soul is a separate substance in its entirety. See pp. 354 and 358.

[†]See Aristotle on *nous,* pp. 183–184.

of itself, not dependent on the body. (*PDS,* art. 1; *SPW,* pp. 187–188)

You can see Aquinas, like Augustine, struggling to unify two strands of thought that are not easy to harmonize. On the one hand, a man or woman is one substance, and the soul is its form. On the other hand, a human soul, by virtue of its capacity to abstract universals and reason with them, its ability to know virtually anything, is an intellectual substance in its own right, able to subsist even when the body is destroyed.*

On the one hand, a soul gets a content, becomes a determinate, individual soul only by virtue of its intimate relation to the body because whatever is in a soul is conveyed there by the specific bodily sense experience of some individual human. On the other hand, it is the soul's possible subsistence without the body that gives it immortality. Although Aquinas has rational arguments for each part of this view, in the end it may be a matter of faith that these demands can be reconciled. He calls on the Christian doctrine of the resurrection of the body to do the job.

> Firstly, if we deny the resurrection of the body it isn't easy—indeed it becomes very difficult—to defend the immortality of the soul. The union of body and soul is certainly a natural one, and any separation of soul from body goes against its nature and is imposed upon it. So if soul is deprived of body it will exist imperfectly as long as that situation lasts. . . . Secondly, what human beings desire by nature is their own well-being. But soul is not the whole human being, only part of one; my soul is not me. So that even if soul achieves well-being in another life, that doesn't mean I do or any other human being does. (*CC,* 15 : 17–19; *SPW,* pp. 192–193)

"My soul is not me." This definitive rejection of Platonism means that even if my soul is a substance capable of existing after my body dies, *I* may not survive. For *my* survival, that soul must be the form

of a body—my body. And to buttress this hope of immortality, Aquinas looks not to reason, but to the resurrection of Christ. Just as Christ's body was transformed into a heavenly body, so, the Christian saint believes, will our bodies be also.

Humans: Their Knowledge

We have seen how humans can know something of God by (1) reasoning from effects to causes, and (2) using analogies from common experience to partially describe this cause of existing things. But how do we come to have knowledge of those effects in the first place? We need to pay some attention to Aquinas' theory of knowledge. As we have noted, knowing begins with sensing. How does sensing work? Take the eye, for example. An eye has the power to receive images of external things —their shape, color, texture, motion. It's not the substance being perceived that enters the eye, of course, but its sensible form.

Imagine you are stroking a cat that is purring contentedly on your lap. You see the cat stretch with pleasure, feel the softness of its fur, and hear the purr. Each of these sensible forms is received by the appropriate sense. Yet it is not three experiences you are having, but one. So these images must be united in what Aquinas (following Aristotle) calls your "common root sensitivity." The unified complex image formed in you is a particular item that mirrors a determinate, particular substance outside you: contented Tabby at a certain moment in time. When the cat jumps off your lap, your current sensory experience changes, but something is left behind in you. The proof is that you can later remember that experience, bring its images back into consciousness, and, as it were, run the experience again. So images are stored in you somewhere; Aquinas (again following Aristotle) calls this storehouse *the imagination.*

Thus far described, our minds do not differ much from the minds of the higher animals, which also have sensitivity, imagination, and (limited) memory. But we have an additional capacity called *intellect.* Using intellect, we can form *ideas* from the

---

*See the fuller discussion in the following section, "Humans: Their Knowledge."

images stored in imagination. And ideas are not just more images, not copies of images, but what the medievals called "universals."* *Universals* are features of things that can be expressed in language and formulated in definitions. So while our senses can take in the sensible form of Tabby and the imagination can store that image, it is the intellect that can abstract the universal features of this cat and all other cats and formulate the *idea* of a *cat*.

> The senses are bodily powers and know singular objects tied down by matter, whereas mind [intellect] is free from matter and knows universals, which are abstract from matter and contain limitless instances. (*ST,* 1a.2ae. 2.6; *PT,* p. 231)

When this happens we have the form of the cat actually resident in the intellect itself. That's what a concept or idea of a cat is: the actual presence in the intellect of the very *form* that makes a cat a cat—only without making the intellect into a cat because the usual *material* for cats (flesh, bone, fur) is missing.

There might be a problem here. If our intellect deals in universals such as "small domestic feline" or "rational animal," which are true of limitless individuals, how is it possible for us to know particular things—Tabby or Socrates—that aren't pure forms? It is, after all the *matter* composing this cat or this human that make them the particular things that they are. But matter as such is unknowable; matter is what the intellect abstracts *from*. Aquinas solves this problem by noting that sensory images have two uses. They are the originals from which knowledge starts, but they are also needed when we think about particular things. We may be able to know a lot about cats-as-such in terms of forms or universals, but if we want to direct our thought to Tabby in particular, we need to recall an image of Tabby to tie our thought down to her. The image, remember, is as particular as the individual that produced it and will ensure that we are indeed thinking about that specific cat. Knowledge of particulars, then, is possible; it will involve both universals and images, as when we say that Tabby is gray or that Socrates is wise.

Intellect has two distinguishable operations. In the first of these the intellect enjoys a simple apprehension of some object; it grasps, more or less adequately, the *whatness* of the object, its *nature,* or what Aquinas calls its **quiddity** (from the Latin for "what it is"). So a child learns to identify a cat and distinguish it from a dog. The child's idea of a cat is not false to the reality, but it is pretty incomplete. An adult's idea is more adequate, and a biologist's concept more adequate still. Our idea of what a cat is can expand and improve; typically, it does improve with continued experience of cats. In such a simple grasp of a nature, there is, properly speaking, no truth or falsity. It's just there in the intellect. (Compare Aristotle on truth not being applicable to *terms,* but only to *statements,* p. 161.)

In the second operation, which Aquinas calls "making connections and disconnections," the intellect unites ideas to make judgments about the things apprehended. Such judgments may be affirmative or negative. So we say, "All cats meow," or "Socrates is not stupid." With respect to judgments the concept of truth is in place.

> For the meaning of true consists in a matching of thing and understanding, and matching presupposes diversity, not identity. So the notion of truth is first found in understanding when understanding first starts to have something of its own which the external thing doesn't have, yet which corresponds to the thing and can be expected to match it. Now when articulating what things are, understanding possesses only a likeness of the external thing, just as the senses do when they take in the appearance of what they sense. But when understanding starts to make judgements about the thing it has taken in, then those are the understanding's own judgements not found in the thing outside, yet called true judgements in so far as they match what is outside. Now understanding makes judgements about the thing it takes in when it says something about how it is or is not, and that we call understanding making connections and disconnections. . . . So that is why truth is found first in understanding making connections and disconnections. (*PDT,* 1.2; *SPW,* p. 59)

---

*Contrast David Hume, who thinks ideas just are faint copies of images. See pp. 401–402.

Truth, then, just as in Aristotle, is a matter of correspondence or matching between judgments made by the intellect and the thing being judged. To say "Socrates is wise" is true, provided Socrates is wise. Otherwise, the statement is false.*

There also seem to be two powers in the intellect: an active power and a receptive power. The former does the abstracting; the latter stores the abstract ideas, functioning for the active intellect as imagination does for the senses. There must be such a passive power, Aquinas argues, because we can bring back into active consideration ideas that have not been present to the conscious mind for some time; these ideas have not completely disappeared but are potentially present, ready once again to play a role in current thinking. It is the active power of intellect that Aquinas believes is not and cannot be tied down to any bodily organ. It is to this agent intellect that he looks when he searches for a proof of the immortality of the soul. But the receptive intellect is equally important, lest our minds be restricted solely to awareness of the present moment.

It is very important to note that although intellect gets its material from the images stored in imagination, it is not those images that we know (at least not in the first instance). What we know are those hylomorphic objects that produced the images—the cat, the chair, the person sitting in the chair holding the cat. We know them by virtue of, or by means of, these images. But the images are not the primary objects of knowledge.† True, we can reflect on our own mental operations, draw back and pay attention to the image as such. In general, however, what we know is not limited to the contents of our minds. We know Tabby and Socrates and the fact that fire causes water to boil. None of these are mental phenomena.

This, then, is the account Aquinas gives of our knowledge of the material world. All our knowledge begins with what our senses reveal about it.

This explains how we can know that the premises of his arguments for the existence of God are true. We begin from simple facts about the world—that things change, that one thing causes another, and so on. Starting there, Aquinas believes we can work back to that cause, which is its own existence, and the cause of whatever else there is.

Humans: Their Good

Following Aristotle again, Aquinas holds that every finite substance tends naturally toward its perfection, toward realizing its potential. Actualization of a thing's potential is in fact the *good* for that thing. This natural teleology of final causes is present even in the inanimate world, but it is strikingly apparent in animals; they are always seeking something. This is especially true of human beings, who can scarcely sit still an hour without planning what to do next. We regard what we seek—rightly or wrongly—as good, as contributing to our perfection. We want dinner, or a movie, or exercise. These things are goals that move us to action, so we go to the kitchen or head toward the theater or change into our running shoes. Such actions are chosen as means to reach the goal, and we wouldn't engage in them if the goal didn't seem good to us.

This much seems mere common sense. But Aquinas pushes these thoughts in two directions. First, suppose we ask why we want exercise. We might answer, for the sake of health, which also seems good to us. Why do we want health? It must be for the sake of some further good. That such questions can be repeated leads us to ask, Is there any goal that we want simply for itself, not for the sake of something beyond it? Aquinas answers, yes, of course. Again following Aristotle, he identifies the goal as happiness (*eudaemonia*) or beatitude.* Whatever else seems good to us does so because it seems either to be a part of happiness or to contribute to our happiness. That it is good to be

---

*See Aristotle's definition of truth, pp. 162–163.

†Contrast this "realism" about knowledge with the "empiricism" of John Locke, who says that the mind has "no other immediate object but its own ideas," p. 380.

---

*Note that happiness is no more just the *feeling* of happiness for Aquinas than it was for Socrates, Plato, or Aristotle. It is a condition of the person. Compare pp. 103, 148, 187.

happy or blissful is beyond proving, but also beyond question.

Second, humans differ from other animals in being able to frame ideas in terms of universal concepts. We want dinner, but that concept can be filled out in a great many ways. Do we want steak, or chicken, or vegetables? Do we want to eat out or at home? Alone or with others? Simple or fancy? Dinner is good, but that rather empty concept cries out for a multitude of decisions. A sheep that is hungry and is put in a green pasture faces no such quandaries; it simply starts eating the nearest grass. The sheep's actions are pretty closely determined by what its senses reveal in its immediate environment. Human action is unlike that because our universalizing intellect presents possibilities to us. Among these possibilities we must choose. And if you think "dinner" is a concept that can be filled out in numerous ways, consider "happiness."

We all want to be happy, then—to flourish, to fare well. This is a desire implanted in us by nature; whether that *should* be our goal is not up to us. (Though I have asked many students, I have never found a single one who confessed to having as a goal being unhappy in life!) Happiness is a natural good.* We don't have to consider whether to take happiness as a goal, but we do have to think about how to achieve that goal. This thinking eventuates in acts of will that produce actions.

> There is a desire for good in everything: good, the philosophers tell us, is what all desire. In things without awareness this desire is called natural desire: the attraction a stone has for downwards, for instance. In things with sense-awareness it is called animal desire, and divides into capabilities of affective and aggressive feeling. In things with understanding it is called intellectual or rational desire: will. So created intellectual substances have wills. (*SCG,* 2.47; *SPW,* p. 169)

Strictly speaking, a sheep does not have a will, though it does have desires. Nonetheless, Aquinas maintains, will is a species of desire. It is differentiated from desire in general by being rational desire, desire that is informed by intellectual knowledge

and reason. True, like the sheep we may simply be attracted to food that is before us. But we can also apply universal concepts in reasoning about food; we can say, "That's filled with saturated fats, and though I'm sure I would like it, I will not eat it." Such a decision, made in the light of rational knowledge, in the light of some goal that reason approves (such as health), is an act of will. Humans, by virtue of their intellectual nature, have wills.

What that means is that human beings are not at the mercy of their desires. They can choose which desires to satisfy and which to leave unsatisfied— and that means the will is free.

> Things lack freedom to decide either because they lack all judgement, like stones and plants which lack awareness, or because their judgements are fixed by nature, like nonreasoning animals. . . . But wherever judgement of what to do is not fixed by nature, there is freedom to decide. And all creatures with understanding are of this sort. For understanding takes in not only this or that good but the notion of good as such. . . . So all things with understanding have freedom of will deriving from understanding's judgement, and that is freedom of decision, which is defined as free judgement of reason. (*SCG,* 2.48; *SPW,* pp. 170–171)

Aquinas means that we can evaluate particular goods (such as this rich, dark, sweet, chocolate cake) in the light of "good as such" and decide in the light of our more general good whether *this* good is one that should be chosen. The fact that we can do this means we are responsible for our actions. Unlike sheep, we are not simply determined to act by our immediate surroundings.

Aquinas distinguishes between *acts of a human* and *human acts.* I do, in a sense, grow a beard every night. But whether I shave it off in the morning or let it grow is a matter for decision and the exercise of my will. Only the latter is properly called a *human act.* Why? Because only that is under the control of the form that makes me human: my rational nature. Suppose I really would like to have a beard but my wife just hates beards. Then I am faced with incompatible goods—having a beard or pleasing my wife—and I have to decide. I am free to decide either way. Whichever I do will be voluntary. What I decide will be willed in the light of intellectual

---

*Compare Plato's argument for morality in the *Republic,* which depends on precisely this premise. See p. 150.

reflection on overall goodness, and that will not only be something I am responsible for, but it will also be a revelation of my character.

Before we discuss character (virtue and vice), however, we should ask, What makes an individual action good or bad?

> We should judge actions good and bad in the same way we do things, since what things do reflects what they are. Now a thing's goodness is measured by how fully it exists; for . . . good and existent are interchangeable terms. . . .* Full human being, for example, demands a complex of soul and body endowed with every ability and organ needed for knowledge and movement, and if an individual lacks any of this he would not exist fully. As existing he would be good, but as not fully existing he would lack goodness and be called bad: thus for blind men it is good to be alive, but bad to be without sight. . . .
>
> In a similar way then actions must be called good in so far as they exist, but in so far as they exist less fully than human actions should they will lack goodness and be called bad: if, for example, we don't do as much as we reasonably should, or do something out of place or the like. (ST, 1a2e.18.1; SPW, pp. 343–344)

What actions would "exist less fully than human actions should"? Clearly, actions would not exist as fully human if they were not under the control of our intellectual, rational faculties—because those faculties are what make us distinctively human. Those actions, then, would lack goodness and would be called bad. Good actions are actions that flow from our nature, fulfilling and perfecting that nature.

This principle allows Aquinas to formulate the notion of a *natural law*. Everything in the created world, of course, expresses the divine reason, according to which it was designed. God's reason can be called an *eternal law*, and nothing can happen that is not permitted to happen by God's eternal law. In creating the world, however, God brought substances into being that have natures or essences of their own, and these natures incorporate within themselves something of the eternal law. A stone,

for instance, naturally falls to Eart wolves naturally act out their nature. grass, and wolves eat sheep; they have no c Human beings also have a given nature. But, as have seen, our nature includes the capacity to formulate universals and to think about what to do in terms of them. This provides us with a freedom of action that stones and sheep and wolves lack. Unlike sheep and wolves, then, we can act in ways that are contrary to our nature, detrimental to it—and when we do, the saint tells us, we sin.

But we also have the capacity to know what the law of our nature is, together with a partial ability (even apart from the special grace of God) to act in accordance with it. How do we know what the natural law says? Its first principle, Aquinas tells us, is this: "Good should be done and evil avoided." Now this is not something that can be proved from more general principles, or it wouldn't be first. It is a practical parallel to that principle of intellectual life in general, the principle of noncontradiction, which says that two contradictory propositions cannot both be true. Though it cannot be proved, there does seem to be something incoherent in its denial. Since I always act for the sake of some good, for me to say, "Let me do evil," is equivalent to saying, "Let evil be good."*

Can we know anything of natural law beyond this self-evident first principle? Yes. How? By observing the natural inclinations or propensities of things. For example, all human beings experience the drive to continue in existence. Our reason apprehends this universal drive as good. It is good to continue to live—so murder is wrong. And it is part of our nature to eat when hungry—so feeding the hungry is good. Humans have a natural tendency to mate and care for their children—so marriage, intended to provide a safe and lasting environment to meet these goals is a good thing. In general, law is what reason declares to be fitting in

---

*This is, you will recall, one of the principles of the Great Chain of Being idea.

---

*Notice that the first natural law does *not* say, "What I think is good should be done and what I take to be evil should be avoided." Aquinas does think that we have no alternative but to do the best we know, so if, after reflection, our conscience tells us to do something that is in fact wrong, that is what we should do. But that doesn't mean we are doing the right thing.

f something. By using our
he nature of human beings
can discern the image of
is resident in the things he
believes that in addition to
reason tells us that drunken-
, lying, homosexuality, and
ises are contrary to nature.
The argument all of these, in one way or another, violate the natural inclinations of a being
with a nature like ours.

> Now since everything subjected to God's provi-
> dence is measured by the standards of his eternal
> law, as we have said, everything shares in some way
> in the eternal law, bearing its imprint in the form
> of a natural tendency to pursue the behaviour and
> goals appropriate to it. Reasoning creatures are
> subject to God's providence in a special, more pro-
> found way than others, by themselves sharing the
> planning, making plans both for themselves and
> for others; thus sharing in the eternal reasoning it-
> self that is imprinting them with their natural ten-
> dencies to appropriate behaviour and goals. And
> it is this distinctive sharing in the eternal law by
> reasoning creatures that we call the law we have in
> us by nature. (*ST,* 1a2ae.91.2; *SPW,* p. 418)

In addition to the eternal law, which is part of
the nature of God, and the natural law, which is resident in our own natures, Aquinas distinguishes two
further kinds of law. The third kind is *human law.*
This is law that is devised and promulgated by an
authority in a community for the good of that community—or, at least, that is its essence. When human law is in accord with that goal, it also mirrors
the eternal and natural law. But, as humans are subject to sin—rulers no less than the rest of us—human law may deviate from natural goodness and often does. Where human law deviates from natural
law, Aquinas says, it is not truly law at all, but lawlessness. Why? Because it is not in accord with reason, which is the source of all law.

Human law, then, must meet four conditions
to be true law: (1) It must issue from a legitimate
authority that has responsibility for a community;
(2) it must be promulgated publicly so that people
can know what is and is not acceptable; (3) it must
further the good of that community; and (4) it must

be in conformity with reason. In terms of these criteria, Aquinas distances himself from any notion of
law as simply what the sovereign declares, or whatever is customarily accepted.[*]

Finally, there is *divine law.* This is law that is beyond our natural capacities to discover but is revealed to us in the Scriptures. An example might
be the New Testament commandment to believe in
the Lord Jesus Christ in order to be saved. Reason
cannot figure this out for itself; but, Aquinas holds,
it is necessary to enable us to reach our final bliss.
Here we have something on the third floor of the
house.

We can now return to the issue of character. Like
Aristotle, Aquinas holds that we shape our characters by developing habits or dispositions to act in
certain ways. And we build such habits by actually
acting in those ways. These habits of character are
virtues and vices. *Virtues* incline us to act in ways
that reason approves of; when you have a virtue, it
is easy to do what otherwise is difficult. *Vices* are
contrary habits, which incline us to ignore or neglect the discernment of good by our reason.

Virtues are important to us. The reason is that,
though we are naturally oriented toward bliss or
happiness, it is not so clear what contributes to that
blessed state. Our rational faculties have (in addition to the task of finding truth) the practical role of
choosing actions suitable to promoting our blessedness. But we are not, as the angels are, pure intellectual beings. We also feel the attractions of the
senses and the pleasures of the body, and these animal propensities have some independence of our
intellect. Thus, they need to be habituated to the
good—trained, if you like, to obey their rightful
master, reason. That's just what a virtue is: a habit
of choosing wisely in light of the ultimate end of
blessedness. Aquinas, again following Aristotle, says
that the soul rules the body like a tyrant. He means
that if I will to raise my arm, my arm (other things

---

[*] Aquinas thereby aligns himself with those who claim that there
is a criterion for judging human laws, from Heraclitus and Antigone, through Plato, Aristotle, and the Stoics. He sets himself
against Sophist understandings of law and justice as wholly conventional, and against notions of law as simply what the ruler
declares. Compare Hobbes, p. 371.

being equal) simply obeys and goes up. But our desires and emotions

> don't obey my reason's slightest signal, but have their own ways of acting, which are sometimes at odds with reason: reason rules my affections and my aggressions, Aristotle goes on to say, *democratically,* like free people are ruled, who have their own will in certain areas. (*ST,* 1a2ae.56.4; *SPW,* p. 406)

As we see in this quote, Aquinas divides our desires and emotions into two large classes: the *affective* and the *aggressive.**

> The object of our affective ability [is] anything sensed as straightforwardly good or bad, pleasurable or painful. But sometimes the animal has a hard struggle attaining such good or avoiding such bad things, because they are not within its immediate power, and then good or bad, seen as challenging or requiring effort, becomes an object of our aggressive ability. . . .
>
> . . . the function of aggressive feelings in animals is to remove obstacles preventing affective feelings from pursuing their objective, obstacles that make good difficult to attain or bad difficult to avoid. So all aggressive feelings end up in affective feeling, so that even aggressive feelings *are accompanied by* the affective feelings of *joy or sadness.* (*ST,* 1a2ae.23; *SPW,* pp. 163–164)

One function of virtue is to order these emotions and desires toward the good—that is, toward blessedness. So we have, Aquinas says, a virtue specific to the affective emotions, those that are immediately attracted by pleasure and repelled by pain. This virtue is *temperance,* which brings the impulse to pursue the pleasant and avoid the painful under the tutelage of practical reason. Temperance prevents us from indulging too much in pleasures, keeping us on an even keel and aimed at the blessed state.

With respect to the aggressive feelings, we have a second virtue: *fortitude* or *courage.* Fortitude makes us tenacious in pursuing what our reason determines to be truly good, so that we don't give up easily in the face of obstacles. It is firmness or re-

solve when temptations arise to distract us from our ultimate good by promising some minor gain. Fortitude is being steadfast rather than wimpy, determined rather than reckless. It keeps us from being overpowered by fear, on the one hand, or being rashly bold on the other.

In addition to these two virtues governing our emotional life, there is *justice,* which ensures that we are not inclined to take more than our share of goods, or to favor ourselves in some distribution of such goods. Distributive justice does not apply so much to what we feel as to what we do. It has an intrinsic reference to others. To be just is to be fair and equitable in allotting to each person what is due to him or her. A just person, for instance, will not even be tempted to steal money lying in plain sight on someone's desk; to a just person, the possibility of stealing simply doesn't appear in the list of options for action. To truly have the virtue of justice is for it to be *easy* to leave the money there.

Finally, there is *prudence,* a virtue that pertains more directly to the intellect than do the others. Prudence involves habits that lead us to think again when we are being hasty and keep in mind the overall good when we are deliberating.*

These four (temperance, fortitude, justice, and prudence) do not exhaust all the virtues there are, but Aquinas calls them the *cardinal virtues,* the principal or most important of them. If human beings were simply animal beings, with no hope of immortality, these would be sufficient to produce whatever degree of happiness is attainable in this life. If we were restricted to the first two floors of the house, there would be nothing to add. But if it is rational to believe that our good is not exhausted by such bliss as this life offers, blessedness also requires the *theological virtues* of faith, hope, and love.

Here Aquinas self-consciously goes beyond Aristotle. He says that Aristotle understands perfectly well what we require for *eudaemonia* (happiness). But then, confined to this world, he resigns himself to making do with less. Happiness, Aristotle says, is activity of soul, in accord with reason, over an entire lifetime, which cannot be taken away from us,

---

*The traditional terms for these are the *concupiscible* and the *irascible* desires and feelings.

*Compare Aristotle on "practical wisdom," pp. 191–193.

together with modest external goods—the most satisfying activity being that of intellectual contemplation. But Aristotle realizes that happiness in this world is fragile, as his reference to Priam makes clear.* In this life, we are ever subject to fortune, and though he rightly says our highest happiness is in contemplation, he acknowledges that even this cannot be continuously engaged in. So if this life is all there is, we can at best approximate the goal that we all have.

What would true happiness consist in, then? It would have to be total immersion in absolute goodness forever—in the presence of and being suffused by that original energy or existence that *is* goodness and is the source of all good. Nothing else would do. That's what we all want, though we don't usually realize it. That's the goal of all our desiring. But we are talking of the mystical vision of God, perhaps of what Aquinas himself tasted briefly during that December mass, after which he could write no more. Philosophy can perhaps point to that bliss, but philosophy cannot supply it. That's a gift reserved for God's grace.

Because we are not self-sufficient in our existence, Aquinas writes, we have a "twofold ultimate goal." We are aiming at an internal perfection, which can only come when we deeply and wholeheartedly love God above all else and love our neighbors as ourselves. And we are aiming at unity with God, the source of all goodness and so also of that very perfection within.

> Bliss then, the ultimate human goal, will be twofold: one within, the ultimate perfection human beings can attain, a created bliss; and one without, union with which causes that bliss within, and this is God himself, an uncreated bliss. (*CPLS,* Bk. 4, 49; *SPW,* p. 328)

> Now the activity of seeing God, which we hold human bliss to be, cannot be measured by time: neither in itself, since it has no before and after, nor on the side of the seer or the seen, since both exist outside change, . . . for seeing God transcends the native power of all creatures and is something no creature can attain by nature. What properly measures it is eternity itself; and the see-

ing of God, bliss itself, is thus eternal life. (*CPLS,* Bk. 4, 49; *SPW,* p. 332)

Ockham and Skeptical Doubts—Again

Since Augustine rebutted skepticism in the late fourth century, there had been a broad consensus that human minds were capable of knowing the truth.* Thinkers disagreed, often sharply, about what constituted the truth, but these disagreements were almost always conducted on this epistemological common ground. God had created the world, and he created human beings in his own image. It would not have been suitable for God to mismatch reality and the mind. In any case, it was through Wisdom, the *logos,* the second person of the Trinity, that everything was created. So it was natural to suppose that the patterns in reality could be reproduced in the mind.

It is true that our minds are finite and limited. We cannot discover the whole truth on our own. But God has graciously come to our aid; he has revealed to us the truths necessary for our salvation, which are beyond our finite grasp. These revealed truths, which we accept on the authority of the Scriptures and the Church, are not in conflict with the truths we can discover on our own. How could they be, since both come ultimately from the same God? Revealed truth supplements our rational knowledge, completes it, and provides an overall framework within which all correct believing and knowing are carried on.

We must add two further notes to this happy picture.

1. Knowledge is understood in that very strong classical sense delineated by Plato when he distinguishes it from opinion.† In medieval philosophy, the requirement that knowledge "stays put" or "endures" is understood to mean that it involves *absolute certainty.* If you *know* something, you are certain of it; you are not about to be shaken by any

---

*See p. 189.

*Review his arguments on pp. 233–234.
†See pp. 118–119.

stray wind that might blow some doubts your way. As with Plato, this feature is correlated with the fact that knowledge is something for which reasons can be given. The reasons are sometimes based on logic, sometimes on experience, and sometimes on the Scriptures — often on a combination of them. But there is always "an account" that can be given.

2. Knowledge, and the certainty that goes with it, is crucially important. It is absolutely essential to get it right, because your eternal salvation depends on getting it right. That is why heresy — erroneous belief — is so terrifying. The difference between correct, or orthodox, belief and heresy is the difference between *heaven* and *hell*. So it is not just an attempt to satisfy Aristotelian "wonder" that motivates the medieval theologians and philosophers.* Getting it right has an intensely personal and practical aspect.

All this is common ground in the thirteenth century. On these foundations Thomas Aquinas builds a remarkably comprehensive system of thought. We can call it a system because it is cleanly ordered, its parts are interdependent, and it aspires to completeness. The kind of confidence in the intellect that Aquinas expresses has perhaps not been seen since the time of Aristotle himself.

It is surprising to learn that this systematic synthesis, so marvelous in its way, is being undermined already in the fourteenth century. Doubts raise their ugly heads once again: doubts not about some detail, but about the very foundation that has been taken for granted in the centuries since Augustine. It is even more surprising to learn that these doubts have their source not, as you might suspect, among some atheist or agnostic folks who can't accept the claims about revealed truth, but among theologians whose orthodoxy (at least on central issues) is beyond question.[5]

Two condemnations of heretical opinions, issued in 1270 and 1277 by the bishop of Paris, Etienne Tempier, have a dramatic effect on the thought of Christian philosophers. Avicenna and Averroës had written impressive commentaries on Aristotle, which are greatly admired among Chris-

tian thinkers. They bring out, however, certain Aristotelian opinions that are in conflict with Christian doctrine. Among the Aristotelian/Arab views that are condemned are these:

- The opinion that the world is eternal (which conflicts with Christian views of creation)

- The view that, with the possible exception of certain human actions, everything happens for sufficient natural causes (which conflicts with the possibility of miracles)

- The opinion that substances are necessarily connected with their incidental properties or "accidents" (which conflicts with Catholic interpretations of the eucharist, wherein the bread and the wine are said to *become* the body and blood of Christ while retaining the "accidents" of bread and wine)

- The view that the soul is the form of a living body (which seems to conflict with individual immortality)

Aquinas, of course, struggles with these problems. He either transforms Aristotle in ways consistent with Christian doctrine or rejects certain Aristotelian views. But the condemnation has the following general effect: thinkers come to suspect that there might be a conflict between the best-reasoned view of some matter and the teachings of the Church. The authority of Aristotle in logic, natural philosophy, metaphysics, and ethics is substantial by this time. But if what Aristotle teaches can conflict with what the Church clearly teaches, thinkers will have to be much more cautious about relying on classical thought to interpret Christian doctrine.

It is important also to note that these views are not argued against. They are not shown to be mistaken by a close rational critique; they are *condemned as heretical.** Given this, it is obvious that one has to be mighty careful about relying on natural reason. Even the most conscientious use of it might lead one astray. A gulf begins to yawn between revealed truth (which these thinkers do not question)

---

*See Aristotle on wonder, p. 173.

*Compare the contrast drawn earlier between the philosopher and the prophet, p. 216.

and what the human mind could show to be true. It is not that there are two truths; it is that what seems evidently true to unaided reason might in fact not—according to the "measure" of revelation—be true. And revelation might pronounce what *seems* untrue to *be* true. The celebrated harmony between faith and reason seems on the brink of dissolving, and the message is: Philosophers beware!

In conjunction with these condemnations, increased attention is paid to one basic doctrine: the *omnipotence* of God. "I believe in one God, the Father Almighty," begins the Nicene Creed. What does this mean? During the medieval period, God's omnipotence is understood to mean that he can do anything that is not self-contradictory. He cannot make a cube with only five sides, since by definition a cube has six sides. Nor can he make something that did happen not happen; for in this case it would be true of some event *x* that *x* both happened and did not happen—and that is contradictory. But since contradictory expressions do not describe real possibilities, this is no real limitation on God's power. God can do anything that is possible. For any state of affairs that can be given a consistent description, then, God can realize that state of affairs. This doctrine is important partly because it protects the possibility of miracles.

Among those who derive some surprising consequences from this doctrine is William of Ockham (born in the 1280s and died about 1349). Ockham was English, taught at Oxford, and was embroiled in some nasty confrontations between his Franciscan order and the pope. Like all the major philosophers of the period, he thinks of himself first and foremost as a theologian. He is also a very acute logician who makes some important contributions concerning the status of logical principles and the structure of knowledge. Any adequate treatment of Ockham's thought would have to include his logic. But we will concentrate on what he says about the omnipotence of God—specifically, on the impact this doctrine has on views of the world and our knowledge of it.

Consider the following kind of case. You are sitting at a table, in good light, looking directly at a tangerine about three feet in front of your eyes. You are wide awake, not under the influence of any drugs, and are paying attention to what is before you. This seems to be the most favorable sort of case we can imagine for knowing something. We would ordinarily say that you know that there is a tangerine on the table.

But what does your knowledge consist in? It is clearly some state of yourself—what Ockham calls an "intuitive cognition." In standard cases, we think, this state is caused in part by the tangerine and in part by your sense organs and intellect. The first part of the cause is a matter of how the world is—that there happens to be a tangerine on the table. The second part is a matter of how you are—where you are, whether your eyes are open, whether you have learned what a tangerine is, and so on. In the standard case, your "intuitive cognition" of the tangerine depends both on the actual existence of a tangerine on the table and on a suitable state within you. Ockham does not deny this.

But now consider the impact that the doctrine of God's omnipotence has on this case. God, remember, can do anything that is not self-contradictory. This means that he can cause to happen anything that does not have an inconsistent description. God has created a world that operates as we have described in the foregoing standard case. But could God *directly* cause you to have that "intuitive cognition" of the tangerine? In the standard case, your experience is caused by the presence of the tangerine, but could God cause this experience without the mediation of the actual piece of fruit?

To answer this question, we must ask whether that would be self-contradictory. And it is easy to see that it is not. The presence of that piece of fruit on the table neither entails nor is entailed by your "intuitive cognition" of it. Either, so far as logic goes, could exist without the other. So, God could cause you to have such an experience even in the absence of the tangerine.

What is the consequence of this line of reasoning? Evidently, our conviction that we *know* that the tangerine exists—even in this most favorable case—is mistaken. For knowledge, remember, involves absolute certainty that could not possibly be mistaken. But if God can produce in us the internal state that is usually caused by the tangerine even in the absence of the tangerine, there is a possibility that our "intuitive cognition" is mistaken.

At best, our belief that there is a tangerine in front of us is merely *probable* belief. It amounts to no more than what Plato calls "opinion." But since all our knowledge of the world rests ultimately on such favorable cases of "intuitive cognition," the claim to know is seriously undermined.

Ockham does not draw the completely skeptical conclusion that knowledge is impossible for us. But these reflections deal a serious blow to confidence in our ability to find such absolute knowledge. And, as you can see, the blow comes from a consideration of what God's omnipotence implies.

A similar conclusion follows about the causality we claim to find in the world independent of ourselves. A piece of cloth is brought near a flame and starts to burn. How are we to explain the burning? It might be possible for God to cause it directly, so that our usual account in terms of the causal efficacy of the fire would be mistaken.* Again, the best we can do is to give probable explanations of why things happen in the world. It seems that our explanations might always be mistaken. And if that isn't skepticism itself, it surely seems to move us toward skeptical doubts, especially if one insists at the same time that knowledge must involve absolute certainty.

This produces a very interesting situation. For a thousand years thinkers assumed that reason and revelation are compatible, that reason can supply foundations—with certainty—for revelation to build upon. Philosophy, the pursuit of wisdom by our human wits, has been treated as the "handmaiden" of theology, which in turn is the "queen" of the sciences. And suddenly the suspicion arises that perhaps natural reason and experience are not well suited for this task!

Let us ask what effect this has on attempts to prove the existence of God. Such proofs are a main part of the service that philosophy is supposed to provide to theology. Ockham himself thinks that a certain form of proof is still possible, but let us consider some propositions put forward in the late fourteenth century by Pierre d'Ailly, a cardinal of the Church. He is discussing Aristotle's argument for a first mover (which was adapted by Aquinas in his "first way").[†] And he considers what a "captious debater" could say.

1. It is not unqualifiedly evident that something is moved; movement may be only apparent. . . .

2. Even if we grant that an object is in motion, we do not have to grant that it comes from some other object.

3. Granted that all motion originates in another thing and granting that there is no infinite series of movers, we cannot infer a first unmoved mover, for the first mover might be unmoved for the present but not absolutely unmovable.

4. We cannot exclude the possibility that there is a circularity of causes and effects, i.e., A causes B, B causes C, and C causes A.

5. We cannot be sure that there is no infinity of essentially ordered causes. For God by His absolute power could create such an infinite series.

6. It is not evident that if something exists anew, it was produced.

7. It is very difficult to explain what it means for one thing to be effected or produced by another thing.[6]

This piling up of alternative possibilities that have not been definitively excluded seriously undermines our confidence in the "proof." At the very least, it shows us that a defender of the argument will have to do a lot more work if the argument is to succeed. It appears much less than certain that there must be a first mover, which all men call God.

It is important to note that d'Ailly does not intend to call the existence of God into question. Far

---

*We have here an anticipation of one of the most influential of all treatments of causality, that by David Hume in the eighteenth century. Hume does not depend on the doctrine of God's omnipotence; and the skeptical consequences are more determinedly drawn. See "Causation: The Very Idea," in Chapter 15.

†See again p. 276.

from it. That God exists we know on the authority of the Scriptures and the Church. Rather, such reflections serve to undermine confidence in our natural ability to substantiate such truths apart from authority—at least with the certainty necessary for faith. (The cardinal allows that a *probable* argument for God's existence can be constructed.) Skepticism such as this, then, casts us more firmly than ever into the arms of the Church, which has such truths in its care. The moral is this: Aristotle and those who, like him, rely on our natural reason, should be approached with caution.

It seems then that the late Middle Ages is busily undoing what the earlier Middle Ages has done. It is engaging in a critique of the basic assumptions that have made the grand synthesis of classical and Christian thought possible. When several more ingredients are added to this furiously boiling pot—namely, the scientific revolution, the humanism of the Renaissance, and the impact of the Reformation on the Church—the modern era in philosophy will begin.

1. What assumptions about knowledge do thinkers in the late Middle Ages commonly make?
2. What Aristotelian views were condemned as heretical?
3. What effect did this condemnation have?
4. What impact does Ockham's reflection on God's omnipotence have on our claim to know something?
5. What impact does it seem to have on proofs for the existence of God?

For Further Thought

1. If you think Anselm's argument is faulty, write a brief explanation of what, exactly, is wrong with it.

2. What do you think about the prospects for proving that there is a God? (Don't just react. Give a reasoned explanation for your answer.)

3. Can God make a stone so heavy that he can't lift it? If he can't, does that mean his power is limited?

4. If our life is limited to this world, does that mean true happiness is impossible?

Notes

1. Jasper Hopkins, *A Companion to the Study of St. Anselm* (Minneapolis: University of Minnesota Press, 1972), 17.
2. Quotations from Anselm's *Proslogium*, in *St. Anselm: Basic Writings*, trans. S. N. Deane (La Salle, IL: Open Court, 1962), are cited in the text by chapter number.
3. Quotations from Thomas Aquinas are from one of the following:
   St. Thomas Aquinas: Philosophical Texts, trans. Thomas Gilby (London: Oxford University Press, 1951), abbreviated as *PT,* or
   Aquinas: Selected Philosophical Writings, trans. Timothy McDermott (New York: Oxford University Press, 1993), abbreviated as *SPW.*
   References are first to the source in Aquinas, then to page numbers in these collections. References to the works of Aquinas are as follows:
   ST: *Summa Theologica*
   DT: *Commentary on Boethius' De Trinitate*
   BE: *On Being and Essence*
   DPG: *Disputations on the Power of God*
   PDS: *Public Disputations on the Soul*
   CC: *Commentary on St. Paul's First Letter to the Corinthians*
   PDT: *Public Disputations on Truth*
   CPLS: *Commentary on Peter Lombard's Sentences*
   SCG: *Summa Contra Gentiles*
4. Patterson Brown, "Infinite Causal Regression," in *Aquinas: A Collection of Critical Essays,* ed. Anthony Kenny (London: Macmillan, 1969), 234–235.
5. I am especially indebted in this section to Julius R. Weinberg's *Short History of Medieval Philosophy* (Princeton, NJ: Princeton University Press, 1964).
6. Cited in Weinberg, *Short History of Medieval Philosophy,* 287–288.

CHAPTER

12

MOVING FROM MEDIEVAL TO MODERN

It is not clear just when the modern era begins. But it cannot be denied that something of
immense significance happens in the sixteenth
and seventeenth centuries that changes life and
thought startlingly. In philosophy the beginnings of
modernity are usually attributed to René Descartes
(1596–1650). Though there are other plausible
candidates for the title of "father of modern philosophy," it is the work of Descartes that sets the
agenda for most of what we call "modern" in philosophy. Despite the fact that he shares with medieval philosophers many concerns and convictions,
Descartes sees clearly that a new beginning is required. He dramatically poses fundamental questions. And, although his own answers to these
questions will satisfy few of his successors, they all
see that an answer is required. Generations of philosophers will worry about solving the problems
Descartes uncovers.

We can classify these problems under three
heads.

1. Descartes, himself a distinguished mathematician and contributor to physics, sees with blinding
clarity the need to assimilate the methods and results of the *new sciences* into our picture of the world.
Copernicus, Kepler, and Galileo had reoriented
thinking about both Earth and the heavens. Their
new conceptions clash badly with the old, so some
tearing down and rebuilding is called for.

2. Paradoxically, and to some extent accidentally, *skepticism* has arisen once more from its
ashes—this phoenix that first Plato and then Augustine sought to slay.* Fueled by Reformation
quarrels among the churches and lack of agreement
among philosophers and scientists, the doubts of
Sextus Empiricus spread rapidly among Renaissance intellectuals.† Descartes sees that skepticism
cuts at the root of the claims made by science, philosophy, and religion alike. If we are going to rely
on any one of them to tell us how things are, skepticism will have to be taken on again—and this
time killed for good.

---

*For Plato's attempt at refutation, see p. 120; for Augustine's,
pp. 233–234.
†For a discussion of ancient skepticism, featuring the views of
Sextus, see "The Skeptics," in Chapter 8.

3. Both of the first two problems mean that much closer attention will have to be paid to *knowledge*. Epistemological questions begin to take center stage. Can we know anything at all? And if so, by what means? Do the sciences give us knowledge of reality? If they do, how can we be sure of that? This preoccupation with epistemological questions is the principal heritage of Descartes. In ancient and medieval philosophy, questions about knowledge are just one sort of question among many others. But after Descartes they seem absolutely preeminent. *Unless you can solve these problems, no other problems can be solved.*

Those are Descartes' problems: the problems of modern philosophy. But to feel the force of them as problems we need to back up a bit and sketch the context. His age is intellectually, and in other ways as well, one of the most tumultuous we have ever lived through. Though we are interested primarily in the intellectual ferment, we cannot help but note some of the social, political, and economic factors that make this an age of change. It is useful to start with a review of the medieval picture of the world.

The World God Made for Us

Though there was by no means unanimity in the late Middle Ages about details, there was broad agreement about a certain picture of the world.[1] The universe, people thought, is a harmonious and coherent whole, created by an infinite and good God as an appropriate home for human beings, for whose sake it was made. It is difficult for us now to put ourselves into the place of medieval men and women and to see the world as they saw it. But let us try.

It will help if we try to set aside all we have learned in school about the structure of the universe and attempt to recapture a more direct and naive interpretation of our experience. Consider the sky as you see it on a clear day or night. If you look *at* it, rather than *through* it, as those with our picture of the world tend to do, you will almost certainly conclude that it has a certain shape. It is *something* (as our term "the sky" tends to suggest), and it has roughly the shape of an upside-down bowl. It is the roof of the earth, the "firmament" of Genesis 1 that God created to separate the primeval waters and make a place for dry land and living creatures. This view of the heavens is very common among primitive people and among children, too. We have to *learn* that the sky is not a thing.

This primitive view of the sky undergoes a great deal of rather sophisticated development by the later Middle Ages, but two things remain constant. It is still considered a thing, and its nature is defined in terms of its relation to the earth. The development is largely due to the efforts of ancient philosophers (particularly Plato and Aristotle) and astronomers, especially an Egyptian astronomer of the second century A.D., named Ptolemy. How do they modify this primitive view?

For one thing, the earth is recognized to be roughly a sphere, so the heavens can't be completely analogous to the roof of a house or a tent. They, in fact, are spherical, too. The basic picture is of two spheres, the smaller one solid and stationary directly in the center of a much larger sphere, which is hollow and moving. The sphere in the center is, of course, the earth. And the outer sphere, composed of aether, a crystalline, weightless solid, is that of the stars, which revolve around the inner sphere once each day.

Astronomical observations complicate this picture considerably. Neither the sun nor the moon fits neatly into such a scheme, and they are given spheres of their own. Even more recalcitrant to neatness are those wanderers in the heavens, the planets. They seem to move in more complicated patterns, both speed and direction varying at irregular times. Much astronomical ingenuity had been devoted to the mathematical description of their paths; postulations of circles revolving around centers that are themselves revolving on circles are used to solve these problems. But the basic pattern is the same: Each planet is assigned an etherial sphere. Saturn occupies the sphere just below that of the fixed stars, and the moon occupies that nearest to the earth, with the sun and the other planets arranged between.

This universe is said to be finite. Aristotle holds that beyond the outer sphere there is literally nothing—no matter, no space, not even a void.* For medieval Christians, however, there is something beyond the sphere of the stars. It is often called simply heaven, but sometimes also the Empyrean, the place of perfect fire or light; it is the dwelling place of God and the destination of saved souls. (Note that heaven, in this view, has a physical location. From the earth, it is *up*.)

In this universe, everything has its natural place. The earth is the center toward which heavy objects naturally fall. The heavy elements, earth and water, find their natural place as near this center as they can. The lighter elements, air and fire, have a natural home between the earth and the sphere of the moon. But these four elements are continually being mixed up with one another and suffer constant change.

This change is explained by the motions of the heavens.† Aristotle supplies a mechanism to explain such change. The outermost celestial sphere rotates at great speed, as it must to return to the same position in only twenty-four hours. (Compare the speed at the inside of a merry-go-round with that at its edge.) This motion drags the sphere of Saturn (just inside it) along by friction; and this process is repeated all the way to the spheres of the sun and moon. These then produce changes in the air and on the earth: the tides, the winds, and the seasons, for example, and the generation of plants and animals. We may wonder, though: Why does the sphere of the stars move? Dante, whose *Divine Comedy* is a perfect expression of this view of the world,

offers an Aristotelian explanation in terms of final causes.

> Beyond all these [crystalline spheres], the Catholics place the Empyrean Heaven . . . , and they hold it to be immovable, because it has within itself, in every part, that which its matter demands. And this is the reason that the *Primum Mobile* [or ninth sphere] moves with immense velocity; because the fervent longing of all its parts to be united with those of this most quiet heaven, makes it revolve with so much desire that its velocity is almost incomprehensible.[2]

The celestial spheres are quite different from anything on Earth. Here on Earth, all is subject to change, generation, and decay. But the spheres in which the heavenly bodies are located revolve in immutable splendor. Only one conclusion can be drawn: Terrestrial and celestial substances are made of different stuff and governed by different laws. Spiritual beings—angels, for instance, whom Aquinas holds to be pure forms without matter—have their home in these more perfect regions.

It is obvious—consider only the sun—that what happens in these spheres affects conditions on earth. Medievals drew the conclusion that signs in the heavens—comets and eclipses, for instance—are omens that need interpretation. What they mean is scarcely distinguishable from what the spiritual beings that dwell in those regions mean to convey. Virtually every astronomer is also an astrologer; as late as the seventeenth century, Kepler, recognized to possess unusually accurate astronomical data, is consulted for horoscopes, and reference to astrological phenomena is common in the work of Dante and Chaucer. Everything in the heavens is significant because it all exists for the sake of man.

Here we come to the heart of the medieval worldview. The earth is not only the physical center of the universe; it is also the religious center. For on this stationary globe lives the human race, made in the image of God himself, the summit of his creative work. Around human beings everything revolves, both literally and symbolically. The earth is the stage whereon is enacted the great drama of salvation and damnation. It is on the earth that human beings fall from grace. It is to the earth that

---

*Aristotle does not accept the atomists' conception of a *void*, that is, a space in which nothing exists. His reasoning depends on the notion of potentiality. Wherever there is space, there is potentially some substance. But potentiality is just the possibility of having some form; and what is formed into a substance is matter. So wherever there is space there is matter; matter never exists unformed; so the idea of empty space is a contradiction in terms. There could not be other worlds out in space beyond this world; this world is not just the only world there is, but the only world there *could be*.

†See the pre-Socratic speculations about the vortex, pp. 13–14.

God's Son comes to redeem fallen men and women and lead them to that heavenly realm in which they can forever enjoy blessedness in light eternal.

Nothing expresses this drama in its intimate connection with the medieval picture of the world better than Dante's great poem.* The journey on which he is led, first by Virgil and later by Beatrice, traverses the known universe. As we follow that journey we learn both physical and religious truths, inextricably linked. Let us trace the outline of that journey.

Dante begins his great poem by telling us that he had lost his way and could not find it again. (Suggestion: read the poetry aloud.)

> Midway life's journey I was made aware
> That I had strayed into a dark forest,
> And the right path appeared not anywhere.
> Ah, tongue cannot describe how it oppressed,
> This wood, so harsh, dismal and wild, that fear
> At thought of it strikes now into my breast.
> —*Inferno* 1.1–6[3]

The pagan poet Virgil appears and offers to lead him down through hell and up through purgatory as far as the gates of heaven. There he will be supplanted by another guide, as Virgil is not allowed into paradise. A vision of these moral and religious realities, embedded as they are in the very nature of things, should resolve Dante's crisis and show him the way again. It may also serve as a guide to the blessed life for all who read the poem.

We can read this complex allegory with an eye only to the values it expresses, but there is little doubt that Dante means its cosmology to be taken with equal seriousness. The point we need to see is that the cosmos, as envisaged by late medieval thinkers, is not an indifferent and valueless place; every detail speaks of its creator, and the "right path" is inscribed in the very structure of things.

We can do no more than briefly indicate that structure. There are three books in the poem: *Inferno, Purgatorio,* and *Paradiso.* In each a portion of the

physical and moral/religious universe is explored. The first thing to note is that to get to hell (the inferno), one goes *down*—deep into the earth. Hell is a complex place of many layers; as one descends, the sins of its occupants become more serious, the punishments more awful, and the conditions more revolting. After an antechamber in which the indifferent reside (offensive both to God and to Satan), Dante and Virgil cross the river Acheron and find hell set up as a series of circles, descending ever deeper into the earth. The first circle is limbo, in which are found the virtuous pagans, including Homer and Aristotle; this is Virgil's own home. Here there is no overt punishment; only the lack of hope for blessedness.

Descending from limbo, they find the damned in circles of increasingly awful punishments, corresponding to their sins:

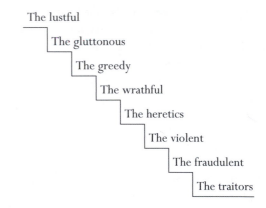

These last are frozen up to their necks in ice at the very center of the earth, guarded over by Satan—the arch traitor—in whose three mouths are the mangled bodies of Judas, Brutus, and Cassius.

Virgil and Dante climb down past Satan and climb up again through a passage in the earth until they come out on the opposite side from which they began. There they find themselves on a shore, facing a mountain that rises to the sky. This is the mountain of purgatory, where those who will ultimately be saved are purified of their remaining faults. Here there are seven levels (corresponding to the "seven deadly sins"), each populated by persons whose

---

*Dante's *Divine Comedy* was written in the first decades of the fourteenth century.

loves are not yet rightly ordered.* These have re-
pented and will be saved, but they still love earthly
things too much, or not enough, or in the wrong
way. From the lower levels to the higher, the un-
purged sins are ranked from more to less serious,
those highest on the mountain being farthest from
hell and closest to heaven. Let us list them in that
"geographical" order, so that we can imagine Virgil
and Dante mounting from the bottom of the list to
the top:

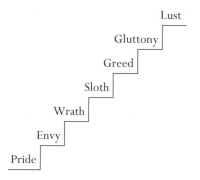

Those who dwell at each level are purging
their predominant passion by suffering penances of
an appropriate kind. The proud, for example, are
bowed down by carrying heavy stones, so that they
can neither look arrogantly about nor look down
on their fellows. It is worth noting that the "spiritual" sins of pride, envy, and anger are judged to
be more serious (farther from heaven) than the
"fleshly" sins of gluttony and lust; this ranking
roughly corresponds to the evaluations of church
fathers such as Augustine, for whom pride is the
root of all sin.†

At the top of the purgatorial mountain, Virgil
disappears, and Beatrice, who represents Christian
love, takes his place. She transports Dante through
the sphere of fire above the earth to the lowest celestial sphere, that of the moon. She answers Dante's
question about why the moon seems to have shad-

ows on it and in the process gives a fine description
of the celestial realm, which looks roughly like this:

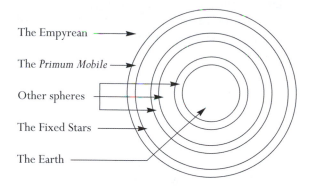

You can see that it conforms nicely to the Aristotelian / Ptolemic astronomical view we sketched
earlier. Motion (energy) is imparted from outside
toward the center, each of the spheres displaying in
its own magnificent way the glory of God. This vision of the heavens as the visible image of the creator is summed up in the first canto of *Paradiso*.

> The glory of Him who moveth all that is
>   Pervades the universe, and glows more bright
>   In the one region, and in another less. . . .
>
> "All things, whatever their abode, [*Beatrice says*]
>   Have order among themselves; this Form it is
>   That makes the universe like unto God.
> Here the high beings see the imprint of His
>   Eternal power, which is the goal divine
>   Whereto the rule, aforesaid testifies.
> In the order I speak of, all natures incline
>   Either more near or less near to their source
>   According as their diverse lots assign.
> To diverse harbors thus they move perforce
>   O'er the great ocean of being, and each one
>   With instinct given it to maintain its course."
>   —*Paradiso* 1.1–3, 103–114

The spheres of paradise which Beatrice leads
Dante through correspond to the various virtues,
though Dante is careful to say that the appearance
of the souls of the virtuous in each sphere is not to
be taken literally. One and all, blessed souls inhabit
the Empyrean realm with God himself.

The key notions in Dante's vision of the universe are order, harmony, justice, and, finally, love.

---

*For the concept of a proper ordering of one's loves, see Augus-
tine, p. 247.
†For Augustine on pride, see pp. 249–250.

The poem ends with Dante trying to describe, inadequately he admits, the vision of God. This vision is both intelligible and emotional. Its object both explains the universe and draws Dante's soul toward itself. In the end, imagination fails to communicate the glory.

> But like to a wheel whose circling nothing jars
> Already on my desire and will prevailed
> The Love that moves the sun and the other stars.
> —*Paradiso* 33.143–145

Such is the world for late medieval man: harmonious, ordered, finite, displaying the glories of its creator. Physics, astronomy, and theology are one in a marvelous integration of life and knowledge. Everything in the universe embodies a goal and purpose set within it by the divine love, which governs all. To understand it is to understand this purpose, to gain guidance for life, and to see that absolutely everything depends on and leads to God.

---

1. Describe the Aristotelian / Ptolemaic picture of the universe.
2. Why, given that picture of the universe, is it appropriate for Virgil and Beatrice to take Dante on a tour of the world in order to show him "the right path"?
3. What do the levels in hell and purgatory show us about virtue and vice?

The Humanists

That magnificent flowering of arts and letters we call the Renaissance is greatly influenced by the rediscovery of classical literature—poetry, histories, essays, and other writings—that followed the recovery of Aristotelian philosophy.* These Greek and Roman works breathe a spirit quite different from the extreme otherworldliness of monk's vows, on the one hand, and the arid disputations of scholastic theologians on the other. They present a model of style, both in language and life, that seems worthy of emulation. And a rather diffuse movement called "humanism" spreads gradually northward from Italy.

Some of the humanists are churchmen, but many are not. They belong to that aristocratic stratum of society that has leisure to cultivate the arts, paint, compose, or write. They are not, on the whole, antagonistic to the Church; nor do most of them pit the old pagan classical works against Christianity. On the contrary, they tend to see a profound harmony between Christianity and the classics. In this they are, of course, following in the steps of Augustine and Aquinas.* But there is a difference. These theologians hold that pagan philosophy can be a servant to Christian understanding—but never its equal. Many humanists, however, equate faith with virtue and move toward a kind of universalism: The virtuous sage is blessed, whether he knows of Christ as savior or not.

In a dialogue called "The Godly Feast," printed in 1522, Erasmus (the "prince of humanists") has one of the characters say,

> Whatever is devout and contributes to good morals should not be called profane. Sacred Scripture is of course the basic authority in everything; yet I sometimes run across ancient sayings or pagan writings—even the poets—so purely and reverently and admirably expressed that I can't help believing their authors' hearts were moved by some divine power. And perhaps the spirit of Christ is more widespread than we understand, and the company of saints includes many not in our calendar.[4]

One of his partners in the conversation, on being reminded of Socrates' attitude at his death, exclaims,†

---

*For the Renaissance see http://en.wikipedia.org/wiki/Renaissance.

*To see how Augustine used Platonic philosophy in the service of the faith, see pp. 238–241. Aquinas did much the same for Aristotle.

†Contrast this with Dante's vision two hundred years earlier, in which virtuous pagans are consigned—at best—to limbo. See *Inferno,* canto IV. For the last moments of Socrates' life, see *Phaedo,* pp. 113–116.

An admirable spirit, surely, in one who had not known Christ and the Sacred Scriptures. And so, when I read such things of such men, I can hardly help exclaiming, "Saint Socrates, pray for us!"[5]

In another dialogue, "The Epicurean," Erasmus argues that those who spend their lives pursuing fine food, sex, wealth, fame, and power in a quest for pleasure actually miss the greatest pleasures: those of righteousness, moderation, an active mind, and a calm conscience. It is Epicurus, of course, who holds that pleasure is the one true good.[*] It follows that the *successful* Epicurean—the one who gets the most pleasure out of life—will live righteously and moderately, preferring the approval of God to the satisfaction of bodily appetites. But these are precisely the virtues cultivated by the Christian!

> If people who live agreeably are Epicureans, none are more truly Epicurean than the righteous and godly. And if it's names that bother us, no one better deserves the name of Epicurean than the revered founder and head of the Christian philosophy [Christ], for in Greek *epikouros* means "helper." He alone, when the law of Nature was all but blotted out by sins, when the law of Moses incited to lusts rather than cured them, when Satan ruled in the world unchallenged, brought timely aid to perishing humanity. Completely mistaken, therefore, are those who talk in their foolish fashion about Christ's having been sad and gloomy in character and calling upon us to follow a dismal mode of life. On the contrary, he alone shows the most enjoyable life of all and the one most full of true pleasure.[6]

This gives us an insight into why these thinkers are called humanists.[†] Their concern is the development of a full and rich human life—the best life for a human being to live. Their quest is stimulated by the works of classical antiquity, which they read, edit, translate, and imitate with eagerness. They live, of course, in a culture dominated by Christianity and express that quest in basically Christian terms, but their interests focus on the human. To that end they recommend and propagandize for what they call "humane studies": an education centering on the Greek and Latin classics, on languages, grammar, and rhetoric. They are convinced that "the classics represent the highest level of human development."[7]

The ideal is a person who can embody all the excellences a human being is capable of: music, art, poetry, science, soldiery, courtesy, virtue, and piety. This renewed passion for human excellence is expressed in the art of Bellini, Titian, Tintoretto, Raphael, Holbein, Dürer, and Michelangelo. In these Renaissance painters and sculptors, one finds the ideal human form, often in an idealized natural setting—whether the subject is the Christian Madonna and child or Greek gods and heroes. And sometimes classical and biblical themes are found in the same painting.[*] The man who embodies this Renaissance ideal most completely is perhaps Leonardo da Vinci. His many accomplishments show what humans are capable of. He represents what humanists admired and worked for: a celebration of the human being as the central fact in all the created world.

In the 1480s, a twenty-four-year-old Italian wrote a preface to nine hundred theses that he submitted for public debate. As it turned out, the debate was never held, but the *Oration on the Dignity of Man* by Giovanni Pico della Mirandola has seldom been equalled as a rhetorical tribute to the glory of being human. We could say it is the apotheosis of humanism. Pico finds the unique dignity of man in the fact that human beings alone have no "archetype" they are predetermined to exemplify. Everything else has a determinate nature, but it is man's privilege to be able to *choose* his own nature. He imagines God creating the world. All is complete, from the intelligences above the heavens to the lowest reaches of earth.

---

[*]See pp. 199–200.

[†]Note that Erasmus here follows the lead of much Greek thought, from Homer to Epicurus. Pursuit of virtue is recommended on ground of *self-interest*. Why be moral? Because you will be happier that way. See the following pages: for Plato, pp. 145–148; for Aristotle, pp. 195–196; for Epicurus, pp. 203–204.

---

[*]We already find this unification in Dante, but there the classical is still severely subordinated to the Christian.

But, when the work was finished, the Craftsman kept wishing that there were someone to ponder the plan of so great a work, to love its beauty, and to wonder at its vastness. Therefore, when everything was done. . . . He finally took thought concerning the creation of man. But there was not among His archetypes that from which He could fashion a new offspring, nor was there in His treasurehouses anything which He might bestow on His new son as an inheritance, nor was there in the seats of all the world a place where the latter might sit to contemplate the universe. All was now complete. . . .

At last the best of artisans ordained that that creature to whom He had been able to give nothing proper to himself should have joint possession of whatever had been peculiar to each of the different kinds of being. He therefore took man as a creature of indeterminate nature and, assigning him a place in the middle of the world, addressed him thus: "Neither a fixed abode nor a form that is thine alone nor any function peculiar to thyself have we given thee, Adam, to the end that according to thy longing and according to thy judgment thou mayest have and possess what abode, what form and what functions thou thyself shalt desire. The nature of all other beings is limited and constrained within the bounds of laws prescribed by Us. Thou, constrained by no limits, in accordance with thine own free will, in whose hand We have placed thee, shalt ordain for thyself the limits of thy nature. We have set thee at the world's center that thou mayest from thence more easily observe whatever is in the world. We have made thee neither of heaven nor of earth, neither mortal nor immortal, so that with freedom of choice and with honor, as though the maker and molder of thyself, thou mayest fashion thyself in whatever shape thou shalt prefer. Thou shalt have the power to degenerate into the lower forms of life, which are brutish. Thou shalt have the power, out of thy soul's judgment, to be reborn into the higher forms, which are divine."

O supreme generosity of God the Father, O highest and most marvelous felicity of man! To him it is granted to have whatever he chooses, to be whatever he wills.[8]

Man as "maker and molder" of himself, able "to have whatever he chooses, to be whatever he wills." What a concept! Pico exclaims, "Who would not admire this our chameleon?"[9] With such possibilities open to them, it is no wonder that human beings should develop in so many different ways. Along with the theme of an essential unity that runs through humanity, the diversity of individuals comes to be valued more and more. Individualism, the idea that there is value to sheer uniqueness, begins to counter the uniformity of Christian schemes of salvation. Portrait painters strive to capture the unique character of each of their subjects, and variety and invention flourish in music and literature.

Finally, the humanists recapture some of the confidence that had characterized Athenians of the Golden Age. Human failings are more apt to be caricatured as foolishness (as Erasmus satirically did in *Praise of Folly*) than to be condemned as sins. And this reveals a quite different attitude and spirit. Though the humanists do not deny sin and God's grace, they tend to focus on our capability to achieve great things. As often happens in such cases, they thereby help to make great things happen.

1. What rediscoveries stimulate the movement we know as Renaissance humanism?
2. Describe the ideal human life, as pictured by the humanists.
3. In what feature of human beings does Pico della Mirandola find their "dignity"?

Reforming the Church

The worldview Dante expresses in his great poem was institutionalized in the Church. The Church was the keeper and protector of Christian truths and the harbor of salvation for those at sea in sin. But the institutional Church had strayed far from the precepts of humility and love enjoined by Jesus. It had become a means of securing worldly prestige, power, and wealth for those who were clever and ruthless enough to bend it to their will.

The Church in the West was dominated by the papacy in Rome, whose occupants had, through the centuries, succeeded in bringing under their control a great variety of incomes, privileges, and powers. Popes were continually engaged in political intrigues to establish and extend their power. More than one pope during this period exceeded in influence, wealth, and power any secular prince, king, or emperor. His court was more splendid, his staff more extensive, and his will more feared than theirs. For a king could, if need be, torture and kill the body; but the pope had the power to cast the soul into hell. If displeased with a monarch, the pope could put an entire land under the "interdict," which meant that no masses and no sacraments could be celebrated there—a dire threat indeed for those who depended on them for their eternal salvation.

No one doubts—and few doubted even then—that the Church had grown corrupt. Already in the fourteenth century Dante had set several popes, bishops, friars, and priests in the Inferno. There had been numerous attempts at reform. The establishment of new monastic orders by Saint Francis and Saint Dominic had been motivated by a desire to recapture the purity of Christian life by renouncing wealth and power. Unfortunately, their very success ensured the acquisition of wealth and power, with all the inevitable outcomes. Heretical groups, such as the Albigenses in southern France, mixed moral rigor with unacceptable theologies. (The Albigenses were exterminated after a twenty-year "crusade" called for by Pope Innocent III.)

The notorious Inquisition was established in 1231 under Pope Gregory IX, and heresy hunting gained official sanction. Heresy was considered "the greatest of all sins because it was an affront to the greatest of persons, God; worse than treason against a king because it was directed against the heavenly sovereign; worse than counterfeiting money because it counterfeited the truth of salvation; worse than patricide and matricide, which destroy only the body." If a heretic recanted under torture, he "might be granted the mercy of being strangled before being burned at the stake."[10]

From a philosophical point of view, we should note that the institution known as the Inquisition rests on several presuppositions: (1) that truth about God and man not only can be known, but is clearly identifiable and available to all; (2) that it is the Church who is the custodian of this truth; and

(3) that whether one affirms these truths or not *matters terribly*. Perhaps even these assumptions do not suffice to justify such extreme measures, but it is clear both that these were actually in the background and that nothing less than these will do. These assumptions are the heritage of that blend of Judeo–Christian prophetism and classical Greek philosophy worked out first by Augustine using the Platonic tradition and later by Thomas Aquinas using the Aristotelian. A further (but not irrelevant) question is to what extent the Inquisition was simply a technique used by those in power for consolidating their power and suppressing dissent.

Unless they could be assimilated into the structure of the Church, as the monastic orders were, reformers were harshly dealt with. The followers of John Wycliffe in England (the Lollards) were sent to the stake in 1401. Jan (John) Hus of Bohemia was burned in 1415. Savonarola of Florence was hanged and then burned in 1498. Meanwhile the Church, clutching its pomp and privileges, went from corruption to corruption. Here are a few examples. Pope Alexander VI had four illegitimate children (including Cesare and Lucrezia Borgia), though clerical celibacy was the rule. Pope Julius II led his own troops in armor to regain certain papal territories. And Leo X, made a cardinal through family influence at the age of thirteen, is said to have exclaimed after his election as pope, "The papacy is ours. Let us enjoy it."[11]

Albert of Brandenburg, already bishop of two districts, aspired to be also Archbishop of Mainz, which would make him the top cleric in Germany. The price demanded by the pope was high—ten thousand ducats. Because his parishes could not supply that fee, he paid it himself, borrowing the money at 20 percent interest from the banking house of Fugger. It was agreed that "indulgences" (more about these later) would be sold in his territories; half of the income he could use to repay the loan and half would go to Rome to help build Saint Peter's Cathedral.

Such examples, which could be multiplied indefinitely, called forth a steady stream of critical responses. In the eyes of many, they discredited the claim of the Church to be the repository of truth about God and man. But it was not until the protests of Martin Luther (1483–1546) that the situation was ripe for such moral objections to make a real difference. Luther's appeal for reform coincided with a new assertion of the rights of nations against domination by the Church. Princes heard not only the cry for religious reform but also an opportunity to stop wealth and power from flowing interminably to Rome.*

It was religious reform that Luther was interested in, but he could address the German nobility in terms that encouraged them to think of papal taxes, fees, and benefits as exploitation of the German people. For example,

> If ninety-nine per cent of the papal court were abolished and only one per cent were left, it would still be large enough to deal with questions of Christian faith. At present there is a crawling mass of reptiles, all claiming to pay allegiance to the pope, but Babylon never saw the like of these miscreants. The pope has more than 3,000 secretaries alone, and no one can count the others he employs, as the posts are so numerous. It is hardly possible to number all those that lie in wait for the institutions and benefices of Germany, like wolves for the sheep. . . . It is not at all astonishing if princes, aristocracy, towns, institutions, country, and people grow poor. We ought to marvel that we still have anything left to eat.[12]

This is strong stuff, and it had its effect. But it is a *consequence* of Luther's views and not the heart of them. We need to understand the religious center from which such protests arose.

Luther was a monk troubled about his sins and in mortal terror of God's justice. His sins did not in fact seem so terrible in the eyes of the world, for he was a monk of a most sincere and strict kind. But he had early seen the point that God looks not at externals, but at motivations; and he could not be sure that his motives were pure.[†] No matter how much he confessed, he was never confident that he had searched out every tinge of selfishness, greed,

lust, and pride. And these sins the righteous God would judge. Luther did penances of a rigorous sort, going so far as to scourge himself. But he could never be sure: Had he done enough to make himself worthy of salvation? He suffered agonies of doubt and self-accusation.

> Though I lived as a monk without reproach, I felt that I was a sinner before God with an extremely disturbed conscience. I could not believe that he was placated by my satisfaction. I did not love, yes, I hated the righteous God who punishes sinners, and secretly, if not blasphemously, certainly murmuring greatly, I was angry with God.[13]

He was assigned by his superior to study the Bible and become a professor of theology. As he wrestled with the text of the Psalms and the letters of Saint Paul, it gradually dawned on him that his anxieties about sin were misplaced. He was, to be sure, a sinner. But the righteous God, whom Luther had so much feared, had sent Jesus, his Son, the Christ, precisely to win forgiveness for such sinners. This was an undeserved gift of grace and needed only to be believed to be effective. Even though one was not just, God "justified" the unjust person by means of the cross and resurrection of Christ, who had taken upon himself the sins of the world. Salvation did not have to be *earned!* It was a *gift!*

> I began to understand that the righteousness of God is that by which the righteous lives by a gift of God, namely by faith. And this is the meaning: the righteousness of God is revealed by the gospel, namely, the passive righteousness with which merciful God justifies us by faith, as it is written, "He who through faith is righteous shall live." Here I felt that I was altogether born again and had entered paradise itself through open gates. . . .
>
> Thus that place in Paul was for me truly the gate to paradise. Later I read Augustine's *The Spirit and the Letter,* where contrary to hope I found that he, too, interpreted God's righteousness in a similar way, as the righteousness with which God clothes us when he justifies us.[14]

With this insight, the Reformation was born. The power of this idea was first demonstrated in relation to the indulgences being sold under the authority of the pope and Archbishop Albert of Mainz.

---

*For the Reformation, see http://www.newgenevacenter.org/west/reformation.htm.

†See the discussion of Jesus on pp. 222–223, and the similar point made by Augustine on pp. 247–248 and 256. It is perhaps significant that Luther was a monk of the Augustinian order.

An *indulgence* was a piece of paper assuring the purchaser of the remission of certain penalties—perhaps in this life, perhaps in purgatory, and perhaps escape from hell itself. The practice of promising such spiritual benefits in return for worldly goods can be traced back to the Crusades. Popes offered heavenly blessings in return for military service in the Holy Land against the Turks. But for those who could not serve or were reluctant to go, a payment in cash to support the effort was accepted instead. This practice had proved so lucrative that, as we have seen, it was extended for other purposes—including the repayment of loans for the purchase of an archbishopric!

The set of indulgences sponsored by Albert were peddled in 1517 by a Dominican monk named Tetzel, who advertised his wares with a jingle:

> As soon as the coin in the coffer rings,
> The soul from purgatory springs.[15]

Although prohibited in Wittenberg, where Luther was both parish priest and teacher of theology, indulgences were sold near enough that his parishioners traveled to buy them. They came back boasting that they could now do what they liked, for they were guaranteed heaven. Luther was troubled. Was this Christianity—to buy salvation for a few gold coins? Didn't this make a mockery of repentance and the attempt to reform one's life? Indeed, didn't it make a mockery of God's grace, which was sold for worldly gain like any other commodity? On the eve of All Saints' Day, 1517, Luther posted ninety-five theses on the door of the Castle Church. He had drafted them quickly and meant them only to form the substance of a scholarly debate among theologians. But they caused a sensation, escaped his control, and were published and disseminated widely. Among the theses were these:

> 27. There is no divine authority for preaching that the soul flies out of purgatory immediately the money clinks in the bottom of the chest.
> . . .
> 36. Any Christian whatsoever, who is truly repentant enjoys plenary remission from penalty and guilt, and this is given him without letters of indulgence.
> . . .

> 43. Christians should be taught that one who gives to the poor, or lends to the needy, does a better action than if he purchases indulgences.
> . . .
> 44. Because, by works of love, love grows and a man becomes a better man; whereas, by indulgences, he does not become a better man, but only escapes certain penalties.[16]

Let us think about Thesis 27 for a moment. Here Luther says there is no "divine authority" for Tetzel's rhyme. What does he mean by this? There clearly was ecclesiastical authority for it, at least in the sense that the selling of the indulgences was sponsored by an archbishop and the pope. But for Luther, who had spent five years trying to understand the Bible and who knew well the works of the early Church fathers, particularly Augustine, this does not settle the matter at all. It didn't take a great deal of historical knowledge to discover that popes and councils of the Church had disagreed with one another and were often flatly in disagreement with the words of Scripture. So the fact that the practice was backed by the highest Church authority is just that for Luther—a fact. It does not make the practice *right*. Only a *divine* authority can determine that.*

What, then, does Luther mean by "divine authority"? Above all, he means the words and deeds of Christ. But secondarily, he means the testimony of the apostles who had known Jesus or of those (like Paul) to whom Christ had specially revealed himself. So Luther appeals to the Bible, that collection of the earliest records we have of the life and impact of Jesus. This was Luther's authority, against which the words of archbishops and popes alike had to be measured.

It is precisely here that his conflict with the established Church is sharpest. In a certain sense, the Church does not deny that Scripture is the ultimate authority; however, Scripture needs to be interpreted. And the proper interpretation of Scripture, according to the Church, is that given by the Church itself in the *tradition* that reaches back in a long, unbroken historical sequence to the apostles.

---

*Compare the speech in which Antigone defends her action defying the king's command, p. 47.

Ultimately the authority to interpret Scripture resides in the pope, the successor of the apostle Peter, of whom Jesus had said, "You are Peter, and on this rock I will build my church" (Matt. 16:18).

In an interview with Cardinal Cajetan (during the tumult over indulgences) the cardinal reminded Luther of these points. Luther was unmoved. "'His Holiness abuses Scripture,' retorted Luther. 'I deny that he is above Scripture.' The cardinal flared up and bellowed that Luther should leave and never come back unless he was ready to say, '*Revoco*'—'I recant.'"[17]

In a great debate at Leipzig in 1519, Luther went as far as to say,

> A simple layman armed with Scripture is to be believed above a pope or a council without it.

His opponent in the debate replied,

> When Brother Luther says that this is the true meaning of the text, the pope and councils say, "No, the brother has not understood it correctly." Then I will take the council and let the brother go. Otherwise all the heresies will be renewed. They have all appealed to Scripture and have believed their interpretation to be correct, and have claimed that the popes and the councils were mistaken, as Luther now does.[18]

This exchange gives the tenor of the arguments that continued for about four years while the Church was trying to decide what to do about the rebel. Luther appeals to the Scriptures against the pope and the ecclesiastical establishment. They in turn point out the damaging consequences—heresy and the destruction of the unity of Christendom—if Luther is allowed to be right.

In 1521 Luther was formally excommunicated from the Church, and the split between "Protestants" and "Roman Catholics" became official. There is much more to this story, but we have enough before us to draw some lessons relevant to our philosophical conversation.

For more than a thousand years there had been a basic agreement in the West about how to settle questions of truth. Some questions could be settled by reason and experience; the great authority on these matters for the past few centuries had been Aristotle, whom Aquinas had called simply "the

philosopher." But above these questions were others—the key questions about God and the soul and the meaning of life—which were answered by *authority,* not reason. And the authority had been that of the Church, as embedded in the decision-making powers of its clergy, focused ultimately in the papacy.

When Luther challenges this authority, he attacks the very root of a whole culture. It is no wonder that there is so much opposition. His appeal to the authority of Scripture sets up a standard for settling those higher questions that is different from the accepted one. And we can now see that the crisis Luther precipitates is a form of the old skeptical *problem of the criterion,* one of the deepest and most radical problems in our intellectual life.* By what criterion or standard are we going to tell when we know the truth? If a criterion is proposed, how do we know that it is the right one? Is there a criterion for choosing the criterion?

In the religious disputes of the following century, each side busies itself in demolishing the claims of the other side. On the one hand, Protestants show that if we accept the Catholic criterion, we can be sure of nothing because—as Luther points out—popes and councils disagree with one another. If there are contradictions in the criterion itself, how can we choose which of the contradictory propositions to accept? Moreover, popes had certainly sanctioned abuses contrary to the spirit of the Scriptures, so the claim that the interpretations of the Church constitute the criterion seems more and more hollow.

Catholics, on the other hand, argue that reliance on one's individual conscience after reading Scripture could not produce certainty, for the conscience of one person may not agree with the conscience of another. Indeed, it is not long before the Protestants are as divided among themselves as they are united in opposing the Catholics. Luther's assumption that Scripture speaks unambiguously enough to serve *of itself* as a criterion begins to look rather naive, and the Roman Catholic insistence on

---

*For a discussion of the problem about the criterion, see pp. 211–213.

the need for an authoritative interpreter of Scripture seems to be supported by the chaotic course of events.

The consequence is that each side appeals to a criterion that is not accepted by the other side, but neither can find a criterion to decide which of these criteria is the correct one!

This quarrel, moreover, is not just an intellectual and religious debate. A series of savage and bloody quasi-religious wars ensues, in which princes try not only to secure territories, but also to determine the religion of the people residing in them.* Indeed, one outcome of these wars is that southern Germany is to this day overwhelmingly Catholic, whereas northern Germany is largely Protestant.

What the Reformation does, philosophically speaking, is to unsettle the foundations. Though the reformers only intend to call an erring Church back to its true and historical foundations, the consequences are lasting divisiveness, with those on each side certain of their own correctness and of the blindness (or wickedness) of their opponents. This unsettling of the foundations by the reformers is one of the factors that lies behind Descartes' attempt to sink the piles so deep that beliefs built on them could never again be shaken.

But these disputes of the Reformation are not the only source of Descartes' concern. We must consider next the revival of skeptical thought in the sixteenth century.

---

1. In what ways had the Church grown corrupt?
2. What does Luther find in the New Testament that leads to his objection to indulgences?
3. To what authority does Luther appeal?
4. How did the challenge posed by the Reformation raise again the problem of the criterion?

---

*Here you may be reminded of Socrates' point in *Euthyphro* 7b–d: The gods do not quarrel about length and weight and such matters, but about good and justice. Where there are accepted criteria (rules of measurement, for instance) for settling disputes, wars are unlikely. But where there are apparently irresolvable disagreements, involving appeal to differing standards, might may seem like the only thing that *can* make right.

Skeptical Thoughts Revived

As we have noted, the recovery of ancient scientific and philosophical texts (in particular, the works of Aristotle) was followed by the recovery of Greek and Roman poetry, histories, and essays. Somewhat later still, another rediscovery exerted an influence.[19] In 1562 the first Latin edition of a work by Sextus Empiricus was published, and within seven years all his writings were available.* Sextus calls his views "Pyrrhonism," after one of the earliest Greek skeptics, Pyrrho. In this period of divisiveness and strife between Catholics and Protestants, Pyrrhonism strikes a responsive chord in more than one thinker who considers that an impasse has been reached, but we will focus on just one man: Michel de Montaigne.

Montaigne (1533–1592) was a Frenchman of noble birth who, after spending some years in public service as a magistrate, retired at the age of thirty-eight to think and write. His essays are one of the glories of French literature. We are interested not in his style, however, but in his ideas—ideas that a great many people begin to find attractive in the late sixteenth and early seventeenth centuries.

His point of view comes out most clearly in a remarkable essay called *Apology for Raymond Sebond*. Sebond had been a theologian of the fifteenth century who had exceeded the claims of Augustine, Anselm, and Aquinas by claiming not only that the existence and nature of God could be proved by reason, but that rational proofs could be given for *all* the distinctive doctrines of Christianity. This is an astonishing claim; if true, it would mean that clear thinking alone would suffice to convince us all (Jews, Muslims, and pagans alike) that we should be Christians. No one had ever gone so far before. And, as you can imagine, Sebond attracted critics like clover attracts bees.

In his youth, Montaigne had translated Sebond's book into French, at his father's request. Much later, he set out to defend Sebond's thesis. ("Apology" here means "defense," as it does in the title of

---

*For a discussion of the skeptical philosophy of Sextus, see Chapter 8.

Plato's account of Socrates' trial.) It is an unusual defense, however; and Sebond, had he been alive, might well have exclaimed that he needed no enemies with friends like this!

Montaigne's strategy is to demonstrate extensively that Sebond's "proofs" of Christian beliefs are not in the slightest inferior to reasons offered for any other conclusion whatsoever. He claims that Sebond's arguments will

> be found as solid and as firm as any others of the same type that may be opposed to them. . . .
>
>   Some say that his arguments are weak and unfit to prove what he proposes, and undertake to shatter them with ease. These must be shaken up a little more roughly. . . .
>
>   Let us see then if man has within his power other reasons more powerful than those of Sebond, or indeed if it is in him to arrive at any certainty by argument and reason. (*ARS,* 327–328)[20]

Montaigne, then, is going to "defend" Sebond's claim to prove the doctrines of the faith by showing that his arguments are as good as those of his critics—because *none* of them are any good at all!

The essay is a long and rambling one, but with a method in its madness. It examines every reason that has been given for trusting our conclusions and undermines each with satire and skeptical arguments. Are we capable of knowing the truth because of our superiority to the animals? In example after example, Montaigne causes us to wonder whether we are superior at all. Have the wise given us insight into the truth? He collects a long list of the different conceptions of God held by the philosophers and then exclaims,

> Now trust to your philosophy . . . when you consider the clatter of so many philosophical brains! (*ARS,* 383)

He adds,

> Man is certainly crazy. He could not make a mite, and he makes gods by the dozen. (*ARS,* 395)

Can we not at least rely on Aristotle, the "master of those who know"? But why pick out Aristotle as our authority? There are numerous alternatives.

The god of scholastic knowledge is Aristotle. . . . His doctrine serves us as magisterial law, when it is peradventure as false as another. (*ARS,* 403)

Surely, however, we can depend on our senses to reveal the truth about the world.

> That things do not lodge in us in their own form and essence, or make their entry into us by their own power and authority, we see clearly enough. Because, if that were so, we should receive them in the same way: wine would be the same in the mouth of a sick man as in the mouth of a healthy man; he who has chapped or numb fingers would find the same hardness in the wood or iron he handles as does another. . . .
>
>   We should remember, whatever we receive into our understanding, that we often receive false things there, and by these same tools that are often contradictory and deceived. (*ARS,* 422–424)

Can't we at least depend on science? Haven't scientists discovered the truth about things? Montaigne reminds us that in old times most people thought that the sun moved around the earth, though some thought the earth moved.

> And in our day, Copernicus has grounded this doctrine so well that he uses it very systematically for all astronomical deductions. What are we to get out of that, unless we should not bother which of the two is so? And who knows whether a third opinion, a thousand years from now, will not overthrow the preceding two? (*ARS,* 429)

Well, maybe it is difficult or impossible to know the truth about the universe. But surely reason can demonstrate truth about right and wrong?

> Truth must have one face, the same and universal. If man knew any rectitude and justice that had body and real existence, he would not tie it down to the condition of this country or that. It would not be from the fancy of the Persians or the Indians that virtue would take its form. . . .
>
>   But they are funny when, to give some certainty to the laws, they say that there are some which are firm, perpetual and immutable, which they call natural, which are imprinted on the human race by the condition of their very being. And of those one man says the number is three, one man four, one

more, one less: a sign that the mark of them is as doubtful as the rest. . . .

It is credible that there are natural laws, as may be seen in other creatures; but in us they are lost; that fine human reason butts in everywhere, domineering and commanding, muddling and confusing the face of things in accordance with its vanity and inconsistency. . . .*

See how reason provides plausibility to different actions. It is a two-handled pot, that can be grasped by the left or the right. (*ARS*, 436–438)

Finally Montaigne gives us a summary of the chief points of skeptical philosophy. Whenever we try to justify some claim of ours, we are involved either in a *circle* or in an *infinite regress* of reason giving. In neither case can we reach a satisfactory conclusion.

To judge the appearances we receive of objects, we would need a judicatory instrument; to verify this instrument, we need a demonstration; to verify the demonstration, an instrument: there we are in a circle!

Since the senses cannot decide our dispute, being themselves full of uncertainty, it must be reason that does so. No reason can be established without another reason; there we go retreating back to infinity. . . .†

Finally, there is no existence that is constant, either of our being or of that of objects. And we, and our judgment, and all mortal things go on flowing and rolling unceasingly. Thus nothing certain can be established about one thing by another, both the judging and the judged being in continual change and motion. (*ARS*, 454)

Montaigne remarks that if the senses do not simply record external realities (as Aristotle assumes, using the image of a seal impressing its form on the wax), then our ideas may not correspond at all to those realities.* Even worse, we are never in a position to find out whether they do or not. We may be in the position of having only pictures, without ever being able to compare these pictures to what they are pictures of. Here is that depressing and familiar image of the mind as a prisoner within its own walls, constantly receiving messages but forever unable to determine which of them to trust, and utterly incapable of understanding what is really going on. This image plagues many modern thinkers, not least of all Descartes.

Like all radical skeptics, Montaigne is faced with the question of how to manage the business of living. To live, one must choose, and to choose is to prefer one course as better than another. But this seems to require precisely those beliefs (in both facts and values) that skeptical reflections undermine. Montaigne accepts the solution of Protagoras and Sextus Empiricus before him of simply adapting himself to the prevailing opinions. We see, he says, how reason goes astray—especially when it meddles with divine things. We see how

when it strays however little from the beaten path and deviates or wanders from the way traced and trodden by the Church, immediately, it is lost, it grows embarrassed and entangled, whirling round and floating in that vast, troubled, and undulating sea of human opinions, unbridled and aimless. As soon as it loses that great common highroad it breaks up and disperses onto a thousand different roads. (*ARS*, 387)

. . . since I am not capable of choosing, I accept other people's choice and stay in the position where God put me. Otherwise I could not keep myself from rolling about incessantly. Thus I have, by the grace of God, kept myself intact, without agitation or disturbance of conscience, in the ancient beliefs of our religion, in the midst of so many sects and divisions that our century has produced. (*ARS*, 428)

You can see that skepticism is here being used as a defense of the status quo. Montaigne was born and brought up a Catholic. No one can bring forward reasons for deserting Catholic Christianity that are

---

*Note that Montaigne is making essentially the same point as Pico (p. 304). There are no determinate laws for human nature. But whereas Pico takes this to be the *glory* of man, Montaigne draws from it a *despairing* conclusion: The truth is unavailable to us.

†Here we have a statement of that problem of the criterion that was identified by Sextus. For a more extensive discussion of it, see pp. 211–213.

---

*For a discussion of Aristotle's view of sense experience, see p. 167. See also the elaboration by Aquinas, pp. 285–287.

any better than Raymond Sebond's reasons for supporting Catholic Christianity. Reason supports the Roman view just as strongly as it supports the Protestant view or, indeed, any other view—which is, of course, not at all! So to keep from "rolling about incessantly," the sensible course is to stick with the customs in which one has been brought up.* In one of his sharpest aphorisms, Montaigne exclaims:

> The plague of man is the opinion of knowledge. That is why ignorance is so recommended by our religion as a quality suitable to belief and obedience. (ARS, 360)

It is not knowledge, note well, that Montaigne decries as a plague, but the opinion that one possesses it. If you are reminded of Socrates, it is no coincidence.† He was known to his admirers as "the French Socrates."

Such is Montaigne's "defense" of the rational theology of Raymond Sebond. In an age when everyone's conscience seems to demand that those who disagree are either blind or wicked, the view has a certain attractiveness. While despairing and pessimistic in one way, it seems at least to promote tolerance. Someone who is a Catholic in Montaigne's sense is unlikely to have any incentive to burn someone who differs. This is no doubt one, but only one, of the reasons for the spread of Pyrrhonism among intellectuals and even among some members of the clergy.

---

1. What is Montaigne's strategy in "defending" Raymond Sebond?
2. What does Montaigne have to say about depending on authority? Our senses? Science? Reason?

---

*Note how different this religiosity is from both that of the Catholic Dante (for whom the "indifferent" are rejected by both God and Satan) and the reformer Luther (for whom commitment and certainty are essential to Christianity). Can it count as being religious at all? What do you think?

†For the claim that Socrates is the wisest of men because he knows that he doesn't know, see Plato's Apology, 20e–23b. Socrates, however, is not a Pyrrhonian skeptic; he does not doubt that knowledge is possible; he just confesses that (with some possible few exceptions), he does not possess it.

3. How does Montaigne try to show that we are involved either in a circle or in an infinite regress?
4. How does he recommend we live?

Copernicus to Kepler to Galileo: The Great Triple Play*

Renaissance humanism, the Reformation, and the undermining of accepted certainties by the new Pyrrhonists all contribute to a general sense of chaos and lost unity. But there is also a spirit of expectation. Something new is in the air; the tumults and controversies of the time are a testimony to it. The newly invented printing press spreads the new ideas. Imagination is enlarged by the discovery of the New World, and a sense of excitement is generated by voyages around the globe. New wealth flowing into Europe from America and the East stimulates growth and a powerful merchant class. The isolation of Europe is coming to an end and the reverberations are felt on every side—not least in the sphere of the intellect. The ancient authorities had been wrong about geography. Perhaps they were wrong about other things as well, and better understanding might lie in the future rather than in the past.

But nothing else can compare, in its long-term impact, with the development of the new science. More than all these other factors combined, this changes people's view of themselves, of the world, and of their place in it. Before we examine the philosophy of Descartes, who was himself a contributor to these new views, we need to look briefly at one tremendously significant shift in perspective—one that decisively overturns the entire medieval worldview and undermines forever the authority of its philosophical bulwark, Aristotle. It is traditionally called the Copernican Revolution. Though there were anticipations of it before Copernicus, and the revolution was carried to completion only in the time of Newton, it is the name of Copernicus we honor. For his work is the turning point.

---

*When your team is in the field, a triple play is a great success.

The key feature of that work is the displacement of the earth from the center of the universe.

We saw earlier how the centrality of the earth had been embedded in the accepted astronomical and physical theories. A stationary earth, moreover, had intimate links with the entire medieval Christian view of the significance of man, of his origins and destiny, and of God's relation to his creation. If the earth is displaced and becomes just one more planet whirling about in infinite space, we can expect consequences to be profound. And so they are, though the more radical consequences are not immediately perceived.

The earth-centered, multisphere universe had dominated astronomy and cosmology for eighteen hundred years. As developed by Ptolemy, with a complex system of epicycles to account for the "wanderings" of the planets, it was an impressive mathematical achievement, and its accuracy in prediction was not bad. But it never quite worked. And Copernicus (1473–1543) tells us that this fact led him to examine the works of previous astronomers to see whether some other system might improve accuracy. He discovered that certain ancient thinkers had held that the earth moved.

> Taking advantage of this I too began to think of the mobility of the Earth; and though the opinion seemed absurd, yet knowing now that others before me had been granted freedom to imagine such circles as they chose to explain the phenomena of the stars, I considered that I also might easily be allowed to try whether, by assuming some motion of the Earth, sounder explanations than theirs for the revolution of the celestial spheres might so be discovered.[21]

It is important to recognize that the heart of Copernicus' achievement is in the mathematics of his system—in the geometry and the calculations that filled most of his 1543 book, *De Revolutionibus*. As he himself puts it, "Mathematics are for mathematicians."[22] He expects fellow astronomers to be the ones to appreciate his results; from nonmathematicians he expects trouble.

We cannot go into the mathematical details. But we should know in general what Copernicus does—and does not—do. He does not entirely abolish the Ptolemaic reliance on epicycles cen-

tered on circles to account for apparent motion. His computations are scarcely simpler than those of Ptolemy. He retains the notion that all celestial bodies move in circles; indeed, the notion of celestial spheres is no less important for Copernicus than for the tradition. And he accepts the idea that the universe is finite—though considerably larger than had been thought. Even the sun is not located clearly in the center, as most popular accounts of his system state.[23]

But his treatment of the apparently irregular motions of the planets is a breakthrough. The planets appear to move, against the sphere of the fixed stars, slowly eastward. But at times they reverse course and move back westward. This "retrograde" motion remains a real puzzle as long as it is ascribed to the planets themselves. But Copernicus treats it as merely an *apparent* motion, the appearance being caused by the *actual* motion of the observers on an earth that is not itself stationary. And this works; at least, it works as well as the traditional assumptions in accounting for the observed phenomena. Moreover, it is aesthetically pleasing, unlike the inexplicable reversals of earlier theory. Copernicus' view, though not less complex and scarcely more accurate in prediction, allows for a kind of unity and harmony throughout the universe that the renegade planets had previously spoiled. Until the availability of better naked-eye data and the invention of the telescope (about fifty years later) these "harmonies" are what chiefly recommend the Copernican system to his astronomical successors.

At first some of them simply use his mathematics without committing themselves to the truth of this new picture of the universe. Indeed, in a preface to Copernicus' major work, a Lutheran theologian, Osiander, urges this path. Copernicus' calculations are useful, but to give up the traditional picture of the universe would mean an overhaul of basic beliefs and attitudes that most are not ready for. So if one could treat the system merely as a calculating device, without any claims to truth, one could reconcile the best of the new science with the best of ancient traditions.*

---

*Here is foreshadowed one of the intense debates in current philosophy of science: Should we understand terms in explanatory

Johannes Kepler (1571–1630), however, is not content with this restricted view of the theory. A lifelong Copernican, he supplies the next major advance in the system by taking the sun more and more seriously as the true center. Oddly enough, his predilection for the sun as the center has its roots not so much in observation, or even in mathematics, as in a kind of mystical Neoplatonism, which takes the sun to be "the most excellent" body in the universe.* Its essence, Kepler says

> is nothing else than the purest light, than which
> there is no greater star; which singly and alone is
> the producer, conserver, and warmer of all things;
> it is a fountain of light, rich in fruitful heat, most
> fair, limpid, and pure to the sight, the source of
> vision, portrayer of all colours, though himself
> empty of colour, called king of the planets for his
> motion, heart of the world for his power, its eye
> for his beauty, and which alone we should judge
> worthy of the Most High God, should he be
> pleased with a material domicile and choose
> a place in which to dwell with the blessed
> angels.[24]

It may be somewhat disconcerting to hear this sort of rhetoric from one we honor as a founder of the modern scientific tradition; but it is neither the first nor the last time that religious or philosophical views function as a source of insights later confirmed by more exact and pedestrian methods.

Part of Kepler's quasi-religious conviction is that the universe is fundamentally mathematical in nature. God is a great mathematician, and his creation is governed by mathematically simple laws. This view can be traced back through Plato to the Pythagoreans, who hold (rather obscurely) that all things are numbers. In the work of Kepler and his successors, this conviction is to gain an unprecedented confirmation. Mathematics must be devised to fit the phenomena, and the phenomena are given a mathematical description.

Drawing on more accurate data compiled by the great observer of the heavens, Tycho Brahe, Kepler makes trial after trial of circular hypotheses, always within the Copernican framework, but none of them exactly fit the data. He tries various other kinds of ovals without success. For the greater part of ten years he works on the orbit of Mars. At last, he notices certain regularities suggesting that the path of a planet might be that of an ellipse, with the sun at one of the two foci that define it. And that works; the data and the mathematical theory fit precisely.

This becomes the first of Kepler's famous three laws. The second offers an explanation of the varying speeds that must be postulated in the planets' movement around these ellipses: The areas swept out by a line from the sun to the planet are always equal in equal intervals of time. The third law is more complicated, and we need not bother about its details; it concerns the relation of the speeds of planets in different orbits. In fact, Kepler formulates a great many laws; posterity has selected these three as particularly fruitful.

The significance of Kepler's work is that for the first time we are presented with a simple and elegant mathematical account of the heavens that matches the data; and it is sun-centered. For the first time we have a really powerful alternative to the medieval picture of the world. Its ramifications are many, however, and will take time to draw out. Part of this development is the task of Galileo.

Galileo Galilei (1564–1642) was, in 1609, the first to view the heavens through a telescope. The result was a multitude of indirect but persuasive evidences for the Copernican view of the universe. New stars in prodigious numbers were observed. The moon's topography was charted; it resembled the earth remarkably, a fact that cut against the distinction between terrestrial imperfection and celestial perfection. Sun spots were observed; it was not perfect either! And it rotated—it was not immutable! The moons of Jupiter provided an observable model of the solar system itself. The phases of Venus indicated that it moved in a sun-centered orbit.

Encouraged by the successful application of mathematics to celestial bodies, Galileo sets him-

---

theories in a "realistic" way, or take such terms as mere "instruments" for calculation and prediction?

*In *Republic* 506d–509b, Plato uses the sun as a visible image of the Form of the Good (see p. 132). And in his later work *Laws,* he recommends a kind of sun worship as the heart of a state-sponsored religion.

self to use these same powerful tools for the description and explanation of terrestrial motion. Previous thinkers, influenced by Aristotle, had asked primarily *why* bodies move. Why do objects fall to earth when unsupported? Aristotelian answers were at hand. A body falls because it is seeking its *natural place.* The significance of this answer can be seen by a thought experiment. Imagine that the earth is where the moon now is and that you let go of a rock some distance above the surface of the earth. What would happen? If Aristotle's answer were correct, the rock would not fall to the earth but would travel to the place where the center of the earth *used to be;* it would fly away from the earth.[25]

Place, not space, is primary in an Aristotelian world; place is a qualitative term, each place having its own essential character. The place at the center of the celestial spheres is the place of heavy elements. The concept of space, by contrast, which plays such a crucial role in the new science, is the concept of an infinitely extended neutral container with a purely mathematical description.

Note also that the Aristotelian explanation in terms of final causes gives no answer at all as to *how* an object falls; no specification of laws that describe its speed and trajectory is given.* But this is just what Galileo supplies in terms of a mathematical theory of motion. It is a theory that applies to *all* motion, terrestrial and celestial alike. For him, as for his two predecessors, the great book of nature is written in mathematical language. And we, by using that language, can understand it.

Let us set down some of the consequences of the new science. First, our sense of the size of the universe changes. Eventually it will be thought to be infinitely extended in space. This means it has *no center* because in an infinite universe every point has an equal right to be considered the center. As a result, it becomes more difficult to think of human beings as the main attraction in this extravaganza, where quite probably there are planets similar to the earth circling other suns in other galaxies. The universe no longer seems a cozy home in which

everything exists for our sake. Blaise Pascal, himself a great mathematician and contributor to the new science, would exclaim a hundred years after Copernicus, "The eternal silence of those infinite spaces strikes me with terror."[26]

Second, our beliefs about the nature of the things in the universe change. Celestial bodies are thought to be made of the same lowly stuff as we find on the earth, so that the heavens are no longer special— eternal, immutable, and akin to the divine. Furthermore, matter seems to be peculiarly *quantitative.* For Aristotle and medieval science alike, mathematics had been just one of the ways in which substances could be described. Quantity was only one of the ten categories, which together supplied the basic concepts for describing and explaining reality. Substances were fundamentally qualitative in nature, and science had the job of tracing their qualitative development in terms of changes from potentiality to actuality.*

But now mathematics seems to be a privileged set of concepts in terms of which to describe and explain things. Only by the application of geometry and mathematical calculation has the puzzle of the heavens been solved; and it is mathematics that can describe and predict the fall of rocks and the trajectory of a cannonball. Mathematics, it seems, can tell us what *really* is. The result is a strong push toward thinking of the universe in purely quantitative terms, as a set of objects with purely quantitative characteristics (size, shape, motion) that interact with each other according to fixed laws. It is no surprise that the implications of the new science move its inventors in the direction of atomism or, as they call it, "corpuscularism."† We will see this at work in Descartes' philosophy.

In the third place, the new science does away with teleological explanations, or final causes. The question about what end or goal a planet or a rock realizes in behaving as it does is simply irrelevant. Explanations are framed in terms of mathematical laws that account for *how* it behaves. Why does it behave in a certain way? Because it is a thing of just

---

*For a discussion of final causes, see pp. 171–173.

*See Aristotle's development of these ideas on pp. 169–173.
For Aristotle's categories, see pp. 160–162.
†The key notions of ancient atomism are discussed on pp. 32–35.

this precise quantity in exactly these conditions, and things of that quantity in those conditions necessarily behave in accordance with a given law. It is no longer good enough to explain change in terms of a desire to imitate the perfection of God.*

As you can see, this way of viewing the universe puts values in a highly questionable position. If we assume that the valuable is somehow a goal, something desirable, what we all want—and this is the common assumption of virtually all philosophers and theologians up to this time—where is there room for such goals in a universe like this? A goal seems precisely to be a final cause, something that draws us onward and upward toward itself. But if everything simply happens as it must in the giant machine that is the universe, how can there be values, aspirations, goals?

It looks as though knowledge and value, science and religion are being pulled apart again after two thousand years of harmony. Plato, and Aristotle after him, opposes the atomism of Democritus to construct a vision of reality in which the ultimate facts are not indifferent to goodness and beauty. Christian thinkers take over these schemes and link them intimately to God, the creator. But all this, expressed so movingly in Dante's *Divine Comedy,* seems to be in the process of coming unstuck again.

One more consequence of the new science will prove to be perhaps the most perplexing of all. Galileo sees that the quantitative, corpuscular universe makes the qualities of experience highly questionable. If reality is captured by mathematics and geometry, then the real properties of things are just their size, shape, velocity, acceleration, direction, weight: those characteristics treatable by numbers, points, and lines. But what becomes of those fuzzy, intimate, and lovable characteristics, such as warm, yellow-orange, pungent, sweet, and harmonious to the ear? It is in terms of such properties that we make contact with the world beyond us; it is they that delight or terrify us, attract or repel us. But what is their relation to those purely quantitive things revealed by Galilean science as the real stuff of the universe?

---

*Compare the teleological explanations of Aristotle (pp. 170–173) and Dante (pp. 300–302).

Our instinctive habit is to consider the apple to be red, the oatmeal hot, cookies sweet, and roses fragrant. But is this correct? Do apples and other such things really have these properties? Here is Galileo's answer:

> that external bodies, to excite in us these tastes, these odours, and these sounds, demand other than size, figure, number, and slow or rapid motion, I do not believe; and I judge that, if the ears, the tongue, and the nostrils were taken away, the figure, the numbers, and the motions would indeed remain, but not the odours nor the tastes nor the sounds, which, without the living animal, I do not believe are anything else than names, just as tickling is precisely nothing but a name if the armpit and the nasal membrane be removed; . . . having now seen that many affections which are reputed to be qualities residing in the external object, have truly no other existence than in us, and without us are nothing else than names; I say that I am inclined sufficiently to believe that heat is of this kind, and that the thing that produces heat in us and makes us perceive it, which we call by the general name fire, is a multitude of minute corpuscles thus and thus figured, moved with such and such a velocity; . . . But that besides their figure, number, motion, penetration, and touch, there is in fire another quality, that is heat—that I do not believe otherwise than I have indicated, and I judge that it is so much due to us that if the animate and sensitive body were removed, heat would remain nothing more than a simple word.[27]

Galileo is here sketching a distinction between two different kinds of qualities: those that can be attributed to things themselves and those that cannot. The former are often called **primary qualities** and the latter **secondary qualities.** Primary qualities are those that Galilean mathematical science can handle: size, figure, number, and motion. These qualities are now thought to characterize the world—or what we might better call the *objective* world—exhaustively. All other qualities exist only *subjectively*—in us. They are caused to exist in us by the primary (quantitative) qualities of things.

Heat, for example, experienced in the presence of a fire, no more exists in the fire than a tickle exists in the feather brushing my nose. If we try to use the term "heat" for something out there in the world, it turns into "nothing but a name"—that is, it does not describe any reality, since the reality is just the motion of "a multitude of minute corpuscles." The tickle exists only in us; and if the term "heat" (or for that matter "red" or "sweet" or "pungent") is to be descriptive, then what it describes is also only in us. Take away the eye, the tongue, the nostrils, and all that remains is figure and motion.

Democritus, the ancient atomist, draws the same conclusion. He remarks in a poignant phrase, "By this man is cut off from the real."* The problem that Galileo's distinction between primary and secondary qualities bequeaths to subsequent philosophers is this: If, in order to understand the world, we must strip it of its experienced qualities, where do those experienced qualities exist? If they exist only in *us,* what then are *we?* If they are mental, or subjective, what is the *mind?* And how is the mind related to the corpuscular world of the new science? Suppose we agree, for the sake of the mastery of the universe given us by these new conceptions, to kick experienced qualities "inside." Then how is this "inside" related to the "outside"? Who is this man who, in Democritus' phrase, is cut off from reality? Galileo, concerned as he is with the objective world, can simply relegate secondary qualities to some otherwise specified subjective realm. But the question will not go away.

It is a new world, indeed. The impact of all these changes on a sensitive observer is registered in a poem by John Donne in 1611.

> And new philosophy calls all in doubt,
> The element of fire is quite put out;
> The sun is lost, and th' earth, and no man's wit
> Can well direct him where to look for it.
> And freely men confess that this world's spent,
> When in the planets, and the firmament
> They seek so many new; they see that this
> Is crumbled out again to his atomies.
> 'Tis all in pieces, all coherence gone;
> All just supply, and all relation:
> Prince, subject, father, son, are things forgot,
> For every man alone thinks he hath got
> To be a phoenix, and that then can be

> None of that kind, of which he is, but he.
> This is the world's condition now.[28]

Here is a lament founded on the new developments. Point after point recalls the detail we have just surveyed; Pyrrhonism, secondary qualities (why is the sun, source of light, heat, and color "lost"?), the moving earth, the expanding universe, corpuscularism, and in the last few lines, the new individualism, which seems to undermine all traditional authority. The medieval world has vanished: "'tis all in pieces, all coherence gone."

It did not go quietly, of course. The Roman Catholic Counter-Reformation tried to preserve as much as it could. The argument about Copernicanism, which seemed to be the key, was long and fierce; we all know the story of the Church's condemnation of Galileo's opinions and his recantation and house arrest. In 1633, the Church prohibited teaching or believing that the earth moved around the sun. And many Protestants were no more friendly, citing biblical passages that seemed to support the claim that the earth was stationary.* These conservative forces were not interested in the new science per se, but in the fact that it seemed subversive of the "coherence" Christian society had enjoyed for so long. It questioned everything and seemed to turn it all upside down. When one part of a coherent worldview is undermined, all the rest seems suddenly unstable.

But the new science proves irresistible, and in one way or another, religion, morality, worldview, and the structure of society would have to make peace with it. The question of what to make of this science is perhaps the major preoccupation of philosophers in the modern era.

If we wanted to sum up, we could say that the new science bequeaths to philosophers four deep and perplexing problems:

1. What is the place of mind in this world of matter?

2. What is the place of value in this world of fact?

---

*See p. 34.

*For example, Joshua 10:13, Ecclesiastes 1:4, 5, and Psalms 93:1.

3. What is the place of freedom in this world of mechanism?

4. Is there any room left for God at all?

Descartes, among others, sees the radical nature of these problems and sets himself to solve them.

---

1. How does Copernicus resolve the puzzle about the apparent irregularity in the motions of the planets?

2. What is the impact of a moving earth on Dante's picture of the world?

3. What does Kepler add to the Copernican picture?

4. Contrast Aristotelian explanations of motion with those of Galileo.

5. What impact does giving up final causes have on values?

6. What happens to the qualities we think we experience in objects? Explain the difference between primary and secondary qualities.

7. What questions does the new science pose to the philosophical quest for wisdom?

For Further Thought

Imagine that you are a philosopher living at the beginning of the seventeenth century. You are acquainted with the writings of the humanists, with Luther's reforming views of Christianity, with Montaigne's skeptical arguments, and with the new science. A friend asks you, "What should I live for? What is the point of life?" How do you reply?

Notes

1. I am indebted for much in this chapter to the excellent book by Thomas Kuhn, *The Copernican Revolution* (Cambridge, MA: Harvard University Press, 1957).

2. Quoted in Kuhn, *Copernican Revolution,* 112.

3. Quotations from Dante, *The Divine Comedy,* in *The Portable Dante,* ed. Paolo Milano (New York: Penguin Books, 1947), are cited in the text by canto and line numbers.

4. Erasmus, "The Godly Feast," in *The Colloquies of Erasmus,* trans. Craig R. Thompson (Chicago: University of Chicago Press, 1965), 65.

5. Erasmus, "Godly Feast," 68.

6. Erasmus, "The Epicurean," in *Colloquies,* 549.

7. Ernst Cassirer, Paul Oskar Kristeller, and John Herman Randall, Jr., *The Renaissance Philosophy of Man* (Chicago: University of Chicago Press, 1948), 4.

8. Giovanni Pico della Mirandola, *Oration on the Dignity of Man,* in Cassirer, Kristeller, and Randall, *Renaissance Philosophy of Man,* 224–225.

9. Pico, *Oration,* 225.

10. Roland H. Bainton, *Christendom: A Short History of Christianity and Its Impact on Western Civilization* (New York: Harper and Row, 1964), 218.

11. Bainton, *Christendom,* 249.

12. Martin Luther, "An Appeal to the Ruling Class of German Nationality as to the Amelioration of the State of Christendom," in *Martin Luther: Selections from His Writings,* ed. John Dillenberger (New York: Anchor Books, 1981), 418–421.

13. Quoted in Dillenberger, "Preface to the Complete Edition of Luther's Latin Writings," in *Martin Luther,* 11.

14. Quoted in Dillenberger, *Martin Luther,* 11–12.

15. Quoted in Roland H. Bainton, *Here I Stand: A Life of Martin Luther* (London: Hodder and Staughton, 1951), 78.

16. Luther, "The Ninety-Five Theses," in Dillenberger, *Martin Luther,* 493–494.

17. Bainton, *Here I Stand,* 96.

18. Quoted in Bainton, *Here I Stand,* 117.

19. I rely here on Richard H. Popkin's *History of Scepticism from Erasmus to Descartes* (Assen, Netherlands: Van Gorcum, 1960).

20. Quotations from Michel de Montaigne, *Apology for Raymond Sebond,* in *The Complete Works of Montaigne,* trans. Donald M. Frame (Palo Alto, CA: Stanford University Press, 1958), are cited in the text, using the abbreviation *ARS.* References are to page numbers.

21. Quoted from Copernicus, *De Revolutionibus,* in Kuhn, *Copernican Revolution,* 141.

22. Quoted in Kuhn, *Copernican Revolution,* 142.

23. Kuhn, *Copernican Revolution,* 164–170.

24. Quoted in Edwin Arthur Burtt, *The Metaphysical Foundations of Modern Physical Science* (London: Routledge and Kegan Paul, 1924), 48.

25. Kuhn, *Copernican Revolution,* 86.

26. Blaise Pascal, *The Pensées,* trans. J. M. Cohen (New York: Penguin Books, 1961), sec. 91, p. 57.

27. Quoted in Burtt, *Metaphysical Foundations,* 78.

28. John Donne, "An Anatomy of the World," in *John Donne: The Complete English Poems* (New York: Penguin Books, 1971), 276.

13

RENÉ DESCARTES

Doubting Our Way to Certainty

When he is just twenty-three years old, René Descartes (1596–1650) experiences a vision in a dream. He writes down,

> 10, November 1619; I discovered the foundations of a marvellous science.[1]

This discovery decisively shapes the intellectual life of the young man. Before we focus on the philosophy of his *Meditations,* we need to understand something about that discovery and its importance for his method of approaching problems.

Descartes had received a good education, as he himself acknowledges. But he is dissatisfied. He had expected to obtain "a clear and certain knowledge . . . of all that is useful in life." Instead, he tells us,

> I found myself beset by so many doubts and errors that I came to think I had gained nothing from my attempts to become educated but increasing recognition of my ignorance. (*DM* 1.4, p. 113)[2]

Mathematics delights him "because of the certainty of its demonstrations and the evidence of its reasoning," though he is surprised that more has not been done with it. As for philosophy, he says,

Seeing that it has been cultivated for many centuries by the most excellent minds, and yet there is still no point in it which is not disputed and hence doubtful, I was not so presumptuous as to hope to achieve any more in it than others had done. (*DM* 1.8, pp. 114–115)

What is a serious young man, who has always had "an earnest desire to learn to distinguish the true from the false" to do? (*DM* 1.10, p. 115).

> I entirely abandoned the study of letters. Resolving to seek no knowledge other than that which could be found in myself or else in the great book of the world, I spent the rest of my youth travelling, visiting courts and armies, mixing with people of diverse temperaments and ranks, gathering various experiences, testing myself in the situations which fortune offered me, and at all times reflecting upon whatever came my way so as to derive some profit from it. (*DM* 1.9, p. 115)

A striking move! He does not give up learning, but he does give up "letters"—learning what other men had written. In this, Descartes is both a reflection of the age and an immense influence furthering the individualism we earlier remarked on. Where would he seek truth? Not in the writings of the ancients, but in *himself* and in *the great book of the world.* Because he concludes—echoing Socrates—that hardly anyone knows anything worth learning, he would have to *discover* the truth.[*] If he is going to "learn to distinguish the true from the false," he would have to look to himself.

He joins an army (a traditional way to "see the world") and in his travels meets a Dutchman interested in mathematics and the new physics. Descartes' interest is sparked, and he begins to think about using mathematics to solve problems in physics. While working on these problems, he has his dream.

What is this "marvellous science" that forms the content of his "vision"? Apparently it is analytic geometry.[†] Descartes sees in a flash of insight that there is an isomorphism between algebraic symbols and geometry. He sees, moreover, that this opens the door to a mathematical treatment of everything that can be geometrically represented. But nature seems to be something that can be geometrically represented, natural things having size, figure, volume, and geometrical relations to each other. Suppose that the things in the world were just objects having such geometrical properties; suppose that whatever other properties they have can in one way or another be reduced to purely geometrical properties; then the stunning prospect opens up of a science of nature—a physics—that is wholly mathematical. Mathematics, the only discipline that impressed him in his college days as clear and certain, would be the key to unlock the secrets of nature. Surely this is a vision fit to motivate a research program! And that is exactly what it does.

For the rest of his life Descartes works on this program, in constant communication with the best minds at work on similar problems. In 1633 he is about to publish a *Treatise on the World,* when he learns of the Catholic Church's condemnation of

Galileo and the burning of his books. He holds the treatise back, for in it he has endorsed the Copernican view of the moving earth. Four years later, however, he ventures to publish several works on light, on meteors, and on geometry. These are accompanied by a *Discourse on Method,* which we will examine in more detail shortly.

He writes on a wide variety of topics: on the sun, moon, and the stars; on comets; on metals; on fire; on glass; on the magnet; on the human body, particularly on the heart and the nervous system (for which he gathers observations from animal bodies at a local slaughterhouse). He formulates several "laws of nature." Here are two influential ones:

> that each thing as far as in it lies, continues always in the same state; and that which is once moved always continues to move.
> . . . that all motion is of itself in a straight line; and thus things which move in a circle always tend to recede from the centre of the circle that they describe. (*PP* 2.37–39, p. 267)[3]

Newton will later adopt both of them, and so they pass into the foundations of classical physics; but they were revolutionary in Descartes' day. Both laws contradict Aristotelian assumptions built into the worldview of medieval science. It had been thought that rest (at or near the center of the universe) is the natural state of terrestrial things, while the heavenly spheres revolve naturally in perfect circles. To say that rest is not more "natural" than motion and that motion is "naturally" in a straight line is radical indeed. It could make sense only in a world of infinite space, where there is no such thing as a natural center. And it fits only with a moving earth.

Descartes applies these principles to a world that he takes to be geometrical in essence. He tries to do without concepts of weight and gravity, for these seem to be "occult" qualities like those in the nonmathematical science of Aristotle. To say that a body falls because it has weight or because it is naturally attracted to another body seems to him no explanation at all; it is just attaching a name to a phenomenon and supposing that we thereby learn something.

For Descartes, bodies are sheer extended volumes. They interact according to mechanical prin-

---

[*]Do you find it surprising that two thousand years after Socrates someone should still echo the same complaint? Could we say the same today? If not, why not?
[†]So-called Cartesian coordinates are, of course, named for Descartes.

ciples that can be mathematically formulated. Given that a single body in motion would continue in that motion unless interfered with, and given the laws of interaction, the paths and positions of interacting bodies can be plotted and predicted. Since extension is the very essence of body, there can be no vacuum or void. (You can see that if bodies are just extended volumes, the ideal of such a volume containing *no body* is self-contradictory.) So the universe is full, and motion takes place by a continual recirculation of bodies, each displacing another as it is itself displaced. The fall of bodies near the earth is due to the action on them of other bodies in the air, which in turn are being pressed down by others out to the edges of the solar system. This system forms a huge vortex tightly bound in by the vortices of other systems, which force the moving bodies in it to deviate from otherwise straight paths into the roughly circular paths traced by the planets.*

The key idea, as you can see, is that everything in the material world can be treated in a purely geometrical and mathematical fashion. Descartes is one of the most vigorous promoters of that "corpuscularism" noted earlier.† Although he criticizes Democritus and the ancient atomists (for thinking that atoms are indivisible, for positing a void, for believing in gravity, and for not specifying the laws of interaction precisely), it is clear that the general outlines of Descartes' universe bear a striking resemblance to that earlier theory.‡ In particular, the *mechanistic* quality of the picture is identical. He states explicitly that "the laws of mechanics . . . are identical with the laws of Nature" (*DM* 5.54, p. 139).

The radical nature of this conception can be appreciated by noting a thought experiment Descartes recommends. Imagine, he says, that God creates a space with matter to fill it and shakes it up until there is thorough chaos. All that God then adds is a decree that this matter should behave according to the laws of Nature. What would be the result?

> I showed how, in consequence of these laws, the greater part of the matter of this chaos had to become disposed and arranged in a certain way, which made it resemble our heavens; and how, at the same time, some of its parts had to form an earth, some planets and comets, and others a sun and fixed stars. Here I dwelt upon the subject of light, explaining at some length the nature of the light that had to be present in the sun and the stars. . . . From that I went on to speak of the earth in particular: how, although I had expressly supposed that God had put no gravity into the matter of which it was formed, still all its parts tended exactly towards its centre; . . . how mountains, seas, springs and rivers could be formed naturally there, and how metals could appear in mines, plants grow in fields, and generally how all the bodies we call "mixed" or "composite" could come into being there. (*DM* 5.43–44, p. 132)

Of course, Descartes does not actually succeed in demonstrating all that. No one yet has solved all these problems, and they are in fact insoluble with the limited resources that Descartes allows himself. But it is the conception and the daring it expresses that counts. This vision of a universe evolving itself in purely mechanistic ways has been enormously influential; and we haven't yet finished exploring its ramifications.

Descartes is quick to add that he does not infer from this thought experiment that the world was actually formed in that way, only that it could have been. Careful still about charges of heresy, he says it is "much more probable" that God made it just as it now is. But in either case, it is pretty clear that God is excluded from the day-to-day operations of the universe, which in Descartes' view proceeds as it must according to purely mathematical and mechanistic laws.

---

*The notion of a cosmic vortex, a huge, swirling mass of matter, is already found in the speculations of Anaximander; see pp. 13–14. Compare also Parmenides' arguments against the existence of a void, pp. 27–28.

†See p. 315.

‡For the views of the atomists, see Chapter 4. Descartes' criticisms may be found in Part IV, CCII, of *The Principles of Philosophy*.

The Method

While working on these physical problems, and feeling certain that progress is being made virtually every day, Descartes asks himself why more progress hadn't been made in the past. It is surely not, he thinks, that he is more clever or intelligent than earlier thinkers. No, the problem is that they lacked something. And it gradually becomes clear to him that what they lacked is a *method*. They did not proceed in as careful and principled a way as they might have. Acceptance of obscurity, the drawing of hasty conclusions, avoidable disagreements, and general intellectual chaos are the results.

Descartes sets himself to draw up some rules for the direction of the intellect. It is of some importance to recognize that these rules of method formulate what Descartes takes himself to be doing in his scientific work. In particular, they are indebted to his experience as a mathematician. They are not picked arbitrarily, then, but are an expression of procedures that actually seem to be producing results. If only other thinkers could be persuaded to follow these four rules, he thinks, what progress might be made!

> The first was never to accept anything as true if I did not have evident knowledge of its truth: that is, carefully to avoid precipitate conclusions and preconceptions, and to include nothing more in my judgments than what presented itself to my mind so clearly and distinctly that I had no occasion to doubt it.
>
> The second, to divide each of the difficulties I examined into as many parts as possible and as may be required in order to resolve them better.
>
> The third, to direct my thoughts in an orderly manner, by beginning with the simplest and most easily known objects in order to ascend little by little, step by step, to knowledge of the most complex, and by supposing some order even among objects that have no natural order of precedence.
>
> And the last, throughout to make enumerations so complete, and reviews so comprehensive, that I could be sure of leaving nothing out. (*DM* 2.18–19, p. 120)

He says of these four rules that he thought they would be "sufficient, provided that I made a strong and unswerving resolution never to fail to observe them" (*DM* 2.18, p. 120). They are difficult to follow, as any attempt to do so will convince you immediately. But let us explore their content more carefully.

The first one has to do with a condition for accepting something as true. It is pretty stringent. You want to avoid two things: "precipitate conclusions" (hastiness) and "preconceptions" (categorizing something before you have good warrant to do so). How do you do this? By accepting only those things that are *so clear and distinct that you have no occasion to doubt them.* Descartes obviously has in mind such propositions as "3 + 5 = 8" and "the interior angles of a triangle are equal to two right angles." Once you understand these, you really cannot bring yourself to doubt that they are true. Can you?

What do the key words "clear" and "distinct" mean? In *The Principles of Philosophy* (*PP* 1.45, p. 237) he explains them as follows. Something is "clear" when it is "present and apparent to an attentive mind, in the same way as we assert that we see objects clearly when, being present to the regarding eye, they operate upon it with sufficient strength." Seeing an apple in your hand in good light would be an example. We are not to accept any belief unless it is as clear as that. Nothing obscure, fuzzy, dim, indefinite, indistinct, vague—only what is *clear!*

By "distinct" he means "so precise and different from all other objects that it contains within itself nothing but what is clear." An idea not only must be clear in itself but also impossible to confuse with any other idea. There must be no ambiguity in its meaning. Ideas must be as distinct as the idea of a triangle is from the idea of a square.

Ask yourself how many of *your* beliefs are clear and distinct in this way. Descartes is under no illusions about the high standard he sets. "There are even a number of people who throughout all their lives perceive nothing so correctly as to be capable of judging it properly." But the first rule of the method is to *accept nothing as true* that does not meet that high standard. In the first of the *Meditations* we shall see how much that excludes.

The second rule recommends analysis. Problems are typically complex, and an essential step in their solution is to break them into smaller problems. Anyone who has tried to write a computer program to solve a problem will have an excellent feel for this rule. Often more than half the battle is to discover smaller problems we already have the resources to solve, so that by combining the solu-

"It is much easier to have some vague notion about any subject, no matter what, than to arrive at the real truth about a single question."

—RENÉ DESCARTES

tions to these more elementary problems we can solve the big problem. We move, by analysis, not only from the complex to the simple, but also from the obscure to the clear and distinct, and so we follow the first rule as well.

The third rule recognizes that items for consideration may be more or less simple. It recommends beginning with the simpler ones and proceeding to the more complex. Here is a mathematical example. If we compare a straight line to a curve, we can see that there is a clear sense in which the straight line is simple and the curve is not; no straight line is more or less straight than another, but curves come in all degrees. If we know a line is straight, we know something perfectly definite about it; if we know it is curved, we do not. And it is in fact possible to analyze a curve into a series of straight lines at various angles to each other, thus "constructing" the more complex curve from the simple straights.

For Descartes, this serves as a model of all good intellectual work. There are two basic procedures: a kind of *insight* or *intuition* of simple natures (which must be clear and distinct), and then *deduction* of complex phenomena from perceived relations among the simples. A deduction, too, is in fact just an insight: insight into the connections holding among simples. Geometry, again, provides many examples. Theorems are proved by deduction from the axioms and postulates. The latter are simply "seen" to be true; for example, through two points in a plane, one and only one straight line can be drawn. The same kind of "seeing" is required to recognize that each step in a proof is correct.

Deductions, of course, can be very long and complex, even though each of the steps is clear and distinct. That is the reason for the fourth rule: to set out all the steps completely (we all know how easily mistakes creep in when we take something for granted) and to make comprehensive reviews.

Descartes is extremely optimistic about the results we can obtain if we follow this method:

> These long chains composed of very simple and easy reasonings, which geometers customarily use to arrive at their most difficult demonstrations, had given me occasion to suppose that all the things that can fall under human knowledge are interconnected in the same way. And I thought that, provided that we refrain from accepting anything as true which is not, and always keep to the order required for deducing one thing from another, there can be nothing too remote to be reached in the end or too well hidden to be discovered. (*DM* 2.19, p. 120)

We will see this optimism at work when Descartes tackles knotty problems such as the existence of God and the relation between soul and body. But first we need to ask, Why does Descartes feel a need to address these *philosophical* problems at all? Why doesn't he just stick to mathematical physics?

For one thing, he is confident that his method will allow him to succeed where so many have failed. But a deeper reason is that he needs to show that his physics correctly describes the world, that it is more than just a likely story. In short, he needs to demonstrate that his physics is *true*. He is quite aware of the skeptical doubts of the Pyrrhonists, of the way they undermine the testimony of the senses and cast doubt on our reasoning. In particular, he is aware of the problem of the criterion.* Unless this can be solved, no certainty is possible.

Descartes thinks he has found a way to solve this problem of problems. He will outdo the Pyrrhonists at their own game; when it comes to doubting, he will be the champion doubter of all time. The first rule of his method already gives him the means to wipe the slate clean—unless, perhaps, there remains something that is *so clear and distinct that it cannot possibly be doubted.* If there were something like that (and, as we shall see, Descartes thinks that there is), the rest of the method could gain a foothold, deductions could lead us to further truths, and perhaps, from the depths of doubting despair, we could be raised to the bliss of certainty.

This is Descartes' strategy. And it is this attempt to justify his physics that makes Descartes not just a great scientist, but a great philosopher as well. We are now ready to turn to this philosophy as expressed in the *Meditations*.

Meditations: **Commentary and Questions**

The *Meditations on First Philosophy* is Descartes' most famous work. We focus our attention on the text itself, as we did earlier with certain dialogues of Plato. It is a remarkably rich work; and if you come to understand it, you will have mastered many of the concepts and distinctions that philosophers use to this day. So it will repay careful study. I cannot emphasize too much that in this section it is the *text,* the words of Descartes himself you must wrestle with. It is he who is your partner in this conversation, and you must make him speak to you and—as far as possible—answer your questions. What I do is offer some commentary on particularly difficult aspects, fill in some background, and ask some questions.

Though it is usually known just as the *Meditations,* the full title of the work is *Meditations on First Philosophy in Which the Existence of God and the Distinction of the Soul from the Body Are Demonstrated.* The title gives you some idea what to expect. But as you will see, his experience as a mathematician and physicist is everywhere present. It was first published in 1641.

Although not represented in our text, the *Meditations* are prefaced by a letter to "the Wisest and Most Distinguished Men, the Dean and Doctors of the Faculty of Theology in Paris." The motivation behind this letter is fairly transparent. It had been just eight years since the condemnation of Galileo's opinions, and, as we have seen, Descartes has allied himself with the basic outlook of Galileo. The Faculty of Theology in Paris had indeed been an illustrious one for some centuries. If he could secure their approval, he could almost certainly escape Galileo's fate. The *Meditations* was examined carefully by one of the theologians, who expressed his approval, but twenty-two years later it was placed on the *Index Librorum Prohibitorum* of books dangerous to read.*

Descartes had also asked one of his close friends, the priest and scientist Mersenne, to circulate the text to some distinguished philosophers, who were then invited to write criticisms of it. These criticisms, including some from his English contemporary Thomas Hobbes, were printed along with Descartes' replies at the end of the volume.†

In the letter to the theologians, Descartes refers to "believers like ourselves." He professes to be absolutely convinced that it is sufficient in these matters to rely on Scripture. But there is a problem. On the one hand, God's existence, he says, is to be believed because it is taught in Scripture. Scrip-

---

*For a discussion of this problem by the ancient skeptics, see pp. 211–213. For the impact of skepticism nearer to Descartes' time, see p. 311.

---

*The *Index* was created in 1571 by Pope Pius V, after approval by the Council of Trent; the latter was a general council of the Roman Catholic Church, called to deal with problems created by the Protestant Reformation. It set in motion the Catholic Counter-Reformation, and the *Index* was one of its tools.
†We discuss the views of Hobbes in the next chapter. For his criticisms of the *Meditations,* see the "Third Set of Objections" in Haldane and Ross, *The Philosophical Works of Descartes,* Volume 2.

ture, on the other hand, is to be believed because God is its source. Now it doesn't take a lot of thought to realize that there is a circle here, a pretty tight circle. It comes down to believing that God exists because you believe that God exists. (Recall skeptics such as Sextus and Montaigne, who maintain that all our claims to know are either involved in such circular thinking or are strung out in an infinite regress.)

To break into the circle, Descartes thinks it necessary to *prove rationally* that God exists and that the soul is distinct from the body. His claim that reason should be able to do this is no innovation; Augustine, Anselm, Aquinas, and others had said as much before. Descartes, however, claims to have proofs superior to any offered by these thinkers.

He refers to some thinkers who hold that it is rational to believe the soul perishes with the body. Aristotle seems in the main to think so (though he waffles).* Christian Aristotelians like Thomas Aquinas labor mightily, but inconclusively, to reconcile this view with the tradition of an immortal soul. Descartes thinks he has a proof of the soul that is direct, simple, and conclusive.† He claims, in fact, that his proofs will "surpass in certitude and obviousness the demonstrations of geometry." A strong claim indeed! You will have to decide whether you agree.

These are meditations on *first philosophy.* This is a term derived from Aristotle, who means by it a search for the first principles of things. First philosophy is also called *metaphysics.* Descartes uses a memorable image.‡

> Thus the whole of philosophy is like a tree; the roots are metaphysics, the trunk is physics, and the branches that issue from the trunk are all the other sciences.⁴

---

*For Aristotle's view of the soul as "the form of a living human body" see pp. 181–183.

†Descartes tends to use the terms "soul," "mind," and "spirit" interchangeably. They are all terms for "the thing that thinks." Some philosophers and theologians make distinctions among them.

‡In the twentieth century this image of the tree is used by Martin Heidegger, who claims to be inquiring into the soil that nourishes the roots. See p. 676.

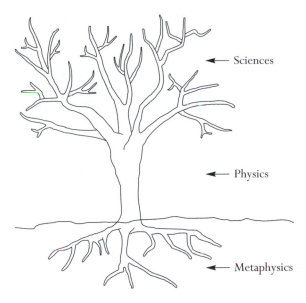

Metaphysics, then, is thought to be more fundamental even than physics. Physics and the other sciences give us detailed knowledge of material things; first philosophy inquires whether material things are the only things there are. What Descartes is seeking is a set of concepts that will give us an inventory of the *basic kinds of being.** As it turns out, his inventory of what there is looks fairly simple. We can diagram it this way:

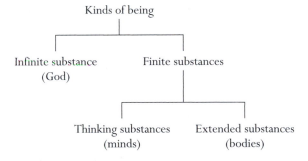

But by itself this chart isn't very informative. It is time to turn to the *Meditations* themselves, to see how Descartes fills in this schema and why it turns out just that way.

The text of *Meditations on First Philosophy* is printed at the end of this chapter, beginning on

---

*Aristotle calls such fundamental concepts "categories." See p. 160. It is interesting to note that in 1641 all the sciences are still counted as parts of philosophy, the love of wisdom.

page 336.[5] You should read through one of the meditations quickly to get a general feel for the argument. After reading it, come back to the commentary and the accompanying questions, using them as a guide to go through the text again, this time paying close attention to Descartes' exact words. He is a careful and clear writer and says exactly what he means. If you proceed in this way, you will not only learn some philosophy but also gain skill in reading a text of some difficulty—a valuable ability. Writing out brief answers to the questions will increase your understanding. Repeat this procedure for each of the six meditations.

It may be helpful to have a preview of this dramatic little work. I offer an outline that sketches the progression from the first *Meditation* to the last.

Meditation I.   The Problem:
Can anything be known?

Meditations II–VI. The Solution: I can know
   II.   that I exist.
   III. that God exists.
   IV.   why we make mistakes and how to avoid them.
   V.   that material things *might* exist; and again, that God exists.
   VI.   that material things *do* exist and are distinct from souls.

Read Meditation I: On What Can Be Called into Doubt   Note the personal, meditative character of the writing. Descartes is inviting us to join him in thinking certain things through, asking us to mull them over and see whether we agree. He is not making authoritative pronouncements. Just as he reserves the right to be the judge of what *he* should believe, so he puts you on the spot. You will have to be continually asking yourself: Do I agree with this or not? If not, why not? This familiar first-person style is quite different from most of medieval philosophy; it harks back to Augustine's *Confessions* in the late fourth century. Descartes is, as it were, having a conversation with himself, so the structure of *Meditation I* is dialectical: proposal, objection, reply, objection, reply. . . . Try to distinguish the various "voices" in this internal dialogue.

Note that there are three stages in the "tearing down" of opinions, and one principle running throughout. The principle is that we ought to withhold assent from anything uncertain, just as much as from what we see clearly to be false. This is simply a restatement of the first rule of his method but is of the greatest importance.* The three stages concern (1) the senses, (2) dreams, and (3) the evil demon hypothesis.

Q1. Aren't you strongly inclined to think, just like Descartes by the fire, that you can't deny that you are now reading this book, which is "right there" in your hands? Should you doubt it anyway?

Q2. What do you think of Descartes' rule that we shouldn't completely trust those who have cheated us even once? Does this rule apply to the senses?

Q3. *Could* you be dreaming right now? Explain.

Q4. What is the argument that even in dreams some things—for example, the truths of mathematics—are not illusory?

Q5. How does the thought of God, at *this* stage, seem to reinforce skeptical conclusions—even about arithmetic?†

Here Descartes avails himself of the techniques of the Pyrrhonists, who set argument against plausible argument until they find themselves no more inclined to judge one way than another. But he acknowledges that this equilibrium or suspension of judgment is difficult to achieve. "Habit" strongly inclines him to believe some of these things as "probable." Like Descartes, you almost certainly take it as *very* probable that you are now looking

_____

*A brief look back at the four rules of the method will be of use at this point. See p. 322. Compare the principle Aquinas notes about big mistakes from small beginnings on p. 275. Once, when a friend of mine stumbled on an unusually high first step of a staircase, I formulated what came jokingly to be known as Norman's First Law: Watch that first step; it's a big one—good advice for appraising philosophical systems. For an alternative to Descartes' view, see the critique by C. S. Peirce on pp. 568–570.
†Review the consequences William of Ockham draws from the doctrine of God's omnipotence (pp. 294–295).

at a piece of paper, which is located a certain determinate distance before your eyes, that you indeed have eyes, and that 2 plus 3 really does equal 5. And you almost certainly find it very hard *not* to believe these things. You probably find yourself so committed to them that you almost *can't* doubt them. (Ask yourself whether this is the case.) How can we overcome these habits of believing? We now know, if Descartes is right so far, that we *should* doubt them. As a remedy against these habitual believings, Descartes determines *deliberately* (as an act of will) to suppose that all his prior beliefs are false.

Q6. How does the hypothesis of the evil demon help?

Descartes now thinks that he has canvassed every possible reason for doubting. We cannot rely on our senses; we cannot even rely on our rational faculties for the simplest truths of mathematics, geometry, or logic. All our beliefs, it seems, are dissolved in the acid of skeptical doubt.

Q7. Before going on to *Meditation II,* ask yourself the question, Is there anything at all that I am *so certain* of that I could not *possibly* doubt it? (Meditate on this question awhile.)

Read **Meditation II: On the Nature of the Human Mind, Which Is Better Known Than the Body** Descartes seems to have gotten nowhere by doubting. What to do? He resolves to press on, suspecting that the terrors of skepticism can be overcome only by enduring them to the end. The monster in the child's closet will disappear only if the child can muster the courage to look at it directly. If we avert our eyes in fear, we will not conquer.

The particular horror, of course, is that all our beliefs might be false—that nowhere would they connect at all with reality. If Descartes has carried us with him to this point, we know that we have lots of ideas and beliefs, but whether any one of them represents something that really *exists* must seem quite uncertain. Perhaps they are just webs of illusion, like those spun by a master magician—or the evil demon.

Descartes here represents a pattern of thought that deserves a name. Let us call it the representational theory of knowledge and perception, or the **representational theory** for short. The basic ideas of this theory are very widely shared in modern philosophy. We can distinguish five points:

1. We have no immediate or direct access to things in the world, only to the world of our ideas.*

2. "Ideas" must be understood broadly to include all the contents of the mind, including perceptions, images, memories, concepts, beliefs, intentions, and decisions.

3. These ideas serve as *representations* of things other than themselves.

4. Much of what these ideas represent, they represent as "out there," or "external" to the mind containing them.

5. It is in principle possible for ideas to represent these things correctly, but they may also be false and misleading.

In *Meditation I,* Descartes draws a certain consequence of the representational theory. It seems that mind and world could be disconnected in a perplexing way, that even the most solid ideas might represent things all wrong—or maybe even not represent anything at all! This possibility, foreshadowed by the ancient skeptics and by William of Ockham

---

*The American philosopher John Searle calls this view that we only perceive our *ideas* of objects "the greatest single disaster in the history of philosophy over the past four centuries." In *Mind: A Brief Introduction* (Oxford: Oxford University Press, 2004), 23.

in his reflections on God's omnipotence, provokes thinkers to try to find a remedy. What we need is a bridge across the chasm between mind and world, and it is clear that it will have to be built by inference and argument. We want *good reasons* to believe that our ideas represent the "external" world truly. But the good reasons must be of a peculiar sort. We have to start this construction project while isolated on one side, restricted in our choice of materials to those available there. It is from the vantage point of the mind that we try to stretch the girders of our argument across the gulf to the world.

We will examine Descartes' effort to build such a rational bridge. The difficulty of that task is emphasized in the dramatic rehearsal of skeptical worries about knowledge in *Meditation I.* And we can now see that these worries hover around the representational theory. The gulf between mind and external reality seems immense.* We might remember Archimedes, who says, "Give me a lever long enough, and a place on which to rest it, and I can move the earth." Descartes thinks that if he can find just one certainty, he might, like Archimedes, do marvels. He might just build that bridge.

Q8.   To what certainty does Descartes' methodical doubt lead? Is he right about that?†

The principle "I think, therefore I am" is often referred to as the *cogito,* from the Latin "I think" and we will use that shorthand expression from time to time. It is worth emphasizing that in the *cogito* Descartes has an example of *knowledge,* of knowledge about *reality,* and so of *metaphysical* knowledge. He has thrown the first plank of his bridge across the chasm.

Note that Descartes rejects the standard, long-accepted way of answering the question, What am I? (p. 338). According to a tradition that goes back

to Socrates (and is codified by Aristotle), the way to answer such a question is to give a *definition.* The traditional way to define something will tell you (a) what *genus* it belongs to and (b) the *difference* between it and other things in that genus. Not surprisingly, this is called *definition by genus and difference.* A human being is said to belong to the genus *animal;* and the difference between a human and other animals is that a human is *rational.* Human beings, Aristotle says, are *rational animals.*

Descartes objects to such a definition because it simply calls for more definitions; you need next a definition of *animal* and a definition for *rational.* Then, presumably, you will require definitions for the terms used to define *them.* And so on.

This whole process has to come to ground somewhere. There must be some terms, Descartes thinks, that do not need definition of this sort, but whose meaning can just be "seen." These will be the *simple* terms. From them, more complex terms can be built up. We see in Descartes' rejection of the traditional definition procedure an application of the second and third rules of his method. He is searching for something so simple, clear, and distinct that it just presents itself without any need for definition. He is looking for something *self-evident.* If that can be found, he can use it as a foundation on which to build more complex truths.

Q9.   What, then, does Descartes conclude that he is?

Note that Descartes briefly considers the view that he may after all *be* a body, or some such thing, even though he does not *know* he is (p. 339).* But he does not try to refute it here; that proof comes in *Meditation VI.* Here he is interested in what he knows that he *is*—not in what he can infer that he *is not.*

Q10.   Why does Descartes rule out the use of the imagination in answering the question, What am I?

Q11.   What is included in "thinking," as Descartes understands the term? (See p. 339.) Note how broad the term is for him.

---

*Other thinkers after Descartes also wrestle with this problem. Locke recognizes the gulf but papers it over, Berkeley settles down on one side of it, Hume despairs of a solution, Kant redefines the problem so as to make the gulf (partially) disappear, Hegel denies there is a gulf at all, and Kierkegaard opens it up again. The problem is not dead today.

†Descartes' central idea here is anticipated by Augustine in his refutation of the skeptics. See pp. 233–235.

*This is the view that Thomas Hobbes urges against Descartes. See "Minds and Motives" in Chapter 14.

Both inferences seem to be correct. What reason is there to prefer Bridget's formulation?

Q12.   Suppose I feel certain that I see a cat on the mat. Is it certain that there is a cat on the mat? What, in this situation, *can* I be certain of?

How difficult it is to stay within the bounds of what I know for certain! As Descartes says, his "mind enjoys wandering." And so it is with us. I, too, keep slipping back into the error of thinking that I know *sensible* things best—this desk, this computer keyboard, this hand. (Do you find that too?)

It is to cure this inclination to rely on the senses that Descartes considers the bit of wax. Read that passage once more (pp. 339–340). All the sensible qualities by means of which we recognize the wax can change. But we still judge that it is the same wax. What does that mean?

The distinction between *ordinary perception* and *judgment* is crucial for Descartes. It is illustrated by the hats and coats we see through the window. We say that we *see* men passing, but this is inaccurate, for they may be just robots dressed like men. What is actually happening in ordinary perception is that our intellect is drawing an *inference* on the basis of certain *data* (supplied by the senses) and issuing a judgment. Judging is an activity of the mind—indeed, as we'll see in *Meditation IV,* of the will.

Perceiving, then, is not a purely passive registration by the senses. Implicit in all perception is judgment, or *giving assent.* In ordinary perception, these judgments are apt to be obscure, confused, and just plain wrong. But fortunately they can be corrected by the application of ideas that are clear and distinct—for example, the mathematical simples. (These points will be crucial in *Meditation IV,* where Descartes explains how it is possible for us to err.)

With respect to the bit of wax, the moral is that it is "grasped, not by the senses or the power of having mental images, but by the understanding alone." When based wholly on sense, our perception is "imperfect and confused." When directed, however, to "the things of which the wax consists" (the mathematically determinable simples of extension, figure, and motion), knowledge of the wax can be *clear and distinct.*

Now we can understand why Descartes introduces the wax example. If even here knowledge cannot be found in sensation, but only in a "purely mental inspection," then we should have less difficulty remembering that knowledge of *what we are* must also be approached in this way. Our tendency to think of ourselves as what we can *sense* of ourselves—these hands, this head, these eyes—is considerably undermined. Indeed, I must know myself "much more truly and certainly" even than the wax.

And there follows a remarkable conclusion: "I can't grasp anything more easily or plainly than my mind." (What would Freud have said to that?)

Q13.   What qualities, then, belong to the wax essentially? (Look again at the basic principles of Descartes' physics on pp. 320–321.)

Q14.   Why is our imagination incapable of grasping these qualities of the wax? By what faculty do we grasp it?

Q15.   How does the wax example help to cure our habitual inclination to trust the senses?

Q16.   How does our language tend to mislead us?

Read Meditation III: On God's Existence   In the first paragraphs, Descartes resolves to explore more carefully his own mind. But then what alternative does he have, now that he has resolved to consider everything else "as empty illusions"?

A momentous step is taken: He *solves* (or at least he thinks he solves) the problem of the criterion! Here are the steps.

1. He is certain that he exists as a thinking thing.

2. He asks himself, What is it about this proposition that accounts for my certainty that it is true?

3. He answers, The fact that I grasp it so clearly and distinctly that I perceive it could not possibly be false.

4. He concludes, Let this then be a general principle (a *criterion*): Whatever I grasp with *like* clarity and distinctness must also be true.

He then reviews (yet again) the things he had at one time thought were true and reminds himself that no matter how sure he feels about them, he can't be absolutely certain.

Q17.   Why does he feel a need to inquire about the existence and nature of God?

Descartes now tries to make clear a crucial distinction between *ideas* on the one hand and *volitions, emotions,* and *judgments* on the other (pp. 341–342). This distinction is embedded in an inventory of the varied contents of the mind (which is all that we can so far be certain of). You will find a schematic representation of that inventory above.

Q18.   What is the key difference between ideas and judgments?

Q19.   What is the key difference between judgments on the one hand, and volitions and emotions on the other?

Q20.   What question arises with respect to the ideas that seem to be acquired from outside myself?

Q21.   What (provisional) examples does Descartes give of each class of ideas?

We need to comment on the notion of **innate ideas.** In calling them "innate," Descartes does not mean to imply that they are to be found in babies and mentally defective adults, as some of his critics suppose. He merely means that there are some ideas we would have even if nothing existed but ourselves. These ideas do not require external causes for their existence in us; every developed rational mind will possess them from its own resources. Thus, the idea of a *thing* can originate with the *cogito,* which gives me the certainty that I exist as a thing that thinks — even if nothing else exists. Perhaps my idea of an antelope is caused in me by seeing antelopes in a zoo (though this remains to be proved). But we would have the ideas of thing, thought, and truth in any case.

Q22.   Why do you think Descartes believes that the ideas of truth and thought are innate?

Q23.   Why is he inclined to believe that some ideas do originate from objects outside himself? He gives two reasons (p. 342).

Q24.   Are these two reasons conclusive?

Q25.   What is the difference between being taught "by nature" and being taught "by the light of nature"? (See p. 342.) What is the **light of nature**?*

----

*It is interesting to compare this with what Augustine says about the Interior Teacher and the light within. (See Chapter 10.) Descartes' view is less explicitly theological and is a step on the road to secularization. It should also be compared to what Heidegger says about "the clearing" (pp. 657–658).

We come now to a point of terminology. Descartes distinguishes *subjective reality* on the one hand from *formal* and *eminent reality* on the other. If we are going to understand Descartes' argument, we must be clear about how he uses these terms and keep his use firmly in mind.

It is easier to begin with formal reality. Something has formal reality if it is, in our terms, actual or existing. If there really are giraffes and angels, then giraffes and angels have formal reality. You also, because you exist, have formal reality. And when you form an image of a giraffe in your mind, that image also has formal reality—that is, it actually exists *as an image* in your mind. So any idea actually present in a mind is formally real. This means that (if there are giraffes) both the idea of a giraffe (when being thought) and the giraffe you are thinking of are formally real. They are distinct realities, but related: The one *represents* the other.

What you are thinking about when you entertain an idea has subjective reality, reality "for you." Giraffes and angels have subjective reality whenever you think of them, but there are ideas whose objects have *only* subjective reality: the tooth fairy, for instance, or unicorns. These, of course, are examples of ideas "produced by us." But if we look carefully, we can see that they have not been invented out of nothing. The idea of a unicorn comes from the ideas of a horse and a single horn. And (though Descartes has not proved it yet) it may be that horses and horns are formally real. Already he remarks (p. 343) that although one idea may be derived from others, this cannot go on to infinity: There must eventually be a cause for these ideas; and the reality of that cause must be more than "merely subjective." If this were not so, we would have gotten something "from nothing." And the light of nature assures us that this is impossible. There is an old Latin saying: *ex nihilo nihil fit,* or "from nothing, nothing comes."

Descartes does not, of course, make these distinctions for their own sake. There is a problem he is trying to solve: Given that I can be certain that *I* exist (together with all my ideas), can I be certain of the *formal* existence of anything else? Although thoroughgoing skepticism may have been refuted (we do know something in the *cogito*), we have not got beyond solipsism. **Solipsism** is a view that

each of you (if there is anyone out there!) must state for yourself in this way: "I am the only thing that actually (formally) exists; everything else is only real *for me.*"

Another step in solving that problem is to note that there are *degrees of reality:* some things have more reality than others. This is the cardinal principle of the Great Chain of Being.* Descartes gives two examples, framed in terms of subjective reality (p. 342), though the same is true for formal reality, as well.

Q26.   Why does the idea of *substance* contain more subjective reality than that of *modification* or *accident?* (Think of a fender and the dent in it.)†

Q27.   Why does the idea of infinite substance have more subjective reality than that of finite substance?

On the basis of these distinctions, Descartes formulates a *causal principle:* There must be at least as much reality in the cause as there is in the effect. A cause is said to be *formally real* when it has the same degree of reality as the effect it produces; it is said to be *eminently real* when it has even more reality than its effect.

Q28.   What examples does Descartes offer to illustrate this causal principle?

Once more Descartes canvasses the various kinds of ideas he finds in himself as a thinking thing. He is looking for some idea of which he himself could not possibly be the cause. Such an idea must have a cause (since nothing comes from nothing). If (1) he is not the cause, and (2) there is a cause, then (3) he knows that he is not alone in the universe. Something else exists!

Descartes thinks his meditations to this point give him the materials with which to prove that God exists. Let us see what it looks like:

1. I have an idea of an infinitely perfect substance.

2. Such an idea must have a cause.

---

*See pp. 239–241.

†I owe this nice example to Ronald Rubin, the translator of these *Meditations.*

3. *Ex nihilo nihil fit.*

4. So the cause of an idea must have at least as much *formal* reality as there is *subjective* reality in the idea.

5. Though I am a substance, I am not infinitely perfect.

6. So I could not be the cause of this idea.

7. So there must be a formal reality that is an infinitely perfect substance.

8. So God exists.

Q29.   Is this argument valid?

Q30.   Are there premises in the argument that are less than certainly true?

Meditation III contains two separate arguments for God's existence. The first one, which we have now examined, begins with the fact that each of us has an *idea* of God. The second one begins (on p. 344) with the fact that it is certainly true that I exist. The argument then addresses whether I could exist if God does not. It is an argument by exclusion; it considers the other plausible candidates for the cause of my existence and shows in each case that it won't do. Note that both of these arguments are *causal* arguments. The first inquires about the cause of my *idea* of God, the second about the cause of my own *existence*. Both make use of the causal principle Descartes has formulated.

Let us sketch the principal steps in this argument.

1. I exist.

2. There must be a cause for my existence.

3. The cause must be one of the following: (a) myself, (b) my always having existed, (c) my parents, (d) something else less perfect than God, or (e) God.

4. Not a, or I would have given myself perfections I now lack—because creating the properties of a substance is not as hard as creating the substance itself.

5. Not b, because my existing now does not *follow from* my having existed in the past.

6. Not c, for this leads to an infinite regress.

7. Not d, for this couldn't account for the unity of the idea of God that I have.

8. So e, and God exists.

Q31.   Is there a weak point in this argument? Is there more than one?

Q32.   Why does Descartes think his idea of God must be innate?

Q33.   Explain why Descartes says we cannot "comprehend" God but can "reach" him in thought. (Compare touching an elephant and wrapping your arms around it.)*

At the end of the third *Meditation,* Descartes feels he has achieved his aim. He now knows that he is not alone. In addition to himself there is at least one other being—a substance infinite in intelligence and power, and perfect in every way. This latter fact will prove to be of very great significance, for Descartes will use it to defeat the hypothesis of the evil demon; a perfect being could not be a deceiver. Thus he thinks he can overcome the deepest ground for skepticism about knowledge of the external world. But that is a line of argument pursued in the remaining meditations.

Read **Meditation IV: On Truth and Falsity** Note the transitional character of the first paragraph. Descartes sums up the argument so far, expresses his confidence that God's existence is more certain than anything else (except the *cogito*), and looks forward to further progress.

Q34.   Is Descartes' assertion (p. 346) that deception is an evidence of weakness rather than power plausible? Explain your answer.

Before God's existence was proved, it was unclear whether any of our beliefs were true. Now there is a new puzzle: How can any of them be false? (Do you see why this puzzle arises?) So Descartes has to provide an explanation of the obvious fact that we can and do make mistakes.

For the basic framework he depends again on the idea of the Great Chain of Being. He finds that

---

*Compare the similar thought by Aquinas, p. 280.

he is an "intermediate" between God and nothingness, having less reality than God, whose perfection excludes error, but more reality than sheer nonbeing. Error, in any case, is not a positive reality; it is only a defect, as weakness is only the absence of strength and cold the absence of heat. So it should not be too surprising that Descartes, and we, too, should be susceptible to error.

Two points he makes in passing are worth noting.

1. Why did God create me so that I could make mistakes? I don't know, he says, but if I could see the world as God sees it, it is quite possible that I would judge it to be for the best.*

Q35. How does recognizing that I am only a part of a larger whole help answer this question?

2. Among the many things we do not know are God's purposes. It follows that Aristotelian final causes—the what for—are not appropriate in the explanations given by physics. Thus Descartes buttresses the mechanistic character of his (and the modern world's) scientific work. We can come to know *how* things happen, but not *why*.

A more detailed analysis of error can be given. It depends on another distinction: that between entertaining a belief, or having it in mind (which is the function of the *understanding*), and assenting to that belief, or accepting it (which is the function of the *will*).

Q36. How does this distinction between *understanding* and *will* explain the possibility of error?

Q37. In what way is the will more perfect than the understanding?

---

*Here is one expression of that attitude expressed in Leibniz and other later writers to the effect that "this is the best of all possible worlds." It is this optimism that Voltaire caricatures so savagely in *Candide.* These reflections of Descartes form part of a project known as *theodicy*—the justification of the ways of God to man. For another attempt at theodicy, see Hegel (pp. 484–486). You might also review the Stoic notion that evil does not exist in the world, but only in our perception of it (p. 206).

Q38. Can God be blamed for our errors?

Q39. How can we avoid error?

Read Meditation V: On the Essence of Material Objects and More on God's Existence This brief meditation is a transition to the more important sixth meditation. Though Descartes says at the beginning that he wants to investigate whether anything can be known about material things (so far, only God and the soul are known), he doesn't solve that problem here. But he does take a significant step toward its solution. And, along the way, he discovers a third proof that God exists.

Again we find the typical Cartesian strategy at work. He wants to know whether material things exist independently of himself. How can he proceed? He can't just look to see because he has put the testimony of the senses in doubt. So he must consider more carefully the *idea* of material things, which is all that is available to him. And again he finds that some of these ideas are confused and obscure, while others are clear and distinct. The latter are those of extension, duration, and movement—the qualities that can be treated geometrically or mathematically. Material things, if there are any, are essentially extended volumes.* Once we are clear about their *essence,* it makes sense to inquire about their *existence;* and that is the subject of *Meditation VI.*

Note that these mathematical ideas are not just imaginary inventions. I cannot put them together any way I like, as I can construct fantastic creatures by combining heads, bodies, and hides at will. I may not yet know whether there are any triangular things outside myself, but the idea of a triangle "can't be said to be nothing" (p. 349). It has a *nature* that is "immutable and eternal." This nature does not depend on me.

The point can be put in this way. Suppose you imagine a creature with wings covered with scales, a long furry tail, six legs, and an elephantlike nose covered with spikes. Then I ask you, does this creature have a liver? You will have to *invent* the answer. You cannot discover it. But if you imagine a triangle

---

*Review the discussion of the bit of wax in *Meditation II* and on p. 329.

and I ask you whether the interior angles equal two right angles, you do not have to invent an answer. Even if you had never thought about that question before, you could investigate and discover that the answer is yes. With respect to these geometrical properties, there are *truths*.* And these, remember, are the very properties that determine the essence of material things.

Since the idea of a material thing is the idea of something extended, and since extended things can be treated geometrically, it follows that the *idea* of a material thing is clear and distinct. Material substances have an essence or nature that would make a *science* of them a possibility—if only we could be assured that they exist. And we know that such a science is a possibility merely from an examination of their ideas. So, provided we can discover a proof that some *formal* reality corresponds to the *subjective* reality of our ideas of material things, we can have a science of material things. In this way, then, he hopes to give a metaphysical foundation to his mechanistic physics.

The discovery that certain ideas have a nature or essence of their own, quite independent of our inventions, also supplies Descartes with material for a third proof of God's existence.† If we simply pay close attention to what is necessarily involved in our idea of *what* God is (his essence or nature), we can discover, Descartes argues, *that* God is (that he exists). God's existence is included in his essence. Notice that, unlike the first two arguments, this is not a *causal* proof. In its bare essentials, it looks like this:

1. God, by definition, is a being of infinite perfection.
2. Existence is a perfection (that is, no being could be perfect that lacked it).
3. So God exists.

Q40.   Is the argument valid?

Q41.   Can the premises be questioned?

This last proof of God's existence allows Descartes to lay to rest a final worry that has been tormenting him. You really cannot help believing, he suggests, that your clear and distinct thoughts are true—while you are thinking them. But later you may not be so sure! You may then think you were dreaming what earlier seemed so certain. But now this worry can be dealt with. And *Meditation V* closes on a note of reassurance.

Q42.   How are the dream and demon worries finally disposed of?

Q43.   Can an atheist do science? (See the last paragraph.)

***Read* Meditation VI: On the Existence of Material Objects and the Real Distinction of Mind from Body**   We now know what the essence of material things is: To be such a thing is to be extended in space in three dimensions, to have shape and size, to endure, and to be movable and changeable in these dimensions. This is what a material thing would be—if there were any. At last we face the haunting question: Are there any?

The first thing to note is that they *can* exist.

Q44.   What is Descartes' reason for thinking this?

If, moreover, we examine our *images* of material things, it seems that the imagination produces these images by turning "to the body" and looking "at something there" (p. 352). It is as though a representation of a triangle were physically stored in the body (or brain); and imagination is looking, not at a real triangular thing, but at that stored representation. Because we can undoubtedly form mental images, it certainly seems as though some material things exist—namely, our bodies.

---

*Socrates thinks that we can never be taught anything other than what we in some sense already know; what we call "learning" is in fact just remembering. (See p. 142.) Descartes alludes to this doctrine here; in discovering the properties of a triangle I am "noticing for the first time something that had long been in me without my having turned my mind's eye towards it." Descartes is not, however, committed to the Socratic doctrine of the preexistence of the soul as an explanation of this phenomenon, since he thinks God's creation of a soul possessing certain innate ideas will suffice.

†This proof is a version of the ontological argument first worked out by Anselm of Canterbury in the eleventh century. See Chapter 11.

But to make this clearer, Descartes draws a sharp distinction between *imagining* something and *conceiving* it.

Q45.   How does the example comparing the triangle with the chiliagon help to clarify this distinction? (See p. 351.)

We still have no proof, of course, that there are any bodies. But again, progress has been made; for we now have an account of how one of the faculties of the mind works — on the assumption that there really are bodies. If we can find a proof of this assumption, it will "fit" with what we know about our mental capacities.

Descartes now turns from imagining to sensing. On pages 352–353, he reviews again his reasons for confidence in the senses and then his reasons for doubt.* At the end of this review he concludes again that what he is taught "by nature" does not deserve much credence.

However, the situation is now very different from that of the first *Meditation.* For now he knows that God exists and is not a deceiver. And in short order Descartes offers proofs that the soul is distinct from the body and that material things exist. Both of these depend on clear ideas of the essence of material things, which he arrived at in the fifth *Meditation.*

Here, in outline, is his proof for the distinctness of soul from body.

1.   God can create anything that I can clearly and distinctly conceive — there being no impossibility in it.

2.   If God can create one thing independently of another, the first thing is distinct from the second.

3.   I have a clear and distinct idea of my essence as a thinking thing.

4.   So God can create a thinking thing (a soul) independently of a body.

5.   I also have a clear and distinct idea of my body as an extended thing — its essence.

6.   So God can create a body independently of a soul.

7.   So my soul is a reality distinct from my body.

8.   So I, as a thinking thing (soul), can exist without my body.

Q46.   How sound is this argument? What are the weak points, if any?

Q47.   Is there a tension between the conclusion of this argument and Descartes' assertion (p. 354) that I am *not* in my body the way a sailor is in his ship?*

Descartes' proof for the reality of material things goes roughly like this:

1.   I have a "strong inclination" to believe in the reality of the material (extended) things that I seem to sense. (To put it another way, their independent reality seems to be one of the things I am "taught by nature.")

2.   God must have created me with this inclination.

3.   If material things do not exist independently, then God is a deceiver.

4.   But God is not a deceiver.

5.   So material things exist with those properties I conceive to be essential to them.

Q48.   Evaluate the soundness of this argument.

At this point, Descartes has, he thinks, achieved his main objectives. Skepticism and solipsism have been defeated. The basic structure of reality has been delineated: God, souls, and material things. Reality, then, is composed of infinite substance and two kinds of finite substances — thinking and extended. The bridge has been built. Knowledge has

---

*In the course of this review he paraphrases one of the basic principles of Thomas Aquinas, who derives it from Aristotle: There is no idea in the intellect, which was not previously in the senses. This is, for instance, the foundation for Aquinas' rejection of the ontological argument (see p. 275). Descartes allows that this principle is superficially plausible, but in the light of his skeptical doubts he considers it naive. Not only do we know that we have ideas before we know we have senses, we know that some of these ideas must be innate — that is, they could not plausibly be derived from sensible experience. Such are the ideas of thing, thought, truth, and God.

*Compare the use that Aquinas makes of this same image, p. 284.

been shown to be possible. Physics has been supplied with a foundation in metaphysics. And all this with a certainty that rivals that of geometry!

The rest of *Meditation VI* attends to a few details that are still left.

Q49.   Compare what Descartes says on p. 354 with Galileo's view of "secondary qualities" (pp. 316–317).

Q50.   If the senses present external things in such an inadequate way, what use are they?

Q51.   How are we to account for certain errors the senses seem to lead us to—such as the pain in an amputated limb or the desire of a person with dropsy (edema) to drink?

Q52.   What is the final disposition of the problem arising from dreams?

MEDITATIONS ON FIRST PHILOSOPHY
Meditation I: On What Can Be Called into Doubt

For several years now, I've been aware that I accepted many falsehoods as true in my youth, that what I built on the foundation of those falsehoods was dubious, and accordingly that once in my life I would need to tear down everything and begin anew from the foundations if I wanted to establish any stable and lasting knowledge. But the task seemed enormous, and I waited until I was so old that no better time for undertaking it would be likely to follow. I have thus delayed so long that it would be wrong for me to waste in indecision the time left for action. Today, then, having rid myself of worries and having arranged for some peace and quiet, I withdraw alone, free at last earnestly and wholeheartedly to overthrow all my beliefs.

To do this, I don't need to show each of them to be false; I may never be able to do that. But, since reason now convinces me that I ought to withhold my assent just as carefully from what isn't obviously certain and indubitable as from what's obviously false, I can justify the rejection of all my beliefs if in each I can find some ground for doubt. And, to do this, I need not run through my beliefs one by one, which would be an endless task. Since a building collapses when its foundation is cut out from under it, I will go straight to the principles on which all my former beliefs rested.

Of course, whatever I have so far accepted as supremely true I have learned either from the senses or through the senses. But I have occasionally caught the senses deceiving me, and it's prudent never completely to trust those who have cheated us even once.

But, while my senses may deceive me about what is small or far away, there may still be other things that I take in by the senses but that I cannot possibly doubt—like that I am here, sitting before the fire, wearing a dressing gown, touching this paper. And on what grounds might I deny that my hands and the other parts of my body exist?—unless perhaps I liken myself to madmen whose brains are so rattled by the persistent vapors of melancholy that they are sure that they're kings when in fact they are paupers, or that they wear purple robes when in fact they're naked, or that their heads are clay, or that they are gourds, or made of glass. But these people are insane, and I would seem just as crazy if I were to apply what I say about them to myself.

This would be perfectly obvious—if I weren't a man accustomed to sleeping at night whose experiences while asleep are at least as far-fetched as those that madmen have while awake. How often, at night, I've been convinced that I was here, sitting before the fire, wearing my dressing gown, when in fact I was undressed and between the covers of my bed! But now I am looking at this piece of paper with my eyes wide open; the head that I am shaking has not been lulled to sleep; I put my hand out consciously and deliberately and feel. None of this would be as distinct if I were asleep. As if I can't remember having been tricked by similar thoughts while asleep! When I think very carefully about this, I see so plainly that there are no reliable signs by which I can distinguish sleeping from waking that I am stupefied—and my stupor itself suggests that I am asleep!

Suppose, then that I am dreaming. Suppose, in particular, that my eyes are not open, that my head is not moving, and that I have not put out my hand. Suppose that I do not have hands, or even a body. I must still admit that the things I see in sleep are like painted images which must have been patterned after real things and, hence, that things like eyes, heads, hands, and bodies are real rather than imaginary. For, even when painters try to give bizarre shapes to sirens and satyrs, they are unable to give them completely new natures; they only jumble together the parts of various animals. And, even if they were to come up with something so novel that no one had ever seen anything like it before, something entirely fictitious and unreal, at least there must be real colors from which they composed it. Similarly, while things like eyes, heads, and hands may be imaginary, it must be granted that some simpler and more universal things are real—the "real colors" from which the true and false images in our thoughts are formed.

Things of this sort seem to include general bodily nature and its extension, the shape of extended things, their quantity (that is, their size and number), the place in which they exist, the time through which they endure, and so on.

Perhaps we can correctly infer that, while physics, astronomy, medicine, and other disciplines that require the study of composites are dubious, disciplines like arithmetic and geometry, which deal only with completely simple and universal things without regard to whether they exist in the world, are somehow certain and indubitable. For, whether we are awake or asleep, two plus three is always five, and the square never has more than four sides. It seems impossible even to suspect such obvious truths of falsity.

Nevertheless, the traditional view is fixed in my mind that there is a God who can do anything and by whom I have been made to be as I am. How do I know that He hasn't brought it about that, while there is in fact no earth, no sky, no extended thing, no shape, no magnitude, and no place, all of these things seem to me to exist, just as they do now? I think that other people sometimes err in what they believe themselves to know perfectly well. Mightn't I be deceived when I add two and three, or count the sides of a square, or do even simpler things, if we can even suppose that there is anything simpler? Maybe it will be denied that God deceives me, since He is said to be supremely good. But, if God's being good is incompatible with His having created me so that I am deceived always, it seems just as out of line with His being good that He permits me to be deceived sometimes—as he undeniably does.

Maybe some would rather deny that there is an omnipotent God than believe that everything else is uncertain. Rather than arguing with them, I will grant every-thing I have said about God to be fiction. But, however these people think I came to be as I now am—whether they say it is by fate, or by accident, or by a continuous series of events, or in some other way—it seems that he who errs and is deceived is somehow imperfect. Hence, the less power that is attributed to my original creator, the more likely it is that I am always deceived. To these arguments, I have no reply. I'm forced to admit that nothing that I used to believe is beyond legitimate doubt—not because I have been careless or playful, but because I have valid and well-considered grounds for doubt. Hence, I must withhold my assent from my former beliefs as carefully as from obvious falsehoods if I want to arrive at something certain.

But it's not enough to have noticed this: I must also take care to bear it in mind. For my habitual views constantly return to my mind and take control of what I believe as if our long-standing, intimate relationship has given them the right to do so, even against my will. I'll never break the habit of trusting and giving in to these views while I see them for what they are—things somewhat dubious (as I have just shown) but nonetheless probable, things that I have much more reason to believe than to deny. That's why I think it will be good deliberately to turn my will around, to allow myself to be deceived, and to suppose that all my previous beliefs are false and illusory. Eventually, when I have counterbalanced the weight of my prejudices, my bad habits will no longer distort my grasp of things. I know that there is no danger of error here and that I won't overindulge in skepticism, since I'm now concerned, not with action, but only with gaining knowledge.

I will suppose, then, not that there is a supremely good God who is the source of all truth, but that there is an evil demon, supremely powerful and cunning, who works as hard as he can to deceive me. I will say that sky, air, earth, color, shape, sound, and other external things are just dreamed illusions that the demon uses to ensnare my judgment. I will regard myself as not having hands, eyes, flesh, blood, and senses—but as having the false belief that I have all these things. I will obstinately concentrate on this meditation and will thus ensure by mental resolution that, if I do not really have the ability to know the truth, I will at least withhold assent from what is false and from what a deceiver may try to put over on me, however powerful and cunning he may be. But this plan requires effort, and laziness brings me back to my ordinary life. I am like a prisoner who happens to enjoy the illusion of freedom in his dreams, begins to suspect that he is asleep, fears being awakened, and deliberately lets the enticing illusions slip by unchallenged. Thus, I slide back into my old views, afraid to awaken and to find that after my peaceful rest I must toil, not in the light, but in the confusing darkness of the problems just raised.

Meditation II:
On the Nature of the Human Mind,
Which Is Better Known Than the Body

Yesterday's meditation has hurled me into doubts so great that I can neither ignore them nor think my way out of them. I am in turmoil, as if I have accidentally fallen into a whirlpool and can neither touch bottom nor swim to the safety of the surface. I will struggle, however, and try to follow the path that I started on yesterday. I will reject whatever is open to the slightest doubt just as though I have found it to be entirely false, and I will continue until I find something certain—or at least until I know for certain that nothing is certain. Archimedes required only one fixed and immovable point to move the whole earth from its place, and I too can hope for great things if I can find even one small thing that is certain and unshakeable.

I will suppose, then, that everything I see is unreal. I will believe that my memory is unreliable and that none of what it presents to me ever happened. I have no senses. Body, shape, extension, motion, and place are fantasies. What then is true? Perhaps just that nothing is certain.

But how do I know that there isn't something different from the things just listed that I do not have the slightest reason to doubt? Isn't there a God, or something like one, who puts my thoughts into me? But why should I say so when I may be the author of those thoughts? Well, isn't it at least the case that I am something? But I now am denying that I have senses and a body. But I stop here. For what follows from these denials? Am I so bound to my body and to my senses that I cannot exist without them? I have convinced myself that there is nothing in the world—no sky, no earth, no minds, no bodies. Doesn't it follow that I don't exist? No, surely I must exist if it's me who is convinced of something. But there is a deceiver, supremely powerful and cunning whose aim is to see that I am always deceived. But surely I exist, if I am deceived. Let him deceive me all he can, he will never make it the case that I am nothing while I think that I am something. Thus having fully weighed every consideration, I must finally conclude that the statement "I am, I exist" must be true whenever I state it or mentally consider it.

But I do not yet fully understand what this "I" is that must exist. I must guard against inadvertently taking myself to be something other than I am, thereby going wrong even in the knowledge that I put forward as supremely certain and evident. Hence, I will think once again about what I believed myself to be before beginning these meditations. From this conception, I will subtract everything challenged by the reasons for doubt that I produced earlier, until nothing remains except what is certain and indubitable.

What, then, did I formerly take myself to be? A man, of course. But what is a man? Should I say a rational animal? No, because then I would need to ask what an animal is and what it is to be rational. Thus, starting from a single question, I would sink into many that are more difficult, and I do not have the time to waste on such subtleties. Instead, I will look here at the thoughts that occurred to me spontaneously and naturally when I reflected on what I was. This first thought to occur to me was that I have a face, hands, arms, and all the other equipment (also found in corpses) which I call a body. The next thought to occur to me was that I take nourishment, move myself around, sense, and think—that I do things which I trace back to my soul. Either I didn't stop to think about what this soul was, or I imagined it to be a rarified air, or fire, or ether permeating the denser parts of my body. But, about physical objects, I didn't have any doubts whatever: I thought that I distinctly knew their nature. If I had tried to describe my conception of this nature, I might have said this: "When I call something a physical object, I mean that it is capable of being bounded by a shape and limited to a place; that it can fill a space so as to exclude other objects from it; that it can be perceived by touch, sight, hearing, taste, and smell; that it can be moved in various ways, not by itself, but by something else in contact with it." I judged that the powers of self-movement, of sensing, and of thinking did not belong to the nature of physical objects, and, in fact, I marveled that there were some physical objects in which these powers could be found.

But what should I think now, while supposing that a supremely powerful and "evil" deceiver completely devotes himself to deceiving me? Can I say that I have any of the things that I have attributed to the nature of physical objects? I concentrate, think, reconsider—but nothing comes to me; I grow tired of the pointless repetition. But what about the things that I have assigned to soul? Nutrition and self-movement? Since I have no body, these are merely illusions. Sensing? But I cannot sense without a body, and in sleep I've seemed to sense many things that I later realized I had not really sensed. Thinking? It comes down to this: Thought and thought alone cannot be taken away from me. I am, I exist. That much is certain. But for how long? As long as I think—for it may be that, if I completely stopped thinking, I would completely cease to exist. I am not now admitting anything unless it must be true, and I am therefore not admitting that I am anything at all other than a thinking thing—that is, a mind, soul, understanding, or reason (terms whose meaning I did not previously know). I know that I am a real, existing thing, but what kind of thing? As I have said, a thing that thinks.

What else? I will draw up mental images. I'm not the collection of organs called a human body. Nor am I some rarified gas permeating these organs, or air, or fire, or vapor, or breath—for I have supposed that none of these things exist. Still, I am something. But couldn't it be that these things, which I do not yet know about and which I am therefore supposing to be nonexistent, really aren't distinct from the "I" that I know to exist? I don't know, and I'm not going to argue about it now. I can only form judgments on what I do know. I know that I exist, and I ask what the "I" is that I know to exist. It's obvious that this conception of myself doesn't depend on anything that I do not yet know to exist and, therefore, that it does not depend on anything of which I can draw up a mental image. And the words "draw up" point to my mistake. I would truly be creative if I were to have a mental image of what I am, since to have a mental image is just to contemplate the shape or image of a physical object. I now know with certainty that I exist and at the same time that all images—and, more generally, all things associated with the nature of physical objects—may just be dreams. When I keep this in mind, it seems just as absurd to say "I use mental images to help me understand what I am" as it would to say "Now, while awake, I see something true—but, since I don't yet see it clearly enough, I'll go to sleep and let my dreams present it to me more clearly and truly." Thus I know that none of the things that I can comprehend with the aid of mental images bear on my knowledge of myself. And I must carefully draw my mind away from such things if it is to see its own nature distinctly.

But what then am I? A thinking thing. And what is that? Something that doubts, understands, affirms, denies, wills, refuses, and also senses and has mental images.

That's quite a lot, if I really do all of these things. But don't I? Isn't it me who now doubts nearly everything, understands one thing, affirms this thing, refuses to affirm other things, wants to know much more, refuses to be deceived, has mental images (sometimes involuntarily), and is aware of many things "through his senses"? Even if I am always dreaming, and even if my creator does what he can to deceive me, isn't it just as true that I do all these things as that I exist? Are any of these things distinct from my thought? Can any be said to be separate from me? That it's me who doubts, understands, and wills is so obvious that I don't see how it could be more evident. And it's also me who has mental images. While it may be, as I am supposing, that absolutely nothing of which I have a mental image really exists, the ability to have mental images really does exist and is a part of my thought. Finally, it's me who senses—or who seems to gain awareness of physical objects through the senses. For example, I am now seeing light, hearing a noise, and feeling heat. These things are unreal, since I am dreaming. But it is still certain that I seem to see, to hear, and to feel. This seeming cannot be unreal, and it is what is properly called sensing. Strictly speaking, sensing is just thinking.

From this, I begin to learn a little about what I am. But I still can't stop thinking that I apprehend physical objects, which I picture in mental images and examine with my senses, much more distinctly than I know this unfamiliar "I," of which I cannot form a mental image. I think this, even though it would be astounding if I comprehended things which I've found to be doubtful, unknown, and alien to me more distinctly than the one which I know to be real: my self. But I see what's happening. My mind enjoys wandering, and it won't confine itself to the truth. I will therefore loosen the reigns on my mind for now so that later, when the time is right, I will be able to control it more easily.

Let's consider the things commonly taken to be the most distinctly comprehended: physical objects that we see and touch. Let's not consider physical objects in general, since general conceptions are very often confused. Rather, let's consider one, particular object. Take, for example, this piece of wax. It has just been taken from the honeycomb; it hasn't yet completely lost the taste of honey; it still smells of the flowers from which it was gathered; its color, shape, and size are obvious; it is hard, cold, and easy to touch; it makes a sound when rapped. In short, everything seems to be present in the wax that is required for me to know it as distinctly as possible. But, as I speak, I move the wax toward the fire; it loses what was left of its taste; it gives up its smell; it changes color; it loses its shape; it gets bigger; it melts;

it heats up; it becomes difficult to touch; it no longer makes a sound when struck. Is it still the same piece of wax? We must say that it is: not one denies it or thinks otherwise. Then what was there in the wax that I comprehended so distinctly? Certainly nothing that I reached with my senses — for, while everything having to do with taste, smell, sight, touch, and hearing has changed, the same piece of wax remains.

Perhaps what I distinctly knew was neither the sweetness of honey, nor the fragrance of flowers, nor a sound, but a physical object that once appeared to me one way and now appears differently. But what exactly is it of which I now have a mental image? Let's pay careful attention, remove everything that doesn't belong to the wax, and see what's left. Nothing is left except an extended, flexible, and changeable thing. But what is it for this thing to be flexible and changeable? Is it just that the wax can go from round to square and then to triangular, as I have mentally pictured? Of course not. Since I understand that the wax's shape can change in innumerable ways, and since I can't run through all the changes in my imagination, my comprehension of the wax's flexibility and changeability cannot have been produced by my ability to have mental images. And what about the thing that is extended? Are we also ignorant of its extension? Since the extension of the wax increases when the wax melts, increases again when the wax boils, and increases still more when the wax gets hotter, I will be mistaken about what the wax is unless I believe that it can undergo more changes in extension than I can ever encompass with mental images. I must therefore admit that I do not have an image of what the wax is — that I grasp what it is with only my mind. (While I am saying this about a particular piece of wax, it is even more clearly true about wax in general.) What then is this piece of wax that I grasp only with my mind? It is something that I see, feel, and mentally picture — exactly what I believed it to be at the outset. But it must be noted that, despite the appearances, my grasp of the wax is not visual, tactile, or pictorial. Rather, my grasp of the wax is the result of a purely mental inspection, which can be imperfect and confused, as it was once, or clear and distinct, as it is now, depending on how much attention I pay to the things of which the wax consists.

I'm surprised by how prone my mind is to error. Even when I think to myself non-verbally, language stands in my way, and common usage comes close to deceiving me. For, when the wax is present, we say that we see the wax itself, not that we infer its presence from its color and shape. I'm inclined to leap from this fact about language to the conclusion that I learn about the wax by eyesight rather than by purely mental inspection. But, if I happen to look out my window and see men walking in the street, I naturally say that I see the men just as I say that I see the wax. What do I really see, however, but hats and coats that could be covering robots? I *judge* that there are men. Thus I comprehend with my judgment, which is in my mind, objects that I once believed myself to see with my eyes.

One who aspires to wisdom above that of the common man disgraces himself by deriving doubt from common ways of speaking. Let's go on, then, to ask when I most clearly and perfectly grasped what the wax is. Was it when I first looked at the wax and believed my knowledge of it to come from the external senses — or at any rate from the so-called "common sense," the power of having mental images? Or is it now, after I have carefully studied what the wax is and how I come to know it? Doubt would be silly here. For what was distinct in my original conception of the wax? How did that conception differ from that had by animals? When I distinguish the wax from its external forms — when I "undress" it and view it "naked" — there may still be errors in my judgments about it, but I couldn't possibly grasp the wax in this way without a human mind.

What should I say about this mind — or, in other words, about myself? (I am not now admitting that there is anything to me but a mind.) What is this "I" that seems to grasp the wax so distinctly? Don't I know myself much more truly and certainly, and also much more distinctly and plainly, than I know the wax? For, if I base my judgment that the wax exists on the fact that I see it, my seeing it much more obviously implies that I exist. It's possible that what I see is not really wax, and it's even possible that I don't have eyes with which to see — but it clearly is not possible that, when I see (or, what now amounts to the same thing, when I think I see), the "I" that thinks is not a real thing. Similarly, if I base my judgment that the wax exists on the fact that I feel it, the same fact makes it obvious that I exist. If I base my judgment that the wax exists on the fact that I have a mental image of it or on some other fact of this sort, the same thing can obviously be said. And what I've said about the wax applies to everything else that is outside me. Moreover, if I seem to grasp the wax more distinctly when I detect it with several senses than when I detect it with just sight or touch, I must know myself even more distinctly — for every consideration that contributes to my grasp of the piece of wax or to my grasp of any other physical object serves better to reveal the nature of my mind. Besides, the mind has so much in it by which it can make its conception of itself distinct that what comes to it from physical objects hardly seems to matter.

And now I have brought myself back to where I wanted to be. I now know that physical objects are grasped, not by the senses or the power of having mental images, but by understanding alone. And, since I grasp physical objects in virtue of their being understandable rather than in virtue of their being tangible or visible, I know that I can't grasp anything more easily or plainly than my mind. But, since it takes time to break old habits of thought, I should pause here to allow the length of my contemplation to impress the new thoughts more deeply into my memory.

Meditation III: On God's Existence

I will now close my eyes, plug my ears, and withdraw all my senses. I will rid my thoughts of the images of physical objects—or, since that's beyond me, I'll write those images off as empty illusions. Talking with myself and looking more deeply into myself, I'll try gradually to come to know myself better. I am a thinking thing—a thing that doubts, affirms, denies, understands a few things, is ignorant of many things, wills, and refuses. I also sense and have mental images. For, as I've noted, even though the things of which I have sensations or mental images may not exist outside me, I'm certain that the modifications of thought called sensations and mental images exist in me insofar as they are just modifications of thought.

That's a summary of all that I really know—or, at any rate, of all that I've so far noticed that I know. I now will examine more carefully whether there are other things in me that I have not yet discovered. I'm certain that I am a thinking thing. Then don't I know what's needed for me to be certain of other things? In this first knowledge, there is nothing but a clear and distinct grasp of what I affirm, and this grasp surely would not suffice to make me certain if it could ever happen that something I grasped so clearly and distinctly was false. Accordingly, I seem to be able to establish the general rule that whatever I clearly and distinctly grasp is true.

But, in the past, I've accepted as completely obvious and certain many thoughts that I later found to be dubious. What were these thoughts about? The earth, the sky, the stars, and other objects of sense. But what did I clearly grasp about these objects? Only that ideas or thoughts of them appeared in my mind. Even now, I don't deny that these ideas occur in me. But there was something else that I used to affirm—something that I used to believe myself to grasp clearly but did not really grasp at all: I affirmed that there were things besides me, that the ideas in me came from these things, and that the ideas perfectly resembled these things. Either I erred here, or I reached a true judgment that wasn't justified by the strength of my understanding.

But what follows? When I considered very simple and easy points of arithmetic or geometry—such as that two and three together make five—didn't I see them clearly enough to affirm their truth? My only reason for judging that I ought to doubt these things was the thought that my God-given nature might deceive me even about what seems most obvious. Whenever I conceive of an all-powerful God, I'm compelled to admit that, if He wants, He can make it the case that I err even about what I take my mind's eye to see most clearly. But, when I turn to the things that I believe myself to grasp very clearly, I'm so convinced by them that I spontaneously burst forth saying, "Whoever may deceive me, he will never bring it about that I am nothing while I think that I am something, or that I have never been when it is now true that I am, or that two plus three is either more or less than five, or that something else in which I recognize an obvious inconsistency is true." And, since I have no reason for thinking that God is a deceiver—indeed since I don't yet know whether God exists—the grounds for doubt that rest on the supposition that God deceives are very weak and "metaphysical." Still, to rid myself of these grounds, I ought to ask as soon as possible whether there is a God and, if so, whether He can be a deceiver. For it seems that, until I know these two things, I can never be completely certain of anything else.

The structure of my project seems to require, however, that I first categorize my thoughts and ask in which of them truth and falsity really reside. Some of my thoughts are like images of things, and only these can properly be called ideas. I have an idea, for example, when I think of a man, of a chimera, of heaven, of an angel, or of God. But other thoughts have other properties: while I always apprehend something as the object of my thought when I will, fear, affirm, or deny, these thoughts also include a component in addition to the likeness of that thing. Some of these components are called volitions or emotions; others, judgments.

Now, viewed in themselves and without regard to other things, ideas cannot really be false. If I imagine a chimera and a goat, it is just as true that I imagine the chimera as that I imagine the goat. And I needn't worry about falsehoods in volitions or emotions. If I have a perverse desire for something, or if I want something that doesn't exist, it's still true that I want that thing. All that remains, then, are my judgments; it's here that I must be careful not to err. And the first and foremost of the errors that I find in my judgments is that of assuming that the ideas in me have a similarity or conformity to things outside me. For, if I were to regard ideas merely as modifications of thought, they could not really provide me with any opportunity for error.

Of my ideas, some seem to me to be innate, others acquired, and others produced by me. The ideas by which I understand reality, truth, and thought seem to have come from my own nature. Those ideas by which I hear a noise, see the sun, or feel the fire I formerly judged to come from things outside me. And the ideas of sirens, hippogriffs, and so on I have formed in myself. Or maybe I can take all of my ideas to be acquired, all innate, or all created by me: I do not yet clearly see where my ideas come from.

For the moment, the central question is about the ideas that I view as derived from objects existing outside me. What reason is there for thinking that these ideas resemble the objects? I seem to have been taught this by nature. Besides, I find that these ideas are independent of my will and hence of me—for they often appear when I do not want them to do so. For example, I now feel heat whether I want to or not, and I therefore take the idea or sensation of heat to come from something distinct from me: the heat of the fire by which I am now sitting. And the obvious thing to think is that a thing sends me its own likeness, not something else.

I will now see whether these reasons are good enough. When I say that nature teaches me something, I mean just that I have a spontaneous impulse to believe it, not that the light of nature reveals the thing's truth to me. There is an important difference. When the light of nature reveals something to me (such as that my thinking implies my existing) that thing is completely beyond doubt, since there is no faculty as reliable as the light of nature by means of which I could learn that the thing is not true. But, as for my natural impulses, I have often judged them to have led me astray in choices about what's good, and I don't see why I should regard them as any more reliable on matters concerning truth and falsehood.

Next, while my sensory ideas may not depend on my will, it doesn't follow that they come from outside me. While the natural impulses of which I just spoke are in

me, they seem to conflict with my will. Similarly, I may have in me an as yet undiscovered ability to produce the ideas that seem to come from outside me—in the way that I used to think that ideas came to me in dreams.

Finally, even if some of my ideas do come from things distinct from me, it doesn't follow that they are likenesses of these things. Indeed, it often seems to me that an idea differs greatly from its cause. For example, I find in myself two different ideas of the sun. One, which I "take in" through the senses and which I ought therefore to view as a typical acquired idea, makes the sun look very small to me. The other, which I derive from astronomical reasoning (that is, which I make, perhaps by composing it from innate ideas), pictures the sun as many times larger than the earth. It clearly cannot be that both of these are accurate likenesses of a sun that exists outside me, and reason convinces me that the one least like the sun is the one that seems to arise most directly from it.

All that I've said shows that, until now, my belief that there are things outside me that send their ideas or images to me (perhaps through my senses) has rested on blind impulse rather than certain judgment.

Still, it seems to me that there may be a way of telling whether my ideas come from things that exist outside me. Insofar as the ideas of things are just modifications of thought, I find no inequality among them; all seem to arise from me in the same way. But, insofar as different ideas present different things to me, there obviously are great differences among them. The ideas of substances are unquestionably greater—or have more "subjective reality"—than those of modifications or accidents. Similarly, the idea by which I understand the supreme God—eternal, infinite, omniscient, omnipotent, and creator of all things other than Himself—has more subjective reality in it than the ideas of finite substances.

Now, the light of nature reveals that there is at least as much in a complete efficient cause as in its effect. For where could an effect get its reality if not from its cause? And how could a cause give something unless it had it? It follows both that something cannot come from nothing and that what is more perfect—that is, has more reality in it—cannot come from what is less perfect or has less reality. This obviously holds, not just for those effects whose reality is actual or formal, but also for ideas, whose reality we regard as merely subjective. For example, it's impossible for a non-existent stone to come into existence unless it's produced by something containing, either formally or eminently, everything in the stone. Similarly, heat can only be induced in something that's not already hot by something having at least the same degree of perfection as heat. Also, it's impossible for the *idea* of heat or of stone to be in me unless it's been put there by a cause having at least as much reality as I conceive of in the heat or the stone. For, although the cause doesn't transmit any of its actual or formal reality to the idea, we shouldn't infer that it can be less real than the idea; all that we can infer is that by its nature the idea doesn't require any formal reality except what it derives from my thought, of which it is a modification. Yet, as the idea contains one particular subjective reality rather than another, it must get this reality from a cause having at least as much formal reality as the idea has subjective reality. For, if we suppose that an idea has something in it that wasn't in its cause, we must suppose that it got this thing from nothing. However imperfect the existence of something that exists subjectively in the understanding through an idea, it obviously is something, and it therefore cannot come from nothing.

And, although the reality that I'm considering in my ideas is just subjective, I ought not to suspect that it can fail to be in an idea's cause formally—that it's enough for it to be there subjectively. For, just as the subjective existence of my ideas belongs to the ideas in virtue of their nature, the formal existence of the ideas' causes belongs to those causes—or, at least, to the first and foremost of them—in virtue of the causes' nature. Although one idea may arise from another, this can't go back to infinity; we must eventually arrive at a primary idea whose cause is an "archetype" containing formally all the reality that the idea contains subjectively. Hence, the light of nature makes it clear to me that the ideas in me are like images that may well fall short of the things from which they derive, but cannot contain anything greater or more perfect.

The more time and care I take in studying this, the more clearly and distinctly I know it to be true. But what follows from it? If I can be sure that the subjective reality of one of my ideas is so great that it isn't in me either formally or eminently and hence that I cannot be the cause of that idea, I can infer that I am not alone in the world—that there exists something else that is the cause of the idea. But, if I can find no such idea in me, I will have no argument at all for the existence of anything other than me—for, having diligently searched for such an argument, I have yet to find one.

Of my ideas—besides my idea of myself, about which there can be no problem here—one presents God, others inanimate physical objects, others angels, others animals, and still others men like me.

As to my idea of other men, of animals, and of angels, it's easy to see that—even if the world contained no men but me, no animals, and no angels—I could have composed these ideas from those that I have of myself, of physical objects, and of God.

And, as to my ideas of physical objects, it seems that nothing in them is so great that it couldn't have come from me. For, if I analyze my ideas of physical objects carefully, taking them one by one as I did yesterday when examining my idea of the piece of wax, I notice that there is very little in them that I grasp clearly and distinctly. What I do grasp clearly and distinctly in these ideas is size (which is extension in length, breadth, and depth), shape (which arises from extension's limits), position (which the differently shaped things have relative to one another), and motion (which is just change of position). To these I can add substance, duration, and number. But my thoughts of other things in physical objects (such as light and color, sound, odor, taste, heat and cold, and tactile qualities) are so confused and obscure that I can't say whether they are true or false—whether my ideas of these things are of something or of nothing. Although, as I noted earlier, that which is properly called falsehood—namely, *formal* falsehood—can only be found in judgments, we can still find falsehood of another sort—namely, *material* falsehood—in an idea when it presents what is not a thing as though it were a thing. For example, the ideas that I have of coldness and heat are so unclear and indistinct that I can't tell from them whether coldness is just the absence of heat, or heat just the absence of coldness, or both are real qualities, or neither is. And, since every idea is "of something," the idea that presents coldness to me as something real and positive could justifiably be called false if coldness were just the absence of heat. And the same holds true for other ideas of this sort.

For such ideas, I need not posit a creator distinct from me. I know by the light of nature that, if one of these ideas is false—that is, if it doesn't present a real thing—it comes from nothing—that is, the only cause of its being in me is a deficiency of my nature, which clearly is imperfect. If one of these ideas is true, however, I still see no reason why I couldn't have produced it myself—for these ideas present so little reality to me that I can't even distinguish it from nothing.

Of the things that are clear and distinct in my ideas of physical objects, it seems that I may have borrowed some—such as substance, duration, and number—from my idea of myself. I think of the stone as a substance—that is, as something that can exist on its own—just as I think of myself as a substance. Although I conceive of myself as a thinking and unextended thing and of the stone as an extended and unthinking thing so that the two conceptions are quite different, they are the same in that they both seem to be of substances. And, when I grasp that I exist now while remembering that I existed in the past, or when I count my various thoughts, I get the idea of duration or number, which I can then apply to other things. The other components of my ideas of physical objects—extension, shape, place, and motion—can't be in me formally, since I'm just a thinking thing. But, as these things are just modes of substance, and as I am a substance, it seems that they may be in me eminently.

All that's left is my idea of God. Is there something in this idea of God that couldn't have come from me? By "God" I mean a substance that's infinite, independent, supremely intelligent, and supremely powerful—the thing from which I and everything else that may exist derive our existence. The more I consider these attributes, the less it seems that they could have come from me alone. So I must conclude that God necessarily exists.

While I may have the idea of substance in me by virtue of my being a substance, I who am finite would not have the idea of infinite substance in me unless it came from a substance that really was infinite.

And I shouldn't think that, rather than having a true idea of infinity, I grasp it merely as the absence of limits—in the way that I grasp rest as the absence of motion and darkness as the absence of light. On the contrary, it's clear to me that there is more reality in an infinite than in a finite substance and hence that my grasp of the infinite must somehow be prior to my grasp of the finite—my understanding of God prior to my understanding of myself. For how could I understand that I doubt and desire, that I am deficient and imperfect, if I didn't have the idea of something more perfect to use as a standard of comparison?

And, unlike the ideas of hot and cold which I just discussed, the idea of God cannot be said to be materially false and hence to come from nothing. On the contrary, since the idea of God is completely clear and distinct and contains more subjective reality than any other idea, no idea is truer *per se* and none less open to the suspicion of falsity. The idea of a supremely perfect and infinite entity is, I maintain, completely true. For, while I may be able to suppose that there is no such entity, I can't even suppose (as I did about the idea of coldness) that my idea of God fails to show me something real. This idea is maximally clear and distinct, for it contains everything that I grasp clearly and distinctly, everything real and true, everything with any perfection. It doesn't matter that I can't fully comprehend the infinite—that there are innumerable things in God which I can't comprehend

fully or even reach with thought. Because of the nature of the infinite, I who am finite cannot comprehend it. It's enough that I think about the infinite and judge that, if I grasp something clearly and distinctly and know it to have some perfection, it's present either formally or eminently—perhaps along with innumerable other things of which I am ignorant—in God. If I do this, then of all my ideas the idea of God will be most true and most clear and distinct.

But maybe I am greater than I have assumed; maybe all the perfections that I attributed to God are in me potentially, still unreal and unactualized. I have already seen my knowledge gradually increase, and I don't see anything to prevent its becoming greater and greater to infinity. Nor do I see why, by means of such increased knowledge, I couldn't get all the rest of God's perfections. Finally, if the potential for these perfections is in me, I don't see why that potential couldn't account for the production of the ideas of these perfections in me.

None of this is possible. First, while it's true that my knowledge gradually increases and that I have many as yet unactualized potentialities, none of this fits with my idea of God, in whom absolutely nothing is potential; indeed, the gradual increase in my knowledge shows that I am *imperfect*. Besides, I see that, even if my knowledge were continually to become greater and greater, it would never become actually infinite, since it would never become so great as to be unable to increase. But I judge God to be actually infinite so that nothing can be added to his perfection. Finally, I see that an idea's subjective being must be produced, not by mere potentiality (which, strictly speaking, is nothing), but by what is actual or formal.

When I pay attention to these things, the light of nature makes all of them obvious. But, when I attend less carefully and the images of sensible things blind my mind's eye, it's not easy for me to remember why the idea of an entity more perfect than I am must come from an entity that really is more perfect. That's why I'll go on to ask whether I, who have the idea of a perfect entity, could exist if no such entity existed.

From what might I derive my existence if not from God? Either from myself, or from my parents, or from something else less perfect than God—for nothing more perfect than God, or even as perfect as Him, can be thought of or imagined.

But, if I derived my existence from myself, I wouldn't doubt, or want, or lack anything. I would have given myself every perfection of which I have an idea, and thus I myself would be God. And I shouldn't think that it might be harder to give myself what I lack than what I already have. On the contrary, it would obviously be much harder for me, a thinking thing or substance, to emerge from nothing than for me to give myself knowledge of the many things of which I am ignorant, which is just an attribute of substance. But surely, if I had given myself that which is harder to get, I wouldn't have denied myself complete knowledge, which would have been easier to get. Indeed, I wouldn't have denied myself *any* of the perfections that I grasp in the idea of God. None of these perfections seems harder to get than existence. But, if I had given myself everything that I now have, these perfections would have seemed harder to get than existence if they were harder to get—for in creating myself I would have discovered the limits of my power.

I can't avoid the force of this argument by supposing that, since I've always existed as I do now, there's no point in looking for my creator. Since my lifetime can be divided into innumerable parts each of which is independent of the others, the fact that I existed a little while ago does not entail that I exist now, unless a cause "re-creates" me—or, in other words, preserves me—at this moment. For, when we attend to the nature of time, it's obvious that exactly the same power and action are required to preserve a thing at each moment through which it endures as would be required to create it anew if it had never existed. Hence, one of the things revealed by the light of nature is that preservation and creation differ only in the way we think of them.

I ought to ask myself, then, whether I have the power to ensure that I, who now am, will exist in a little while. Since I am nothing but a thinking thing—or, at any rate, since I am now focusing on the part of me that thinks— I would surely be aware of this power if it were in me. But I find no such power. And from this I clearly see that there is an entity distinct from me on whom I depend.

But maybe this entity isn't God. Maybe I am the product of my parents or of some other cause less perfect than God. No. As I've said, there must be at least as much in a cause as in its effect. Hence, since I am a thinking thing with the idea of God in me, my cause, whatever it may be, must be a thinking thing having in it the idea of every perfection that I attribute to God. And we can go on to ask whether this thing gets its existence from itself or from something else. If it gets its existence from itself, it's obvious from what I've said that it must be God—for it would have the power to exist on its own and hence the power actually to give itself every perfection of which it has an idea, including every perfection that I conceive of in God. But, if my cause gets its existence from some other thing, we can go on to ask whether this other thing gets its existence from itself or

from something else. Eventually, we will come to the ultimate cause, which will be God.

It's clear enough that there can't be an infinite regress here—especially since I am concerned, not so much with the cause that originally produced me, as with the one that preserves me at the present moment.

And I can't suppose that several partial causes combined to make me or that I get the ideas of the various perfections that I attribute to God from different causes so that, while each of these perfections can be found somewhere in the universe, there is no God in whom they all come together. On the contrary, one of the chief perfections that I understand God to have is unity, simplicity, inseparability from everything in Him. Surely the idea of the unity of all God's perfections can only have been put in me by a cause that gives me the ideas of all the other perfections—for nothing could make me aware of the unbreakable connection of God's perfections unless it made me aware of what those perfections are.

Finally, even if everything that I used to believe about my parents is true, it's clear that they don't preserve me. Insofar as I am a thinking thing, they did not even take part in creating me. They simply formed the matter in which I used to think that I (that is, my mind, which is all I am now taking myself to be) resided. There can therefore be no problem about my parents. And I am driven to this conclusion: The fact that I exist and have an idea in me of a perfect entity—that is, God—conclusively entails that God does in fact exist.

All that's left is to explain how I have gotten my idea of God from Him. I have not taken it in through my senses; it has never come to me unexpectedly as the ideas of sensible things do when those things affect (or seem to affect) my external organs of sense. Nor have I made the idea myself; I can't subtract from it or add to it. The only other possibility is that the idea is innate in me, like my idea of myself.

It's not at all surprising that in creating me God put this idea into me, impressing it on His work like a craftsman's mark (which needn't be distinct from the work itself). The very fact that it was God who created me confirms that I have somehow been made in His image or likeness and that I grasp this likeness, which contains the idea of God, in the same way that I grasp myself. Thus, when I turn my mind's eye on myself, I understand, not just that I am an incomplete and dependent thing which constantly strives for bigger and better things, but also that He on whom I depend has all these things in Himself as infinite reality rather than just as vague potentiality and hence that He must be God. The whole argument comes down to this: I know that I could not exist with my present nature—that is, that I could not exist with the idea of God in me—unless there really were a God. This must be the very God whose idea is in me, the thing having all of the perfections that I can't fully comprehend but can somehow reach with thought, who clearly cannot have any defects. From this, it's obvious that He can't deceive—for, as the natural light reveals, fraud and deception arise from defect.

But before examining this more carefully and investigating its consequences, I want to dwell for a moment in the contemplation of God, to ponder His attributes, to see and admire and adore the beauty of His boundless light, insofar as my clouded insight allows. As I have faith that the supreme happiness of the next life consists wholly of the contemplation of divine greatness, I now find that contemplation of the same sort, though less perfect, affords the greatest joy available in this life.

Meditation IV:
On Truth and Falsity

In the last few days, I've gotten used to drawing my mind away from my senses. I've carefully noted that I really grasp very little about physical objects, that I know much more about the human mind, and that I know even more about God. Thus, I no longer find it hard to turn my thoughts away from things of which I can have mental images and toward things completely separate from matter, which I can only understand. Indeed, I have a much more distinct idea of the human mind, insofar as it is just a thinking thing that isn't extended in length, breadth, or depth and doesn't share anything else with physical objects, than I have of physical objects. And, when I note that I doubt or that I am incomplete and dependent, I have a clear and distinct idea of a complete and independent entity: God. From the fact that this idea is in me and that I who have the idea exist, I can clearly infer both that God exists and that I am completely dependent on Him for my existence from moment to moment. This is so obvious that I'm sure that people can't know anything more evidently or certainly. And it now seems to me that, from the contemplation of the true God in whom are hidden all treasures of knowledge and wisdom, there is a way to derive knowledge of other things.

In the first place, I know that it's impossible for Him ever to deceive me. Wherever there is fraud and deception, there is imperfection, and, while the ability to deceive may seem a sign of cunning or power, the desire to deceive reveals malice or weakness and hence is inconsistent with God's nature.

Next, I find in myself an ability to judge which, like everything else in me, I've gotten from God. Since He doesn't want to deceive me, He certainly hasn't given me an ability which will lead me wrong when properly used.

There can be no doubt about this—except that it may seem to imply that I don't err at all. For, if I've gotten everything in me from God and He hasn't given me the ability to err, it doesn't seem possible for me ever to err. Thus, as long as I think only of God and devote all my attention to Him, I can't find any cause for error and falsity. When I turn my attention back to myself, however, I find that I can make innumerable errors. In looking for the cause of these errors, I find before me, not just the real and positive idea of God, but also the negative idea of "nothingness"—the idea of that which is completely devoid of perfection. I find that I am "intermediate" between God and nothingness, between the supreme entity and nonentity. Insofar as I am the creation of the supreme entity, there's nothing in me to account for my being deceived or led into error, but, insofar as I somehow participate in nothingness or the nonentity—that is, insofar as I am distinct from the supreme entity itself and lack many things—it's not surprising that I go wrong. I thus understand that, in itself, error is a lack, rather than a real thing dependent on God. Hence, I understand that I can err without God's having given me a special ability to do so. Rather, I fall into error because my God-given ability to judge the truth is not infinite.

But there's still something to be explained. Error is not just an absence, but a deprivation—the lack of knowledge that somehow ought to be in me. But, when I attend to God's nature, it seems impossible that He's given me an ability that is an imperfect thing of its kind—an ability lacking a perfection that it ought to have. The greater the craftsman's skill, the more perfect his product. Then how can the supreme creator of all things have made something that isn't absolutely perfect? There's no doubt that God could have made me so that I never err and that He always wants what's best. Then is it better for me to err than not to err?

When I pay more careful attention, I realize that I shouldn't be surprised at God's doing things that I can't explain. I shouldn't doubt His existence just because I find that I sometimes can't understand why or how He has made something. I know that my nature is weak and limited and that God's is limitless, incomprehensible, and infinite, and, from this, I can infer that He can do innumerable things whose reasons are unknown to me. On this ground alone, I regard the common practice of explaining things in terms of their purposes to be useless in physics: it would be foolhardy of me to think that I can discover God's purposes.

It also seems to me that, when asking whether God's works are perfect, I ought to look at all of them together, not at one in isolation. For something that seems imperfect when viewed alone might seem completely perfect when regarded as having a place in the world. Of course, since calling everything into doubt, I haven't established that anything exists besides me and God. But, when I consider God's immense power, I can't deny that He has made—or, in any case, that He could have made—many other things, and I must therefore view myself as having a place in a universe.

Next, turning to myself and investigating the nature of my errors (which are all that show me to be imperfect), I notice that these errors depend on two concurrent causes: my ability to know and my ability to choose freely—that is, my understanding and my will. But, with my understanding, I just grasp the ideas about which I form judgments, and error therefore cannot properly be said to arise from the understanding itself. While there may be innumerable things of which I have no idea, I can't say that I am deprived of these ideas, but only that I happen to lack them—for I don't have any reason to think that God ought to have given me a greater ability to know than He has. And, while I understand God to be a supremely skilled craftsman, I don't go on to think that He ought to endow each of his works with all the perfections that He can put in the others.

Nor can I complain about the scope or perfection of my God-given freedom of will—for I find that my will doesn't seem to me to be restricted in any way. Indeed, it seems well worth noting that nothing in me other than my will is so great and perfect that it couldn't conceivably be bigger or better. If I think about my ability to understand, for example, I realize that it is very small and restricted and I immediately form the idea of something much greater—indeed, of something supremely perfect and infinite. And, from the fact that I can form the idea of this thing, I infer that it is present in God's nature. Similarly, if I consider my other abilities, like the abilities to remember and to imagine, I clearly see that they all are weak and limited in me, but boundless in God. My will or freedom of choice is the only thing I find to be so great in me that I can't conceive of anything greater. In fact, it's largely for this reason that I regard

myself as an image or likeness of God. God's will is incomparably greater than mine, of course, in virtue of the associated knowledge and power that make it stronger and more effective, and also in virtue of all its greater range of objects. Yet, viewed in itself as a will, God's will seems no greater than mine. For having a will just amounts to being able either to do or not to do (affirm or deny, seek or avoid)—or, better, to being inclined to affirm or deny, seek or shun what the understanding offers, without any sense of being driven by external forces. To be free, I don't need to be inclined towards both alternatives. On the contrary, the more I lean towards one alternative—either because I understand the truth or goodness in it, or because God has so arranged my deepest thoughts—the more freely I choose it. Neither divine grace nor knowledge of nature ever diminishes my freedom; they increase and strengthen it. But the indifference that I experience when no consideration impels me towards one alternative over another is freedom of the lowest sort, whose presence reveals a defect or an absence of knowledge rather than a perfection. For, if I always knew what was good or true, I wouldn't ever deliberate about what to do or choose, and thus, though completely free, I would never be indifferent.

From this I see that my God-given ability to will is not itself the cause of my errors—for my will is great, a perfect thing of its kind. Neither is my power of understanding the cause of my errors; whenever I understand something, I understand it correctly and without the possibility of error, since my understanding comes from God. What then is the source of my errors? It is just that, while my will has a broader scope than my understanding, I don't keep it within the same bounds, but extend it to that which I don't understand. Being indifferent to these things, my will is easily led away from truth and goodness, and thus I am led into error and sin.

For example, I've asked for the last few days whether anything exists in the world, and I've noted that, from the fact that I ask this, it follows that I exist. I couldn't fail to judge that which I so clearly understood to be true. This wasn't because a force outside me compelled me to believe, but because an intense light in my understanding produced a strong inclination of my will. And, to the extent that I wasn't indifferent, I believed spontaneously and freely. However, while I now know that I exist insofar as I am a thinking thing, I notice in myself an idea of what it is to be a physical object and I come to wonder whether the thinking nature that's in me—or, rather, that *is* me—differs from this bodily nature or is identical to it. Nothing occurs to my reason (I am supposing) to convince me of one alternative rather than the other. Accordingly, I am completely indifferent to affirming either view, to denying either view, and even to suspending judgment.

And indifference of this sort is not limited to things of which the understanding is completely ignorant. It extends to everything about which the will deliberates in the absence of a sufficiently clear understanding. For, however strong the force with which plausible conjectures draw me towards one alternative, the knowledge that they are conjectures rather than assertions backed by certain and indubitable arguments is enough to push my assent the other way. The past few days have provided me with ample experience of this—for I am now supposing each of my former beliefs to be false just because I've found a way to call them into doubt.

If I suspend judgment when I don't clearly and distinctly grasp what's true, I obviously do right and am not deceived. But, if I either affirm or deny in a case of this sort, I misuse my freedom of choice. If I affirm what is false, I clearly err, and, if I stumble onto the truth, I'm still blameworthy since the light of nature reveals that a perception of the understanding should always precede a decision of the will. In these misuses of freedom of choice lies the deprivation that accounts for error. And this deprivation, I maintain, lies in the working of the will insofar as it comes from me—not in my God-given ability to will, or even in the will's operation insofar as it derives from Him.

I have no reason to complain that God hasn't given me a more perfect understanding or a greater natural light than He has. It's in the nature of a finite understanding that there are many things it can't understand, and it's in the nature of created understanding that it's finite. Indeed, I ought to be grateful to Him who owes me absolutely nothing for what He has bestowed, rather than taking myself to be deprived or robbed of what God hasn't given me.

And I have no reason to complain about God's having given me a will whose scope is greater than my understanding's. The will is like a unity made of inseparable parts; its nature apparently will not allow anything to be taken away from it. And, really, the wider the scope of my will, the more grateful I ought to be to Him who gave it to me.

Finally, I ought not to complain that God concurs in bringing about the acts of will and judgment in which I err. Insofar as these acts derive from God, they are completely true and good, and I am more perfect with the ability to perform these acts than I would be without it. And, the deprivation that is the real ground of falsity and error doesn't need God's concurrence, since it's not a thing. When we regard God as its cause, we should say that it is an absence rather than a deprivation. For it clearly is no imperfection in God that He has given me the freedom to assent or not to assent to things of which He hasn't given me a clear and distinct grasp. Rather, it is undoubtedly an imperfection in me that I misuse this freedom by passing judgment on things that I don't properly understand. I see, of course, that God could easily have brought it about that, while I remain free and limited in knowledge, I never err: He could have implanted in me a clear and distinct understanding of everything about which I was ever going to make a choice, or He could have indelibly impressed on my memory that I must never pass judgment on something that I don't clearly and distinctly understand. And I also understand that, regarded in isolation from everything else, I would have been more perfect if God had made me so that I never err. But I can't deny that, because some things are immune to error while others are not, the universe is more perfect than it would have been if all its parts were alike. And I have no right to complain about God's wanting me to hold a place in the world other than the greatest and most perfect.

Besides, if I can't avoid error by having a clear grasp of every matter on which I make a choice, I can avoid it in the other way, which only requires remembering that I must not pass judgment on matters whose truth isn't apparent. For, although I find myself too weak to fix my attention permanently on this single thought, I can—by careful and frequent meditation—ensure that I call it to mind whenever it's needed and thus that I acquire the habit of avoiding error.

Since the first and foremost perfection of man lies in avoiding error, I've profited from today's meditation, in which I've investigated the cause of error and falsity. Clearly, the only possible cause of error is the one I have described. When I limit my will's range of judgment to the things presented clearly and distinctly to my understanding, I obviously cannot err—for everything that I clearly and distinctly grasp is something and hence must come, not from nothing, but from God—God, I say, who is supremely perfect and who cannot possibly deceive. Therefore, what I clearly and distinctly grasp is unquestionably true. Today, then, I have learned what to avoid in order not to err and also what to do to reach the truth. I surely will reach the truth if I just attend to the things that I understand perfectly and distinguish them from those that I grasp more obscurely and confusedly. And that's what I'll take care to do from now on.

Meditation V:
On the Essence of Material Objects
and More on God's Existence

Many questions remain about God's attributes and the nature of my self or mind. I may return to these questions later. But now, having found what to do and what to avoid in order to attain truth, I regard nothing as more pressing than to work my way out of the doubts that I raised the other day and to see whether I can find anything certain about material objects.

But, before asking whether any such objects exist outside me, I ought to consider the ideas of these objects as they exist in my thoughts and see which are clear and which confused.

I have a distinct mental image of the quantity that philosophers commonly call continuous. That is, I have a distinct mental image of the extension of this quantity—or rather of the quantified thing—in length, breadth, and depth. I can distinguish various parts of this thing. I can ascribe various sizes, shapes, places, and motions to these parts and various durations to the motions.

In addition to having a thorough knowledge of extension in general, I grasp innumerable particulars about things like shape, number, and motion, when I pay careful attention. The truth of these particulars is so obvious and so consonant with my nature that, when I first think of one of these things, I seem not so much to be learning something novel as to be remembering something that I already knew—or noticing for the first time something that had long been in me without my having turned my mind's eye toward it.

What's important here, I think, is that I find in myself innumerable ideas of things which, though they may not exist outside me, can't be said to be nothing. While I have some control over my thoughts of these things, I do not make the things up: they have their own real and immutable natures. Suppose, for example, that I have a mental image of a triangle. While it may be that no figure of this sort does exist or ever has existed outside my thought, the figure has a fixed nature (essence or form), immutable and eternal, which hasn't been produced by me and isn't dependent on my mind. The proof is that I can demonstrate various propositions about the tri-

angle, such as that its angles equal two right angles and that its greatest side subtends its greatest angle. Even though I didn't think of these propositions at all when I first imagined the triangle, I now clearly see their truth whether I want to or not, and it follows that I didn't make them up.

It isn't relevant that, having seen triangular physical objects, I may have gotten the idea of the triangle from external objects through my organs of sense. For I can think of innumerable other figures whose ideas I could not conceivably have gotten through my senses, and I can demonstrate facts about these other figures just as I can about the triangle. Since I know these facts clearly, they must be true, and they therefore must be something rather than nothing. For it's obvious that everything true is something, and, as I have shown, everything that I know clearly and distinctly is true. But, even if I hadn't shown this, the nature of my mind would have made it impossible for me to withhold my assent from these things, at least when I clearly and distinctly grasped them. As I recall, even when I clung most tightly to objects of sense, I regarded truths about shape and number—truths of arithmetic, geometry, and pure mathematics—as more certain than any others.

But, if anything whose idea I can draw from my thought must in fact have everything that I clearly and distinctly grasp it to have, can't I derive from this a proof of God's existence? Surely, I find the idea of God, a supremely perfect being, in me no less clearly than I find the ideas of figures and numbers. And I understand as clearly and distinctly that eternal existence belongs to His nature as that the things which I demonstrate of a figure or number belong to the nature of the figure or number. Accordingly, even if what I have thought up in the past few days hasn't been entirely true, I ought to be at least as certain of God's existence as I used to be of the truths of pure mathematics.

At first, this reasoning may seem unclear and fallacious. Since I'm accustomed to distinguishing existence from essence in other cases, I find it easy to convince myself that I can separate God's existence from His essence and hence that I can think of God as nonexistent. But, when I pay more careful attention, it's clear that I can no more separate God's existence from His essence than a triangle's angles equaling two right angles from the essence of the triangle, or the idea of a valley from the idea of a mountain. It's no less impossible to think that God (the supremely perfect being) lacks existence (a perfection) than to think that a mountain lacks a valley.

Well, suppose that I can't think of God without existence, just as I can't think of a mountain without a valley. From the fact that I can think of a mountain with a valley, it doesn't follow that a mountain exists in the world. Similarly, from the fact that I can think of God as existing, it doesn't seem to follow that He exists. For my thought doesn't impose any necessity on things. It may be that, just as I can imagine a winged horse when no such horse exists, I can ascribe existence to God when no God exists.

No, there is a fallacy here. From the fact that I can't think of a mountain without a valley it follows, not that the mountain and valley exist, but only that whether they exist or not they can't be separated from one another. But, from the fact that I can't think of God without existence, it follows that existence is inseparable from Him and hence that He really exists. It's not that my thoughts make it so or impose a necessity on things. On the contrary, it's the fact that God does exist that necessitates my thinking of Him as I do. For I am not free to think of God without existence—of the supremely perfect being without supreme perfection—as I am free to think of a horse with or without wings.

Now someone might say this: "If I take God to have all perfections, and if I take existence to be a perfection, I must take God to exist, but I needn't accept the premise that God has all perfections. Similarly, if I accept the premise that every quadrilateral can be inscribed in a circle, I'm forced to the patently false view that every rhombus can be inscribed in a circle, but I need not accept the premise." But this should not be said. For, while it's not necessary that the idea of God occurs to me, it is necessary that, whenever I think of the primary and supreme entity and bring the idea of Him out of my mind's "treasury," I attribute all perfections to Him, even if I don't enumerate them or consider them individually. And this necessity ensures that, when I do notice that existence is a perfection, I can rightly conclude that the primary and supreme being exists. Similarly, while it's not necessary that I ever imagine a triangle, it is necessary that, when I do choose to consider a rectilinear figure having exactly three angles, I attribute to it properties from which I can rightly infer that its angles are no more than two right angles, perhaps without noticing that I am doing so. But, when I consider which shapes can be inscribed in the circle, there's absolutely no necessity for my thinking that all quadrilaterals are among them. Indeed, I can't even think that all quadrilaterals are among them, since I've resolved to accept only what I clearly and distinctly understand. Thus my false sup-

positions differ greatly from the true ideas implanted in me, the first and foremost of which is my idea of God. In many ways, I see that this idea is not a figment of my thought, but the image of a real and immutable nature. For one thing, God is the only thing that I can think of whose existence belongs to its essence. For another thing, I can't conceive of there being two or more such Gods, and, having supposed that one God now exists, I see that He has necessarily existed from all eternity and will continue to exist into eternity. And I also perceive many other things in God that I can't diminish or alter.

But, whatever proof I offer, it always comes back to the fact that I am only convinced of what I grasp clearly and distinctly. Of the things that I grasp in this way, some are obvious to everyone. Some are discovered only by those who examine things more closely and search more carefully, but, once these things have been discovered, they are regarded as no less certain than the others. That the square on the hypotenuse of a right triangle equals the sum of the squares on the other sides is not as readily apparent as that the hypotenuse subtends the greatest angle, but, once it has been seen, it is believed just as firmly. And, when I'm not overwhelmed by prejudices and my thoughts aren't besieged by images of sensible things, there surely is nothing that I know earlier or more easily than facts about God. For what is more self-evident than there is a supreme entity—that God, the only thing whose existence belongs to His essence, exists?

While I need to pay careful attention in order to grasp this, I'm now as certain of it as of anything that seems most certain. In addition, I now see that the certainty of everything else so depends on it that, if I weren't certain of it, I couldn't know anything perfectly.

Of course, my nature is such that, when I grasp something clearly and distinctly, I can't fail to believe it. But my nature is also such that I can't permanently fix my attention on a single thing so as always to grasp it clearly, and memories of previous judgments often come to me when I am no longer attending to the grounds on which I originally made them. Accordingly, if I were ignorant of God, arguments could be produced that would easily overthrow my opinions, and I therefore would have unstable and changing opinions rather than true and certain knowledge. For example, when I consider the nature of the triangle, it seems plain to me—steeped as I am in the principles of geometry—that its three angles equal two right angles: I can't fail to believe this as long as I pay attention to its demonstration. But, if I were ignorant of God, I might come to doubt its truth as soon as my mind's eye turned away from its demonstration, even if I recalled having once grasped it clearly. For I could convince myself that I've been so constructed by nature that I sometimes err about what I believe myself to grasp most plainly—especially if I remember that, having taken many things to be true and certain, I had later found grounds on which to judge them false.

But now I grasp that God exists, and I understand both that everything else depends on Him and that He's not a deceiver. From this, I infer that everything I clearly and distinctly grasp must be true. Even if I no longer pay attention to the grounds on which I judged God to exist, my recollection that I once clearly and distinctly knew Him to exist ensures that no contrary ground can be produced to push me towards doubt. About God's existence, I have true and certain knowledge. And I have such knowledge, not just about this one thing, but about everything else that I remember having proven, like the theorems of geometry. For what can now be said against my believing these things? That I am so constructed that I always err? But I now know that I can't err about what I clearly understand. That much of what I took to be true and certain I later found to be false? But I didn't grasp any of these things clearly and distinctly; ignorant of the true standard of truth, I based my belief on grounds that I later found to be unsound. Then what can be said? What about the objection (which I recently used against myself) that I may be dreaming and that the things I'm now experiencing may be as unreal as those that occur to me in sleep? No, even this is irrelevant. For, even if I am dreaming, everything that is evident to my understanding must be true.

Thus I plainly see that the certainty and truth of all my knowledge derives from one thing: my thought of the true God. Before I knew Him, I couldn't know anything else perfectly. But now I can plainly and certainly know innumerable things, not only about God and other mental beings, but also about the nature of physical objects, insofar as it is the subject-matter of pure mathematics.

Meditation VI:
On the Existence of Material Objects and the Real Distinction of Mind from Body

It remains for me to examine whether material objects exist. Insofar as they are the subject of pure mathematics, I now know at least that they can exist, because I grasp them clearly and distinctly. For God can undoubt-

edly make whatever I can grasp in this way, and I never judge that something is impossible for Him to make unless there would be a contradiction in my grasping the thing distinctly. Also, the fact that I find myself having mental images when I turn my attention to physical objects seems to imply that these objects really do exist. For, when I pay careful attention to what it is to have a mental image, it seems to me that it's just the application of my power of thought to a certain body which is immediately present to it and which must therefore exist.

To clarify this, I'll examine the difference between having a mental image and having a pure understanding. When I have a mental image of a triangle, for example, I don't just understand that it is a figure bounded by three lines; I also "look at" the lines as though they were present to my mind's eye. And this is what I call having a mental image. When I want to think of a chiliagon, I understand that it is a figure with a thousand sides as well as I understand that a triangle is a figure with three, but I can't imagine its sides or "look" at them as though they were present. Being accustomed to using images when I think about physical objects, I may confusedly picture some figure to myself, but this figure obviously is not a chiliagon—for it in no way differs from what I present to myself when thinking about a myriagon or any other many sided figure, and it doesn't help me to discern the properties that distinguish chiliagons from other polygons. If it's a pentagon that is in question, I can understand its shape, as I can that of the chiliagon, without the aid of mental images. But I can also get a mental image of the pentagon by directing my mind's eye to its five lines and to the area that they bound. And it's obvious to me that getting this mental image requires a special mental effort different from that needed for understanding—a special effort which clearly reveals the difference between having a mental image and having a pure understanding.

It also seems to me that my power of having mental images, being distinct from my power of understanding, is not essential to my self or, in other words, to my mind—for, if I were to lose this ability, I would surely remain the same thing that I now am. And it seems to follow that this ability depends on something distinct from me. If we suppose that there is a body so associated with my mind that the mind can "look into" it at will, it's easy to understand how my mind might get mental images of physical objects by means of my body. If there were such a body, the mode of thinking that we call imagination would differ from pure understanding in only one way: when the mind understood something, it would turn "inward" and view an idea that it found in it-self, but, when it had mental images, it would turn to the body and look at something there which resembled an idea that it had understood by itself or had grasped by sense. As I've said, then, it's easy to see how I get mental images, if we supposed that my body exists. And, since I don't have in mind any other equally plausible explanation of my ability to have mental images, I conjecture that physical objects probably do exist. But this conjecture is only probable. Despite my careful and thorough investigation, the distinct idea of bodily nature that I get from mental images does not seem to have anything in it from which the conclusion that physical objects exist validly follows.

Besides having a mental image of the bodily nature that is the subject-matter of pure mathematics, I have mental images of things which are not so distinct—things like colors, sounds, flavors, and pains. But I seem to grasp these things better by sense, from which they seem to come (with the aid of memory) to the understanding. Thus, to deal with these things more fully, I must examine the senses and see whether there is anything in the mode of awareness that I call sensation from which I can draw a conclusive argument for the existence of physical objects.

First, I'll remind myself of the things that I believed really to be as I perceived them and of the grounds for my belief. Next, I'll set out the grounds on which I later called this belief into doubt. And, finally, I'll consider what I ought to think now.

To begin with, I sensed that I had a head, hands, feet, and the other members that make up a human body. I viewed this body as part, or maybe even as all, of me. I sensed that it was influenced by other physical objects whose effects could be either beneficial or harmful. I judged these effects to be beneficial to the extent that I felt pleasant sensations and harmful to the extent that I felt pain. And, in addition to sensations of pain and pleasure, I sensed hunger, thirst, and other such desires—and also bodily inclinations towards cheerfulness, sadness, and other emotions. Outside me, I sensed, not just extension, shape, and motion, but also hardness, hotness, and other qualities detected by touch. I also sensed light, color, odor, taste, and sound—qualities by whose variation I distinguished such things as the sky, earth, and sea from one another.

In view of these ideas of qualities (which presented themselves to my thought and were all that I really sensed directly), I had some reason for believing that I sensed objects distinct from my thought—physical objects from which the ideas came. For I found that these ideas came to me independently of my desires so that, however much I tried, I couldn't sense an object when it wasn't present to an organ of sense or fail to sense one when it was present. And, since the ideas that I grasped by sense were much livelier, more explicit, and (in their own way) more distinct than those I deliberately created or found impressed in my memory, it seemed that these ideas could not have come from me and thus that they came from something else. Having no conception of these things other than that suggested by my sensory ideas, I could only think that the things resembled the ideas. Indeed, since I remembered using my senses before my reason, since I found the ideas that I created in myself to be less explicit than those grasped by sense, and since I found the ideas that I created to be composed largely of those that I had grasped by sense, I easily convinced myself that I didn't understand anything at all unless I had first sensed it.

I also had some reason for supposing that a certain physical object, which I viewed as belonging to me in a special way, was related to me more closely than any other. I couldn't be separated from it as I could from other physical objects; I felt all of my emotions and desires in it and because of it; and I was aware of pains and pleasant feelings in it but in nothing else. I didn't know why sadness goes with the sensation of pain or why joy goes with sensory stimulation. I didn't know why the stomach twitchings that I call hunger warn me that I need to eat or why dryness in my throat warns me that I need to drink. Seeing no connection between stomach twitchings and the desire to eat or between the sensation of a pain-producing thing and the consequent awareness of sadness, I could only say that I had been taught the connection by nature. And nature seems also to have taught me everything else that I knew about the objects of sensation—for I convinced myself that the sensations came to me in a certain way before having found grounds on which to prove that they did.

But, since then, many experiences have shaken my faith in the senses. Towers that seemed round from a distance sometimes looked square from close up, and huge statues on pediments sometimes didn't look big when seen from the ground. In innumerable such cases, I found the judgments of the external senses to be wrong. And the same holds for the internal senses. What is felt more inwardly than pain? Yet I had heard that people with amputated arms and legs sometimes seem to feel pain in the missing limb, and it therefore didn't seem perfectly certain to me that the limb in which I feel a pain is always the one that hurts. And, to these grounds for doubt, I've recently added two that are very general:

First, since I didn't believe myself to sense anything while awake that I couldn't also take myself to sense in a dream, and since I didn't believe that what I sense in sleep comes from objects outside me, I didn't see why I should believe what I sense while awake comes from such objects. Second, since I didn't yet know my creator (or, rather, since I supposed that I didn't know Him), I saw nothing to rule out my having been so designed by nature that I'm deceived even in what seems most obviously true to me.

And I could easily refute the reasoning by which I convinced myself of the reality of sensible things. Since my nature seemed to impel me toward many things that my reason rejected, I didn't believe that I ought to have much faith in nature's teachings. And, while my will didn't control my sense perceptions, I didn't believe it to follow that these perceptions came from outside me, since I thought that the ability to produce these ideas might be in me without my being aware of it.

Now that I've begun to know myself and my creator better, I still believe that I oughtn't blindly to accept everything that I seem to get from the senses. Yet I no longer believe that I ought to call it all into doubt.

In the first place, I know that everything that I clearly and distinctly understand can be made by God to be exactly as I understand it. The fact that I can clearly and distinctly understand one thing apart from another is therefore enough to make me certain that it is distinct from the other, since the things could be separated by God if not by something else. (I judge the things to be distinct regardless of the power needed to make them exist separately.) Accordingly, from the fact that I have gained knowledge of my existence without noticing anything about my nature or essence except that I am a thinking thing, I can rightly conclude that my essence consists solely in the fact that I am a thinking thing. It's possible (or, as I will say later, it's certain) that I have a body which is very tightly bound to me. But, on the one hand, I have a clear and distinct idea of myself insofar as I am just a thinking and unextended thing, and, on the other hand, I have a distinct idea of my body insofar as it is just an extended and unthinking thing. It's certain, then, that I am really distinct from my body and can exist without it.

In addition, I find in myself abilities for special modes of awareness, like the abilities to have mental images and to sense. I can clearly and distinctly conceive of my whole self as something that lacks these abilities, but I can't conceive of the abilities' existing without me, or without an understanding substance in which to reside. Since the conception of these abilities includes the conception of something that understands, I see that these abilities are distinct from me in the way that a thing's properties are distinct from the thing itself.

I recognize other abilities in me, like the ability to move around and to assume various postures. These abilities can't be understood to exist apart from a substance in which they reside any more than the abilities to imagine and sense, and they therefore cannot exist without such a substance. But it's obvious that, if these abilities do exist, the substance in which they reside must be a body or extended substance rather than an understanding one—for the clear and distinct conceptions of these abilities contain extension but not understanding.

There is also in me, however, a passive ability to sense—to receive and recognize ideas of sensible things. But, I wouldn't be able to put this ability to use if there weren't, either in me or in something else, an active power to produce or make sensory ideas. Since this active power doesn't presuppose understanding, and since it often produces ideas in me without my co-operation and even against my will, it cannot exist in me. Therefore, this power must exist in a substance distinct from me. And, for reasons that I've noted, this substance must contain, either formally or eminently, all the reality that is contained subjectively in the ideas that the power produces. Either this substance is a physical object (a thing of bodily nature that contains formally the reality that the idea contains subjectively), or it is God or one of His creations that is higher than a physical object (something that contains this reality eminently). But, since God isn't a deceiver, it's completely obvious that He doesn't send these ideas to me directly or by means of a creation that contains their reality eminently rather than formally. For, since He has not given me any ability to recognize that these ideas are sent by Him or by creations other than physical objects, and since He has given me a strong inclination to believe that the ideas come from physical objects, I see no way to avoid the conclusion that He deceives me if the ideas are sent to me by anything other than physical objects. It follows that physical objects exist. These objects may not exist exactly as I comprehend them by sense; in many ways, sensory comprehension is obscure and confused. But these objects must at least have in them everything that I clearly and distinctly understand them to have—every general property within the scope of pure mathematics.

But what about particular properties, such as the size and shape of the sun? And what about things that I understand less clearly than mathematical properties, like light, sound, and pain? These are open to doubt. But, since God isn't a deceiver, and since I therefore have the God-given ability to correct any falsity that may be in my beliefs, I have high hopes of finding the truth about even these things. There is undoubtedly some truth in everything I have been taught by nature—for, when I use the term "nature" in its general sense, I refer to God Himself or to the order that He has established in the created world, and, when I apply the term specifically to *my* nature, I refer to the collection of everything that God has given *me*.

Nature teaches me nothing more explicitly, however, than that I have a body which is hurt when I feel pain, which needs food or drink when I experience hunger or thirst, and so on. Accordingly, I ought not to doubt that there is some truth to this.

Through sensations like pain, hunger, and thirst, nature also teaches me that I am not present in my body in the way that a sailor is present in his ship. Rather, I am very tightly bound to my body and so "mixed up" with it that we form a single thing. If this weren't so, I—who am just a thinking thing—wouldn't feel pain when my body was injured; I would perceive the injury by pure understanding in the way that a sailor sees the leaks in his ship with his eyes. And, when my body needed food or drink, I would explicitly understand that the need existed without having the confused sensations of hunger and thirst. For the sensations of thirst, hunger, and pain are just confused modifications of thought arising from the union and "mixture" of mind and body.

Also, nature teaches me that there are other physical objects around my body—some that I ought to seek and others that I ought to avoid. From the fact that I sense things like colors, sound, odors, flavors, temperatures, and hardnesses, I correctly infer that sense perceptions come from physical objects that vary as widely (though perhaps not in the same way) as the perceptions do. And, from the fact that some of these perceptions are pleasant while others are unpleasant, I infer with certainty that my body—or, rather, my whole self which consists of a body and a mind—can be benefited and harmed by the physical objects around it.

There are many other things that I seem to have been taught by nature but that I have really accepted out of a habit of thoughtless judgment. These things may well be false. Among them are the judgments that a space is empty if nothing in it happens to affect my senses; that a hot physical object has something in it resembling my idea of heat; that a white or green thing has in it the same whiteness or greenness that I sense; that a bitter or sweet thing has in it the same flavor that I taste; that stars, towers, and other physical objects have the same size and shape that they present to my senses; and so on.

If I am to avoid accepting what is indistinct in these cases, I must more carefully explain my use of the phrase "taught by nature." In particular, I should say that I am now using the term "nature" in a narrower sense than when I took it to refer to the whole complex of what God has given me. This complex includes much having to do with my mind alone (such as my grasp of the fact that what is done cannot be undone and of the rest of what I know by the light of nature) which does not bear on what I am now saying. And the complex also includes much having to do with my body alone (such as its tendency to go downward) with which I am not dealing now. I'm now using the term "nature" to refer only to what God has given me insofar as I am a composite of mind and body. It is this nature that teaches me to avoid that which occasions painful sensations, to seek that which occasions pleasant sensations, and so on. But this nature seems not to teach me to draw conclusions about external objects from sense perceptions without first having examined the matter with my understanding—for true knowledge of external things seems to belong to the mind alone, not to the composite of mind and body.

Thus, while a star has no more effect on my eye than a flame, this does not really produce a positive inclination to believe that the star is as small as the flame; for my youthful judgment about the size of the flame, I had no real grounds. And, while I feel heat when I approach a fire and pain when I draw nearer, I have absolutely no reason for believing that something in the fire resembles the heat, just as I have no reason for believing that something in the fire resembles the pain; I only have reason for believing that there is something or other in the fire that produces the feelings of heat and pain. And, although there may be nothing in a given region of space that affects my senses, it doesn't follow that there aren't any physical objects in that space. Rather I now see that, on these matters and others, I used to pervert the natural order of things. For, while nature has given sense perceptions to my mind for the sole purpose of indicating what is beneficial and what harmful to the composite of which my mind is a part, and while the perceptions are sufficiently clear and distinct for that purpose, I used these perceptions as standards for identifying the essence of physical objects—an essence which they only reveal obscurely and confusedly.

I've already explained how it can be that, despite God's goodness, my judgments can be false. But a new difficulty arises here—one having to do with the things that nature presents to me as desirable or undesirable and also with the errors that I seem to have found in my internal sensations. One of these errors seems to be committed, for example, when a man is fooled by some food's pleasant taste into eating poison hidden in that food. But surely, in this case, what the man's nature impels him to eat is the good tasting food, not the poison of which he knows nothing. We can draw no conclusion except that his nature isn't omniscient, and this conclusion isn't surprising. Since a man is a limited thing, he can only have limited perfections.

Still, we often err in cases in which nature does impel us. This happens, for example, when sick people want food or drink that would quickly harm them. To say that these people err as a result of the corruption of their nature does not solve the problem—for a sick man is no less a creation of God than a well one, and it seems as absurd to suppose that God has given him a deceptive nature. A clock made of wheels and weights follows the natural laws just as precisely when it is poorly made and inaccurate as when it does everything that its maker wants. Thus, if I regard a human body as a machine made up of bones, nerves, muscles, veins, blood, and skin such that even without a mind it would do just what it does now (except for things that require a mind because they are controlled by the will), it's easy to see that what happens to a sick man is no less "natural" than what happens to a well one. For instance, if a body suffers from dropsy, it has a dry throat of the sort that regularly brings the sensation of thirst to the mind, the dryness disposes the nerves and other organs to drink, and the drinking makes the illness worse. But this is just as natural as when a similar dryness of throat moves a person who is perfectly healthy to take a drink that is beneficial. Bearing in mind my conception of a clock's use, I might say that an inaccurate clock departs from its nature, and, similarly, viewing the machine of the human body as designed for its usual motions, I can say that it drifts away from its nature if it has a dry throat when drinking will not help to maintain it. I should note, however, that the sense in which I am now using the term "nature" differs from that in which I used it before. For, as I have just used the term "nature," the nature of a man (or clock) is something that depends on my thinking of the difference between a sick and a well man (or of the difference between a poorly made and a well-made clock)—something regarded as extrinsic to the things. But, when I used "nature" before, I referred to something which is *in* things and which therefore has some reality.

It may be that we just offer an extrinsic description of a body suffering from dropsy when, noting that it has a dry throat but doesn't need to drink, we say that its nature is corrupted. Still, the description is not purely extrinsic when we say that a composite or union of mind and body has a corrupted nature. There is a real fault in the composite's nature, for it is thirsty when drinking would be harmful. It therefore remains to be asked why God's goodness doesn't prevent *this* nature's being deceptive.

To begin the answer, I'll note that mind differs importantly from body in that body is by its nature divisible while mind is indivisible. When I think about my mind—or, in other words, about myself insofar as I am just a thinking thing—I can't distinguish any parts in me; I understand myself to be a single, unified thing. Although my whole mind seems united to my whole body, I know that cutting off a foot, arm, or other limb would not take anything away from my mind. The abilities to will, sense, understand, and so on can't be called parts, since it's one and the same mind that wills, senses, and understands. On the other hand, whenever I think of a physical or extended thing, I can mentally divide it, and I therefore understand that the object is divisible. This single fact would be enough to teach me that my mind and body are distinct, if I hadn't already learned that in another way.

Next, I notice that the mind isn't directly affected by all parts of the body, but only by the brain—or maybe just by the small part of the brain containing the so-called "common sense." Whenever this part of the brain is in a given state, it presents the same thing to the mind, regardless of what is happening in the rest of the body (as is shown by innumerable experiments that I need not review here).

In addition, I notice that the nature of body is such that, if a first part can be moved by a second that is far away, the first part can be moved in exactly the same way by something between the first and second without the second part's being affected. For example, if A, B, C, and D are points on a cord, and if the first point (A) can be moved in a certain way by a pull on the last point (D), then A can be moved in the same way by a pull on one of the middle points (B or C) without D's being moved. Similarly, science teaches me that, when my foot hurts, the sensation of pain is produced by nerves distributed throughout the foot which extend like cords from there to the brain. When pulled in the foot, these nerves pull the central parts of the brain to which they are attached, moving those parts in ways designated by nature to present the mind with the sensation of a pain "in the foot." But, since these nerves pass through the shins, thighs, hips, back, and neck on their way from foot to brain, it can happen that their being touched in the middle, rather than at the end of the foot, produces the same motion in the brain as when the foot is hurt and, hence, that the mind feels the same pain "in the foot." And the point holds for other sensations as well.

Finally, I notice that, since only one sensation can be produced by a given motion of the part of the brain that directly affects the mind, the best conceivable sensation for it to produce is the one that is most often useful for the maintenance of the healthy man. Experience teaches that all the sensations put in us by nature are of this sort and therefore that everything in our sensations testifies to God's power and goodness. For example, when the nerves in the foot are moved with unusual violence, the motion is communicated through the middle of the spine to the center of the brain, where it signals the mind to sense a pain "in the foot." This urges the mind to view the pain's cause as harmful to the foot and to do what it can to remove that cause. Of course, God could have so designed man's nature that the same motion of the brain presented something else to the mind, like the motion in the brain, or the motion in the foot, or a motion somewhere between the brain and foot. But no alternative to the way things are would be as conducive to the maintenance of the body. Similarly, when we need drink, the throat becomes dry, the dryness moves the nerves of the throat thereby moving the center of the brain, and the brain's movements cause the sensation of thirst in the mind. It's the sensation of thirst that is produced, because no information about our condition is more useful to us than that we need to get something to drink in order to remain healthy. And the same is true in other cases.

This makes it completely obvious that, despite God's immense goodness, the nature of man (whom we now view as a composite of mind and body) cannot fail to be deceptive. For, if something produces the movement usually associated with an injured foot in the nerve running from foot to brain or in the brain itself rather than in the foot, a pain is felt as if "in the foot." Here the senses are deceived by their nature. Since this motion in the brain must always bring the same sensation to mind, and since the motion's cause is something hurting the foot more often than something elsewhere, it's in accordance with reason that the motion always presents the mind a pain in the foot rather than elsewhere. And, if dryness of the throat arises, not (as usual) from drink's being conducive to the body's health, but (as happens in dropsy) from some other cause, it's much better that we are deceived on this occasion than that we are gener-

ally deceived when our bodies are sound. And the same holds for other cases.

In addition to helping me to be aware of the errors to which my nature is subject, these reflections help me readily to correct or avoid these errors. I know that sensory indications of what is good for my body are more often true than false; I can almost always examine a given thing with several senses; and I can also use my memory (which connects the present to the past) and my understanding (which has now examined all the causes of error). Hence, I need no longer fear that what the senses daily show me is unreal. I should reject the exaggerated doubts of the past few days as ridiculous. This is especially true of the chief ground for these doubts—namely, my inability to distinguish dreaming from being awake. For I now notice that dreaming and being awake are importantly different: the events in dreams are not linked by memory to the rest of my life like those that happen while I am awake. If, while I'm awake, someone were suddenly to appear and then immediately to disappear without my seeing where he came from or went to (as happens in dreams), I would justifiably judge that he was not a real man but a ghost—or, better an apparition created in my brain. But, if I distinctly observe something's source, its place, and the time at which I learn about it, and if I grasp an unbroken connection between it and the rest of my life, I'm quite sure that it is something in my waking life rather than in a dream. And I ought not to have the slightest doubt about the reality of such things if I have examined them with all my senses, my memory, and my understanding without finding any conflicting evidence. For, from the fact that God is not a deceiver, it follows that I am not deceived in any case of this sort. Since the need to act does not always allow time for such a careful examination, however, we must admit the likelihood of men's erring about particular things and acknowledge the weakness of our nature.

What Has Descartes Done?

It is possible to argue whether Descartes is the last of the medievals or the first of the moderns. Like most such arguments about transitional figures, there is truth on both sides. But that both philosophy and our general view of the world have been different ever since is indisputable. Descartes develops a philosophy that reflects the newly developing sciences and, in turn, gives them a legitimacy they otherwise lack. A measure of his lasting influence is the fact that a significant part of philosophy since World War I has been devoted to showing that he was crucially wrong about some basic things (which would not be worth doing unless his influence was still powerfully felt).* Descartes is *our* ancestor.

Let us sum up several key features of his thought and then indicate where certain problems crop up.

A New Ideal for Knowledge

One commentator says of the Cartesian revolution that it "stands for the substitution of free inquiry for submission to authority, for the rejection of Faith without reason for faith *in* reason, and the replacement of Faith by Demonstration."[6] Though Descartes is far from trying to reject religious belief (indeed, he thinks he can rationally justify its two most important parts, God and the soul), in the last analysis everything comes down to what the rational mind finds clear and distinct enough to be indubitable. Nothing else will be accepted, regardless of its antiquity or traditional claims to authority. We each contain within ourselves the criterion for truth and knowledge. This radical individualism is qualified only by the conviction that rationality is the same for every individual (just as mathematics is the same for all). No longer can we put the responsibility for deciding what to believe on someone else, whether priest, pope, or king. It lies squarely on each of us.

Moreover, the ideal for such belief is the clarity and certainty of mathematics. Probability or plausibility is not enough. Being vaguely right is not enough. The habits of thought developed in us by nature are not enough. By analysis we can resolve problems into their simple elements; by intuition we can see their truth; and by demonstration we can move to necessary consequences. Knowledge has the structure of an axiomatic system. All this is

possible. Anything less is unacceptable. To be faithful to this ideal is to free oneself from error and to attain truth.

In all this Descartes deserves his reputation as Prince of the Rationalists.* The ultimate court of appeal is reason—the light of nature. We ought to rely on intellect rather than sense, on intuition and deduction rather than imagination; "for true knowledge of external things seems to belong to the mind alone, not the composite of mind and body" (p. 354).

A New Vision of Reality

Descartes' metaphysics makes explicit and complete the worldview that was emerging already in the work of Copernicus, Kepler, and Galileo. Our world is a giant mechanism, not unlike a clock (see Descartes' analogy on p. 355). It was, to be sure, created by God. But now it runs on the principles of mechanics, and our science is mechanistic in principle. If we abstract from the fact of creation, the entire material universe, including the human body, is just a complex machine. The world has become a *secular* world. What happens can be explained and predicted without reference to any purposes or intentions of the creator. We are, we might say, worlds away from the intrinsically purposive, inherently value-laden, God-directed world of the medievals. Dante now begins to look like a fairy tale or, at best, a moral allegory with no literal truth value at all. It is, perhaps, no great surprise that the *Meditations* ends up on the index of forbidden books.

There are, to be sure, human minds or souls, and they are not caught up in the mechanism of the material world. They are, in fact, radically free. Even God does not have more freedom than a soul (see *Meditation IV*). But as we'll see, this disparity between soul and body is not so much the solution to a problem as it is a problem in itself.

---

*Among the critics are C. S. Peirce, Martin Heidegger, Ludwig Wittgenstein, Willard Quine, and Richard Rorty. See the chapters on their philosophies.

---

*Though (almost) all philosophers try to reach their conclusions rationally, a rationalist is one who emphasizes the exclusive role of reason in the formation of knowledge. For one of Descartes' most distinguished predecessors in this tradition, see the discussion of the pre-Socratic thinker, Parmenides, in Chapter 2.

Problems

Great as Descartes' achievement is, he bequeaths to his successors a legacy of unsolved problems. There are those who refuse to accept his radical beginning point and remain true to a more traditional approach, usually Aristotelian. But his methodological doubt has been powerfully persuasive to many, and the continued progress of physics seems to be evidence that his basic view of the world is correct. For the next hundred and fifty years, Cartesianism, together with its variants, will be the dominating philosophy on the European continent. As we'll see, different assumptions are at work in Britain, but even here the Cartesian spirit of independence is pervasive. Still, there are nagging worries. Let us note three of them.

The Place of Humans in the World of Nature   Descartes is intent on legitimizing the new science. And this he does. But what place is there for us in the universe of the new physics? Is it plausible to think that we, too, are just cogs in this universal machine? We assume that we have purposes and act to realize certain values. But where is there room for purposes and values in this mechanistic world? Is our assumption just an illusion? We assume that we can make a difference in the outcome of physical processes. But if the world is a closed mechanism, how can this be? We experience ourselves as conscious beings, aware of ourselves and the world around us. But can a machine be conscious? These are very contemporary questions, the sort cognitive science aims to sort out and solve.

All these questions force themselves on us once we take Descartes' vision of the universe seriously. Descartes is not unaware of them. His basic strategy for dealing with them consists in the radical split that he makes between mind and body. Bodies, he holds, are parts of the mechanical universe; minds are not. Physics can deal with the body, but not with the mind. We know that we are not merely automata because (1) we can use language, and (2) we are flexible and adaptable in a way no machine could be; reason, Descartes says, "is a universal instrument which can be used in all kinds of situations." It is quite possible, he says, that we

could construct a machine that utters words—even one that utters words corresponding to movements of its body. But it is not possible, he thinks, for a machine to "give an appropriately meaningful answer to whatever is said in its presence, as the dullest of men can do" (*DM* 6.56–57, p. 120).*

But merely dividing mind from body does not completely solve the problem. The question arises, How are they related?

The Mind and the Body   Descartes concludes that the mind is one thing and the body another; each is so independent of the other that either could exist without the other. They are, moreover, of a radically different character. The essence of a mind is thinking; minds are in no sense extended objects. The essence of a material thing is extension; but extended things such as bodies cannot think. Still, he says, mind and body are so intimately related as to form "a single unified thing" (p. 354).

But how can I be two things and yet one single thing? No explanation is given. Clearly he must insist that what happens to the body affects the mind, as when I get hungry, or am hurt, or open my eyes to a blue wall in daylight. And what the mind decides, the body may do, as when I choose to walk or eat an ice cream cone. There seems to be a two-way causal relation between mind and body. This view is called *interactionism*.

Yet it is completely puzzling how this can be. How can something that is not extended reach into the closed system of the mechanical world and work a change there, where all changes are governed by mechanical principles? And how can an alteration in the shape or position of certain material particles cause us to feel sad or think of Cleveland? No explanation is forthcoming. It seems entirely mysterious. To save the integrity of his physics, Descartes pushes the mental out of the physical world entirely. But then it is inexplicable how physics itself can be done at all, since it seems to depend on interactions between nonphysical minds and physical bodies. Here is the problem that Schopenhauer

---

*This, of course, is precisely the aim of research on artificial intelligence. Will it be successful? Descartes bets not.

would later call "the world knot." It is safe to say that a philosophy that does not solve the mind—body problem cannot be considered entirely acceptable.

God and the Problem of Skepticism   As we have seen, Descartes takes the skeptical problem very seriously. He pushes skeptical arguments about as far as they can be pushed, and he thinks that in the *cogito* he has found the key to overcoming skepticism. But even if we grant that each of us knows, by virtue of the *cogito,* that we exist, knowledge of the *world* depends on the fact that God is not a deceiver. And that depends on the proofs for the existence of God.

What if those proofs are faulty? Then I am back again in solipsism, without a guarantee that anything exists beyond myself. Are the proofs—or at least one of them—satisfactory? Descartes is quite clear that everything depends on that question; "the certainty and truth of all my knowledge derives from one thing: my thought of the true God" (p. 351). He is sure that the proofs are as secure as the theorems of geometry. But is he right about that?

The Preeminence of Epistemology

In earlier philosophies there are many problems—the one and the many, the nature of reality, explaining change, the soul, the existence of God—and the problem of knowledge is just one among the rest. Descartes' radical skepticism changes that. After Descartes and until very recent times most philosophers have thought that epistemological problems are absolutely foundational. Among these problems of knowledge, the problem about knowing the external world is the sharpest and most dangerous. Can we know anything at all beyond the contents of our minds? Unless this skeptical question can be satisfactorily answered, nothing else can be done. Epistemology is, for better or worse, the heart of philosophy for the next several hundred years.

These are problems that Descartes' successors wrestle with, as we'll see. Next, however, we want to look at a figure who is often neglected in the history of modern philosophy: Thomas Hobbes. Hobbes is more interesting to us than to previous generations, perhaps, because he presents an alternative response to the new science. Some recent thought about the mind—that associated with artificial intelligence—can be regarded as a struggle to replace the paradigm of Descartes with that of Hobbes.

For Further Thought

Descartes argues that there is no way you could tell that your ideas about the external world were correct unless there were a nondeceptive God to guarantee their basic rightness. Can you think of any way you might be able to know there is a world corresponding to your ideas? Try to construct a view that provides this reassurance without depending on God.

Notes

1. Quoted in S. V. Keeling, *Descartes* (London: Oxford University Press, 1968).
2. Quotations from René Descartes' *Discourse on the Method of Rightly Conducting One's Reason and Seeking the Truth in the Sciences,* in *The Philosophical Writings of Descartes,* ed. John Cottingham, Robert Stoothoff, and Dugald Murdoch (Cambridge: Cambridge University Press, 1985), are cited in the text using the abbreviation *DM.* References are to part numbers and page numbers in the classic French edition, followed by page numbers in this edition.
3. Quotations from René Descartes, *The Principles of Philosophy,* in *The Philosophical Works of Descartes,* vol. 1, ed. Elisabeth S. Haldane and G. R. T. Ross (n.p.: Dover Publications, 1955), are cited in the text using the abbreviation *PP.* References are to the classic French edition, followed by the page numbers in this edition.
4. Quoted by Martin Heidegger in *The Way Back into the Ground of Metaphysics,* reprinted in *Existentialism from Dostoevsky to Sartre,* ed. Walter Kaufmann (New York: Merchant Books, 1957).
5. Trans. Ronald Rubin, *Meditations on First Philosophy* (Claremont, CA: Areté Press, 1641/1986).
6. Keeling, *Descartes,* 252.

CHAPTER

14

HOBBES, LOCKE, AND BERKELEY

Materialism and the Beginnings of Empiricism

Descartes' new beginning in philosophy was dramatic and arresting. Many thought this was just what was needed. It swept away all the old rubbish, legitimated the new science, and seemed a breath of fresh air in its clarity and apparent simplicity. But—there were those nagging problems. If mind and body are as distinct as Descartes claims, how do they ever communicate? Does the will really escape the causal net? Do we really have all those innate ideas? Are Descartes' proofs for God's existence really *proofs*? And if not, can we escape skepticism about the external world?

Across the English Channel, thinkers were impressed and influenced by Descartes, but they were not entirely convinced. In this chapter, we look at three of these philosophers, examining their response to the challenges of Cartesian thought: Thomas Hobbes, who refuses to exclude human beings from the new scientific principles; John Locke, who is determined to trace all our ideas to their source in experience; and George Berkeley, who tries to apply empiricist principles more consistently than Locke does. A consideration of these

three will prepare us for that most radical of empirical thinkers in the next chapter: David Hume.

Thomas Hobbes: Catching Persons in the Net of the New Science

For various reasons, Descartes, one of the heroes of the new science, stops short of supposing that his geometrical mechanics can account for everything. The most obvious exceptions are mental activities: thinking, imagining, doubting, feeling, and willing. Because Descartes believes it is beyond question that each of us is first and foremost a thinking thing—and as free in our decisions as God himself—there can be no Cartesian physics of human beings. As thinkers, we escape the web of mechanical causality.*

---

*For Descartes' reasons, see his argument for the distinctness of mind and body in *Meditation VI*. He is also convinced that our minds, being rational, are *infinitely adaptable*. This, he thinks, distinguishes us from any conceivable automaton, no matter how cleverly designed. See p. 358.

But are Descartes's reasons for thinking so really conclusive? What would be the result if we tried to understand human beings as just bits of matter in motion, completely enclosed in the natural world described by mechanical physics? Thomas Hobbes (1588–1679) makes the experiment. We will not survey the whole of Hobbes' philosophy, but it will prove useful to bring into our sense of the great conversation what he has to say about human beings—our place in the world and our life together. So we focus our attention on his views about mind and morals.

Hobbes accepts without reservation the new physics of the nonhuman world and embraces the rejection of that medieval/Aristotelian picture of the world we examined earlier. Let us review some of the salient features of this new science and contrast them with that earlier view.

- Whereas for Aristotle and his medieval disciples, motion is development toward some fulfilling goal (a change from potentiality to actuality), for the new science, motion is simply a body's change of place in a neutral geometrical space.

- Galileo substitutes the distinction between accelerated motion and constant motion for the Aristotelian distinction between motion and rest. For Galileo, rest is simply a limiting case of motion. In no sense is rest the culmination or fulfillment or goal of a motion.

- Motion is the normal state of things; it does not require explanation, as in the medieval view. Only changes in motion (in direction or rate) need to be explained, and they are explained in terms of other motions.

- Therefore, there is no natural center to the universe where things "rest." Since something in motion continues in a straight line to infinity unless interfered with, the universe is conceived to be infinite rather than finite, and there are no privileged places in it.

- Scientific explanation can no longer mention the final causes of things—those essences toward which development has been thought to strive. Final causes are derided as explanatorily barren, obscure, and even occult. In the geometrical world of Galileo and Descartes, all explanation is in terms of *contact,* of some prior impetus or push. It is as if the rich Aristotelian world with its four causes is stripped down to only the "efficient cause." Purposiveness is eliminated from the physical world.*

In his comments on the *Meditations,* Hobbes claims to be unconvinced by Descartes' arguments concerning the independence of the mind from the body. For all Descartes has said, Hobbes thinks, the thing that thinks may just as well be a physical body! Indeed, Hobbes is convinced that "the subject of all activities can be conceived only after a corporeal fashion."[1] If so, then the mind cannot be thought of as a thing independent of the body. It becomes just one of the ways that bodies of a certain sort function.† Can this claim be plausible?

Method

Hobbes is as convinced as Descartes that method is the key to progress. He calls his method—which he claims to have learned from Galileo and his friend William Harvey (who discovered the circulation of the blood)—the method of *resolution and composition.* The first stage, resolution, consists in the analysis of complex wholes into simple elements. It resembles Descartes' second rule.‡ In the second stage, the elements are reassembled, or

---

*Compare Hobbes in this respect to the Greek atomists ("The World," in Chapter 2). You might also like to remind yourself of Plato's critique of this kind of nonpurposive explanation, pp. 131–132.
†Hobbes, like nearly all the moderns, is a great opponent of Aristotle. And yet this conclusion is basically Aristotelian. (See p. 182.) Likewise, his account of how we gain knowledge about the world is Aristotelian in spirit, if not in detail. In more than one way, Hobbes must be counted a "critical Aristotelian." Descartes, by contrast, clearly stands in the Plato–Augustine tradition. The principal difference between Hobbes and Aristotle is the former's repudiation of final causes, of potentiality, and of the essences that make them work, but this difference transforms everything it touches.
‡See pp. 322–323.

composed again into a whole. This is analogous to Descartes' third rule. When we have both resolved and composed the complex whole we began with, we understand it better than we did before we applied the method. Both Galileo and Harvey offer impressive examples of successes attained by this method.

Galileo explains the path taken by a cannonball by imagining a projectile moving on a frictionless horizontal plane that suddenly comes to an end. At that point, the cannonball will tend both to move in the same direction (since things in motion tend to remain in motion) and to drop (since unsupported objects fall at a specific rate). The path is then *resolved* into these two tendencies, each of which can be mathematically expressed. And when synthesized or *composed* by the laws of motion, it can be seen that the path is that of a semiparabola. This principle can then be used to make predictions about the actual paths cannonballs take. These predictions (for instance, that the greatest distance is reached when the gun is at 45 degrees) are found to agree with the observations made by gunners in the field.

A somewhat different example is that of Harvey's work on the circulatory system. Here *resolution* is actually taking apart a complex object—dissecting the body of a human or other mammal. The elements figuring in the explanation of the behavior of the blood are the heart together with its chambers and valves, the arteries and veins, and the blood itself. When all these are understood in their complex relations to each other, that is, when they are *composed* again into a whole, we understand what was previously puzzling to us.

We will see Hobbes trying to use these methods to understand both mind and society. His aim is to analyze human beings into their simplest elements—which he takes to be bits of matter in motion—and then understand a community of persons in terms of the way these elements interact. Hobbes aspires to be the Galileo or the Harvey of the human world. He is convinced that a scientific understanding of human nature will be both a contribution to knowledge and a practical benefit. If we could but organize society on the basis of truths about ourselves, rather than on the basis of ignorance and superstition, we could avoid conflict and live together in peace.

Minds and Motives

Life, says Hobbes,

> is but a motion of limbs, the beginning whereof is in some principle part within; why may we not say, that all *automata* (engines that move themselves by springs and wheels as doth a watch) have an artificial life? For what is the heart, but a spring; and the nerves, but so many strings, and the joints, but so many wheels, giving motion to the whole body, such as was intended by the artificer? (L, 129)[2]

The distinction, in other words, between living and nonliving things is not to be found in a soul, or a life principle, or in anything nonmaterial. Living things are just those things that *move* because they have a source of motion *within* them. They are not in principle different from automata or robots that we ourselves might make. In fact, we could say that robots are alive, too; it is just that their life is *artificially created*. That doesn't make it any the less life. The internal motions causing the movements of automata are, in principle, no different from the heart, nerves, and joints of the human body. Living things, whether natural or artificial, are just matter in motion.

In a way, Descartes does not yet disagree. For he thinks that animals are just "machines"; and animals are undoubtedly alive. But what about the life of the mind? What of thought and feeling? What of desire, imagination, and memory? Can these too be plausibly considered just matter in motion? We have seen Descartes' negative answer. Can Hobbes make a positive answer plausible?

Let us begin with thinking. What are thoughts?

> They are everyone a *representation* or *appearance,* of some quality or other accident of a body without us, which is commonly called an *object.* (*L,* 131)

Note that Hobbes expresses no doubt that there are indeed bodies — objects — independent of ourselves. He seems simply not to take the Cartesian reasons for doubting seriously.* Descartes, notoriously, thinks there is a serious problem here — that all our experience might be just as it is while *nothing at all* corresponds to it in the world beyond our minds. That there are bodies, Descartes holds, is something that needs to be proved. Hobbes offers no proofs. It is as though he thinks it beyond question. *Of course* our thoughts represent bodies. *Of course* bodies really exist. To be sure, we are sometimes mistaken about them, but these mistakes give us no reason to withhold belief in external things altogether. In fact, if it were not for those objects, we would not have any thoughts at all!

> The original of them all is that which we call *sense,* for there is no conception in a man's mind which hath not first, totally or by parts, been begotten upon the organs of sense. The rest are derived from that original. (*L,* 131)

The source of all our thoughts is to be found in sensation.[†] And sensation is an effect in us of the action of those external bodies upon our eyes, ears,

"The light of human minds is perspicuous words . . . ; reason is the pace, increase of science, the way and the benefit of mankind, the end."

—THOMAS HOBBES

nose, skin, and tongue. Motions are communicated to our sense organs from these bodies; these motions set up other motions in the sense organs; and these motions are in turn propagated by the nerves "inwards to the brain and heart." There the pressure of these motions meets a "counter-pressure, or endeavor of the heart to deliver itself" (*L,* 131). Because this counterpressure is directed outward, we take the disturbance set up to be a representation of the object from which the motions originated. Here, then, are the origins of our experiences of colors, sounds, tastes, smells, hardness and softness, and so on. These experiences we call sensations, or, to use Hobbes' seventeenth-century term, "fancy."

But what of these experiences themselves? Can a sensation of red or the smell of a rose really be "resolved" into motions? Here is what Hobbes says. In the objects that cause them, these qualities are

---

*Here again Hobbes stands to Descartes as Aristotle to Plato. See p. 158.

[†]For all Hobbes' tirades against Aristotle, this is a very Aristotelian view. It is the dead opposite of Descartes' belief in innate ideas (see p. 330). It means that he can have no tolerance for Descartes' first proof for the existence of God. Compare Thomas Aquinas' rejection of the ontological argument of Saint Anselm on essentially similar Aristotelian grounds (see p. 275).

but so many several motions of the matter, by which it presseth our organs diversely. Neither in us that are pressed, are they anything else but divers motions; for motion produceth nothing but motion. But their appearance to us is fancy. (*L,* 131)

It will pay us to consider this passage carefully, for it contains a crucial ambiguity. On the one hand, Hobbes says that sensations are themselves nothing but motion; "for motion produceth nothing but motion." If we take that seriously, then Hobbes is what we call a **materialist.** The entire life of the mind is nothing more than matter in motion. For sensations are motions, and all the rest is built up out of sensations. There are no distinctive mental qualities at all. Mind is just matter that is moved in certain distinctive ways.

On the other hand, Hobbes says of these motions that "their appearance to us is fancy." Now if it is not the motions themselves that constitute the sensations, but their *appearance* to us, then the sensations must be distinct from the motions. Under this interpretation Hobbes is not a materialist at all; he is what we call an **epiphenomenalist.** An epiphenomenalist thinks there are unique mental qualities, that they are causally dependent on physical states, but that they do not in turn affect the physical world. They more or less ride piggyback on the physical, but they have no physical effects.

Is Hobbes a materialist or an epiphenomenalist about the mind? It is probably impossible to decide. He talks both ways, perhaps because he is simply unaware of the distinction. His intentions, however, are fairly clear. He wants to be a materialist, to resolve everything—including all aspects of mental life—into matter in motion. We consider him, therefore, to be a materialist about the mind. In this way, he stands in dramatic opposition to Descartes, for whom mind is a radically different kind of substance from body. Descartes, then, is a metaphysical **dualist,** Hobbes a **monist.** For Hobbes, there is only one kind of finite substance.

Sensations, the "original" of thought, are motions. But this poses a problem. Paraphrasing Galileo's laws of inertia, Hobbes admits that "when a body is once in motion, it moveth, unless something else hinder it, eternally" (*L,* 133). Why is it, then, that sensations do not remain with us? The answer is that in a way they do—but in a diminished way only. For new sensations are ever pouring in on us; and by these succeeding motions the previous ones are weakened. This *"decaying sense,"* as Hobbes calls it (*L,* 133), is *imagination* and *memory.*

In this way, Hobbes can give an account of dreams. The old motions that constitute imagination and memory are reactivated in us during sleep by some condition of the body. He allows, what Descartes makes so much of, that it is a hard matter sometimes to distinguish dreams from waking life. But he finds in this fact quite a different implication. It does not, for Hobbes, constitute a reason to doubt everything. What it does provide is an explanation for belief in satyrs, nymphs, fairies, ghosts, goblins, and witches. Because of the similarity to wakeful experience, the presence of such entities in dreams leads to belief in their reality. Superstitions, false prophecies, and purely private religious certainties have the same source and constitute a threat, Hobbes thinks, to civil peace and well-being.

But let us return to thinking. When an image (the decayed motion left by a sensation) is combined with a sign, he says, we have *understanding.* And this is common to both humans and the higher animals. For instance, a dog who comes when his master whistles gives evidence that he understands what is wanted of him. The whistle is a sign connected in this case to tendencies to act. Hobbes, unlike Descartes, is quite content to speak of a dog as thinking this or that. The difference between the dog and ourselves is not absolute (that we have a soul, which the dog completely lacks) but is a matter of degree.

Because sense is the origin of all thinking, it is not possible for us to think of something we have not experienced. We can, of course, combine sense elements in novel ways to produce purely imaginative thoughts of unicorns or centaurs. But things that are neither sensed nor invented on the basis of sensations are *inconceivable.* This has an important consequence: We can have, Hobbes says, no positive thought of God. "Whatsoever we imagine," he says, "is *finite.* Therefore there is no idea or conception of anything we call *infinite*" (*L,* 140). We do, of course, have *words* for God; we can call him a "being of infinite perfection"—as Descartes does. But these terms do not really function to describe God; rather, says Hobbes, they are signs of our intention to honor him.

Our thoughts, then, are derived from sense; they too are just motions in the matter of our brains. If we examine them, we find that they can roughly be grouped into two classes: *unregulated* (as when we daydream) and *regulated* thoughts. The first kind may seem to follow each other in a wholly random way. But it is not so. Upon careful observation, Hobbes tells us, we can see that their order mirrors a prior order of sense experiences. The appearance of randomness comes from the variety of our experiences. If at one time we *see* Mary with John, and then again with Peter, the *thought* of Mary may be accompanied by either that of John or that of Peter. But it will be associated in some way dependent on earlier experiences. In trying to find a pattern to unregulated thoughts, Hobbes is making a suggestion that will be developed into the doctrine of the *association of ideas*.*

More interesting, however, are regulated thoughts. These do not even have an appearance of randomness but exhibit a quite definite order. One thing Hobbes has in mind is the kind of thinking that looks for means to attain a certain end; a young woman wants to attract a certain man, and she thinks about how she might bring that about. Another kind of regulated thought consists in inquiry about the consequences of taking a certain action; a student considers what her life will be like if she changes her curriculum from history to engineering. In regulated thought about the world, we are always searching for either causes or effects.

Such a hunt for causes is usually carried out in *words,* which are useful both as aids to memory and as signs representing our thoughts to others. Hobbes is acutely conscious of the benefits we derive from having such objective signs of our inner thoughts, but he also warns us about the errors into which they can easily trap us.

> Seeing then the truth consisteth in the right ordering of names in our affirmations, a man that seeketh precise truth had need to remember what every name he uses stands for, and to place it accordingly,

or else he will find himself entangled in words, as a bird in lime twigs, the more he struggles the more belimed. (*L,* 142)

The cure for these evils of confusion is to be found in *definition,* to which Hobbes attributes the success of geometry, "the only science that it hath pleased God hitherto to bestow on mankind" (*L,* 142). Words need to be carefully defined, lest we find ourselves "entangled" in them like the bird in the lime twigs. In an often quoted phrase, Hobbes tells us that

> words are wise men's counters, they do but reckon by them; but they are the money of fools, that value them by the authority of an Aristotle, a Cicero, or a Thomas. (*L,* 143)

Only a "fool" thinks that we can buy truth with the words of some authority.* A "wise man" realizes that they are only *signs* that, if properly used to "reckon" with, may possibly yield us a science.

We use words to *reason,* to think rationally about some matter. What is reasoning? Hobbes has a view of reasoning that some artificial intelligence researchers these days look back to as prophetic. Reasoning, he tells us, is "nothing but *reckoning,* that is adding and subtracting, of the consequences of general names agreed upon for the marking and signifying of our thoughts" (*L,* 133–134). As the cognitive scientist nowadays says, reasoning is computation.

Whether we reason about the theoretical consequences of some geometrical axiom, about means to attain a certain end, or about the practical consequences of some course of action, these regulated thoughts are governed by *desire*. We wouldn't bother if we didn't want to find out the answer. So the motivation behind all our rational thinking is passion. Hobbes must now ask, Can these desires and wants, these likes and dislikes, themselves be accounted for in terms of the metaphysics of motion?†

---

*See the use to which David Hume puts this notion, Chapter 15.

*Augustine makes a similar point in a quite different context. See pp. 237–238.

†What is at stake here is whether *purpose* and *intention* can be given a mechanistic explanation. We have seen that Plato and, following him, Aristotle, think not. For this reason, Aristotle believes we need to ask about *final* causes in addition to the other three kinds. This question is still hotly debated.

We have seen that living things are distinguished from nonliving things by having the origins of some of their motions within them. Hobbes must now give a more careful account of this. He distinguishes two sorts of motions peculiar to animals: vital and voluntary motions. *Vital motions* are such things as the circulation of the blood, the pumping of the heart, breathing, and digestion. *Voluntary motions,* by contrast, are those for which the cause is to be found in some imagination. John imagines how pleasant it would be to go with Jane to the movies; he walks out of his way in the hope that their paths will cross. It is clear that if imagination itself is nothing but the diminished motions of sense, voluntary motions such as walking in a certain direction have their origin in internal motions.

These small, perhaps infinitesimally small beginnings of motion Hobbes calls *endeavor.* Endeavor can either be toward something (in which case it is called *desire*) or away from something (which is called *aversion*). In desire and aversion we find the sources of all human action.

Desire and aversion allow Hobbes to introduce certain value notions. What we desire, he says, we call good; what we wish to avoid we call evil. And these value distinctions are invariably founded on pleasure and pain, respectively: What gives us pleasure we call good; what causes pain we call evil.* It is important to realize that good and evil are not thought to attach absolutely to things. They are not properties that things have independently of our relation to them. The words "good" and "evil," Hobbes tells us,

> are ever used with relation to the person that useth them; there being nothing simply and absolutely so; nor any common rule of good and evil to be taken from the nature of the objects themselves; but from the person of the man, where there is no common-wealth; or, in a commonwealth, from the person that representeth it; or from an arbitrator or judge, whom men disagreeing shall by consent set up, and make his sentence the rule thereof. (*L,* 150)

The idea that in a "commonwealth," or state, good and evil are not relative to *individuals* is one

we will explore shortly. But in what Hobbes calls a "state of nature," where there are no monarchs and judges, good and evil strictly depend on "the person of the man." The *only* judgment possible is that of the individual; if she desires *X,* she judges *X* to be good; if he dislikes *Y,* he considers *Y* evil. And from those judgments there is (in the state of nature) no appeal.*

This analysis is an important step in Hobbes' materialistic program. Goodness is not a Platonic Form or an unanalyzable property that some things have. Everything is just body and motion. But some (living) bodies are related in certain ways to other bodies in such a way that the former bodies utter the words "That is good" about those latter bodies. They do so when the latter produce motions in the former that are pleasurable.

What is pleasure? Pleasure, Hobbes tells us, is just "a corroboration of vital motion, and a help thereunto," while pains are a "hindering and troubling [of] the motion vital" (*L,* 150). Feeling good, in other words, is just having all our normal bodily processes working smoothly; the more active and untroubled they are, the better we feel—and what we all want is to feel good.

It seems, then, that regulated thoughts are regulated by desire, that desire is always for the good, and that "good" is our name for whatever produces pleasure. The end point of a train of regulated thoughts is some action on our part—an action we think will gain us some good. These actions, when caused by thoughtful desires in this way, are called "voluntary."

At this point, Hobbes meets a natural objection. It is not, someone might claim, *desire* that is the cause of voluntary action; it is *will.* And willpower can override our desires. I desperately want another slice of that dark, rich chocolate cake, but I exercise my will and say, "Thank you, but no." Can Hobbes deal with this common experience?

He does so by asking what we mean by "will." It cannot be anything else, he thinks, than "*the last appetite in deliberating*" (*L,* 154). Will, then, *is* a desire. I do desire that slice of cake, but I also have desires that run counter to that desire: I want not to look

---

*It is clear that Hobbes is a hedonist. See Epicurus, p. 199.

piggish; I want not to gain too much weight. On this occasion, these latter desires outweigh the former; they are the ones that dictate my action, and so these are what we *call* my will. Will is nothing but *effective desire*. It is the desire that *wins*. Since we have already seen that Hobbes believes desire and aversion can be given an analysis in terms of matter in motion, there is no need (as Descartes thinks) to bring in nonmaterial factors to explain the origin of voluntary actions.*

Our voluntary actions, then, are governed in the last analysis by passion—by our desires and aversions, our loves and hates. And since the good we seek and the evil we try to avoid are rooted in our own pleasures and pains, action is always egoistic. It is my own good that I seek, if Hobbes is right—not yours. As Hobbes puts it, "of the voluntary acts of every man, the object is some *good to himself*" (*L*, 165).

Moreover, we seek such good *continually*. It is not enough to act once for our own pleasure; the next moment demands other acts that have the same end. Happiness—or felicity, as Hobbes calls it—is just a life filled with the satisfaction of our desires.

> *Continual success* in obtaining those things which a man from time to time desireth, that is to say, continual prospering, is that men call *felicity;* I mean the felicity of this life. For there is no such thing as perpetual tranquility of mind, while we live here; because life itself is but motion, and can never be without desire, nor without fear, no more than without sense. (*L*, 155)

In this life there can be no resting, no "tranquility." No sooner has one desire been fulfilled than another takes its place. The reason Hobbes gives for this is that life itself is nothing but motion. (We have here a kind of principle of inertia for living things; just as things in motion tend to remain in motion, so the life of desiring tends to perpetuate itself.) So there is a perpetual striving for the satisfaction of desires; when this is successful over some period of time, we say that during that period a person is happy.*

All of us desire this felicity, Hobbes says. But it is easy to see that if we are not to be mere pawns of fortune, we must also control access to it; that is, we must be guaranteed the *power* to satisfy whatever desires we may happen to have.

> I put for a general inclination of all mankind, a perpetual and restless desire of power after power, that ceaseth only in death. And the cause of this, is not always that a man hopes for a more intensive delight, than he has already attained to; or that he cannot be content with a moderate power: but because he cannot assure the power and means to live well, which he hath present, without the acquisition of more. (*L*, 158–159)

This kind of power is, of course, a relative matter. In a world of limited resources, if I gain more power to guarantee the satisfaction of *my* desires, I naturally diminish *your* power to satisfy your desires. In seeking to assure my own felicity, I threaten yours. So we are naturally competitors. I seek my good. You seek yours. And we each seek to increase our own power to assure that we at least do not lose those goods we now have.†

---

*It is clear that Hobbes is a *determinist*—that is, one who thinks that for every event, including all human actions, there is a set of sufficient conditions guaranteeing its occurrence. All actions are caused; and the causes of these causes themselves have causes. This poses a problem, of course: the problem of freedom of the will. We saw that Descartes, who is not a materialist, can hold that our decisions escape this universal determinism that holds for the material world; even God, Descartes says, is not more free than we are. Hobbes cannot think so. He has a solution to this problem, but because the same solution is more elegantly set out by Hume, we consider it in the next chapter. If you want a preview, see "Rescuing Human Freedom," in Chapter 15.

*Compare this notion of happiness to that of Epicurus ("The Epicureans," in Chapter 8). Note that there is a fundamental agreement: pleasure is the good. But note also that Hobbes makes no distinction between those desires it is and is not wise to try to fulfill. It is hard to see how he could—at least for the state of nature. Desires are just facts—any and all of them; they all, equally, demand satisfaction. And the strongest wins. That, Hobbes might say, is just how it is.

†If this seems unrealistic to you as a model of relations among individuals, consider political and economic rivalries among nations. As we will see, Hobbes has an explanation of how we have gotten beyond this competitive situation on the individual level. It is instructive to compare this picture of restless competitiveness to Augustine's two cities, pp. 257–259.

FRANCIS BACON

Although Francis Bacon (1561–1626) was both a jurist and a statesman (rising as high as lord high chancellor in the England of James I) he was most passionately interested in reforming intellectual life and creating a new kind of science. His principal philosophical works are *The Advancement of Learning* (1605) and *Novum Organum* (1620).

Bacon believed that old habits had to change; it was a bad mistake to look to the authorities of the past because nearly everything about the natural world remained to be discovered. Traditional philosophers, he said, are like spiders, spinning out intricate conceptions from their own insides. Alchemists and other early investigators were like ants, scurrying about collecting facts without any organized method. We should rather follow the example of the bees; let scientists cooperate in acquiring data, offering interpretations, conducting experiments, and drawing judicious conclusions.

Bacon identified four "idols" that, he said, have hindered the advance of knowledge: (1) idols of the tribe—tendencies resident in human nature itself, such as imagining that the senses give us a direct picture of their objects or imagining there is more order in experience than we actually find; (2) idols of the den—people's inclination to interpret experiences according to their private dispositions or favorite theories; (3) idols of the marketplace— language that subverts communication through ambiguities in words or in names that are assumed to name something but actually do not; and (4) idols of the theater—the dogmas of traditional philosophy, which portray the universe no more accurately than stage plays portray everyday life.

How can we counter these tendencies to revere the past and idolize the wrong things? Bacon recommended a method of careful experimentation and induction. Supporting a theory by simple enumeration of positive instances, however, is not good enough. We must look particularly, he said, for negative instances—especially if the theory is one we are fond of—and for variations in the degrees of presence and absence of factors so that we can find correlations between then.

Nature, Bacon told us, can be commanded only by obeying her; by submitting to nature's own ways through carefully designed experiments, we can gain knowledge. Knowledge, he said, is power. And the result of a reformed science will be mastery of nature, leading to a higher quality of human life.

Although there are natural differences in our power, we are equal enough in natural gifts that each of us has reason to fear the other. As Hobbes says, even "the weakest has strength enough to kill the strongest" (*L*, 159). Because of this equality, the egoistic desire for happiness—plus the need to be assured of it by a continual increase of power— leads human beings to be enemies. So our *natural* condition (i.e., before any artificial arrangements or agreements among us) is one of *war*. Indeed, it is "such a war as is of every man against every man." In such a condition, Hobbes argues,

> there is no place for industry, because the fruit thereof is uncertain; and consequently no culture of the earth; no navigation, nor use of the commodities that may be imported by sea; no commodious building; no instruments of moving and removing, such things as require much force; no knowledge of the face of the earth; no account of time; no arts; no letters; no society; and which is worst of all, continual fear, and danger of violent death; and the life of man, solitary, poor, nasty, brutish, and short. (*L*, 161)

Solitary, poor, nasty, brutish—and short! Such is our life in a state of nature.

Let us remind ourselves of what Hobbes claims to be doing here. He is trying to use the same method on human nature and society that Galileo and Harvey use on the nonhuman world. He resolves human beings into their component elements—the motions characteristic of living things—and finds this competitive and restless striving to be the result.

This analysis is supported, he believes, by observation. Hobbes lived during extremely troubled times in England.* There was a long struggle between king and Parliament over the right to make laws and to collect taxes. This struggle reflected a broader quarrel between the old nobility and the established Church of England on the one hand and the rising middle classes and religious dissenters of a more radical Protestant sort on the other. Those on each side, in Hobbes' view, were trying to preserve against the other side the means of their own happiness.

The outcome was a protracted and bloody civil war, the execution of King Charles I, a period of government without a king under the Protectorate of Oliver Cromwell, and finally the Restoration of the monarchy under Charles II (to whom Hobbes had been a tutor in mathematics). The "state of nature" into which Hobbes resolves human society was very nearly the actual state of affairs during a good part of the seventeenth century in England. The war of all against all was not just a theoretical construct; it was an observed actuality.

Still, Hobbes does not intend his description of the state of nature to be a description of society at all times and places. Nor is it supposed to be a historical description of the state of society at some time in the distant past. It is intended to picture the results of an analytical decomposition of human society into its elements. Left to their own devices, the theory says, individuals will always act egoistically for their own good, and the inevitable consequence is a state of war—each of us fearing our neighbor and striving to extend our sphere of control at our neighbor's expense. This is the result of the *resolution phase* of Hobbes' method.

We now need to look at the *composition phase,* where the elements are put back together again. And here we are interested primarily in Hobbes' view of the ethical consequences.

The Natural Foundation of Moral Rules

Hobbes has "resolved" human society into its elements. Let us see how he thinks it can be "com-

posed" back again into a whole. If Hobbes succeeds in this stage, we will have an explanation of the human world, including its ethical and political aspect, in purely mechanistic terms.

In the state of nature, human beings are governed by their egoistic passions, their endeavor to ensure their own happiness. And we have seen how this leads to the "war of everyone against everyone," a deadly competition for the power to guarantee for each person what he considers good. If this is our natural state, how can it be overcome? Partly, Hobbes says, by passion itself, and partly by reason.

One of the strongest passions is the *fear of death.* It is this fear, together with the desire for happiness, that motivates us to find a way to end the state of nature. We must remember that in the state of nature there are no rights and wrongs, no goods and bads, except where an individual thinks there are. We each take as much as we have power to take and keep. An individual's liberty extends as far as his power. But if a person in this state of nature realizes how unsatisfactory this condition is, he will see that

> it is a precept, or general rule of reason, *that every man ought to endeavor peace, as far as he has hope of obtaining it; and when he cannot obtain it, that he may seek and use all helps and advantages of war.* The first branch of which rule containeth the first and fundamental law of nature; which is, to *seek peace and follow it.* The second, the sum of the right of nature; which is, *by all means we can, to defend ourselves.* (L, 163)

Hobbes speaks here of a *right* of nature and of a *law* of nature. What can he mean? In a universe composed merely of matter in motion, how can there be rights and laws *in nature?* Hasn't Hobbes already denied that there is any right or wrong independent of some monarch or judge to declare what is right and wrong?

There has been much debate about how Hobbes means these notions to be understood. If we interpret him sympathetically, however, it seems that a law of nature must simply be an expression of the way things go. Jones, who by nature seeks his own happiness and fears death, is worried about his future. This is just how it is. In reasoning about his situation, Jones sees that if peace were to replace war,

---

*For the English Civil War, see http://www.open2.net/civilwar/.

then his fear of death would be relieved; and if he didn't have to be so afraid of his neighbors, he could more satisfactorily fill his own life with "felicity." The rule to "seek peace" is a rule that an egoistic but rational creature such as Jones will inevitably—naturally—come upon. He will reason that if he is going to have any chance of a good life, he has to get beyond this state of war. A *law of nature* for Hobbes is simply a rule of prudence that results from the shrewd calculation of a scared human being.

A *right of nature* must have a similar foundation. In the state of nature there are no "rights" in the usual sense. If, in a state of nature, someone injures me, I cannot complain that my "rights" have been infringed. All I can say is that I don't like it and will do whatever I can to see that it doesn't happen again! But precisely because there are no rules, I am *at liberty* to use whatever means I can muster to preserve my life and happiness. Hobbes uses the term "right" to refer to this liberty everyone has in the state of nature. So Jones having the "right" to defend himself is simply the fact that there are no rules that curtail his tendency to preserve his life and happiness. If, however, Jones (and everyone else) exercises this liberty without limit, the results will be, as we have seen, uniformly bad: the war of all against all.

This suggests to the rational person that some of the liberty we have in the state of nature must be given up. To give it up entirely, however, would make no sense at all; if Jones gave up the liberty of defending himself altogether, he would become the prey of everyone—and an egoistic agent could not rationally allow that. So this "right" of self-defense remains something that Jones will always retain.

We have, then, one right and one law, which are used by Hobbes as the foundation for a series of deductions. Once we have these, others "follow" in almost geometrical fashion. For instance, the second law, Hobbes tells us, is

> that a man be willing, when others are so too, as far forth as peace and defense of himself he shall think it necessary, to lay down this right to all things; and be contented with so much liberty against other men, as he would allow other men against himself. (*L,* 163–164)

Each of us, according to this second law, should be content with as much liberty with respect to others as we are willing to allow with respect to ourselves. There should be—in order to end the state of war—a mutual limiting of rights, as far as this is of mutual benefit to each. (Note that Hobbes does not suppose that anyone would do this altruistically, or out of sheer goodwill. The motivation throughout is hedonistic and egoistic.)

This agreement to limit one's claims has the flavor of a contract. And, indeed, Hobbes' view is one version of a **social contract** theory,* but you can see that there is a difficulty at this point. Suppose Jones and Smith, in a state of nature, each agree to limit their own liberty to the extent that the other does as well. Why should they believe each other? What reason do they have to trust each other to keep the promise? Is there anything to keep Smith from violating the contract if she thinks it is in her interest to do so and calculates that she can get away with it? It seems not. Hence, in a state of nature, contracts and promises are useless. They are just words! This is a serious problem. It looks as if you cannot get here from there—that is, to a moral community from a state of nature. Can Hobbes solve this problem?

What is necessary to make the contract operative, Hobbes says, is "a common power set over them both, with right and force sufficient to compel performance" (*L,* 167). Only then, when punishment threatens, can Jones trust Smith to keep her promise. For only then will it clearly be in Smith's self-interest not to break it. There is, then, a necessity for

> some coercive power, to compel men equally to the performance of their covenants . . . and such power there is none before the erection of a commonwealth. (*L,* 168)

---

*The idea of a contract or agreement as the basis for society is taken up by a number of other political thinkers: Spinoza, Rousseau, and—most importantly for the founding of the American Republic—John Locke (see the following section). They differ about the powers such a contract bestows on a government, about whether such a contract could or could not be revoked, and about the grounds on which a citizen might withdraw allegiance. Nonetheless, social contract theories generally stress both the rights of individuals and the necessity of consent as the basis of legitimate government. Thus, they are both a reflection of and an influence on the individualism of the times.

This is the rationale for that "great *Leviathan*," that "artificial man," that "mortal god," the state. It is the state, together with the power of enforcement that we agree to give it, that gets us beyond the state of nature. Only in such a community can moral and legal rules exist and structure our lives.

The great danger in any community, Hobbes believes, is that it might fall back again into the state of nature, where everyone thinks he or she has the right to be judge of everything. So a state cannot allow individuals to follow their own consciences, to decide for themselves what is good and evil. The sovereign established by the contract, whether king or governing assembly, must be absolute; its word must be law. The sovereign declares what is good, what is evil—and even what those terms shall mean. Lacking this absolute power in the sovereign, we stare chaos and civil war in the face again.

In setting up a government for the purpose of escaping the dangers of the state of nature, then, we are bound to treat its actions as our own. So once a sovereign power is established, there can be no right of rebellion against it, for it cannot be right to rebel against ourselves. Nor can any subject claim that the sovereign power has acted unjustly, no matter what it does, for whatever it does is done by the citizens themselves who established it. Moreover, because the sovereign is not a party to the contract, but is established by it, it follows that the sovereign cannot violate the contract. A government may do bad things, Hobbes allows, but it can never be accused of injustice.

Because the aim of government is to secure a condition of peace among the citizens, it must have all the powers that are necessary to this end. And because individual actions are governed by opinions, the sovereign must have the power to determine which opinions and doctrines may be taught in the state. Finally, the sovereign power must be one and undivided. Hobbes thought one lesson of the civil war was that power divided between king and parliament made conflict inevitable. So a unified sovereign must have the power to make the law, to judge cases according to the law, and to administer the application of law—including the power to appoint judges and cabinet ministers—otherwise the whole

point of establishing a government by limiting individual natural rights would be lost.

You might think that this is a rather extreme position, but you have to remember that Hobbes' analysis of human beings leads to a rather extreme view of the problem: the war of all against all. For extreme situations, extreme solutions may be required. In any case, we have here an example of a worldview built on the foundations of the new science, a view that *includes* human beings, together with their mental and moral life. Let us summarize a few of the main points:

- Sensation, thought, motivation, and voluntary action are all analyzed in terms of matter in motion.

- All events, including human actions, are subject to the same laws of motion that Galileo has discovered.

- Only egoistic desires are recognized as motivators, so all actions are performed for the welfare of the agent.

- If you peel off the veneer of civilization, what you are left with is individuals in conflict.

- This conflict can be resolved on the basis of the very passions that produce it, provided people reason well about their individual long-term interest.

- Morality and law are simply the best means available, the *only* means to stave off imminent death and the possible loss of felicity. Being moral and law-abiding is no more than a smart strategy for self-preservation.

- Unless these rules are enforced by a powerful ruler, everything will collapse again into the state of nature.

It is a stark vision that Hobbes gives us. He thinks that acceptance of modern science forces that view upon us. Is that correct, or are there less forbidding alternatives?

---

1. Contrast the world-picture we get from the Galileo–Descartes–Hobbes gang with that of Aristotle and his medieval followers with respect to

- a description of the universe
- what needs explaining
- kinds of explanation desired
- the place of values in the world

2. How does Hobbes try to explain thinking? Compare his views, if you can, with recent work in artificial intelligence.

3. How are good and evil explained by Hobbes? Compare with the view of Augustine (e.g., pp. 238–241).

4. How do Hobbes and Descartes differ on the nature of the will? Relate this to the metaphysics of each.

5. Describe what Hobbes calls "the state of nature," and explain why it has the character it does have.

6. How does Hobbes think we can have gotten, or can get, beyond the state of nature?

7. What makes Hobbes think that a "social contract" will require the "coercive power" of a state?

John Locke: Looking to Experience

Although a clear implication of Cartesian method is that "first" philosophy is really epistemology, Descartes' own meditations are still in the metaphysical mode. Hobbes, too, is primarily a metaphysician — the metaphysician of matter in motion, in contrast to Descartes' dualism. The credit (or blame) for taking seriously the idea that theory-of-knowledge issues must come first in philosophical thought belongs to the English philosopher John Locke (1632–1704). With Locke the lesson is drawn: Unless we are clear about our capacities for gaining knowledge, we are likely to waste our time in controversies over matters that are beyond our grasp and end in confusion. Understanding how our kind of mind works and whence its contents come has to be the first order of business. So he writes, over a period of years, the famous *Essay Concerning Human Understanding.* This long and complex treatise, in four books, is usually thought to mark the proper beginning of **empiricism** in philosophy.* Locke begins the *Essay* with these words:

---

*There are, of course, forerunners of the empirical trend. Francis Bacon is a distinguished empiricist (see the profile on p. 368), and Hobbes also, to some extent. There is an immense amount of detail in Locke's long and rambling *Essay,* much of it having only historical interest. We will focus our attention on those parts that have made a lasting impact on the great conversation.

"It is ambition enough to be employed as an under-labourer in clearing the ground a little, and removing some of the rubbish which lies in the way to knowledge."
—JOHN LOCKE

Since it is the *understanding* that sets man above the rest of sensible beings, and gives him all the advantage and dominion which he has over them; it is certainly a subject, even for its nobleness, worth our labour to inquire into. The understanding, like the eye, whilst it makes us see and perceive all other things, takes no notice of itself: and it requires art and pains to set it at a distance and make it its own object. . . .

If by this inquiry into the nature of the understanding, I can discover the powers thereof; how far they reach; to what things they are in any degree proportionate; and where they fail us, I suppose it may be of use to prevail with the busy mind of man to be more cautious in meddling with things exceeding its comprehension; to stop when it is at the utmost extent of its tether; and to sit down in a quiet ignorance of those things which, upon examination, are found to be beyond the reach of our capacities. (*Essay,* Intro, 1, 3; vol. 1, pp. 25–28)[3]

You can see that Locke intends to recommend a certain modesty with respect to our capacity for knowledge. Moreover, he thinks that circumscribing the scope of our understanding will be a very *useful* thing to do; he is not writing just to satisfy curiosity on this score, but to mitigate the quarrels—religious, political, or what have you—leading even to wars, that arise when men believe they have certainty about things that are actually beyond our powers to know.

How shall he proceed? He states his purpose more precisely in these words:

> to inquire into the original, certainty, and extent of *human knowledge.* (*Essay,* Intro, 2; vol. 1, p. 26)

He says that he will use a "historical, plain method" in this investigation. By this, he means that he will try to trace our ideas to their origin, using no more esoteric technique than directing our attention to what should be obvious to any careful inquirer. So we find him again and again asking us to look and see whether we do not agree with what he finds.

He notes in the introduction that he will use the word "idea" in a very broad sense: for "whatsoever is the *object* of the understanding when a man thinks" (*Essay,* Intro, 8; vol. 1, p. 32). He means to include everything from sensations of red and warm, through the contents of memory and imagination, to abstract ideas of a circle or an animal species, and even to our idea of God. That there are such ideas in our minds, Locke says, we all admit. The first question is this: How do they get there?

Origin of Ideas

Book I of the *Essay* is devoted to destroying one possible answer: that ideas, any or all of them, are innate. Locke's argument is that if there are innate ideas, they must be universally held in all minds. Perhaps the most plausible cases are trivialities such as "Whatever is, is." But Locke argues that (1) not even such ideas are universal (e.g., they are not present in the minds of children or idiots), and (2) universality would prove innateness only if there were no other way such ideas could be acquired.* Locke

is convinced that there is another way, and to that he turns in Book II, the longest and most influential book of the *Essay.*

If the mind is not innately supplied with ideas and knowledge, where do they come from?

> Let us then suppose the mind to be, as we say, white paper, void of all characters, without any ideas: —How comes it to be furnished? Whence comes it by that vast store which the busy and boundless fancy of man has painted on it with an almost endless variety? Whence has it all the *materials* of reason and knowledge? To this I answer, in one word, from EXPERIENCE. In that all our knowledge is founded; and from that it ultimately derives itself. (*Essay,* II, I, 2; vol. 1, pp. 121–122)

There are two sources of such experience. On the one hand, there is the experience of external objects via our senses; this is the first and greatest source of ideas. Locke calls this source *sensation.* Here we get the ideas of yellow, hot, cold, hard, soft, bitter, sweet, and so on. On the other hand, we can reflect internally on how our minds work, garnering ideas of mental operations. Locke calls this source *reflection.* From reflection we get the ideas of perceiving, thinking, doubting, believing, reasoning, knowing, willing, and so on. These two sources supply the raw materials for all our knowledge.

> The understanding seems to me not to have the least glimmering of any ideas which it doth not receive from one of these two. *External objects* furnish the mind with the ideas of sensible qualities, which are all those different perceptions they produce in us; and *the mind* furnishes the understanding with ideas of its own operations. (*Essay,* II, I, 5; vol. 1, p. 124)

It is worth noting that Locke takes for granted, as Hobbes also does but Descartes does not, that there *are* "external objects" supplying us with ideas of themselves.* This supposition sits uneasily with other parts of Locke's view, and Berkeley (later in this chapter) and Hume (Chapter 15) exploit this tension.

---

*Locke is attacking a very crude version of innate ideas; it is not clear that it applies to Descartes' version of innateness as an idea that a thinking being would possess even if nothing else but that being existed. See p. 330.

*Locke does offer some arguments on behalf of this assumption much later in the *Essay* (see Book IV, Chapter XI), but they seem to be no stronger than the arguments Descartes destroys in *Meditation I.*

Ideas can be classified as either simple or complex. A *simple idea* is one that, "being in itself uncompounded, contains in it nothing but *one uniform appearance, or conception in the mind*" (*Essay,* II, II, 1; vol. 1, p. 145). What might seem to be a single experience may be composed of several simple ideas; touching a piece of ice, for instance, produces not one idea but the two distinguishable ideas of cold and hard. Simple ideas are the *elements* of all our thinking.

> When the understanding is once stored with these simple ideas, it has the power to repeat, compare, and unite them, even to an almost infinite variety, and so can make at pleasure new complex ideas. But it is not in the power of the most exalted wit, or enlarged understanding, by any quickness or variety of thought, to *invent* or *frame* one new simple idea in the mind, not taken in by the ways before mentioned. (*Essay,* II, II, 2; vol. 1, p. 145)

Even with respect to simple ideas, however, the mind carries on certain operations. For instance, (1) we have the power to *distinguish* one clearly from another; (2) we can *compare* them, noting their likenesses and differences; (3) we can *put them together* in various ways; (4) we can *name* them; and most important, (5) we can *frame abstract ideas*. How do we do that? Locke gives this example. Seeing the same color today, in chalk or snow, which we yesterday observed in milk, we consider that appearance alone (disregarding the crumbly nature, the coldness, or the liquidity it is associated with) and give it the name *whiteness*. We *abstract* the color from the other qualities by paying selective attention to it, neglecting its surroundings. That is the way, Locke says, "universals, whether ideas or terms, are made" (*Essay,* II, XI, 9; vol. 1, p. 207). It is this power to abstract that distinguishes us from the other animals. All of these powers are known to us by reflection on the operations of our own minds.

We come now to *complex ideas,* which can be classified under three heads, Locke tells us: modes, relations, and substances. There is a long and complicated chapter on our ideas of *modes* (what the medievals called "accidents" or "incidental properties"). These do not exist on their own, but only as modifications of a substance. Locke strives to show that our ideas of space, time, and infinity are modes, built by adding simple ideas to simple ideas.

Relations are of many kinds and are very important in our knowledge. Examples are knowing that one thing occurs before another, that this is next to that, that *a* causes *b,* that *x* is identical with *y,* and that two numbers added make a third number. But because Locke's discussion of the general nature of relations is both complex and confused, we pass it by— though we will examine what he says about certain particular relations, such as are involved in our idea of personal identity and in our knowledge of things external to us.

Of more lasting significance is what Locke has to say about *substances*.

Idea of Substance

The notion of substance, as we have seen, plays a significant role in philosophical thought from the time of Aristotle onward. Let's briefly review that tradition. Substance is what can exist on its own, not dependent on another. A lizard, for instance, is a substance; its tan color, its scaliness, its being long-tailed and dry-skinned—these are not substances, but properties of a substance. Some of its properties are incidental to its nature—its weight, for example—but some of them make up the *essence* of a lizard—are what make the lizard a lizard. Any such substance is a composite of *form* (making it the kind of thing it is) and *matter* (which makes it the particular instance of that kind of thing). Thomas Aquinas adds that existence is something added to the essence of any actual substance (except for God, whose essence is his existence). According to the tradition, substances are knowable; they are knowable in terms of their forms, and particularly in terms of their essential forms.

What does Locke, the empiricist, say about substance? Clearly he will want to explain in terms of his "historical plain method" how we come to have that idea. We already know that there are just two sources for ideas—sensation and reflection—and that all ideas can be traced back to simple ideas. Now the mind, Locke says, takes notice

> that a certain number of these simple ideas go constantly together; which being presumed to belong to one thing, . . . we are apt afterward to talk of and consider as one simple idea, which indeed is

a complication of many ideas together: because . . . not imagining how these simple ideas *can* subsist by themselves, we accustom ourselves to suppose some *substratum* wherein they do subsist, and from which they do result, which therefore we call *substance.*

. . . If any one should be asked, what is the subject wherein colour or weight inheres, he would have nothing to say, but the solid and extended parts; and if he were demanded, what is it that solidity and extension adhere in, he would not be in a much better case than the Indian . . . who, saying that the world was supported by a great elephant, was asked what the elephant rested on; to which his answer was—a great tortoise: but being again pressed to know what gave support to the broadbacked tortoise, replied—*something, he knew not what.* (*Essay,* II, XXIII, 1,2; vol. 1, pp. 390–392)

Something—we know not what! That, according to Locke, is what we can know of substance. We know there are substances, but we don't know what they are. The reason we don't has to do with Locke's account of the way we get our ideas. In our experience, certain simple ideas always seem to appear together: a yellow color, for instance, together with solidity, malleability, and an unusual heaviness. And

because we cannot conceive how they should subsist alone, nor in one another, we suppose them existing in and supported by some common subject; which support we denote by the name substance, though it be certain we have no clear or distinct idea of that thing we suppose a support. (*Essay,* II, XXIII, 4; vol. 1, p. 395)

How could these qualities just happen to hang together this way? There must, we think, be something that *has* them. So we invent a name for that thing—that support, that substratum, that *substance*—and call it "gold." It isn't any of those qualities. Gold isn't yellowness; it isn't heaviness; nor is it just the collection of all those qualities together. Gold is the thing that has those qualities; *it* is yellow, solid, malleable, and so on. But what it is, in itself, we have no idea.*

An important part of our idea of substance is made up of our idea of the substance's powers. By "power," Locke means something like a disposition to affect other things, given suitable circumstances. A magnet, for instance, has the (active) power to attract iron filings and will do so if there are iron filings in the neighborhood; similarly, iron filings have the (passive) power to be attracted. These powers or dispositional properties are part of what makes a magnet a magnet, and of what makes iron filings what they are.

Among the powers of substances, a particularly important set are their powers to affect our minds.

For, to speak truly, yellowness is not actually in gold, but is a power in gold to produce that idea in us by our eyes, when placed in a due light: and the heat, which we cannot leave out of our ideas of the sun, is no more really in the sun, than the white colour it introduces into wax. These are both equally powers in the sun, operating, by the motion and figure of its sensible parts, so on a man, as to make him have the idea of heat; and so on wax, as to make it capable to produce in a man the idea of white. (*Essay,* II, XXIII, 10; vol. 1, pp. 400–401)

From this, we see that Locke accepts that division of qualities into primary and secondary that we first met in Galileo.* The properties that are actually in gold are its extension, shape, motion, and impenetrability. These are gold's primary qualities, the qualities it really has. Locke puts it this way: Our ideas of the primary qualities of a substance *resemble* the qualities the object actually has. So a physical object we experience as rectangular, say, or hard, may actually *be* rectangular or hard.

Properly speaking, however, gold is not yellow; that color is not one of its primary qualities, does not belong to it as it is—apart from us. Gold does have a secondary quality: the power to produce yellow sensations in creatures such as ourselves. The idea is that the primary qualities of gold, when joined with the primary qualities of light, of the eye, and of the nervous system of a human being, bring about (somehow) an experience of color. But we

---

*Note how different this view is from that of Aristotle and Aquinas. For them what we know is *precisely* the substance; we know it in terms of its characteristics, and primarily in terms of its substantial form—which defines *what it is.*

*See pp. 316–317.

would be mistaken to read that sensation back into the substance itself.

Idea of the Soul

Substances, then, are unknown in themselves but can be known to exist as the *causes* of the ideas they produce in us. But this means, Locke holds, that we have just as good an idea of spiritual substance as of material. Just as we frame the idea of a material substance from the ideas of sensation, so from ideas of reflection,

> we are able to frame the *complex idea of an immaterial spirit.* And thus . . . we have as clear a perception and notion of immaterial substances as we have of material. . . . The one is as clear and distinct an idea as the other. . . . For whilst I know, by seeing or hearing &c., that there is some corporeal being without me, the object of that sensation, I do more certainly know, that there is some spiritual being within me that sees and hears. (*Essay,* II, XXIII, 15; vol. 1, pp. 406–407)

What applies in the one case applies in the other, however. In neither case do we have any knowledge of what such a substance is in itself. We know only that there must be such a substance to serve as the substratum for physical properties in the one case and mental properties in the other. So Locke comes to agree with Descartes—and to disagree with Hobbes—in believing that there are minds *and* bodies, and that they are radically different kinds of things.[*]

Locke takes some pains to try to show us that the notion of an immaterial substance is no more obscure than that of a material thing. He does *not* do it, as you might suppose, by arguing for the clarity of our idea of an immaterial soul. No, instead, he argues that our notions of how *each* works will bottom out in unintelligibility. Take the power of moving a material thing, for example. I decide to dig in the garden, and I lift a spade full of dirt: The spade moves the dirt; I move the spade by exercising my will; and in each case we can go some distance in explaining why the mover moves the moved. For instance, we can explain why the spade lifts the dirt in terms of relations between the molecules in the spade; and those relations in terms of relations between atoms; and those in turn. . . . But there will come a point where we will have to say, "Well, those kinds of things just do this," and that will be that. The case is exactly the same with respect to how the will moves the body. Ultimately, there can be no more a final understanding of why the spade moves the dirt than of how my will gets the spade to move.[*]

> The communication of motion by thought, which we attribute to spirit, is as evident as that by impulse, which we ascribe to body. Constant experience makes us sensible of both these, though our narrow understandings can comprehend neither. For, when the mind would look beyond those original ideas we have from sensation or reflection, and penetrate into their causes. . . . it discovers nothing but its own short-sightedness. (*Essay,* II, XXIII, 28; vol. 1, p. 414)

In sum, although we have clear ideas of some of the primary qualities of both bodies and souls (for instance, solidity on the one hand and thinking on the other), the substance of each is unknown to us—and is bound to remain so.

> For whensoever we would proceed beyond these simple ideas we have from sensation and reflection, and dive further into the nature of things, we fall presently into darkness and obscurity, perplexedness and difficulties, and can discover nothing further but our own blindness and ignorance. (*Essay,* II, XXIII, 32; vol. 1, p. 418)

Idea of Personal Identity

Still, Locke holds that there are such immaterial substances as souls. And it is of some interest to ask

---

[*]Actually Locke does not think it possible to *demonstrate* that thinking cannot go on in material substances, "since we know not wherein thinking consists, nor to what sort of substances the Almighty has been pleased to give that power" (*Essay,* IV, III, 6; p. 193).

[*]We have here an anticipation of David Hume's much more famous analysis of causation. Locke still takes it for granted that we have a meaningful idea of "power," even though it is mysterious in the end. Hume will claim such a notion is a mere "fiction" and gives an account of how it arises. See "Causation: The Very Idea" in Chapter 15.

whether my continuing as the same person over a period of time consists in the enduring existence of the same soul. I, in my maturity, possess very different qualities from those I had at ten years old. What is it that makes me the same person throughout? Is this the rule: same person, same soul? That had been, in fact, the traditional answer. Locke's answer to this question is novel and has had great influence.

You might guess, given Locke's skeptical attitude toward knowledge of substances, that he could not accept the traditional rule. Since I know nothing about the spiritual substance underlying my experiences, how could I judge that it was the same from year to year—or even, for that matter, from moment to moment? In fact, it turns out to be completely irrelevant whether the soul substance present in me at age ten is the same soul substance as I now have. In keeping with his determination to trace all our ideas to experience, Locke asks, What is it that gives me the *idea of myself* at all? and he answers, consciousness.

> For, since consciousness always accompanies thinking, and it is that which makes every one to be what he calls self, . . . as far as this consciousness can be extended backwards to any past action or thought, so far reaches the identity of that person; it is the same self now it was then; and it is by the same self with this present one that now reflects on it, that that action was done. (*Essay,* II, XXVII, 11; vol. 1, p. 449)

If I ask what makes me the self I am at this moment, the answer has to be this: my consciousness of myself. If I were not conscious of myself, I would be no more a self than a stone is. Then if I ask what makes the self I now am identical with the self I was yesterday, the answer has to be in conformity with this. I must be conscious of that self—remember having the experiences of yesterday's self.

Personal identity, then, cannot consist in sameness of substance. For all we know, it might be that a succession of soul substances could constitute a self, provided each were connected to the last by memories of what was thought and done in it. To take the contrary view, if a single substance were "wholly stripped of all consciousness of its past existence . . . beyond the power of ever retrieving it again," that

would constitute the end of one person and the beginning of another (*Essay,* II, XXVII, 14; vol. 1, p. 455).

Imagine, Locke says, that one and the same soul substance was present in you and in Nestor, the wise counselor of the Greeks at Troy, but that not a trace of memory connects you to him.

> This would no more make [you] the same person with Nestor, than if some of the particles of matter that were once a part of Nestor were now a part of [you]; the same immaterial substance, without the same consciousness, no more making the same person, . . . than the same particle of matter, without consciousness, . . . makes the same person. But [if you] once find [yourself] conscious of any of the actions of Nestor, [you] then find [yourself] the same person with Nestor. (*Essay,* II, XXVII, 14; vol. 1, p. 456)

What is true over time is true also in space.

> Thus every one finds that, whilst comprehended under that consciousness, the little finger is as much a part of himself as what is most so. Upon separation of this little finger, should this consciousness go along with the little finger, and leave the rest of the body, it is evident the little finger would be the person, the same person; and self would then have nothing to do with the rest of the body. (*Essay,* II, XXVII, 17; vol. 1, p. 459)

Locke remarks that "person" is a *forensic* term, the sort of term that appears in courts of law. It has to do with what we can be held responsible for, praised and blamed for, rewarded and punished for. Imagine a man who is being punished for what he did in another life, where he is not at all conscious of that other life. What is the difference between this, he asks, and being *created* miserable? None at all, if Locke is right about personal identity. My person

> extends itself beyond present existence to what is past, only by consciousness,—whereby it becomes concerned and accountable; owns and imputes to itself past actions, just upon the same ground and for the same reason as it does the present. (*Essay,* II, XXVII, 26; vol. 1, p. 467)

We own up to our present actions as ours because we are conscious of doing them. We own up to having done past actions on exactly the same grounds.

Locke thinks it is "probable" that one and the same consciousness is always attached to the same soul. He does not mean that these alternatives he has been exploring should be taken as serious possibilities; they are what we sometimes call *thought experiments*—imaginative trials forcing us to clarify our concepts. And Locke thinks they decisively refute the claim that our identity as the persons we are is founded in the continued sameness through time of a thinking substance. Personal identity has a psychological rather than a metaphysical basis.*

Language and Essence

Book III of the *Essay* has to do with words.† It is in words, by and large, that we express our knowledge, so an examination of the "origins, extent, and certainty" of our knowledge ought to clarify how language works. According to Locke, words are necessary for "sociable" creatures such as ourselves, language being "the great instrument and common tie of society" (*Essay,* III, I, 1; vol. 2, p. 3). Their principal function is to stand as signs for ideas.

> The comfort and advantage of society not being to be had without communication of thoughts, it was necessary that man should find out some external sensible signs, whereof those invisible ideas, which his thoughts are made up of, might be made known to others. . . . Thus we may conceive how *words,* which were by nature so well adapted to that purpose, came to be made use of by men as the signs of their ideas; not by any natural connexion that there is between particular articulate sounds and certain ideas, for then there would be but one language amongst all men; but by a voluntary imposition, whereby such a word is made arbitrarily the mark of such an idea. The use, then, of words, is to

be sensible marks of ideas; and the ideas they stand for are their proper and immediate signification. (*Essay,* III, II, 1; vol. 2, pp. 8–9)

Words, then, "in their primary or immediate signification, stand for nothing but *the ideas in the mind of him that uses them*" (*Essay,* III, II, 2; vol. 2, p. 9). And the aim of speaking is to make hearers understand these ideas by awakening similar ideas in them. The connection between a word and the idea it stands for—a few words such as "meow" aside—is completely arbitrary. The word "black" no more resembles my idea of black than the word "schwarz" does. But if hearing one of these words brings an idea into my mind which is similar to the idea in the speaker's mind, the word has done its job. Locke takes pains to deny that words stand directly for things in the world. It is not entirely wrong to think this, he says, but *precisely put,* words represent such things only indirectly, by representing ideas, which in turn stand for these things.

Again there is a wealth of detail in Locke's discussion, and again we pass by most of it. Let us look, though, at what Locke has to say about words for essences. As we have seen, knowledge in the Aristotelian tradition is knowledge of substance, and principally of the form of a substance that is its essence. Such knowledge tells us what it is to be a thing of a certain kind. Essences determine kinds of things: horses, clouds, tides, memories, thefts, and so on.

Now our ideas for kinds of things are, as Locke has told us, formed by abstraction, and we understand how that works. We consider a theft, say, and ignore everything that makes it this *particular* theft; we are then left with the general idea of theft. And general words represent general ideas. Most of our words—proper names aside—are general in this sense and represent abstract ideas.

But where in the world do we find essences or universals?

> It is plain, by what has been said, that *general* and *universal* belong not to the real existence of things; but are the inventions and creatures of the understanding, made by it for its own use, and concern only signs, whether words or ideas. Words are general . . . when used for signs of general ideas, and so are applicable indifferently to many particu-

---

*In recent decades the concept of personal identity has been given extended consideration, often in terms of science-fiction examples. The work of Bernard Williams, Derek Parfit, and Peter Unger makes clear the philosophers' debt to Locke. You might look at the delightful little book by John Perry, *A Dialogue on Immortality and Personal Identity* (Indianapolis: Hackett, 1978).

†Here is another way in which Locke is a forerunner of things to come; much twentieth-century philosophy has been preoccupied with linguistic matters. See for instance, Chapters 22 and 23, in which the thought of Ludwig Wittgenstein is featured.

lar things; and ideas are general when they are set up as the representatives of many particular things. . . . (*Essay*, III, III, 11; vol. 2, pp. 21–22)

This is a conclusion of considerable importance. If Locke is right here, the whole tradition stemming from Plato and Aristotle has been mistaken in thinking of universality as a feature of reality—whether in the Platonic heaven of Forms or in Aristotelian real essences embedded in things. Everything is particular. Universality is to be found only in the way certain particular things (mental ideas and words) *function*. Ideas and words are universal in their use, but not in their nature. My idea of a raven is as particular a thing as any individual raven. The way it differs is this: I *use* it to represent this raven and that raven—and indeed all the ravens there are or could be.

It is true that nature produces things that are similar to each other: ravens, for example. And it is even true, Locke admits, that a particular raven has a *real essence,* meaning by that those elements that are the ultimate foundation of the qualities we are aware of through our senses. But such real essences of things are completely unknown to us. Whatever it is in a given substance that causes our simple ideas of black, feathered, and winged is forever beyond our ken.

Moreover, though the things we call ravens are undeniably similar to each other, there is nothing that all ravens have that forces this similarity: no form or essence that *determines* the existence or co-existence of those qualities. Locke cites natural variations in individuals as evidence of this. Nature produces "monsters" of various kinds, deformed individuals without what we normally take to be properties essential to a kind. If we just pay attention to our experience, it seems clear that *any* property of a thing, no matter how "essential" we deem it, may, in a given instance, be lacking. How could that happen if nature were arranged in species where each particular instance of the species were determined to be the kind of thing it is by a universal form?

We do, of course, have abstract ideas and words, and they do present essences to us. But these are what Locke calls **nominal essences.** As the word suggests, nominal essences are attached to names. Nominal essences, while not entirely arbitrary, are

our own creations; they are not read off directly from nature itself. We do not consider the ultimate constitution of things in forming our ideas of essences because we cannot. Nor do we consider substantial forms, since those are mere inventions of the philosophers. What we do consider are the sensible qualities of things—those clusters of qualities that seem to hang together with some regularity and get a name.

> And if this be so, it is plain that *our distinct species* are *nothing but distinct complex ideas, with distinct names annexed to them.* It is true every substance that exists has its peculiar constitution, whereon depend those sensible qualities and powers we observe in it; but the ranking of things into species (which is nothing but sorting them under several titles) is done by us according to the ideas that *we* have of them: which, though sufficient to distinguish them by names, . . . yet if we suppose it to be done by their real internal constitutions, . . . by real essences, . . . we shall be liable to great mistakes. (*Essay,* III, VI, 13; vol. 2, p. 69)

Nominal essences, then, are not "copied from precise boundaries set by nature," but are "made by man with some liberty" (*Essay*, III, VI, 27; vol. 2, p. 77). They may be more or less carefully constructed, given our experience of things. And, no doubt, they can be improved by more careful observation. But they are one and all creatures of their creator and cannot be thought to be a simple mirror of reality.

> This, then, in short, is the case: Nature makes many *particular things,* which do agree one with another in many sensible qualities, and probably too in their internal frame and constitution: but it is not this real essence that distinguishes them into species; it is men who, taking occasion from the qualities they find united in them . . . range them into sorts, in order to their naming, for the convenience of comprehensive signs. (*Essay,* III, VI, 36; vol. 2, p. 86)

It is, then, Locke says, "evident that *men* make sorts of things" (*Essay*, III, VI, 35; vol. 2, p. 85). Nature produces particular beings in great abundance; many of them resemble each other. But "it is nevertheless true, that the boundaries of the species, whereby men sort them, are made by men" (*Essay*, III, VI, 37; vol. 2, p. 87). That science of the real essences of things that Aristotle and his followers dreamed of is not possible.

The Extent of Knowledge

Locke told us in the beginning of the *Essay* that his purpose was to determine the origins, the certainty, and the extent of our knowledge. His method has been to examine our understanding, getting clear about the materials it has to work with and how it operates with them. Now, in the fourth book of the *Essay,* he is at last ready to address the questions about knowledge directly. It begins this way:

> Since the mind, in all its thoughts and reasonings, hath no other immediate object but its own ideas, which it alone does or can contemplate, it is evident that our knowledge is only conversant about them.
>
> *Knowledge* then seems to me to be nothing but *the perception of the connexion of and agreement, or disagreement and repugnancy of any of our ideas.* In this alone it consists. (*Essay,* IV, I, 1; vol. 2, p. 167)
>
> We can have knowledge no further than we have ideas. (*Essay,* IV, III, 1; vol. 2, p. 190)*

This might not seem to be a very promising beginning. Surely, you want to say, we want to know more than how our ideas are related to *each other.* We want to know about reality, the world—what there actually is! In fact, Locke himself states such an objection, but he thinks he can meet it—in a characteristically modest fashion. Let us see how.

First we should note that he accepts that view of knowledge common in the tradition from Plato to Descartes—when we know, we have certainty. "The highest probability amounts not to certainty, without which there can be no true knowledge," Locke says (*Essay,* IV, III, 14; vol. 2, p. 203). This, of course, sets the standard very high.† The higher you set the standard, the fewer propositions will pass muster, so we mustn't be surprised when Locke again and again laments the small extent of our knowledge.

By the agreement and disagreement of ideas, he means the way ideas are put together in propositions. Again there are many distinctions. Let us focus on several of the most important. He notes four kinds of agreement or disagreement.

1. Concerning the *identity or diversity of ideas.* This seems more a preamble to knowledge than knowledge itself, having to do with making sure our ideas are both clear and distinct from one another.* Examples are "Whatever is, is" and "Blue is not yellow."

2. Concerning *relations between ideas.* Locke's clearest examples here are mathematical: for instance, the relation between the idea of a triangle and the idea of the sum of the interior angles being equal to two right angles. Such relations among ideas are the bread and butter of arithmetic, geometry, algebra, and so on. He also thinks that certain moral truths fall into this class, such as "Where there is no property there is no injustice." By and large, what Locke has in mind here is that class of truths later philosophers would call *analytic:* propositions we can know because one idea is "included" in another.† But he is not as clear about the nature of such truths as we might hope.

3. Concerning *coexistence or necessary connection.* This kind of knowledge, Locke says, pertains largely to substances. Now we already know that he thinks our knowledge of substance is extremely limited. What we can know of gold, he says, is just that certain simple ideas—yellow, malleable, heavy—tend to *coexist* or come always together in our experience. We don't see any necessary connection between these qualities; we don't understand why they *have* to appear together in that way.‡ And we certainly don't understand the connection between the primary qualities of gold and the subjective sensation of yellow. Why should just those minute elements in gold, via the light acting on our eyes and

---

*See again the remark about "disaster" by John Searle, footnote, p. 327.

†For a critique of this demand for certainty, see C. S. Peirce, p. 583. See also Ludwig Wittgenstein, pp. 635–641.

---

*The Cartesian language here is surely no accident. Locke talked philosophy extensively with followers of Descartes while spending some time on the European continent.

†See the distinctions drawn by Kant, for instance, pp. 429–431.

‡Compare David Hume, who says, "all events seem entirely loose and separate," p. 408.

then on the bits of stuff in our central nervous systems, make us see yellow? That is, and Locke suspects will ever remain, a mystery to us. It would be nice if we could discern necessary connections between qualities, he says, but it is unlikely that we will be able to advance much along this line, and we will be left with those coexistences that our experience testifies to.

4. Concerning *real existence*. To this point, Locke has stuck to his program of analyzing knowledge in terms of relations among our ideas. But here, apparently without entirely realizing it, he strikes a new note. He explains this kind of knowledge as "of *actual real existence* agreeing to any idea" (*Essay*, IV, I, 7; vol. 2, p. 171). Now the existence of something that "agrees to" one of our ideas cannot just be a matter of the relations *among* ideas. Yet it is only in this way that Locke can meet that natural objection to his principles that we noted previously.

What then can we know to "really" exist? Like Descartes and Augustine before him, Locke believes we have a clear *intuitive* knowledge of our own existence. This "we perceive . . . so plainly and so certainly, that it neither needs nor is capable of any proof. For nothing can be more evident to us than our own existence" (*Essay*, IV, IX, 3; vol. 2, pp. 304–305). We can know *demonstratively* that God exists. Locke rejects Descartes' first proof of God, which depends on an innate idea of God in us, but he offers an argument based on our own existence and the *nihilo nihil fit* principle: From nothing, you get nothing.

The knowledge of other things we have by *sensation*. Other than ourselves and God, we can know of the existence of any other thing

only when, by actual operating upon [us], it makes itself perceived by [us]. For the having the idea of anything in our mind, no more proves the existence of that thing, than the picture of a man evidences his being in the world, or the visions of a dream make thereby a true history.

It is therefore the *actual receiving* of ideas from without that gives us notice of the existence of other things, and makes us know, that something doth exist at that time without us, which causes that idea in us. . . . And of this, the greatest assurance I can

possibly have . . . is the testimony of my eyes, . . . whose testimony . . . I can no more doubt, whilst I write this, that I see white and black, and that something really exists that causes that sensation in me, than that I write or move my hand. . . .

The notice we have by our senses of the existing of things without us, though it be not altogether so certain as our intuitive knowledge, or the deductions of our reason employed about the clear abstract ideas of our own minds; yet it is an assurance that deserves the name of *knowledge*. (*Essay*, IV, XI, 1–3; vol. 2, pp. 325–327)

Several questions press themselves upon us: (1) If our knowledge does not reach further than our ideas, as Locke has repeatedly insisted, how do we know these ideas are being received from something outside ourselves? (2) Isn't his confidence in the testimony of the senses simply naive, given Descartes' first meditation? (3) Locke has told us that knowledge requires certainty, but now he says that though it is not as certain as intuition or demonstration, the assurance of the senses amounts to knowledge anyway. We will see other philosophers exploring these problems.*

It is clear that Locke has accepted the main themes in the *representational theory of perception and knowledge*.† The mind is a storehouse of ideas. These ideas are the immediate or direct objects of our knowledge. We suppose them to be representations or signs of things beyond themselves. They are such, we think, by virtue of their being produced in the mind by the causal powers of those external things. So we can know "real existence" indirectly, by virtue of the "correspondence" of our ideas with those really existing items in the world beyond the mind. This is a pattern of thought that ever totters on the brink of skepticism—How do you check the correspondence?—and we see Locke struggling against drawing the skeptical conclusion.‡ He piles reason upon inconclusive reason for resisting the plunge, but it is not clear that anything will rescue him.

---

*See especially Berkeley and David Hume, pp. 389 and 424.
†Review the discussion of these themes in the chapter on Descartes, p. 327.
‡Compare the view of Aquinas, who does not make ideas the objects of our mental acts, pp. 285–287.

1. What is Locke's aim in the *Essay Concerning Human Understanding?*
2. What are Locke's arguments against innate ideas?
3. What are the two sources of our ideas?
4. How do we get abstract ideas?
5. How do we come to have the idea of substance?
6. What can we know of substance?
7. What is the idea of a soul? How does it arise?
8. What is, and what is not, the origin of our idea of personal identity?
9. Contrast real essences with nominal essences. Why is it important to Locke to make this distinction?
10. How do we know real things existing outside our minds?

Of Representative Government

Locke's influence extends far beyond his epistemology. In fact, he may be best known in America for his political thought, which had a decisive impact on Thomas Jefferson and the other founders of the United States. Though trained as a physician, Locke was near the centers of power in late seventeenth-century England, serving in several official posts himself and being a close friend and associate of Lord Shaftesbury, who rose to be Lord Chancellor. Because of the intrigues of the time, he left England on several occasions for his safety and lived for some years in France and in Holland. He lived through the "glorious revolution" of 1688, which brought William and Mary to the English throne and established the rights of an independent parliament. So he had reason to be interested in political matters.

Like Hobbes, Locke begins his theory of government with speculations about a state of nature. But unlike Hobbes, he doesn't end up justifying an absolute sovereign. If his solution to the human predicament in a state of nature is less extreme, the reason is that he thinks the "inconveniences" in that state are less dire. He does not think that life in such a state would be a war of all against all, though there might be some danger of collapsing into that. For Locke follows Thomas Aquinas in thinking that even before government is instituted, human beings, through their reason, have access to the natural law.[*] So he does not see men in a state of nature as mere calculating desire-machines, the way Hobbes does. In a natural state, humans have a sense for justice and injustice, right and wrong, independently of any law declared by a sovereign. And this makes a difference.

Locke does not discuss the contents of this natural law to any great extent. It seems to be more or less coextensive with the Golden Rule: Do unto others as you would have them do unto you.

> The state of Nature has a law of Nature to govern it, which obliges every one, and reason, which is that law, teaches all mankind who will but consult it, that being all equal and independent, no one ought to harm another in his life, health, liberty, or possessions; for men being all the workmanship of one omnipotent and infinitely wise Maker; . . . they are made to last during His, not one another's pleasure. . . . Every one as he is bound to preserve himself, . . . so by the like reason, when his own preservation comes not in competition, ought he as much as he can to preserve the rest of mankind. (*Gov't*, II, II, 6; pp. 119–120)

Locke realizes, of course, that not everyone will conform to this natural law, even though it is present in their reason. So, like law under government, it needs to be enforced. But who will do it where there is no government? The answer is—everyone.

> And that all men may be restrained from invading others' rights, and from doing hurt to one another, and the law of Nature be observed, which willeth the peace and preservation of all mankind, the execution of the law of Nature is in that state put into every man's hands, whereby every one has a right to punish the transgressors of that law to such a degree as may hinder its violation. (*Gov't*, II, II, 6; p. 120)

Violations of the natural law, together with this universal right to punish violations of it, produce the "inconveniences" men hope a government will save them from. For in the state of nature, there is no avoiding the situation where men will be judges in their own cause; and we know that in such cases,

---

[*]See the fuller discussion of natural law in the chapter on Aquinas, pp. 289–290.

self-love will make men partial to themselves and their friends; and, on the other side, ill-nature, passion, and revenge will carry them too far in punishing others, and hence nothing but confusion and disorder will follow. . . . I easily grant that civil government is the proper remedy for the inconveniences of the state of Nature, which must certainly be great where men may be judges in their own case, since it is easy to be imagined that he who was so unjust as to do his brother an injury will scarce be so just as to condemn himself for it. (*Gov't,* II, II, 13; p. 123)

It is to restrain the "partiality and violence of men" that God instituted government, Locke says.

Obviously, however, there is a problem here. For absolute rulers are men, too. What is there in absolute sovereignty to restrain *their* partiality and violence? So Hobbes' solution won't work; it won't solve the problem of partiality and violence but, at best, will locate it at one very powerful point in a community. What would work? Because men are

by nature all free, equal, and independent, no one can be put out of this estate and subjected to the political power of another without his own consent, which is done by agreeing with other men, to join and unite into a community for their comfortable, safe, and peaceable living, one amongst another, in a secure enjoyment of their properties. . . . When any number of men have so consented to make one community or government, they are thereby presently incorporated, and make one body politic, wherein the majority have a right to act and conclude the rest. (*Gov't,* II, VIII, 95; pp. 164–165)

Locke envisages a "contract" as the basis for government. Note that this is not a contract of the people with a sovereign, but a contract made with each other. Each agrees to give up the right to punish violations of the natural law, provided the others do so too. And each agrees to abide by majority rule. So they institute a government with political power, which Locke defines as

a right of making laws, with penalties of death, and consequently all less penalties for the regulating and preserving of property, and of employing the force of the community in the execution of such laws, and in the defence of the commonwealth from foreign injury, and all this only for the public good. (*Gov't,* II, I, 3; p. 118)

Note that Locke assumes that there is such a thing as property before there is a government; in fact, one of the chief functions of a government is to guarantee persons security in the enjoyment of their property.* But property entails rights; for something to be my property means that I have a right to its use and you do not. How could there be such rights before the institution of positive law backed by political power?

Locke imagines that in a state of nature the fruit on the trees, the water in the streams, and the animals in the forest are common to all. What could make part of that mine rather than yours? Locke gives some examples. If I fill a bucket with water from the common source and take it to my dwelling, and if you then take that water rather than fetch some for yourself, you have injured me and have done me an injustice. Why? Because I have mixed my labor with this water; and my labor belongs to me. Anyone can fish in the ocean and bring back a catch, but the catch then belongs to the one who fishes, and whoever takes it away without permission does wrong.

He that is nourished by the acorns he picked up under an oak, or the apples he gathered from the trees in the wood, has certainly appropriated them to himself. Nobody can deny but the nourishment is his. I ask, then, when did they begin to be his? when he digested? or when he ate? or when he boiled? or when he brought them home? or when he picked them up? And it is plain, if the first gathering made them not his, nothing else could. That labour put a distinction between them and common. That added something to them more than Nature, the common mother of all, had done, and so they became his private right. (*Gov't,* II, V, 27; p. 130)

Private property, then, antedates the institution of government; it is not created by positive law, but recognized by it.†

---

*It should be noted that Locke uses "property" in a broad sense to include life and liberty, as well as possessions (see *Gov't.* II, IX, 123; p. 180), but he definitely does mean to include possessions as things to which we have a natural right.

†This "labor theory of value" was adopted by the political economist Adam Smith and used by Karl Marx in his critique of capi-

What sort of government is it, then, that can best protect life, health, liberty, and possessions? To avoid the dangers of anarchy at the one extreme and tyranny at the other, it must be a government of limited powers. And to ensure that it resists the temptation to make itself an exception to the laws it passes for others, it must be responsible to the people who established it. So Locke envisions a representative government with two powers: the legislative, to enact laws for the good of the whole, and the executive, to enforce the laws and protect the commonwealth against external enemies. It is most important, however, not to think of these powers as having the ultimate or supreme authority in a community. They are established by the people for certain ends, so they exist by the will of the people— and only for so long as they serve those ends.

The legislative power, Locke says,

> being only a fiduciary power to act for certain ends, there remains still in the people a supreme power to remove or alter the legislative, when they find the legislative act contrary to the trust reposed in them. For all power given with trust for the attaining an end being limited by that end, whenever that end is manifestly neglected or opposed, the trust must necessarily be forfeited, and the power devolve into the hands of those who gave it, who may place it anew where they shall think best for their safety and security. And thus the community perpetually retains a supreme power of saving themselves from the attempts and designs of anybody, even of their legislators, whenever they shall be so foolish or so wicked as to lay and carry on designs against the liberties and properties of the subject. (*Gov't*, II, XIII, 149; p. 192)

It was thoughts like these that inspired the American revolutionaries in the late eighteenth century and laid the foundations for the Constitution of the United States of America.

Of Toleration

We bring our brief consideration of Locke's thinking to a close by taking a look at another influential view

of his, concerning religious toleration. In Locke's day, political struggles were entangled with religious quarrels. If the king was Roman Catholic, he sought to enact privileges for Catholics and restrictions on Anglicans. If Parliament was dominated by the Church of England, it decreed penalties on dissenters—Baptists, Presbyterians, and Quakers. Wars were fought over such issues. So while in exile in Holland, Locke wrote *A Letter Concerning Toleration,* which did more to change that situation than anything else ever did.

He draws a distinction between the civil commonwealth, the state, and a church. The commonwealth is

> a Society of Men constituted only for the procuring, preserving, and advancing of their own *Civil Interests.*
>
> *Civil Interests* I call Life, Liberty, Health, and Indolency of Body; and the Possession of outward things, such as Money, Lands, Houses, Furniture, and the like.
>
> It is the Duty of the Civil Magistrate, by the impartial Execution of equal Laws, to secure unto the People in general, and to every one of his Subjects in particular, the just Possession of these things belonging to this Life. (*Toleration,* p. 26)

A church, on the other hand, is

> a voluntary Society of Men, joining themselves together of their own accord, in order to the publick worshipping of God, in such a manner as they judge acceptable to him, and effectual to the Salvation of their Souls. (*Toleration,* p. 28)

Locke argues that it is not the business of the civil authorities to prescribe the way in which God is to be worshipped; they have no wisdom in this sphere. Nor is it appropriate to ecclesiastical authorities to try to gain worldly power.

> The Boundaries on both sides are fixed and immovable. He jumbles Heaven and Earth together, the things most remote and opposite, who mixes these two Societies; which are in their Original, End, Business, and in every thing, perfectly distinct, and infinitely different from each other. (*Toleration,* p. 33)

For this reason the civil power is obliged to tolerate differences in the ways men seek to relate to God and organize their worship.

---

talism. Marx, of course, does not agree that private property is a natural right. See pp. 509–514.

The care . . . of every man's Soul belongs unto himself, and is to be left unto himself. (*Toleration,* p. 35)

Locke piles up a variety of arguments in favor of religious toleration by the state. Here is an influential one. It is said that religious dissenters from the established church are dangerous to civil order, that they breed sedition and rebellion. Historically, there was truth to this. But, Locke asks, why is this? It is *because* they are adversely discriminated against by the civil authority that they are a threat to that authority. Take away their oppression, and they will be as loyal as any other subjects.

> Just and moderate Governments are every where quiet, every where safe. But Oppression raises Ferments, and makes men struggle to cast off an uneasie and tyrannical Yoke. I know that Seditions are very frequently raised, upon pretence of Religion. But 'tis as true that, for Religion, Subjects are frequently ill treated, and live miserably. Believe me, the Stirs that are made, proceed not from any peculiar Temper of this or that Church or Religious Society; but from the common Disposition of all Mankind, who when they groan under any heavy Burthen, endeavour naturally to shake off the yoke that Galls their Necks.
>
> . . .
>
> It is not the diversity of Opinions, (which cannot be avoided) but the refusal of Toleration to those that are of different Opinions, (which might have been granted) that has produced all the Bustles and Wars, that have been in the Christian World, upon account of Religion. (*Toleration,* pp. 52, 55)

If we in the West now take such toleration and religious liberty pretty much for granted, it is to Locke we owe a debt of gratitude as much as to any man.

---

1. How does Locke's notion of a state of nature differ from Hobbes' notion?
2. What are the "inconveniences" in a state of nature that lead to the formation of a government?
3. Why can't Locke adopt Hobbes' view of an absolute sovereignty as the solution for these problems?
4. What is the origin of private property, according to Locke?
5. What sort of government does Locke recommend?

6. How does Locke distinguish the two spheres of church and state?
7. Why should governments be tolerant of religious differences?

George Berkeley: Ideas into Things

Born near Kilkenny, Ireland, to a family in comfortable circumstances, George Berkeley (1685– 1753) became a cleric and later a bishop. While at Trinity College, Dublin, which he entered at the youthful age of fifteen, he became acquainted with the latest science of the day, including the work of Isaac Newton, and with Locke's *Essay Concerning Human Understanding.* He had a decidedly negative reaction to much in the *Essay.* He came to think that the doctrines Locke taught there were mistaken in their fundamentals and pernicious in their effects. In short, Berkeley thought Locke's views led directly to the errors of *skepticism* and the evils of *atheism.* By his midtwenties he had worked out a view that he believed would save us from these two errors. It is a view, moreover, that allows Berkeley to present himself as a determined defender of *common sense* against the meaningless jargon of the philosophers and the unnecessary materialism of the scientists.*

Perhaps the best place to begin is with a characterization of common sense, as Berkeley understands it. Two principles characterize what we might call *commonsense realism* about the world.[4]

1. Things exist independently of our perceiving that they do.
2. Things have the qualities they seem to have: The rose we see is really red, the sugar on our tongue is really sweet, and the fire we approach is really hot.

---

*Not everyone agrees that Berkeley's views are harmonious with commonsense views of the world. In some respects they obviously are; in others, perhaps not. You will have to make up your own mind. His philosophy is set forth mainly in two small, clearly written books: *The Principles of Human Knowledge* (1710) and the charming *Three Dialogues Between Hylas and Philonous* (1713).

"What do we perceive besides our own ideas or sensations?"
—George Berkeley

Surely he is right that before we study philosophy, this is what we do think. Berkeley wants to defend our natural belief in both of these claims.

Let us try to get a sense for why he thinks they need defending. According to Locke, material substances do exist independently of our perception of them.* Moreover, they have qualities of their own—the primary qualities of extension, figure, solidity, and motion. However, Locke insists that the true nature of substance is unknowable. Berkeley asks: How does this differ from skepticism?

Furthermore, we have seen that Galileo, Descartes, and Locke deny the second principle and hold that color, taste, and feeling are not in things at all! They exist only in us, as a result of the action of material things on our senses. According to them, the rose is not literally red; in reality, it is an

uncolored extended substance with a power to produce a sensation of red in us. Nor is sugar sweet, nor fire hot.

But this means that the accepted philosophical view (in contrast to the view of the man on the street) is only half committed to common sense—and with respect to that half teetering on the edge of skepticism. This might not be so bad if the arguments for departing from commonsense convictions about things were sound and persuasive, but Berkeley thinks these arguments are a tissue of confusions that make the view literally senseless. With respect to views such as Locke's, Berkeley's fine comment is, "We have first raised a dust and then complain we cannot see" (*Principles,* Intro, p. 8).[5]

Berkeley, then, sets himself to defend common sense. But you will be surprised at the way he does it.

Abstract Ideas

At the root of the confusion into which Berkeley believes modern philosophy has fallen is what he calls "Abuse of Language." In particular, philosophers have not understood how general terms work. That we have words general in their meaning is beyond doubt; *most* words are like that—tiger, snow, woman, rainbow, planet, wood, word, and so on. But in what does their universality consist?

Locke tells us that general words function as *names for abstract ideas.* So the word "tiger" stands not for this tiger or that one, nor for the idea of this or that particular tiger, but for the abstract idea of a tiger. And we get the abstract idea of a tiger by selective attention, focusing on only those features of a thing that make it a tiger, or by noting what particular tigers have in common. So it is not an idea of a male tiger or a female tiger, nor of an old or a young tiger, nor of a large or a small tiger. And yet it must be an idea of all of these.

To Berkeley, this is just nonsense. A "chief part in rendering speculation intricate and perplexed," producing "innumerable errors and difficulties in almost all parts of knowledge," is

the opinion that the mind hath a power of framing *abstract ideas* or notions of things. (*Principles,* Intro, 6; p. 9)

---

*Locke, of course, believes in spiritual substance, as well as material, but for the time being, we focus on what he says about matter.

We are supposed to be able to look at Peter, James, and John and abstract from them *the idea of man*. But then, Berkeley notes, in this idea

> there is included colour, because there is no man but has some colour, but then it can be neither white, nor black, nor any particular colour, because there is no one particular colour wherein all men partake. So likewise there is included stature, but then it is neither tall stature, nor low stature, nor yet middle stature, but something abstracted from all three. (*Principles*, Intro, 9; p. 10)

What kind of idea can this be—with a color that is no particular color and a height that is no specific height? It seems to embody a contradiction. Berkeley is certain he has no such ideas and asks us to examine and see whether we do.*

Moreover, once you allow abstract ideas, where do you stop? The idea of a material substance is clearly an abstract idea. It is constructed to play the role of support or substratum for qualities that need such support. Because such qualities are of widely different kinds—inanimate, animal, and human, for instance—the idea of a substance has to be the idea of something neither animate nor inanimate, neither human nor nonhuman—and yet all these at once. As Locke admits, it is the idea of *something, we know not what*. Is it even *possible* that there should be such ideas? Berkeley thinks not.

The idea of existence, too, is supposed to be an abstract idea. So we think we have an idea that substances exist, even though substances lie beyond all possible experiencing. We also suppose that we have abstract ideas of the extension, motion, and solidity of those substances. But these would have to be ideas of an object having some size, but no determinate size; moving at some speed, but no specific speed; and so on. Do we have—*could* we have—such ideas?

Berkeley actually quotes a passage from Locke to illustrate his point that abstract ideas are impossible. Locke says,

> when we nicely reflect upon them, we shall find that *general ideas* are fictions and contrivances of the mind, that carry difficulty with them, and do not so easily offer themselves as we are apt to imagine. For example, does it not require some pains and skill to form the general idea of a triangle, . . . for it must be neither oblique nor rectangle, neither equilateral, equicrural, nor scalenon; but all and none of these at once. In effect, it is something imperfect, that cannot exist; an idea wherein some parts of several different and inconsistent ideas are put together. (*Essay*, IV, VII, 9; vol. 2, p. 274)

Berkeley could only wonder why Locke himself did not jettison such a monster.*

Berkeley does not, of course, deny that we have general words. We may even have general ideas, Berkeley says. But these are not *abstract* general ideas. Their generality lies in the way we *use* them, not in their intrinsic nature. He gives an example. Suppose a math teacher is showing you how to bisect a line using intersecting arcs. She draws a line on the chalkboard. Then she takes a piece of string with chalk attached to one end of it and cuts two arcs, the first with the fixed point at one end of the line and the second with the fixed point at the other end. Then she takes a straightedge and connects the points of intersection in the arcs. Notice that what you have in your perception of this performance is completely particular. It is an image of one specific line and two arcs. But the point is completely general: This method will work for lines of *any* length.

Suppose you ask, how do we know that the method will work for lines of other lengths, since you have only demonstrated it for a line of this given

---

*In asking ourselves this question, we must keep in mind that Berkeley agrees with Locke that the origin of all our ideas is in sensation or reflection. Whatever other ideas we have are derived from that source as pale copies or images of sensation. So we are being asked whether we have an *image* of something colored, but without any particular color. You probably have to confess that you do not. Whether such images exhaust what we can properly mean by "ideas," however, is an important question. If they do not, perhaps abstract ideas are not in such disrepute as Berkeley claims. See Kant on the distinction between *intuitions* and *concepts*, pp. 434–436.

---

*It is not entirely clear whether Berkeley is being fair to Locke here. Obviously he is supposing that any idea that is not itself a sensation is a definite specific image; and it is obvious that no *image* could have the inconsistent properties Locke ascribes to the abstract idea of a triangle. But is that what Locke means? Perhaps not, but it is hard to say.

length? Berkeley replies that we know it will work for other lines because there is nothing in the demonstration that depends on the length of this line. The length is arbitrarily chosen, so it doesn't matter what it is. So it will work for any line at all.

The example shows how universality works in our words and ideas. Nowhere do we need to appeal to abstract ideas. Every word and every idea can be as particular as that line.

> It is, I know, a point much insisted on, that all knowledge and demonstration are about universal notions, to which I fully agree: but then it does not appear to me that those notions are formed by *abstraction* in the manner premised—*universality,* so far as I can comprehend, not consisting in the absolute, positive nature or conception of anything, but in the relation it bears to the particulars signified or represented by it; by virtue whereof it is that things, names, or notions, being in their own nature *particular,* are rendered *universal.* (*Principles,* Intro, 15; pp. 15–16)

The word "tiger," then, has a universal significance not because it stands for an abstract idea of a tiger (there is no such idea), but because those letters or sounds are used to refer indifferently to this tiger and that tiger—and indeed to any tiger at all. It really is an abuse of language to think that all words have to be *names,* like "Socrates," and that they must name ideas that are abstract. To think so is just part of that dust we raise that makes it hard for us to see.

Another part of the dust, closely connected to abstract ideas, is Locke's view that the sole function of language is to communicate ideas from my mind to yours—that it is a kind of code for transporting ideas across an otherwise incommunicable gap. Berkeley says there are two things wrong with that. First, even where words *are* names that stand for ideas, it is not necessary that these ideas be brought to mind on every occasion of their use. He gives algebra as an example. Though in an algebraic equation each letter may in fact represent a particular quantity, it is not at all necessary to the understanding of the equation that we have those quantities explicitly in mind. Many of our words work like that. Second, it is a mistake to think that language is restricted to the function of communicating ideas.

> There are other ends, as the raising of some passion, the exciting to or deterring from an action, the putting the mind in some particular disposition. . . . Even proper names themselves do not seem always spoken with a design to bring into our view the ideas of those individuals that are supposed to be marked by them. For example, when a schoolman tells me *Aristotle hath said it,* all I conceive he means by it is to dispose me to embrace his opinion with the deference and submission which custom has annexed to that name. (*Principles,* Intro, 20; pp. 19–20)

Language has multiple functions, then, the communicating of ideas being just one. And even when that is what I intend to do, I cannot communicate to you my *abstract* ideas because there aren't any. Words for them—including "material substance"—are just meaningless noise.

> He that knows he has no other than particular ideas, will not puzzle himself in vain to find out and conceive the abstract idea annexed to any name. And he that knows names do not always stand for ideas will spare himself the labour of looking for ideas where there are none to be had. (*Principles,* Intro, 24; p. 22)

In these reflections, Berkeley sounds quite contemporary, playing notes that help constitute familiar melodies in twentieth-century philosophy of language.*

Ideas and Things

If the problem is abuse of words, the solution must be a careful use of words. If it is the reliance on abstract ideas that has led philosophers astray, there must be a strict adherence to *non*abstract ideas. And here Berkeley confesses a debt to Locke. In fact, he thinks, Locke begins in just the right way, by pointing to experience as the source of all our ideas. Locke's problem, according to Berkeley, is that he doesn't rigorously stick to his principle that the

---

*See the discussion regarding analytic and ordinary language philosophy in Chapters 22 and 23. See also the aims of phenomenology in Chapter 24, pp. 647–649.

mind knows nothing but its own ideas; Berkeley is determined to be more consistent.*

> It is evident to anyone who takes a survey of the objects of human knowledge, that they are either ideas actually imprinted on the senses; or else such as are perceived by attending to the passions and operations of the mind; or lastly, ideas formed by help of memory and imagination. (*Principles*, I, 1; p. 24)

Here we have Locke's simple ideas of sensation and reflection, together with complex ideas we put together as we like. Note that Berkeley also agrees with Locke that these ideas are the *objects* of our knowledge.

In addition to these ideas, however,

> there is likewise something which knows or perceives them; and exercises divers operations, as willing, imagining, remembering, about them. This perceiving, active being is what I call *mind, spirit, soul,* or *myself*. By which words I do not denote any one of my ideas, but a thing entirely distinct from them, wherein they exist, or, which is the same thing, whereby they are perceived—for the existence of an idea consists in its being perceived. (*Principles*, I, 2; p. 24)

Here we have Locke's spiritual substance. Note that Berkeley says we do not, strictly speaking, have an *idea* of it, yet the mind or spirit or soul is so evident to us at every moment that it cannot be doubted. If ideas are the objects of knowledge, spirit is its subject. If ideas are what we have, spirit is what has them. Berkeley sometimes says that though we do not have an idea of it, we do have a *notion* of spirit.

So far, then, we have two kinds of items in our inventory of reality: spirits and their ideas. What makes Berkeley distinctive is his claim that *that's all there is*. Whatever exists is either a mind or an idea in such a mind. And Berkeley thinks he can show us that anything else is strictly *inconceivable*—that is, involves a contradiction.

——————
*It is traditional to see Locke, Berkeley, and Hume as three philosophers who more and more thoroughly apply empiricist principles in philosophy. This is a bit too schematic to be wholly correct, but there is a lot of truth in it.

But then there is a puzzle. Is that what you commonsensically believe? I don't think so! Surely this violates principle 1 (mentioned earlier) which says that things exist *independently* of our minds. So it looks like Berkeley is as guilty of violating common sense as are Locke and the modern scientists who violate principle 2 by talking about secondary qualities. If we are to understand Berkeley, we have to solve this puzzle. We need to answer three questions: (1) How is Berkeley's view consistent with common sense? (2) How does it defeat skepticism? and (3) How does it kill atheism?

The first point to note is that Berkeley insists that ideas exist only *as perceived*. Even sensations "cannot exist otherwise than in a mind perceiving them" (*Principles*, I, 3; p. 25). He thinks that this will be evident to us if we just pay attention to what we mean when we say something *exists*.

> The table I write on I say exists, that is, I see and feel it; and if I were out of my study I should say it existed—meaning thereby that if I was in my study I might perceive it, or that some other spirit actually does perceive it. There was an odour, that is, it was smelt; there was a sound, that is, it was heard; a colour or figure, and it was perceived by sight or touch. This is all I can understand by these and the like expressions. For as to what is said of the absolute existence of unthinking things without any relation to their being perceived, that is to me perfectly unintelligible. Their *esse* is *percipi*, nor is it possible they should have any existence out of the minds or thinking things which perceive them. (*Principles*, I, 3; p. 25)

This is an extremely important set of claims for Berkeley. Let us make sure we understand what he is saying. The first claim is that there is no abstract idea of existence, such as might be applied to things even beyond our experience like Locke's material substances. The existence (*esse*) of things consists in their being perceived (*percipi*). For ideas, including simple sensations, to be *is* to be perceived. To exist is to be experienced. (Actually, Berkeley should say, and sometimes does say, that to be is *either* to be an idea perceived *or* to be a perceiver of ideas—a spirit.) Ideas have, in other words, only a relative, not an absolute being. The supposition that ideas might exist on their own, apart from a knower, Berkeley claims to be "unintelligible."

The second thing to note is that Berkeley talks about "the table I write on." Now a table, we usually think, is a thing, not an idea. But its inclusion here is not, as you might suspect, a slip on his part. For Berkeley, the table is also an idea — or rather, a complex of ideas presented to the various senses: sight and touch predominantly. So the table as experienced has its being only in being perceived. We will examine Berkeley's argument for this claim subsequently.

Third, note that Berkeley says of the table, when it is not in my presence, that its existence consists in its being either *actually* perceived by another spirit, or in a *hypothetical* condition such as this: *If I were in my study, then* I would perceive it. In fact, Berkeley thinks both halves of this disjunction are the case. If my table actually exists in my absence, then it *is* being perceived by another spirit, *and* it is true that if I were there in my study, I would perceive it. (This will become clearer in a moment.)

But a table is a *thing,* we say. What can we make of Berkeley's claim that it is an idea? Here is the argument:

> It is indeed an opinion strangely prevailing amongst men that houses, rivers, and in a word all sensible objects, have an existence, natural or real, distinct from their being perceived by the understanding. But, with how great an assurance and acquiescence soever this principle may be entertained in the world, yet whoever shall find it in his heart to call it in question may, if I mistake not, perceive it to involve a manifest contradiction. For, what are the forementioned objects but the things we perceive by sense? and what do we perceive besides our own ideas or sensations? and is it not plainly repugnant that any one of these, or any combination of them, should exist unperceived? (*Principles,* I, 4; p. 25)

What is the contradiction in thinking that sensible things exist unperceived? Let us set out the argument, using the table as an example.

1. A table is a sensible thing.
2. Sensible things are perceived by sense.
3. Whatever is perceived by sense is a sensation.
4. No sensation can exist unperceived.

5. So, no table can exist unperceived.
6. So, to say that a table exists even when not perceived is to say, This table, which exists only as perceived, exists unperceived.

And 6 is contradictory. Berkeley holds that it is only because of the confused doctrine of abstract ideas that we can separate existence from appearance in our experience. "For can there be a nicer strain of abstraction than to distinguish the *existence* of sensible objects from their *being perceived,* so as to conceive them existing unperceived?" (*Principles,* I, 5; p. 25).

You may still not be convinced. In particular, you may balk at proposition 3 in the preceding argument. You may say that you do perceive tables by means of your senses, but what you perceive that way is *not* a sensation — it is a table — that is, a thing. And Berkeley would want to reply that you are partly right and partly wrong. True, he says, it is indeed a thing you sense. That part is right. But you are wrong if you assume that a thing exists independently of perception. For what do we mean by the term "thing"? If this is to be a meaningful term, it must be filled out in terms of experience. And what do we experience the table *as*?

Well, for one thing, we experience a table as colored. But the philosophers have demonstrated that neither color nor any other secondary quality can exist independently of us. It is too variable, too dependent on the light, the condition of the eyes, and the proper functioning of the nervous system to be a property of the thing. Berkeley presents a well-known experiment in his dialogue. Hylas has been arguing that heat is really present in fire, and Philonous (who usually speaks for Berkeley) replies,*

PHIL.: Can any doctrine be true that necessarily leads a man into an absurdity?
HYL.: Without doubt it cannot.
PHIL.: Is it not an absurdity to think that the same thing should be at the same time both cold and warm?

_____

*The name "Hylas" comes from the Greek word for matter, *hyle.* And "Philonous" obviously means *lover of mind or spirit.* So Berkeley gives us in the dialogue a conversation between a would-be materialist and a champion of the spirit.

HYL.: It is.

PHIL.: Suppose now one of your hands hot, and the other cold, and that they are both at once put into the same vessel of water, in an intermediate state; will not the water seem cold to one hand, and warm to the other?

HYL.: It will.

PHIL.: Ought we not therefore, by our principles, to conclude it is really both cold and warm at the same time, that is, according to your own concession, to believe an absurdity?

HYL.: I confess it seems so.

PHIL.: Consequently, the principles themselves are false, since you have granted that no true principle leads to an absurdity.

—*Dialogues*, pp. 115–116

The principle proved false by this experiment is that secondary qualities have an existence outside the mind that perceives them. The same goes for all such qualities, including the color of the table. For secondary qualities, then, the tradition has it right: To be is to be perceived.

But you, having learned of the distinction between secondary qualities and primary qualities, now say: "That may be true of the color of the table, but its size, its extension, its solidity—these qualities it *really has*. These qualities may be *represented* by ideas in my mind, but their *existence* is not *percipi*." When you say this, you are in distinguished company—the company of Galileo, Descartes, and John Locke, to say nothing of Hylas in Berkeley's dialogue. But Berkeley and his alter ego, Philonous, argue that whatever goes for odors, tastes, colors, sounds, and textures goes also for the primary qualities of extension, solidity, and motion. Let's take the argument concerning extension as illustrative:

It is said that heat and cold are affections only of the mind, and not at all patterns of real beings existing in the corporeal substances which excite them, for that the same body which appears cold to one hand seems warm to another. Now, why may we not as well argue that figure and extension are not patterns or resemblances of qualities existing in Matter, because to the same eye at different stations, or eyes of a different texture at the same station, they appear various, and cannot therefore

be the images of anything settled and determinate without the mind? (*Principles*, I, 14; p. 29)

Berkeley's point can be illustrated in your own experience. Take a piece of paper and lay it on the desk before you. Then move around it, looking at it from this angle, now that. Move away from it, then close. Then very, very close. Pay careful attention to your experience of what we call "the paper." Is there anything in that experience that remains constant from one moment to the next? No, the ideas or sensations you are provided with vary continuously in both size and shape. Wherever did you get the idea that the size of the paper was something constant and unchanging, a given absolute property of the paper? Not from any experience you ever had. All you know of the paper is supplied by your experience; and nothing in that experience testifies to such a permanent and immutable property. It must be that the idea you *think* you have of the paper's extension is an *abstract* idea. But there are no abstract ideas, so you don't really have a proper idea of that at all! To talk about an objective, mind-independent, absolute property of extension is just meaningless jargon, an empty abuse of words.

In this way Berkeley argues that the distinction between secondary and primary qualities breaks down. What is true of the former is true also of the latter: They too have their being only in being perceived. But now we may begin to feel dizzy. What has happened to our familiar world? It looks as though all the everyday, stable, commonsense, dependable things we thought we were dealing with have been dissolved into a giddy whirl, where nothing remains the same from moment to moment—a chaos of changes. It looks as though *the world* has been lost, and all we are left with is a flux of ever-shifting sensations.

But at this point, Berkeley, the defender of common sense, comes back and says,

I do not argue against the existence of any one thing that we can apprehend either by sense or reflection. That the things I see with my eyes and touch with my hand do exist, really exist, I make not the least question. The only thing whose existence we deny is that which philosophers call matter or corporeal substance. And in doing of this there is no damage done to the rest of mankind, who, I dare say, will never miss it.

. . .

If any man thinks this detracts from the existence or reality of things, he is very far from understanding what hath been premised in the plainest terms I could think of.

. . .

. . . if the word *substance* be taken in the vulgar sense—for a combination of sensible qualities, such as extension, solidity, weight, and the like—this we cannot be accused of taking away; but if it be taken in a philosophic sense, for the support of accidents or qualities without the mind, then indeed I acknowledge that we take it away, if one may be said to take away that which never had any existence, not even in the imagination. (*Principles*, I, 35, 36, 37; pp. 38–39)

Does the paper on your desk really exist? Really, *really?* Yes, says Berkeley. Of course. In fact, it exists with all those qualities that it *seems* to have—just that whiteness, that combination of shapes, that coolness to the touch, that flexibility, and so on that you perceive it to have. The piece of paper is not a mysterious something behind or beyond our experience of it but is itself just a *combination* of the qualities we attribute to it. We *call* such a combination that is regularly ordered by the laws of nature "a thing," or "a substance", and that's the only sense the term "thing" could meaningfully have for us. This is the way Berkeley defends the second principle of common sense: that things have just the properties they appear to have.

Still, we may have an uneasy feeling, expressed clearly by a question Hylas asks in the dialogues: "Can anything be plainer than that you are for changing all things into ideas?" (*Dialogues,* III, p. 188). But to this Philonous replies,

You mistake me. I am not for changing things into ideas, but rather ideas into things; since those immediate objects of perception, which, according to you, are only appearances of things, I take to be the real things themselves. . . . In short, you do not trust your senses, I do. (*Dialogues,* III, p. 188)

But we still may not be satisfied. How can Berkeley avoid the charge that he destroys the independent existence of things, making them wholly relative to our perceiving of them? That is, can he show that principle 1 (cited at the outset of this section) is also true on his account—that things *do* exist independently of our perceiving them? He makes several points.

1. He echoes Descartes, Locke, and others in observing that while I can, in my imagination, arrange ideas pretty much as I like, I cannot do that with my senses. What I see when I open my eyes is not in my control. I cannot decide not to feel heat when I put my hand near a fire. With respect to my sensations (which are, remember, the origin of all my ideas) I am *passive.*

2. Moreover, ideas are *inert.* That is, they are causally inactive. It is never the case that one idea *causes* another idea to appear.

There is nothing of Power or Agency included in them. So that one idea or object of thought cannot produce or make any alteration in another. —To be satisfied of the truth of this, there is nothing else requisite but a bare observation of our ideas. For, since they and every part of them exist only in the mind, it follows that there is nothing in them but what is perceived: but whoever shall attend to his ideas, whether of sense or reflection, will not perceive in them any power or activity; there is, therefore, no such thing contained in them. (*Principles*, I, 25; p. 34)

What Berkeley has in mind here is this: The *sensation* of water boiling is not caused by the *sensation* of the kettle on the fire. True, the one follows the other with regularity, according to the laws of nature. But this just shows that the laws of nature are not *causal* laws. They don't tell us that *x causes y;* they just describe the uniformities in our experience: Kettles left on a fire long enough are followed by water boiling.

The connexion of ideas does not imply the relation of *cause* and *effect,* but only of a mark or *sign* with the thing *signified.* The fire which I see is not the cause of the pain I suffer upon my approaching it, but the mark that forewarns me of it. In like manner the noise that I hear is not the effect of this or that motion or collision of the ambient bodies, but the sign thereof. (*Principles,* I, 65; p. 52)

Sensations and ideas, then, do not *act*. (Berkeley takes this as an additional proof that a secondary quality such as color could not be *caused* in us by primary qualities such as extension and motion; *no such qualities are causes!*)

3. Do we have any experience, then, of something active, of something with causal power? Yes, virtually every moment of our lives. I stand, I sit, I raise my arm, I walk, I write. In all these ways activity is evident—the activity of the *will*. We have been thinking almost exclusively of ideas or things (things being just ideas that are connected in the right ways). And the constant theme has been that *their being* consists in their being perceived. But we must now turn our attention to the perceivers of these ideas. Spirits are not merely passive receivers of sensations; they also have control over some of their ideas—and even over some sensations. Not only can I decide to recall the capital of Ohio and (usually) do so, but I can also decide to move my finger and (usually) my finger moves. The finger—that combination of ideas we call "a finger"—does not itself contain anything active, no powers or causal energies; Berkeley takes it that he has proved that. But my will does. True, I cannot decide what I will see when I open my eyes, but it is up to my will when and in what circumstances they open. Here, in spirit or mind, which we know not by sense but by reflection, we discover causal power. Philonous says,

> How often must I repeat, that I know or am conscious of my own being; and that I myself am not my ideas, but something else, a thinking, active principle that perceives, knows, wills, and operates about ideas? I know that I, one and the same self, perceive both colours and sounds: that a colour cannot perceive a sound, nor a sound a colour: that I am therefore one individual principle, distinct from colour and sound; and for the same reason, from all other sensible things and inert ideas. (*Dialogues,* III, p. 176)

> I have no notion of any action distinct from volition, neither can I conceive volition to be anywhere but in a spirit; therefore, when I speak of an active being, I am obliged to mean a spirit. (*Dialogues,* III, pp. 182–183)

And now we are near the point where Berkeley thinks that his way of looking at things refutes atheism. What makes atheism both possible and attractive, Berkeley holds, is the hypothesis of matter or corporeal substance as the bearer of real existence. We do need to explain the regular, uniform course that our sensations take, and matter seems to provide an explanation. The reason we see what we see, hear what we hear, and touch what we touch is that there is an objectively existing, material world out there affecting us, producing these sensations in our minds. But if it is matter that is doing it, who needs God?

> How great a friend material substance has been to *atheists* in all ages were needless to relate. All their monstrous systems have so visible and necessary a dependance on it that, when this corner-stone is once removed, the whole fabric cannot choose but fall to the ground. (*Principles,* I, 92; p. 65)

But we have seen that Berkeley has proved, or at least has argued, that the abstract idea of a material substance independent of mind is a grotesque construction, full of contradiction. And in any case, the qualities we are acquainted with in sensation are none of them causes. So materialism is broken-backed as an explanation for the course of our experience. It cannot do the job it is supposed to do.

God

We do, however, need an account of why our experience is as regular and well ordered as it is. For a sensation to *be* is for it to be *perceived*—but not necessarily by us. Since we are not in control of the course of those ideas we call the world, and yet they must exist in a spirit, and only a spirit could cause these ideas in our minds, it follows that there must be a spirit in which these ideas exist and which produces them in us. So, Berkeley thinks, if we get our epistemology and metaphysics straight, we are presented with a new and extremely simple proof for the existence of God.

I know my own existence as a spirit by a kind of immediate intuition. I know your existence only indirectly. That is, I observe in the course of my experience certain conjunctions of sensations, which act as a *sign* of the presence of other finite spirits like myself; to put it colloquially, some of what I observe I take to be *behavior* expressing other minds.

But, though there be some things which convince us *human* agents are concerned in producing them, yet it is evident to every one that those things which are called the Works of Nature—that is, the far greater part of the ideas or sensations perceived by us—are not produced by, or dependent on, the wills of men. There is therefore some other Spirit that causes them; since it is repugnant that they should subsist by themselves. . . . But, if we attentively consider the constant regularity, order, and concatenation of natural things, the surprising magnificence, beauty and perfection of the larger, and the exquisite contrivance of the smaller parts of the creation, together with the exact harmony and correspondence of the whole; but above all the never-enough-admired laws of pain and pleasure, and the instincts or natural inclinations, appetites, and passions of animals—I say if we consider all these things, and at the same time attend to the meaning and import of the attributes One, Eternal, Infinitely Wise, Good, and Perfect, we shall clearly perceive that they belong to the aforesaid Spirit, "who works all in all," and "by whom all things consist." (*Principles*, I, 146, pp. 139–140)

So we see how Berkeley means to support commonsense principle 1 as well as 2. Principle 1 says that things have a reality independent of our perceiving them—and so they do. Their reality may not be what we in our scientific culture have been led to believe; theirs is not the reality of material substance, but the reality of ideas perceived by an infinite Spirit. But given the difficulties attaching to the idea of matter, together with the apparent impossibility of explaining how matter can cause ideas in us, this might seem like a good trade. After all, we do have a clear notion, Berkeley assures us, of an active mind or self, and we do need an account of the regular course of nature. The providential guidance of an Almighty Spirit is near at hand to supply it.

We can perhaps sum up Berkeley's argument in this way:

1. The regular succession of changes in ideas must be caused by either
   a. The ideas themselves.
   b. Material substances.
   c. Myself or some other finite Spirit.
   d. God.

2. Not *a,* for ideas, unlike spirits, are inert and have no causal power.

3. Not *b,* since material substances are (necessarily) nonexistent.

4. Not *c,* because I and all other finite spirits are largely passive with respect to this succession.

5. So *d,* and this succession is caused to be what it is because it is perceived by an infinitely powerful Spirit, which (as Aquinas might say) we all call *God.*

Thus we have an answer to an obvious question: If to be is to be perceived, what happens to my desk when I'm not perceiving it? Does it jump in and out of existence when I open and close my eyes? No, of course not. It continues to exist in both of those senses we distinguished earlier: the hypothetical sense (*If* I were to open my eyes, *then* I would perceive it) and the absolute sense (It is all the while being perceived by God).

This feature of Berkeley's thought has been memorialized in a pair of limericks.[6]

> There was a young man who said, "God
> Must think it exceedingly odd
>   If he finds that this tree
>   Continues to be
> When there's no one about in the Quad."
>
> Dear Sir:
>   Your astonishment's odd;
> *I* am always about in the Quad.
>   And that's why the tree
>   Will continue to be,
> Since observed by
>   *Yours faithfully,*
>   God.

You have probably noticed something that Hylas also remarks about near the end of his dialogue with Philonous. All along, it has been Philonous who has been trotting out arguments characteristic of the skeptics, showing again and again how anything we perceive is relative to the perception of it—how it has no objective, absolute existence at all. Then at the end, like a judo master, he turns the tables, using the strength of the skeptical arguments against themselves to show that what, on traditional principles, was merely appearance is in fact the reality itself!

HYL.: You set out upon the same principles that Academics, Cartesians, and the like sects usually do, and for a long time it looked as if you were advancing their philosophical scepticism; but, in the end, your conclusions are directly opposite to theirs.

PHIL.: You see, *Hylas,* the water of yonder fountain, how it is forced upwards, in a round column, to a certain height; at which it breaks, and falls back into the basin from whence it rose: its ascent as well as descent proceeding from the same uniform law or principle of *gravitation.* Just so, the same principles which at first view lead to scepticism, pursued to a certain point, bring men back to common sense.

—*Dialogues,* III, p. 259

Skepticism, then, is refuted in virtue of the fact that the things of our experience are actually just as we perceive them to be. And atheism is refuted in virtue of these things having a necessary dependence on God. Common sense is vindicated, Berkeley believes, in both of its main tenets. And he considers himself to be altogether successful in dispelling the dust that previous philosophers' thoughts had raised, leaving us with a clear and coherent vision of things.

1. What two principles of common sense does Berkeley hope to defend?
2. How does the distinction between primary and secondary qualities undermine common sense?
3. Why does Berkeley think that abstract ideas are impossible?
4. How, according to Berkeley, do general words and ideas work?
5. What's wrong with the notion that language is for the communication of ideas?
6. In what basic way does Berkeley agree with Locke, despite his criticisms?
7. Explain the slogan that "*esse* is *percipi.*"

8. What does it mean, for Berkeley, that my bicycle exists even when neither I nor any other person is observing it?
9. What does he say we must mean when we use the word "thing"?
10. What is the argument that shows that the existence of primary qualities is *percipi* just as truly as is the existence of secondary qualities?
11. What does it mean to say ideas are "inert"?
12. Where do we experience causal power?
13. Why does God need to be brought into the picture?
14. How is skepticism defeated?
15. How is atheism defeated?
16. Sketch the argument by which Berkeley would claim to be a defender of common sense.

For Further Thought

1. Write a dialogue in which Descartes and Hobbes (who were contemporaries and met at least once) debate about the nature of human beings.

2. Imagine that your soul left your body and went to heaven, but your consciousness (including your memories and your basic character traits) remained here on Earth in your body. Where would *you* be? Why? (Or couldn't you imagine that? Why not?)

3. Berkeley says that a *thing*—your left running shoe, for instance—is just a combination of ideas. I doubt that you believe this. Try to construct a critique of this claim, which doesn't allow Berkeley an immediate comeback.

Notes

1. Quoted in *Objections III with Replies* in *The Philosophical Works of Descartes,* vol. 2, ed. Elisabeth S. Haldane and G. R. T. Ross (n.p.: Dover Publications, 1955), 62.
2. Quotations from Thomas Hobbes, *Leviathan, or The Matter, Form, and Power of a Commonwealth, Ecclesiastical and Civil,* in *The English Philosophers from Bacon to Mill,* ed. Edwin A. Burtt (New York: Modern Library, 1939), are cited in the text using the abbreviation *L.* References are to page numbers.
3. Quotations from Locke are cited as follows: *Essay: An Essay Concerning Human Understanding,* ed. Alexander Campbell Fraser (New York: Dover

Publications, 1959), by book, chapter, and section number, followed by the volume and page number in this edition.

Gov't: Of Civil Government, Two Treatises (London: J. M. Dent and Sons, 1924), cited by book, chapter, and section number, followed by the page number in this edition.

Toleration: A Letter Concerning Toleration (Indianapolis: Hackett, 1983).

4. I am indebted to A. C. Grayling, who frames the puzzle of Berkeley's commonsense claims in this way in his book *Berkeley: The Central Arguments* (London: Duckworth, 1986).

5. Quotations from Berkeley are from *George Berkeley: Principles of Human Knowledge and Three Dialogues,* ed. Howard Robinson (Oxford: Oxford University Press, 1996), cited as:

Principles, by book and section number, followed by the page number in this edition

Dialogues, by page number in this edition

6. In Bertrand Russell's *History of Western Philosophy* (London: Allen and Unwin, 1946), 623; Russell attributes it, or at least the first stanza, to Ronald Knox.

CHAPTER

15

DAVID HUME

Unmasking the Pretensions of Reason

The eighteenth century is often called the Age of Enlightenment. Those who lived through this period felt that progress was being made almost daily toward overthrowing superstition and arbitrary authority, replacing ignorance with knowledge and blind obedience with freedom. It is an age of optimism. One of the clearest expressions of this attitude is found in a brief essay by Immanuel Kant (the subject of our next chapter). Writing in 1784, eight years after the death of David Hume, Kant defines what the age understands by "enlightenment."

Enlightenment is man's emergence from his self-imposed immaturity. Immaturity is the inability to use one's understanding without guidance from another. This immaturity is self-imposed when its cause lies not in lack of understanding, but in lack of resolve and courage to use it without guidance from another. Sapere Aude! "Have courage to use your own understanding!"—that is the motto of enlightenment.[1]

This call to think for oneself, to have the courage to rely on one's own abilities, is quite characteristic of the age. For Kant, the lack of courage is

"self-imposed." To overcome it we need only the resolve not to be bound any more by those who set themselves up as our guardians.

It is so easy to be immature. If I have a book to serve as my understanding, a pastor to serve as my conscience, a physician to determine my diet for me, and so on, I need not exert myself at all. I need not think, if only I can pay. . . . The guardians who have so benevolently taken over the supervision of men have carefully seen to it that the far greatest part of them (including the entire fair sex) regard taking the step to maturity as very dangerous, not to mention difficult. Having first made their domestic livestock dumb, and having carefully made sure that these docile creatures will not take a single step without the go-cart to which they are harnessed, these guardians then show them the danger that threatens them, should they attempt to walk alone. Now this danger is actually not so great, for after falling a few times they would in the end certainly learn to walk; but an example of this kind makes men timid and usually frightens them out of all further attempts.

Thus, it is difficult for any individual man to work himself out of the immaturity that has all but become his nature. He has even become fond of this state and for the time being actually incapable of using his own understanding.[2]

Working oneself out of this immaturity is "difficult," but not impossible—as had been clearly shown in the triumphs of the scientific revolution from Copernicus to that most admired of thinkers, Isaac Newton (1642–1727). It was Newton's unified explanatory scheme for understanding both terrestrial and celestial movements that symbolized what human efforts could achieve—if only they could be freed from the dead hand of the past. And thinkers throughout the eighteenth century busy themselves applying Newton's methods to other subjects: to the mind, to ethics, to religion, and to the state of society.

Yet none of them would claim to have arrived at the goal. Here again is Kant:

> If it is now asked, "Do we presently live in an *enlightened* age?" the answer is, "No, but we do live in an age of *enlightenment*."[3]

The key word is "progress." Newton showed that progress is really possible. And the conviction spreads that this progress can be extended indefinitely if only we can muster the courage to do what Newton had done in physics and astronomy. We were not yet mature, but we were becoming mature.

How Newton Did It

It is almost impossible to exaggerate Newton's impact on the imagination of the eighteenth century. As a towering symbol of scientific achievement, he can be compared only to Einstein in the twentieth century. The astonished admiration his work evoked is expressed in a couplet by Alexander Pope.

> Nature and Nature's laws lay hid in night;
> God said, Let Newton be, and all was light.[*]

_____
[*]Epitaph intended for Sir Isaac Newton. John Bartlett, *Familiar Quotations,* 14th ed. (Boston: Little, Brown, 1968).

Everyone has some idea of Newton's accomplishment, of how his theory of universal gravitation provides a mathematically accurate and powerful tool for understanding not only the motions of heavenly bodies but also such puzzling phenomena as the tides. We don't go into the details of this theory here, but every science is developed on the basis of certain methods and presuppositions that may properly be called philosophical. It is these philosophical underpinnings that we must take note of, for they are crucially important to the development of thought in the eighteenth century—not least to the philosophy of David Hume.

How had Newton been able to pull it off? His methods are in fact not greatly different from those of Galileo and Hobbes. There are two stages (like Hobbes' resolution and composition), which he calls *analysis* and *synthesis*. But there is a particular insistence in some of his pronouncements that strike a new note. He does not, he says, *frame hypotheses*. What does this mean? By a hypothesis he means a principle of explanation not derived from a close examination of the facts. The key to doing science, he believes, is to stay close to the phenomena; the big mistake is to jump prematurely to an explanation. Newton's own long and persistent series of experiments with the prism exemplifies this maxim. The fact that white light is not a simple phenomenon (as it seems to naive sight) is disclosed only by an immensely detailed series of investigations, which reveal its composition out of the many simpler hues of the rainbow.

> I frame no hypotheses; for whatever is not deduced from the phenomena is to be called an hypothesis; and hypotheses, whether metaphysical or physical, whether of occult qualities or mechanical, have no place in experimental philosophy.[4]

Principles of explanation are to be "deduced from the phenomena." This emphasis on paying attention to the facts of experience can be traced back through John Locke to Francis Bacon—and, indeed, it is Aristotelian in character. But in Newton its fruitfulness pays off in a way that had never been seen before. Newton expresses a deep suspicion of principles not derived from a close experimental examination of the sensible facts. We cannot *begin* with what *seems* right to us. Hypotheses not arrived at by way of careful analysis of the sensible facts are arbitrary—no matter how intuitively convincing they may seem. And Newton's success is, to the eighteenth-century thinker, proof that his methods are sound.

Note how different this is from the rationalism of Descartes. Always the mathematician, Descartes seeks to find starting points for science and philosophy that are intuitively certain, axioms that are "so clear and distinct" that they cannot possibly be doubted. He is confident that reason, the "light of nature," will certify some principles as both knowable and known. So the structure of wisdom, for Descartes, is the structure of an axiomatic, geometrical system. Intuitive insight and deduction from first principles will get you where you want to go.

But for eighteenth-century thinkers inspired by Newton, this smells too much of arbitrariness. One man's intuitive certainty, they suspect, is another man's absurdity.* The only cure is to stick closely to the facts. The *rationalism* of Descartes is supplanted by the *empiricism* of Locke, Berkeley, and David Hume.

To Be the Newton of Human Nature

David Hume (1711–1776) aspires to do for human nature what Isaac Newton did for nonhuman nature: to provide principles of explanation both simple and comprehensive.[5] There seem to be two motivations. First, Hume shares with many other Enlightenment intellectuals the project of debunking what they call "popular superstition." By this they usually mean the deliverances of religious enthusiasm, together with the conviction of certainty

that typically accompanies them.* (The era of religious wars based on such certainties is still fresh in the memory.) But they also mean whatever cannot be demonstrated on a basis of reason and experience common to human beings. Hume's prose betrays his passion on this score. Remarking on the obscurity, uncertainty, and error in most philosophies, he pinpoints the cause:

> They are not properly a science; but arise either from the fruitless efforts of human vanity, which would penetrate into subjects utterly inaccessible to the understanding, or from the craft of popular superstitions, which, being unable to defend themselves on fair ground, raise these entangling brambles to cover and protect their weakness. Chased from the open country, these robbers fly into the forest, and lie in wait to break in upon every unguarded avenue of the mind, and overwhelm it with religious fears and prejudices. The stoutest antagonist, if he remit his watch a moment, is oppressed. And many, through cowardice and folly, open the gates to the enemies, and willingly receive them with reverence and submission, as their legal sovereigns.
>
> But is this a sufficient reason, why philosophers should desist from such researches, and leave superstition still in possession of her retreat? Is it not proper to draw an opposite conclusion, and perceive the necessity of carrying the war into the most secret recesses of the enemy? (*HU,* 91–92)[6]

The basic strategy in this war is to show what the human understanding is (and is not) capable of. And this is what a science of human nature should give us. If we can show that "superstition" claims to know what no one can possibly know, then we undermine it in the most radical way.

Hume's second motivation is his conviction that a science of human nature is, in a certain way, fundamental.

> Even *Mathematics, Natural Philosophy, and Natural Religion,* are in some measure dependent on the

---

*They feel confirmed in this suspicion by the example of rationalist philosophy after Descartes. First-rate intellects such as Malebranche, Spinoza, and Leibniz developed remarkably different philosophical systems on the basis of supposedly "self-evident" truths.

---

*"Enthusiasm" is the word eighteenth-century thinkers use to describe ecstatic forms of religion involving the claim that one is receiving revelations, visions, or "words" directly from God. This form of religion is far from dead.

science of Man; since they lie under the cognizance of men, and are judged of by their powers and faculties. 'Tis impossible to tell what changes and improvements we might make in these sciences were we thoroughly acquainted with the extent and force of human understanding, and could explain the nature of the ideas we employ, and of the operations we perform in our reasonings. (*T*, Intro, p. 4)

Because all our intellectual endeavors are *products* of human understanding, an examination of that understanding should illumine them all. Such an inquiry will reveal how the mind works, what materials it has to operate on, and how knowledge in any area at all can be constructed.

Hume is aware that others before him have formulated theories of the mind (or human understanding), but they have not satisfactorily settled matters.

> There is nothing which is not the subject of debate, and in which men of learning are not of contrary opinions. . . . Disputes are multiplied, as if every thing was uncertain; and these disputes are managed with the greatest warmth, as if every thing was certain. (*T*, Intro. p. 3)

Consider the wide disagreement between Descartes and Hobbes, for instance. Descartes, as we have seen, believes that the freedom and rationality of our minds exempts them from the kind of causal explanation provided for material bodies. A mind, he concludes, is a thing completely distinct from a body. Hobbes, on the other hand, includes the mind and all its ideas and activities within the scope of a materialistic and deterministic science. "Mind," for Hobbes, is just a name for certain ways a human body operates. Who is right here?

From Hume's point of view, neither one prevails. Hobbes simply *assumes* that our thoughts represent objects independent of our minds and that whatever principles explain these objects will also explain the mind. But surely Descartes has shown us that this is something we should not assume. Whatever our experience "tells" us about reality, things could actually be different. That is the lesson of Descartes' doubt. Hobbes' assumption that sensations and thoughts generally represent realities accurately is nothing but a "hypothesis." And,

"As the science of man is the only solid foundation for the other sciences, so the only solid foundation we can give to this science itself must be laid on experience and observation."

—David Hume

Hume says (following Newton), we must avoid framing hypotheses.

Descartes' positive doctrine of a separate mind-substance, however, is just as "hypothetical" as that of Hobbes. It is derived from principles that may *seem* intuitively obvious but have not been "deduced from the phenomena." The problem is that neither pays close attention to the data available. Both of them fail because they did not have the example of Newton to learn from. We do not have, Hume thinks, any insight into the "essence" of either material bodies or minds. We have made progress in the former realm only by sticking close to the experimental facts; we can hope to progress in the latter realm only if we do the same.

> For to me it seems evident, that the essence of the mind being equally unknown to us with that of external bodies, it must be equally impossible to form any notion of its powers and qualities otherwise than from careful and exact experiments, and the observation of those particular effects, which result from its different circumstances and situations. And tho' we must endeavour to render all our principles as universal as possible, by tracing up our experiments to the utmost, and explaining all effects from the simplest and fewest causes, 'tis still certain we cannot go beyond experience; and any hypothesis, that pretends to discover the ultimate original qualities of human nature, ought at first to be rejected as presumptuous and chimerical. (*T,* Intro p.5)

The Newtonian tone is unmistakable. What, then, are the *data* that scientists of human nature must "observe" and from which they may draw principles "as universal as possible"? Hume calls them "perceptions," by which he means all the contents of our minds when we are awake and alert.* Among perceptions are all the ideas of the sciences, as well as ideas arbitrary and superstitious. Hume aims to draw a line between legitimate ideas and ideas that are confused, unfounded, and nonsensical. The first thing to do is to inquire about the *origin* of our ideas.

The Theory of Ideas

A science of human nature must concentrate on what is peculiarly human. A woman's height, weight, and shape are characteristics of a human being, but these are properties shared with the nonhuman objects Newtonian science explains so well. It is human ideas, feelings, and actions that are distinctive and require special treatment. Ideas are particularly important because they are involved in nearly all the activities that are characteristically human. What are ideas, and how do we come to have them?

Perceptions, Hume claims, can be divided into two major classes: *impressions* and *ideas.*

> The difference betwixt these consists in the degrees of force and liveliness with which they strike upon the mind, and make their way into our thought or consciousness. Those perceptions, which enter with most force and violence, we may name *impressions;* and under this name I comprehend all our sensations, passions and emotions, as they make their first appearance in the soul. By *ideas* I mean the faint images of these in thinking and reasoning. (*T,* I, 1, 1 p.7)

You can get a vivid illustration of the difference between the two classes if you slap the table smartly with your hand (the sound you hear is an impression), and then, a few seconds later, recall that sound (the content of your memory is an idea).

Hume thinks that we are all familiar with this difference. There may be borderline cases such as a terrifying dream, in which the ideas are very nearly as lively as the actual impressions would be. But on the whole, the distinction is not only familiar, but clear. One other important distinction must be observed: that between *simple* and *complex* perceptions. The impression you have when you slap the table is simple; the impression you have when you hear a melody is complex. Complex impressions and ideas are built up from simple ones.

Hume is trying to pay close attention to the data. The next thing he notices is "the great resemblance betwixt our impressions and ideas" (*T,* I, 1, 1, p.8). It seems as though "all the perceptions of the mind are double, and appear both as impressions and ideas" (*T,* I, 1, 1, p.8). No, he adds, this is not quite correct. For you have the idea of a unicorn, but you have never experienced a unicorn impression. (Ah, you say; but I have seen a *picture* of a unicorn! True enough, but your experience on that occasion did not constitute an impression of a unicorn, but of a unicorn picture. Your idea of a unicorn is not the idea of a picture.) So you do have an idea that does not correspond to

---

*Here Hume shows that he, like Descartes (and Locke and Berkeley, too), is committed to the basic principle of the representational theory (p. 327)—that what we know first and best are our ideas. Unlike Descartes, as we will see, Hume believes there are no legitimate inferences from ideas to things.

any impression; so not all our perceptions are "double."

But a closer look, Hume thinks, will convince us that although this principle does not hold for *complex* ideas, it does hold for all *simple* ideas. We need not analyze the idea of a unicorn very far to notice that it is made up of two simpler ideas: that of a horse and that of a single horn. Impressions do correspond to these simpler ideas, for we have all seen horses and horns. So the revised principle is that to every *simple idea* corresponds a *simple impression* that resembles it.

If impressions and simple ideas come in pairs like this, so that there is a "constant conjunction" between them, the next question is, Which comes first? Hume again notes that in his *experience,* it is always the impression that appears first; the idea comes later.

> To give a child an idea of scarlet or orange, of sweet or bitter, I present the objects, or in other words, convey to him these impressions; but proceed not so absurdly, as to endeavour to produce the impressions by exciting the ideas. . . . We cannot form to ourselves a just idea of the taste of a pine-apple, without having actually tasted it. (*T*, I, 1, 1, p.9)

This suggests that there is a relation of *dependence* between them; Hume concludes that every simple idea has some simple impression as a causal antecedent. Every simple idea, in fact, is a *copy* of a preceding impression.* What is the origin of all our ideas? The impressions of experience. The rule is this: *no impression, no idea.*

This is an apparently simple principle, but Hume warns us that taking it seriously will have far-reaching consequences. It is, in fact, a rule of procedure that Hume makes devastating use of.

> All ideas, especially abstract ones, are naturally faint and obscure: The mind has but a slender hold

of them: They are apt to be confounded with other resembling ideas; and when we have often employed any term, though without a distinct meaning, we are apt to imagine it has a determinate idea, annexed to it. On the contrary, all impressions, that is, all sensations, either outward or inward, are strong and vivid: The limits between them are more exactly determined: Nor is it easy to fall into any error or mistake with regard to them. When we entertain, therefore, any suspicion, that a philosophical term is employed without any meaning or idea (as is but too frequent), we need but enquire, *from what impression is that supposed idea derived?* And if it be impossible to assign any, this will serve to confirm our suspicion. (*HU*, 99)

Every meaningful term (word), Hume tells us, is associated with an idea. Some terms, however, have no clear idea connected with them. We get used to them and think they mean something, but we are deceived. Hume in fact thinks this happens all too frequently! How can we discover whether a term really means something? Try to trace the associated *idea* back to an *impression.* If you can, it is a meaningful word that expresses a real idea. If you try and fail, then all you have are meaningless noises or nonsensical marks on paper.

Hume has here a powerful critical tool. It seems innocent enough, but Hume makes radical use of it. The rule is a corollary to Hume's Newtonian analysis of phenomena. It is a result of the theory of ideas.

The Association of Ideas

The results so far constitute the stage of analysis. What we find, on paying close attention to the contents of the human mind, are impressions and ideas, the latter in complete dependence upon the former. Hume now needs to proceed to the stage of synthesis: What are the principles that bind these elements together to produce the rich mental life characteristic of humans? Like Newton, he finds that the great variety of phenomena can be explained by a few principles, surprisingly simple in nature. These are principles of *association,* and they

---

*Compare Hobbes, p. 363, and Locke, p. 374. Hume's theory of the origin of ideas is similar, but without Hobbes' mechanistic explanation, and also without the assumption that external objects are the cause of our impressions. Hume considers both these claims to be merely "hypotheses." The perceptions of the mind are our data; beyond them we may not safely go.

correspond in the science of human nature to universal gravitation in the purely physical realm.

> It is evident that there is a principle of connexion between the different thoughts or ideas of the mind, and that, in their appearance to the memory or imagination, they introduce each other with a certain degree of method and regularity. . . . Were the loosest and freest conversation to be transcribed, there would immediately be observed something, which connected it in all its transitions. Or where this is wanting, the person, who broke the thread of discourse, might still inform you, that there had secretly resolved in his mind a succession of thought, which had gradually led him from the subject of conversation. (*HU*, 101)

Whether this observation is correct or not you should be able to test by observing your own trains of thought, or noting how one topic follows another in a conversation you are party to.

If Hume is right here, the next question is, What are these principles of association?

> To me, there appear to be only three principles of connexion among ideas, namely *Resemblance, Contiguity* in time or place, and *Cause* or *Effect.*
>   That these principles serve to connect ideas will not, I believe, be much doubted. A picture naturally leads our thoughts to the original [Resemblance]: The mention of one apartment in a building naturally introduces an enquiry or discourse concerning the others [Contiguity]: And if we think of a wound, we can scarcely forbear reflecting on the pain which follows it [Cause and Effect]. (*HU*, 101–102)

There is some question about whether this list of three principles is complete; Hume thinks it probably is and invites you to try to find more if you think otherwise. The world of ideas, then, is governed by the "gentle force" of association. He likens it to "a kind of ATTRACTION, which in the mental world will be found to have as extraordinary effects as in the natural, and to shew itself in as many and as various forms" (*T*, I, 1, 4, pp. 12, 14).

It is important to note that this "gentle force" operates entirely without our consent, will, or even consciousness of it. It is not something in our control, any more than we can control the force of gravity. If Hume is right, it just happens that this is

how the mind works. He does not think it possible to go on to explain *why* the mind works the way it does; explanation has to stop somewhere, and, like Newton, he does not "frame hypotheses." But these principles, he thinks, can be "deduced from the phenomena."

---

1. Using the quotations from Immanuel Kant as a cue, explain the notion of *enlightenment.*
2. Contrast rationalism, materialism, and empiricism, and relate each to Newton's rule about not framing hypotheses.
3. How does Hume explain the origin of our ideas? (Distinguish complex from simple ideas.)
4. What principles govern transitions from one idea or impression to another?

Causation: The Very Idea

We now have the fundamental principles of the science of human nature Hume is trying to construct: an analysis into the elements of the mind (impressions and ideas), the relation between them (dependence), and the principles that explain how ideas interact (association). We are now ready for the exciting part: What happens when this science is applied?

One more distinction will set the stage.

> All the objects of human reason or enquiry may naturally be divided into two kinds, to wit, *Relations of Ideas,* and *Matters of Fact.* Of the first kind are the sciences of Geometry, Algebra, and Arithmetic; and in short, every affirmation, which is either intuitively or demonstratively certain. *That the square of the hypothenuse is equal to the square of the two sides,* is a proposition, which expresses a relation between these figures. *That three times five is equal to the half of thirty,* expresses a relation between these numbers. Propositions of this kind are discoverable by the mere operation of thought, without dependence on what is anywhere existent in the universe. Though there never were a circle or triangle in nature, the truths, demonstrated by Euclid, would forever retain their certainty and evidence.

Matters of fact, which are the second objects of human reason, are not ascertained in the same manner; nor is our evidence of their truth, however great, of a like nature with the foregoing. The contrary of every matter of fact is still possible; because it can never imply a contradiction, and is conceived by the mind with the same facility and distinctness, as if ever so conformable to reality. *That the sun will not rise to-morrow* is no less intelligible a proposition, and implies no more contradiction, than the affirmation, *that it will rise*. We should in vain, therefore, attempt to demonstrate its falsehood. Were it demonstratively false, it would imply a contradiction, and could never be distinctly conceived by the mind. (*HU,* 108)

The contrast drawn in these paragraphs is an important one. Let's be sure we understand it. Suppose we contrast these two statements:

A: Two plus three is not five.

B: The sun will not rise tomorrow.

Assume that the sun does rise tomorrow. Then both statements are false. But what Hume draws our attention to is that they are *false in different ways*. *A* is false simply because of the way in which the ideas "two," "plus," "three," "five," and "equals" are related to each other. To put them together as *A* does is not just to make a false statement; it is to utter a *contradiction,* to say something that cannot even be clearly conceived. As Hume puts it, we can know it is false "by the mere operation of thought." We do not have to make any experiments or look to our experience. The opposite of *A* can in turn be known to be true, no matter what is "anywhere existent in the universe."

However, we can clearly conceive *B* even though it is false. It is not false because the ideas in it are related the way they are; given the way they are related, it might possibly be true. We can clearly conceive what that would be like: We wake up to total and continuing darkness. Whether *B* is true or false depends on the *facts,* on what actually happens in nature. And to determine its truth or falsity we need to do more than just think about it. We need to consult our experience. The falsity of *B*, Hume says, cannot be *demonstrated.* Reason alone will not suffice to convince us of matters of fact; here only experience will do.

And he suggests one further difference between them: About relations of ideas like *A* we can be certain, but with respect to propositions stating matters of fact, our evidence is never great enough to amount to certainty.*

At this point we need to remind ourselves once again that Hume is committed to sticking to the phenomena: the perceptions of the mind, its impressions and ideas. These are the data that need explaining in a science of human nature. But now it is obvious that a question forces itself on us. Is that all we can know about?

We don't usually think so. We talk confidently of things beyond the reach of our senses and memory—of what's going on in the next room or on the moon, of what happened long before we were born, of a whole world of objects that exist (we think) quite independently of our minds, and many of us think it quite sensible to talk of God and the soul. All this is common sense, and yet it all goes far beyond the narrow bounds of Hume's data. What can we make of this? Or rather, what can Hume make of it? He considers some examples:

- A man believes that his friend is in France. Why? Because he has received a letter from his friend.

- You find a watch on a desert island and conclude that some human being had been there before you.

- You hear a voice in the dark and conclude there is another person in the room.

In each of these cases, where someone claims to know something not present in his perceptions,

---

*Hume is here suggesting a revolutionary understanding of the kind of knowledge we have in mathematics. A contrast with Plato will be instructive. For Plato (see pp. 120–122), mathematics is the clearest case of knowledge we have. Not only is it certain and enduring, but it is also the best avenue into acquaintance with absolute reality, for its *objects* are independent of the world of sensory experience—eternal and unchanging Forms. What Hume is suggesting is that mathematics is certain not because it introduces us to such a world of realities, but simply because of how it relates *ideas* to one another. Mathematics *has no objects.* This suggestion undermines in a radical way the entire Platonic picture of reality. It is further developed in the twentieth century by Ludwig Wittgenstein and the logical positivists. See pp. 604–606 and 614.

you will find that a connection is being made by the relation of *cause and effect*. In each case a present impression (reading the letter, seeing the watch, hearing the voice) is *associated* with an idea (of the friend's being in France, of a person's dropping the watch, of someone speaking). The way we get beliefs about matters of fact beyond the present testimony of our senses and memory is by relying on our sense of causal relations. The letter is an *effect* of our friend's having sent it; the watch was *caused* to be there on the beach by another person; and voices are *produced* by human beings. Or so we believe. It is causation that allows us to reach out beyond the limits of present sensation and memories.

> All reasonings concerning matter of fact seem to be founded on the relation of *Cause and Effect*. By means of that relation alone we can go beyond the evidence of our memory and senses. (*HU,* 109)

This seems like progress, though it is hardly very new. Descartes, you will recall, escapes solipsism by a causal argument for the existence of God.* But Hume now presses these investigations in a novel direction. How, he asks, do we arrive at the knowledge of cause and effect?

The first part of his answer to this question is a purely negative point. We do not, and cannot, arrive at such knowledge independently of experience, or **a priori.** To put this in a now familiar way, our knowledge of causality is not a matter of the *relations of ideas.*

Consider two events that are related as cause and effect. To use a typical eighteenth-century example, think about two balls on a billiard table, the cue ball striking the eight ball, causing the eight ball to move. Suppose we know all about the cue ball— its weight, its direction, its momentum—but have never had any experience whatsoever of one thing striking another. Could we predict what would happen when the two balls meet? Not at all. For all we would know, the cue ball might simply stop, reverse its direction, pop straight up in the air, go straight through, or turn into a chicken. Our belief

that the effect will be a movement of the second ball is *completely* dependent on our having observed that sort of thing on prior occasions. Without that experience, we would be at a total loss.

> No object ever discovers, by the qualities which appear to the senses, either the causes which produced it, or the effects which will arise from it; nor can our reason, unassisted by experience, ever draw any inference concerning real existence and matter of fact. . . . *causes and effects are discoverable, not by reason, but by experience.* (*HU,* 110)

My expectation that the second ball will move when struck is based entirely on past experience. I have seen that sort of thing happen before. This seems entirely reasonable: I make a prediction on the basis of past experience. But if that prediction is reasonable, we ought to be able to set out the reason for it. Reasons can be given in arguments. Let us try to make the argument explicit.

1. I have seen one ball strike another many times.
2. Each time, the ball that was struck has moved. Therefore,
3. The struck ball will move this time.

If we look at the matter this way, however, it is easy to see that proposition 3 does not *follow* from propositions 1 and 2. It seems quite possible that this time, something else could happen. To be sure, none of us believes that anything else will happen, but it is precisely this belief, the belief that the first one *causes* the second to move, that needs explanation. Hume is searching for what, if anything, makes this a *rational* thing to believe. Because this time could be very different from all those past times, the argument is invalid and does not give us a *good reason* to believe that the second ball will move. Can we patch up the argument?

Suppose we add a premise to the argument.

1a. The future will (in the relevant respect) be like the past.

Now the argument looks valid. Propositions 1a, 1, and 2 do indeed entail proposition 3. If we know that 1a is true, then, in the light of our experience summed up in 1 and 2, it is rational to believe that

---

*You might review the argument in *Meditation III,* noting especially the role played by the causal principle that nothing comes from nothing.

the second billiard ball will move when struck by the first one. We could call proposition 1a the principle of *the uniformity of nature.*

But how do you know that proposition 1a is true? Think about that a minute. How *do* you know that the future will be like the past? It is surely not *contradictory* to suppose that the way events hang together might suddenly change; putting the kettle on the fire after today *could* produce ice. So 1a is not true because of the relation of the ideas in it.* Whether 1a is true or false must surely be a *matter of fact*. So if we know it, we must know it on the basis of experience. What experience? If we look back, we can see that the futures we were (at various points) looking forward to always resembled the pasts we were (at those points) recalling. This suggests an argument to support 1a.

1b. I have experienced many pairs of events that have been constantly conjoined in the past.

1c. Each time I found that similar pairs of events were conjoined in the future. Therefore,

1a. The future will (in these respects) be like the past.

But it is clear that this argument is no better than the first one; we are trying to justify our general principle 1a in *exactly* the same way as we tried to justify the expectation that the struck billiard ball would move (proposition 3). If it didn't work the first time, it surely won't work now. The fact that past futures resembled past pasts is simply no good reason to think that future futures will resemble their relevant pasts.

Yet we all think that is so, don't we? Our practical behavior surely testifies to that belief; we simply have no hesitation in walking about on the third floor of a building, believing that it will support us now just as it always has in the past. We all believe in the uniformity of nature. But why? For what *reason?*

Let us review. Hume is inquiring into the foundation of ideas about things that go beyond the

contents of our present consciousness. These ideas all depend on relations of cause and effect: They are effects caused in us by impressions of some kind. But what is the foundation of these causal inferences? It can only be experience. But now we see that *experience cannot supply a good reason* for believing that my friend is in France. No former correlations of letters with friends in France could do the job. There is a gap between the premise and the conclusion; I might have such a letter even though she is not in France but is taking a holiday in Istanbul. The gap is certainly there; and it seems there is no possible *reason* that can fill that gap.

And so we have the first part of Hume's answer to the question about what justifies us in believing in so many things independent of our present experience: *not any reason!*

We must be careful here. Hume is not advising us, on that ground, to give up such beliefs; he thinks we could not, even if we wanted to. "Nature will always maintain her rights," he says, "and prevail in the end over any abstract reasoning whatsoever" (*HU,* 120). The fact that these beliefs do not rest on any rational foundation is an important result in his science of human nature, and, as we'll see, its philosophical consequences are dramatic. But he acknowledges that these are beliefs we really cannot do without. Our survival depends on them.

If we allow that these beliefs about the world are not rationally based, the next obvious question is this: What *is* their foundation? Hume suggests a thought experiment.

> Suppose a person, though endowed with the strongest faculties of reason and reflection, to be brought on a sudden into this world; he would, indeed, immediately observe a continual succession of objects, and one event following another; but he would not be able to discover any thing farther. He would not, at first, by any reasoning, be able to reach the idea of cause and effect; since the particular powers, by which all natural operations are performed, never appear to the senses; nor is it reasonable to conclude, merely because one event, in one instance precedes another, that therefore the one is the cause, the other the ef-

---

*You should review the discussion of the distinction between relations of ideas and matters of fact, pp. 403–404.

fect. Their conjunction may be arbitrary and casual. . . .

Suppose again, that he has acquired more experience, and has lived so long in the world as to have observed similar objects or events to be constantly conjoined together; what is the consequence of this experience? He immediately infers the existence of one object from the appearance of the other. (*HU,* 120–121)

This seems plausible. But what is the difference between the first and the second supposition? The only difference is that in the first case the man lacks sufficient experience to notice which events are "constantly conjoined" with each other. But what difference does this difference make? What allows him in the second case to make inferences and have expectations, when he cannot do that in the first case? If it is not a matter of reasoning, then there must be

some other principle, which determines him to form such a conclusion. This principle is CUSTOM or HABIT. (*HU,* 121)

Note carefully what Hume is saying. Our belief that events are related by cause and effect is a completely *nonrational* belief. We have no good reason to think this. We *do* believe in causation. We cannot help it. But we believe in it by a kind of natural instinct. That is just how human nature works: When we experience the *constant conjunction* of events, we form a habit of expecting the second when we observe the first, and we believe the first causes the second.

Custom, then, is the great guide of human life. It is that principle alone, which renders our experience useful to us, and makes us expect, for the future, a similar train of events with those which have appeared in the past. Without the influence of custom, we should be entirely ignorant of every matter of fact, beyond what is immediately present to the memory and senses. (*HU,* 122)

Hume is here turning upside down the major theme of nearly all philosophy before him. Almost everyone in the philosophical tradition has agreed that a person has a right to believe something only if a good reason can be given for it. This goes back at least to Plato.* The major arguments among the philosophers concern what can (and what cannot) be adequately supported by reason. This commitment to the rationality of belief is most prominent, of course, in a rationalist such as Descartes, who determines to doubt everything that cannot be certified by the "light of reason." The skeptics, on precisely these same grounds, argue that virtually no belief in matters of fact can be known because virtually nothing can be shown to be reasonable. Hume seems to agree that virtually no belief in matters of fact can be shown to be reasonable; is he, then, a skeptic? We return to this question later in this chapter.

For now, let us note his conclusion that almost none of our most important beliefs (all of which depend on the relation between cause and effect) can be shown to be rational. We hold them simply out of habit. Our tendency to form beliefs about the external world is just a *fact* about us; this is the way human nature works. Hume does not try to explain *why* human nature functions this way—it just does. We should not frame hypotheses!

There is a corollary, which Hume is quick to draw. Sometimes a certain event is *always* conjoined with another event. But in other cases two events are more loosely connected in our experience, so that it is only *often* the case that when the one occurs the other follows. Water always boils when put on a hot fire, but it only sometimes rains when it is cloudy. These facts are the foundation of *probabilistic* expectations. Our degree of belief corresponds to the degree of connection that our experience reveals between the two events. The more constant the conjunction between event *A* and event *B*, the more probable we think it that a new experience of *A* will be followed by *B*. Again, note that for Hume this is not the result of a rational calculation. We do not *decide* to believe with a particular degree of assurance. It just happens. We *find ourselves* believing those things most confidently which are

---

*Review Plato's distinction of knowledge from opinion in terms of the former being "backed up by reasons" (pp. 118–119).

most regular in our experience. That is how we are made.[*]

One more fact about our causal beliefs needs to be accounted for. We have seen that they are founded on a habit, or custom, of expecting one event whenever we have observed it to be constantly conjoined with another event. But this does not seem to exhaust the notion of causality. When we say that *X* causes *Y,* we don't just mean that whenever *X* occurs *Y* also occurs. We mean that if *X* occurs, *Y* *must* occur, that *X produces Y,* that *X* has a certain *power* to bring *Y* into being. In short, we think that in some sense the connection between *X* and *Y* is a *necessary connection.* This is part of what we mean by the idea of a cause. We could express this idea in a formula:

CAUSE = CONSTANT CONJUNCTION + NECESSARY CONNECTION

Hume now owes us an account of this latter aspect of the idea.

How can he proceed? The idea of cause is one of those metaphysical ideas we are all familiar with, but whose exact meaning is obscure. Hume has already given us a rule to deal with these cases: Try to trace the idea back to an impression. What happens if we try to do that?

Think again about the billiard balls on the table. Try to describe with great care your exact experience when seeing the one strike the other. Isn't it your impression that the cue ball moves across the table, it touches the eight ball, and the eight ball moves? Is there anything else you observe? In particular, do you observe the *force* that *makes* the second ball move? Do you observe the *necessary connection* between the two events? Hume is convinced that you do not.

> We are never able, in a single instance, to discover any power or necessary connexion; any quality

which binds the effect to the cause, and renders the one an infallible consequence of the other. We only find, that the one does actually, in fact, follow the other. . . . Consequently, there is not, in any single, particular instance of cause and effect, any thing which can suggest the idea of power or necessary connexion. (*HU,* 136)

Mental phenomena are no different. If I will to move my hand, my hand moves. If I try to recall the first line of "The Star Spangled Banner," I can (usually) do it. But no matter how closely I inspect these operations, all I can observe is one thing being followed by another. I never get an impression of the *connection* between them. All relations of cause and effect must be learned from experience; and experience can show us only "the frequent CONJUNCTION of objects, without being ever able to comprehend any thing like CONNEXION between them" (*HU,* 141).

Where then do we get this second part of our idea of cause? Is it one of those ideas that is simply meaningless? Should we discard it or try to do without it? That seems hardly possible. Yet a close inspection of all the data seems to confirm Hume's conclusion:

> Upon the whole, there appears not, throughout all nature, any one instance of connexion, which is conceivable by us. All events seem entirely loose and separate. One event follows another; but we can never observe any tie between them. They seem *conjoined,* but never *connected.* And as we can have no idea of any thing, which never appeared to our outward sense or inward sentiment, the necessary conclusion *seems* to be, that we have no idea of connexion or power at all, and that these words are absolutely without any meaning, when employed either in philosophical reasonings, or common life. (*HU,* 144)

"All events seem entirely loose and separate." And the conclusion *seems* to be that we have no idea of cause at all—because there is no corresponding impression of necessary connections. But then it is really puzzling why this idea should be so natural, so pervasive, and so useful. It is an idea we all have, and one we can hardly do without.

This puzzle, Hume thinks, can be solved. To solve it, we have to go back to the fact that exposure

---

[*]A qualification needs to be made here. While our degree of confidence in our beliefs is usually governed by this principle, there are exceptions. We can be misled by thinking that certain ideas have meaning when they do not. Or we can generalize too soon on the basis of limited information. These mistakes lead to what Hume calls "superstition." Most superstitions are erroneous beliefs about causes and effects. Think about the bad luck supposedly associated with breaking a mirror or walking under a ladder.

to constant conjunctions builds up an associationistic *habit* of expecting one event on the appearance of the other. This habit is the key to understanding the full concept of a cause.

> After a repetition of similar instances, the mind is carried by habit, upon the appearance of one event, to expect its usual attendant, and to believe that it will exist. This connexion, therefore, which we *feel* in the mind, this customary transition of the imagination from one object to its usual attendant, is the sentiment or impression, from which we form the idea of power or necessary connexion. (*HU,* 145)

As we have seen, there are two things that go into the concept of a cause. One component is a constant conjunction of events. Of that we have experience, and on that basis Hume offers the following definition of a cause:

> an object, followed by another, and where all the objects, similar to the first, are followed by objects similar to the second. (*HU,* 146)

Notice that this is a reduced, cautious, pulled-back definition of "cause." It is not a definition of the *full* notion of cause, which includes the idea of a necessary connection between events. We cannot, Hume says, "point out that circumstance in the cause, which gives it a connexion with its effect. We have no idea of this connection" (*HU,* 146).

But we do experience something relevant to our *belief* in necessary connection. We cannot help but *feel* that there is a connection. Built on habit, our *expectation* leads us to feel that the water *must* boil, given the fire beneath the kettle. It is on the basis of this kind of subjective experience that we *project* a necessary connection into the relation between objective events. And Hume gives us a second definition of cause:

> an object followed by another, and whose appearance always conveys the thought to that other. (*HU,* 146)

Hume has done two things, then. (1) He has provided an account of the basis on which we have the idea of cause at all—the observed constant conjunctions between kinds of events. (2) He has given an explanation of why we attribute a necessary connection to those pairs of events—even though such necessary connections are never experienced. The full concept of a cause is a kind of *fiction.** So far as our experience goes, there are no necessary connections anywhere. But we cannot help applying that notion to observed events, even though nothing in our impressions ever gives us a warrant for doing so.

Remembering that we rely on cause and effect for all our inferences to realities beyond present consciousness, we now see that all such beliefs are simply based on habit. We have *no reason* for belief in an external world, in the reality of other persons, or even in past events. If knowledge is based on reason, as the philosophical tradition has held, there is precious little we can claim to know!

Again we should ask, Is this just skepticism all over again—this time on the foundation of an attempt to construct a science of human nature? Again, let us put off the question.

---

1. Contrast relations of ideas with matters of fact. Give some examples of your own.
2. What is Hume's argument for the conclusion that causes and effects are discoverable not by reason but by experience?
3. If our beliefs about causation are dependent on experience, what experiences are of the relevant kind?
4. How does Hume explain our judgments of probability?
5. Granted that the idea of *necessary connection* is an important part of our idea of a cause, how does Hume account for that?
6. What part of our idea of causation is a fiction, according to Hume? What part is not?

The Disappearing Self

Philosophers since Plato have struggled with the question about the nature of human beings. This metaphysical problem is puzzling and difficult be-

---

*Hume does not apply the term "fiction" to his account of causality; but he does use it when talking of (1) the identity of objects through time, (2) the existence of objects independent of experience, and (3) personal identity in a continuing self. Since the pattern of analysis is similar in all these cases, I think it is justified to use the term here. I am indebted to Matthew McKeon for additional clarity on this topic.

cause the phenomena of mind—consciousness, thinking, feeling, willing, deciding to act—seem to be so different from nonmental phenomena—size, motion, weight, inertia. Plato argues that a person is really an entity distinct from the body, a *soul;* residence in a body is a temporary state, and the soul survives the body's death. The tradition in the West generally follows him, though there are dissenters. The atomists and Epicureans think of the soul as material and mortal; Aristotle holds (with qualifications) that the soul is a functional aspect of a living body; the skeptics, of course, suspend judgment on the whole question.

In modern times, Descartes follows Plato's lead, holding not only that the soul or mind is a distinct substance and immortal, but also that it is better known than any body could be. Hobbes, by contrast, interprets human beings in a thoroughly materialistic way. Locke believes in spiritual substances, though he emphasizes our lack of knowledge concerning their real nature. And, as we have seen, Berkeley argues that spirits and their ideas make up the whole of reality.*

Hume can hardly avoid dealing with the problem since he claims to be constructing a science of human nature. The first thing we need to do, to the extent possible, is to clarify the meaning of the central term. What Plato called "soul" and Descartes the "mind," Hume names the "self." A *self* is supposedly a substance or thing, simple (not composed of parts), and invariably the same through time. It is the "home" for all our mental states and activities, the "place" where these characteristics are "located." (The terms in quote marks are, of course, used metaphorically.) My self is what is supposed to account for the fact that I am one and the same person today as I was at the age of four, even though nearly all my characteristics have changed over the years. I am larger, stronger, and smarter; I have different hopes and fears, different thoughts and

memories; my interests and activities are remarkably different. Yet I am the *same self.* The thing that I most deeply am has not changed. This selfsame, identical thing—this is *I.* Or so the story goes.*

It is clear what Hume will ask here. Remember his rule: If there is a term that is in any way obscure, or about which there is much controversy, try to trace it back to an impression.

> From what impression cou'd this idea be derived? This question 'tis impossible to answer without a manifest contradiction and absurdity; and yet 'tis a question, which must necessarily be answer'd, if we wou'd have the idea of self pass for clear and intelligible. It must be some one impression, that gives rise to every real idea. But self or person is not any one impression, but that to which our several impressions and ideas are suppos'd to have a reference. If any impression gives rise to the idea of self, that impression must continue invariably the same, thro' the whole course of our lives; since self is suppos'd to exist after that manner. But there is no impression constant and invariable. (*T,* I, 4, 6, p.164)

Let us be clear about the argument here. The term "self" is supposed to represent an idea of something that continues unchanged throughout a person's life. Since the idea is supposed to be a simple one, there must be a simple impression that is its "double." But there is no such impression, Hume claims, "constant and invariable" through life. It follows, according to Hume's rule, that *we have no such idea!* The term is one of those meaningless noises that we suppose (through inattention or confusion) means something, when it really doesn't.

This is a most radical way of undermining belief in the soul or self. Some philosophers claim to have such an idea and to be able to prove the self really exists. Others claim to be able to prove that it doesn't exist. But Hume undercuts both sides; they are just arguing about words, he holds, because neither side really knows what it is talking

---

*Discussions of these various doctrines can be found as follows: Plato, pp. 141–144; Aristotle, pp. 179–184; atomism, pp. 33–35; Descartes in *Meditation VI;* Hobbes on pp. 362–366; Locke, pp. 376–378; and Berkeley, pp. 389–393. A contemporary treatment of this problem is discussed on pp. 736–742.

*It would be helpful at this point to review what Locke says about personal identity, pp. 376–378. Note that he argues that my identity cannot *consist* in sameness of soul or self, though he doesn't find those terms meaningless.

about. Literally! There simply is no such idea as the (supposed) idea of the self, so it doesn't make sense to affirm it *or* to deny it.

This claim, of course, rests on the theory of ideas. It is only as strong as that theory is good. Is that a good theory? This is an important question; in later chapters, we meet other philosophers who investigate this question.* But for now, let us explore in a bit more depth why Hume thinks there is no impression that corresponds to the (supposed) idea of the self. In a much-quoted passage, Hume says,

> For my part, when I enter most intimately into what I call *myself,* I always stumble on some particular perception or other, of heat or cold, light or shade, love or hatred, pain or pleasure. I never can catch *myself* at any time without a perception, and never can observe any thing but the perception. When my perceptions are remov'd for any time, as by a sound sleep; so long am I insensible of *myself,* and may truly be said not to exist. And were all my perceptions remov'd by death, and cou'd I neither think, nor feel, nor see, nor love, nor hate after the dissolution of my body, I shou'd be entirely annihilated, nor do I conceive what is farther requisite to make me a perfect non-entity. If any one upon serious and unprejudic'd reflexion, thinks he has a different notion of *himself,* I must confess I can reason no longer with him. All I can allow him is, that he may be in the right as well as I, and that we are essentially different in this particular. (*T,* I, 4, 6, p.165)

Again, Hume tries to pay close attention to the phenomena and tries not to frame hypotheses. If we look inside ourselves, do we find an impression of something simple, unchanging, and continuing? He confesses that *he* can find no such impression, and his suggestion that maybe *you* can, that maybe *you* are "essentially different" in this regard, is surely ironic. His claim is that none of us ever finds more in ourselves than fleeting perceptions—ideas, sensations, feelings, and emotions.

So we have no reason to suppose that we are selves, or minds, or souls, if we understand those terms to refer to some simple substance that underlies all our particular perceptions. But what, then, are we?

> I may venture to affirm of the rest of mankind, that they are nothing but a bundle or collection of different perceptions, which succeed each other with an inconceivable rapidity, and are in a perpetual flux and movement. . . . The mind is a kind of theatre, where several perceptions successively make their appearance; pass, re-pass, glide away, and mingle in an infinite variety of postures and situations. There is properly no *simplicity* in it at any one time, nor *identity* in different; whatever natural propensity we may have to imagine that simplicity and identity. The comparison of the theatre must not mislead us. They are the successive perceptions only, that constitute the mind; nor have we the most distant notion of the place, where these scenes are represented, or of the materials, of which it is compos'd. (*T,* I, 4, 6, 165)

Thinking that we have an idea of the self, then, is a mistake, but one that is natural and inevitable. As in the case of causation, Hume offers an explanation of why it is so easy to fall into this error (we confuse similarity with identity), but like the idea of cause, the idea of the self is a fiction. As selves or minds, we are nothing but a "bundle" of perceptions. Anything further is sheer, unsupported hypothesis. We have not only no reason to believe in a world of "external" things independent of our minds, but also no reason to believe in mind as a thing.*

In thinking of ourselves, Hume suggests, the analogy of a theater is appropriate. In this theater, an amazingly intricate and complex play is being performed. The players are just all those varied perceptions that succeed each other, as Hume says, with "inconceivable rapidity." But if we are to understand the analogy correctly, we must think away the walls of the theater, think away the stage, think away the seats and even the audience. What is left is

---

*Kant, for instance, denies a key premise of the theory of ideas: that all our ideas (Kant calls them "concepts") arise from impressions. Some of our concepts, Kant claims, do not *arise* out of experience, though they may *apply* to experience. See pp. 434–439.

*Compare Berkeley on a thing being no more than a combination of sensations. What Berkeley does to the idea of material substance, Hume does to spirit or mind.

THE BUDDHA

Siddhartha, whose family name was Gautama, was born into a royal family in the north of India in the sixth century B.C. As a youth he lived a sheltered life in the greatest luxury. Eventually, however, he confronted the realities of sickness, old age, suffering, and death, and determined to find a way out of the pain that seemed a universal aspect of life.

He left home and became an ascetic, seeking to find the way in traditional religious disciplines, denying himself everything but the barest necessities. He did not find satisfaction. After six years, he gave up the ascetic life and while sitting under a tree one evening attained enlightenment, and thereafter was known as "the Buddha," or "the Enlightened One."

The wisdom of the Buddha involves recognizing (1) the nature of suffering, (2) the origins of suffering, (3) the possibility of escape from suffering, and (4) the path to attain that end. These are known as the Four Noble Truths. Enlightenment is not just learning these formulas, but seeing for oneself that things are as the Buddha has said, coming to know that this is Truth.

What produces suffering is desire or thirst—desire for things, for pleasure, thirst for life itself. The cessation of suffering, therefore, requires the extinction of desire. And this is possible if we come to see that there is no self, no permanent soul or spirit that is doing the desiring—no "I" to have or experience or possess what is desired. There are just states of matter, states of sensation and perception, of volition and consciousness succeeding each other according to laws of cause and effect. There is thinking but no thinker, seeing without one who sees, desiring but no substantial *I* which desires.

Enlightenment consists in detachment from this conditioned series of appearances. One who is enlightened is said to have attained nirvana, a state of absolute freedom from craving, hatred, and resentment. It is a state of untroubled bliss. And yet it is not *someone* who has attained nirvana, for in reality there is no self to attain anything. The idea of a continuing, permanent self that is *me* is an illusion.

---

just the performance of the play. Such a performance each of us *is*.

But what distinguishes one performance from another—the bundle of perceptions that I am from the bundle that you are? We might think that my bundle is distinguished from others by the fact that it is associated with my body. But this can't be the right answer, in Hume's terms. My awareness of my body is through an impression. So the question arises for that impression, too: What makes *that* perception one of mine? Hume's answer is that personal identity must be a matter of the *relations between* the perceptions I call mine. But since Hume himself is never satisfied with this answer, we don't discuss it in detail.

However, we do need to see how the bundle theory of the self bears on Descartes' *cogito*, "I think, therefore I am." Descartes takes this as something each of us knows with certainty. And in answer to the question, "What, then, am I?" he says, "I am a thing (a substance) that thinks." Hume is in effect saying that Descartes is going beyond what the phenomena reveal. A twentieth-century Humean, Bertrand Russell, puts it this way: The most that Descartes is entitled to claim is that there is thinking going on. To claim that there is a mind or self—a thing—doing the thinking is to frame a hypothesis, to go beyond the evidence available.[7] If this criticism is correct, it clearly undermines Descartes' dualistic metaphysics, to say nothing of Berkeley's spiritual monism; we cannot know that the mind is a substance distinct from the body because we cannot know it is a substance at all! All we have is acquaintance with that bundle of perceptions.

Rescuing Human Freedom

Another topic a science of human nature must address is whether human actions are in some sense *free*. This question takes on a new urgency with the adoption of the mechanistic physical theories of Galileo and Newton. As long as the entire world is conceived in Aristotelian terms, where a key mode of explanation is teleological,* the question of freedom is not pressing. If *everything* acts for the sake of some end, pursuing its good in whatever way its nature allows, human actions would fit the general pattern neatly. Humans have more alternatives available than do petunias and snails, and they make choices among the available goods. But the pattern of explanation would be common to all things.

In the mid-eighteenth century, however, the situation is quite different. Explanation in terms of ends or goals has been banished; explanation by prior causes is "in." The model of the universe is mechanical; the world is compared to a gigantic clock. Stones do not fall *in order to* reach a goal (their natural place); and oak trees do not grow because of a *striving* to realize the potentiality in them. Everything happens as it *must happen,* according to laws that make no reference to any end, goal, or good. Every movement takes place with the same inexorability as we find in the hands of a clock.

What about human actions in a world like this? Are they as strictly determined by law and circumstance as the fall of the stone? How are we to think of our lives, now that we think of everything else in this mechanical way? The view that human actions constitute no exception to the universal rule of causal law is known as **determinism.** The successes of modern science give it plausibility. But it seems to clash with a deeply held conviction that sometimes we are *free* to choose, will, and act.†

Descartes shows us one way to deal with this problem: Make an exception for human beings! Mechanical principles might govern material bodies, but they can get no leverage on a nonmaterial mind. The will, Descartes says, is completely free; even the will of God could not conceivably be more free than the human will. And by "free" he means "not governed by causal laws."

But Hume cannot take this way, for he is convinced we have no idea of a substantial self, so we can have no reason to think such a nonmaterial mind or soul exists. Hume's solution to this puzzle is quite different from Descartes', and it is justly famous. Its basic pattern is defended by numerous philosophers (but not all) even today.

He begins by asserting that "all mankind" is of the same opinion about this matter. Any controversy is simply due to "ambiguous expressions" used to frame the problem. In other words, if we can get our terms straight, we should be able to settle the matter to everyone's satisfaction. What we need is a set of *definitions* for what Hume calls "necessity" on the one hand and "liberty" on the other.

> I hope, therefore, to make it appear, that all men have ever agreed in the doctrine both of necessity and of liberty, according to any reasonable sense, which can be put on these terms; and that the whole controversy has hitherto turned merely upon words. (*HU,* 149)

We already know what Hume says about *necessity.* The idea of necessity is part of our idea of a cause but is a kind of fiction. It arises, not from impressions, but from that habit our minds develop when confronted with regular conjunctions between events. All we ever observe, when we believe that one event causes another, is the constant conjunction of events of the first kind with events of the second.

Are human actions caused? If we understand this in what Hume thinks is the only possible way, we are simply asking whether there are *regularities* detectable in human behavior.* And he thinks we all must admit that there are. He gives some examples (*HU,* 150, 151):

- Motives are regularly conjoined to actions: Greed regularly leads to stealing, ambition to the quest for power.

- When we do things together, I depend on the regularity of your behavior.

- If a foreigner acts in unexpected ways, there is always a cause — some condition (educa-

---

*An explanation is *teleological* if it makes essential reference to the realization of a goal or end state. Aristotle's discussion of "final causes" provides a good case study (see pp. 170–173).
†See the anticipation of modern deterministic views by Democritus, pp. 32–33.

*Look again at Hume's two definitions of "cause" on p. 409.

tion, perhaps) that regularly produces this behavior.

- Where we are surprised by someone's action, a careful examination always turns up some unknown condition that allows it to be fit again into a regular pattern.

If all that we can possibly mean by "caused" is that events are regularly connected, we should all agree that human behavior is caused. Why do some of us resist this conclusion? Because, Hume says,

> men still entertain a strong propensity to believe, that they penetrate farther into the powers of nature, and perceive something like a necessary connexion between the cause and the effect. When again they turn their reflections towards the operations of their own minds, and *feel* no such connexion of the motive and the action; they are thence apt to suppose, that there is a difference between the effects, which result from material force, and those which arise from thought and intelligence. (*HU,* 156, 157)

But this is just a confusion! Causality on the side of the objects observed is just regularity, and on the side of the observer it is the generation of a habit based on regularities. In neither case, material or intelligent, is there any necessity observed. Human actions are "caused" in exactly the same sense as events in the material world.

What then of freedom or liberty?

> It will not require many words to prove, that all mankind have ever agreed in the doctrine of liberty as well as in that of necessity, and that the whole dispute, in this respect also, has been hitherto merely verbal. For what is meant by liberty, when applied to voluntary actions? We cannot surely mean, that actions have so little connexion with motives, inclinations, and circumstances, that one does not follow with a certain degree of uniformity from the other, and that one affords no inference by which we can conclude the existence of the other. For these are plain and acknowledged matters of fact. By liberty, then, we can only mean a *power of acting or not acting, according to the determinations of the will;* that is, if we choose to remain at rest, we may; if we choose to move, we also may. Now this hypothetical liberty is universally allowed

to belong to everyone, who is not a prisoner and in chains. (*HU,* 158–159)

This requires some comment. Perhaps the most accessible way to understand Hume's point is to think of cases where a person is said to be *unfree.* Hume's example is that of a man in chains. What is it that makes this a case of unfreedom? Isn't it just this: that he cannot do what he *wants* to do? Even if he *yearns* to walk away, *wills* to walk away, *tries* to walk away, he will be *unable* to walk away. He is unfree because his actions are *constrained*—against his will, as we say.

Suppose we remove his chains. Then he is free, at liberty to do what he wants. And isn't this the very essence of freedom: to be able to do whatever it is that you want or choose to do? We could put this more formally in the following way:

> A person *P* is *free* when the following condition is satisfied: *If P chooses to do action A, then P does A.*

If this condition were *not* satisfied (if *P* should choose to do *A* but be *unable* to do it), then *P* would *not be at liberty* with respect to *A.*

Now we can see what Hume is up to. He wants to show us that it is possible to *reconcile* our belief in causality with our belief in human freedom. We do not have to choose between them. We can have both modern science and human freedom. Newtonian science and freedom to act would clash only if freedom entailed exemption from causality. But causes are simply regularities; and freedom is not an absence of regularity, but the "hypothetical" power to do something *if* we choose to do it. It is, in fact, a certain kind of regularity. It is the regularity of having the actions we choose to do follow regularly upon our choosing to do them.

There is no reason, then, in human liberty, to deny that a science of human nature—a causal science of a Newtonian kind—is possible. And Newtonian, mechanistic science is no reason to deny or doubt human freedom. In particular, human freedom gives us no reason to postulate a Cartesian mind, independent in its substance and operations of the basic laws of the universe. Hume's **compatibilism,** as it is sometimes called, is an important part of a kind of **naturalism,** a view that takes the human being to be a natural fact, without remainder.

---

1. What does Hume fail to find when—as he says—he enters most intimately into what he calls *himself*?
2. What conclusions does Hume draw about the nature of a "self"?
3. Explain how Hume thinks the necessity of actions (i.e., that they have causes) is compatible with the fact of liberty in actions (i.e., that sometimes we act freely).

Is It Reasonable to Believe in God?

After doubting everything doubtable, Descartes finds himself locked into solipsism—unless he can demonstrate that he is not the only thing that exists. The way he does this, you recall, is to try to demonstrate the existence of God. He looks, in other words, for a good reason to believe that something other than his own mind exists. If he can prove that God exists, he knows he is not alone; and, God being what God is, he will have good reason to trust at least what is clear and distinct about other things as well. Thus everything hangs, for Descartes, on whether it is reasonable to believe that there is a God.*

What does Hume say about this quest to show that belief in God is more reasonable than disbelief? We review briefly two of the arguments Descartes presents, together with a Humean response to each, and then we look at a rather different argument that was proving very popular in the atmosphere after Newton.

Descartes' first argument begins from the fact that we have an idea of God—an idea of an infinite and perfect being. Descartes argues roughly in the following way:

1. Such an idea requires a cause.
2. The cause must be equal in "formal" reality to the "subjective" reality of the idea.
3. I myself could not possibly be the cause.
4. The only plausible alternative cause is God himself. Therefore,
5. God exists.

Where could Hume attack this argument? Consider premise 3. This premise concerns the *origin* of a certain idea. As we have seen, Hume has a theory about the origin of ideas: Each and every one stems from some impression. What impression could be the origin of the idea of God?

> The idea of God, as meaning an infinitely intelligent, wise, and good Being, arises from reflecting on the operations of our own mind, and augmenting, without limit, those qualities of goodness and wisdom. (*HU*, 97–98)

The idea of God, Hume says, does have its origin in impressions. We reflect on ourselves and find impressions of intelligence and a certain degree of goodness—not perfect intelligence or complete goodness, of course. But we also have, from our impressions, the ideas of more and less. If we combine the idea of more with the ideas of intelligence and goodness, we get the idea of a being more intelligent and good than we are. We can reiterate this operation, over and over again, until we get the idea of a being that is perfectly intelligent and completely good. And this is the idea of God.*

If Hume is correct, you can see that he has undercut one of the premises Descartes uses in his first argument. He *can* be the origin of his idea of God, contrary to premise 3. Since Descartes' argument absolutely depends on the correctness of that premise, it no longer can give us a good reason to believe in God.

---

*Earlier thinkers, too, from Aristotle on, think they can give good reasons for concluding that some ultimate perfection exists and is in one way or another responsible for all other things. Review the proofs given by Augustine (p. 235), Anselm (pp. 264–268), and Aquinas (pp. 275–280). The arguments of Descartes are in *Meditations III* and *V*.

*Descartes foresees this line of argument and tries to block it. See his discussion in *Meditation III*, p. 344.

Think about Descartes' third argument, which goes something like this:

1. You cannot think of God without thinking that God exists, any more than you can think of a mountain without a valley or a triangle without three sides.

2. You do have the thought of God.

3. You must, therefore, think (believe) that God exists. Therefore,

4. God exists.

The first premise states a set of relations between ideas we have. The idea of a mountain necessarily involves the idea of a valley (or at least of a plain). In the same way, Descartes says, you cannot have the idea of God without also having the idea that he exists. You should remember, however, that Hume has drawn a sharp contrast between *relations of ideas* on the one hand and *matters of fact* on the other. Propositions concerning the relations of ideas, he holds, are independent in their truth value of "what is anywhere existent in the universe." It may be that thinking of God entails thinking that he exists; but that concerns only how those *ideas* are related to each other. It has nothing whatever to do with whether God *in fact* exists. Yet it is the latter that Descartes is vitally concerned with; unless God exists *in fact,* he is stuck in solipsism. Likewise, it is this question that we, believers and nonbelievers alike, are interested in. Does God *in fact* exist? Simply pointing out that one thought involves another does not answer that question—even if one of the thoughts is the thought of God's existence.

If we analyze the argument this way, it may be quite correct through step 3, but the transition from step 3 to step 4 is illegitimate, for a relation among ideas—even a necessary relation—gets no grip on how things actually are in the world. If it did, then the truth of matters of fact could be discovered "by the mere operation of thought." And that cannot be done, Hume is convinced, because "the contrary of every matter of fact is still possible" (*HU,* 108). In the realm of fact, it is just as possible that God does not exist as that God does exist—no matter how the ideas are logically related in our conceptual scheme. If it is God's ex-

istence as a matter of *fact* that we are interested in (and surely it is), then logical proof moving only within the realm of our ideas will not get us there. Belief in God's existence cannot be made reasonable, then, simply by considering the idea of God. Relations of ideas can't be used to prove matters of fact. About matters of fact we must consult *experience.*

The most popular argument for God during the Enlightenment, among common folk and intellectuals alike, does begin from experience. It can be called the *argument from design.** If there had ever been suspicions that the universe was not a perfectly ordered, magnificently integrated piece of work, Newton set such suspicions at rest. The image of a great machine, or clockwork, dominates eighteenth-century thought about the nature of the world. And it suggests a powerful analogy. Just as machines are the effects of intelligent design and workmanship, so the universe is the work of a master craftsman, supremely intelligent and wonderfully skilled. Machines don't just happen, and neither does the world.

In a set of dialogues that Hume did not venture to publish during his lifetime, one of the participants sets out this argument:

> Look round the world: Contemplate the whole and every part of it: You will find it to be nothing but one great machine, subdivided into an infinite number of lesser machines, which again admit of subdivisions to a degree beyond what human senses and faculties can trace and explain. All these various machines, and even their most minute parts, are adjusted to each other with an accuracy which ravishes into admiration all men who have ever contemplated them. The curious adapting of means to ends, throughout all nature, resembles exactly, though it much exceeds, the productions of human contrivance; of human design, thought, wisdom, and intelligence. Since therefore the effects resemble each other, we are led to infer, by all the rules of analogy, that the causes also resemble, and that the Author of Nature is somewhat similar to the mind of man, though possessed of much larger

---

*Compare the fifth way of Thomas Aquinas, pp. 279–280. See also Berkeley, p. 394.

faculties, proportioned to the grandeur of the work which he has executed. By this argument *a posteriori,* and by this argument alone, do we prove at once the existence of a Deity and his similarity to human mind and intelligence. (*D,* II, 45)

Before considering Hume's appraisal of this argument, let us note several points. It is an argument, Hume says, **a posteriori;** that is, it is an argument that depends in an essential way upon experience. Our experience of the world as an ordered and harmonious whole provides one crucial premise; our experience of how machines come into being provides another. Note also that it is an argument *by analogy.* Its structure looks like this (*M* = a machine; *I* = intelligence; *W* = the world):

1. *M* is the effect of *I.*
2. *W* is like *M.* Therefore,
3. *W* is the effect of something like *I.*

Finally, you should recognize that this, like Descartes' first two arguments, is a *causal* argument. Both the first premise and the conclusion deal with causal relations.

Hume says many interesting things about this argument, partly through his spokesmen in the dialogue. Here we are brief, simply listing a number of the points he makes.

1. No argument from experience ever can establish a certainty. The most that experience can yield is probability (since experience is always limited and cannot testify to what is beyond its limits). So even if the argument is a good one (of its kind), it does not give us more than a probability that the "Author of Nature" is analogous to a human designer.

2. There is a sound principle to be observed in all causal arguments: that "the cause must be proportioned to the effect."

A body of ten ounces raised in any scale may serve as a proof, that the counterbalancing weight exceeds ten ounces; but can never afford a reason that it exceeds a hundred. . . . If the cause be known only by the effect, we never ought to ascribe to it any qualities, beyond what are precisely requisite to produce the effect. (*HU,* 190)

If we look around at the world, can we say that it is perfectly good? That is hard to believe. If we think of this proof as an attempt to demonstrate the existence of God as he is traditionally conceived— infinite in wisdom and goodness—it surely falls short. For the proportion of goodness we are *justified* in ascribing to the cause (God) cannot far exceed the proportion of goodness (in the world) that needs to be explained.

3. The analogy is supposed to exist between the productions of intelligent human beings and the world as an effect of a supremely intelligent designer. But a number of consequences follow if we take the analogy seriously.

• Many people cooperate to make a machine; by analogy, the world may have been created through the cooperation of many gods.

• Wicked and mischievous people may create technological marvels; by analogy, the creator(s) of the world may be wicked and mischievous.

• Machines are made by mortals; by analogy, may not the gods be mortal?

• The best clocks are a result of a long history of slow improvements; by analogy,

Many worlds might have been botched and bungled, throughout an eternity, ere this system was struck out; much labor lost; many fruitless trials made; and a slow but continued improvement carried on during infinite ages in the art of world-making. (*D,* 36)

The point here is not that any of these possibilities is likely but that analogies always have resemblances in certain respects and differences in others. How do we know which are the similarities in this case and which are the differences? Unless we have some principled way to make this distinction, any one of these conclusions is as justified as the one theists wish to draw.

4. Finally, we have to ask what we can learn from a single case. Here Hume applies his analysis of the idea of causality to the case of the cause of the world.

It is only when two *species* of objects are found to be constantly conjoined, that we can infer the one from the other; and were an effect presented, which was entirely singular, and could not be comprehended under any known *species,* I do not see, that we could form any conjecture or inference at all concerning its cause. If experience and observation and analogy be, indeed, the only guides which we can reasonably follow in inferences of this nature; both the effect and cause must bear a similarity and resemblance to other effects and causes, which we know, and which we have found, in many instances, to be conjoined with each other. (*HU,* 198)

There is one respect in which this universe is entirely *unlike* the clocks and automobiles and stereos of our experience: It is, in our experience, "entirely singular." We can infer that the cause of a new computer is some intelligent human because we have had past experience of the constant conjunction of computers and intelligent designers. We experience *both* the effects *and* the causes. To apply this kind of analogical reasoning to the universe, we would need past experience of the making of worlds; and in each instance there would have to have been a conjoined experience of an intelligent being. On the basis of such a constant conjunction, we could infer justly that this world, too, is the effect of intelligence. But since the universe is, in our experience, "entirely singular," we can make no such inference. These, and more, are the difficulties Hume finds in the design argument.

You can see that according to Hume's principles *any* causal argument for God is subject to this last criticism. But now we are in a position to see that our situation is much worse than we ever imagined. These reflections not only undercut causal arguments for God's existence, but also undermine all causal arguments for the existence of *anything at all* beyond our own impressions!* For causal judgments are always founded on the constant conjunction of pairs of events *within our experience.* To judge that some extra-mental object is the cause of a perception, we would need to be able to observe a constant conjunction of that perception with its

extra-mental cause. But to do that we would need to jump out of our own skins, observe the perception from outside, and compare it with the external thing correlated with it. And that is something we surely cannot do.

Descartes thinks we need to prove the existence of God in order to ground our belief that the material world (described by his physics) is more than merely a set of ideas. His argument involves the claim that God is the (extra-mental) cause of an idea he has. But if Hume is right about the origin of the concept of causality *within* experience, we could never have the evidence required to validate this claim. All we can do is relate perceptions to perceptions. And if Descartes is right that without *good reason* to believe in God we are caught within the web of our own ideas, then solipsism seems (rationally) inescapable*—a dismal and melancholy conclusion.

After reviewing these attempts to make belief in God reasonable, it seems that this must be our conclusion: We have so far not found good reason to believe in God. Now we must add that neither have we found good reason to believe in the existence of a material world independent of our perceptions. We can think of this as a radical consequence of the representational theory (p. 327). Hume shows us that if we begin from ideas in the mind, there is no way to build that bridge to the world beyond.

This is not, however, Hume's last word on the subject of religion. In a passage that has puzzled many commentators, one of Hume's characters goes on to say,

> A person, seasoned with a just sense of the imperfections of natural reason, will fly to revealed truth with the greatest avidity: While the haughty dogmatist, persuaded that he can erect a complete system of theology by the mere help of philosophy, disdains any further aid and rejects this adventitious instructor. To be a philosophical skeptic is, in a man of letters, the first and most essential step towards being a sound, believing *Christian.* (*D,* XII, 130)

---

*Here we see how—accepting the starting points of Locke and Berkeley—Hume presses their empiricist principles to radical and (apparently) skeptical conclusions.

*Solipsism is explained on p. 331.

What can we make of this? Is Hume serious here? Or, more importantly, is this a serious possibility, this combination of religious faith and philosophical skepticism? What would this be like?*

---

1. How, according to Hume, does the idea of God originate? Compare Hume's view to Descartes' view.
2. How does Hume use the notion of relations of ideas to block the ontological arguments of Anselm (pp. 264–268) and Descartes (*Meditation V*)?
3. State clearly the argument from design, and sketch several of Hume's criticisms.

Understanding Morality

You and I find ourselves making judgments like this: "That was a bad thing Jones did," "Smith is a good person," "Telling the truth is the right thing to do," and "Justice is a virtue." You see twenty dollars on a desk in a room down the hall; no one is around, and you could pick it up; you say to yourself, "That would be wrong," and walk away. Such "moral" judgments are very important to us, both as evaluations of the actions of others and as guides to our own behavior. They are no less important to society. A science of human nature ought to have something to say about this feature of human life, so Hume tries to understand our propensity to make judgments of this kind. As we might anticipate by now, he puts his question this way: Are these judgments founded in some way on reason, or do they have some other origin?

Reason Is Not a Motivator

Nothing is more usual in philosophy, and even in common life, than to talk of the combat of passion and reason, to give the preference to reason, and to assert that men are only so far virtuous as they conform themselves to its dictates. Every rational

---

Fideism, as this view is sometimes called, is explored in the work of Søren Kierkegaard. See "The Religious," in Chapter 18.

creature, 'tis said, is oblig'd to regulate his actions by reason; and if any other motive or principle challenge the direction of his conduct, he ought to oppose it, 'till it be entirely subdu'd, or at least brought to a conformity with that superior principle. . . . In order to shew the fallacy of all this philosophy, I shall endeavour to prove *first,* that reason alone can never be a motive to any action of the will; and *secondly,* that it can never oppose passion in the direction of the will. (*T,* II, 3, 3, p. 265)

Hume's claim that "reason alone" can never motivate any action has clear moral implications, for moral considerations can be motivators. We sometimes refrain from doing something simply because we judge that it would be *wrong.* If reason alone cannot motivate an action, it seems to follow that morality cannot be a matter of reason alone.

But what does this mean, that reason alone can neither motivate an action nor oppose passion (e.g., desire or inclination)? Recall Hume's claim that "all the objects of human reason or enquiry may naturally be divided into two kinds, to wit, *Relations of Ideas* and *Matters of Fact*" (*HU,* 108). If reason is going to motivate action, it must do so in one of these two ways. Let us examine each possibility.

Consider adding up a sum, which Hume takes to be a matter of the relations of ideas. Suppose I am totaling up what I owe to my dentist, Dr. Payne. Will this reasoning lead to any action? Not by itself, says Hume. If I *want* to pay Payne what I owe her, this reasoning will contribute to what I do: I will pay her the total and not some other amount. But in the absence of that (or another) want, the reasoning alone will not produce an action. The motivator is the want; and a want is what Hume calls a *passion.*

Consider next these examples:

Ask a man *why he uses exercise;* he will answer *because he desires to keep his health.* If you then enquire *why he desires health,* he will readily reply *because sickness is painful.* If you push your enquiries further and desire a reason *why he hates pain,* it is impossible he can ever give any. This is an ultimate end, and is never referred to any object.

Perhaps to your second question, *why he desires health,* he may also reply that *it is necessary for the exercise of his calling.* If you ask *why he is anxious on that head,* he will answer, *because he desires to get money.* If you demand why? *It is the instrument of pleasure,* says he. And beyond this it is an absurdity to ask for a reason. It is impossible there can be a progress *in infinitum;* and that one thing can always be a reason why another is desired. Something must be desirable on its own account, and because of its immediate accord or agreement with human sentiment and affection. (*PM,* 163)

Here we have reasoning about matters of fact; it is a matter of fact that exercise is conducive to health, that health is required to pursue a profession successfully, and so on. But mere knowledge of these matters of fact will not motivate action unless one cares about the end to which they lead. And this caring is not itself a matter of reason. It is a matter of *sentiment* or *passion.* Hume draws this conclusion:

> It appears evident that the ultimate ends of human actions can never, in any case, be accounted for by *reason,* but recommend themselves entirely to the sentiments and affections of mankind, without any dependence on the intellectual faculties. (*PM,* 162–163)

So reason alone can never motivate us to action. But Hume goes even further; he claims that reason can never oppose passion although one passion can oppose another. For example, as I contemplate the roller coaster ride, fear fights with the desire for thrills. Likewise, one rational proposition can be opposed to another when they are contradictory. But for reason to oppose passion, it would have to be a motivator in itself, and Hume argues that it is not. Reason, we might say, is *inert.*

> We speak not strictly and philosophically when we talk of the combat of passion and of reason. Reason is, and ought only to be the slave of the passions, and can never pretend to any other office than to serve and obey them. (*T,* II, 3, 3, 266)

Reason can instruct us how to satisfy our desires, but it cannot tell us what desires to have.*

Reason can only be the "slave" of the passions. In a few dramatic sentences, Hume drives this point home.

> Where a passion is neither founded on false suppositions, nor chuses means insufficient for the end, the understanding can neither justify nor condemn it. 'Tis not contrary to reason to prefer the destruction of the whole world to the scratching of my finger. (*T,* II, 3, 3, 267)

What would Plato have said about this?* Plato's idea that reason can grasp the Good, and therefore should *rule* the passions, simply misses the point if Hume is right here. Reason is motivationally impotent; it cannot rule. Its role is that of a slave! The master says, "I want that," and it is the job of the slave to figure out how it can be got. The slave deals with *means.* Reason has an important place in action, since if we calculate wrong or make a mistake about the facts, we will be likely to miss our ends. But those ends are dictated by the nonrational part of our nature, the wants and desires, the passions and sentiments, that are simply given with that nature. If I truly prefer the destruction of the world to the scratching of my finger, reason cannot oppose me. There is nothing *irrational* about that.

The Origins of Moral Judgment

What, then, of morality? It is clear that if moral judgments are to have any effect on actions, they cannot be purely rational judgments. They must be the expression of passions of some sort. This is just what Hume claims.

Let us again consider the two classes of things subject to reason. Could morality be simply a matter of the relations between ideas? It is plausible to think that there is a conceptual relation between the ideas of murder and wrong. All murder is wrong—because what "murder" means is "wrongful killing." So the connection in this case *is* a matter of relations of ideas. But this can hardly be all that is involved in morality because morality is supposed to be applied to the facts. Just pointing

---

*You might think there is an obvious exception: Can't reason tell me that it would be better for me if I didn't have this desire to smoke cigarettes? And isn't this a case of reason opposing a desire I have? What would Hume say?

*See Plato's discussion of the role of reason in the life of the just and happy person, pp. 145–150.

out that murder involves the idea of wrongful killing is no help at all when we are asking of a certain action, Is this murder—that is, is this a wrongful killing? So morality, if it is going to have any practical effects, cannot be merely a matter of the relations between ideas.

Can morality be a matter of fact (the second province of reason)?

> Take any action allow'd to be vicious: Wilful murder, for instance. Examine it in all lights, and see if you can find that matter of fact, or real existence, which you call *vice*. In whichever way you take it, you find only certain passions, motives, volitions and thoughts. There is no other matter of fact in the case. The vice entirely escapes you, as long as you consider the object. You can never find it, till you turn your reflexion into your own breast, and find a sentiment of disapprobation, which arises in you, towards this action. Here is a matter of fact; but 'tis the object of feeling, not of reason. It lies in yourself, not in the object. So that when you pronounce any action or character to be vicious, you mean nothing, but that from the constitution of your nature you have a feeling or sentiment of blame from the contemplation of it. Vice and virtue, therefore, may be compar'd to sounds, colours, heat and cold, which, according to modern philosophy, are not qualities in objects, but perceptions in the mind. (*T*, II, 3, 1, 301)

This analysis should be compared to Hume's discussion of causation. When we observe carefully any instance of a causal relation, we never observe the causing itself. We claim that one event causes another on the basis of building up a habit (in ourselves) of expecting the one on the appearance of the other; the concept of "necessary connection" we attribute to the relation between the events is founded on a "feeling" in our minds. Moral judgments, Hume is saying, are perfectly parallel to judgments of causality. Here, too, we project onto the facts an idea with an origin that is simply a feeling in the mind. In this case, the feelings are those of approval and disapproval, which are expressed in terms of the concepts "right/good" and "wrong/bad." No matter how closely you examine the facts of any action, you will never discover in them its goodness or badness. The moral quality of the facts is not read off them; it is a matter of how

the author of the moral judgment "feels" about them.

In a famous passage that widely influences subsequent moral philosophy, Hume marks out clearly the distinction between *the facts* on the one hand (expressible in purely descriptive language) and *the value qualities of the facts* on the other (expressible in evaluations).

> In every system of morality, which I have hitherto met with, I have always remark'd, that the author proceeds for some time in the ordinary way of reasoning, and establishes the being of a God, or makes observations about human affairs; when of a sudden I am surpriz'd to find, that instead of the usual copulations of propositions, *is,* and *is not,* I meet with no proposition that is not connected with an *ought,* or *ought not.* This change is imperceptible; but is, however, of the last consequence. For as this *ought* or *ought not,* expresses some new relation or affirmation, 'tis necessary that it shou'd be observ'd and explain'd; and at the same time that a reason should be given, for what seems altogether inconceivable, how this new relation can be a deduction from others, which are entirely different from it. But as authors do not commonly use this precaution, I shall presume to recommend it to the readers; and am persuaded, that this small attention wou'd subvert all the vulgar [i.e., common] systems of morality, and let us see, that the distinction of vice and virtue is not founded merely on the relations of objects, nor is perceiv'd by reason. (*T*, II, 3, 1, 302)

Hume is here pointing to what is often called the *fact/value gap,* or the *is/ought problem.*[*] Reason can tell us what the facts are, but it cannot tell us how to value them. And from premises that mention only the facts, no conclusions about value may be derived.

---

[*] Reflection should tell you that this problem, too, is a consequence of the change produced by the development and acceptance of modern science. Dante's world contained no such gap; he could find the "right way" by discovering the facts about the universe. In general, where *final causes* are an intrinsic part of the *way things are* no such gap exists. For the ends of things are part of their very being. When final causes are cast out, however, values lose their rootedness in the way things are.

A contrast with Augustine may help clarify what Hume is insisting on here. For Augustine and other believers in the Great Chain of Being, everything that exists has a value. Being and goodness always come together. Some things—those nearer to God and farther from nothingness—have more value than others.* That's just a fact, Augustine believes. There is value *in* things, and it is incumbent on us to adjust our desires to the degree of value that things *in fact* have.

For Hume there are no value-facts. Value has its origin in *valuing*—in feelings of desire, aversion, love, hate, and so on. Values are projections onto the facts, all of which have the same value—i.e., none. A diagram may illustrate this contrast. We do, of course, make value judgments; it is hard to imagine human life without them. And Hume is not advising us to refrain from doing so, any more than he advises against making causal judgments. But a science of human nature tries to understand both kinds of judgment; what it discovers, Hume thinks, is that neither of them is founded on reason. Neither is a matter of fact. Both have their origins in sentiment or feeling; both are projections onto a world in which they cannot be dis-covered.

The foundation, or "origin," of morality, then, is to be found in sentiment—in feelings of approval and disapproval—not in reason. A scientific examination of morality ought to do more than discover these foundations, however. It ought also to reveal what *kinds of things* we approve and disapprove, and why. Hume has many interesting things to say about this matter, but we'll be brief.

Hume claims that we tend to approve of those things which are either *agreeable* or *useful,* either to *ourselves* or to *others*. Some things naturally elicit our immediate approval (e.g., white sand on a warm beach); those are the agreeable things. Others do not but are valued as means, useful in promoting the occurrence of agreeable things (e.g., a visit to Dr. Payne). Hume believes that we often feel a kind of approval for things agreeable to others, as well as to ourselves; for example, we can take pleasure in another person's enjoyment of a good meal. If

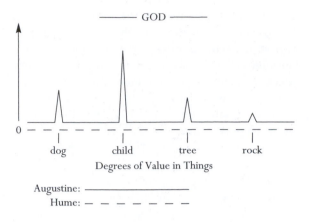

Degrees of Value in Things

Augustine: ———————
Hume: — — — — — —

Hume is right, an egoistic account of human motivation (such as that of Hobbes) is inadequate.* A Hobbesian might claim, of course, that when we approve of another's enjoyment we do so because such approval is a *means* to our own pleasure. But Hume argues that this can't be right. The pleasure or satisfaction we feel on viewing another's enjoyment *is* our approval of it, so it could not possibly be that for the sake of which we approve.

There is a passion in human beings that makes possible this "disinterestedness" of moral judgments. Hume calls it *sympathy* or *humanity* or *fellow feeling*. Sympathy plays a large role in our moral judgments, since it is characteristic of moral judgments not to be purely self-interested. As evidence, Hume notes that we make moral judgments about figures in past history, where there is no possible impact on our present or future interests. So we tend to approve of benevolent or generous acts, even when they are not directed toward ourselves.

We will not follow the development of Hume's ideas about the particular virtues, but we should note one aspect. His insistence that morality is not founded on reason would seem to catapult him directly into moral relativism because feelings seem so personal. What I approve, we may think, might be quite different from what you approve. But the insistence on sympathy as an original passion in human nature—within every individual—works

---

*Take another look at the diagram of the Great Chain on p. 241.

*Compare Hobbesian egoism, pp. 367–368.

toward a commonality in the moral sense of us all. It does not make moral disagreements between cultures or individuals impossible, but it is a pressure built into us all that explains the large agreement in moral judgment we in fact find.

---

1. Explain what Hume means when he says that reason is the slave of the passions.
2. How does Hume explain our judgment that a certain action is bad or wrong or vicious? In what do we find the viciousness of a vicious action?
3. What keeps Hume from complete moral relativism?

Is Hume a Skeptic?

On topic after topic, Hume sets himself against the majority tradition in the West. No doubt he feels this is only to be expected. Galilean and Newtonian science had overthrown traditional views about the nonhuman world; it should be no surprise that an attempt to apply the same methods to human nature should have the same result. Aristotle had defined man as a rational animal; ever since, the emphasis had been on the "rational" aspect. In deciding what to believe, what to do, how to live, and how to judge, philosophers had looked to reason. The prerogatives of reason had lately been exalted in an extreme way by Descartes, who held that we shouldn't accept *anything* unless it was attested by rational insight or rational deduction. What Hume thinks he has shown is that *if this is the right rule,* then there is *virtually nothing* we should accept.

Let us review:

- The principles governing the way ideas succeed each other are nonrational principles— those of sheer mechanical association, analogous in their function to the principle of gravitation.
- All knowledge of anything beyond our perceptions depends on the relation of cause and effect, but the origin of our idea of causality is a nonrational custom or habit that builds up in our minds whenever impressions succeed each other in a constant conjunction.

- We have no reason to believe in a substantial self; any such belief is a fiction foisted on us by detectable mistakes.
- We have no reason to believe in God.
- Our actions are governed by nonrational passions.
- Our liberty in action is not a matter of reason freeing us from the causal order, but simply a matter of nothing standing in the way of following our passions.
- Moral judgments, too, whether used as guides to our own action or as evaluations of the actions of others, are founded on nonrational sentiments that are simply a given part of human nature.

In every area, Hume discovers the passivity, the limits, the impotence of reason. There is no good reason to believe in an objective causal order, in the existence of a material world independent of our perceptions, in God, in a soul or self, or in objective moral values. These certainly seem to be skeptical themes. Is Hume, then, a skeptic?

He makes distinctions among several kinds of skepticism. Let us examine two. There is Descartes' type, which Hume calls "antecedent" skepticism because it is supposed to come *before* any beliefs are deemed acceptable. About this sort, he says,

> It recommends an universal doubt, not only of all our former opinions and principles, but also of our very faculties; of whose veracity, say they, we must assure ourselves, by a chain of reasoning, deduced from some original principle, which cannot possibly be fallacious or deceitful. But neither is there any such original principle, which has a prerogative above others, that are self-evident and convincing: Or if there were, could we advance a step beyond it, but by the use of those very faculties, of which we are supposed to be already diffident. The CARTESIAN doubt, therefore, were it ever possible to be attained by any human creature (as plainly it is not) would be entirely incurable; and no reasoning could ever bring us to a state of assurance and conviction upon any subject. (*HU,* 199)

His criticism of Descartes' project is twofold. First, you cannot *really* bring yourself to doubt everything; belief is not that much under your control. You find yourself believing in the reality of the world whether you want to or not. Second, if you could doubt everything, there would be no way back to rational belief; to get back, you would have to use your reasoning faculties, the competence of which is one of the things you are doubting.* So Hume dismisses Cartesian "antecedent" skepticism as both unworkable and barren.

There is another kind of skepticism, however, which Hume thinks is quite useful. This is not an attempt to doubt everything in the futile hope of gaining something impossible to doubt, but an attempt to keep in mind "the strange infirmities of human understanding."

> The greater part of mankind are naturally apt to be affirmative and dogmatical in their opinions. . . . But could such dogmatical reasoners become sensible of the strange infirmities of human understanding, even in its most perfect state, and when most accurate and cautious in its determinations; such a reflection would naturally inspire them with more modesty and reserve, and diminish their fond opinion of themselves, and their prejudice against antagonists. . . . In general there is a degree of doubt, and caution, and modesty, which, in all kinds of scrutiny and decision, ought for ever to accompany a just reasoner. (*HU,* 207–208)

This "mitigated" skepticism, Hume says, makes for modesty and caution; it will "abate [the] pride" (*HU,* 208) of those who are haughty and obstinate. It will teach us the limitations of our human capacities and encourage us to devote our understanding, not to abstruse problems of metaphysics and theology, but to the problems of common life.

In sponsoring such modesty about our intellectual attainments, Hume reflects Enlightenment worries about the consequences of dogmatic attachments to creeds that have only private backing. And if reason is really as broken-backed as Hume says, then dogmatic attachment to what appears rational is just as worrisome. One of the virtues of his examination of human nature, he feels, is that it makes such dogmatism impossible.

There might be an opposite worry, however. Could the consistently skeptical conclusions of Hume's philosophy undermine our lives to the point of paralysis? Hume himself reports, in an introspective moment, that after pursuing his research for a while, he finds himself

> ready to reject all belief and reasoning, and [to] look upon no opinion even as more probable or likely than another. Where am I, or what? From what causes do I derive my existence, and to what condition shall I return? Whose favor shall I court, and whose anger must I dread? What beings surround me? and on whom have I any influence, or who have any influence on me? I am confounded with all these questions, and begin to fancy myself in the most deplorable condition imaginable, invi-ron'd with the deepest darkness, and utterly depriv'd of the use of every member and faculty. (*T,* I, 4, 7, 175)

Reason has no answer to these questions. Depressing indeed!

What is the solution?

> Most fortunately it happens, that since reason is incapable of dispelling these clouds, nature herself suffices to that purpose, and cures me of this philosophical melancholy and delirium, either by relaxing this bent of mind, or by some avocation, and lively impression of my senses, which obliterate all these chimeras. I dine, I play a game of back-gammon, I converse, and am merry with my friends; and when after three or four hours' amusement, I wou'd return to these speculations, they appear so cold, and strain'd, and ridiculous, that I cannot find in my heart to enter into them any farther. (*T,* I, 4, 7, 175)

We need not worry, he assures us, that the results of philosophical study will paralyze us by taking away all our convictions. "Nature," he says, "is always too strong for principle" (*HU,* 207). Custom and habit, those nonrational instincts that are placed in our natures, will ensure that we don't sit shivering in terror at our lack of certainty.

But Hume does not mean that we should cease to pursue philosophy. Indeed, his conviction that nothing is more useful than the science of human

---

*Hume seems to be saying that we must be content with the things we are "taught by nature," as Descartes would say. See *Meditation III*. Is this criticism of Descartes correct? Compare also the critique of Descartes by Charles Peirce, pp. 569–570.

nature remains untouched. Only such an inquiry into the nature and limits of human understanding can free us from the natural tendency toward dogmatism and superstition that plagues human society. All our knowledge falls into one of two camps: relations of ideas or matters of fact. The former concern logical and mathematical matters; these, Hume thinks, are irrelevant to real existence. The latter are based wholly on experience, can get us probability at best, and are founded in any case on mere instinct, which we cannot prove is reliable. Here are Hume's last words in *An Enquiry Concerning Human Understanding*.

> When we run over libraries, persuaded of these principles, what havoc must we make? If we take in hand any volume of school metaphysics, for instance; let us ask, *Does it contain any abstract reasoning concerning quantity or number?* No. *Does it contain any experimental reasoning concerning matter of fact and existence?* No. Commit it then to the flames: For it can contain nothing but sophistry and illusion. (*HU*, 211)

Hume represents a kind of crisis point in modern philosophy. Can anyone build anything on the rubble he leaves behind?

---

1. What sort of skepticism does Hume criticize? What sort does he advocate?
2. What does Hume hope his philosophizing will accomplish? Does it do that for you?

For Further Thought

1. Both Descartes and Hume can be compared to Robinson Crusoe. Each tries to construct "a world" out of the resources available only to an isolated individual. Sketch the similarities and differences in their projects, noting the materials they have available and the tools with which they work.

2. Does Hume's view of human liberty leave room for *responsibility*? Compare Descartes on free will.

Notes

1. Immanuel Kant, "An Answer to the Question: What Is Enlightenment?" in *Perpetual Peace and Other Essays,* trans. Ted Humphrey (Indianapolis: Hackett, 1983), 41.
2. Kant, "What Is Enlightenment?" 41.
3. Ibid., 44.
4. From Newton's *Principia Mathematica,* General Scholium to Book III, reproduced in John Herman Randall, *The Career of Philosophy,* vol. 1 (New York: Columbia University Press, 1962), 579.
5. I have benefited from the excellent study of Hume by Barry Stroud: *Hume* (London: Routledge and Kegan Paul, 1977).
6. References to Hume's works are as follows:
   HU: Enquiry Concerning Human Understanding, ed. Tom L. Beauchamp (Oxford: Oxford University Press, 1999).
   D: Dialogues Concerning Natural Religion, in *Principal Writings on Religion,* ed. J. C. A. Gaskin (Oxford: Oxford University Press, 1993), cited by part and page number.
   T: A Treatise of Human Nature, ed. David Fate Norton and Mary J. Norton (Oxford: Oxford University Press, 2000). Citations are by book, part, section, and page number.
   PM: An Enquiry Concerning the Principles of Morals, ed. Tom L. Beauchamp (Oxford: Oxford University Press, 1998).
7. Bertrand Russell, *A History of Western Philosophy* (New York: Simon and Schuster, 1945), 567.

CHAPTER

16

IMMANUEL KANT

Rehabilitating Reason (within Strict Limits)

David Hume had published *A Treatise of Human Nature* at the youthful age of twenty-three, whereas Immanuel Kant (1724–1804) published the first of his major works, *The Critique of Pure Reason,* in 1781, when he was fifty-seven. He enters the great conversation rather late in life because it has taken him some time to understand the devastating critique of Hume, "that acute man."

> Since the beginning of metaphysics, . . . no event has occurred which could have been more decisive in respect of the fate of this science than the attack which David Hume made on it. (*P,* 64)[1]

> I freely admit: it was David Hume's remark that first, many years ago, interrupted my dogmatic slumber and gave a completely different direction to my enquiries. (*P,* 67)

Kant sets himself to solve what he calls "Hume's problem": whether the concept of cause is indeed objectively vacuous, a fiction that can be traced to a merely subjective and instinctive habit of human nature. We have seen the skeptical consequences Hume draws from his analysis; these, we can imagine, are what wake Kant from his "dogmatic slumber."

Human thought seems naturally to recognize no limits. It moves easily and without apparent strain from bodies to souls, from life in this world to life after death, from material things to God. One aspect of Enlightenment thought is the acute consciousness of how *varied* thoughts become when they move out beyond the ground of experience—and yet how *certain* most people feel about their own views. This is the dogmatism (or superstition) that Hume tries to debunk. Stimulated by Hume, Kant, too, feels this is a problem. It is true that in mathematics we have clear examples of knowledge independent of experience. But it does not follow (as thinkers such as Plato suppose) that we can extend this knowledge indefinitely in a realm beyond experience. Kant uses a lovely image to make this point.*

> The light dove, cleaving the air in her free flight, and feeling its resistance, might imagine that its

---

*Plato believes that the nonsensible, purely intelligible world of Forms is not only knowable but also more intelligible than the world of experience, and more real, too. See pp. 121–126.

flight would be still easier in empty space. It was thus that Plato left the world of the senses, as setting too narrow limits to the understanding, and ventured out beyond it on the wings of the ideas, in the empty space of the pure understanding. He did not observe that with all his efforts he made no advance—meeting no resistance that might, as it were, serve as a support upon which he could take a stand, to which he could apply his powers, and so set his understanding in motion. (*CPR*, 47)

Could the dove fly even better in empty space? No, it could not fly there at all; it absolutely depends on some "resistance" to fly. In the same way, Kant suggests, human thought needs a medium that supplies "resistance" to work properly. In a resistance-free environment, everything is equally possible (as long as formal contradiction is avoided), and the conflicts of dogmatic believers (philosophical, religious, or political) are inevitable.

Kant is convinced that Hume is right to pinpoint *experience* as the medium that disciplines reason, as the limit within which alone reason can legitimately do its work. But Kant doubts that Hume has correctly understood experience. Why? Because Hume's analysis has an unacceptable consequence. We did not explicitly draw this consequence when discussing Hume (because he does not draw it). But if Hume is right, Newtonian science itself is basically an irrational and unjustified fiction.* Recall that for Hume *all* our knowledge of matters of fact beyond present perception and memory is founded on the relation of cause and effect. And causes are nothing more than projections onto a supposed objective world from a feeling in the mind.

Kant is convinced that in Newtonian science we do have rationally justified knowledge. And if Hume's examination of reason forces us to deny that we have this knowledge, something must be wrong with Hume's analysis. What we need, Kant says, is a more thorough and accurate *critique of reason*—a

critique that will lay out its *structure*, its *relationship to its objects*, and inscribe precisely the line that sets the *limits* within which it can legitimately work. Hume thinks that what we need is a science of human nature. Kant agrees, but he thinks it must be done better than Hume manages to do it. This is the project Kant sets for himself, now that he has awakened from his dogmatic slumber and is no longer, like the dove, trying to fly in empty space.

He makes an absolutely revolutionary suggestion:

> Hitherto it has been assumed that all our knowledge must conform to objects. But all attempts to extend our knowledge of objects by establishing something in regard to them *a priori*, by means of concepts, have, on this assumption, ended in failure. We must therefore make trial whether we may not have more success in the tasks of metaphysics, if we suppose that objects must conform to our knowledge. . . . We should then be proceeding precisely on the lines of Copernicus' primary hypothesis. Failing of satisfactory progress in explaining the movements of the heavenly bodies on the supposition that they all revolved round the spectator, he tried whether he might not have better success if he made the spectator to revolve and the stars to remain at rest. A similar experiment can be tried in metaphysics, as regards the *intuition* of objects. (*CPR*, 22)

This requires some explanation. Nearly all previous philosophy (and science and common sense, too) has made a very natural assumption—as natural as the assumption that the heavenly bodies revolve around us. But perhaps it is just as wrong.

What is that assumption? It is that we acquire knowledge and truth when our thoughts "conform to objects." According to this assumption, objects are *there*, quite determinately *being* whatever they are, completely independent of our apprehension of them. To know them our beliefs must be brought to *correspond* to these independently existing things. Aristotle's classical definition of truth expresses this assumption perfectly: to say of what *is* that it is, and of what *is not* that it is not, is true.* The assumption

---

*You can see that Hume ends up exactly where Descartes fears to be, with science indistinguishable from a dream. In order to escape this fate, Descartes thinks you need to prove the existence of a nondeceptive God. But by undermining such proofs, Hume finds himself unable to escape from solipsism—except by joining a game of backgammon and ignoring the problem.

*See Aristotle's discussion of this on pp. 162–163.

is a basic part of the representational theory of knowledge and perception (p. 327).

But Hume has argued that you can't think about representation in this way. Ideas that have their origin in experience (e.g., green, warm, solid) can go no further than experience. And ideas that don't (e.g., cause) are mere illusions. By using such concepts we can know nothing at all about objects. All this follows if (1) we are acquainted only with the ideas in our experience, (2) objects are thought to exist independently of our experience, and (3) knowledge requires that we ascertain a correspondence between ideas and objects.*

But what if this assumption has it exactly backwards? What if, to be an object at all, a thing has to conform to certain concepts? What if objects couldn't exist—simply couldn't *be* in any sense at all—unless they were related to a rational mind, set in a context of rational concepts and principles? Think about the motion of the planets in their zigzag course across the sky. On the assumption that this motion is *real,* accurate understanding proves to be impossible. Copernicus denies this assumption and suggests that the motion is only *apparent.* It is *contributed by us,* the observers. On this new assumption, we are able to understand and predict the behavior of these objects.

Perhaps, Kant is suggesting, the same is true in the world of the intellect. Perhaps the objects of experience are (at least in part) the result of a construction by the rational mind. If so, they have no reality independent of that construction. Like the apparent motions of the planets, the objects of our experience are merely apparent, not independently real. If this is so, it may well be that concepts such as causation, which cannot be *abstracted* from experience (the lesson of Hume), still *apply* to experience, simply because objects that are *not* structured by that concept are *inconceivable.* The suggestion is that the rational mind has a certain structure, and whatever is knowable by such a mind must necessarily be known in terms of that structure. This structure is not derived from the objects known; it is *imposed*

on them—but not arbitrarily, because the very idea of an object not so structured makes no sense.

This is Kant's "Copernican Revolution" in philosophy. To the details of this novel way of thinking we now turn.

Critique

If we are going to take seriously this possibility that objects are partially constituted by the rational mind, we must examine how that constitution takes place. We need to peer reflectively behind the scenes and catch a glimpse of the productive machinery at work. So we are interested in the *processes* involved in knowing anything at all. A prior question, of course, is whether we *can* know anything at all, but Kant thinks that Newton's science has definitely settled that question. Assuming, then, that a rational mind can have some knowledge, we want to ask, How does it manage that? We need to engage in what Kant calls "critique." A "critical" philosophy is not one that criticizes, in the carping, censorious way where "nothing is ever right." *Critique* is the attempt to get behind knowledge claims and ask, What makes them possible?

The objects of human knowledge seem to fall into four main classes. We can see what Kant is up to if we frame a question with respect to each of these classes.

1. How is *mathematics* possible?
2. How is *natural science* possible?
3. How is *metaphysics* possible?
4. How is *morality* possible?

These are, in Kant's sense, "critical" questions. We are not going to develop mathematics, physics, metaphysics, or morality. But in each case we are going to look at the rational foundations on which these disciplines rest. What is it, for instance, about human reason that makes it possible to develop mathematics? What *structure, capacities,* and *concepts* must reason have for it to be *able* to do mathematics?

These are *reflective questions,* which together constitute a *critique of reason,* a critical examination of the way a rational mind works. Kant also calls

---

*Montaigne compares the problem to that of a man who does not know Socrates and is presented with a portrait of him. How can he tell whether it resembles Socrates?

this kind of investigation **transcendental.**[*] A *transcendental inquiry* reaches back into the activities of the mind and asks how it produces its results. If this kind of investigation succeeds, we'll know what the powers of reason are——and what they are not. We can, Kant thinks, determine the *limits* of rational knowledge. And this is most important. For if we can determine both the capacities and the limitations of human reason, we may be able to escape both of those evils between which philosophy has so often swung: *dogmatism* on the one hand, and *skepticism* on the other. From Kant's point of view, these extremes are well illustrated by Descartes and Hume, respectively.

---

1. What is the problem with the *representational theory of knowledge and perception* that Kant thinks can be resolved by imitating Copernicus?. How does a "Copernican turn" help?
2. What does a critique of reason try to uncover? In what sense will the answers be transcendental?

Judgments

Because all our claims to know are expressed in the form of judgments, the first task is to clarify the different kinds of judgments there are. Hume had divided our knowledge into relations of ideas and matters of fact.[†] Kant agrees that this is roughly right, but not precise enough. Hume's distinction runs together two quite different kinds of consideration. (1) There is an *epistemological* question involved: Does a bit of knowledge rest on experience, or not? (2) There is also a *semantic* question: How do the meanings of the words we use to express that knowledge relate to each other? Kant sorts these matters out, and the result is a classification of judgments into *four* groups rather than into Hume's two.

1. Epistemological
   1a. A judgment is *a priori* when it can be known to be true without any reference to experience. "7 + 5 = 12" is an example.
   1b. A judgment is *a posteriori* when we must appeal to experience to determine its truth or falsity. For instance, "John F. Kennedy was assassinated" cannot be known independently of experience.

2. Semantic
   2a. A judgment is **analytic** when its denial yields a contradiction. Here is an example Kant gives: "All bodies are extended." This is analytic because the predicate "extended" is already included as part of the subject, "bodies." To say that there is some body that is *not* extended is, in effect, to claim there can be some extended thing that is not extended. And that is contradictory. If an analytic judgment is true, it is necessarily true. The opposite of an analytic judgment is not possible. Since it is analytic that every father has a child, it is not possible that there should be a father without a child. And every father necessarily has a child.
   2b. A judgment is **synthetic** when it does more than simply explicate or analyze a concept. Here are some examples: "Every event has a cause," "Air has weight," and "John F. Kennedy was assassinated." Consider the first example. The concept *having a cause* is not part of the concept *being an event*. This is something Hume teaches us.[*] We can imagine that an event might simply occur without any cause. Even if we don't believe that ever happens, there is no contradiction in supposing it might. The opposite of synthetic judgments is always possible.

"Two things fill the mind with ever new and increasing admiration and awe . . . the starry heavens above me and the moral law within me."

—Immanuel Kant

These two pairs can be put together to give us four possibilities. In Kant's view, every judgment that is a candidate for being knowledge will belong to one or another of these four classes. Let us give some examples.

- *Analytic a priori:* "All bodies are extended." This is analytic, as we have seen, because "extended" is part of the definition of "body." It is a priori because we don't have to examine our experience of bodies to know it is true; all we need is to understand the meanings of the terms "body" and "extended."

- *Analytic a posteriori:* This class seems empty; if the test for analyticity is examining a judgment's denial for contradiction, it seems clear

that we do not also have to examine experience. Every analytic judgment must be a priori.

- *Synthetic a posteriori:* Here belong most of our judgments about experience, judgments of science and common sense alike, from particular judgments (e.g., "The water in the tea kettle is boiling") to general laws (e.g., "Water always boils at 100°C at sea level").

- *Synthetic a priori:* This is a puzzling and controversial class of judgments. If we were to know such a judgment as true, we would have to be able to know it quite independently of experience. This means that if such a judgment is true, it is true no matter what our experience shows us. Even if the events of experience were organized in a completely different way, a true judgment of this kind would remain true. And yet it is *not* true because it is analytic; its denial expresses a logical possibility.

We can represent these types in a matrix:

	A priori	*A posteriori*
Analytic	"Every mother has a child."	
Synthetic	"?"	"There is a Waterloo in both Iowa and Wisconsin."

There is something very odd about synthetic a priori judgments. Consider a judgment that is about experience. Suppose that it is synthetic, but that we can know it a priori. Because it is synthetic, its opposite is (from a logical point of view) a real possibility. And yet we can know—without appealing to experience—that this possibility is never realized! How can this be?

Kant believes that the solution to the dilemmas of past philosophy lies precisely in the recognition that we are in possession of synthetic a priori judgments. It is his Copernican revolution in philosophy that makes this recognition possible. Think: On the assumption that objects are realities independent of our knowing them, it would be crazy to suppose that we could know them without experiencing them in some way; our thoughts about them would be one thing, the objects something quite different; and they could vary independently.* What could possibly guarantee that things would match our thoughts a priori? On the traditional correspondence assumption, then, a priori knowledge that is synthetic would be impossible.

But suppose that objects *are* objects only because they are structured in certain ways by the mind in the very act of knowing them. Then it is plausible to think that there might be *principles* of that structuring and that some of these principles might be synthetic. And those principles could be known a priori—independently of the objects they are structuring. So if Kant's Copernican revolution makes sense, there will be a priori synthetic principles for every domain of objects.

It is time to give some examples of judgments Kant considers to be both a priori and synthetic. You may be surprised by some of them.

- All the judgments of mathematics and geometry
- In natural science, such judgments as "Every event has a cause"
- In metaphysics, "There is a God," and "The soul is a simple substance, distinct from the body"
- In morality, the rule that we should not treat others merely as means to our own ends.

I do not mean to suggest that we *know* all these judgments, or that they are all true. That remains to be seen. But if you examine them, you should be able to see that they are all examples of judgments which would have to be known a priori (i.e., not from experience), if at all. And examination should also confirm, Kant thinks, that they are all synthetic. None of them is true simply in virtue of how the terms are related to each other.

Kant wants to understand how mathematics, natural science, metaphysics, and morality are possible. In the light of his Copernican revolution, we can see that he is asking how the rational mind structures its objects into the objects of mathematics, natural science, metaphysics, and morality. It must be that implicit in the foundations of all these disciplines are some judgments that do not arise out of experience but *prescribe* how the objects of experience *must be*. All four of these areas are constituted by synthetic a priori judgments. The objects we encounter are—in part—*constructions*. And these judgments are *principles for the construction of objects*.

Kant sometimes calls a priori judgments "pure." By this, he means that they are not "contaminated" by experience. We can now restate his questions with a transcendental twist:

1. How is *pure* mathematics possible?
2. How is *pure* natural science possible?
3. How is *pure* metaphysics possible?
4. How is *pure* morality possible?

Let's examine his answers.

---

1. Give examples of your own for each of the four types of judgment.
2. Explain the idea of a synthetic a priori judgment, showing clearly both its semantic and its epistemological aspects.
3. What makes a priori synthetic judgments puzzling?

Geometry, Mathematics, Space, and Time

It would be useful to have a criterion by which we could distinguish a priori knowledge from a posteriori knowledge. Kant suggests that there are two tests we can use: *necessity* and *universality*.

Experience teaches us that a thing is so and so, but not that it cannot be otherwise. First, then, if we

---

*Compare Ockham's reflections on God's omnipotence, pp. 294–295.

have a proposition which in being thought is thought as *necessary,* it is an *a priori* judgment. . . . Secondly, experience never confers on its judgments true or strict, but only assumed and comparative *universality,* through induction. . . . Necessity and strict universality are thus sure criteria of *a priori* knowledge, and are inseparable from one another. (*CPR,* 43–44)

As Hume has taught us, necessity cannot be discovered by means of experience; as far as experience tells us, all events are "entirely loose and separate." Further, because experience is limited in extent, it cannot guarantee that a proposition is universally true (i.e., true everywhere and at all times). It follows that if we find a judgment that is either necessarily true or universally true, we can be sure that it does not have its justification in experience. Such a judgment must be a priori.

Mathematical truths are both necessary and universal. They are, therefore, clear examples of a priori judgments. But are they analytic or synthetic?

> One might indeed think at first that the proposition 7 + 5 = 12 is a merely analytic proposition, which follows according to the principle of contradiction from the concept of a sum of seven and five. But if we look more closely, we find that the concept of the sum of 7 and 5 contains nothing further than the unification of the two numbers into a single number, and in this we do not in the least think what this single number may be which combines the two . . . and though I may analyze my concept of such a possible sum as long as I please, I shall never find the twelve in it. We have to go outside these concepts by resorting to the intuition which corresponds to one of them, our five fingers for instance . . . and thus add to the concept of seven, one by one, the units of five given in intuition. . . .
>
> Nor is any principle of pure geometry analytic. That the straight line between two points is the shortest is a synthetic proposition. My concept of the straight contains nothing of magnitude but only a quality. The concept of the shortest is therefore wholly an addition, and cannot be drawn by any analysis from the concept of the straight line. Intuition, by means of which alone the synthesis is possible, must therefore be called in here to help. (*P,* 74)

Hume suggests that the truths of mathematics are simply matters of how ideas are related to each other—that they are analytic and can be known by appeal to the principle of contradiction. Kant argues that this is not so. For "7 + 5 = 12" to be analytic, the concept "12" would have to be included in the concept "7 + 5." But all that concept tells us, if Kant is right, is that two numbers are being added. It does not, of itself, tell us what the sum is.

What can tell us what the sum is? Only some *intuition,* Kant says.* An intuition is not anything mysterious or occult. By "intuition" Kant simply means the presentation of some sensible object to the mind. That is why we need the five fingers. We must "add successively" the units presented in the intuition: We count, one finger at a time. Knowing that 7 + 5 = 12 is a *process.* We *construct* mathematics by inscribing it on a background composed of objects or sets of objects.

But we need to understand these objects more clearly. If mathematics were only about the objects of experience, it could be neither necessary nor universal. We might know that these five oranges and those seven oranges happen to make twelve oranges. But we wouldn't know that *all* such groups of oranges (examined or not) make twelve and *must* make twelve. If we know this with necessity and universality (as we surely do), the objects that justify mathematical truths must themselves be known in a purely a priori manner. There must be *pure* intuitions, forms of *pure sensibility.* But what could they be?

> Now space and time are the two intuitions on which pure mathematics grounds all its cognitions and judgements. . . . Geometry is grounded on the pure intuition of space. Arithmetic forms its own concepts of numbers by successive addition of units in time. (*P,* 90)

Think about space a moment. According to our ordinary experience, space is filled with things. But

---

*Kant is the ancestor of a school in the philosophy of mathematics that still has distinguished adherents. The viewpoint is called "intuitionism" but might more accurately be termed "constructivism."

suppose you "think away" all these things—all the household goods, the clothes, the houses, the earth itself, sun, moon, and stars. Have you thought away space? Kant thinks not. (Newton would have agreed.) But you have "subtracted" everything *empirical*—that is, everything that gives particular content to our experience. All that is left is a kind of container, a form or structure, in which empirical things can be put. But, since you have gotten rid of everything empirical, what is left is *pure.* And it can be known a priori. Geometry is the science of this pure intuition of space.[*]

But what is the status of the intuition itself? Could space simply be one more (rather abstract and esoteric) object independent of our perception of it? Kant doesn't think so. And the reason is this: The truths of geometry, like those of mathematics, are *necessary.* If you ask, "How *likely* is it that any given straight line is the shortest distance between its end points?" you demonstrate that you haven't understood geometry! Moreover, that a straight line in a plane is the shortest distance between two points is something we know to be universally true. If space were an object independent of our minds, knowing this would be impossible. We would have to say that this is true *for all the spaces we have examined,* but beyond that—who knows? Geometers do not proceed in this manner. They neither make experiments concerning space nor suppose that unexamined space could have a different structure. Yet geometry is the science of space. How can this be?

The explanation must be this: Space is not something "out there" to be discovered; space is a form of the mind itself. It is a pure intuition providing a "structure" into which all our more determinate perceptions *must fit.* When you handle an apple, your experience is constituted on the one hand by sensations (color, texture, weight, and so on) and on the other hand by a form or structure into which these sensations fit (the pure intuition of space). The apple is not an object entirely independent of our perception of it. Part of that perception is constituted by the intuition of space, which we do not *abstract from* the experience, but *bring to* the experience.

This has an important consequence. We cannot experience the apple as it is in itself, independent of our perception of it. Why not? Because part of what it is to *be* an apple is to be in space; and space is an aspect of our experience that comes from the side of the subject. So we know the apple as it *appears to us,* not the apple as it *is in itself.* What goes for the apple goes for the entire world. We can only know how things *appear.*

> Things are given to us as objects of our senses situated outside us, but of what they may be in themselves we know nothing; we only know their appearances, i.e. the representations which they bring about in us when they affect our senses. Consequently I do indeed admit that there are bodies outside us, i.e. things which, although wholly unknown to us, i.e. as to what they may be in themselves, we know through the representations which their influence on our sensibility provides for us, and to which we give the name of bodies. This word therefore merely means the appearance of that for us unknown but nonetheless actual object. (*P,* 95)[*]

Just as space is the pure intuition that makes geometry possible, time is the pure intuition that makes mathematics possible. Geometrical figures are constructed on the pure (spatial) intuition in which *external* objects are experienced. Numbers and their relations are constructed on the pure (temporal) intuition in which *any* objects (including mental events) are experienced. An elementary example of constructing in time is counting, where we construct one number *after* another.

Kant has now answered his first question. Pure geometry and mathematics are possible because their objects—space and time—are not independent of the mind that knows them; space and time are pure forms of sensible intuition. He has shown, moreover, that geometry and mathematics essen-

---

[*]Kant is referring to Euclidean geometry, of course. Various non-Euclidean geometries were discovered—or constructed—in the nineteenth century.

[*]Note that this conclusion squares with Locke's belief about the unknowability of substance. Here, however, that conviction is set in a much more rigorous framework and is much more adequately argued for. See pp. 374–376 for Locke on substance.

tially involve judgments that are synthetic (because they are constructive) and a priori (because they are necessary and universal).

Because experience is always in time—and in space as well if it is of external objects—it is experience of the *appearances* of things; it is a *product* of contributions from two sides: the objective and the subjective. Nowhere can we know things as they are in themselves. It is not as Descartes thinks, that we know things-in-themselves in a confused and inadequate way that can be continually improved. We do not know them at all! Of the objects we do experience, we can know a priori just what we ourselves, as rational minds, necessarily supply in experiencing them.

1. Explain why Kant thinks that mathematical and geometrical propositions are both a priori and synthetic.
2. What is Kant's argument that space and time must be "pure" or a priori forms of intuition?
3. How do Kant's reflections on space and time lead to the conclusion that we can know things only as they appear to us, not as they are in themselves?

Common Sense, Science, and the A Priori Categories

Pure mathematics does not exhaust our knowledge. We know many things in the course of our ordinary life and through Newtonian science. What is the application of Kant's Copernican revolution in these spheres? One thing we know already. Whatever common sense and science may reveal, they will not be able to penetrate the veil of our pure sensible intuitions, which structure all possible objects in space and time. In these fields, too, we will be unable to reach to things in themselves; all our knowledge will concern how these things *appear* to us.

To deal with his second question, how pure natural science is possible, Kant needs to clarify a distinction between two aspects or powers of the mind. He calls them *sensibility* and *understanding*. The former is a passive power, the ability to receive impressions. The latter is an active power, the power to think objects by constructing a representation of them using concepts.

What is it to have a concept anyway—any kind of concept? At this point, Kant makes a significant advance over the empiricists. They all think that our "ideas" *derive* from sense experience. Exactly what this means for Locke is none too clear, but it is crystal clear in Berkeley and Hume. Ideas, they say, are faint copies or images of sensations, a kind of less vivid imprint left on the mind when the sensation itself fades. According to this way of thinking, we are as passive with respect to ideas as we are in our sense experience. (True, we can put ideas together in complex ways, but the ideas themselves are simply there—feeble impressions.)

Kant doesn't deny that we have such images, but a Kantian concept is a different kind of thing altogether. A *concept*, Kant tells us, is a kind of rule for operating on intuitions. In itself, it needn't have any sensuous content at all. To have a concept is to have an ability. And in the use of concepts the understanding is *active*, not passive. Think of the concept *viper*. To be in possession of this concept is to be able to sort snakes (or maybe cars!) into vipers and nonvipers. Having the concept is *not* having an image or a Lockean abstract idea in your mind. To have the concept is to be able to use a rule for dividing the snakish parts of our experience into categories or classes of things. Kant says,

Our knowledge springs from two fundamental sources of the mind; the first is the capacity of receiving representations (receptivity for impressions), the second is the power of knowing an object through these representations (spontaneity [in the production] of concepts). Through the first an object is *given* to us, through the second the object is *thought*. . . . Intuition and concepts constitute, therefore, the elements of all our knowledge, so that neither concepts without an intuition in some way corresponding to them, nor intuition without concepts, can yield knowledge. Both may be either pure or empirical. When they contain sensation (which presupposes the actual presence of the object), they are empirical. When there is no min-gling of sensation with the representation, they are pure. (*CPR*, 92)

Kant's general term for the contents of the mind is "representation." He is here telling us that our representations can be of several different kinds: pure or empirical, intuitive or conceptual. In fact, this gives us a matrix of four possibilities; let us set them out with some examples:

Representations

	Pure	Empirical
Intuitions (from sensibility)	Space and time	Sensations of red, warm, hard, etc.
Concepts (from understanding)	Straight, cause, substance, God, the soul	Cherry pie, otter, water, the sun, unicorn, etc.

We have not determined whether all these representations actually *represent* something, but we know that any concept that does represent something will have to do it in tandem with some intuition. For "neither concepts without an intuition . . . nor intuition without concepts, can yield knowledge." The dove cannot fly in empty space.

Kant has contrasted sensibility with understanding, intuitions with concepts. But he is also convinced that they must work together.

> To neither of these powers may a preference be given over the other. Without sensibility no object would be given to us, without understanding no object would be thought. Thoughts without content are empty, intuitions without concepts are blind. It is, therefore, just as necessary to make our concepts sensible, that is, to add the object to them in intuition, as to make our intuitions intelligible, that is, to bring them under concepts. . . . The understanding can intuit nothing, the senses can think nothing. Only through their union can knowledge arise. (*CPR*, 93)

In addition to the *pure* intuitions that can be known a priori (i.e., space and time), we have em-

pirical intuitions—what Locke calls "sensations" and Hume calls "impressions." Kant thinks of sensations as the *matter* of sensible objects. We can illustrate by imagining a square cut out of wood. The spatial properties of a square (four equal straight lines, four right angles) can be known a priori, quite independent of whether it is red or brown, warm or cold, smooth or rough. But it can only be some *particular* square if it is either red or some other color, either warm or not, either smooth or less than smooth. Our sensations determine which it is. They provide the "filling" or content for the purely formal intuition of a square.*

Are concepts like this, too? Do we have pure concepts, as well as empirical concepts? Well, suppose there were concepts that we *necessarily* made use of whenever we thought of any object at all. Remembering that necessity is one of the marks of the a priori, we would have to conclude that we have pure or a priori concepts. This is, in fact, just what Kant thinks; he is convinced that we make use of pure concepts all the time. In fact, these concepts—these *a priori rules*—do for our understanding exactly what the pure intuitions of space and time do for sensibility: They give it structure and organization. They make it possible for us to experience *objects* and not just a chaos of impressions.

Just as there are empirical intuitions, there are empirical concepts. Just as there are pure intuitions, there are pure concepts.† Like sensibility, the understanding brings something of its own to experience. In neither dimension is the mind just "white paper" on which experience writes, as Locke claimed. It is this rich source of structure in our experience, this transcendental organizing power, that Kant wants to uncover through his critique of reason.

The question then forces itself upon us: What concepts do we have that *apply* to objects but are

---

*The pattern of thought here should remind you of the distinction between matter and form in Aristotle and Aquinas; *sensation* plays the role of matter, and *concepts* play the role of form. Though there is a structural similarity, there is a fundamental difference: In Kant both members of the pair have their being only *relative to a mind*. In this Kant shows his debt to Locke and his successors. And in this Kant is characteristically "modern."
†Check the examples again in the chart above.

not *derived* from them? We are searching for a set of concepts we use necessarily in thinking of an object. These will be a priori concepts. Kant calls them "categories" because they will supply the most general characteristics of things: the characteristics it takes to qualify as a thing or object at all.*

How can we discover these concepts? Critical philosophy, you will remember, is reflective or transcendental in nature. So we need to reflect on our thinking, to see whether there are some features of our thinking about objects that must be present no matter what the object is.

Let's begin by asking, What is it to think of an *object,* anyway? Consider the contrast between these two judgments:

A: "It seems as if there is a heavy book before me."

B: "The book before me is heavy."

What is the difference? In a certain sense, they both have the same content: book, heavy, before me. Yet there is a crucial difference. What is it? Isn't it just that *B* is a judgment about an *object,* whereas *A* pulls back from making a judgment about that object? *A* is a judgment, not about the book, but about *my perception;* it has only what Kant calls "subjective validity." *B,* however, is a judgment about *the book.* It is an "objective" judgment; whether true or false, it makes a claim that an object has a certain characteristic.

What makes this difference? It can't be the empirical concepts involved, because "book" and "heavy" and "before me" are the same in *A* and *B.* Nor can the difference be anything derived from

my experience in the two cases, since my experience may be exactly the same in each. So the difference must be an a priori one. It seems to be a difference in the *manner* in which the judgments are made, or in the *form* of the judgments. If we can isolate the feature that distinguishes *B* from *A,* we will have put our finger on something necessary for objective judgments—that is, for thinking about a world of objects. We will have isolated the contribution the *understanding* makes to our experience of an objective world.

In this case, Kant tells us, the distinguishing feature is that in *B* we are thinking in terms of a *substance* together with its *properties.* These concepts are not derived from what is given in my sensations (since the sensations are exactly the same in *A*). These concepts are brought to the experience by the understanding in the very form of thinking of the book as an object. The book is a substance that has the property of being heavy. But this means that the concepts "substance" and "property" are a priori concepts—and that is just what we are looking for.

The point is this: In thinking of an objective world, thinking necessarily takes certain forms of organization. One of these forms consists of a kind of logical function or rule: *Structure experience in terms of substances having properties.* Unless thoughts take this logical form, Kant says, a world of objects simply cannot be conceived at all. Without the application of these a priori concepts, there can be no objective world for common sense or science to know. So a world of objects is, like the world of sensible intuitions, a composite. There is an empirical aspect to it (expressed in empirical concepts such as "book" and "heavy"). But there is also an a priori aspect to it (expressed in nonempirical concepts such as "substance" and "property"). Experience of an objective world requires both.

Kant works out an entire system of such a priori concepts or categories. He thinks he can do this by canvassing all the possible forms objective judgments can take. And he thinks he can do that because he assumes that logic (the science of the forms of judgment) is a closed and finished science; no essential changes, he observes, have occurred in

---

*You can see that Kant is embarked on a project similar to that of Aristotle: to discover the characteristics of being qua being. Aristotle also produces a set of categories, displaying the most general ways in which something (anything) can *be.* (See p. 160.) Kant goes about the project in a roughly similar way: He looks at the language in which we talk about objects. Between Kant and Aristotle, however, there stands the Kantian Copernican revolution—and that makes a tremendous difference. Kant's "categories," the universal and necessary features of objects, originate in the structure of *thinking* about those objects. They apply not to being *as such,* but to being *as it is knowable* by rational minds such as ours—that is, to appearance.

it since Aristotle.* For each possible form of judgment (he thinks there are twelve such forms) he finds an a priori concept that we bring to bear on sensations. In each case, the application of this concept produces an a priori characteristic of the objective world of our experience. So Kant identifies twelve categories—twelve general ways we know that any objective world *must* be. The fact that the world of our experience must be structured in terms of substances-having-properties is just one of these ways. We will examine only one other, passing over much of the detail of Kant's treatment.

The a priori concept of substance gets an opportunity, so to speak, to apply to experience because sensations come grouped together in various ways in *space*. Considered just as sensations, my experience of what I call the book hangs together in a certain way; the color, texture, shape, and so on move together across my field of vision.† If this were not so, I could scarcely unify these sensations under one concept and experience one object, the book. In a similar way, sensations also appear *successively in time*. This provides a foothold for another of the categories: *causation*.

We have examined Hume's powerful argument that our idea of cause is not an empirical idea—that it is not abstracted from our experience.‡ Because it contains the notion of a necessary connection between cause and effect, Hume concludes that the idea is a fiction, a kind of illusion produced in us by custom. So we cannot really know that objects are related to each other by cause and effect.

But what if there simply couldn't *be* objects at all unless they were set in causal relations with each other? What if the concept of causation (like the concept of substance) is a necessary aspect of any world of objects? This is the possibility that Kant's Copernican revolution explores. If nothing could *be* objective for us without *appearing* in a context of causal relations, we could know that every event has a cause—and avoid Hume's skeptical conclusions.

Can Kant convince us that this is so? Again Kant shows us that there is a difference between judgments that refer only to our perceptions and objective judgments. It may *seem* to us that one thing follows necessarily upon another, but once we affirm the idea of a world of objects, we are committed to there being a rule that it *must* be so. Suppose that something unusual happens. What will we do? We will ask why. We will search for its cause. Will we allow the possibility that this event had no cause? Certainly not. But what if we search and search and do not discover its cause (e.g., the cause for a certain kind of cancer)? Will we finally conclude that it has no cause? Of course not. No degree of failure in finding its cause would ever convince us that it has no cause. *Every* event has a cause.

How do we know that? We have seen that it is not analytic. How do we know that this conviction is not a mere prejudice on our part? Our confidence cannot be based on an induction from past successes in finding causes, for that would never justify our certainty that even unexamined events must have causes. That we learned from Hume. If we know that every event has a cause, we know it because part of the very idea of an objective world is that events in it are structured by rules of succession we don't control. There *could not be* an objective world that was not organized by cause and effect.

Think of it this way: If there were no necessary order in the succession of events, this succession could not be distinguished from sheer fancy, dream, or imagination. Its being subject to a rule determining that when *X* happens, *Y* must necessarily happen is just what *makes* it objective. Objective worlds (as opposed to subjective fancies) are just those that do have such a causal structure in time.*

---

*We now know that Kant's list of the possible forms of judgments is not, as he thinks, complete. Logic has gone through a revolution since Kant's time.

†Appearing together that way constitutes what Berkeley calls a "combination" of ideas and Hume a "bundle" of impressions. (See pp. 392, 412.) For Berkeley, such a combination *is* a thing; for Kant it is the *appearance* of a thing (which in itself is unknown to us).

‡Review this argument on pp. 403–409.

---

*Think again about Descartes' final dismissal of the dream-threat (p. 356). Dreams, he says, do not have that "unbroken connection" to the rest of life that real things have. Kant would love

BARUCH SPINOZA

Expelled with curses from the Amsterdam synagogue in 1656, Baruch Spinoza (1632–1677) has been characterized both as a "God-intoxicated man" and as an atheistic naturalist. Fundamentally, he is one of the most rationalistic of philosophers. His major work, *The Ethics,* published posthumously, is written in geometrical form; that is, its propositions are deduced from definitions and axioms. Spinoza's aim is to attain a secure happiness by approaching as closely as possible an adequate understanding of absolutely everything.

He defines "substance" as what exists "in itself" and requires nothing beyond itself for its being. He argues that substance must be infinite and that there cannot be two such substances (otherwise each would limit the other and defeat the infinity). So there can be but one substance, which can equally well be called God or Nature. This means that the individuals of our experience—from stones to ourselves—are not substances, but modifications of the one infinite substance.

Mind and body are not substances, as Descartes thought, but attributes under which the one substance can be conceived. In fact, for every natural body, there is an idea; the idea corresponding to a human body is what we call the mind. It follows that every bodily change is a mental change, and vice versa.

Because everything that happens is a necessary expression of the immutable divine nature, there is no free will in the ordinary sense. Freedom, Spinoza claims, is just the power to act from one's own nature, unconstrained by anything outside oneself. God (or Nature), then, is the only completely free being, since God is the only thing for which there is nothing outside itself.

We, for the most part, are in "bondage," since we are controlled by emotions (desire, love, hate) that we passively suffer; emotions are *caused* in us. But our freedom expands as we act from "adequate ideas" that are part of our own nature. Since the only truly adequate ideas are those in God's mind, we move toward freedom by the intellectual love of God, coming to see the necessities of the world as God sees them. Such knowledge is the source of power to act (rather than react), of virtue, and of joy. Thus we can approximate the blessed life of God.

The concept of causality *does* apply to the world we experience—not because we discover it there, but because we bring it with us to the experience.

> This complete solution to the Humean problem . . . thus rescues their a priori origin for the pure concepts of the understanding, and their validity for the universal laws of nature . . . but in such a way that it limits their use to experience only. (P, 117–118)

Let us sum up. The principle that every event has a cause is, as we have seen, synthetic (the concept of causation is not included in the concept of an event but is added to it). And Hume is right that the causal principle cannot be known a posteriori, from experience. But we know that the principle applies universally and necessarily to all experience. We know that because, as Kant says, experience is derived from it. The principle that every event has a cause is, then, one of the synthetic a priori judgments. Such purely rational, nonempirical principles, Kant believes, lie at the root of both commonsense knowledge and Newtonian science.

Now we can see that Kant has answered the question as to how science of nature is possible. It is possible because nature itself (the objective world that is there to be known) is partially constituted by the concepts and principles that a rational mind must use in understanding it. We know a priori that nature is made up of substances-having-properties, though only through experience can we know which substances have what properties. We know a priori that the world is a causally ordered whole, though only through experience can we know which particular events cause what other events. Science, to-

---

this; it is just such unbroken connections of causality— in contrast to dreams—that *constitute* a world as an objective world.

gether with its pure or a priori part, is possible only because it is the knowledge of an objective world that is not independent of our minds. Natural science is possible only on the basis of Kant's Copernican revolution.

Let us just remind ourselves once more of the consequence: We have, and can have, no knowledge whatever about things as they are "in themselves." Do things-in-themselves—independently of how we know them—occupy space? *We have no idea.* Are they located in time, so that one event really does happen after another? *We have no idea.* Are there things (substances) at all? Does one event really cause another? *We have no idea.* Our knowledge is solely about the way things appear to us.

But, we must add, it does not follow that our knowledge is in any way illusory. It is not like a dream or a fancy of our imagination. The distinction, in fact, between illusion and reality is one drawn by us *within* this objective world of appearance—not *between* it and something else. Dreams and illusions are just sequences that cannot be ordered by the regularity of causal law; that is why they lack objectivity and are taken to be purely subjective phenomena. We are not capable of knowing anything *more real* than the spatiotemporal world of our experience, structured as it is by the categories of the pure understanding. This world may be "transcendentally ideal" (that is, its basic features are not independent of the knowing mind), but it is *empirically real.*

This, perhaps, needs a bit more explanation.

Phenomena and Noumena

"Thoughts without content are empty," Kant says, and "intuitions without concepts are blind" (*CPR,* 93). Thoughts are made up of concepts united in various ways. But unless those concepts are given a content through some intuition, either pure (as in geometry) or empirical (as in physics), they are "empty"—sheer rules that for all we know may apply to nothing. They provide us with no knowledge. However, merely having an intuition of space, or of blue-and-solid, provides no knowledge either. Intuitions without concepts are "blind." To

know, or to "see" the truth, we must have concepts that are applied to some matter.

> We demand in every concept, first, the logical form of a concept (of thought) in general, and secondly, the possibility of giving it an object to which it may be applied. . . . Therefore all concepts, and with them all principles, even such as are possible *a priori,* relate to empirical intuitions, that is, to the data for a possible experience. Apart from this relation they have no objective validity, and in respect of their representations are a mere play of imagination or of understanding. (*CPR,* 259)

Kant insists on this point again and again, for we are

> subject to an illusion from which it is difficult to escape. The categories are not, as regards their origin, grounded in sensibility, . . . and they seem, therefore, to allow of an application extending beyond all objects of the senses. (*CPR,* 266)

We have ideas of "substance," for example, and "cause." And it seems there is no barrier to applying them even beyond the boundaries of **possible experience.** In fact, nearly all previous philosophers think we can do that! Plato, for example, is convinced that reality is composed of *substances* (the Forms) that cannot be sensed but are purely intelligible. Descartes asks about the *cause* of his idea of God. One of the assumptions of traditional metaphysics is that these concepts *can* take us beyond the sphere of experience.* But, if Kant is right, these concepts

> are nothing but *forms of thought,* which contain the merely logical faculty of uniting *a priori* in one consciousness the manifold given in intuition; and apart, therefore, from the only intuition that is pos-

---

*Notice how Kant has turned completely upside down Plato's claim that knowledge is restricted to the purely intelligible world of Forms. For Kant, this realm beyond any possible sensory experience cannot be known at all; what we can know is the changing world of the senses, about which Plato thinks we can have only opinions. Here we have yet another example of the radical consequences of modern science for traditional epistemology and metaphysics; for Kant's confidence in knowledge of the sensory world rests ultimately on the achievement of Newton.

GOTTFRIED WILHELM VON LEIBNIZ

Mathematician, physicist, historian, theologian, and diplomat, Gottfried Wilhelm von Leibniz (1646–1714) wrote voluminously; among his most philosophically important works are *Discourse on Metaphysics* (1686) and *Monadology* (1714).

As an inventor of calculus, Leibniz was poised to make use of the principles of continuity and infinity in his philosophical work. He objected to the purely quantitative, geometrical account of matter (as extension) given by Descartes and Spinoza. Sheer extension does not account for resistance, solidity, and impenetrability, he argued, so there must be some real qualitative thing to be extended. A new concept of substance was needed, and Leibniz offered one: A substance is a being capable of action. This makes reality intrinsically dynamic; the ultimate substances are points of activity (force), each with an inherent tendency toward motion (in his view, rest is just infinitesimally small movement). He called these simple substances *monads*.

Though each monad is intrinsically simple, each has infinitely many properties—namely, the ways it is related to each of the infinitely many other monads. So each monad, in a way, mirrors or reflects the entire universe; in certain monads, this reflection is perception and the mind. If you knew any monad completely, you would know everything.

Because each monad mirrors all the others, a change in one would necessitate a change in all the others. The sum total of all the substances that are possible along with a given monad—mirrored in it—constitute a *possible world*. There are many possible worlds, many families of possible monads; this actual world is just one of the possibilities. Contrary to Spinoza, then, Leibniz held that the actual universe does not exist of necessity.

Why is it *this* world, out of all the many possible worlds, that is the actual one? We can figuratively imagine God—the one being that is not merely possible, but necessarily existing—contemplating all the possible worlds and choosing one to actualize. He would clearly choose the "best" one, the one most like God himself, who is perfectly actual. This would be the universe that combines the most actuality (the richest variety of content) with the greatest simplicity of laws. In that sense, Leibniz believed, we live in the best of all possible worlds.

---

sible for us, they have even less meaning than the pure sensible forms [space and time]. (*CPR*, 266)

The categories, Kant claims, cannot be used apart from sensible intuitions to give us knowledge of objects. Why not? Because they are merely "forms of thought." Compare them to mathematical functions, such as x^2. Until some number is given as x, we have no object. If a content for x is supplied, say 2 or 3, then an object is specified—in these cases the numbers 4 or 9. The categories of substance, cause, and the rest are similar. They are merely operators, the function of which is to unite "in one consciousness the manifold given in intuition." If a certain manifold of sensations is given, our possession of the concept "substance" allows us to produce the thought of a book; a different manifold of sensations produces the thought of a printing press; and the category of "causation" allows us to think a causal relation between the two. Objects are the result of the application of the categories as operators to some sensible material.

As we have seen, a concept is just a formal rule for structuring some material. The material is supplied by our intuitions. Without the sensible intuitions, there are no *objects*. But it can *seem* as though there are. This is the illusion.

> The categories . . . extend further than sensible intuition, since they think objects in general, without regard to the special mode (the sensibility) in which they may be given. But they do not thereby determine a greater sphere of objects. (*CPR*, 271)

The category of substance, for instance, is not inherently limited to the objects of sensory experience, or even, for that matter, to space and time. It seems we can have the idea of a nonmaterial, nonspatial, nontemporal substance. Nothing easier! But

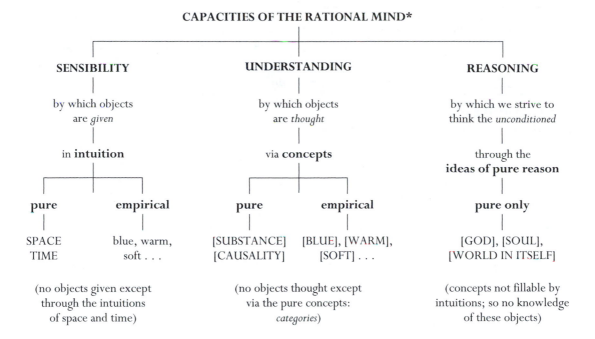

CAPACITIES OF THE RATIONAL MIND*

SENSIBILITY	UNDERSTANDING	REASONING
by which objects are *given*	by which objects are *thought*	by which we strive to think the *unconditioned*
in **intuition**	via **concepts**	through the **ideas of pure reason**

pure	**empirical**	**pure**	**empirical**	**pure only**
SPACE TIME	blue, warm, soft . . .	[SUBSTANCE] [CAUSALITY]	[BLUE], [WARM], [SOFT] . . .	[GOD], [SOUL], [WORLD IN ITSELF]

(no objects given except through the intuitions of space and time)	(no objects thought except via the pure concepts: *categories*)	(concepts not fillable by intuitions; so no knowledge of these objects)

this is profoundly illusory, if Kant is right. Why? Because the concept "substance" is not a complete concept in its own right. It is only a kind of *rule* for organizing some content or other. And the content must be given by intuition.

It is perhaps not impossible for there to be other forms of intuition than those available to us. We human beings, however, are limited to space, time, and sensation. To treat the categories as concepts that can give us knowledge beyond these limitations is to suppose that we have types of intuition that we do not have. And that is to fall into the illusion.

One common form of the illusion is the claim that we can know things as they are, apart from the way they appear to us. This is the illusion of speculative metaphysics. The illusion is reinforced because we do have the concept of **things-in-themselves.** Kant even gives it a name: Something as it is in itself, independently of the way it reveals itself to us, is called a **noumenon.** This contrasts with a **phenomenon,** its appearance to us.

But it is crucial to observe that this concept of a noumenon is not a concept with any positive meaning. Its role in our intellectual life is purely negative; it reminds us that there are things we cannot know—namely what the things affecting our sensibility are *really* like (if by "really" we mean what they are like independently of our intuitions of them). The phenomenal world of appearance is all we can ever know.

Kant once more drives home the moral:

Understanding and *sensibility,* with us, can determine objects *only when they are employed in conjunction.* When we separate them, we have intuitions without concepts, or concepts without intuitions— in both cases, representations which we are not in a position to apply to any determinate object. (*CPR,* 274)

1. What does it mean that the dove cannot fly in empty space? Relate this aphorism to the notions of concept and intuition.
2. Explain the role Kant assigns to the categories, illustrating it with the examples of substance/properties and cause/effect. How are these a priori concepts related to the objects of our common experience?
3. Explain the famous Kantian dictum: "Thoughts without content are empty, intuitions without concepts are blind."

---

*Concepts are indicated by square brackets.

4. Explain the notion that our a priori concepts are the source of a powerful illusion—the illusion of speculative metaphysics.

Reasoning and the Ideas of Metaphysics: God, World, and Soul

Kant's third question concerns metaphysics. The term "metaphysics" has a precise meaning for Kant. Metaphysics contrasts sharply with both common sense and science. We have seen that the entire range of possible experience is governed by the *pure intuitions* of space and time, as well as by the *pure categories* of the understanding. These, together with *sensations,* constitute the way things appear to us, the realm of phenomena. Beyond this realm, our understanding is without footing. We know there are things that appear to us, but we are completely at sea about what they may be in themselves. "Out there," the dove cannot fly.

Metaphysics looks in two directions. Understood in the traditional way, it is the discipline that tries to gain knowledge about things apart from their appearance to us. It is the attempt to go beyond experience in a *transcendent* direction, toward the *noumenal world,* which *transcends* all possible experience. But metaphysics can also look in the opposite direction: to the structures on the side of the subject that condition the being of objects. In this case, Kant calls it *transcendental.* It is just that critique of pure reason we have been examining; it tries only to discern the a priori conditions of experience. Such a transcendental investigation, looking back into the knowing subject, Kant also calls *immanent.*

Not surprisingly, Kant thinks the transcendent kind of metaphysics is impossible. But his discussion of the reasons for the impossibility are full of interesting insights. First, Kant claims to be able to explain why the quest for metaphysical knowledge recurs with such inevitability and why it is so difficult to give up. Second, he finds a positive use for the fundamental metaphysical ideas—God, the world, and the soul—even though he denies that these ideas can give us knowledge. Finally, Kant's examination of these ideas propels us into the fourth of

his major concerns, the practical use of reason, or morality.

The notion we can get knowledge of things-in-themselves is, Kant says, "a *natural* and inevitable *illusion*" (*CPR,* 300). Something in the very structure of rationality gives us that notion; it has to do with *reasoning.* The aim of reasoning is to supply "the reason why" something is true. As we have seen numerous times already, the why question can always be repeated; we can ask for the reason for the reason. Kant talks of this process as one that seeks the *conditions* that account for a given truth. Grass is green. Why? In answering this question, we refer to some condition in the world that explains that fact. Why is that condition the way it is? Again, we can supply a condition that explains that condition. And we could go on.

As you can see, the quest for reasons will not be satisfied until it finds some condition that doesn't need to be explained by a further condition. Reason is always searching for the *unconditioned.* We can think of this as Kant's version of the search for first principles. This has always been the task of first philosophy, or metaphysics. The search is for something intelligible in itself, which explains or makes intelligible all the rest.

> Reason can never be completely satisfied by any use of the rules of the understanding in experience, this use always remaining conditioned; and when reason demands completion of this chain of conditions, it drives the understanding out of its sphere, partly to represent objects of experience in a series so far extended that no experience whatever can comprehend it, partly even (in order to complete it), to seek *noumena* quite outside experience, to which the chain can be fastened; whereby reason, independent at long last of the conditions of experience, can nevertheless make its hold complete. (*P,* 137)

We can understand only what lies within the bounds of possible experience. But reason cannot be content with that. If those bounds are reached, reason still wants to ask why. Why is experience as a whole the way it is? Why is there experience at all? But this question can be answered only by transcending those boundaries. To ask for the condition that explains the absolute totality of all possible experience is no longer asking for the explanation of one phenomenon in terms of another—about which we might then ask the same question. It is asking for something absolute, for the unconditioned, which will necessarily involve knowledge of things-in-themselves.

And so arise, naturally and inevitably, those concepts of God, the world in itself, and the knowing subject or soul. These concepts are very different from all others. They are not empirical concepts abstracted from sensations. Nor are they a priori concepts structuring our experiences. Kant gives them a special name: *Ideas of Pure Reason.**

> Ideas lie in the nature of reason, as categories in the nature of the understanding, and if ideas carry with them an illusion which can easily mislead, this illusion is unavoidable, although "that it shall not seduce into error" can very well be achieved. (*P,* 133)

Reason can try to trace out the ultimate conditions in three different directions: back into the *subject* (trying to construct an absolute psychological Idea), out into the *world* (trying to discover the cosmological Ideas), and toward the *absolute condition of anything at all* (searching for the theological Idea). And so we find reason inevitably constructing the ideas of soul, world, and God.

The Soul

The outcome of Descartes' strategy of methodical doubt is that he cannot doubt his own existence. And when he asks himself what he is, the answer seems obvious: a thing that thinks. He "knows" that he is a substance whose essential characteristic is to think. Descartes, as we have seen, further claims that this substance is simple (indivisible), distinct from the body, unchanging through time, and immortal.

It is clear that Descartes is not doing empirical psychology here; there are no experiments, and he gathers no data. Kant calls this kind of thing **rational psychology.** Rational psychology is an attempt to understand the fundamental nature of the self by rational reflection on what the self *must* be if experience is to be possible. It is a quest for the *unconditioned condition* on the side of the subject. Kant is convinced that rational psychology is illusory, that there can be no such knowledge. But he also thinks that the illusion is a powerful one and difficult to resist. It arises from what Kant calls "the sole text of rational psychology," the judgment "I think" (*CPR,* 330). Reflection on this judgment alone seems to be enough to yield all the conclusions desired by the rational psychologist.

Is the soul a substance? It seems as though I can conclude that I am a substance. Here is the argument. Every thought I have can be preceded (at least implicitly) by the phrase, "I think." I think roses are lovely; I think eggs come from chickens; I think Kant is a great philosopher. All these thoughts belong to me; they are qualities or properties of myself. But what about the "I"? Could this "I" be simply a property or characteristic? Of what? The idea that *I* might be just a property of some other substance doesn't seem to make sense. *I* am the absolute subject of all these determinations. But this is just what we mean by substance; a substance is, by definition, that which cannot be predicated of anything else but is the subject of properties.* So I, as a thinking thing, must be a substance.

This seems a persuasive argument, but, if Kant is right, it is a mere sophism. Remember that "substance" is one of the a priori categories. This means that it is a concept that is purely formal in itself, without any content. Its whole function is to serve as a kind of rule for organizing sensible intuitions into experience. But where is the intuition that corresponds to the "I"? Kant agrees with Hume, who claims not to be able to find any perception of the self when he introspects.† When you say "I think,"

---

*Kant has Plato explicitly in mind here. In Plato the "Forms" or "Ideas" are purely intelligible entities that can be understood but not sensed. For Kant, of course, the Ideas are concepts, not realities; and they can give us no knowledge. But they are concepts that *aim* to present realities beyond sensory experience. For Plato on the Forms, see pp. 121–126.

*This idea of substance can be traced back to Aristotle's discussion of the categories of being. Substance is basic in the sense that all other modes of being (qualities, relations, and so on) depend on substance. See p. 161 for a brief discussion of this point.
†For Hume on the self, see "The Disappearing Self," in Chapter 15.

you are not peering at or describing your self. The whole content of what you think is expressed in what comes *after* that phrase.

> The "I" is indeed in all thoughts, but there is not in this representation the least trace of intuition, distinguishing the "I" from other objects of intuition.
>   We do not have, and cannot have, any knowledge whatsoever of any such subject. (*CPR,* 334)

Reason is always searching for the conditions that make experience possible. In looking back and back into myself, I seem to come upon the idea that there is a substance to which all these mental activities belong. But this is a kind of grammatical or logical illusion. Just because I need to express my thinking by using subject/predicate forms in which the "I" occurs, I cannot infer that *noumenal reality* is structured that way. I cannot transform a *semantic* necessity in the way I represent myself into a *metaphysical* necessity concerning my nature.

Kant says that the "I" in "I think" is just a kind of formal marker. Concepts such as this (others are "now" and "here" and "this") are sometimes called "indexicals"; what is peculiar about them is that they have no determinate content but merely indicate something relative to the circumstances of utterance. About the term "I," Kant says, "we cannot even say that this is a concept, but only that it is a bare consciousness which accompanies all concepts" (*CPR,* 331). All knowledge, however, is through concepts. So the "I" is nothing more than an empty representation of an unknown *X,* "this I or he or it (the thing) which thinks" (*CPR,* 331). What I am in myself is completely unknown to me. For all that rational reflection can tell me, this *X* that I am may be anything at all. I do not know that I am a substance. The self or soul, then, is merely that unknown *X* to whom the world appears and by which it is structured into objects.[*]

Kant calls this *X* the "transcendental unity of apperception." This mouthful needs a bit of explaining. There is a *unity* in conscious experience—as

though we see everything at a given moment from a single point of view. Consciousness, moreover, is not merely passive reception of data (*a la* writing on Locke's white paper) but is intensely active. When we perceive, we are *aware* that we are perceiving—hence *apperceiving.* And this *X* is *transcendental* in the sense that it is a condition of experience that cannot itself be experienced. Hence, it cannot be given in intuition or brought under the categories; and so it cannot be known to be a substance.

Similar reflections undermine the claims about the soul's simplicity, its unchanging nature, and its immortality. In each case a *merely subjective condition* of thinking is transformed into a concept of a *noumenal object.* The "I," however, the transcendental ego, is not an object and cannot be known as an object. The "I" is a *subject* and *resists objectification.* As far as rational knowledge goes, the subject of thinking remains merely an *X,* which must express itself *as if* it were a simple substance, continuously the same through time, and so on. But what it is in itself remains a complete mystery.[*] The concept of "soul" is an empty idea.

Kant's denial of rational psychology is not a denial of the possibility of an *empirical* psychology. Such a psychology, based on experience, is just as legitimate as Newtonian science of nature. Only let psychologists be aware that they are examining appearance, the world of phenomena—in this case, the world of inner phenomena in time. Let them not think that they can discern the ultimate nature of the *subject* of consciousness!

The World and the Free Will

When we reason about the world, our reasoning seeks completeness, closure. Whatever we experi-

---

[*]Remember that Locke says we do have the idea of ourselves as spiritual substances, but we don't know the real nature of those substances. (See p. 376.) Kant's analysis of a priori concepts forces him to go one step further: We don't know that the metaphysical concept of substance or soul applies to us at all!

[*]Some thinkers have taken this lack of direct insight into the nature of the self to open the door to the Hobbesian possibility that the subject might be a material body after all—perhaps just a human body with a certain type of brain. To see how this interesting possibility might be worked out, see pp. 736–742. There is no evidence that Kant takes this view, though he does point out that the *supposed* simplicity of the soul is the only ground on which it can be distinguished from matter.

ence in the realm of phenomena is conditioned by other things; reason seeks the final condition, a foundation on which it can rest. It is seeking a point where its why-questions can stop. But Kant believes our reason can find no satisfaction in its search for the totality of the world; in fact, it develops internal conflicts. For example, he tries to demonstrate that we cannot decide whether the world had a beginning in time—whether it is temporally finite or infinite. In fact, he has arguments that seem to show that each alternative is false! When reason runs into such a contradiction—he calls it an "antinomy"—this is a sign that reason is overreaching its own powers. In trying to complete the search for the unconditioned, reason frustrates itself. The moral of the story is that the origins of the world *in itself* are unknowable.

A second question, one more pertinent to our concerns here, asks whether we can know that the world in itself is ordered causally. Phenomena are subject to causal ordering, as we have seen, but only because phenomenal objects are constituted *as objects* by the category of causality. Does this category extend to noumena? No. But then an interesting possibility arises: that our wills might—in themselves—be free.

As we have seen, this problem arises with particular insistence in the modern era. The scientific revolution, which leads to thinking of the world in mechanistic ways, raises the question about human actions: Are they, too, just a part of the mechanism?

Descartes takes one possible tack here: Mind and all its manifestations are excluded from the universal determinism governing material bodies. For Descartes, will is as free in man as it is in God: absolutely free. It escapes the causal network; when I will to raise my arm, there is no worldly cause in existence sufficient to produce that action. It is my doing—mine alone!

Hobbes and Hume take another tack. Universal determination of events is not denied. Actions, too, have causes: The laws of nature determine what we do just as surely as they determine the fall of a stone. These philosophers try to rescue human freedom, however, by offering a hypothetical analysis of what it is to act freely: *If* you can do what you

want to do, *then* you are free. This is a *conditional* account of freedom. In a free action, they say, there are no conditions to constrain us, to keep us from doing what we want. They believe that this view of freedom is quite compatible with the view that (1) our wants themselves have causes and (2) our wants cause our actions. So they hope to reconcile freedom of action with the new physics.*

We should not be surprised if Kant's Copernican revolution in philosophy were to transform the shape of this problem. For, from Kant's point of view, Descartes and Hobbes/Hume share an important presupposition: Both sides assume that they are describing things (in this case the will, or human action) as they are, independent of our knowing them. What happens if we recognize that things-in-themselves are unknown to us and that all we can know is their appearance?

Critical philosophy, Kant thinks, will resolve this puzzle in the nicest possible way.

- We can agree with Descartes that freedom is exemption from causality. Kant calls it "the power of beginning a state *spontaneously*" (*CPR*, 464).

- But we do not have to carve out a part of the world in which causal law does not apply. We can agree with Hobbes and Hume that Newtonian science applies without limits to everything we can possibly experience.

This surely seems like the best of both views! Kant thinks he can give us all this without the questionable moves of Descartes and Hume. Descartes' exemption of the will from causal determination is dubious; it seems like special pleading, a stratagem designed simply to preserve something we are loath to give up. And the definition of "free" that Hobbes and Hume offer is equally questionable; can our actions really be free if they have causes that reach back and back and back in an unbroken chain to some period before we were even born? If Kant can avoid both shortcomings, effectively preserve

---

*Review the discussion by Descartes in *Meditation IV,* p. 347. For Hume's view, see "Rescuing Human Freedom," in Chapter 15.

human freedom, and still allow science unlimited scope, what more could we ask?

What makes this possible, of course, is the distinction between phenomena and noumena, between things as they appear to us and things-in-themselves.

> Is it a truly disjunctive proposition to say that every effect in the world must arise *either* from nature *or* from freedom; or must we not rather say that in one and the same event, in different relations, both can be found? That all events in the sensible world stand in thoroughgoing connection in accordance with unchangeable laws of nature is an established principle. . . . The question, therefore, can only be whether freedom is completely excluded by this inviolable rule, or whether an effect, notwithstanding its being thus determined in accordance with nature, may not at the same time be grounded in freedom. (*CPR,* 466)

Every action, even every act of will, has two aspects: (1) It is something that appears in the world of our experience, and (2) it is something in itself. As an appearance, part of the world of nature, it is governed by all the principles that constitute that realm. It appears in time and is related by the category of causality to other events that precede and follow it. In this aspect, every action is causally determined. But as a thing in itself, we cannot even say that it occurs in time! And the category of causality does not extend to what occurs beyond the bounds of experience. So it may well be that in itself an act of will is free in that *absolute* sense of Descartes'; that is, there are no causal conditions sufficient for producing it.

Both Descartes and Hume think you have to choose between a strong noncausal view of freedom and a weaker compatibilist view. If you choose the former, you are committed to events that are exceptions to scientific laws. If you choose the latter, you believe the will is not free (in this absolute sense). Descartes chooses the former, Hume the latter (but adds that acts can be free in another, weaker, hypothetical sense). Kant argues that if we keep in mind the distinction between phenomena and things in themselves, we don't have to choose! An act can be both free and determined: free in it-

self (since the category of causality does not reach so far) and yet causal as it appears to us. The notion that an act couldn't possibly be both is simply due to considering the things we experience as things in themselves. And that is a mistake that critical philosophy can keep us from making.

> All actions of rational beings, insofar as they are appearances . . . stand under natural necessity; the same actions however, merely with respect to the rational subject and to its faculty of acting according to reason alone, are free. . . . Freedom thus hinders the law of nature . . . by as little as the law of nature takes away from the freedom of the practical use of reason. (*P,* 148)

Most of this should now be intelligible to you. The "practical use of reason" is freedom in action, freedom to decide what events should occur in the world. This freedom, Kant is convinced, is closely tied to reason and acting for reasons. We can act freely when we act *for a reason* and not just in response to nonrational causes. You can see that Kant is thinking of reason itself, in the form of a rational will, as a certain kind of (spontaneous) causality. When you act for good reasons, you bring into being events that *appear* in the causal order of the world, but *in themselves* may have a completely noncausal—but rational—origin. The order of reasons is not the same as the order of causes.

We need to be very careful, however. Kant does not claim he has proved that there are free actions, or that he has evidence that such free actions exist. Remember, the will as free is the will considered noumenally, and about the noumenal world we can know nothing at all. Kant does not even claim to have proved that such freedom is possible; the most he will say is that "causality through freedom is at least *not incompatible with* nature" (*CPR,* 479). There is no contradiction in thinking of an act as free in itself, but determined as appearance.

This means that, from the viewpoint of critical theory, freedom remains merely an Idea of Reason. It is the Idea to which reason is driven when it asks (this time) about how it can itself make a difference in the world. Although no empirical filling of that concept is available to give us knowledge, we can say something more positive about freedom when we come to the topic of morality.

God

We have seen how reason, in asking the why question, runs through a series of conditions that aims at completeness. The endpoint of each such series must be the concept of some being that is, *in itself,* a foundation for phenomena and a natural stopping place. We have seen how this process generates the Ideas of the soul and of the world in itself. Kant's conclusion in both cases is, of course, that these Ideas are *merely ideas.* Because we have no intuitions providing content for these concepts, knowledge of them is impossible. Experience is the only soil our intellect can cultivate. And experience is essentially open ended; no closure, no completeness will be found there. So the Ideas are sources of illusion. We are drawn to think we can know something about them, but we are mistaken.

There is one more pattern of reasoning we simply cannot avoid. It leads to the concept of God. Let us see how Kant understands this. He agrees with Descartes and the tradition that the idea of God is the idea of an all-perfect being, but he has a very interesting analysis of the way reasoning leads us to that idea. Like the ideas of soul and world, the idea of God is not an arbitrary invention. Nor is it something we might or might not invent, as Hume claims. Nor is it, as some in the Enlightenment hold, a priestly or political trick foisted on people to keep them in subjection. For any being that reasons, it is an absolutely unavoidable concept.

Every thing, a philosopher once said, is what it is and not another thing.[2] Very sensible. But what determines what a thing is? In the broadest possible perspective (which is what our reasoning seeks), a thing is only a determinate thing if, given *every possible property* together with its *contradictory opposite,* one out of each pair of such opposites belongs to the thing. This looks complicated, but the idea is really quite simple. Let's take an example.

Think of an egg, an ordinary chicken egg you might have for breakfast. It has certain properties and lacks others. That is what makes it the thing it

is. But it isn't fully *determinate* unless every possible question about it has an answer; if there are questions without answers, it isn't any definite thing. Questions can be put in terms of *predicates* that express all the possible properties there are. So we can ask about the egg:

- Is it living, or not living?
- Is it white, or not white?
- Does it weigh thirty pounds, or does it not?
- Is it fragile, or is it not fragile?

And the list goes on and on and on. If the egg is to be a single, determinate thing, then to each such question there must be an answer. And there must be as many questions as there are possible predicates.

To get a clear understanding of even one thing, such as our egg, reason would have to encompass in understanding the complete system of *all* the properties there could possibly be. Again we have the notion of completeness, finality. And because our egg is a real egg, this sum total of all possibilities cannot be merely imaginary. There must actually be *some being* that makes all these possibilities *possible*—a being that is the foundation for the determinate nature of all things, by being the foundation of that enormously long list of possibilities that accounts for things being the things they are.* Such a being, as Thomas Aquinas might say, we call "God."

This is how reason inevitably comes upon the Idea of God. But the Idea is empty.† The emptiness of the Idea is clear when we realize that finding the sum total of all possible properties is an infinite task we could never complete. No experience, no intuition could ever fulfill the requirements of this Idea. Moreover, it is the Idea of something that cannot

---

*Even this is not enough, for we can imagine other worlds than this one. And they too would need determinacy. So the being we are led to conceive must be the foundation not only for the actual world but also for any other possible world, as well. God, if there is a god, must account not only for what the world *is* but also for what it *could be.* But this is just to emphasize that such a being could not lack any *possible* perfection.

†Remember the slogan, "Thoughts without content are empty, intuitions without concepts are blind." (See p. 439.) The Ideas are thoughts without content.

just be another phenomenal being; since it is the foundation for the determinate character of all phenomenal things, it must be noumenal—a thing-in-itself. As we are now abundantly aware, Kant argues that things-in-themselves are unknowable. So the concept of God is *just* an Idea of Reason. If we keep the principles of critical philosophy firmly in mind, Kant says, "the dialectical illusion which arises from taking the subjective conditions of our thought for objective conditions of the things themselves" can be easily exposed (*P*, 150).

Kant adds a critique of the major arguments that purport to prove the existence of God. He divides the arguments into three types: cosmological, design, and ontological. He argues that each of the first two types makes use of the principle of the ontological argument at a crucial stage. So let us focus on that.

The Ontological Argument

We met Descartes' version of this argument in the fifth *Meditation;* the argument is originally presented by Anselm of Canterbury in the eleventh century.* You will remember that this argument presupposes nothing but our idea of God as a most perfect being. From that idea alone, a priori, as Kant would say, the existence of God is supposed to follow; it follows just as surely (so Descartes tells us) as a theorem about the interior angles of a triangle follows from the concept of a triangle. Kant's critique of this argument is famous, and we examine it with some care.

He begins with a general point:

In all ages men have spoken of an *absolutely necessary* being, and in so doing have endeavoured, not so much to understand whether and how a thing of this kind allows even of being thought, but rather to prove its existence. There is, of course, no difficulty in giving a verbal definition of the concept, namely, that it is something the non-existence of which is impossible. But this yields no insight into the conditions which make it necessary to regard

the non-existence of a thing as absolutely unthinkable. It is precisely these conditions that we desire to know, in order that we may determine whether or not, in resorting to this concept, we are thinking anything at all. (*CPR,* 501)

Kant is again insisting on the need for critical philosophy. Previous thinkers have rushed to prove the existence of a supremely perfect being, without examining in a reflective way "how a thing of this kind allows even of being thought." What we need to do, Kant says, is to examine the status of such a concept in our thought. We may find that we are not "thinking anything at all," that the concept has only a "verbal definition."*

If we give the concept this kind of examination, what do we find? We find that it is supposed to be illuminated by several analogies. God is supposed to have necessary existence in just the same way that a triangle necessarily has three angles. Kant's first criticism shows that these are not in fact analogous.

All the alleged examples are, without exception, taken from *judgments,* not from *things* and their existence. But the unconditioned necessity of judgments is not the same as the absolute necessity of things. . . . The above proposition does not declare that three angles are absolutely necessary, but that, under the condition that there is a triangle (that is, that a triangle is given), three angles will necessarily be found in it. . . .

If, in an identical proposition, I reject the predicate while retaining the subject, contradiction results; and I therefore say that the former belongs necessarily to the latter. But if we reject subject and predicate alike, there is no contradiction; for nothing is then left that can be contradicted. (*CPR,* 501–502)

The ontological argument is supposed to show us that the judgment "God does not exist" is self-

---

*For a discussion of the original argument as given by Anselm, see pp. 264–268. Review the argument as presented by Descartes in *Meditation V.*

---

*Kant's doubts here recall the reason that Thomas Aquinas does not accept the ontological argument. Thomas says that the argument assumes we have an adequate grasp of the "essence" of God, but that this is not something we can assume. (See p. 275.) The reason Thomas gives (that all our concepts originate in the senses) is not exactly Kant's reason, but both of them require an examination of our *title* to such a concept, and in that way, both are doing "critical" philosophy.

contradictory because existence is one of the perfections of God. (It is supposed to be like saying, "Something that exists does not exist.") The aim of the argument is to show that the atheist is just not thinking coherently. But, Kant says, even if we grant that "God exists" is necessarily true, this is simply a fact about our *concepts*. If the concept of God is given, then the concept of existence is given, and we cannot consistently deny God's existence. But it is quite open to the atheist to simply reject the concept. And if he does, the argument can get no hold on him. As Kant says, "Nothing is then left that can be contradicted."*

You can probably see that defenders of the argument might have a comeback to this point. They might say it is not so clear that the atheist *can* reject the concept. An atheist, in denying God's existence, must understand what it is he is denying, in which case he does have the concept. But Kant has a second and deeper criticism of the argument, one that will reinforce the first. The deeper criticism rests on an analysis of what we are doing when we say that something exists.

> "Being" is obviously not a real predicate: that is, it is not a concept of something which could be added to the concept of a thing. It is merely the positing of a thing, or of certain determinations, as existing in themselves. (*CPR,* 504)

This is a difficult thought, but we can make it clear by reflecting on definitions. Suppose we have a certain concept *x*. If we want to know what that concept is, we are asking for a definition. And the definition will be given in terms of certain predicates, say *f, g, h*. So we will be told that an *x* is something that is *f, g,* and *h*. A triangle, for example, is a closed plane figure bounded by three straight lines. Could "being" or "existence" be on such a list of predicates? This is what Kant denies. To say that *a triangle is a figure* is one thing. To say that *a triangle exists* is to say something of an altogether different *kind*. If we say that a triangle exists, we are not expressing one of the properties of the triangle; existence is not the kind of thing that should be named

in a list of those properties. To say that a triangle exists is to "posit" something that has *all* the properties of a triangle. It is to say that the concept (together with the properties that define it) *applies* to something.

If Kant is right, it follows that every judgment of existence is *synthetic*. None of them is simply analytic of the concept expressed by the subject of the judgment—because existence is not a normal predicate and cannot be part of the subject term's definition. And that means that *in no case* is the denial of a judgment asserting existence a contradiction. But this is exactly what the ontological argument claims.*

The fundamental mistake of the argument is the assumption that existence is a predicate like others and that the concept of a perfect being would have to include it.

> If, now, we take the subject (God) with all its predicates . . . , and say "God is," or "There is a God," we attach no new predicate to the concept of God, but only posit the subject in itself with all its predicates, and indeed posit it as being an *object* that stands in relation to my *concept*. The content of both must be one and the same; nothing can have been added to the concept, which expresses merely what is possible, by my thinking its object . . . as given absolutely. Otherwise stated, the real contains no more than the merely possible. A hundred real thalers do not contain the least coin more than a hundred possible thalers. (*CPR,* 505)

If I say that God does not exist, I am not denying in the predicate part of the sentence what I have implicitly asserted in the subject part. I am simply refusing to "posit" an object of the sort the subject describes. Atheism may be wrong, but it is at least not a logically incoherent view. So the ontological argument fails.

> The attempt to establish the existence of a supreme being by means of the famous ontological argument of Descartes is therefore so much labour and effort

---

*So far the analysis is similar to that given by Hume. Look again at Hume's discussion on p. 416.

*Modern logic agrees with Kant here. The two propositions "Dogs bark" and "Dogs exist" may look very much alike, but their logic is very different. In symbolic notation, the first is $(x)(Dx \supset Bx)$. The second is $(\exists x)(Dx)$.

lost; we can no more extend our stock of [theoretical] insight by mere ideas, than a merchant can better his position by adding a few noughts to his cash account. (*CPR*, 507)

Is it Kant's purpose to make atheism possible? Not at all. In another famous line, Kant says,

I have therefore found it necessary to deny *knowledge,* in order to make room for *faith.* (*CPR*, 29)

What sort of faith he has in mind we will discover in examining his moral philosophy.

Let us sum up this section with some reflections on the positive function of these Ideas of Reason: soul, world, and God. We have seen that in no case can we have knowledge of the things-in-themselves these Ideas point to. Taken as sources of knowledge, the Ideas are illusory. But they do express an *ideal* that reason cannot disregard: the ideal of knowledge as a complete, unified, and systematic whole, with no loose ends and nothing left out. It is this that drives reason forward in asking its why-questions; and it is this goal that, in their various ways, the Ideas of soul, world, and God express. *If reason could complete its search, it would have to end with such concepts.* Because experience, the field in which reason can successfully labor, is essentially open ended, the search cannot be completed. But these ideals can serve a regulative purpose, representing the goal toward which rational creatures like ourselves are striving. We want to understand *completely.*

---

1. What is it about reasoning, in Kant's view, that drives us inevitably to the concepts of God, the soul, and the world in itself?
2. How does Kant attack the Cartesian claim that we are thinking things?
3. Explain how the distinction between noumena and phenomena allows Kant to claim that we can reconcile causality with freedom.
4. Why is it, according to Kant, that the idea of God is an unavoidable idea for any reasoning being?
5. Kant says, "'Being' is obviously not a real predicate." What does this mean? How does Kant use this principle to criticize the ontological argument for the existence of God?

6. If the Ideas of Pure Reason (God, the soul, the world in itself) are such powerful sources of illusion, what good are they?

Reason and Morality

So far, we have seen Kant examining in his critical way our capacities for knowing. The critical investigation into knowledge looks at reason in its *theoretical* aspect; it is concerned with the a priori foundations of mathematics and physics, together with the temptations of transcendent metaphysics. As we have seen, it uncovers space and time as pure forms of intuition, the pure concepts (categories) that structure experience, and the Ideas. We are now turning to see what Kant has to say about our actions. The critical inquiry into action concerns reason in its *practical* aspect. It deals with the a priori foundations of morality.

Kant takes pains to distinguish his treatment from a common way to look at morality—as just one more empirical phenomenon to be understood. If we take this point of view, we examine what people *in fact* praise and blame, and what motivations (e.g., sympathy) explain these facts. To look at morality this way, Kant says, is to do "*practical anthropology*" (*G,* 190). This is the way Hume looks at morality.*

There is nothing wrong with studying practical life this way, but Kant is convinced that a merely empirical study of morality will miss the contribution of *reason* to our practice; and it will be impossible to find the *moral law.* All you will get is a collection of different, probably overlapping, practices or customs. No *universality* can be found this way; nor will the *necessity* that attaches to duty appear.† (In fact, Kant is right about this; anthropology seems to reveal nothing but customs that vary from culture to culture. Compare the story told by Herodotus on

---

*To make sure you understand the contrast, look back at the way Hume does moral philosophy—as part of his science of human nature, pp. 419–423.

†For *universality* and *necessity* as marks of the a priori contributions of reason to experience, see p. 432. What goes for experience goes for action, too.

page 45, in the light of which he says that custom—*nomos*—is "king of all.")

Kant, of course, wants to apply his Copernican revolution to practice, as well as to theory. We need a transcendental inquiry into the foundations of our practical life to complement the critique of our theoretical life. Morality, he believes, is not just a set of practices in the phenomenal world. It has its foundation in *legislation by pure reason*. Morality, like mathematics and natural science, is constituted in part by a priori elements originating in the nature of reason itself. Therefore it is necessary to work out

> a pure moral philosophy, completely cleansed of everything that may be only empirical and that really belongs to anthropology. (*G, 191*)

In pursuing such a philosophy, Kant aims

> to seek out and establish *the supreme principle of morality*. (*G, 193*)

This is an ambitious aim. You can see that if Kant succeeds, he will have undercut the moral relativism that seems to be the result of empirical anthropology. He will have found a *criterion* of moral value that is *nonrelative*.

The Good Will

One way into such a "pure moral philosophy" is to ask whether there is anything at all that could be called *good* without qualification. Now there are many good things in the world.

> Intelligence, wit, judgement, and the other mental talents, whatever we may call them, or courage, decisiveness, and perseverance, are, as qualities of *temperament*, certainly good and desirable in many respects; but they can also be extremely bad and harmful when the will which makes use of these *gifts of nature* . . . is not good. It is exactly the same with *gifts of fortune*. Power, wealth, honour, even health and that total well-being and contentment with one's condition which we call *"happiness,"* can make a person bold but consequently often reckless as well, unless a good will is present to correct their influence on the mind. (*G, 195*)

You can see Kant's line of argument. Money, for example, is surely something good, but it is not good *without qualification;* it is good only if used well. Likewise, intelligence is surely good, but dangerous if put to bad use. Think of a healthy, wealthy, and smart terrorist!

> It is impossible to imagine anything at all in the world, or even beyond it, that can be called good without qualification—except a *good will*. (*G, 195*)

Many earlier philosophers have suggested a connection between being a morally good person and being happy. Plato, for instance, argues that the just man *is* the happy man.* Kant, more realistic perhaps, disagrees. If happiness correlates (as Hobbes claims) with the satisfaction of desires, there is no guarantee that moral goodness will match perfectly with happiness. Think of the image in Plato's *Republic* of the perfectly just man languishing in prison; it is just too hard, Kant seems to suggest, to imagine that he is also perfectly happy! There is a relationship, however.

> It goes without saying that the sight of a creature enjoying uninterrupted prosperity, but never feeling the slightest pull of a pure and good will, cannot excite approval in a rational and impartial spectator. Consequently, a good will seems to constitute the indispensable condition even of our worthiness to be happy. (*G, 195*)

It may not be the case that happiness correlates perfectly with a good will in this world, but it *should* be so. Any "impartial spectator" will feel uneasy at the sight of some really rotten person who is really happy. Goodness may not guarantee happiness, but it seems to constitute the condition for deserving it. This opinion is reflected in common sayings, such as, "She deserves better."†

We cannot, then, solve the problem about the nature of moral goodness by inquiring (as Aristotle, Epicurus, and Augustine do) into happiness.‡ If the

---

*See pp. 145–150. Plato is not the only one to pursue this tack. We find it in Aristotle (pp. 185–189), Epicurus (pp. 199–201), the Stoics (pp. 204–206), and Augustine (pp. 232–236).

†This connection between moral goodness and happiness is important for what Kant calls "rational religion." See pp. 458–460.

‡For another view on this issue, see the utilitarians, Chapter 19.

only thing good without qualification is a *good will,* we must examine that directly. So let us ask, What is a good will? And what makes a good will *good?*

We need first to clarify the notion of will. We will not go far wrong if we think of an *act of will* as a kind of internal command with a content of this kind: "Let me now do *A*!" But not every such imperative qualifies as an act of will. If I do *A* on a whim, or because I want to, or for no reason at all, this will be acting from *inclination,* not from will. Only internal commands that come at the end of a process of rational deliberation qualify as acts of will. In fact, it is not too much to say that *will is just reason in its practical employment.* Dogs and cats have inclinations, but only a rational being can have a will.* In its theoretical employment, the outcome of a process of reasoning is a descriptive statement (e.g., "Bodies fall according to the formula $v = \frac{1}{2} gt^2$"). But when reason deliberates about practical matters, the outcome is an imperative (e.g., "Let me now help this suffering person").

As this example makes clear, every act of will has a certain content. If we spell out the "*A*" in one of the will's commands, we get what Kant calls a *maxim. Maxims* are rules that express the *subjective intention* of the agent in doing an action. For instance, we might get maxims of the following sort: "Let me now keep the promise I made yesterday," or "Let me now break the promise I made yesterday."

We can think of Kant's moral philosophy as the search for a criterion, a rule for sorting maxims into two classes: those that are morally okay, and those that are not. If he can find such a rule (really a *metarule,* since it is a rule for deciding about maxims, which are themselves rules), he will have found "the supreme principle of morality."

Now we return to the question, What makes an act of will *good?* Kant first makes a negative point. It is not the *consequences* of a good will that make it good. In determining what makes it good, we must altogether set aside what it accomplishes in the world.

Even if it were to happen that, because of some particularly unfortunate fate or the miserly bequest of a step-motherly nature, this will were completely powerless to carry out its aims; if with even its utmost effort it still accomplished nothing, so that only good will itself remained, . . . even then it would still, like a jewel, glisten in its own right, as something that has its full worth in itself. (*G,* 196)

If Jane acts out of a truly good will, our estimation of her moral worth is unaffected even if an uncooperative nature frustrates the intended outcome. Her will sparkles "like a jewel," even if the action it produces goes wrong.*

But this just raises the question with more urgency. What makes a will good? If a good will cannot be defined by anything external to it, something about the *willing itself* must make it good. Now we have seen that every act of will has an intelligible content, expressible as the maxim of that act. Only the maxim, in fact, differentiates one act of will from another. So a good will must be one with a certain kind of maxim. But what kind?

Here we have to distinguish the *form* of a maxim from its *content.* The content of a maxim always refers to some outcome, such as a promise kept or someone helped. But since we must abstract from all outcomes to evaluate its goodness, it is clear that a good will cannot be defined in terms of content. So something about the *form* of a maxim must make it morally okay or not okay. What could it be?

Kant finds a clue in the concept of *duty.* We act out of a good will when we try to do the right thing. In trying to do what is morally right, we do not have our eyes on some advantage to ourselves, but only on the rightness of the action.[†] We want nothing else but to do our duty. What is duty?

Duty is the necessity of an act done out of respect for the law. (G, 202)

---

*Compare the similar view of Aquinas, pp. 288–289. Contrast this notion of will with that of Hobbes, pp. 366–367.

---

*Compare the Stoic story of the two slaves, p. 207.

[†]In T. S. Eliot's play *Murder in the Cathedral,* Thomas Becket, the archbishop of Canterbury, is meditating about his possible martyrdom. He says, "The last temptation is the greatest treason: / To do the right deed for the wrong reason." A very Kantian sentiment.

Duty and law go together. The law tells us what our duties are. The law says, "You *must* do *A*"—the "must" expressing the "necessity" Kant refers to. If an action is done out of a good will, then, it is one that has a peculiar motivation: "respect for law." What law? The moral law, of course. But what does that law say? The answer to this question is the heart of Kant's moral philosophy, but we are not quite ready for it yet.

Let us note that actions can be motivated in two quite distinct ways. We often act out of desires of various kinds. These are the kinds of motivations that Hobbes and Hume recognize.* Kant groups all these motivations under *inclinations.* But he recognizes one other motivator: *respect for law.* This is a purely rational motivation, quite different from and possibly opposed to even the strongest desire. For Kant, unlike Hume, reason is not just the slave of the passions. Like Plato, Kant thinks that reason can rule, can motivate us to override and control the desires.† And he believes his critical philosophy explains how this can be.

On the assumption that rational respect for law can motivate persons to do their duty, we can classify actions in four ways:

1. *As done from inclination, but contrary to duty:* I do not repay the ten dollars I borrowed because my friend has forgotten about it, and I would rather keep it.

2. *As done from calculated self-interest, but according to duty:* Common proverbs, such as "Honesty is the best policy," often express this (partial) overlap of prudence and morality.

3. *As done from a direct inclination, but according to duty:* If I act to preserve my life out of fear, or I am kind simply because I am overwhelmed with pity, I am doing the right thing, but not *because* it is right.

4. *As done from duty, even if it runs contrary to inclinations:* I keep my promise to take my children on a picnic, whether I want to or not.

Only the last is a case of acting from a good will.

We have an answer, then, to the question about what makes a will good. It is neither the outcome nor the particular content of the maxim implicit in it. We act from a good will when we act out of a sense of duty, doing what is right solely because it is right, from respect for the moral law. Only such acts have true moral worth.

The Moral Law

We now need to know what the moral law says. We already know that we cannot discover it by empirical investigation; the most we can get that way is anthropology—a description of the rules people *do* live by. We cannot get rules they *ought* to live by.* At best, one might be able to cite examples to imitate. But no one, Kant says, could

> give morality worse advice than by trying to derive it from examples. For every example of morality presented to me must itself first be assessed with moral principles to see whether it deserves to be used as an original example, i.e., as a model. By no means can it have the authority to give us the concept of morality. Even the Holy One of the Gospels must first be compared with our ideal of moral perfection before we can acknowledge Him to be such. (*G,* 210)

If there is going to be a moral law, its origin must be independent of experience. It must be a priori; it must be an aspect of practical reason itself.

In order to understand the content of the moral law, we need one more distinction, that between two kinds of *imperatives:*

1. An imperative is *hypothetical* when it has this form: "If you want *x* in circumstance *C,* do *A.*"

---

*For Hobbes, you will recall, desire for pleasure and aversion to pain are the sole motivators. Hume adds a nonegoistic source of action in sympathy, but this, too, is simply a passion. See pp. 366–368 and 422.

†See pp. 419–420 for Hume's views of passion and reason. Plato's opposed views are discussed on pp.143–144.

---

*Note that once more Kant is trying to solve a problem that Hume poses. He is trying to answer the question, Where does the "ought" come from? Review Hume's famous challenge on p. 421.

Kant distinguishes two types of hypothetical imperative:[*]

1a. *Technical imperatives,* such as those of medicine and engineering (e.g., if you want to cure a patient with these symptoms, use this drug); Kant calls these *rules of skill.*

1b. *Pragmatic imperatives,* such as advice about how to be happy; "Dear Abby" is filled with examples; Kant calls these *counsels of prudence.*

There are also categorical imperatives.

2. A *categorical imperative* has this form: "Do *A* (in circumstance *C*)."

Note that there is no reference to your wishes, wants, desires, ends, or goals in a **categorical imperative.** This is what it means to call it "categorical." Given that you are in *C,* it simply says, "Do *A.*" It is not "iffy" or conditional.

If the moral law expresses our duty and if there is something necessary about our duty, then it seems the moral law must be *categorical.* Hypothetical imperatives are neither necessary nor universal; they apply to you only if your wants are those specified in the if-clause. If you don't want to build a bridge, then the technical imperatives of engineering get no grip on you. But the moral law applies regardless of your wants.

We can sum up in this way. The moral law must

- Abstract from everything empirical
- Make no reference to consequences of actions
- Be independent of inclinations
- Be capable of inspiring respect

Now if we examine hypothetical imperatives, we find that they one and all

- Make reference to empirical facts
- Concern consequences of actions
- Express our inclinations
- Inspire, at most, approval, not respect

Therefore, the moral law must be a categorical imperative.

We are getting close. The moral law is a rule for choosing among maxims. It is supposed to be a sorting device, separating the morally acceptable maxims from those not acceptable. Because all empirical content must be left behind, it cannot refer to the *content* of maxims, so it must refer to their *form.* As an imperative, it has the character of law, and the essential feature of a law is that it has a *universal* form.[*]

> There is therefore only one categorical imperative and it is this: "Act only on that maxim by which you can at the same time will that it should become a universal law." (*G,* 222)

Kant has reached his goal: "the supreme principle of morality." This is the first formulation of the famous categorical imperative. Note several features of this rule:

- It is clearly synthetic; no contradiction is produced by denying it.
- It is clearly a priori; it has no empirical content.
- It is therefore an example of pure reason at work—this time legislating for actions.

If pure reason in its theoretical employment provides principles according to which things *do in fact happen,* we can now see that in its practical employment pure reason provides a principle according to which things *ought to happen.*

Let us see how it works. There are two cases.[†] Here is the first. You are considering making a promise, but you have in mind not keeping it if it runs counter to your inclinations. The maxim of your action might be expressed this way: "Let me make this promise, intending not to keep it if I don't want to."

How does the categorical imperative get a grip on this? It tells you that this is a morally acceptable maxim only if you can *universalize* it. To universal-

---

[*]Hypothetical imperatives, when they function as the conclusions of arguments, are instances of reason being "the slave of the passions." (See Hume, p. 420.) They tell you how to get what you want.

[*]Think of laws in science; if a proposition is claimed to be a law, but a counterinstance is found, we conclude that it is not a law after all—because it does not hold universally. Review what Kant says about universality and necessity being the criteria for the a priori. (See p. 432.)

[†]Kant actually considers four cases, but we will simplify.

JEAN-JACQUES ROUSSEAU

"Man is born free, and is everywhere in chains." Thus Rousseau (1712–1778) begins *The Social Contract,* one of his most famous works. He has in mind not just actual slavery, but also the constraints, expectations, oppressions, and inequalities generated in civilized societies. How did the transition from freedom to chains come about?

Rousseau paints a picture of "natural man" living a simple life, largely isolated from others, devoted to satisfying his few needs in an environment that makes that easy to do. His self-interest moderated by compassion, he oppresses no one, and is exploited by none.[*] He feels no need to satisfy another's expectations. He is free.

But natural inequalities in strength, wit, or enterprise are amplified when men begin to live in society. Property ("mine," not "thine") comes into being. Inequalities in wealth and power are generated. Comparison raises its ugly head and everyone wants to appear esteemed by others. Hence arise vanity and contempt, shame and envy—and all the pretenses and hypocrisies of modern societies. Some become rulers, others slaves.

It is not enough, however, to understand the degradation of man in society. Rousseau wants to find a remedy. In *Emile* he describes an education that will allow the preservation of a man's freedom and natural goodness. And in *The Social Contract* he searches for principles that will legitimate a government that will be neither oppressive nor corrupt.

Since might does not make right, actual control by force cannot justify a state. Only an agreement among free individuals could do that. This agreement would have to be one in which each individual surrenders his private right to do as he pleases to the whole community, which then expresses through law the "general will" of the community—that is, what is in the common interest.

No one individual will be privileged by laws that everyone must agree to, so the laws will tend toward equality. Such a contract each will enter into freely, and therefore in obeying the laws each will obey only himself, thus expressing in society the freedom of the natural man.[*]

_____

[*] Kant admired Rousseau, and it is easy to see why. The idea of laws agreed to freely by all—obedience to which is freedom itself because they express the fundamental nature of human beings—is obviously a foreshadowing of the categorical imperative.

_____

[*] Contrast this version of the state of nature with that of Hobbes, pp. 366–368.

---

ize a maxim is to consider the case in which *everyone* acts according to it: "Let us all make promises, intending not to keep them if we don't want to."

Now the question to ask is, Could this be a universal law? It could not; for if everyone acted according to this rule, no one would trust others to keep their promises. And if no one ever trusted others to keep a promise, the very meaning of promising would vanish. Saying "I promise" would become indistinguishable from saying "Maybe." So your original maxim is not one that can be universalized; you cannot will that everyone should act on the principle you are considering for your own action. It could not be a *law,* and it must be rejected as an acceptable moral principle. Whenever you act according to this maxim, you are acting *immorally.*

Here is the second case. You are in the presence of someone who desperately needs your help, and you are considering the maxim: "Let me not help this person." Could you universalize this maxim? The first thing to note is that, unlike the promising case, universalizing this maxim will not produce incoherence; universal failure to provide help does not undermine the very maxim we are considering. A world where no one offers another person help is a possible, if unattractive, world. There is no *logical* contradiction in considering it.

But if you universalize the maxim in question, you are in effect willing that *you* should not be helped, no matter how desperately you might need it. Since it is perfectly rational to will that another should help when you need it, your will is engaged in a kind of *practical* contradiction; you are saying, "Help me and don't help me." And that is not a rational thing to say. You *couldn't* universalize the promise-breaking maxim; you *wouldn't* universalize the no-aid maxim. Neither is in conformity with the moral law. Reason—in different ways—stands against both.

In either case it becomes clear that the essence of acting immorally is deciding to make an *exception for yourself* from rules that you (at the same time) will should be *obeyed by others*. You can see how close the categorical imperative comes to the traditional Golden Rule.

There is only one categorical imperative, but Kant thinks it can be expressed in a variety of ways. One of the most interesting makes use of the notion of an *end in itself*. All our actions have ends; we always act for the sake of some goal. If our end is prompted by desire, the end has only *conditional value*. That is, it is worth something *only* because someone desires it. Diamonds have that sort of worth. If no one wanted them, they would be worthless; and how much they are worth depends exactly on how much people want them (taking a certain supply of them for granted). All these ends are relative, not absolute.

> Suppose, however, there were something *whose existence in itself* had an absolute worth, something that, as an end *in itself*, could be a ground of definite laws. . . .
>
> Now, I say, a human being, and in general every rational being *does exist* as an end in himself, *not merely as a means* to be used by this or that will as it pleases. (G, 228–229)

Rational beings—including extraterrestrial rational beings, if there are any—are different from the ends that have worth only because somebody desires them. How could they fail to be different? They are the *source* of all the relative values there are. How could they just be another case of relative values? They are ends in themselves. In terms of value, then, there are two classes of entities:

1. Things, which have only a *conditional* value, which we can call *price;* their value is *relative* to the desires for them and correlates to their *use* as *means* to the satisfaction of those desires.

2. Persons, who have *absolute* worth, which we can call *dignity;* their value is *not relative* to what someone desires from them; they have value as *ends* and command *respect*.

In terms of this distinction, the categorical imperative can be stated this way:

> Act in such a way that you treat humanity, whether in your own person or in any other person, always at the same time as an end, never merely as a means. (G, 230)

Don't treat persons like things. Don't *use* people. Don't think of others simply as means to your own ends. These are all admonitions in the spirit of Kant's categorical imperative. You can see that this form of it is merely a variant of the first (universalizing) form: By restricting the maxims of your own actions to those to which *anyone* could subscribe (the first form), you are extending to *everyone* the dignity of personhood (the second form) by respecting them as equal sources of the moral law.

Autonomy

The moral law as categorical imperative arises from pure reason. It imposes itself imperiously upon me, saying, Do this—choose your maxims according to whether they can be universalized. But since it is a principle of reason, and I am a rational being, I am not just subject to it. I am also the *author* of it. It expresses my nature as a rational being. And we are led naturally to

> the Idea of the *will of every rational being as a will that legislates universal law.* . . . The will is therefore not merely subject to the law, but subject in such a way that it must be considered as also *giving the law to itself.* (G, 232)

This leads Kant to the momentous conclusion that with regard to the moral law, each of us is **autonomous.** We each give the law to ourselves. A law to which I cannot give my rational consent according to the universalization principle cannot be a *moral* law.

There are nonmoral (and even immoral) laws; Kant calls them *heteronomous*—having their source outside ourselves. What is characteristic of such laws is that I have no intrinsic reason to obey them.

If I find them binding on me, it is only because they appeal to some interest (perhaps by threatening punishment for violations). But with respect to the moral law, no such appeal to the inclinations can work. Not even promises of heaven or threats of hell are relevant. With respect to the moral law, I do not feel bound from without, for the moral law expresses my inmost nature as a rational creature.

As an autonomous legislator of the moral law, I find myself a member of a community of such legislators. Kant calls this community a *kingdom of ends.*

> For rational beings all stand under the *law* that each of them should treat himself and all others *never merely as a means* but always at *the same time as an end in himself.* But from this there arises a systematic union of rational beings through shared objective laws—that is, a kingdom. Since these laws aim precisely at the relation of such beings to one another as ends and means, this kingdom may be called a kingdom of ends (admittedly only an ideal).
>
> A rational being, however, belongs to the kingdom of ends as a *member,* if, while legislating its universal laws, he is also subject to these laws. He belongs to the kingdom as its *head,* if, as legislating, he is not subject to the will of any other being. (*G,* 234)

Note that Kant here calls certain laws "objective." These laws contrast with "subjective" rules. A *subjective rule* or *maxim* is relative to inclination, and inclinations differ from person to person. Consider the maxim, "Let me run six miles per day." Is that a good maxim? We would all agree that this depends on what you *want;* it is a good maxim for someone who wants eventually to compete in a marathon, but it is a poor maxim for someone who wants only to maintain basic fitness. Such maxims are neither objective nor universal; they are implicitly hypothetical, relative, and personal. There are many such personal maxims, and Kant has no objection to them.

But, if Kant is right, not all rules are relative and subjective like this. A law legislated by the rational will, according to the categorical imperative, is "objective." He means it is a law that *any rational being* will agree to. The moral law for me is the moral law for you. Any maxim approved by the universalization test will be the same for all; it is simply

not acceptable unless it is fit to be a *universal* law, one that each rational being can legislate for itself. Reason is not, despite Hume, just the "slave of the passions"; reason is the source of a criterion for judging the passions. The inclinations may propose actions, together with their maxims, but reason judges which are acceptable. Reason is legislative; it is autonomous; and its laws are *absolute.**

We can come back at last to the notion of a good will, the only thing good without qualification. We now see that a good will is governed by the categorical imperative; a good will is one that can be universalized. We can even imagine a will so much in harmony with reason that all its maxims are in natural conformity with the moral law. Such a will Kant calls a "holy" will. A holy will would never feel that it *ought* to do something it didn't want to do because it would always *want* to do what was right. It would never feel duty to be a constraint. Though we can imagine such a will, we must confess that it is not the will we have. We experience a continual struggle between inclination and duty. So a good will is something we may aspire to, but we can never be completely confident that we have attained it.

> We like to flatter ourselves with the false claim to a nobler motive but in fact we can never, even with the most rigorous self-examination, completely uncover our hidden motivations. For when moral worth is the issue, what counts is not the actions which one sees, but their inner principles, which one does not see.
>
> I am willing to grant that most of our actions are in accord with duty; but if we look more closely at the devising and striving that lies behind them, then everywhere we run into the dear self which is always there; and it is this and not the strict command of duty . . . that underlies our intentions. (*G,* 209)

As Aristotle said, "It is a hard job to be good."†

---

*Note that in a certain way, Kant again agrees with Hume, this time about the fact/value distinction. There are no values just in facts per se. Value comes from the side of the subject. But it does not follow that it is always bestowed by desire or passion; reason has a crucial role that provides a kind of objectivity in morality parallel to the objectivity in science.

†See p. 192.

Freedom

Finally, we need to situate Kant's moral theory in the general critique of reason, to see how the moral law fits with his epistemology and metaphysics. The notion of *autonomy* is the key. An autonomous will must be one that is *free*.

> *The will* is a kind of causality that living beings have so far as they are rational. *Freedom* would then be that property whereby this causality can be active, independently of alien causes *determining* it. . . . (*G, 426*)

> What else then can freedom of the will be but autonomy—that is, the property that a will has of being a law to itself? (*G, 246*)

You are not truly free when you are merely free to follow the whim of a moment, to indulge your desires, or to act capriciously. To act in these ways is to yield control to "alien causes," because in a *rational being* like yourself, *will* (reason in its practical employment) should be in control, not inclination. Freedom is "a kind of causality"—a power of producing actions according to a rule that you (rationally) legislate for yourself. To be free is to be true to your nature as a rational being by giving the law for your actions to yourself. This law is the moral law. So freedom is not lawlessness; nor is it freedom from duty. But then, duty is not something alien either, not something externally (heteronomously) imposed on you. So freedom is really autonomy, and "a free will and a will under moral laws are one and the same" (*G, 246*).

You should remember that from a theoretical point of view, freedom was declared to be one of the Ideas of Pure Reason, and Kant confessed that he couldn't prove we were free. Let us use the distinction between the phenomenal and noumenal worlds to remind ourselves of how the question of freedom might look from that point of view.

Phenomenally	*Noumenally*
I *appear* to myself as an *object* in the world.	I *am* the unknown *subject* to whom the world appears.
All objects are organized by the a priori category of causality.	The category of causality does not apply.
I appear to act under causal laws that I do not legislate for myself (*heteronomy*).	I may act under rational laws I legislate for myself (*autonomy*).
I do not appear to be free.	I am free, in that I can act on laws that I give to myself.

Given that the noumenal world is strictly unknowable, we do not know the propositions on the right to be true. We do know, however, that there is a world of things-in-themselves to which the category of causality does not apply. So those propositions are *possibly* true. From a theoretical point of view, then, Kant's Copernican revolution *creates room* for autonomy, freedom, and the moral law.

We are now in a position to go another step. As agents, Kant says, we

> cannot act except *under the Idea of freedom*. . . .

> Reason must regard itself as the author of its own principles independently of alien influences. It follows that reason, as practical reason, or as the will of a rational being, must regard itself as free. (*G, 247–248*)

Whenever you face a decision, you cannot help but think that it is up to you to decide. You cannot help but believe in your freedom, regard yourself as free. Now this still doesn't *prove* that you are free. Freedom of the will remains a mere Idea of Pure Reason. But it makes it not unreasonable to *believe* you are free. Recall Kant saying that he "found it necessary to deny *knowledge,* in order to make room for *faith* (*CPR, 29*). Faith in freedom is one thing he has in mind—not an arbitrary faith, but one founded in that practical necessity to think of ourselves as agents "under the Idea of freedom." It is not knowledge, but it is a *rational faith*. And the distinction between things as they are in themselves and things as they appear to us is the metaphysical foundation that makes this faith possible. We *must assume* we are free; and we *may do so*. The assumption of freedom is a *practical necessity* and a *theoretical possibility*.

Morality is the foundation of other articles of a rational faith as well. We can think of morality as giving us the command, "*Do that through which thou*

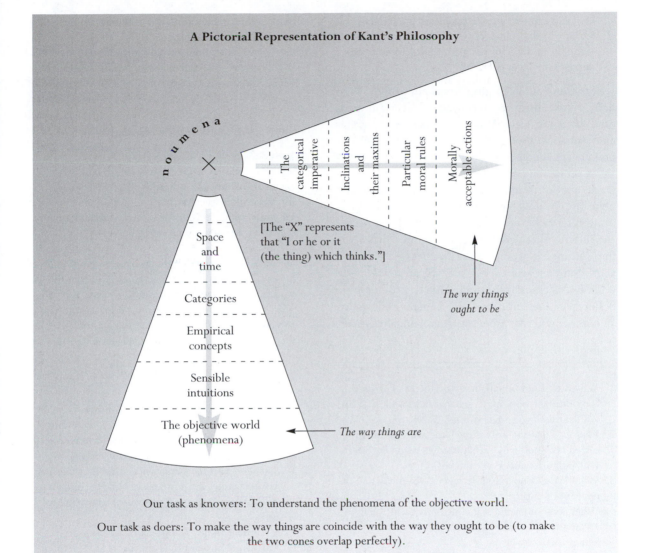

A Pictorial Representation of Kant's Philosophy

noumena

×

The categorical imperative
Inclinations and their maxims
Particular moral rules
Morally acceptable actions

[The "X" represents that "I or he or it (the thing) which thinks."]

The way things ought to be

Space and time

Categories

Empirical concepts

Sensible intuitions

The objective world (phenomena)

The way things are

Our task as knowers: To understand the phenomena of the objective world.

Our task as doers: To make the way things are coincide with the way they ought to be (to make the two cones overlap perfectly).

becomest worthy to be happy" (*CPR*, 638). As we have seen, being worthy of happiness does not guarantee that we will be happy, at least not in the world of our experience. Yet goodness and happiness *ought* to go together. It wouldn't make good sense if we were urged by reason to qualify for a condition that would ultimately be denied to us. It seems that reason is telling us that we have *a right to hope* for happiness. The fact that we belong to the noumenal, purely intelligible world opens up a possibility that it might be more than a mere hope.

For it to be more than a futile hope, however, it seems that a future life must be possible (since we see that goodness and happiness do not coincide in this life). It follows that we must believe in the immortality of the soul (which is, from the point of view of theoretical knowledge, a mere Idea of Reason). And we must also believe that a power exists sufficient to guarantee the eventual happiness of those who strive for moral goodness. This power, of course, is God (also, from the point of view of theory, merely an Idea).

God and a future life are two postulates which, according to the principles of pure reason, are inseparable from the obligation which that same reason imposes upon us. (*CPR,* 639)

So Kant rounds off his critical philosophy. Wisdom, Kant tells us, requires indeed a certain modesty about our rational powers—as both Socrates and Hume, in their different ways, insist. But our powers are adequate to do mathematics and empirical science, and they provide a sure and certain guide for our practical life. For the rest, faith and hope are at least not irrational. But *knowledge* is limited to the realm of possible experience. After the incisive skeptical probes of Hume, "that acute man," Kant has grounds to claim that he has indeed rehabilitated reason—but only within strict limits.

Kant's critical philosophy has a profound influence on the course of subsequent philosophy, and, as we will see, aspects of it are still alive today.

---

1. Why can't Kant be satisfied with the kind of view "practical anthropology" gives us of morality? What will be missing in such a view?
2. Kant says that the only thing good without qualification is a good will. What is the relation between will and rationality?
3. What is the connection between a good will and the concept of duty?
4. What is the supreme principle of morality? Why is it categorical (not hypothetical)? And why must it be a priori?
5. In what way does the distinction between conditional value and absolute value play a role in the moral law?
6. In what way am I autonomous (rather than heteronomous) in the realm of morality? Why doesn't individual autonomy precipitate social chaos?
7. Explain the connections among autonomy, rationality, and human freedom.
8. Kant says he has demonstrated the limits of knowledge, but that this makes room for faith. Faith in what? And on what grounds?

For Further Thought

1. Kant does seem to resolve certain puzzles concerning knowledge that are bequeathed to him by Descartes and Hume. But there is a high price to pay for these successes: We have to give up the hope of knowing reality as it really is. Can you think of a way to avoid paying this price?

2. Suppose you are talking things over with Kant and he says, "Lying is wrong, you know." And, in the way undergraduates are apt to these days, you reply, "Who's to say?" What would Kant have to say to you? And would you need to think again about that flippant, but very popular, question?

Notes

1. References to Kant's works are as follows:
   P: Prolegomena to Any Future Metaphysics, ed. Günter Zöller, trans. Peter G. Lucas and Günter Zöller (Oxford: Oxford University Press, 2004).
   G: Groundwork for the Metaphysics of Morals, trans. Arnulf Zweig, ed. Thomas E. Hill, Jr., and Arnulf Zweig (Oxford: Oxford University Press, 2002).
   CPR: Immanuel Kant's Critique of Pure Reason, trans. Norman Kemp Smith (New York: St. Martin's Press, 1956).
2. Joseph Butler, *Fifteen Sermons* (London: G. Bell and Sons, 1949), 23.

17

GEORG WILHELM FRIEDRICH HEGEL
Taking History Seriously

Since early Greek times, it has been the ambition of those seeking wisdom to give a general account of the universe and our place in it. One after another, philosophers announce to the world that they have succeeded in solving the riddle. But each attempt, though it builds on preceding efforts and tries to correct their shortcomings, seems to raise new occasions for doubt. The persistent jabs of Sophists and Skeptics always find a target and keep generations of philosophers in business. Some assumptions, however, are taken for granted by most of these thinkers and by Western culture in general. We can set them out in the following way:

- There is a *truth* about the way things are.
- This truth is *eternal* and unchanging.
- This truth can, in principle, be *known* by us.
- It is the job of the *philosopher,* relying on reason and experience, to discover this truth.
- Knowing the truth about ourselves and the universe in which we live is *supremely important,* for only such truth can serve as a secure

foundation on which culture can be built: science, religion, ethics, the state, and a good life for all.

As we have seen, both Hume and Kant argue for a severe limitation on these ambitions. Hume drives us toward a skeptical attitude regarding the powers of human reason, and Kant, though he rescues Newtonian science and offers us a rational morality, concedes that we can know things only as they appear to us, structured by our sensibility and rational faculties. What we really are, and what reality is in itself, is completely and forever hidden from us.

Still, in one important respect, Kant accepts the assumptions common to most of the Western philosophical tradition: that there is a truth about the way things are and that this truth is eternal. He thinks he has found it. Kant's central truths, of course, focus on what it is to be rational. The structures of a rational mind are the same for all rational creatures (and so, of course, for all humans). They are unchanging over time—the same for ancients and moderns, primitives and enlightened philosophers. The receptive structures of sensibility, the pattern-imposing categories of understanding, and the insatiable logical drive of reason are the given features of mind, identical in every age and every place.

Nineteenth-century thinkers transform this picture in surprisingly far-reaching ways. Chief among them is Georg Wilhelm Friedrich Hegel (1770–1831), a German philosopher of encyclopedic range who is sensitive to the exciting changes surrounding him in his world. It will be worth spending a little time in setting the scene.

Historical and Intellectual Context

The French Revolution

July 14, 1789: A Paris mob storms the fortress-prison known as the Bastille, hated symbol of royal absolutism. Hegel is nineteen. Like youths all over Europe, he is enthralled. The revolution seems like a new start, an overthrow of the dead weight of centuries. Reason is triumphant over tradition. The people are in control.*

It is true that this control turns into the Reign of Terror, that it spawns a series of wars, and that it leads to Napoleon's coup d'etat and his assumption of the title of emperor. But something deep and remarkable has happened, and Europe will never be the same again. Hegel imbibes the sense of history being made, of real change, of the possibility of progress toward a more rational society. And he never loses it.

> It is not difficult to see that ours is a birth-time and a period of transition to a new era. Spirit has broken with the world it has hitherto inhabited and imagined, and is of a mind to submerge it in the past. Spirit is indeed never at rest but always engaged in moving forward. But just as the first breath drawn by a child after its long, quiet nourishment breaks the gradualness of merely quantitative growth—there is a qualitative leap, and the child is born—so likewise the Spirit in its formation matures slowly and quietly into its new shape,

"What is rational is actual and what is actual is rational."

—G. W. F. Hegel

> dissolving bit by bit the structure of its previous world, whose tottering state is only hinted at by isolated symptoms. The frivolity and boredom which unsettle the established order, the vague foreboding of something unknown, these are the heralds of approaching change. The gradual crumbling that left unaltered the face of the whole is cut short by a sunburst which, in one flash, illuminates the features of the new world. (PS, 6–7)[1]

Hegel's references to the revolution are obvious here, as is his sense of something new bursting into history. It is not, of course, absolutely new, any more than,

> a new-born child; it is essential to keep this in mind. It comes on the scene for the first time in its immediacy or its Notion. Just as little as a building is finished when its foundation has been laid, so

---

*For the French Revolution, see http://en.wikipedia.org/wiki/French_Revolution.

little is the achieved Notion of the whole the whole itself. When we wish to see an oak with its massive trunk and spreading branches and foliage, we are not content to be shown an acorn instead. (*PS, 7*)

Several crucial concepts are introduced in these two quotations, and it is important to get some preliminary understanding of them. The word translated as "Spirit" is the German *Geist*. Scholars disagree about whether the best English equivalent is "spirit," as this translator has it, or "mind." Hegel's use of *Geist* surely includes everything we mean by mind, but it has implications that allow Hegel to see the revolution as spirit breaking with past traditions and maturing as it moves forward in history. The term "Notion" is a translation of *Begriff* and is often rendered "concept." It is the term Kant uses for concepts, including the a priori concepts he calls *categories*. Sometimes I use "concept" where it seems appropriate, and sometimes "notion." In this second quotation we can understand Hegel to be saying that the *concept* of a people united in "Liberty, Equality, and Fraternity" has come on the scene. But that is not yet the *reality* of a society organized by those principles. That may take a long time, just as it takes a long time for the acorn to develop into the giant oak. Development, movement toward maturity, the sense of history going on —history with direction, purpose, aim—are central characteristics of Hegel's thought.

The Romantics

Hegel lives at what is arguably the high point of German culture. Goethe is just twenty years his senior, Schiller ten. Hegel is a close friend of the poet Hölderlin. Beethoven is almost his exact contemporary. Novalis, Herder, the Schlegel brothers—all react against what they feel is the dry and cold rationality of the Enlightenment. In England it is the time of Wordsworth, Shelley, Keats, Byron, and Blake. They are called the Romantics. What do the Romantics stand for?*

They champion imagination and feeling. They are suspicious of science and the picture of the world

it provides. They resist "analysis" and the application of logical methods to living things. They agree with Kant that science and reason cannot reveal reality, but they look to other faculties to take us where reason falters: to intuition, to love, to passion.

The Romantics look back to classical Greece— once again! The inexhaustibility of that heritage is remarkable. There they see a somewhat idealized version of what they come to admire. It is the *unity* and *harmony* of Greek life that impresses them. As they see it, there is no conflict in these Greeks between reason and inclination, science and religion, rationality and feeling. Their morality seems to grow naturally out of their sense of being at home in the world and in their society.

This is what the Romantics hold against Kant: that he divides human beings, so that their reason is eternally at odds with their passions. For Kant, as we have seen, morally right actions cannot be motivated by inclination, passion, or feeling—not even the feeling of love. The only acts that are morally good, Kant tells us, are done out of that austere motivation of rational respect for the moral law. This strikes the Romantics as an almost schizophrenic divisiveness. Are all of our impulses to be dismissed as of no account? Or worse—as evil? Many of them oppose the Christianity they are familiar with, setting its pessimism about sin and evil in humanity against what they perceive as the sunny, optimistic outlook of the Greeks.* Kant's austere morality seems to them merely a remnant of a tradition that has outworn its usefulness. Some, including the young Hegel, explore the possibilities for a new folk religion that would express more adequately the ideals they hold dear.

Hegel cannot be classed as a Romantic; indeed, in some respects he criticizes the movement severely. As we'll see, he is himself a great champion of reason. But this ideal of harmony within and among human beings he makes thoroughly his own. Nothing will satisfy him that leaves conflicts unresolved, that pits one aspect of a human being against another—or against a neighbor.

Hegel's thought is notoriously difficult, and what you will read here is a considerable simplification.

---

*For Romanticism, see http://en.wikipedia.org/wiki/ Romanticism.

*But see Nietzsche, pp. 534–535.

But in an introduction to philosophy, that is quite in order. The main themes and something of Hegel's contribution to the great conversation should be intelligible. As you will surely see, the very idea of the history of philosophy *as* a great conversation owes much to Hegel. For him, this conversation *is* philosophy, and to study its history is to immerse oneself in the development of reason itself.

Epistemology Internalized

Hume calls for the construction of a science of human nature, and Kant attempts a critique of pure reason. In each case, the motivation is to examine the "instrument" by which we gain knowledge in order to understand the nature and limits of our cognitive capacities. This seems, on the face of it, a very reasonable thing. But Hegel has an objection.

> In the case of other instruments, we can try and criticize them in other ways than by setting about the special work for which they are destined. But the examination of knowledge can only be carried out by an act of knowledge. To examine this so-called instrument is the same thing as to know it. But to seek to know before we know is as absurd as the wise resolution of Scholasticus, not to venture into the water until he had learned to swim.[2]

If we want to know whether a chisel is an adequate instrument, we can use our sense of touch as a criterion, or we can observe with our eyes how easily it parts the wood. But if we want to know whether our knowledge is an adequate instrument—whether it gets us the truth—we have only our own knowledge to depend on. For coming to know how (and what) we know is an *instance* of knowing and cannot therefore *precede* it.

Since Descartes, the rule has been this: To know whether we can know anything, we have to *know* what knowing is. But that *presupposes* we can know something. And so we are involved in a circle and cannot answer the question. How do we know that our "knowledge" about knowledge really is—*knowledge*?

Hegel sees a second difficulty in Kant's project: It concedes too much to skepticism. Our aim at the outset is to know the way things *really are,* to discover the truth about reality as it exists *in itself.* But if our reason imposes its categories on things, so that objects can exist only for us, then this ambition of knowing what is real and true must be given up. Kant bravely draws the consequence: All we can know is how things appear to us. The truth about reality is forever hidden from our sight. But this leaves us skeptical about things-in-themselves.

Some of Kant's successors find this unsatisfactory—indeed, self-contradictory. To claim to know that there are things-in-themselves but to deny that we can know anything about them does seem odd. If we don't know anything about them, how do we know there are such things? Hegel agrees with this criticism and works out an alternative view in which the distinction between consciousness and its objects is seen to be a distinction *internal* to consciousness. This is a difficult notion, but a crucial one. Let us see if we can understand it.

Amazingly, Hegel thinks he can solve both problems at once: the problem of circularity and the problem of skepticism. The key to his solution is the idea of *development.* As long as we think of a mind as *one* complete and finished entity and the object of knowledge as a *second* complete and finished entity, there can be no solution to these problems. As long as subject and object are thought to be inherently unrelated, there can be no guarantee that they will correspond, and skepticism always looms large. Descartes and Locke do not defeat it, Hume resigns himself to it, and Kant cultivates the garden of phenomena in the midst of a vast sea of unknowables. What Hegel proposes to show is that consciousness moves through *stages* (he sometimes calls them "moments"), that it does this with a kind of *necessity,* driven by inadequacies at each stage, and that we can "watch" as it develops itself from the simplest and most inadequate consciousness to one that is completely adequate to its object. To "watch" in this way is to do what he calls **phenomenology**—to observe the *internal dialectic* through which consciousness moves toward ever more satisfactory relations with its objects. Phenomenology of mind (spirit) takes consciousness itself as a phenomenon; it tries to set out the *logos*—the logic or internal rationale—of its development.

ARTHUR SCHOPENHAUER

Known for his pessimism, Arthur Schopenhauer (1788–1860) accepts the Kantian distinction between the phenomenal world presented to our understanding and the world as it is in itself. Schopenhauer holds that phenomena are organized by a *principle of sufficient reason,* which guarantees that everything we can experience has a cause or ground explaining why it must be as it is. This principle corresponds to the Kantian a priori machinery of the mind and entails that the experienced world, including even my body, is "my idea."

In *The World as Will and Idea* (1818), Schopenhauer claims to go beyond Kant; that is, he claims to be able to identify the character of the world as it is in itself. We ourselves, he argues, are part of the noumenal world, so we have the most direct and immediate knowledge of its nature. In us the world reveals itself to be "will," a blind, ceaseless striving, the desire for existence. The whole of the phenomenal world, with all its varied individuals, is but a manifestation in time and space of this will. Beneath the surface appearances of things, we see a never-ending struggle for existence, desire succeeding desire, until life finally ends in death.

Unsatisfied desire is painful, but when desire is satisfied, boredom sets in—until we want something else. So life continually swings between pain and ennui. Is there any cure for the disease of life? Schopenhauer holds that art, and music in particular, can provide a temporary release from this cycle of frustration. In the peculiarly disinterested character of aesthetic experience, the clamor of the will is quieted. We are freed for a time from the wheel of suffering and lose ourselves in the contemplation of a beautiful object.

A more permanent salvation can be attained only by a denial of the will to live itself. Schopenhauer believes this is the goal of all religions and is found most explicitly in Buddhism. If we realize that individuality (including our own bodily life in the phenomenal world) is *merely* idea—a kind of illusion, and not reality—our striving for individual ends will cease, egoism will be defeated, and we can dwell in a kind of will-less, ascetic, compassionate harmony with all.

Development, for Hegel, is not chaotic or random; though it zigzags toward its goal, it does have a direction. Consciousness, history, forms of life, and reality all develop

- from *implicit* forms to *explicit*
- from the *potential* to the *actual*
- from the *abstract* to the *concrete*
- from *notion* to *reality*
- from *partial truth* to *absolute knowledge*
- from *less rational* to *more rational*

Development, in short, is progress.

I have several times used the word "internal." This needs to be explained. You can see the significance of what Hegel is doing by comparing it to our "ordinary" way of thinking. For most of us, knowledge (if we think of it at all) is a certain state of mind that *represents* or *corresponds to* some object ex-

ternal to it. I have this idea that my bicycle is in the garage. That is one thing. I also have this bicycle. That is a second thing. These two things, idea and object, seem quite independent of one another and can vary independently.* That is why knowledge is a problem. I can believe my bicycle is in the garage when in fact it has been stolen. In the possibility of this discrepancy we have the origins of skepticism.†

Notice, though, that every time we are aware of an object, we take it *really to be* (in itself) what it *seems to be* (for us). As long as we are satisfied in our contemplation of this object, no dichotomy be-

---

* Again we note the key elements of the representational theory. See p. 327.

† You should review Descartes' first *Meditation* at this point. It is the classic modern source for the way skeptical problems arise. Note that it all depends on the absolute independence of idea and object.

tween what it really is and how it appears to us arises in our consciousness. But then how does the idea of *appearance* ever arise? How does the idea of the way something *is for us* ever get distinguished from the idea of what it *is in itself*? Hegel argues that this can happen because consciousness is conscious not only of the object but also of itself (as related to the object); and it *does* happen whenever we become aware of some discrepancy between our "knowledge" of the object and our "experience" of the object.

> For consciousness is, on the one hand, consciousness of the object, and on the other, consciousness of itself; consciousness of what for it is the True, and consciousness of its knowledge of the truth. Since both are *for* the same consciousness, this consciousness is itself their comparison; it is for this same consciousness to know whether its knowledge of the object corresponds to the object or not. (*PS*, 54)

The crucial phrase here is this: "both are *for* the same consciousness." The object and our awareness of that object are given *together*—in the same consciousness! This is why Hegel thinks a critique of knowledge can be *internal* to consciousness and why it can proceed by means of phenomenology. The comparison between concept and object is made by the same consciousness that is aware of both. The object of consciousness is not, never has been, and *could not be* some completely independent thing-in-itself. Every object is an object *for a subject.** The slogan "no object without a subject" expresses the key idea in what is called **idealism.**

What we discover if we just "watch" consciousness at work is that it reveals—by itself, and with a certain kind of inevitability—the discrepancies between its own awareness and its objects. It corrects itself to make its awareness more adequate to the object, but in changing itself, it finds that the object has not stayed put but has changed correspondingly. And what the object was previously taken to *be*, we now see it only *appears* to be. Its former status as thing-in-itself (a status it had only because the former consciousness *ascribed* that status to it) is now withdrawn, and it is now seen

as having been only an object *for us*. Thus arises *within consciousness* the distinction between appearance and reality, that very distinction we naively thought existed between the realm of consciousness as a whole and something entirely independent of consciousness.

As an example, think of a movie in which you "see" Smith kill Jones. As the plot develops, more facts are assembled, a larger context is elaborated, and new evidence comes to light. Eventually it becomes clear that it was not Smith, but Brown dressed up like Smith, who was the killer. What you had taken to be reality is now seen to be merely appearance. But, of course, you are now taking something else to be real. And it is always possible that a larger picture may upset your convictions yet again.

Phenomenology is the discipline that traces the dialectical succession of these ever more adequate stages of consciousness.

> Consequently, we do not need to import criteria, or to make use of our own bright ideas and thoughts during the course of the inquiry; it is precisely when we leave these aside that we succeed in contemplating the matter in hand [knowledge] as it is *in and for itself*. (*PS*, 54)

There is no need for philosophers to come up with the criterion for knowledge, Hegel tells us, because the problem of the criterion is in the process of solving itself! Nor should we despair because it seems we cannot compare our thoughts with their objects and test them definitively for their correctness. In examining its own adequacy, consciousness is continually engaged in such comparison and testing; "all that is left for us to do is simply to look on" (*PS*, 54). Hegel claims that by pursuing philosophy this way, by simply "looking on," we will see the criterion for knowledge develop naturally and necessarily *from within consciousness itself;* consciousness corrects itself!

Hegel's *Phenomenology of Spirit* can be thought of as a kind of biography of consciousness, the story of its development toward maturity. As consciousness develops, it grows ever more adequate to its object (and its object to consciousness), until at the end we discover a stage that deserves to be called **ab-**

---

*Here Hegel agrees with Kant—indeed with Berkeley!

solute knowledge. At this point there will be no more discrepancy between reality and the knower; what there is will *be* what it is *known to be;* and what we *know* will correspond perfectly to *what there is*—because there has been a long process of mutual adjustment of each to the other. At that point, reason will be satisfied because it will see that *what is real is what is rational,* and *what is rational is the real.*

> The series of configurations which consciousness goes through along this road is, in reality, the detailed *education* of consciousness itself to the standpoint of Science. (*PS*, 50)

There is an ambiguity in the way I have presented Hegel to this point, but it is an ambiguity present in Hegel's thought. Is this development to be thought of as a series of stages within the life of *each human consciousness,* as it matures toward adequacy, or is it to be regarded as a historical process, through which the *human race* travels from stages of primitive culture to the most advanced science, religion, and philosophy? The answer is that it is both. And in some sense it is a *logical* progression as well. Individuals are manifestations of Spirit, but so are civilizations and cultures. And throughout all, Hegel holds, there is present the *World Spirit,* which develops in individuals and cultures toward self-knowledge, rationality, and freedom. But of this, more later.

So far, this is all rather abstract. We need to look at several examples. Let us begin where Hegel does in his book *Phenomenology of Spirit,* with the simplest sort of knowledge—what he calls **sense-certainty.***

Think of the simple presence of some object to your consciousness—for example, the paper

on which this sentence is written. Now, as Hegel warns, you have to be very careful here. You may now be *thinking* of this experience. But in the *consciousness* of the piece of paper itself, there is no thinking going on. There is just the presence of the paper to your consciousness. You are just *sensing* the paper. The fact that there is no thinking involved—no use of concepts to characterize the paper—is crucial for the *certainty* of this kind of experience. It is a very basic, extremely elementary kind of experience—an experience of the sheer presence of something to consciousness without any "work" being done on it by the consciousness. This sort of consciousness is wholly *receptive.* It is like one of Hume's impressions. There seem to be no Kantian "conceptual filters" at work organizing, relating, and structuring the material. The knowledge is "unmediated" by any interpretive scheme of the mind that has it. That is why this kind of experience seems to exclude the possibility of mistake. Hegel calls this kind of experience *immediate.*

We, of course, are using language and quite sophisticated concepts in doing this phenomenology of sense-certainty. But we want to characterize it "from the inside," so to speak, as it experiences itself. So we must be careful not to import our external descriptions into that consciousness. What, then, is it like? All we can say by way of description is that there is a "this" presented to an "I." And perhaps, to make the "this" more clear, we can add that it is presented *now* and *here.* Sense-certainty presents what philosophers have called a *particular* (the "this") in its sheer particularity, without attributing any *universal* characteristics to it.* Sense-certainty does not know this page *as* white, or *as* dotted with black marks—or, for that matter, *as* a page. Such characterizations import interpretive concepts into the experience, but it is wholly bare of such no-

---

*Philosophers have often looked to something like this to serve as the *foundation for knowledge.* It may be that you are deceived that there is a dagger before you. But, apparently, you cannot be mistaken that it is *as if* there were a dagger before you. How things *seem* to you, what you *sense* (as opposed to what objects you *perceive*), seems immune from doubt and so is fit to be a foundation. Recall what Descartes claims to be certain of even if his senses deceive him about external objects. Hume's impressions also play this role (p. 402). There are later examples as well, right into the twenty-first century. But if Hegel is right in his critique of sense-certainty, a lot of modern epistemology is simply based on a mistake.

---

*The distinction between particulars and universals goes back at least to Plato, who notes that some things have properties in common—squareness, redness, humanity, and so on. These common features, Plato thinks, are (peculiar) things themselves; he calls them "Forms." (See p. 123.) Aristotle and the medieval philosophers call the common properties of things "universals." For Kant, it is *concepts* that supply this universal aspect. Hegel has this part of the great conversation clearly in mind here.

tions. There is just that sheer presence in your visual field. (Take a minute to see whether this description does capture an elementary aspect of your current experience.)

But now we notice that this "I" might direct its attention elsewhere, and a new "this" is presented—a can of Coke, perhaps. But the Coke can be characterized by "this" just as well as the paper. And there is a new "now" and "here," as well. The "this," "now," and "here" have not changed; they just apply to a different object. But what this shows us is that these are themselves *concepts;* they are, in fact, universals. And they are among the *most universal* of all universals because they can apply to *every* object.

Moreover, another consciousness might become aware of this piece of paper. In that case, there is another "I" involved. It is no less an "I" than the first. And this shows that the "I" is also a universal. Like the others, it is *universally* universal. And so it is essentially empty.* It reveals nothing at all about the nature of the "I" in question.

What does all this mean? We can observe, Hegel says, that this most fundamental kind of consciousness turns into its opposite. It seemed to be the most concrete, rich, dense, real kind of knowledge there is. It seemed to be "immediate," by which Hegel means uninterpreted, unconceptualized, and unmodified by any conscious activity. It seemed to be an apprehension of the pure particularity of things. But it turns out that this "knowledge" is the most bare, most abstract, most universal, and most empty of content imaginable.

> Because of its concrete content, sense-certainty immediately appears as the *richest* kind of knowledge. . . . Moreover, sense-certainty appears to be the *truest* knowledge; for it has not as yet omitted anything from the object, but has the object before it in its perfect entirety. But, in the event, this very *certainty* proves itself to be the most abstract and poorest *truth.* (*PS,* 58)

What does such a consciousness *know?* It *cannot say.* But is knowledge that cannot be expressed really knowledge at all? Imagine a world in which the

only consciousnesses that exist are instances of such brute awareness; there would be no classification, no characterization, no comparison, no relating of one thing to another, no narratives, no laws, no explanations, no remembrance of things past or expectations of things to come—and virtually no language! Consciousness could not even be aware of a tree *as a tree,* for that involves the application of the concept "tree" and a classification of it with like things. Would such a world qualify as one in which *knowledge* exists? Hegel, for one, is sure that it would not.

So sense-certainty, which seemed to be the most secure form of knowledge, immune from the ravages of doubt, turns out not to be knowledge at all. And consciousness is impelled to go beyond it. Note well: It is consciousness itself that is forced beyond this minimal stage. Indeed, in necessarily using the universal concepts of "this" and "I," it is already beyond this stage. *We* are not imposing this from the outside. *We* are not supplying some criterion according to which this stage is unsatisfactory. There is an internal dialectic at work, forcing consciousness to recognize the inadequacy of sense-certainty and to move to a new level of sophistication. We are just "looking on."

Suppose that we "personalize" consciousness for a moment (as Hegel tends to do anyway) and think of it as having intentions and goals. We can then ask, What is it that "motivates" consciousness to develop beyond this primitive stage? Hegel answers this question in a somewhat peculiar, but characteristic, way. Consciousness, in its "attempt to be" simply sense-certainty, *negates itself.* In the stage of sense-certainty, it "intends" to be nothing more than a knowledge of what is immediately present to it. But, as we have seen, it fails. The insufficiency of this attempt is *displayed* to consciousness itself in its very attempt. It *cannot* be what it tries to be because it necessarily interprets even this minimal experience in terms of universal concepts ("this," "here," "now," and "I"), which, moreover, are completely inadequate to capture the experience.

But, Hegel points out, this negation of itself as certain knowledge is not a kind of blank rejection. It is not equivalent to skepticism (which can be thought of as a *general* sort of negation of

---

*There are echoes here of Kant's critique of rational psychology. Review pp. 443–444.

knowledge). It is a quite determinate and specific negation: the negation of the sufficiency of sense-certainty for knowledge. And this drives consciousness not into skepticism, but into a quite determinate new form.

What consciousness has learned is that it cannot find the certainty of true knowledge by retreating to elementary beginning points.* So it has no other alternative but to plunge ahead, make use of concepts, interpret its experience, and hope that somehow a correspondence of subject and object lies in the direction of conceptual elaboration. If knowledge is to be possible, consciousness cannot be merely receptive, for what it has discovered is that any attempt to merely "register" what is present to it already makes use of universal concepts, but these are concepts so poor that *what* is being sensed cannot be expressed. Mind *must* play a more active role.†

We can learn one more thing from this first bit of the dialectic of consciousness. Sense-certainty is negated. Its pretentions to knowledge are false. But when consciousness goes on to another stage, it will not leave the contents of sense behind, to start afresh. When consciousness begins to interpret in terms of richer concepts, it will interpret *precisely what has been negated:* the sense experience that does not itself suffice for knowledge. So the earlier stage is not lost; what is *true* in it is preserved and incorporated in the next level.

Hegel finds this dialectical pattern repeated again and again, both in the progress of consciousness toward absolute knowledge and in the sequence of stages the human race goes through in history. A "moment" develops until it displays its own inadequacy. It is then negated and supplanted by a second (as the universally universal supplants the purely particular in sense-certainty). Then a

stage emerges that incorporates the valuable and true in each of these stages. That stage then begins to develop, and the process repeats itself.* It is this *internal* dialectic that he thinks will supply at last the criterion for knowledge and close off the possibility of skepticism.

We cannot here follow the immensely elaborate and complex dialectic Hegel displays for us. Let us instead sketch briefly the progress of the next few stages, then discuss more fully several of the most famous and influential of them.

The inadequacy of sense-certainty leads consciousness on to the stage Hegel calls

- *Perception,* in which objects (things) are characterized using concepts (universals) that describe their properties. But what is a thing? Is it a mere collection of the properties?† That hardly seems right since it misses the *unity* of a thing. Is it then something lying behind all the properties?‡ But then it becomes an unknowable *X,* since we perceive things only in terms of their properties. That can't be right either. This dilemma forces consciousness on to the next stage of

- *Understanding,* in which things are understood in terms of laws, as in Newtonian science. These laws are thought to express the *truth of things*—their inner nature or essence. They explain the properties we ascribe to things in perception and give us an account of the unity of things—of why a given thing has just the properties it does have. But in producing such explanations, consciousness is *active,* not merely passive.§ In recognizing this contribution by itself, consciousness reaches the stage of explicit

- *Self-consciousness.*

What Hegel says here is justly famous; let's examine it more carefully.

---

* Contrast Descartes' project of discovering a foundation in simple certainties and Hume's recommendation to trace ideas back to impressions.
† Here Hegel agrees with Kant's Copernican revolution and supplies an argument to back it up. Knowledge cannot be like the wax tablet that passively receives impressions from objects. The knower cannot help but play an active role in conceptualizing the object.

---

* Hegelians have often called these moments the *thesis,* the *antithesis,* and the *synthesis.* Hegel does not often use these terms, but this triadic structure is common in his analyses.
† That is Berkeley's proposal. See pp. 390–393.
‡ That is Locke's idea. See pp. 374–375.
§ Here we have Kant's contribution. See p. 428.

1. How does the problem of the "instrument" called knowledge involve us again in circular reasoning?
2. In what sense does Hegel think Kant concedes too much to the Skeptics?
3. How does the distinction between appearance and reality arise within consciousness, if Hegel is right?
4. What is phenomenology?
5. What would absolute knowledge be—if we could get it?
6. What is sense-certainty? What is it "certain" about? Can it say? Sketch Hegel's critique of sense-certainty.
7. Define the term "immediate," as Hegel uses it. Why is immediacy something that has to be surpassed?
8. Explain how perception and understanding are dialectical developments from sense-certainty.

Self and Others

There is, within the stage of self-consciousness, a dialectic that structurally resembles the one in sense-certainty. In a passage that is the despair of commentators, Hegel seems to suggest that the most basic form of self-consciousness is *desire*. Why should this be? Any answer, in view of the obscurity of Hegel's text here, is somewhat speculative, but perhaps this is what he has in mind.

Consciousness faces a world of objects that is *other* than itself. Yet, in the stage of understanding, it recognizes that the essence or truth of these objects (as revealed in scientific laws) is its own work. So the other isn't really other after all. And yet it obviously isn't just itself, either. It both *is* and *is not* other. What to do? Consciousness tries to resolve this unsatisfactory situation by making the other wholly its own. And isn't that exactly what desire is—a project to make mine what is not yet mine?

Such desire is not just conscious of the object, however. It is also, in a minimal way, *self*-conscious. Think about what it is like to want something. You say, "I want a fast car." The "I" (which doesn't have a fast car) is present explicitly in the expression of your desire for the car. In desiring something I experience a poignant contrast between myself and what is not myself.

But there is something incomplete about this stage of self-consciousness because although I am present in it, I am not conscious of myself as a self that *is* self-conscious. All we have are these two poles—I and the other—together with a project to close the gap between them. But what this I *is,* that is still unclear.

It might help to think of the way a child develops a consciousness of herself. At first no distinction is made between herself and the other. What breaks this seamless unity of the child's world is frustration (unsatisfied desire). She becomes aware of the difference between herself and Mama, herself and the bottle, herself and Teddy. But she is not yet conscious of herself *as a self-conscious being.* This comes much later, and requires—as Hegel is among the first to recognize—another self-conscious being with which to contrast herself.

> Self-consciousness achieves its satisfaction only in another self-consciousness. (*PS,* 110)

Like everything in Hegel's world, self-consciousness doesn't appear complete at its first appearance; it *develops.* What is required for its development is recognition by another self-consciousness. It is this sort of recognition that *creates* self-conscious beings. I become self-conscious when I am acknowledged as such by another self-conscious being and recognize this acknowledgment. Self-consciousness is a *social* fact.*

Again like everything else, this development does not go smoothly; in fact it is filled with conflict of the most desperate sort. It is a dialectical achievement that involves—no surprise—radical negation. How does it work? Let's consider two individuals, Jones and Smith.

Suppose that Jones, who has achieved self-consciousness, comes to recognize Smith as like himself—a self-consciousness constituted by desire. This is not a happy recognition. In a certain

---

*Contrast this with the view of Descartes, who holds that it is possible that *he alone* exists (the specter of solipsism—see p. 331). If Hegel is right, this individualism is simply impossible. Humans are made into self-conscious individuals, persons in the full sense, by their interactions with other human beings. No one is self-made.

sense, it means that Jones has "lost himself," for he now recognizes himself as an "other"—for Smith. Who is he now? He is what Smith takes him to be. He is an *object* for Smith. Moreover, remember that desire is an attempt to make one's own what is felt to be alien. The ominous aspect of this can be brought out in terms of *control*. Jones experiences Smith as someone who is trying to control him, define him, make him into what Smith wants him to be. Naturally, Jones resists this objectification and control.

Meanwhile, from the other side, Smith is having analogous experiences. He feels himself to be the object of a hostile takeover attempt by Jones—to be nothing more than what Jones takes him to be and under the threat of control by Jones. He, too, struggles against this status.[*]

But even this does not bring out the full complexity of the situation. In recognizing each other as self-conscious beings, "They *recognize* themselves as *mutually recognizing* each other" (*PS,* 112). So their consciousness of each other is of a distinctive kind —different from their consciousness of things like stones or pencils.

Again there is development, and again it is tortuous because this mutual recognition is still inadequate. From each side, the situation is this: One is doing the *recognizing* and the other is *being recognized*. Look at it from the side of Jones, remembering that the same can be said for Smith's point of view. Jones recognizes Smith as both like himself and as other than himself, but he does not yet recognize Smith as a *pure* self-consciousness.[†] Smith

appears as an embodied, living conscious individual—one who wants to control Jones. So Jones thinks:

- Smith is like me, an independent, self-conscious being.
- Smith is aware of me.
- Smith recognizes that I am aware of him.
- He realizes that *for me,* he is just another object in the world.
- Like me, Smith is constituted by desire.
- Hence, Smith will not be content to leave me in my independence because that will mean I may come to control him.
- So I had better not leave Smith in his independence, lest he control me.
- Therefore, if I cannot absolutely control him, I must kill Smith.

Smith, of course, has exactly parallel thoughts. Each consciousness is driven to negate the other, to control it, to turn it into a mere means for the satisfaction of its own desire.[*] And it is this negating that reveals to each consciousness its true nature as a *pure self-consciousness.*

> Thus the relation of the two self-conscious individuals is such that they prove themselves and each other through a life-and-death struggle. They must engage in this struggle, for they must raise their certainty of being *for themselves* to truth, both in the case of the other and in their own case. And it is only through staking one's life that freedom is won; only thus is it proved for self-consciousness . . . that there is nothing present in it which could not be regarded as a vanishing moment, that it is only

---

[*]Kant's second formulation of the categorical imperative (p. 456) commands us to treat others as ends, not as means only. What Hegel is identifying here is an unavoidable tendency in self-conscious beings to treat each other precisely as means. Relations between the sexes often take this dialectical form, and complaints that someone is perceived only as a "sex object," or is being "used," get a natural interpretation in this Hegelian context. Hegel agrees, of course, with the rationality and rightness of Kant's imperative, but he is pointing out how difficult it is to achieve the state in which it is actualized.

[†]Hegel has a strong sense of "self-consciousness" in mind here. Think of it like this. You can become conscious of your height and weight, but that is a minimal self-consciousness indeed. You can go farther and become aware of your inclinations, of your

character, of your personality, of your thoughts. Indeed, for *any fact* about yourself, you could become conscious of it—make it into an *object* for yourself. By making every such fact into an object for yourself, you attain a kind of *pure* self-consciousness. To use the title of a book by Thomas Nagel, this is *The View from Nowhere* (New York: Oxford University Press, 1986).

[*]There are echoes here of Hobbes' description of the state of nature. See again pp. 366–369. In Jean-Paul Sartre's play *No Exit,* we find three people engaged in just such control games. Eventually we discover they are in hell, from which there is "no exit," since they cannot die. One of the characters says, "Hell is other people."

pure *being-for-itself*. The individual who has not risked his life may well be recognized as a *person,* but he has not attained to the truth of this recognition as an independent self-consciousness. (*PS,* 113–114)

Hegel's thought here is an extreme one. *Spirit* comes on the scene explicitly for the first time in pure self-consciousness; it cannot *realize itself* (become an actuality) except in mutual recognition by independent and free self-conscious individuals. But such mutual recognition is hazardous and tricky; it involves tearing oneself—and the other—away from everything immediate and merely natural. The only proof that I am not just an object for another, but a subject—a spirit, a being-for-myself, a person—is my willingness to risk everything worldly to gain such recognition.

But what happens next is a surprise. Suppose Jones wins the struggle and kills Smith. Has he achieved what he wanted? Not at all. For in eliminating Smith, he deprives himself of precisely that source of recognition that he needs to realize himself as a self-conscious being! He has shattered the mirror in which he might have discovered who he is. In some fashion (either in the course of history or in some dim way within each developing consciousness, or perhaps in both), self-conscious individuals become aware of this self-defeating character of the life-and-death struggle. And the result is a compromise.

What happens is this: The stronger makes the weaker into his slave.* Let us imagine that Jones makes himself the master. Then he has, in relation to Smith, a very real independence and freedom; and he experiences Smith as recognizing that independence. Jones, then, exists *for himself* and has apparently achieved what he needs: the recognition of himself as a free and independent self-consciousness. But has he really? Strangely enough, he has not. For consider the consciousness of the slave. It is a *dependent* consciousness—unfree and subject to the will of the master. But such a consciousness is not fit to provide the recognition that the master needs to confirm himself as free and independent. That can only be given by another free and independent individual. From Jones' own point of view, Smith (his slave) is almost indistinguishable from a mere brute. What could "recognition" by such a creature mean?

Consider now the consciousness of the slave. The slave must work at the master's bidding. Smith's work is not done for Smith's sake, but for the sake of Jones, who rules him. It would seem that Smith, too, has failed to achieve that self-consciousness that spirit is driving toward. But again something odd happens.

Think of Smith's work. Suppose he is a cobbler; he takes leather and nails and changes them until they become shoes. He does this not to satisfy his own desire, of course, but to satisfy the desire of his master, Jones. But in working on the things of the world, he expresses himself; he *puts himself into the products of his labor.** These products exist independently of him; he recognizes himself in them and so achieves in his *work* a kind of self-realization that is denied the master. He *objectifies* himself and so can recognize himself in what he produces. "I," he can say, "am the one who made this; this object reveals what I can do and who I am; I have put *myself* into this object." Thus he achieves a definite kind of self-consciousness. In the independence of these objects, in the products of his labor, he recognizes his own independence.†

But that is not all. In addition to this "positive moment" in Smith's attainment of self-consciousness, there is a pervasive fear in the slave that constitutes a "negative moment."

---

*It is worth noting that ancient societies, including Greek, Roman, Hebrew, and Muslim, were all slave societies. Indeed, as we know, slavery was not abolished even in America until relatively recently. Hegel's discussion here has a historical cast that the earlier, more purely epistemological studies lack.

*Compare Locke, on the origin of property, pp. 383–384.
†Some forty years later, Karl Marx would take up this dialectic of master and slave. For Marx, of course, it is not consciousness that is at stake, but real material life and well-being. He accepts Hegel's point that one objectifies oneself in one's labor and goes on to emphasize that if the product of one's labor is not one's own, if it belongs to another, then one becomes alienated *from oneself.* From this point arises his critique of capitalism. See "Marx: Beyond Alienation and Exploitation," in Chapter 18.

For this consciousness has been fearful, not of this
or that particular thing or just at odd moments,
but its whole being has been seized with dread.
In that experience it has been quite unmanned, has
trembled in every fibre of its being, and everything
solid and stable has been shaken to its foundations.
But this pure universal movement, the absolute
melting-away of everything stable, is the simple,
essential nature of self-consciousness, absolute negativity, *pure being-for-itself,* which consequently is
implicit in this consciousness. (*PS,* 117)

The fear of the slave, a kind of universal dread,
drives Smith back into himself, distances him from
the master and even from the things on which he
works. The entire material world is "negated"; the
slave in his fear says "no" to it all—and discovers
himself as a pure self-consciousness. In this way,
too, he becomes aware of himself as something
other than everything else that exists. Moreover,
he has objectively before him an example of self-
consciousness in the master. He becomes what the
master can never become: a being who exists as an
object *for himself.* He, rather than the master, is the
bearer of spirit in its progress toward new heights
of development!

And yet all is not well in the self-consciousness
of the slave. It recognizes itself in the products of
its labor and it has an image of itself in the self-
conscious independence of the master. But, as Hegel
says, these two "moments" *fall apart.* They are not
brought together in one unified self-consciousness.
And the dialectical story must go on.

---

1. Why does Hegel think desire is the first stage of
   self-consciousness?
2. Explain the role that recognition plays in the development of self-consciousness.
3. In the dialectic of master and slave, in what sense
   does the slave win?

Stoic and Skeptical Consciousness

Hegel thinks that the next stage in the development
of spirit first appeared at a definite point in our his-

torical past. After the death of the Greek city-states
came the era of empires, first Alexander's, then, after a period of uncertainty, the empire of Rome.
The vastness of the empire, its impersonality and
bureaucracy, and the sheer weight of established
institutions caused most people to feel helpless to
shape their destiny in this world. In this context,
spirit, now acutely conscious of itself, withdraws
from everything that it cannot control; in effect, it
withdraws *into itself,* finding there an independence
and freedom that is denied it in the hostile world.

This is the key idea in Stoic thought, which distinguishes *what is in one's power* from *what is not in
one's power;* it identifies as in one's power such conscious states as "opinion, aim, desire, aversion."[*]
These Hegel calls "thinking." Why? Note that with
respect to absolutely any experience—pain, pleasure, boredom, and so on—the Stoic will ask,
"Now, what shall I do about that? How shall I consider that? What opinion shall I have of it?" The *immediacy* of sensory experience is completely tran-
scended, and the self-conscious Stoic must *think*
about how to respond.[†] This reflective self is apparently in complete control of its own happiness because it can always "negate" or consider *as
nothing* anything that threatens it. Consequently, it
experiences itself as perfectly free. The Stoic claims
that this way of life produces both happiness and
freedom.

> This freedom of self-consciousness when it ap-
> peared as a conscious manifestation in the history
> of Spirit has, as we know, been called Stoicism. Its
> principle is that consciousness is a being that *thinks,*
> and that consciousness holds something to be es-
> sentially important, or true and good only in so far
> as it *thinks* it to be such. (*PS,* 121)

As you might have guessed by now, Hegel is not
content just to describe the Stoic form of consciousness. He proposes to show that it, too, is
one-sided and inadequate, that spirit has not yet

---

[*] See p. 205.
[†] Epictetus says, "Men are disturbed not by things, but by the
view they take of things." And what view we take is something,
he says, that is in our own control. It would be helpful to review
the discussion of Stoicism in Chapter 8.

found a satisfactory resting place. His critique of Stoicism is that its form of self-consciousness is still too abstract.

> The freedom of self-consciousness is *indifferent* to natural existence and has therefore *let this equally go free*: the *reflection* is a *twofold* one. Freedom in thought has only *pure thought* as its truth, a truth lacking the fullness of life. Hence freedom in thought, too, is only the Notion of freedom, not the living reality of freedom itself. (*PS*, 122)

Stoic thought, Hegel tells us, frees the Stoic from "natural existence"; but by the same token, it lets natural existence "go free". Consequently, there is a lack of *reality* in the Stoic's freedom, and his much-prized thinking lacks "the fullness of life." That is why Hegel says the Stoic has only the notion (the concept) of freedom, not its "living reality." What is still required is that this concept be embedded in the Stoic's life, so that he does not *need* to abstract himself from it in order to find his happiness. The Stoic mode of life does have a certain "truth" to it; it is possible to withdraw into "pure thought." But this truth is a partial truth, an *abstraction* from what would be the whole truth about conscious existence. This truth—perhaps *the Truth*—lies in the unity of a life where what thinking declares to be valuable is *actually realized in natural existence*. And this integration the Stoic conspicuously lacks.*

Again, the road toward such unity is tortuous and indirect. Things have to get worse before they can get better. Consciousness has to *experience* itself as the negation of all reality. It is not enough, as with Stoicism, to realize that one *could* set the value of everything as nothing. This stage must actually be lived through. Such a life is that of the skeptic.

> *Scepticism* is the realization of that of which Stoicism was only the Notion, and is the actual experience of what the freedom of thought is. This is *in itself* the negative and must exhibit itself as such. (*PS*, 123)

Skeptics actually *live* this negation of the world by thinking; they suspend judgment about each and every claim concerning reality. Indeed, they actively use the resources of thought to make this possible by constructing equally plausible arguments on each side of every question.*

But once again, this stratagem on the part of Spirit proves unstable. Notoriously, Skeptics need to find a way to *live*. They cannot make judgments about the true, the real, and the good. So how are they to manage it? The standard skeptical line at this point is to "adhere to appearances," as Sextus Empiricus puts it, to "live in accordance with the normal rules of life, undogmatically, seeing that we cannot remain wholly inactive."† Hegel's analysis of this tactic lays it bare as a sham. Skeptical self-consciousness at one time

> recognizes that its freedom lies in rising above all the confusion and contingency of existence, and at another time equally admits to a relapse into occupying itself with what is unessential. . . . It affirms the nullity of seeing, hearing, etc., yet it is itself seeing, hearing, etc. It affirms the nullity of ethical principles, and lets its conduct be governed by these very principles. Its deeds and its words always belie one another. (*PS*, 124–125)

In short, skeptical self-consciousness is mired deep in self-deception. Priding itself on its freedom, it becomes slave to the customs of the society in which it finds itself, whatever they happen to be. This purely accidental life cannot, Hegel is convinced, be the goal of reason and spirit.

Hegel's Analysis of Christianity

The next transition arises naturally—necessarily, Hegel would say—out of this unsatisfactory state.‡

---

*It is worth comparing this critique of Stoicism with that of Saint Augustine. See p. 262. Note also that Hegel's internal critique of Stoicism (that it splits a person into two halves) is akin to the Romantics' critique of Kant (p. 463).

---

*For an example of the techniques of the Skeptics, see p. 211.

†See p. 213. For a modern version of the same principle, recall Montaigne's "defense" of Raymond Sebond and its outcome, pp. 310–312. A somewhat similar pattern is found in David Hume; see pp. 424–425.

‡It is perhaps time to pause a moment and reflect. Recall that Hegel's strategy is to discover the criterion for knowledge *from within*. The dialectic we have been tracing can be thought of as a process of sloughing off one proposed but clearly unsatisfactory

Again, as Hegel sees it, something very interesting happens.

> In Scepticism, consciousness truly experiences itself as internally contradictory. From this experience emerges a *new form* of consciousness which brings together the two thoughts which Scepticism holds apart. Scepticism's lack of thought about itself must vanish, because it is in fact *one* consciousness which contains within itself these two modes. This new form is, therefore, one which *knows* that it is the dual consciousness of itself, as self-liberating, unchangeable, and self-identical, and as self-bewildering and self-perverting. (*PS,* 126)

Spirit recognizes its split nature, and it recognizes the split as a duality *within itself.* It no longer identifies itself only with the thinking, rational side but incorporates into itself both of the opposed aspects. This, too, is a process that takes agonizingly long. Once again, things have to get worse before they can get better. This self-divided consciousness, aware nonetheless that it is *one,* Hegel calls the *Unhappy Consciousness.** On the one side there is the experience of free and rational thinking, of pure universality, which nothing merely contingent or natural can touch. Hegel calls this the *Unchangeable.* On the other side, consciousness experiences itself as a changeable, unessential, "self-bewildering and self-perverting" particular individual, subject to the sheerest happenstance of accident. These two sides are "alien to one another" (*PS,* 127).

Under psychological pressure to resolve this dilemma, consciousnesss identifies itself with the changeable and experiences the unchangeable as "an alien Being," as *not itself* (*PS,* 127). The Unhappy Consciousness is essentially a *religious* consciousness; as you can see, Hegel has in mind the two poles around which Augustine's thought revolves: God and the soul.* But there is an obviously radical twist in Hegel's story. The Unchangeable (experienced as God) is not *actually* a being independent of an individual's consciousness; it only seems so. Actually, it is one *pole* of Spirit's consciousness of itself in this unhappy stage of its dialectical development. And the desperately unhappy individual, cut off from the Unchangeable, does not *actually* exist independently; he only seems to. Still, it does really seem so! It is not an illusion to be brushed aside as trivial.

Christianity appears to Hegel as a subtle and ingenious construction on the part of Spirit to reunite what has been split. What is needed is supplied: a *mediator.* This mediator must participate in both sides of the duality—that is, he must be both God and man. The (supposed) actuality of this mediator demonstrates that *in principle* the two sides of spirit—eternal and temporal, infinite and finite, unchangeable and changeable—are one. This, Hegel holds, is what the Christian doctrine of the *incarnation* really means: Jesus as truly man and truly God manifests the unity of the Spirit. The believer participates in the Unchangeable through devotion, sacrifice, and thanksgiving and hopes for the completion of this process in the life to come. The Holy Spirit is the sign that the gulf can be bridged, that sinners can become saints, and individuals can participate in the life divine.†

---

criterion after another. And by now the goal should be getting clearer, too, though the details still need to be filled in. Nothing will do but a state in which Spirit is not *alienated* from reality, but *identifies* with it, and can see *itself* expressed in whatever it knows to be real. Moreover, you can see that we have moved from a purely theoretical sense of knowledge to one that incorporates the entire life of a knower. This correlates with the increasingly historical cast to the story Hegel is telling. Hegel, for whom the truth is always the whole, will be satisfied with nothing less: *Reason governs all.*

*Compare Augustine's flirtation with Manicheanism (which located evil outside himself) and the essential move in its rejection—his recognition that the problem was his own divided will (pp. 228–229).

*Hegel's characterization of this stage as an *Unhappy Consciousness* brings to mind Saint Paul's despairing cry in Romans 7: "When I want to do the right, only the wrong is within my reach. In my inmost self I delight in the law of God, but I perceive that there is in my bodily members a different law, fighting against the law that my reason approves and making me a prisoner under the law . . . of sin." A quick review of Chapter 9 would be helpful at this point.

†Is Hegel a Christian theologian, explaining "the true meaning of the faith"? Or is he an atheist, proposing a secular interpretation of a religious tradition he does not accept? As is characteristic with Hegel, it is hard to answer this question unambiguously. He is convinced that every stage of consciousness has its truth (as well as its falsity) and that what is true in it will be preserved in

So Hegel regards Christianity as expressing truth, or at least partial truth. But it does so in mythological and imaginative forms. It takes philosophy—that is, reason—to understand its real significance.

---

1. What is the "truth" in Stoicism? Why is Stoicism, in Hegel's view, nonetheless inadequate?
2. How does Stoicism lead to the pure negativity of Skepticism? Why does Hegel think Skepticism, too, is inadequate?
3. How does the inadequacy of Skepticism lead to the unhappy consciousness? How does Hegel utilize this concept to try to understand Christianity?

Reason and Reality: The Theory of Idealism

Consciousness, by its own internal development, has now reached the stage of reincorporating its *other* into itself. It recognizes that what it took to be alien—the thing sensed and perceived, the world as understood by science, the object of desire and labor, the self-consciousness of the master and the dependence of the slave, the negatively valued world of Stoic and skeptic, and finally the projection of itself into the heavens as God—is all its own work. Wherever consciousness looks, it sees nothing but *itself!**

---

successor stages. But there *are* successor stages, which will do more justice to the phenomena than the earlier ones do. Christianity, for Hegel, is one necessary, fruitful stage in the history of spirit. But it is no more than that. Marx and his followers will emphasize the aspect of surpassing religion and proclaim themselves atheists. Others—"liberal" theologians—will emphasize what is true and must be preserved. Kierkegaard takes offense at the whole notion that finite individuals could ever "surpass" the truth in Christianity. See Chapter 18.

*Our natural resistance to this conclusion, our conviction that consciousness cannot be all there is, has its basis in "sense-certainty"—in the apparent brute-fact character of sensation. It seems absolutely *not up to us* to determine what we sense when we open our eyes. And the sense of something independent of our awareness—something *other,* something *alien*—is very powerful. Hegel does not deny this, but he asks you to consider

In grasping the thought that the *single* individual consciousness is *in itself* Absolute Essence, consciousness has returned into itself. (*PS,* 139)

Hegel calls this stage *reason.* It will help to understand why if we think back to Kant. For Kant, reason is the faculty that asks and tries to answer why-questions. You will remember that the propensity to ask such questions sets us off in a search for the "condition" that explains the subject we are asking about. Because we can always ask again, we find ourselves driven toward the Idea (a technical term, for Kant, you recall) of a condition that is *unconditioned,* that neither has nor needs any further explanation. But in the realm of phenomena, nothing unconditioned can be found, and noumena are closed to our inspection. So reason is a drive that must remain forever unsatisfied. This is how Kant limits knowledge to make room for faith.*

But for Hegel there is no need for faith. His elaborate dialectic *from within* has, he thinks, covered all the possibilities that any consciousness could ever be aware of. And everywhere, absolutely everywhere, consciousness discovers *itself;* in every explanation of an *other,* it finds meanings, laws, truths, values it has itself supplied. It is true that there is process involved, but it is a process that consciousness now knows must have a close; for it knows that it—it, itself—is the Unconditioned. And that is why Hegel calls the stage in which this truth is recognized *reason.* It is Kantian reason with this difference: It can achieve its aim!

Now that self-consciousness is Reason, its hitherto negative relation to otherness turns round into a positive relation. Up till now it has been concerned only with its independence and freedom, concerned to save and maintain itself for itself at the expense of the *world,* or of its own actuality, both of which appeared to it as the negative of its essence. But as Reason, assured of itself, it is at peace with them, and can endure them; for it is

---

that as soon as you try to say what it is that you sense, you are in the realm of concepts, interpretation, and reason. *What it is*— even this apparently independent fact—is relative to the consciousness that comprehends it.

*Kant's concept of reason is discussed on pp. 442–443.

certain that it is itself reality, or that everything actual is none other than itself; its thinking is itself directly actuality, and thus its relationship to the latter is that of idealism. . . .

Reason is the certainty of consciousness that it is all reality; thus does idealism express its Notion. (*PS*, 139–40)

To put it in another typically Hegelian way, the *substance* of the world is a *subject* of consciousness!

This conclusion might seem to be outrageous. How could *I,* a "*single* individual consciousness," be *all reality?* Is this some sort of mysticism? Even if we grant Hegel's controversial claim that whatever I can be aware of is something I have constituted myself, *I* am certainly not conscious of *all reality!*

Two things can be said in Hegel's defense. First, his claim is to be understood only as the outcome of the entire dialectical story that has been told up to this point. It is not something that you in your common sense should be expected to immediately assent to. Our feeling of outrageousness may be simply a manifestation of that stage of consciousness in which most of us mostly live; we may occupy a rather lowly rung on the dialectical ladder. Common sense may have its limits, and the question we need to address is this: How sound is the dialectical path that Hegel has sketched for us?

Anyone who has not trodden this path finds this assertion incomprehensible when he hears it in this pure form—although he does as a matter of fact make the assertion himself in a concrete shape [i.e., the assertion is implicit in his behavior]. (*PS*, 141)

What Hegel means by this last remark is that whenever we act, we implicitly assume that the world is intelligible, rational, and meaningful. We bank on it. But to do that is to "make the assertion" that it is not alien to reason—that the reason in it is the same reason as is in us. We are all, he seems to say, *practical* idealists, whether we admit it or not.

The second reply has to do with the *subject* of consciousness. My outrage is predicated on the assumption that I am merely a single, finite, limited individual. If that were so, of course, the outrage would be justified. But is that so? One thing to consider is our earlier conclusion that mind and

forms of consciousness are inherently social.* A completely isolated individual consciousness is not possible. So I, as a conscious subject, represent or manifest a more general consciousness: that of my community, those who share the same language and instruments of interpretation (concepts).

Moreover, Hegel agrees with Kant that reason is a principle of universality. What is rational cannot differ from mind to mind. If it is rational in *these* circumstances to do just exactly *that,* then it is rational for me, for you, and for anyone else. So when Hegel says that consciousness in its mode of reason is *all reality,* he does not mean the consciousness that you happen to display today. After all, the dialectic he has led us through has shown us one after another inadequate form of consciousness. And your form of consciousness today is no doubt inadequate in many ways. Hegel means that consciousness, reason *in itself* or *in its essence,* is identical with all reality. This consciousness is *implicit* in you and me, and we are part of the historical process in which it is *becoming explicit.* In that (implicit) sense, even the single consciousness that *you* are is *all reality.*†

In this connection, Hegel often talks in terms of a *World Spirit.* The term has clear religious connotations, but it would be a mistake to identify it with the Christian concept of God. (Recall Hegel's critique of the "alienation" characteristic of traditional religious—unhappy—consciousness.) The World Spirit is consciousness and reason manifesting itself in the world. Indeed, Hegel thinks history is a process in which "God" is coming to comprehend itself through us. In a sense, then, you and I are God—but potentially, implicitly, and in essence, not yet in actuality.

Consciousness will determine its relationship to otherness or its object in various ways, according to the precise stage it has reached in the development of the World Spirit into self-consciousness. How it *immediately* finds and determines itself and its object at any time, or the way in which it is *for*

---

*See p. 470.

†For an enlightening analogy, compare Aristotle's notion of potentiality. The tadpole is not yet actually a frog, but it already is a frog *potentially* (see p. 172).

itself, depends on what it has already *become,* or what it already is *in itself.* (*PS,* 141–142)

The endpoint of this process, when subject and object correspond perfectly, the stage of perfect self-consciousness, is the stage Hegel calls *absolute knowledge.*

What is known in absolute knowledge? The Kantian *Idea*—the unconditioned explainer of all reality. But it is now known not just as an ever-receding goal serving to regulate our inquiries. It is known as it is *in itself.* For it is the World Spirit's rational consciousness of itself as constituting all reality. This means that the process of gaining knowledge is not like an infinitely long path we can never hope to traverse. It is more like a loop; it closes and comes back on itself. In absolute knowledge the problem of the criterion will be solved, because all possible grounds for skeptical doubt will have been analyzed and *surpassed* in the dialectical progression that gets us to that point. Spirit will not just know reality; it will know that it knows. It will *be* what it knows.

It is not for you and me, but for the World Spirit that objects are (or rather, will be) completely intelligible. For us there remains opacity and darkness and an alien character to the things of the world. They continue to be experienced as *other.* But if Hegel is right, this otherness is merely appearance; even now it is in the process of being surpassed. In themselves, things are illuminated by the light of reason and are comprehensible without remainder. There are no dark and unintelligible Kantian noumena hiding behind the face of appearance. Apart from being known, things do not even exist—*could not* exist; things have their reality only *for a subject.* That is what idealism means. Hegel's idealism is an *absolute idealism* because reality is thought to be constituted in the self-consciousness of the Absolute—in God, Reason, the World Spirit. For the World Spirit is all of reality.

---

1. Explain idealism as the theory of how reason and reality are related.
2. Relate, as Hegel might, the World Spirit, absolute knowledge, and yourself.

Spirit Made Objective: The Social Character of Ethics

The recognition on the part of reason that it encompasses all reality is not yet the end of the dialectic. For this is, as we might say, "mere" recognition and has a formal or abstract character to it. Hegel would say it merely expresses the *notion* of reason.* It remains for reason to *make itself* into what it truly is; reason must *objectify* itself. It must come out of itself and express itself in its objects so that these objects are made to display explicitly the rationality that, so far, is theirs only implicitly. Reason must become practical reason and actually shape the life of the community of self-conscious beings. Reason must become ethics.

The realm of **objective spirit,** as Hegel calls it, is the realm of culture—of art, religion, custom, morality, the family, and law. Here Spirit externalizes itself into worldly objects and can comprehend itself in contemplating its products. But this, too, is a process involving complication, negativity, and inadequacy. Again we will simplify.

Hegel looks back to ancient Greece before the controversy between Socrates and the Sophists for an example of unity and harmony.† At this time, the judgments of individuals about what should and should not be done, what is valuable, and what the good life consists in reflect the "ethos" of the Greek city-state. Individuals simply absorb the standards of their city; these standards are theirs without question and without reflection. Citizens do not experience a conflict between their individual conscience and what is required of them by the state because they cannot be said to have an "individual" conscience at all.‡ Their desires are simply molded

---

*Compare the passage about the French Revolution, p. 463.
†Hegel would not want to deny that there have been many such "traditional societies" (as they are often called); but the Greeks, whom Hegel here interprets in line with the Romantic view of them, are unique because they seem to have been the first to move away from the "immediacy" of traditional modes of community to a more rational and reflective mode.
‡Hegel says, "An Athenian citizen did what was required of him, as it were from instinct" (*RH,* 53). Compare Heidegger on "the One" ("The 'Who' of Dasein," in Chapter 24).

by the customs of the community, which they take for granted. We must not think that there is anything sinister about this process. It is the most natural thing in the world since children grow up *necessarily* internalizing the standards of the society in which they live.

There are consequences: (1) Citizens do not experience the welfare of their community as hostile to their own welfare, but naturally identify their own good with the good of the state to which they belong, so there is harmony between individual and community; and (2) they experience themselves as free in their actions—so free, indeed, that they need not even remark on it. We can call this the stage of *custom.*

But this stage, Hegel notes, is marked by an *immediate* identity between an individual and the community. And, as we should now know, immediacy is a state that needs to be overcome and will be overcome by producing some negative to itself. Immediacy is always simplistic, naive, and abstract, for Hegel. In this case, it lacks the character of being *for itself,* which is essential to a developed consciousness; it is not a *self-conscious* harmony and freedom. It does not represent a rational decision, just an unexamined way of life that is taken for granted.

The negative "moment" in Greek history is represented by the Sophists and Socrates. Influenced by the wider knowledge of the non-Greek world brought about through trade and warfare, the Sophists express the view that Greek customs are not "natural," not matters of *physis,* but mere matters of "convention" or *nomos.** This represents a giant step toward becoming self-conscious, for it suggests that customs and traditions have been invented and can be changed. Socrates, for his part, engages in his ceaseless questioning in order to discover the *reason why* something is considered just or pious or courageous.† It is self-consciousness as reason that comes on the scene with Socrates. The detachment of consciousness from its immersion in

the traditional customs of the Greeks is a fateful step; it detaches the individual from that sense of natural solidarity with his community, and Western civilization is never the same again. Our history since has been an exploration of the consequences of this step.

This negative stage of increasing individual self-consciousness reaches a culmination, according to Hegel, in modern times, when the Reformation affirms the criterion of individual conscience, Enlightenment thinkers debunk everything based only on tradition and privilege, and the French Revolution tries overnight to reconstruct society according to the dictates of reason.* Philosophically speaking, Hegel sees this stage reaching a climax in the ethical thinking of Immanuel Kant. He calls this stage *morality.* We need to pay some attention to Hegel's discussion of Kant because he takes Kant to "typify" this second, self-conscious stage.

Hegel accepts much of Kant's analysis. Morality, he agrees, must be founded on reason, not desire. Reason, moreover, gives us universal laws telling us what our duties are. And to do one's duty is to act in a way that is both autonomous and free:†

> I should do my duty for duty's sake, and when I do my duty it is in a true sense my own objectivity which I am bringing to realization. In doing my duty, I am by myself and free. To have emphasized this meaning of duty has constituted the merit of Kant's moral philosophy and its loftiness of outlook. (*PR,* 253)

In all these respects, Kant's thought is the culmination of that tradition of self-reflective rationality begun by Socrates. In fact, Hegel gives the Kantian emphasis on the role of reason additional support.

Think about the claim that you are free when you can do—without hindrance or constraint—

---

* See the discussion of the debate about *nomos* and *physis* (Chapter 3).
† Any of the earlier dialogues of Plato will give you the flavor of his questions, *Euthyphro* being a particularly good example.

* Take a quick look back at the discussions of conscience in the Reformation (p. 308), Kant on enlightenment (p. 397), and Hume on superstition (p. 399). The French revolutionaries consciously aimed at a rational society; to this end, they introduced a new religion of reason, rationalized the calendar, adopted the metric system, and cut off the king's head.
† For Kant's theory of morality, see "Reason and Morality," in Chapter 16.

what you want to do.* It is a view of freedom that has been espoused by many "liberal" thinkers, from Hume and John Stuart Mill to present-day "liberal" economists. What is characteristic of the view is that desires are simply accepted as a given; according to this view, the question a person faces in seeking happiness is just this: What shall I do to satisfy maximally the desires I in fact have? I am free to the degree that no one interferes with my pursuit of that satisfaction.

It is Hegel's view that this is a very shallow kind of freedom, no more satisfactory than the abstract view of Stoic and Skeptic. Indeed, it is equally abstract, but in a precisely opposite direction.† Just as the Stoic and Skeptic abstract themselves from "living reality" and identify themselves with pure thought, so the "liberal" theorists about freedom identify themselves solely with their nonreflective, given desires. The former experience themselves as possessing an "infinite will," since their decisions range freely over any alternatives presented to them.‡ The will of the latter is wholly finite, being simply a set of naturally given (or culturally instilled) inclinations, yearnings, hankerings, wants, and so on. Hegel calls this an "arbitrary will."

> Arbitrariness implies that the content is made mine not by the nature of my will but by chance. Thus I am dependent on this content, and this is the contradiction lying in arbitrariness. The man in the street thinks he is free if it is open to him to act as he pleases but his very arbitrariness implies that he is not free. When I will what is rational, then I am acting not as a particular individual but in accordance with the concepts of ethics in general. (PR, 230)

To be truly free, Hegel claims, we must not be at the mercy of whatever happens to influence and form us, lest we be simply the pawns and dupes of irrational interests and forces. (Think, in this connection, of the ways advertisers or politicians try to mold and persuade us.) To be free we must be *rational*. And, since rationality is intrinsically *universal*, to be rational is to be *ethical*. This is already argued by Kant, and Hegel emphatically agrees. Reason is not, and cannot be, simply the slave of the passions; reason must be a determining factor in action.

Hegel thinks that the Stoic/Skeptic view on the one hand and the "liberal" Humean view on the other constitute *two abstract moments* that need to interact and interpenetrate each other. Abstract reason must become concrete in action, and the arbitrary will needs to be disciplined by reason. In this way, Hegel buttresses the Kantian view of reason, freedom, morality, and action.

But, in Hegel's view, Kant does not show us how to make reason actual in the world. Though Kant correctly identifies reason as the key to morality and freedom alike, his discussion, too, remains abstract and, therefore, inadequate as a guide for life. We need to examine Hegel's critique of Kant's ethics.

Recall that Kant's criterion for the moral acceptability of a principle of action is the categorical imperative.* Suppose we are thinking of acting on a certain maxim; the categorical imperative bids us examine it by asking, Can it be universalized? The maxim will be morally acceptable as a basis for acting only if it passes this universalization test. Otherwise, it would be morally wrong to act on that principle. It is important to note that the categorical imperative is a purely formal rule; by itself, it does not bid us do anything in particular. What it does is to test proposed maxims (and hence actions) for moral acceptability.

One of Kant's clearest examples is the proposal to make a promise, intending all the while to break it if it proves inconvenient to keep. Kant argues that this cannot be a moral maxim because if universalized, promising would simply disappear.

This seems a strong argument. What is Hegel's objection? In effect, Hegel asks, And then what?

---

*See Hume's endorsement of this view, pp. 412–414. It is the natural companion of the view that reason is and must be the slave of the passions.

†"The development we are studying is that whereby the abstract forms reveal themselves not as self-subsistent but as false" (PR, 233).

‡Compare Descartes' claim in *Meditation IV* that even God's will is not more free than our own.

*The content of the categorical imperative, together with an examination of two examples, is set out on pp. 454–456.

Suppose we grant the entire argument; what are we to do now? We see that the practice of false promising cannot be institutionalized in a society, but that still leaves us with two options:

1. We can make promises, intending sincerely to keep them.

2. We can dispense with the institution of promising altogether.

There seems to be no way the categorical imperative, as a purely formal rule, can decide between these two possibilities, for there seems nothing impossible or contradictory about a society that simply does not have the institution of promising. Kant's formal principle is *too abstract* because it cannot choose between these two alternatives.*

The criticism can be put in a more politically sensitive way if we consider another example: stealing. Can a maxim that I may steal what is my neighbor's property be universalized? It again seems clear that it cannot, for were it universalized the institution of private property would disappear. Hegel grants that there is a contradiction between the institution of private property and the maxim "Thou mayest steal." You cannot consistently have both. But again, the question is this: Shall we have the institution or not? And again we seem to be left with two consistent possibilities:

3. A society with private property and rules against stealing

4. A society without private property

Kant's purely formal imperative, Hegel argues, is helpless to choose between them.† And the reason is that in itself it has no *content*.

_____

*Would a Kantian be able to reply to this argument? Might one say that if faced with the prospect of legislating for society a set of practices that either includes or excludes the practice of promising, the rational choice would be in favor of promising? If so, the same move might be possible for stealing and private property (see the following). In either case, however, rationality would probably have to mean more than just absence of contradiction.

†This is obviously another one of the points Karl Marx picks up from Hegel. If a purely formal and individualistic morality like Kant's cannot be a guide in selecting institutions, then a guide for life must be given by society, and doing that is politics.

The absence of property contains in itself just as little contradiction as the non-existence of this or that nation, family, etc., or the death of the whole human race. But if it is already established on other grounds and presupposed that property and human life are to exist and be respected, then indeed it is a contradiction to commit theft or murder; a contradiction must be a contradiction of something, i.e., of some content presupposed from the start as a fixed principle. (*PR*, 90)

The inadequacy of this stage of morality was made dramatically clear, Hegel believes, in the French Revolution. This was an attempt to impose on society abstract principles of a universal sort, to *force* recalcitrant reality to be rational and free. But this freedom was a purely *negative* freedom; and the result was the Reign of Terror. When negative freedom

turns to actual practice, it takes shape in religion and politics alike as the fanaticism of destruction—the destruction of the whole subsisting social order—as the elimination of individuals who are objects of suspicion to any social order, and the annihilation of any organization which tries to rise anew from the ruins. Only in destroying something does this negative will possess the feeling of itself as existent. Of course it imagines that it is willing some positive state of affairs, such as universal equality or universal religious life, but . . . what negative freedom intends to will can never be anything in itself but an abstract idea, and giving effect to this idea can only be the fury of destruction. (*PR*, 22)

The stage of morality is supplanted by what Hegel calls *ethics*. (These terms are often used synonymously, but they are quite distinct for Hegel.) Ethics is the next dialectical step in the objectification of spirit. Let us pause a moment to review. At first there was *custom*, where an unreflective and uncritical harmony existed between the life of the individual and the life of his society. This broke down in the Socratic/Stoic/Skeptic realization of oneself as pure reason, distinct from any natural or social realities; the apex of this stage is to be found in the *morality* of Kant.

What is required for Spirit to become what it is, however—fully rational, self-conscious, and free—is for it to be able to recognize itself in its cultural expressions. So the next step, *ethics,* is the recognition of rationality in institutions—in property, contracts, the family, and the state. Spirit, alienated from its products by setting itself apart from them, must reappropriate them, see itself in them, express itself in the social dimension—but now critically, rationally, freely. The abstraction of Kantian morality is to be overcome by the objectification of reason in society.

CUSTOM $\longrightarrow$	MORALITY $\longrightarrow$	ETHICS
pre-rationality	abstract rationality	concrete rationality
nonreflective	reflective	reflection satisfied
individual identifies with community	individual alienated from community	individual identifies with rational community
individual feels free	individual is free (in abstract sense)	individual is free (in actuality)

For Hegel, ethics is virtually indistinguishable from social and political philosophy. Or rather, it is not philosophy at all, but the *realization* of philosophy in an actual community. As he says, "the system of right is the realm of freedom made actual, the world of mind brought forth out of itself like a second nature" (*PR,* 20). What kind of social system will this incarnation of Spirit be? How will right, duty, rationality, and freedom all manage to coalesce in the society of Spirit objectified?

We won't go into the details of Hegel's social thought; he tends too much to see his own society as approaching or having reached the ideal, and much of his discussion is thus of interest only to historians. But we need to indicate his general idea and to point out one of its consequences.

As we have already noted, an individual must be thought of as socially shaped and constructed; no one is an island. Hobbes' view that the state originates in a contract made by isolated individuals is, for Hegel, simply another instance of undue ab-

straction.* The relation between an individual and the community is more like that between a leg and the body it belongs to. If the leg were to say, "I am an independent entity, and I will go my own way," this would be manifestly absurd. It is no less absurd for individuals to consider themselves distinct from the community that nourishes, educates, shapes and forms them. Indeed, an individual per se is an *abstraction* (there's that word again) from the whole. As separate from the community, a person lacks reality. It is the community, which Hegel calls the *State,* that is the bearer of the objective reality of spirit and as such is "higher" than the individual. The state is like an organism, and individuals are like its organs. Hegel goes as far as to say,

> A single person . . . is something subordinate, and as such he must dedicate himself to the ethical whole. Hence if the state claims life, the individual must surrender it. . . .
>
> It is false to maintain that the foundation of the state is something at the option of all its members. It is nearer the truth to say that it is absolutely necessary for every individual to be a citizen. (*PR,* 241–242)

But what kind of state is it that can rightly subordinate persons like this? It must be, Hegel says, a rational state. And that means that it must be one in which laws are universal and impartial, one to which free and rational individuals can give their free and rational consent.[†] Citizens will be able to live freely and rationally in such a state because the state is the objective correlate of that reason which is the essence of their very being. Here we see how Hegel thinks to surpass, and yet incorporate, the "moments" of unthinking harmony (custom) and rational abstraction from that harmony by individuals (morality). There is to be a new harmony, one now founded self-consciously on rational principles. Af-

---

*For Hobbes' view of the social contract, see pp. 370–371. See also Locke, pp. 382–384.

[†]It does not necessarily mean one in which each citizen has a vote; Hegel's picture of a rational state is a constitutional monarchy where decisions are made by discussion among large-scale interests, such as the landed class and corporations.

ter being merely implicit in traditional societies, and after long estrangement from a reality that was less than fully rational, Spirit is now to find itself mirrored in the institutions and laws of the organic community.

> If men are to act, they must not only intend the good but must know whether this or that particular course is good. What special course of action is good or not, right or wrong, is determined, for the ordinary circumstances of private life, by the laws and customs of a state. It is not too difficult to know them. . . . Each individual has his position; he knows, on the whole, what a lawful and honorable course of conduct is. To assert in ordinary private relations that it is difficult to choose the right and good, and to regard it as a mark of an exalted morality to find difficulties and raise scruples on that score indicates an evil and perverse will. It indicates a will that seeks to evade obvious duties or, at least, a petty will that gives its mind too little to do. (*RH,* 37)

The empty form of Kantian morality is thus to be given content by the laws and customs of the state one grows up in. It is true that "each individual is also the child of a people at a definite stage of its development" (*RH,* 37) and that none of us lives in a perfectly rational society. But Hegel seems to say that this is no excuse for trying to go off on our own individualistic tangents. Our ethical life is only realized by actualizing the norms of our society. An individual "*must bring the will demanded by his people to his own consciousness, to articulation*" (*RH,* 38).

The moral of the French Revolution (and of other revolutions since then, we might add) is that reason cannot (like Descartes in the sphere of ideas) sweep the board clean and begin anew. That way leads only to destruction. What is necessary is to recognize what is already rational in the present and to nurture and strengthen that. And there is *always* some rationality in current circumstances; Spirit is always already implicit in some stage of realization, though it is usually inadequate, one-sided, and (of course) abstract.

When Spirit becomes fully *concrete,* when its objective expression in culture matches perfectly its rational essence, then individuals—the subjec-

tive bearers of self-consciousness—will recognize themselves in the institutions of their society without hesitation. At that point they will be fully free. They will not be constrained either by their own nonrationally given desires or by the arbitrariness of irrational laws and institutions. All will be, as in the stage of custom, a harmony. But now it will be a rationally founded harmony, approved by the self-conscious, rational citizens of that state.

You can see that there is an uneasy ambiguity in Hegel's treatment of the ideal community. On the one hand, there is some basis for a radical critique of nearly any given society; insofar as its institutions lack rationality—and when will they not?—they are subject to criticism and potential change. On the other hand, Hegel can seem terribly conservative, for whatever there is in the way of social arrangements has *some* rationality to it, is in some way a stage on the way to the absolute. The state at that stage, moreover, is the shaper of all the individuals who make it up; apart from it, they are mere abstractions, unrealities. Moreover, that stage is in some sense, he tells us, necessary. If it is necessary and is simply working its own way out toward a more adequate embodiment of reason and freedom, what sense does it make to interfere? His emphasis that the philosopher must not prescribe, but must simply "look on," seems to indicate that in the social setting, as in epistemology, Spirit takes care of itself.

This ambiguity runs throughout Hegel's thought and explains how after his death there could form two groups of Hegelians, radical and conservative, each claiming to represent the master.[*] It permeates, moreover, his thought about history, with which we will end our much simplified consideration of this complex system of ideas.

---

1. What does Hegel mean by *objective spirit?*
2. What transition in our history does Hegel believe Socrates represents?

---

[*]The most famous of the "left-wing," or radical, Hegelians is of course Karl Marx.

3. What does Hegel praise in Kant's account of morality? What, nonetheless, is his critique of the categorical imperative?
4. What is Hegel's critique of an arbitrary will?
5. How does Hegel understand ethics?
6. How does Hegel think that individuals are related to the state?
7. What is there in Hegel's thought that explains why both conservatives and radicals could claim him as their ancestor?

History and Freedom

We have seen that a central concept in Hegel's thought is that of development. Development in the realm of spirit is complex and dialectical because spirit, unlike nature, is intrinsically in relation to itself; that is why there is always negativity involved: always (1) an object standing in opposition to the subject, (2) typically experienced as *other* (alien), and (3) needing to be recovered so that the subject can recognize itself in its object. As an observer of the development of spirit, Hegel sees this dialectical process at work everywhere: in the consciousness of the individual, in society, even in concepts themselves. Unlike nearly all previous philosophers, Hegel sees *reason itself* developing its own tools, its concepts and notions, in this dialectical and historical process. That is why it has not been possible previously to solve the problem of the criterion: Each philosopher has necessarily been working in a certain stage of the development of reason and necessarily expresses the way things look at that stage. But each of these stages has been abstract (that is, not yet the whole, the true) and therefore inadequate. The criterion for knowledge and action, Hegel believes, is in the process of *working itself out in history*. And we "phenomenological" observers need only "look on" to see it happening.

History is meaningful; it has a direction and a purpose; it is going somewhere. And Hegel claims to know where it is going. Its goal is *freedom*. In a schematic (and surely oversimple) way, Hegel claims we can actually see this process going on. In ancient Asian societies (for example, the Persian), he says, only *one* was free (the ruler); in Greek and Roman societies, *some* were free (the citizens, but not the slaves); and in his own time, it has been realized that *all* are free (though the working out of this realization may take a long time yet). But to understand this fully, we need to say a bit more about freedom and its relation to reason.

> The sole thought which philosophy brings to the treatment of history is the simple concept of *Reason*: that Reason is the law of the world and that, therefore, in world history, things have come about rationally. (*RH*, 11)

Hegel discusses reason in exalted terms, saying it is "both *substance and infinite power*" (*RH*, 11), and suggesting that it is what people really mean when they speak of God. Let us see whether we can understand this.

Reason is *substance*, Hegel says, because it is "that by which and in which all reality has its being" (*RH*, 11). This should make some sense to us by now because we have seen that Hegel believes the universal concepts of rational thought determine *what something is*. Its very being (as that kind of thing) is a function of reason—and *nothing* can have a nonrational existence.

Reason is *power*, he says,

> for Reason is not so impotent as to bring about only the ideal, the ought, and to remain in an existence outside of reality—who knows where?—as something peculiar in the heads of a few people. . . . [Reason] is its own exclusive presupposition and absolutely final purpose, and itself works out this purpose from potentiality into actuality, from inward source to outward appearance, not only in the natural but also in the spiritual universe, in world history. (*RH*, 11)

Parts of this "working out" we have traced in following the dialectical stages from implicit to explicit self-consciousness, and from a naively traditional to a self-consciously rational and organic society. Reason, then, seems to be simply another term for the Absolute, for the World Spirit.

How is reason related to freedom? Well, what is freedom? Freedom, Hegel tells us, is

> self-contained existence. . . . For when I am dependent, I refer myself to something else which I am not; I cannot exist independently of something ex-

ternal. I am free when I am within myself. This self-contained existence of Spirit is self-consciousness, consciousness of self. (*RH,* 23)

You can see that if there isn't anything in reality *but* Spirit (or reason)—its objects having existence only relative to it,* so that when Spirit becomes conscious of them, it is becoming conscious of itself in them—and if to be free is to be "self-contained," then Spirit is essentially free. But being *essentially* free and being *actually* free are two different things. The former is merely the abstract essence, the latter is the concrete reality. History is the dialectical tale by which the former becomes the latter.

> World history is the exhibition of spirit striving to attain knowledge of its own nature.
> World history is the progress of the consciousness of freedom. . . .
> We have established Spirit's consciousness of its freedom, and thereby the actualization of this Freedom as the final purpose of the world. (*RH,* 23–24)

This sounds glorious, and perhaps it is. But how does it fit the facts of history, where there is so much that seems irrational and evil? Is Hegel just a "cockeyed optimist" about history? On the contrary, Hegel is acutely conscious of the negative side of the story, only, as always, he sees this negativity as an essential aspect of the dialectic leading to freedom. Reason does not conquer easily, but only with agonizing slowness and indirection. He is under no illusions about the motivations behind the acts that make history.

> Passions, private aims, and the satisfaction of selfish desires are . . . tremendous springs of action. Their power lies in the fact that they respect none of the limitations which law and morality would impose on them; and that these natural impulses are closer to the core of human nature than the artificial and troublesome discipline that tends toward order, self-restraint, law, and morality.
> When we contemplate this display of passions and the consequences of their violence, the unreason which is associated not only with them, but even— rather we might say *especially*—with *good* designs and righteous aims; when we see arising therefrom the evil, the vice, the ruin that has befallen the

most flourishing kingdoms which the mind of man ever created, we can hardly avoid being filled with sorrow at this universal taint of corruption. And since this decay is not the work of mere nature, but of human will, our reflections may well lead us to a moral sadness, a revolt of the good will (spirit)—if indeed it has a place within us. Without rhetorical exaggeration, a simple, truthful account of the miseries that have overwhelmed the noblest of nations and polities and the finest exemplars of private virtue forms a most fearful picture and excites emotions of the profoundest and most hopeless sadness, counterbalanced by no consoling result. We can endure it and strengthen ourselves against it only by thinking that this is the way it had to be—it is fate; nothing can be done. (*RH,* 26–27)

Hegel compares history to a "slaughter bench," at which the happiness, wisdom, and virtue of countless individuals and peoples have been sacrificed. When this image takes hold, the question forces itself upon us:

> To what principle, to what final purpose, have these monstrous sacrifices been offered? (*RH,* 27)

Hegel's answer, of course, is freedom. But we need to say a bit more about how he thinks freedom will come out of this protracted and bloody process.

He is under no illusions, as we have noted, about individuals acting from reason. In fact, he goes as far as to say,

> We assert then that nothing has been accomplished without an interest on the part of those who brought it about. And if "interest" be called "passion" . . . we may then affirm without qualification that *nothing great in the world* has been accomplished without passion. (*RH,* 29)

But that is only half the story. The other half is equally important: reason, or what Hegel calls the *Idea.**

> Two elements therefore enter into our investigations: first the Idea, secondly, the complex of human passions; the one the warp, the other the woof of the vast tapestry of world history. (*RH,* 29)

---

*This is the key element in Hegel's absolute idealism.

*Remember that Idea, for Hegel, represents the unconditioned explainer of everything and that the nature of Spirit (self-conscious, universal reason) is that it functions as the Idea.

Individuals, then, act out of their passions and desires. Like the threads in a tapestry that run in one direction only, they are unaware that they are held in place by a rationality that, fixing their actions into a pattern they can scarcely discern, works out a purposeful progress toward absolute knowledge and freedom.

The burden of historical development is carried particularly, Hegel thinks, by certain persons, whom he calls "world-historical individuals." Alexander, Caesar, and Napoleon are examples he cites. What is true of them is that

> their own particular purposes contain the substantial will of the World Spirit.
>
> Such individuals have no consciousness of the Idea as such. They are practical and political men. But at the same time they are thinkers with insight into what is needed and timely. They see the very truth of their age and their world, the next genus, so to speak, which is already formed in the womb of time. It is theirs to know this new universal, the necessary next stage of their world, to make it their own aim and put all their energy into it. (*RH,* 40)

They do not pursue this "new universal" consciously, of course. They may simply seek to consolidate their own power. And they may do so quite ruthlessly; "so mighty a figure must trample down many an innocent flower, crush to pieces many things in its path" (*RH,* 43). But in pursuing their private aims, they unknowingly serve a larger purpose. There are unintended effects to their actions, and whether they will it or not, they serve the purposes of reason. This Hegel calls the

> *cunning of Reason*—that it sets the passions to work for itself, while that through which it develops itself pays the penalty and suffers the loss. . . . The particular in most cases is too trifling as compared with the universal; the individuals are sacrificed and abandoned. The Idea pays the tribute of existence and transience, not out of its own funds but with the passions of the individuals. (*RH,* 44)

Individuals, then, are the *means* by which the World Spirit actualizes its reason in the world. And if we see this, we can be reconciled to the agony and the tragedy of world history. It is all worthwhile because it is necessary to realize the goal.

> The insight then to which . . . philosophy should lead us is that the actual world is as it ought to be, that the truly good, the universal divine Reason is the power capable of actualizing itself. This good, this Reason, in its most concrete representation, is God. God governs the world. (*RH,* 47)

What Hegel gives us in his reflections on history is a **theodicy,** a justification of the ways of God to human beings; it is one solution to the old problem of evil. Hegel's is perhaps the most elaborate theodicy since Augustine wrote *The City of God* in the early fifth century.* But notice the price that is paid: The actual world *is as it ought to be.* Remembering Hegel's own lament over the "slaughter bench" of history, this is a remarkable conclusion. All this is worthwhile because it leads to a supremely valuable end.

And what, in particular, is that end to be? We already know. It is "the union of the subjective with the rational will; it is the moral whole, the *State*" (*RH,* 49). Once again, note that the state does not exist for the sake of satisfying the desires of its citizens.

> Rather, law, morality, the State, and they alone, are the positive reality and satisfaction of freedom. The caprice of the individual is not freedom. It is this caprice which is being limited, the license of particular desires.
>
> The subjective will, passion, is the force which actualizes and realizes. The Idea is the interior; the State is the externally existing, genuinely moral life. It is the union of the universal and essential

---

* See the discussion of Augustine's view of history, pp. 257–259. One crucial difference is that for Augustine the justification of history lies *beyond* it in the life to come, whereas for Hegel it lies *within* history itself in an attainable historical condition. A second difference is that Augustine looks for the *peace* of the blessed, whereas Hegel justifies everything in terms of the rational *freedom* to be enjoyed by citizens of a rational state. A third difference is in the conception of God. For Augustine, God is a being quite independent of the world he created, having his being even outside of time; for Hegel, the world *is* God coming to self-actualization in time through self-conscious knowers such as ourselves.

with the subjective will, and as such it is *Morality*. (*RH, 50*)*

It is the realization of Freedom, of the absolute, final purpose, and exists for its own sake. All the value man has, all spiritual reality, he has only through the state. . . . For the True is the unity of universal and particular will. And the universal in the state is in its laws, its universal and rational provisions. The state is the divine Idea as it exists on earth. (*RH, 52–53*)

Here again we feel that ambiguity we noted before. When Hegel says the state is the "divine Idea as it exists on earth," does he mean *any* state or does he mean only the ideal, perfectly rational state? On the one hand, as we have seen, the actual world is as it ought to be. This suggests that if things are not as good as they *might* be, still they are as good as they realistically *can* be (at this stage), and there is no sense complaining. On the other hand, there is the ideal of a rational state in which individuals will actually find themselves at home because it expresses perfectly their inner nature as rational beings. No actually existing state seems to measure up. Again we find the ambivalence between conservative and radical points of view.

But perhaps this ambivalence can be reduced if we note that Hegel is quite self-consciously *not* a "world-historical individual." He is a philosopher. And it is not the job of philosophy, he holds, to change the world; it is the philosopher's job simply to understand it. Remember that we began our consideration of Hegel's philosophy with the problem of the criterion. Hegel suggests that this problem does not need to be solved by the philosopher because it is in process of solving itself; all the philosopher needs to do is "look on" and describe. Near the end of his life, Hegel comes back to that same point in a memorable image.

_____
*Hegel here uses the term "morality" to designate what he elsewhere has called "ethics," perhaps to indicate that only in the actuality of the state does Kantian morality realize its inner nature.

One more word about giving instruction as to what the world ought to be. Philosophy in any case always comes on the scene too late to give it. As the thought of the world, it appears only when actuality is already there cut and dried after its process of formation has been completed. . . . When philosophy paints its grey in grey, then has a shape of life grown old. By philosophy's grey in grey it cannot be rejuvenated but only understood. The owl of Minerva spreads its wings only with the falling of the dusk. (*PR, 12–13*)

_____

1. What is the goal of history, according to Hegel? What all does it justify?
2. Explain the notion of the *cunning* of reason. What are world-historical individuals?
3. How does Hegel think of God? How is God related to the world? To us?
4. Explain the image of the owl of Minerva. What does it say about the task of the philosopher?

For Further Thought

If you were to understand yourself in terms of Hegel's philosophy, how would you characterize (a) your real nature, (b) your relation to society, and (c) your place in history? Would you find this satisfactory?

Notes

1. References to Hegel's works are as follows:
   PS: Phenomenology of Spirit, trans. A. V. Miller (Oxford: Clarendon Press, 1977).
   PR: Hegel's Philosophy of Right, trans. T. M. Knox (Oxford: Oxford University Press, 1952).
   RH: Reason in History, trans. Robert S. Hartman (New York: Liberal Arts Press, 1953).
2. Quoted from *The Logic of Hegel,* trans. William Wallace (Oxford: Clarendon Press, 1892), in Richard Norman, *Hegel's Phenomenology: A Philosophical Introduction* (Published for Sussex University Press by Chatto and Windus, London, 1976), 11.

18

KIERKEGAARD AND MARX

Two Ways to "Correct" Hegel

The influence of Hegel was enormous. Everywhere, he was read and discussed, dissected and analyzed, damned and admired. The synthesis of so much learning and the forging of so many insights could hardly help but shape the next generation of philosophers.

Despite the range and depth of Hegel's thought, some readers had the sense (which perhaps you share) that this magnificent system was extravagant, that it promised more than it could deliver. In a certain way, moreover, and contrary to Hegel's explicit intentions, it seemed too *abstract;* it did not seem to deal concretely enough with the actuality of people's lives as they led them, making specific choices in specific circumstances. This was an ironic complaint indeed, because abstraction is Hegel's great enemy.

In this chapter, we glance at two thinkers who are deeply in Hegel's debt. They can both be considered Hegelians, but they are renegade Hegelians, each in his own way. Both have contributed in lasting ways to our thinking in many spheres of human life, from religion to politics, from art to economics, from the anxieties of individual psychology

to the sociology of class struggle. Their intellectual progeny in our time go by the names of **existentialist** and Marxist. Thus, we examine some of the central contributions of Søren Kierkegaard and Karl Marx to the great conversation.

Kierkegaard: On Individual Existence

The authorship of Søren Kierkegaard (1813–1855) is exceedingly varied and diverse. For one thing, about half of it is pseudonymous (written under other names—and quite a number of them, too). Why? Not for the usual reason, to hide the identity of the author; nearly everyone in little Copenhagen knew Kierkegaard, and they knew he had written these books. There is a deeper reason: the various "authors"—a romantic young man known simply as A; Judge William (a local magistrate), Johannes *de silentio* (John the silent), the Seducer (who writes a famous diary), Victor Eremita (the Hermit), Johannes Climacus (the Climber), to name only a few—represent different views. Through their voices, Kierkegaard expresses certain possibilities for managing the problem of having to exist as a human being. This is a problem, he believes, that we all face. Moreover, it is a problem that cannot be solved in the abstract, by thinking about it—though it cannot be solved without thinking about it either!* A solution is worked out in one's life by the choices one actually makes, thereby defining and creating the self one becomes. His pseudonymous authors "present themselves" to the reader as selves in the process of such self-creation. They thereby function as models for possibilities that you or I might also actualize in our own lives; they awaken us to alternatives and stimulate us to self-examination.

Kierkegaard calls this technique "indirect communication." His motive for adopting it is his conviction that most of us live in varying forms and degrees of self-deception. We are not honest with ourselves about the categories that actually structure our lives. He attempts to provoke the shock of self-recognition by offering characters with which the reader may identify and then revealing slowly, but inexorably, what living in that way really means. He is particularly concerned with an "illusion" he discerns in many of his contemporaries in nineteenth-century Denmark: the impression that they are *Christians.* He wants to clarify what it means actually to live as a Christian. And it is his particular concern to distinguish such a life from two things: (1) from the average bourgeois life of a citizen in this state-church country, where everyone is baptized as a matter of course, and (2) from the illusion that intellectual speculation of the Hegelian type is a modern successor to faith.

In the course of this elaborate literary production, Kierkegaard offers us insights that many recent philosophers, psychologists, and theologians have recovered and used in their own work.† For our present purposes, we sketch several of these life possibilities and then draw some conclusions about how Hegel needs to be modified if Kierkegaard is right. Following Kierkegaard, we call these possibilities the **aesthetic,** the ethical, and the religious.

The Aesthetic

In the first part of a two-part work called *Either/ Or,** we find the somewhat chaotic papers of an unknown young man whom the editor of the volume (himself a pseudonymous character) elects simply to call "A." The fond desire of A's life is simply to *be* something. His ideal is expressed in a line by the twentieth-century poet T. S. Eliot: "You are the music while the music lasts."[1] This kind of complete absorption, which we experience occasionally in pleasurable moments, seems wonderful to him. If only the whole of life could be like that! If only he could evade reflection, self-consciousness, thought, the agony of choice, and this business of always having to *become* something! If he could just enjoy life in its *immediacy.*† A's dream is to live unreflectively a life of pleasure.

But A is a clever and sophisticated young man. He realizes that this is not possible. For one thing, immediacy never exists where it is sought; to take it as one's aim or ideal entails directly that one has missed the goal. As soon as you think, "What I really want is a life of pleasure," you prove that you are already beyond simply *having* such a life. You are reflecting on how nice that would be. No human, in fact, can attain the placid, self-contained immediacy of the brutes. And it is clear to A that pleasure is not his life, but the chief preoccupation of his life.

---

*Kierkegaard, who thinks of himself as the "gadfly of Copenhagen," agrees with Socrates' dictum that "the unexamined life is not worth living." (See Plato's *Apology,* 38a.)

†We later examine a twentieth-century thinker who owes much to Kierkegaard: Martin Heidegger; see Chapter 24.

*Already in the title of this early work, we see an attack on central themes in Hegel, for whom "both/and" might be an appropriate motto. As we have seen, the progress of Hegelian dialectic is a successively reiterated synthesis, gathering in the truth contained in earlier stages until we reach in the end a stage of absolute knowledge. Kierkegaard is convinced that such a stage is impossible for existing human beings. We'll see why.

†"Immediacy," of course, is a Hegelian category. Look back to pp. 467–469 for Hegel's phenomenological critique of immediacy as a foundation for knowledge.

This becomes clear to A through his reflections on the figure of Don Juan. As A imagines him, he is pure, undifferentiated, unreflective desire—nothing more than embodied sensuality. Don Juan wants women wholesale, and he gets what he wants. In Mozart's opera, *Don Giovanni,** the Don's servant keeps a list of his conquests, which he displays in a comic aria, informing us that they number 1003 in Spain alone! Don Juan represents something analogous to a force of nature—an avalanche or hurricane—but for this very reason there is something subhuman about him.† A thereby concludes that this "pure type" can exist only in art and that music is the appropriate vehicle for its expression. Sensuality (together with its associated pleasure) is not human reality, but an aspect of human reality. Considered in itself, it is an abstraction.‡

What, then, to do? To A, there seems to be one obvious solution: to make one's life itself into a work of art. Then one could enjoy it as one enjoys any fine aesthetic object. The pleasures of immediacy may be vanishing, but the pleasures of aesthetic appreciation are all the more available. The most damning comment on a movie or novel is—boring! So one wants above all to keep life interesting. Toward this end, A writes a little "how-to" manual called *Rotation of Crops*.

> People with experience maintain that proceeding from a basic principle is supposed to be very reasonable; I yield to them and proceed from the basic principle that all people are boring. Or is there anyone who would be boring enough to contradict me in this regard? . . . Boredom is the root of all evil.
>
> This can be traced back to the very beginning of the world. The gods were bored; therefore they created human beings. Adam was bored because he was alone; therefore Eve was created. Since that

"The biggest danger, that of losing oneself, can pass off in the world as quietly as if it were nothing; every other loss, an arm, a leg, five dollars, a wife, etc. is bound to be noticed."

—SØREN KIERKEGAARD

moment, boredom entered the world and grew in quantity in exact proportion to the growth of population. Adam was bored alone; then Adam and Eve were bored together; then Adam and Eve and Cain and Abel were bored *en famille*. After that, the population of the world increased and the nations were bored *en masse*. To amuse themselves, they hit upon the notion of building a tower so high that it would reach the sky. This notion is just as boring as the tower was high and is a terrible demonstration of how boredom had gained the upper hand. (*EO* 1, 285–286)²

Here we have an expression of the categories under which A organizes his life. Everything is evaluated in terms of the pair of concepts,

interesting/boring.

---

*Kierkegaard admired this opera extravagantly, attending many performances of it.

†The figure of Don Juan can be understood as a representation of the aspect of reality Nietzsche calls "Dionysian" in his *Birth of Tragedy*. See pp. 536–538, but also compare Nietzsche's later (and different) concept of the Dionysian on p. 562.

‡Here A is echoing, of course, Hegel's own critique of immediacy. These considerations also constitute a criticism of the hedonistic ideal of Epicurus and Hobbes. See pp. 199–200, 366.

The rotation method is a set of techniques for keeping things interesting. Let us just note a few of the recommendations.

Variety, of course, is essential because nothing is as boring as the same old thing. But it is no use trying to achieve variety by varying one's surroundings or circumstances, though this is the "vulgar and inartistic method."

> One is weary of living in the country and moves to the city; one is weary of one's native land and goes abroad; one is europamüde [weary of Europe] and goes to America, etc; one indulges in the fanatical hope of an endless journey from star to star. (*EO* 1, 291)

What one must learn to do is vary *oneself,* a task that A compares to the rotation of crops by a farmer. The key idea is a developed facility for remembering and forgetting. To avoid boredom, we need to remember and forget artistically, not randomly as most of us do. Whoever develops this art will have a never-ending source of interesting experiences at hand.

> No part of life ought to have so much meaning for a person that he cannot forget it any moment he wants to; on the other hand, every single part of life ought to have so much meaning for a person that he can remember it at any moment. (*EO* 1, 293)

In addition, one requires absolute freedom to break away at any time from anything, lest one be at the mercy of something or someone boring. Thus, one must beware of entanglements and avoid commitments. The rule is no friendships (but acquaintances aplenty), no marriage (though an occasional affair adds to the interest), and no business (for what is so boring as the demands of business?).

The key notion is to stay in control. As A writes in one of a series of aphoristic paragraphs,

> Real enjoyment consists not in what one enjoys but in the idea. If I had in my service a submissive jinni who, when I asked for a glass of water, would bring me the world's most expensive wines, deliciously blended, in a goblet, I would dismiss him until he learned that the enjoyment consists not in what I enjoy but in getting my own way. (*EO* 1, 31)

This project of living for the interesting is explored in a variety of ways in A's papers, but its apex is surely the lengthy manuscript known as *The Seducer's Diary.* In some prefatory remarks, A claims to have stolen the diary from the desk of an acquaintance, though the "editor" of *Either/Or,* in which it appears, doubts this. He speculates that it was written by A himself, in which case it may represent a kind of dream on the part of A, in which A explores possibilities that he knows he is capable of—and perhaps we are, too.[*]

The essentials of the plot are simple. Johannes, the diarist, sees a young girl, Cordelia, and is fascinated. He insinuates himself into her family. While paying little attention to her, but much to her fussy old aunt, he sets things up so that he appears interesting to Cordelia. He promotes Edward, a rather conventional and boring young man in love with Cordelia, as a suitable match; but slowly and cleverly he brings her to see Edward—in comparison with himself—as boorish and common. He manipulates an engagement with himself. But then, so subtly that she seems to be making the decisions, he leads her to believe that a marriage is merely an external impediment to true love. *She* breaks the engagement. There is a passionate night together, and then he leaves her.

Everything is arranged by Johannes to intensify the interesting. As a result, the diary is a far cry from those novels of sexual athleticism whose characters are as thin as their bodies are voluptuous. The focus is on the psychological rather than the physical. And it must be so, for the seducer is the polar opposite of Don Juan (within the sphere of the aesthetic).[†] Whereas the latter is supposed to be wholly nonreflective, an embodiment of pure im-

---

[*]Note how possibilities are piled up here. Kierkegaard presents Victor Eremita (the nonreal, merely possible editor of the volume), who presents A (the literary embodiment of certain possibilities), who (possibly) presents the seducer. Everything conspires to hold the reader at a distance, as if to say, *This* is not your life; it is merely a reflection of it. By its very intensification of possibility, it accentuates—by contrast—the actual. The medium is itself part of the message.

[†]Remember that the aesthetic is defined as that style of life in which everything is judged in terms of the pair of categories, interesting/boring.

mediacy, the seducer lives so completely in reflection that he seems to touch down in reality only occasionally. All is planning, arranging, scheming, plotting, and enjoying the results, as one would enjoy a play at the theater. Johannes is at once the playwright, the actor, and the audience in the drama of his life. It is not the actual seduction that matters to him (one moment of physical conquest is much like another), but the drama leading up to that moment. That is where the art lies. That is what is really interesting. And to preserve the aesthetic character of his experience, he must keep the necessary aesthetic distance, even from himself.

> I scarcely know myself. My mind roars like a turbulent sea in the storms of passion. If someone else could see my soul in this state, it would seem to him that it, like a skiff, plunged prow-first down into the ocean, as if in its dreadful momentum it would have to steer down into the depths of the abyss. He does not see that high on the mast a sailor is on the lookout. Roar away, you wild forces, roar away, you powers of passion; even if your waves hurl foam toward the clouds, you still are not able to pile yourselves up over my head— I am sitting as calmly as the king of the mountain. (EO 1, 324–325)

Other aspects of this project to treat one's life like an aesthetic object reveal themselves subtly in the diary. The project must be carried out in secret. To reveal his intentions to Cordelia would bring the whole enterprise to ruin, so he must, necessarily, deceive Cordelia. He is, in terms Kant and Hegel would find appropriate, *using* her for ends she not only does not consent to, but of which she has not the slightest hint.

Does Johannes love Cordelia? He asks himself this question.

> Do I love Cordelia? Yes! Sincerely? Yes! Faithfully? Yes—in the esthetic sense. (EO 1, 385)

He flatters himself that he is benefiting her. In what sense? Why, in the only sense he recognizes: He is making her life more interesting! He found her a naive young girl; he will leave her a sophisticated woman. She was innocent, uninitiated into *possibility*; he has taught her the delights and the ter-

rors of the possible. He found her nature; he will leave her spirit. So, at least, he tells himself.

Whether Cordelia agrees is another matter. A includes a letter she sent to Johannes after the break, which Johannes had returned unopened (EO 1, 312):

> Johannes,
>   Never will I call you "my Johannes," for I certainly realize you have never been that, and I am punished harshly enough for having once been gladdened in my soul by this thought, and yet I do call you "mine": my seducer, my deceiver, my enemy, my murderer, the source of my unhappiness, the tomb of my joy, the abyss of my unhappiness. I call you "mine" and call myself "yours," and as it once flattered your ear, proudly inclined to my adoration, so shall it now sound as a curse upon you, a curse for all eternity. . . . Yours I am, yours, yours, your curse.
>
>   Your Cordelia

It appears that even within the sphere of the aesthetic there might be no clear answer to whether Johannes has benefited Cordelia. But, as we'll see, that is not the only kind of question that can be asked.

---

1. What is "indirect communication"? Why did Kierkegaard write so much under pseudonyms?
2. Under what categories does an aesthete organize his or her life? Describe two ways this might work out, using the examples of Don Juan and the seducer.

The Ethical

The bulk of the second part of *Either/Or* is composed of several long letters from a magistrate in one of the lower courts, a certain Judge William. They are addressed to A. The main topic is love, but the judge has his eye on a larger issue: what it means for an existing human being to be a *self*.

To see the relevance of this issue, let us look back to another of A's aphorisms. He says,

My life is utterly meaningless. When I consider its various epochs, my life is like the word *Schnur* in the dictionary, which first of all means a string, and second a daughter-in-law. All that is lacking is that in the third place the word *Schnur* means a camel, in the fourth a whisk broom. (*EO* 1, 36)

A recognizes that there is no continuity in his life. It is as if he were a succession of different people, one interested in this, another in that. The different periods of his life have no more relation to each other than do the meanings of the word *Schnur*. In a sense, A has no self—or rather, he is splintered into a multiplicity of semi-selves, which comes to much the same thing. The judge has a remedy.

Taking his cue from A's own preoccupations, the judge gives us an analysis of romantic love. Its "mark" is that it is *immediate*. Its watchword is "To see her was to love her." And indeed, that is how we think about love, too; we talk about "falling in love"—something that can *happen* to one, a condition in which one may, suddenly, just find oneself. Falling in love is not something one *does* deliberately after reflection.

> Romantic love manifests itself as immediate by exclusively resting in natural necessity. It is based on beauty, partly on sensuous beauty. . . . Although this love is based essentially on the sensuous, it nevertheless is noble by virtue of the consciousness of the eternal which it assimilates, for it is this that distinguishes all love from lust: that it bears a stamp of eternity. The lovers are deeply convinced that in itself their relationship is a complete whole that will never be changed. (*EO* 2, 21)

This conviction, however, because it is based merely on something natural, on *what happens to one,* is an illusion. If you can fall into love, you can fall out of it again. For this reason, it is easy to make romantic love look ridiculous; it promises what it cannot deliver: faithfulness, persistence, *eternity.* (Just listen to popular love songs.) The judge notes that a lot of modern literature expresses cynicism about love. The culmination of this cynicism is either (1) giving in to the transience of nature, resigning the promise of lasting love, and making do with a series of affairs; or (2) the marriage of convenience, which gives up on love altogether.

The judge deplores both alternatives. He believes A is right in valuing romantic love. But, he says to A, What you want, you can't have on your terms. The promise of eternity in romantic love can be realized, but not if you simply "go with the flow" (as we say). What is required is choice, a determination of the will.

The judge is a defender of conjugal love, a defender of marriage, the mark of which is precisely the engagement of the will. The bride and groom *make promises* to each other. They promise to *love.* The judge argues that what one hears from the Romantic poets, that marriage is the enemy of romantic love, is simply false. For what romantic love seems to offer, but cannot deliver, is exactly what the engagement of the will can provide: the continuity and permanence of love. Marriage, as an expression of the will, is not the death of romantic love; it comes to its aid and provides what it needs in order to endure. Without the will, love is simply inconstant and arbitrary nature.*

It is true, the judge admits, that conjugal love is not a fit subject for art. Love stories usually go like this: The handsome prince falls in love with the beautiful princess, and after much opposition and struggle (ogres and dragons, wicked uncles and unwilling fathers), they are married; the last line of the story is "And they lived happily ever after." But, says the judge, these stories end just where the really interesting part begins. Nevertheless, the marriage cannot be represented in art, "for the very point is time in its extension." The married person "has not fought with lions and ogres, but with the most dangerous enemy—with time."

> The faithful romantic lover waits, let us say for fifteen years; then comes the moment that rewards him. Here poetry very properly perceives that the fifteen years can easily be concentrated; now it hastens to the moment. A married man is faithful for fifteen years, and yet during these fifteen years he has had possession; therefore in this long succession

---

*Compare what Hegel has to say about the "arbitrariness" of a will (by which he means merely natural or conditioned desires) that has not been subjected to reason. See p. 480.

he has continually acquired the faithfulness he possessed, since marital love has in itself the first love and thereby the faithfulness of the first love. But an ideal married man of this sort cannot be portrayed, for the point is time in extension. . . .

And although this cannot be portrayed artistically, then let your consolation be, as it is mine, that we are not to read about or listen to or look at what is the highest and the most beautiful in life, but are, if you please, to live it.

Therefore, when I readily admit that romantic love lends itself much better to artistic portrayal than marital love, this does not at all mean that it is less esthetic than the other—on the contrary, it is more esthetic. (*EO* 2, 138–139)

The judge is defending the *aesthetic* validity of marriage and, with it, the self. For the judge sees marriage as an example of a style of life quite other than that which A has been leading. The ethical life requires the development of the *self*.

The crucial difference between the aesthetic and the ethical is *choice*. In a certain sense, of course, the aesthetic life is full of choices. But, with that clear-sighted irony that an intelligent aesthete brings to his experience, A sees that none of them are significant choices. Any choice might as well have been the opposite—and can be tomorrow. After all, if your aim is "the interesting," you must not get stuck in commitments. None of these aesthetic choices really mean anything for the self doing the choosing. Among A's papers, this is expressed in "An ecstatic lecture."

> Marry, and you will regret it. Do not marry, and you will also regret it. . . . Whether you marry or do not marry, you will regret it either way. Laugh at the stupidities of the world, and you will regret it; weep over them, and you will also regret it. . . . Whether you laugh at the stupidities of the world or weep over them, you will regret it either way. Trust a girl, and you will regret it. Do not trust her, and you will also regret it. . . . Whether you trust a girl or do not trust her, you will regret it either way. Hang yourself, and you will regret it. Do not hang yourself, and you will also regret it. . . . Whether you hang yourself or do not hang yourself, you will regret it either way. This, gentle-

men, is the quintessence of all the wisdom of life. (*EO* 1, 38–39)

In a certain sense, "either/or" is A's watchword. But *how* one says this makes all the difference. And the judge urges that A's manner of saying it means the loss of the self.

> Imagine a captain of a ship the moment a shift of direction must be made; then he may be able to say: I can do either this or that. But if he is not a mediocre captain he will also be aware that during all this the ship is ploughing ahead with its ordinary velocity, and thus there is but a single moment when it is inconsequential whether he does this or does that. So also with a person . . . there eventually comes a moment where it is no longer a matter of Either/Or, not because he has chosen, but because he has refrained from it, which also can be expressed by saying: Because others have chosen for him—or because he has lost himself. (*EO* 2, 164)

And so it is with us; if we drift, if we fail to decisively take hold of our lives, if we treat every either/or as indifferent, we will lose our selves; there will be nobody who we are.*

So the judge pleads with A to adopt a different either/or, the mark of which is *seriousness of choice*. When one chooses seriously, when one *engages oneself*, one chooses *ethically*.†

> Your choice is an esthetic choice, but an esthetic choice is no choice. On the whole, to choose is an intrinsic and stringent term for the ethical. Wherever in the stricter sense there is a question of an Either/Or, one can always be sure that the ethical has something to do with it. The only absolute Either/Or is the choice between good and evil, but this is also absolutely ethical. (*EO* 2, 166–167)

---

*This thought is developed by Martin Heidegger, who holds that without a resolute seizing of oneself, one's life is dominated by what "they" say, or what "One" does or doesn't do. See "The 'Who' of Dasein," in Chapter 24.

†This does not mean that one necessarily chooses the right, but that one's choice, whether right or wrong, lies within the domain of the ethical; it is a choice subject to ethical evaluation. From the aesthetic point of view, such evaluation is simply not meaningful (since the categories of evaluation are restricted to "interesting/boring").

And yet the judge is not—at least not directly—urging A to choose the good. He just wants him to *choose*.

> What, then, is it that I separate in my Either/Or? Is it good and evil? No, I only want to bring you to the point where this choice truly has meaning for you. . . .
>
> Rather than designating the choice between good and evil, my Either/Or designates the choice by which one chooses good and evil or rules them out. Here the question is under what qualifications one will view all existence and personally live. That the person who chooses good and evil chooses the good is indeed true, but only later does this become manifest, for the esthetic is not evil but the indifferent. And that is why I said that the ethical constitutes the choice. Therefore, it is not so much a matter of choosing between willing good or willing evil as of choosing to will, but that in turn posits good and evil. (*EO* 2, 168–169)

The judge's either/or, then, has to do with the categories under which things are evaluated. One will lead a radically different life if everything is decided according to

good/evil (ethical choice)

rather than

interesting/boring (aesthetic choice).

And the basic either/or, the really significant or deep one, is not either one of these alternatives, but that which poses this question:

aesthetic *or* ethical?

If the judge is right, the mark of making that choice is the *way* one chooses: with the entire seriousness and passion of the will (in which case the categories of good and evil *automatically* arise), or in that ironic, detached, amoral way in which one can say, "Choose either, you will regret both."

We can now see why marriage is, for the judge, an example and symbol of the ethical. What one says at the altar is a decisive expression of the will, a choice that one makes for the future, a choice of *oneself*. One chooses to be the sort of self who will continue to nurture and come to the aid of romantic love. It is no longer a matter of what happens to you; it is a matter of what you do with what happens to you.[*] The ethical person gives up the futile project of simply trying to *be* something, and takes up the project of *becoming* something—of becoming a *self*.

It will be helpful before moving on to summarize some of the chief differences between these two ways of life. It is striking how different everything looks from the two perspectives.

- *Immediacy,* which in the aesthetic stage has the status of a condition to be aspired to, looks from the ethical point of view like *nature*— that is, material for the will to act upon, to shape and form.

- The possibility of *reflection* in the aesthetic (the spectator's view of one's own life) takes on in the ethical the aspect of *practical freedom* (the ability to take the givens of one's life and make something of them).

- The necessity for *secrecy* in the aesthetic life (remember the seducer) is supplanted by a requirement of *openness* in the ethical.

- The prominence of the *accidental* in the aesthetic (what happens to one) finds its ethical contrast in the notion of the *universal* (what duty requires of every human being).

- The *abstraction* of the aesthetic, hung as it is between the impossible immediacy of Don Juan and the incredible reflectiveness of the seducer, is contrasted with the *concreteness* of an individual's self-construction, where the accidental givens are taken over and shaped by the universal demands of duty.

- The attempt to *be* is given up in favor of the striving to *become*.

- The emphasis on the *moment* is superseded by the value of the *historical* (as in an affair versus a marriage).

---

[*]Notice the similarity to Stoic notions of self-control. See pp. 205–207.

- The *fragmentariness* of an aesthetic life stands in contrast to the *continuity* of the ethical.

These contrasts pave two distinct avenues for human life. The question arises, Are there any other possibilities?

---

1. Explain Judge William's fundamental Either/Or. How does it relate to choice? And how is this choice different from the many choices made by an aesthete?
2. What is the judge's view of the relation between romantic love and marriage?

The Religious

If the key characteristic of the aesthetic style of life is enjoying (and perhaps arranging) what happens to one, and that of the ethical stage is taking oneself in hand and creating oneself, it seems apparent that human existence involves a tension between two poles. Kierkegaard characterizes them differently in various works: immediacy and reflection; nature and freedom; necessity and possibility; the temporal and the eternal; the finite and the infinite. On the one hand, we simply *are* something: a collection of accidental facts. "I am American, five feet ten inches tall, and balding." On the other hand, we are an awareness of this, together with some attitude toward these facts and the need to do something about them. This aspect of ourselves seems to elude all limitation, since it is not definitely this or that. It seems to be a capacity for distancing ourselves from anything finite, temporal, and given.*

From the ethical point of view, this duality defines the task facing an individual: to *become oneself*. The task is to bring these two poles together so that they interpenetrate and inform each other: The immediate and finite takes a definite shape, and the reflective and infinite loses its abstract indefi-

niteness. One becomes a definite and unique thing: oneself.*

If you listened only to the judge, you might think that this is an achievable, if difficult, task. Further reflection, however, casts doubt on that optimistic assumption. These two sides of a person, the raw material from which a self is to be constructed, have a disconcerting tendency to drift apart. We slide into identifying ourselves now with one aspect, now with another. Indeed, this is not something that just happens to us; it is a tendency we acquiesce in, cooperate with. We refuse the anxiety-filled role of having to hold the two poles together. Our problem is that we are *not willing to be ourselves* and always want to be something more or something less: *either* something approaching God *or* something analogous to an unthinking brute.

As soon as we discover this tendency, we are beyond the ethical. What use is more determination to succeed in the task of being yourself if you continually undermine this determination by your unwillingness to be yourself?† All this huffing and puffing and moral seriousness begin to look like impossible attempts to lift yourself by your own bootstraps. You might as well try to raise yourself off the ground by wrapping your arms around your chest and lifting!

Even the judge seems to have an inkling of this; the last thing we hear from him concerns a "sermon" that he sends along to A. The judge tells A that the sermon has caused him to think about himself, and also about A. The sermon was composed by an "older friend" of the judge's, a pastor out on

---

*See the note on p. 471, where I discuss Hegel's notion of pure self-consciousness. See also Pico della Mirandola on the dignity of human beings, pp. 303–304.

---

*We need to be careful here. Kierkegaard does not present the ethical self as unique in the sense that it defines itself as *different from other selves*, for that would be to define it in terms external to itself. Becoming oneself involves the embodiment of those rational and universally human aspects that Kant and Hegel focus on in their treatment of morality and ethics. These are shared by all. But the *way* in which these are embodied will depend on the particular given facts about oneself, and in that respect, no one individual will be exactly like any other.

†Compare what Augustine has to say about the bondage of the will. See pp. 231 and 250. The "unhappy consciousness" of Hegel, at once self-liberating and self-perverting, is another expression of this stage. See p. 475.

the heaths of Denmark; it is a meditation on the thought that "as against God, we are always in the wrong." The pastor says that this is an edifying thought, a helpful thought, a thought in which we can find rest. Struggling with the ethical task, we inevitably discover ourselves failing. What then should we do? Perhaps, the pastor says, we try to console ourselves by saying, "I do what I can." But, he asks, doesn't that provoke a new anxiety?

> If a person is sometimes in the right, sometimes in the wrong, to some degree in the right, to some degree in the wrong, who, then, is the one who makes that decision except the person himself, but in the decision may he not again be to some degree in the right and to some degree in the wrong?
>
> Doubt is again set in motion, care again aroused; let us try to calm it by deliberating on: THE *UPBUILDING* THAT LIES IN THE THOUGHT THAT IN RELATION TO GOD WE ARE ALWAYS IN THE WRONG. (*EO* 2, 345–346)

These thoughts take us into the domain of religion; it is no coincidence that they are presented in a sermon. Kierkegaard's views on religion are complex and extensive; he expresses some of them under still other pseudonyms and some under his own name. He distinguishes two levels of religion: a basic level of religious consciousness in general (shared by pagan figures such as Socrates, and Old Testament patriarchs, such as Abraham) and a more intense level distinctive, he thinks, of Christianity. One of his "authors" calls the first "religiousness A" and the second "religiousness B." Let us look at each in turn.

In a haunting little book by Johannes *de silentio* (John the silent) called *Fear and Trembling,* he poses this question: Is there anything beyond the ethical? If so, what would it be like? Johannes meditates on Abraham, in particular on a story in Genesis 22, where God asks Abraham to take his only son, Isaac, to Mount Moriah and there offer him up as a sacrifice. Abraham does what God asks, and only at the last moment, as Abraham raises the knife, is Isaac spared. If there is a stage of life beyond the ethical, this seems an appropriate story to contemplate. As Johannes makes clear, from a strictly eth-

ical point of view,* Abraham is the moral equivalent of a murderer; he was willing to do the deed. Yet he is remembered as the *father of faith.* What can this mean?

Johannes says that he cannot understand Abraham, cannot explain him. Before Abraham he is "silent." The reason is that Abraham seems to do two contradictory things at once. On the one hand, he apparently gives up Isaac, resigns any claim to him, emotionally lets him go; how else could he travel those three long days to Moriah? On the other hand, he clearly continues to love Isaac as dearly as ever and even to believe that the sacrifice of Isaac will not be required of him! The proof, Johannes says, is that Abraham was not embarrassed before Isaac after having raised the knife—that he received him back with joy. How could anyone do both things, simultaneously make both these "movements" of the spirit? It seems impossible, paradoxical, absurd.

But, Johannes suggests, this absurdity is precisely the secret life of faith. If there is anything beyond the ethically human, it must be something like this. It must be a state in which one lives in an absolute relationship to God, where even the universally human requirements of the ethical drop away into relative insignificance.† Yet it is not an escape from this world, but a life wholly engaged in the concrete finitude of one's earthly being.

Johannes illustrates these two internal movements by describing two "knights." The Knight of Infinite Resignation withdraws into the interior chambers of the spirit, makes no claims on anyone, asks for nothing worldly. He no longer identifies

---

*The ethical is here understood as the highest that human thought can reach with respect to our duties to one another. Johannes, like Kant, takes ethics to be composed of rules that we rationally understand to be binding on us all. From the ethical standpoint, then, taking one's son out to slaughter him is clearly forbidden. No one could rationally universalize this rule.
†It is not, of course, that a religious life of faith is an *unethical* life. Just as the judge argues that an ethical life is *more* aesthetic than a life lived specifically for aesthetic enjoyments, so does a relation to God preserve and enhance whatever is of value in the ethical life. As Johannes points out, Abraham did not become the father of faith by *hating* his son.

himself with his possessions, his worldly relationships, or even his body. Like the Stoic philosopher or the monk, this knight identifies with the infinite, reflective side of himself, with his "eternal consciousness":

> In infinite resignation there is peace and rest; every person who wills it . . . can discipline himself to make this movement, which in its pain reconciles one to existence. Infinite resignation is that shirt mentioned in an old legend. The thread is spun with tears, bleached with tears; the shirt is sewn in tears—but then it also gives protection better than iron or steel. The defect in the legend is that a third person can work up this linen. The secret in life is that each person must sew it himself, and the remarkable thing is that a man can sew it fully as well as a woman. (*FT,* 45)

Johannes stresses how difficult it must be to make this movement. It would seem to require absolutely all one's energy, all one's strength, all one's passion. What could be left over to make still another movement? Yet that is just what the Knight of Faith does. He also resigns everything, sets himself adrift from the world, takes refuge in the eternal side of himself. But as he is making the movements of infinite resignation, the Knight of Faith comes back again into the world. How does he do that? Where does he find the strength? Johannes doesn't know. He can't understand it.

He admires the Knight of Resignation extravagantly; he can understand, he says, how someone could resign everything, thinks he might even be capable of it himself, difficult though it is. But faith he can't understand. It seems absurd to him that this should be possible. And yet, if there is to be anything beyond the ethical, it would have to be something like this paradoxical life, simultaneously beyond and totally within this world. Johannes imagines that he meets a Knight of Faith.

> The instant I first lay eyes on him, I set him apart at once; I jump back, clap my hands, and say half aloud, "Good Lord, is this the man, is this really the one—he looks just like a tax collector!" But this is indeed the one. I move a little closer to him, watch his slightest movement to see if it reveals a bit of heterogeneous optical telegraphy from the infinite, a glance, a facial expression, a gesture, a

sadness, a smile that would betray the infinite in its heterogeneity with the finite. No! I examine his figure from top to toe to see if there may not be a crack through which the infinite would peek. No! He is solid all the way through. . . . He belongs entirely to the world; no bourgeois philistine could belong to it more. . . . He finds pleasure in everything, takes part in everything. . . . He attends to his job. . . . He goes to church. . . . In the afternoon, he takes a walk to the woods. He enjoys everything he sees, the swarms of people, the new omnibuses. . . . Toward evening, he goes home, and his gait is as steady as a postman's. On the way, he thinks that his wife surely will have a special hot meal for him when he comes home—for example, roast lamb's head with vegetables. If he meets a kindred soul, he would go on talking all the way to Østerport about this delicacy with a passion befitting a restaurant operator. It so happens that he does not have four shillings to his name, and yet he firmly believes that his wife has this delectable meal waiting for him. If she has, to see him eat would be the envy of the elite and an inspiration to the common man, for his appetite is keener than Esau's. His wife does not have it—curiously enough, he is just the same. . . . And yet, yet—yes, I could be infuriated over it if for no other reason than envy—and yet this man has made and at every moment is making the movement of infinity. He drains the deep sadness of life in infinite resignation, he knows the blessedness of infinity, he has felt the pain of renouncing everything, the most precious thing in the world, and yet the finite tastes just as good to him as one who never knew anything higher. (*FT,* 38–40)

Several points stand out in this portrait. The first is that faith is not something to be understood, not a doctrine to be memorized and accepted. Faith is something to be lived. Second, the life of faith is not an otherworldly or particularly ascetic sort of life. There are, of course, many sorts of lives that someone who is every moment making the movement of infinite resignation would simply not be interested in, but it is definitely a life *in* the world. Third, it is not easy to recognize a knight of faith. What distinguishes such knights from other people is not external but a matter of their "inwardness"; it concerns not so much what they do but how and why they do what they do. Fourth, because of its interiority, it may seem easy to "have faith"; it may seem to be something everybody and her brother has already got. But that is an illusion. In fact, no other sort of life is as difficult, as demanding, as strenuous as the life of faith. For, Johannes tells us, faith is a *passion,* the highest passion of all.

Johannes is full of scorn for Hegelian philosophers who think they have "understood" faith, and now want to "go further." Here, he says, there is nothing to understand, nothing that can be learned in a formula from someone else. It is not like a theorem that has been proved, which you can use to prove still other theorems. Here we have a way of life. To aspire to get beyond it is to show that you haven't the slightest idea what sort of life is lived by knights of faith. In an entire lifetime, he says, Abraham did not get further than faith. If it is possible at all, it is apparent that the life of faith is the greatest and most arduous life one could live.

In a large and difficult book, *Concluding Unscientific Postscript,* the philosopher among the pseudonyms, Johannes Climacus, offers an intriguing image. An existing individual, he says, cannot be in two places at the same time; "when he is nearest to being in two places at the same time he is in passion" (*CUP,* 178). What does he mean?

Suppose you are facing a chemistry exam tomorrow and it is important to you to do well. Here are two possibilities: (1) You have been attending class, doing the homework, and have easily passed the quizzes so far; (2) you have been neglecting the course but are hoping an all-nighter will pull you through. It is as if you were in two places at once, the place you actually are and the place you want to be. And it is clear that the "distance" between these two points is greater in situation (2) than in (1). Correspondingly, passion is heightened in situation (2): fear, anxiety, desperation, and panic make themselves felt. The greater the distance between where you are and where you want to be, the greater the passion.

We can apply this principle to the sorts of lives that Kierkegaard's pseudonymous authors are presenting for our consideration. There is certainly passion in the aesthete's life, but there is no *great* passion because the aesthete is wholeheartedly committed to nothing. If we live this way, we fritter life away pursuing momentary passions, always ready to move on if interest flags; there is nothing for which we are willing to live or die.

There is much greater passion, much greater intensity in the life the judge recommends. Why? Because the distance between where the judge is and where he genuinely wants to be is much greater: His aim is to construct himself as a concrete ethical individual over a lifetime, making his moment-to-moment particularity an exemplary instance of what is universally required of all. Now that's reaching pretty far; that's a task! And that's why the judge insists that the way to reach it is committed, passionate, whole-hearted choice.

Johannes *de silentio* tells us, as we have seen, that faith is the highest of the passions. Can we understand what he means by this? Let us take Socrates as an example, remembering that the first religious stage is exemplified in paganism as well as in Old Testament patriarchs such as Abraham. Socrates wants the truth, the truth about human excellence. He wants to understand courage, piety, justice, and what makes a life worth living. We see him still pursuing the same goal daily at the age of seventy, still asking questions, not satisfied that he *knows.* Now that's passion!

Is Socrates wise? The oracle at Delphi had said there was no one wiser, and after his long search, Socrates concludes that the god was right. Those persons are wisest who know that they don't know, who understand that true wisdom belongs to the god alone. But Socrates never relaxes into a "who's to say?" or "true-for-me" mode. Thinking that something is true doesn't in itself *make* it true, he holds. And so, though he is never satisfied, he keeps his faith in truth. For humans, Socrates believes, it is the search for truth that is the very best way of life.[*]

Johannes Climacus understands Socratic passion in this way: There is a disparity between individuals who exist in time and what is eternally true; it is paradoxical to think that existing individuals such as you and I could actually grasp that truth. So if that is what we want, we are in two places that

---

[*] For a discussion of Socrates' character and philosophical convictions, see Chapters 4 and 5.

are very far from each other—much farther from each other than you are from an "A" in chemistry, even if you haven't been studying. So the passion is intensified. Like Abraham's faith in God (maintained though he can't understand God's asking for the sacrifice of his son), Socrates' life exemplifies a passionate faith in the existence of a truth about human existence. This faith manifests itself in a lifelong search.

Is it possible that the passion guiding a life should be still more intense than that? Yes, says Climacus. The sermon that caused the judge to rethink his own life has already given us a hint. Suppose, he says, that the situation is worse than it seems to Socrates. Suppose that we are not just lacking the truth but that we are continually engaged in obscuring the truth—hiding it from ourselves, deceiving ourselves, pretending that we are other than in fact we are. If that were our situation, we would be even further from the eternal truth than Socrates thinks. Once again, passion would be intensified.

Now this is precisely, he says, the possibility Christianity puts before us; this is what distinguishes Christianity from all sorts of paganism, from mysticism, from Socratic and Abrahamic religion, and (he might add today) from New Age optimism. Christianity (religiousness B) tells us that we are sinners. But what is sin? It is a very shallow view of sin to think of it as rule-breaking, as occasional lapses from the straight and narrow. No, sin is a condition of the self. *Sin is despair.* And what is despair? We already know; despair is *not being willing to be oneself.*

The many varieties of despair are examined in a little book by Anti-Climacus, *The Sickness unto Death.** Being able to be in despair is our advantage over the other animals, but actually to be in despair is "the greatest misfortune and misery" (*SUD,* 45). Despair is a sickness in the self; unless cured, it leads to death—not the death of the body, but the

death of the self. And that is the worst sort of death there is, for if we are not a self, what are we?

We usually think of despair as something that overcomes us, something produced in us by unfavorable events.

> Someone in despair despairs over *something.* So, for a moment, it seems, but only for a moment. That same instant the true despair shows itself, or despair in its true guise. In despairing over *something* he was really despairing over *himself,* and he now wants to be rid of himself. (*SUD,* 49)

My wife leaves me or the stock market crashes, and I am in despair. Am I in despair over my wife leaving or over the market crash? No, Anti-Climacus says; that is a shallow view. I am in despair over myself; my despairing is my not being willing to be this self that I now am—this self whose wife has left him, whose stock portfolio is worthless. I would rather be someone else, perhaps almost anyone else. That is my sickness. That is the essence of despair.

But what is a self? In a passage often cited for obscurity, Anti-Climacus says,

> The self is a relation which relates to itself, or that in the relation which is its relating to itself. The self is not the relation but the relation's relating to itself. A human being is a synthesis of the infinite and the finite, of the temporal and the eternal, of freedom and necessity. In short a synthesis. (*SUD,* 43)

Here we have our old friends, the duality of (1) what we immediately, factually, are, and (2) the possibility of reflecting on that and (freely) doing something about it. But we are not yet selves, Anti-Climacus says, just in virtue of this duality in us, this synthesis of two opposing factors. No, being a self is having to relate these factors to each other, bringing them into balance, creating a harmony between them. Being a self, as the judge also says, is a task. It is a task we can fail at. And our failure is despair, an imbalance in the factors of the synthesis that manifests our unwillingness to be ourselves.

The analysis of despair by Anti-Climacus is subtle and complex. Here we can examine only a few examples. Thinking about the factors that make up a human being, we note that there can be

---

* Johannes Climacus tells us that he is not a Christian, but he claims to know what it is to be or become a Christian. Anti-Climacus writes from the point of view of a sort of super-Christian. Together they give us a view from beneath and a view from above of what a Christian life would be like.

a despair of infinitude and a despair of finitude. Let's see what each is like.

1. *The Despair of Infinitude*. If I fall into this kind of despair, I lack finitude. I drift off into never-never land and become "fantastic." My *emotions* slide into fantasy in a kind of abstract sentimentality; I absolutely melt with sympathy for suffering mankind, but I cannot stand my next-door neighbor. My *understanding* becomes fantastic when it squanders itself in the pursuit of useless knowledge or in satisfying idle curiosity; I know all about the lives of the movie stars, but don't care to know about the troubles of my roommate. My *will* fantasizes by building castles in the air; I am full of all the many wonderful things I will do, but do not focus on the nearest act at hand that would move me one step along the way. All this is despair. All this is not being willing to be myself. All this is sin.

2. *The Despair of Finitude*. Falling into this kind of despair means I lack possibility, distance from myself, open vistas. I just go along with the crowd, doing what is expected, assuming that my path is already set by "the others."*

> By seeing the multitude of people around it, by being busied with all sorts of worldly affairs, by being wise to the ways of the world, such a person forgets himself, in a divine sense forgets his own name, dares not believe in himself, finds being himself too risky, finds it much easier and safer to be like the others, to become a copy, a number, along with the crowd.
>
> Now this form of despair goes practically unnoticed in the world. Precisely by losing oneself in this way, such a person gains all that is required for a flawless performance in everyday life, yes, for making a great success out of life. Here there is no dragging of the feet, no difficulty with his self and its infinitizing, he is ground smooth as a pebble, as exchangeable as a coin of the realm. Far from anyone thinking him to be in despair, he is just what a human being ought to be. Naturally the world has generally no understanding of what is truly horrifying. . . .

---

*Martin Heidegger's more recent discussion of human existence as "falling-in-with-the-One" is obviously indebted to Kierkegaard's discussion of despair. See Chapter 24.

> Yes, what we call worldliness simply consists of such people who, if one may so express it, pawn themselves to the world. They use their abilities, amass wealth, carry out worldly enterprises, make prudent calculations, etc., and perhaps are mentioned in history, but they are not themselves. (*SUD*, 63–65)

All this is despair. All this is not being willing to be myself. All this is sin.

There is another form that despair can take—a rather surprising one given the general definition of despair. I can in defiance will to be myself. What is that like?

3. *The Despair of Defiance*. We can perhaps light up this form of despair by contrasting *being willing* to be oneself with *willing* to be oneself. In the latter there is something proud, arrogant, Promethean. Here

> the self wants in despair to rule over himself, or create himself, make this self the self he wants to be, determine what he will have and what he will not have in his concrete self. . . . That is to say, he wants to begin a little earlier than other people, not at and with the beginning, but "in the beginning"; he does not want to don his own self, does not want to see his task in his given self, he wants . . . to construct it himself. (*SUD*, 99)

"In the beginning" is obviously a reference to the first words of Genesis; this self wants to be its own god, to create itself completely. That is why Anti-Climacus says such a person "does not want to don his own self" but to construct it—out of nothing, as it were.

Defiance can take several forms.

3a. *Active Defiance*. I will make myself whatever I want to be. I am self-made, and if I don't like what I turn out to be, I'll become something else. In this mode, the self

> can, at any moment, start quite arbitrarily all over again. . . . So, far from the self succeeding increasingly in being itself, it becomes increasingly obvious that it is a hypothetical self. The self is its own master, absolutely (as one says) its own master; and exactly this is the despair, but also what it regards as its pleasure and joy. But it is easy on closer examination to see that this absolute ruler is a king

without a country, that really he rules over nothing; his position, his kingdom, his sovereignty, are subject to the dialectic that rebellion is legitimate at any moment. Ultimately it is arbitrarily based upon the self itself.

Consequently, the despairing self is forever building only castles in the air. (*SUD*, 100)

In that old television comedy, *The Honeymooners*, Ralph tells his wife, Alice, "Remember, I'm the king, and you're nothing. *I'm* the king; *you're* nothing." To which she replies, "Big deal, king over nothing."

3b. *Passive Defiance.* Perhaps I find something objectionable about myself. I notice a flaw, perhaps in my character, perhaps in my physical constitution, and because of it I am filled with resentment. I am offended. But I don't want to be changed or healed—oh no! That would deprive me of my case against existence—against God himself. In passive defiance the self uses the flaw

> as an excuse to take offense at all existence; he wants to be himself in spite of it. (*SUD*, 102)

> The demonic despair . . . wants to be itself in hatred toward existence, to be itself according to its misery. . . . Rebelling against all existence, it thinks it has acquired evidence against existence, against its goodness. The despairer thinks that he himself is this evidence. . . . It is, to describe it figuratively, as if a writer were to make a slip of the pen, and the error became conscious of itself as such—perhaps it wasn't a mistake but from a much higher point of view an essential ingredient in the whole presentation—and as if this error wanted now to rebel against the author, out of hatred for him forbid him to correct it, and in manic defiance say to him: "No, I will not be erased, I will stand as a witness against you, a witness to the fact that you are a second-rate author." (*SUD*, 104–105)*

In wanting to be its own creator, to begin "a little earlier than other people," the defiant self imagines that it can establish itself from the ground up. But

no one can do that. There is much about each of us that we simply have to accept. So even defiance is despair. Even this is not being willing to be myself—the self that I actually am. Even this is sin.

But all this analysis raises an urgent question: What would a self be like that did not despair?

> This then is the formula which describes the state of the self when despair is completely eradicated: in relating to itself and in wanting to be itself, the self is grounded transparently in the power that established it. (*SUD*, 43)

What does Anti-Climacus mean by saying that such a self is "grounded transparently in the power that established it"? We can call this power *God*. But what does *transparent grounding* come to? I think he means to say that there are not *two* things to do: (1) be willing to be oneself, and (2) establish a relationship with God. No, doing the first *is* doing the second, and vice versa. You cannot do one without doing the other.

What should we call this state of a self without despair? Virtue? No, says Anti-Climacus, not virtue. The proper name for the state of the self opposite to despair is *faith*. So we come back again to that passion of inward intensity we met earlier in the Knight of Faith. Only now the passion is ever so much more intense because now we can see how much we are actually despairing—how far from a true way of life we really are.

But how could we come to accept ourselves as we are, knowing what we now know about despair, about sin? Isn't this just as impossible as the judge actually living the perfectly ethical life? What we require is forgiveness. And this, too, Christianity has a word about. But it is a word that once more intensifies the passion, for it is the word about Christ, the God-Man who makes our forgiveness possible. Kierkegaard and his pseudonyms all agree that this pushes the truth out beyond all understanding. If, with Socrates, the relation between an existing individual and the eternal truth had an element of paradox about it, Christianity makes it far worse. If there is any truth in Christianity, it is absolutely paradoxical, paradoxical in itself. If we know anything about God, we know God is not

---

*This passively defiant despair is perfectly captured in the spiteful voice that speaks in Dostoevsky's *Notes from Underground*.

human; and if we know anything about humans, we know they are not God. Yet Christianity proclaims our healing through the life and death of the God-Man.

What does this mean? It means, Kierkegaard is certain, that faith should never be confused with knowledge. (Philosophy is just confused, a subject for ridicule, if it thinks that by human reason it can "go further" than faith; faith is not a matter of understanding anything, for the absolute paradox rebuffs our understanding.) It means that proofs for the existence of God and evidence for the divinity of Jesus are beside the point; faith is not a matter of accepting certain propositions as true, but of *existing* in a certain manner. (Christianity resists being understood; it invites a certain form of life.) It means that a life trusting in the forgiveness of sins, a life in imitation of Christ, is inherently risky——that there are no guarantees that it will "pay off." Such a life is the ultimate risk, stretched as it is between recognition of one's sinfulness and the paradox of possible forgiveness. But such is the life of faith; for faith is the highest passion.

But does Christianity present us with the truth about ourselves, about our sickness and its healing——or not? That is not a question Kierkegaard thinks he can answer for us. That is something we all have to answer for ourselves. And answer it we will——one way or another——in our lives.

-----

1. What two "movements" does the Knight of Faith make? Why does Johannes *de silentio* think this is "absurd," or beyond human understanding?
2. Characterize in several ways the two aspects of human life that fascinate Kierkegaard and his "authors."
3. How do these two aspects look to the aesthete, to the ethical person, and to someone who lives in religious categories?
4. What is despair? What is the condition of a self when despair is completely eradicated? How can this be attained?
5. What, according to Kierkegaard and Johannes Climacus, is distinctive about Christianity? Why is it characterized as "the highest passion"?

The Individual

You might think that the pattern we have seen in the relations between aesthetic, ethical, and religious forms of life is just the Hegelian pattern all over again. Inadequacies in earlier stages are exposed and remedied by later stages, toward which consciousness moves with a kind of inexorable logic. But this would be a serious mistake. To see why, we must examine the way Kierkegaard understands the position of the individual human being.

One reason he resorts to indirect communication is to combat the Hegelian view of the natural and necessary evolution of consciousness to ever higher levels. Each pseudonymous "author" presents to the reader a "possibility" for life; in that respect, they are all on the same level. Each invites the reader to identify with him.

- *The aesthete:* You have only one life to live, so you might as well arrange to make it enjoyable. It is true that the kind of ironic detachment this requires means that life is ultimately meaningless and that there are no serious choices, but that's just how life is.

- *The ethicist:* Life *is* neither this way nor that; it all depends on what you *do* with it. And that is a matter of choice, the sort of serious choice that constitutes a continuing self. You *are* what you *make* of yourself. And far from being meaningless, nothing could possibly matter more.

- *The Christian:* You can't successfully create yourself. We are all failures at this task. What is required is acknowledgment of this fact, together with faith in God's forgiveness through Christ. In this way we can come to accept ourselves in spite of our unacceptability; only thus can we be free simply to *be* ourselves.*

-----

*It is worth noting that Kierkegaard's stage of *faith* is worlds away from the sort of "self-acceptance" urged upon us by so much contemporary psychology (and advertising!). The "I'm OK, you're OK" syndrome is one that is basically aesthetic, in Kierkegaard's terms. What it lacks is both the seriousness of the

It is Kierkegaard's claim that among these three possibilities (and they may not be the only ones) existing human beings must *choose*. And they must choose without being able to attain a position in which they could know for certain which choice was the right or best one. For existing human beings, the key concepts are choice, decision, and *risk*. A move from one kind of life to another is less like the result of rational persuasion and more like conversion. If one makes such a move, it is by a *leap*.

It is true that *within* each of these frameworks each occupant thinks he can characterize and explain the others. To the judge, A looks like a man who has lost himself; to A, the judge's marriage looks overwhelmingly boring. The Christian sees them both as examples of despair—of not willing to be oneself; and no doubt the Christian could be accused, from some other framework, of irrationality and of going beyond the evidence. Where does the truth lie? In order to determine this, it seems one would have to take up a point of view outside them all and consider them all *objectively*. But it is Kierkegaard's conviction that no such point of view is available to an existing human being. There is no such vantage point for us as Hegel imagines absolute knowledge to be—no coincidence of subjectivity and objectivity, no identification of ourselves with Absolute Spirit, no *good reason* to choose one life rather than another, and no *knowledge* here at all. You and I, he thinks, are free to choose among the possibilities, but we are not free to choose for good reasons—from an objective point of view. Neither are we free *not* to choose. Simply by living, we are making our choices; we cannot help it.

Hegel and the Hegelians whom Kierkegaard knew suppose that the process of living well can be organized in an objective and rational way. In particular, they think that philosophy can construct a *system* in which every aspect of life and reality is given its necessary and proper place. To this supposition Johannes Climacus responds in scathing tones:

> I shall be as willing as the next man to fall down in worship before the System, if only I can manage to set eyes on it. Hitherto I have had no success; and though I have young legs, I am almost weary from running back and forth. . . . Once or twice I have been on the verge of bending the knee. But at the last moment, when I already had my handkerchief spread on the ground, to avoid soiling my trousers, and I made a trusting appeal to one of the initiated who stood by: "Tell me now sincerely, is it entirely finished; for if so I will kneel down before it, even at the risk of ruining a pair of trousers (for on account of the heavy traffic to and from the system, the road has become quite muddy),"—I always received the same answer: "No, it is not yet quite finished." And so there was another postponement—of the System, and of my homage.
>
> System and finality are pretty much one and the same, so much so that if the system is not finished, there is no system. . . . A system which is not quite finished is an hypothesis; while on the other hand to speak of a half-finished system is nonsense. (*CUP,* 97–98)

Climacus makes a distinction between a *logical system* and what he calls an *existential system*. And he claims that a logical system is possible, but an existential system is not. Geometry is a good example of a logical system; it is founded on axioms, postulates, and definitions, from which we can prove theorems using the rules of logic. Characteristic of a logical system is that all the theorems are already implicit in the premises. That is the respect in which "finality" is an essential characteristic of a system—if a proposition that cannot be deduced from the axioms is introduced, it follows that a mistake has been made. Given a certain set of axioms, the set of derivable theorems is also given; no new truths can be added later, and none of the theorems can be altered. In particular, Climacus says, nothing must be incorporated into such a logical system "that has any relation to existence, that is not indifferent to existence" (*CUP,* 100). Existence, after all, makes headway, like the ship in the judge's image, and may always falsify any "system" that pur-

---

ethical and the consciousness of sin. Dietrich Bonhoeffer, a German theologian influenced by Kierkegaard and killed by the Nazis, would have called it "cheap grace."

ports to describe it. So far as its relation to existence goes, a logical system merely presents a possibility, a hypothesis.*

The reason why an existential system is not possible (at least for us) is that "existence is precisely the opposite of finality." (*CUP*, 107)

> Respecting the impossibility of an existential system, let us then ask quite simply . . . "Who is to write or complete such a system?" Surely a human being; unless we propose again to begin using the strange mode of speech which assumes that a human being becomes speculative philosophy in the abstract, or becomes the identity of subject and object. So then, a human being—and surely a living human being, i.e., an existing individual. . . . It is from this side . . . that objection must be made to modern philosophy; not that it has a mistaken presupposition, but that it has a comical presupposition, occasioned by its having forgotten in a sort of world-historical absentmindedness, what it means to be a human being. Not indeed, what it means to be a human being in general; for this is the sort of thing that one might even induce a speculative philosopher to agree to; but what it means that you and I and he are human beings, each one for himself. (*CUP*, 109)

The problem is that in constructing a system that supposedly captures existence, the speculative philosopher supposes that he can be finished with existence before existence is finished with him! As long as he lives, he must choose; his own existence is precisely not something finished. To suppose that at some point in his life, he (or we, or the human race in its history) could attain the finality that comes with a system is simply comic.† Such a philosopher,

Climacus says, "has gradually come to be so fantastic a being that scarcely the most extravagant fancy has ever invented anything so fabulous" (*CUP*, 107).

We have seen that the problem of the criterion has plagued philosophers since Sextus Empiricus, who first formulates it clearly. By what mark can we tell when we have latched onto truth and goodness? Hegel's answer to this problem is that we will know *in the end*—that is, when we see how everything hangs together in a systematic way. What Kierkegaard is denying is that this kind of sight is possible for existing human beings. Perhaps that *would* do as a criterion, but we can't get there from here. So we have to live without a criterion, without certainty, without good reason. We live by a *leap*.

The essential task for an existing human being, then, is not to speculate philosophically about absolute knowledge, but to become himself. As we have seen, this is a task involving risky choices, choices that must be made without the comfort of objective certainty. Speculative philosophers who try to present a *system* explaining existence imagine they can reach such a degree of objectivity that they revoke the risk in living; but this is sheer illusion. As Climacus plaintively asks, "Why can we not remember to be human beings?" (*CUP*, 104).

The tendency of modern philosophy is entirely toward objectivity. Kierkegaard sets himself absolutely against this tendency. He deplores

> the objective tendency, which proposes to make everyone an observer, and in its maximum to transform him into so objective an observer that he becomes almost a ghost, scarcely to be distinguished from the tremendous spirit of the historical past. (*CUP*, 118)

He endorses a saying by G. E. Lessing (a noted eighteenth-century German dramatist) to this effect: If God held in his right hand the truth and in his left hand the striving for the truth, and asked the

---

*About this point, Climacus seems to be more correct than he could have known. Since the discovery of non-Euclidean geometries in the latter part of the nineteenth century, any system of geometry has to be regarded, as far as its application goes, as a hypothesis about the nature of space. For all these systems themselves can tell us, space may be either Euclidean or non-Euclidean.

†There is some reason to believe Kierkegaard's criticism here may be more apt against some enthusiastic "right-wing" Hegelians than against Hegel himself. You will recall that we noted

---

several times a deep ambivalence running through Hegel's thoughts. For a strain that sounds very Kierkegaardian, see again the famous "Owl of Minerva" passage on p. 487.

existing individual to choose one, the appropriate choice would be the left hand.

With respect to the individual's relation to the truth, there are two questions: (1) whether it is indeed the truth to which one is related; and (2) whether the mode of the relationship is a true one. Call the former an *objective question* and the latter a *subjective question*. The former concerns *what* is said or believed, the latter *how* it is said or believed.

For an existing individual, there is no way to settle that first question definitively. As a result, the *how* is accentuated.* For an individual, the quality of life depends on the intensity, the passion, the decisiveness with which this relation is maintained. (Remember the advice of the judge to A about choice; remember also the way in which the consciousness of sin—of actually being already in error and separated from the truth—intensifies the situation in the Christian framework.) Climacus offers a formula that expresses the appropriate knowledge relation of the individual to the truth.

> *An objective uncertainty held fast in an appropriation-process of the most passionate inwardness is the truth,* the highest truth available for an *existing individual.* (*CUP,* 182)

Objectively speaking, the individual never has more than "uncertainty"; this uncertainty correlates subjectively with the riskiness of the choice made, and the riskier the choice the more intense the "passionate inwardness" with which it is made. For the individual, living in this subjectivity *is* living in the truth.

Kierkegaard is interested in two questions: (1) What is it to be an existing human being? and (2) What is it to be a Christian? He is convinced that unless we get an adequate answer to the first question, we will get the second answer wrong. He

believes most people do get it wrong. In an age in which everyone considers himself a Christian as a matter of course, Kierkegaard means to unsettle this complacency by drawing our attention back to the first question.

If the problem that faces each individual is this problem of how to manage the duality implicit in being a self, then it becomes evident that being a Christian must be a certain way of solving the problem. It cannot be just a matter of church membership, or of being baptized, or of having the right (i.e., orthodox) beliefs, or of "understanding" oneself and one's place in the "system" (in the manner of Hegelian philosophy). It is a problem that cannot be solved in any other way than by the construction of the self through the choices, momentous and trivial, that one makes when faced with life's multifarious possibilities.

In a whimsical passage, Johannes Climacus tells us the story of how he became an author. He was smoking his cigar on a Sunday afternoon in a public garden and ruminating on how he might best spend his life to be of benefit to mankind. He was thinking about all those

> "celebrated names and figures, the precious and much heralded men who are coming into prominence and are much talked about, the many benefactors of the age who know how to benefit mankind by making life easier and easier, some by railways, others by omnibuses and steamboats, others by the telegraph, others by easily apprehended compendiums and short recitals of everything worth knowing, and finally the true benefactors of the age who make spiritual existence in virtue of thought easier and easier, yet more and more significant. And what [he asks himself] are you doing?" Here my soliloquy was interrupted, for my cigar was smoked out and a new one had to be lit. So I smoked again, and then suddenly this thought flashed through my mind: "You must do something, but inasmuch as with your limited capacities it will be impossible to make anything easier than it has become, you must, with the same humanitarian enthusiasm as the others, undertake to make something harder." This notion pleased me immensely, and at the same time it flattered

---

*Here Climacus is thinking of truth about the best life choices. But an analogy from general epistemology might be helpful. Knowledge is commonly defined as *justified true belief.* Unless our belief is true—that is, objectively correct—it cannot constitute knowledge. But the best we can do is believe for good reasons. Nothing we can do will guarantee truth.

me to think that I, like the rest of them, would be loved and esteemed by the whole community. For when all combine in every way to make everything easier, there remains only one possible danger, namely, that the ease becomes so great that it becomes altogether too great; then there is only one want left, though it is not yet a felt want, when people will want difficulty. Out of love for mankind, and out of despair at my embarrassing situation, seeing that I had accomplished nothing and was unable to make anything easier than it had already been made, . . . I conceived it as my task to create difficulties everywhere. (*CUP,* 165–166)

What sort of difficulties? Those that remind us of what a hazardous and risky business it is, this business of having to be an existing human individual.

---

1. What is characteristic of a system? What would an existential system be? How does Kierkegaard attack this notion?
2. What, according to Johannes Climacus, is the proper relation of an existing human individual to the truth?

Marx: Beyond Alienation and Exploitation

As we have noted, several themes become prominent at the close of the Enlightenment and the beginning of the nineteenth century. They are most systematically developed in Hegel. We can summarize these themes as follows:

- *The significance of history.* The classical quest for eternal truths, knowable at any time and in any circumstances, is replaced by the notion of the development of culture and of reason itself. Moreover, this development is thought of as *progress* toward a more encompassing truth, rationality, and freedom.

- *The role of opposition and antagonism in this progress.* Hegel notices, indeed emphasizes the role

of the *negative* in development—that is, that struggle and loss are an essential part of any move forward.* William Blake, the English Romantic poet, puts it this way: "Without contraries is no progression."[3]

- *The attainment of the goal by the race, not the individual.* Because the progress is a historical one and individuals cannot jump out of their own cultural setting, the goal (self-consciousness, rationality, freedom) must be one toward which the race is moving, rather than one that an individual could completely attain.

- *The justification of the evil that accompanies this progression.* Hegel, as we have seen, acknowledges the suffering that individuals endure on the "slaughter bench" of history but argues that all is worthwhile because of the incomparable value of the end: the realization of Absolute Spirit in the wholly rational state. As Lenin was later to put a similar point: You can't make an omelette without breaking some eggs.

Karl Marx (1818–1883) accepts these views. Indeed, he accepts them in their Hegelian guise; as a young man, Marx was self-consciously one of the left-wing Hegelians. Like Kierkegaard, whom he did not know, he complains that Hegelian philosophy is speculative and abstract. But unlike Kierkegaard, his remedy for this abstraction is not to focus on the plight of the anxious individual, forced to make choices without rational warrant; such a focus on "subjectivity" would seem to him an abstraction of a different, but no less deplorable, kind. Marx develops his critique along other lines.

Hegel believes (1) that reality is Spirit, (2) that the human being is Spirit unknown to itself, alienated from its objects (and so from itself), and (3) that the cure for this **alienation** is the knowledge that there is nothing in the object that is not put there by the subject—by Spirit itself. The human being is God coming to consciousness of himself through history. Marx comes to believe that this is exactly

---

*In a way, this is a very old thought. See Heraclitus on the necessity for opposition and strife, pp. 19–20.

right, but only in a funny kind of way. For what Hegel has done, Marx thinks, is to take reality and "etherealize" it. It is as though the real world has been transposed into another key and played back to us—all there, but with everything looking weirdly distorted. Hegel, Marx believes, has taken philosophy off its feet and turned it upside down on its head. It is Marx's determination to put philosophy back on its feet again. In an early work written with Friedrich Engels, Marx expresses this determination:

> In direct contrast to German philosophy which descends from heaven to earth, here we ascend from earth to heaven. That is to say, we do not set out from what men say, imagine, conceive, nor from men as narrated, thought of, imagined, conceived, in order to arrive at men in the flesh. We set out from real, active men, and on the basis of their real life-process we demonstrate the development of the ideological reflexes and echoes of this life-process. The phantoms formed in the human brain are also, necessarily, sublimates of their material life-process, which is empirically verifiable and bound to material premises. Morality, religion, metaphysics, all the rest of ideology and their corresponding forms of consciousness, thus no longer retain the semblance of independence. They have no history, no development; but men, developing their material production and their material intercourse, alter, along with this their real existence, their thinking and the products of their thinking. Life is not determined by consciousness, but consciousness by life. (*GI,* 118–119)[4]

Consider the last sentence. Hegel writes as if the forms of consciousness, traced in his phenomenology of Spirit, are independent of the material world. Forms of life, Hegel holds, depend on forms of consciousness, the level to which knowledge has evolved: sense-certainty, perception, understanding, desire, the unhappy consciousness, morality, and so on. But to Marx and Engels, this puts the cart before the horse. Those forms of consciousness do not have the kind of independence Hegel ascribes to them, so they do not, in themselves, have a history. There is, however, an underlying reality that does have a history. This *material reality* has to do first and foremost with *economic* matters—

with putting bread on the table. It is the reality of "men in the flesh," of "real, active men" and their "life processes." Hegel's forms of consciousness are simply "sublimates" or ideological reflections of this more basic reality.

The most essential need of real people is the sustenance of their material life. Marx calls this the

> first premise of all human existence, and therefore of all history, the premise, namely, that men must be in a position to live in order to be able to "make history." But life involves before everything else eating and drinking, a habitation, clothing and many other things. The first historical act is thus the production of the means to satisfy these needs, the production of material life itself. (*GI,* 119–120)

This premise is followed by other no less basic points: that producing the means of subsistence requires instruments of production; that this multiplies needs; that people propagate their own kind and so create families; and, most important, that these activities involve people from the start in social relationships.

> It follows from this that a certain mode of production or industrial stage is always combined with a certain mode of co-operation, or social stage, and this mode of co-operation is itself a "productive force." (*GI,* 121)

It is Marx's intention, then, to substitute for Hegelian speculative philosophy a discipline that looks carefully at the actual, empirically ascertainable facts about human beings. Marx is an influential figure in the history of both sociology and economics. He holds that if you want to understand a certain form of consciousness—of religion, perhaps, or of literature—you need to understand the material (economic and social) conditions in which it is produced. It is no good simply looking at texts or practices in isolation; you need to understand the context in which they arise.* He also believes that certain forms of intellectual and spiritual life are

---

*Vigorous controversies exist among literary critics over precisely this point, the "New Critics" arguing that the text itself must speak, and more or less Marxist opponents replying that the text is not an independent entity that has a voice of its own.

"From each according to his ability, to each according to his needs!"

—KARL MARX

merely compensations for an unsatisfactory life here on earth; religion, for instance, an opiate of the people, will simply vanish if we can get society straightened out.

Understanding is not enough, however, even for the intellectual. What Marx calls for is action. Perhaps no one has put the philosopher in such a central role since Plato had proposed that philosophers should become kings and kings philosophers.* In a famous line, Marx writes,†

> The philosophers have only *interpreted* the world, in various ways; the point, however, is to *change* it. (*TF*, 109)

In what ways is philosophy supposed to change the world? To answer this question, we must consider what Marx sees when he undertakes to describe "real" people in their actual existence.

Alienation, Exploitation, and Private Property

In an early work (1844), unknown until the 1930s, Marx presents an analysis of the condition these "real" people had reached in the middle of the nineteenth century. We need to remind ourselves that this is the heyday of the Industrial Revolution—of the steam engine, the coal mine, and the knitting mill, of the twelve- or fourteen-hour workday, of child labor, and of a widening gap between those who own the means of production and the masses who give their labor in factories they have no stake in.* In understanding these conditions, Marx relies heavily on the major political economists who analyze the new industrial situation: Adam Smith and David Ricardo.

Here is how Marx sees things.

> *Wages* are determined through the antagonistic struggle between capitalist and worker. Victory goes necessarily to the capitalist. The capitalist can live longer without the worker than can the worker without the capitalist. (*EPM*, 65)

The capitalist, of course, owns the means of production—the factories and tools. A separation of ownership from labor is characteristic of the industrial age. In the days when cobblers made shoes, virtually all cobblers had their own shops and tools; perhaps they had an apprentice or two and maybe even a servant, but ownership and labor were typically combined in the same person. In the nineteenth century, however, there is a split between the class of people who own the very large and expensive means of industrial production and the class that provides the labor, a split that takes on the characteristics of a "struggle."

To increase their profits and meet the competition of other industrial entrepreneurs, the capital-

---

*For the rationale behind this proposal of Plato's, see "The State," in Chapter 6. In a way, Marx proposes a similar role for the intellectual in the struggles of his time.

†Look once more at the "Owl of Minerva" passage in Hegel (p. 487). This is what Marx is attacking.

*For the Industrial Revolution, see http://mars.acnet.wnec. edu/~grempe1/courses/wc2/lectures/industrialrev.html.

ists pay the workers no more than is necessary to keep the workers alive, working, and reproducing. This is possible in part because there are typically more workers than jobs. So the worker takes on the characteristic of a *commodity* in the system; like all commodities, the capitalist tries to buy it as cheaply as possible. As a commodity, of course, the worker is not thought of as a human being, but "only as a working animal—as a beast reduced to the strictest bodily needs" (*EPM,* 73). The worker could be (and often is) replaced by a machine.

The worker must face not only the capitalist but also the landlord. Formerly, the landed gentry could live solely by the productivity of the land. But the vigorous activity of the capitalist has forced competition here, too; and landowners are either driven out of this class altogether or become capitalists in their own right, seeking a profit from the land. They, therefore, seek to make rents as high as possible, and tenant farmers join the industrial workers as commodities on the market.

Private property is one fact political economy takes for granted, Marx says. But that should not be taken for granted; it needs an explanation. Marx's explanation leans heavily on his Hegelian background. For example, suppose you take a piece of wood from the floor of the forest, sit down, and painstakingly carve into it the face of Lincoln. We can say that you have "put something of yourself into it." No longer raw nature, it now is an expression of yourself. It is, in fact, your labor *objectified*. In confronting it, you are confronting yourself: You are the person who *did that*. In contemplating this object, you become aware at one and the same time of it and of yourself, for part of what you are stands there in objectified form before you. Before you put your labor into it, you would not have been harmed had someone taken it, but now, if it is stolen, the thief steals part of *you*.*

We humans are active, productive, creative beings. In producing objects, we create not only

them, but also ourselves. The products of our labor show us to ourselves as in a mirror. Do you want to know what humans are? Don't examine just their physiology and individual psychology. Look at their art, their laws, their religion, their societies, their technologies, their industrial products; these things will tell you because they are humanity itself in objectified form. It is in such *externalization* that we make ourselves fully human, that is, self-consciously human.

But in the industrial age, this process has become perverted, for the worker labors and produces a *commodity*. What does that mean?

1. It means that workers do not experience their work as an affirmation of themselves. On the contrary, they feel *alienated* from their work. Their labor is not an expression of their lives but external to their lives. As Marx puts it, the worker

> does not affirm himself but denies himself, does not feel content but unhappy, does not develop freely his physical and mental energy but mortifies his body and ruins his mind. . . . His labor is therefore not voluntary, but coerced; it is *forced labor*. It is therefore not the satisfaction of a need; it is merely a *means* to satisfy needs external to it. Its alien character emerges clearly in the fact that as soon as no physical or other compulsion exists, labor is shunned like the plague. (*EPM,* 110–111)

Rather than being fulfilled in their work, workers experience a loss of themselves. They are *dehumanized;* they feel active and productive only in their animal functions. In what should be their highest human functions (productive, creative labor), they become no more than animals, or worse, machines.*

2. Workers are alienated not only from their labor but also from the products of their labor, which belong not to them but to the capitalist. The workers have just their wages, which are necessarily only enough for bare subsistence. The products they make stand over against them as independent pow-

---

*This is, of course, a development of Locke's views on property. See pp. 383–384. Compare also Hegel on master and slave, p. 472.

*Those of you who have worked on an assembly line can perhaps verify from your own experience Marx's description of such work.

ers; although they have put themselves into these products, they have no control over them. They put their lives into the objects they produce but then find that their lives no longer belong to them.

3. In the early days of the Industrial Revolution, there was no solidarity among workers, no labor union, no force to rival the superior power of the employer. Workers competed against each other for jobs, and there were too many workers. For every worker who faltered or expressed dissatisfaction with working conditions, there were a dozen waiting at the employer's door. As a result, workers were also alienated from each other and, of course, from the capitalist, who was making money from exploiting them.

This is all more intelligible if we note that according to the economists of the day, *value* is defined in terms of labor. The value of something (including money) represents a certain amount of labor. The worker produces value, but value in the hands of another: the one with the means to purchase the labor of the worker—that is, the capitalist. In plain words, what the worker is producing is capital, and with it the capitalist.

Workers, then, are alienated from their labor and from the products of their labor; in neither can they find themselves. If we return now to the question about the origin of private property, we can see, Marx says, that it has its foundation in *alienated labor.* Because the classical political economists formulate their laws in terms of private property, we can see that they are formulating the laws of estranged labor—the laws of a condition of society in which workers are exploited, dehumanized.*

All these consequences result from the fact that the worker is related to the *product of his labor* as to an *alien* object. For on this premise it is clear that the more the worker spends himself, the more powerful becomes the alien world of objects which he

creates over and against himself, the poorer he himself—his inner world—becomes, the less it belongs to him as his own. . . . The *alienation* of the worker in his product means not only that his labor becomes an object, an *external* existence, but that it exists *outside him,* independently, as something alien to him. It means that the life which he has conferred on the object confronts him as something hostile and alien. . . .

It is true that labor produces for the rich wonderful things—but for the worker it produces privation. It produces palaces—but for the worker, hovels. It produces beauty—but for the worker, deformity. It replaces labor by machines, but it throws a section of the workers back to a barbarous type of labor, and it turns the other workers into machines. It produces intelligence—but for the worker stupidity, cretinism. (*EPM,* 108–110).

In the condition of alienated labor—of private property—the natural human needs of people become perverted. "Man becomes ever poorer as man, his need for *money* becomes ever greater if he wants to overpower hostile being" (*EPM,* 147). The need for money, of course, is insatiable; schemes for multiplying human needs are devised to increase one's money wealth. The process is fueled by *greed.* Greed and the money system, Marx says, are corollaries; devotion to money becomes a kind of secular religion.

1. What does Marx mean when he says that "life is not determined by consciousness, but consciousness by life"?
2. Characterize the struggle between capitalist and worker.
3. What is the origin of private property, according to Marx?
4. Describe some forms of worker alienation.

Communism

Private property, then, has a history; it is not a natural, given fact. Private property is the result of

---

*Notice how Marx differs here from Locke, who believes there would be property even in a state of nature where no exploitation existed.

alienated labor. And this alienation of labor itself has a history. Marx's view of this history is sketched in the first part of the *Manifesto of the Communist Party,* which he wrote with Engels in 1848.

> The history of all hitherto existing society is the history of class struggles.
>
> Freeman and slave, patrician and plebeian, lord and serf, guild-master and journeyman, in a word, oppressor and oppressed, stood in constant opposition to one another, carried on an uninterrupted, now hidden, now open fight, a fight that each time ended, either in a revolutionary reconstitution of society at large, or in the common ruin of the contending classes. . . .
>
> Our epoch, the epoch of the bourgeoisie, possesses, however, this distinctive feature: it has simplified the class antagonisms. Society as a whole is more and more splitting up into two great hostile camps, into two great classes directly facing each other: Bourgeoisie and Proletariat. (*CM,* 3)

The *bourgeoisie* is the class of owners, including both capitalists (in the narrower sense) and landlords. Marx characterizes it in the following way:

> The bourgeoisie, wherever it has got the upper hand, has put an end to all feudal, patriarchal, idyllic relations. It has pitilessly torn asunder the motley feudal ties that bound man to his "natural superiors," and left remaining no other nexus between man and man than naked self-interest, than callous "cash payment." It has drowned the most heavenly ecstasies of religious fervor, of chivalrous enthusiasm, of philistine sentimentalism, in the icy water of egotistical calculation. It has resolved personal worth into exchange value, and in place of the numberless indefeasible chartered freedoms, has set up that single, unconscionable freedom—Free Trade. In one word, for exploitation, veiled by religious and political illusions, it has substituted naked, shameless, direct, brutal exploitation. (*CM,* 5)

In pursuit of wealth, the bourgeoisie constantly revolutionizes the instruments of production and thus transforms relations among people in society into competitive relations. It produces a world market and interdependence among nations. It converts all other nations, on pain of extinction, into

bourgeoisie as well. It concentrates property in a few hands, and it produces its own opposition: the proletariat.

> In proportion as the bourgeoisie, *i.e.,* capital, is developed, in the same proportion is the proletariat, the modern working class, developed—a class of labourers, who live only so long as they find work, and who find work only so long as their labour increases capital. (*CM,* 9)

The proletariat is the class of nonowners, of workers who have nothing but their labor to call their own. We have already characterized the life of the worker, as Marx sees it. We can now add that the lower strata of the middle classes—small tradespeople, shopkeepers, craftsmen, peasants—tend to sink gradually into the proletariat. As the proletariat grows in size, it begins to feel its strength and becomes the only really revolutionary class. As Marx sees it,

> The development of Modern Industry . . . cuts from under its feet the very foundation on which the bourgeoisie produces and appropriates products. What the bourgeoisie, therefore, produces, above all, is its own grave diggers. Its fall and the victory of the proletariat are equally inevitable. (*CM,* 15–16)

Historical development, as Marx sees it, has led us to the point where society is divided into two great classes whose interests are diametrically opposed. The interests of the proletariat, Marx believes, are best represented by the communists, "the most advanced and resolute section of the working class parties of every country," who have "the advantage of clearly understanding the line of march, the conditions, and the ultimate general results of the proletarian movement" (*CM,* 17). (This insight is the result of taking Hegelian dialectical philosophy off its head and setting it back on its feet.) What communism stands for, then, is the abolition of private property. About this claim, Marx and Engels make the following remarks:

> The distinguishing feature of Communism is not the abolition of property generally, but the abolition of bourgeois property. But modern bourgeois

private property is the final and most complete expression of the system of producing and appropriating products, that is based on class antagonisms, on the exploitation of the many by the few. . . .

Hard-won, self-acquired, self-earned property! Do you mean the property of the petty artisan and of the small peasant, a form of property that preceded the bourgeois form? There is no need to abolish that; the development of industry has to a great extent already destroyed it, and is still destroying it daily. . . .

You are horrified at our intending to do away with private property. But in your existing society, private property is already done away with for nine-tenths of the population; its existence for the few is solely due to its non-existence in the hands of those nine-tenths. You reproach us, therefore, with intending to do away with a form of property, the necessary condition for whose existence is, the non-existence of any property for the immense majority of society.

In one word, you reproach us with intending to do away with your property. Precisely so; that is just what we intend. . . .

Communism deprives no man of the power to appropriate the products of society; all that it does is to deprive him of the power to subjugate the labour of others by means of such appropriation. (*CM*, 18–20)

If the history of the world has, as Marx says, been the history of class struggles, then there seems to be something final and apocalyptic about this division of society into bourgeoisie and proletariat, into the few who have all and the many who have nothing. If this picture is taken seriously, it seems as though a final revolution, in which the workers take control of the means of production, might be the goal toward which history is moving. This is, in fact, the "theoretical advantage" that the communists claim—that they can see this line of development.

Marx agrees with Hegel about the character of the end: All this suffering is worthwhile only for *freedom*.* But it is not the freedom of pure self-

consciousness—knowing itself to be all there is, both subject and object—that Marx praises. Rather, it is the freedom of real, active, working men and women, who no longer find themselves alienated from their work, the products of their work, and their fellow workers.

> When, in the course of development, class distinctions have disappeared, and all production has been concentrated in the hands of a vast association of the whole nation, the public power will lose its political character. Political power, properly so called, is merely the organized power of one class for oppressing another. If the proletariat during its contest with the bourgeoisie is compelled, by the force of circumstances, to organize itself as a class, if, by means of a revolution, it makes itself the ruling class, and, as such, sweeps away by force the old conditions of production, then it will, along with these conditions, have swept away the conditions for the existence of class antagonisms and of classes generally, and will thereby have abolished its own supremacy as a class.
>
> In place of the old bourgeois society, with its classes and class antagonisms, we shall have an association, in which the free development of each is the condition for the free development of all. (*CM*, 26)

It is indeed not enough to understand the world; what is required is to change it. The *Manifesto* ends with a ringing call to action (*CM*, 39):

> The Communists disdain to conceal their views and aims. They openly declare that their ends can be attained only by the forcible overthrow of all existing social conditions. Let the ruling classes tremble at a Communistic revolution. The proletarians have nothing to lose but their chains. They have a world to win.
> WORKING MEN OF ALL COUNTRIES, UNITE!

If things have not worked out as Marx and Engels expected, it must nonetheless be allowed that their vision of a world where the "free development of each is the condition for the free development of all," a world without exploitation and without class antagonisms, has done as much actually to change

---

*See Hegel's discussion of freedom as the goal of history, pp. 484–487.

the world (in one way and another) as any system of thought has ever done.

---

1. Characterize the bourgeoisie and the proletariat as Marx saw them in the mid-nineteenth century. How did he think they were related?
2. What does communism intend? Why?

For Further Thought

1. Does the pattern of your life seem to match (more or less) that of any of Kierkegaard's pseudonymous writers? Write a brief story to illustrate.

2. Argue for one or another of the following theses:
   a. If we could satisfactorily meet people's material needs (whether through communism or in some other way), the sorts of concerns expressed by Kierkegaard would seem merely neurotic symptoms to us and would probably vanish.
   b. Even if we completely satisfied everyone's material and bodily needs, the spiritual and existential questions that concerned Kierkegaard would be as lively as ever.

3. Argue for one of the following propositions:
   a. In a state of nature without exploitation, rights of private property would naturally develop (Locke).
   b. Private property essentially depends on the exploitation of some by others (Marx).

Notes

1. T. S. Eliot, *Four Quartets: The Dry Salvages,* V, in *The Complete Poems and Plays 1909–1950* (New York: Harcourt, Brace, 1958), 136.

2. References to the works of Søren Kierkegaard are as follows:
   EO: Either/Or, vols. 1 and 2, trans. Howard V. Hong and Edna H. Hong (Princeton: Princeton University Press, 1987). References are to volume numbers and page numbers.
   FT: Fear and Trembling, trans. Howard V. Hong and Edna H. Hong (Princeton: Princeton University Press, 1983).
   SUD: The Sickness unto Death, trans. Alistair Hannay (London: Penguin Books, 1989).
   PF: Philosophical Fragments, trans. Howard V. Hong and Edna H. Hong (Princeton: Princeton University Press, 1985).
   CUP: Concluding Unscientific Postscript, trans. David F. Swenson and Walter Lowrie (Princeton: Princeton University Press, 1944).

3. William Blake, "The Marriage of Heaven and Hell," in *William Blake,* ed. J. Bronowski (New York: Penguin Books, 1958), 94.

4. References to the works of Karl Marx are as follows:
   GI: The German Ideology, in *The Marx–Engels Reader,* ed. Robert C. Tucker (New York: W. W. Norton, 1972).
   TF: Theses on Feuerbach, in Tucker (ed.), *The Marx–Engels Reader.*
   EPM: The Economic and Philosophic Manuscripts of 1844, ed. Dirk J. Struik (New York: International Publishers, 1964).
   CM: The Communist Manifesto (with Friedrich Engels), trans. Samuel Moore, ed. David McLellan (Oxford: Oxford University Press, 1992).

19

THE UTILITARIANS

Moral Rules and the Happiness of All (Including Women)

At about the same time that Kant is working out his views on duty and the rational justification of the moral law, a quite different orientation for ethics is being developed in England. The utilitarians, as they come to call themselves, are much more empirical than Kant or Hegel, and in their own way nearly as radical in their critique of society as Marx; however, they advocate reform rather than revolution. They draw on sources in their own English-speaking history, particularly on Hobbes, Locke, and Hume, but they develop these themes in quite a distinctive fashion.

The Classic Utilitarians

Two thinkers stand out in connection with **utilitarianism,** though others contribute to the doctrine: Jeremy Bentham (1748–1832) and John Stuart Mill (1806–1873) together set out its principal tenets, though there are some basic points on which they disagree. We can begin our investigation of this still influential view of morality with a quotation from Mill's booklet *Utilitarianism* (1861).

All action is for the sake of some end, and rules of action, it seems natural to suppose, must take their whole character and color from the end to which they are subservient. When we engage in a pursuit, a clear and precise conception of what we are pursuing would seem to be the first thing we need. (*U,* 132)[1]

Note the *teleological* orientation here.* Suppose I want to know what I ought to do, or what would be the right thing to do. Because everything I do is intended to accomplish something—is "for the sake of some end"—it seems sensible to pay attention to that end. Mill suggests that the end I have in view determines whether what I do is the morally right thing. The consequences I intend to bring about by my action fix its rightness and wrongness.†

---

* You may recall that this word comes from the Greek *telos,* meaning "end" or "goal." Something is *teleological* if it points to an outcome. See the earlier discussion on p. 172. See also pp. 187–188.

† For Kant, the morally relevant facts concern not only our intentions, but also our motives: *Why* do I want to bring about these consequences? Is it because I respect the moral law—or for some other reason? See pp. 452–453.

But what consequences do we look to? Every act always has many, many consequences. Which of them are morally relevant? Bentham and Mill answer this question by claiming that in everything we do, no matter what the particular end, we are aiming at a single thing: happiness. But does this help? Aristotle has already noted that people disagree widely over what happiness is.* If happiness means one thing to Jones and another to Smith, how will it help to note that all their actions are aiming at happiness?

Bentham and Mill are convinced, however, that this variability is only superficial; at its core, happiness is everywhere alike. As Bentham puts it,

> Nature has placed mankind under the governance of two sovereign masters, *pain* and *pleasure*. It is for them alone to point out what we ought to do, as well as to determine what we shall do. On the one hand the standard of right and wrong, on the other the chain of causes and effects, are fastened to their throne. They govern us in all we do, in all we say, in all we think: every effort we can make to throw off our subjection, will serve but to demonstrate and confirm it. (*PML,* 1) [2]

Our goal in whatever we do, Bentham says, is to avoid pain and to secure pleasure. And that is what happiness is.† Note that Bentham here makes two distinct claims. The first is a thesis about motivation; this is a psychological thesis, proposing that considerations of pain and pleasure always determine our actions. This psychological or causal thesis has a name: *psychological hedonism.*‡

The second is an ethical or moral thesis, which holds that right and wrong are tied to pleasure and pain. That is, in judging the moral rightness of an action, we must consider the pleasure and pain that action produces. This claim is called *ethical hedonism.* As you can see, it is distinct from the former; it is a claim, not about what we in fact do, but about what we ought to do. It is in these terms that Bentham and Mill formulate the principle of utility.

> By the principle of utility is meant that principle which approves or disapproves of every action

"The happiness which forms the utilitarian standard of what is right in conduct is not the agent's own happiness, but that of all concerned."

—John Stuart Mill

whatsoever, according to the tendency which it appears to have to augment or diminish the happiness of the party whose interest is in question: or what is the same thing in other words, to promote or oppose that happiness. (*PML,* 2)

So far this doesn't have a moral ring to it. If the "party whose interest is in question" is I, then I follow this principle in doing what will make me happy, that is, what will provide me the greatest proportion of pleasure over pain. That may be prudent, but not, it seems, especially moral. It doesn't seem to have that peculiar moral *bite;* after all, pursuing my own interests may sometimes be held to be wrong. The utilitarians, however, give the principle of utility a moral character by insisting that what is ethically relevant is not my happiness or yours, but happiness itself. In this form it is some-

---

*See pp. 186–188.
†This is what Hobbes calls "felicity." See p. 367.
‡The term "hedonism" is discussed on p. 199.

times also called the greatest happiness principle and is summed up in the slogan "The greatest happiness for the greatest number." So the utilitarian standard, as Mill tells us,

> is not the agent's own greatest happiness, but the greatest amount of happiness altogether. (*U,* 142)

Suppose you are facing a choice between actions and wondering which, morally speaking, you ought to do. Here is what the utilitarian advises. Estimate how much total pleasure and pain each alternative action will produce for you and everyone concerned. The action that produces the best pleasure/pain ratio overall is the one you ought to perform. Note that it is not more important that *you* should be happy as a result of your action than other people. But neither is it less important. The utilitarian principle is an *impartial* principle. The happiness of each is to be weighed equally.

It is of great importance to see that the utilitarians were not thinking just of private actions by individual citizens. They were one and all active in politics, in the reform of law, and in trying to produce better legislation. The principle of utility was to function not just as a moral guide, but as a tool of social criticism and reform. In the early nineteenth century, many felt that the law in England was a mess—a tangled skein of contradictory precedents originating in forms of society very different from the one in which these thinkers were living. The law seemed designed chiefly to secure a livelihood for the lawyers.* All the utilitarians, Bentham in particular, used the principle of utility to criticize this maze by asking, Does this law, this institution, this way of doing things contribute to happiness or misery? This tool was sufficiently sharp to earn them the appellation "philosophical radicals." In the name of general happiness, they demanded parliamentary reform, prison reform, the extension of the right to vote, full legal rights for women, greater democracy, ways of making government officials accountable, changes in punishments, and so

on. The principle of utility is a sharp tool for reformers; it can pinpoint social evils and suggest remedies.

But how is this tool to be used? Bentham believes that one of the great advantages of the principle of utility is the detail and precision of thought it makes possible in these moral and political issues. In fact, he tries to work out something like a calculus of pleasures and pains, so that one can simply *calculate* the right thing to do by taking into account the various amounts of happiness each alternative course of action or law would produce. Though Mill and other utilitarians have doubts about how strictly this method can work, a brief glance will help us get an understanding of the movement.

One part of Bentham's project is to list the various kinds of pleasures and pains that need to be taken into account. There are a great many; among the pleasures are those of sense, wealth, skill, a good name, piety, power, happy memories, and so on. Among the pains are those of privation, the senses, awkwardness, a bad name, unhappy memories, expectation, and so on. Each of these is explained in sufficient degree, Bentham thinks, so that it can be recognized and taken account of by the judge, the legislator, or the private citizen in dealing with other persons.

In considering any given pleasure, however, we see that it differs in several ways from another pleasure of the same kind; the same is true of pains. Pleasures and pains differ in

- *Intensity* (some toothaches hurt worse than others)
- *Duration* (some last longer)
- *Certainty* or *uncertainty* (some are avoidable, others not)
- *Propinquity* or *remoteness* (some are expected tomorrow, others not for several years)
- *Fecundity* (some pleasures or pains bring further pleasures or pains in their wake; others do not)
- *Purity* (the degree to which a pleasure [or pain] is *not* tainted by accompanying pain [or pleasure])
- *Extent* (how many people are affected by it)

---

*Charles Dickens, Mill's contemporary, details the terrible effects of interminable suits dragging through the courts in his novel *Bleak House.*

You can see how these considerations might be brought to bear on a practical problem. A more intense pleasure is preferable to one less intense. The longer pains last and the more people they affect, the worse they are judged to be. So if a law will produce quite intense pleasure for a few people but condemn a great many to pains of long duration, it is sure to be a very bad law. Actual cases are usually more complicated, but this gives the basic idea.

The utilitarians believe that legislation and moral judgment alike can approximate a science. Given the principle of utility and these rules, one should not have to *guess* which law or action is best; one can *discover* it. These thinkers assume that pleasure can be quantified; if this assumption is correct, the legislator or moral agent need only add up the sums to arrive at the right answer. Bentham allows that it may be difficult or too time-consuming to engage in this deliberation before every decision. But, he says, it should be kept in view; the closer we can come to it, the more exactly correct our choices will be.

But can pleasures and pains be quantified in this exact way? Here is a point on which Mill differs from Bentham.* Though full of admiration for the older man, Mill says that Bentham is like a "one-eyed man," who sees clearly and far, but very narrowly.[3] To Bentham, pleasure is pleasure, and that's the end of it. In a famous line, Bentham declares that "quantity of pleasure being equal, push-pin [a children's game] is as good as poetry."[4] But Mill thinks this is obviously not true. Some pleasures are worth more than others, even if the *amount* of pleasure in each is the same. Pleasures, he wants to say, differ not only in quantity, but also in quality.

> It is quite compatible with the principle of utility to recognize the fact that some kinds of pleasure

are more desirable and more valuable than others. It would be quite absurd that, while in estimating all other things quality is considered as well as quantity, the estimation of pleasure should be supposed to depend on quantity alone. (*U,* 138–139)

This may well be right, but it raises two problems. First, it seems to undermine Bentham's claim that legislation and morality might be made scientific, for even if you agree that one could compare *amounts* of pleasure and pain, it seems hard to imagine that *qualities* are likewise quantifiable. If they were, they would just be quantities again, and we would be back with Bentham. The second problem is whether there is any way to *tell* which pleasures are more desirable. To this question, Mill has an answer:

> Of two pleasures, if there be one to which all or almost all who have experience of both give a decided preference, irrespective of any feeling of moral obligation to prefer it, that is the more desirable pleasure. (*U,* 139)

Consult the person of experience, Mill tells us, someone who has tried both. Setting aside moral considerations, that person's preference is a sign that one exceeds the other in quality and is more desirable.*

But, you might object, is there any reason to think that people will agree about which pleasure is better? Suppose we take a survey of those who have experienced each of two kinds of pleasure—a day in an amusement park, let us say, and a day spent reading poetry. Do you think we will find anything approaching unanimity? If we don't, how are we going to take the principle of utility as a practical rule to make decisions? We are supposed to maximize happiness, but if happiness varies so much among individuals, how are we going to decide whether to build more amusement parks or more libraries?

---

*To understand why, it helps to know something of Mill's life. You may enjoy Mill's very readable *Autobiography,* in which he recounts his childhood and remarkable education at the hands of his father, his nervous breakdown and the cure of it, and his twenty-year Platonic love of Harriet Taylor, who became his wife only after the death of her husband. Mill's active involvement with the intellectual and political movements of the day are also detailed.

---

*We have to set moral consideration aside in making this judgment, lest we beg the question. After all, we are trying to discover where the greatest happiness lies precisely in order to determine what our moral obligations are!

From this verdict of the only competent judges, I apprehend there can be no appeal. On a question which is the best worth having of two pleasures, or which of two modes of existence is the most grateful to the feelings, . . . the judgement of those who are qualified by knowledge of both, or if they differ, that of the majority among them, must be admitted as final. (*U*, 141)

So, Mill tells us, democratic politics is the way to decide about quality in pleasures. In fact, he thinks there will be a large measure of agreement because of the similarities among people. But where there are differences, the majority must rule.

When deciding on a course of action, then, we should (1) try to foresee the consequences of each action open to us, (2) compare the total happiness produced by each, and (3) choose the one that produces the most happiness overall (understood as pleasure in this qualitative sense).

A key concept of utilitarian moral philosophy is its *consequentialism:* Actions are sorted into the morally acceptable and the morally unacceptable by virtue of their consequences. The early utilitarians identify as relevant the consequences bearing on happiness, understanding happiness to be pleasure and the absence of pain. More recent utilitarians, while preserving the consequentialism, have sometimes looked to other features than pleasure to justify moral judgments.*

Suppose we ask whether the principle of utility is the right one to use in making a choice. Is it, as the utilitarians hold, the criterion for the morally right? It is not the only option available, as we already know. Aristotle would ask whether the action contributes to our excellence (virtue). Jesus, Saint Paul, and Augustine would have us ask whether what we propose to do is in accord with the will of God. Kant would urge us to submit the maxim of our action to the test of universalization. And He-

gel would presumably have us look to the standards present in our current cultural situation.* Is there anything the utilitarian can say that should convince us that the principle of utility is what Kant said he was searching for: the "supreme principle of morality"?†

Both Bentham and Mill address this question. Both insist that because the principle of utility is held to be the *first* principle of morality, it is not subject to ordinary kinds of proof. Nonetheless, each thinks he can provide arguments to convince us. Let us examine them in turn.

Bentham believes we will be converted to utilitarianism if we just consider the alternatives to it. There are only two, he thinks, though these two may appear in various versions and disguises. The clearest opposite to the principle of utility is what he calls the principle of asceticism. An adherent of this principle would judge many actions to be right, which involve a denial of pleasure for themselves and, perhaps, for others. A vivid illustration is Luther in the monastery beating himself for his sins.

Bentham has two arguments against the principle of asceticism. First, it is never applied consistently. A monk does not torture himself because he thinks it is good in itself, but because he judges it necessary to gain the incomparable pleasures of heavenly bliss. Thus, he bears witness against his will to the principle of utility. Second, asceticism has never been applied to government. Even if one thought it would be good to minimize one's own pleasures, or perhaps to increase one's pains, no legislator has ever consciously aimed at stocking the body politic with highwaymen, housebreakers, or arsonists.

Basically, Bentham argues that the ascetic principle cannot be consistently pursued.

> The principle of utility is capable of being consistently pursued; and it is but tautology to say, that the more consistently it is pursued, the better it must ever be for humankind. The principle of ascetism never was, nor ever can be, consistently

---

*G. E. Moore, for instance, holds that a certain quality of *goodness* is what the moralist is to look to; while pleasure is one good thing, he says, there are numerous other goods, such as knowledge, not reducible to pleasure. R. M. Hare takes as fundamental what people *prefer;* whether that is always a matter of pleasure is an open question.

*See pp. 187–189 (Aristotle); p. 221 (Jesus); pp. 253–254 (Augustine); p. 454 (Kant); and p. 483 (Hegel).
†See p. 451.

pursued by any living creature. Let but one tenth part of the inhabitants of the earth pursue it consistently, and in a day's time they will have turned it into a hell. (*PML,* 13)

The other alternative to utility Bentham calls the principle of sympathy and antipathy. Most of the other proposed criteria for morality reduce, he thinks, to this.

I mean that principle which approves or disapproves of certain actions, . . . merely because a man finds himself disposed to approve or disapprove of them. (*PML,* 15–16)

In a way, Bentham remarks, this is not a principle, but the denial that a principle is needed. All that is required is a sentiment of approval or disapproval on the part of the moral agent. People, of course, seldom are content to say that an action is right simply because they approve of it, so they cloak their decisions in fine words. They attribute their approvals and disapprovals to common sense, to a special moral sense, to understanding, to the law of nature, to reason, to good order, to the voice of God, and more. But all such appeals come down in the final analysis to what the individual in question approves or disapproves. And this seems to Bentham excessively arbitrary.*

Bentham ends this defense of utility with a rhetorical flourish. Suppose you say, "Action A is morally right; I know it is, though I do not know whether it will bring happiness or misery." Bentham asks you to assume it will bring unmitigated misery. Then he urges you to bring that misery clearly before your mind, to feel it, become sensible of it. Can you still, in the face of that fact, persist in your conviction that doing A is the right thing?

Mill adds arguments of his own. Though he agrees that questions of ultimate ends do not admit of proof, he thinks convincing considerations can be brought forward. Among these considerations, unfortunately, are two arguments that nearly all subsequent philosophers have held to be remark-

ably poor. They are famous (perhaps even infamous) for that reason alone. We examine them briefly.

The only proof capable of being given that an object is visible is that people actually see it. The only proof that a sound is audible is that people hear it; and so of the other sources of our experience. In like manner, I apprehend, the sole evidence it is possible to produce that anything is desirable is that people do actually desire it. (*U,* 168)

What Mill needs to show is that the general happiness is desirable, that it is what we ought to strive for. But his analogies do not work. "Visible" means "can be seen," and "audible" means "can be heard." But "desirable" is not parallel. It does not mean "can be desired," but "should be desired." So the fact that something *is* desired doesn't mean it *ought* to be desired.

Mill's second argument is no better. The conclusion he needs to support is that each of us should (morally speaking) take the general happiness as our end; when we act, that is what we ought to be trying to bring about. He argues that

happiness is a good, that each person's happiness is a good to that person, and the general happiness, therefore, a good to the aggregate of all persons. (*U,* 169)

We can, perhaps, grant the premises of this argument: Happiness is a good, and for each person, that person's own happiness is a good to that person. But all that follows from this premise is that each person's happiness is a good to *someone*. It does not follow that *your* happiness is a good to *me,* just because my own is. Each and every bit of the general happiness is a good to *some* person, but it may not be, for all the premises tell us, that the general happiness is a good to *each and every* person. Yet that is what the principle of utility claims.*

How important are these errors? Both Bentham and Mill, after all, admit that their first principle cannot be proved. Perhaps, then, it is a mistake to

---

*You might wonder whether Bentham's claim that pleasure is picked out *by nature* as the criterion is any less arbitrary than the proposals he dismisses.

*Logicians have a name for this kind of mistake. They call it a *fallacy of composition* because what applies to every part is erroneously applied to the whole.

try to prove it. We may feel that their consequentialist morality is pointing to something important even if it cannot be proved correct. The lack of proof does leave open the possibility that there is more to morality than utility, but it may be hard to deny that utility plays an important role.

Let us set aside this attempt at a positive proof and look at another kind of defense of the utilitarian creed. Mill considers various sorts of objections to it and tries to show that they all rest on misunderstandings. It is worth reviewing some of those objections; we will gain a clearer view of the utility principle by seeing what it does *not* mean.

1. Some accuse utilitarians, especially utilitarians who set pleasure as the good, of aiming too low. It is the old objection aimed already at the Epicureans. Since pleasure and pain are something we share with the animals, to make these the standard of right and wrong is to espouse a philosophy for pigs.* To this, Mill replies that human beings, having higher faculties than pigs, require more to make them happy; but their happiness is still just pleasure and their unhappiness pain. In this connection, Mill pens a famous line:

> It is better to be a human being dissatisfied than a pig satisfied; better to be a Socrates dissatisfied than a fool satisfied. And if the fool, or the pig, are of a different opinion, it is because they only know their own side of the question. (*U,* 140)

2. Some hold that the utilitarian standard is unrealizable. Is it possible that everyone should be happy? First, Mill replies, even if that were impossible, the principle of utility would still be valid. We can do much to minimize unhappiness, even if we cannot attain its opposite. Second, it is an exaggeration to say that happiness—even the general happiness—is impossible. The happiness that utilitarians favor is not, after all, a life of constant rapture, but

> moments of such, in an existence made up of few and transitory pains, many and various pleasures,

with a decided predominance of the active over the passive, and having as the foundation of the whole not to expect more from life than it is capable of bestowing. (*U,* 144)

He believes that even now a great many people live this way. If it were not for the "wretched education and wretched social arrangements" prevailing in his society, he thinks, such a life would be attainable by almost all. And he adds,

> When people who are tolerably fortunate in their outward lot do not find in life sufficient enjoyment to make it valuable to them, the cause generally is caring for nobody but themselves. (*U,* 144)

This point is actually so important to Mill that it is a little surprising he doesn't make more of it in *Utilitarianism.* In his *Autobiography,* Mill tells us about a period of severe depression that he suffered in his early twenties. He came out of it, he says, with a new certainty.

> I never, indeed, wavered in the conviction that happiness is the test of all rules of conduct, and the end of life. But I now thought that this end was only to be attained by not making it the direct end. Those only are happy (I thought) who have their minds fixed on some object other than their own happiness; on the happiness of others, on the improvement of mankind, even on some pursuit, followed not as a means, but as itself an ideal end. Aiming thus at something else, they find happiness by the way. The enjoyments of life (such was now my theory) are sufficient to make it a pleasant thing, when they are taken *en passant,* without being made a principal object. Once make them so, and they are immediately felt to be insufficient. . . . Ask yourself whether you are happy, and you cease to be so. The only chance is to treat, not happiness, but some end external to it, as the purpose of life. . . . This theory now became the basis of my philosophy of life.[5]

If this is Mill's considered view, it must make quite a difference when we try to estimate the happiness that our actions produce. For if we cannot ensure our own happiness by aiming directly at it, we cannot produce the happiness of others in any direct way, either. At least when thinking about other people's lives as a whole, the most we may be

---

*See the discussion of Epicurus on pp. 199–200. You might also look at Aristotle's remark about pleasure on p. 187.

able to do is to produce conditions in which people can work toward their own "ideal ends."*

3. Some critics object that in making happiness the end, utilitarians undercut the most noble motives and the most admirable character. Do we not, they ask, admire the individual who is willing to sacrifice personal happiness? Wouldn't this human virtue be destroyed if we all became happiness seekers?

Mill admits that we admire those who give up their personal happiness for the sake of something they prize even more. But what do they renounce their happiness *for*?

> After all, this self-sacrifice must be for some end; it is not its own end; and if we are told that its end is not happiness but virtue, which is better than happiness, I ask, would the sacrifice be made if the hero or martyr did not believe that it would earn for others immunity from similar sacrifices? . . . All honor to those who can abnegate for themselves the personal enjoyment of life when by such renunciation they contribute worthily to increase the amount of happiness in the world; but he who does it or professes to do it for any other purpose is no more deserving of admiration than the ascetic mounted on his pillar. (*U,* 147)

Utilitarians, Mill says, can admire such self-sacrifice as much as any. They only refuse to recognize that it is good in itself. It is admirable only if it tends to increase the total amount of happiness in the world. And that is exactly what the principle of utility urges.

4. Other critics object that it is asking too much of people to aim at general happiness in all their actions. You can think of this as the opposite of the first objection; instead of holding that the standard is too low, some claim it is impossibly high.

To this Mill replies that it is the business of ethics to tell us what our duties are, what is right and what is wrong. But ethics does not go as far as to re-

quire that everything we do should be done from a certain *motive.** From a utilitarian point of view, the rightness of an action is judged by what it brings about; why the agent acted in that way is irrelevant. Mill gives an example:

> He who saves a fellow creature from drowning does what is morally right, whether his motive be duty or the hope of being paid for his trouble. (*U,* 149)

Does this make ethics seem altogether *too external?* Are people's motives really that irrelevant to what is right and wrong? In a footnote added in response to criticism of that sort, Mill allows that the agent's *intention* (his aim to bring about the consequence of a person saved from drowning) is morally relevant. And our estimate of the *worth of the agent* may vary, depending on whether he was motivated by duty or greed. In the latter case we will think less of the man and be less likely to trust him in similar circumstances. But, Mill insists, the right thing was done, whatever the motive.

5. The preceding objection easily turns into another. It would seem that utilitarianism

> renders men cold and unsympathizing; that it chills their moral feelings toward individuals; that it makes them regard only the dry and hard consideration of the consequences of actions, not taking into their moral estimate the qualities from which those actions emanate. (*U,* 151)

Here Mill reiterates that we have to distinguish *actions* as good or bad from *persons* as good or bad. It is possible, of course, that a good person occasionally performs a morally bad action, just as a really bad person may do a good thing. And though some utilitarians may stress the moral estimation of action almost to the exclusion of "the other beauties of character which go toward making a human being lovable or admirable" (*U,* 152)—Mill is surely thinking of Bentham here—utilitarianism

---

*Mill's point that happiness is a by-product of other aims, strivings, and successes is one that utilitarians often neglect. If taken seriously, this point would to some extent reconcile the differences between utilitarians and those who (like Kant, Aristotle, and the Stoics) stress virtue as the key to ethics.

---

*This is exactly what Kant thinks morality does require; that every morally right action be one that is done out of duty, from respect for the moral law. Actions done out of mere inclination are not worth anything, morally speaking. See p. 453.

itself does not forbid valuing character. Moreover, although goodness of character and the rightness of action do not always coincide, "in the long run the best proof of a good character is good actions" (*U*, 152). So utilitarianism need have no chilling effect on us.

6. To the objection that utilitarianism, which counts only worldly happiness as the mark of moral rightness, is a "godless" doctrine, Mill replies that it all depends on how you think of God.

If it be a true belief that God desires, above all things, the happiness of his creatures, and that this was his purpose in their creation, utility is not only not a godless doctrine, but more profoundly religious than any other. (*U*, 153)

7. It seems as if the principle of utility is impractical. It requires something there is usually no time to do. Very often we are called on to act quickly in making a choice; there is no time to do the exhaustive calculations required to determine the consequences of all the alternatives available. To this, Mill has a very interesting reply:

This is exactly as if anyone were to say that it is impossible to guide our conduct by Christianity because there is not time, on every occasion on which anything has to be done, to read through the Old and New Testaments. The answer to the objection is that there has been ample time, namely the whole past duration of the human species. During all that time mankind have been learning by experience the tendencies of actions. (*U*, 155)

The fact that utility functions as a first principle does not in any way rule out secondary principles. These intermediate generalizations, Mill holds, are readily available to us in the common wisdom of our culture and in the law. We do not need to calculate each time whether *this* murder would be all right, or whether *that* lie would be justified, or whether making *this* contribution to the relief of the homeless fits with the first principle. We learn the basic moral rules as children. Such secondary rules may be subject to gradual improvement. They may be more and more perfectly adapted to produce happiness. There may be occasional excep-

tions to them, too, but a *moral* justification for an exception must be decided by appeal to utility.*

Nobody argues that the art of navigation is not founded on astronomy because sailors cannot wait to calculate the Nautical Almanac. Being rational creatures, they go to sea with it ready calculated; and all rational creatures go out upon the sea of life with their minds made up on the common questions of right and wrong. (*U*, 157)

It is indeed not possible to calculate the utility of each of our actions on the occasion of their performance. But we don't need to. We cannot do without secondary rules in society, which can be learned and relied on. But these can be improved only by bringing them more closely in line with the first principle: utility. For Mill, Bentham's great value lies in his attempt to improve these subordinate principles, particularly in social institutions and the law.

8. There is a final objection, perhaps the most important of all, and Mill devotes an entire chapter to it. The objection concerns justice. Can the demands of justice be incorporated into the utilitarian framework, or is justice something different, something that resists the calculation of consequences?

It is easy to dream up cases where there is at least the appearance of conflict between justice and utility. Executing an innocent person may, in certain circumstances, quell a riot and prevent the death of hundreds. It is clear that to execute the innocent is *unjust*. Yet a utility calculation seems to tell us that in this circumstance, executing the person is the morally right thing to do because it would produce more pleasure and less pain overall.† So it seems there is a clash between the claims of justice

---

*Relying on rules to determine right and wrong rather than on direct calculations of utility is called *rule utilitarianism*—provided the rules themselves are justified in terms of their utility in producing the desired consequences.

†Discussion of such cases has made it clear that from a utilitarian standpoint, it is not so easy to be sure that the circumstances justifying an innocent person's execution ever exist. For instance, we would have to be virtually certain that the fact of the person's innocence would never be known, lest even worse events ensue. And could we ever be certain enough of that?

and the claims of utility. In circumstances like this, justice tells us one thing, utility another. Mill tries to argue that this clash is merely apparent and that justice rightly understood can be seen to be just a special case of utility. If his argument is successful, justice and utility are reconciled.

Mill allows that the subjective feeling attached to judgments about justice is different from, and stronger than, feelings about utility. We think it more serious to violate justice than to fail to bring about as much happiness as we can. Why? Because, Mill believes, justice is associated with *rights*. In normal circumstances it is unjust to violate someone's *legal rights*. Perhaps, however, there is a law that gives some people rights they really shouldn't have. It may not be unjust to violate such a law. But to deal with such cases we need the notion of a *moral right*—a right that the law should protect, but may not. A person may have moral rights even in the absence of any legal protection. And now we can say that doing injustice is violating a person's moral rights. We usually have a very strong reaction to injustice. We resent the violation of rights and want the perpetrator to be punished.

But what is it to have a right, anyway?

> When we call anything a person's right, we mean that he has a valid claim on society to protect him in the possession of it. (*U*, 189)

I have a right to walk peaceably down a city street without being molested. To have such a right, Mill tells us, is to have a "valid claim" to protection in the exercise of this right. Society *owes* it to me to see that this right is not violated, has a *duty* to guarantee my safety in such circumstances.

But where do rights like this come from? Can they really originate in utility? And on what grounds can I claim that society owes me such protection? Mill's argument is that there is one part of utility that is so basic, so fundamental, that in its absence everything else making for happiness is in jeopardy: *security*.

> All other earthly benefits are needed by one person, not needed by another; and many of them can,

if necessary, be cheerfully foregone or replaced by something else; but security no human being can possibly do without; on it we depend for all our immunity from evil and for the whole value of all and every good, beyond the passing moment, since nothing but the gratification of the instant could be of any worth to us if we could be deprived of everything the next instant by whoever was momentarily stronger than ourselves. (*U*, 190)

Security, being safe in our persons and possessions, is the "most indispensable of all necessaries," Mill says (*U*, 190).* Because it is so basic to our happiness, the feelings that attach to its protection are particularly strong. That is why it may *seem* that justice is different from utility. But far from being different from utility, let alone opposed to it, justice is its deepest and most fundamental form.

> I account the justice which is grounded on utility to be the chief part, and incomparably the most sacred and binding part, of all morality. Justice is a name for certain classes of moral rules which concern the essentials of human well-being more nearly, and are therefore of more absolute obligation, than any other rules for the guidance of life; and the notion which we have found to be of the essence of the idea of justice—that of a right residing in an individual—implies and testifies to this more binding obligation. . . . a person may possibly not need the benefits of others, but he always needs that they should not do him hurt. (*U*, 195–196)

In this way, Mill argues there is no conflict between justice and utility. If we return to our example of executing an innocent man for the sake of avoiding a riot, we can see what Mill would say. It is unjust to take his life, so it ought not to be done. To acquiesce in the violation of that man's security imperils the security of us all. And that none of us will tolerate.† The appearance of conflict can

---

*You would be right to hear echoes of Hobbes here. See Hobbes on the deplorable "state of nature" in which no one can feel safe (pp. 367–368).

†Critics of utilitarianism will push the point, however, that it is *possible*—however unlikely—that such an execution will actually increase the general happiness. And if one could be sure that the circumstances were right, then utility would prescribe the

be overcome if we reflect that justice is the name we give to the deepest condition for securing our happiness.

Bentham and Mill, together with utilitarians to the present day, urge that there is only one way to decide the morally right thing to do. Think about the consequences of all the actions open to you, estimate (if you can't literally calculate) the effect each action would have on the happiness of all the persons affected (or on the goodness of their lives, or on what they would prefer), and the right thing will become apparent. What remains is simply to do it.

1. What makes utilitarianism a teleological theory?
2. What general features of an action determine whether it is morally right or wrong? Contrast this utilitarian view with Kant's account of what makes actions right or wrong.
3. What makes classic utilitarianism a form of hedonism? Distinguish the two hedonic theses that form the core of Bentham's version of utilitarianism.
4. What is happiness, according to the utilitarians, and what does it have to do with morality? (Pieces of their view of happiness are scattered through the chapter; gather them together to form your answer.)
5. Explain the principle of utility. What makes this a moral principle, rather than just prudence or self-interest?
6. How does a person apply the principle of utility to determine whether a particular action is morally right or wrong?
7. How do Bentham and Mill differ in their methods of calculating happiness? How does Mill propose to determine the quality of pleasures?
8. Mill presents two arguments in favor of utilitarianism. Explain each argument. Identify the fallacy in each.

9. How does Mill defend utilitarianism against the charges that (a) pleasure is too low a standard to be appealed to in morality, and (b) the general happiness is too high a standard?
10. Contrast Mill and Kant on the question of whether an agent's motivation is relevant to an appraisal of the morality of an action.
11. What problem is justice thought to raise for the utilitarians? How does Mill argue that, at bottom, there is no conflict between justice and utility?

The Rights of Women

By the time Mill wrote *The Subjection of Women*[6] in 1869, slavery had been abolished in the United States and, indeed, in most of the world. But one form of bondage, Mill said, remained: that in which half the world's population, the female half, was still held. Our situation today is so much changed from the circumstances in which Mill wrote (though it may still be far from ideal) that we need to exert our imaginations to grasp the "Woman Question," as it was then known. Together with Mill's little book, we consider an earlier work by Mary Wollstonecraft, *A Vindication of the Rights of Women* (1792). Wollstonecraft is not clearly a utilitarian, though much of what she writes is in the same spirit.* Mill and Wollstonecraft take a similar view of the "Woman Question," and they recommend similar remedies.[7]

Writing in 1869, Mill reminds us of the state of English law concerning women. (It was scarcely better anywhere else.) Society assumed that women generally would marry, and most did. For this rea-

---

execution. Since this could in no case be a just act, there is in principle an unresolved conflict between justice and utility, and Mill's attempt at reconciliation fails. The principle of justice must have other, independent grounds—perhaps in something like the Kantian imperative that one is never to use a person as a means to an end. See again Kant's discussion of this on p. 456.

*Bentham had published *Introduction to the Principles of Morals and Legislation* just three years earlier, in 1789. Wollstonecraft's arguments vary. There are consequentialist arguments of a utilitarian cast, appeals to reason as the arbiter of morality, claims about what is suitable for an individual destined for immortality, and arguments from justice and the will of God. Even though it is a bit hard to find any theoretical unity in the essay, there is no denying its power.

"Let there be then no coercion established in society, and the common law of gravity prevailing, the sexes will fall into their proper places."

—Mary Wollstonecraft

son, the laws concerning marriage were the crucial ones. Here is what those laws held (*SW,* 502–506):

- A married woman can have no property except in her husband; anything she inherits immediately becomes his.

- There is a way for a woman to secure "her" property from her husband, but even so, she is not allowed the use of it; if he by violence takes it from her, he cannot be punished or compelled to return it to her.

- Husband and wife are called "one person in law," but that means only that whatever is hers is his (not vice versa).

- Her children are by law *his* children. She can do nothing with them except by his delegation. On his death, she does not become their legal guardian, unless he by will makes her so.

- If she leaves her husband, she can take nothing with her, not even her children. He can—by

force, if it comes to that—compel her to return.

And, of course, women were excluded from voting, from running for Parliament, and (at least by custom) from nearly all nondomestic professions. Mill considers the question of why this should be so. Is it, he asks, because society has experimented with alternative social arrangements and discovered that, all in all, this is best? Of course not. The adoption of this system

> never was the result of deliberation, or forethought, or any social ideal, or any notion whatever of what conduced to the benefit of humanity or the good order of society. It arose simply from the fact that from the very earliest twilight of human society, every woman (owing to the value attached to her by men, combined with her inferiority in muscular strength) was found in a state of bondage to some man. (*SW,* 475)

Mill stresses that the situation now sanctioned by law was simply the situation that was actually in place when laws were first written. This amounts to an adoption of the *law of the strongest,* a law that led to kingship and slavery, as well as to the subjection of women. So the fact that the subjection of women has been a custom nearly everywhere for ages is no more an argument in its favor than is a similar argument in support of absolute monarchy or slavery—both of which have been done away with in the modern world.

Moreover, it is not hard to explain why this custom has outlasted monarchy and slavery. Each of these had the attractions of power; the same is true of the relation between women and men. But there is an important difference:

> Whatever gratification of pride there is in the possession of this power, and whatever personal interest in its exercise, is in this case not confined to a limited class, but common to the whole male sex. . . . It comes home to the person and hearth of every male head of a family, and of everyone who looks forward to being so. The clodhopper exercises, or is to exercise, his share of the power equally with the highest nobleman. . . . We must consider, too, that the possessors of the power have facilities in this case, greater than in any other, to

prevent any uprising against it. Every one of the subjects lives under the very eye, and almost, it may be said, in the hands, of one of the masters—in closer intimacy with him than with any of her fellow-subjects; with no means of combining against him, and, on the other hand, with the strongest motives for seeking his favour and avoiding to give him offence. (*SW,* 481, 482)

The fact that women don't complain about this inequality might constitute an argument in its favor; women consent to it, it is said, and even contribute to its continuance. But Mill notes several things: (1) Some women do complain. (2) The common pattern is that those subjected to power of an ancient origin begin by complaining not about the power itself, but only about its abuse; and there is plenty of complaint by women about their husbands' ill use of them. But most important, (3)

Men do not want solely the obedience of women, they want their sentiments. All men, except the most brutish, desire to have, in the woman most nearly connected with them, not a forced slave but a willing one, not a slave merely, but a favourite. They have therefore put everything in practice to enslave their minds. The masters of all other slaves rely, for maintaining obedience, on fear, either fear of themselves, or religious fears. The masters of women wanted more than simple obedience, and they turned the whole force of education to effect their purpose. (*SW,* 486)

To us, this may sound exaggerated. But Wollstonecraft cites passages from popular books about how to bring up young women that suggest this is no exaggeration. Let's look at some of her evidence.

The theme running through the popular literature is that a woman exists for the sake of a man. Because of that, a woman's virtues are different from a man's and a woman's daily life is oriented toward pleasing. One of Wollstonecraft's sources is *Émile,* an influential book on education by Jean-Jacques Rousseau.* Here is Rousseau on the education of women. (I cite Wollstonecraft's quota-

tions from Rousseau at some length to stimulate the imagination we need to re-create the situation of the time.)

"It being once demonstrated that man and woman are not, nor ought to be, constituted alike in temperament and character, it follows, of course, that they should not be educated in the same manner. . . .

"Woman and man were made for each other, but their mutual dependence is not the same. The men depend on the women only on account of their desires; the women on the men both on account of their desires and their necessities. We could subsist better without them than they without us. . . .

"For this reason the education of women should be always relative to the men. To please, to be useful to us, to make us love and esteem them, to educate us when young, and take care of us when grown up, to advise, to console us, to render our lives easy and agreeable—these are the duties of women at all times, and what they should be taught in their infancy. . . .

"Boys love sports of noise and activity; to beat the drum, to whip the top, and to drag about their little carts; girls, on the other hand, are fonder of things of show and ornament; such as mirrors, trinkets, and dolls: the doll is the peculiar amusement of the females; from whence we see their taste plainly adapted to their destination. . . . And, in fact, almost all of them learn with reluctance to read and write; but very readily apply themselves to the use of their needles. They imagine themselves already grown up, and think with pleasure that such qualifications will enable them to decorate themselves. . . .

"Girls . . . should also be early subjected to restraint. This misfortune, if it really be one, is inseparable from their sex; nor do they ever throw it off but to suffer more cruel evils. They must be subject, all their lives, to the most constant and severe restraint, which is that of decorum; it is, therefore, necessary to accustom them early to such confinement, that it may not afterwards cost them too dear; and to the suppression of their caprices, that they may the more readily submit to the will of others. . . .

"There results from this habitual restraint a tractableness which women have occasion for during their whole lives, as they constantly remain

---

* See the profile of Rousseau on p. 455.

either under subjection to the men, or to the opinions of mankind; and are never permitted to set themselves above those opinions. The first and most important qualification in a woman is good nature or sweetness of temper: formed to obey a being so imperfect as man, often full of vices, and always full of faults, she ought to learn betimes even to suffer injustice, and to bear the insults of a husband without complaint; it is not for his sake, but her own, that she should be of a mild disposition. . . .

"Woman has everything against her, as well our faults as her own timidity and weakness; she has nothing in her favour, but her subtilty and her beauty. Is it not very reasonable, therefore, she should cultivate both? . . .

"A man speaks of what he knows, a woman of what pleases her; the one requires knowledge, the other taste; the principal object of a man's discourse should be what is useful, that of a woman's what is agreeable. There ought to be nothing in common between their different conversation but truth.

"We ought not, therefore, to restrain the prattle of girls, in the same manner as we should that of boys, with that severe question, *To what purpose are you talking?* but by another, which is no less difficult to answer, *How will your discourse be received?* In infancy, while they are as yet incapable to discern good from evil, they ought to observe it, as a law never to say anything disagreeable to those whom they are speaking to." (Quoted in *VRW,* 88–95)

There is more to the same effect in Wollstonecraft, quoted from other popular authors of the time. Mill and Wollstonecraft not only agree that this subjection of women to men is unjust, but also argue that it has many bad consequences. Let us examine what they say.

The idea that there are special virtues for a woman, and that these are all oriented around pleasing men, results in morality being

very insidiously undermined, in the female world, by the attention being turned to the show instead of the substance. A simple thing is thus made strangely complicated; nay, sometimes virtue and its shadow are set at variance. (*VRW,* 148)

A woman is persuaded to value trivial things: attractiveness, dress, decorum, the short-term plea-

sures of sex. Thus are women turned toward sensuality and away from understanding.

They who live to please—must find their enjoyments, their happiness, in pleasure! (*VRW,* 129–130)

It is this emphasis on pleasing—and pleasing men particularly—that accounts for the fact that the term "a virtuous woman" has such a narrow connotation. Why should that term direct the mind immediately to sexual behavior, when the term "a virtuous man" does not? Because a woman is regarded as first and foremost a pleaser!

How then can the great art of pleasing be such a necessary study? it is only useful to a mistress. The chaste wife and serious mother should only consider her power to please as the polish of her virtues, and the affection of her husband as one of the comforts that render her task less difficult, and her life happier. But whether she be loved or neglected, her first wish should be to make herself respectable, and not to rely for all her happiness on a being subject to like infirmities with herself. (*VRW,* 32)

Everything is focused on the opinions of others, on how a woman is *regarded.* This constant attention to keep the "varnish" of character fresh often supersedes actual moral obligations. With respect to reputation, Wollstonecraft says,

The attention is confined to a single virtue—chastity. If the honour of a woman, as it is absurdly called, be safe, she may neglect every social duty; nay, ruin her family by gaming and extravagance; yet still present a shameless front—for truly she is an honourable woman! (*VRW,* 150)

Thus the social order makes women worse than they ought to be; this narrow view of their nature gives them the status of secondary beings whose very existence is justifiable only in terms of a relation to another.

Pleasure is the business of woman's life, according to the present modification of society; and while it continues to be so, little can be expected from such weak beings. Inheriting in a lineal descent from the first fair defect in nature—the sovereignty of beauty—they have, to maintain their power, resigned the natural rights which the exercise of reason might have procured them, and chosen rather to be short-lived queens than labour to obtain the sober pleasures that arise from equality. (*VRW*, 61)

Not much can be expected from such weak beings, Wollstonecraft says. But, of course, they have been deliberately created weak. Mill puts the argument this way:

All women are brought up from the very earliest years in the belief that their ideal of character is the very opposite to that of men; not self-will, and government by self-control, but submission, and yielding to the control of others. All the moralities tell them that it is the duty of women, and all the current sentimentalities that it is their nature, to live for others; to make complete abnegation of themselves, and to have no life but in their affections. And by their affections are meant the only ones they are allowed to have—those to the men with whom they are connected, or to the children who constitute an additional and indefeasible tie between them and a man. When we put together three things—first, the natural attraction between the sexes; secondly, the wife's entire dependence on the husband, every privilege or pleasure she has being either his gift, or depending entirely on his will; and lastly, that the principal object of human pursuit, consideration, and all objects of social ambition, can in general be sought or obtained by her only through him, it would be a miracle if the object of being attractive to men had not become the polar star of feminine education and formation of character. And, this great means of influence over the minds of women having been acquired, an instinct of selfishness made men avail themselves of it to the utmost as a means of holding women in subjection, by representing to them meekness, submissiveness, and resignation of all individual will into the hands of a man, as an essential part of sexual attractiveness. (*SW*, 486–487)

Wollstonecraft speaks of women having to resign reason and their natural rights "to maintain their power" (*VRW*, 61). And this leads to further bad consequences. Women become, of necessity, *cunning.*

Only employed about the little incidents of the day, they necessarily grow up cunning. My very soul has often sickened at observing the sly tricks prac-

tised by women to gain some foolish thing on which their silly hearts were set. Not allowed to dispose of money, or call anything their own, they learn to turn the market penny; or, should a husband offend, by staying from home, or give rise to some emotions of jealousy—a new gown, or any pretty bauble, smooths Juno's angry brow.

But these *littlenesses* would not degrade their character, if women were led to respect themselves, if political and moral subjects were opened to them; and, I will venture to affirm that this is the only way to make them properly attentive to their domestic duties. An active mind embraces the whole circle of its duties, and finds time enough for all. (*VRW*, 187)

Thus understanding, strictly speaking, has been denied to woman; and instinct, sublimated into wit and cunning, for the purposes of life, has been substituted in its stead. . . .

I shall not go back to the remote annals of antiquity to trace the history of woman; it is sufficient to allow that she has always been either a slave or a despot, and to remark that each of these situations equally retards the progress of reason. The grand source of female folly and vice has ever appeared to me to arise from narrowness of mind; and the very constitution of civil governments has put almost insuperable obstacles in the way to prevent the cultivation of the female understanding; yet virtue can be built on no other foundation. (*VRW*, 59–60)

On this same narrowness of education another female fault is built: meddlesomeness. Wollstonecraft argues that

women cannot by force be confined to domestic concerns: for they will, however ignorant, intermeddle with more weighty affairs, neglecting private duties only to disturb, by cunning tricks, the orderly plans of reason which rise above their comprehension. (*VRW*, 12)

Mill adds that men who are considerate of their wives' opinions are often made worse, not better, by the wife's influence.

She is taught that she has no business with things out of that [domestic] sphere; and accordingly she seldom has any honest and conscientious opinion on them; and therefore hardly ever meddles with them for any legitimate purpose, but generally for an interested one. She neither knows nor cares which is the right side in politics, but she knows what will bring in money or invitations, give her husband a title, her son a place, or her daughter a good marriage. (*SW, 512*)

Many women do manage to "govern" their husbands, of course. Their weakness and lack of straightforward rationality, however, cause them to do this indirectly, sneakily, with what Rousseau calls "subtility." In fact, Wollstonecraft argues, it is this very weakness that entices women to become tyrants in their families.

> Women are, in fact, so much degraded by mistaken notions of female excellence, that I do not mean to add a paradox when I assert that this artificial weakness produces a propensity to tyrannize, and gives birth to cunning, the natural opponent of strength, which leads them to play off those contemptible infantine airs that undermine esteem even whilst they excite desire. (*VRW, 7*)

Either women use their beauty, their desirability, to tyrannize men, or they become shrewish. But what is the alternative?

> "Educate women like men," says Rousseau, "and the more they resemble our sex the less power will they have over us." This is the very point I aim at. I do not wish them to have power over men; but over themselves. (*VRW, 69*)

In this last remark we come near to the heart of the matter. Such, then, are the consequences of restricting the education and dulling the reason of women, of teaching them that their only concern must be to please a man.

What do Wollstonecraft and Mill want for women? Equality with men before the law, independence, freedom to make their own decisions, strength of body, a real education that broadens understanding and doesn't just heighten sensitivity, and the capacity for friendship with men rather than submissive fawning. Wollstonecraft sums it up by declaring that there should be no sexually based virtues. Virtue—moral goodness—is a *human* matter; only evil comes from assuming that there is one virtue for a man and another for a woman, with its corollary that the woman's virtue exists only relative to the man's. True, men and women may to some extent have different duties, but they are one and all, she says, human duties.

> I here throw down my gauntlet, and deny the existence of sexual virtues, not excepting modesty. For man and woman, truth, if I understand the meaning of the word, must be the same. (*VRW, 57*)

As things are, a woman is denied the independent use of reason and must see everything through her husband's eyes. But the question is, does she have as much capacity for reason and understanding as a man?

> If she have, which, for a moment, I will take for granted, she was not created merely to be the solace of man, and the sexual should not destroy the human character. (*VRW, 59*)

Very well. But should we take that for granted? How could we tell whether her reason would be as strong as a man's if it were given a chance? Both Mill and Wollstonecraft argue that you can't tell by looking at contemporary society or history because both are tainted by the corrupting influence of the education and upbringing women have received. The only way to tell is to make the experiment. Wollstonecraft says,

> I have not attempted to extenuate their faults; but to prove them to be the natural consequence of their education and station in society. If so, it is reasonable to suppose that they will change their character, and correct their vices and follies, when they are allowed to be free in a physical, moral, and civil sense.
>
>   Let woman share the rights, and she will emulate the virtues of man; for she must grow more perfect when emancipated, or justify the authority that chains such a weak being to her duty. (*VRW, 214–215*)

Mill adds,

> I consider it presumption in anyone to pretend to decide what women are or are not, can or cannot be, by natural constitution. They have always hitherto been kept, as far as regards spontaneous development, in so unnatural a state, that their nature cannot but have been greatly distorted and disguised; and no one can safely pronounce that if women's nature were left to choose its direction

as freely as men's, and if no artificial bent were attempted to be given to it except that required by the conditions of human society, and given to both sexes alike, there would be any material difference, or perhaps any difference at all, in the character and capacities which would unfold themselves. (*SW,* 532)

There are no means of finding what either one person or many can do, but by trying. (*SW,* 499)

Suppose the trial is made and we find that women are not by nature the inferior beings they have been made to be. Suppose that the reforms in law and custom Mill and Wollstonecraft urge come to pass. What good can we expect to come of them? First of all, Mill says, we will have justice rather than injustice, and that is no insignificant gain (*SW,* 558). Second, we would virtually double "the mass of mental faculties available for the higher service of humanity" (*SW,* 561). Third, women would have a more beneficial influence, though not necessarily a greater influence, on general belief and sentiment (*SW,* 563).* Fourth, there will surely be a great gain in happiness for women (*SW,* 576).

We can close this brief consideration of the "Woman Question" in the nineteenth century with an appeal by Wollstonecraft:

I then would fain convince reasonable men of the importance of some of my remarks; and prevail on them to weigh dispassionately the whole tenor of my observations. I appeal to their understandings; and as a fellow-creature, claim, in the name of my sex, some interest in their hearts. I entreat them to assist to emancipate their companion, to make her a *helpmeet* for them.

Would men but generously snap our chains, and be content with rational fellowship instead of slavish obedience, they would find us more observant daughters, more affectionate sisters, more faithful wives, more reasonable mothers—in a word, bet-

ter citizens. We should then love them with true affection, because we should learn to respect ourselves. (*VRW,* 164)

If our situation is very different from the situation in which these two philosophers wrote, one reason is the impact their thoughts have had on successive generations down to the present day.

---

1. What principles for the education of women does Rousseau advocate?
2. What bad consequences do Wollstonecraft and Mill see flowing from the differential treatment of women?
3. What ideals do they recommend in place of the current beliefs about the position of women in society?
4. What benefits will result from such a change, according to Wollstonecraft and Mill?

For Further Thought

1. Bentham argues that the only alternatives to utilitarianism are asceticism and the "principle of sympathy and antipathy." Look again at Kant's ethics, and try to determine whether it escapes this critique.

2. To a considerable degree, we have made the experiment that Wollstonecraft and Mill recommend. Look at what they anticipate the outcome to be, and estimate to what degree we have achieved their ends.

Notes

1. References to John Stuart Mill's *Utilitarianism,* in *On Liberty and Other Essays,* ed. John Gray (Oxford: Oxford University Press, 1991), are cited in the text by the abbreviation *U.* References are to page numbers.
2. References to Jeremy Bentham, *An Introduction to the Principles of Morals and Legislation* (Oxford: Clarendon Press, 1907), are cited in the text by the abbreviation *PML.* References are to page numbers.
3. John Stuart Mill, "Bentham," in *Utilitarianism and Other Essays,* ed. Alan Ryan (New York: Penguin Books, 1987), 151.

---

*As an example of bad consequences caused by narrowness of vision and domination by sentiment, Mill cites the charity given by "ladies" of the upper classes; this does more harm than good, he believes, by making the recipients dependent rather than independent. Opening the minds of women to a broader perspective will forestall such shortsighted response to emotion (*SW,* 566–567).

4. Quoted in *The Encyclopedia of Philosophy,* vol. 1, ed. Paul Edwards (New York: Macmillan, Free Press, 1967), 283.

5. John Stuart Mill, *Autobiography,* in *Essential Works of John Stuart Mill,* ed. Max Lerner (New York: Bantam Books, 1961), 88.

6. References to John Stuart Mill's *The Subjection* of *Women,* ed. John Gray (Oxford: Oxford University Press, 1991), are cited by the abbreviation *SW.* References are to page numbers.

7. References to Mary Wollstonecraft, *A Vindication of the Rights of Women,* ed. Mary Warnock (London: J. M. Dent, Everyman's Library, 1986), are cited by the abbreviation *VRW.* References are to page numbers.

20

FRIEDRICH NIETZSCHE

The Value of Existence

Born to a German Lutheran minister's family, Friedrich Nietzsche (1844–1900) lost his father when he was five years old. He was strictly brought up in a household of five women (his mother, sister, grandmother, and two aunts), where religion was, according to reports, less practiced than preached. He went to excellent schools and studied classical philology at the universities of Bonn and Leipzig. At the unheard-of age of twenty-four, on an extravagant recommendation by a great scholar, Nietzsche became a full professor in philology at the University of Basel, Switzerland.

He served as a medical orderly in the Franco-Prussian War and returned in poor health, but he continued working and published his first book in 1872. In 1879, he resigned his professorship on grounds of ill health and spent the next nine years in lonely apartments or flats in Switzerland and Italy. He was severely ill for a long time, racked with pain and weakness that would have put most men in the hospital. But throughout his illness he kept working, producing book after book. He was deeply disappointed in the reception of his work; very few copies of his books were purchased, the few re-

views were based mostly on misunderstandings, and he was generally ignored. In the late winter of 1888, he broke down and spent the next eleven years insane, cared for by his sister.*

Nietzsche is famous, or infamous, as an influence on the Nazi movement. There is no doubt that he wrote things that rather easily lent themselves to the distortions of Nazi propagandists, and he is certainly no friend of Christianity, democracy, or equal rights for all. But there is also no doubt that he would have been sickened by the whole Nazi business. He was no friend of nationalism, thinking of himself always as a "good European." Scarcely any other writings contain such malicious attacks

---

*Walter Kaufmann, famous as a Nietzsche translator, writes: "His madness was in all probability an atypical general paresis. If so, he must have had syphilis; and since he is known to have lived a highly ascetic life, it is supposed that, as a student, he had visited a brothel once or twice. This has never been substantiated, and any detailed accounts of such experiences are either poetry or pornography—not biography. Nor has the suggestion ever been disproved that he may have been infected while nursing wounded soldiers in 1870" (*The Portable Nietzsche* [New York: Viking Press, 1954], 13–14).

on "the Germans." And anti-Semitism was diagnosed by Nietzsche as a particularly reprehensible form of resentment (about as bad a thing as he could say about anything). But the Nazis made him over in their own image and used perverted versions of his concepts of the *overman* and *will to power* to their advantage.

Like Kierkegaard (whom he did not know), Nietzsche is concerned primarily with the individual, not with politics. His basic question is this: In a fundamentally meaningless world, what sort of life could justify itself, could show itself to be worth living? Around that issue all his work circles.*

Pessimism and Tragedy

Appropriately enough for a classically trained philologist, Nietzsche's first book, *The Birth of Tragedy,*† is about the Greeks. Both its style and content were shocking to his scholarly colleagues. It is not a dry historical treatise filled with footnotes and Greek quotations; it is a passionately argued account of how tragedy allowed an ancient people to solve the problem of "the value of existence" (*BT,* 17), together with a plea for the relevance of that solution today.[1] Nietzsche challenges the received view of

"We want to be the poets of our life."
—FRIEDRICH WILHELM NIETZSCHE

the Greeks, that everything they did expressed a noble simplicity and grandeur, a calm and measured naïveté, a spirit in which everything was harmonious and beautiful. Greek statues and temples do reflect such a spirit, and many people had taken this to be the classical ideal. But Nietzsche argues that this spirit doesn't fit tragedy—in particular, it doesn't fit what we know of the origins of tragedy.*

What is the problem that tragedy is supposed to solve? Nietzsche finds it expressed by Sophocles in the play *Oedipus at Colonus.*

---

*Interest in Nietzsche is intense these days, and controversy rages over the proper interpretation of his thought. Perhaps no single rendering can claim to be the authentic Nietzsche. One source of dispute concerns what weight to give to the mass of notes that were published posthumously under the title *Will to Power;* to put my cards on the table, I believe it best to stick to what Nietzsche himself approved for publication, using the rest only to illuminate that. Just as "in the end we must all have to some extent our own Socrates" (p. 59), so we may all have to have our own Nietzsche. Let me encourage you to read widely in Nietzsche, but with the warning that it is easy to get him wrong if you just dip in here and there.

†Published in 1872, its title was originally *The Birth of Tragedy from the Spirit of Music.* In the second half of the book, Nietzsche praises Richard Wagner's music dramas as an indication that the spirit of tragedy might be reborn. But by 1886, when a later edition came out, Nietzsche had despaired of Wagner as a "romantic" and a "decadent." This edition contains Nietzsche's severe appraisal of the book in a preface called "Attempt at a Self-criticism."

---

*By tragedy Nietzsche means above all the dramas of Aeschylus and Sophocles. Representative examples are the *Oresteia* trilogy by Aeschylus (which tells the tale of Agamemnon's return from Troy and his murder by his wife, Clytemnestra; the vengeance of their son Orestes; and how the law of blood-guilt was replaced by the establishment of courts of justice in Athens) and the well-known plays of Sophocles, *Oedipus Rex* and *Antigone.* The third great Athenian tragedian, Euripides, is thought by Nietzsche to preside over the death of tragedy.

According to an ancient legend, King Midas had long hunted the forest for the wise *Silenus,* the companion of Dionysus, without catching him. When Silenus finally fell into his hands, the king asked him what is the very best and most preferable of all things for man. The stiff and motionless daemon refused to speak; until, forced by the king, he finally burst into shrill laughter and uttered the following words: "Miserable ephemeral race, children of chance and toil, why do you force me to tell you what is best for you not to hear? The very best of all things is completely beyond your reach: not to have been born, not to *be,* to be *nothing.* But the second best thing for you is—to meet an early death." (*BT,* 3, 27)

The problem is pessimism. Contrary to the accepted view of Greek cheerfulness, Nietzsche believes that the Greeks looked into the abyss of human suffering without blinking, that they experienced the terrors and misery of life—and they *did not look away.* All things considered, said Greek folk wisdom, Silenus is right; the best of all is not to be. And yet the Greeks found a way to live, to affirm life, even to rejoice in life. How did they do that? Nietzsche finds the key to this puzzle in their art, especially in their tragedies.

The first thing to note is that the tragedies were performed at religious festivals. Attending these performances was serious business, more like going to a papal mass than taking in the latest hit movie. The second thing to note is that prizes were given for the best plays at each festival, so playwrights were continually challenged to excel.* But the most important feature of the tragedies is the way they unite two opposing powers in human life. Nietzsche designates these powers with the names of two Greek gods, Apollo and Dionysus; each is the patron of a certain kind of art.

Apollo is the god of order and measure, the god of restraint and calm composure. He is the god who says, "Nothing too much," and "Know thyself." It is the spirit of Apollo that reigns supreme in the harmonious sculptures on the Parthenon, where each individual being reaches a divine perfection without denying the perfection of any other. This spirit also pervades the Homeric epic: Homer's portrayal of Olympus, with its radiant gods, glows with those powers Apollo represents. Zeus, Hera, Athena, Poseidon, and the rest are a magnificent dream of the human spirit.*

> Everything here speaks to us of a sumptuous, even triumphant existence in which everything is deified, regardless of whether it is good or evil. And so the spectator might stand full of consternation before this fantastic exuberance of life, wondering what magic potion these arrogant men took in order to have enjoyed life in such a way that wherever they look, Helen, the ideal image of their own existence "hovering in sweet sensuality" smiles back at them, laughing. (*BT,* 3, 27)

In the Homeric epic, then, the wisdom of Silenus was

> continually overcome anew, in any case veiled and removed from view by the Greeks through that artistic *middle world* of the Olympians. In order to be able to live, the Greeks were obliged to create these gods, out of the deepest necessity. . . . So the gods justify the life of men by living it themselves—the only adequate theodicy! (*BT,* 3, 28)†

In this way, Nietzsche accounts for the epic, for the glories of Homer's *Iliad* and *Odyssey.* But tragedy is something else. In tragedy, the suffering in human life is not "veiled and removed from view"; it is presented, explored, and given weight. Tragedy *shows* us the terror.

---

*Nietzsche says that for the Greeks, everything was a contest. Characteristically, he sees envy, ambition, and the struggle to prevail flaring out in every sphere of Greek life, from athletics to poetry. What distinguishes the Greek ethos from our own, he thinks, is that this competitive spirit is *affirmed* and not condemned; "Every talent must unfold itself in fighting" ("Homer's Contest" in *PN,* 37).

---

*See Chapter 1 on the Homeric gods as portrayed in *The Iliad.*
†In his later thought, after all gods have disappeared, Nietzsche reaffirms this principle. The only satisfactory justification for human life lies in *living* it. The question then becomes, What sort of life could constitute such a justification? The answer turns out to be a life rather like the one the Greek gods themselves lived.

To account for tragedy, Nietzsche believes we need to bring in another kind of god. Dionysus (Bacchus) is the god of wine, of intoxication, of excess and loss of control. Where Dionysus lives, all order, form, and measure break down. Women are caught up in long lines, dancing beyond the civilized towns to orgies in the countryside.* Individual consciousness is drowned in a sea of feelings; conventions are left behind as primal nature rules. This god, too, has his art. In lyric poetry and folk song the passions—desire, anguish, hate, contempt, frenzy, joy—are expressed without reserve. But lyric and folk song are no more tragedy than is the epic. For the birth of tragedy, Dionysus must meet Apollo.

To understand how Nietzsche thinks tragedy solves the problem of the value of existence, we need to grasp one more thing: the metaphysics of Schopenhauer.† In *The Birth of Tragedy* Nietzsche accepts Schopenhauer's view of reality, though not Schopenhauer's evaluation of it. For Schopenhauer, as for Kant, the world of our experience is merely appearance, not reality. But unlike Kant, Schopenhauer thinks he knows what it is that appears. *In itself,* this world we are so familiar with is nothing but *will*—endless striving, desiring, wanting. The principles that *individuate* things—that make you different from me, one stone different from another—are space, time, and causality (as Kant taught). But these principles apply only in the realm of phenomena. Reality in itself is not cut up into individual things by our intuitions and concepts.

As you should be able to see, Schopenhauer's realm of individuated, orderly phenomena fits pretty neatly with Apollo, the god of order, measure, and knowledge. And his image of the raging depths of urgent reality accords with Dionysus, whose intoxications break down all distinctions and overwhelm all rules. Apollo governs the world of *appearance.* Dionysus represents the *in itself.*

We are now ready to understand how Nietzsche thinks tragedy can at one stroke, solve the problem of existence and overcome pessimism. The key, he believes, is the role of the chorus in Greek tragedy.

If you are familiar with these plays, you know that in them a chorus often speaks (or chants) in unison. Three facts, Nietzsche believes, must be accounted for. (1) In early Greek drama there were no actors; there was only the chorus. (2) The chorus was composed of *satyrs,* those half-human, half-goat companions to Dionysus. (3) Tragedy has a religious dimension. In some way that we need to understand, tragedy *redeems.* Through tragedy we can be *saved.*

What does it mean that the chorus was originally made up of satyrs?

> Nature before knowledge has set to work on it, before the bolts of culture have been broken open—that is what the Greek saw in his satyr. . . . What he saw was the archetype of man, the expression of his highest and strongest impulses, as excited enthusiast, . . . as wise prophet from the depths of . . . nature, as symbol of the sexual omnipotence of nature, which the Greek habitually regards with reverence and astonishment. The satyr was something sublime and divine. (*BT,* 8, 47)

In the songs, the chants, the dances of the satyrs, Greek spectators recognized something deep and natural in themselves. Their spirits sang, too, in the Dionysian rhythms of the chorus, which seemed to well up directly from primordial reality—from the *will.**

But tragedy as we have it is not just music and dance. There is drama, a story, individual characters who act and suffer. So far we have not accounted for that. But the explanation is not far away: The drama, Nietzsche tells us, is the *dream of the chorus.* The Dionysian chorus dreams an Apollonian dream, and the spectators, identifying with the chorus, dream it too.

> Under the influence of its spell, the Dionysian enthusiast sees himself as satyr, *and as satyr he in turn beholds the god,* that is, transformed in this way he sees a new vision outside himself, as the Apollonian completion of his state. With this vision, the drama is complete. (*BT,* 8, 50)

---

*Such festivals are chronicled in Euripides' late play, *The Bacchae.*
†See the profile of Schopenhauer on p. 465.

*For a modern counterpart, you might think of the audience at a rock concert. In Oliver Stone's movie *The Doors,* one of the musicians says to Jim Morrison, "I played with Dionysus, man."

A play, after all, is rather like a dream, isn't it? It's all imagination, appearance, phenomenon. The tragedies present (apparent) individuals whose (apparent) actions have (apparent) effects. Oedipus searches out the riddle of the Sphinx, Jocasta hangs herself, Clytemnestra murders Agamemnon in the bath. Yet no one rushes on stage to prevent Agamemnon's death or to save Antigone from being buried alive. Experiencing a tragic drama, Nietzsche says, is like having a dream in which you say to yourself, "This is a dream! I want to dream on!" (*BT*, 1, 21)

And now at last we are ready to understand how Nietzsche thinks tragedy solves the problem of existence, how it overcomes the pessimistic wisdom of Silenus. Tragedy does not deny the pessimism. Oh no; look at what happens in the tragedies. Oedipus blinds himself with his wife's brooches and goes into exile. Clytemnestra dies at the hand of her son. Prometheus is chained to a mountain peak where every day, an eagle eats at his liver. What happens in the tragedies is the *destruction of individuals.*

But now we can see that tragedy acts as a window into reality. Just as the drama is the Apollonian dream of the Dionysian chorus, so—given Schopenhauer's metaphysics—*our individual lives are merely appearance* and not reality. We ourselves are a dream—a dream of the will. Reality is found in the Dionysian depths, where no individuation by space, time, or causality is possible. And just as the chorus affirms the dream, *including* the suffering and destruction, so the spectators affirm life. They affirm it passionately and joyously, including the suffering and destruction, for they know themselves to be other than, more than—infinitely more than—the petty individualities of the apparent world. They experience themselves in fusion with primal being as the eternal, nonindividualized, primordial root of the world. They experience themselves as willing the creation of the drama—and the creation of their lives.

Tragedy is terror and ecstasy in one. Everything that pessimism can say is true—and yet those truths concern only the dream world of appearance. There is also another truth,

and this is the most immediate effect of Dionysian tragedy, that state and society, indeed the whole chasm separating man from man, gives way to an overpowering feeling of unity which leads back to the heart of nature. The metaphysical consolation—with which . . . all true tragedy leaves us—that life at the bottom of things, in spite of the passing of phenomena, remains indestructibly powerful and pleasurable, this consolation appears in embodied clarity in the chorus of satyrs, of creatures of nature who live on as it were ineradicably behind all civilization and remain eternally the same in spite of the passing of generations and of the history of peoples. (*BT*, 7, 45)

The metaphysical joy in the tragic is a translation of the instinctively unconscious Dionysian wisdom into the language of images: the hero, the greatest phenomenon of the will, is negated for our pleasure, because he remains only phenomenon and the eternal life of the will remains untouched by his annihilation. "We believe in eternal life," such is the cry of tragedy . . . In Dionysian art and in its tragic symbolism, this same nature speaks to us in its true undistorted voice: "Be as I am! Beneath the incessantly changing phenomena, I am the eternally creative original mother, eternally compelling people to exist, eternally finding satisfaction in this changing world of phenomena!" (*BT*, 16, 90)

Nietzsche thinks there are two kinds of pessimism: a pessimism of weakness and a pessimism of strength. The former he finds exemplified in Schopenhauer, who wants nothing more than Buddhist relief from willing—rest, escape from life. But in their tragedies the Greeks show us another way, the way of *joyous affirmation in the face of the terror.* Like a primordial artist, the will ceaselessly creates the dreamscape of the phenomenal world. And we, identifying with this Dionysian power, can experience our lives, too, as art. Our lives may, of course, turn out as tragic as the lives of Oedipus and Agamemnon; there is no guarantee that they won't. This art work, in which we individuals are like actors on a stage, is not created for our happiness or our improvement. And yet we

have our greatest dignity in our meaning as works of art—for only as an *aesthetic phenomenon* are existence and the world *justified* to eternity. (*BT*, 5, 38)

In what do we find our dignity and value? What is it that makes life worth living? Not anything moral, Nietzsche says, not *another* life (the "life of the world to come"), nor our relation to God. Only its *aesthetic* value justifies our life and makes it worth living. There is something intrinsic to *Oedipus Rex* that leads us to value it, to continue to perform and experience it even after 2,500 years. If *our lives* had that same sort of aesthetic value, that would be enough to justify the living of them. If we come to experience ourselves as images and artistic projections for the true author of our lives—for the primordial unity, the will, that Dionysian power projecting the dream of the world drama—pessimism can be overcome. We can accept our lives even if our eyes are wide open to the wisdom of Silenus. We are works of art! Nothing else, Nietzsche tells us, could suffice. That is the way to solve the problem of "the value of existence." That is the only way it *could* be solved.* And that is what tragedy shows us.

---

1. What is the "wisdom" of Silenus?
2. Distinguish the human powers symbolized by the gods Apollo and Dionysus.
3. How does Nietzsche use the metaphysics of Schopenhauer in his analysis of tragedy?
4. What is the role of the chorus in a Greek tragedy, according to Nietzsche?
5. What "metaphysical consolation" does tragedy provide?

Good-bye Real World

In *The Birth of Tragedy,* Nietzsche solves the problem of existence with the help of a metaphysical theory. Spectators at a tragedy, he thinks, experience the "metaphysical consolation" of realizing that they are infinitely more than the limited and suffering individuals they normally appear to be. Behind the appearance they discover *reality* in the Dionysian exu-

berance of the one true will's self-affirmation. They identify with their "true" self and rejoice. This solution is *metaphysical* in its appeal to "another world," a "real world" beyond, behind, or beneath the familiar world of everyday experience. Philosophers have long assured us that things are not really as they seem; from Heraclitus and Parmenides, through Plato and Augustine, to Descartes, Kant, and Hegel, we hear that reality is not what we think—that *we* are not what we think! And Nietzsche's reliance on Schopenhauer's metaphysics of the will is just another example of the same pattern.

But in the period after writing *The Birth of Tragedy,* Nietzsche comes to believe that no such metaphysics is possible for us. So another solution has to be found for the problem of the value of existence. All of Nietzsche's later work is oriented around this problem. Before we can grasp that solution, however, we need to understand why he thinks we must abandon the traditional philosophers' dream: to tell us what there really is.

> Little by little I came to understand what every great philosophy to date has been: the personal confession of its author, a kind of unintended and unwitting memoir; and similarly, that the moral (or immoral) aims in every philosophy constituted the actual seed from which the whole plant invariably grew. Whenever explaining how a philosopher's most far-fetched metaphysical propositions have come about, in fact, one always does well (and wisely) to ask first: "What morality is it (is he) aiming at?" (*BGE*, 6, 8–9)

What we need is a psychology of the great philosophers, a psychology that uncovers the real drives and interests that motivate their work. Nietzsche prides himself on his psychological acuity and thinks he has discovered that it is not *reality* that philosophical theories display, but the *philosophers themselves:* what sorts of people they are, how weak or strong they are, how sick or how healthy. Philosophy is "confession." Philosophers, Nietzsche says, want us to believe that they want truth, that their sole interest is knowledge. But

> they are not honest enough, however loud and virtuous a racket they all make as soon as the problem

---

*Compare Kierkegaard's aesthetic mode of life, pp. 489–492.

Good-bye Real World   **539**

of truthfulness is touched upon, even from afar. For they act as if they had discovered and acquired what are actually their opinions through the independent unraveling of a cold, pure, divinely unhampered dialectic. . . . They are using reasons sought after the fact to defend a pre-existing tenet, a sudden idea, a "brainstorm," or in most cases a rarefied and abstract version of their heart's desire. They are all of them advocates who refuse the name, . . . in most cases wily spokesmen for their prejudices, which they dub "truths"; and they are *very* far from having a conscience brave enough to own up to it. (*BGE*, 5, 8)

Nietzsche means to apply this critique to all the central conceptions of traditional philosophy: to "soul," "free will," "the 'real' world," "God," "immortality," and "morality"—to say nothing of "cause," "substance," "unity," and "sameness of things." Nietzsche is suspicious of such notions; in them he senses dishonesty, the lack of an intellectual conscience, even lying.* What philosophers create is a world that satisfies "their heart's desire"; their "reasons" come later.

> But this is an old, eternal story . . . [Philosophy] always creates the world according to its own image, it cannot do otherwise; philosophy is this tyrannical drive itself, the most spiritual form of the will to power, to "creation of the world" to the *causa prima* [first cause]. (*BGE*, 9, 11)

Nietzsche's notion of "will to power," that "tyrannical drive" displayed in philosophizing, is a central idea for him; we explore it more fully later. Here we only need to note that this will to power expresses itself in philosophers through their attempts to create the world in their own image—and that means according to what they value, and that means according to what they *need*. The Stoics, for example, needed order, law, control; they needed to be safe from disorder, chaos, and help-lessness. So they created the world as they needed it: a world of providential orderliness, perfectly organized by the *logos,* the divine reason present in it. To cohere with such a world was virtue, happiness, and perfect freedom. But is nature really like that? Nietzsche doesn't think so. So the Stoics read into nature what they *need* it to be. And *all* the philosophers have done the same.

In addition to such personal needs, Nietzsche thinks there are *common* factors that influence metaphysical views. These factors may be grounded in the language we speak or simply in our human nature.

> Over immense periods of time the intellect produced nothing but errors. A few of these proved to be useful and helped to preserve the species. . . . Such erroneous articles of faith, which were continually inherited, until they became almost part of the basic endowment of the species, include the following: that there are enduring things; that there are equal things; that there are things, substances, bodies; that a thing is what it appears to be; that our will is free; that what is good for me is good in itself. It was only very late that truth emerged—as the weakest form of knowledge. (*GS*, 110)

Even today, these "articles of faith" seem to be just common sense. But Nietzsche tells us they are *errors.* Kant's famous *categories,* Nietzsche holds, are also errors.* The concept of substance, for instance,

> is indispensable for logic, although in the strictest sense nothing real corresponds to it. . . . The beings that did not see so precisely had an advantage over those that saw everything "in flux." At bottom, every high degree of caution in making inferences and every skeptical tendency constitute a great danger for life. No living beings would have survived if the opposite tendency—to affirm rather than suspend judgment, to err and *make up* things rather than wait . . .—had not been bred to the point where it became extraordinarily strong. (*GS*, 111)

The same is true of the a priori concept of causality.

---

*This suspicion toward traditional philosophizing, which Nietzsche in the nineteenth century shares with Kierkegaard, finds numerous echoes in the twentieth century. Compare the variously motivated rejections by Peirce (p. 577), Dewey (pp. 580–582), Wittgenstein (pp. 612, 624, 635–641), Heidegger (pp. 676–683), and Rorty (pp. 714–719).

*See pp. 434–439.

Cause and effect: such a duality probably never exists; in truth we are confronted by a continuum out of which we isolate a couple of pieces, just as we perceive motion only as isolated points and then infer it without ever actually seeing it. The suddenness with which many effects stand out misleads us; actually it is sudden only for us. In this moment of suddenness there is an infinite number of processes that elude us. An intellect that could see cause and effect as a continuum and a flux and not, as we do, in terms of an arbitrary division and dismemberment, would repudiate the concept of cause and effect and deny all conditionality. (*GS,* 112)

You can see that in a sense Nietzsche accepts the Kantian point. It *is* necessary for us to judge the world in terms of such very general concepts. But Nietzsche's view is radically different from Kant's on two scores: (1) These concepts do *not* apply correctly to the phenomenal world, and (2) there is no noumenal world of things-in-themselves that these concepts fall short of. Their necessity for us is a purely practical necessity; without such "errors" we couldn't survive in the world as it is.* So these errors are not arbitrary or capricious inventions; they serve *life*. But the fact that they are useful doesn't mean that they are true.

> *Life no argument.*—We have arranged for ourselves a world in which we can live—by positing bodies, lines, planes, causes and effects, motion and rest, form and content; without these articles of faith nobody now could endure life. But that does not prove them. Life is no argument. The conditions of life might include error. (*GS,* 121)

Human beings as they now are have been formed by their errors; we depend on them. Expanding on the general character of these errors, Nietzsche writes,

> *The four errors.*—Man has been educated by his errors. First, he always saw himself only incompletely; second, he endowed himself with fictitious attributes; third, he placed himself in a false order of rank in relation to animals and nature; fourth, he invented ever new tables of goods and always accepted them for a time as eternal and unconditional. (*GS,* 115)

Note that all four errors concern our knowledge of ourselves. Though they have taken "Know thyself" as their motto, philosophers go wrong most often just here. They see themselves "incompletely," they endow themselves with "fictitious attributes," they conclude that they are higher in "rank" than the other animals. They endow themselves with souls—immortal souls, no less. And they call this wisdom. But we, Nietzsche says,

> have learned differently. We have become more modest in every way. We no longer derive man from "the spirit" or "the deity"; we have placed him back among the animals. We consider him the strongest animal because he is the most cunning: his spirituality is a consequence of this. On the other hand, we oppose the vanity that would raise its head again here too—as if man had been the great hidden purpose of the evolution of the animals. Man is by no means the crown of creation: every living being stands beside him on the same level of perfection. And even this is saying too much: relatively speaking, man is the most bungled of all the animals, the sickliest, and not one has strayed more dangerously from its instincts. But for all that, of course, he is the most *interesting*. (*A,* 14)

It is clear that Nietzsche accepts a naturalistic, scientific picture of the world and of our place in it—with the qualification that science, too, must use those falsifying concepts: thing, equal, cause, line, plane, and so on. Science cannot avoid this degree of error because it must be expressed in language, and language necessarily simplifies and falsifies. The universe of which we are a part, is indifferent to good and evil, wasteful beyond measure, without mercy and justice, fertile and desolate, without purpose or reason, composed of mere processes in continuous flux. And we are just animals

---

*Nietzsche here anticipates a movement in late twentieth-century philosophy called "evolutionary epistemology." The key idea is that we are natural parts of the natural world and our capacities for knowing this world have been developed by natural-selection pressures over vast periods of time. Donald Campbell and Willard Quine are two recent exponents of this line of thought. See pp. 732–736.

of a sickly sort, mechanisms governed by instincts that we are scarcely conscious of. Consciousness itself is scarcely our "essence"; it is "the last and latest development of the organic and hence also what is most unfinished and unstrong" (*GS*, 11).* To focus on consciousness is bound to mislead.

This view of things, Nietzsche thinks, is the result of centuries of training in truthfulness; *honesty* has brought us to this point. Philosophers have thought otherwise, but

> how could we reproach or praise the universe? Let us beware of attributing to it heartlessness and unreason or their opposites: it is neither perfect nor beautiful, nor noble, nor does it wish to become any of these things; it does not by any means strive to imitate man. None of our aesthetic and moral judgments apply to it. . . . When will all these shadows of God cease to darken our minds? When will we complete our de-deification of nature? When may we begin to "*naturalize*" humanity in terms of a pure, newly discovered, newly redeemed nature? (*GS,* 109)

The last words in this quotation are extremely important to Nietzsche, but we are not yet ready to understand them. For the moment, let us focus on the situation Nietzsche thinks we have come to: the view of the universe that—unless we continue to deceive ourselves—we *must* come to. Nature is completely "de-deified," vacant of all purposiveness and value; "nature is always value-less, but has been *given* value at some time as a present—and it was *we* who gave and bestowed it" (*GS,* 301).† In such a world we live; of such a world are we a part.

In *Twilight of the Idols,* Nietzsche gives us a capsule history of philosophical conceptions of reality. He calls it "HOW THE 'REAL WORLD' FINALLY BECAME A FABLE: *History of an Error*":

1. The real world attainable for the wise man, the pious man, the virtuous man—he lives in it, *he is it.*

(Most ancient form of the idea, relatively clever, simple, convincing. Paraphrase of the proposition: "I, Plato, *am* the truth.")*

2. The real world unattainable for now, but promised to the wise man, the pious man, the virtuous man ("to the sinner who repents").

(Progress of the idea: it becomes more cunning, more insidious, more incomprehensible—*it becomes a woman,* it becomes Christian . . .)†

3. The real world unattainable, unprovable, unpromisable, but the mere thought of it a consolation, an obligation, an imperative.

(The old sun in the background, but seen through mist and skepticism; the idea become sublime, pale, Nordic, Königsbergian.)‡

4. The real world—unattainable? At any rate unattained. And since unattained also *unknown.* Hence no consolation, redemption, obligation either: what could something unknown oblige us to do? . . .

(Break of day. First yawn of reason. Cockcrow of positivism.)

5. The "real world"—an idea with no further use, no longer even an obligation—an idea become useless, superfluous, *therefore* a refuted idea: let us do away with it!

(Broad daylight; breakfast; return of *bon sens* and cheerfulness; Plato's shameful blush; din from all free spirits.)

6. The real world—we have done away with it: what world was left? the apparent one, perhaps? . . . But no! *with the real world we have also done away with the apparent one!*

(Noon; moment of the shortest shadow; end of the longest error; pinnacle of humanity; INCIPIT ZARATHUSTRA.) (*TI,* 20)

Little by little, the "real world" vanishes: Parmenides' One, Plato's Forms, Aristotle's God, Augustine's soul, the Christian heaven, Descartes'

---

*Nietzsche has many interesting things to say about consciousness; he sounds very contemporary. See, for instance, *GS,* sections 11, 179, 333, 354, and 360; and *BGE,* sections 3, 16, 32.
†Compare the early Wittgenstein, pp. 607–610. The difference is that for Wittgenstein we are *not* a part of the world.

---

*In *The Antichrist,* Nietzsche interprets Jesus according to the same formula. The kingdom of God, Jesus says, is "within you." And it is, of course, Jesus who says, "I am the way, the truth, and the life" (John 14:6).
†Christianity, Nietzsche thinks, has *betrayed* the spirit of Jesus.
‡Kant lived in Königsberg. Nietzsche obviously is thinking of the unknowable noumenal world and the categorical imperative.

free and immortal mind, Kant's world of things-in-themselves, Hegel's Absolute Spirit, Schopenhauer's will. All gone. Vapors. Evaporated by a heightened honesty about ourselves and our place in the scheme of things. But what is left? Only the "apparent" world? Proposition 6 tells us that when the contrast between real and apparent vanishes, so does all reason to disparage this world—the one and only world—by calling it "apparent" (or, as many philosophers have said, "*merely* apparent"). There is just the world, and we a part of it.

> The "true world" and the "apparent world"—that means: the mendaciously invented world and reality. (*EH*, 218)

Nietzsche's estimate of his own importance can be gathered from the phrase that characterizes stage 6, the stage of his own philosophy; he calls it the "pinnacle of humanity." He truly believes that he has seen through the shams and pretenses of all our previous philosophical history. Zarathustra, as we shall see soon, is the fictional "prophet" in whose mouth Nietzsche puts his own deepest philosophical thoughts. "INCIPIT ZARATHUSTRA" means "Zarathustra begins." And the time of Zarathustra is noon—when the shadows are shortest, when everything is in light and can be seen for what it is.*

So now we see why Nietzsche has to rethink the problem of the meaning of life. In *The Birth of Tragedy,* he had relied on one version of the "real world" to solve the problem of pessimism. But now the real world has disappeared. And the question about the value of existence is posed anew, in an even more stark and dramatic way. How *can* life have any meaning in a world such as we now believe in? But before we can get ourselves out of this hole, we

have to dig it still deeper. We must *look into the chasm* if we are to be saved.

The Death of God

The disappearance of the "real world"—our inability to take it seriously any longer—is not an obscure and remote event that is of interest only to a few philosophers. We all need a sense for the meaning of life, and for centuries most people have found it in religion*—in the West, primarily through Christianity. We have solved the problem of meaninglessness by setting our lives in the larger context of creation and salvation, God's plan, immortality, heaven and hell. So the whole culture—and certainly every Christian Jew, and Muslim—has been committed to a metaphysics involving a "real world." If "real worlds" vanish like smoke in a clear sky, what will happen?

In one of his best known parables, Nietzsche gives us his answer:

> *The madman.*—Have you not heard of that madman who lit a lantern in the bright morning hours, ran to the market place, and cried incessantly: "I seek God! I seek God!"—As many of those who did not believe in God were standing around just then, he provoked much laughter. Has he got lost? asked one. Did he lose his way like a child? asked another. Or is he hiding? Is he afraid of us? Has he gone on a voyage? emigrated?—Thus they yelled and laughed.
>
> The madman jumped into their midst and pierced them with his eyes. "Whither is God?" he cried; "I will tell you. *We have killed him*—you and I. All of us are his murderers. But how did we do this? How could we drink up the sea? Who gave us the sponge to wipe away the entire horizon? What were we doing when we unchained this earth from its sun? Whither is it moving now? Whither are we mov-

---

*"Among my writings my *Zarathustra* stands to my mind by itself. With that I have given mankind the greatest present that has ever been made to it so far. This book, with a voice bridging centuries, is not only the highest book there is, the book that is truly characterized by the air of the heights—the whole fact of man lies *beneath* it at a tremendous distance—it is also the *deepest,* born out of the innermost wealth of truth, an inexhaustible well to which no pail descends without coming up again filled with gold and goodness" (*EH*, 219).

---

*Remember that the Greek tragedies had precisely this function—to answer the question (in the face of pessimism) about the value of existence. Remember, too, that they were performed at *religious* festivals. Note also the religious language Nietzsche uses when he talks about this problem. Art "saves" us, he says; our lives are "redeemed" when we see them in an aesthetic perspective.

ing? Away from all suns? Are we not plunging continually? Backward, sideward, forward, in all directions? Is there still any up or down? Are we not straying as through an infinite nothing? Do we not feel the breath of empty space? Has it not become colder? Is not night continually closing in on us? Do we not need to light lanterns in the morning? Do we hear nothing as yet of the noise of the gravediggers who are burying God? Do we smell nothing as yet of the divine decomposition? Gods, too, decompose. God is dead. God remains dead. And we have killed him.

"How shall we comfort ourselves, the murderers of all murderers? What was holiest and mightiest of all that the world has yet owned has bled to death under our knives: who will wipe this blood off us? What water is there for us to clean ourselves? What festivals of atonement, what sacred games shall we have to invent? Is not the greatness of this deed too great for us? Must we ourselves not become gods simply to appear worthy of it? There has never been a greater deed; and whoever is born after us—for the sake of this deed he will belong to a higher history than all history hitherto."

Here the madman fell silent and looked again at his listeners; and they, too, were silent and stared at him in astonishment. At last he threw his lantern on the ground, and it broke into pieces and went out. "I have come too early," he said then; "my time is not yet. This tremendous event is still on its way, still wandering; it has not yet reached the ears of men. Lightning and thunder require time; the light of the stars requires time; deeds, though done, still require time to be seen and heard. This deed is still more distant from them than the most distant stars—*and yet they have done it themselves.*"

It has been related further that on the same day the madman forced his way into several churches and there struck up his *requiem aeternam deo.* Led out and called to account, he is said always to have replied nothing but: "What after all are these churches now if they are not the tombs and sepulchers of God?" (*GS, 125*)

Perhaps what Nietzsche means to say in these dramatic paragraphs is clear enough, but some questions and answers might be in order.

- Why is the message concerning the death of God put into the mouth of a madman? Be-

cause anyone who brings this message to a culture dominated by Christianity is bound to seem mad.

- Why does the madman announce the "death" of God rather than merely his nonexistence? Because a death is something that *happens.* It can be dated; it happens at one time and not another. Nonexistence is just not ever having been. God's death, Nietzsche thinks, is something that happened recently.

- What does it mean that God died? It means that people no longer believe—though they may not have noticed this fact. (God "lives" in the prayers of the people.) "The greatest recent event—that 'God is dead,' that the belief in the Christian god has become unbelievable—is already beginning to cast its first shadows over Europe" (*GS,* 343).

- Who are the clowns standing around that make fun of the madman? Those who don't take these things seriously; they think God can disappear and everything can go along as it always has.

- Who are the murderers of God? We all are.

- What are the consequences of God's death? We have lost our moorings. We don't know anymore where we are, where we are going—or where we should be going. We are without a goal. The one who for centuries supplied the rules for living, the goal to strive for, has died. We are adrift.

- Why does the madman say, "I have come too early"? Because though the deed is done, people are not ready to recognize what they have done. And they certainly are not aware of the consequences. "God is dead; but given the way of men, there may still be caves for thousands of years in which his shadow will be shown" (*GS,* 108).

Can we say anything more precise about how God died? Zarathustra says, "When gods die, they always die several kinds of death" (*Z 4,* 373). Nietzsche offers a number of explanations. For example, in the account we canvassed in the last section,

Nietzsche claims that the whole idea of a metaphysical "real world" simply became incredible to us. Christianity, which Nietzsche calls "Platonism for the 'common people'" (*BGE,* preface, 4), disappears with the rest of the "real worlds" killed by "the decline of the faith in the Christian god, the triumph of scientific atheism" (*GS,* 357).

But there are other explanations. In the fourth book of *Thus Spoke Zarathustra,* the prophet meets "the last pope," who says that though he is now "retired," he served the old god "until his last hour." Zarathustra asks him how God died: "Is it true what they say, that pity strangled him, that he saw how *man* hung on the cross and that he could not bear it, that love of man became his hell, and in the end his death?" (*Z* 4, 372). The old pope replies,

> "When he was young, this god out of the Orient, he was harsh and vengeful and he built himself a hell to amuse his favorites. Eventually, however, he became old and soft and mellow and pitying, more like a grandfather than a father, but most like a shaky old grandmother. Then he sat in his nook by the hearth, wilted, grieving over his weak legs, weary of the world, weary of willing, and one day he choked on his all-too-great pity." (*Z* 4, 373)

As Zarathustra understands pity, it is the opposite of a life-affirming emotion. In pity, one *deplores* the condition of someone's existence.* Because the Christian God is one who pities mankind, it is possible that his "all-too-great" pity might in the end undermine even his own will to live, and he might simply wither away. Pity, Zarathustra thinks, is a very bad thing.

Zarathustra tells the old pope that "it might have happened that way—that way, and also in some other way." And he offers another explanation:

> "I love all that looks bright and speaks honestly. But he—you know it, you old priest, there was something of your manner about him, of the priest's

_____

*The thing Nietzsche holds most adamantly against Christianity is that it is (as he sees it) a religion of pity. If pity is the appropriate reaction to human life as a whole—is even the reaction of *God!*—then one is virtually saying it would be better if life did not exist at all. And then one is back with Silenus. Nietzsche condemns Christianity for giving in to pessimism instead of overcoming it.

manner: he was equivocal. He was also indistinct. How angry he got with us, this wrath-snorter, because we understood him badly! But why did he not speak more cleanly? And if it was the fault of our ears, why did he give us ears that heard him badly? If there was mud in our ears—well, who put it there? He bungled too much, this potter who had never finished his apprenticeship. But that he wreaked revenge on his pots and creations for having bungled them himself, that was a sin against *good taste.* There is good taste in piety, too; and it was this that said in the end, 'Away with *such* a god! Rather no god, rather make destiny on one's own, rather be a fool, rather be a god oneself!'" (*Z* 4, 373–374)

Zarathustra's claim here is that integrity, intellectual conscience, cleanliness of spirit, honesty—and finally just good taste—eventually reject the comforts of such a god. And where did we learn such honesty? From Christianity itself. Nietzsche calls this atheism

> a triumph achieved finally and with great difficulty by the European conscience, being the most fateful act of two thousand years of discipline for truth that in the end forbids itself the *lie* in faith in God.
>
> You see what it was that really triumphed over the Christian god: Christian morality itself, the concept of truthfulness that was understood ever more rigorously, the father confessor's refinement of the Christian conscience, translated and sublimated into a scientific conscience, into intellectual cleanliness at any price. (*GS,* 357)

Paradoxically, God, the source of Christian morality, is finally done in by that morality itself!

There are also less praiseworthy explanations for the death of God. Nietzsche puts one of them into the mouth of "the ugliest man," whom Zarathustra meets and recognizes as *"the murderer of God"* who "took revenge on this witness" (*Z* 4, 376). The ugliest man confesses,

> "But he *had* to die: he saw with eyes that saw everything; he saw man's depths and ultimate grounds, all his concealed disgrace and ugliness. His pity knew no shame: he crawled into my dirtiest nooks. This most curious, overobtrusive, overpitying one had to die. He always saw me: on such a witness I wanted to have revenge or not live myself. The god who saw everything, *even man*—this

god had to die! Man cannot bear it that such a witness should live." (*Z* 4, 378–379)

Nietzsche does not admire such motives for killing off the Christian god; it is, after all, the "ugliest man" who says these words. Nietzsche wants a life that, unlike the ugliest man's life, can bear examination—especially one's own examination. Moreover, he considers revenge a particularly bad motive (although one that is hard to get beyond). Motives such as these, Nietzsche tells us, have also played a role in the death of God.

Reactions to this great event will, of course, differ. Some people will deny that it has happened; others will despair. But, Nietzsche says, the consequences for himself and others like him

> are quite the opposite of what one might perhaps expect: They are not at all sad and gloomy but rather like a new and scarcely describable kind of light, happiness, relief, exhilaration, encouragement, dawn.
>
> Indeed, we philosophers and "free spirits" feel, when we hear the news that "the old god is dead," as if a new dawn shone on us; our heart overflows with gratitude, amazement, premonitions, expectation. At long last the horizon appears free to us again, even if it should not be bright; at long last our ships may venture out again, venture out to face any danger; all the daring of the lover of knowledge is permitted again; the sea, *our* sea, lies open again; perhaps there has never yet been such an "open sea." (*GS,* 343)

Despite such cheerful thoughts, Nietzsche sees that the death of God poses a serious problem. If our culture has for two thousand years been nourished by these religious roots, what happens when the roots no longer sustain its life? When the source of our values dries up, what happens to them? When the lawgiver disappears, what happens to our law? As the madman says, "Is there still any up or down? Are we not straying as through an infinite nothing?" The threat is **nihilism.** Zarathustra meets a soothsayer who expresses the danger of nihilism this way:

> "—And I saw a great sadness descend upon mankind. The best grew weary of their works. A doctrine appeared, accompanied by a faith: 'All is empty, all is the same, all has been!' And from all

the hills it echoed: 'All is empty, all is the same, all has been!' Indeed we have harvested: but why did all our fruit turn rotten and brown? What fell down from the evil moon last night? In vain was all our work; our wine has turned to poison; an evil eye has seared our fields and hearts. We have all become dry; and if fire should descend on us, we should turn to ashes; indeed, we have wearied the fire itself. All our wells have dried up; even the sea has withdrawn. All the soil would crack, but the depth refuses to devour. 'Alas, where is there still a sea in which one might drown?' thus are we wailing across shallow swamps. Verily, we have become too weary even to die. We are still waking and living on—in tombs." (*Z* 2, 245)

When Zarathustra hears the soothsayer, he himself becomes "sad and weary"; he becomes "like those of whom the soothsayer had spoken" (*Z* 2, 246). Weariness of life—finding everything empty, dry, shallow, meaningless, the same,—that is the mood of nihilism.* Into such a state we might be cast by the death of God. It is against nihilism that Zarathustra and Nietzsche struggle. A new meaning must be forged for life. But the fight for meaning, as we shall see, will take a surprising turn: Christianity itself—the factor that until now had saved us from nihilism—is accused of the greatest nihilism of all.

---

1. Philosophers claim to tell us about reality, but what do they really reveal, if Nietzsche is right?
2. In what ways can errors be useful? What are some of the errors Nietzsche identifies?
3. What is Nietzsche's "nonmetaphysical" view of the world and human nature?
4. Sketch the stages by which Nietzsche thinks the "real world" became a fable.
5. What does Nietzsche mean when he says "God is dead"?
6. In what ways might God have died?

---

*Theodore Dalrymple refers to a "bitter Argentinian tango" that includes the words "everything is the same, nothing is better"—a doctrine, he says, "as barbaric and untruthful . . . as has yet emerged from the fertile mind of man" (*Life at the Bottom* [Chicago: Ivan R. Dee, 2001], 194).

Revaluation of Values

As we have seen, Nietzsche believes that nature is "value-less." Whatever values we might think are present have been "bestowed" on nature by us.* He claims that

> *there are no moral facts at all.* Moral judgement has this in common with religious judgement, that it believes in realities which do not exist. Morality is merely an interpretation of certain phenomena, more precisely a *mis*interpretation. . . . In this respect moral judgement should never be taken literally. (*TI,* 33)

Our current values and moral judgments are *interpretations* that were formed in a context that takes God and a "real world" for granted. But if God is dead for us and we no longer believe in any world but the one revealed by our senses and interpreted by the sciences, we surely need to look again at the received values. Nietzsche asks himself, "*In what do you believe?*" and answers, "In this, that the weights of all things must be determined anew" (*GS,* 269).

But how do we do this? Nietzsche thinks that philosophers have not been much help; they have typically busied themselves with the task of providing rational foundations for morality.† But in doing so they have simply taken a certain morality for granted. This prevented them from even laying eyes on

> the real problems of morality—all of which come to light only by comparing *many* moralities. As strange as it may sound, in every previous "science of morality" the problem of morality itself was *missing;* there was no suspicion that it might be something problematic. (*BGE,* 186, 74–75)

---

*Contrast this view with that of Plato, Aristotle, and (especially) Augustine. Compare the diagram on p. 240.

†Think of Plato (pp. 145–150) and Aristotle (pp. 185–193), who try to show that living virtuously is the way to live happily; of the Stoics (pp. 204–209), who try to demonstrate that the good life is integration into the order of the universe; of Aquinas (pp. 287–292), who argues for a natural moral law; of Kant (pp. 450–456), who claims that morality is a requirement of pure reason alone; of Hegel (pp. 478–483), for whom morality is realized in a perfectly rational state; and of the arguments for utilitarianism (pp. 519–520).

If we are going to determine the "weights" of things anew, we obviously cannot just take the present "weights" for granted.

> If one would like to see our European morality for once as it looks from a distance, and if one would like to measure it against other moralities, past and future, then one has to proceed like a wanderer who wants to know how high the towers in a town are: he *leaves* the town. "Thoughts about moral prejudices," if they are not meant to be prejudices about prejudices, presuppose a position *outside* morality, some point beyond good and evil to which one has to rise, climb, or fly—and in the present case at least a point beyond *our* good and evil, a freedom from everything "European," by which I mean the sum of the imperious value judgments that have become part of our flesh and blood. (*GS,* 380)

So Nietzsche calls for "a *taxonomy* of morals" (*BGE,* 186, 74) and makes a contribution to this project in his book *On the Genealogy of Morals.* A genealogy, of course, traces the ancestry of a person; a genealogy for a certain type of morality will shed light on its ancestry by revealing the historical and psychological conditions out of which it grew. Nietzsche thinks that our present morality is actually the result of a "revaluation of values" that took place a long time ago. And he believes he can tell us the story of how that happened.

Master Morality/Slave Morality

It is a mistake, Nietzsche says, to identify the good with the useful or beneficial, as the utilitarians do. It is equally a mistake to identify it with good will or right intention, as Kantians do. Besides, neither utilitarians nor Kantians ask the radical questions about morality that Nietzsche wants to press: Why have morality at all? What good is it? Would we be better off without it?

Pursuing his genealogical project, Nietzsche asks: What did the word "good" originally mean?

> The judgement "good" does *not* derive from those to whom "goodness" is shown! Rather, the "good" themselves—that is, the noble, the powerful, the superior, and the high-minded—were the ones who felt themselves and their actions to be good—

that is, as of the first rank—and posited them as such, in contrast to everything low, low-minded, common, and plebeian. (*GM*, 1, 2, 12)

Here is a morality—the morality of the aristocrats, the well-born, the powerful, the masters. These people of the "first rank" call themselves "noble," "commanders," "the rich," the "happy," the "truthful"—what *need* do they have to lie? They affirm their lives; they say yes to their being. They *feel* themselves to be good. To them, "good" means "what *we* are."

> The knightly-aristocratic value-judgements presuppose a powerful physicality, a rich, burgeoning, even overflowing health, as well as all those things which help to preserve it—war, adventure, hunting, dancing, competitive games, and everything which involves strong, free, high-spirited activity. (*GM*, 1, 7, 19)

> The noble type of person feels *himself* as determining value—he does not need approval, he judges that "what is harmful to me is harmful per se," he knows that he is the one who causes things to be revered in the first place, he *creates values*. (*BGE*, 260, 154)

This is the morality of conquerors. They may "help the unfortunate, but not, or not entirely, out of pity" (*BGE*, 260, 154). Among themselves, they are held in check "by custom, respect, usage, gratitude, even more by circumspection and jealousy," and in their relations with one another they express "consideration, self-control, tenderness, fidelity, pride, and friendship" (*GM*, 1, 11, 25). But once they go beyond their community where foreigners are found, they behave

> in a manner not much better than predators on the rampage. There they enjoy freedom from all social constraint, in the wilderness they make up for the tension built up over a long period of confinement and enclosure within a peaceful community, they *regress* to the innocence of the predator's conscience, as rejoicing monsters, capable of high spirits as they walk away without qualms from a horrific succession of murder, arson, violence, and torture, as if it were nothing more than a student prank, something new for the poets to sing and celebrate for some time to come. (*GM*, 1, 11, 25–26)

Nietzsche obviously has the heroes of Homer's great poems in mind.* These magnificent and terrible human beings claim the right to define goodness. *They* are good, they say. There is, of course, a contrast. Those who are not good are *below* them—the common, plebeian, pitiable, unhappy, lying ones. The nobles call these weak, shifty, untrustworthy people "bad." They are despicable, contemptible, almost beneath notice. They are slaves or fit to be slaves. Toward them the nobles have no duties. The "bad" have no dignity, no worth—no *goodness*.

So we have a first type of morality, that of the masters. It is characterized by a certain sort of value discrimination. Its categories are

good/bad,

and moral judgments are made in those terms. Notice that all the weight lies in the first term. "Bad" is just a contrast term; it designates only a shadow of the good. The masters affirm themselves and find themselves good; others hardly matter. The noble mode of valuation

> acts and grows spontaneously, it only seeks out its antithesis in order to affirm itself more thankfully and more joyfully. Its negative concept, "low," "common," "bad," is only a derived, pale contrast to its positive basic concept which is thoroughly steeped in life and passion—"we the noble, we the good, we the beautiful, we the happy ones!" (*GM*, 1, 10, 22)

It is clear that this sort of moral evaluation is made *from the point of view* of the masters.

Nietzsche also identifies a second type of morality: that of the slaves. Here there is a value contrast, too—not "good/bad," but

good/evil,

and its psychological dynamics are very different. Here "evil" is the primary concept and is driven not by affirmation, but by negation—not by a yes to life, but by a no. So "evil" and "bad" are very different from each other. Correspondingly, the "goods" in the two moralities are also different. But this requires explanation.

---

*See Chapter 1.

Slaves are by definition the powerless. They find themselves at the mercy of those noble "predators on the rampage" who call themselves "the good." They suffer from them—and they *resent* it.

> —The slave revolt in morals begins when *ressentiment** itself becomes creative and ordains values: the *ressentiment* of creatures to whom the real reaction, that of the deed, is denied and who find compensation in an imaginary revenge. While all noble morality grows from a triumphant affirmation of itself, slave morality from the outset says no to an "outside," to an "other," to a "non-self": and *this* no is its creative act. The reversal of the evaluating gaze—this *necessary* orientation outwards rather than inwards to the self—belongs characteristically to *ressentiment*. In order to exist at all, slave morality from the outset always needs an opposing, outer world;—its action is fundamentally reaction. (*GM,* 1, 10, 22)

So the slave basically says, "No!" And to whom does the slave say no? Why, to the masters, of course—to those who say of themselves that they are the *good*. There is no way a slave will agree with the master's self-evaluation; such rapacious monsters are experienced as *evil*.

This negation of what is other than themselves, Nietzsche says, is the "creative deed" in slave morality. The fundamental concept is that of the enemy, the *evil* man. As a kind of afterthought, the slave derives its opposite—the *good* one, himself. Just as "bad" is the shadow of "good" for the masters, so is "good" a shadow of the primary word "evil" for the slaves.

Let us ask: What is such a good person like? Can there be any doubt? The good would have to be such as they themselves are: poor, weak, humble, serving. Being powerless, slaves cannot overtly express their outrage over the actions of the strong. So their resentment simmers in them. It becomes a longing for revenge and colors their lives with rancor. What sort of revenge, Nietzsche asks, would be most appropriate for those who cannot simply overpower their enemies? What sort would be *pos-*

*Nietzsche consistently uses the French term because there is no German word with just that nuance. I will use the corresponding English term, "resentment."

sible? The most subtle, shrewd, and insidious revenge of all would be this: to persuade the strong they should adopt the values of the weak, to give them a bad conscience about their "goodness," to get *them* to say of their natural impulses, "These are evil; they must be suppressed. We are sinful. We must become 'good' (as the slaves define good)." What a triumph that would be! How delicious the revenge! How satisfying! And, Nietzsche tells us, *that is just what happened.*

Nietzsche identifies the Jews as the source of this slave revaluation of values. Having actually been slaves in Egypt and thereafter continually dominated by the powerful nations around them (Egypt, Assyria, Babylon, Greece, Rome), the Jews are the world-historical origin of the most powerful revision in moral values the Western world has seen.

> It has been the Jews who have, with terrifying consistency, dared to undertake the reversal of the aristocratic value equation (good = noble = powerful = beautiful = happy = blessed) and have held on to it tenaciously by the teeth of the most unfathomable hatred (the hatred of the powerless). It is they who have declared: "The miserable alone are the good; the poor, the powerless, the low alone are the good. The suffering, the deprived, the sick, the ugly are the only pious ones, the only blessed, for them alone is there salvation. You, on the other hand, the noble and the powerful, you are for all eternity the evil, the cruel, the lascivious, the insatiable, the godless ones. You will be without salvation, accursed and damned to all eternity!" (*GM,* 1, 7, 19–20)

This act of "*most intelligent revenge*" originated a tremendous revaluation of values, a "revolt which has a two-thousand-year history behind it and which has today dropped out of sight only because it—has succeeded" (*GM,* 1, 7, 19). And Nietzsche adds:

"There is no doubt as to *who* inherited this Jewish transvaluation" (*GM,* 1, 7, 20). He means, of course, the Christians.

> From the trunk of that tree of revenge and hatred, Jewish hatred—the deepest and most sublime hatred, that is, the kind of hatred which creates ideals and changes the meaning of values, a hatred the like of which has never been on earth—from this tree grew forth something equally incomparable,

a *new love,* the deepest and most sublime of all the kinds of love. . . . But let no one think that it somehow grew up as the genuine negation of that thirst for revenge, as the antithesis of Jewish hatred! No, the opposite is the case! Love grew forth from this hatred, as its crown, as its triumphant crown, spreading itself ever wider in the purest brightness and fullness of the sun, as a crown which pursued in the lofty realm of light the goals of hatred—victory, spoils, seduction. . . . This Jesus of Nazareth, as the gospel of love incarnate, this "redeemer" bringing victory and salvation to the poor, the sick, the sinners—did he not represent the most sinister and irresistible form of the very same temptation, the indirect temptation to accept those self-same *Jewish* values and new versions of the ideal?* (*GM*, 1, 8, 20)

Jesus' love, of course, takes him to the cross—for the salvation of mankind. But, Nietzsche asks, in the service of what values? Certainly not on behalf of master morality! In this way, through the influence of Christianity, "Israel's revenge and transvaluation of all values has so far continued to triumph over all other ideals, over all *nobler* ideals" (*GM*, 1, 8, 21). Our values, Nietzsche believes, are Judeo–Christian values.

And now we are ready for the big question, the question Nietzsche thinks he is the first to ask: *What value do these values have?*

Our Morality

Think again about Kant and the utilitarians, the sponsors of the two most powerful moral theories of modern times. Although they have many differences, they have something in common: Both assert the equal dignity and value of each individual human being. For Kant, this equality is grounded in the fact that every one of us is equally rational and that the *same moral law* is legislated categorically for each of us. Utilitarianism specifies that when we calculate the greatest happiness, *each one is to count for one.* In either case, no basic inequality of value is

allowed to exist between humans; there is no "order of rank" that would allow moral privileges to certain persons and not others. This emphasis on basic equality in our values, Nietzsche believes, can be traced back to the slave revolt in morality; after all, it is the slaves, not the masters, who have an interest in leveling things out. This insistence on equality is a (more or less secular) consequence of the Christian theme that we are equally children of God, equally precious in his sight.

But is this egalitarianism something we should prize, or is it a symptom of decadence, weakness, illness, resentment—of a basic dissatisfaction with life? Our morality, Nietzsche thinks, is the morality of the *herd.*

> It is obvious that Europeans nowadays *know* that which Socrates thought he did not know, and what that famous old serpent once promised to teach—people "know" what is good and evil. It must sound harsh and trouble the ears, then, if we insist over and over that it is the instinct of man the herd animal that thinks it knows, that glorifies itself and calls itself good whenever it allots praise or blame. This instinct has had a breakthrough, has come to predominance. . . . *Morality in Europe today is herd animal morality*—and thus, as we understand things, it is only one kind of human morality next to which, before which, after which many others, and especially *higher* moralities, are or should be possible. But this morality defends itself with all its strength against such "possibilities," against such "should be's." Stubbornly and relentlessly it says, "I am Morality itself, and nothing else is!" (*BGE,* 202, 89)

In this context, Nietzsche calls himself an "immoralist" (*BGE,* 32, 33; 226, 117; *EH,* 327, 328, 331) and a **free spirit** (*HA,* 6–8; *GS,* 343, 347; *TI,* 74; *EH,* 280, 283). Nietzsche assails "modern ideas" and "modern men," with their claims to equality and equal rights and their advocacy of democracy and socialism. Zarathustra says,

> I do not wish to be mixed up and confused with these preachers of equality. For, to *me* justice speaks thus: "Men are not equal." Nor shall they become equal! (*Z* 2, 213)

Why should men not *become* equal? Because the only way that could happen is by leveling down to

---

*For Nietzsche's interpretation of Jesus as someone *incapable* of resisting evil, see *The Antichrist,* sections 27–35. The sections following 35 give Nietzsche's view of how Christianity betrayed the spirit of Jesus.

the average or below the average: to the level of the herd. And to do that is to give in to the morality of resentment, of revenge—the morality of slaves.

Zarathustra's story begins with the prophet high on a mountain, outside his cave, where he has lived alone for ten years. He believes he has some wisdom to share and descends from the heights to impart it to men. He speaks to a crowd in a village marketplace about a superior kind of human being he calls "the overman" (see the next section), but they don't want to hear it. Then he tries to motivate their interest with a description of "what is most contemptible." Zarathustra calls this "the *last man*":

> "Alas, the time is coming when man will no longer give birth to a star. Alas, the time of the most despicable man is coming, he that is no longer able to despise himself. Behold, I show you the *last man*.
>
> "'What is love? What is creation? What is longing? What is a star?' thus asks the last man, and he blinks.
>
> "The earth has become small, and on it hops the last man, who makes everything small. His race is as ineradicable as the flea-beetle; the last man lives longest.
>
> "'We have invented happiness,' say the last men, and they blink. They have left the regions where it was hard to live, for one needs warmth. One still loves one's neighbor and rubs against him, for one needs warmth.
>
> "Becoming sick and harboring suspicion are sinful to them: one proceeds carefully. A fool, whoever still stumbles over stones or human beings! A little poison now and then: that makes for agreeable dreams. And much poison in the end, for an agreeable death.
>
> "One still works, for work is a form of entertainment. But one is careful lest the entertainment be too harrowing. One no longer becomes poor or rich: both require too much exertion. Who still wants to rule? Who obey? Both require too much exertion.
>
> "No shepherd and one herd! Everybody wants the same, everybody is the same: whoever feels differently goes voluntarily into a madhouse.
>
> "'Formerly, all the world was mad,' say the most refined, and they blink.
>
> "One is clever and knows everything that has ever happened: so there is no end of derision. One still

quarrels, but one is soon reconciled—else it might spoil the digestion.
>
> "One has one's little pleasure for the day and one's little pleasure for the night: but one has a regard for health.
>
> "'We have invented happiness,' say the last men, and they blink." (*Z* 1, 129–130)

Zarathustra is obviously full of contempt for such a safe, cautious, careful, timid, excessively prudent form of life. He sneers at the idea that *here* one finds happiness. But what happens? The crowd interrupts him with "clamor and delight":

> "Give us this last man, O Zarathustra," they shouted. "Turn us into these last men! Then we shall make you a gift of the overman!" (*Z* 1, 130)

Our morality, Nietzsche believes, has turned us into such "last men." Or, if we are not yet quite "last men," that is what we long to be: comfortable, easily satisfied, without pain and suffering—"happy." Everyone has an equal right to this, we think. Nietzsche's Zarathustra means to teach us (or those of us with ears to hear) to *despise* such a life.

Zarathustra compares the preachers of equality to tarantulas. He says of them:

> Revenge sits in your soul: wherever you bite, black scabs grow; your poison makes the soul whirl with revenge.
>
> Thus I speak to you in a parable—you who make souls whirl, you preachers of *equality*. To me you are tarantulas, and secretly vengeful. But I shall bring your secrets to light; therefore I laugh in your faces with my laughter of the heights. Therefore I tear at your webs, that your rage may lure you out of your lie-holes and your revenge may leap out from behind your word justice. For *that man be delivered from revenge*, that is for me the bridge to the highest hope, and a rainbow after long storms. (*Z* 2, 211)

Nietzsche hopes to bring to light the dark and dirty secrets hidden in our highest values—to show us that behind such words as "equality" and "justice for all" stand hatred, revenge, resentment, weakness, and spite. And why does he want to expose those secrets? So that we might at last "be delivered from revenge," from negation and saying, "No!"

Our "highest values" have been inherited from that first revaluation of values, but now we can see that they are based on lies.

> If, out of the vindictive cunning of impotence, the oppressed, downtrodden, and violated tell themselves: "Let us be different from the evil, that is, good! And the good man is the one who refrains from violation, who harms no one, who attacks no one, who fails to retaliate, who leaves revenge to God, who lives as we do in seclusion, who avoids all evil and above all asks little of life, as we do, the patient, the humble, the just." When listened to coldly and without prejudice, this actually means nothing more than: "We weak men are, after all, weak; it would be good if we refrained from doing anything *for which we lack sufficient strength*". . . as if the weakness of the weak man itself . . . were a free achievement, something willed, chosen, a *deed*, a merit. (*GM*, 1, 13, 30)

The "virtues" of slave morality are really just what the weak *cannot help* but do. The weak, however, interpret these virtues as something they choose—something for which they deserve credit. But, Nietzsche says, this is self-deception. He invites us to peer into the workshop where ideals are made. Here is the voice of someone who looks carefully:

> "It seems to me that lies are being told; a sugary sweetness clings to every sound. Weakness is to be transformed into a *merit* through lies, there is no doubt—it is just as you said."—
> —Go on!
> —"And the impotent failure to retaliate is to be transformed into 'goodness'; craven fear into 'humility'; submission to those one hates into 'obedience.'. . . The inoffensive appearance of the weak man, even the cowardice which he possesses in abundance, his hesitation on the threshold, the inevitability of his being made to wait—all assume a good name here, as 'patience,' that is, as virtue *as such;* the inability to take revenge is called the refusal to take revenge, perhaps even forgiveness. . . . There is also talk of 'loving one's enemies'—accompanied by much perspiration."
> —Go on! . . . .
> —"Now they give me to understand that they are not only better than the powerful, . . . but also

'have it better,' or will 'have it better' one day. But enough! enough! I can stand it no longer. Bad air! Bad air! This workshop where ideals are fabricated—it seems to me to stink of nothing but lies." (*GM*, 1, 14, 32–33)

This morality, Nietzsche claims, is *our* morality. Jerusalem has overcome Rome; "consider before whom one bows down today in Rome itself" (*GM*, 1:16).

There is one additional, absolutely crucial, lie that Nietzsche believes the weak and impotent tell. They tell it to themselves—and to their enemies. It is the lie about *free will*. In truth, Nietzsche holds, there is no such thing as a free will. Human beings are body entirely; they are animals. As we have seen, he even calls us mechanisms. But unless there were a free will, how could the weak take credit for their "virtues"? And, even more important, how could they blame the strong for their "crimes"? Nietzsche holds that the concept of "free will" is

> the most disreputable piece of trickery the theologians have produced, aimed at making humanity "responsible" in their sense, i.e. at *making it dependent on them*. . . . Wherever responsibilities are sought it is usually the instinct for *wanting to punish and judge* that is doing the searching. Becoming is stripped of its innocence once any state of affairs is traced back to a will, to intentions, to responsible acts: the doctrine of the will was fabricated essentially for the purpose of punishment, i.e. of *wanting to find guilty*. . . . People were thought of as "free" so that they could be judged and punished—so that they could become *guilty:* consequently every action *had* to be thought of as willed, the origin of every action as located in consciousness. (*TI*, 31)

But consciousness, as we have seen, is altogether too superficial to contain the causes for actions, which actually lie in the physiological conditions of the body. So actions could not be due to "free will" for the very good reason that they are not due to will at all. The idea of "free will" is an invention, an interpretation of the facts by those who wanted very much to be able to hold people accountable, to persuade people they were guilty, sinful, and evil in the sight of God—because *they could have done otherwise!*

The truth is quite to the contrary, Nietzsche believes:

No one is responsible for simply being there, for being made in such and such a way, for existing under such conditions, in such surroundings. . . . *No one* is the result of his own intention, his own will, his own purpose. . . . One is necessary, one is a piece of fate, one belongs to the whole, one *is* in the whole—there is nothing which could judge, measure, compare, condemn our Being. . . . We deny God, we deny responsibility in God: *this* alone is how we redeem the world.— (*TI, 32*)

One of Nietzsche's aims is to restore a sense of the "innocence" of life, freed from the slanders of sin and guilt. "Atheism and a kind of *second innocence* belong together" (*GM, 2*:20, 71). Christians believe the world is redeemed by the sacrifice of Christ on the cross for human sin. Nietzsche thinks to redeem the world by denying sin, Christ, and God altogether. As he sees it, the concepts of free will, sin, guilt, and responsibility are part and parcel of the revolution in values he calls "slave morality." And Nietzsche calls for a new "revaluation of values" in which none of these concepts that taint existence has a place.

We would get Nietzsche wrong, however, if we thought that he simply wants to get back again to the master morality of Homer's epic heroes. Despite their love of life, their self-affirmation and yes-saying, there is something simple-minded, naive, and slightly stupid about these "nobles." The long history of resentment and self-deception has also been a history of self-examination, self-discipline, training, obedience, and hardness toward oneself and others. Through it we have become subtler, deeper, more—human. Through this long process, Nietzsche says, everything became more dangerous,

not only cures and therapies, but also arrogance, revenge, perspicacity, extravagance, love, the desire to dominate, virtue, illness. With some fairness, admittedly, it might also be added that it is only on the basis of this *essentially dangerous* form of human existence, the priestly form, that man has at all developed into an *interesting animal,* that it is only here that the human soul has in a higher sense taken on *depth* and become *evil*—and these have certainly been the two fundamental forms of man's

superiority over other animals up to now! (*GM,* 1, 6, 18)

There is no going back. We need to go forward— "beyond good and evil." And with that thought we are ready to consider Nietzsche's concept of the overman.

---

1. In what ways might God have died?
2. What does Nietzsche understand by a "genealogy" of morals?
3. What is master morality like? Who devised it? What do the central terms "good" and "bad" mean?
4. What is slave morality like? Who devised it? What do the central terms "good" and "evil" mean?
5. What is *our* morality like?
6. In what ways does Nietzsche criticize our morality?
7. Who is the "last man"?
8. How did the idea of free will arise?

The Overman

"Dead are all gods," Zarathustra says; *"now we want the overman to live"* (*Z 1,* 191). When Zarathustra arrives at the village, fresh from his ten-year retreat on the mountain, his first words to the crowd in the marketplace concern the overman.*

"*I teach you the overman.* Man is something that shall be overcome. What have you done to overcome him?

"All beings so far have created something beyond themselves; and do you want to be the ebb of this great flood and even go back to the beasts rather than overcome man? What is the ape to man? A laughing-stock or a painful embarrassment. And man shall be just that for the overman: a laughing

---

*This is the point at which it must be acknowledged that "overmen" do not seem to include women. Only males, for instance, are among the "higher men" in Zarathustra's cave at the end of his quest for wisdom. Nietzsche writes quite a lot about women, of which this is a representative sample: "Women want to be autonomous: and to that end they have begun to enlighten men about 'women per se'—*that* is one of the worst signs of progress in Europe's overall *uglification*" (*BGE,* 232, 124).

stock or a painful embarrassment. You have made your way from worm to man, and much in you is still worm. Once you were apes, and even now, too, man is more ape than any ape. . . .

"Behold, I teach you the overman. The overman is the meaning of the earth. Let your will say: the overman *shall be* the meaning of the earth! I beseech you, my brothers, *remain faithful to the earth,* and do not believe those who speak to you of otherworldly hopes!" (*Z* 1, 124–125)

Let us remind ourselves of the drama so far. In his early book, *The Birth of Tragedy,* Nietzsche tries to solve the problem of the meaning of life (the value of existence) by using Schopenhauer's metaphysical theory—that reality in itself is *will.* The idea is that through tragedy, we identify ourselves with the surging, nonindividualized, eternal reality of the will and are saved from pessimism about life. Later Nietzsche comes to believe that philosophy cannot guarantee any metaphysical theory and Schopenhauer's real world disappears. But though God is dead, otherworldly values continue to hold sway; the morality of "good and evil" is still our morality. By saying no to life as it expresses itself in the strong, this morality levels down to the mediocre herd and so sets itself *against life itself.* The result: Pessimism and nihilism remain undefeated, and the problem of the meaning of life is still unsolved.

Zarathustra proposes to solve it, and the overman is the key. The overman, he says, "is the meaning of the earth." Human beings as they now are —*you and I*—cannot be what all these eons of evolution have been for. That would be too petty, too small, too absurd. It could not be that all the while *life* has been driving at *us!* No, "man is something that shall be overcome."

"Man is a rope, tied between beast and overman—a rope over an abyss. A dangerous across, a dangerous on-the-way, a dangerous looking-back, a dangerous shuddering and stopping.

"What is great in man is that he is a bridge and not an end: what can be loved in man is that he is an *overture* and a *going under.*" (*Z* 1, 126–127)

Nietzsche clearly has in mind some mode of life that is not "human, all-too-human" (as our lives typically are) but human, *more than human.* Zarathustra is the prophet of the overman. In the life of the overman, the earth itself will find its meaning, and the problem of "the value of existence" will find its solution.

We need to try to understand what sort of life Nietzsche imagines this to be. What is an overman like? Nietzsche returns to this question again and again, though not always under the rubric of "overman"; for instance, the last section in *Beyond Good and Evil,* "What Is Noble," addresses this same issue. What he says is exceptionally rich and complex, often expressed in poetic form that a brief treatment can hardly do justice to. But here we set out a number of the principal themes:

1. An overman will "remain faithful to the earth." There will be no hankerings for a "real world"—for the soul, God, immortality, heaven. None of these fictions can solve the problem of the value of existence.

It was suffering and incapacity that created all afterworlds—this and that brief madness of bliss which is experienced only by those who suffer most deeply.

Weariness that wants to reach the ultimate with one leap, with one fatal leap, a poor ignorant weariness that does not want to want any more: this created all gods and afterworlds. . . .

Many sick people have always been among the poetizers and God-cravers; furiously they hate the lover of knowledge and that youngest among the virtues, which is called "honesty." . . .

Listen rather, my brothers, to the voice of the healthy body: that is a more honest and purer voice. More honestly and purely speaks the healthy body that is perfect and perpendicular:* and it speaks of the meaning of the earth. (*Z* 1, 143–145)

Belief in "afterworlds" is a symptom of suffering and sickness and weariness with life. The overman will have none of it.

2. There is a "physiological presupposition" for the overman (*EH,* 298). The overman will be possessed of "*the great health,* . . . a new health, stronger, more seasoned, tougher, more audacious, and gayer than any previous health" (*GS,* 382). The

---

*"Perpendicular," no doubt, because it is not on its knees praying.

healthy body, Zarathustra says, speaks true, and what it says reveals the meaning of the earth. But how can that be? How can a *body* say anything at all?

> "Body am I, and soul"—thus speaks the child. And why should one not speak like children?
>
> But the awakened and knowing say: body am I entirely, and nothing else; and soul is only a word for something about the body.
>
> The body is a great reason, a plurality with one sense, a war and a peace, a herd and a shepherd. An instrument of your body is also your little reason, my brother, which you call "spirit"—a little instrument and toy of your great reason. . . .
>
> Behind your thoughts and feelings, my brother, there stands a mighty ruler, an unknown sage—whose name is self. In your body he dwells; he is your body.
>
> There is more reason in your body than in your best wisdom. (*Z* 1, 146–147)

If we are "body entirely," then in all our thinking and reasoning, the *body* thinks and reasons. Beneath the surface of our conscious life, there are tendencies opposing one another ("war"), quarrels resolved ("peace"), some forces dominant ("shepherd"), others submissive ("herd"). What we experience as our reasoning, our deliberation, our oh-so-highly-prized rationality (our "little reason," Nietzsche says) is nothing more than the body at work—our "great reason."

Why would a *body* invent stories about a soul and an afterlife? Because it is at war with itself; it is ill, "angry with life and the earth" (*Z* 1, 147). Sick bodies create "real worlds" as compensation. A body possessing "the great health," by contrast, would need no compensation. An overman would trust the body, and in so doing would trust himself—but then the body of someone who could be called an overman would be a body that *could* be trusted.

Someone possessed of this "great health" would be able to experience in his own body all the drives and pretenses to wisdom that *any* body could experience—the tendencies to lie and deceive oneself, as well as the exuberance of great health and strength. Such a person could diagnose illness, expose the actors, distinguish the true from the false. Nietzsche says of such a person,

> whoever wants to know from the adventures of his own most authentic experience how a discoverer and conqueror of the ideal feels, and also an artist, a saint, a legislator, a sage, a scholar, a pious man, a soothsayer, and one who stands divinely apart in the old style—needs one thing above everything else: *the great health*. . . .
>
> And now, after we have long been on our way in this manner, we argonauts of the ideal . . . —it will seem to us as if, as a reward, we now confronted an as yet undiscovered country whose boundaries nobody has surveyed yet, something beyond all the lands and nooks of the ideal so far, a world so overrich in what is beautiful, strange, questionable, terrible, and divine that our curiosity as well as our craving to possess it has got beside itself—alas, now nothing will sate us any more.
>
> After such vistas and with such a burning hunger in our conscience and science, how could we still be satisfied with *present-day man?* (*GS*, 382)

This "undiscovered country . . . beyond all the lands and nooks of the ideal so far" is where the overman lives. A prerequisite for living there—indeed, even for discovering its existence—is the great health. Nietzsche clearly thinks of himself as one of those "argonauts of the ideal" who has sailed many a sea to find this place.* He describes it this way:

> Another ideal runs ahead of us, a strange, tempting, dangerous ideal to which we should not wish

---

*The first section of Nietzsche's quasi-autobiographical book *Ecce Homo* (which means, "Behold, the man"—the phrase taken from Pilate's words as he presents the scourged Jesus to the crowd) is titled, "Why I Am So Wise." Here Nietzsche tells us of his long illness, of his weakness, of the incredible pains he suffered. But never to complain. No, he is *grateful* for it. "I took myself in hand, I made myself healthy again: the condition for this—every physiologist would admit that—is *that one be healthy at bottom*. A typically morbid being cannot become healthy, much less make itself healthy. For a typically healthy person, conversely, being sick can even become an energetic *stimulus* for life, for living *more*. This, in fact, is how that long period of sickness appears to me *now*: as it were, I discovered life anew, including myself; I tasted all good and even little things, as others cannot easily taste them—I turned my will to health, to *life*, into a philosophy. For it should be noted: it was during the years of my lowest vitality that I *ceased* to be a pessimist; the instinct of self-restoration *forbade* me a philosophy of poverty and discouragement" (*EH*, 224).

to persuade anybody because we do not readily concede *the right to it* to anyone: the ideal of a spirit who plays naively—that is, not deliberately but from overflowing power and abundance—with all that was hitherto called holy, good, untouchable, divine . . . ; the ideal of a human, superhuman well-being and benevolence that will often appear *inhuman*—for example, when it confronts all earthly seriousness so far. (*GS,* 382)

Note that Nietzsche is not eager to persuade you and me to adopt this ideal. We probably do not have the right to it. The chances are overwhelming that you and I are not overmen, and if we tried to put on this ideal, if *we* thought we could easily go "beyond good and evil," we would almost certainly become mere "actors" of that ideal. And for such "actors" Nietzsche has the greatest contempt.*

3. The notion that the overman "plays naively" with what has hitherto been called good and divine, parallels what Zarathustra says about the necessary "metamorphoses of the spirit." He tells us "how the spirit becomes a camel; and the camel, a lion; and the lion, finally, a child" (*Z* 1, 137).

> What is difficult? asks the spirit that would bear much, and kneels down like a camel wanting to be well loaded. What is most difficult, O heroes, asks the spirit that would bear much, that I may take it upon myself and exult in my strength? (*Z* 1, 138)

The easy path, the soft life of pleasure and indulgence, is not for an overman. An overman seeks out what is "most difficult" and loads it on his back. Discipline, obedience, and bearing heavy burdens is part of an overman's training. An overman is someone who is hard on himself and others. A spirit that would attain great heights cannot *begin* there, any more than an apprentice cabinetmaker can begin as a master craftsman.†

---

*It has happened that people read Nietzsche, decide to go "beyond good and evil," to become overmen, and end up merely absurd—and sometimes as murderers (not exactly what Nietzsche has in mind).

†Nietzsche began his career by learning the demanding craft of philology. Students sometimes think they should be able to skip the camel phase—not have to bear the burden of tracing out the arguments of Plato, Aristotle, and Kant—and become philosophers immediately, without effort. But one way or another, in

In the loneliest desert, however, the second metamorphosis occurs: here the spirit becomes a lion who would conquer his freedom and be master in his own desert. Here he seeks out his last master: he wants to fight him and his last god; for ultimate victory he wants to fight with the great dragon.

> Who is the great dragon whom the spirit will no longer call lord and god? "Thou shalt" is the name of the great dragon. But the spirit of the lion says, "I will." "Thou shalt" lies in his way, sparkling like gold, an animal covered with scales; and on every scale shines a golden "thou shalt."
>
> Values, thousands of years old, shine on these scales; and thus speaks the mightiest of all dragons: "All value of all things shines on me. All value has long been created, and I am all created value. Verily, there shall be no more 'I will.'" (*Z* 1, 138–139)

The spirit that would attain to overman status cannot be content with bearing the burdens of the camel. In the guise of a lion, the spirit says "No!" to all "Thou shalts" and thus opens up a space for freedom—a space in which new values can be created.

> But say, my brothers, what can the child do that even the lion could not do? Why must the preying lion still become a child? The child is innocence and forgetting, a new beginning, a game, a self-propelled wheel, a first movement, a sacred "Yes." For the game of creation, my brothers, a sacred "Yes" is needed: the spirit now wills his own will, and he who had been lost to the world now conquers his own world. (*Z* 1, 139)

The "naive play" of the overman is the play of a child—a yes to his own life that grows out of great health. It is the "innocence" of the child "willing his own will."* The child plays "the game of creation." And what does the child create? Values.

4. So the overman is a creator of values. And creation cannot take place without a corresponding destruction—the "No!" of the lion. "Whoever must be a creator always annihilates" (*Z* 1, 171). But the overman does not create heedlessly or arbitrarily. The child does not play dice with values.

---

everything worthwhile, one must first be a camel. Great pianists have practiced many scales.

*But see Augustine on the "innocence" of children, p. 247.

The principal thing the overman creates is *himself*. And his values are simply expressions of who he is.*

> We, however, *want to become those we are*—human beings who are new, unique, incomparable, who give themselves laws, who create themselves. (*GS*, 335)

In *Ecce Homo,* Nietzsche says a surprising thing.

> To become what one is, one must not have the faintest notion *what* one is. . . .
>
>   The whole surface of consciousness—consciousness *is* a surface—must be kept clear of all great imperatives. Beware even of every great word, every great pose! So many dangers that the instinct comes too soon to "understand itself"—. Meanwhile the organizing "idea" that is destined to rule keeps growing deep down—it begins to command; slowly it leads us *back* from side roads and wrong roads; it prepares *single* qualities and fitnesses that will one day prove to be indispensable as a means toward a whole—one by one, it trains all *subservient* capacities before giving any hint of the dominant task, "goal," "aim," or "meaning." (*EH*, 254)

The danger is that one gets an idea of *what one is* and then tries to conform to that idea. But in that case one has almost certainly got it *wrong,* and one will become merely the ape of an ideal that is not one's own—again, merely an actor. One must not decide too soon what one is or take the idea of what one is from others; this is good advice for everyone, Nietzsche thinks. And it is absolutely essential advice for those few who are possessed of the great health and are capable of becoming overmen. For it is *themselves* they want to create, not some cracked and misshapen image of themselves.

It is not the case, however, that an overman can just lie back and wait for what he is to unfold itself. That way one will get nothing worthwhile. All creators, Nietzsche tells us, are *hard*—most of all, hard on themselves.

> "Among the conditions for a *Dionysian* task are, in a decisive way, the hardness of the hammer, the *joy even in destroying.* The imperative, 'become hard!'

the most fundamental certainty *that all creators are hard,* is the distinctive mark of a Dionysian nature."* (*EH,* 309)

An overman demands much, has a right to demand much. He demands most of all *from himself.* Zarathustra warns,

> But the worst enemy you can encounter will always be you, yourself; you lie in wait for yourself in caves and woods.
>
>   Lonely one, you are going the way to yourself. . . . You must wish to consume yourself in your own flame: how could you wish to become new unless you had first become ashes! . . .
>
>   Lonely one, you are going the way of the lover: yourself you love, and therefore you despise yourself, as only lovers despise. The lover would create because he despises. What does he know of love who did not have to despise precisely what he loved? (*Z* 1, 176–177)

Not for the overman a sweet contentment with his present state—no easy self-esteem. He climbs over himself on his way to himself. Love of himself is inseparable from contempt—contempt of whatever in himself has not yet become perfect. The overman overcomes himself, "giving style" to his character:

> A great and rare art! It is practiced by those who survey all the strengths and weaknesses of their nature and then fit them into an artistic plan until every one of them appears as art and reason and even weaknesses delight the eye. Here a large mass of second nature has been added; there a piece of original nature has been removed—both times through long practice and daily work at it. Here the ugly that could not be removed is concealed; there it has been reinterpreted and made sublime. Much that is vague and resisted shaping has been saved and exploited for distant views; it is meant to beckon toward the far and immeasurable. In the end, when the work is finished, it becomes evident how the constraint of a single taste governed and formed everything large and small. (*GS,* 290)

---

*Compare Kierkegaard on being willing to be oneself, pp. 500–503.

*Here we see that Dionysus does not disappear when the "real worlds" of *The Birth of Tragedy* are left behind. But the conception of the god deepens and changes substantially, as we shall see. An overman is clearly a "Dionysian nature." In his last book, *Ecce Homo,* Nietzsche identifies *himself* with Dionysus.

So the overman is the poet of his life, the artist who both creates the work and lives it. In *The Birth of Tragedy,* Nietzsche says that existence and the world can be justified only as an aesthetic phenomenon. On this point Nietzsche has not changed his mind. If the overman is going to become the meaning of the earth, he will do it by creating himself as a work of art. Zarathustra considers those who are "sublime." By the "sublime," he means those who have struggled hard for the heights and have attained them, but who still have "tense souls" filled with the exertion of control. He admires them but considers that they have not yet reached the pinnacle.

> To stand with relaxed muscles and unharnessed will: that is most difficult for all of you who are sublime.
>
> When power becomes gracious and descends into the visible—such descent I call beauty.
>
> And there is nobody from whom I want beauty as much as from you who are powerful: let your kindness be your final self-conquest.
>
> Of all evil I deem you capable: therefore I want the good from you.
>
> Verily, I have often laughed at the weaklings who thought themselves good because they had no claws. (Z 2, 230)

It is the *beauty* of the overman that makes life worthwhile.

5. The overman loves himself. In deliberate opposition to the morality of "good and evil," Nietzsche praises selfishness. Zarathustra, for the first time,

> pronounced *selfishness* blessed, the wholesome, healthy selfishness that wells from a powerful soul—from a powerful soul to which belongs the high body, beautiful, triumphant, refreshing, around which everything becomes a mirror—the supple, persuasive body, the dancer whose parable and epitome is the self-enjoying soul. The self enjoyment of such bodies and souls calls itself "virtue." (Z 3, 302)

It is worth noting that it is the selfishness of "a powerful soul" in a "high body" that is praised—not every kind of selfishness. Only an overman has a *right* to such selfishness.

There is also another selfishness, an all-too-poor and hungry one that always wants to steal—the selfishness of the sick: sick selfishness. With the eyes of a thief it looks at everything splendid; with the greed of hunger it sizes up those who have much to eat; and always it sneaks around the table of those who give. Sickness speaks out of such craving and invisible degeneration; the thievish greed of this selfishness speaks of a diseased body. (Z 1, 187)

Because we know what Nietzsche thinks of sickness and diseased bodies, there is no question about his attitude toward this kind of selfishness. But what can we say of the higher selfishness, the kind appropriate to the higher man?

Perhaps above all, the higher selfishness is the overman's determination not to be drawn *away from himself.* If the *task* is to become who we are, then all sorts of enticements to betray that task must be resisted—for the sake of the self! In the same passage (Z 3, 302–303) where Zarathustra praises selfishness, he contrasts it with

- "whatever is cowardly"
- "anyone who always worries, sighs, is miserable"
- "anyone who picks up even the smallest advantages"
- "all wisdom that wallows in grief"
- "the subservient, the doglike, who immediately lie on their backs, the humble"
- "those who never offer resistance, who swallow poisonous spittle and evil glances, the all-too-patient, all-suffering, always satisfied; for that is servile"
- "especially the whole wicked, nitwitted, witless foolishness of priests"
- the "'selfless'"

There is one mode of being drawn away from oneself that Zarathustra particularly pillories: what Christians call love of the neighbor.[*]

> You crowd around your neighbor and have fine words for it. But I say unto you: your love of the

---

[*]Compare Jesus' parable of the good Samaritan, p. 221.

neighbor is your bad love of yourselves. You flee to your neighbor from yourselves and would like to make a virtue out of that: but I see through your "selflessness." . . .

Do I recommend love of the neighbor to you? Sooner I should even recommend flight from the neighbor and love of the farthest. . . . But you are afraid and run to your neighbor. (Z 1, 172–173)

As Zarathustra interprets it, neighbor love is another one of those virtues "lied" into existence by the weak; they are dissatisfied with themselves, and they "flee" to the neighbor. Being occupied with the sufferings of others, Zarathustra thinks, is a way of avoiding the hard task of creating oneself. Selflessness is praised by those who have no self worth prizing. Neighbor love is part of the "morality of timidity" that the herd praises to thwart "everything that raises an individual above the herd and causes his neighbor to fear him" (BGE, 201, 88).

But once again, as with selfishness generally, there can be a bad and a good form of loving one's neighbor.

"Do love your neighbor as yourself, but first be such as *love themselves*—loving with a great love, loving with a great contempt." Thus speaks Zarathustra the godless. (Z 3, 284)

As we have seen, loving yourself is being *hard* on yourself, loving yourself "with a great contempt" for all in your life that has not yet been "given style."* Loving your neighbor "as yourself" would involve the same hardness and contempt.

6. Zarathustra praises not the accidental and anonymous "neighbor," but the friend.

I teach you not the neighbor, but the friend. The friend should be the festival of the earth to you and an anticipation of the overman. I teach you the friend and his overflowing heart. . . .

Let the future and the farthest be for you the cause of your today: in your friend you shall love the overman as your cause. (Z 1, 173–174)

A friend is not *someone who needs you,* and you should not "flee" to your friend out of need. A true friend is one with an "overflowing heart," which, of course,

requires the "great health." A friend shares what is highest—the passion for self-overcoming. Friends are not just good-time buddies, occasions for enjoyment. Friends stimulate each other to excel; each demands more and ever more from the other—more, that is, of the other's nobility and self-mastery.

In a friend one should have one's best enemy. You should be closest to him with your heart when you resist him. (Z 1, 168)

Let us be enemies too, my friends! Let us strive against one another like gods. (Z 2, 214)

7. As the prophet of the overman, Zarathustra is also the prophet of the *will to power.*

Where I found the living, there I found will to power; and even in the will of those who serve I found the will to be master. . . .

And life itself confided this secret to me: "Behold," it said, "I am *that which must always overcome itself.* Indeed, you call it a will to procreate or a drive to an end, to something higher, farther, more manifold: but all this is one, and one secret. . . .

"Whatever I create and however much I love it— soon I must oppose it and my love; thus my will wills it. And you too, lover of knowledge, are only a path and footprint of my will; verily, my will to power walks also on the heels of your will to truth." (Z 2, 226–227)

In every kind of overcoming, every will to a higher state, in every valuation and esteeming, Zarathustra detects the will to power.* It is will to power that seeks truth.† It is will to power that cre-

---

*You may be wondering how Nietzsche can identify will to power as the key drive in all existence, when he has attacked the will as superficial and hardly the sort of thing that can serve as a cause. The answer is that will to power is not the *conscious* will; it is not the intention to which we normally ascribe action. Will to power is simply *life itself* climbing over itself, overcoming every plateau, always seeking mastery and control—whether consciously or not. Needless to say, this is not Schopenhauer's *metaphysical will,* either; will to power is meant to be a characterization of life in *this* world.

†In an important speech called "On Immaculate Perception," Zarathustra attacks the idea that there can be any disinterested, purely contemplative, spectatorlike knowledge. *All* of our knowing and pursuit of truth is driven by desire, interest, will. The trick is not to pare these passions away, but to multiply

ates tablets of values—as a means to self-control and mastery, to more power!

> A tablet of the good hangs over every people. Behold, it is the tablet of their overcomings; behold, it is the voice of their will to power. (*Z* 1, 170)

Will to power drives the revenge of the weak and motivates the slave rebellion in morality. And will to power points us toward the overman as the one in whom power is at its peak. That is why the overman can be the meaning of the earth. Overman is what life—all life—is driving toward.

The power of the overman is primarily *self*-mastery, *self*-overcoming; it is the enjoyment of an overfull, overflowing, abundant life in which one is no longer dominated by need, aching, longing, or wishing that things might be otherwise. The life of an overman is a life *beyond revenge* and *without resentment*.

> One needs only to do me some wrong, I "repay" it—you may be sure of that: soon I find an opportunity for expressing my gratitude to the "evildoer" (at times even for his evil deed). (*EH*, 229)

No blaming, no accusations, no complaining. No victim-think. No self-pity. *No pity at all*. The life of an overman will not be without suffering, pain, and struggle, but an overman is strong enough for that, too. More to the point, an overman is *grateful* for it. That, too, can be overcome.

All this may sound attractive; we might like to be overmen, too. But we should not be naive about the power of an overman. It is a life, after all, *beyond good and evil*. And Nietzsche on numerous occasions takes pains to tell us how dangerous overmen can be. In the chapter on "What Is Noble," Nietzsche says,

> To refrain from injuring, abusing, or exploiting one another; to equate another person's will with our own: in a certain crude sense this can develop into good manners between individuals, if the pre-

conditions are in place (that is, if the individuals have truly similar strength and standards and if they are united within one single social body). But if we were to try to take this principle further and possibly even make it the *basic principle of society*, it would immediately be revealed for what it is: a will to *deny* life, a principle for dissolution and decline. We must think through the reasons for this and resist all sentimental frailty: life itself *in its essence* means appropriating, injuring, overpowering those who are foreign and weaker. . . . "Exploitation" is not part of a decadent or imperfect, primitive society: it is part of the *fundamental nature* of living things, . . . a consequence of the true will to power, which is simply the will to life.* (*BGE*, 259, 153)

An aristocracy of overmen will *of course* exploit those beneath them. Again Nietzsche displays his hostility to "modern ideas" of equality and equal rights for all. All this is superficiality and sentimental weakness. Worse, it is "a will to *deny* life, a principle for dissolution and decline." Men are *not* equal. And a clear view of the very "*essence*" of life should convince us of that.

8. An overman will know what he is worth. Under no illusions about equality, the noble soul of an overman will sense the immense distance between himself and others. He will be conscious of the "*order of rank*, and of how power and right and spaciousness of perspective grow into the heights together" (*HA*, preface, 9). Very much like Plato,[†] Nietzsche thinks there are roughly three classes of human beings.

> The highest caste—I call them *the fewest*—being perfect, also has the privileges of the fewest: among them, to represent happiness, beauty, and graciousness on earth. Only to the most spiritual human beings is beauty permitted: among them alone is graciousness not weakness. . . .
> The *second*: they are the guardians of the law, those who see to order and security, the noble warriors, and above all the king as the highest formula of warrior, judge, and upholder of the law. . . .

---

them (as "great health" makes possible), to add perspectives so as to gain the *height* from which an overman can survey the truth. "How much truth does a spirit *endure*, how much truth does it *dare*? More and more that became for me the real measure of value. Error (faith in the ideal) is not blindness, error is *cowardice*" (*EH*, 218).

---

*Remember Nietzsche's description of the "uncaged beasts of prey" who created master morality (pp. 546–547). Is Nietzsche here celebrating what Marx deplores?

†For Plato's ideal ordering of a state, see pp. 150–151.

A high culture is a pyramid: it can stand only on a broad base; its first presupposition is a strong and soundly consolidated mediocrity. Handicraft, trade, agriculture, *science,* the greatest part of art, the whole quintessence of *professional* activity, to sum it up, is compatible only with a mediocre amount of ability and ambition. (*A, 57*)

Nietzsche emphasizes that in this pyramid, with the few at the top, there is nothing unnatural.

In all this, to repeat, there is nothing arbitrary, nothing contrived; whatever is *different* is contrived—contrived for the ruin of nature. The order of castes, the *order of rank,* merely formulates the highest law of life; the separation of the three types is necessary for the preservation of society, to make possible the higher and the highest types. The *inequality* of rights is the first condition for the existence of any rights at all. (*A, 57*)

The overman, then, will look *down*. The *many* will be below him—perhaps far below. But what attitude will these highest few have toward those who are lower in the order of rank? The overman will be filled with contempt, loathing, and nausea wherever he sees resentment and revenge in those lower ranks, deception and self-deception, the rancor of the ill-constituted, the demand for equality (where there *is* none)—in short, the morality of good and evil. But for those mediocre ones who are content, who find their happiness in mediocrity, the situation is different:

It would be completely unworthy of a more profound spirit to consider mediocrity as such an objection. In fact, it is the very *first* necessity if there are to be exceptions: a high culture depends on it. When the exceptional human being treats the mediocre more tenderly than himself and his peers, this is not mere politeness of the heart—it is simply his *duty.* (*A, 57*)

There is certainly more to be said about the life of an overman, but in a word, the overman is one who says "Yes!" to his life, to life itself—who is strong enough for such a yes, healthy enough for such a yes. In such self-affirmation and in continual self-overcoming, the overman finds his joy. And in individuals like that the earth finds its meaning.

There is one problem still facing the overman, a problem Zarathustra faces, too. Can one who has reached these heights really say "Yes!" to *everything?* With that question we come to the crucial test for those who aspire to greatness.

1. What does it mean that man is "a bridge and not an end"?
2. What does it mean to "remain faithful to the earth"?
3. Explain the parable of the camel, the lion, and the child.
4. How does one "become what one is"?
5. In what sense is selfishness a virtue? In what sense not?
6. What is the contrast Nietzsche draws between the neighbor and the friend?
7. Explain the notion of an "order of rank."

Affirming Eternal Recurrence

Thus Spoke Zarathustra tells us not only of Zarathustra's speeches but also of his visions, dreams, and adventures. Most importantly, it chronicles Zarathustra's own growth toward overman status. By the end of the book, if Zarathustra is not yet an overman, he is close. As we have seen, an overman says "Yes!" to his life; an overman turns his back on spite and revenge and all no-saying; an overman remains faithful to the earth. But how could one tell whether one has done that? Self-deception is such a common human characteristic; perhaps one is kidding oneself.

In *The Gay Science,* Nietzsche devises a test.

The greatest weight.—— What, if some day or night a demon were to steal after you into your loneliest loneliness and say to you: "This life as you now live it and have lived it, you will have to live once more and innumerable times more; and there will be nothing new in it, but every pain and every joy and every thought and sigh and everything unutterably small or great in your life will have to return to you, all in the same moonlight between the trees, and even this moment and I myself. The eternal hourglass of existence is turned upside down again and again, and you with it, speck of dust!"

Would you not throw yourself down and gnash your teeth and curse the demon who spoke thus? Or, have you once experienced a tremendous moment when you would have answered him: "You are a god and never have I heard anything more divine." If this thought gained possession of you, it would change you as you are or perhaps crush you. The question in each and every thing, "Do you desire this once more and innumerable times more?" would lie upon your actions as the greatest weight. Or how well disposed would you have to become to yourself and to life *to crave nothing more fervently* than this ultimate eternal confirmation and seal? (*GS,* 341)

The eternal recurrence of all things:* At one point, Zarathustra faces that prospect (*Z* 3, 269–272), but he sets it aside. He speaks of an "abysmal thought," which, apparently, he cannot bear to face. Some time later he calls it forth.

Up, abysmal thought, out of my depth! I am your cock and dawn, sleepy worm. Up! Up! My voice shall crow you awake! . . .

I, Zarathustra, the advocate of life, the advocate of suffering, the advocate of the circle; I summon you, my most abysmal thought!

Hail to me! You are coming, I hear you. My abyss speaks. I have turned my ultimate depth inside out into the light. Hail to me! Come here! Give me your hand! Huh! Let go! Huhhuh! Nausea, nausea, nausea—woe unto me! (*Z* 3, 327–328)

What could this thought be that so terrifies Zarathustra, that fills him with such nausea? Remember the prospect that the demon puts before us: that *all* things should recur—eternally—exactly as they are. Zarathustra's abysmal thought is that this means the small man, the herd man, the

"last" man, the man of resentment and revenge, the weak, the priest, the slaves with their nihilistic morality, Christianity—all this would recur again and again and again. . . .

The great disgust with man—*this* choked me and had crawled into my throat; and what the soothsayer said: "All is the same, nothing is worth while, knowledge chokes." A long twilight limped before me, a sadness, weary to death, drunken with death, speaking with a yawning mouth. "Eternally recurs the man of whom you are weary, the small man"—thus yawned my sadness and dragged its feet and could not go to sleep. . . . "Alas, man recurs eternally! The small man recurs eternally!"

Naked I had once seen both, the greatest man and the smallest man: all-too-similar to each other, even the greatest all-too-human. All-too-small, the greatest!—that was my disgust with man. And the eternal recurrence even of the smallest—that was my disgust with all existence. Alas! Nausea! Nausea! Nausea! (*Z* 3, 331)

The prospect of eternal recurrence brings the soothsayer's nihilism back with a vengeance. What is life for, if it isn't going anywhere? If there is no hope for ultimate improvement, for progress, for getting beyond the small and the great—for *overcoming man* once and for all—what would be the point? Man would be a bridge leading nowhere! If it all repeats itself, how could one bear it? But that is just the question the demon asks, isn't it? Suppose this prospect of the eternal recurrence of everything were offered to you. Would you "throw yourself down and gnash your teeth," or would you say, "Never have I heard anything more divine"? The way you answer this question shows "how well disposed" you are "to yourself and to life." It is a test of your yes-saying. Would you say "Yes!" even to this? Would you affirm the eternal recurrence of all things?*

What the thought of eternal recurrence teaches Zarathustra is that the meaning of life cannot be sought in anything beyond it. Eternal recurrence

---

*Scholars are divided about whether Nietzsche actually believed in recurrence as a fact. There is some evidence that he did, but many think it inconclusive. Whether he did or did not, however, it is clear that its principal importance for him is not as a *truth,* but as a thought experiment to test the level of yes-saying in a person's life.

---

*Of the Holocaust, too, you ask? Of the events on 9/11? Yes, even of those.

is the ultimate denial of all "real worlds"; there is just *this world*—over and over and over again. With "real worlds" gone, life must justify itself *as it is,* or it cannot be justified at all. Not every life, Nietzsche thinks, can stand this thought. Only the strongest can bear this "greatest weight"—only an overman who says "Yes!" to everything, who affirms life and remains faithful to the earth, who overcomes himself, who gives style to his life, who creates his own values in the very living of his life. The overman says "Yes!" to eternal recurrence. And it is in the life of the overman that the problem of the meaning of life is solved. In *that* life, it doesn't seem a problem!

In *Ecce Homo,* a late work, Nietzsche says, "I am a disciple of the philosopher Dionysus" (*EH,* 217). The *philosopher* Dionysus? When we meet Dionysus in *The Birth of Tragedy,* he is a god; in fact, he is just *one* of the gods, symbolizing a certain feature of human life, but certainly not the whole of it. He is contrasted with Apollo, you will remember, and represents passion unconstrained by reason, measure, and order (these being Apollo's domain). But something interesting has happened in the course of Nietzsche's development. With the disappearance of "real worlds," any contrast between "opposite values"—by which Nietzsche means values grounded in different realities (see *BGE,* 2, 5–6)—also vanishes. Every aspect of human life, therefore—virtues, vices, values, science—has to be accounted for in terms of the same fundamental reality. And what is that? Will to power.

We have seen that Nietzsche interprets intelligence and "spirit" as no more than an aspect of body. And each body (slave and master alike) expresses the will to power, the will to overcome, the will to achieve a higher, stronger, more masterful condition. So what Nietzsche thinks of as Apollo in *The Birth of Tragedy*—the powers of reason, order, measure (and philosophy, too)—is now seen to be just a manifestation of a body's will to power: its "little reason." (The will to truth, remember, is just will to power—one form the will to mastery can take.) So all these Apollonian powers are *not* opposed to Dionysus; they are an aspect of Dionysus, a manifestation of the power of Dionysus—of the will to power. Will to power *sublimated into rea-*

son—that is how Dionysus can be a philosopher and not just the god of irrational intoxication. And that is why at the end only Dionysus remains. A philosophy that remains *faithful to the earth* must be a philosophy of the will to power that says yes to everything earthly—and so is willing to affirm the eternal recurrence of everything. But to affirm life, to rejoice in life, *is* Dionysian.

The affirmation of eternal recurrence is identical with a formula that Nietzsche calls "my formula for greatness in a human being: *amor fati*" (*EH,* 258), that is, love of fate. He explains it in this way:

> that one wants nothing to be different, not forward, not backward, not in all eternity. Not merely bear what is necessary, still less conceal it . . . but *love* it. (*EH,* 258)

Because everything that happens in this world is, Nietzsche believes, necessary and a manifestation of the will to power, to love it is to affirm it. And to affirm it is to say yes even to its eternal recurrence. Whoever can truly do that is an overman—and a disciple of the god and philosopher Dionysus.

Not even death can subvert the gratitude and joy with which an overman experiences life. At one point Zarathustra romances life, declaring his love. But life says softly to him,

> "O Zarathustra, you are not faithful enough to me. You do not love me nearly as much as you say; I know you are thinking of leaving me soon. . . ."
> "Yes," I answered hesitantly, "but you also know—" and I whispered something into her ear, right through her tangled yellow foolish tresses.
> "You *know* that, O Zarathustra? Nobody knows that."
> And we looked at each other and gazed on the green meadow over which the cool evening was running just then, and we wept together. But then life was dearer to me than all my wisdom ever was. (*Z* 3, 339–340)

What does Zarathustra whisper in life's ear? Presumably that life and death recur eternally in a never-ending cycle, and to say yes to one is to affirm the other. That thought may be an occasion for sadness, but it does not dim in the slightest Zarathustra's love of life.

Zarathustra meets a number of "higher men" who have risen above the herd in one way or another but have not yet reached Zarathustra's level of development. Among them are the soothsayer, the retired pope, and the ugliest man. Zarathustra invites them to his cave, where they have a feast (a sacrilegious parody of Jesus' "last supper") and are merry. The dreaded "spirit of gravity" retreats and they laugh together. Zarathustra notes,

> Nausea is retreating from these higher men. Well then! That is my triumph. In my realm they feel safe, all stupid shame runs away, they unburden themselves. They unburden their hearts, good hours come back to them, they celebrate and chew the cud: they become grateful. *This* I take to be the best sign: they become grateful. (Z 4, 423)

Gratitude is the "best sign" of a "redeemed" life. Gratitude for *everything*—just as Nietzsche himself was grateful for his illness and pain, and for those who did him wrong. That gratitude covers everything is a sign of affirming life—even to the point of willing it all again.

At the banquet, the ugliest man (the murderer of God) says,

> "My friends, all of you, . . . what do you think? For the sake of this day, *I* am for the first time satisfied that I have lived my whole life. And that I attest so much is still not enough for me. Living on earth is worth while: one day, one festival with Zarathustra, taught me to love the earth.
> "'Was *that* life?' I want to say to death. 'Well then! Once more!'" (Z 4, 429–430)

Meanwhile, Zarathustra overcomes his "last temptation"—pity for the higher men, pity that they had not come—perhaps *could not* come—still higher. Pity is the last, subtlest, most seductive form of no-saying. To pity is to say, *would it were not so.* "Pity is the *practice* of nihilism" (A, 7). To pity is to give in to suffering, to hallow suffering, to suffer oneself. But Zarathustra believes that suffering and pain are no objection to life! They are, rather, stimulants to self-overcoming, and for them, too, one must be grateful. Zarathustra is like a convalescent recovering from a long illness—from his wandering in search of wisdom, from his nausea, his pity,

his lack of ability to affirm life. Zarathustra is approaching the life of an overman.

Nietzsche tells us, out of his own experience, what such a convalescence is like.

> The free spirit again draws near to life—slowly, to be sure, almost reluctantly, almost mistrustfully. It again grows warmer about him, yellower, as it were; feeling and feeling for others acquire depth, warm breezes of all kind blow across him. It seems to him as if his eyes are only now open to what is *close at hand.* He is astonished and sits silent: where *had* he been? These close and closest things: how changed they seem! what bloom and magic they have acquired! He looks back gratefully—grateful to his wandering, to his hardness and self-alienation, to his viewing of far distances and bird-like flights in cold heights. What a good thing he had not always stayed "at home," stayed "under his own roof" like a delicate apathetic loafer! He had been *beside himself:* no doubt of that. Only now does he see himself—and what surprises he experiences as he does so! What unprecedented shudders! What happiness even in the weariness, the old sickness, the relapses of the convalescent! How he loves to sit sadly still, to spin out patience, to lie in the sun! Who understands as he does the happiness that comes in winter, the spots of sunlight on the wall! They are the most grateful animals in the world, also the most modest, these convalescents and lizards again half turned towards life:—there are some among them who allow no day to pass without hanging a little song of praise on the hem of its departing robe. And to speak seriously: to become sick in the manner of these free spirits, to remain sick for a long time and then, slowly, slowly, to become healthy, by which I mean "healthier", is a fundamental *cure* for all pessimism. (HA, 8–9)

Such a convalescent could wish for it all again.

---

1. What does it mean to affirm eternal recurrence? What does one's reaction to the prospect of eternal recurrence reveal about oneself?
2. How has the conception of Dionysus changed from Nietzsche's early work to his late work?
3. Explain *amor fati* and indicate how this could be Nietzsche's "formula for greatness in a human being."

For Further Thought

1. Suppose that you want to resist Nietzsche's attacks on equality and equal rights. How much else in Nietzsche would you have to reject?

2. Nietzsche believes the interpretation of human beings as sinful is based on a lie, whereas Kierkegaard takes it to be the very truth. Nietzsche pins his hopes for "redemption" on *amor fati* and affirming eternal recurrence; Kierkegaard, on faith. Compare these analyses of the problem of human life and its solution.

Notes

1. References to Nietzsche's works are as follows:

   PN: The Portable Nietzsche, trans. Walter Kaufmann (New York: Viking Press, 1954). References are to page numbers.

   BT: The Birth of Tragedy, trans. Douglas Smith (Oxford: Oxford University Press, 2000). References are to sections and page numbers.

   HA: Human, All Too Human, trans. R. J. Hollingdale (Cambridge: Cambridge University Press, 1986). References are to page numbers.

   GS: The Gay Science, trans. Walter Kaufmann (New York: Vintage Books, 1974). References are to sections.

   Z: Thus Spoke Zarathustra, in *The Portable Nietzsche.* References are to part and page number.

   BGE: Beyond Good and Evil, trans. Marian Faber (Oxford: Oxford University Press, 1998). References are to section and page numbers.

   GM: On The Genealogy of Morals, trans. Douglas Smith (Oxford: Oxford University Press, 1996). References are to essay, section, and page numbers.

   A: The Antichrist, in *The Portable Nietzsche.* References are to sections.

   TI: Twilight of the Idols, trans. Duncan Large (Oxford: Oxford University Press, 1998). References are to page numbers.

   EH: Ecce Homo, in *On the Genealogy of Morals and Ecce Homo,* trans. Walter Kaufmann (New York: Vintage Books, 1967). References are to page numbers.

CHAPTER

21

THE PRAGMATISTS
Thought and Action

The nineteenth century is a tumultuous century, socially, politically, and intellectually. It is the century of the railroad, the newspaper, and the factory. It is the century of the British Empire, colonialism, and the conquest of the American continent. And it is the century of the principle of the conservation of energy, of non-Euclidean geometries, of non-Aristotelian logic, and of evolution. A topsy-turvy century, indeed, but one convinced on the whole that progress is being made every day.

Nothing bolsters this conviction more substantially than the progress of science, and among the accomplishments of science, none stands out more prominently than that of Darwin. A cause for controversy down to our own day, Darwin's theory of evolution claims to give a scientific account of *life,* in much the same way that Newton masters space, time, and gravitational forces. A basically mechanistic explanation is given for the forms of living things, for their variety, and for their tendency to alter over long spans of time. The basic outlines of Darwin's theory of evolution are well known: Sexual selection and the mechanisms of inheritance

produce small variations in offspring; some of these changes are beneficial to individuals who possess them; under the pressures of population and scarce resources, these individuals are more likely to reproduce, passing their advantage to their offspring, thus leading eventually to differentiation of species in different ecological niches. The core ideas are those of *random variation* and *natural selection.* Darwinian thought is a momentous and influential shift, affecting intellectuals of all kinds—not least those philosophers who come to call themselves pragmatists.

Charles Sanders Peirce

Charles Sanders Peirce (1839–1914), the son of a Harvard mathematician, was trained in the techniques of science from an early age. He used to claim that he had been brought up in a laboratory. For a good part of his adult life, he worked as a scientist for the United States Coast and Geodetic Survey. He made some contributions to the theory of the pendulum and was much concerned with problems of accurate measurement. But he was early attracted to problems in logic and probability theory and made a close study of the philosophies of Kant and Hegel. His research in logic is highly original, contributing to the expansion of logic beyond the Aristotelian syllogism.* In addition to extending the theory of *deductive inferences,* Peirce does much to clarify *inductive inferences;* he also explores the sort of inference that starts from certain facts and leaps to a hypothesis that explains them. He calls this last sort *abductive inference,* a term that has not caught on; it is nowadays usually called *inference to the best explanation.*

Peirce is also a metaphysician of some power, combining in his later thought a version of evolutionary theory with absolute idealism.† But it is not his metaphysics that has been influential, so we concentrate on what he calls his **pragmatism.** The word comes from a Greek root meaning "deed" or "act" and is chosen to accentuate the close ties that Peirce sees between our intellectual life (concepts, beliefs, theories) on the one hand and our practical life of actions and enjoyments on the other. Peirce also occasionally calls it *practicalism,* and sometimes *critical common-sensism.* We'll see that John Dewey thinks of **instrumentalism** as a term nearly equivalent in force, this term bringing out the toollike character of the intellectual conceptions we use.

Others, including most prominently the psychologist and philosopher William James, adopt the term "pragmatism"; it comes to mean a number of subtly different things to different people. In 1908, an American philosopher, Arthur Lovejoy, wrote an article entitled "The Thirteen Pragmatisms." It seemed there were almost as many versions of the doctrine as there were philosophers who adopted the name. Because many of them diverged significantly from what Peirce meant by the

term, he invented the term *pragmaticism* for his own views—a word, he said, ugly enough to be safe from kidnappers. He was correct, and in fact, history knows his views by the more common term "pragmatism." It is under that heading that we examine what he has to say.

Fixing Belief

In the late 1870s, Peirce published a series of articles in *Popular Science Monthly,* in which the influence of scientific practice on this lifelong researcher is evident. He distinguishes four ways of coming to a fixed belief about some subject matter, four methods of settling opinion. These are techniques that can be used (indeed, are used) to arrive at what we *think* is true. They are ways of resolving doubt.

First there is the *method of tenacity.* If the aim is settlement of opinion, one might ask oneself,

> Why should we not attain the desired end, by taking as answer to a question any we may fancy, and constantly reiterating it to ourselves, dwelling on all which may conduce to that belief, and learning to turn with contempt and hatred from anything that might disturb it? (*FB,* 233–234)[1]

Those who adopt this technique enjoy certain benefits. For one, they avoid the uncomfortable state of indecision and doubt. It cannot be denied, Peirce says, "that a steady and immovable faith yields great peace of mind" (*FB,* 249). Moreover, there seems to be nothing that can *rationally* be said in objection, for such persons are content to set rationality aside, and reasons against their beliefs will be (from their point of view) beside the point.

Nonetheless, Peirce believes that this is not a satisfactory method of settling opinion. His reason is an interesting one and sheds light on his pragmatism. One might think that the proper objection to the method of tenacity is that it is bound to leave one with too many false beliefs. But that is not Peirce's objection. The trouble with this method is that it

> will be unable to hold its ground in practice. The social impulse is against it. The man who adopts it will find that other men think differently from him, and it will be apt to occur to him, in some saner

---

*For a brief account of Aristotle's conception of logic, which dominates Western thought for 2,400 years, see pp. 159–166; the syllogism is discussed on pp. 163–166.

†For an account of absolute idealism in its Hegelian guise, see pp. 476–478. The key feature in Peirce's version is that the entire universe has the distinguishing features of mind and that it is moving toward a rational end out of love. But such a brief account hardly does it justice.

moment, that their opinions are quite as good as his own, and this will shake his confidence in his belief. (*FB*, 235)

The right objection is that tenacity *doesn't work!*[*] This thought, that others may well be as right as oneself, arises from the "social impulse," Peirce says, "an impulse too strong in man to be suppressed" (*FB*, 235). We are in fact influenced by the opinions of others. So some method must be found that will fix belief not only in the individual, but also in the community.

This thought leads us to the second method: *authority*.

> Let an institution be created which shall have for its object to keep correct doctrines before the attention of the people, to reiterate them perpetually, and to teach them to the young; having at the same time power to prevent contrary doctrines from being taught, advocated, or expressed. Let all possible causes of a change of mind be removed from men's apprehensions. Let them be kept ignorant, lest they should learn of some reason to think otherwise than they do. Let their passions be enlisted, so that they may regard private and unusual opinions with hatred and horror. Then, let all men who reject the established belief be terrified into silence. Let the people turn out and tar-and-feather such men, or let inquisitions be made into the manner of thinking of suspected persons, and, when they are found guilty of forbidden beliefs, let them be subjected to some signal punishment. When complete agreement could not otherwise be reached, a general massacre of all who have not thought in a certain way has proved to be a very effective means of settling opinion in a country. (*FB*, 235−236)

This method, Peirce judges, is much superior to the first; it can produce majestic results in terms of culture and art. He even allows that for the mass of humankind, there may be no better method than that of authority. But this method is also unstable: There will always be some people who see that in other ages or countries, different doctrines have been held on the basis of different authorities. And

"The whole function of thought is to produce habits of action."

—CHARLES SANDERS PEIRCE

they will ask themselves whether there is any reason to rate their beliefs higher than the beliefs of those who have been brought up differently.[*] These reflections "give rise to doubts in their minds" (*FB*, 238). In the long run, authority does not work any better than tenacity in settling opinion.

The unsatisfactory character of the first two methods gives rise to the third, which Peirce calls both *the method of natural preferences* and the *a priori method*. Here we accept what seems "obvious," or "agreeable to reason," or "self-evident," or "clear and distinct." Our opinions are neither those we just happen to have nor those imposed by an authority; they are those we arrive at after reflection, conversation with others, and taking thought.

The best examples of such a method, Peirce thinks, are the great metaphysical systems from Plato through Hegel. But history seems to show that one person's self-evidence is another's absurdity, and the method

---

[*]Experience with certain sorts of "fanatics" may make one doubt whether Peirce is altogether correct here.

[*]Compare once again the example cited by Herodotus so long ago, p. 45. Peirce, however, does *not* draw the conclusion of Herodotus, that "custom is king over all."

makes of inquiry something similar to the development of taste; but taste, unfortunately, is always more or less a matter of fashion, and accordingly metaphysicians have never come to any fixed agreement, but the pendulum has swung backward and forward between a more material and a more spiritual philosophy, from the earliest times to the latest. (*FB,* 241)

Again we have an unstable and hence unsatisfactory method for settling our opinions.*

What we need is some method

by which our beliefs may be determined by nothing human, but by some external permanency—by something upon which our thinking has no effect. . . . It must be something which affects, or might affect, every man. And, though these affections are necessarily as various as are individual conditions, yet the method must be such that the ultimate conclusion of every man shall be the same. Such is the method of science. Its fundamental hypothesis, restated in more familiar language, is this: There are Real things, whose characters are entirely independent of our opinions about them; those Reals affect our senses according to regular laws, and, though our sensations are as different as our relations to the objects, yet, by taking advantage of the laws of perception, we can ascertain by reasoning how things really and truly are, and any man, if he have sufficient experience and he reason enough about it, will be led to the one true conclusion. (*FB,* 242–243)

Several features of the fourth method, the *method of science,* are distinctive. First, there is the attempt to make our beliefs responsive to something *independent* of what any of us thinks—or would like to think; in various ways, the first three methods lack precisely this feature. Second, we see that the method of science is decidedly a *public* method: There is to be no reliance on what is peculiar to you or to me; our beliefs are to be determined by what can affect you *and* me *and* anyone else who inquires. Again, this public character is lacking in the first three methods. Third, because of this essentially

public character, the *social impulse* (which wrecks the first three methods) will not undermine opinion that is settled in this scientific way.

According to Peirce's conception of science, however, it rests on an assumption, or "hypothesis" that there actually is some reality independent of our thinking about it. Suppose we ask, Why should we grant this assumption?* For one thing, the practice of science does not lead us to doubt the assumption; indeed, Peirce holds, the method "has had the most wonderful triumphs in the way of settling opinion" (*FB,* 249). In this regard, too, it is strikingly different from the other methods: It works! But the fundamental reason to grant this assumption has to do with the very nature of belief and doubt. Peirce's thoughts on this score are original and deep. We need to look at them.

Belief and Doubt

We have been examining methods of "fixing" belief or settling our opinions. But what is it to have a belief? And what is it like to doubt? Doubting and believing are clearly different, but how? Peirce finds three differences: (1) The sensation of believing is different from that of doubting; they just feel different. (2) We are strongly disposed to escape doubt but are content when we have a belief—at least until we are led to doubt it again by some surprise the world has in store for us. (3) The most profound difference, however, gets us to the very nature of belief and doubt, for a belief is a *habit,* and doubt is the lack of such a habit. This needs explaining.

Do you believe the world is (roughly) round? Let's assume you do. What is it to have this belief? It is not a matter of having a thought in your mind; presumably, you have believed this for a long time, although you have not been constantly thinking that thought. And it would be wrong to say that you believe it only when you have this thought actively in mind. Belief, Peirce says, "is not a momentary

---

*Compare Hume's impatience with intuition as a foundation for knowledge, pp. 399–401.

*After all, this seems to be the central issue in modern epistemology; it is what Descartes' methodical doubt undermines and what Hegel's idealism denies. How can Peirce be so naive?

mode of consciousness" (*WPI,* 279). Nor does it "make us act at once, but puts us into such a condition that we shall behave in a certain way, when the occasion arises" (*FB,* 231). So if you believe the world is round, you are in a "condition" that leads you to behave in the following ways: If someone asks you whether the world is flat, you say, "No, it is round"; if you win a trip "around the world," you accept it gladly; if you see a picture of the world taken from a satellite, you say, "Yes, that is what I expected it would look like." If you are on the interstate highway in Kansas, you drive confidently and do not worry about running your car off the edge. Being *disposed to behave* in these various ways —and more—is what it is to have the belief that the world is round. To have a belief is to have a habit that allows you to act confidently in the world, expecting that your actions in given circumstances will fulfill their purposes.

Doubting, on the other hand, is being in an uncertain state; it is the lack of a settled habit and so involves not knowing what to do in a given situation. That is why we struggle to escape doubt; it is essentially an anxious and irritating state. Peirce calls the struggle to escape doubt and attain the condition of belief *inquiry,* though he admits that sometimes it is not a very apt term. Inquiry, then, is an attempt to recover the calm satisfactoriness of *knowing what to do when,* which is characteristic of belief. And Peirce is convinced, as we have seen, that only the public, intersubjective methods of scientific inquiry will work in the long run to carry us from doubt to fixed belief.

Three things are essential to inquiry: a stimulus, an end or goal, and a method. Here is how Peirce thinks about these things:

- Stimulus: doubt
- End: settlement of opinion
- Method: science

We need to explore further each of the first two factors. Let us begin with some reflections on doubt.

According to all the pragmatists, inquiry (indeed, thinking in general) always begins with a felt problem. But, they say, not everything that has been thought by philosophers to be problematic really is so.

> Some philosophers have imagined that to start an inquiry it was only necessary to utter a question whether orally or by setting it down upon paper, and have even recommended us to begin our studies with questioning everything! But the mere putting of a proposition into the interrogative form does not stimulate the mind to any struggle after belief. There must be a real and living doubt, and without this all discussion is idle. (*FB,* 232)

Peirce obviously has Descartes in mind.* Perplexed by the contradictory things he had been taught, Descartes decides to "doubt everything" until he should come upon something "so clear and distinct" that he could not possibly doubt it. Descartes is embarked on what Dewey is to call "the quest for certainty."

But Peirce simply cannot take this project of methodical doubt seriously. This is not, he thinks "a real and living doubt"; it is only a "make-believe" (*WPI,* 278). To propose that one begin by doubting everything, Peirce remarks, is to suppose that doubting is "as easy as lying."

> We cannot begin with complete doubt. We must begin with all the prejudices which we actually have when we enter upon the study of philosophy. These prejudices are not to be dispelled by a maxim, for they are things which it does not occur to us *can* be questioned. Hence this initial skepticism will be a mere self-deception, and not real doubt; and no one who follows the Cartesian method will ever be satisfied until he has formally recovered all those beliefs which in form he has given up. It is, therefore, as useless a preliminary as going to the North Pole would be in order to get to Constantinople by coming down regularly upon a meridian.† A person may, it is true, in the course of his studies, find reason to doubt what he began by believing; but in

---

*Review Descartes' first *Meditation.*

†Peirce's sarcastic comment about the detour to the North Pole refers to the fact that Descartes, shortly after "doubting everything," had once again proved—now on a certain foundation!—the existence of God and the distinctness and immortality of the soul, the existence and nature of the external world, and much more that he claimed he had "suspended judgment" about.

that case he doubts because he has a positive reason for it, and not on account of the Cartesian maxim. Let us not pretend to doubt in philosophy what we do not doubt in our hearts. (*SCFI,* 156–157)

Do you call it *doubting* to write down on a piece of paper that you doubt? If so, doubt has nothing to do with any serious business. But do not make believe; if pedantry has not eaten all the reality out of you, recognize, as you must, that there is much that you do not doubt, in the least. (*WPI,* 278)

What is the basis of Peirce's condemnation of "make-believe" doubt? It rests on his analysis of what it is to believe something. To believe, as we have seen, is to be possessed of a habit, to have a disposition to behave in certain ways in certain situations; to doubt is to be without such a habit—not to know what to do when. But if that is so, to say "I doubt everything" while going about eating bread rather than stones, opening doors rather than walking into them, and carrying on all the normal business of living is "a mere self-deception." There is much we do not doubt at all, and we should not "pretend to doubt in philosophy what we do not doubt in our hearts."

It is quite possible, of course, that our experiences will lead us to doubt things that we had not doubted before; the world often surprises us. But then these are *real doubts,* doubts that pose real problems and urge us on to inquiry because we no longer know how to act. This is very different from a philosopher who sits in his dressing gown before the fire and says, "I doubt everything."

Peirce's critique of Descartes' starting point, then, comes to this: (1) It is impossible, since we cannot suspend judgment about everything while continuing to live; and (2) it is futile.* What we need is not an absolutely certain starting point, but a method of improving the beliefs that, to begin with, we do not imagine *can* be doubted. We must start where we are, with all the beliefs we actually have; only *real* doubts are to count in nudging us away from them. As long as our beliefs work for us, we will have no motivation to question them.

_____

*Compare Hume's critique of "antecedent skepticism," p. 423. The similarities are striking, but Peirce's criticism is based on a deeper conception of belief.

You can perhaps appreciate why Peirce occasionally thinks "practicalism" would be a suitable term for his thought.

We might also wonder whether Peirce has correctly identified the end of inquiry. Can the settlement of opinion really suffice as the end or goal of our inquiries? Isn't that being satisfied with too little? Surely, we are inclined to think, What we are after in science and philosophy is the *truth.* Couldn't we settle our opinions and still be *wrong?*

Truth and Reality

Peirce points out first that we invariably think each of our beliefs to be true as long as we have no cause to doubt it.* It is only in that uneasy state of doubt that we wonder about the truth of our beliefs. Second, when doubt ceases, so does inquiry. If we are satisfied with the belief we come to, what sense does it make to wonder, abstractly, whether it might still be false? If our belief is fixed, we wouldn't know what else to do to determine whether it is true or false.

Finally, Peirce asks us to consider what we mean by "true":

If your terms "truth" and "falsity" are taken in such senses as to be definable in terms of doubt and belief and the course of experience (as for example they would be if you were to define the "truth" as that to a belief in which belief would tend if it were to tend indefinitely toward absolute fixity), well and good: in that case, you are only talking about doubt and belief. But if by truth and falsity you mean something not definable in terms of doubt and belief in any way, then you are talking of entities of whose existence you can know nothing, and which Ockham's razor would clean shave off. (*WPI,* 279)

What motivates those "doubts" that we raise occasionally even when we are, for all practical purposes, satisfied with our beliefs? It is the suspicion that our beliefs may not, for all their practical usefulness, *correspond* with reality—that reality may, for all our care and investigation, still be quite different. And this might be the case, we suspect,

_____

*Compare Hegel for a similar point, pp. 465–466.

even if we could in no way discover the discrepancy. But if that is what we mean, Peirce says, then we "are talking of entities of whose existence [we] can know nothing." **Ockham's razor,** that principle of parsimony in theorizing, would shave them clean off.*

We do not and cannot stabilize our beliefs, Peirce argues, by noticing they are true—by seeing that they correspond with a fact. We never do see this. Peirce's argument for this is complicated, but we can get the gist of it quite simply by using an example he gives. Consider a triangle with one side horizontal at the top and its apex pointing down. And now think of it being dipped into still water.

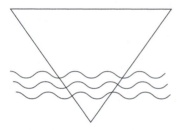

Let the water represent some fact, and let the waterline across the triangle represent some cognition of that fact. Dipping the triangle deeper into the water represents a more and more adequate understanding of the fact, and the horizontal base of the triangle may represent a highly developed understanding of that fact (as we might have in some science). The waterline will be such that, no matter how little the triangle is dipped into the water, other horizontal lines can be drawn between it and the apex. If the distance from the apex up to the waterline is a, then other lines could be drawn at $\frac{1}{2}a$, $\frac{1}{4}a$, and so on—no matter how small a is.

The question is this: Can we get a *pure* conception of the fact, untainted by any previous theorizing? Can we see the fact *bare,* or *uncontaminated* by any previous cognitions? This is what would be necessary to settle our beliefs by seeing whether they correspond to reality. We would have to be able to

apprehend the fact quite independently of any beliefs we already have and then compare that fact with our beliefs. But we can no more do this, Peirce argues, than we can find a waterline on the triangle below which no other line can be drawn. All our cognitions, beliefs, hypotheses, theories, and understandings are dependent on other items of that same kind; none of them provides a *test* of correspondence with a fact independent of the beliefs we already have when we experience that fact.*

It would be easy to draw the wrong conclusion from this claim, however.† It would be easy to suppose that this makes impossible the understanding of those "external permanencies" that it is supposed to be the genius of science to discern—of those things "upon which our thinking has no effect" (*FB,* 242). But Peirce remarks that although

> everything which is present to us is a phenomenal manifestation of ourselves, this does not prevent its being a phenomenon of something without us, just as a rainbow is at once a manifestation both of the sun and the rain. (*SCFI,* 169)

What Peirce's argument does do, however, is to undercut any claim to be *certain* about a belief on the ground that it represents a "pure intuition," uncontaminated by prior beliefs. This is an implication Peirce is happy to welcome since, as we have seen, he has given up the project of basing our knowledge on a foundation of certain truths in any case. What counts, again, is whether we have a method to *improve* our beliefs, not whether we can be *certain* of them.‡

---

*William of Ockham, the fourteenth-century theologian and philosopher, formulates this principle: Do not multiply entities beyond necessity. It is a rule that bids us to make do with the simplest hypothesis in explaining the facts. For a brief look at some of Ockham's views, see pp. 292–295.

*Here Peirce agrees with Hegel's attack on immediacy. To try to say what an experience is *of* without relying on the concepts and theories we bring to that experience is quite impossible. There is no unmediated knowledge, no "theory-free" apprehension of "the facts." Wilfrid Sellars has called the opinion to the contrary "the myth of the given." For the Hegelian view, see pp. 467–469. For Sellars', see pp. 732–733.

†So easy that it is quite regularly done these days.

‡You may be reminded here of the saying of Xenophanes, the pre-Socratic. "The gods have not revealed all things from the beginning to mortals; but, by seeking, men find out, in time, what is better. No man knows the truth, nor will there be a man who has knowledge about the gods and what I say about everything. For even if he were to hit by chance upon the whole truth, he himself would not be aware of having done so, but each forms

But now we must ask, How does Peirce think of truth? If we cannot understand fixation of belief in terms of attaining truth, he suggests we try to define truth in terms of belief and doubt. He offers several attempts at such a definition:

> The opinion which is fated to be ultimately agreed to by all who investigate, is what we mean by the truth. (*HMIC,* 268)

> that to a belief in which belief would tend if it were to tend indefinitely toward absolute fixity. (*WPI,* 279)

> a state of belief unassailable by doubt. (*WPI,* 279)

Note that each of these definitions makes truth dependent on the states of belief and doubt, not the other way around. A true belief, according to them, is a fixed belief—not fixed just for the moment, but *absolutely* fixed, not just undoubted, but *unassailable* by doubt. The truth about some subject matter is what investigators using scientific methods, if they were persistent, would eventually come to agree upon. That is what truth *means.*

Let's draw out some consequences. The truth is a kind of *ideal,* one for which we strive in our inquiries. Because it is what investigators *will* agree upon, no present agreements (no matter how broad and deep) can suffice to give us absolute confidence that what we *now* believe is true. It is always possible that further investigation will upset present beliefs. Nonetheless, it is quite possible that many of our present beliefs are true. What does this mean? It means that many of our beliefs are ones that future investigators will continue to reaffirm in the light of their inquiries; these beliefs are in fact "unassailable by doubt" because the world holds no surprises that will upset them, though again we cannot ever be certain that this is so for any given belief.

Note, moreover, the truth is something *public.* It is not the case that truth is relative to individuals or cultures. *Evidence* may be relative in such a way, and what one individual has good reason to believe may differ from what another has good reason to believe—because the one may have access to evidence that the other lacks. But it is the *community of inquirers* that defines what is true, not any individual.

We can see how this understanding of truth fits in with Peirce's practicalism by noting a further implication:

> For truth is neither more nor less than that character of a proposition which consists in this, that belief in the proposition would, with sufficient experience and reflection, lead us to such conduct as would tend to satisfy the desires we should then have. To say that truth means more than this is to say that it has no meaning at all.[2]

Beliefs, being habits, invariably lead to conduct in conjunction with desires that move us to act. For example, we believe there is a hamburger before us and, being hungry, pick it up and take a bite. The belief is a true one if, when we act on it, our desire can be satisfied and not frustrated. If I experience the mouth-watering flavor of a Big Mac, then the belief that it was indeed a hamburger is a true one. If my teeth meet a rubber imitation, my belief is a false one; the falsity is testified to by the fact that my action does not satisfy my desire to eat.[*] True beliefs, then, are those that can be relied on in our practical activity in the world (including the world of the scientific laboratory). William James puts it this way: They are the beliefs that *pay.* But Peirce would be quick to add that they must pay *for the community of inquirers* and in the *long run.*

It is in terms of truth, so understood, that Peirce thinks we must also understand the concept of reality. What do we mean by "the real"? Peirce says that we may define it as

---

his own opinion." For a discussion of this saying, see pp. 17–18. Peirce would add two caveats: (1) Xenophanes is right about no one's knowing the truth only if knowing the truth entails having certainty about it; (2) the "seeking" must be by scientific methods if we are to find out "what is better"; that is how each is to form "his own opinion."

*This notion of satisfaction is an important one for the pragmatists. In the thought of William James, it is subject to certain ambiguities and provoked the outcry of critics: "What? Do you mean to say that any belief that *satisfies you* is to be counted a true one?" But you can see that in Peirce's hands the public nature of truth, together with the requirement of agreement by a community of scientific inquirers, makes this rebuke inapplicable to him.

that whose characters are independent of what anybody may think them to be. (*HMIC,* 266)

But though that is a perfectly correct definition, it is not, he thinks, a very helpful one. It does not tell us how to recognize reality or give us any instructions about how to find it.

A more satisfactory explanation can be given in terms of truth (which, remember, is itself defined in terms of belief fixed by the methods of scientific investigation). Peirce remarks that scientists are convinced that different lines of inquiry into the same subject matter will come eventually to the same result:

> One man may investigate the velocity of light by studying the transits of Venus and the aberration of the stars; another by the oppositions of Mars and the eclipses of Jupiter's satellites; a third by the method of Fizeau; a fourth by that of Foucault; a fifth by the motions of the curves of Lissajous; a sixth, a seventh, an eighth, and a ninth, may follow the different methods of comparing the measures of statical and dynamical electricity. They may at first obtain different results, but, as each perfects his method and his processes, the results are found to move steadily together toward a destined centre. So with all scientific research. Different minds may set out with the most antagonistic views, but the progress of investigation carries them by a force outside of themselves to one and the same conclusion. This activity of thought by which we are carried, not where we wish, but to a fore-ordained goal, is like the operation of destiny. No modification of the point of view taken, no selection of other facts for study, no natural bend of mind even, can enable a man to escape the predestinate opinion. This great hope is embodied in the conception of truth and reality. The opinion which is fated to be ultimately agreed to by all who investigate, is what we mean by the truth, and the object represented in this opinion is the real. That is the way I would explain reality. (*HMIC,* 268)

According to this view, reality is *what true opinion says it is*. And true opinion is an opinion that further scientific inquiry will never upset. But here is a problem. Doesn't this understanding of reality make it dependent on us in a way that the former definition (in terms of what is independent of what anyone may think) does not? Hasn't Peirce contra-

dicted himself here? He considers this objection and says that

> reality is independent, not necessarily of thought in general, but only of what you or I or any finite number of men may think about it,* . . . though the object of the final opinion depends on what that opinion is, yet what that opinion is does not depend on what you or I or any man thinks. Our perversity and that of others may indefinitely postpone the settlement of opinion; it might even conceivably cause an arbitrary proposition to be universally accepted as long as the human race should last. Yet even that would not change the nature of the belief, which alone could be the result of investigation carried sufficiently far; and if, after the extinction of our race, another should arise with faculties and disposition for investigation, that true opinion must be the one which they would ultimately come to. "Truth crushed to earth shall rise again," and the opinion which would finally result from investigation does not depend on how anybody may actually think. But the reality of that which is real does depend on the real fact that investigation is destined to lead, at last, if continued long enough, to a belief in it. (*HMIC,* 269)

Reality, then, can be independent of the inquiries of any finite number of individuals and yet be what would be revealed in inquiry, provided inquiry is scientific and carried "sufficiently far." For Peirce, then, *science* is the *criterion of the real*; not science as it exists at any given stage, of course, but that ideal science toward which scientific activity is even now moving.[†]

---

*Compare Parmenides saying that "thought and being are the same," p. 26.

†Here we have a decisively different conception of the problem of the criterion; it is not a criterion from which to start—as though we had to solve that problem first, before we could do any intellectual work. Peirce would agree that if we think of the problem of the criterion in that way, it is unsolvable; it requires that we know something before we can know something, and skepticism will be the result. According to Peirce's view, however, we know enough about the nature of the criterion to know that we do not now have it in hand; yet we also know how to make definite and regular progress toward it. Peirce's view has certain similarities to Hegel's idea that "absolute knowledge" lies at the end of a process of historical development and that nothing prior to that point can be certain; it differs in recommending

The real, then, is that which, sooner or later, information and reasoning would finally result in, and which is therefore independent of the vagaries of me and you. Thus the very origin of the conception of reality shows that this conception essentially involves the notion of a COMMUNITY, without definite limits, and capable of a definite increase of knowledge. And so those two series of cognition—the real and the unreal—consist of those which, at a time sufficiently future, the community will always continue to reaffirm; and of those which, under the same conditions, will ever after be denied. Now, a proposition whose falsity can never be discovered, and the error of which therefore is absolutely incognizable, contains, upon our principle, absolutely no error. Consequently, that which is thought in these cognitions is the real, as it really is. There is nothing, then, to prevent our knowing outward things as they really are, and it is most likely that we do thus know them in numberless cases, although we can never be absolutely certain of doing so in any special case. (*SCFI*, 186–187)

Two comments: (1) Peirce is here denying the Kantian doctrine that we *cannot* know things as they really are, but only as they appear to us.* There is no essentially hidden thing-in-itself; things are as they reveal themselves to inquiry. (2) His ground for affirming that we can know things "as they really are" is the "principle" that there is no error possible where it is impossible to discover it. Why does he believe this? To understand his reasoning here, we must turn to what Peirce has to say about *meaning*.

First let us summarize a main theme in all we have examined so far. It goes by the name of **fallibilism:** a readiness to acknowledge that one's knowledge is not yet completely satisfactory, together with an intense desire to find things out.†

Peirce would wholeheartedly agree with an aphorism formulated in the early twentieth century by Otto Neurath, one of a group of thinkers known as logical positivists.

> We are like sailors who must rebuild their ship on the open sea, never able to dismantle it in dry-dock and to reconstruct it there out of the best materials.[3]

There is, perhaps, no belief of ours immune from possible revision. But, like the sailors on the open sea, we cannot replace all our beliefs at once. If we revise certain convictions, we do it only by standing on some others, which, for the time being, we must regard as stable.

1. Why, according to Peirce, is the method of science superior to the methods of tenacity, authority, and natural preferences for arriving at fixed beliefs?
2. What is it, actually, to believe something? To doubt something? And what is the function of intellectual inquiry?
3. What is Peirce's critique of Descartes' project of arriving at certainty through doubting?
4. How does Peirce understand truth? How is this different from the way, say, Aristotle (and most of the tradition) understands it? (See pp. 162–163.)
5. How does Peirce understand reality? If you asked him, "Do we now know reality?" what would he say?
6. What is fallibilism? How is it related to the quest for certainty?

Meaning

Peirce says that

> pragmatism is, in itself, no doctrine of metaphysics, no attempt to determine any truth of things. It is merely a method of ascertaining the meanings of hard words and of abstract concepts. (*SP,* 317)

We have already, as a matter of fact, seen this method at work on the concepts of belief and doubt, truth and reality. But now we must examine it directly.

---

empirical science as the method by which to arrive at "fixed beliefs." (See the discussion of Hegel, pp. 464–470).

*Review Kant's distinction between noumena and phenomena, pp. 439–441.

†Once more you should look over that fragment of Xenophanes discussed on pp. 17–18. Compare also Socrates' confession of ignorance, together with his passionate search for the truth, pp. 63–66. And note the similarity to Kierkegaard's view of our relation to the truth, p. 506.

Peirce restricts his doctrine of meaning to what he calls *intellectual concepts,* which he contrasts with *mere subjective feelings.* An intellectual concept is any concept "upon the structure of which, arguments concerning objective fact may hinge" (*SP,* 318). Examples are concepts such as "hard," "ten centimeters," "lithium," and "believes." We may get a better feel for what is distinctive about them by looking at how Peirce characterizes subjective feelings.

> Had the light which, as things are, excites in us the sensation of blue, always excited the sensation of red, and *vice versa,* however great a difference that might have made in our feelings, it could have made none in the force of any argument. In this respect, the qualities of hard and soft strikingly contrast with those of red and blue; because while red and blue name mere subjective feelings only, hard and soft express the factual behaviour of the thing under the pressure of a knife-edge. . . . My pragmatism, having nothing to do with qualities of feeling, permits me to hold that the predication of such a quality is just what it seems, and has nothing to do with anything else. Hence, could two qualities of feeling everywhere be interchanged, nothing but feelings could be affected. Those qualities have no intrinsic significations beyond themselves. (*SP,* 318)

Peirce here presents a version of a thought experiment called the *inverted spectrum.* It is often given in a two-person setting. Suppose the sensation I have when I see a ripe tomato is qualitatively identical to the sensation you have when you look at the sky on a clear day, and vice versa. Could we discover this? Apparently we could not, since you cannot directly access my sensations, nor I yours—and everything else would be the same. I would have learned to call ripe tomatoes "red" (doesn't everybody?) despite the fact that the sensation they produce in me is the sensation you call blue. If someone asked me to bring them something red, I might bring a tomato. And I would call the sky "blue," even though the sensation I have when I look at it is the same as the sensation you have when looking at a ripe tomato. Such an inversion of qualities would make absolutely no difference to our behavior, our language, our reasoning, or our sci-

ence. They are "mere subjective feelings only." In a fairly clear sense, such sensations have no *meaning.* Nothing else depends on them.

Contrast such a sensation with the quality of hardness (to use Peirce's example). Whether something is hard makes a difference to all those things sensations do not affect: our behavior (we will not be able to crush it in our hand like a sponge), our language (if we call something hard, we communicate something quite definite to our hearers), our reasoning (from the premise that an item is hard, we can conclude that a knife edge will not easily divide it), and our science. "Hard" is a good example of an intellectual concept. It has *implications* that must be understood if we are to understand the concept. If you do not understand that a knife edge will not easily divide a hard object, you do not understand what "hard" means.

These implications have to do with the *behavior* of the objects that are correctly called "hard." They will behave in certain ways under certain circumstances. Indeed, even if a knife edge is never actually drawn across an object, to call it "hard" is to imply that *if* a knife edge *were* put to it, it *would not* divide easily. So the implications of an intellectual concept include what Peirce calls the "would-be's" and the "would-do's" of objects. These would-be's and would-do's, are of course, nothing else than habits or dispositions. The rock has a disposition to resist a knife edge; and by virtue of this disposition it is rightly called "hard."

We have looked at one example of an intellectual concept and have noted the ways in which it contrasts with pure subjective sensations. But now we should ask, How can we decide what an intellectual concept means? And this is the same as to ask, How can we make our ideas clear?

> The very first lesson that we have a right to demand that logic shall teach us is, how to make our ideas clear; and a most important one it is, depreciated only by minds who stand in need of it. To know what we think, to be masters of our own meaning, will make a solid foundation for great and weighty thought. . . . It is terrible to see how a single unclear idea, a single formula without meaning, lurking in a young man's head, will sometimes act like an obstruction of inert matter in an artery,

hindering the nutrition of the brain, and condemning its victim to pine away in the fullness of his intellectual vigor and in the midst of intellectual plenty. (*HMIC*, 251–252)

Peirce distinguishes three grades of clearness in ideas. We may first "have such an acquaintance with the idea as to have become familiar with it, and to have lost all hesitancy in recognizing it in ordinary cases" (*HMIC*, 252). If we can identify samples of quartz, for example, from among a variety of stones presented to us, then "quartz" is clear to us to this first degree. A second grade of clearness is provided by a verbal definition, such as one finds in a dictionary and could memorize (or write down in an exam, perhaps). But to attain the third grade of clearness we must follow this rule:

> Consider what effects that might conceivably have practical bearings, we conceive the object of our conception to have. Then, our conception of these effects is the whole of our conception of the object. (*HMIC*, 258)

Let us examine this rule carefully. The first thing to note is that the meaning of an intellectual concept is always something that itself has meaning. Meanings are not things; they are not brute facts; they are not sensations or actions. If you ask what "hard" means, it is not a proper answer for me to clunk you on the head with a rock. Or, if I do, then the meaning of "hard" is still not the rock; nor is it the sensation you felt when you were struck. The word "hard" is a *sign,* and its meaning must be another sign. (We will examine the nature of signs in a moment.)

Next, consider the idea of "effects, which might conceivably have practical bearings." If we ask what "hard" means, we are asking for a conception that can apply to objects that are hard; we are asking what effects these objects have that we can notice, that is, have some impact upon us—for instance, that they will not be scratched by many other substances.

Finally, note that Peirce holds that the whole of our conception of these effects is the whole of the conception we are trying to clarify. There is nothing in our conception of "hard" beyond our conception of these effects. Peirce offers a procedure for identifying these effects:

> Proceed according to such and such a general rule. Then, if such and such a concept is applicable to such and such an object, the operation will have such and such a general result; and conversely. (*SP,* 331)

This is a formula for what is sometimes called *operational definition*. Note that applications of this procedure will always have two parts: There will be an operation performed and a result observed. Let us see how it might work in the case of "hard." We can define "*x* is hard" in this way:

- If you apply a knife edge to *x,* you will not cut it.
- If you throw *x* forcefully at a window, the window will (probably) break.
- If you press your hand on *x, x* will resist the pressure of your hand.

Note that in each case the structure is the same; an operation is specified, and a result is observed. Some action is performed and in consequence we have an experience of some kind. Note also that an indefinite number of such tests can be made, and all of them together make up the meaning of the concept "hard."

By employing such operational definitions, we can attain the third grade of clearness in ideas. With such clarity we can not only apply the concept to familiar examples or give a verbal definition, but also clear away the fogginess that so often seems to surround our ideas. We sometimes hear that we know how gravity *works*—that is, we know its laws—but we don't know what it *is*. The same is sometimes said of force—that we understand its effects, but not what it *is*. But if Peirce is right about the structure of clear ideas, this is just confusion. Once you know the laws of gravity and the equations of force, once you can predict the results of certain operations correctly so that your experience confirms your predictions, you *do know* what gravity and force are; for there is nothing more in your ideas of them than these effects, which you admit you are clear about. What else could you possibly mean?

The idea which the word force excites in our minds has no other function than to affect our actions, and these actions can have no reference to force otherwise than through its effects. Consequently, if we know what the effects of force are, we are acquainted with every fact which is implied in saying that a force exists, and there is nothing more to know. (*HMIC*, 265)

We have already seen this procedure at work, clarifying our ideas of belief and doubt, truth and reality. Let's review. In what does your *belief* that the earth is round consist? The answer is given in terms of operation and result: If you are offered a trip around the world, you will not say, "What? Are you crazy?" What does it mean to *doubt* whether a certain food is spoiled? If it is offered to you, you will be uncertain whether to eat it. What is it for a belief to be *true*? If the community were to inquire sufficiently long about it, there would come a point where the belief would stabilize. What do we mean when we claim that something is *real*? That inquiry concerning it would survive all possible tests. In each case, Peirce has been striving all along for that third grade of clearness, and in each case he applies that hypothetical structure of operation and result. In each case, the operations are such as any member of the community might (in principle) perform, and the results are public in the sense that anyone might observe them. There might, of course, be private associations or feelings associated with these terms—especially with "truth" and "reality"—but these are not part of the meaning of the terms. Language, after all, is a social convention we learn as children and teach others. Were its meanings not founded in something public and common, neither the learning nor the teaching of language would be explicable.

We should note one other consequence of Peirce's discussion of meaning. Consider two beliefs that seem to be different; perhaps they just have a different feel to them or are expressed in different words. Are they really different? If the practical consequences of the two are not different, "then no mere differences in the manner of consciousness of them can make them different beliefs, any more than playing a tune in different keys is

playing different tunes" (*HMIC*, 255). William James was later to put this point in terms of a slogan:

Every difference must make a difference.

If there is no difference in practical effects, then there is no difference in meaning. Peirce draws out the radical consequence of this principle:

It will serve to show that almost every proposition of ontological metaphysics is either meaningless gibberish—one word being defined by other words, and they by still others, without any real conception ever being reached—or else is downright absurd; so that all such rubbish being swept away, what will remain of philosophy will be a series of problems capable of investigation by the observational methods of the true sciences. (*WPI*, 282)

This seems to be an announcement of the end of philosophy, its true work being taken over by the empirical sciences. Indeed, some twentieth-century thinkers draw just that conclusion from similar premises about meaning.[*] Peirce himself, however, goes on to argue for a metaphysics of absolute idealism in which mind is the fundamental fact in reality. Because he thinks this conclusion can be warranted on the basis of methods continuous with those of the sciences, he believes that his metaphysics conforms to this radical principle.

To understand the essentials of Peirce's view better, let us contrast it with that of David Hume.[†] There are some clear similarities to be noted first. Both are interested in getting rid of what they see as fakery and quackery in metaphysics, and both are convinced that clarity about meaning will be helpful in dismissing much of it as sophistry and illusion.

But the differences are more striking than the similarities:

- Hume's method of certifying the meaning of a term is essentially *contemplative*. The philosopher sits in his study and muses over his expe-

---

[*] Compare the logical positivists, pp. 614–618. See also Martin Heidegger for a differently motivated but similar conclusion on p. 680.
[†] See "The Theory of Ideas," in Chapter 15.

riences; if he finds some sensation in his memory from which the idea in question has arisen, it is accepted—otherwise not. For Peirce, on the other hand, the method of clarifying our ideas is *active*. To find out what a term means, we have to *do* something and then experience the consequences.

- Hume's criterion tends to be *individualistic* and *private;* the sensations I have had are not likely to be exactly the sensations you have had. Peirce's criterion is emphatically *public;* he will admit as a practical consequence nothing that could not be experienced by *anyone.**

- Whereas Hume's investigation of the meaning of our ideas is oriented toward the *past,* toward their origin, Peirce's is *future-looking,* toward use.

- These differences have a consequence. Whereas for Hume the meanings of words are pretty much *fixed* in the light of our past experience, Peirce is able to think of us as much more flexible and *creative* with respect to language. What we do (together with the effects of those actions) determines the meanings of words. And what we do is under our control (though the result is not). This consequence is quite in line with Peirce's acceptance of evolution and the possibility of progress. Language, too, evolves.

In fact, therefore, men and words reciprocally educate each other; each increase of a man's information involves, and is involved by, a corresponding increase of a word's information. (*SCFI,* 189)

The meanings of our words are not cut from stone once and for all; they change as relevant information about their objects changes—because for them to have meaning at all is for them to be part of a network of implications. As information changes, so do these implications. The meaning of "heat," for example, is no longer what it was in the days before modern thermodynamics.

Signs

A consideration of some elements of Peirce's doctrine of signs will bring us full circle. The entities that have meaning Peirce calls "signs." Here again Peirce is extremely original; he calls himself a "pioneer," a "backwoodsman," and "first-comer" in this area. His discussion is very complex and never systematically worked out. We concentrate only on several central features.

Peirce gives the term "sign" (as he does "habit") a very wide sense. He means to include the simplest cases of communication in the animal world as well as the most sophisticated language of science. He believes there is one property that is common to all signs and that differentiates them from anything not a sign. All signs have a certain *triadic structure:* A *sign* stands for an *object* to an *interpretant.** Being a sign, then, requires all three of these elements. We do, of course, sometimes just say that "*a* means *b,*" but Peirce holds this is an incomplete formulation; if it is spelled out in full, we must say that "*a* means *b* to *c.*" For *a* couldn't *mean b* except to some interpreter of *a.*

It is from this triadic structure that modern linguistics and philosophy of language has grown. We may consider language simply as a set of markers or tokens and investigate the permissible relations among them; such an investigation of rules relating signs to each other is called *syntax.* Second, we may

---

*In addition, remember that Peirce does not count subjective sensations as part of meaning in any case; when he refers to what anyone can experience, he is talking about something that is already interpreted, already a sign. It is not the pure *sensation* of blue that counts as the relevant experience, but the *judgment* "That is blue" elicited from us in the presence of certain objects, together with all the implications concerning its relations to other colors, to light, to what we know of the surfaces of objects, to our sensory apparatus, and so on.

*We would normally speak here of an "interpreter," thinking primarily, no doubt, of a human who understands the sign. Peirce uses this odd term "interpretant" because he wants to be able to say that there are a variety of ways in which the meaning of a sign can be apprehended, interpretation by a human mind being only one. The behavior of bees in response to a bee dance indicating the direction of nectar (they fly in a certain direction) is, in his terms, an interpretant of the dance. But it would be strange to think of the flight of bees as an "interpreter" of the dance.

pay attention to the relation between words and what they are about—that is, what they stand for: the "word-world" relation. When we do this, we are considering the *semantics* of language. Finally, we may think about the way signs affect their users and hearers, and this is known as *pragmatics*.

Let us think for a moment of the semantic aspect of signs. Peirce notes three different ways that a sign can be related to its object. (1) The significance of the sign may depend on an actually existing *causal relation* between it and what it signifies. For example, dark clouds are a sign of rain and smoke a sign of fire. Thus does Robinson Crusoe infer that he is not alone on his island, for footprints in the sand *mean* another person. Signs that work in this way Peirce calls *indexes*. A weather vane, for example, is an index of the direction of the wind. (2) Some signs work because they *resemble* their object. Peirce calls these *icons*. The face in the rock at the Delaware Water Gap is an icon of an Indian. Photographs, as you should be able to see, are both indexes and icons. (3) Some signs are related to their objects in purely *conventional* or *arbitrary* ways. Peirce calls such signs *symbols*. Most of the words in human languages are like this. There is no natural relation between the color red and the word "red"—or, for that matter, "rot" or "rouge." These words stand for red things, rather than for square or heavy things, because a custom or convention of using them in that way has grown up.*

But they stand for red things only *to* some interpretant. Without an interpretant, a sign is just a brute fact; nothing, in short, is a sign unless it is used as a sign. What kinds of interpretants can there be? Peirce distinguishes three important kinds. (1) There are *emotional interpretants* for signs. Some words, for instance, produce a lot of feeling when heard or uttered ("freedom," for example), others very little. But the feeling itself is not just a brute fact; it has itself the nature of a sign; it is itself significant. A feeling of pride on observing the flag refers to one's nation just as surely as does the

flag itself. (2) There are also *energetic interpretants*. Peirce gives the example of a drill sergeant's order, "Ground arms!" One interpretant of this command is the actual movement by the troops as they lower their muskets to the ground. But by far the most important kind of interpretant is (3) the *logical*. And we need to examine this in more detail.

The first thing to be noted about a logical interpretant is that it is itself a sign. In fact, it is a sign that has the same meaning as the sign it interprets. A dictionary definition might be a good example: "vixen" is defined as "female fox." The latter is the interpretant, and you can see it is about the same class of objects as the former. But, Peirce says, such an interpretant cannot be the *final* or *ultimate* interpretant; because it is itself a sign, it calls for further interpretants of the same kind. And those interpretants require still others, and so on. Can this potential regress be brought to a halt?*

There is an ultimate interpretant, Peirce says. It is a *habit*. Though Peirce's discussion of these matters is somewhat obscure, we can understand his point in this way. One understands a word best when one goes beyond the first and second grades of clearness to the third.† That third grade of clearness, you recall, is given by a set of "if-then" sentences that specify a series of operations together with the results experienced in consequence of performing them. "*x* is hard" means "if you try to cut *x* with a knife, you will fail," and so on. A habit or disposition is itself precisely such a set of "if-thens." So having the *third grade of clearness* with respect to a concept is having a *habit with respect to the word* that expresses the concept. For example, if I really do understand "hard," then my behavior is such that *if* I want something I can cut with my knife, *then* I will select a stick rather than a stone to practice my whittling.

---

*This is a point Locke already made. See p. 378. But Peirce does not think such general terms stand for *ideas* in the mind—unless, of course, they are terms *for* such ideas.

*You should be reminded here of Descartes' second rule, which prescribes analysis into simples that are clear and distinct ideas requiring no further analysis (p. 322). And Hume, worried about the same problem, traces ideas back to their origin in sensations. Both are ways to halt the regress of meaning-giving. Peirce's way to halt this regress is distinctively different.
†See p. 576.

Consequently, the most perfect account of a concept that words can convey will consist in a description of the habit which that concept is calculated to produce. But how otherwise can a habit be described than by a description of the kind of action to which it gives rise, with the specification of the conditions and of the motive? (*SP*, 342)

We saw earlier that belief has the nature of a habit; we now see that coming to master the meaning of a word is itself a matter of attaining a habit. So the meaning of an intellectual concept is given by a logical interpretant, and each logical interpretant is subject to further interpretations until anchored finally in a habit of behavior. Two things follow: (1) A linguistic or conceptual sign can function *as a sign* only in the context of an entire working system of signs; nothing can be a sign in isolation; all by itself, a word has *no meaning.* This view is often called "holism." (2) Our entire intellectual life is tied to matters of behavior and experience, to action, and to the quest to establish habits (concepts and beliefs) that will serve us well. To this end, we modify the concepts and beliefs we begin with (and cannot help having), hoping to attain intellectual concepts that will prove ever more adequate to living in our community and in the world. As we have seen, Peirce recommends the methods of science as the way to attain more adequate habits—to "fix" our beliefs. And with this thought we have come full circle.

---

1. Contrast intellectual concepts with what Peirce calls mere subjective feelings. Could you be experiencing something different from what I am experiencing when we both look at lush grass? Would that matter? Could we find out?
2. What is Peirce's rule for attaining the "third grade of clearness" about our ideas?
3. What does James' slogan "Every difference must make a difference" mean?
4. Contrast Peirce's theory of meaning with that of Hume.
5. Distinguish syntax, semantics, and pragmatics.
6. Distinguish various kinds of signs. Of what sort is most of language composed?

John Dewey

Intellectually speaking, John Dewey was born in the year that Darwin published *On the Origin of Species by Means of Natural Selection.* He took seriously Darwin's incorporation of human life into nature and tried to work out its consequences for epistemology, metaphysics, and ethics. He lived a long life, from 1859 to 1952, and wrote voluminously on social, educational, and political matters, as well as on these more traditional philosophical topics. He was born in Vermont on the eve of the Civil War and lived through the time of tremendous industrial growth in America, the expansion westward, and both world wars. He lived through the revolution in physics that we associate with Einstein and contributed to theories that made scientific methods applicable also in sociology and psychology. He said of himself that the forces that influenced him and stimulated him to think came not from books, but "from persons and from situations" (*FAE,* 13).[4] He is one of the classic sources of pragmatic ideas in philosophy.

The Impact of Darwin

We are scarcely able to canvas everything Dewey contributed, even to pragmatic philosophy. But an examination of his *naturalism* in epistemology and metaphysics, together with his *theory of value,* will supplement our discussion of Peirce and give a good overview of the leading pragmatic themes. A 1909 lecture, "The Influence of Darwinism on Philosophy," sets the stage:

That the publication of the "Origin of Species" marked an epoch in the development of the natural sciences is well known to the layman. That the combination of the very words origin and species embodied an intellectual revolt and introduced a new intellectual temper is easily overlooked by the expert. The conceptions that had reigned in the philosophy of nature and knowledge for two thousand years, the conceptions that had become the familiar furniture of the mind, rested on the assumption of the superiority of the fixed and final; they rested upon treating change and origin as signs of defect and unreality. In laying hands upon the sacred ark of absolute permanency, in treating the forms that had been regarded as types of fixity and perfection as originating and passing away, the "Origin of Species" introduced a mode of thinking that in the end was bound to transform the logic of knowledge, and hence the treatment of morals, politics, and religion. (*IDP,* 3)

The ancient Greeks assume that to really know something, one has to grasp its essence, its form (*eidos*).* Scholastic philosophy in the Middle Ages, sharing this assumption, translates *eidos* as "species." The cardinal principle is that species (forms) are *fixed,* an assumption that would shape philosophy, science, ethics, and theology for two thousand years.

> The conception of *eidos,* species, a fixed form and final cause, was the central principle of knowledge as well as of nature. Upon it rested the logic of science. Change as change is mere flux and lapse; it insults intelligence. Genuinely to know is to grasp a permanent end that realizes itself through changes. . . . Completely to know is to relate all special forms to their one single end and good: pure contemplative intelligence. . . . The influence of Darwin upon philosophy resides in his having conquered the phenomena of life for the principle of transition, and thereby freed the new logic for application to mind and morals and life. When he said of species what Galileo had said of the earth, *e pur se muove,* he emancipated, once for all, genetic and experimental ideas as an organon of asking questions and looking for explanations. (*IDP,* 6–8)

Obviously Dewey sees a much broader significance to the achievement of Darwin than the merely biological. Dewey thinks there are just two

"At the best, all our endeavors look to the future and never attain certainty."

—JOHN DEWEY

fundamentally different ways to look at knowledge and our place in nature; either we must find "the appropriate objects and organs of knowledge in the mutual interactions of changing things," or we must "seek them in some transcendent and supernal region" (*IDP,* 6). It is Darwin's great merit, Dewey believes, that he has shown us the former path.

In the wake of Darwin's work, a great shift of attention and emphasis opens up. Intelligence becomes more concrete, more down-to-earth, more practical. And the new philosophy

> forswears inquiry after absolute origins and absolute finalities in order to explore specific values and the specific conditions that generate them. . . . Interest shifts from the wholesale essence back of special changes to the question of how special

---

*This is most clear in the work of Plato (see "Knowledge and Opinion," in Chapter 6); for him, knowledge has to be certain and its objects eternal and unchanging: the Forms. For Aristotle, form is always embedded in concrete substances, but he is no less insistent than his teacher Plato that the object of knowledge is always the form of a thing, and, as we have noted before, the dominant form is the one toward which a substance develops: its *final cause.* The final cause of all things, for Aristotle, is that pure actuality he calls the *unmoved mover,* or God.

changes serve and defeat concrete purposes. . . . To idealize and rationalize the universe at large is after all a confession of inability to master the courses of things that specifically concern us. As long as mankind suffered from this impotency, it naturally shifted a burden of responsibility that it could not carry over to the more competent shoulders of the transcendent cause. But if insight into specific conditions of value and into specific consequences of ideas is possible, philosophy must in time become a method of locating and interpreting the more serious of the conflicts that occur in life, and a method of projecting ways for dealing with them: a method of moral and political diagnosis and prognosis. (*IDP,* 10–13)

Dewey sees the result of Darwin's evolutionary theory as the prospect of applying scientific, experimental methods to all the pressing, practical human problems. This can't happen overnight, he acknowledges; but he does see it happening and devotes himself to helping the process along.

Old ideas give way slowly; for they are more than abstract logical forms and categories. They are habits, predispositions, deeply engrained attitudes of aversion and preference. Moreover, the conviction persists—though history shows it to be a hallucination—that all the questions that the human mind has asked are questions that can be answered in terms of the alternatives that the questions themselves present. But in fact intellectual progress usually occurs through sheer abandonment of questions together with both of the alternatives they assume—an abandonment that results from their decreasing vitality and a change of urgent interest. We do not solve them: we get over them. Old questions are solved by disappearing, evaporating, while new questions corresponding to the changed attitude of endeavor and preference take their place. (*IDP,* 14)

We have not solved all the old problems of philosophy, but that's all right. Those are problems, Dewey says, that we should just "get over." When we see how the "new methods" of the latest scientific revolution can be applied to the practical problems we already face, the old problems will simply "disappear" or "evaporate."

Dewey thus sets himself against any philosophy that would pose an impassable gulf between know-

ers and what is known, between subject and object, self and nonself, experience and nature, action and the good.[*] Human beings are to be understood as embedded without residue in the flux of natural processes—indeed, as a product of such processes. The vaunted cognitive abilities of the human species, including its capacity for sophisticated science, are to be understood as abilities developed through the evolutionary process. This view is often called *naturalism,* and John Dewey is one of its most vigorous exponents.

An epistemological corollary of this naturalistic vision in metaphysics is *giving up the quest for certainty.* All our knowledge is understood to be hypothetical and revisable in the light of future experience. What we know depends as much on our interests and capacities as it does on the objects of knowledge; if our interests shift, so will our concepts, and with them the "world" of our experience.

The same is true of our *values,* Dewey believes. Here, too, no certainty is possible, but it does not follow that all values are on a par, or that whatever an individual happens to like is valuable. Dewey believes that some views about value are superior to others and that we can improve our opinions about morals and values. The situation here is parallel to that in the sciences. Let us explore these matters in more detail.

Naturalized Epistemology

Dewey thinks of intelligence or inquiry as a matter of problem solving. Like Peirce, he understands problem solving as the endeavor to remove doubt and establish habits we can use to advantage.

The function of reflective thought is to transform a situation in which there is experienced obscurity, doubt, conflict, disturbance of some sort, into a situation that is clear, coherent, settled, harmonious. (*HWT,* 100–101)

This is the process: We face a difficulty or perplexity; we take stock of the situation (the facts of the case); we imagine possible courses of action.

_____

[*]This theme Dewey adapts from Hegel; see p. 463.

WILLIAM JAMES

Often called America's greatest psychologist, William James (1842–1910) was also a distinguished contributor to pragmatist philosophy. In addition to the classic *Principles of Psychology* (1890), James is noted for *The Will to Believe* (1896), *The Varieties of Religious Experience* (1902), *Pragmatism* (1907), and *The Meaning of Truth* (1909).

Like the other pragmatists, James stressed the connection between our beliefs and our practical life. But more than the others, he emphasized the practical consequences of actually believing one thing or another. Because our beliefs are shaped as much by our needs and interests as by the world, we are justified in taking those needs and interests into account when deciding what to believe. With respect to our conception of reality as a whole, James held that the crucial question is this: Does our conception give us cause to hope or cause to despair?

The great philosophical systems, James believed, are in part a reflection of the temperaments of those who devised them, and in this light he sorted philosophies into the *tender-minded* (rationalistic, idealistic, optimistic, religious, and free-willist) and the *tough-minded* (empiricist, materialist, pessimistic, irreligious, and fatalistic). James viewed pragmatism as a middle way between these extremes. The key to pragmatism is a revised notion of truth.

Truth, James said, is a human thing; to an unascertainable degree, our truths are a product of our interests. A belief is true, then, when it works for us, when it satisfies our needs; the true is just the useful in the way of ideas. In cases where the evidence does not clearly decide the issue (and he thought nearly all the large questions of philosophy are like that), we are within our rights to believe what will make for a more satisfying life. The question of fatalism is such a case. We are justified in believing that the universe is open to new possibilities of improvement, not a closed system where each future event is already determined by the ancient past, because this belief will have better consequences in our lives than the other.

Nor is there any reason, according to James, why religious faith should be rationally forbidden. If belief in God works to make life more satisfying—offering hope rather than despair—then it is true. And James thought it does work that way.

This leads in turn to further reflection on the facts; this may lead to considering other possibilities for action, and then to further investigation of the situation. This interaction between the discovered facts and suggested solutions goes on until we find what moves us toward a more satisfactory state.

Suppose you are walking where there is no regular path. As long as everything goes smoothly, you do not have to think about your walking; your already formed habit takes care of it. Suddenly you find a ditch in your way. You think you will jump it (supposition, plan); but to make sure, you survey it with your eyes (observation), and you find that it is pretty wide and that the bank on the other side is slippery (facts, data). You then wonder if the ditch may not be narrower somewhere else (idea), and you look up and down the stream (observation) to see how matters stand (test of idea by observation). You do not find any good place and so are thrown back upon forming a new plan. As you are casting about, you discover a log (fact again). You ask yourself whether you could not haul that to the ditch and get it across the ditch to use as a bridge (idea again). You judge that idea is worth trying, and so you get the log and manage to put it in place and walk across (test and confirmation by overt action). . . .

The two limits of every unit of thinking are a perplexed, troubled, or confused situation at the beginning and a cleared up, unified, resolved situation at the close. . . . (*HWT,* 105–107)

Dewey means this example to represent the pattern of *all* our intellectual endeavors. Three points are particularly important. First, human knowers are not passive spectators of the world they come to know. They are involved participants, part of the world. It is one of Dewey's complaints that traditional theories of knowledge make the knower an entity separate from the known, thus erecting barriers between knower and known that could not be bridged again. Dewey rejects the key idea in the representational theory of knowledge (p. 327): that we have direct access only to the world of our own mental states. His own theory, by setting human beings firmly within the natural world, claims to avoid many of the traditional problems of epistemology.* Second, there is a conscious rejection of the rule that we should "not frame hypotheses."† The mind "leaps forward" to possible solutions. Such leaps should not be condemned, but encouraged. We cannot do without framing hypotheses. Third, what is crucial is not whether a proposition represents a leap beyond present evidence, but whether it stands up to future tests by experience and action. A good hypothesis is one that *works*.

You can see that there is an intimate connection between this way of conceiving human knowledge and the futility of a quest for certainty. If the correctness of our beliefs lies open to future tests, to possible correction by future experience (mediated by actions we have not yet taken), then any claim to certainty *now* must be unjustified. Even the most firmly grounded beliefs of science and common sense may need to be modified as human experience grows more extensive and complex.‡

Dewey carries on a constant dialectical debate with traditional philosophy and especially with empiricism. Like William James, he believes that pragmatism is a middle way between the extremes of empiricism and rationalism, incorporating what is best in both. The main problem with these traditional rivals, he believes, is that each operates with an impoverished notion of what experience is. In an essay of 1917, Dewey contrasts the traditional concept of experience with one he thinks more adequate:

> (i) In the orthodox view, experience is regarded primarily as a knowledge-affair. But to eyes not looking through ancient spectacles, it assuredly appears as an affair of the intercourse of a living being with its physical and social environment. (ii) According to tradition experience is (at least primarily) a psychical thing, infected throughout by "subjectivity." What experience suggests about itself is a genuinely objective world which enters into the actions and sufferings of men and undergoes modifications through their responses. (iii) So far as anything beyond a bare present is recognized by the established doctrine, the past exclusively counts. Registration of what has taken place, reference to precedent, is believed to be the essence of experience. Empiricism is conceived of as tied up to what has been, or is, "given." But experience in its vital form is experimental, an effort to change the given; it is characterized by projection, by reaching forward into the unknown; connection with a future as its salient trait. (iv) The empirical tradition is committed to particularism. Connections and continuities are supposed to be foreign to experience, to be by-products of dubious validity. An experience that is an undergoing of an environment and a striving for its control in new directions is pregnant with connections. (v) In the traditional notion experience and thought are antithetical terms. Inference, so far as it is other than a revival of what has been given in the past, goes beyond experience; hence it is either invalid, or else a measure of desperation by which, using experience as a springboard, we jump out to a world of stable things and other selves. But experience, taken free of the restrictions imposed by the older concept, is full of inference. There is, apparently, no conscious experience without inference; reflection is native and constant. (*NRP,* 23)

Important points are made here. Let us review them in order.

- Point (i) is the denial that the knower is a disinterested spectator.

---

*The solipsism and skepticism that haunt Descartes and Hume, for instance, simply cannot arise in this view; they *begin* with the possibility that *my* experience might be all there is and face the problem of justifying belief in anything else. For Dewey, this is not a real possibility because we are in *constant interaction* with the world around us from the very start.

†For the role of this thought in the views of Newton and David Hume, see pp. 398–401.

‡You can see that Dewey, like Hegel, takes time seriously. Not only our beliefs but also our methods, concepts, and logical tools are part of history. But unlike Hegel, he does not envision a stage in which the progression comes to completion; there is no such thing as *absolute knowledge* for Dewey. In this regard, he resembles Kierkegaard more than Hegel (though he would not have liked Kierkegaard's supernatural religion or the emphasis on nonrational choice). Compare pp. 503–506.

- Point (ii) rejects any notion of experience that would locate it exclusively in a subject, leaving the question of an objective world up in the air.

- Point (iii) captures the inherent purposiveness of experience, the fact that it is always oriented toward the future and concerned about the implications of the present on that future.*

- Point (iv) attacks the Humean notion that experience presents all events as "loose and separate."†

- Point (v) notes that if reason were a faculty for making inferences distinct from experience, the result would be the restriction of experience to a purely subjective realm. Then, as long as we wanted to base our knowledge on experience, we would be unable to escape the skepticism plaguing traditional empiricism. But if experience is adequately characterized, it shows itself to be a matter of interactions between an organism and its environment; it is "full of inference" and presents itself in intimate contact with the objective world. There is no such thing as experience that is not already involved in the world.

And once we see that, many of the traditional problems of philosophy (such as the problem of the "reality" of the "external" world) simply "evaporate"; we "get over" them.

Nature and Natural Science

Experience, then, is an affair of nature because human beings are wholly natural creatures. But what is nature? Dewey resists the imperialism, so to speak, of certain sciences that claim a unique title to reveal the essence of nature. Galileo and Descartes agree that (material) reality is what mathematical physics can tell us about, and Hobbes tries

to extend that claim to human nature. The result seems to Dewey an unpalatable dichotomy: Either human experience is not a part of the world of nature at all (as in Descartes' dualism), or Hobbesian materialism reigns. But neither seems able to do justice to all we value and hold dear. We saw that "secondary qualities"—the felt, sensory, reds and blues, warms and colds, feelings of hope, love, or despair—are "kicked inside" by the early scientific revolutionaries as being merely effects *in us* of the geometrical, extended things that make up the realm of nature; many philosophers, acknowledging that physics gives us knowledge of what really is, feel compelled to join them.* This seems wholly inadequate to Dewey. If we identify science with the physical sciences (as traditionally understood), we will cut ourselves off from the uses of intelligence in the more human spheres. The problem, as he sees it, is once again a *spectator theory of knowledge*. It springs from

> the assumption that the true and valid object of knowledge is that which has been prior to and independent of the operations of knowing, . . . [from] the doctrine that knowledge is a grasp or beholding of reality without anything being done to modify its antecedent state—the doctrine which is the source of the separation of knowledge from practical activity. (QC, 196)

But as we have seen, experience and knowledge are a matter of interactions (transactions) between the knower and the known; neither is left at the end exactly as it was at the beginning of the affair. What counts as intelligent intervention, Dewey holds, is a matter of *method*. And a method is legitimate if it succeeds in transforming confused situations into clear ones.

> The result of one operation will be as good and true an object of knowledge as any other, provided it is good at all: provided, that is, it satisfies the

---

*Contrast Hume's rule about ideas: To discover whether a purported idea is a genuine one, trace it *back* to an impression. Here experience is assumed to be *given* whole and complete at any moment, and "the past exclusively counts." Compare Peirce, pp. 577–578.

†See p. 408.

---

*The loss is poignantly expressed in the poem by John Donne. (See p. 317.) The pattern is an ancient one. Democritus, the contemporary of Socrates, is convinced that reality is made up of atoms and the void, but he recognizes that our access to the world is through the sensory qualities of our experience and laments that "man is cut off from the real." (See p. 34.) Dewey struggles against this conclusion.

conditions which induced the inquiry. . . . One might even go as far as to say that there are as many kinds of valid knowledge as there are conclusions wherein distinctive operations have been employed to solve the problems set by antecedently experienced situations. . . .

There is no kind of inquiry which has a monopoly of the honorable title of knowledge. (*QC,* 197, 220)

Along these lines, Dewey attacks what some call "scientism."

Thus, "science," meaning physical knowledge, became a kind of sanctuary. A religious atmosphere, not to say an idolatrous one, was created. "Science" was set apart; its findings were supposed to have a privileged relation to the real. In fact the painter may know colors as well as the meteorologist; the statesman, educator and dramatist may know human nature as truly as the professional psychologist; the farmer may know soils and plants as truly as the botanist and mineralogist. For the criterion of knowledge lies in the method used to secure consequences and not in metaphysical conceptions of the nature of the real. . . .

That "knowledge" has many meanings follows from the operational definition of conceptions. There are as many conceptions of knowledge as there are distinctive operations by which problematic situations are resolved. (*QC,* 221)

If we add one more ingredient, we will be ready to see why Dewey thinks that intelligence can be as effective in the realms of value and morality as it is in science. That ingredient is his *instrumentalism.* Because the basic cognitive situation is the problem situation, and because hypotheses are created to resolve such situations satisfactorily, the concepts involved in hypotheses are necessarily relative to our concerns and interests. Without interests and concerns there would be no problems! Ideas, concepts, and terms, then, are intellectual *tools* we use as long as they serve our purposes and discard when they no longer do. They are *instruments* for solving problems.

Physicists and chemists create concepts that serve the purposes of these sciences: explanation, prediction, and control. But these concepts, too, are merely instruments serving certain purposes;

there is nothing prior or more basic about them that should cast a disparaging shadow on concepts serving other purposes. Dewey believes that many philosophers have been misled in thinking that modern physics alone reveals the true nature of reality. Making that assumption seems to shunt the qualities manifest in experience (all those "secondary qualities," whose loss was mourned by John Donne) off the main line onto a siding. But, Dewey says, that is to mistake the purport of scientific knowledge:

Only when the older theory of knowledge and metaphysics is retained, is science thought to inform us that nature in its true reality is but an interplay of masses in motion, without sound, color, or any quality of enjoyment and use. What science actually does is to show that any natural object we please may be treated in terms of relations upon which its occurrence depends, or as an event, and that by so treating it we are enabled to get behind, as it were, the immediate qualities the object of direct experience presents, and to regulate their happening, instead of having to wait for conditions beyond our control to bring it about. Reduction of experienced objects to the form of relations, which are neutral as respects qualitative traits, is a prerequisite of ability to regulate the course of change, so that it may terminate in the occurrence of an object having desired qualities. (*QC,* 104–105)

From the point of view of physical science, then, the world appears to be just a sequence of events in certain relations to each other. But we needn't conclude that the world *really* is just such a sequence of events, bare of every quality we prize and delight in. Scientific concepts, like all concepts, are merely tools we use to satisfy certain interests. But the interests served by physical science are not all the interests we have; they are not even our primary interests. In fact, treating nature as physics does (in terms of events and relations between events) serves larger purposes: our interest in controlling change, "so that it may terminate in the occurrence of an object having desired qualities." The concepts of science owe their very being to *values* we have.

"Event" is a concept about as bare and stripped of all that is precious to us as we can find. Yet it applies to everything that happens. Even tables and chairs can be considered extended, slowly unfolding events. But as we experience them, they are not "bare" events, but *events with meanings.* And the meanings are multiple. Consider, Dewey suggests, a piece of paper. We call it "a piece of paper," when we are interested in it in a certain way—as something to write on, perhaps, or something to wrap the fish in. But if we consider it in terms of an event (a kind of extended happening), it is clear that it

> has as many other explicit meanings as it has important consequences recognized in the various connective interactions into which it enters. Since the possibilities of conjunction are endless, and since the consequences of any of them may at some time be significant, its potential meanings are endless. It signifies something to start a fire with; something like snow; made of wood-pulp; manufactured for profit; property in the legal sense; a definite combination illustrative of certain principles of chemical science; an article the invention of which has made a tremendous difference in human history, and so on indefinitely. There is no conceivable universe of disclosure in which the thing may not figure, having in each its own characteristic meaning. And if we say that after all it is "paper" which has all these different meanings, we are at bottom but asserting that . . . paper is its ordinary meaning for human intercourse. (*EN, 7*)

Suppose we insist on asking, But what is it *really?* Is it really wood pulp? Or a white surface for writing on? Or atoms and the void? What would Dewey say? He would tell us that we were asking a question to which there is no answer. It is all of these things—and more—because the applicability of any of these concepts merely reflects certain purposes and interests. No one of them can be singled out as the *essence* of the event.

We can see that for Dewey there is no sharp line demarcating science from common sense, any more than there is a gap between knower and the known. Both are ways of dealing with recalcitrant situations and making us better able to cope; science and common sense are different because they serve different purposes, but they are alike in using concepts as *tools* for the realization of those

purposes. The same is true of philosophy. Dewey proposes

> a first-rate test of the value of any philosophy which is offered us: Does it end in conclusions which, when they are referred back to ordinary life-experiences and their predicaments, render them more significant, more luminous to us, and make our dealings with them more fruitful? Or does it terminate in rendering the things of ordinary experience more opaque than they were before, and in depriving them of having in "reality" even the significance they had previously seemed to have? (*EN, 319–320*)

1. What, according to Dewey, is the significance of Darwin for philosophy?
2. What is naturalism? Should we be naturalists? Are you one?
3. What are the stages in problem solving?
4. Why must we give up the quest for certainty?
5. What are Dewey's criticisms of empiricism? Of spectator theories of knowledge?
6. What is Dewey's critique of scientism?
7. What is instrumentalism?
8. In what way are tables and chairs events with meanings? Is there one meaning, or are there more?

Value Naturalized

Let us apply this criterion to Dewey's own philosophy by looking finally at what he has to say about values.

He notes that the modern problem about values arises with the expulsion of ends and final causes from nature, which takes place with the rise of modern science.

> For centuries, until, say, the sixteenth and seventeenth centuries, nature was supposed to be what it was because of the presence within it of *ends.* . . . All natural changes were believed to be striving to actualize these ends as the goals toward which they moved by their own nature. Classical philosophy identified *ens* [being], *verum* [truth], and *bonum* [goodness], and the identification was taken to be

an expression of the constitution of nature as the object of natural science. In such a context there was no call and no place for any *separate* problem of valuation and values, since what are now termed values were taken to be integrally incorporated in the very structure of the world. But when teleological considerations were eliminated from one natural science after another, and finally from the sciences of physiology and biology, the problem of value arose as a separate problem. (*TV,* 2–3)

Our earlier discussions of Dante and the consequences of Galilean science fit this analysis. The problem of how to understand values in a world of sheer fact is acute. As Dewey sees it, there are two tendencies in modern thought that accept the value-neutral character of nature. On the one hand, value is thought to originate in something above or beyond nature: in God, perhaps, or in pure reason, as Kant claims. At the other extreme, value is identified with purely subjective satisfactions, such as pleasure.

> There is either a basic distrust of the capacity of experience to develop its own regulative standards, and an appeal to what philosophers call eternal values, in order to ensure regulation of belief and action; or there is acceptance of enjoyments actually experienced irrespective of the method or operation by which they are brought into existence. Complete bifurcation between rationalistic method and an empirical method has its final and most deeply human significance in the ways in which good and bad are thought of and acted for and upon. (*QC,* 256)

Neither of these alternatives is attractive to Dewey, who wants to account for values in a wholly *naturalistic* way, but without identifying goodness with the arbitrary preference of an individual. What he wants is a way of treating values parallel to the way a scientist treats hypotheses—a way that will make *progress* in valuations possible but without claiming *certainty* at any point.

> The problem of restoring integration and cooperation between man's beliefs about the world in which he lives and his beliefs about the values and purposes that should direct his conduct is the deepest problem of modern life. (*QC,* 255)

It is this "integration and cooperation" between facts and values that is disturbed by the rise of modern science in the sixteenth and seventeenth centuries.* Dewey thinks a pragmatic approach can best restore such integration and solve this "deepest problem." The key idea is this:

> Escape from the defects of transcendental absolutism is not to be had by setting up as values enjoyments that happen anyhow, but in defining value by enjoyments which are the consequences of intelligent action. Without the intervention of thought, enjoyments are not values but problematic goods, becoming values when they re-issue in a changed form from intelligent behavior. (*QC,* 259)

Let us explore this idea. Like Peirce, who holds that we must begin reflection with the beliefs we already have, Dewey thinks we all begin with certain values and cannot help doing so. We do so simply by virtue of the fact that there are things we *like* or *prize.* Some of these likings may be biologically determined, some culturally produced. But there can be no doubt that at any stage of our lives, we do have such likings, desirings, and prizings. How are these to be understood? In accord with his general theory of experience, Dewey denies that these are purely subjective states. To *like* something is to have a certain disposition to behavior; if I like chocolate ice cream, I have tendencies to choose it when buying ice cream, to eat it when it is served to me, and so on. Liking is a matter of interactions between an organism and its environment; it is a transactional matter. To like *X* is to be disposed to try to get it; or, if we already have *X,* liking it is a matter of attempts to preserve, keep, or protect it.

Now, given that we all have such likings, do they constitute values? In one sense they do, Dewey says, but in another sense not. They do represent what we antecedently or *immediately* value (to use a word of Hegel's); but it would be a big mistake to identify these values with values per se. And the reason is that there is a big difference between what

---

*See, for instance, Hume on the gap between fact and value, pp. 421–422.

we find *satisfying* and that which is *satisfactory,* between what we *desire* and what is *desirable,* between those things we *think good* and the things that *are good.* Dewey is here trying to do justice to the fairly common experience of wanting a certain thing, getting it, and discovering (once we have it) that it does not live up to its advance notices.

What makes the difference between the satisfying and the satisfactory is the intervention of intelligence.

> The fact that something is desired only raises the *question* of its desirability; it does not settle it. Only a child in the degree of his immaturity thinks to settle the question of desirability by reiterated proclamation: "I want it, I want it, I want it." . . . To say that something satisfies is to report something as an isolated finality. To assert that it is *satisfactory* is to define it in its connections and interactions. The fact that it pleases or is immediately congenial poses a problem to judgment. How shall the satisfaction be rated? Is it a value or is it not? Is it something to be prized and cherished, *to be* enjoyed? Not stern moralists alone but everyday experience informs us that finding satisfaction in a thing may be a warning, a summons to be on the lookout for consequences. To declare something *satisfactory* is to assert that it meets specifiable conditions. It is, in effect, a judgment that the thing "will do." It involves a prediction; it contemplates a future in which the thing will continue to serve; it *will* do. It asserts a consequence the thing will actively institute; it will *do.* (QC, 260–261)

The ultimate sources of value, then, are our likings, prizings, esteemings, desirings. If we never liked anything, value would not even be on our horizon. But the things we like are always involved in a network of relations to other things. It might be that if we could just have Y, we would be satisfied. But Y never comes isolated and alone. It requires X as a precondition and brings along Z as a consequence. And X might require such effort and sacrifice that the luster of Y is considerably diminished. And Z might be so awful that it disqualifies Y as a value altogether. (The use of cocaine might be a good example.) Discovering these relations is the work of inquiry, intelligence, and scientific methods, for causal conditions and consequences are

matters of fact. So science and values are not two realms forever separated from each other. Finding what is valuable involves the use of methods of intelligence similar to those used in the sciences.[*]

It follows, then, that value judgments can be true and false, for they involve a prediction. To say that something is *good* or to urge that an action *ought* to be done is to say that it *will do.* And that means that we will continue to like it in the light of the entire context in which it is embedded. To call something satisfactory is to say that it will satisfy, given its causal conditions and consequences. And whether that is so is a matter of fact. What is desirable, then, is what is desired after intelligent inquiry and experience have had their say. So not only can value judgments be true and false, they can also be supported by methods of intelligent inquiry analogous to scientific methods.

Let us consider a typical objection to this way of looking at things. Suppose we allow that intelligence and the methods of science might have bearing on *means* and on *consequences;* we might nonetheless hold that this does not show how these methods can get any grip at all on what is *good in itself,* what is *intrinsically valuable.*[†] Or we might say that science (sociology or anthropology) can indeed

----

[*]Note that in a way, Dewey agrees here with the classical tradition from Socrates through Aquinas that it is *reason* that judges what is good. There are two differences: (1) He understands reason in terms of scientific inquiry; (2) The ultimate "measure" of the good is what we like, not a value inherent in things.

[†]This objection is a version of Hume's principle that reason is and can only be the slave of the passions. (See p. 420.) According to this principle, reason can tell you how to get what you want (means), but it cannot tell you what to want (ends). We have already seen, however, that Dewey challenges just this exclusivity of reason and experience; if he is right, there is no experience that is not already interpreted in terms of certain concepts, and no reason apart from experience. In a way, this echoes Kant's famous motto about concepts and intuitions (see p. 439), but with this difference: that there are no absolutely a priori concepts; all concepts are instruments invented to serve certain purposes—which themselves are not absolute but develop reciprocally as a result of the application of the methods of intelligence. Again the closest historical parallel is Hegel (see "Epistemology Internalized," in Chapter 17).

tell us what people do in fact value, but it cannot tell us what is valuable.

What is Dewey's reply? To suppose that there are such things as *ends in themselves* or things that are good no matter what is to make an illegitimate abstraction from the real context in which things are liked and enjoyed. Every end is itself a means to some further end, simply because it is located in time and has consequences. Ends, then, are never absolute; they are what Dewey calls *ends-in-view*. We may take a certain state of affairs to be an end, but that is always provisional and subject to revision in the light of further experience—of the conditions and consequences of that state of affairs. In fact, there is a *continuum* of ends and means, each means being a means in the light of some end, and each end a means to some further end. Furthermore, there is a *reciprocity* between ends and means; any actual end is what it is only as the culmination of those specific means that lead to it, and the means are means only as they lead to that particular end.

Dewey uses the story by Charles Lamb about the origin of roast pork to illustrate these points.

> The story, it will be remembered, is that roast pork was first enjoyed when a house in which pigs were confined was accidentally burned down. While searching in the ruins, the owners touched the pigs that had been roasted in the fire and scorched their fingers. Impulsively bringing their fingers to their mouths to cool them, they experienced a new taste. Enjoying the taste, they henceforth set themselves to building houses, enclosing pigs in them, and then burning the houses down. Now, if ends-in-view are what they are entirely apart from means, and have their value independently of valuation of means, there is nothing absurd, nothing ridiculous in this procedure, for the end attained, the *de facto* termination, *was* eating and enjoying roast pork, and that was just the end desired. Only when the end attained is estimated in terms of the means employed—the building and burning-down of houses in comparison with the other available means by which the desired result in view might be attained—is there anything absurd or unreasonable about the method employed. (*TV,* 40–41)

You simply cannot have ends apart from means, and every means qualifies the end you actually get.* This fact has implications, Dewey believes, for the maxim "the end justifies the means" and also for the popular objection to it. The maxim clearly involves the notion of something which is an end-in-itself, apart from the conditions and consequences of its actual existence. That end is supposed to justify the use of whatever means are necessary to its attainment—no matter how awful they may be. The maxim is plausible, however, only because we assume that only *that* end will be brought into existence. And that assumption is a mistake. You always get more than you intend—for better or worse. A recognition that the relation of ends and means is reciprocal and ongoing clarifies the sense in which the maxim is true (nothing *could* justify a means except a certain end) and the sense in which it is false (no end in isolation from its context could ever justify terrible means to it, simply because there are no such ends). Dewey says that

> nothing happens which is *final* in the sense that it is not part of an ongoing stream of events. . . . Every condition that has to be brought into existence in order to serve as means is, *in that connection,* an object of desire and an end-in-view, while the end actually reached is a means to future ends as well as a test of valuations previously made. Since the end attained is a condition of further existential occurrences, it must be appraised as a potential obstacle and potential resource. If the notion of some objects as ends-in-themselves were abandoned, human beings would for the first time in history be in a position to frame ends-in-view and form desires on the basis of empirically grounded propositions of the temporal relations of events to one another. (*TV,* 43)

It is clear that Dewey has no use for the idea of something good in itself—at least not prior to in-

---

*This is a fact that nations are apt to forget in wartime, to their own detriment. And individuals who take it as their end to be, let us say, rich, sometimes discover that in the process they have created themselves as persons they are not happy to be. Means enter into, that is, help determine, the character of the ends you actually get.

telligent reflection. If any pragmatic sense can be made of that notion at all, it will have to be along Peircean lines: that which the intelligent community ultimately comes to agree upon as desirable or good.* We have no hot line to either truth or goodness, and certainty has to be given up with respect to values, as well as knowledge. But by inquiring into the conditions and consequences of ends-in-view, we bring our values more and more into line with what we ultimately *would* be satisfied with, if we knew everything there is to know about the facts. If we were to treat our values the same way we treat our scientific beliefs, then

> standards, principles, rules . . . and all tenets and creeds about good and goods, would be recognized to be hypotheses. Instead of being rigidly fixed, they would be treated as intellectual instruments to be tested and confirmed—and altered— through consequences affected by acting upon them. They would lose all pretense of finality— the ulterior source of dogmatism. It is both astonishing and depressing that so much of the energy of mankind has gone into fighting for (with weapons of the flesh as well as of the spirit) the truth of creeds, religious, moral and political, as distinct from what has gone into effort to try creeds by putting them to the test of acting upon them. The change would do away with the intolerance and fanaticism that attend the notion that beliefs and judgments are capable of inherent truth and authority; inherent in the sense of being independent of what they lead to when used as directive principles. . . . Any belief as such is tentative, hypothetical; it is not just to be acted upon, but is to be *framed* with reference to its office as a guide to action. Consequently, it should be the last thing in the world to be picked up casually and then clung to rigidly. When it is apprehended as a tool and only a tool, an instrument of direction, the same scrupulous attention will go to its formation as now goes into the making of instruments of precision in technical fields. Men, instead of being proud of accepting and asserting beliefs and "principles" on the ground of loyalty, will be as ashamed of that procedure as they would now be to confess

their assent to a scientific theory out of reverence for Newton. (*QC,* 277–278)

This theme, that thought and action are reciprocally dependent on each other, that no knowledge worth the name is without implications for practice, and that no action is irrelevant to the utility of our intellectual tools, may be considered the distinctive and essential theme of pragmatism.

---

1. What is the origin of value? How does Dewey argue that despite this origin, the valuable is not identical to what I happen to like?
2. What is the difference between ends-in-view and absolute ends? How does Dewey think that means and ends should be related?
3. If modern science gives rise to the peculiarly modern problem about values, how does pragmatism claim to resolve that problem? And what role does science itself have in the resolution?

For Further Thought

1. Peirce and Dewey both urge fallibilism, giving up the quest for certainty. Imagine that our culture took that advice. What would be the result? Do you think that would be mostly good or mostly bad?

2. Naturalism holds that we human beings are, without remainder, parts of the natural world explored by the sciences—not thinking souls (Plato, Descartes), bundles of perceptions (Hume), noumenal selves (Kant), or the World Spirit on its way to self-realization (Hegel). Why should we think so, in the light of all this philosophical history?

Notes

1. References to the works of Charles Sanders Peirce are as follows:
   FB: "The Fixation of Belief"; *HMIC:* "How to Make Our Ideas Clear"; *WPI:* "What Pragmatism Is"; *SCFI:* "Some Consequences of Four Incapacities"; and *SP:* "Survey of Pragmatism," in *Collected Papers of Charles Sanders Peirce,* vol. 5, ed. Charles

---

*Review what Peirce says about truth, p. 572.

Hartshorne and Paul Weiss (Cambridge, MA: Harvard College, 1934).

2. Note added by Peirce in 1903 to "The Fixation of Belief," in Hartshorne and Weiss, *Collected Papers,* 232.

3. Epigraph (translated from the German) to W. V. O. Quine's *Word and Object* (New York: John Wiley and Sons, 1960).

4. References to the works of John Dewey are as follows:
   FAE: "From Absolutism to Experimentalism," and *NRP,* "The Need for a Recovery of Philosophy," in *Dewey: On Experience, Nature, and Freedom,* ed. Richard Bernstein (Indianapolis: Bobbs-Merrill, 1960).

IDP: "The Influence of Darwinism on Philosophy," in *John Dewey: The Middle Works (1899–1924),* vol. 4, ed. Jo Ann Boydston (Carbondale: Southern Illinois University Press, 1977).

QC: The Quest for Certainty: A Study of the Relation of Knowledge and Action (1929; New York: G. P. Putnam's Sons, Capricorn Books, 1960).

HWT: How We Think (Boston: D. C. Heath, 1933).

EN: Experience and Nature (New York: W. W. Norton, 1929).

TV: Theory of Valuation (Chicago: University of Chicago Press, 1939).

22

ANALYSIS

Logical Atomism and the Logical Positivists

One of the major interests in twentieth-century philosophy is language. At first glance, this may seem puzzling, but a second look suggests that it is not so surprising. Our scientific theories, our religious and philosophical views, and our commonsense understandings are all expressed in language. Whenever we try to communicate with someone about a matter of any importance, it is language that carries the freight. What if there were something *misleading* about the language in which we think? What if it set traps for us, catapulted us into errors without our even realizing it? Perhaps we ought not to trust it at all.

Actually, this suspicion is a sort of subtext running through modern philosophy. Descartes notes that we naturally *say* that we "see" men passing by, but the truth is we see only colors and shapes; we "judge" that these are men. So our language misleads us. Hobbes tells us that words are the money of fools who think they can buy truth with them, but that the wise are not deceived. One of the four books of Locke's *Essays* is titled "Of Words." Berkeley claims we have misunderstood how general terms work. Hume thinks that language deludes us

into identifying as ideas what are merely fictions or illusions. Kant holds that we do not understand how words such as "substance" or "cause" or "I" actually work. Nietzsche thinks nearly all of traditional philosophy is a house of cards built from misleading words. Peirce says his pragmatism is nothing but a doctrine of meaning and explores the geography of the land of signs. Only in the twentieth century, however, does attention to language become a major preoccupation of philosophers, both on the European continent and in the Anglo-American world. The interest in language has been so dominant that some speak of "the linguistic turn" in philosophy.

In this chapter and the next we examine two phases of this interest in language. These two phases are often called *analytic philosophy* and *ordinary language philosophy*. Both are complex movements involving many thinkers, and one could get a taste of these styles of doing philosophy in a number of ways. I have chosen to focus on one remarkable thinker, Ludwig Wittgenstein, whom many would cite as one of the greatest philosophers of the twentieth century. He has had, and continues to have, a pervasive influence on philosophical thought. Surprisingly, he can stand as an emblem for *both* of these phases. In Wittgenstein's change of mind and his severe critique of his own earlier analytic thought, we can see how attention to language in its *ordinary* employment tends to supplant the earlier attraction to constructing an *ideal* language. Wittgenstein is also interesting because he is not just interested in language—or even just in traditional philosophical problems; his passionate concern from first to last is, *How shall we live?* But first we need a little background.

Language and Its Logic

To understand analytic philosophy, we need to know at least a bit about modern logic. It is a tool of very great power, incredibly magnified in our day by the speed and storage capacities of the digital computer. Every college and university now teaches this "formal," or "symbolic," logic, which was developed in the period near the beginning of the twentieth century by Gottlob Frege, Bertrand Russell, Alfred North Whitehead, and others.

The power of the new logic derives from abstracting completely from the meaning or semantic content of assertions. It is a *formal* logic in just this sense: The rules governing transformations from one symbolic formula to another make reference only to the syntactical structures of the formulas in question and not at all to their meaning. Aristotle's logic of the syllogism, of course, is formal in this same sense.* But it is oversimple. The new logic provides a symbolism for the internal structure of sentences that is enormously more powerful than Aristotle's. It can also deal with a more complex set of relations among sentences. For the first time, it really seems plausible that whatever you might want to say can be represented in this formalism. Because this logic abstracts entirely from content, it can be used with equal profit in any field, from operations research to theology. It can show us what follows from certain premises, which asser-

tions are inconsistent with each other, and so on. Being formal in this sense, it sets out a kind of logical skeleton that can be fleshed out in any number of ways, while preserving the logical relations precisely.

The prospect opened up by the new logic is that of a language more precise and clear than the language we normally speak—a purified, *ideal language,* in which there is no ambiguity, no vagueness, no dependence on emphasis, intonation, or the many other features of our language that may mislead us and that are inessential for representing the truth. Bertrand Russell expresses the appeal of such a language in this way:

> In a logically perfect language the words in a proposition would correspond one by one with the components of the corresponding fact, with the exception of such words as "or," "not," "if," "then," which have a different function. In a logically perfect language, there will be one word and no more for every simple object, and everything that is not simple will be expressed by a combination of words, by a combination derived, of course, from the words for the simple things that enter in, one word for each simple component. A language of that sort will be completely analytic, and will show at a glance the logical structure of the facts asserted or denied. The language which is set forth in *Principia Mathematica* is intended to be a language of that sort.* It is a language which has only syntax and no vocabulary whatever. Barring the omission of a vocabulary, I maintain that it is quite a nice language. It aims at being that sort of a language that, if you add a vocabulary, would be a logically perfect language. Actual languages are not logically perfect in this sense, and they cannot possibly be, if they are to serve the purposes of daily life.[1]

Two complementary ideas make the new logic of particular interest to philosophers. The first is the conviction that natural language, such as ordinary English, does not in fact possess this sort of perfection. The language we normally speak is full of vagueness, ambiguity, and confusion. It is by no means what Russell calls "a logically perfect lan-

---

Principia Mathematica, written by Bertrand Russell and Alfred North Whitehead between 1910 and 1913, is a classic of modern logic.

guage." The second idea is the suspicion that these tawdry features of our natural languages tend to lead us astray, particularly when we think about philosophical matters, which are always at some conceptual distance from everyday talk "of shoes and ships and sealing wax, of cabbages and kings."

So the dazzling idea of applying the new logic to traditional philosophical problems takes root in the imagination of many philosophers. Perhaps, if we could formulate these problems in terms of the crystalline purity of these formal logical structures, they could finally—after all these centuries—be definitively solved. The excitement is great. And indeed some very impressive analyses of puzzling uses of language are produced.

As an example, let us consider Russell's "theory of definite descriptions." A *definite description* is a phrase of the form, "the so-and-so." Some sentences containing phrases of this form have a paradoxical character. Consider this sentence: "The golden mountain (that is, a mountain wholly made of pure gold) does not exist." We think this is a true sentence, don't we? You couldn't find a mountain made of gold anywhere. But now ask yourself: How can it be *true* that the golden mountain doesn't exist unless this definite description, "the golden mountain," is *meaningful?* (Meaning seems to be a prerequisite for truth; if a term lacks meaning you don't even know *what it is* that is true!) And how can that phrase be meaningful unless there is something that it means? And if there *is* something that it means—why, then, there must be a golden mountain after all. So the original sentence seems to be *false,* not true. So it looks as if the sentence, if true, is false. And that's a paradox.

Russell applies the new logic to this puzzle and shows how it can be made to disappear. The solution goes like this. We go wrong in thinking of the phrase "the golden mountain" as a *name.* It is true that for a name such as "Socrates" or "New York" to be meaningful, there must be something that they name.* Although definite descriptions *look* like

names, they actually have the *logic* of predications. If we can get clear about the logic of such phrases, we will clear up our confusion.

According to Russell, to say, "The golden mountain does not exist," is equivalent to saying, "There exists no thing that has both of these properties: being golden and being a mountain." In the language of formal logic, this is expressed as follows: $\sim(\exists x)(Gx \,\&\, Mx)$. In this formula, it is crystal clear that the G (for golden) and the M (for mountain) are in the predicate position. There are, in fact, no names in it at all—not even the occurrences of the letter $x,$ which function as variables ranging over everything. In effect, the formula invites you to consider each and every thing and assures you with respect to it: This is not both golden and a mountain. And that statement is both true and unparadoxical.

So by getting clear about the *logic* of the language in which the puzzle is stated, we get ourselves into a position to understand the sentence in a clear and unpuzzling way. We see that it is just a confusion to think that this language commits us to the existence of a golden mountain. Of great importance, however, is that we also identify the *source* of the confusion—which lies very naturally in the language itself. Phrases such as "the golden mountain" *do* look like names.

This analysis has a great impact on many philosophers, and a sort of cottage industry develops in which bits of language are analyzed in similar fashion, trying to show how we are misled by misreading the logic of our language. The suspicion grows that many of the traditional problems of philosophy have their origin in such misreadings. The prospect opens up that some, at least, of these problems in epistemology, metaphysics, and ethics can be cleared up and perhaps even made to completely disappear.*

---

*You might think at this point, "Whoa—I know that's not true; 'Santa Claus' is a name, but there isn't anything that it names!" But Russell holds that "Santa Claus" is not a true name; it is shorthand for "the fat, jolly, bearded man who flies through the

air on a sleigh and brings presents to children at Christmas time." And that is a definite description, subject to the same analysis as "the golden mountain." True names *do* name something. (In some moods, Russell thinks that even "Socrates" is not a true name, but a disguised description; when he is thinking along these lines, he is inclined to say that the only true names are terms such as "this" and "that.")

*Think, for example, of what might happen to Plato's semantic argument for the reality of the Forms (p. 123), if understood

BERTRAND RUSSELL

Over a long lifetime (1872–1970), Bertrand Russell wrote on nearly every conceivable topic. His books range from *The Principles of Mathematics* (1903) and *Human Knowledge, Its Scope and Limits* (1948) to *The Conquest of Happiness* (1930) and *Common Sense and Nuclear Warfare* (1959). In 1950 he was awarded a Nobel Prize for literature. A pacifist during World War I, Russell was active in social causes all his life. Three passions, he said, governed his life: a longing for love, the search for knowledge, and unbearable pity for the suffering of mankind.

Though his views changed and developed on some topics, he was consistent in wishing philosophy to become more scientific. As one of the major contributors to the new logic, he held that traditional philosophical problems either are not properly the business of philosophy at all (and should be farmed out to the sciences) or are problems of logic. As a maxim for scientific philosophizing, Russell recommended that logical constructions replace inferences whenever possible.

Consider, for example, our knowledge of the external world; suppose I think I am now seeing a table. What I have directly in my acquaintance is a "sense datum"—some brownish, trapezoidal, visual figure or a tactual feeling of resistance. Common sense (and philosophy, too) characteristically *infers* from such data the existence of a table quite independent of my evidence for it. But such inferences are notoriously unreliable and lead easily to skeptical conclusions.

Russell suggested that my knowledge of the table should rather be *constructed* in terms of logical relations among all the sense data (actual and possible) that, in ordinary speech, we would say are "of" the table. Thus the inference to the table external to my evidence is replaced by a set of relations among the data constituting that evidence. About those items, skeptical problems do not arise.

In matters of ethics, Russell took a utilitarian line, holding that right actions are those that produce the greatest overall satisfaction. With respect to religion, he was an agnostic. He was once asked what he would say if after his death he found himself confronted with his Maker. He replied that he would say, "God, why did you make the evidence for your existence so insufficient?"

Ludwig Wittgenstein:
Tractatus Logico-Philosophicus

In 1889 a son was born into the wealthy and talented Wittgenstein family of Vienna. He grew up in an atmosphere of high culture; the most prominent composers, writers, architects, and artists of that great city were regular visitors to his home. His father was an engineer and industrialist, his mother was very musical, and Ludwig was talented both mechanically and musically. It was also, however, a troubled family; there were several suicides among his siblings. He himself seems to have struggled against mental illness most of his life.

Having decided to study engineering, he went first to Berlin and then to Manchester, England, where he did some experiments with kites and worked on the design of an airplane propeller. This work drew his interests toward pure mathematics and eventually to the foundations of mathematics. The early years of the twentieth century, as we have seen, were a time of exciting developments in logic and the foundations of mathematics.

It was apparently Frege who advised Wittgenstein to go to Cambridge, England, to study with Russell, which he did in the fall of 1911.

---

in this light. His argument is that terms such as "square" and "equal" do not name anything in the visible world, yet they are meaningful. So they must name something in the intelligible world. But if what Plato takes to be a *name* has the logic of a *predicate,* the whole argument for the Forms on this basis falls to the ground.

Russell tells a story about Wittgenstein's first year there.

> At the end of his first term at Cambridge he came to me and said: "Will you please tell me whether I am a complete idiot or not?" I replied, "My dear fellow, I don't know. Why are you asking me?" He said, "Because, if I am a complete idiot, I shall become an aeronaut; but if not, I shall become a philosopher." I told him to write me something during the vacation on some philosophical subject and I would then tell him whether he was a complete idiot or not. At the beginning of the following term he brought me the fulfillment of this suggestion. After reading only one sentence, I said to him: "No, you must not become an aeronaut."[2]

When the war broke out in 1914, Wittgenstein was working on a manuscript that was to become the *Tractatus Logico-Philosophicus.* He served in the Austrian army and spent the better part of a year in an Italian prisoner-of-war camp, where he finished writing this dense, aphoristic little work that deals with everything from logic to happiness. After the war, he gave away the fortune he had inherited from his father, designating part of it for the support of artists and poets. He considered that he had set out in the *Tractatus* the final solution of the problems addressed there and left philosophy to teach school in remote Austrian villages. He lived, at that time and afterward, in severe simplicity and austerity.

His days as a schoolmaster did not last long, however, and for a time he worked as a gardener in a monastery. Then he took the lead in designing and building a mansion in Vienna for one of his sisters. Eventually, through conversations with friends, he came to recognize what he thought were grave mistakes in the *Tractatus* and to think he might be able to do good work in philosophy again. He was invited back to Cambridge in 1929, where he submitted the *Tractatus*—by then published and widely read—as his dissertation.

He lectured there (except for a time during the Second World War) until shortly before his death in 1951. He published nothing else in his lifetime, though several manuscripts circulated informally.

"At some point one has to pass from explanation to mere description."

—LUDWIG WITTGENSTEIN

A second major book, *Philosophical Investigations,* was published posthumously in 1953. This work is the subject of our next chapter. Since then, many other works have been published from notes and writings he left.

Subsequent developments leave no doubt that Wittgenstein is one of the century's deepest thinkers. He is also one of the most complex and fascinating human beings to have contributed to philosophy since Socrates.[3] Wittgenstein's concerns early in life are fundamentally moral and spiritual; the most important question of all, he believes, is *how to live.* As we'll see, however, he also believes there is very little one can *say* about that problem. In fact, he thinks getting clear about what one *cannot* say is just about the most important thing we can do.

Like a number of other Viennese in the early decades of the twentieth century, he is repelled by the degree to which the hypocritical, the artificial, the ornate and merely decorative, the false and pretentious, and the striving for *effect* characterize politics, daily life, and art. He is a kindred spirit of the revolt that includes Arnold Schönberg in music and Adolf Loos in architecture. An austere lucidity and ruthless honesty are the values Wittgenstein sets against the confusion of the age. It is not, perhaps, accidental that he masters the new logic of Frege and Russell and becomes an important contributor to it. He sees in it the key by which certain fundamental problems of life and culture can be definitively solved. He also shares the feeling that the new logic might make *all* the difference for philosophy. In the preface to the *Tractatus,* he writes,

> The book deals with the problems of philosophy, and shows, I believe, that the reason why these problems are posed is that the logic of our language is misunderstood. The whole sense of the book might be summed up in the following words: what can be said at all can be said clearly, and what we cannot talk about we must pass over in silence. (*Tractatus,* preface, 3)[4]

Wittgenstein's thought here is a radical one indeed: The posing of the problems of philosophy is itself the problem! If we can just get clear about "the logic of our language," these problems will disappear. They will be part of "what we cannot talk about." About them we must be silent.*

How will getting clear about the logic of our language produce such a startling result? If we get clear about the logic of our language, Wittgenstein thinks, we will see what the *limits* of language are. We will also see that thinkers violate those limits whenever they pose and try to answer the sorts of problems we call philosophical.

> Thus the aim of the book is to set a limit to thought, or rather—not to thought, but to the expression of thoughts: for in order to be able to set a limit to thought, we should have to find both sides of the limit thinkable (i.e., we should have to be able to think what cannot be thought).
>
> It will therefore only be in language that the limit can be set, and what lies on the other side

of the limit will simply be nonsense. (*Tractatus,* preface, 3)

This has a somewhat Kantian ring to it, and it is worth taking a moment to compare it to Kant's view of the limits of knowledge. You will recall that Kant sets himself to uncover the limits of rational knowledge and thinks to accomplish that by a critique of reason. Knowledge, Kant holds, is a product of a priori concepts and principles supplied by reason on the one hand and of intuitive material supplied by sensibility on the other. Its domain is *phenomena,* the realm of possible experience. Beyond this are things-in-themselves (*noumena*), thinkable, perhaps, but unknowable by us. Knowledge, Kant believes, has definite limits; and we can know what these are.*

Wittgenstein's strategy in the *Tractatus* bears a family resemblance to this Kantian project, but it is more radical on two counts: (1) It aims to set a limit not just to knowledge, but to thought itself; and (2) what lies on the other side of that limit is *not in any way thinkable.* Wittgenstein calls it "nonsense."

He refers, rather opaquely, to a problem standing in the way of such a strategy. In drawing boundaries, we draw a line and say, for example: Here, on this side, is Gary's land; there, on that side, is Genevieve's. But as this example shows, drawing ordinary boundaries or setting ordinary limits presupposes that both sides are thinkable, perhaps even experienceable or knowable. How, then, is it possible to set a limit to *thought?* To do so, it would seem we would have to "think what cannot be thought," survey what is on the other side of the boundary line, if only to know what it is we intend to exclude. Wittgenstein's ingenious notion, which we explore in the next section, is that this limit setting must be done in language—and *from inside* language. He thinks he has found a way to draw the line, which doesn't require having to *say* in language what is excluded, what lies outside the limit. One can set the limit, he thinks, by working outward from the center through what *can* be said. The cen-

---

*Those of you who know something of Zen may detect a familiar note here. So far as I know, Wittgenstein never discusses Zen—his concern is for problems, not schools of thought. But you would not go far wrong to think of him as a kind of Zen master for the West—especially in his later thought, the subject of the next chapter.

---

*A quick review of Kant's Copernican revolution and the idea of critique will bring this back to mind. See pp. 427–429.

ter is defined by what a language *is,* by the *essence of* language. What lies out beyond the boundary simply *shows itself* to be linguistic nonsense.

Here are the first two sentences in Wittgenstein's youthful work, the *Tractatus Logico-Philosophicus:*

1.   The world is all that is the case.

1.1   The world is the totality of facts, not of things.*

These sayings, announced so bluntly, may seem dark, but the key to unlock these mysteries is at hand: the new logic. Wittgenstein believes that he can use this logic to reveal the *essence of language,* and the essence of language *shows* us what the world must be. But this needs explanation.

Picturing

What is language? We are told that Wittgenstein's thinking about this question takes a decisive turn when he sees a diagram in a magazine story about an auto accident. Let us suppose it looked like this:

This diagram, we can say, pictures a *state of affairs.* It may not, of course, accurately represent what really happened. Let us call the actual state of affairs the *facts.* We can then say that this is a picture

of a **possible state of affairs**—a picture of what might have been the facts. (We can imagine the lawyers on each side presenting contrasting pictures of the accident.)

2.1	We picture facts to ourselves.
2.12	A picture is a model of reality.
2.131	In a picture the elements of the picture are the representatives of objects.
2.14	What constitutes a picture is that its elements are related to one another in a determinate way.
2.141	A picture is a fact.

The preceding diagram is itself a fact: It is made up of actual elements (lines on the page) that are related to each other in certain ways. Moreover, each element in the diagram *represents* some object in the world (the edges of the streets, cars). So this fact pictures another (possible) fact: the way the objects here represented were actually (or possibly) related to each other at a certain time and place.

Every picture has a certain *structure.* By "structure," Wittgenstein means the way its elements are related to each other. Two pictures that are different in many ways might still have a similar structure. Imagine, for instance, a color photograph taken from a helicopter hovering over the corner just after the accident. The elements of this picture (blobs of color) are quite different from the elements of our drawing (black lines on a white background). But if our drawing is accurate, the two pictures have similar structures: Their elements are related to each other in similar ways.

Furthermore, the two pictures not only have similar structures but also have something in common: what Wittgenstein calls **pictorial form.** It is important to note that pictorial form is not another element in addition to the lines in our drawing or the colors in the photograph, nor is it the actual structure of these two pictures. Rather, pictorial form is the *possibility* that a picture might actually have just this structure, that elements of some sort might actually be arranged in just this way. There needn't ever have been a picture, or a fact, with elements related to each other like this. But even if there never had been, there *could* have been. This

---

*The *Tractatus* is arranged in short, aphoristic sentences, or small groups of sentences that express a complete thought. These sentences are numbered according to the following scheme. There are seven main aphorisms, 1, 2, 3, and so on. 1.1 is supposed to be a comment on or an explanation of 1; 1.11 is to play the same role with respect to 1.1. It must be admitted that this elegant scheme is sometimes difficult to interpret.

possibility, actualized in our diagram, might also be actualized in many more pictures of the same state of affairs. All these pictures would have the *same* pictorial form.

But it is not just similar pictures that share the same form.

> 2.16   If a fact is to be a picture, it must have something in common with what it depicts.
>
> 2.161   There must be something identical in a picture and what it depicts, to enable the one to be a picture of the other at all.
>
> 2.17   What a picture must have in common with reality, in order to be able to depict it — correctly or incorrectly — in the way it does, is its pictorial form.

Pictures and *what is pictured* by them (e.g., the possible accident itself) must also share the same form.

So far we have been thinking of spatial pictures of spatial objects. But there are other kinds of pictures, too. We can, for instance, think of an orchestra score as a picture; this is a spatial picture (the notes are laid out next to each other on a page), but what it primarily pictures is not spatial, but temporal: the succession of sounds the orchestra plays in a performance. Yet a score is also a picture, in Wittgenstein's sense, of the grooves in a recording of the work and of the magnetic tracings on a tape or compact disc. And we could think of the grooves in a recording as in turn a picture of the sound produced when it is played (see *Tractatus,* 4.0141). So while we tend to use the word "picture" rather narrowly, the concept applies very widely. Wherever there are objects in relation representing other objects, there is a Wittgensteinian picture.

Every picture, Wittgenstein claims, is a *logical* picture. And logical pictures can depict the world (*Tractatus,* 2.19). As we have seen, a picture may represent reality correctly or incorrectly. That is why Wittgenstein says that logical pictures *can* depict the world: They depict ways the world might be — possible states of affairs.

If we think of a certain two-dimensional space, such as a desk top, we can see that there are a vari-

ety of possible ways the books on it can be arranged. Analogously, we can think of *logical space.* Logical space consists of all the *possibilities* there are for all the *objects* there are to be related to each other in all the *possibly different* ways there are. Logical space, then, comprises the form not only of all the actual states of affairs but also of all possible states of affairs. Given this notion of logical space, we can say,

> 2.202   A picture represents a possible situation in logical space.

Some pictures represent reality correctly, and others don't. How can we tell whether what a picture tells us is true?

> 2.22   What a picture represents it represents independently of its truth or falsity, by means of its pictorial form.
>
> 2.223   In order to tell whether a picture is true or false we must compare it with reality.
>
> 2.224   It is impossible to tell from the picture alone whether it is true or false.
>
> 2.225   There are no pictures that are true *a priori.*

You can't tell just by looking at our accident diagram, no matter how microscopically you inspect it, whether it represents the accident correctly. And this is the case with *all* pictures, Wittgenstein says. A *true* picture is one that represents a possible state of affairs that is also actual. And actual states of affairs are *facts.* So a true picture depicts the facts. If there were a picture that was true a priori (independent of experience), you wouldn't have to "compare it with reality" to tell whether it was true; you could discover the facts just by examining the picture. But that, Wittgenstein says, is precisely what is not possible. To tell whether a picture is true (represents the facts correctly), you have to check its fit with the facts. In no case can we tell a priori whether a picture is true. This is an extremely important feature of pictures.*

---

*If Wittgenstein is right, rationalist attempts to say what the world must be like based on reason alone must be mistaken. No matter how "clear and distinct" one of Descartes' ideas is, for instance, one can't deduce from this that it is true. By stress-

Thought and Language

Among the logical pictures, there is one sort that is of particular significance:

3.   A logical picture of facts is a thought.

3.001   "A state of affairs is thinkable": what this means is that we can picture it to ourselves.

3.01   The totality of true thoughts is a picture of the world.

3.02   A thought contains the possibility of the situation of which it is the thought. What is thinkable is possible too.

Our thoughts, then, are pictures, too. And, being pictures, they have all the characteristics of pictures we noted earlier: They are composed of elements in a certain arrangement, so they are facts with a certain structure; in virtue of that, they possess pictorial form; they represent possible states of affairs; and they share their pictorial and logical form with what they represent.

And now comes a crucial point:

3.1   In a proposition a thought finds an expression that can be perceived by the senses.

3.11   We use the perceptible sign of a proposition (spoken or written, etc.) as a projection of a possible situation.

So thought finds its expression in perceptible signs, or sentences—that is, in *language*. Now we can understand why Wittgenstein thinks he can set a limit to thought by finding the limits of language. It is in language that thought is expressed. If there are limits to what language can express, these will be the limits of thought as well.

But what is a propositional sign, a sentence? Like all pictures, it is a fact, an arrangement of objects.

3.1431   The essence of a propositional sign is very clearly seen if we imagine one composed of spatial objects (such as

tables, chairs, and books) instead of written signs.
Then the spatial arrangement of these things will express the sense of the proposition.

For instance, suppose you want to picture the fact that Sarah is standing to the east of Ralph. You might use a table to represent Sarah and a chair to represent Ralph. By putting the table to the east of the chair, you can picture the fact in question. This shows us, Wittgenstein says, "the essence of a propositional sign." What he means is that written or spoken sentences are like this, too; they are made up of elements standing in certain relations.

But it is not obvious that they are like this.

4.002   Everyday language is a part of the human organism and is no less complicated than it.
It is not humanly possible to gather immediately from it what the logic of language is.
Language disguises thought.

The *essence* of language is hidden, "disguised." Yet it is something that can be disclosed, or shown. What reveals the hidden essence of language? *Logic.* Wittgenstein agrees with Russell that the superficial grammar of what we say may not be a good indication of the logic of what we say. And he holds that the new logic displays for us the internal structure, the essence of language. Still, he is not tempted to discard our natural languages (German or English, for example) in favor of some artificially created "ideal" language. Nor does he have any inclination to reform our language in the direction of some postulated ideal. Because the languages we speak are *languages,* they too must exemplify the essence of language. So logic must reside even there, in the heart of our confusing, vague, and ambiguous languages. What we need is not to junk them in favor of some ideal, but to understand them.

5.5563   In fact, all the propositions of our everyday language, just as they stand, are in perfect logical order.

If they weren't, they wouldn't constitute a language!
But because "language disguises thought," the logical structure of our language is not apparent. To

---

ing that there are no pictures that are true a priori, Wittgenstein expresses one version of empiricism. Compare Hume, pp. 403–405.

bring it to light we need *analysis*. What sort of analysis, then, can we give of a sentence? We already have the elements of an answer in hand. A sentence is a picture, and we know that a picture, like all facts, is composed of elements set in a certain structure. So there must be elements and a structure in every sentence. It only remains to determine what they are.

Let's consider again the sentence "Sarah is to the east of Ralph." We saw that this could be represented by one object in relation to another, a table and a chair, for instance. The table would in effect be a kind of name for Sarah, and the chair a name for Ralph. Wittgenstein concludes that the *only* elements needed in a language are names. Everything else—all the adjectives and prepositions, for instance—are inessential. If sentences were completely analyzed into their basic elements, all this would disappear. What would be left would be names in a structure.[*]

> 3.202   The simple signs employed in propositions are called names.
>
> 3.203   A name means an object. The object is its meaning. . . .
>
> 3.26   A name cannot be dissected any further by means of a definition: it is a primitive sign.

As you can see, there would be a very great difference between the "look" of a completely analyzed propositional sign and our ordinary sentences. One might have a hard time even recognizing the complete analysis of a familiar sentence, particularly because the names in question have to be *simple* signs. What we take to be names in ordinary language are invariably complex; they can be "dissected . . . by means of a definition." "George Washington," for instance, is a shorthand expression for "the first president of the United States" (and many other descriptions). These descriptions

themselves need to be analyzed if we are to get to the roots of things to understand how language pictures the world.

If we could get to that level of clarity, Wittgenstein thinks, we would see that sentences are composed of names in a logical structure. And names are *simple*. They cannot be further analyzed or "dissected." The meaning of a name cannot be given in a definition using other linguistic elements; the meaning of a name is the object it stands for.[*]

Now we are ready to go back to the beginning and understand those first mysterious propositions of the *Tractatus*. Just as sentences represent possible states of affairs, true sentences represent facts. True sentences, moreover, are made up of names, and names stand for objects. But a sentence isn't just a list of names; it has an internal structure. And a fact isn't just a jumble of things; it has the same structure as the true sentence that pictures it. Why? Because the pictorial form of sentences mirrors the logical form of facts. The *world* is what is pictured in the totality of true *sentences*. The world, then, is not just a random collection of objects; it is "the totality of facts, not of things" because it shares the same logical form as the true sentences.

> 1.13   The facts in logical space are the world.

So the world is "all that is the case."

But we do not yet see how to solve the main problem Wittgenstein poses: to set a limit to thought. To do this, we have to look more closely at the logic of propositions.[†] As Russell shows, ordinary language often disguises the logical form of our sentences, but analysis can reveal it. A complete analysis would leave us with sentences that

---

[*] Here is a rough analogy. Certain notations in mathematics are merely a convenience and could be eliminated without diminishing the science. For instance, x^3 is just $x \cdot x \cdot x$, and $4y$ can be defined as $y + y + y + y$. So Wittgenstein thinks names standing in certain relations will express whatever we want to express, though we usually use more economical means.

[*] It is worth noting that Wittgenstein does not offer any examples of these simple names in the *Tractatus*. He argues that such names must be implicit in our language and ultimately reachable by analysis; but just what they are—and what they name—is something of a mystery.

[†] For our purposes, I do not distinguish sentences from propositions, though some philosophers do; a *proposition* is often thought of as an abstract feature several sentences can share when they mean the same thing. For example, "Mary hit Sally" and "Sally was hit by Mary" are different sentences but can be said to express the same proposition. Another example is "Snow is white" and "Schnee ist weiss."

could not be further analyzed—simple sentences sometimes called *atomic propositions*. They would have constituents (names in a structure of possibility), but they could not be further broken down into other sentences.

> 4.221 It is obvious that the analysis of propositions must bring us to elementary propositions which consist of names in immediate combination.

But how are these simple sentences related to each other? Wittgenstein holds that

> 5.134 One elementary proposition cannot be deduced from another.

What this means is that the truth-value of each is independent of the truth-value of any other. An elementary proposition can remain true while the truth-values of any others (or even all the others) change. This has consequences for our view of the world as well.

> 2.061 States of affairs are independent of one another.
>
> 2.062 From the existence or non-existence of one state of affairs, it is impossible to infer the existence or non-existence of another.

Recall once more the beginning of the *Tractatus*:

> 1.2 The world divides into facts.
>
> 1.21 Each item can be the case or not the case while everything else remains the same.

This view, called **logical atomism,** is reminiscent of Hume's remark that "all events seem entirely loose and separate."[*] It means that relations existing between atomic facts cannot be *logical* relations. Given one true elementary proposition, it is never *necessary* that another one be true—or false.

There are, of course, logical relations between complex propositions. If we are given the truth-value of *p* and of *q*, we can infer something about the truth of the conjunction, *p and q*. To display these logical relations, Wittgenstein devises *truth tables*. A truth table for a complex proposition sets

---

[*]See p. 408.

forth all the logically possible combinations of truth-values for its components and then displays the corresponding truth-values for the whole. Here, for example, are truth tables for conjunctive, disjunctive, and negative propositions.

p	q		p and q	p or q	not p
T	T		T	T	F
T	F		F	T	F
F	T		F	T	T
F	F		F	F	T

The two columns on the left set out the possibilities: They show us that two propositions may both be true, one or the other may be true, or neither one may be true. The truth table for the conjunction shows us that the conjunction is true only when both of the components are true, and false otherwise. The truth table for the disjunction (an "or" statement) shows us that the disjunction is true unless both of the components are false. And the truth table for negation shows that negating a proposition changes its truth-value.

Propositions may be of any degree of complexity. There may be a very large number of elementary propositions in its makeup, and the logic of their relations may be extremely complicated. The truth table for a proposition such as

> *if [if (p and q) then not (r or s)]*
> *then (t if and only if not u)*

is very large, but it is calculable. The truth-value of a complex proposition is a function of the truth-values of the component parts; this feature is called *truth functionality*. The logic of the *Tractatus* is a truth-functional logic.

Logical Truth

We noted before that no pictures are true a priori. To determine whether a proposition is true or false, then, we must compare it to the world. From the point of view of logic, any elementary proposition might be true, or it might be false. Such propositions are called *contingent:* Their truth depends on the facts. The contingency of elementary propositions has another implication: However the world is, whatever the facts are, they *might have been dif-*

ferent. There is never any necessity in the facts. The negation of any true elementary proposition always pictures a possibility. Suppose it is true that it is now raining where I am; then it is false that it is not raining here and now (see the preceding truth table), but it is not necessarily false. It is a coherent possibility that it should not be raining here and now, even if it is. Given the configuration of the objects in the world, it is raining. But the objects of the world *could have been* otherwise configured.

We might like to ask, Just how far do these unrealized possibilities extend? How many possibilities are there? The answer is that this is what logic shows us. Our experience of the world can tell us what the actual facts are. Logic shows us what they *might be.* Logic is the science of the possible. And everything that it shows us is *necessary* (i.e., not contingent).*

Consider, for example, the truth table for a proposition like this:

Either it is raining, or it is not raining.

p	not p	p or not p
T	F	T
F	T	T

The first column gives us the possibilities for the truth of p. The next column shows us what is the case when p is negated. And the third displays the results of disjoining the first two. The crucial thing to notice is that whatever the truth of p (and there are just these two possibilities), *p or not p* is true. In other words, there is no possibility that this proposition could be false. It is *necessarily* true; it is a **logical truth.** Such a proposition Wittgenstein calls a **tautology.**†

There are three important points to notice here.

---

*If something is possible, it cannot be merely contingent that it is possible, since whatever actually exists must already be possible; so what is possible couldn't depend on what the facts are.
†There are two limiting cases of propositions. Tautologies are one case; contradictions are the other. While *tautologies* are necessarily true, *contradictions* are necessarily false. Tautologies do not rule out any possibilities, contradictions rule them all out. In a sense, it is not strictly correct to call tautologies and contradictions "propositions" because propositions are pictures of reality; tautologies and contradictions do not picture states of affairs. They have a different, and very important, role to play.

1. The sentence represented by *p or not p* is a complex, not an elementary, proposition; *p* may or may not be elementary, but in this complex proposition, it is set in a structure defined by the logical operators, "not" and "or."* Only propositions that are logically complex in this way can be necessarily true or false. (That is just another way to say that the truth of an elementary proposition is always contingent.)

2. Logical words such as "not," "and," "or," and "if-then" are not *names.* These terms do not stand for objects; they have an entirely different function. They are part of the *structure* of sentences, not part of the content.†

> 4.0312   My fundamental idea is that the "logical constants" are not representatives; that there can be no representatives of the *logic* of facts.

Wittgenstein illustrates this "fundamental idea" by considering double negation. There is a law of logic stating that negating the negation of a proposition is equivalent to asserting the proposition:

(not not p) if and only if p.

To say that it is not the case that it is not raining is equivalent to saying that it is raining. If the logical operator "not" were a name of something, the left side of this equivalence would picture something quite different from what the right side pictures, and the law would be false. But it doesn't. And the proof of this is that a truth table for this principle is a tautology. So the logical operators are not names.

3. Suppose we interpret *p* as "It is raining"; then the tautology *p or not p* says, "Either it is raining, or it is not raining." But while "It is raining" gives us some information, the tautology tells us nothing. It says nothing; it is not a *picture.* Why is it that the proposition *p* can tell us something? It can be informative because it picks out one of several possibilities and says: That is how things are. In picking

---

*A *logical operator* is a term that has the function of producing propositions from other propositions. Additional examples are "and" and "if-then."
†Compare Russell's description of a logically perfect language on p. 594.

out that possibility, it excludes another. It tells us something about the world by shutting out one possibility and allowing another; *p or not p,* by contrast, excludes nothing. It does not rule out any possibilities, so it does not *say* anything.

> 4.461   Propositions show what they say: tautologies and contradictions show that they say nothing. A tautology has no truth conditions, since it is unconditionally true: and a contradiction is true on no condition.

> 4.462   Tautologies and contradictions are not pictures of reality. They do not represent any possible situations. For the former admit *all* possible situations, and the latter *none.*

Saying and Showing

In 4.461, Wittgenstein makes use of a distinction that is very important to him: the distinction between *saying* and **showing.** Propositions do two things; they show something and they say something.

> 4.022   A proposition *shows* its sense.
> A proposition *shows* how things stand *if* it is true, and it *says that* they do so stand.

The proposition "All crows are black" shows or presents its sense. We can see what this means if we ask what would be required to *understand* it. To understand this proposition is to grasp its sense; to grasp its sense is to understand what *would be* the case if it *were true.* When we understand the sentence, we know that *if* it is true, any crow we come across will be black. Notice that understanding the sentence is not yet knowing that all crows are black. Given that we understand it, we might wonder whether it is true or doubt that it is true. It is, after all, possible that some crows aren't black; the proposition might present a possible state of affairs only, not a fact. But we grasp its sense in *knowing what would make it either true or false.* That—its sense—is what a proposition *shows.*

But a proposition such as this plays another role. It not only shows its sense but also *says* that things are this way, that crows actually are black. It makes

an assertion and so is true or false, depending on the facts of the world. According to Wittgenstein, this is the most general propositional form—that is, what all propositions have in common:

> 4.5   This is how things stand.

Propositions *show* (display) their sense; they *say* how things are.

But tautologies and contradictions *show* that they *say nothing.* If these limiting cases of propositions say nothing, however, we might wonder whether they have any importance. Couldn't we just ignore or neglect them? No. They are of the very greatest importance. They show us what is possible and what is impossible. They display for us the structure of logical space.

But they have another importance as well.

> 6.1   The propositions of logic are tautologies.

What Wittgenstein here calls the "propositions" of logic are sometimes called the laws of logic. Consider as an example the very basic law called the *principle of noncontradiction:* No proposition can be both true and false. We can represent this as

not both p and not p.

If we write a truth table for this formula, we can see that it is a tautology—that is, necessarily true no matter what the truth-values of p are.

p	not p	p and not p	not (p and not p)
T	F	F	T
F	T	F	T

So the device of truth tables provides a justification for the laws of logic. Showing they are tautologies is equivalent to demonstrating their necessary truth. The truth table shows that there is no alternative to the laws of logic—no possibility that they might be false.[*] The *Tractatus* doctrine is that every principle of logical inference can be reduced to a tautology.[†]

---

[*]Of course this also shows that the laws of logic *say* nothing—that is, are *about* nothing. The laws of logic are purely formal and empty of content. And that is exactly why they can be noncontingently true.

[†]In fact this claim is not correct. Truth tables constitute a decision procedure for validity only in *propositional logic,* where the

Moreover,

> 6.113   It is the peculiar mark of logical propo-
> sitions that one can recognize that they
> are true from the symbol alone, and
> this fact contains in itself the whole
> philosophy of logic.

What this means is that the propositions of logic
can be known a priori. As we saw previously, we
can know about the actual world only by comparing a proposition with reality. It is the mark of logical propositions that this is not only unnecessary,
but also impossible; because they say nothing, they
cannot say anything we could check out by examining the facts.

So the propositions of logic are one and all tautologies. And every valid form of inference can be
expressed in a proposition of logic. This means that
all possible logical relations between propositions
can be known a priori. And in knowing them, we
know the logical structure of the world—logical
space, what Wittgenstein calls "the scaffolding of
the world" (6.124).

> 6.1251   Hence there can *never* be surprises in
> logic.

> 6.127   All the propositions of logic are of
> equal status: it is not the case that
> some of them are essentially primitive
> propositions and others essentially de-
> rived propositions.
> Every tautology itself shows that it is a
> tautology.

Setting the Limit to Thought

Finally, we are ready to understand how Wittgenstein thinks he can show us the limits of language.
An operation discovered by Wittgenstein can be
performed on a set of elementary propositions to
produce all the possible complex propositions
(truth functions) that can be expressed by that set.
Suppose we have just two elementary propositions,
p and *q*. Using this operator, we can calculate that

there are just sixteen possible truth functions combining them: *not p, not q, p or q, p and q, if p then q,*
and so on. Now imagine that we were in possession
of *all* the elementary propositions there are; using
this operation on that enormous set, one could simply calculate all the possible truth functions there
are and so *generate each and every possible proposition.*

Remembering the picture theory of meaning,
we can see that this set of propositions pictures all
the possible states of affairs there are, and in all
their possible combinations. So, it represents the
entirety of logical space; it pictures everything that
there could possibly be in reality—every "possible
world." Notice that there would be no proposition
saying that these are all the possible facts; in fact,
there couldn't be such a proposition. But there also
doesn't need to be. That these are all the facts there
are *shows itself* in these propositions being all there
are—in there simply being no more propositions
that are possible, calculable, formulable. And we
can see there are no more possible propositions,
because all the possible ones are part of this set produced by this operator.

This very large set of propositions contains *everything it is possible to say,* plus the tautologies and contradictions (which say nothing). Beyond this set of
possible propositions lies only *nonsense.* So the limit
of thought is indeed set from inside. Thought is expressed in language. The essence of language is picturing. And, given this, we can work out from the
center to the periphery of language by means of
logic. We do not need to take up a position outside
the thinkable in order to draw a line circumscribing it. The limit *shows itself* by the lack of sense that
pseudopropositions display when we try to say
something unsayable. It is indeed, then, only "in
language that the limit can be set, and what lies on
the other side of the limit will simply be nonsense"
(*Tractatus,* preface, 3).

> 5.61   Logic pervades the world: the limits of
> the world are also its limits.
> So we cannot say in logic, "The world
> has this in it, and this, but not that."
> For that would appear to presuppose
> that we were excluding certain possibili-
> ties, and this cannot be the case, since it
> would require that logic should go be-

---

analysis of structure does not go deeper than whole propositions. In *quantificational* (or *predicate*) *logic,* where the analysis
reveals the internal structure of propositions, Alonzo Church
later proves there is no such decision procedure.

yond the limits of the world; for only in that way could it view those limits from the other side as well. We cannot think what we cannot think; so what we cannot think we cannot *say* either.

---

1. What is Wittgenstein's aim in his *Tractatus*? And what motivates that aim—that is, why does he want to do that? If he had succeeded, would that have been significant?

2. Explain how a picture is a "model of reality." In what sense is a picture itself a fact?

3. Explain the concepts of pictorial form, possible state of affairs, and logical space.

4. Why are there no pictures that are true a priori?

5. In what way does language "disguise" thought? What is the essential nature of a proposition?

6. What is the meaning of a simple name? What are atomic propositions composed of? And why is this view correctly called "logical atomism"?

7. What, then, is the world? And how is it related to logic? To language? To the truth?

8. How do truth tables work? What is truth functionality?

9. What domain does logic reveal to us? In what way does logic "show itself"?

10. Contrast contingent truth with necessary truth. How do necessary truths reveal themselves in a truth table?

11. Why do tautologies and contradictions "say nothing"? What do they "show"?

12. Explain: "A proposition *shows* its sense" and it *says* "This is how things stand." Give an example.

13. How is the limit to thought set?

Value and the Self

We noted earlier that the young Wittgenstein's concerns were mainly spiritual and moral, but we have just seen that the bulk of the *Tractatus* deals with quite technical issues in logic and the philosophy of language. How are we to understand this apparent discrepancy? In a letter to a potential publisher for the *Tractatus,* Wittgenstein writes,

> The book's point is an ethical one. I once meant to include in the preface a sentence which is not in

fact there now but which I will write out for you here, because it will perhaps be a key to the work for you. What I meant to write, then, was this: My work consists of two parts: the one presented here plus all that I have *not* written, and it is precisely this second part that is the important one. My book draws limits to the sphere of the ethical from the inside as it were, and I am convinced that this is the ONLY *rigorous* way of drawing those limits. In short, I believe that where many others today are just *gassing,* I have managed in my book to put everything firmly in place by being silent about it.[5]

What could this mean—that the really important part of the book is the part he did not write? Why didn't he write it? Was he too lazy? Did he run out of time? Of course not. He didn't write the important part because he was convinced it *couldn't be written*. What is most important—the ethical point of the book, the "key" to the work—is something that *cannot be said*.

Nonetheless, and again paradoxically, he does have some things to "say" about this sphere, which he also calls "the mystical."[*] Before we examine his remarks—brief and dark sayings, as many have noted—it will be helpful to set out a consequence of what we have already learned.

> 4.1　Propositions represent the existence and non-existence of states of affairs.
>
> 4.11　The totality of true propositions is the whole of natural science (or the whole corpus of the natural sciences).

The essence of language is picturing; and to picture is to say, "This is how things stand." The job of natural science is to tell us how things are, to give us a description of the world. And if natural science could finish its job, we would then have a complete picture of reality.[†] Nothing—no object, no fact—would be left out. It would include the *totality* of true propositions.

But natural science does not contain any propositions like these: one ought to do *X;* it is wrong to

---

[*]It is obviously a problem how we are to understand what he "says" about the unsayable. He makes a suggestion we consider later.

[†]Compare Peirce's similar conviction, pp. 573–574.

Y; the meaning of life is *Z.* It follows that these are not really propositions at all; they look a lot like propositions, but, if Wittgenstein is right, they lie *beyond the limits of language.* Strictly speaking, they are unsayable. Those who utter them may be "just *gassing.*" Or they may be trying to say the most important things of all but failing because they "run against the boundaries of language." In a "Lecture on Ethics" Wittgenstein gave in 1929 or 1930 (not published until 1965), he says,

> This running against the walls of our cage is perfectly, absolutely hopeless. Ethics so far as it springs from the desire to say something about the ultimate meaning of life, the absolute good, the absolute valuable, can be no science. What it says does not add to our knowledge in any sense. But it is a document of a tendency in the human mind which I personally cannot help respecting deeply and I would not for my life ridicule it.[6]

Ethics "can be no science" because science consists of propositions, and

6.4 All propositions are of equal value.

6.41 The sense of the world must lie outside the world. In the world everything is as it is, and everything happens as it does happen: *in* it no value exists—and if it did exist, it would have no value. If there is any value that does have value, it must lie outside the whole sphere of what happens and is the case.

6.42 And so it is impossible for there to be propositions of ethics. Propositions can express nothing that is higher.

6.421 It is clear that ethics cannot be put into words. Ethics is transcendental.

We can think of the *Tractatus* as the absolute endpoint of that road that begins with Copernicus and leads to the expulsion of value from the framework of the world.* The vision of the *Tractatus* is one where everything in the world is flattened out, where nothing is of any more significance than anything else because nothing is of any significance at all. In the world is no value at all, nothing of importance. There are just the facts. And even if there were such a thing in the world as a value, that thing would itself just be another fact. It would *have* no value.

In Samuel Beckett's play *Endgame,* a character named Hamm, blind and unable to move from his chair, commands his servant, Clov, "Look at the earth." Clov gets his telescope, climbs a ladder, and looks out of the high window.

CLOV:
Let's see.
(He looks, moving the telescope.)
Zero . . .
(he looks)
. . . zero . . .
(he looks)
. . . and zero.

HAMM:
Nothing stirs. All is—

C:
Zer—

H: *(violently):*
Wait till you're spoken to!
(Normal voice.)
All is . . . all is . . . all is what?
(Violently.)
All is what?

C:
What all is? In a word? Is that what you want to know? Just a moment.
(He turns the telescope on the without, looks, lowers the telescope, turns toward Hamm.)
Corpsed.[7]

Beckett's vision could not be more like Wittgenstein's. At the same time, it could not be more unlike it. Turn the telescope to the earth (the world) and the verdict is "Zero, zero, zero." "Corpsed." In it, no value exists. For Beckett, that is all there is;

---

*Look back again to the discussion of how *final causes,* purposes and goals, are excluded from explanations in the new science. See p. 316. So far as the *world* goes, Wittgenstein agrees with Hume and disagrees with Augustine. See the diagram on p. 240.

In spirit, though, he may be closer to Augustine. Compare also Nietzsche, p. 546.

and that accounts for the sense of desolation and despair you find in his work. But Wittgenstein also knows another "reality."*

Ethics, Wittgenstein says, "cannot be put into words." But what does it mean that ethics is something "higher," that it is "transcendental"? To understand this saying, we need to consider Wittgenstein's views of the subject, the self, the "I." He suggests that if you wrote a book called *The World As I Found It,* there is one thing that would not be mentioned in it: *you.* It would include all the facts you found, including all the facts about your body. And it would include psychological facts about yourself as well: your character, personality, dispositions, and so on. But you—the subject, the one to whom all this appears, the one who *finds* all these facts— would not be found.†

> 5.632 The subject does not belong to the world; rather, it is a limit of the world.
>
> 5.641 The philosophical self is not the human being, not the human body, or the hu-

man soul, with which psychology deals, but rather the metaphysical subject, the limit of the world—not a part of it.

It seems, then, that there are two "realities" in correlation: the world and the self; however, in the strict sense, the self or subject cannot be said to be a reality. The self is not a *fact.* Wittgenstein compares the situation to the relation between an eye and its visual field. The eye is not itself part of the visual field; it is not seen. In the same way, all content, all the facts, are "out there" in the world, which is the "totality of facts" (1.1).

> 5.64 Here it can be seen that solipsism, when its implications are followed out strictly, coincides with pure realism. The self of solipsism shrinks to a point without extension, and there remains the reality co-ordinated with it.
>
> 5.62 For what the solipsist *means* is quite correct; only it cannot be *said,* but makes itself manifest.*

What the solipsist wants to say is that only he exists, and the world only in relation to himself. But this cannot be *said.* Why not? Because to say it would be to use language—propositions—to picture facts. And in picturing facts we are picturing the world, *not* the transcendental self to whom the world appears. So this self "shrinks to a point without extension." And if we ask *what there is,* the answer is the world—"all that is the case" (*Tractatus,* proposition 1). And this is just the thesis of radical **realism,** the antithesis of solipsism.

The concern of ethics is good and evil. But, as we have seen, there is no room for good and evil in the world, where everything just is whatever it is. What application, then, do these concepts have? Ethics must concern itself with the transcendental: the self, the subject. But how? Here is a clue.

---

*In a phrase as opposed as possible to Beckett's conclusion that the earth is "corpsed," Wittgenstein says, "The world and life are one" (5.621). But in the light of his claim that the world consists wholly of valueless facts, this is a dark saying. It does seem, though, to be related to the idea that the self is the "limit" of the world and to the complementarity of solipsism and realism. We examine these ideas subsequently.

†Among thinkers we have studied, this should remind you most of Kant, for whom the ego is also transcendental. It is not identical with Kant's view, however. Kant believes that, though we can't come to know the nature of "this I or he or it (the thing) which thinks," we could come to know a lot about it—that it is the source of the pure intuitions, the categories, the a priori synthetic propositions, all of which explain the structure of the empirical world. And all this can be stated in meaningful propositions. For Wittgenstein, none of this is possible. The structure of the world is not dictated by the structure of rational minds because the structure of reality is just logic; and logic, consisting as it does of empty tautologies, neither has nor needs a source. Kant's world needs a structure-giver because its fundamental principles are thought to be synthetic. For Wittgenstein, logic is *analytic.* It requires no source beyond itself because it has no content requiring explanation. This "scaffolding of the world" is not itself a fact in the world, nor is it a fact about the world or about rational minds. It is not a fact at all! It shows *itself.* Look again at the relevant discussions of Kant on pp. 443–444, including the diagram on p. 459.

---

*Compare Descartes' struggles to overcome solipsism by proving the existence of God in *Meditation III;* see also pp. 331 and 359. Wittgenstein acknowledges there is a truth in solipsism, but such truth as there is already involves the reality of the world—of which the self is aware. So there is no need to *prove* the world's existence—or that of God, about whom in any case nothing can be said.

6.373   The world is independent of my will.

6.374   Even if all that we wish for were to happen, still this would only be a favour granted by fate, so to speak.

I may will or intend to do something, such as write a check to pay a telephone bill. And usually I can do it. But it is clear that paying a bill by check depends on the cooperation of the world: The neurons have to fire just right, the nerves must transmit the neural signals reliably, the muscles must contract in just the right way, the bank must not suddenly crash, and so forth. And none of that is entirely in my control. That is what Wittgenstein means when he says the world is independent of my will. If I intend to pay my telephone bill, getting it done is, in a way, a "favour granted by fate."*

Good and Evil, Happiness and Unhappiness

Wittgenstein seems to have proved that good and evil cannot lie in the world. Everything just happens as it does happen. So good and evil must pertain to the will. What I will is in my control, even if the outcome of my willing in the world is not. In a strict sense, my willing *is* my action: The rest is just the result of my action. But now we have to ask what good and evil could be, if they pertain to the will only.

6.422   When an ethical law of the form, "Thou shalt . . .", is laid down, one's

───────────

*If these reflections are going to make any sense to you at all, you will have to pause a bit and try to sink into this way of viewing things. It will not be any good to just try to learn the words, or even memorize the sentences. Wittgenstein would insist that if you are able only to parrot the words, you will have understood *nothing*. Here is an exercise that might help. Pick out some fact about your present experience. Focus on it. Try to regard it as merely a fact in the world, one fact among others. Now try to focus on some psychological state in the same way. Practice in this should make even your own psychological states have the same status as any other fact in the world; they will not be "privileged," as it were, but just facts that are *there*. Then ask yourself, For whom are they there? For ideas that are in some ways similar, see the discussion of the Stoics on pp. 205–206.

first thought is, "And what if I do not do it?" It is clear, however, that ethics has nothing to do with punishment and reward in the usual sense of the terms. So our question about the *consequences* of an action must be unimportant. At least those consequences should not be events. For there must be something right about the question we posed. There must indeed be some kind of ethical reward and punishment, but they must reside in the action itself. (And it is also clear that the reward must be something pleasant and the punishment something unpleasant.)

Good action (good willing) is rewarded with something pleasant, and evil action is punished with the unpleasant. But these are not rewards and punishments "in the usual sense"; they cannot be external to the action itself. They cannot, in other words, be something added by the world. How could a "favour granted by fate" have anything to do with *ethical* rewards? Such rewards and punishments must be intrinsic to the actions themselves. But what could they be?

6.43   If the good or bad exercise of the will does alter the world, it can alter only the limits of the world, not the facts— not what can be expressed by means of language.
In short the effect must be that it becomes an altogether different world.
It must, so to speak, wax and wane as a whole.
The world of the happy man is a different one from that of the unhappy man.

These are difficult sayings, indeed. And I do not claim to understand fully what Wittgenstein means by them. It does seem clear that the reward for good willing is happiness and the punishment for bad is unhappiness. The good person, as Plato also thinks, is the happy person.* But this obviously does not mean that Jones, who lives righteously and well,

───────────

*See Plato's discussion of the happiness of the moral person, pp. 145–150.

will get whatever she wants in life. That kind of connection between willing and the world doesn't exist. (This fact is also recognized by Kant.) Goodness does not produce *that kind* of happiness.* What kind does it produce, then?

Strictly speaking, this question cannot be answered. In the *Notebooks, 1914–1916,* Wittgenstein asks,

> What is the objective mark of the happy, harmonious life? Here it is again clear that there cannot be any such mark, that can be *described*. This mark cannot be a physical one but only a metaphysical one, a transcendental one. (*N,* 78)[8]

And we know that nothing can be *said* about the transcendental. Still, there are clues and hints. What could it mean, for instance, that the world of the happy person is a different world from that of the unhappy one? That the world waxes and wanes as a whole? Here is a possibility.

Most of us, most of the time, do not occupy the position of the transcendental subject, even though that is what we essentially are—the limit of the world, not some entity within the world. We identify ourselves with a body, with certain desires, with a set of psychological facts. This is, we think, what we are. And in so identifying ourselves, our world narrows, *wanes*. We are concerned with *this* body, with satisfying *these* desires. And *our* world is just the world relevant to these concerns. It is as though the rest didn't exist. If we could, however, identify with the transcendental self, our world would wax larger. Indeed, we would see it just as it is—a limited whole and the totality of facts, none of which are of such importance that they crowd out any other. *Our* world would become *the* world. Only the world of the happy person is identical with the world as it is.†

The happy see the world with that disinterested enjoyment we experience when we appreciate a fine work of art. In Wittgenstein's words,

> 6.421   (Ethics and aesthetics are one and the same.)

and

> The work of art is the object seen *sub specie aeternitatis;* and the good life is the world seen *sub specie aeternitatis.* This is the connection between art and ethics.
>   The usual way of looking at things sees objects as if it were from the midst of them, the view *sub specie aeternitatis* from outside. (*N,* 84e)

and

> Aesthetically, the miracle is that the world exists. That what exists does exist.
>   Is it the essence of the artistic way of looking at things, that it looks at the world with a happy eye? (*N,* 86e)

To live one's life "from the viewpoint of eternity" is to live in the present.* And here we have another clue:

> Whoever lives in the present lives without fear and hope. (*N,* 76e)

What could this mean? The thought seems to be that fear and hope essentially refer to time; one fears what may happen, and one hopes for the future. But if one lives entirely in the present, there is no past and future about which to fear and hope. If there is nothing one fears—absolutely nothing—and if there is nothing one hopes (presumably because one lacks nothing), how could one fail to be happy? In his "Lecture on Ethics," Wittgenstein tells us that when he tries to think of something with absolute value, two "experiences" come to mind.

> I will describe this [first] experience in order, if possible, to make you recall the same or similar ex-

---

*It might help to remember here that Wittgenstein gave away the considerable fortune he inherited when his father died and lived the rest of his life simply and austerely. What the world can supply cannot *make* you happy!

†Compare Heraclitus, who says, "To those who are awake the world order is one, common to all; but the sleeping turn aside each into a world of his own." The *Tractatus* might almost be read as an extended commentary on this and related sayings by

---

Heraclitus, with logic—the "scaffolding" of the world—playing the role of the *logos.* See the discussion of these matters on pp. 19–24.

*Compare Augustine on God's eternity, pp. 243–244.

periences, so that we may have a common ground for our investigation. I believe the best way of describing it is to say that when I have it *I wonder at the existence of the world.* And I am then inclined to use such phrases as "how extraordinary that anything should exist" or "how extraordinary that the world should exist." I will mention another experience straight away which I also know and which others of you might be acquainted with: it is, what one might call, the experience of feeling *absolutely* safe. I mean the state of mind in which one is inclined to say "I am safe, nothing can injure me what ever happens."[9]*

Wittgenstein adds that the expression of these "experiences" in language is, strictly speaking, nonsense. One can wonder that the world contains kangaroos, perhaps, but there is no proposition that can express the "fact" that the world exists. Why not? Because this "fact" is obviously not one of the facts that make up the totality that *is* the world, and beyond that totality, there is nothing. It is equally nonsense to say that one feels *absolutely* safe. One can be safe from tigers, or protected from polio, but to say, "Nothing whatever can injure me," is just a misuse of language. Yet, that is the only satisfactory expression, Wittgenstein thinks, for what is of absolute value. Here we have an example of running against the boundaries of language.

To "wonder at the existence of the world" is to experience it as a limited whole. And that Wittgenstein calls "the mystical."

6.44   It is not *how* things are in the world that is mystical, but *that* it exists.

6.45   To view the world *sub specie aeterni* is to view it as a whole—a limited whole. Feeling the world as a limited whole—it is this that is mystical.

To live the life of the philosophical self, the metaphysical self that is not a part of the world but its limit, is to have a sense for "the mystical." This

life is also the good life, the beautiful life, and the happy life. It is a life of absolute safety.

Remember, though, that none of this can properly be said. It cannot even really be asked about. It is tempting to think that we can ask, Why does the world exist? or Why is there anything at all rather than nothing? But

6.5   When the answer cannot be put into words, neither can the question be put into words.
The riddle does not exist.
If a question can be framed at all, it is also *possible* to answer it.

The *answer* cannot be put into words because to say why the world exists would be to state a fact—and the world itself is already the *totality of facts*. So the question, "Why does the world exist?" which has exercised so many philosophical minds and has produced so many arguments for God's existence, is *no question at all*. It seems like a question—but that is an *illusion* generated by language.

What we can say is *how* the world is. And that is the job of natural science. But

6.52   We feel that even when *all possible* scientific questions have been answered, the problems of life remain completely untouched. Of course there are then no questions left, and this itself is the answer.

6.521   The solution of the problem of life is seen in the vanishing of the problem. (Is not this the reason why those who have found after a long period of doubt that the sense of life became clear to them have then been unable to say what constituted that sense?)

6.522   There are, indeed, things that cannot be put into words. They *make themselves manifest.* They are what is mystical.

The Unsayable

If you have been following carefully, you have no doubt been wondering how Wittgenstein can manage to say all this stuff that he so explicitly "says"

---

*Such a powerful echo of Socrates! In his defense at his trial, Socrates says, "A good man cannot be harmed either in life or in death" (*Apology* 41d).

cannot be said. This is indeed a puzzle we must address. What he has been writing is clearly philosophy. But if, as he (philosophically) says, the totality of true propositions is science, what room is there for philosophy?

4.111   Philosophy is not one of the natural sciences.
(The word "philosophy" must mean something whose place is above or below the natural sciences, not beside them.)
Philosophy aims at the logical clarification of thoughts.
Philosophy is not a body of doctrine but an activity.
A philosophical work consists essentially of elucidations.
Philosophy does not result in "philosophical propositions," but rather in the clarification of propositions.
Without philosophy thoughts are, as it were, cloudy and indistinct: its task is to make them clear and to give them sharp boundaries.

The key thought here is that philosophy is an activity; its business is clarification. It follows that we should not look to philosophy for *results,* for truths, or for "a body of doctrine." To do so is to mistake the nature of philosophizing altogether. It has been one of the major failings of the philosophical tradition, Wittgenstein believes, that it has tried to produce "philosophical propositions"—that it has thought of itself as something "beside" the sciences, in the same line of work as science. But it is *altogether different* from science. It lies, one might say, at right angles to science. Wittgenstein's view of his predecessors is severe:

4.003   Most of the propositions and questions to be found in philosophical works are not false but nonsensical.
Consequently we cannot give any answer to questions of this kind, but can only establish that they are nonsensical. Most of the propositions and questions of philosophers arise from our failure to understand the logic of our language.

(They belong to the same class as the question whether the good is more or less identical than the beautiful.)
And it is not surprising that the deepest problems are in fact *not* problems at all.

6.53   The correct method in philosophy would really be the following: to say nothing except what can be said, i.e., propositions of natural science—i.e., something that has nothing to do with philosophy—and then, whenever someone else wanted to say something metaphysical, to demonstrate to him that he had failed to give a meaning to certain signs in his propositions. Although it would not be satisfying to the other person—he would not have the feeling that we were teaching him philosophy—*this* method would be the only strictly correct one.

Plato and Aristotle, Hume and Kant all think they are revealing or discovering truth. But, if Wittgenstein is right, all of their most important claims are nonsensical. They aren't even *candidates* for being true! Their theories—to the extent that they are not absorbable by empirical science—are pseudo-answers to pseudoquestions. Just *gassing.* Such theories arise because these philosophers don't understand the logic of our language; Wittgenstein thinks he has, for the first time, clearly set this forth.

But there is still a worry. Wittgenstein is himself not utilizing "the correct method" in writing the *Tractatus.* How, then, are we to take his own "propositions" here?

6.54   My propositions serve as elucidations in the following way: anyone who understands me eventually recognizes them as nonsensical, when he has used them—as steps—to climb up beyond them. (He must, so to speak, throw away the ladder after he has climbed up it.)
He must transcend these propositions, and then he will see the world aright.

To "see the world aright" is to see it from the viewpoint of eternity, from the point of view of the philosophical self. It is not too far-fetched to be reminded of that ladder the mystics talk about as leading to oneness with God. Having climbed Wittgenstein's ladder, we too can wonder at the existence of the world, feel absolutely safe, experience happiness and beauty—and do our science. But we would always have to keep in mind the last "proposition" of the *Tractatus:*

> 7.   What we cannot speak about we must pass over in silence.

Yet, the things we must "pass over in silence" are the most important of all.

In Wittgenstein's *Tractatus,* then, we have an excellent example of analytic philosophy. He uses the new logic in an analysis of our language and finds the result to be a kind of logical atomism. In Wittgenstein, however, this logical analysis of language is placed in the service of larger ends. His problem, from first to last, concerns the meaning of life. If he had not thought that applying logic to thought and language would clarify *that* problem, we cannot imagine he would have devoted himself to philosophy in the way he did. He might just have become an aeronaut.

---

1. Why couldn't the "important" part of the *Tractatus* be written?
2. Why must the sense of the world lie outside the world? Why cannot there be "propositions of ethics"?
3. Suppose you wrote a book entitled *The World As I Found It*. Would you appear in the book?
4. How does solipsism coincide with pure realism?
5. In what way is the world of the happy person different from the world of the unhappy person? What does it mean to see the world *sub specie aeternitatis*?
6. Could a person be absolutely safe? (Compare Socrates in his defense to the jury in *Apology* 41c–d, pp. 100–101.)
7. What is the "mystical"? Why does it have absolutely nothing to do with the "occult"?
8. Why won't science solve the problems of life? Why does "the riddle" not exist?
9. What is philosophy? What is its "correct method"? What is the ladder analogy?

Logical Positivism

In the preface to the *Tractatus,* Wittgenstein writes,

> Perhaps this book will be understood only by someone who has himself already had the thoughts that are expressed in it—or at least similar thoughts. (*Tractatus,* preface, 3).

This was to prove prophetic. Russell supplied an introduction that Wittgenstein thought so misunderstood his intentions that he refused to have it printed in the German edition. And his book was studied painstakingly by a group of scientifically oriented philosophers in Vienna (a group that came to be known as the Vienna Circle) who admired its logic and philosophy of language but had no sympathy with what Wittgenstein himself thought most important. Because this latter group proved extremely influential, at least for a time, we briefly note their major theses here. The movement they began had a significant impact on scientists (both natural and social), on philosophy of science, and on the general public. These philosophers are called *logical positivists.*

Logical positivism can be identified with three claims, all of which have recognizable roots in the *Tractatus.* The first is that logic and mathematics are *analytic.* The positivists accept Wittgenstein's analysis of the basic truths of logic: The truths are tautological in nature. Both mathematics and logic are empirically or factually empty, providing no knowledge of nature at all.* They are, however, extremely important: They provide a framework in which we can move from one true factual state-

---

*Thus they correspond roughly to what Hume calls relations of ideas (see pp. 403–405) and Kant's notion of the analytic a priori (see p. 430). Note how different a philosophy of mathematics this is from that of Kant, who believes that arithmetic, while a priori, is not analytic.

ment to another; that is, they license inferences, just as Wittgenstein says they do.*

The second principle is a criterion for judging the meaningfulness of all nontautological assertions. It is called the **verifiability principle.** The positivists believe they can use it to sweep away not only the confusions of past philosophy, but also everything Wittgenstein holds most dear. Here is Moritz Schlick's explanation of verifiability:

> When, in general, are we sure that the meaning of a question is clear to us? Evidently when and only when we are able to state exactly the conditions under which it is to be answered in the affirmative, or as the case may be, the conditions under which it is to be answered in the negative. By stating these conditions, and by this alone, is the meaning of a question defined.
>
> The meaning of a proposition consists, obviously, in this alone, that it expresses a definite state of affairs. One can, of course, say that the proposition itself already gives this state of affairs.† This is true, but the proposition indicates the state of affairs only to the person who understands it. But when do I understand a proposition? When I understand the meanings of the words which occur in it? These can be explained by definition. But in the definitions new words appear whose meanings cannot again be described in propositions, they must be indicated directly: the meaning of a word must in the end be *shown*, it must be *given*. This is done by an act of indication, of pointing; and what is pointed at must be given, otherwise I cannot be referred to it.[10]

The definitions Schlick refers to are Wittgenstein's analyses of complex propositions into elementary or atomic propositions and ultimately into words that are not further definable. For Wittgenstein, as we have seen, elementary propositions are composed of names in a logical syntax. The names stand for objects. He never specifies exactly what objects the names name. He once said, much later, that when he wrote the *Tractatus,* he thought of himself as a logician and believed that it wasn't his

business to identify the objects that he deduced on logical grounds would have to be there.

But for the positivists, the truth conditions for elementary sentences are given in *perception*. The simple objects designated by the indefinable words must be the kind of thing you can point to. Schlick uses the Wittgensteinian word "shown" and paraphrases it by "given." The meaning of a word must be something you can point to or indicate in some way. You have to be able to *show* me what you mean. What Schlick means by "given" is "given in sense experience." This, then, is the bite of the verifiability principle. Unless you can explain what perceptual difference the truth or falsity of your assertion would make, the proposition you are asserting is *meaningless.* Clearly, logical positivism is a kind of empiricism.*

The positivists have no sympathy for a "good" kind of nonsense, no tolerance for "running against the boundaries of language." All this they want to *exterminate*. They talk about the *elimination* of metaphysics. (One gets the image of lining metaphysical ideas up against the wall and gunning them down.) What is to be left as meaningful is science—science alone! Out with Plato's Forms, Aristotle's entelechy, Augustine's God, Descartes' mind, Kant's noumena, Hegel's Absolute Spirit—and Wittgenstein's mystical! Out with metaphysics altogether—that attempt to know something beyond what our senses can verify. It is to be purged from human memory.† And the instrument of this purging is the principle of meaningfulness. Since none of these notions are verifiable by sense experience, they are all meaningless.

Note that the positivists are not committed, for example, to the atheist's claim that there is no God. Such a claim they consider to be as much a meta-

---

*Review the discussion of the principles of logic on p. 605.

†Wittgenstein says, "A proposition *shows* its sense" (4.022).

---

*Like David Hume, prince of empiricists, the positivists want to base all nonanalytic knowledge on the data our senses provide. See again the discussion of "the theory of ideas" and Hume's rule, "No impression, no idea" (p. 402).

†For a similar sentiment, see David Hume's trenchant remarks at the end of his *Enquiry* (p. 425). It has been said, with some justice, that logical positivism is just Hume plus modern logic.

physical statement as the claim that there is a God. Both claims are shut out from the realm of meaning altogether; if the verifiability criterion is correct, both the believer and the atheist are uttering meaningless noises. Because their claims are without sense, one cannot sensibly ask which is true: Neither one is even a possible candidate for truth. So arguments for (or against) the existence of God are completely worthless!

The positivists work at refining the verifiability principle to avoid obvious counterexamples. For instance, verifiability needn't be *direct,* as when I see something with my own eyes; it can be *indirect,* as when I rely on instrumentation, or (more important) when I test the observable consequences of a hypothesis that is not itself directly testable. It is enough, they say, for propositions to be verifiable *in principle.* They obviously want to allow for the meaningfulness of propositions that are not now verifiable only because of technological limitations. Moreover, something doesn't have to be conclusively verifiable for it to be meaningful. They draw a contrast between *strong* (conclusive) verification and *weak* verification (verification by evidence indicating that something is likely to be true or probably true). The positivists hold that weak verifiability is enough to qualify a statement as meaningful. But unless a proposition is at least indirectly verifiable, verifiable in principle, and weakly verifiable, it is declared to have no sense.

The third plank of the positivist platform concerns the nature of philosophy. Like Wittgenstein, they hold that philosophy is not in the business of providing knowledge about the supersensible; its task is the clarification of statements. So it is an activity, as Wittgenstein says. But they are convinced that philosophy doesn't have to be classified as nonsense. If the activity of philosophy is clarification, it has certain statable results: It issues in definitions. Much of the writing of the logical positivists is devoted to clarifying what they call "the logic of science," so they are interested in the concepts of *law* and *theory,* of *hypothesis* and *evidence,* of *confirmation* and *probability.* Much good work is produced in understanding these concepts and how they relate to each other. Under their influence the *philosophy of*

science becomes a recognized and important part of philosophy; without their work in this area, it is unlikely that most academic departments would now be teaching courses in this field.[*]

The fate of ethical statements on positivist principles is particularly interesting. Moral judgments do not seem to be verifiable—even weakly, indirectly, and in principle. So they don't seem to meet the criterion for factual meaningfulness. That raises the question: What kind of statement is a judgment that stealing is wrong?[†] In an explosive book titled *Language, Truth, and Logic,* published in 1936, the English philosopher A. J. Ayer sets out the positivist view of ethics. Ethical concepts, he says, are "mere pseudoconcepts."

> Thus if I say to someone, "You acted wrongly in stealing that money," I am not stating anything more than if I had simply said, "You stole that money." In adding that this action is wrong I am not making any further statement about it. I am simply evincing my moral disapproval of it. It is as if I had said, "You stole that money," in a peculiar tone of horror, or written it with the addition of some special exclamation marks. The tone, or the exclamation marks, adds nothing to the literal meaning of the sentence. It merely serves to show that the expression of it is attended by certain feelings in the speaker.
>
> If now I generalize my previous statement and say, "Stealing money is wrong," I produce a sentence which has no factual meaning—that is, expresses no proposition which can be either true or

---

[*]Like most of the distinctive theses of logical positivism, the positivists' understanding of the logic of science is now largely surpassed. It now seems too abstract, too prescriptive, and not mindful enough of how science is actually done. The complaint is, ironically, that positivists are not empirical enough about science itself. Historical studies in the past several decades have significantly modified our understanding of that important cultural institution we call science. One of the milestones in this development is Thomas Kuhn's 1962 work, *The Structure of Scientific Revolutions.*

[†]Recall Wittgenstein's claim that in the world there is no value—and if there were a value in the world, it would *have* no value. The realm of facts excludes the realm of values. You should also look back to Hume's famous discussion of the distinction between *is* and *ought* (pp. 421–422).

false. It is as if I had written "Stealing money!!"—where the shape and thickness of the exclamation marks show, by a suitable convention, that a special sort of moral disapproval is the feeling which is being expressed. It is clear that there is nothing said here which can be true or false. Another man may disagree with me about the wrongness of stealing, in the sense that he may not have the same feelings about stealing as I have, and he may quarrel with me on account of my moral sentiments. But he cannot, strictly speaking, contradict me. For in saying that a certain type of action is right or wrong, I am not making any factual statement, not even a statement about my own state of mind. I am merely expressing certain moral sentiments. And the man who is ostensibly contradicting me is merely expressing his moral sentiments. So that there is plainly no sense in asking which of us is in the right. For neither of us is asserting a genuine proposition. . . .

. . . If a sentence makes no statement at all, there is obviously no sense in asking whether what it says is true or false. And we have seen that sentences which simply express moral judgments do not say anything. They are pure expressions of feeling and as such do not come under the category of truth and falsehood. They are unverifiable for the same reason as a cry of pain or a word of command is unverifiable—because they do not express a genuine proposition.[11]

This is pretty radical stuff, at least as judged by the philosophical tradition. Its ancestry lies in the views of the Sophists, that things (at least in the moral sphere) just are as they seem to the individual human being.* If Ayer is right, there are no objective truths about the good life or about right and wrong, so reason (obviously) cannot help us find them. It follows that Socrates' search for the nature of piety, courage, and justice is misguided. And all the philosophers who build on that assumption are mistaken in what they are doing. Plato's Form of the Good, Aristotle's virtues as human excellences,

Epicurus' pleasure, the Stoics' keeping of the will in harmony with nature, Augustine's ordered loves, Hobbes' social contract, Kant's categorical imperative, Mill's greatest good for the greatest number—all these are not, if Ayer is right, contributions to a theory of the right and the good for humans, but merely expressions of how these individuals feel about things.*

If we use a different measure, however, Ayer's view isn't so radical. In fact, it is the underpinning of what seems to many these days the sheerest common sense. Nearly every college freshman, in my experience, arrives with the opinion that this view of moral judgments is so obvious that it is very nearly absurd to question it.† (That, of course, is not a very strong argument in its favor.)

Ayer's view, sometimes called the *emotivist theory of ethics,* is stated in a brash and bold fashion. Other thinkers in the same tradition qualify and complicate it to meet obvious objections, but it is good to see it stated in its bare essentials, especially since it has been so widely adopted by the public. It is important to note that the emotivist theory of ethics depends on a stark contrast between the realm of facts and all the rest. This contrast, at least as the positivists develop it, is based on the verifiability principle's adequacy as a theory of meaning. If that theory of meaning is flawed, we may not be able to get by with such a radically subjectivist theory of morality. We will reexamine the question

---

*See the motto of Protagoras on p. 44, and the relevance of rhetoric to justice as developed by Gorgias, Antiphon, and Callicles, discussed on pp. 47–49. A major portion of rhetoric might be thought of as techniques for "expressing moral sentiments" in persuasive ways.

---

*It is important to note that the Wittgenstein of the *Tractatus* would think this turn of events about as awful as could be imagined. While he would agree that value is not a matter of fact, he wants to locate ethics—what really matters—in the life of the transcendental or philosophical self. Positivist ethics construes value as no more than the way some empirical self happens to feel about things. What greater difference could there be? Wittgenstein says, "God does not reveal himself *in* the world" (*Tractatus* 6.432). The positivists make each of us a little god. From Wittgenstein's point of view, if Ayer is right, all we ever get in morality is "just *gassing.*" See again Wittgenstein's views on ethics, pp. 607–612.

†This fact is one of the centerpieces of Alan Bloom's complaint about today's university education, addressed in his book *The Closing of the American Mind* (New York: Simon and Schuster, 1988).

about meaning when we turn to Wittgenstein's later philosophy, in Chapter 23.

To their credit, it should be noted that certain difficulties in the verifiability principle are noted and examined by the positivists themselves. For instance, by dividing the analytic statements of logic and definition so sharply from verifiable statements of fact, they provoke the question, What sort of statement is the verifiability principle itself? There seem to be three possibilities:

1. The verifiability principle might be a factual statement. But—by its own terms—the principle, to be factual, must itself be verifiable by sense experience. But what sense experiences could constitute the truth conditions for this principle? The possibility of seeing red roses might constitute the meaning of "Some roses are red." And experiences in a laboratory might (in a complicated and indirect way) verify "Copper conducts electricity." But what experience could show that the only meaningful statements are those verifiable by experience? As Wittgenstein was to later remark, the standard meter bar in Paris cannot be said either to be or not to be one meter long. A criterion cannot guarantee itself, so it seems clear that it is not factual.

2. It might be analytic, a definition of "meaningful." But it doesn't seem to capture the *ordinary* sense of meaningfulness. There are lots of unverifiable propositions we think we understand perfectly well. Consider this example: "The last word in Caesar's mind, unuttered, before he died, was 'tu.'" This seems obviously sensible and it is either true or false, but the possibility of verifying it, even weakly, indirectly, and in principle, seems zero. The fact that we cannot in any way *find out* whether it is true, does not subtract from its meaningfulness in the slightest.

3. There seems only one possibility left, given the positivist framework. If it doesn't fit either of the two main favored categories, perhaps the principle functions as a kind of recommendation that this is how we *should* use the word "meaningful," or a proposal that it would be *good* to use the word "meaningful" in this way. This understanding of the verifiability principle would associate it with the positivist view of ethical propositions. Its enunciation would express feelings of approval about this way of understanding meaning and perhaps urge others to feel the same way. But if this is what the verifiability principle amounts to, then there is no *reason* why we all should adopt it, and nonpositivists can (on positivist grounds) simply say, "Well, I feel different about it." And that is not very satisfactory.

---

1. Explain the verifiability principle of factual meaningfulness.
2. In what ways can verification be indirect? Weak? In principle?
3. What is the positivist's analysis of ethical judgments? Compare to Hume; to Kant; to the utilitarians.
4. What difficulties do the positivists identify in the verifiability criterion?

For Further Thought

The young Wittgenstein thought he had found a unique solution to the problem of the meaning of life. The solution is found in the disappearing of the problem—but not through thoughtlessness or inattention. Try to explain this "solution" in terms that could be meaningful to your own life—and then decide whether you accept it.

Notes

1. Bertrand Russell, "Logical Atomism," in *Logic and Knowledge* (London: Allen and Unwin, 1956), 197–198.
2. Bertrand Russell, "Philosophers and Idiots," *Listener* 52, no. 1354 (February 10, 1955): 247. Reprinted in Russell's *Portraits from Memory* (London: Allen and Unwin, 1956), 26–27.
3. A brief and very readable account of Wittgenstein's life can be found in Norman Malcolm's *Ludwig Wittgenstein: A Memoir* (Oxford: Oxford University Press, 1958).
4. Ludwig Wittgenstein, *Tractatus Logico-Philosophicus,* trans. D. F. Pears and B. F. McGuinness (London: Routledge and Kegan Paul, 1961). Quotations from the main text of the *Tractatus*

are identified by the paragraph numbers found in that work.

5. Paul Englemann, *Letters from Ludwig Wittgenstein, with a Memoir* (Oxford: Basil Blackwell, 1967), 143–144.

6. Ludwig Wittgenstein, "Lecture on Ethics," *Philosophical Review* 74 (1965): 12.

7. Samuel Beckett, *Endgame* (New York: Grove Press, 1958), 29–30.

8. Quotations from Ludwig Wittgenstein's *Notebooks, 1914–1916* (Oxford: Basil Blackwell, 1961), are cited in the text using the abbreviation *N*. References are to page numbers.

9. Wittgenstein, "Lecture on Ethics," 8.

10. Moritz Schlick, "Positivism and Realism," in *Logical Positivism,* ed. A. J. Ayer (New York: Macmillan, 1959), 86–87.

11. A. J. Ayer, *Language, Truth, and Logic* (New York: Dover, n.d.), 107–108.

23

ORDINARY LANGUAGE
"This Is Simply What I Do"

The analysis of language in terms of the new logic yields some impressive results, but not everyone is convinced that this is the way to go. Logical atomism, whether in the form developed by the early Wittgenstein or in a phenomenalistic version by Russell,* has some problems (see the following section). And the ambitious program of the logical positivists doesn't seem to be working out even for their favorite case of meaningful discourse: science.

These problems suggest to certain thinkers that instead of looking to some "ideal" language inspired by logic, we might be better advised to pay closer attention to how our own language actually functions. Perhaps the lack of definite results and clear progress in previous philosophy is due to the fact that we *misunderstand* our language. Maybe it's not that language itself is to blame so much as that we—philosophers particularly—misuse it or misdescribe its use. Perhaps all goes smoothly when we talk about minds in everyday life, for instance, but when the philosopher reflectively asks himself, "Just what is a mind?" things start to go all wobbly.

Gilbert Ryle gives expression to this suspicion in contrasting the philosopher's use of language with that of other professionals and specialists:

> The experts who use the technical terms of bridge, law, chemistry and plumbing learn to employ these terms partly from official instructions but largely by directly engaging in the special techniques and by directly dealing with the special materials or ob-

*Russell suggests that we take as Wittgenstein's simple objects what he calls "sense data." These are the phenomenally given, particular instances of *orange, warm, hard, sweet,* and so on. He proposes that instead of *inferring* that something is the cause of those phenomena in us, we should try to *construct* our knowledge of things out of these elements and the formal structures of logic. (See, for instance, Russell's book, *Our Knowledge of the External World.*) This project obviously owes a debt to the early empiricists, especially Berkeley and Hume, though without the former's commitment to spiritual substance as the "home" for these data. See pp. 388–393.

jects of their specialism. They familiarise themselves with the harness by having to drive their (to us unfamiliar) horses.

But the terms of art of philosophy itself (save for those of formal logic) are not like this. . . . We know by what special sorts of work mastery is acquired of the concepts of *finesse, tort, sulphanilamide* and *valve-seating.* But by what corresponding special sorts of work do philosophers get their supposed corresponding mastery of the concepts of *Cognition, Sensation, Secondary Qualities* and *Essences?* What exercises and predicaments have forced them to learn just how to use and how not to misuse these terms?

Philosophers' arguments which turn on these terms are apt, sooner or later, to start to rotate idly. There is nothing to make them point north rather than nor'-nor'-east.[1]

Ryle thinks that the concepts we use to think about the mind tend to "rotate idly" in just this way, especially since Descartes. In a now-classic work titled *The Concept of Mind,* Ryle attacks Cartesian dualism, calling it "Descartes' Myth" and describing it "with deliberate abusiveness, as 'the dogma of the Ghost in the Machine.'"[2] To think that there are minds *and* bodies, is to commit a "category mistake," Ryle tells us, to suppose that the concept of mind belongs to the category of *thing,* just as bodies do. In a series of chapters dealing with knowing how and knowing that, the will, emotion, self-knowledge, sensation and observation, imagination, and so on, Ryle exposes this "dogma" to withering criticism, showing over and over again how it misrepresents the way we actually employ these concepts.

If philosophical mistakes are so easy to slip into, what is the remedy? J. L. Austin, another distinguished contributor to this way of looking at philosophy, advises us to pay close attention to "what we should say when." Austin engages in a set of careful descriptions of the ordinary use of philosophically interesting words, trying to elicit their meaning—which is not, as Locke thought, the idea they stand for, but the rules for their proper use. In one of the most famous of these, the short essay, "A Plea for Excuses,"* he offers a justification for proceeding in this way.

First, words are our tools, and, as a minimum, we should use clean tools: we should know what we mean and what we do not, and we must forearm ourselves against the traps that language sets us. Secondly, words are not (except in their own little corner) facts or things: we need therefore to prise them off the world, to hold them apart from and against it, so that we can realize their inadequacies and arbitrariness, and can re-look at the world without blinkers. Thirdly, and more hopefully, our common stock of words embodies all the distinctions men have found worth drawing, and the connexions they have found worth marking, in the lifetimes of many generations: these surely are likely to be more numerous, more sound, since they have stood up to the long test of the survival of the fittest, and more subtle, at least in all ordinary and reasonably practical matters, than any that you or I are likely to think up in our arm-chairs of an afternoon—the most favoured alternative method. . . .

When we examine what we should say when, what words we should use in what situations, we are looking again not *merely* at words (or "meanings," whatever they may be) but also at the realities we use the words to talk about: we are using a sharpened awareness of words to sharpen our perception of, though not as the final arbiter of, the phenomena.[3]

The last phrase is of some importance. Austin is not arguing that an understanding of the use of ordinary language will definitively settle philosophical questions. It may not be the last word—but, he

---

*The topic here is *responsibility,* or, more broadly, theory of action. But characteristically, instead of trying to address those big issues directly, Austin concentrates on a narrow aspect of the problem, focusing a bright light on the circumstances in which various kinds of excuses are in order, how excuses differ from justifications for actions, and how excuses are appraised. Austin takes himself to be dealing with the same issues as Aristotle in his famous discussion of responsibility (see pp. 193–195), but doing so in a way less subject to the dangers Ryle (and Wittgenstein, as we shall see) points out.

insists, it should be the *first* word. That is where we should begin, but that is where philosophers, all too often, have been deficient.

The Later Wittgenstein:
Philosophical Investigations

This way of thinking about philosophical problems is given a decisive push by Wittgenstein. In the preface to that youthful work, *Tractatus Logico-Philosophicus,* Wittgenstein had written,

> The *truth* of the thoughts that are here set forth seems to me unassailable and definitive. I therefore believe myself to have found, on all essential points, the final solution of the problems.[4]

With great consistency and in perfect conformity with his inexpressible ethics, he then leaves philosophy to teach elementary school in a remote Austrian village. As the years pass, though, he engages in conversations with other philosophers and scientists, including members of the Vienna Circle. Eventually he comes to believe that he has not, after all, found "the final solution" of all the problems he had addressed. The vision expressed in his *Tractatus* is powerful and elegant, but Wittgenstein gradually becomes convinced that it is not *true*. In the first fifty pages of *Philosophical Investigations* he subjects his earlier views to devastating criticism.[*]

There are certainly difficulties in the *Tractatus.* For one thing, his view that logic consists solely of tautologies is proved by Alonzo Church to be too simple.[†] Furthermore, there is that strange conse-

quence of the picture theory—that all his own philosophical propositions are nonsensical, despite the fact that many of us seem to understand at least some of them rather well. But it is neither of these things that moves Wittgenstein to criticize the doctrines of the *Tractatus*. Indeed, he is already dissatisfied before the publication of Church's Theorem. Wittgenstein begins to feel difficulties in connection with the central thesis of the *Tractatus*—that a proposition is a picture, together with the correlated doctrine of names and simple objects. Norman Malcolm tells a story about a conversation between Wittgenstein and P. Sraffa, a lecturer in economics at Cambridge.

> One day (they were riding, I think, on a train) when Wittgenstein was insisting that a proposition and that which it describes must have the same "logical form," the same "logical multiplicity," Sraffa made a gesture, familiar to Neapolitans as meaning something like disgust or contempt, of brushing the underneath of his chin with an outward sweep of the fingertips of one hand. And he asked: "What is the logical form of *that?*" Sraffa's example produced in Wittgenstein the feeling that there was an absurdity in the insistence that a proposition and what it describes must have the same "form." This broke the hold on him of the conception that a proposition must literally be a "picture" of the reality it describes.[5]

A meaningful gesture, surely! It communicates something very effectively. Or think of "Phooey!" or "Nuts!" Bits of language? Of course. But what is their logical form? And of what simple names are they composed? And what possible states of affairs do they picture? Just to ask such questions shows up

---

[*] Published posthumously in 1953, two years after his death, *Philosophical Investigations* is written in two parts, the first of which is organized in numbered sections, most of which are a paragraph or two long. Like the *Tractatus,* it is a difficult book, but in quite a different way. Whereas you can read a sentence in the *Tractatus* half a dozen times and still be puzzled about what it means, the *Investigations,* for the most part, reads with some ease. But then you find yourself asking, What does this all amount to?

[†] Wittgenstein had held that sentences containing quantifiers were capable of analysis into elementary propositions and so were truth functions of elementary propositions. This meant

that truth tables could function as a decision procedure for determining the truth of all logically true propositions. For instance, $(\exists x)Fx$ (there exists something that has the property F) was to be analyzed as (*Fa* or *Fb* or *Fc*. . .) (i.e., object *a* is *F*, or object *b* is *F*, or object *c* is *F*, or . . .). And $(x)Fx$ became (*Fa* and *Fb* and *Fc* . . .). This meant that in principle there could be a truth table written for any generalized sentence, and we would have a *decision procedure* for determining the truth of these sentences. But in 1930, Alonzo Church proved that no such decision procedure is possible for domains that are possibly infinite. (This is called Church's Theorem.)

a deficiency in the *Tractatus* doctrine—if it is to be taken as a description of the very *essence* of language. Even if you were to grant that the picture theory correctly analyzes an important part of language (e.g., the propositions of natural science), it would be at best only partial; it would not reach the essence of language.*

Philosophical Illusion

Wittgenstein allows that his *Tractatus* does express a possible way of seeing things. We can climb the ladder of his "nonsensical" propositions and get a certain vision of things. He had said in the *Tractatus* that we would then "see the world aright" (*Tractatus* 6.54). But he now thinks this way of seeing things is a mistake. Yet, "mistake" is not quite the right word; it is more like an illusion, he suggests, or even a superstition that held him in thrall (*PI,* 97, 110).[6] But how could he have been so deceived? What is the source of this illusion that the *Tractatus* presents with such clarity and power? Philosophers, he thinks, are especially subject to this illusion, but all of us can easily be seduced into this kind of error. Here is one way that the seduction can work.

We sometimes find that others misunderstand what we mean when we talk to them. These misunderstandings can often be removed by paraphrasing, by substituting one form of expression for another. It is often helpful to use simpler terms to explain what we mean:

> This may be called an "analysis" of our forms of expression, for the process is sometimes like one of taking a thing apart. (*PI,* 90)

> But now it may come to look as if there were something like a final analysis of our forms of language, and so a *single* completely resolved form of every expression. That is, as if our usual forms of expression were, essentially, unanalyzed; as if there were something hidden in them that had to

be brought to light. When this is done the expression is completely clarified and our problem is solved.

> It can also be put like this: we eliminate misunderstandings by making our expressions more exact; but now it may look as if we were moving towards a particular state, a state of complete exactness; and as if this were the real goal of our investigation. (*PI,* 91)

The Wittgenstein of the *Tractatus* was committed to all these notions: to the idea that there is "something hidden" in our ordinary language that can be "completely clarified" by a "final analysis" into "a *single* completely resolved form of every expression," which would gain us our "real goal"—"a state of complete exactness." The slide to these conclusions is so subtle we scarcely notice it, but it is a slide into illusion.

> This finds expression in questions as to the essence of language, of propositions, of thought. . . . For they see in the essence, not something that already lies open to view and that becomes surveyable by a rearrangement, but something that lies *beneath* the surface. Something that lies within, which we see when we look *into* the thing, and which an analysis digs out.
> "*The essence is hidden from us*": this is the form our problem now assumes. We ask: "*What is* language?", "*What is* a proposition?" And the answer to these questions is to be given once for all; and independently of any future experience. (*PI,* 92)

Language, propositions—these seem mysterious, strange. We are encouraged to suppose that there *must* be an essence of language—one essence—because it is all called by one name, "language." Further, we assume that every instance of it must have something in common with all the rest. This is a supposition that goes way back; Socrates, in asking about piety, is not content with answers that give him examples of pious behavior. What he wants is the essence of piety—that is, something common to all examples that *makes* them instances of piety.*

---

*The positivists recognize this deficiency, too; Ayer's emotivist theory of moral language (that it does nothing more than express and influence feelings) is an attempt to accommodate other uses of language than the literal and descriptive. Wittgenstein's critique, however, is far deeper and more radical.

*See Plato's *Euthyphro* 5d—6e and p. 81.

About this seductive idea, Wittgenstein now says,

> A *picture* held us captive. And we could not get outside it, for it lay in our language and language seemed to repeat it to us inexorably. (*PI,* 115)

This picture is not a *Tractatus* picture. It is a picture in an ordinary, though metaphorical, sense, as when we say, "I can't help but picture her as happy." It is a picture of language as a *calculus,* as something possessing "the crystalline purity of logic" (*PI,* 107). This picture, Wittgenstein says, "held us captive."

> It is like a pair of glasses on our nose through which we see whatever we look at. It never occurs to us to take them off. (*PI,* 103)

> We predicate of the thing what lies in the method of representing it. (*PI,* 104)

> (*Tractatus Logico-Philosophicus* 4.5): "The general form of a proposition is: This is how things are."— That is the kind of proposition that one repeats to oneself countless times. One thinks that one is tracing the outline of the thing's nature over and over again, and one is merely tracing round the frame through which we look at it. (*PI,* 114)

Captive to a picture, we cannot shake off the conviction that language *must* have an essence, that hidden in the depths of our ordinary sentences must be an exact logical structure in which simple names stand for simple objects. Logic, which is the "scaffolding of the world" (*Tractatus* 6.124), *requires* that. Propositions *must* have pictorial form and an isomorphism with what they picture. Never mind that they don't actually look like that! That is the way it *must* be—we think.

But that is just what is wrong with the *Tractatus* vision. The *Tractatus* doesn't *describe* the way language works; it *prescribes.* Once we become aware of that, we can also see our way out of the illusion. We can get out of the grip of this superstition by confining ourselves solely to *description.*

> It was true to say [in the *Tractatus*] that our considerations could not be scientific ones. . . . And we may not advance any kind of theory. There must not be anything hypothetical in our considerations. We must do away with all *explanation,* and description alone must take its place. And this description

gets its light, that is to say its purpose, from the philosophical problems. These are, of course, not empirical problems; they are solved, rather, by looking into the workings of our language, and that in such a way as to make us recognize those workings: *in despite of* an urge to misunderstand them. The problems are solved, not by giving new information, but by arranging what we have always known. Philosophy is a battle against the bewitchment of our intelligence by means of language. (*PI,* 109)

There are clear echoes of the *Tractatus* here. Note that philosophy is still something quite different from the sciences: Its problems are "not empirical." And philosophy's job is not to produce theories or explanations. Philosophy is still an activity of clarification rather than a set of results. But Wittgenstein no longer thinks that all philosophical problems can be solved at once, by analyzing "the essence of language." We must proceed in a piecemeal fashion, working patiently at one problem after another by "looking into the workings of our language," by "arranging what we have always known." It is not "new information" that we need to resolve philosophical problems. We need the ability to find our way through the many temptations to misunderstand.[*]

> When philosophers use a word—"knowledge," "being," "object," "I," "proposition," "name"—and try to grasp the *essence* of the thing, one must always ask oneself: is the word ever actually used in this way in the language-game which is its original home?—
>
> What *we* do is to bring words back from their metaphysical to their everyday use. (*PI,* 116)

The notion of a *language-game* is one we will have to examine closely. It is clear that philosophical *theories* of knowledge, reality, the self, and the external world are regarded with great suspicion by Wittgenstein, just as they were in the *Tractatus.* Such theories, we may imagine, he still regards as

---

[*]In the introduction to *The Concept of Mind,* Ryle says the purpose of his book is not to give us new information about minds, but "to rectify the logical geography of the knowledge which we already possess" (p. 9).

"just *gassing*." But the reason for suspicion is now different. The words that are being used in these theories—"know," "object," "I," "name"—all are words with common uses. Wittgenstein now suspects that as they are used in these philosophical theories, the words lose their anchors in the uses and activities that make them meaningful. They float free, without discipline, and lose their meaning; yet, it is just *because* they have no anchors in concrete life that they seem to indicate deep problems. This appearance of depth, however, is just part of the illusion. What is needed is to "bring words back from their metaphysical to their everyday use."

Here is another point of similarity and contrast with Wittgenstein's view in the *Tractatus*. There he held that the "correct method" in philosophy was to show someone who thinks he is saying something philosophical and deep that "he had failed to give a meaning to certain signs" (*Tractatus* 6.53) and so was not saying anything at all. Here, the alternative to saying something metaphysical is not restricting oneself to the propositions of natural science, as the *Tractatus* recommends. The alternative is to come back to home ground in our *ordinary* ways of talking.

Philosophical problems are *baffling*:

A philosophical problem has the form: "I don't know my way about." (*PI*, 123)

But the solution is not to construct a philosophical theory about the baffling topic. What we need is to clarify the language in which the problem is posed.

Philosophy may in no way interfere with the actual use of language; it can in the end only describe it.
For it cannot give it any foundation either.
It leaves everything as it is. (*PI*, 124)

Philosophy simply puts everything before us, and neither explains nor deduces anything. —Since everything lies open to view there is nothing to explain. For what is hidden, for example, is of no interest to us.
One might also give the name "philosophy" to what is possible *before* all new discoveries and inventions.
The work of the philosopher consists in assembling reminders for a particular purpose.

If one tried to advance *theses* in philosophy, it would never be possible to question them, because everyone would agree to them. (*PI*, 126–128)

This is surely a radical view of philosophy, as radical in its way as that of the *Tractatus*. According to this view, the aim of the philosopher is not to solve the big problems about knowledge, reality, God, the soul, and the good. These are not real problems at all; they arise only out of misunderstanding our language. The task of the philosopher is to unmask the ways in which these problems are generated, and by putting "everything before us" and "assembling reminders" bring us back to home ground. What is the purpose of the reminders? To show us how the language in which these "deep" questions are framed is actually used in those human activities in which they get their meaning. If we understand that, we will be freed from the temptation to suppose these are real questions. Wittgenstein offers the following rule:

Don't think, but look! (*PI*, 66)

Here are two more striking remarks on this theme.

The philosopher's treatment of a question is like the treatment of an illness. (*PI*, 255)

What is your aim in philosophy? To shew the fly the way out of the fly-bottle. (*PI*, 309)

The first remark suggests that philosophy is itself the illness for which it must be the cure. There is that old saying by Bishop Berkeley about raising a dust and then complaining that we cannot see. The posing of philosophical problems, Wittgenstein is saying, is like that. Being possessed by a philosophical problem is like being sick; only it is we who make ourselves sick—confused, trapped, perplexed by paradoxes. We foist these illusions on ourselves by misunderstanding our own language. It is so very *easy* to do that because language itself suggests these illusions to us. Philosophy, then, is a kind of therapy for relieving mental cramps.

With the second remark we get the unforgettable image of a fly having gotten itself trapped in a narrow-necked bottle, buzzing wildly about and slamming itself frantically against the sides of the bottle, unable to find the way out that lies there open and clear if only the fly could recognize it. We get into philosophical problems so easily but then can't find our way out again.

> "But *this* isn't how it is!"—we say, "Yet *this* is how it has to *be!*" (*PI*, 112)

Just like the fly in the bottle! It is Wittgenstein's aim to show the fly the way out of the bottle—to help us put philosophical problems behind us, not to devise theories to solve them.

Language-Games

Let us look in more detail at the way Wittgenstein uses the prescription "Don't think, but look!" in criticizing the characteristic theses of the *Tractatus*. We begin with one of the most basic notions in that work, the notion of a *name*.

Wittgenstein makes use of a device he calls "language-games." A **language-game** is an activity that involves spoken (or written) words. These words have a natural place in the activity; it is this place, the role they play in the activity, that makes them mean what they do mean. It is sometimes helpful, Wittgenstein suggests, to imagine a language-game more primitive than the ones we engage in.

> It disperses the fog to study the phenomena of language in primitive kinds of applications in which one can command a clear view of the aim and functioning of the words. (*PI*, 5)

Here is such a primitive language-game.

> The language is meant to serve for communication between a builder A and an assistant B. A is building with building-stones: there are blocks, pillars, slabs and beams. B has to pass the stones, and that in the order in which A needs them. For this purpose they use a language consisting of the words "block," "pillar," "slab," "beam." A calls them out; —B brings the stone which he has learnt to bring at such-and-such a call.   —Conceive this as a complete primitive language. (*PI*, 2)

The words in this language-game can very naturally be thought of as names. To each word there corresponds an object. Here we have an example of a language that the theory of the *Tractatus* fits. This theory

> does describe a system of communication; only not everything that we call language is this system. And one has to say this in many cases where the question arises "Is this an appropriate description or not?" The answer is: "Yes, it is appropriate, but only for this narrowly circumscribed region, not for the whole of what you were claiming to describe."
>
>   It is as if someone were to say, "A game consists in moving objects about on a surface according to certain rules . . ."   —and we replied: You seem to be thinking of board games, but there are others. You can make your definition correct by expressly restricting it to those games. (*PI*, 3)

There are language-games in which all the words are names, in which the function of each name is to stand for an object. But not all language is like that. In the following language-game, the *Tractatus* view that names exhaust the meaningful symbols shows itself to be inadequate—if we only *look*.

> I send someone shopping. I give him a slip marked "five red apples." He takes the slip to the shopkeeper, who opens the drawer marked "apples"; then he looks up the word "red" in a table and finds a colour sample opposite it; then he says the series of cardinal numbers—I assume that he knows them by heart—up to the word "five" and for each number he takes an apple of the same colour as the sample out of the drawer.   —It is in this and similar ways that one operates with words. (*PI*, 1)

What is interesting in this little example is the very different way in which the shopkeeper operates with each of the three words. "Apple" seems to be a name, like "slab." But what of "red"? And, even more significantly, what of "five"? Both of them are used in ways completely different from "apple" and completely different from each other. Can they all be *names?** Suppose we ask,

---

*Consider again Plato's theory of Forms (pp. 121–126). Is Plato someone who falls into the trap of thinking that meaningful

But what is the meaning of the word "five"?
—No such thing was in question here, only how the word "five" is used. (*PI,* 1)

The suggestion that "five" is a name, and that it names a number, is resisted. The point of this language-game, this little "reminder," is to cure us of the hankering to ask about the *meaning* of this word, especially since we are inclined to think its meaning must be an object analogous to apples—only a very mysterious one. We are brought back to the way in which we actually use the word. We say the numbers and take an apple for each number. And there is nothing deep or mysterious here to puzzle us. Note that this example shows us Wittgenstein doing just what he says the job of the philosopher is: dispelling puzzlement by bringing words "back from their metaphysical to their everyday use" (*PI,* 116). There is no explanation given, just description. Wittgenstein is merely "arranging what we have always known" (*PI,* 109).

Still, the idea that all words *signify* something is hard to resist. We do feel the temptation to ask, But what does the word "five" *mean*? And we can just feel the slide toward asking, "What *really* is a number, anyway?" (Don't you feel it?) If we like, Wittgenstein says, we can agree that every word signifies something. But what is gained thereby? Assimilating

> the descriptions of the uses of words in this way cannot make the uses themselves any more like one another. For, as we see, they are absolutely unlike.
>
> Think of the tools in a tool-box: there is a hammer, pliers, a saw, a screw-driver, a rule, a glue-pot, glue, nails and screws.   —The functions of words are as diverse as the functions of these objects. (And in both cases there are similarities.)
>
> Of course, what confuses us is the uniform appearance of words when we hear them spoken or meet them in script and print. For their *application* is not presented to us so clearly. Especially not, when we are doing philosophy!

> It is like looking into the cabin of a locomotive. We see handles all looking more or less alike. (Naturally, since they are all supposed to be handled.) But one is the handle of a crank which can be moved continuously (it regulates the opening of a valve); another is the handle of a switch, which has only two effective positions, it is either off or on; a third is the handle of a brake-lever, the harder one pulls on it, the harder it brakes; a fourth, the handle of a pump: it has an effect only so long as it is moved to and fro.
>
> When we say: "Every word in language signifies something" we have so far said *nothing whatever;* unless we have explained exactly *what* distinction we wish to make. (*PI,* 10–13)

The quest for general explanations of meaning is fruitless. Like the handles in the cabin of the locomotive, what counts is how words *work;* and they work in very different ways. "Five" works in an altogether different way from "red." The quest for general explanations is likely to make us forget that and to lead us into illusions about meaning and language—illusions into which the author of the *Tractatus* was led.

In his *Tractatus,* Wittgenstein had claimed to give us the *essence* of language. This claim had two implications that he now believes are baseless. The first is that language is *everywhere all alike;* we have just been examining some reasons to give up this claim. The second is that the account of language he gave was *complete.* We might be inclined to say that these primitive language-games Wittgenstein describes are, by contrast, incomplete. But Wittgenstein now says,

> Ask yourself whether our language is complete; —whether it was so before the symbolism of chemistry and the notation of the infinitesimal calculus were incorporated in it; for these are, so to speak, suburbs of our language. (And how many houses or streets does it take before a town begins to be a town?) Our language can be seen as an ancient city: a maze of little streets and squares, of old and new houses, and of houses with additions from various periods; and this surrounded by a multitude of new boroughs with straight regular streets and uniform houses. (*PI,* 18)

---

words—"eagle," "square," "equal"—are names and that there must be something each one names? Or think of Locke on general terms, pp. 378–380.

Language is something living and growing; creative language users are always adding to it. And there is no rule that new additions have to be like the old. The calculus, for instance (and the new logic, for that matter) are like "new boroughs with straight regular streets." But we must not assume that all language is like that; it is an "ancient city," with all the twists and turns of narrow streets and houses from different eras—like London or Vienna.

In the *Tractatus,* Wittgenstein had held that the proposition was the basic unit and that each proposition pictured a possible state of affairs. Now he asks,

> But how many kinds of sentence are there? Say assertion, question, and command?   —There are *countless* kinds: countless different kinds of use of what we call "symbols," "words," "sentences." And this multiplicity is not something fixed, given once for all: but new types of language, new language-games, as we may say, come into existence, and others become obsolete and get forgotten. (We can get a *rough picture* of this from the changes in mathematics.)
>   Here the term "language-*game*" is meant to bring into prominence the fact that the *speaking* of language is part of an activity, or of a form of life.
>   Review the multiplicity of language-games in the following examples, and in others:
>   Giving orders, and obeying them—
>   Describing the appearance of an object, or giving its measurements—
>   Constructing an object from a description (a drawing)—
>   Reporting an event—
>   Speculating about an event—
>   Forming and testing a hypothesis—
>   Presenting the results of an experiment in tables and diagrams—
>   Making up a story; and reading it—
>   Play-acting—
>   Singing catches [i.e., rounds]—
>   Guessing riddles—
>   Making a joke; telling it—
>   Solving a problem in practical arithmetic—
>   Translating from one language into another—
>   Asking, thanking, cursing, greeting, praying.
> (*PI,* 23)

In all these ways—and more—we use language. It is absolutely unhelpful—and worse, dangerous!—to suppose that language is everywhere all alike. It leads into pseudoproblems and illusions, the sorts of dead ends where we are likely to say, This isn't how it *is, but this is how it must be.*

---

1. How is philosophy now conceived? What are "philosophical problems" like? What is to happen to them?
2. What is a language-game? What does Wittgenstein think the notion can do for us, and why does he think this is important?
3. How does the example of shopping for five red apples undermine some basic theses of the *Tractatus*? And what is the moral of the tool and locomotive examples?
4. What now happens to the notion of an essence of language? How many kinds of sentences are there, anyway?

Ostensive Definitions

Let's think again about names. We are tempted to think that the process of naming is fundamental and that the rest of language can be built on that foundation. We teach the child "ball," "blue," "water." But how do we do this? And when has the child mastered the meaning of these words? We present a ball to a child and get the child to pay attention to it, while we repeat, "ball, ball." This might lead us to generalize again and claim that language gets attached to the world by means of *ostensive definitions* such as this. So we might formulate a *theory* of naming.

But if we look carefully, we see that this assumption cannot be right.

> Now one can ostensively define a proper name, the name of a colour, the name of a material, a numeral, the name of a point of the compass and so on. The definition of the number two, "That is called 'two'"—pointing to two nuts—is perfectly exact.   —But how can two be defined like that? The person one gives the definition to doesn't

know what one wants to call "two"; he will suppose that "two" is the name given to *this* group of nuts! . . . an ostensive definition can be variously interpreted in *every* case. (*PI*, 28)

Note that Wittgenstein is not denying that ostensive definitions are often useful. What he is attacking is the notion that they are a key to the essence of language, to what is basic in language use. He denies that ostensive definitions can be the simple foundation stone on which all else is built. If I try to show you what a watch is (supposing you don't know) by pointing to the device on my wrist, you may take it that "watch" means a color, a material, a device for keeping time, or a direction. My intention can be "variously interpreted." And what is true for this case is true for every case.

How do ostensive definitions work, then? Well, I could help you out by saying, "This device on my wrist is a watch." But that presumes, as you can clearly see, that you already are in possession of large portions of the language. You have to understand "device" and "on" and "wrist" if what I say is going to be helpful. So it seems clear that language cannot *begin* with ostensive definitions. And names cannot themselves be absolutely primitive: To understand a name, you have to understand what role it is supposed to play in the language-game.

> So one might say: the ostensive definition explains the use—the meaning—of the word when the overall role of the word in the language is clear. . . .
> One has already to know (or be able to do) something in order to be capable of asking a thing's name. But what does one have to know?
> When one shews someone the king in chess and says: "This is the king," this does not tell him the use of this piece—unless he already knows the rules of the game up to this last point: the shape of the king. . . .
> We may say: only someone who already knows how to do something with it can significantly ask a name. (*PI*, 30–31)

An ostensive definition is of use only *within* a language-game. It is of no help in getting into the game in the first place.

But that leaves us with a problem. How do we ever get started with language, if acquiring the use of even names such as "ball" and "milk" presupposes an understanding of language in general? Here Wittgenstein again advises us to *look*.

> A child uses such primitive forms of language when it learns to talk. Here the teaching of language is not explanation, but training.
> (I do not want to call this "ostensive definition," because the child cannot as yet *ask* what the name is. I will call it "ostensive teaching of words.". . . This ostensive teaching of words can be said to establish an association between the word and the thing. (*PI*, 5–6)

Suppose that such an "association" is established between "apple" and apples by "training" little Jill in that way. Does she now *understand* the word "apple"? Well, does your dog understand "Come!" when it comes at that command? The process is similar, Wittgenstein suggests, and so are the results. The difference between Jill and Rover is that Jill can eventually go on to learn a lot more about apples by internalizing an ever more complex language in which to talk about them. Understanding comes in degrees; Jill is capable of understanding more than Rover, but they start in the same way. It is not by definitions (ostensive or not) that we enter the gate of language, but by *training*.

Objects

We are tempted to think, as the *Tractatus* suggests, that "a name means an object. The object is its meaning." But if that were so, Wittgenstein "reminds" us, a word would have no meaning if nothing corresponded to it.

> It is important to note that the word "meaning" is being used illicitly if it is used to signify the thing that "corresponds" to the word. That is to confound the meaning of a name with the *bearer* of the name. When Mr. N. N. dies one says that the bearer of the name dies, not that the meaning dies. And it would be nonsensical to say that, for if the name ceased to have meaning it would make no sense to say, "Mr. N. N. is dead." (*PI*, 40)

It does, of course, make sense to say that John F. Kennedy is dead, so the name is not meaningless, even though its bearer is no longer in existence. It follows that the meaning of a name cannot be the object it names. What, then, is the meaning of a name? It is having a place in a particular language-game, a certain role in a form of life.

> For a *large* class of cases—though not for all—in which we employ the word "meaning" it can be defined thus: the meaning of a word is its use in the language. (*PI*, 43)

And that is why it is important not to think, but to look and see how a word is being used.

In the *Tractatus,* names stand for objects, and these objects are said to be *simple.* In fact, at the time he wrote the *Tractatus,* Wittgenstein held that there *must* be simple objects; otherwise, the definition of names could go on forever, and nothing would have any determinate sense. Definitions must come to an end! And they can only end in the absolutely simple.[*]

> But what are the simple constituent parts of which reality is composed?   —What are the simple constituent parts of a chair?   —The bits of wood of which it is made? Or the molecules, or the atoms? —"Simple" means: not composite. And here the point is: in what sense "composite"? It makes no sense at all to speak absolutely of the "simple parts of a chair." (*PI,* 47)

When talking of simple and composite, we must pay attention to the game we are playing with these words. To suppose that they have meaning quite independently of some concrete activity in which they are being used is to let language "go on holiday" (*PI,* 38), a sure way to generate unsolvable philosophical problems.

> If I tell someone without any further explanation: "What I see before me now is composite," he will

have the right to ask: "What do you mean by 'composite?' For there are all sorts of things that can mean!" . . .

> But isn't a chessboard, for instance, obviously, and absolutely, composite?   —You are probably thinking of the composition out of thirty-two white and thirty-two black squares. But could we not also say, for instance, that it was composed of the colours black and white and the schema of squares? (*PI,* 47)

There are circumstances in which we analyze composite things in one way and circumstances in which we analyze them in another way. This is what we find, if we *look.* Why should we insist that there must be one way in which composite things can be analyzed into elements that are absolutely simple, quite independent of context or language-game? This insistence looks like a prime case of thinking and not looking—a case of prescribing to language and the world. Once again, Wittgenstein invites us to resist the temptation.[*]

Family Resemblances

Here we come up against the great question that lies behind all these considerations.   —For someone might object against me: "You take the easy way out! You talk about all sorts of language-games, but have nowhere said what the essence of a language-game, and hence of language, is: what is common to all these activities, and what makes them into language or parts of language. So you let yourself off the very part of the investigation that once gave you yourself most headache, the part about the *general form of propositions* and of language."

And this is true.   —Instead of producing something common to all that we call language, I am saying that these phenomena have no one thing in common, which makes us use the same word for all—but that they are *related* to one another in many different ways. And it is because of this relationship, or these relationships, that we call them all "language." I will try to explain this.

---

[*]The commitment to simples has a long history. We find it already in Plato, and versions of it are found in many other thinkers—including Locke, Berkeley, Hume, and Russell, who hold that although not every idea has to be traceable to a corresponding impression, the simple ones do. (See p. 402.)

[*]Compare Dewey on the analysis of a concept such as "a piece of paper," p. 587.

Consider for example the proceedings that we call "games." I mean board-games, card-games, ball-games, Olympic games, and so on. What is common to them all? —Don't say: "There *must* be something common, or they would not be called 'games'"—but *look and see* whether there is anything common to all. —For if you look at them you will not see something that is common to *all*, but similarities, relationships, and a whole series of them at that. To repeat: don't think, but look! —Look for example at board-games; here you find many correspondences with the first group, but many common features drop out, and others appear. When we pass next to ball-games, much that is common is retained, but much is lost. —Are they all "amusing"? Compare chess with noughts and crosses [tic-tac-toe]. Or is there always winning and losing, or competition between players? Think of patience [solitaire]. In ball-games there is winning and losing; but when a child throws his ball at the wall and catches it again, this feature has disappeared. Look at the parts played by skill and luck; and at the difference between skill in chess and skill in tennis. Think now of ring-a-ring-a-roses; here is the element of amusement, but how many other characteristic features have disappeared! And we can go through the many, many other groups of games in the same way; can see how similarities crop up and disappear.

And the result of this examination is: we see a complicated network of similarities overlapping and criss-crossing: sometimes overall similarities, sometimes similarities of detail.

I can think of no better expression to characterize these similarities than "family resemblances"; for the various resemblances between members of a family: build, features, colour of eyes, gait, temperament, etc. etc. overlap and criss-cross in the same way. —And I shall say: "games" form a family. (*PI,* 65–67)

I have quoted this well-known passage at length because it is extremely important. The notion of **family resemblances** has been a freeing notion of great significance for thought. Recall that at the beginning of the Western philosophical tradition, dominating it with the kind of power that only unexamined assumptions can have, stands Socrates with his questions: What is piety? Courage? Justice?

And what Socrates wants is a definition, the *essence* of the thing. What he wants to discover are those features that (1) any act of justice has, (2) any non-just act lacks, and (3) *make* the just act just. Are acts *A* and *B* both just? Then it seems natural to suppose that there must be something they have *in common,* something they share, some feature by virtue of which they are just. Unless we understand what that is, we will not understand justice.*

It is difficult to exaggerate the impact this assumption has had. It certainly lies beneath the *Tractatus* quest for the essence of language; it accounts for the author's certainty that there must be such a thing. But now that we are looking rather than thinking, we discover that, in very many cases, there is no such thing. There is no essence of games, nor of language. And almost surely there is no essence of justice or piety. All are matters of instances, examples, and cases loosely related to each other by crisscrossing and overlapping similarities. What we find when we look are family resemblances. What we find is exactly the kind of thing that Socrates so curtly dismisses when it is offered by Euthyphro!

It follows from this new picture that there may be no sharp boundaries for many of our concepts.

How should we explain to someone what a game is? I imagine that we should describe *games* to him, and we might add: "This *and similar things* are called 'games.'" And do we know any more about it ourselves? Is it only other people whom we cannot tell exactly what a game is? But this is not ignorance. We do not know the boundaries because none have been drawn. To repeat, we can draw a boundary— for a special purpose. Does it take that to make the concept usable? Not at all! (Except for that special purpose.) No more than it took the definition:

Euthyphro on piety is a good example. For other examples, see Plato on knowledge (pp. 118–120) and Descartes on clear and distinct ideas (p. 322). The assumption pervades nearly all of our philosophical tradition. I recall some years ago being on a committee to rethink the requirements for a bachelor of arts degree. We expended a lot of energy in trying to discern the *essence* of a bachelor of arts, just what it is that makes a certain degree a bachelor of arts degree—as though this were somehow laid up in the Platonic heaven of Forms. That this discussion was fruitless would not have surprised Wittgenstein.

1 pace = 75 cm. to make the measure of length "one pace" usable. And if you want to say, "But still, before that it wasn't an exact measure," then I reply: very well, it was an inexact one.   —Though you still owe me a definition of exactness. (*PI,* 69)

One might say that the concept "game" is a concept with blurred edges.   —"But is a blurred concept a concept at all?"   —Is an indistinct photograph a picture of a person at all? Is it even always an advantage to replace an indistinct picture by a sharp one? Isn't the indistinct one often exactly what we need?

Frege compares a concept to an area and says that an area with vague boundaries cannot be called an area at all. This presumably means that we cannot do anything with it.   —But is it senseless to say: "Stand roughly there"? (*PI,* 71)

We may understand Wittgenstein's point more clearly by examining another example. What, people sometimes ask, is a religion? Is belief in a supreme being essential to religion? Then early Buddhism is not a religion. How about belief in life after death? But early Judaism seems to lack that feature. Some people suggest that communism is essentially religious in character. But how can that be, if it lacks so many of the features of Presbyterianism? If we search for the conditions that are both necessary and sufficient to define "religion," we will probably search in vain. But suppose we proceed this way: Do you want to know what a religion is? Consider Roman Catholicism; this and similar things are called "religions." To treat the question this way is to think of "religion" as a family resemblance concept.

Someone might ask, "How 'similar' to Roman Catholicism does something have to be if it is to qualify as a religion?" We would be right to reply that there is no exact answer to that question.

Suppose someone objects, "But then you haven't drawn a sharp boundary!" We can reply, "That is true. If you want, you can draw a boundary for a special purpose; but don't suppose that in doing so you are answering the original question. It is not our ignorance that makes this way of replying to the question about religion an appropriate one. We don't know more about it ourselves; no one does." The concept "religion" functions in our language in this family resemblance kind of way. And the ab-

sence of a set of necessary and sufficient conditions to mark off religions from other things does not mean that the concept is not useful and serviceable, any more than "Stand roughly there" is a useless instruction just because it isn't perfectly precise.*

When he was writing the *Tractatus,* Wittgenstein thought that every proposition had to have a determinate sense and that therefore a completely analyzed proposition would be free of all vagueness and ambiguity. (Remember the ideal presented by Russell's notion of a logically perfect language; see p. 594.) How could it be otherwise, when it was composed of simple names, each standing for a simple object? But if we look, without seeking to prescribe how it *must* be, we see that language is not everywhere exact, like a logical calculus. Like "game," many of our concepts are governed by relationships of family resemblance rather than essences.† And they are none the worse for that. So Wittgenstein assembles his reminders of how our language actually functions, bringing us back to the activities (forms of life) in which it does its varied jobs. And in so doing, he shows us the way out of various fly bottles we get ourselves into by misunderstanding the logic of our language.

---

1. Why cannot ostensive definitions be basic in language use? And if they are not, how do language-games get started? (How do children learn a language?)
2. What argument purports to show that the meaning of a word cannot be the object to which it refers?

---

*Notice how this sort of thing undercuts Descartes' requirement (*Meditation IV*) that we should assent only to ideas that are clear and distinct. Most of our ideas, Wittgenstein holds, are not clear and distinct. And that is not something we should try to fix. On the contrary, our concepts are "in order" as they are.
†But not all. We do have concepts that are governed by strict rules. Many scientific concepts—"triangle," for example, or "force"—are like that. We should not think of the family resemblance claim as a *theory* about the essence of meaning! It is worth noting that contemporary studies by cognitive psychologists about how people categorize objects have strongly supported Wittgenstein's views about the family resemblance character of many of our concepts.

Explain, in contrast, the motto "The meaning of a word is its use in the language."

3. Why does it make no sense to speak absolutely of "the simple parts of a chair"?

4. Must usable concepts have sharp boundaries? What are family resemblances? What are we supposed to learn from the example of games?

The Continuity of Wittgenstein's Thought

As you can see, virtually every one of the principal theses of the *Tractatus* is undermined and rejected by the later Wittgenstein.

- There is an essence of language.
- The essence of language is picturing facts.
- There is a complete and exact analysis of every sentence.
- The basic elements of language are names.
- The meaning of a name is its bearer.
- Names are simple.
- Names name simple objects.
- The world is pictured as the totality of facts in logical space.

Other thinkers have changed their ways of thinking—Augustine after his conversion to Christianity, Kant after reading Hume—but Wittgenstein's turnabout is as deep and dramatic as any. Is there any line of continuity that one can trace through this shift? Let me suggest that three interrelated themes and a motivation persist.

The first theme is an opposition, amounting almost to a personal revulsion, to what Wittgenstein calls "just *gassing*." A more contemporary term for this phenomenon might be "bullshitting."[7] The second is the idea that one might "set a limit to thought" (*Tractatus*, preface, 3). The third is the notion that some things cannot be said, but only shown. The motivation that persists is a quest for a life that is worth living.

1. The whole point of the *Tractatus*, you will recall, was to "set a limit to thought" by delineating what can and cannot be said. Whatever can be said can be said clearly. The rest is "nonsense," which we must "pass over in silence" (*Tractatus*, preface, 3). Wittgenstein felt that most talk about the meaning of life, about value and God and the soul, was "just *gassing*"—an attempt to put into words questions and answers that cannot be put into words. But it is crucial to remember that he also thought that these matters were *far and away the most important*. The revulsion he felt was grounded in his conviction that prattle about them demeans them, takes them out of the realm in which they properly exist. A good man, for instance, is not someone who *talks* about goodness, but someone who "shows" it, displays it in his life. "It is clear that ethics cannot be put into words" (*Tractatus* 6.421). But it *can* be put into a life!

2. That project—to set a limit to thought by identifying nonsense, gassing, and bullshit—is still a driving force in Wittgenstein's later thought. The aim has not changed, but the method by which he thinks it can be done has changed. In the *Tractatus*, he tried to do it all at once—with one stroke, as it were—by constructing a *theory* of language and meaning that would expose nonsense for what it is. But now having come to see that he had been prescribing to language, that he had been held captive by the picture of language as a logical calculus, he gives up the attempt to create a theory. Instead, he "assembles reminders" (*PI*, 127) that bring us back from nonsense to the actual uses of language in those varied activities (forms of life) in which words get their meaning. This is something that cannot be done all at once; it requires the careful examination of case after case where language "goes on holiday" (*PI*, 38) and misleads us. And so we get the little stories, the language-games, the questions and answers, and the multitudinous examples of the *Philosophical Investigations*.

3. The *Tractatus* tells us there are some things that cannot be said: These things *show* themselves. Among them are these:

- The logical structure of language (which displays itself in every proposition)
- The nature of logical truth (manifest in tautologies)

- The relation of the philosophical subject to the world (the coincidence of solipsism and realism)
- The happiness of the good person (who has a different world from that of the unhappy person)
- "The mystical" (that the world is)

Are there still, in *Philosophical Investigations,* things that can only be shown, not said? There are, and one suspects they are still the most important things. But it is no longer so easy to list them. Rather, the *showing* has become identical with the *style* of the book. Even the samples we have examined display a most unusual style.* The book is full of questions (often unanswered), conversations between the author and an interlocutor, instructions ("Compare . . . ," "Imagine . . ."), little stories, suggestions, reminders, and so on. Surely no other book in the history of philosophy contains so many questions! Wittgenstein is reported to have said that he thought an entire book of philosophy could be written containing nothing but *jokes.*

The aim of all this is still, as in the *Tractatus,* to get us to "see the world aright" (*Tractatus,* 6.54). But that no longer means a flight of the metaphysical self to that point without extension from which the entire world looks like a limited whole of valueless facts. Seeing the world aright now means to see it, and language especially, in all its incredible variety and lush richness. And we are invited to see it that way—or, better, to let it *show itself* to us—through the very structure of the book. It is no accident that in the preface Wittgenstein compares his book to an album of sketches:

> The philosophical remarks in this book are, as it were, a number of sketches of landscapes which were made in the course of . . . long and involved journeyings.

. . . Thus this book is really only an album. (*PI,* ix)

We could compare what Wittgenstein is doing in the *Investigations* to the work of an artist. He is trying in as many ways as he can think of to get us to appreciate the "landscapes" of our language—and so of our forms of life—so that we no longer get *lost* in them. There are few doctrines, if any, to be learned here. The book *shows* us a way of investigating puzzles and problems.

> It is not our aim to refine or complete the system of rules for the use of our words in unheard-of ways.
>
> For the clarity that we are aiming at is indeed *complete* clarity. But this simply means that the philosophical problems should *completely* disappear.
>
> The real discovery is the one that makes me capable of stopping doing philosophy when I want to. —The one that gives philosophy peace, so that it is no longer tormented by questions which bring *itself* in question.   —Instead, we now demonstrate a method, by examples; and the series of examples can be broken off.   —Problems are solved (difficulties eliminated), not a *single* problem.
>
> There is not a philosophical method, though there are indeed methods, like different therapies. (*PI,* 133)

Here we come to the motivation that persists from the early work through the last: to give philosophy *peace.* There can be little doubt that Wittgenstein is doing more than trying to dispel illusions. By bringing our words back from their metaphysical to their everyday use, he wants to show us how to be *content* here—in the everyday. It's not just that we misunderstand our language; because language is part of a form of life, we also fail to understand our *lives.* Yet this is not a simple mistake, Wittgenstein holds. There is in us an "urge" to misunderstand (*PI,* 109). We are *driven* to these illusions because we are not satisfied with our lives. Metaphysical theories are a kind of compensation, an attempt to find peace beyond the world because we have not been able to find it here. (The *Tractatus* was an attempt to find peace that way.)*

---

*One is reminded of Kierkegaard's indirect communication, or of Nietzsche's aphorisms, or maybe of Heraclitus, or perhaps of the stories about how Zen masters proceed. It is not accidental that the earlier book is called a *treatise* and the later book *investigations.* The former suggests completeness and a theoretical character that is altogether lacking in the latter.

*Compare Nietzsche on "real worlds," pp. 538–542. See also Kierkegaard's characterization of the "Knight of Faith," pp. 497–499. Wittgenstein once said that Kierkegaard was the greatest

Wittgenstein wants to show us a form of life that is so worthwhile we can simply stop doing philosophy when we want to—free of this metaphysical "urge." As in the *Tractatus*, characteristically "philosophical" problems should simply *disappear*. But the form of life shown us in the *Investigations* is not something "unheard-of." It is our own life! A student asks a Zen master, "What must I do to gain enlightenment?" The master asks, "Have you eaten?" "Yes," says the student. "Then wash your bowl."

In Wittgenstein's later work, we find a number of attempts to show us how traditional philosophical problems disappear if we look carefully at the language in which they are framed. There are discussions relevant to understanding something, to meaning, to the status of sensations. We find sections dealing with seeing something, with interpreting something, with following rules. A summary of these investigations would stand to them in somewhat the same way that a brief description of a van Gogh painting would stand to the painting itself. Just as you really need to immerse yourself in the painting if you are going to appreciate it, so you need to follow the text of the *Investigations* if it is to have the proper effect on you.

But we can say that these investigations are profoundly subversive of the traditional ways of doing philosophy. Doctrines found in Plato, Descartes, Locke, Hume, Kant, Hegel, and so on are undercut, not by *argument* but by the examples, stories, questions, and language-games—all designed to get us to *see* things in a different (though familiar) light. Wittgenstein aims to show us how to give up the temptation to formulate philosophical *theories* about reality, mind, perception, or understanding. He aims to show the fly the way out of the bottle.

There is one theme in Wittgenstein's later work, closely connected to the idea of a language-game, that we can perhaps pull out. It is a theme directly relevant to a matter that has come up repeatedly in our account of the great conversation: the question

about relativism. Recall that this issue originates in the dispute between Socrates and the Sophists (see those earlier chapters) and is expanded on by most of our philosophers. Can Wittgenstein throw any new light on that old perplexity?

1. What continuities exist between the thoughts of the early and the late Wittgenstein
2. How has the project of setting a limit to thought changed in Wittgenstein's later philosophy?

Our Groundless Certainty

Think about the ubiquitous arrow, indicating to us which way to go—to the exit, on the one-way street, to Philadelphia. The arrow is a kind of rule. Let us ask a question you may never have asked before: How do I know which way I am being directed to go? I do know. I am to go in the direction of the arrow's point. But how do I know this? Why, for instance, don't I go toward the tail of the arrow? Or why don't I go in different directions on different days of the week?

Here are some possible answers: (1) I *decide* in each case to go toward the arrow's head; (2) I *intuit* which way it is directing me to go; (3) I *follow* the *rule,* Go toward the arrow's head. But (1) is crazy; (2) seems just to put a label on what I do without giving any account of it; and (3) promises an infinite regress—for exactly the same question arises in regard to this rule! Is there a "metarule" that explains to me how *this* rule is to be obeyed?

Wittgenstein suggests a fourth possibility:

> What has the expression of a rule—say a signpost—got to do with my actions? What sort of connexion is there here? —Well, perhaps this one: I have been trained to react to this sign in a particular way, and now I do so react to it. (*PI,* 198)

Training. Rather like we train a dog to heel, perhaps. But can that be right? An objection is raised by Wittgenstein's "interlocutor," the voice that so often presents our own hesitations to suggestions he makes.

But that is only to give a causal connexion; to tell how it has come about that we now go by the sign-post; not what this going-by-the-sign really consists in. (*PI,* 198)

The objection is that this does not tell us what rule following *is,* but only how we come by it. To explain how we acquire a practice, it seems, is not to explain the practice itself. But Wittgenstein replies,

> On the contrary; I have further indicated that a person goes by a sign-post only in so far as there exists a regular use of sign-posts, a custom. (*PI,* 198)

Without such a custom, such a "regular use," there would be no such thing as obeying the sign. If that is right, some interesting consequences follow.

> It is not possible that there should have been only one occasion on which someone obeyed a rule. It is not possible that there should have been only one occasion on which a report was made, an order given or understood; and so on.   —To obey a rule, to make a report, to give an order, to play a game of chess, are *customs* (uses, institutions). (*PI,* 199)

Rules are embedded in institutions, customs, and ways of doing things. There are no rules apart from that kind of setting. We are not to understand this as an empirical remark, as something that we conclude on the basis of observing rules. Rather, he means to say that it is *not possible* that there should be a purely private rule.* Because obeying a rule is part of a custom, it presupposes a community in which such practices exist.

Suppose, then, that you were asked, "But why do you go in the direction of the arrow's point?"

What would you say? How *do* you know that is the way to go?

> Well, how do I know?   —If that means "Have I reasons?" the answer is: my reasons will soon give out. And then I shall act, without reasons. (*PI,* 211)
>
> "How am I able to obey a rule?"   —If this is not a question about causes, then it is about the justification for my following the rule in the way I do.
>
> If I have exhausted the justifications I have reached bedrock, and my spade is turned. Then I am inclined to say: "This is simply what I do." (*PI,* 217)

In this striking metaphor, Wittgenstein brings us back to the communal practices in which our language-games have their home. It is as if the Platonic and Kantian why-questions have made us dig deeper and deeper. But there comes a point when we can dig no more, find no more justifications for our beliefs, our knowledge claims, or our scientific methods. At that point we reach bedrock, and our "spade is turned." What is bedrock? Is it some Cartesian clear and distinct idea? Is it some Humean private impression? Is it a Kantian synthetic a priori truth? Or is it the Hegelian culmination of reason's inexorable development into Absolute Spirit made explicit for itself? No. None of these things. Bedrock is "simply what I do." And what I do is part of what *we* do, we who live this form of life, engage in these activities, play these language-games, grow up in these customs. There comes a point where explanations and justifications for behaving in a certain way come to an end. Then one just acts. We do as our linguistic community has trained us to do. In the end, it comes down to this:

> When I obey a rule, I do not choose.
> I obey the rule *blindly.* (*PI,* 219)

Custom, practice, the activities that make up a form of life—these have an almost sophistic ring to them, reminding us of Protagoras, who says, "Of all things the measure is man."* Does Wittgenstein mean that agreeing among ourselves *makes* things true?

> "So you are saying that human agreement decides what is true and what is false?"   —It is what hu-

---

*In a section of the *Investigations* we do not discuss, Wittgenstein uses this principle of the essentially public character of rules to show that there could not be a language in which I give ostensive (private) definitions for my sensations. The supposition that such a language is possible is remarkably pervasive, both in common life and in philosophy. (Think of Descartes, Locke, Berkeley, Hume, Kant, Russell, and the early logical positivists, as well as the common thought that "everybody has his own ideas.") Accordingly, if Wittgenstein is correct, a great deal of confusion is dismissed, and numerous philosophical theories of the mind are shown to be untenable. The sections in which this view is set out (roughly 243–351) are as famous as they are difficult.

*For a comparison with the Sophists' version of relativism, see "Relativism," in Chapter 3.

man beings *say* that is true and false; and they agree in the *language* they use. That is not agreement in opinions but in form of life. (*PI*, 241)

Think of measuring the length of a table. I do it and report my results: 30. You do it and report 76. Is one of us right and the other wrong? It turns out that my rule is graduated in inches and yours in centimeters. So what we both say can be true; the difference is that we were using different measures. If you use my measure, agree in my "language for measuring," we will (usually) agree in "opinion," too. Still, it is not our agreement on 30 that *makes* that opinion true; the length of the table does that. But there is an agreement in language-game that *makes it possible* for us to agree and disagree about opinions. So the "measure" both is and is not ourselves. It is *not* ourselves in Protagoras' sense. Human agreement doesn't *make* things true. But it *is* ourselves in the sense that all our measures are conventional; they all depend on customs, uses of language, forms of life.

In the *Tractatus,* we found the distinction between what can be said and what can only be shown. In the *Investigations,* we find that when we get to bedrock, there is no more to say. At that point I can only *display* my form of life, the language-game I play. Here, where the spade is turned, I just *show* you what I do: This is what I do—how I live, the way I understand, mean things, and follow rules; this is my (our) form of life. In the *Tractatus,* it was the logical hardness of tautologies that turned the spade, that could only be shown. Here it is the practice of a certain set of language-games.

But this bedrock cannot, as we have seen, be a purely private form of life, governed by private rules. And Wittgenstein now pushes this point by asking, "What does it mean to "agree in language"?

> If language is to be a means of communication there must be agreement not only in definitions but also (queer as this may sound) in judgments. (*PI*, 242)

Imagine that when we measure the table, our results are inconsistent, even if we use the same rule each time. At first we report 30, then 17, then 54, then 1,003, and so on. Whatever it was we were doing, could we call that *measuring?* No. That,

whatever it is, is not measuring. A measure (the yardstick) is analogous to a language. It allows us to say certain things. And just as there has to be some agreement in "results" if we are to have a measure, so also there has to be some agreement in "opinions" or "judgments" if we are to have a language. We have to hold many of the same things true and false.

But which things? Are there any judgments in particular that we need to agree about in order to communicate with one another in a language? Is there a *foundation* of agreement? And if there is, can we identify it?

In an essay titled "A Defense of Common Sense," English philosopher G. E. Moore claims to "know with certainty" a large number of propositions.[8] And he thinks we all know them, too. For instance, he claims each of us knows that

- There exists a living human body that is *my* body.
- My body was born at a certain time in the past.
- My body has existed continuously ever since.
- My body has changed in many ways.
- Since my birth, my body has been close to the surface of the earth.
- My body has been at various distances from other things, which also exist.

And we know with certainty that

- The earth existed many years before I was born.
- There have been many other human bodies like my own.
- I have had many different experiences.
- So have other human beings.

This is not Moore's complete list, but you get the idea. It is a list of what seem to be *truisms.*

Wittgenstein says many interesting things about the claim that we *know with certainty* that these propositions are true. (He tends to think the word "know" is inappropriately used here.) But our interest is directed to his idea that these "judgments" might form the basis for an agreement defining a language or a form of life.

How is it that we are so *certain* of these "facts"? Have we carefully investigated each of them and found that the evidence is in their favor? No. They do not have that kind of status. Taken together they are more like a picture we accept.[*]

> But I did not get my picture of the world by satisfying myself of its correctness; nor do I have it because I am satisfied of its correctness. No: it is the inherited background against which I distinguish between true and false. (*OC,* 94)[9]

Wittgenstein compares this "inherited background" to a kind of mythology, by which he means that though the truisms of the picture are empirical, they are not acquired by empirical investigation.[†] He also compares our world picture to the banks of a river within which the water of true and false propositions can flow. The mythology can change; the banks of the river are not unalterable. And in some ways, at least, different pictures are possible for us even at a given time.

> Very intelligent and well-educated people believe in the story of creation in the Bible, while others hold it as proven false, and the grounds of the latter are well known to the former. (*OC,* 336)

How are we to account for this? Suppose the doubter talks to the believer. If the reasons for doubt are already well known to someone who believes the biblical story, what could the doubter say to convince the believer? All the doubter's reasons are already on the table—and they don't convince! Moore believes that the earth has existed for many, many years. But

> why should not a king be brought up in the belief that the world began with him? And if Moore and this king were to meet and discuss, could Moore really prove his belief to be the right one? I do not say that Moore could not convert the king to his view, but it would be a conversion of a special kind; the king would be brought to look at the world in a different way. (*OC,* 92)

Different language-games (different forms of life) are possible. And arguments in favor of one of them *presuppose* the standards of argument and evidence characteristic of that very form of life. So reasons do not get a grip on a different form of life with different standards and rules of reasoning.

But again we are tempted to think there *must* be something that would constitute a definitive justification, if not for our present view, then for some future one.[*] Is "conversion" really the final word? What about *science?* Can that be just a matter of "what we do"? Suppose I justify my actions by the propositions of physics; for example, I do not perform rain dances because science tells me dancing is ineffective in bringing rain.

> Supposing we met people who did not regard that as a telling reason. Now, how do we imagine this? Instead of the physicist, they consult an oracle. (And for that we consider them primitive.) Is it wrong for them to consult an oracle and be guided by it? —If we call this "wrong" aren't we using our language-game as a base from which to *combat* theirs?
>
> And are we right or wrong to combat it? Of course there are all sorts of slogans which will be used to support our proceedings.
>
> Where two principles really do meet which cannot be reconciled with one another, then each man declares the other a fool and heretic.
>
> I said I would "combat" the other man,   —but wouldn't I give him *reasons?* Certainly; but how far

---

[*]Not a *Tractatus* picture, of course; this kind of picture is holistic rather than atomistic, imprecise rather than exact, a system of mutually supporting judgments. It doesn't occur to us, moreover, that this picture *can* be doubted. These matters are explored in another posthumously published book by Wittgenstein, *On Certainty.*

[†]Throughout this discussion of the "background" for our beliefs, you should keep in mind the Kantian a priori synthetic principles. Wittgensteinian "world pictures" play a similar role. They define a world for us. They are as anchored for us as the categories. But they are neither universal nor necessary—nor are they unchangeable. They function like the *paradigms* in Thomas Kuhn's influential book, *The Structure of Scientific Revolutions* (Chicago: University of Chicago Press, 1962).

[*]Compare Peirce's definition of truth as the opinion investigators will eventually come to agree upon, if they continue to investigate according to scientific methods (p. 572).

do they go? At the end of reasons comes *persuasion.* (Think what happens when missionaries convert natives.) (*OC,* 609–12)[*]

Combat does not seem to be a form of justification, and conversion is not being convinced by good reasons. Reasons, Wittgenstein reminds us, come to an end.

World pictures, then, may differ; but there is *always* a framework within which we come to believe and think certain things.

> I have a telephone conversation with New York. My friend tells me that his young trees have buds of such and such a kind. I am now convinced that his tree is. . . . Am I also convinced that the earth exists?
>
> The existence of the earth is rather part of the whole *picture* which forms the starting-point of belief for me.
>
> Does my telephone call to New York strengthen my conviction that the earth exists? (*OC,* 208–210)

Wittgenstein wants us to answer no; it does not strengthen that conviction. That conviction is already as strong as it could possibly be! Is there anything of which I am *more* certain?[†] Moore's truisms, to which we all consent, are not *known* by us to be true; a claim to know is in order only where doubt is in order, and where one is ready to trot out one's evidence to resolve the doubt.

> If you tried to doubt everything you would not get as far as doubting anything. The game of doubting itself presupposes certainty. (*OC,* 115)
>
> Why do I not satisfy myself that I have two feet when I want to get up from a chair? There is no why. I simply don't. That is how I act. (*OC,* 148)
>
> How does someone judge which is his right and which his left hand? How do I know that my judgment will agree with someone else's? How do I

know that this colour is blue? If I don't trust *myself* here, why should I trust anyone else's judgment? That is to say: somewhere I must begin with not-doubting; and that is not, so to speak, hasty but excusable; it is part of judging. (*OC,* 150)

> I should like to say: Moore does not *know* what he asserts he knows, but it stands fast for him, as also for me; regarding it as absolutely solid is part of our *method* of doubt and enquiry. (*OC,* 151)

The world picture we have is not something we have checked out; nor is it something we could check out. What would I do to assure myself that *this* is my right hand? Ask somebody? But if I have a doubt here, why would I credit a second person's reassurance? (This is not to deny that in certain special circumstances I might have such a doubt and be reassured; perhaps I have put on distorting spectacles.) Can I doubt—Descartes notwithstanding—that I have a body? That I have parents? That I have never been to the moon? These things "stand fast" for us. It is hard to imagine anything *more certain* than these judgments that could cast doubt on them. Is it, for example, more certain that my senses have sometimes deceived me than that the sky I'm looking at is blue?[*]

> Might I not believe that once, without knowing it, perhaps in a state of unconsciousness, I was taken far away from the earth—that other people even know this, but do not mention it to me? But this would not fit into the rest of my convictions at all. Not that I could describe the system of these convictions. Yet my convictions do form a system, a structure. (*OC,* 102)
>
> And now if I were to say "It is my unshakeable conviction that etc.," this means in the present case too that I have not consciously arrived at the conviction by following a particular line of thought, but that it is anchored in all my *questions and answers,* so anchored that I cannot touch it. (*OC,* 103)
>
> All testing, all confirmation and disconfirmation of a hypothesis takes place already within a system. And this system is not a more or less arbitrary and

---

[*]Compare these views with the contrast Plato draws between *knowledge* and *opinion* (pp. 118–120). Do Wittgensteinian certainties fall neatly into *either* category?

[†]Compare Descartes' doubt in *Meditations I* and *II.* He thinks we can be more certain that we are thinking, understanding, doubting. But is that so?

---

[*]Wittgenstein's critique here should remind you of Peirce on doubt and belief. (See again pp. 568–570.)

doubtful point of departure for all our arguments: no, it belongs to the essence of what we call an argument. The system is not so much the point of departure, as the element in which arguments have their life. (*OC*, 105)

Much seems to be fixed, and it is removed from the traffic. It is so to speak shunted onto an unused siding. (*OC*, 210)

Now it gives our way of looking at things, and our researches, their form. Perhaps it was once disputed. But perhaps, for unthinkable ages, it has belonged to the *scaffolding* of our thoughts. (Every human being has parents.) (*OC*, 211)

The use of the *Tractatus* word "scaffolding" in this connection cannot be an accident. In his earlier view, logic (that transparent and absolutely rigid medium) was the scaffolding of the world. Now, in dramatic contrast, what grounds our system of beliefs are such apparently empirical and logically accidental facts as that I have parents, or even that motor cars don't grow out of the earth (*OC*, 279). If certain people believed that, we would suppose they are so different from us as to have entirely different standards of reasonableness; it is not clear we could even understand those who seriously persisted in this belief; they would seem mad. The person who claims—in the face of all our certainties about Chrysler and Honda and engineering and production lines—that cars grow out of the earth is not making a *mistake*. This person would seem *demented*.

In order to make a mistake, a man must already judge in conformity with mankind. (*OC*, 156)

The complex system of certainties that make up a world picture does not function like an ordinary foundation. The foundation of a house is that on which everything else rests, but the foundation could stand alone. Our certainties form a system of interrelated judgments.

When we first begin to *believe* anything, what we believe is not a single proposition, it is a whole system of propositions. (Light dawns gradually over the whole.) (*OC*, 141)

I have arrived at the rock bottom of my convictions. And one might almost say that these foun-

dation-walls are carried by the whole house. (*OC*, 248)

Here the atomism of the *Tractatus* is most thoroughly repudiated. We do not first believe a single isolated proposition, then a second, a third, and so on. "Light dawns gradually over the whole." In a striking metaphor, Wittgenstein suggests that the foundation walls are themselves borne up by their connection with the rest of the house.

We may still want to ask, What makes us so certain of this picture? What guarantees for us that these judgments are fixed, that they do stand fast? Wittgenstein's answer is that *nothing* guarantees this. There is no guarantee. We are, indeed, certain of these things; but our certainty cannot be anchored in anything objective, in anything more certain than they.

To be sure there is justification; but justification comes to an end. (*OC*, 192)

And in what does it come to an end?

At the foundation of well-founded beliefs lies belief that is not well-founded. (*OC*, 253)

The difficulty is to realize the groundlessness of our believing. (*OC*, 166)

Giving grounds . . ., justifying the evidence, comes to an end;   —but the end is not certain propositions' striking us immediately as true, i.e., it is not a kind of *seeing* on our part; it is our *acting*, which lies at the bottom of the language-game. (*OC*, 204)*

My *life* consists in my being content to accept many things. (*OC*, 344)

If the Western philosophical tradition has been a quest for certainty, we can say that Wittgenstein satisfies that quest, for he acknowledges that there are many, many things of which we are certain (many more things than most philosophers ever imagined!). But if philosophy is a quest for objective certainty, for a foundation that guarantees the *truth* of the edifice of knowledge, then, in a certain sense, if Wittgenstein is right, philosophy is

---

*See Kierkegaard on the unavoidability of a leap (pp. 504–505).

over. Epistemology is *over.* For there comes a point where the spade is turned, where one cannot dig any deeper. And bedrock comes sooner than most philosophers have wanted it to come. We find it in our form of life. Our life *consists* in "being content to accept many things." This is, Wittgenstein holds, a difficult realization; we keep wanting to ask that good old why-question. Can't we, we yearn to ask, *somehow justify our form of life?* No, says Wittgenstein. It is *groundless.* It is "simply what we do." And what *we* do may not be what *they* do. Philosophy cannot dig deeper than the practices and customs that define our form of life. We do have our certainties, but they are groundless.[10]

> Philosophy may in no way interfere with the actual use of language; it can in the end only describe it.
> For it cannot give it any foundation either.
> It leaves everything as it is. (*PI,* 124)

1. When we see the sign EXIT, how do we know which way to go to find the exit?
2. Could there be just one occasion on which someone obeyed a certain rule? Explain.
3. When reasons give out, what do we do then? In what sense do we obey rules blindly?
4. What is bedrock? And what does Wittgenstein mean by "agreement in language"? Why is that important?
5. What kind of status does my "world picture" have? Am I certain about it? What guarantees its correctness?
6. How is persuasion related to the giving of reasons? And what does it mean to say that our believing is groundless?

For Further Thought

1. If Wittgenstein is right, philosophy as a quest for foundations, for the absolute truth of things, has suffered shipwreck. Do you think he is right? If so, what should we do now?

2. Several times, a similarity to Zen themes has been suggested. See whether you can work out this parallel more fully. Are there differences, too?

Notes

1. Gilbert Ryle, "Ordinary Language," in *Philosophy and Ordinary Language,* ed. Charles E. Caton (Urbana: University of Illinois Press, 1963), 123–124.
2. Gilbert Ryle, *The Concept of Mind* (Harmondsworth, England: Penguin Books, 1963), 17.
3. J. L. Austin, "A Plea for Excuses," in Austin, *Philosophical Papers* (Oxford: Oxford University Press, 1979), 181–182.
4. Ludwig Wittgenstein, *Tractatus Logico-Philosophicus,* trans. D. F. Pears and B. F. McGuinness (London: Routledge and Kegan Paul, 1961), preface, 5.
5. Norman Malcolm, *Ludwig Wittgenstein: A Memoir* (Oxford: Oxford University Press, 1958), 69.
6. Quotations from Ludwig Wittgenstein's *Philosophical Investigations* (New York: Macmillan, 1953) are cited in the text using the abbreviation *PI.* References are to section numbers.
7. Wittgenstein is mentioned in Harry D. Frankfurt's very interesting piece, "On Bullshit," in his *The Importance of What We Care About* (Cambridge: Cambridge University Press, 1988). Frankfurt identifies the essence of *bullshit* as the lack of any concern for truth.
8. G. E. Moore, "A Defense of Common Sense," in *Contemporary British Philosophy,* 2nd ser., ed. G. Muirhead (London: Allen and Unwin, 1925).
9. Quotations from Ludwig Wittgenstein's *On Certainty* (Oxford: Basil Blackwell, 1969) are cited in the text using the abbreviation *OC.* References are to paragraph numbers.
10. I have learned much about reading Wittgenstein from Gordon Bearn's *Waking to Wonder: Wittgenstein's Existential Investigations* (New York: State University of New York Press, 1996).

24

MARTIN HEIDEGGER

The Meaning of Being

Martin Heidegger was born in the southern German village of Messkirch, near the Swiss border, in 1889. He seldom went far from that area. He felt close to the earth and treasured the fields and woods among which he lived. One can almost hear in his writing the weary tread of peasant shoes. As a youth, he considered studying for the priesthood but turned instead toward philosophy, which he took to be devoted to more fundamental matters. In his adult life he was a professor, mainly at Freiburg, not far from where he was born.

Heidegger lived through both world wars and for a time in the 1930s supported the Nazi party. This disreputable episode has been the occasion for much debate: Was it, or was it not, essentially connected to his philosophy? Opinion is divided. Although Heidegger was not in all respects an admirable person, he is nevertheless a philosopher of great power. He died in 1976.*

The difficulty of his writing is legendary. Heidegger's aim is to try to say things that our tradition—the great conversation since Plato—has made it hard to say. Our language has been formed by this tradition; since Heidegger thinks the tradition has "hidden" precisely what he is most interested in, he finds it inadequate. So he devises new terms to express what he wants to say.* Often these inventions have Greek etymological roots. Sometimes they are ordinary words put together in extraordinary ways or given extraordinary meanings.

The difficulty is compounded because translators do not always agree on the best English rendering of a German term. So the same term may be translated several ways.†

---

*For a brief discussion of the Heidegger/Nazi case, see http://www.molloy.edu/academic/philosophy/sophia/heidegger/case_txt.htm

*Early in our story we see thinkers struggling to find (or invent) language adequate to what they want to say. Compare Anaximander (p. 13), Heraclitus (p. 19), and Democritus (p. 31). Though we usually assume our language is satisfactory, we see that the struggle to find the right words continues.

†I have had to make some terminological decisions; where a translation is at variance with my decision, I have put the translation I am using in brackets.

In 1927, Heidegger published a book called *Being and Time*. Actually, the work Heidegger projected was in two parts, and *Being and Time* constituted just two-thirds of the first part. The rest was never published. Why? Apparently he came to believe that the edifice for which *Being and Time* was to provide a foundation could not be built on that foundation. Consequently, there was a "turn" in his thinking, so that (as with Wittgenstein) we can speak of the early and the late philosophy. He never gave up the pursuit of the issue he announced as his concern in *Being and Time,* however; in 1962, he gave a lecture titled *Time and Being*. We will explore this "turn," but we begin with—and give most of our attention to—the analysis of human existence as it is worked out in that partially completed 1927 book.

What Is the Question?

Tortuous though it is, Heidegger's thought has from the beginning a remarkable single-mindedness. There is one question, and only one, to which all his intellectual effort is directed. Heidegger calls it the question of the meaning of **Being.**[*] How to understand this question is itself a question. The concern it expresses will become richer and clearer as we explore his philosophy, but we should now address it in a preliminary way.

You have before you a piece of paper on which some words are written. The paper can be described in a variety of ways.[†] When we describe it, we are saying *what* it is—what kind of thing it is, what its characteristics and functions and uses are. But there is also this curious fact: *that* it is. I call it a curious fact because it tends to remain in the background, taken for granted—even, perhaps,

hidden. But it is just this fact Heidegger wishes to ask about. What does it mean for the piece of paper to *be*? Kant, you will recall, urges that "being" is no ordinary predicate, and we have noted that this insight is incorporated into the quantifier of modern logic.[*] To say that the piece of paper *exists,* Kant claims, is not further to describe it, nor to elaborate its concept, but to assert that something corresponds to the description we have given.

So far, so good. But what does this "corresponding" come to? What is it for the piece of paper to *be*? It is hard, perhaps, to get that question clearly in mind, to focus it, to pay attention to it. Heidegger is convinced that Kant doesn't satisfactorily answer this question, nor has anyone else in Western philosophy answered it. But that is precisely the question Heidegger is addressing. What does that *mean* —that the paper *is*?

Heidegger begins *Being and Time* with a quotation from Plato's dialogue *The Sophist,* in which a stranger remarks,

> For manifestly you have long been aware of what you mean when you use the expression "being."
> We, however, who used to think we understood it, have now become perplexed. (*BT,* 1)[1]

That, Heidegger thinks, precisely describes *our* situation. You might think that this is odd. Even if Plato is perplexed, how can it be that all the intervening centuries of thought haven't cleared the matter up? Heidegger's answer is that philosophical reflection about Being has *hidden* as much as revealed the phenomenon—and for deep and interesting reasons, as we will see.

We tend to have conflicting intuitions about the nature of Being. On the one hand, it seems the most obvious thing in the world: It applies to everything! We ourselves and every entity we meet *are*. How could we not know what Being is? On the other hand, if you are asked to define it, your response will probably be like that of Augustine when asked about the nature of time.[†] One thing is clear,

---

[*]I will follow the usual convention and capitalize the word when it is *Being* that is in question. The word "being" of course has other uses in English. Occasionally I may speak of *a being* or of *beings;* when uncapitalized, the term is the equivalent of "entity" or "item" or "thing" in a very broad sense (not just a physical thing)—that is, whatever can *be,* or have *Being*.

[†]You might look again at all the ways that John Dewey finds for describing such an item (p. 587).

[*]See again Kant's discussion of the ontological argument (pp. 448–450).

[†]See p. 243.

Heidegger says: Being is not itself an entity; it is not one more thing along with all the other things in the world. Imagine that you write down on a long, long list all the things that there are. Would you write down "apples, planets, babies, dirt, . . . , and Being"? No, you would not. Each of the entities on that list, in a strange way, has carried its Being along with it.* But what is this Being that puts humans and hammers and rocks and stars on the list but unicorns and square circles off? That is the question.

In saying that Being—the object of his inquiry—is not itself *a* being (not a thing, an entity, one of the items that exist), Heidegger means to make clear that he is not engaging in that traditional quest for *the* being who is responsible for all the rest. Heidegger is not searching for or trying to prove the existence of God—at least as God has traditionally been conceived. Heidegger is not asking about the *highest being,* but about what it is that accounts for the fact that there is *anything at all* (rather than nothing). This question seems on the one hand to be so abstract and distant from us as to be of purely academic interest. Yet because we ourselves exist, it seems so intimate and near to us as to be almost too close to examine.† How could we make any progress in answering this question about the meaning of Being?

The Clue

Any inquiry, as an inquiry about something, has *that which is asked about.* But all inquiry about some-

thing is somehow a questioning of something. So in addition to what is asked about, an inquiry has *that which is interrogated.* . . . Furthermore, in what is asked about there lies also *that which is to be found out by the asking.* (*BT,* 24)

The inquiry about the meaning of Being is *asking about* Being; that is the focus of our question. And what we want to find out by our asking is the meaning of Being. But what will we examine? Where will we look? If our investigation is to be a real, concrete one, it can't just hang in the air; it must tie down to something. There must be something that we *interrogate.*

"Being is always the Being of an entity." (*BT,* 29)

Being, in other words, is not like the smile of the Cheshire cat, which can remain mysteriously after the cat has vanished. As we have seen, Being comes along with the entities that *are.* What Heidegger is now saying is that apart from entities, there "is" no Being. If we wanted to put this in a slangy slogan, we might say: No *be-ing* without a *be-er.** So if we want to investigate Being, we must do it in connection with some entity. But which entity do we choose? In principle, any might do, from quarks to gophers to black holes. But is there some entity that would be *best* to interrogate with respect to its Being?

At this point, Heidegger notes that an inquiry like this is itself something that has Being. (Asking questions is not just *nothing,* after all.) And we would not have answered our question about the meaning of Being unless we also got clear about the Being of items such as inquiries—and of the entities that inquire! This suggests that *we ourselves* might be the entity we interrogate in our inquiry, the focus of our investigation.

Heidegger recognizes, of course, that many sorts of investigation concern themselves with human beings. Many sciences have something to say about us: physics, chemistry, biology, history, psychology, anthropology. But none of these sciences

---

*The early Wittgenstein's contrast between (a) the totality of facts that make up the world and (b) *that* the world exists is essentially the same as Heidegger's contrast between entities (beings) and Being. (See p. 612.) Wittgenstein, of course, believes nothing can be said about this "*that* it is"; this is the "unsayable" about which we must be silent—the *mystical.* But it is just this that Heidegger commits all his intellectual energy to trying to say. A caution: What Heidegger means by "world" is very different from what the *Tractatus* means by it, and our relationship to it is correspondingly different.

†Again Wittgenstein comes to mind: Recall the analogy of the visual field that does not include the eye that sees it (see p. 609). *Being* is so "close" to us as to be invisible to us. It is one of Heidegger's aims to get us some "distance" from it so that it can appear to us as it is.

*Heidegger's notion of *Being*—something distinct from *beings*—is obviously indebted to the claim by Aquinas that existence (*esse*) is "something added." (See pp. 272–275.) But Aquinas would not agree that there can be no Being without *a* being, because that's precisely what *God* is!

"What is strange in the thinking of Being is its simplicity. Precisely this keeps us from it."

—Martin Heidegger

takes the perspective on humans that is relevant to our question. To focus attention on the relevant aspect, he refers to the entity we will interrogate by a term that is usually left untranslated: **Dasein.** This German term can be used to refer to almost any kind of entity, though it is usually used for human beings. Literally the term means "being there." ("Da" means "there" or sometimes "here"; "sein" is "being.") And Heidegger chooses this term to highlight the aspect of humans he is interested in: not the chemistry of the body nor the history of human society, but their Being.*

The suggestion that Dasein should be the focus of our investigation—the entity to be interrogated—is further supported by noting that we are distinctive among entities in an interesting way.

---

*Like the term "person" in Kant, this term doesn't specify whether human beings are the only beings with the particular *way of Being* we have. Perhaps in other galaxies. . . .

Dasein is an entity which does not just occur among other entities. Rather it is ontically distinguished by the fact that, in its very Being, that Being is an *issue* for it. But in that case, this is a constitutive state of Dasein's Being, and this implies that Dasein, in its Being, has a relationship towards that Being—a relationship which itself is one of Being. And this means further that there is some way in which Dasein understands itself in its Being, and that to some degree it does so explicitly. It is peculiar to this entity that with and through its Being, this Being is disclosed to it. *Understanding of Being is itself a definite characteristic of Dasein's Being.* Dasein is ontically distinctive in that it *is* ontological. (*BT,* 32)

This important paragraph no doubt needs some explanation. Heidegger employs a distinction between two levels at which an entity can be described; he calls them **ontic** and **ontological.** We can think of the *ontic level* as that of ordinary facts. Each Dasein has a certain physical size, grows up in a certain culture, experiences moods, uses language and tools, remembers and intends, often fears death, and usually thinks its way of life is the right way: These are all ontic facts.

But there is also a deeper level at which Dasein can be described: in its *way of Being*—in the way it is "there," present to things, in the world, together with others. We can think of this level as a matter of structural features of Dasein that make possible all the ontic facts we are ordinarily aware of.* This is the *ontological level.*

Heidegger holds that, ontically considered, Dasein is unique among entities. And what makes it distinctive is that its own Being "is an *issue* for it." What he means is that Dasein is the being that is

---

*It might be helpful to recall Kant's four questions, for example, "What makes natural science possible?" Kant is asking about the "transcendental" conditions on the side of the subject that must be assumed, given that science (or mathematics, or morality, or metaphysics) actually exists. In a similar way, Heidegger is inquiring about Dasein's basic mode of Being: What must Dasein be for the ontic facts to be what they are? As we will see, Heidegger's project differs from Kant's in two distinct ways: (1) He is not asking about a *subject,* as opposed to an object; (2) he thinks he has a way to reveal to us the very Being of Dasein. So there is no unknowable noumenal entity that has the character of a transcendental ego. Compare Kant on the soul, pp. 443–444.

concerned about its own Being; it *matters* to Dasein how things are going with it, how it is doing, what the state of its Being is and will become. So Dasein already has a certain understanding of Being. Its own Being is always, at any given point, "disclosed to it." Because this feature of Dasein is so fundamental, Heidegger asserts that Dasein "*is ontological.*" What does this mean? Ontology is the discipline concerned with Being. So to say that Dasein *is* ontological is to say that Dasein's way of Being involves having an *understanding* of its own Being. This openness to itself is what makes Dasein Da-sein.

This feature of Dasein is so central that Heidegger points to it as the *essence* of Dasein. In each case—yours, mine—Dasein "has its Being to be" (*BT*, 33). It is as though Dasein can't just *be* (the way spiders are, for example); Dasein has to *decide* about its Being. How it will *be* is an *issue;* its Being this way or that is not just a given fact. Being, for Dasein, is a *problem* to be solved; but it cannot be solved in a disinterested and theoretical way; it is solved only by living—by existing.*

Heidegger searches for a term to designate the way of Being that is characteristic of Dasein. He settles on "existence." Dasein *exists.* As he uses this term, dogs and cats *are,* but they do not *exist.* Stones and stars are, but they do not exist. They have a different *kind* of Being. "Existence," then, is a technical term for Dasein's way of being. The term "exist" has etymological roots that suggest a kind of projection out from or away from the given situation. Heidegger sometimes writes it as "ek-sist" to emphasize this transcending of the given.† As we will see, Dasein ek-sists: It is always projecting itself beyond the present circumstance to future possibilities. We are aware of the *present* in the light of what we have been (the past) and could become (the future); we are not simply confined in it. It is this feature that makes it possible for Dasein to be concerned about its own Being. (Already we hear intimations of the importance of *time* to the question about the meaning of Being.)

Heidegger can say, then, that the essence of Dasein—what Dasein most essentially is—is its existence. And his first task is an "analytic" of Dasein. If we can get clear about Dasein's way of Being, this should be a step toward the larger question of the meaning of Being in general. Dasein is the best entity to interrogate because Dasein, in existing, already has an understanding of Being. To some degree, Being is "in the open" in Dasein, available in a way it would not be in a chemical compound. Dasein's self-understanding does not yet amount to the clear and comprehensive ontological understanding Heidegger is seeking; it is only an average, everyday kind of understanding, which (as we will see) may hide as much as it discloses. But Heidegger has found the clue as to where to begin.*

Heidegger calls an analysis of Dasein's existence a *fundamental* ontology. The ontological analysis of Dasein (the description of Dasein's basic structures) provides "the condition for the possibility of any ontologies" (*BT*, 34). Since the essence of Dasein is its existence, this will be an *existential* analysis. And what Heidegger will be looking for is something analogous to the traditional *categories,* that is, concepts setting out the most basic sorts of ways that things can be.† Heidegger uses the term *existentials* for the existential concepts that correspond to the traditional categories.

Let us summarize:

- What we are after is the meaning of Being. The name for such an inquiry is "ontology."

---

*Compare Kierkegaard, pp. 503–504.
†"Ek" is a Greek particle that suggests a standing out away from some origin, as in "ecstasy"—standing outside one's normal self.

*Heidegger's reason for turning to Dasein in his attempt to discern the meaning of Being is responsive to the puzzle Plato discusses about searching for the truth: If we don't know the truth, how will we know where to look? And how will we know when we have found it? If we do know the truth, what sense does it make to search for it? See p. 102. Plato thinks learning the truth is "recollecting" what the soul had known in some preexistence. Heidegger thinks Dasein has a "preontological" understanding of Being as part of its essence. This understanding can be deepened into a genuine ontology.
†Compare Aristotle on the categories, p. 160, and Kant, p. 436. Heidegger agrees that "Being can be said in many ways." But he thinks neither of them has discovered the appropriate "categories" for Dasein, the language adequate to our existence.

- The place to begin is where Being is "in the open."
- Dasein, because it is constituted by an understanding of its own Being, is such a "place."
- So, Dasein is the entity to be interrogated.
- Dasein's way of Being is existence.
- So we want an existential analysis of Dasein.
- This analysis will be formulated in terms of concepts called "existentials," which play the role for Dasein that the traditional categories play for other entities—that is, they give the most general characterizations of its way of Being.
- And this analysis will provide a fundamental ontology, from which the meaning of Being in general can be approached.

This focus on Dasein and its existence has led many to classify Heidegger as an *existentialist*. And perhaps there is no harm in that. But it must be clearly kept in mind that the analysis of existence is not what he is mainly interested in. Heidegger is, from first to last, intent on deciphering the meaning of Being.

Phenomenology

We now know what the aim is. But we do not yet have a very clear idea of how to pursue that goal. Even though Dasein is the kind of being that has an understanding of its own Being, we must not think that philosophy can just take over that understanding—far from it. For one thing, there are many ways in which Dasein has been interpreted in the great conversation, and any of these are available for Dasein to use: as a soul temporarily imprisoned in a body (Plato), as a rational animal (Aristotle), as a creature of God (Augustine), as the *ego cogito* (Descartes), as a material mechanism (Hobbes), as a transcendental ego (Kant), or as the absolute subject (Hegel). *None* of these interpretations, Heidegger thinks, is adequate. In one way or another, they all miss the *existence* of Dasein. And even the average, everyday, unsophisticated way in which Dasein

understands itself may hide as much as it reveals about Dasein's true existential nature.

You can see, however, that we have a serious problem. How are we going to approach Dasein? With what method? Heidegger suggests that the analysis should proceed in two stages. In the first stage, we should set aside all the sophisticated theories of the tradition and try just to look at Dasein's "average everydayness."* We want to grasp Dasein as it exists most obviously and naturally. Still, the results of this analysis of everyday Dasein will be merely provisional, because we suspect that Dasein understands itself to some degree *inauthentically,* self-deceptively, hiding its way of Being from itself.

For this reason, the second stage is necessary; we must ask what it would be for Dasein to grasp itself, to own up to what it really is, to exist and understand itself *authentically.* In such an adequate self-understanding of its Being, Dasein will reveal the existentials that define it, and we will have an authentic fundamental ontology. This second stage will reveal *temporality* as the meaning of the Being of Dasein; thus we'll see that *time* is of central importance for the main question. In fact, Heidegger suggests time as the "horizon" within which the meaning of Being must be understood. If that is correct, Being itself is fundamentally temporal in nature.

But this is getting far ahead of our story. We are still faced with the problem of how to go about investigating everyday existence. This must be done, Heidegger tells us, *phenomenologically.* Hegel's use of the term "phenomenology" can serve as a clue to its meaning here.† There, the key idea is that we can "watch" consciousness as it develops through its stages toward more adequate forms. This idea of observing is central for Heidegger, too.‡ It has

---

*Compare the later Wittgenstein's motto "Don't think, but look!" (p. 625).

†See p. 464.

‡Heidegger's phenomenological method actually owes most to his teacher, Edmund Husserl, who develops phenomenological methods of inquiry. For Husserl, phenomenology is (1) a *science* that is (2) purely *descriptive,* rather than deductive or explanatory, (3) that *sets aside in a systematic way* all prior assumptions and *presuppositions,* (4) the subject matter of which is *consciousness*—its structure, its contents, and its "intended" objects—and

JEAN-PAUL SARTRE

Perhaps the best known of the existentialist philosophers, Jean-Paul Sartre (1905–1980) was a novelist, playwright, biographer, and short-story writer, as well as a philosopher. His major philosophical work is *Being and Nothingness* (1943). His literary works include the novel *Nausea* (1938) and the plays *The Flies* (1943) and *No Exit* (1944).

Influenced by the phenomenology of Husserl and Heidegger, Sartre investigated the structures of consciousness. He noted that in ordinary unreflective awareness, the ego or self does not appear; what is present is just an object. We can reflect, of course, and then the ego appears—but then it is an object, too! Consciousness itself is apparently *not any thing*. It is, Sartre said, a pure function, an emptiness, a wind blowing toward being: nothingness. All being is located in the object of consciousness, which is full, opaque, dense: the *in-itself*.

Yet even unreflective consciousness has a kind of diaphanous self-awareness. It is always *for-itself*. As such, no consciousness is ever completely coincident with itself; there is nothing that it definitively *is*. Human reality is the place where in-itself and

for-itself meet. You and I are undeniably objects; we do have Being. But we are also awareness of ourselves and not just a collection of facts. So we *are not* what we are, and we *are* what we are not.

One of Sartre's most famous claims was that "existence precedes essence," by which he meant that there is no given essential nature to a human being; we first exist, and then by our free choices and actions make ourselves into something. But we are tempted to evade the anxiety and responsibility of having to create ourselves, so we identify with our in-itself or with our for-itself, and thus we slide into various forms of self-deception. (Compare Kierkegaard on despair. pp. 500–503.)

In various ways we try to justify or make meaningful our lives. Ultimately we want simultaneously to *be* something and for that something to be the result of our conscious choice: to be an in-itself/for-itself. But this concept of a self-caused being is just the traditional notion of God. The ultimate project of human beings is to be God. Unfortunately, Sartre believes, the concept of God is self-contradictory. So man, he concludes, is a futile passion.

---

nothing to do with bodily eyes, of course; this "watching" is more a matter of attitude, of not imposing preconceived notions on the subject in question. Phenomenology is the disclosing, or uncovering, of a phenomenon by means of discourse about it. We can think of it as the attempt to *let* entities manifest themselves as they truly are.

Phenomena are understood to be "the totality of what lies in the light of day or can be brought to light" (*BT*, 51). A phenomenon, Heidegger says, is "*that which shows itself in itself,* the manifest" (*BT*, 51). Phenomena are not "mere appearances," then. They are not just illusions. Nor are they signs for

something else. They are "the things themselves" as they show themselves—and not by means of something else, but "in themselves." And that is why phenomenology can be ontology—for what we want to do is to let Being itself appear, as it is.

Notice that Heidegger makes a subtle distinction: Some matters, he says, "lie in the light of day," and others "can be brought to light." Roughly speaking, entities are what lie in the light of day—the tableware we use at lunch, the daily newspaper, the family dog, your brother. But (and this should be no surprise by now) their Being is not so clearly apparent to us. Their Being must be brought to light, uncovered, disclosed. And this is just what phenomenology is designed to do.

Heidegger suggests three ways in which the phenomenon of Being might be hard to discern: (1) Being might be "hidden," in the sense that it is just too close to us for us to focus on it easily; (2) it

---

(5) the outcome of which is a *description of essences*—for example, an account of *what it is to be* an act of perception or the object of a remembering. Husserl's motto is "to the things themselves!" Heidegger takes this over, but he understands it in quite a different way.

might be "covered up," an idea that suggests Being was once known but has been made inaccessible by the tradition; and (3) Being might be "disguised," in the sense that Dasein, unable to face the awful truth about its existence, might draw a veil of camouflage over it (*BT*, 59–60). So the data we are after might not simply be there "in the light of day," manifesting themselves for us to see. We will have to engage in some *interpretation* to bring the phenomena to light. This interpretation Heidegger calls "hermeneutics," drawing this term from the tradition of interpreting texts, particularly Scripture. The meaning of a text is often obscure; to understand it requires an interpretation. Similarly, the meaning of Being is obscure. To get to the meaning of Dasein, then, will require a method that is phenomenological and hermeneutical at the same time. Our aim is to let the phenomenon of Being shine forth, as it is in itself.

---

1. Indicate the difference between Being and beings. Why does Heidegger say that Being is not *a* being?
2. Why does Heidgger choose *us* as the beings to "interrogate" in his quest for the meaning of Being? And why does he designate us with the term "Dasein"?
3. What does it mean to say that Dasein exists? And what will an existential analysis provide for us?
4. How will a fundamental ontology help in the quest for the meaning of Being?
5. Why does Heidegger recommend we begin our search by examining Dasein's average everydayness? And why is phenomenology the appropriate method?
6. What is hermeneutics? And why must our phenomenology of existence be hermeneutical?

Being-in-the-World

We are now ready to begin the analysis of Dasein's existential structure. Remember, what we are aiming at is an explicit understanding of Dasein's way of Being, the way that Heidegger calls "existence." The *basic state* of Dasein, he tells us, is this: Dasein essentially, necessarily, *is-in-the-world*. The hyphens

in this odd phrase are not accidental; they tell us that we are dealing here with a *unitary* phenomenon. It is not possible to understand Dasein apart from its world; indeed, Dasein without the world would not be "da"—that is, *there*. To be in a world—to "have" a world—is constitutive for Dasein.

We can already see that Heidegger's phenomenological analysis of Dasein's Being is completely at variance with the view expressed most clearly by Descartes, that it is a real possibility—one that needs to be ruled out by argument—that I might be the only thing that exists.* As we have seen, this ego (or mind), which Descartes thinks could exist independently of the world, gets trapped inside itself and has a hard time finding the world again. In supposing that such an independent existence is possible for the soul, Heidegger claims, Descartes misses precisely the *Being* of Dasein—namely, its **Being-in-the-world.** Heidegger thinks that Descartes' notion of the *ego,* of "the *thing* which thinks," in fact attributes to Dasein a kind of Being that belongs rather to a different sort of entity, which he calls the **present-at-hand.**[†] This is just one dramatic example of how the Western philosophical tradition has gone wrong—one example, Heidegger thinks, of how our forgetfulness of Being has warped our perception of things. One finds this pattern, he believes, in the whole history of the conversation since Descartes.[‡] But its roots can be traced back to Plato's interpretation of the true Being of entities in terms of the Forms.

Our tradition, Heidegger holds, has succumbed to a tendency toward *objectification*. As a result, we have taken the world to be made up of substances, things, objects; and the self or soul or mind has been understood as just another substance or thing.

---

*Review *Meditation I* with its skeptical arguments from sense deceptions, dreams, and the evil demon. Descartes thinks he can defeat solipsism only by *proving* the existence of God.

[†]We discuss this notion of the present-at-hand subsequently.

[‡]Heidegger would think that Locke's spiritual substance, Berkeley's spirit, Hume's bundle theory of the self, Kant's transcendental ego, and Hegel's infinite subject (Spirit) as the substance of the world all miss the phenomenon of the Being of Dasein. All are dominated by the heritage of Descartes, for whom the subject is a peculiar kind of *thing* (though they differ about the kind of thing it is).

No wonder the crucial question seemed to be the epistemological one: whether the subject (a thinking thing, the mind) can *know* the object (a different kind of thing). Can a subject *transcend* its subjectivity and know the truth about objects existing independently of it? We have seen how Kant's Copernican revolution "solves" this problem by making the knowable objects dependent on the knowing subject, but at the price of leaving things-in-themselves unknowable. All this, Heidegger believes, is a result of our having "covered over" the phenomenon of Being. And, most crucially, it has distorted our understanding of *our own* Being. This covering over is what Heidegger means to combat. And the first shot in this battle is the notion that the basic state of Dasein (which, you will recall, is in each case *mine*) is Being-in-the-world.

What does this mean? For one thing, it means that the fundamental relation between Dasein and the world is not epistemological, but ontological. Knowing is not basic; Being is. We *are* in-the-world, and we are so in a way that is deeper and richer than any propositional knowledge could completely express. What is it to be *in* the world? We can't fully answer this question until we understand more clearly what a "world" is. But in a preliminary way, we can say this: It is not the same as the coffee being *in* the cup, or the pencil being *in* the box. In these cases, we have one "present-at-hand" thing spatially contained in another. Heidegger does not want to deny that for certain purposes the entity that is Dasein can be regarded like this: Right now, for instance, I am *in* my study, which is *in* my house in exactly this sense.

But this is not the basic fact about the way I am in the world. (It is not the basic fact, for that matter, about the way I am in my study.) Dasein is *in*-the-world more in the sense in which my brother was *in* the Navy, or my son is *in* love. Dasein's way of Being-in-the-world is a matter of being engaged in projects, involved with others, using tools. Dasein *dwells* in the world; it is not just *located* there. Dasein's

> Being-in-the-world has always dispersed itself or even split itself up into definite ways of Being-in. The multiplicity of these is indicated by the following examples: having to do with something, pro-

ducing something, attending to something and looking after it, making use of something, giving something up and letting it go, undertaking, accomplishing, evincing, interrogating, considering, discussing, determining. . . . All these ways of Being-in have *concern* as their kind of Being—a kind of Being we have yet to characterize in detail. (*BT,* 83)

Concernfully—that is the way Dasein is *in*-the-world. What this means is that there is a more basic mode of relating to the things in the world than knowing them. Knowledge we might have or lack. But Being-in is something we cannot *be* without.

> From what we have been saying, it follows that Being-in is not a "property" which Dasein sometimes has and sometimes does not have, and *without* which it could be just as well as it could with it. It is not the case that man "is" and then has, by way of an extra, a relationship-of-Being towards the "world"—a world with which he provides himself occasionally. (*BT,* 84)

Being-in-the-world, in other words, is one of the *existentials* that characterizes the fundamental ontology of Dasein. It is one aspect of the essence of Dasein. The world is *given with* Dasein. But what a *world* is we are not yet clear about.

Remember that we are trying to disclose the Being of Dasein by an investigation of "average everydayness." So we now have to ask, How does this phenomenon of Being-in-the-world show itself in Dasein's average everydayness? What form does our Being-in normally take? We can get an answer, Heidegger suggests, via an interpretation of the *entities in the world* "closest" to us.

> We shall call those entities which we encounter in concern "*equipment*." In our dealings we come across equipment for writing, sewing, working, transportation, measurement. The kind of Being which equipment possesses must be exhibited. (*BT,* 97)

If we try to give a phenomenological description of our everyday mode of Being, what we find is that we dwell in a world of gear, of equipment for use. We do not first understand a pen as a "mere thing," and thereafter apprehend its use as a writing instrument. We grasp it *to write with,* usually without a thought. It is "on hand," or, as Heidegger puts it, **ready-to-hand.**

We simply turn the knob to open the door, often with our mind entirely on other matters—don't we? We deal with the things around us in an engaged, not a detached, manner. We cope with them in a variety of ways. They are elements in our ongoing projects. The things that are phenomenologically "closest" to us are not, then, neutral "objects" that we first stare at in a disinterested way and to which we must subsequently assign some "value."

It is in this engaged manner that we are most primordially in-the-world. Descartes worries about the problem of a transcendent reality: Is there anything "out there" beyond my mind's ideas? But if Heidegger is right, that is not a problem at all. Dasein *is* a kind of transcendence—in its very Being! Dasein is essentially *in-the-world,* engaged with the entities of the world in a concernful fashion. Kant says that the scandal of philosophy is that philosophers have not solved this problem of transcendence. Heidegger thinks the scandal is that philosophy has thought there is a problem here! That there seems to be a problem about "the reality of the external world" is just a sign of how distant we are from an understanding of our own mode of Being.*

But we still need to clarify the mode of Being of these entities "closest" to us in-the-world. Let us ask, What is it to *be* a hammer? In what does its *being-a-hammer* consist? There is a certain characteristic shape for a hammer, and a hammer is usually made out of certain definite materials, though both shape and materials can vary. But it is neither shape nor composition that *makes* a hammer a hammer. What it is for something to be a hammer is for it to have a certain definite use—a function, a purpose. A hammer is (to oversimplify slightly) *to-drive-nails-with.* That is what a hammer *is.* A hammer *hammers.*

It is important to note that the Being of the hammer involves a reference to something else—to nails. What is it to be a nail? To be a nail is to be something that can be driven into boards to fasten them together. Another reference!

> Taken strictly, there "is" no such thing as *an* equipment. To the Being of any equipment there always belongs a totality of equipment, in which it can be this equipment that it is. Equipment is essentially "something in-order-to . . ." A totality of equipment is constituted by various ways of the "in-order-to," such as serviceability, conduciveness, usability, manipulability.
> In the "in-order-to" as a structure there lies an *assignment* or *reference* of something to something. (*BT,* 97)

It is not possible, in other words, that there should exist just one item of equipment. Being a hammer involves a context of other equipment and, ultimately, the world.*

Let us ask a related question. When do we *understand* something to be a hammer? In what does this understanding consist? Most basically, I understand a hammer when I know how to hammer with it—when I can use it to drive the nails into the boards. The Being of the hammer does not reveal itself to a disinterested observation of its appearance or to a scientific investigation of its weight and material properties. Its Being is manifest primarily and fundamentally in a skill I have, particularly when I actualize this skill in actually hammering. That is how the hammer shows itself to be what it is. Hammers are understood in virtue of a kind of "know-how," not (primarily) by way of a "theory of hammers." Its being a hammer reveals itself to my *circumspective concern*—to my care-full involvements with it in the projects I am engaged in. Heidegger calls this kind of Being "readiness-to-hand."

Tools, gear, and equipment in general have this kind of Being. And dealing with the ready-to-hand is the most fundamental mode of our Being-in-the-world. We find it on all sides if we only have eyes to look. It is easy to miss, because it is so "close" to us,

---

*Heidegger's analysis of Being-in-the-world is a radical rejection of what we have called the *representational theory* (p. 327), the central claim of which is that we are directly or immediately acquainted only with ideas in the mind. If Heidegger is right, what we are directly and immediately acquainted with are functionally understood items in the world around us.

---

*Compare the anti-atomistic remarks of the later Wittgenstein, pp. 639–641.

almost too familiar to notice. But our skillful coping with nearly everything we encounter during a day's dealings is a matter of encountering over and over again the ready-to-hand. Our fundamental mode of understanding is not theoretical or scientific, but practical. We *understand how* to drive a car, use a fork, put on a pair of pants, open a can. And we manifest that understanding in actually driving, hammering, using the computer, combing our hair, and so on.

It cannot be emphasized too much that this concernful dealing with the ready-to-hand is *basic.* If Heidegger is right about this, the question of whether there "really" are hammers and cars and cans simply cannot arise. Philosophers have thought this is a real problem only because they have missed the Being of Dasein as Being-in-the-world and Dasein's relation to the ready-to-hand.

We are making some progress, but we do not yet know what it is to be a world. A clue can be derived from the fact that the ready-to-hand never comes alone, but always in a context of references and assignments to other entities. The hammer is to pound the nails; there would be no nails if there were no boards to join; the boards are shaped the way they are to build a house; houses are for sheltering and for dwelling in. All these things are meaningful together — or not at all. Each has the structure of an in-order-to. But if we pay close attention to this phenomenon of interlocking in-order-tos, we can see that three other things are also manifest.

1. Though we do not usually pay attention to the hammer directly — what we are involved in is the *work,* and the hammer is used "transparently" — the work involves *making use of something* for a purpose. Consider a cobbler making shoes.

> In the work there is also a reference or assignment to "materials": the work is dependent on leather, thread, needles, and the like. Leather, moreover, is produced from hides. These are taken from animals, which someone else has raised. . . . Hammer, tongs, and needle, refer in themselves to steel, iron, metal, mineral, wood, in that they consist of these. In equipment that is used, "Nature" is discovered along with it by that use — the "Nature" we find in natural products. (*BT,* 100)

As Heidegger is careful to point out, the "Nature" that presents itself in this way is nature as a resource: "the wood is a forest of timber, the mountain a quarry of rock; the river is water-power, the wind is wind 'in the sails'" (*BT,* 100). This nature is part of the world of equipment "in" which Dasein essentially is. So it is not quite the "Nature" of the scientist (to which we will come shortly). Along with the ready-to-hand Being of equipment, then, there is revealed the world of nature.

2. Other entities having the same kind of being as Dasein are also manifest. I, after all, did not make the hammer I pound with, nor did I manufacture the nails, nor did I shape the boards I join with them. These entities reveal that I am not alone in the world but live in the world with others who are like me.* This world, moreover, shows itself to be a *public* world. Hammers are mass produced; they are designed specifically so that *anyone* can hammer with them. The instruments in a car are intentionally designed so that the *average person* can easily read them. It would be a big mistake (we will soon see just how big) to understand Heidegger as saying that each Dasein lives in his own little world. Far from it. While we can quite properly speak of the chicken farmer's world, or the magazine publisher's world, or the cyclist's world, these are not fundamental. Each is carved out of the larger public world. These smaller worlds are not the world in which Dasein most fundamentally dwells; that world is the one and only public world — the world I have in common with others.

3. There is a third phenomenon that is evident together with the ready-to-hand: Heidegger calls it a "for-the-sake-of-which." Let's go back to the hammer. The hammer has its Being as equipment; it is ready-to-hand for hammering. As we have seen, there is a whole series of references or assignments in which the hammer is involved: It is essentially related to nails, which "refer" to boards, which "point" toward building houses. Does this set of functional

---

* Just as the "external world" problem seems like a pseudo-problem from Heidegger's point of view, the same is true of the problem of "other minds." It just doesn't arise!

relations have a terminus? Does it come to an end somewhere? Is there anything *for the sake of which* this whole set of relations exists? Yes. The totality of these involvements

> goes back ultimately to a "towards-which" in which there is *no* further involvement: this "towards-which" is not an entity with the kind of Being that belongs to what is ready-to-hand within a world; . . . The primary "towards-which" is a "for-the-sake-of-which". But the "for-the-sake-of-which" always pertains to the Being of *Dasein,* for which in its Being, that very Being is essentially an issue. (*BT,* 116–117)

Dasein, concerned for its own Being, understands the possibility that it might freeze in the winter and provides for itself a house. It is in terms of the possibilities of Dasein's Being that the entire set of functional relations attains its structure and Being. We get the image of an immensely complicated, crisscrossing network of functional assignments in which all the entities in the world are caught up and have their Being. This network is anchored in the Being of Dasein, that Being for whom its own Being is a matter of concern and whose Being has the structure of Being-in-the-world.

It is important to note that the *world* is not an entity; nor is it a collection of entities; nor is it a totality of facts, as the early Wittgenstein thinks.[*] Heidegger's thought is as far removed from the atomism of the *Tractatus* as you can imagine. It is only within the context of the world that something can *be* a hammer. The world is a prior whole, presupposed by the Being of the ready-to-hand; it is not the *sum* of lots and lots of things, each of which might equally well exist alone. There would be no hammers in a world without nails to drive; there would be no nails without boards to join; there would be no boards without houses to build; and there would be none of these entities without Dasein—that for-the-sake-of-which they all exist and whose mode of Being is Being-in-the-world.

But if we are clear about what the world is *not,* we are still not clear about what it *is.* The world in which Dasein has its Being is one of those all-too-familiar, too-close-to-be-observed phenomena. The world is not, for instance, the earth. It would sound very odd indeed to talk about Being-in-the-earth (as though one lived underground). Nor is the world the same as the universe. (Christians talk of the "sins of the world," but "sins of the universe" makes no sense at all.) What, then, is this familiar, but strange, phenomenon of the world?

Though our immediate focus is usually on the things *in* the world, Heidegger suggests that there are certain experiences in which the phenomenon of the world itself—the *worldhood* of the world—comes to the fore. Consider working with a lever, trying to move a large and heavy box. What is manifest is the work, the project—to get *this* over *there*—and in a subsidiary (but not explicitly focused) way, the lever. Suddenly the lever breaks. It is no longer ready-to-hand. It takes on the character of *conspicuousness.* Whereas we had hardly noticed the lever before, just using it in that familiar transparent way, suddenly it announces itself, forces itself into awareness.

Two things happen. For one thing, "pure presence-at-hand announces itself in such [damaged] equipment" (*BT,* 103). There occurs a transition to another mode of Being. The functionality that defined the lever *as* a lever vanishes; the item is disconnected from that series of references and involvements that made it be—as a lever. It no longer *is* a lever. It just *lies there.* We no longer seize hold of it in that familiar way to use in our project. It is no longer alongside us in our work. Rather, it stands over against us. We observe it, stare at it. It has become an *object.* It now *is* merely *present-at-hand.*

Heidegger allows that in the course of our everyday lives, this moment of pure presence-at-handedness may not last very long; the item soon takes up a new place in our system of functional involvements, with the meaning of "to-be-fixed" or "to-be-discarded." But this glimpse into the present-at-hand is a revelation of another whole *mode of Being:* a realm of pure objects, suitable for contem-

---

[*]See the discussion of the first sentences of the *Tractatus,* pp. 599 and 602–603.

plation and scientific investigation. It is important to note that in some sense, it is the same entity as before: but revealed in this way, it can be a theme for investigation by the natural sciences. In fact, nature—in the sense dealt with by modern physics now first makes its appearance. This is not nature as a resource, part of the equipment of the world; it is nature disconnected from Dasein's concern—a sheer presence.

Here we have the *origin* of that objectifying way of understanding the world, which has so dominated our tradition. The important thing to note is that the present-at-hand is not primordial, or basic. The objects of natural science have their Being in a *modification* of the more fundamental entities that are ready-to-hand.

This claim has its bite in the notion that no matter how much of the world we "objectify," we always, necessarily, do so on a background of circumspective concern, of practices that involve the ready-to-hand. Dasein cannot, if Heidegger is right, totally objectify itself. Yet, that is just the way our tradition has treated Dasein—as an *object* with *properties* of a certain sort (distinctive properties, perhaps, but an object nonetheless). That is why we tend to think that explanations of a *scientific* sort can be given for human behavior: explanations in terms of conditioning, or complexes, or drives, or peer "pressure," or any number of other analogues to explanation in physical science. And that is why the question of the meaning of Being is so obscure to us; in assimilating our own Being to that of the present-at-hand, we have lost the sense of what it is to *exist*. Because existence is our own mode of Being, a misunderstanding here turns everything topsy-turvy. It is no wonder that clarifying the meaning of Being is so difficult a task.

But we still have not clarified the meaning of "the world." What is it to be a world? That is the second thing that shows up in those experiences where tools go wrong in some way. When the lever breaks, not only does the present-at-hand light up, but the whole network of relations in which it was transparently embedded now comes into view. The *worldhood of the world* is constituted by this system of references, within which Dasein and the ready-to-hand have their Being. To be a world, in other words, is to be a structure within which entities *are* and have their meaning.[*] This entire *network of in-order-tos and toward-whichs and for-the-sake-ofs*—that is the phenomenon of the world. So the world is neither a thing nor a collection of things. It is that wherein entities have their Being, whether that Being is existence, readiness-to-hand, or presence-at-hand.

You should now have a fairly clear understanding of that basic *existential,* that most fundamental characteristic of Dasein: Dasein's Being-in-the-world.

The "Who" of Dasein

Who is Dasein?

That may sound like a strange question, and in fact it is. Not because the term "Dasein" is a strange one, but because the answer seems so straightforward. If Dasein is in each case "mine," then it would seem that, in my case anyway, the answer would be *I myself,* this *person* named Norman Melchert, this *individual,* this *self* or *subject; I* am who Dasein is in this case. And each of you should be able to answer in the same way. What could be more obvious?

But Heidegger thinks this easy and familiar answer covers up or disguises the ontological reality. To talk of self or subject is to fall prey to the temptation to suppose that I am a *thing,* a kind of "soul substance" (perhaps in the way Descartes thinks). But the *Being* of Dasein in its everydayness is not illuminated by this kind of answer; rather, it is hidden.[†] This question is then in order: Who is Dasein

---

[*] Heidegger's conception of "the world" is something like that "scaffolding of the world" that the early Wittgenstein thinks logic provides. (See p. 606.) The enormous difference, of course, is that Wittgenstein's scaffolding supports only sheer meaningless facts—what Heidegger would call the present-at-hand—whereas the worldhood of the world is rich in functionality, usefulness, meaning.

[†] We can interpret Kant and Hegel as denying that a person is an object; A person, they would say, is subject! (See pp. 444 and 477). But Heidegger thinks that nonetheless—and despite Kant's explicit denial—they both implicitly assimilate the Being of Dasein to that of the present-at-hand, and they both miss the ontological character of Dasein's Being—its existence. Heideg-

as it exists in its averageness? The answer Heidegger gives to this question is extraordinary.

> It could be that the "who" of everyday Dasein just is *not* the "I myself." (*BT*, 150)

Heidegger's phenomenological answer to the question about the "who" of Dasein in everydayness is *das Man*. This phrase is based on an ordinary German term that occurs in contexts such as "*Man sagt,*" which can be rendered as "One says," or "It is said that," or perhaps as "They say." While in the detergent aisle of the supermarket one day, I heard one woman say to another, "I think I'll try this; they say that's good." You might ask, Who is this "they"? If you had put this question to her, she probably wouldn't have been able to tell you.*

So Heidegger finds that Dasein in its average everydayness is this "They" or "the One."† But what does that mean? We have already seen that *Others* are "given" along with the ready-to-hand (e.g., with this shirt, which was cut and sewn in a factory somewhere). And if our account is to be phenomenologically adequate, it must record the fact that Others are encountered as themselves Being-in-the-world. The Others, too, *exist* with that same concernful Being-in-the-world as I do.

Moreover, the existence of Others like me is not something that has to come as the conclusion of an argument, as the old problem of "other minds" suggests. I do not first start with *myself* and then conclude on the basis of similarity between observ-

able aspects of myself and Others that they must be persons, too.* That would not be an accurate description of my experience of Others.

> By "Others" we do not mean everyone else but me—those over against whom the "I" stands out. They are rather those from whom, for the most part, one does *not* distinguish oneself—those among whom one is too. . . . The world of Dasein is a *with-world*. Being-in is *Being-with* Others. (*BT*, 154–155)

Being-with, like Being-in-the-world, is an *existential*—one of the characteristics that defines Dasein's Being. This means that Dasein could not exist without Others, any more than it could exist without the world. It is part of Dasein's very *Being* to be with-Others-in-the-world. This is true even when Dasein is alone or neglects the Others or is indifferent to them. The anchorite in the cave is *with* Others, if only in the mode of seeking to avoid them. The anchorite carries the Others with her into the cave in her ability to speak a language, to think, to meditate in the way she does; this "carrying with" is what it means to say that Being-with is an *existential*.

The discovery of Being-with is an important step. But it does not yet get us clearly to the "who" of Dasein. There is a clue, however, in the phrase, "those from whom . . . one does *not* distinguish oneself." We could paradoxically put it this way: One is, oneself, one of the Others. In fact, Heidegger tells us, we are so much one of the "they" that we are constantly concerned lest we differ too much from them.

> In one's concern with what one has taken hold of, whether with, for, or against, the Others, there is constant care as to the way one differs from them, whether that difference is merely one that is to be evened out, whether one's own Dasein has lagged behind the Others and wants to catch up in relation to them, or whether one's Dasein already has

---

ger agrees with Kierkegaard in thinking of the Self as a *task,* not something given. That is part of what it means that Dasein's own Being is an *issue* for it; how it is to be constituted is a matter for *decision.* See pp. 495 and 504.

*The translators of *Being and Time* render "*das Man*" as "the They." Hubert Dreyfus argues in an unpublished commentary that it is much better to bring it into English as "the One" (*Being-in-the-World: A Commentary on Heidegger's Being and Time, Division I,* June 1988). I will sometimes use one locution, sometimes the other.

†Dreyfus argues convincingly that Heidegger does not always distinguish clearly two facets of his own account of "the One": a positive function Dreyfus calls "conformity" or "Falling-in-with," and a negative function he calls "conformism" or "Falling-away-from." The latter, but not the former, correlates with Dasein in the mode of *inauthentic existence.* I try to keep these aspects distinct.

---

*To proceed in this way would be to assume that I *first* have an ontologically adequate grasp of myself and *thereafter* extend this understanding to others. But that is just the (very Cartesian) assumption that Heidegger says we cannot make.

some priority over them and sets out to keep them suppressed. (*BT,* 163–164)

We can think of this as the existential foundation for the familiar phenomenon of "keeping up with the Joneses." Heidegger calls it *distantiality* (still another of those invented words!); he uses this term to signify the constant concern of Dasein that it might get too far away from the norm—from what "they say," or what "one does." (Compare: "One just doesn't *do* that!") Either one doesn't want too large a "distance" to open up between oneself and the Others, or one takes care to preserve a certain "appropriate distance."

Heidegger suggests that this phenomenon is "hidden" from Dasein. And, indeed, I think that is so. When I have suggested to young people that an enormous part of their lives is governed by norms they participate in but are hardly aware of, I usually get a lot of resistance. They all want to think of themselves as unique, self-made individuals! But we all hold our forks the same way, a way different from that of the English; and we North Americans all stand roughly the same distance from others when we converse with them, a distance farther away than Latin Americans stand. If you spell "existence" as "existance," I correct you. And if you want to "be your own person" by dyeing your hair green or wearing a ring in your nose, you are merely rejecting one They for another, falling in with Others who say, "That's cool."

> This distantiality which belongs to Being-with, is such that Dasein, as everyday Being-with-one-another, stands in *subjection* to Others. It itself *is* not; its Being has been taken away by the Others. Dasein's everyday possibilities of Being are for the Others to dispose of as they please. These Others, moreover, are not *definite* Others. On the contrary, any Other can represent them. . . . One belongs to the Others oneself and enhances their power. . . . The "who" is not this one, not that one, not one-self, not some people, and not the sum of them all. The "who" is the neuter, the *"they"* [the One]. . . .
>
> We take pleasure and enjoy ourselves as *they* take pleasure; we read, see, and judge about literature and art as *they* see and judge; likewise we shrink back from the "great mass" as *they* shrink back; we

find "shocking" what *they* find shocking. The "they" [the One], which is nothing definite, and which all are, though not as the sum, prescribes the kind of Being of everydayness. (*BT,* 164)

Let's take one of these "they" phenomena from everydayness and examine it: Consider the "proper" distance to stand from someone you are talking with. Social scientists will tell you that there is a "norm" here based on your cultural background. You almost certainly behave according to your cultural norm, and you are uncomfortable if it is violated. Is this something you *decided?* Certainly not. What is its ground, its reason, its justification—its *logos?* There really doesn't seem to be any. Is it "natural"? No, though it feels natural to us, just as other distances feel natural to people of other cultures. Where does it come from, this "naturalness"—this "rightness," even—that we are uncomfortable violating? Can there be any other answer than "that is what we do?"* This is how it is done, how *One* does it. That is all the foundation it has!

Along with distantiality, the phenomenon of *averageness* is an existential characteristic of the One. And this involves a kind of *leveling down,* in which every kind of uniqueness, oddness, or priority is smoothed out as much as possible. We noted the *public* character of the world as manifest in ready-to-hand items. Now we see that the world is a common, public world in another sense, too. The "way things are done" is set by the One, not by each Dasein privately for itself. The world of the One is a *public* world from the start. It is into that world, moreover, that Dasein comes from the very beginning; it is the One that shapes it and makes Dasein's "who" what it is. We are all *das Man.* In a striking phrase, Heidegger puts it this way:

> Everyone is the other, and no one is himself.
> (*BT,* 165)

The public character of the world of the One—the world of everyday Dasein (our world)—has an interesting consequence:

---

*Compare the later Wittgenstein, pp. 635, 638, and 640.

It deprives the particular Dasein of its answerability. The "they" . . . can be answerable for everything most easily, because it is not someone who needs to vouch for anything. It "was" always the "they" who did it, and yet it can be said that it has been "no one." . . .

Thus the particular Dasein in its everydayness is *disburdened* by the "they." (*BT,* 165)

Who is responsible for the way everyday life goes? No one. It is just the way One does it. Dasein conforms to this *way of Being; Dasein Falls-in-with-it*. Notice that this is not—so far—something for which Dasein is to *blame; distantiality* and *averageness* are *existentials; that is, they are aspects of the very *essence* of Dasein's existence. It couldn't be otherwise for Dasein. And isn't this fortunate? To have to bear the burden of responsibility for the whole of the way one lives would be too much; the "they" is there to help out.

It is important to note that Heidegger distinguishes three modes in which Dasein can relate itself to itself: **inauthenticity, authenticity,** and an undifferentiated mode, which is neither. We have so far been trying to describe the undifferentiated mode of Dasein's existence—though the eagerness with which Dasein accepts the "disburdening" is a hint of what inauthenticity amounts to. As a being for whom its own Being is always at issue, Dasein is always facing the *decision* between existing inauthentically and existing authentically; it always exists predominantly in one mode or the other. We will explore these modes more fully later, but we can now say that authentic existence is not a grasping of some nature or essence of oneself quite different from the "they-self"; it is, rather, a matter of coming to terms with the fact that this is what one is and that one is *no more than this.* And inauthentic existence is a way of hiding this truth from oneself. Existing as "the One" is not yet inauthentic. But "the One" constantly presents to Dasein the possibility of evading the disquieting aspects of *having to Be the being that it is* by fleeing into the security of what "they say." Thus the One is both a constitutive factor in Dasein and a temptation to inauthenticity.

For now, though, we can see that the answer to the question about the "who" of Dasein is this: In its average everydayness, Dasein exists in the mode of "the One." Dasein (you and I in our way of existing) belongs to "the They."

1. How does the notion of Dasein's Being-in-the-world undercut the philosophical tradition about the nature of the self or subject? What does it mean to be in-the-world? And why is epistemology not fundamental?
2. Contrast, using an example, the ready-to-hand with the present-at-hand. Which is basic?
3. What is the world? Contrast Heidegger's answer with that of Wittgenstein's *Tractatus.*
4. What does it mean to say that Dasein is (in its average everydayness) the One? Explain in terms of distantiality and averageness.
5. Explain how the One is both an existential (i.e., is essential to or constitutive of Dasein) and a temptation to inauthenticity.

Modes of Disclosure

Dasein has an understanding of its own Being, though it is not explicitly worked out. But what sort of understanding is this? In what ways is Dasein *always* already disclosed to itself? Think of a dense and dark forest, and in the midst of it imagine a clearing. The clearing opens up a space within which flowers and trees can appear; in fact, it is the clearing that is the condition for anything at all being visible. And now, with this analogy in mind, let us ask, Is there such a clearing in the *world?* Does Dasein exist in such a clearing? Not exactly, Heidegger answers. Rather, he wants to say, Dasein *is* such a clearing.*

---

*The German word here translated as "clearing" is "Lichtung." It is important that the word comes from the word for *light*— "Licht." Dasein is in itself the "light of nature" (Descartes, *Meditation III*), the condition for uncovering the truth. Compare also Augustine on the interior illumination of the soul (p. 238) and Plato on the Image of the Sun (p. 132). What Augustine attributes to the Interior Teacher (Christ) and Plato to the Form of

Dasein brings its "there" along with it. If it lacks its "there," it is not factically* the entity which is essentially Dasein; indeed, it is not this entity at all. *Dasein is its disclosedness.* (*BT,* 171)

A human that was not this kind of openness to beings and to Being would, perhaps, be a corpse. In any case, it would not be "there." Disclosedness is part of the existential constitution of Dasein. And that is what we now have to bring more clearly to light.

Heidegger discusses this "thereness" of Dasein under three headings: **attunement,** understanding, and discourse.† These are very rich pages in *Being and Time,* and we must be content with omitting much. But it is essential to grasp something of these modes of disclosure.

Attunement

We are sometimes asked, "How are you doing?" The surprising thing is that we can always answer. And in answering, we report our *mood.* We say, "Fine," or "Awful—I think I failed the calculus exam." Heidegger holds that moods don't *just happen;* they are not just meaningless present-at-hand items we undergo, the way our heart sometimes beats faster and sometimes slower. Moods are *cognitive.* They are disclosive. But what do they disclose? They reveal how we are coping with this business of having to exist—that is, how we are bearing the burden of having to be here. Dasein is "attuned" to its own Being.

Moreover, moods are not experienced as private states or feelings, independent of the world

out there. Suppose you are in a bad mood, that (as we say) you got out of bed on the wrong side this morning. Where, phenomenologically speaking, does this mood reveal itself? In your head, while the world goes on its sunny way? Not at all. *Nothing,* you are likely to say, is going right. *Everything* seems to be against you. Your *world* is dark. And why should it not be so, if your Being is indeed Being-in-the-world? Moods are pervasive, coloring everything. Suppose you have been watching a horror movie on a DVD all alone, late at night. Thereafter, every creak in the house, every hoot of an owl, and every gust of wind in the trees takes on an ominous quality. You anxiously check the locks and make sure the windows are closed. The *world* is now a scary place! How are you now bearing the burden of having to be there? Not very well.

Dasein never exists without a mood. Even the flat, calm, easygoing character of an average day is a mood. Dasein *is,* remember, its disclosedness. In revealing its "thereness," Dasein's mood discloses how Dasein is attuned to its world. In this disclosure is revealed a further aspect of Dasein's Being: **thrownness.** We find ourselves "thrown" into our Being-in-the-world in the following sense. None of us chose to be born. Nor did we decide to be born in the twentieth century, rather than the thirteenth. Nor were we consulted about whether we would be American or Chinese or Mexican. Nor if we preferred being male or female. Nor black nor white nor any other color. Nor to be born to just *these* parents in just *that* town with just *those* relatives and neighbors, with a certain very specific kind of housing, transportation, and tools at hand. (Lucy says to Snoopy: "You've been a dog all your life, haven't you? I've often wondered what made you decide to become a dog." Snoopy, lying on his doghouse roof, replies, "I was fooled by the job description." But that is a joke, isn't it? It *belongs* in the comics!) We just *find ourselves* in existence—in a world of a particular sort, having one language rather than another and one characteristic way of looking at things, rather than another. We are, as Heidegger says, "delivered over" to our "there," to our world (*BT,* 174).

We could put this idea in another way: *Who* we are is a very particular sort of *One;* there is no help

the Good, Heidegger takes to be the very essence of Dasein itself—that it is *there.*

*See p. 659 and the Glossary for a discussion of facticity.

†The term I am bringing into English as "attunement" (following Dreyfus) is *Befindlichkeit.* There is no very good English equivalent; the translators of *Being and Time* translate it as "state-of-mind." But that plays right into the hands of Heidegger's opponents in the conversation who interpret the modes of disclosure as "states" belonging to a present-at-hand entity—for example, as properties of something like Descartes' mind-substance. It is such "subjectivism" that Heidegger is combating through and through. A commentator suggests "situatedness," which captures part of it but misses the experiential feel of the thing.

for it, for we are "thrown" into one "they" rather than another. Even if we eventually reject certain features of this One, as characteristically happens when human beings mature, we do so drawing on the resources available in *this* world; we cannot make use, for instance, of the psychological and technological discoveries of the twenty-third century. We are *thrown* into the world.

This thrownness is a fact. It is a fact about our Being. So it is an *ontological* fact. Heidegger uses two words for facts. Ordinary facts (that the kiwi is a bird native to New Zealand, for instance, or that this book is written in English, or that I am five feet, ten inches tall) he calls *factual*. Facts about things present-at-hand, for instance, are factual. Ontological facts about Dasein, facts about us not as beings, but about our Being (or *way* of Being), he calls *factical*. Our being a "clearing," for instance, is factical; our Being-in-the-world is factical; our thrownness is part of our **facticity.** In attempting a "fundamental ontology" of Dasein, then, Heidegger is investigating its facticity: the facts about its Being. The facticity of our being thrown is one of the things that moods reveal.

A phenomenologist could go through mood after mood and display the character of each as revealing an aspect of Dasein's Being. But Heidegger focuses on one mood in particular, which he thinks has far-reaching implications. Let us sketch his analysis of *anxiety*.

Like all moods, anxiety is cognitively significant; that is, it discloses something. Anxiety is rather like fear, but it would be a big mistake to confuse them. Fear discloses the fearful: some particular threat to a future possibility of Dasein (the charging bull, the assassin relentlessly hunting one down). Anxiety, by contrast, reveals a very general feature of Dasein's Being. Anxiety is directed, not to a particular threatening entity, but to something more fundamental and far-reaching.

> That in the face of which one has anxiety is Being-in-the-world as such. (*BT,* 230)

What is Being-in-the-world? We already know; it is the most basic existential characteristic of Dasein. So what Dasein is anxious-in-the-face-of is *itself!* Heidegger is suggesting that anxiety reveals in

a peculiarly conspicuous way Dasein's having-to-Be. Ordinarily, average Dasein goes along "absorbed" in the world of its concern, engaged in projects that seem unquestionably to have a point and meaning. But if we remember that the self of everyday Dasein is the *One,* we can see that these projects are those set down by the public world; they have their meaning dictated by the "they." And normally Dasein does not notice this. In its average everydayness, Dasein is delivered over to Being-in-the-public-world-of-already-assigned-significances. Dasein has "fallen-in" with the world of what "One says," what "One does and doesn't do."*

If a person suffering from anxiety is asked what she is afraid of, she replies, "Nothing." And that, Heidegger says, is exactly right; nothing *in the world* is the object of this mood. Rather,

> what is environmentally ready-to-hand sinks away, and so, in general, do entities within-the-world. The "world" can offer nothing more, and neither can the Dasein-with of Others. Anxiety thus takes away from Dasein the possibility of understanding itself, as it falls, in terms of the "world" and the way things have been publicly interpreted. Anxiety throws Dasein back upon that which it is anxious about——its authentic potentiality-for-Being-in-the-world. Anxiety individualizes Dasein. . . .
>
> Anxiety makes manifest in Dasein its *Being towards* its ownmost potentiality-for-Being——that is, its *Being-free* for the freedom of choosing itself and taking hold of itself. (*BT,* 232)

The world doesn't exactly become meaningless; it is still the *world* (i.e., a set of in-order-tos). But in anxiety, one is detached from it; it means nothing to the particular Dasein gripped by anxiety. One can still see others going through the motions, but it seems absurd.† Anxiety distances us from our or-

---

*It is important to remember that this feature is an *existential;* it is not something Dasein could be without, so it is not something to *blame* Dasein for or to *regret.*

†"Absurd" is a word that I don't believe Heidegger uses in this context, but it plays a large role in the thought of French existentialist thinkers, such as Sartre and Camus. See, for instance, Sartre's novel *Nausea* and Camus' *The Myth of Sisyphus* and *The Stranger.* Heidegger does not like Sartre's version of existentialism; it essentially preserves rather than overcomes Cartesian

dinary everyday *Being-in*. It makes clear that how I am to be is a matter of *choice*—that I am *responsible* for my Being. As Heidegger says, anxiety "individualizes." It separates us out from the One.

Wrenched out of the familiar "falling-in" with the way of the world, Dasein experiences itself as *not-at-home-in-the-world*. Yet, it is essentially nothing but Being-in-the-world! Dasein has no other reality; it cannot repair to its own "substance" or enjoy its own "essence" apart from the world. "Just be *yourself*," we are often advised. But, if Heidegger is right, there is no one for us to be apart from our falling in with the world of the One! In anxiety, then, Dasein is made aware of that fact, but in the mode of not being absorbed in that world. There is no home but that home, yet, anxiously, we are homeless.*

On the one hand, anxiety reveals with penetrating clarity the nature of Dasein's Being. But on the other hand, it provides a powerful motivation for Dasein to hide itself from itself—to flee back into the comfortable, familiar, well-ordered, meaningful world of the One, to avoid the risky business of taking up responsibility for one's own Being. That is why Heidegger says that Dasein is anxious about its "authentic potentiality-for-Being-in-the-world." Anxiety presents Dasein with the clear choice between existing authentically or inauthentically. The temptation is to flee back into the world, to be reabsorbed in it, to shut one's eyes to the fact that a *decision* about one's way of life is called for. The temptation is to think that our lives are as antecedently well ordered as the career of a hammer—that the meaning of life is *given* and doesn't have to be *forged*. To flee back into the predecided life of the One would "disburden" Dasein and quiet anxiety. But such fleeing on the part of

Dasein would be "falling-away-from" itself, the *inauthentic* kind of **falling**.* Falling-away-from oneself is the same as falling-prey-to the One. So Dasein "tranquilizes" itself in the familiar world of significance, fleeing *away from* its freedom and its not-at-homeness *into* the world of the One; thus it disguises from itself its true Being (that its Being is an *issue*). We crave a world in which we can say, "I had no choice." And behold, in the world of the One, all crucial decisions are already made, dictated by the norms of what One does and doesn't do. The possibilities open to Dasein are "disposed of" beforehand. One's life is *settled*. And anxiety is covered up.

Moods, then, are cognitively significant; they always tell us something about ourselves and, in particular, about our Being. Among the moods, anxiety most clearly reveals the Being of Dasein—that it is thrown-Being-in-the-world-of-the-One. And in doing so, it both distances Dasein from that Being and provides a motivation for falling back into that world in an inauthentic way.

Understanding

In one way or another, Dasein is always "attuned" to its world. But every attunement carries with it an understanding of that world (and every understanding has its mood); understanding, Heidegger says, is *equiprimordial* with attunement (meaning that they come together and that neither can be derived from the other). We have already met "understanding," of course. Dasein from the beginning has been held to be that being who—simply by virtue of Being—has an understanding of its Being. To be "there," in fact, *is* to understand. But this is hard to—understand. Let us see if we can do so.

---

dualism, he maintains. But the Heideggerian influence in these thinkers is strong.

*The German word here is "Unheimlichkeit," literally "not-at-homeness." The translators of *Being and Time* bring it into English as "uncanniness." It is perhaps this same sense of homelessness that Augustine has in mind when he prays, "Our hearts find no peace until they rest in you" (p. 254). Unlike Augustine, Heidegger cannot believe that there is a home for us *beyond* the world.

---

*Remember that there are two kinds of "falling": *falling-in-with* is one of the essential characteristics of Dasein, an *existential*. Dasein's "who" is invariably and inevitably the *One*. The second kind of falling, *falling-away-from,* is Dasein's fleeing from the anxious realization of its own essential homelessness into the illusory security that the life of the One seems to offer. Such fleeing is the mark of *inauthentic* existence, of not appropriating the Being that is *one's own*. Simone de Beauvoir calls this flight from authenticity "seriousness." (See pp. 685–687)

We can begin in a very familiar way by examining what we mean when we say that Jane understands carburetors. We mean that she is competent with respect to carburetors, that she can adjust, tune, and repair them. It need not be that Jane could write a book about carburetors; perhaps she couldn't. But if you are having carburetor troubles, Jane is the one for you. She really *understands* carburetors! Now it is crucial to note that *possibility* or *potentiality* is involved in this kind of understanding. Jane can do more than just describe the current present-at-hand state of your carburetor; she can see *what's wrong* with it. And this means that she has in view a potential state of the device that is different from its current state; a possibility that it might function properly. And she has the *know-how* to produce that state. Jane's understanding is a matter of being able to bring it from a condition of not working well to one of satisfactory performance, a possibility not now realized.

This notion of possibility is also involved in the existential understanding that belongs to Dasein. For what does Dasein essentially understand? Itself, in its own Being. Suppose someone (God, maybe) had a list of everything factually true of you at this moment: every hair on your head, the state of every neuron in your brain, and every thought and feeling. Would this list tell us who you are? It would not. It wouldn't, even if it listed every fact about you since you were born. Why not? Because you, as a case of Dasein, are not something present-at-hand, a mere collection of facts; you are essentially *what you can be.* You are a certain "potentiality-for-Being," to use Heidegger's language. Unless I understand your *possibilities,* I will not understand you.

> Dasein is constantly "more" than it factually is, supposing that one might want to make an inventory of it as something-at-hand and list the contents of its Being. . . . But Dasein is never more than it factically is, for to its facticity its potentiality-for-Being belongs essentially. (*BT,* 185)

But now let's shift the perspective. Rather than thinking of what would be required for a third party to understand you, think about what is needed for you to understand yourself. Here is the somewhat startling answer: nothing—beyond your Being-

there. To exist *is* to understand.* Understanding (as an *existential*) is having competence over one's Being; that is not something added on "by way of an extra" (*BT,* 183). That is what it is to exist. And this understanding is an understanding of possibility. Right now, at this very moment, you *are* a certain understanding of your possibilities (e.g., the possibility of continuing to read this chapter, of underlining this phrase, of going to the refrigerator for a cold drink, of calling a friend, of becoming an engineer or accountant, perhaps of dropping out of school and bumming around the world). You exist these potentialities in your every thought and movement. And this understanding, which you *are,* is not something that you need to conceptualize or explicitly think about. It just is a certain *competence* with respect to your Being that you cannot help manifesting.

Understanding has the structure of *projection.* We are always projecting ourselves into possibilities. Again, we must be careful not to think of this as a matter of reflecting on possibilities, of reviewing or deliberating, or of having them "in mind." It is more primordial than that. To understand a chair, for instance, is to be prepared to sit in it rather than wear it. To understand oneself as a student is to *project* oneself into potentially mastering Chinese or statistics or into the possibility of becoming a college graduate. Understanding oneself as a student *permeates* one's Being. To exist in a specific situation *is* to have an understanding (or a misunderstanding) of the promise or menace of what is impending. Understanding in this fundamental sense is a matter of our *Being.* It is an aspect of what it means to *exist.* Since we are what we *can be,* possibility is even more fundamental to our Being than the actuality of the facts about us. And these possibilities are not something external to our Being. They are possibilities that we *are.*

This understanding, as a kind of preparedness to act, tends to be tacit. But it can be developed more explicitly; it then takes the form of *interpretation.* Interpretation is not something different from un-

---

*This is quite compatible, of course, with your *misunderstanding* yourself; a misunderstanding is a kind of understanding. This is why inauthentic existence is one of your possibilities.

derstanding; it is understanding itself come to fruition. Consider the light switch in your room, something you understand very well in one sense; you operate with it in such a familiar way that you scarcely notice it; you probably couldn't tell me what its color is. But suppose one day it fails to function. Now its "place" in the functional ordering of the world is disturbed; you had all along been taking its role as equipment for granted—that is, understanding it implicitly. But now it comes to the fore, and you understand it explicitly—*as* a device to transmit electricity. This "as" structure is already implicit in your everyday and familiar understanding, but now it is expressed; it becomes explicit in an *interpretation*. Interpretation always lays bare "the structure of *something as something*" (*BT*, 189).

The fact that interpretation (whether of a device, a text, the meaning of someone's action, and so on) is always founded on a prior understanding has an important implication for Heidegger. There is no way we can disengage ourselves from our Being-in-the-world sufficiently to guarantee a completely "objective" view of anything. Every interpretation *always* takes something for granted; it is worked out on some background that is not itself available for inspection and decision. That does not mean that truth is unavailable to Dasein, but it does mean that Dasein is involved in a kind of circle it cannot get out of.* Interpreting is understanding *x as y*—for example, the switch *as* a device for controlling the flow of electricity. But interpretation

just makes explicit that prior understanding of it *as* a switch in the first place. That understanding is a matter of having a certain competence with respect to it. Such competent understanding is a matter of (largely unreflective) projection, of ways of behaving toward what *could be*. And all this exists only on the background of our Being-in-the-world in general, which involves understanding the potentialities of such equipment as light switches.

This circle is usually called the **hermeneutic circle;** all interpretation is caught up in what is understood beforehand. It is not a vicious circle, Heidegger maintains,* but it is one that should be recognized.

> If the basic conditions which make interpretation possible are to be fulfilled, this must . . . be done by not failing to recognize beforehand the essential conditions under which it can be performed. What is decisive is not to get out of the circle, but to come into it in the right way. (*BT*, 194–195)

"The right way" is to come without illusions (that is, without imagining that one can get a kind of "bare" look at the object of interpretation) and to be as clear and explicit as possible about what one is bringing to the interpretive task. Part of Heidegger's conviction is that this background can never be made *completely* explicit,[†] for it is this background that Dasein *is*.

---

*It is interesting to compare this point with the pragmatist claim that we must give up the quest for certainty. See Peirce's triangle example on p. 571; the image of sailors on a ship, p. 574; and the summary of Dewey's view of experience, pp. 583–585. Heidegger is here combating the desire of Descartes to find an Archimedean point from which to view the world; there is, Heidegger claims, no "view from nowhere." We can also think of it as an argument against Hume's motto (taken from Newton) to frame no hypotheses (see p. 398ff.). If framing hypotheses is a matter of bringing a certain understanding *to* a situation, then we cannot help framing hypotheses—just as Kant thinks there is no getting around the a priori structures that make knowledge possible. There is some justice in viewing the history of modern philosophy as a conversation between the rationalists, the empiricists, and the pragmatists. In this (oversimplified) schema, Heidegger would line up with the pragmatists. Compare also Nietzsche's critique of "immaculate perception," pp. 558–559.

*Note that Heidegger grants one of the fundamental claims of the skeptic: The structure of our knowledge does involve a circle. He thinks this isn't damaging because Dasein, as he conceives it, does not have to *break* into the clearing (e.g., by means of some *criterion*); Dasein is already the clearing, the revealing of Being. This doesn't mean, of course, that Dasein always knows the truth; both the One and the individual Dasein can conspire to cover it up. For the relevance of this circle to skeptical claims, see the discussion of Sextus Empiricus, p. 212. This same problem comes up in Plato and Aristotle. See pp. 130–133 and 166–168.

†Hubert Dreyfus is the most notable (though not the only) person to apply this point to artificial intelligence. It shows, he believes, that the work in traditional artificial intelligence was bound to fail because it was based on the assumption that all the rules by which an intelligent system operates could be made explicit and operate on items that are context-free (i.e., not in-a-world). If Heidegger is right, this is not true of us and is probably not true for any system that has more than strictly limited capabilities. You might look at Dreyfus' book, *What Computers*

Let us summarize. Understanding, like attunement, is an *existential*. There is no Being-there that does not involve understanding. The primordial mode of understanding is a kind of know-how or competence with respect to things, particularly with respect to Dasein's own Being. This is largely implicit, but it can be spelled out in an interpretation. It is just such an interpretation that Heidegger is striving to construct with respect to the meaning of Dasein's Being and ultimately for the meaning of Being in general.

Discourse

Because the world of Dasein is a world of significations (in-order-tos, toward-whichs, and for-the-sake-ofs, to put it in Heideggerese), Dasein exists in an *articulated* world; like a turkey, it has "joints" at which it may be readily carved. The hammer is distinct from the nails but is *for* pounding them into the boards, which are a third articulated item. In understanding how to use a hammer, Dasein displays a primordial understanding of this articulation. As we have seen, this primitive kind of understanding can be made explicit in interpretation. And now we must add that interpretation itself is a phenomenon *in-the-world* only in terms of *discourse*.

Discourse, Heidegger says, is equiprimordial with attunement and understanding. (Again, this means that while it cannot be reduced to either of them, it is equally basic.) Discourse, too, is an *existential*. It is an essential characteristic of Dasein. There is no Dasein that doesn't *talk*.* In talk, or discourse, the articulations of the world of Dasein are expressed in *language*. Moreover, we talk *with one another,* so discourse essentially involves Being-*with*. Discourse involves communication.

Discoursing or talking is the way in which we articulate "significantly" the intelligibility of Being-in-the-world. Being-with belongs to Being-in-the-world, which in every case maintains itself in some definite way of concernful Being-with-one-another: Such Being-with-one-another is discursive as assenting or refusing, as demanding or warning, as pronouncing, consulting, or interceding, as "making assertions," and as talking in the way of "giving a talk." (*BT,* 204)*

Again, Heidegger warns against a misunderstanding.

Communication is never anything like a conveying of experiences, such as opinions or wishes, from the interior of one subject into the interior of another. Dasein-with is already essentially manifest in a co-state-of-mind [co-attunement] and a co-understanding. In discourse Being-with becomes "explicitly" *shared;* that is to say, it *is* already, but it is unshared as something that has not been taken hold of and appropriated. (*BT,* 205)

This remark should be understood as part of Heidegger's continuing polemic against the Cartesian picture of the isolated subject shut up within the walls of the mind and forced to find some way to "convey" a message across an empty space to another such subject. As Being-with, we already live in a common world with others—the public world of equipment and its structural articulation. In discourse we "take hold" of this common legacy and express it in language.

---

1. What do moods reveal? How are they related to what Heidegger calls *thrownness?*
2. What does anxiety reveal? How is it related to responsibility? To inauthenticity?
3. In what way is possibility or potentiality involved in Dasein's understanding of itself?
4. Explain why understanding is necessarily involved in the hermeneutic circle. Does this have any impli-

---

Can't Do (New York: Harper and Row, 1972), and the book he wrote with his brother Stuart (a computer engineer), *Mind over Machine* (New York: Macmillan, Free Press, 1985).

* What about newborn babies, you ask? The answer seems to be that while they are clearly human, they are not a case of Dasein. They are not (yet) *there* in that way characteristic of Dasein. As they are socialized, Dasein slowly dawns in them.

---

*Compare what Wittgenstein says about the ways we use language (p. 628). Heidegger, like the later Wittgenstein, is convinced that philosophy has often been led astray by supposing that *assertion* has first place in discourse. He takes Berkeley's side against Locke: Language is *not* primarily a code for transferring ideas from one mind to another. See p. 388.

cations for how certain you should feel about your opinions?

Falling-Away

With the analysis of the modes of disclosure, the general shape of Heidegger's fundamental ontology is coming into view. Dasein is

- Being-in-the-world
- Being-with-others
- Falling-in-with-the-One
- Thrown
- A clearing, manifesting itself in attunement, understanding, and discourse

We also know that Dasein has the potentiality for existing in either an authentic or an inauthentic fashion. We need to understand these alternatives more clearly. Let us begin by discussing inauthenticity.

Dasein *is* Being-in-the-world and as such "falls-in-with" the "Others" who constitute "the One." Dasein has no secret, private essence *out of which* it could fall; nor is Dasein initially "innocent," later falling into sin. As long as we are talking about the first kind of falling—falling-in-with—questions of innocence or guilt are not yet in order. This kind of falling is a constitutive, ontological characteristic of what it is to be Dasein.[*]

In discussing anxiety, we noted that Dasein is tempted to flee its anxious homelessness and *lose itself* in the tranquilizing security of the public world. But Heidegger now wants to go a step further and claim that simply Being-in-the-world is itself *tempting*. For the world is, after all, the world of the One. And to understand why this might by its very

nature tempt Dasein toward inauthenticity, we need to understand the modes of disclosure characteristic of the One. How does *One* understand? How are "they" attuned to their Being? What sort of discourse is Dasein thrown into as it takes up its Being-in-the-world?

Idle Talk

As we have seen, discourse has its Being in language, which expresses the articulations making up the world. Discourse is essentially revealing, disclosing. It opens up the world. But in average everydayness, discourse tends toward being just idle talk.

> We do not so much understand the entities which are talked about; we already are listening only to what is said-in-the-talk as such. What is said-in-the-talk gets understood; but what the talk is about is understood only approximately and superficially. (*BT*, 212)

This is something you can test for yourself. Listen carefully to the conversations that go on among your acquaintances; see how much of their "everyday" talk is just a matter of latching on to "what-is-said" as such, without any deep commitment to the subject matter being discussed or to the truth about it. How much of it is just chatter, or an attempt to impose opinions on others? How much is what Wittgenstein calls "just *gassing*"?[*]

> And because this discoursing has lost its primary relationship-of-Being towards the entity talked about, or else has never achieved such a relationship, it does not communicate in such a way as to let this entity be appropriated in a primordial manner, but communicates rather by following the route of *gossiping* and *passing the word along*. What is said-in-the-talk as such, spreads in wider circles and takes on an authoritative character. Things are so because one says so. . . .
>
> Idle talk is the possibility of understanding everything without previously making the thing one's own. (*BT*, 212–213)

When Dasein is thrown into the world, it is into idle talk that Dasein is thrown.

---

[*]Despite Heidegger's protestations, some theologians suggest that we might have here the basis for an interpretation of what the Christian tradition has called "original sin." If there is no "pure" essence of Dasein to be corrupted in the first place, and if—as we will shortly see—the One that becomes the "who" of Dasein is itself inauthentic, how could Dasein *not* be "conceived and born in sin"? Rudolph Bultmann and Paul Tillich are among the theologians who have been strongly influenced by Heidegger. For Augustine on original sin, see pp. 249–251.

---

[*]See pp. 607, 617, and 633.

There are many things with which we first become acquainted in this way, and there is not a little which never gets beyond such an average understanding. This everyday way in which things have been interpreted is one into which Dasein has grown in the first instance, with never a possibility of extrication. In it, out of it, and against it, all genuine understanding, interpreting, and communicating, all re-discovering and appropriating anew, are performed. (*BT,* 213)

Dasein is a talking entity. But when Dasein falls-in-with the others in its world, as it must, it also falls-in-with this degenerate form of discourse. Note that there is no possibility of extricating ourselves from idle talk. It is the milieu in which we exist. The best we can do is to struggle against it—from within it—toward "genuine understanding."* But as long as we remain inauthentically content with what-is-said, idle talk will cover over the meaning of Being, including the meaning of our own Being. That is why Heidegger can say, "Being-in-the-world is in itself tempting" (*BT,* 221).

Curiosity

Dasein, we have said, is a "clearing" in the midst of the world because *understanding* is an aspect of its essence. But in its average everydayness, understanding, too, tends to become shallow and disconnected from Being. As long as we are absorbed in our work, hammering away on the roof, our understanding is engaged in the project. But when we take a rest, understanding idles. And then it becomes *curiosity.* Curiosity is a concern just to see—but not in order to understand what one sees.

> Consequently it does not seek the leisure of tarrying observantly, but rather seeks restlessness and the excitement of continual novelty and changing encounters. In not tarrying, curiosity is concerned with the constant possibility of *distraction.* Curiosity has nothing to do with observing entities and marvelling at them. . . .† To be amazed to the point

of not understanding is something in which it has no interest. Rather it concerns itself with a kind of knowing, but just in order to have known. (*BT,* 216–217)

One is reminded of those folks who visit the Grand Canyon primarily to bring back slides to show their friends. Curiosity and idle talk, Heidegger says, reinforce each other; "*either* of these ways-to-be drags the other one with it" (*BT,* 217). You can see why this is so. If one never tarries anywhere, one's understanding is bound to be expressed in idle talk about what one has "seen." Together, Heidegger wryly remarks, they are supposed to guarantee a "life" that is genuinely "lively."

Ambiguity

Because of the predominance of idle talk and curiosity, ambiguity pervades Dasein's Being-in-the-world. It

> soon becomes impossible to decide what is disclosed in a genuine understanding, and what is not. . . .
> Everything looks as if it were genuinely understood, genuinely taken hold of, genuinely spoken, though at bottom it is not; or else it does not look so, and yet at bottom it is. (*BT,* 217)

Genuine understanding of something is, of course, difficult. It takes time, patience, and careful attention. But in a day when the results of the most mathematically sophisticated physics are reported in the daily paper in a way that is supposed to inform the average person, who can tell what is truly understood and what is not? Since understanding is the "light of nature" in which beings and Being are "cleared," and since understanding is essential to the very Being of Dasein, a deadly ambiguity seeps into Dasein's existence.

In its average everydayness, Dasein is the *One.* But the average everydayness of the One is characterized by idle talk, curiosity, and ambiguity. It follows that Dasein

> has, in the first instance, fallen away from itself as an authentic potentiality for Being its Self, and

---

*Idle talk seems to correspond pretty nearly with the way Plato describes life in the cave. See his myth on pp. 133–135.

†At this point Heidegger makes a reference to Aristotle's remark that all philosophy begins in wonder (p. 173). You should also

review the "rotation method" from the first part of Kierkegaard's *Either/Or* (pp. 490–491).

has fallen into the "world." "Fallenness" into the "world" means an absorption in Being-with-one-another, in so far as the latter is guided by idle talk, curiosity, and ambiguity. (*BT,* 220)

In falling-in-with the way of the world, Dasein tends to fall-away-from itself. While it is important to keep these two notions distinct, one gets the definite impression that Heidegger believes the first invariably brings the second with it. Dasein falls away from itself by failing to grasp its own Being clearly. It understands itself the way "they" understand. It even takes its moods, its way of being attuned, from the One—what matters to Dasein is what "they say" matters. Dasein does not decisively seize itself for itself; it lets itself float, lost in the interpretations of the public "they." It is this *not being one's own,* belonging only to the One, that is the heart of inauthenticity. And we all *are* inauthentic in this way.

This idea is driven home by a further reflection about *thrownness.* To this point, we have talked about being "thrown" into the world as if it were an event that happened to us once, at birth. But Heidegger maintains that we are constantly being thrown into the world.

> Thrownness is neither a "fact that is finished" nor a Fact that is settled. Dasein's facticity is such that *as long as* it is what it is, Dasein remains in the throw, and is sucked into the turbulence of the "they's" inauthenticity. (*BT,* 223)

Dasein remains "in the throw" as long as it is. We are constantly being thrown into the world, and the world is always the world of the One. This has important implications for what *authentic* existence might be.

> *Authentic* existence is not something which floats above falling everydayness; existentially, it is only a modified way in which such everydayness is seized upon. (*BT,* 224)

We will return to that shortly.

Care

Heidegger's interpretation of the ontology of Dasein is rich and complex. We have explored quite a

number of the *existentials,* or "categories" that define its way of Being. At this point, Heidegger asks whether this multiplicity of concepts is founded in a deeper unity. He thinks he can point to a unifying ontological concept, in the light of which all the rest makes sense.

The single phenomenon that lies at the root of Dasein's Being, Heidegger tells us, is *Care.* Care is understood as the ontological structure that makes possible Dasein's everyday *concerns* for its projects, its *solicitude* for Others, even its *willing* and *wishing.* In typical Heideggerian fashion, Care is spelled out as

- Being-ahead-of-itself by projecting toward its possibilities, while

- Being-in-the-world, and

- Being engaged with entities encountered within-the-world.

(This kind of talk should now be making some sense to you; go over these phrases carefully, making sure that it is not simply "idle talk" to you.)

It is important to note that Care is not some special "ontic" attitude that Dasein might occasionally display. Care is the *Being* of Dasein: without Care, no Being-there. Care is manifest in all understanding, from the intensely practical to the most purely theoretical. It is present in attunement and in all discourse. Dasein is not fundamentally the *rational animal,* not basically the *ego cogito,* not primarily a *knower.* What is most fundamental to Dasein's Being is caring: Dasein is the being for whom things *matter.** And that brings us right back to the very beginning, where we noted that Dasein is that being for whom its own Being is an *issue.*

Heidegger supports this interpretation of the unity of Dasein's Being by quoting an old Latin fable about the creation of human beings by the gods:

---

*Some years ago, the rock group Queen recorded a song in which this phrase was repeated: "Nothing really matters." Is this an argument against Heidegger's claim that Care is the essence of Dasein? Not at all. It if were *true* that nothing really mattered, Queen would not bother to sing it in that poignant and nostalgic way they do. They *care* that "nothing matters," thereby proving that something *does* matter.

Once when "Care" was crossing a river, she saw some clay; she thoughtfully took up a piece and began to shape it. While she was meditating on what she had made, Jupiter came by. "Care" asked him to give it spirit, and this he gladly granted. But when she wanted her name to be bestowed upon it, he forbade this, and demanded that it be given his name instead. While "Care" and Jupiter were disputing, Earth arose and desired that her own name be conferred on the creature, since she had furnished it with part of her body. They asked Saturn to be their arbiter, and he made the following decision, which seemed a just one: "Since you, Jupiter, have given its spirit, you shall receive that spirit at its death; and since you, Earth, have given its body, you shall receive its body. But since 'Care' first shaped this creature, she shall possess it as long as it lives." (*BT*, 242)

Some time ago, my wife was recovering from a severe case of flu. Sitting on the sofa in the living room and looking about, she said, "I must be alive; I'm beginning to care that the house is a mess." Heidegger would have liked that.

We have in Care, then, a single, unitary, simple foundation for all the complexities we have so far discovered in the Being of Dasein—and for those still to come. But before we fill in the final bits of the picture, we need to pause a moment to think about *truth*.

Truth

According to the Western philosophical tradition, truth belongs to what is said, to assertions or judgments.* The tradition develops this notion into the idea that in true judgments there is a "correspondence" between the assertion and what it is about; in a similar way, Thomas Aquinas talks about an "adequation" of the intellect to reality, and others about an "agreement." Heidegger does not want to claim that these views are mistaken, exactly. But he does think they are misleadingly formulated and shallow. The problem is one we have met before in

our analysis of everydayness: The items involved (assertion and object) are conceived by the tradition as items *present-at-hand,* when this is not their mode of Being at all.

To mistake their mode of Being makes for insoluble problems; what, after all, *is* it for the assertion "Corn grows in the Midwest" to *agree* with fields of corn in Iowa? As marks on this page, that sentence doesn't seem related at all to what grows around Iowa City. So the tradition feels compelled to *supplement* that present-at-hand item with some mental state (an idea, a concept, an intention, a significant content).* But this presents three further problems: (1) Such states are also conceived as something present-at-hand; they just have a different "locus" (in the subject). (2) How is the *mental state* related to the *marks on the page?* and (3) Doesn't the same question arise with regard to those mental states: What is it for *them* to "agree" with reality? In addition, we always have this nagging problem: How could we ever *tell* whether our judgments corresponded to their objects?†

What is needed, Heidegger is certain, is attention to the *Being* of truth. What mode of Being does truth have? In developing an ontology of truth, Heidegger thinks we can bypass these traditional puzzles and answer the old problem posed so poignantly (or was it cynically?) by Pilate: "What is truth?" (John 18 : 38).

We already have the clue to untangle this mess, for we know that Dasein *is,* in its very Being, disclosure. To "be there" is to *uncover* entities.

> To say that an assertion "*is true*" signifies that it uncovers the entity as it is in itself. Such an assertion asserts, points out, "lets" the entity "be seen" . . . in its uncoveredness. The *Being-true (truth)* of the assertion must be understood as *Being-uncovering.* (*BT*, 261)

---

*See Aristotle's incomparable definition of truth, pp. 162–163.

---

*See Locke, who says that words are signs for ideas in the mind, p. 380.

†This, you will recall, was one of the major motivations leading Kant to his Copernican revolution, in which the problem is "solved" by trying to show that objects are (partially) *constructs* by the judging mind. See pp. 427–428. Representation is a crucial issue in current cognitive science and work in artificial intelligence.

When I say that a picture is askew (supposing that it is), what I say is true. But its being true is not a matter of two present-at-hand items (my saying and the angle of the picture) having some sort of relation holding between them. It is a matter of my actually uncovering it *as it is*. That my assertion is true is demonstrated when I look at the picture; what I have "put forward in the assertion (namely the entity itself) shows itself *as that very same thing*" (*BT,* 261). What the perceiving confirms is that the assertion is indeed an *uncovering;* it is what it purports to be.

Heidegger does not think of this notion as casting away the traditional view of truth. Rather, he says, thinking of truth as *uncovering* is a way of giving that view an ontologically adequate foundation. It is Dasein that uncovers entities by virtue of Being that that disclosedness which comes along with Being-in-the-world understandingly. So Being-true is a way of Being for Dasein.

> *Dasein is "in the truth."* This assertion has meaning ontologically. It does not purport to say that ontically Dasein is introduced "to all the truth" either always or just in every case, but rather that the disclosedness of its ownmost Being belongs to its existential constitution. (*BT,* 263)

If this sounds too optimistic to be true, remember that Dasein is also falling-away-from itself into the world of the One, where idle talk, curiosity, and ambiguity dominate. So Dasein, while essentially "in the truth" in the sense that it is disclosive in its very Being, is also "in untruth." And in fact, because we are "thrown" into the world of the One, it is untruth that is "closer" to us than truth.

> Truth (uncoveredness) is something that must always first be wrested from entities. Entities get snatched out of their hiddenness. The factical uncoveredness of anything is always, as it were, a kind of *robbery*. (*BT,* 265)

Heidegger finds it significant that the Greek word for truth begins with *a* ("not") and that the middle part of the word, *lethe,* is the same as the word for forgetfulness. (Lethe is the river in Hades, whose water produces forgetfulness in those who drink it.) So truth is *not-forgetting,* an idea suggesting that what is uncovered is something that was previously forgotten, covered over, hidden. And Heidegger's view of Dasein as falling (into the world of the One and away from itself) accounts for just such a phenomenon. That is why there is something *violent* about the quest for truth; it is like, he says, robbery. For Dasein must penetrate the fog that rises up around the One—to which fog, remember, each Dasein is also contributing—to "wrest" the truth from entities. Truth is difficult to achieve.

This view of truth as an *existential,* as an essential aspect of Dasein's Being, has interesting consequences for the problem of relativism. Heidegger thinks it enables him to stake out a middle ground between the sophists, skeptics, and relativists on the one hand and the absolutists who talk of eternal truth on the other.

> *"There is"* truth only in so far as Dasein is and so long as Dasein is. Entities are uncovered only *when* Dasein *is;* and only as long as Dasein *is,* are they disclosed. Newton's laws, the principle of contradiction, any truth whatever—these are true only as long as Dasein *is.* Before there was any Dasein, there was no truth; nor will there be any after Dasein is no more. For in such a case truth as disclosedness, uncovering, and uncoveredness, *cannot* be. Before Newton's laws were discovered, they were not "true"; it does not follow that they were false, or even that they would become false if ontically no discoveredness were any longer possible. . . .
>
> To say that before Newton his laws were neither true nor false, cannot signify that before him there were no such entities as have been uncovered and pointed out by those laws. Through Newton the laws became true; and with them, entities became accessible in themselves to Dasein. Once entities have been uncovered, they show themselves precisely as entities which beforehand already were. Such uncovering is the kind of Being which belongs to "truth." (*BT,* 269)

Because Dasein is "in the truth," the uncovering of entities *as they really are in themselves* is a possibility. This possibility, of course, depends on Dasein-like beings: no Dasein, no truth—that is, no uncovering of entities. All truth, as Heidegger says, "*is relative to Dasein's Being*" (*BT,* 270). In a sense, Protagoras was right in saying, "Of all things the measure is man."* But does this mean that truth is *subjective* in the sense that it depends on what a given Dasein happens to think? Not at all. For Dasein, in uncovering entities, comes "face to face with the entities themselves" (*BT*, 270). It is true, of course, that each Dasein is "thrown" into a certain language and culture; and each language and culture already has a certain understanding of entities and Being embedded in it. This understanding is always a mixture of truth and untruth. But the possibility of genuine uncovering is given with Dasein's Being; nothing in principle stands between Dasein and the truth.

Moreover, although truth exists only in conjunction with Dasein (so that there are no eternal truths unless Dasein always existed), what is uncovered is uncovered as *already having been there*. So Heidegger is not an idealist who claims that entities are constructions on the part of a subject. The world is revealed as having antedated the emergence of Dasein, but it is revealed only *to* Dasein. Newton's laws *became* true (i.e., dis-covered) in Newton's day, but what these laws tell us, they tell us about those entities that also existed ages before Newton lived.

---

1. Explain idle talk, curiosity, and ambiguity as inauthentic modes of Dasein's Being.
2. What does it mean to say that Care is the Being of Dasein?
3. What is it for an assertion to be-true? Why does Heidegger think that this ontological understanding of truth recovers a meaning that goes deeper than correspondence between a sentence and a state of affairs?

Death

In spite of the extensive analysis we have been following, Heidegger is not satisfied that he has ex-

---

*See p. 44.

plored all the dimensions of Dasein's Being. In particular, it is not clear that we have an understanding of the *totality* of Dasein. Nor has much been said about the character of *authenticity*. So these topics remain. We first explore the idea of totality.

Is it even possible to understand Dasein *as a whole*? We have seen that Dasein's existence is characterized by projection toward possibilities: at every stage, Dasein is what it is *not yet*; there are always potentialities-for-Being that are yet unrealized. As Heidegger now puts it, this means that there is always "something *still outstanding*," something "*still to be settled*" with respect to Dasein's Being (*BT*, 279). Can that be brought into our understanding in a way that will give us an interpretation of Dasein as a totality? This obviously brings us to the topic of the *end* of Dasein: to death. It is death that makes Dasein a *whole*. Is it possible to understand death?

It seems I cannot experience my own death, since to do so I would have to live through it—and then I wouldn't be dead.*

> When Dasein reaches its wholeness in death, it simultaneously loses the Being of its "there." By its transition to no-longer-Dasein, it gets lifted right out of the possibility of experiencing this transition and of understanding it as something experienced. (*BT*, 281)

Death must be understood in terms of the Being of Dasein; that is, we must understand it in the light of that unitary phenomenon of Dasein's Being: Care. Dasein's death is not just its end in a physical or biological sense. Death, as a *possibility* for Dasein, is something that, in a strange sense, Dasein *lives*. Dasein *is* its possibilities, and among those possibilities is the possibility that Dasein will die. This is, in fact, a strange possibility because it is one that Dasein is *bound* to realize. Unlike other possibilities, this is one about which Dasein has no

---

*There are reported cases, of course, of people who "died" and came back to tell about it. They often tell of experiences they had while they were "dead." But what Heidegger would surely say about these cases is that they are not cases of death but something else. They are not death because the persons involved did not lose their "Being-there."

choice. As Heidegger puts it, death is "not to be outstripped" (*BT,* 294).* We are *thrown* into this possibility, with never a chance of extrication.

One of the aspects of Dasein, however, is *falling.* And in falling-away-from itself into the world of the "they," Dasein exists this possibility of death in the inauthentic mode of fleeing-in-the-face-of-it. Everydayness, in various ways, covers over this possibility. The One hides from Dasein the fact that *it* must die. How does it do this? By interpreting death as a mishap, an event, as something present-at-hand—but not yet!

> Death gets passed off as always something "actual"; its character as a possibility gets concealed. . . . By such ambiguity . . . , the "they" gives its approval, and aggravates the *temptation* to cover up from oneself one's ownmost Being-towards-death. This evasive concealment in the face of death dominates everydayness so stubbornly that, in Being with one another, the "neighbors" often still keep talking the "dying person" into the belief that he will escape death and soon return to the tranquillized everydayness of the world of his concern. Such "solicitude" is meant to "console" him. . . . In this manner the "they" provides a *constant tranquillization about death.* At bottom, however, this is a tranquillization not only for him who is "dying" but just as much for those who "console" him. (*BT,* 297–298)

Everydayness transforms death from one's ownmost possibility into an event that is distant and then says it is nothing to be *afraid* of. But in so tranquilizing Dasein, it closes off the *anxiety* a genuine appropriation of this possibility generates.† Dasein's fleeing in the face of death takes the form of evasion. Our Being is a *Being-toward-death,* but everydayness *alienates Dasein from this Being.* This is one of the modes in which Dasein is "in untruth," since no matter how the One tranquilizes and evades and alienates, Dasein—each of us—will die.

So, our ontological interpretation of Dasein *can* get hold of Dasein as-a-whole; Dasein's Being is a Being-toward-death, in which Dasein's death is understood as a possibility that in each mo-

ment is a defining characteristic of Dasein. Any adequate interpretation of Dasein will necessarily have grasped Dasein's death. Being-toward-death, too, is an *existential.*

The evasion and alienation from oneself typical of absorption in the "they" is a form of inauthentic existence. Is, then, an authentic appropriation of death possible? We know what it would be like. There would be no evasion, no explaining away, no misinterpreting of the mode of Being of death. Death would be steadily apprehended as a possibility of Dasein's Being—not in brooding over it or thinking about it, but existing in every moment in the *anticipation* of death.

> Being-towards-death is the anticipation of a potentiality-for-Being of that entity whose kind of Being is anticipation itself. In the anticipatory revealing of this potentiality-for-Being, Dasein discloses itself to itself as regards its uttermost possibility. (*BT,* 307)

This authentic anticipation of death wrenches Dasein away from the One. It *individualizes* Dasein, brings each Dasein before a possibility that belongs to it alone: It says, "I must die." Anticipation forces the realization that one is *finite* and so lights up all the possibilities that lie between the present and death. Anticipation grasps both the certainty of death and the uncertainty about when it will come. Anticipation is a mode of understanding itself as a limited whole. This understanding of itself on the part of Dasein is accompanied by an attunement. (Remember that every understanding has its mood, every mood an understanding.) The mood that accompanies anticipation is *anxiety.* Again, anxiety is displayed as the mood in which Dasein comes face to face with itself—and *doesn't* flee. Anticipation

> reveals to Dasein its lostness in the they-self, and brings it face to face with the possibility of being itself, primarily unsupported by concernful solicitude, but of being itself, rather in an impassioned freedom towards death—a freedom which has been released from the illusions of the "they" and which is factical, certain of itself, and anxious. (*BT,* 311)

Because anticipation releases us from bondage to the interpretations of the One and puts us "in the truth," we are "freed" to *be* ourselves as a whole—

---

*One of my own professors used to say in his raspy voice, "As soon as a man is born, he is old enough to die."

†See again the contrast between fear and anxiety, pp. 658–660.

but only as Being-toward-death. Any evasion casts us back into the "they" and inauthenticity.

Conscience, Guilt, and Resoluteness

Authentic existence is now our theme. But there is a problem. Dasein is caught up in the life of the One, living wholly by what "they say." Remember that there is no private essence to Dasein, no "interior" self with contents of its own. In everydayness, Dasein acquiesces in the way "they" understand its possibilities; it goes-along with the mood and understanding and discourse of the One; it has not "taken hold" of itself. How then does Dasein know there is anything *but* the life of the "they-self"? How does it become *aware* that it is not being *itself* but is fleeing itself by falling-into-the-world inauthentically? What resources does Dasein have to enable it to come to itself in authentic existence?

> Because Dasein is *lost* in the "they," it must first *find* itself. In order to find *itself* at all, it must be "shown" to itself in its possible authenticity. In terms of its possibility, Dasein is already a potentiality-for-Being-its-Self, but it needs to have this potentiality attested. (*BT,* 313)

What is it that can "show" Dasein to *itself* as a possibly authentic Self? What "attests" to this possibility? The voice of *conscience,* Heidegger says (*BT,* 313). But we have to be careful here, as elsewhere, not to interpret this "voice" in the way it is ordinarily understood. By now we should be sufficiently on guard: conscience, like understanding, attunement, and discourse, has an everyday form that hides as much as it discloses. What we are looking for is the *existential ground* on the basis of which ordinary experiences of conscience are *possible.*

So conscience in this existential or ontological sense is not to be identified with that nagging little voice that occasionally tells us we have done something wrong or that warns us not to do what we might like to do. The deep sense of conscience must have the same sort of Being as Dasein; it is not occasional, but constant. It is, moreover, a mode of disclosure, in which something is presented to be

understood. So we need an interpretation of this phenomenon that makes clear where this "voiceless voice" comes from, to whom it is addressed, and what it "says."

In the mode of average everydayness, Heidegger says, Dasein is constantly listening. But it "listens away" from itself and hears only the voice of the "they." As a result, it "fails to hear" itself. As we have seen, Dasein *is* the One; each of us is one of "the others" (from whom, for the most part, we do not distinguish ourselves); and this indefinite One is what generally determines how life goes in the world.

Conscience is a "call" to this One (who we are).

> *What* does the conscience call to him to whom it appeals? Taken strictly, nothing. The call asserts nothing, gives no information about world-events, has nothing to tell. Least of all does it try to set going a "soliloquy" in the Self to which it has appealed. "Nothing" gets called to this Self, but it has been *summoned* to itself—that is, to its ownmost potentiality-for-Being. (*BT,* 318)

As we have seen, Dasein *is* just such a potentiality-for-Being. But this Being of Dasein is hidden to itself as long as it is governed by the "they." What conscience does is to disclose Dasein to itself as such a potentiality-for-being. So conscience "calls Dasein forth to its possibilities" (*BT,* 319). In effect, it says, "You cannot hide behind the 'they' any longer; *you* are responsible for your existence!" (In putting words in the mouth of conscience, I am of course falsifying somewhat Heidegger's insistence that the call is "wordless," but not in a damaging way, I hope.)

We now know to whom the call of conscience is addressed: to Dasein in its everydayness. And we know what the call "says": *You must become yourself!* [*] The call, then, summons inauthentic Dasein to take hold of itself, to take itself over, and in so doing to be itself authentically. But who is doing the calling?

> *In conscience Dasein calls itself.* (*BT,* 320)

Well, we might have known! Still, that is not exactly clear. How can Dasein call itself in this way? If

---

[*]Compare Nietzsche, p. 556, and Kierkegaard, pp. 500–503.

it is Dasein to whom the call comes, how can it be Dasein who is doing the calling? Indeed, as Heidegger acknowledges, the call typically seems to come from *beyond* oneself. It seems to be

> something which *we ourselves* have neither planned for nor prepared for nor voluntarily performed, nor have we ever done so. "It" calls, against our expectations and even against our will. On the other hand, the call undoubtedly does not come from someone else who is with me in the world. The call comes *from* me and yet *from beyond me.* (*BT,* 320)

This seems phenomenologically accurate; it is the basis, Heidegger suggests, for interpretations of the call as the voice of God or for attempts to give a sociological or biological interpretation of conscience. None of these will do, however, since these causal accounts all try to locate conscience in *something*—that is, in something present-at-hand. And the call has to have the kind of Being of Dasein.

The puzzle can be solved if we recall the not-at-homeness that is revealed in the mood of anxiety. Anxiety, you will remember, individualizes Dasein, pulls it out of the "they," and makes clear that it is its own *having to be.* In anxiety, Dasein feels alienated from the world of the One, yet recognizes that it has no other home. It comes to understand itself as *thrown into existence.* With this contrast between Dasein as *at home in the world on terms set out by the "they"* and Dasein as *cast out of that familiar home* we can solve the problem. The "it" that calls is "uncanny" Dasein in its mode of not-being-at-home-in-the-world; and "it" calls to Dasein in the mode of the "they," summoning it *to itself.*

And now we can also see why authentic existence is not a wholly different kind of existence from inauthentic but just a modified way in which such everydayness is seized upon. To exist authentically is to take responsibility for the self that one is. And that is—inevitably, inextricably, and for as long as one lives—the self that has been (and is being) shaped by the particular "they" into which one has been "thrown." There is no "true self" other than this.

Conscience, then, summons Dasein, lost in the "they," to take up responsibility for itself. It is true

that you are not responsible for yourself "from the bottom up," so to speak; you are not responsible for how and where you were "thrown" into existence. But in authentic existence you shoulder the burden. The authentic self does not excuse itself, blaming parents, society, or circumstance for its shortcomings. Authentic Dasein *makes itself responsible;* it says, "Yes, this is who I am, who I have been; and this is who I will become."*

Conscience summons Dasein to be itself, to turn away from the rationalizations and self-deceptions of the "they." It summons lost Dasein back to its thrownness and forth into existence—into an understanding that projects itself into the peculiar possibilities of its own future. The summons issues from Dasein itself, and Dasein hears the verdict: guilty. Why "guilty"? Because Dasein, in fleeing itself into the world of the "they," has not been what it is called to; Dasein has not been *itself.* Yet we are not summoned to a kind of wallowing around in self-recrimination; we are to realize our essence—that is, for the first time truly to *exist.*

Conscience, then, "attests" to inauthentic Dasein that there is another possibility and calls it to exist authentically by taking over this having-to-be-itself into which it has been thrown. Dasein takes it over in a certain *understanding* of its own authentic possibilities, in the *mood* of anxiety (since the tranquilizing "they" is set aside), and with a reticence that answers to the wordless *discourse* of conscience. There is nothing to be said; there is everything to be done.

> This distinctive and authentic disclosedness, which is attested in Dasein itself by its conscience— *this reticent self-projection upon one's ownmost Being-guilty, in which one is ready for anxiety*—we call "resoluteness." . . .
>
> In resoluteness we have now arrived at that truth of Dasein which is most primordial because it is *authentic.* (*BT,* 343)

---

*Contrast Kierkegaard's despair of defiance, p. 501. Heidegger's *authentic existence* seems a secular interpretation of what Kierkegaard understands by *faith* (pp. 497–499), though it perhaps has more of Pelagius in it than Augustine (see pp. 252–253).

"Resoluteness" is the term for authentic Being-in-the-world. To be resolute is to *be oneself*. In resoluteness, Dasein exists in that disclosedness that puts it "in the truth." But since what Dasein grasps in the understanding of resoluteness is its own Being-guilty, it understands that in truth it has been, and perhaps will soon again be, "in untruth."*

We can put the results of this section and the preceding one together in the following way: In *anticipation,* authentic Dasein grasps its Being-toward-death. In answering the call of conscience, Dasein sets aside the temptations of the One and *resolutely* takes up the burden of Being-itself as thrown, existing, falling, guilty Being-in-the-world. But in resolutely Being-itself, a finite whole, Dasein must anticipate its death. And anticipation, for its part, is not a kind of free-floating imagination, but a way of Being that has come to itself and has become transparent to itself. So anticipation and resoluteness, if understood deeply enough, imply each other.

In **anticipatory resoluteness,** Dasein comes at last authentically to itself. We don't often hear Heidegger speak of "joy," but in the section where he discusses anticipatory resoluteness, he writes,

> Along with the sober anxiety which brings us face to face with our individualized potentiality-for-Being, there goes an unshakable joy in this possibility. (*BT,* 358)

Temporality as the Meaning of Care

Imagine that you know a secret and are very sure that Peter doesn't know it. But on Thursday afternoon he makes an extremely puzzling remark. At first you can't figure out what his remark *means,* nor (which is not the same) what it *means* that Peter made the remark. But as you think about it, you realize that he must know the secret, too. Only on that background does his remark make any sense. What

Peter said is *intelligible* only on that assumption. It is that background—Peter knowing the secret—that made it *possible* for him to say what he did.

This everyday example brings us to Heidegger's sense of *meaning.* Heidegger's interest, of course, is directed to the meaning of Being. That is the fox we have been hunting through all these hills and dales and twisty paths. It is for the sake of uncovering the meaning of Being that Heidegger engages in the analysis of Dasein. But so far we have merely been asking, What is the meaning of *Dasein's* Being? In asking this, we have been constructing an *ontology.* This ontology (the *existentials*) serves as a *background* against which the phenomena of average everydayness become *intelligible.* We can now say that it is the articulated structure of Care that makes everyday Dasein *possible.* And we can summarize this structure:

- Existence (Being-ahead-of-itself-in projecting possibilities)
- Facticity (thrownness into-the-world and toward-death)
- Falling (in-with-the-Others and away-from-itself)

Taken together as a totality, these features define Care as the essence of Dasein's Being. But have we reached rock bottom with the concept of Care? Or can we ask once again, What is the *meaning of Care?* At this point, we need to pay explicit attention to meaning.

> What does "*meaning*" signify? . . . meaning is that wherein the understandability of something maintains itself. . . . "Meaning" signifies the "upon-which" of a primary projection in terms of which something can be conceived in its possibility as that which it is. (*BT,* 370–371)

That is hard to understand. But if you think back to our example, you should be able to grasp it. What did Peter mean by making this remark? To uncover the meaning, we "project" his remark onto a background (or larger context) that makes it understandable—namely, that Peter knows the secret. This background is that "upon which" we project Peter's remark. In this larger context, Peter's remark makes perfect sense; it is meaningful. So meaning is "that wherein the understandability" of the remark "maintains itself." Moreover, it seems that *only* if Peter knows the secret is it possible for him to say what he does.

Here is another analogy. Some people think that human life is meaningful only if it is projected onto a larger background, perhaps of immortality or divine purposes. In that context, life has, perhaps, the meaning of a *test*. Without such a background, they say, life is meaningless—pointless. The meaningfulness of life is possible only if it is embedded in a larger context. Whether this is so is an interesting question we do not directly address (though Heidegger's views are relevant to an answer). But the sense of meaning is the same as the one in Heidegger's question about the meaning of Care—and, ultimately, of the meaning of Being.

So if we are now asking about the meaning of Care, we are asking about a deeper background, or larger context, in the light of which the phenomenon of Care becomes intelligible. We are asking about that upon which Care can be projected to make it understandable and to show it as possible. Is there a still more fundamental (more primordial) structure to Dasein's Being that makes possible existence, facticity, and falling? That is the question.

Heidegger takes as his clue the Being of Dasein when it is most "true," or most itself: authentic existence. We have seen authentic existence spelled out in terms of anticipatory resoluteness. Anticipatory resoluteness, for its part, is

> Being towards one's ownmost, distinctive, potentiality-for-Being. (*BT,* 372)

What makes this "Being towards" possible? Time—and in particular, the future.

For anticipatory resoluteness to be *possible,* it must be that Dasein is in itself, in its very Being, *futural*—temporal. This doesn't mean that Dasein is "located" in time, any more than Dasein's Being-in-the-world means that Dasein is "located" in an objective space.* Dasein is "futural" in that it *comes toward itself* in that projecting of possibilities that

defines existence. Dasein is always ahead-of-itself-in-time.

We have seen that anticipatory resoluteness also fastens onto itself as Being-guilty. Dasein takes over its facticity—makes its thrownness its own—by taking responsibility for itself.

> But taking over thrownness signifies *being* Dasein authentically *as it already was.* . . . Only in so far as Dasein *is* as an "I-am-as-having-been," can Dasein come towards itself futurally in such a way that it comes *back.* Anticipation of one's uttermost and ownmost possibility is coming back understandingly to one's ownmost "been." Only so far as it is futural can Dasein *be* authentically as having been. The character of "having been" arises, in a certain way, from the future. (*BT,* 373)

You "are" your possibilities. But what these possibilities are depends on what you have been. You can only project yourself authentically into the future by "coming back" to yourself as having been something.

What does it mean, though, that this "having been" itself arises from the future? That seems strange. I think we can understand Heidegger's thought here in this way. What you have been (and now are, as a result) is not just a set of dead facts. These facts take life and meaning from your projects. You are now, let us say, a college student; as each moment slips away, this is something you have been. But *have you been* preparing for a job? Or *have you been* learning to understand yourself? Or laying a foundation for a scholarly life? Or inching up the ladder of monetary reward? Four people who answer these questions differently might have taken exactly the same courses and read exactly the same books to this point. But the *meaning* of what they have done is radically different; it is projected against a different background (and notice that each background essentially makes reference to the future!). Because the meaning of what they have done is different, what they "have been" is also different. The difference is defined by the different futures they project. That is how the character of "having been" arises from the future.* We can now see that

---

*Review the discussion of Being-in on p. 650.

*For reasons like this, Sartre claims that we are *radically free* and that any kind of causal determination of our actions is ruled because it is futural, Dasein also essentially has a past. But once again we must be careful. This is an *existential* past, not one that is composed of moments that have added up and then dropped away into nothingness. It is a past that one constantly *is*.

Finally, anticipatory resoluteness plants one firmly in the current situation. It does not live in daydreams or fantasy; it is not lost in nostalgia. Authentic Dasein resolutely takes present action in the light of an attuned understanding of its future potentialities and its past having been. An unblinkered, clear, disclosive *sight* of what is present is essential to Dasein's authentic appropriation of itself.

Those who live in illusion do not act decisively and effectively, because they do not "make present" the entities about them; they veil them over and hide them, fantasize and misunderstand them.* This existential present is not a neutral "now," through a series of which a life must pass. It is not just the knife-edge dividing future from past. It is the rich activity of authentic dealing with things by *making-present* the things that are, in the light of our potentialities and what we have been.

And now we can say that

Temporality reveals itself as the meaning of authentic care. (BT, 374)

So that "upon which" Care becomes intelligible is the structure of temporality. Temporality involves projecting into the future, coming back to one's past, and making present. It is important to note that this structure is not itself an entity; it is not a thing or a being. Most importantly, it is not like an empty container into which temporal items can be placed.† Temporality is the most fundamen-

tal structure of Dasein's Being-there. Dasein is essentially temporal and essentially *finite*, since authentic Dasein anticipates its end in death. Time, in the sense of existential temporality, is the framework within which Care is possible. Time is, to put it in Heidegger's terms, the *horizon* of Dasein's Being. Just as whatever is visible to you now is within the horizon, the framework of temporality defines the horizon for Dasein. All the features of Dasein's Being we have examined are possible only against this background.

Heidegger's analysis of Dasein is now virtually complete. Not much needs to be said about birth as the beginning of Dasein, except that between birth and death Dasein "stretches itself along" (BT, 423). One gets the image of a rubber band fastened down at birth and stretching out toward the future. Dasein is at any moment not just what it is *then*, but also what it has been and will be. This "connectedness" of Dasein in its stretching along Heidegger calls *historicality*. And he thinks the proper understanding of that phenomenon—enlightened by the entire analysis of the Being of Dasein—is essential to the proper writing of "history." These are interesting matters, but we stop here and turn to the big question for which all this has been preliminary: the question about the meaning of Being.

---

1. Why is a consideration of death necessary if we are to understand Dasein as a totality? Why is Being-toward-death one of the existentials?
2. How does average everydayness manage to "tranquilize" itself about death? Contrast with an authentic appropriation of death.
3. In what way does the call of conscience call Dasein to itself? Relate this to authenticity, responsibility, and guilt.
4. "Temporality reveals itself as the meaning of authentic care." Explain.

---

out. If what we have been depends on what it means, and if what it means depends on what we project ourselves to be in the future, then there is no neutral causal description "at-hand" to serve as a basis for deterministic laws. If Heidegger is right, there is no call for the reconciliation projects of Hume and Kant, since the kind of causal determinism with which freedom needs to be reconciled cannot even gain a foothold. But is he right? (See pp. 412–415 for Hume and pp. 444–446 for Kant.)
*Compare Kierkegaard on despair, pp. 500–502.
†Clock time, or ordinary everyday time, which looks rather like this, is the result of a kind of "leveling off" of this rich existential

temporality. It gets a kind of objectivity in much the same way that present-at-hand items do: by abstracting away the meaningfulness of Dasein's Being-in-time.

The Priority of Being

I write about the thought of the later Heidegger with some caution. If you thought things were difficult to this point, try to read some of the later essays, which contain sentences one can read over and over with hardly a glimmer of an idea of what they might mean.* Part of the difficulty, too, is that Heidegger's thought undergoes some development from the early 1930s until the time near his death in 1976, but he almost never acknowledges that it does. Moreover, he looks back to *Being and Time* and reinterprets some of the things he said there—but without admitting that this is what he is doing. He says over and over that the understanding of the *question* is the most important thing and stresses the tentativeness of his formulations. And he uses the same terms in somewhat different ways in different periods, again without telling us that this is what he is doing.

But throughout he insists that he is always trying to say the same thing: to give expression in language to the *meaning of Being*. And he maintains that what he is trying to say is very *simple*. It is its simplicity, in fact, that is the cause of so much obscurity. He even suggests occasionally that the proper way to express what he wants to say is through *silence*.† Yet he writes a great deal, struggling again and again to put it into words. Certain lines of thought do stand out with some clarity, and I will try to give you some idea of how the problem about the meaning of Being fares after the period of *Being and Time*.

I will simplify all this drastically and focus on one central theme. We are reminded of this theme in an image that Heidegger borrows from Descartes: the image of philosophy as a tree.* The roots of the tree, Descartes says, are metaphysics, the trunk is physics, and all the other sciences are the branches. Heidegger accepts this image, but what he wants to ask about (and has been asking about since the first page of *Being and Time*) is the *ground* in which the roots are sunk. Metaphysics is concerned with *beings, entities, substances, things*. It wants to know what kinds of entities there are and whether there is an ultimate explanation for them (perhaps in God, the "highest being"). Metaphysics is more general than the special sciences and goes deeper. Each science deals with a certain *kind* of being and orders it, describes it, and gives an account of how and why it changes. Biology deals with living things, for example, history with historical things; metaphysics, by contrast, deals with things or substances in general. But everywhere, in science and in metaphysics alike, beings (entities) are the focus of attention.

Beings always appear, says Heidegger, in the light of *Being*. Amoebas *are,* and biology can tell us a lot about them, but biology does not tell us what it means for amoebas to *be*. A mountain *is,* and geology can explain how it came to have the shape it has, but geology does not explain what it is for a mountain to *be*. What makes all these entities available for investigation and understanding is that they *are*. But if Heidegger is right, in no case has a metaphysician directly approached the question of *what that means*. This contrast between the *things* there are and the *Being* of those things is given a name: the **ontological difference.** What does it mean for something—anything—to *Be*? This, he thinks, is the question he alone first asks.

Note again that *this* question is not answered by an appeal to God or a first cause understood as the highest being. If such a first cause *is,* the very same question applies to it. What does it mean for God to *Be*? As we have seen, the published parts of *Being and Time* are devoted to what Heidegger calls "fundamental ontology," an analysis of that peculiar entity whose very mode of Being involves an un-

---

*Consider the last sentence in a lecture called "The Turning": "May world in its worlding be the nearest of all nearing that nears, as it brings the truth of Being near to man's essence, and so gives man to belong to the disclosing bringing-to-pass that is a bringing into its own." This work can be found in *The Question Concerning Technology: Heidegger's Critique of the Modern Age,* translated by William Lovitt (New York: Harper and Row, 1977).

†Compare Wittgenstein on the unsayable, pp. 612–614.

*See the illustration on p. 325.

derstanding of what that means—even if that understanding is inadequate and distorted. A quick review of the results will be useful:

- *Temporality* makes possible
- *Care,* which is the essence of
- *Dasein,* which is a
- *Clearing,* in the light of which there come to presence
- *Beings*—(Dasein itself, the ready-to-hand, and the present-at-hand—each of which has a mode of
- *Being* (Care, Functionality, Objectness)

Temporality (primordial time) is the meaning of Dasein's Being—that is, the deepest structure in Dasein through which everything else is seen to make sense. By projecting itself into future possibilities while being firmly anchored in the past of its thrownness, Dasein makes present the situation in which it acts and stretches itself along, caringly, in time. The published parts of *Being and Time* end with the suggestion that this primordial temporality might be the horizon for understanding Being itself. So time might be the meaning not only of Dasein's Being, but also of Being in general. And the title of the book makes one think that this is how the unpublished part would have gone.

Now what's wrong with this? Why does Heidegger not follow out this lead and publish the rest of what he had planned to write? What causes this "turn" in his thinking? I think the answer must be that the pattern in this thinking makes Being too dependent on Dasein. And there are two things wrong with this:

1. It is too *subjective.* Throughout *Being and Time,* Heidegger struggles against subjectivism in philosophy, against the idea that Being is somehow dependent on the subject. The whole analysis of Dasein as a clearing and as Being-in-the-world is designed to show that the terror of being trapped inside our own minds is a "put-up job," the solipsistic consequence of a mistaken starting point. Dasein is *in its very essence* beyond itself, transcendent, *in* the world among entities. But now at the end it suddenly looks as though subjectivism has not been escaped at all. If the meaning of Being is time and if time is a structure of Dasein's Being, then it seems obvious that Being itself is dependent on Dasein's understanding of it.

2. It is too *metaphysical.* Dasein is after all a being, one entity among others. And if Being itself is dependent on Dasein, then it seems the metaphysical pattern of trying to find a ground for Being *in some entity* is repeating itself in Heidegger's thought. And this is intolerable! His objection to traditional metaphysics is that it neglects Being by concentrating on beings, searching *among beings* for a ground or first principle that accounts for them. In a way, this outcome of *Being and Time* is even worse. Traditional metaphysics, in Heidegger's view, is *oblivious* of the question about Being. He, by contrast, devoting all his intellectual energies to clarify the meaning of Being, has fallen directly into the metaphysical trap.

So a new direction is called for. It is not that the work done in *Being and Time* has to be repudiated, but that it all gets transposed into a new key. Without exactly taking anything back, everything is transformed. Let me try to say how. Dasein is no longer thought of as fundamental to discerning the meaning of Being, so the notion of a "fundamental ontology" disappears. The term "Dasein" itself tends to give way to the term "man," or "human being." And the human being now is thought of not as "a clearing," but as one element in a clearing that is now called the *truth of Being.* The other elements of the truth of Being are variously identified but always involve time and Being itself. The idea in *Being and Time* that truth is a kind of "robbery," that it has to be "wrested" resolutely out of its hiddenness, is replaced by the notion that truth is a gift we need only receive. The Open, the Clearing, the Unhiddenness of Being is not something we have to create, just to recognize (not that this is easy). And the initiative is not with us; it is on the side of Being, which "sends" to us various ways of unveiling itself. These various "sendings" of Being constitute historical epochs, which are defined by the understanding of Being they have. And what "they say," the opinion of the faceless "One," is replaced by the very particular and specific understanding of Being in an epoch. Authentic existence, too, is transformed; the focus is not on the anxious individual who has to appropriate the self in anticipatory resoluteness, but on Being, which graciously "calls" or offers itself. And the thought is that if this call could be accepted, the very essence of the human being might alter. The key throughout is that the priority and the initiative shift from the human being to Being.

But we need to fill in at least some of the details that constitute this "turn." A good place to start is Heidegger's understanding of the present age. It is an age dominated, he says, by science and technology. This is a kind of truism, but Heidegger understands this in a peculiar way, one we need to grasp.

We often think of technology as a matter of instruments we can use for one purpose or another. Sometimes we hear that technology in itself is "neutral" and can be used for either good or evil, just as a poison may be used to kill disease-infested rats or one's wealthy aunt Matilda. That is not a mistaken way to think about technology, but, Heidegger claims, it is shallow. It may be "correct," but is it "true"? Does it disclose the *essence* of technology? Today we are battling many ills brought on by technology: air and water pollution, the population explosion, the extinction of species, the depletion of the ozone layer, waste disposal, the threat of nuclear war. But we tend to think that we can master them: What we need is more and better technology! So we equip our cars with catalytic converters and spend much money on antiballistic missile systems. We think we can *master* technology by devising technological "fixes" for technological problems.

But what, Heidegger asks, if the essence of technology is not this business of devising means to desired ends? What if technology is fundamentally something quite different? What if technology is basically a way of revealing, of bringing forth, of unconcealing? What if technology were a "place"—a clearing—where *truth* happens?

And so in fact it is. What is distinctive about *modern* technology is that it does not just use means that nature supplies, as the windmill makes use of the wind. What it does is *store up* energy in a way the older technology could not. It is

a challenging, which puts to nature the unreasonable demand that it supply energy which can be extracted and stored as such.

> . . . a tract of land is challenged in the hauling out of coal and ore. The earth now reveals itself as a coal mining district, the soil as a mineral deposit. . . . Agriculture is now the mechanized food industry. Air is now set upon to yield nitrogen, the earth to yield ore, ore to yield uranium, for example; uranium is set upon to yield atomic energy, which can be released either for destruction or for peaceful use. (*QCT,* 296) [2]

Technology reveals *everything* as what Heidegger calls the **standing-reserve.** What is characteristic of this mode of openness is that everything presents itself as something to be "set upon" and "ordered" and "stored" for *use.* He gives a particular example:

> The hydroelectric plant is set into the current of the Rhine. It sets the Rhine to supplying its hydraulic pressure, which then sets the turbines turning. This turning sets those machines in motion whose thrust sets going the electric current for which the long-distance power station and its network of cables are set up to dispatch electricity. In the context of the interlocking processes pertaining to the orderly disposition of electrical energy, even the Rhine itself appears to be something at our command. . . . What the river is now, namely a water-power supplier, derives from the essence of the power station. In order that we may even remotely consider the monstrousness that reigns here, let us ponder for a moment the contrast that is spoken by the two titles: "The Rhine," as dammed up into the *power* works, and "The Rhine," as uttered by the *art* work, in Hölderlin's hymn by that name. But, it will be replied, the Rhine is still a river in the landscape, is it not? Perhaps. But how? In no other way than as an object on call for inspection by a tour group ordered there by the vacation industry. (*QCT,* 297)

What is "monstrous" about this is not that the Rhine supplies power, but that whatever we behold presents itself as "standing-reserve," something to be mastered and ordered, to be unlocked and exposed, to be set upon and challenged to provide "the maximum yield at the minimum expense" (*QCT,* 297). I used to ride my bike regularly to the university. On the way home there was a substantial hill to climb, and on the way down the other side the road bent to the left and revealed a lovely valley. It was so peaceful—refreshing to view and renewing after a stressful day at school. But of course it was looked on as "standing-reserve" for development and "set upon" by builders who have now nearly filled it with suburban housing. And this is happening everywhere. This is just how "One" sees it today.

Putting it that way makes it seem as though this way of experiencing the world is in our control, as though we can simply change it if we wish to. Heidegger does not believe this is so.

> Man can, indeed, conceive, fashion, and carry through this or that in one way or another. But man does not have control over unconcealment itself, in which at any given time the real shows itself or withdraws. . . .
>
> The unconcealment of the unconcealed has already come to pass whenever it calls man forth into the modes of revealing allotted to him. (*QCT*, 299–300)

I cannot decide to "unconceal" the real; nor can you; nor can we together. Nor can we simply decide to reveal it in a new and different way. That is not something in our power. As soon as we meditate or strive, shape or work, ask or thank, as soon as we do anything at all we are *already* within the clearing of unconcealment. A certain "mode of revealing" has been "allotted" to us. We have not *decided* to see things in this technologically relevant way; that is the way they *present* themselves to us. The origins of a revealing are not more in our control than the thrownness of Dasein.

Heidegger calls this challenging of nature that orders it as standing-reserve **enframing**. Enframing is a mode of disclosure, of revealing the real. It reveals the real as orderable for use. Enframing, while itself nothing technological in the ordinary sense, is the *essence* or *meaning* of technology. It is what makes ordinary technology possible. If you recall our discussion of "meaning," you can see that to call enframing the meaning of technology is to say that enframing is "that wherein the understandability of [technology] maintains itself" (*BT*, 370). We live in a technological world in precisely this

sense: that everything in it is revealed as standing-reserve. This is *our* meaning for Being.

It has not always been so, of course. Other epochs have experienced the world differently. And this fact suggests that the "revealing" characteristic of our time, enframing, hides as much as it discloses. We are "in untruth" as well as in the truth. What accounts for the different ways in which Being presents (and hides) itself in different ages? Heidegger's answer is that there is *no explanation* for this. Whatever explanations we have already presuppose a certain revealing of reality; they are internal to a mode of grasping Being. In our case, explanations have the scientific/technological character they do because they are internal to enframing. They *express* our fundamental relation to reality, so they cannot *explain* it.*

Enframing is our *destiny*. We are ourselves "challenged forth" to order things in the mode of standing-reserve. This *comes* to us; we do not invent it. It is *given* to us. It is "too late" to ask whether we should or should not approach reality this way. These ways of unconcealing are "sent" to us; we participate in them without ever having them totally in our power. And no *reason* can be given for the shifts from one mode of revealing to another.

Heidegger uses the word "monstrous" in his description of the Rhine as a power source. We need to say a bit more about this. Any "destining" of a mode of revealing brings along with it a *danger*. Within a given revealing, much that is correct may be asserted; however, the danger is that "in the midst of all that is correct, the true will withdraw" (*QCT*, 308). With respect to enframing, this danger is intensified; in fact, Heidegger thinks enframing is so dangerous that it is worthy of being called "the supreme danger" (*QCT*, 308).

> This danger attests itself to us in two ways. As soon as what is unconcealed no longer concerns man even as object, but exclusively as standing-reserve,

---

*Compare the later Wittgenstein's remarks about justification coming to an end and about the "spade turning" on "what I do." See pp. 636 and 640. Heidegger sees a kind of "history of Being" in the successive modes of its being revealed. This reminds us of Hegel—except that there is no dialectical necessity posited for the shifts.

and man in the midst of objectlessness is nothing but the orderer of the standing-reserve, then he comes to the very brink of a precipitous fall, that is, he comes to the point where he himself will have to be taken as standing-reserve. Meanwhile, man, precisely as the one so threatened, exalts himself to the posture of lord of the earth. In this way the illusion comes to prevail that everything man encounters exists only insofar as it is his construct. This illusion gives rise in turn to one final delusion: it seems as though man everywhere and always encounters only himself. Heisenberg has with complete correctness pointed out that the real must present itself to contemporary man in this way. *In truth, however, precisely nowhere does man today any longer encounter himself, i.e., his essence. . . .*

Thus, the challenging-enframing . . . conceals revealing itself and with it that wherein unconcealment, i.e., truth, comes to pass. (*QCT,* 308–309)

We are back again to the forgetfulness of Being with which *Being and Time* begins, but now it is in a different guise. The danger in enframing is twofold, Heidegger tells us.

1. We ourselves may be taken simply as standing-reserve, to be ordered forth for use.* But as we relate to ourselves in this technological/scientific way, we miss what is peculiar to us: our essence, our Being-open (what Heidegger earlier calls Dasein). Heidegger goes as far as to say that *nowhere* do we today encounter ourselves in this essence. Enframing is a drastic and extreme mode of *hiding* our Being from ourselves.

2. Because everything looks like material-for-use ordered by our science and technology, it seems we *nowhere* can get beyond ourselves: again, subjectivism triumphs! And this, Heidegger consistently holds, is a "delusion." Enframing exalts man to the position of "lord of the earth" and so *misses* the phenomenon of enframing as itself a mode of reveal-

ing—as a way the truth of Being is made manifest. We are plunged so deep in enframing that it is difficult for us to realize that this is what we are doing. Again we "forget" our Being and the fact that other modes of revealing are possible.

Enframing blocks the shining-forth and holding sway of truth. . . .

The rule of enframing threatens man with the possibility that it could be denied to him to enter into a more original revealing and hence to experience the call of a more primal truth. (*QCT,* 309)

Heidegger is not purely negative about science and technology. For one thing, it *is* a way in which entities become "unhidden." He allows that results in the sciences may be "correct." For another, the technological/scientific way of understanding reality is, he thinks, the legitimate heir of the entire Western philosophical tradition. Philosophy has always been, in Heidegger's view, fundamentally metaphysics. As the individual sciences mature and separate from their mother, as they set up business on their own (or, to use Descartes' image, as the branches of the tree flourish), they take over the task of telling us what entities there are in reality. *This* job can now be done *better* by the scientist in the laboratory than by the metaphysician in an armchair. As Heidegger tells us more than once, philosophy as metaphysics is *finished.* And we are left with enframing, which is the way we have been granted to understand what there is.

So technology and its companion, modern science, have a positive role to play. They constitute the "extreme danger," however, in what we might call their "imperialism": in the claim that there is no other way to reveal reality than this. Remember, this is *our* way of experiencing the world, one we cannot simply step out of, any more than the authentic individual of *Being and Time* has a private reality into which she can repair to "be herself," leaving behind the world of the "One."

But now Heidegger quotes the poet Hölderlin.

But where danger is, grows
The saving power also. (*QCT,* 310)

As the *extreme* danger, enframing seems to close off all modes of revealing but itself. But if we can just concentrate our attention on enframing's *being*

---

*Compare Kant's distinction between persons and things, and his second formulation of the categorical imperative: that rational beings must never be used as means only, but always treated as an end. (See p. 456.) Enframing human beings means taking them to be available as standing-reserve for use, not respecting them as persons. Is it significant that the offices that used to be called "Personnel" are now known as "Human Resources"?

a revealing, we may catch sight of it as a *way of Being.* This attempt to let Being *Be* and to express it in language Heidegger calls *thinking.* This may not seem very illuminating, since we imagine that thinking is something we all do every day. But he (typically) understands thinking in a very particular and peculiar way. Thinking is *recalling Being out of its hiddenness.* It is through this kind of thinking that we may come to understand ourselves as part of that "constellation" in which modes of revealing are "sent" or "granted" to humans, in which beings are lighted up in their becoming *present.* Philosophy and metaphysics, then, must be *replaced* by thinking. And thinking must *supplement* enframing.

And yet this way of putting it is still too subjective. It makes it seem as though this "turning" toward the presence of things is something that is up to us. It makes it seem as though we can just *decide* to "think". But even this turning is a *granting* we cannot manage by ourselves; it is one we can at most be ready for.*

We can ask, though, where we might look for such a revealing of the Being of things and ourselves. Heidegger has two answers to this question: in the thinking of the thinker and in poetry and art. We cannot discuss his understanding of art in detail here. But it is significant, he thinks, that the Greek word for art is *techne.* In the "technology" of the artist, however, what is produced is not something for use, to be stored and transformed and used up. What is produced is a *work.* A work *stands there.* In and through the work, a *world* opens up; and a world is (roughly) the way things present themselves. So art, too, is a mode of unveiling, revealing, unconcealing. But it is not a challenging, a forcing, an imposing and mastering of things. Rather, it *lets things appear* as they are. And in being a *work*—that is, something that has been *worked* into being—it reveals its *presencing* of the world in a way that enframing finds hard to do.

Art is a

> letting happen of the advent of the truth of beings, . . . the setting-into-work of truth. (*OWA,* 184) [3]

Art "opens up a world" (*OWA,* 169); it *lets the truth happen.* Art, moreover, is not concerned (or should not be concerned) with the beautiful, which is just a by-product. In the form of a Greek temple, or in Hölderlin's poetry, art unveils the Being of things. Art is a matter of truth.

But again, we must be careful. For great art is no more a matter for individual decision than any mode of revealing is. Notice that art is understood as the setting-*itself*-into-work of truth. Art is not entirely in the control of the artist, any more than we are in control of enframing. Talk of the "muses" may be an expression of this idea. The work is *given* to the artist, and through the artist to us. Art, too, is a gift, a granting of unveiledness that the human cannot be master of.

We have spoken again and again of a "sending" or a "destining" of a "gift" that must be received and cannot be forced, invented, or created. Every mode of revealing, Heidegger holds, has this character. Let us now, at the end of our consideration, ask, Who does the sending? From whom is this gift received? In asking this question, we approach the clearest answer Heidegger has given as to the *meaning of Being.* Here is his most explicit statement:

> From the dawn of Western-European thinking until today, Being means the same as presencing. . . . Being is determined as presence by time. [4]

Again, Heidegger reminds us that we must not think of Being as a *thing* (or entity). Nor is time a *thing.* Nor is it strictly correct to say that Being *is.** What there *is* are things: This book is, the sun is, your sister is. Being is what these entities *have.* But to say that they have it suggests again that it is a *thing,* like the purse or credit card that you have, or a property they might have or lack, like being brown or heavy. But neither of these can be right.

---

*You might like to compare the contrast between the early and the late Heidegger (anticipatory resoluteness vs. receptive openness) with the contrast between Pelagius and Augustine. See pp. 252–253. There are also obvious echoes of Plato's Myth of the Cave, in which what is required is a turning away from shadows toward the light of the sun (pp. 133–137).

---

*It is interesting to compare here what Plato says about the Form of the Good *surpassing* being, p. 132.

See how hard it is to say what Heidegger wants to express!

Being is not what is present. Being, he tells us, is the *presencing* of things. The notion of "presencing" seems clearly to involve time. Presencing is "making-present" or (better) "letting-be-present." But it would be a mistake, too, to think that Being—presencing—is itself temporal. What is temporal (in time) are entities: this book, the sun, your sister. These things begin, are present for a while, and end. Entities (beings) have a past, a present, and a future.

Nor is time something temporal. Time does not "have" a past, a present, and a future—though my car does. Nor is it strictly correct to say of time that it *is*. Entities *are*. But entities are—*in time*.

Entities *are* precisely in their *presencing*. And presencing is being-present. And being-present is one mode of temporality, or time. So it is *Being* and *Time,* or *Time* and *Being,* after all—but without the priority given to Dasein! And yet presencing must involve that which is open to and receives it; Being involves humans. You can see how Heidegger is struggling to clarify and understand in an authentic way the relations of Being, beings, humans (or Dasein), and time. As he sees it, each one involves the others.

We have seen that entities are present in one mode of revealing or another; currently, the mode is scientific/technological, what Heidegger calls *enframing.* This is how things *present themselves* now to us. This is something not in our control; it is "sent" to us. And we asked, Who does the sending? And now we can see two possible answers: either Being or time.

But neither is adequate, Heidegger thinks. To think of either Being or time as the "giver" of the gift of Being, of presencing, is to turn them back into entities. And that is precisely the wrong way to think. Better, he thinks, is the German phrase *es gibt.* Literally, this means "it gives," but a more idiomatic translation is "there is." So we can say that "it gives Being" or "there is time." There is no "sender" of the gift of Being, if by "sender" we mean "thing that sends." To suppose there is would be to ground Being in *a* being—precisely the error that metaphysics has made all these centuries. We must

just acknowledge that "there is time" and "there is Being."

But that acknowledgment is hidden from us under the domination of enframing. Intent on control and mastery of entities, even thinking of human beings as part of the standing-reserve, we pass right over the mystery and wonder of their *presence.* Were we to "turn" from our preoccupation with "challenging" and "setting-upon," this would be an event—perhaps the event of events! It would be the "gathering together" of (1) Being as presencing, (2) time as the horizon within which presencing occurs, and (3) man. This would be the true clearing, in which Being and time are *appropriated* by man, and by which man could come into his true essence as the entity that is *open to Being.* Heidegger calls this the *event of appropriation.*

If this were to occur, human beings would no longer think of themselves as lords of the earth, but as guardians or shepherds of Being. They would take it as their responsibility to preserve and protect Being, recognizing that *presencing* is a gift they cannot master or control. We are not, Heidegger says, the masters of Being but its "neighbors."

In the age of enframing, where everything is understood as standing-reserve, there is no "room" for God. (Or perhaps even God is thought of as "standing-reserve," a kind of public utility that can be used to gain satisfaction for one's desires; one often gets this impression from the television evangelists.)* Heidegger does not talk much about God. He thinks of the present time as

> the time of the gods that have fled *and* of the god that is coming.[5]

And he is clear that he does not regard Being as God or a god. But in the event of appropriation, where a man opens up to the mystery of presencing, there is also uncovered the "space" in which God (or "the god," as he sometimes says, echoing Socrates), might become meaningful again. He speaks of this as the sphere of "the holy" and suggests that this is what the poet is apt to reveal.

---

* Compare Augustine on the contrast between use and enjoyment, p. 254, and Socrates on "trading-skill" religion.

Only from the truth of Being can the essence of the holy be thought. Only from the essence of the holy can the essence of divinity be thought. Only in the light of the essence of divinity can it be thought and said what the word "God" is to signify. Or must we not first be able to understand and hear these words carefully if we as men, i.e., as existing beings, are to have the privilege of experiencing a relation of God to man? How, then, is the man of the present epoch even to be able to ask seriously and firmly whether God approaches or withdraws when man omits the primary step of thinking deeply in the one dimension where this question can be asked: that is, the dimension of the holy, which, even as dimension, remains closed unless the openness of Being is cleared and in its clearing is close to man.* Perhaps the distinction of this age consists in the fact that the dimension of grace has been closed. Perhaps this is its unique dis-grace.[6]

We await the event of appropriation, a gracious new gift of "sending," a mode of revealing in which Being is not forgotten or hidden, in which man appropriates what is "given," namely, Being as presence. In this *truth of Being,* this disclosedness, people will come to themselves not by force or resolute willing, but in simply *letting Being be.* If this should take place, we will be transformed as we experience

the marvel of all marvels; that what-is *is.*[7]

---

1. How does Heidegger conceive that metaphysics is related to the special sciences? To Being?
2. What is the essence of technology, according to Heidegger? In what sense is seeing the world technologically not in our control?
3. In what sense is enframing the "heir" to traditional metaphysics? Why does Heidegger think of enframing as the "supreme danger"?

---

*You might compare the "dimension of the holy" to what Wittgenstein calls the *mystical* (p. 612).

4. How does Heidegger conceive the relations between art and truth?
5. What is the meaning of Being? How are Being, time, and humans related in presencing?
6. What does it mean that we humans are the "shepherds" or "neighbors" of Being?

For Further Thought

1. Contrast the notion of "world" in the early Wittgenstein and Heidegger. Which do you think is the more basic notion? Why?

2. Write a short story in which the main character exemplifies some aspects of inauthenticity as Heidegger understands that notion.

Notes

1. Quotations from Martin Heidegger's *Being and Time,* trans. John Macquarrie and Edward Robinson (Oxford: Basil Blackwell, 1967), are cited in the text using the abbreviation *BT.*
2. Quotations from Martin Heidegger, *The Question Concerning Technology,* trans. William Lovitt, in *Basic Writings,* ed. David Farrell Krell (New York: Harper and Row, 1977), are cited in the text using the abbreviation *QCT.*
3. Quotations from Martin Heidegger, *The Origin of the Work of Art,* trans. Albert Hofstadter, in *Basic Writings,* are cited in the text using the abbreviation *OWA.*
4. Martin Heidegger, *On Time and Being,* trans. Joan Stambough (New York: Harper and Row, 1972), 2.
5. Martin Heidegger, *Hölderlin and the Essence of Poetry,* trans. Douglas Scott, in *Existence and Being,* ed. Werner Brock (Chicago: Henry Regnery, 1949), 289.
6. Martin Heidegger, *Letter on Humanism,* trans. Edgar Lohner, in *Philosophy in the Twentieth Century,* vol. 2, ed. William Barrett and Henry D. Aiken (New York: Random House, 1962), 294.
7. Martin Heidegger, "Postscript to *What Is Metaphysics?*" in *Existence and Being,* 355.

25

SIMONE DE BEAUVOIR

Existentialist, Feminist

"I am an existentialist," (*ELA,* 307) proclaims Simone de Beauvoir (1908–1986).[1] Deeply influenced by her longtime companion, Jean-Paul Sartre, she wrote novels, essays, a play, and philosophical works, along with many occasional articles, and later in life an autobiography. Her big 1949 book, *The Second Sex,* is generally acknowledged to be one of the classics of feminism. A newspaper headline on the day after her death proclaimed, "Women, you owe her everything."[2]

The extent of her indebtedness to Sartre, and in what ways she went beyond his views (and perhaps influenced them), is much debated, but there is no doubt that they worked together on philosophical problems and that her early writings express a view that is basically Sartrean. It seems, however, that her sense of embodiment is stronger than his (at least as expressed in *Being and Nothingness*) and that she feels more than he does the drag one's situation can have on one's freedom. We shall see this in her discussion of the status of women, but first we need to understand her view of the *human* condition.

Ambiguity

De Beauvoir's term for the human condition is *ambiguity.** By this she means that you and I are

- bodies, objects entrenched in the world of objects, yet transcendence of our objectness toward an open future,
- destined for death, yet aware of that fact,
- embedded in time, yet conscious of that embedding,
- a unique subjectivity, seemingly the center of the world, yet among others who experience themselves the same way,
- an agent who acts in the world, yet faced with our objectified acts which others interpret as it suits them,
- an object for others, as they are for us.

*Note that this is not the Heideggerian ambiguity, one of the modes of inauthenticity. Here ambiguity is a structural feature of human existence.

On every side we find ourselves to be this, yet not this, unstable, drawn between two poles. What are you? A consciousness? Yes. A body? Yes. Free? Yes. Conditioned? Yes. Solitary? Yes. Among others? Yes—all those things, so different from each other, so opposed. You are constantly transcending the very being that you are. Your very existence is ambiguous.

Like Kierkegaard, Heidegger, and Sartre, she realizes that this status poses problems to the human being, and she agrees that these problems cannot be solved just by constructing a theory. They have to be solved by living. "In truth," she says, "there is no divorce between philosophy and life" (*EPW*, 217). Like them, she is aware, too, that there are wrong turns that can be taken.* Let's begin by looking at several.

One is taken by the "hero" of Albert Camus' novel, *The Stranger*. After killing an Arab on an Algerian beach—almost as though he himself were not involved ("The trigger gave, and the smooth underbelly of the butt jogged my palm.")—Meursault is convicted and sentenced to death. A chaplain visits him; Meursault rejects the comfort he is offered and says,

> Nothing, nothing had the least importance, and I knew quite well why. . . . From the dark horizon of my future a sort of slow, persistent breeze had been blowing toward me, all my life long, from the years that were to come. And on its way that breeze had leveled out all the ideas that people tried to foist on me in the equally unreal years I then was living through. What difference could they make to me, the deaths of others, or a mother's love, or his God; or the way a man decides to live, the fate he thinks he chooses?[3]

We hear in these words the unmistakable voice of *nihilism,* and this is one way to resolve the ambiguity: Withdraw into your consciousness, observe passively, make everything into an object, and all importance, all significance, all value flattens out. De Beauvoir comments:

Mr. Camus's Stranger is right to reject all those ties that others want to impose upon him from the outside. . . . No possession is given, but the foreign indifference of the world is not given either. (*PC*, 92–93)

She is saying that this "view from nowhere" is not a privileged point from which to see *the truth* about existence. Rather, it is a vain attempt to evade the ambiguity that we *are* so as not to have to *live* it. It is escape; it is inauthentic.

> The nihilist is right in thinking that the world *possesses* no justification and that he himself *is* nothing [i.e., does not have the solid reality of a rock]. But he forgets that it is up to him to justify the world and to make himself exist validly. (*EA*, 57)

Analogous to the nihilist is the *cynic* who disparages everything equally and the *humorist* who makes everything look comical. De Beauvoir begins one of her philosophical essays with a story about an ancient king of Epirus (in northwest Greece).

> *Plutarch tells us that one day Pyrrhus was devising projects of conquest. "We are going to subjugate Greece first," he was saying. "And after that?" said Cineas. "We will vanquish Africa." —"After Africa?" —"We will go on to Asia, we will conquer Asia Minor, Arabia." —"And after that?" —"We will go on as far as India." —"After India?" —"Ah!" said Pyrrhus, "I will rest." —"Why not rest right away?" said Cineas. (PC, 90)*

It is so easy to make things look absurd! What is the trick here? Cineas takes a series of goals, which Pyrrhus lists one after the other, and interprets them as if he intended to do each of them *in order to* eventually accomplish the last. Since it is so easy to do the last, why go through the trouble of all the rest? Two more examples: "Isn't the tennis player absurd to hit a ball in order for someone to send it back to him and the skier absurd to climb a slope in order to immediately come back down?" (*PC*, 99).*

A more common way of denying the ambiguity of human life is by what de Beauvoir calls *seriousness*. It is more common because we all begin life as children.

---

*Compare Kierkegaard on the varieties of despair (pp. 500–503) and Heidegger on inauthentic existence (pp. 664–666).

---

*Can you find the trick in these examples?

The child's situation is characterized by his finding himself cast into a universe which he has not helped to establish, which has been fashioned without him, and which appears to him as an absolute to which he can only submit. In his eyes, human inventions, words, customs, and values are given facts, as inevitable as the sky and the trees. This means that the world in which he lives is a serious world, since the characteristic of the spirit of seriousness is to consider values as ready-made things. (*EA*, 35)[4]

The child takes his parents to be "the divinities which they vainly try to be," and he thinks that he, too, "has *being* in a definite and substantial way. He is a good little boy or a scamp; he enjoys being it" (*EA*, 35, 36).

Ordinarily, this solid, comfortable world develops cracks during adolescence. The teenager

discovers his subjectivity; he discovers that of others . . . he notices the contradictions among adults as well as their hesitations and weakness. Men stop appearing as if they were gods, and at the same time the adolescent discovers the human character of the reality about him. Language, customs, ethics, and values have their source in those uncertain creatures. The moment has come when he too is going to be called upon to participate in their operation; his acts weigh upon the earth as much as those of other men. He will have to choose and decide. (*EA*, 39)

He discovers his freedom but finds that this is a mixed blessing. While there is joy in his liberation, there is much confusion, too. The adolescent

finds himself cast into a world which is no longer ready-made, which has to be made; he is abandoned, unjustified, the prey of a freedom that is no longer chained up by anything. . . . Freedom is then revealed, and he must decide upon his attitude in the face of it. (*EA*, 39–40)

Because childhood conceals freedom, a man will all his life long be nostalgic for the time when he did not know its demands and anxieties. What happens often enough is that—afraid of his freedom, afraid of having to choose, afraid of *himself*—a man takes refuge again in the serious world.

The serious man gets rid of his freedom by claiming to subordinate it to values which would be un-

conditioned. He imagines that the accession to these values likewise permanently confers value upon himself. Shielded with "rights," he fulfills himself as a *being* who is escaping from the stress of existence. . . .

He chooses to live in an infantile world, but to the child the values are really given. The serious man must mask the movement by which he gives them to himself, like the mythomaniac who while reading a love-letter pretends to forget that she has sent it to herself. (*EA*, 46–47)*

But this is now dishonest. The serious person may think that values are given—authorized perhaps by God, perhaps by the laws of history, perhaps by the Communist Party. But wherever she claims to find them, the truth is that she chooses them.

De Beauvoir accepts Sartre's argument that there is no God, that the very concept of God is incoherent. (See the Sartre profile, p. 648.) But she has arguments of her own.

"Let us listen to the voice of God," says the believer. "He will tell us himself what he expects of us." But such a hope is naive. God could manifest himself only through an earthly voice because our ears can hear no other. But how, then, does one recognize its divine nature? Upon asking a hallucinating woman who that interlocutor was who spoke to her by mysterious waves, she responded cautiously, "He says that he is God, but *I* don't know him." . . . Kafka describes the same uncertainty in *The Castle* [1926]. Man can receive messages and even see the messenger. But isn't this one an impostor? And does *he* know who sends him? Hasn't he forgotten half the message along the way? Is this letter that he hands over to me authentic, and what is its meaning? The Messiah says that he is the Messiah; the false Messiah also says it. Who will distinguish one from the other?

One will be able to recognize them only by their works. But how will we decide whether these works are good or bad? We will decide in the name of a human good. . . . Man cannot enlighten himself through God. . . . Man is never in situation

---

*De Beauvoir uses the term "man" in both the generic and the sexed sense. It is generally easy to tell from the context which is meant. In this chapter I will sometimes, though not always, follow suit.

except before men, and this presence or this absence way up in heaven does not concern him. (*PC,* 104–106)

The serious person claims to subordinate his freedom to values that are of nonhuman origin. He says, "This is serious business," and judges by values he thinks are unconditioned. But he *makes himself* serious; "he is no longer a man, but a father, a boss, a member of the Christian Church or the Communist Party" (*EA,* 48). These identifications supply him with *rights,* and paradoxically he becomes the *slave* of ends that he himself has set up. He serves these values unquestioningly. They become

> inhuman idols to which one will not hesitate to sacrifice man himself. Therefore, the serious man is dangerous. It is natural that he makes himself a tyrant. (*EA,* 49)

Ignoring the subjectivity of his own choice, it comes naturally to him to ignore the subjectivity and freedom of others. He willingly sacrifices them to his ideal, persuading himself that what he sacrifices is nothing compared with it. Seriousness easily leads to fanaticism. It produces the Inquisition, the lynchings of blacks in the Old South, the cruelties of colonialism, the Holocaust, and the gulag. (Today de Beauvoir would certainly add that it produces jihad.)

More or less midway between the nihilist and the serious man is a character de Beauvoir calls *the adventurer.*

> He throws himself into his undertakings with Zest, into exploration, conquest, war, speculation, love, politics, but he does not attach himself to the end at which he aims; only to his conquest. He likes action for its own sake. He finds joy in spreading through the world a freedom which remains indifferent to its content. (*EA,* 58)

Unlike the serious man and the nihilist, the adventurer accepts, affirms his existence in all its inherent ambiguity. He rejoices in its exercise. He does not expect justification of his life from values already given, but he remains "indifferent" to the content of his adventures. How they affect others is no concern of his.

The massacres of the Indians meant nothing to Pizarro; Don Juan was unaffected by Elvira's tears. Indifferent to the ends they set up for themselves, they were still more indifferent to the means of attaining them; they cared only for their pleasure or their glory. . . . Thus, nothing prevents [the adventurer] from sacrificing these insignificant beings to his own will for power. He will treat them like instruments; he will destroy them if they get in his way. (*EA,* 61)

Adventurism seldom appears in its purity, however, for two reasons: (1) The adventurer needs others; he needs money, arms, soldiers; he needs fortune, leisure, and enjoyment. And for these reasons he tends to be "complacent regarding all regimes which defend the privileges of a class or party, and more particularly authoritarian regimes and fascism" (*EA,* 62). Thus, in order to be free for adventure, he becomes the slave of established power. The adventurer, in fact, carries the seed of the dictator within him, since he "regards mankind as indifferent matter destined to support the game of his existence" (*EA,* 62). It requires only fortunate circumstances to make him a tyrant.

(2) Another reason the pure adventurer is seldom found is that he usually pursues certain goals *in all seriousness:* fame, fortune, or glory. Those ends are not just a game for him; they are treated as ends about which he is not lighthearted, but most serious indeed.

De Beauvoir describes still more varieties of inauthenticity, but it is time to see what an authentic life would be like. We already have some negative indications of it in the ways of avoidance we have been discussing. But what can be said positively? Looking back to the sketch of our ambiguous status (see the first paragraph of this section), we can see that we are not correctly described as a *thing* with a given *nature.* De Beauvoir often puts it this way: In comparison with a full and completed thing, like a rock—which just is whatever it is—I am a *lack;* at any given moment I am incomplete. There is always something left to be filled in. I am not just *being,* but *disclosure* of being, consciousness of being.

But—and this is very important for her—this disclosure is not something passive; it is not mere registration of an object, not just a reflection of the world. "I am not first a thing but a spontaneity that desires, that loves, that wants, that acts" (*PC*, 93). Existence is dynamic, active, always engaged in projects. And what is the aim of these projects? To create being, to fill in the lack, to justify my existence by making myself a being of undoubted value, something absolute.* This, of course, I cannot do in its entirety, and in this regard Sartre is correct in calling man "a futile passion." But de Beauvoir insists that this is no cause for despair; nor is it a reason to retreat into apathy. While "I must resign myself to never being entirely saved" (*PC*, 130), I can "take delight in this very effort toward impossible possession" (*EA*, 12).

> This means that man, in his vain attempt to *be* God, makes himself exist *as* man, and if he is satisfied with this existence, he coincides exactly with himself. It is not granted him to exist without tending toward this being which he will never be. But it is possible for him to want this tension even with the failure which it involves. His being is lack of being, but this lack has a way of being which is precisely existence. . . . The failure is not surpassed, but assumed. . . . To attain his truth, man must not attempt to dispel the ambiguity of his being but, on the contrary, accept the task of realizing it. (*EA*, 12–13)

Human life is not inherently absurd. Ambiguity is not absurdity. Nor does death make life absurd. It is not death that makes us finite, either—the existence of others suffices for that. Even our projects are inherently finite.

> Man has to be his being. Every moment he is seeking to make himself be, and that is the project. The human being exists in the form of projects that are not projects toward death but projects toward singular ends. He hunts, he fishes, he fashions instruments, he writes books: these are not diversions or flights but a movement toward being. . . .
>
> Pyrrhus would be absurd if he left in order to return home, but it is the humorist who introduces

"The fact that we are human beings is infinitely more important than all the peculiarities that distinguish human beings from one another."

—Simone de Beauvoir

this finality here. He does not have the right to extend Pyrrhus's project farther than Pyrrhus has settled upon. Pyrrhus is not leaving in order to return; he is leaving in order to conquer. That undertaking is not contradictory. A project is exactly what it decides to be. It has the meaning that it gives itself. (*PC*, 115, 100)

It is by way of these projects that value appears in the world. Renouncing the "given" values of the serious man, the existentialist realizes that

> it is desire which creates the desirable, and the project which sets up the end. It is human existence which makes values spring up in the world on the basis of which it will be able to judge the enterprise in which it will be engaged. (*EA*, 15)*

---

*Augustine and Luther would consider this the apex of "works righteousness." Justified as they believe we are—against all expectation—by the grace of God, proper motivation is not supplied by this futile effort to justify *ourselves,* but by *gratitude* for all we have been given. (See pp. 252–254.)

---

*One might expect that on this basis de Beauvoir would endorse a rather extreme relativism in ethics. As we shall see, that is far from the case.

There is no room for an overall pessimism about life—nor for unconditioned optimism either. We are not in a position to make any such absolute judgments.

> Man exists. For him it is not a question of wondering whether his presence in the world is useful, whether life is worth the trouble of being lived. These questions make no sense. It is a matter of knowing whether he wants to live and under what conditions. (*EA,* 15)

It is a fact that any project of mine can be, and almost certainly will be, surpassed. I invent a new form of internal combustion engine even while I know that eventually it will be improved upon. I devise a scientific theory, sure all the while that it will not be the last word. But this doesn't make invention or theorizing absurd. Here is no good reason for pessimism.

> The paradox of the human condition is that every end can be surpassed, and yet, the project defines the end as an end. In order to surpass an end, it must first have been projected as something that is not to be surpassed. Man has no other way of existing. It is Pyrrhus, and not Cineas, who is right. Pyrrhus leaves in order to conquer; let him conquer, then. "After that?" After that, he'll see.
>   Man's finiteness is therefore not endured; it is desired. . . . The limit of our undertaking is at its very heart, not outside of it. (*PC,* 113)

Human existence just *is* this process of setting goals and striving to achieve them. To want it to be something else, something final and complete, is to wish for the moon.

The key notion in an existentialist understanding of the human being is *freedom*. Man *is* free, but he must also continually be *making* himself free. Although it is not possible to *will ourselves not free,* it is all the more possible to *fail to will ourselves free.* The temptations of nihilism and seriousness exercise a constant pull, and it is so easy to deny our freedom. "In laziness, heedlessness, capriciousness, cowardice, impatience, one contests the meaning of the project at the very moment that one defines it" (*EA,* 25). But in contesting it one undermines himself. Freedom—this active projecting ourselves into the world, seeking this end or another, trying in one

way or another to justify our existence—that is *what we are.*

The adventurer knows this. That is his superiority over the serious person and the nihilist. "If existentialism were solipsistic, as is generally claimed, it would have to regard the adventurer as its perfect hero" (*EA,* 59). But de Beauvoir's existentialism is not solipsistic, and we now have to think about ethics.

1. List some aspects of our ambiguous nature.
2. How do the nihilist, the cynic, and the humorist deny the ambiguity?
3. How does seriousness evade the ambiguity of human life?
4. In what way is the adventurer closer to authenticity than either the nihilist or the serious person?
5. What flaws does de Beauvoir reveal in the adventurer's character?
6. Why cannot we rely on God to set our values?
7. How can one justify one's life? And why cannot we be entirely saved?
8. Why must humans be continually *making* themselves free?

Ethics

As soon as a child has finished a drawing or a page of writing, he runs to show them to his parents. He needs their approval as much as candy or toys; the drawing requires an eye that looks at it. These disorganized lines must become a boat or a horse for someone. . . .

I walk in the country, I break off a stem, I kick a pebble, I climb a hill; all that without witnesses. But no one is satisfied with such solitude for his entire life. As soon as my walk is completed, I feel the need to tell a friend about it. (*PC,* 116)

Our life is always a life with others. Even the adventurer, the hero of his own story, needs others to pursue his goals, to remember his deeds. I need others, of course, because I do not grow my own food or build the house I live in. I do not sew my own clothes or assemble the car that I drive. All this is important, but de Beauvoir has more than this in mind. I act in the world and my action makes something *be*. I decide to write this book. I work over it for six years and finally it *is*. But there was no void in the world shaped exactly like it, crying out in advance for just this production. The book is there, and then we see what *others* will make of it. My life has no antecedent justification; there is no guarantee that my life will be worthwhile; but if others take up my book and use it, my life is (to that extent) vindicated.*

> In order for the object that I founded to appear as a good, the other must make it into his own good, and then I would be justified for having created it. The other's freedom alone is capable of necessitating my being. My essential need is therefore to be faced with free men. (*PC,* 129)

Feeling gratuitous, unnecessary, superfluous, faced with the necessity of creating ourselves by creating objects, we wish to escape the pure contingency of our existence and "need others in order for our existence to become founded and necessary" (*PC,* 129).

Notice that it is *free* human beings that I need. Coerced acceptance, drugged approval, hypnotized, inattentive, or slavish applause mean nothing. Only the tyrant already mired in self-deception will enjoy the crowds who are forced to shout their praises. "Looking for just any approval is another one of the weaknesses of vanity" (*PC,* 130). Moreover, if the other appears only as a limited, finite, and unfree object, the place he creates for me is as contingent and useless as himself. "He needs me, but what need is there for him? How could this unjustifiable existence justify me?" (*PC,* 130).

> For I must have a freedom facing me. Freedom is the only reality that I cannot transcend. How can one surpass what is constantly surpassing itself? (*PC,* 131)
>
> I don't wish to be recognized by just anyone, because in communication with others, we look for

---

*While working on this chapter I was listening to music. Samuel Barber's *Adagio for Strings* was playing. I paused, paying close attention, and this thought came to me: To have written that— that alone would justify a life.

the completion of the project in which our freedom is engaged, and therefore others must project me toward a future that I recognize as mine. For me it would be a bitter failure if my action were perpetuated by becoming useful to my adversaries. The project by which others confer necessity upon me must also be my project. (*PC,* 133)

What I need is that my projects do not die a quick death by being universally ignored, opposed, or used for purposes I do not share. The ideal would be for all of humanity to extend my project into the indefinite future toward ends that I approve of; that would be the ultimate justification. But there is no hope for that; men are separate, opposed, and the goal of making my project last thus takes on the aspect of a struggle.

But how can I struggle here? I can't obtain admiration or love by violence; that would be absurd.

> I can only appeal to the other's freedom, not constrain it. I can invent the most urgent appeals, try my best to charm it, but it will remain free to respond to those appeals or not, no matter what I do. . . . Respect for the other's freedom is not an abstract rule. It is the first condition of my successful effort. (*PC,* 136)

In fact, two conditions must be met: (1) I must be free to appeal to the future for my vindication; and (2) I must have people who are free to respond to my appeals.

> I must therefore strive to create for men situations such that they can accompany and surpass my transcendence. I need their freedom to be available to use and conserve me in surpassing me. I ask for health, knowledge, well-being, and leisure for men so that their freedom is not consumed in fighting sickness, ignorance, and misery. (*PC,* 137)

So here we have the foundation of an ethics. Ethics is grounded in the nature of human existence, in my freedom and yours. I need you to be free to affirm my projects as you need me and my freedom.

> Freedom is the source from which all significations and all values spring. It is the original condition of all justifications of existence. The man who seeks to justify his life must want freedom itself absolutely and above everything else. . . . To will one-

self moral and to will oneself free are one and the same decision. (*EA*, 24)

Morality cannot be obedience to God; there is no God. Nor can it be conformity to an abstract rule like Kant's categorical imperative; abstract rules do not help in particular situations because the *meaning* of the situation is determined by us. Nor can one be moral by seeking another's happiness, as the utilitarians claim; no one can make another person happy. The goal of ethical action is freedom—one's own and the other's.

> Freedom can not will itself without aiming at an open future, . . . but only the freedom of other men can extend [our ends] beyond our life.
>
> Man can find a justification of his own existence only in the existence of other men. Now, he needs such a justification; there is no escaping it. (*EA*, 71–72)

To will myself free is to take up the burden of justifying my life. Since I cannot do that without others who are free to continue to affirm my projects,

> to will oneself free is also to will others free. This will is not an abstract formula. It points out to each person concrete action to be achieved. (*EA*, 73).

This sounds noble and ideal, but de Beauvoir is under no illusions about how difficult this is to realize. Trying to make it work immediately encounters "concrete and difficult problems" (*EA*, 73). Her awareness of these problems was intensified by the situation of France during the Second World War. In May of 1940 the German army invaded France, whose forces were quickly overwhelmed. There was much confusion and debate about what to do, but the outcome was German occupation of the northern two-thirds of France with a collaborationist French government, headquartered in Vichy, nominally controlling the south. Meanwhile, while a "Free French" government-in-exile was proclaimed by Charles de Gaulle in London, the Vichy government, under the leadership of Marshal Petain, cooperated with German policies, including the arrest and deportation of Jews to Nazi concentration camps. Many Frenchmen considered these collaborators to be traitors, and an active Resistance movement played a significant role in sabotage and harassment of the occupiers throughout the rest of the war. Resistance fighters rescued many Allied airmen who were shot down over France and diverted German forces so as to aid the invasion at the beaches of Normandy on June 6, 1944. After the war some of the collaborationist leaders were put on trial and executed for treason and war crimes.*

De Beauvoir was sympathetic to the Resistance and had close contacts with many in that movement. It is important to note that the conflict pitted not just the French against the Germans, but the French against each other. It was a wrenching time for all. Clearly an ethics that made freedom its centerpiece had something to say in these circumstances. But it is equally clear that it couldn't be simple. The goal is freedom for all; but what is one to do when some use their freedom to deny the freedom of others? You can't have both the freedom of the Jew to live her life as she thinks best and also the freedom of the Nazi to deport her to Buchenwald. You have to choose. "A freedom which is interested only in denying freedom must be denied" (*EA*, 91).

As we have seen, freedom for de Beauvoir is nothing abstract; nor is it merely the Stoic freedom to withdraw into one's consciousness and say, "This means nothing to me." Freedom "realizes itself only by engaging itself in the world: to such an extent that man's project toward freedom is embodied for him in definite acts of behavior" (*EA*, 78). Often enough in this world, the free acts of a person meet obstacles and her ends cannot be attained. But there are two different ways this happens. It can happen, first, because of the natural resistance of things: "Floods, earthquakes, grasshoppers, epidemics and plague" can frustrate our desires and turn our projects back on themselves, but these material obstacles do not *oppress* us; "man is never oppressed by things" (*EA*, 81). Even death does not oppress us; it

---

*A discussion of occupied France during World War II, with many links to other sites, can be found at http://en.wikipedia.org/wiki/Vichy_France.

is the natural limit of life—the price we pay for the privilege of being alive.

But oppression does occur when some people's freedom is taken away by the free acts of others.

> Only man can be an enemy for man; only he can rob him of the meaning of his acts and his life because it also belongs only to him alone to confirm it in its existence, to recognize it in actual fact as a freedom. . . . One does not submit to a war or an occupation as he does to an earthquake: he must take sides for or against, and the foreign wills thereby become allied or hostile. (*EA*, 82)

Oppression denies to a person what is most central to human existence; it denies a chance to justify one's life through acts that create oneself by transcending one's current being through projects that others can take up and extend into the indefinite future. Oppression comes in many forms, occupation by a foreign power being only one. Slavery may be the most extreme. Women, too, have been oppressed, de Beauvoir holds (as we shall see in the next section). And workers are oppressed by employers when

> they are condemned to mark time hopelessly in order merely to support the collectivity; their life is a pure repetition of mechanical gestures; their leisure is just about sufficient for them to regain their strength; the oppressor feeds himself on their transcendence and refuses to extend it by a free recognition. (*EA*, 83)

There are echoes of Marx here; de Beauvoir finds the Socialist ideal that Communists supposedly serve congenial, but she is severely critical of the Communist Party, whether in France or the Soviet Union.* It is truly hateful, she says, when life is forced to occupy itself solely with maintaining itself, when there is no chance to reach out toward new vistas, to project oneself toward ends of one's own choosing. This must be resisted. Rebellion is

what ethics requires in circumstances like this, not resignation and humble acquiescence.

Again, rebellion cannot be just *saying*, "I don't accept this." Like every free act, it must be realized in behavior. And this means violence. It would be nice if the oppressor, realizing his own need for the freedom of others, would simply give up oppressing. A purely moral transition away from oppression would have to come by way of a conversion of the oppressors, but de Beauvoir, schooled in the brutality of the Nazi occupation, dismisses this notion as a mere "utopian reverie" (*EA*, 97). To use the title of a play by Sartre, if you want to fight oppression, you have to reconcile yourself to "dirty hands." You cannot "enter into solidarity with all the others, because they do not all choose the same goals. . . . One will always work for certain men against others" (*PC*, 108).

But what can justify violence? Here de Beauvoir uses a word that does not come easily to her; she says there is something that is an "absolute" evil.

> We think that such an evil exists. One can excuse all the offenses, even the crimes by which individuals assert themselves against society. But when a man deliberately tries to degrade man by reducing him to a thing, nothing can compensate for the abomination he causes to erupt on earth. There resides the sole sin against man. When it is accomplished no indulgences are permitted and it belongs to man to punish it. (*EE*, 257)*

These words appear in an essay she wrote following the trial of Robert Brasillach, the French editor of a fascist newspaper who contributed to the arrest and deportation of Jewish citizens during the war. During the trial a petition was circulated among intellectuals pleading for his pardon. De Beauvoir refused to sign it. Brasillach was convicted of treason and executed. The essay "An Eye for an Eye" is a justification of her refusal and of the moral right to punish such evils.

> For to punish is to recognize man as free in evil as well as in good. It is to distinguish evil from good in the use that man makes of his freedom. It is to will the good. (*EE*, 259)

---

*What she objects to is the groupthink demanded of party members, the historical determinism in Communist doctrine that denies individual freedom, and the hypocrisy that doctrine produces in practice when Communists all the while act as though they are free to choose and excoriate their enemies in moral language that makes sense only on the assumption that their opponents' acts are freely chosen.

---

*Compare Kant on treating people as things, p. 456.

She supported the use of violence by Resistance fighters trying to undermine the German occupation, but she does not glorify it and demands in every case that it justify itself. It is true that a kind of paradox is involved in the resort to violence. In order to oppose those who would treat human beings as mere things, they themselves will "have to be treated like things" (*EA,* 97). It is

> necessary to choose to sacrifice the one who is an enemy of man; but the fact is that one finds himself forced to treat certain men as things in order to win the freedom of all.
>
> A freedom which is occupied in denying freedom is itself so outrageous that the outrageousness of the violence which one practises against it is almost cancelled out. . . . (*EA,* 97)
>
> In any event, it is evident that we are not going to decide to fulfill the will of every man. There are cases where a man positively wants evil, that is, the enslavement of other men, and he must then be fought. (*EA,* 136)

Every struggle, moreover, "obliges us to sacrifice people whom our victory does not concern, people who, in all honesty, reject it as a cataclysm: these people will die in astonishment, anger or despair" (*EA,* 108). To put it in contemporary terms, in every struggle there will be "collateral damage." And that is still not the worst, because we will need to sacrifice not only those who oppose us,

> but also those who are fighting on our side, and even ourselves. Since we can conquer our enemies only by acting upon their facticity, by reducing them to things, we have to make ourselves things; in this struggle in which wills are forced to confront each other through their bodies, the bodies of our allies, like those of our opponents are exposed to the same brutal hazard: they will be wounded, killed, or starved. (*EA,* 99)

Here we are faced with the difficult problem of means and ends in action. We know that "the supreme end at which man must aim is his freedom" (*EA,* 113), but is there no limit to the means that can be chosen to achieve it? There is a limit, de Beauvoir says, though it is not possible to give a recipe to decide the matter for every case.

> The means can be understood only in the light of the desired end, but inversely, the end is inseparable from the means by which it is carried out, and it is a fallacy to believe that the end can be achieved by just any means.*
>
> It is not possible to act for man without treating certain men, at certain times, as means.
>
> However, treating man as a means is committing violence against him; it means contradicting the idea of his absolute value that alone allows the action to be fully founded. . . . The moralist who wants both to act and to approve of himself would want to use only means that are in themselves ethical, that is to say, only those whose meaning is in keeping with the end he is aiming for. However, this dream is impossible, and if he insists, he will only vacillate between heaven and earth without being able to engage himself in this world. To come down to earth means accepting defilement, failure, horror; it means admitting that it is impossible to save everything; and what is lost is lost forever. . . .
>
> Whatever I may choose to do, I will be unfaithful to my profound desire to respect human life; and yet, I am forced to choose; no reality exterior to myself can direct me in my choice. (*MIPR,* 184, 189–190)

Ethics can show us what the end is that deserves our unconditional respect: the transcendence and freedom of each individual. But it provides no neat recipes for accomplishing that end, and no guarantee of success. Each situation must be faced with an unblinking eye for the facts and an understanding of their meaning in the light of the ultimate end. And then one must choose. It is only necessary to keep in mind that "an action which wants to serve man ought to be careful not to forget him on the way" (*EA,* 153).

What existentialist ethics recommends is a "lucid generosity" (*PC,* 124): generous in framing our projects so that they maximize freedom for all, but lucid in understanding that others may oppose these projects and in any case—in their own freedom—will make of them what they will. The justification of our lives is ultimately not in our control.

---

*This is similar to John Dewey's view of ends and means. See pp. 589–591. De Beauvoir, however, is less optimistic than Dewey about the possibilities for reconciling means and ends into a morally approvable synthesis.

Thus man can act; he must act. He is only in transcending himself. He acts in risk, in failure. He must assume the risk. By throwing himself toward the uncertain future, he founds his present with certainty. (*PC,* 139)

But despite life's risk and incompleteness, there is joy in existence. Liberation has a concrete meaning only in "individual and living joy." If "the satisfaction of an old man drinking a glass of wine" or "the laugh of a child at play" counts for nothing, then all the rest is worthless. "If we do not love life on our own account and through others, it is futile to seek to justify it in any way" (*EA,* 135–136).

---

1. Why do we need others?
2. Why do we need others who are free?
3. In what way is ethics grounded in the nature of human existence?
4. Why is freedom the supreme value?
5. Define oppression.
6. In what circumstances is violence justified?
7. When is punishment justified?
8. How are means and ends properly related?

Woman

"What is a woman?" de Beauvoir asks. "No one doubts that females exist in the human species. . . . And yet we are told that femininity is in danger; we are exhorted to be women, remain women, become women. It would appear, then, that every female human being is not necessarily a woman" (*SS,* ixx).

The question suggests that there is an *ideal* of woman that actually existing women (biologically speaking) are failing to live up to. But what is that ideal? Where does it originate? Where does it get its power? And is it something that we should cherish or repudiate? These questions are addressed in a large, passionately written, wide-ranging book titled *The Second Sex,* published in 1949.[5] The key to de Beauvoir's answer is summed up in one very influential sentence: "One is not born, but rather becomes, a woman" (*SS,* 267). And the way that happens is the theme of the book.

The first chapter is a survey of the data of biology with respect to male and female. These considerations about a woman's body constitute "an essential element in her situation" and are "extremely important" (*SS,* 32). Like a man, a woman *is* her body; men and women alike experience the world, express themselves, and act through the body. But there are differences; to a much greater degree than a man, a woman feels alienated from her body; she experiences a foreign power at work there. It is the species "gnawing at [her] vitals" (*SS,* 30).

> From puberty to menopause woman is the theater of a play that unfolds within her and in which she is not personally concerned. . . . It is during her periods that she feels her body most painfully as an obscure, alien thing; it is, indeed the prey of a stubborn and foreign life that each month constructs and then tears down a cradle within it; each month all things are made ready for a child and then aborted in the crimson flow. (*SS,* 29)

Pregnancy and gestation, of course, are are female, and both processes demand heavy sacrifices.

> Repeated childbearing will make her prematurely old and misshapen, as often among the rural poor. Childbirth itself is painful and dangerous. . . . The conflict between species and individual, which sometimes assumes dramatic force at childbirth, endows the female body with a disturbing frailty. (*SS,* 30)

A man, of course, is also a bearer of the species; but his species burden is much lighter, and "in comparison with her the male seems infinitely favored: his sexual life is not in opposition to his existence as a person, and biologically it runs an even course, without crises and generally without mishap" (*SS,* 32). The female, in addition to having to bear these extra sexual burdens, is, on average, shorter than the male and lighter, with less muscular strength and with a smaller respiratory capacity. On the whole, women are less robust and more delicate than men.

These facts about a woman's body are important because the body is "the instrument of our grasp upon the world," and the world is bound to seem "a very different thing when apprehended in one manner or another" (*SS*, 32). But de Beauvoir insists that although the biological facts are one key to the understanding of woman, they are not the decisive one.

> I deny that [these facts] establish for her a fixed and inevitable destiny. They are insufficient for setting up a hierarchy of the sexes; they fail to explain why woman is the Other; they do not condemn her to remain in this subordinate role forever. (*SS*, 32–33)

Mere facts have, in themselves, little significance. What matters is what human beings do with the facts. For example, although a woman is in greater bondage to the species than a man, how much that matters depends a great deal on (1) how many children society demands and (2) the quality of care given in pregnancy and childbirth.

Man is defined, de Beauvoir says,

> as a being who is not fixed, who makes himself what he is. As Merleau-Ponty very justly puts it, man is not a natural species: he is a historical idea. Woman is not a completed reality, but rather a becoming, and it is in her becoming that she should be compared with man; that is to say, her *possibilities* should be defined. (*SS*, 34)*

We can see here that existentialist themes are going to play a large role in de Beauvoir's feminism. Individuals are not abandoned to the dictates of their biological nature. Values cannot be based on physiology. It is past choices that have created the situation women find themselves in today, so we have to "find out what humanity has made of the human female" (*SS*, 37).

Woman has been defined, de Beauvoir says, as *the Other*. What does this mean? Otherness, she

---

*Here is a good example of de Beauvoir using the term "man" in both the generic and the sexed senses. Within three sentences she uses the term both ways; you should have no difficulty in understanding which sense is meant in each occurrence. Maurice Merleau-Ponty extended Husserl's phenomenological methods in existentialist directions, producing a phenomenological description of embodiment.

says, is a fundamental category of human thought. No group ever sets itself up as a distinctive group, a One, without setting up an Other by contrast. What has happened in our history, and almost universally, is that male human beings have been understood as human beings par excellence, as the One, while females have been understood only relative to them, as the Other. This is shown in many ways, not least by "the common use of *man* to designate human beings in general," (*SS*, xxi) as de Beauvoir herself does (but which is much less common today). This One/Other pattern is symbolized in Genesis, where Adam is created whole and entire, but Eve is made from Adam's flesh as "a helper" for him. Man is taken to be the representative of humanity, the absolute, while woman has only a relative existence. Philosophers, for their part, have usually reflected this view rather than criticizing it, though there have been a few exceptions; de Beauvoir mentions John Stuart Mill (see pp. 525–531).

In the standard case, this One/Other relationship is reciprocal. Jones, as subject, takes Smith as object, and Smith does the same to Jones. Each tends to consider himself as the essential while thinking of the other as inessential. As Hegel and Sartre both argue, this is a formula for conflict, each trying to dominate the other. (One of the characters in Sartre's play *No Exit* says, "Hell is other people.") But, says de Beauvoir, the male/female case is different; although there is conflict, there is little reciprocity. Woman has always been dependent; the two sexes "have never shared the world in equality" (*SS*, xxvi). This raises an obvious question.

> Why is it that women do not dispute male sovereignty? . . . The Other is posed as such by the One in defining himself as the One. But if the Other is not to regain the status of being the One, he must be submissive enough to accept this alien point of view. Whence comes this submission in the case of woman? (*SS*, xxiv)

Why has male dominance been so widespread and persistent? It is because woman "herself fails to bring about this change." Women "do not authentically assume a subjective attitude" (*SS*, xxv); they do not assert themselves as a One against the male Other. But why is *that?*

De Beauvoir discusses several reasons. For one thing, women have lacked the economic and educational resources allotted to men. For another, they feel the species tie to men. And there are the biological differences in strength and robustness (though these had more importance ages ago than they do today). But two factors are crucial, she says, one on each side of the divide. As we saw in the discussion of *ambiguity,* human beings face constant temptations to evade the anxiety of existing, together with its freedom and its demands for choice and responsibility. From the woman's side it looks like this:

> To decline to be the Other, to refuse to be a party to the deal—this would be to renounce all the advantages conferred upon them by their alliance with the superior caste. Man-the-sovereign will provide woman-the-liege with material protection and will undertake the moral justification of her existence; thus she can evade at once both economic risk and the metaphysical risk of a liberty in which ends and aims must be contrived without assistance. . . . [This is] an easy road; on it one avoids the strain involved in undertaking an authentic existence. (*SS,* xxvii)

Woman has been content to be the "second sex," then, because "she is often very well pleased with her role as the *Other*" (*SS,* xxvii).

From the man's side it can be seen that this arrangement has suited him very well. Not only do men get a "helper" in their projects and a subservient sexual partner, but even "the most humble among them is made to *feel* superior; . . . the most mediocre of males feels himself a demigod as compared with women. . . . Here is a miraculous balm for those afflicted with an inferiority complex" (*SS,* xxx–xxxi).

This pattern of regarding woman as the Other, then, has lasted so long because each party to it has seen advantages in it for itself. Both parties are guilty of "bad faith" (to use Sartre's term), of evading the true nature of their existence by "falling away" (to use Heidegger's term) from their freedom into given roles that allow an escape into "the serious" (to use de Beauvoir's term). However,

> there is no justification for present existence other than its expansion into an indefinitely open future. Every time transcendence falls back into immanence, stagnation, there is a degradation of existence into the "*en-soi*"—the brutish life of subjection to given conditions—and of liberty into constraint and contingence. This downfall represents a moral fault if the subject consents to it; if it is inflicted upon him, it spells frustration and oppression. In both cases it is an absolute evil. (*SS,* xxxv) *

Woman is "a free and autonomous being like all human creatures" (*SS,* xxxv), but she has been—partly through compulsion, partly through her own acquiescence—degraded to the status of an object and doomed to immanence. "The drama of woman lies in this conflict between the fundamental aspirations of every subject . . . and the compulsions of a situation in which she is the inessential. How can a human being in woman's situation attain fulfillment?" (*SS,* xxxv). Consistent with her existentialist ethics, de Beauvoir says that the criterion for fulfillment is not happiness, but liberty. So the question is, how can women become *free?*

By far the larger part of this big book, however, is not devoted to that question (we shall return to it), but to an analysis of the current situation of women (as of 1949), and an account of how things came to be that way. She discusses not only biology, but psychoanalysis and historical materialism. She looks back in history to nomadic peoples, early tillers of the soil, and the situation of women from classical times through the Middle Ages to the French Revolution and beyond. Myths are dissected and the portrayal of women in literature is analyzed. The last two-thirds of the book sketches "woman's life today," from childhood to old age. Because it is

---

* *En-soi* (in-itself) is Sartre's term for the being that is just what it is, with no opening to possibilities, no freedom to choose among them, and no future but the past. He contrasts it with the *pour-soi,* the for-itself that is conscious of itself and its free openness to multiple futures.

impossible to do justice to these riches in this short chapter, I shall just present a sample of her thoughts on a number of topics.

On Psychoanalysis "The axiomatic proposition held in common by all psychoanalysts is this: the human story is to be explained by the interplay of determinate elements" (*SS*, 43). The individual is thus explained "through ties with his past and not in respect of a future toward which he projects his aims" (*SS*, 50–51). Because of this, psychoanalysts "systematically reject the idea of *choice* and the correlated concept of value, and therein lies the intrinsic weakness of the system" (*SS*, 45). Though sexuality plays a substantial role in human life, it is not the basic driving force; "there is in the existent a more original 'quest of being,' of which sexuality is only one of the aspects" (*SS*, 46). The classic psychoanalysts tend to think of psychic life as occurring "inside" the individual; "such words as *complex, tendency,* and so on make that implication. But a life is a relation to the world, and the individual defines himself by making his own choices through the world about him" (*SS*, 49).

Moreover, psychoanalysts simply take over the picture of woman as the Other. It is among them in particular

> that man is defined as a human being and woman as a female—whenever she behaves as a human being she is said to imitate the male. . . . When a little girl climbs trees it is, according to Adler, just to show her equality with boys; it does not occur to him that she likes to climb trees. . . . To paint, to write, to engage in politics—these are not merely "sublimations"; here we have aims that are willed for their own sakes. To deny it is to falsify all human history. (*SS*, 51)

In a final dismissal, de Beauvoir holds that "the psychoanalysts never give us more than an inauthentic picture" (*SS*, 51).

In contrast to the theses of classical psychoanalysis, de Beauvoir says:

> I shall pose the problem of feminine destiny quite otherwise: I shall place woman in a world of values and give her behavior a dimension of liberty. I be-

lieve that she has the power to choose between the assertion of her transcendence and her alienation as object; she is not the plaything of contradictory drives; she devises solutions of diverse ranking in the ethical scale. (*SS*, 50)

(Since 1949 several varieties of psychological analysis have adopted this existentialist emphasis on choice and freedom; these are often called *humanistic* psychologies.)

On Early History The early days of the species were hard, and a man's superior strength must have been of tremendous importance in guaranteeing mere survival. Men, moreover, were oriented beyond themselves in the world, transforming it by means of tools, while women submitted to their biological fate and bore children. Man "put his power to the test; he set up goals and opened up roads toward them; he found self-realization as an existent. . . . This is the reason why fishing and hunting expeditions had a sacred character" (*SS*, 63).

But there was something even more important. Man's activity had a dimension that gave it "supreme dignity; it was often dangerous."

> The warrior put his life in jeopardy to elevate the prestige of the horde, the clan to which he belonged. And in this he proved dramatically that life is not the supreme value for man, but on the contrary that it should be made to serve ends more important than itself. . . . For it is not in giving life but in risking life that man is raised above the animal; that is why superiority has been accorded in humanity not to the sex that brings forth but to that which kills. (*SS*, 63–64)

This is "the key to the whole mystery," she says (*SS*, 64). A species is continued by creating itself anew, but this is only repeating the same again. In transcending mere animal life through existence, a species creates *values;* by contrast with these values mere repetition is diminished to nothing more than a *means.* Thus did men attain a superior status even in the eyes of women, who are biologically destined for the repetition of life.

Yet women, too, feel the urge to surpass and create a new future. "It is regardless of sex that the existent seeks self-justification through transcendence. . . . What [women] demand today is to be recognized as existents by the same right as men and not to subordinate existence to life, the human being to its animality" (*SS*, 65).

On Patriarchy   Many of the most ancient gods are female. This has led some to suppose that there was a time when women ruled, but de Beauvoir says that the "Golden Age of Woman is only a myth. . . . Society has always been male, political power has always been in the hands of men" (*SS*, 70). The time of female gods was a time when men had not yet become masters of technique, tool users, conquerors of the earth. Magic had not yet given way to logic. But even then men understood their equals to be other men; woman has always been the Other. A sure sign of her inferiority is that almost always she goes to live under her husband's roof and often takes his name. In primitive times "marriage is sometimes based on an abduction, real or symbolic, and surely violence done upon another is the most obvious affirmation of that one's alterity. In taking his wife by force the warrior demonstrates that he is capable of annexing the wealth of strangers and of bursting the bounds of the destiny assigned to him by birth" (*SS*, 74). Woman, for her part, "maintained the life of the tribe by giving it children and bread, nothing more" (*SS*, 73).

When men began to work with tools, to *make* tools with which to work, they came to realize responsibility for what they made. A man's

> skill or clumsiness will make or break it; careful, clever, he develops his skill to a point of perfection in which he takes pride: his success depends not upon the favor of the gods, but upon himself. He challenges his fellows, he is elated with success. . . . Man learns his power [and] experiences causation. . . . This world of tools could be embraced within clear concepts: rational thought, logic, and mathematics could now appear. . . . He creates a new world. (*SS*, 75–76)

Woman, by contrast, "was unable to avail herself of the promised benefits of the tool" because she "re-

mained in bondage to life's mysterious processes." So she "did not share [the male's] way of working and thinking." She did not think logically.* In consequence, man did not recognize in her "a being like himself." Given her incapacity, he *had* to recognize her as Other; and given his will to power, he could not be anything but her oppressor (*SS*, 77–78).

When men began to own land, it was natural that they also claimed ownership of women. At the time of patriarchal power, "man wrested from woman all her rights to possess and bequeath property." Because she does not own anything, "woman does not enjoy the dignity of being a person; she herself forms a part of the patrimony of a man. . . . In the patriarchal regime she is the property of her father, who marries her off to suit himself" (*SS*, 82–84). Inheritance passed through the male line and it was important to ensure that sons were legitimate heirs. Thus were women hedged about with restrictions on their movements and behaviors, and the virgin and the faithful wife were honored in both law and religion.

> Thus the triumph of the patriarchate was neither a matter of chance nor the result of a violent revolution. From humanity's beginnings, their biological advantage has enabled the males to affirm their status as sole and sovereign subjects; they have never abdicated this position; . . . woman's place in society is always that which men assign to her; at no time has she ever imposed her own law. (*SS*, 77)

On the Myth of the Feminine   One reason woman is a puzzle is that her image is constantly confused with myth; "as against the dispersed, contingent, and multiple existences of actual women, mythical thought opposes the Eternal Feminine, unique and changeless" (*SS*, 253). Even worse, this myth is itself ambivalent and many-sided. There is woman as "the Praying Mantis, the Mandrake, the Demon," but also "the Muse, the Goddess Mother, Bea-

---

*Here are found the origins of what Derrida and other deconstructionists call "logocentrism," which "privileges" logic, rationality, and objectivity—all traditionally male ways of engaging the world. See pp. 705–707.

trice. . . . The saintly mother has for correlative the cruel stepmother, the angelic young girl has the perverse virgin" (*SS,* 254). She is Eve and Pandora, benefactor and disperser of troubles, life and death, priestess and sorcerer, temptation and release from temptation—each aspect chosen by the fears and desires of the moment. Woman is

> the Other in whom the subject transcends himself without being limited, who opposes him without denying him; she is the Other who lets herself be taken without ceasing to be the Other, and therein she is so necessary to man's happiness and to his triumph that it can be said that if she did not exist, men would have invented her. They did invent her. (*SS,* 188)

But what is she *really?* Men say they can't understand women, but even women do not know. No aspect of the myth is more firmly anchored than the notion of woman as *mystery.* In truth, says de Beauvoir, there is mystery on both sides, male and female. Each subjectivity is impenetrable to the other; no existent can *be* another, experience the world as he or she does. But in another sense, deciding what one *is* is difficult "because in this domain there is no truth. An existent *is* nothing other than what he does; the possible does not extend beyond the real, essence does not precede existence: in pure subjectivity, the human being *is not anything.* He is to be measured by his acts" (*SS,* 257).* This holds for men and women alike. But for women, oppressed through most of history, the mystery is magnified because

> they *do* nothing, they fail to *make themselves* anything. They wonder indefinitely what they *could have* become, which sets them to asking about what they *are.* It is a vain question. If man fails to discover that secret essence of femininity, it is simply because it does not exist. Kept on the fringe of the world, woman cannot be objectively defined

---

* The "existence precedes essence" slogan was made famous by Sartre in his 1945 lecture, "Existentialism Is a Humanism," published as *Existentialism,* trans. Bernard Frechtman (New York: Philosophical Library, 1947).

through this world, and her mystery conceals nothing but emptiness. (*SS,* 258–259)

Perhaps the myth of woman will some day be extinguished; the more women assert themselves as human beings, the more the marvelous quality of the Other will die out in them. (*SS,* 142)

Character and Situation   De Beauvoir is severe in her judgment on woman's character. Woman is

- contrary, prudent, and petty,
- lacking in a sense of fact and accuracy,
- false, theatrical, self-seeking,
- passive,
- without a grasp on reality,
- a believer in magic—in telepathy, astrology, mesmerism, theosophy, table-tipping, clairvoyants, faith healers, answered prayers,
- unfamiliar with the use of logic,
- a believer in intuitions,
- servile, lacking in real pride,
- resigned, but also resentful.

But why is that? It is not because of her hormones or womanly body. It is not because these characteristics manifest the *essence* of woman. It is because of her situation,

> because she is compelled to devote her existence to cooking and washing diapers—no way to acquire a sense of grandeur! It is her duty to assure the monotonous repetition of life in all its mindless factuality. . . . Her life is not directed toward ends: she is absorbed in producing or caring for things that are never more than means, such as food, clothing, shelter. . . . Woman is shut up in a kitchen or in a boudoir, and astonishment is expressed that her horizon is limited. Her wings are clipped, and it is found deplorable that she cannot fly. (*SS,* 604–605)

It is absurd to speak of "woman" in general, as though women in every situation would be the same. There is no eternal essence of woman. If we compare her historically determined situation with that of a man, "we see clearly that man's is far preferable; that is to say, he has many more opportunities to exercise his freedom in the world," with the result that "masculine accomplishment is far superior to that of women, who are practically forbidden to *do* anything" (*SS,* 627).

But "let the future be opened to her, and she will no longer be compelled to linger in the present" (*SS,* 605). Women must "reject the limitations of their situation and seek to open the road of the future. . . . There is no other way out for woman than to work for her liberation" (*SS,* 627). "There is only one way to employ her liberty authentically, and that is to project it through positive action into human society" (*SS,* 678).

Labor and Independence De Beauvoir's claim that throughout history women have not *done* anything, and so have not *become* anything, itself contains the clue to their emancipation.[*]

> It is through gainful employment that woman has traversed most of the distance that separated her from the male; and nothing else can guarantee her liberty in practice. Once she ceases to be a parasite, the system based on her dependence crumbles; between her and the universe there is no longer any need for a masculine mediator.
> (*SS,* 679)

What needs to be changed is women's situation, and nothing more urgently than her economic dependence on men. Let women *do* something and they will transcend their captivity in the immanence of nature, exercise their freedom, and join men in equality as existing human beings—no longer just the Other, no more merely the "second sex." In fact, this has been happening, but it has been a slow process. It was the Industrial Revolution that did more to change women's situation than anything else. With the invention of machine tools,

sheer strength was less important, and manufacturers eagerly sought female labor. True, women workers were shamefully exploited—even more than male workers; they would do more work for less pay and were more docile than male workers. "In 1831 the silk workers labored in summer from three o'clock in the morning until dark, and in winter from five to eleven at night, seventeen hours a day." It was not until 1900 that "the day was limited to ten hours; in 1905 the weekly day of rest was made obligatory; in 1907 the working woman was granted free handling of her income; in 1909 leave with pay was guaranteed to women for childbirth" (*SS,* 114). Woman's status as worker slowly improved, though it was a long and tortuous process. Nonetheless, it is evident that "it is through labor that woman has conquered her dignity as a human being" (*SS,* 114). Only through labor has she become a person in her own right.

Two other developments helped this along. Varieties of birth control allowed woman to "reduce the number of her pregnancies and make them a rationally integral part of her life. . . . Now protected in large part from the slavery of reproduction, she is in a position to assume the economic role that is offered her and will assure her of complete independence" (*SS,* 121). And little by little, woman has gained political equality. Women got the vote in New Zealand in 1893, and in Australia in 1908. It was not until 1920 that woman suffrage became the law of the land in the United States, and not in France until 1945. But it is economic independence that is the key.

Liberty, Equality, Friendship With economic independence, at least for many, women are in a position to do more than simply maintain life. They can devise projects, act on the world, and envision a future that is different from the past. And they can begin, for the first time, to meet men as equals. De Beauvoir is under no illusions that this will be easy and conflict-free, however. Women will now have to struggle with the fate of all human existents— "the tragedy of the unfortunate human consciousness; each separate conscious being aspires to set himself up alone as sovereign subject. Each tries to

---

[*]Some feminists hold that de Beauvoir underestimates what women *do* in rearing children and maintaining a home, and so neglects the choice, responsibility, and self-definition that come with those traditional roles. It must be admitted that it often seems as though only something equivalent to discovering penicillin, changing the course of history, or writing a book counts as action.

fulfill himself by reducing the other to slavery" (*SS*, 140). Women liberated now face the hard work of having to be good human beings.

It is possible to rise above conflict, though never to eliminate it altogether, and some men and women have managed true friendship, whether within marriage or out of it. What is required is that

> each individual freely recognizes the other, each regarding himself and the other simultaneously as object and as subject in a reciprocal manner. But friendship and generosity, which alone permit in actuality this recognition of free beings, are not facile virtues; they are assuredly man's highest achievement, and through that achievement he is to be found in his true nature. But this true nature is that of a struggle unceasingly begun, unceasingly abolished; it requires man to outdo himself at every moment. We might put it in other words and say that man attains an authentically moral attitude when he renounces *mere being* to assume his position as an existent; through this transformation also he renounces all possession, for possession is one way of seeking mere being; but the transformation through which he attains true wisdom is never done, it is necessary to make it without ceasing, it demands a constant tension. And so, quite unable to fulfill himself in solitude, man is incessantly in danger in his relations with his fellows: his life is a difficult enterprise with success never assured. (*SS*, 140)

Although economic independence is a crucial step in securing for women the dignity of human beings, it is not enough. There can be no question, de Beauvoir says, of "abolishing in woman the contingencies and miseries of the human condition." What is required is "giving her the means for transcending them" (*SS*, 727). Only when men and women both assume the ambiguity of the human condition will they be able to live together in amity.

> The fact that we are human beings is infinitely more important than all the peculiarities that distinguish human beings from one another; it is never the given that confers superiorities: "virtue," as the ancients called it, is defined at the level of "that which depends on us." In both sexes is played out the same drama of the flesh and the spirit, of finitude and transcendence; both are gnawed away

by time and laid in wait for by death, they have the same essential need for one another; and they can gain from their liberty the same glory. If they were to taste it, they would no longer be tempted to dispute fallacious privileges, and fraternity between them could then come into existence. (*SS*, 728)

---

1. In what sense is woman more burdened by the demands of the species than man?
2. What does it mean that woman has been defined as "the Other"?
3. How have women and men both fallen into inauthenticity in their relationships with each other?
4. What is de Beauvoir's criticism of classical psychoanalysis?
5. What are some of the features of patriarchy?
6. What is the key to understanding woman as mystery?
7. What aspect of woman's situation must be changed if she is to be liberated from oppression?
8. What challenges will a liberated woman still face?

For Further Thought

1. Write a short story that illustrates the ambiguity of human existence and its temptations.

2. How much of what de Beauvoir hoped for for women has been accomplished, in your view? What remains to be done?

3. Write an essay on some aspect of more recent feminist thought, comparing it to de Beauvoir. A good starting place is the survey by Robin May Schott, *Discovering Feminist Philosophy* (New York: Rowman & Littlefield Publishers, Inc., 2003).

Notes

1. Individual writings collected in *Simone de Beauvoir: Philosophical Writings*, ed. Margaret A. Simons (Urbana: University of Illinois Press, 2004), are referenced by page numbers as follows:
   PC: Pyrrhus and Cineas
   MIPR: Moral Idealism and Political Realism
   EPW: Existentialism and Popular Wisdom

EE: An Eye for an Eye
ELA: An Existentialist Looks at Americans

2. Quoted in Elizabeth Fallaise, ed., *Simone de Beauvoir: A Critical Reader* (London: Routledge, 1998), 7.

3. Quoted in Conor Cruise O'Brien, *Albert Camus of Europe and Africa* (New York: Viking Press, 1970), 17–18.

4. Simone de Beauvoir, *The Ethics of Ambiguity* (New York: Citadel Press, 1948, 1976). References are given as *EA* by page numbers.

5. Simone de Beauvoir, *The Second Sex,* trans. H. M. Parshley (New York: Vintage Books, 1989). References are given as *SS* to page numbers.

26

POSTMODERNISM AND PHYSICAL REALISM

Derrida, Rorty, Quine, and Dennett

In this chapter we will look at two different tendencies in late-twentieth-century philosophy, ways of thinking that owe much to what has gone before and carry the conversation further. I shall call them "postmodernism" and "physical realism," though it is hard to be sure of the best terminology. Let us consider them in that order.[1]

Postmodernism

A diverse group of thinkers are often loosely grouped together as "postmodern"—a term that is extremely vague. Richard Rorty says that it "has been rendered almost meaningless by being used to mean so many different things" (*PSH*, 262), but perhaps we can get some idea of it by noting a few of the things so-called "postmodernists" are against. They criticize or protest many of the central themes of the Enlightenment, a project they are likely to call a failure. Thus they are suspicious of claims to truth, objectivity, rationality, universality, and criteria that purport to be more than local. They are

dubious about the idea that natural science is an apt model for knowledge in general. They doubt that philosophy as it has been practiced in the Descartes, Hume, Kant tradition can serve as a judge of the true and the good. And they want to leave behind (or destroy) the metaphysical pretensions of philosophy to grasp some absolute reality beyond appearance.[*]

Postmodernism is extremely controversial because much of it tends toward subjectivism (there is no objective truth available), relativism (what's "true for me" may not be "true for you"), and irrationalism (supposedly rational arguments are merely masks for attempts at domination). In a recent book, for instance, Thomas Nagel (b. 1937) deplores its influence:

> The worst of it is that subjectivism is not just an inconsequential intellectual flourish or badge of theoretical chic. It is used to deflect argument, or to

---

[*]The postmodern–enlightenment dichotomy is in many ways a reenactment of the Sophist–Socrates quarrel in ancient Greece. For a look at this historical antecedent, see pp. 40–49 and 63–67.

belittle the pretensions of the arguments of others. Claims that something is without relativistic qualification true or false, right or wrong, good or bad, risk being derided as expressions of a parochial perspective or form of life—not as a preliminary to showing that they are mistaken whereas something else is right, but as a way of showing that nothing is right and that instead we are all expressing our personal or cultural points of view. The actual result has been a growth in the already extreme intellectual laziness of contemporary culture and the collapse of serious argument throughout the lower reaches of the humanities and social sciences, together with a refusal to take seriously, as anything other than first-person avowals, the objective arguments of others.[2]

Whether that is a just critique of the movement remains to be seen. To better understand what this controversial thought might be like, we will look at two forms it can take: deconstruction as formulated by Jacques Derrida and Richard Rorty's liberal ironism. Both thinkers are often classified as postmodernists—though neither is really happy with that.

Deconstruction: Jacques Derrida

The idea of "deconstructing texts" has had a very wide influence in the latter part of the twentieth century. On the assumption that language structures all our thought and action—not just speech and literature in all its forms, but also social institutions and political structures—the notion of a "text" seems applicable everywhere. If all our understandings are structured by the specific language we speak, and without that structuring would be impossible, then all our experience is a kind of *text* to be read, interpreted, understood (or misunderstood)—and deconstructed. No one has been more influential in working out the idea of deconstruction than the French philosopher, Jacques Derrida (1930–2004).

To understand deconstruction, it will help to get as clear as we can about what it aims to deconstruct—what the main enemy is taken to be. And to do that let us remind ourselves of certain themes in Heidegger. In *Being and Time* Heidegger adopts (or adapts) Husserl's method of phenomenology to lay bare the essence of human existing—what he calls *Dasein*. To proceed phenomenologically is to try to set aside the assumptions, presuppositions, and interpretations that are normally brought to experience; the aim is to let what is experienced—the phenomenon—simply *show itself as it is,* and then to describe it with care by identifying its essential features.

Although he hopes ultimately to clarify the *meaning of Being,* Heidegger provisionally examines *our* mode of Being—Dasein (our "being here")—to discern the *ontological structure* of human existence. He describes this structure in terms of concepts called "existentials," among which are *Being-in-the-world, the One, attunement, understanding, discourse, inauthentic existence, Being-in-the-truth, Being-toward-death, conscience, care,* and *temporality.** Using these concepts, Heideggerian phenomenology aims to disclose the very essence of human existence, what it is to *Be* in the way that human beings *are.* Notice that he takes for granted that there *is* something—something prior to all description—in which Dasein's Being consists. There is a *truth* about our being here, and that truth is revealed phenomenologically via these existential concepts. Human existence as a phenomenon is laid bare—self-evident, undeniable—a *presence* to be recognized and described. Thus is the aim of phenomenology fulfilled.

In his later work Heidegger turns away from the claim that discovering the essence of human existence will lead us directly to the meaning of Being itself. But he does not turn away from the idea that the goal is still *presence.* Nor does he turn away from the idea that understanding entities, through the sciences, for instance, does not suffice to grasp the meaning of Being. Entities, beings, *are*—and the issue is to grasp what that means, that they *are.* This "ontological difference" between Being itself and the beings that "have Being" remains crucial to the later Heidegger's thought, as does the quest to appropriate Being in its very *presence.* Such appropriation becomes more of a hope for the future than a present reality, however, given that our era is dominated by a scientific/technological way of appre-

---

*Heidegger's existential phenomenology is discussed on pp. 649–675.

hending anything that "blocks the shining-forth and holding sway of truth."* Still, Heidegger says, "From the dawn of Western-European thinking until today, Being means the same as presencing."† If we could allow the *presencing of beings* itself to be present, that might make all the difference—might change us, save us, rescue us from this long era of blindness to Being and deliver us into the "truth of Being."

Now it is precisely this notion of *presence* that Derrida has in his sights. To make it more clear let us cite some other examples.

- In Plato's allegory of the cave, the prisoner turns away from mere shadows of reality and climbs slowly, with difficulty, into the sunlight outside the cave, where she will eventually *see* the truth of things. This "seeing," towards which Plato's epistemology drives, is a case of the Forms being *present* to the knower. The Forms *have Being* in the strictest sense—eternally and unchangeably—and "the eye of the soul" can register them in their *presence*. (See pp. 133–137.)

- In Socrates' discourse about beauty, the final stage on the ladder of love is the "revelation" of a "wondrous vision" of Beauty itself, "an everlasting loveliness." Presence again. (See p. 139.)

- Aristotle argues that not everything can be demonstrated—on pain of an infinite regress—so the first principles just have to be *seen* to be true, seen as they *present* themselves to the mind. (See pp. 166–168.)

- Descartes, seeking something he cannot doubt, finds it in the *cogito,* the "I think, therefore I am" principle. This is so clearly and distinctly *present* to his mind that it can play the role of a first certainty; on this he can build. (See pp. 338–341.)

- Hume may be skeptical about external things, causality, the self, and God; but impressions are just *there!*—present in experience. You can't doubt the blue triangle when it *presents* itself in your visual field. (See pp. 401–402.)

- Kant's transcendental critique of reason *presents* us with the constitutive principles of any rational mind, both theoretical (causality, for example) and practical (the categorical imperative). We simply have to recognize—that the buck stops there. (See pp. 428–431.)

- For Hegel such presence is not available to us here and now, but it is what the dialectic of history is driving toward: absolute knowledge, where the gap between the knower and the known is overcome—pure *presence*. In the end, Spirit will have in full the *presence* denied to us wanderers along the way. (See pp. 464–469, 476–478.)

More examples could be cited, but that is enough to give you the sense that Derrida is concerned with something central in the philosophical tradition. The assumption at work is that at some point we come face to face with undeniable, clear, self-evident truth because the object of that truth is immediately present to our consciousness. At that point we can think the truth, express the truth, speak the truth. The object reveals itself as it is and all we have to do is *signify* its nature in language. Derrida calls this assumption **logocentrism.*** This logocentric presumption, Derrida thinks, pervades our tradition. We could put it this way: *Presence* can guarantee the truth of basic propositions, thus providing *foundations* to build on, and *argument* can guarantee the solidity of the building built on those foundations.† As deconstructionists sometimes put it, logocentrism "privileges" reason as an avenue to truth and goodness.

But of course these truths must be expressed in language, and there's the rub. Derrida notes that

---

*See p. 680.
†See p. 681.

*The Greek term *logos* is rich with connotations, all of which Derrida means to draw on. It can mean "word" or "speech" or "discourse" or "argument" or "rational account."
†As we shall see, Richard Rorty uses the metaphor of the mind as a mirror to express this logocentric assumption. The presence of an object is supposed to be reflected perfectly in a suitably cleaned up and polished mirror. Traditionally, epistemology was the polishing agent.

"There is nothing outside the text."

—Jacques Derrida

language takes two forms, spoken and written. For the most part we think that speaking has a kind of priority over writing, and many philosophers have thought so, too. Plato, for instance, sees writing as a secondary and inherently dangerous form of language. After all (so the thought goes), when I speak I am simply expressing my thought, and what I think is immediately present to my consciousness. There is no *gap,* as it were, between the *presence* of a yellow patch in my visual field and the thought, "Yellow here now." And if I *say* what I think, this speaking is a direct expression of the thought. My language is transparent to my meaning; it doesn't need interpretation. What I mean is obvious on the face of it.* In speech, then, my language is directly

---

*Hegel, of course, long ago expressed doubts about this "immediacy." See pp. 467–469 for his critique of "sense-certainty."

"in touch," so to speak, with my meaning, which is just what it is, unquestionable and present in all its fullness. What I say has an authentic *origin* in what is present to me; with respect to what I *mean,* I have a *privileged access.*

With writing, however, it is different. The link to presence is broken. Writing escapes my control. It is a set of mere marks—arbitrary, lifeless signs—sent out there in the world; who knows what someone will make of them? The reader is not present to what I intend to communicate, but *absent.* This absence is accentuated by the reproducibility of writing. What Plato wrote has been cited, quoted, copied over and over, and is now read by endless numbers of readers unknown to him in contexts unimagined by him. This absence of readers to what Plato intended to say is an essential feature of writing.

> In order for my "written communication" to retain its function as writing, i.e., its readability, it must remain readable despite the absolute disappearance of any receiver, determined in general. My communication must be repeatable—iterable—in the absolute absence of the receiver or of any empirically determinable collectivity of receivers. Such iterability . . . structures the mark of writing itself, no matter what particular type of writing is involved. . . . A writing that is not structurally readable—iterable—beyond the death of the addressee would not be writing. (*SEC,* 7)

In this contrast between speech and writing we have one of a number of **binary oppositions** that Derrida thinks have dominated the Western philosophical tradition.* In each of these oppositions, one of the pair is given primacy; the other is its shadow, derivative from the first and dependent on it. Logocentrism gives priority to speaking (*logos*), thinking of speech as the "good" form of language—basic, secure, mirroring presence—while regarding writing as a derived, secondary, insecure, "bad" form of language. Speaking is good be-

---

*Others are: presence/absence, soul/body, form/matter, one/many, reality/appearance, literal/metaphorical, nature/culture, male/female, light/darkness, good/evil. Such binary oppositions are among the main things that deconstruction aims to deconstruct.

cause it is associated with certainty, with finality, with the truth; when I speak I merely body forth in an external way what I *know* internally; I *represent* the truth in language. Writing lacks this immediate certification in consciousness. All of the philosophers cited in the above list, Derrida thinks, are logocentric in this sense.

If this contrast seems just common sense, that may be because we have been brought up in the Western philosophical tradition. But Derrida now pushes this thought in a radical direction.

> I would like to demonstrate that the traits that can be recognized in the classical, narrowly defined concept of writing are generalizable. They are valid not only for all orders of "signs" and for all languages in general but . . . for the entire field of what philosophy would call experience, even the experience of being: the above-mentioned "presence." (*SEC,* 9)

To demonstrate this, Derrida does two things. He brings to bear certain aspects of the linguistic theory developed by a Swiss linguist, Ferdinand de Saussure, and he tries to show that this opposition undermines itself even in the texts of philosophers who are most "logocentric"—that is, he *deconstructs* their texts. Let us look at each of these in turn.

***Writing, Iterability,* Différance**　　Saussure notes that the signs of which language is composed, whether spoken or written, are arbitrary. There is no natural connection between the word "dog" and dogs. The existence of (what we call) a dog does not necessitate that we have just this word expressing just this concept, for there is no necessity that we parcel up the world in precisely this way: into dogs and all the rest. Because language is arbitrary, that way of classifying, too, is arbitrary. So the word "dog" doesn't mean what it does because of *dogs.* But what, then, makes a word the word that it is, meaning what it does, expressing the concept that it expresses? Saussure's answer is: its *differences* from all other words.

Language forms a system of differences. Its signs are not linked directly to immediately present objects—or even to meanings—but mean what they do because of the way they are related to and differ from other signs. Let us speak of a term like

"dog" as a *signifier.* Then we can call both the meaning of that term (the concept) and an actual dog (the referent) the *signified.* Because language is constituted by a system of differences rather than by direct signification of meanings or objects,

> the signified concept is never present in and of itself, in a sufficient presence that would refer only to itself. Essentially and lawfully, every concept is inscribed in a chain or in a system within which it refers to the other, to concepts, by means of the systematic play of differences. (*D,* 11)

Think of it this way. What makes an utterance or an inscription of the word "dog" refer to dogs is not a simple arrowlike relation between the word and the reality, but a many-faceted, many-layered system of relationships that the word has to other things: to other words like "cat" and "animal" and "pet," to actual critters, to human intentions and behavior, and to the contexts in which the word is uttered or written, heard or read. It is the ways it is *different* from all these related factors that makes it mean what it does. This principle of difference, Derrida says, "affects the *totality* of the sign, that is the sign as both signified and signifier" (*D,* 10). To an unspecifiable degree, both words and their meanings float free of the world we normally think they are anchored to.

If Derrida is right, then the situation is *not* like this: I first have a meaning in mind; then I search for language to express it. On the contrary, meanings are not entities with natures of their own; they do not exist independently of language in some Platonic realm of essences. The *meaning* of the word "dog" (the signified) is completely dependent on the signifier—this conventional sign, "dog," that is part of the language. And this signifier is what it is because of the role it plays in a larger economy of language uses.*

Derrida calls the words I use, even those I use in speaking the "present" contents of my mind, *traces.* A word is not an atomic unity isolated from everything else. Rather, a word is simply a trace of all those relationships in all those networks that

---

*There are similarities here to Wittgenstein's slogan, "The meaning is the use." See p. 630.

make it signify what it does. A word is like a footprint or a mark showing that something else responsible for it is in the neighborhood. So what determines the identity of a word is largely *absent* from the occasion of utterance. And the same is true, for the above reasons, for the meaning it expresses.

Moreover, my language (English in my case) is not something I control; it is a system of signifiers that has a reality independent of me. It shapes me much more than I shape it. Since the words of my language are not constituted by anything I do, but rather by these differential relationships to other things, there can never be what the logocentric tradition assumes: language that expresses directly, in its plenitude or fullness, solely what is *present* to my consciousness. My language is always already caught up in a network of associations that go far beyond the present moment. What determines what I mean is not wholly in my power.

The consequence is that speaking is no better off than writing. In fact, Derrida holds that what has been held to be characteristic of writing is true also of speech: that it is unstable, separated by an unbridgeable gap from what it is about, and subject to various possible interpretations. It is no longer possible to claim that what I say has its origin solely in what is present to me, since what I say depends as well on what I do not say but is in the background of what I say—all of which helps to constitute the meaning of what I say.

Speaking, just like writing, is iterable, repeatable, quotable, capable of being "grafted" into other contexts, its meaning subject to "drift" (*SEC,* 9). Like writing, a spoken utterance can be "repeated in the absence not only of its 'referent,' which is self-evident, but in the absence of a determinate signified or of the intention of actual signification" (*SEC,* 10). It is obvious, Derrida says, that we can use a term in the absence of what it refers to: I can talk about a dog when no dog is present and I can talk about the absent past and the absent future. But he adds that a term can be used even in the absence of intention. What does that mean?

We usually think that the meaning of what I say (given a language) is determined by two factors: my intention and the context. But Derrida argues that neither one can make what I say completely determinate. Meaning something, intending something, is itself language-permeated. I can no more intend to say that I'll return your lawn mower without making use of my linguistic skills than I can manage the actual return without physical skills. Being linguistic in character, however, even intentions are not *wholly present* to the meanings they purport to convey; they, too, are made up of traces of what is absent; so even intentions cannot *anchor* my meaning securely; they cannot eliminate the inevitable drift because they, too, are textlike, requiring interpretation—more like writing than you would ordinarily think. Intentions, too, can be grafted into alternative contexts and get different readings. There is a certain *absence,* then, that permeates even the simplest intending-to-say, a fissure that opens between my intention and my meaning.* This does not mean that my intentions are irrelevant to what I say. The category of intention, Derrida says, "will not disappear; it will have its place, but from that place it will no longer be able to govern the entire scene and system of utterance" (*SEC,* 18).

The same is true of contexts. The contexts that are relevant, of course, are not contexts-in-themselves, contexts that are unknown and unknowable, but contexts as they are understood (by speaker, hearer, quoter, and so on). And so long as understanding comes into it, language comes into it. The same iterability, then, will potentially destabilize any characterization of the context. So neither intention nor context can freeze the flow of meaning into something absolutely, perfectly, completely definite. It's a matter of interpretation all the way down.

This means that the privilege tradition has ascribed to speech over writing is undone, that in fact writing—or the features ascribed to writing—is more fundamental, more "original" than speech.

---

*This is why deconstructionists say an author may not always be the best interpreter of his own works. In a sense, the author occupies exactly the same position with respect to what he has written as the reader; both offer interpretations of a text that escapes their control. Some deconstructionists have gone so far as to speak of "the death of the author," as though what the author intends by what she writes is completely irrelevant and the reader rules. As we see, however, Derrida does not go so far.

Derrida does not mean, of course, to make a historical claim here—to say that writing chronologically pre-dated speech. That would be absurd. The claim is rather that the characteristics of what was held to be secondary and derivative are already, and necessarily, found in what was thought to be basic and primary. It is not, then, that the speech/writing dichotomy is simply overturned, so that it becomes writing/speech, with writing now in the primary spot, but that a deeper sense of "writing" is discovered that underwrites both terms.* Derrida sometimes calls this deeper sense *arche-writing* to signify that the system of differences Saussure found in language infects all of thought and speech—and always has. Thus does Derrida deconstruct the traditional binary opposition between speech and writing.

Derrida's most characteristic term for this non-presence of what is meant by a bit of language is **différance.** The French term for the English "difference" is "différence"—spelled the same but pronounced "dee-fer-ahnz." In a Heidegger-like move, Derrida changes the second "e" to an "a," thus creating a technical term that borrows from the ordinary but—well, differs from it. Derrida delights in the fact that this change of a letter shows up only in writing and doesn't change the pronunciation. As Derrida uses the term, "différance" expresses a certain double meaning. It signifies (1) *to differ* (to be other than) and (2) *to defer* (to postpone, to put off). It is *différance* that accounts for the fact that a word means what it does in virtue of differing from other words; *différance* also separates a word from its meaning, assures its difference from that very meaning. Moreover, what a word means is never absolutely present at the time of its use, so its meaning is deferred, delayed, put off to an interpretation—to a different set of words that, of course, don't *present* its meaning either. If you long to find

what Plato calls "traveller's rest" and "journey's end" (see p. 130), you are bound to be disappointed. There is no point at which "the eye of the soul" can stop and behold truth, or beauty, or Being. *Différance* ensures that that point is indefinitely delayed. Every sign is merely the sign of another sign; every sign is a detour on the way to presence. For the "unveiling of truth," *différance* substitutes "incessant deciphering" (D, 18).

Différance applies to itself, too, of course. Derrida takes some pains to make this point. He says, paradoxically, that *différance* is "neither a word nor a concept" (D, 3, 5), meaning that we should not suppose that here, at last, we have the *truth* about meaning, reference, truth, and Being. *Différance,* he goes on to say, "is never presented as such" and "has neither existence nor essence" (D, 6). He goes so far as to say that *différance* "is not" (D, 6, 21).

> What is written as *différance,* then, will be the playing movement that "produces"—by means of something that is not simply an activity—these differences, these effects of difference. This does not mean that the *différance* that produces differences is somehow before them, in a simple and unmodified—in-different—present. *Différance* is the non-full, non-simple, structured and differentiating origin of differences. Thus, the name "origin" no longer suits it (D, 11).

> It governs nothing, reigns over nothing, and nowhere exercises any authority. It is not announced by any capital letter. Not only is there no kingdom of *différance,* but *différance* instigates the subversion of every kingdom. Which makes it obviously threatening and infallibly dreaded by everything within us that desires a kingdom, the past or future presence of a kingdom. (D, 22)

Note that Derrida isn't claiming that all words are ambiguous or polysemic (having more than one meaning). Even if you straighten out an ambiguity by saying, "No, I mean the sort of bank you put your money in, not the sort that you fish from," *différance* does its work on that clarification. There is nothing in this clarifying sentence that a hearer may not inscribe in other contexts, no words that aren't mere traces of other words, no meaning that isn't deferred, nothing that will escape semantic drift. Derrida's term for this phenomenon is *dissemination*.

---

*This structure is common to deconstructionist treatments of all those binary oppositions mentioned earlier. It is similar to the surpassing of opposites in Hegel (see pp. 468–469 for examples), except that there is not even the temporary illusion of completion in the third term, nor any hope of eventually attaining *presence* via a unity of subject and object. This kind of metaphysical hope Derrida means to put beyond us forever.

Meaning is spread, scattered, distributed widely, disseminated rather than gathered all in one spot to be grasped in a simple act of understanding a word.

> What we know, or what we would know if it were simply a question here of something to know, is that there has never been, never will be, a unique word, a master-name. (*D*, 27)

Not even *différance!*

> There will be no unique name, even if it were the name of Being. And we must think this without *nostalgia*, that is, outside of the myth of a purely maternal or paternal language, a lost native country of thought. On the contrary, we must *affirm* this, in the sense in which Nietzsche puts affirmation into play, in a certain laughter and a certain step of the dance. (*D*, 27)*

One of Derrida's most notorious pronouncements is that "there is nothing outside the text." Some have thought that Derrida means that in offering an interpretation of some text (written or spoken) one should restrict oneself to that text— that in understanding Shakespeare, for instance, one needn't take into account the conditions of life in Elizabethan England. But the dissemination of meaning indicates that there are in principle no limits to what may be relevant in understanding a text. Derrida says that

> the concept of text I propose is limited neither to the graphic, nor to the book, nor even to discourse, and even less to the semantic, representational, symbolic, ideal, or ideological sphere. What I call "text" implies all the structures called "real," "economic," "historical," socio-institutional, in short: all possible referents. [To say that there is nothing outside the text] does not mean that all referents are suspended, denied, or enclosed in a book . . . , but it does mean that every referent, all reality has the structure of a differential trace, and that one cannot refer to this "real" except in an interpretive experience. The latter neither yields meaning nor assumes it except in a movement of differential referring. That's all. (*LI*, 148)

Does "nothing outside the text" amount to a kind of linguistic idealism, then, a theory that there

is nothing more to the world than our language says there is?* Derrida wants to deny that, but the claim that "every referent, all reality has the structure of a differential trace" strongly suggests it. Why, we might ask, should "all reality" have just the structure that Derrida finds in the *language* we use to describe it? He clearly means to say that everything we could possibly understand is infected by undecidability because understanding is necessarily expressed in language. But so understood, the claim comes to this: that language about reality is linguistic in character. And that is a tautology that is neither very interesting nor very exciting. Most commentators remain puzzled by this provocative remark.

Do these reflections support the idea that there is nothing to a text but what a reader finds there— that every text is open to a completely free play of interpretative understandings? Some partisans of deconstruction have read Derrida that way, but he denies that he has ever said anything of the sort. For one thing, the idea of "complete" freedom goes against the grain of his insistence that there can be no completeness anywhere. But more importantly, he emphasizes that not all readings are equally good. To read Rousseau well, for instance (Derrida has a book on Rousseau),

> one must understand and write, even translate French as well as possible, know the corpus of Rousseau as well as possible, including all the contexts that determine it (the literary, philosophical, rhetorical traditions, the history of the French language, society, history, which is to say, so many other things as well). Otherwise, one could indeed say just anything at all, and I have never accepted saying, or encouraging others to say, just anything at all, nor have I argued for indeterminacy as such. (*LI*, 144, 145)

Derrida believes his reflections on language will make possible *better* ways to read texts, *better* ways of discovering both the relative stabilities that exist there and the internal inconsistencies, the gaps, the slips and slides that *différance* makes possible.

---

*Compare Nietzsche, p. 563.

*Compare Hegel's idealism, where being is always *for* a conscious subject (pp. 476–478). If we substitute "language" for "conscious subject" do we get Derrida's idea?

. . . let it be said in passing how surprised I have often been, how amused or discouraged, depending on my humor, by the use or abuse of the following argument: Since the deconstructionist (which is to say, isn't it, the skeptic-relativist-nihilist!) is supposed not to believe in truth, stability, or the unity of meaning, in intention or "meaning to say," how can he demand of us that we read *him* with pertinence, precision, rigor? How can he demand that his own text be interpreted correctly? How can he accuse anyone else of having misunderstood, simplified, deformed it, etc.? In other words, how can he discuss, and discuss the reading of what he writes? The answer is simple enough: this definition of the deconstructionist is *false* (that's right: false, not true) and feeble; it supposes a bad (that's right: bad, not good) and feeble reading of numerous texts, first of all mine, which therefore must finally be read or reread. Then perhaps it will be understood that the value of truth (and all those values associated with it) is never contested or destroyed in my writings, but only reinscribed in more powerful, larger, more statified contexts. And that within interpretive contexts . . . that are relatively stable, sometimes apparently almost unshakeable, it should be possible to invoke rules of competence, criteria of discussion and of consensus, good faith, lucidity, rigor, criticism, and pedagogy. (*LI,* 146)

So it is not the case that anything goes. The recognition of *différance* and all its multifarious effects does not do away with rigor, Derrida urges, but enables a new and enlarged kind of rigor. He does believe, however, that his analysis of language means the end of the logocentric era. This long history of searching for sure and certain foundations, of trying to base a theory of reality and moral goodness on the very presence of Being itself, this reliance on rationality to deliver the *truth,* is now over. Metaphysics is over, finished, done for. There is no firm ground to stand on to distinguish appearance from reality, rhetoric from argument, or metaphor from a literal use of language. If "modernism" is a continuation of that logocentric quest in those who share Enlightenment hopes, then Derrida is definitely a "postmodernist."

Deconstructing a Text We now have the main themes of deconstruction in hand. Let us more briefly turn to an example of what deconstruction looks like when applied to a text. We can think of a text, whether spoken or written or embedded in some institutional context (a constitution, a legal system, a religion) as an attempt to construct an edifice, one that will withstand the winds of criticism and the earthquakes that might shake its foundations. Reading a text is like observing the building under construction. You read Plato or Aristotle or Nietzsche, or you study the United States Constitution or the mores of family life in Fiji, and as you go along it looks good. It looks solid, well-grounded, consistent, and persuasive. It has obviously been well thought out, carefully planned, assembled with attention to detail.

But if you look more closely you begin to see cracks in the walls, parts that do not fit well with other parts, some aspects that tend to undermine others, and you can begin to see that the building trembles. It is not as secure as it first looked. This instability is inevitable, given the structures of *différance,* since nowhere is it possible to find absolutely firm ground to build on. The lack of stability tends to show up in what Derrida calls the "margins," in things that don't seem central to the argument or thesis—in footnotes, prefaces, rhetorical devices, parentheses, metaphors. Just where everything looks firm and solid, things begin to slip and slide.

To stick with the subject we have been focusing on, let us take as an example Derrida's analysis of Plato's dialogue, *Phaedrus.* Plato is certainly one of the central figures in the logocentric tradition, perhaps the most influential one of all.* It is Plato whose love of wisdom puts dialectical reasoning—logic, argument—at the heart of philosophy, and it is Plato who believes that eventually we simply have to *see* the truth for ourselves. Education, remember, is understood as "turning the soul" of the student toward reality so she can apprehend for herself its truth and beauty;† and it is by dialectical argument that the soul is turned. Moreover, it is Socrates who carries on a long controversy with the

---

*Recall Whitehead's remark that all of philosophy is merely a set of footnotes to Plato (p. 117).
†Reread Plato's Myth of the Cave, pp. 133–136.

Sophists, trying to establish the difference between a rational quest for the truth and "mere" rhetoric. It is no surprise to Derrida, then, to find that Plato's Socrates contrasts writing unfavorably with speech and warns in a myth of the dangers of writing.*

In this myth one of the gods of Egypt, Thoth, offers writing to King Thamus as a gift that will benefit his people. Thoth says that writing will make them wiser and improve their memory. But the king refuses the gift. He says that it will on the contrary increase forgetfulness, since people won't have to exercise their memories. Writing will substitute *reminding* for *remembering,* and people will have only a semblance of wisdom rather than the real thing.† They will think they know what they do not really know,‡ and this will make them arrogant and difficult to get along with. Writing, the king says, is composed of marks external to the soul and is a poor substitute for the direct apprehension of the truth. Writing is just a ghost of true knowledge.

All these themes we have already explored above, and here we find them right at the beginnings of the Western philosophical tradition. What can a deconstructive reading of this text reveal? First of all, one is struck by the fact that it is *in writing* that Plato warns of the dangers of writing! Plato writes a myth that tells us that writing (in contrast with speaking) is simply repeating without knowing. So it is the written myth that repeats without knowing the definition of writing—which is to repeat without knowing (*PP,* 75). Here we see a rhetorical device, the writing of a myth, cutting away at the very substance of the argument that the myth is devised to express. Suddenly the argument wobbles.

That's paradoxical enough, perhaps. But Socrates goes on to characterize a more authentic discourse than this external writing that is absent from its origin and subject to varying interpretations.

This interior discourse, Socrates says, is "living and animate," and "written in the soul of the learner" (*Phaedrus,* 276 a,b). Now this is quite extraordinary. "Written" in the soul, Plato writes.

> While presenting writing as a false brother—traitor, infidel, and simulacrum—Socrates is for the first time led to envision the brother of this brother, the legitimate one, as *another sort of writing:* not merely as a knowing, living, animate discourse, but as an *inscription* of truth in the soul. It is no doubt usually assumed that what we are dealing with here is a "metaphor." . . . But it is not any less remarkable here that the so-called living discourse should suddenly be described by a "metaphor" borrowed from the order of the very thing one is trying to exclude from it, the order of its simulacrum. (*PP,* 149)

Derrida *deconstructs* Plato's text here by showing how its meaning implicitly depends on exactly what it aims to exclude, denigrate, and show to be inferior. It seems as if Plato, against his will, is testifying to precisely the sort of thing Derrida has been urging: that *nowhere* is there any discourse that goes straight to the truth, that all knowledge participates in the undecidability characteristic of writing and always, always requires interpretation—even when it is written in the soul.

Derrida sometimes says that deconstruction is not a method and not a technique, by which he seems to mean that there is nothing mechanical or rule-governed about it. Yet it is a certain way of reading a text or of understanding institutions and customs. Deconstruction is above all *suspicious*—suspecting that all is not as cheery and solid as it is made out to be and looking for signs of instability and slip. Often enough, though perhaps not as often as some deconstructionists think, it is right.

---

*See *Phaedrus,* 274cff.

†Compare Heidegger on "idle talk," "curiosity," and "ambiguity" as modes of inauthentic existence (pp. 664–666). Also see Wittgenstein on "just *gassing*" (pp. 607, 633).

‡Recall how Socrates at his trial characterizes his own wisdom: He does not claim to know what he in fact does not know. Socrates calls this "human" wisdom. (See pp. 87–88.)

1. In what sense can everything we experience be thought of as a "text"?
2. Explain the way in which *presence* appears in three or four different philosophies.
3. What are the central features of *logocentrism?*
4. Explain the traditional way of understanding the difference between speaking and writing.

5. Saussure says that language is "a system of differences." Explain.

6. Explain the terms "signified" and "signifier." In what ways, if Derrida is right, does the former depend on the latter?

7. How does *iterability* insert drift and play into language and undercut its ability to represent in full the *presence* of the signified?

8. Why can neither intention nor context completely determine the meaning of a linguistic item?

9. How is the speech/writing binary opposition deconstructed by Derrida?

10. Explain *différance*.

11. What is *dissemination*? Why does he call a word a *trace*?

12. Why do deconstructionists think it is especially profitable to pay attention to the *margins* of a text?

13. What does Derrida find in the margins of Plato's *Phaedrus* that offers a foothold to deconstruction?

Liberal Ironist: Richard Rorty

Richard Rorty (b. 1931) considers Wittgenstein, Heidegger, and Dewey to be the greatest philosophers of the twentieth century; of these three he ranks John Dewey first.* He calls Dewey his "principal philosophical hero," the philosopher he most admires, and the person of whom he should most like to think himself a disciple (*PSH*, xii, xvii). Correspondingly, Rorty's favorite characterization of his own views is "pragmatism," and he thinks of himself as drawing the consequences of that point of view even more consistently than Dewey did. The justification for considering him under the rubric of postmodernism is that he exemplifies most of the major themes of that diffuse movement.

Like Dewey he considers that he is merely working out the consequences for human life of taking Darwin seriously. Most of philosophy, he thinks, has still not caught up with Darwin. He says of his version of pragmatism that is "an attempt to alter our self-image so as to make it consistent with the Darwinian claim that we differ from other animals simply in the complexity of our behavior." We are "exceptionally clever animals," nothing more (*PSH*, 72). As Rorty sees it, Darwin's evolutionary

"A liberal society is one which is content to call 'true' (or 'right' or 'just') . . . whatever view wins in a free and open encounter."

—RICHARD RORTY

theory is one more step in the long process of "de-divinizing" the world. It is Rorty's aim to complete that process.

Here is how the story goes, according to Rorty. People—even the intellectuals—used to believe in God. The pragmatic "cash-value" of such belief was that we felt ourselves responsible to something beyond ourselves, to a being greater than we. When the sciences began to give us more control over the world and our lives, belief in God began to wane.* But there still seemed to be something beyond ourselves to which we had to adjust our beliefs, some-

---

*He also expresses admiration for Derrida.

*Compare Nietzsche's tale of "How the Real World Finally Became a Fable," p. 541.

thing with an "essential nature" that our theories had to "correspond" to. We owed it to reality—to the world and to the self—to make our theories *true* of it. And so was born modern philosophy with its primary focus on epistemology.

Philosophy was now supposed to take over that "priestly" function of religion—mediating between us and reality. Philosophers became the authorities, supplying criteria for "truth" and "knowledge" and "objectivity," thus getting us in touch with the metaphysical depths and revealing who we really are, what the world is, and how we ought to live. But philosophy done on these "metaphysical" assumptions, Rorty thinks, has played itself out; the lesson we should draw from Wittgenstein, Heidegger, and Dewey is that this tradition is over. And in any case we can now see that this history has been a history of immaturity, of infantilism—based on the thought that we humans cannot take responsibility for ourselves but must bow to some power, some reality beyond us. The culture Rorty aspires to is one in which no trace of divinity remains,

> either in the form of a divinized world or a divinized self. Such a culture would have no room for the notion that there are nonhuman forces to which human beings should be responsible. It would drop, or drastically reinterpret, not only the idea of holiness but those of "devotion to truth" and of "fulfillment of the deepest needs of the spirit." The process of de-divinization . . . would, ideally, culminate in our no longer being able to see any use for the notion that finite, mortal, contingently existing human beings might derive the meanings of their lives from anything except other finite, mortal contingently existing human beings. (*CIS*, 45)

Rorty wants us to grow up, and in his view that means getting to the point where "we no longer worship *anything,* where we treat *nothing* as a quasi divinity, where we treat *everything*— our language, our conscience, our community—as a product of time and chance" (*CIS,* 22). It is this determination to see everything about us as subject to this **contingency** that is Rorty's leading theme.

Contingency, Truth, and Anti-Essentialism We have noted Rorty's story of a certain kind of histor-

ical "progress," but he also has arguments.[*] To aspire to the *truth* about things is to assume that we can take truth as a goal. But Rorty argues that this makes no sense. There is no way we could ever determine the difference between a belief that is *true*—in the sense that it corresponds to reality—and a belief we think is *justified by the evidence.* After providing all the justification we can, taking into account what everyone has to say about the matter, what more could we do to discover whether it is true? Citing William James' pragmatic adage that every difference must make a difference,[†] Rorty concludes that

> we cannot regard truth as a goal of inquiry. The purpose of inquiry is to achieve agreement among human beings about what to do, to bring about consensus on the ends to be achieved and the means to be used to achieve those ends. Inquiry that does not achieve coordination of behavior is not inquiry but simply wordplay. (*PSH,* xxv)

This does not mean that we should refrain from using the word "true." Rorty himself uses it freely. But it is one of those words that he thinks we should "drastically reinterpret," bring down to a human scale. And if we do that we can see that it might have two uses. When we call a belief true in the normal course of events, we pay a kind of compliment to the belief, affirming that it is something we can rely on to satisfy our desires. In that sense, Rorty thinks, most of our beliefs are true. Indeed they cannot help but be true (i.e., reliable), since they are formed by an adjustment among ourselves, other persons, and the causal impact of the world on each of us.[‡] Beliefs that are untrue in this sense

---

[*]Not that there is anything wrong with imaginative stories. Rorty thinks that poetically extending the imagination is at least as important as producing arguments. "I think," he says, "that narratives are a perfectly fair means of persuasion" (*RC,* 24).
[†]See p. 577.
[‡]Rorty here relies on the view of Donald Davidson about the connection between beliefs, their meaning, and the truth. Suppose Jane says something that seems obviously false. You have three interpretations to choose from: (1) The sentence uttered means just what it seems to mean, it is false, and Jane has a mistaken belief. (2) The sentence means what it seems to mean, but she doesn't really believe what she seems to believe; she is lying, or kidding, or something of the sort. (3) She is not using words

are beliefs that are not useful; they will soon be extinguished by our continual interaction with the world.

The second use of the word "true" that Rorty recognizes he calls "cautionary." So-called "realists" sometimes think that they can drive a wedge between *being true* and *being justified* by pointing out that the following sentence makes perfect sense: "*P* is justified all right, but it isn't true." The argument is that this shouldn't make sense if truth collapses into justification; but since it does, it follows that truth cannot be "reduced" to justification—not even to Peircean justification by an ideal community of inquirers.* Being true, so the argument goes, cannot be the same as being justified.

But Rorty agrees that the sentence in question makes sense without conceding that this makes truth something independent of justification. When we say that a belief is justified but not true, Rorty says, we are using "true" in a *cautionary* way. In effect we are saying, "Yes, this looks like a belief we can rely on, but its looking that way might be just apparent; further inquiry might show it to be unjustified." There is nothing in this way of thinking about truth that shows it could be a goal independent of further justification. "*The **only** point in contrasting the true with the merely justified is to contrast a possible future with the actual present*" (*PSH*, 39)†— a possible future, that is, in which the belief we *now* think is true is shown to be untrue by further justification.

Rorty's denial that truth is correspondence to some independent reality with a nature of its own is part of a general attack on the notion of representation. We have noted the rise of a *representa-tional theory of knowledge and perception* in the views of Descartes, Locke, and their followers.* According to this theory, ideas in the mind can represent items external to the mind, but can also misrepresent them. Modern epistemology set itself to supply a *criterion* for distinguishing correct from incorrect ideas. Philosophers worked to assure us that, using suitable methods and taking suitable care, we can be confident that our ideas do not misrepresent reality. This image of the mind as a *mirror* of the world beyond it has dominated philosophical imagination from Descartes down to recent times— and Rorty thinks that for the most part it still does.†

> The picture which holds traditional philosophy captive is that of the mind as a great mirror, containing various representations—some accurate, some not—and capable of being studied by pure, nonempirical methods. Without the notion of the mind as a mirror, the notion of knowledge as accuracy of representation would not have suggested itself. Without this latter notion, the strategy common to Descartes and Kant—getting more accurate representations by inspecting, repairing, and polishing the mirror, so to speak—would not have made sense. Without this strategy in mind, recent claims that philosophy could consist of "conceptual analysis" or "phenomenological analysis" or "explication of meanings" or examination of "the logic of our language" . . . would not have made sense. (*PMN*, 12)

A whole nest of terms cluster around this mirror image, this "glassy essence" of the mind: representation, truth, knowledge, objectivity, universal validity, essential nature, appearance versus reality, and rationality. Rorty wants to leave them all behind, or at the very least, to redescribe them in ways consistent with his Darwinian pragmatism. Following Peirce and Dewey, Rorty says that words are tools and beliefs are habits of action. Tools and habits are not the sorts of things that represent; they are not appraised as true or false, but as useful or not useful.

---

with their normal meaning and what she actually believes is true, but that is not what she *seems* to believe. To understand others (and in the last analysis, ourselves) we "triangulate" among truth and falsehood, belief and desire, and meaning. Davidson, however, does not agree that truth is as dispensable as Rorty thinks. See "Truth Rehabilitated" (*RC*, 65–74).
*See Peirce on truth, pp. 570–572.
†It is clear that Rorty cannot accept the Platonic distinction between knowledge and opinion, since Plato assumes knowledge must be backed by reasons (justified) and *also* be true (in a correspondence sense of "true"). See pp. 119–120. Knowledge, for Rorty, collapses into well-justified opinion.

---

*The central theses of this theory can be found on p. 327.
†Using Derrida's terminology, we could say that Rorty aims to *deconstruct* the image of the mind as a mirror.

On this view, when we utter such sentences as "I am hungry" we are not making external what was previously internal, but are simply helping those around us to predict our future actions. Such sentences are not used to report events going on within the Cartesian Theatre which is a person's consciousness. They are simply tools for coordinating our behaviour with those of others. . . . There is no point in asking whether a belief represents reality, either mental reality or physical reality, accurately. That is, for pragmatists, not only a bad question, but the root of much wasted philosophical energy. . . .

The question to ask about our beliefs is not whether they are about reality or merely about appearance, but simply whether they are the best habits of action for gratifying our desires. (*PSH,* xxiv)

Words and beliefs, Rorty says, do not have a representational relationship to the world at all, but merely a causal one. Language is a set of tools for coping with the environment, tools that other animals do not have (or have only minimally). These tools are shaped in part by human purposes and in part by causal interactions with the world, and it is useless to try to disentangle the contributions on each side. Disentangling them is what you would have to do, however, if you wanted to isolate (as Kant wanted to) what we bring to experience from what the world provides, so as to get a picture of the world independent of our contribution to that picture. But Rorty quotes James again, "The trail of the human serpent is over all" (*PSH,* 15), and says it is impossible to separate out the two factors. And unnecessary, too.

No matter whether the tool is a hammer or a gun or a belief or a statement, tool-using is part of the interaction of the organism with its environment. To see the employment of words as the use of tools to deal with the environment, rather than as an attempt to represent the intrinsic nature of that environment, is to repudiate the question of whether human minds are in touch with reality—the question asked by the epistemological sceptic. No organism, human or non-human, is ever more or less in touch with reality than any other organism. The very idea of "being out of touch with reality" pre-

supposes the un-Darwinian, Cartesian picture of a mind which somehow swings free of the causal forces exerted on the body. The Cartesian mind is an entity whose relations with the rest of the universe are representational rather than causal. So to rid our thinking of the vestiges of Cartesianism, to become fully Darwinian in our thinking, we need to stop thinking of words as representations and to start thinking of them as nodes in the causal network which binds the organism together with its environment. (*PSH,* xxiii)

The world, then, in conjunction with our language-using community, causes us to hold certain beliefs; and we continue to hold those beliefs that prove to be reliable guides to getting what we want. That's all there is to it. The very idea of representation is pointless (*CIS,* 4).

Language is not a medium of representation. Rather, it is an exchange of marks and noises, carried out in order to achieve specific purposes. It cannot fail to represent accurately, for it never represents at all. (*PSH,* 50)*

Basic to any language is a vocabulary; it is in terms of that vocabulary that we identify things and distinguish one kind of thing from another. But if we now understand the language we speak in terms of "time and chance," it seems radically *contingent* that we should have just the vocabulary that we have. We speak as we do because of the causal history of the language and not because of the nature of the objects we deal with.† We could be expressing our science and common sense, our law and morality, our literature and religion, in ways quite different from the way we do. In none of those spheres is our vocabulary *dictated* by the realities we mean to talk about.‡

---

* This is Rorty's radical way of dealing with what Derrida calls "logocentrism."

† Other philosophers ask why it should be a matter of "either/ or" at this point. Why cannot we speak as we do *both* because the history of the language *and* because of the objects we deal with? Why cannot a belief be at once a node in a causal network and *also* a repesentation? See Peirce's analogy of the rainbow (p. 571) and Quine on p. 735.

† Again we find a theme common to Rorty and Derrida. See pp. 707–710.

Given that our vocabulary is a contingent set of tools for coping rather than written on the mind by the very nature of things, it is obvious that a variety of such tools may be possible. Rorty takes this to be one of the lessons of history, whether the history of science, of religion, or of culture in general. No vocabulary has any metaphysical backing; there is nothing outside a language by which to judge it. Like any tool, language can be changed, and perhaps improved. If we find that some part of our vocabulary has lost its usefulness, if it is getting in the way of attaining our purposes, we can invent new ways of speaking.

Still, each of us naturally speaks a certain language, employs a certain vocabulary.*

> All human beings carry about a set of words which they employ to justify their actions, their beliefs, and their lives. These are the words in which we formulate praise of our friends and contempt for our enemies, our long-term projects, our deepest self-doubts and our highest hopes. They are the words in which we tell, sometimes prospectively and sometimes retrospectively, the story of our lives. I shall call these words a person's "final vocabulary." (*CIS,* 73)

Suppose we were convinced of the complete contingency of our final vocabulary. We would then be the sort of person Rorty calls an *ironist.* An ironist, he says, fulfills three conditions.

> (1) She has radical and continuing doubts about the final vocabulary she currently uses, because she has been impressed by other vocabularies, vocabularies taken as final by people or books she has encountered; (2) she realizes that argument phrased in her present vocabulary can neither underwrite nor dissolve these doubts; (3) insofar as she philosophizes about her situation, she does not think that her vocabulary is closer to reality than others, that it is in touch with a power not herself. . . .
>
> I call people of this sort "ironists" because their realization that anything can be made to look good or bad by being redescribed, and their renunciation of the attempt to formulate criteria of choice be-

tween final vocabularies, puts them in the position which Sartre called "meta-stable": never quite able to take themselves seriously because always aware that the terms in which they describe themselves are subject to change, always aware of the contingency and fragility of their final vocabularies and thus of their selves. (*CIS,* 73, 74)

To be an ironist in this sense would mean giving up on the old and venerable idea that objects have essential natures to be known. If there are essences in things, dividing the world up into natural kinds, as Aristotle and most other philosophers have thought, then those essences need to be respected, mirrored in descriptions that grasp them. On that assumption, an object demands a specific vocabulary, one that reflects its intrinsic characteristics, its boundaries, and its differences from other things. The object puts severe constraints on the words adequate to describe it.

An ironist, however, believes that nothing has an essence that demands a certain vocabulary. No description is a matter of getting the object's *intrinsic* characteristics correctly registered, since there is no reason to believe in such characteristics. Descriptions always (explicitly or implicitly) relate an object to something else.* In particular, every description is formulated in a vocabulary that is relative to human purposes and interests. For an ironist, not even science should be understood as disclosing the "true nature" of things.† The replacement of Aristotelian final causes by mechanistic explanations, for instance, was not a move to a finally true picture of a mechanical world void of ends or values; it simply replaced a less useful vocabulary by one more useful—for certain purposes, of course, such as prediction and control.

> When we consider examples of alternative language games—the vocabulary of ancient Athenian politics versus Jefferson's, the moral vocabulary of

---

*Compare Dewey's example of the piece of paper: p. 587. Derrida, too, using the notion of *différance,* attacks the notion of knowing the intrinsic natures of things.

†Rorty uses the word "scientism" to describe the temptation to think that science, as opposed to literature or religion, gets us to the nature of things.

---

*Look again at what Heidegger says about "thrownness" (pp. 658–659) and Wittgenstein about "forms of life" (pp. 636–641).

St. Paul versus Freud's, the jargon of Newton versus that of Aristotle, the idiom of Blake versus that of Dryden—it is difficult to think of the world as deciding between them. When the notion of "description of the world" is moved from the level of criterion-governed sentences within language games to language games as wholes, games which we do not choose between by reference to criteria, the idea that the world decides which descriptions are true can no longer be given a clear sense. It becomes hard to think that that vocabulary is somehow already out there in the world, waiting for us to discover it. (*CIS*, 5, 6)

In short, languages are made rather than found (*CIS*, 7, 77). Given a certain vocabulary, speakers will find some sentences expressible in it to be true and others not; but there is no neutral criterion for choosing a language as a whole. Which language we prefer depends on what our purposes are. There is not even any need for all our purposes to mesh harmoniously. One might speak the language of evolutionary biology during a week's work in the laboratory and the language of the Catholic mass on Sundays. Such a person may have a number of purposes, and these may not always fit together neatly. These languages may even be incommensurable—impossible to make a coherent whole of. But there is no requirement in the nature of things that says a final vocabulary has to be coherent.

For an anti-essentialist like Rorty,

> there can be no such thing as a description which matches the way X really is, apart from its relation to human needs or consciousness or language.
>
> The term "objective" is defined by antiessentialists not in terms of a relation to intrinsic features of objects but rather by reference to relative ease of attaining consensus among inquirers. Just as the appearance-reality distinction is replaced by distinctions between relative utility of descriptions, so the objective-subjective distinction is replaced by distinctions between relative ease in getting agreement. To say that values are more subjective than facts is just to say that it is harder to get agreement about which things are ugly or which actions evil than about which things are rectangular. (*PSH*, 50, 51)

Here we have several examples of Rorty's attempt at redescription. The objective notion of *getting it*

right, for instance, is to be "redescribed" as *getting agreement* among inquirers. We have, Rorty says, no distinctive use for the former notion.

Note that Rorty resists giving an *explanation* for why it is harder to get agreement about values than facts. Philosophers are regularly tempted to explain this difference by saying that facts are objective while values are not. But from Rorty's point of view this move is perfectly useless. The only difference that makes a difference is the surface difference. The rest is just unverifiable metaphysics that is better discarded.

Rorty's claim that nothing has an essential nature applies to us humans as well. There are no metaphysical depths to the self, any more than there are metaphysical depths to the world. "On our view," Rorty says, "human beings are what they make themselves" (*PSH*, 61). We cannot, of course, create ourselves de novo. We are as contingent, as much the result of blind causes, as the world around us. And yet, as language users, we have the capacity to imagine new final vocabularies, new ways to understand ourselves, new kinds of lives to live. Choosing, or inventing, a new vocabulary is a way of re-creating ourselves.

> What the Romantics expressed as the claim that imagination, rather than reason, is the central human faculty was the realization that a talent for speaking differently, rather than for arguing well, is the chief instrument of cultural change. What political utopians since the French Revolution have sensed is not that an enduring, substratal human nature has been suppressed or repressed by "unnatural" or "irrational" social institutions but rather that changing language and other social practices may produce human beings of a sort that had never before existed. The German idealists, the French revolutionaries, and the Romantic poets had in common a dim sense that human beings whose language changed so that they no longer spoke of themselves as responsible to nonhuman powers would thereby become a new kind of human beings. (*CIS*, 7)

What if we were to ask, "But is it *true* that human beings are what they make themselves?" Rorty amiably replies that to think of ourselves this way is useful for certain purposes—in particular for the purposes of realizing a certain kind of person or society—but if you don't share those purposes, you won't find it useful. Putting this description of human beings to someone whose interests are religious or metaphysical is like "putting a bicycle pump in the hands of a ditch digger, or a yardstick in the hands of a brain surgeon" (*PSH*, 62).

We can now go back to the beginning and see that Rorty must not intend even his basic claims about the contingency of our vocabulary to be mirroring the facts.* It is not recognition of some objective fact that catapults us into agreeing with Darwin or into an ironic stance with respect to our final vocabulary. To put it that way would be to fall back into thinking that there were facts independent of the way they are described—in this case, facts about the nature of language. But that would be to relapse into the representational, metaphysical kind of thinking from which Rorty is trying to free us. When he recommends irony to us, he is in effect saying that it is more fruitful, more useful, and altogether better to think of ourselves and our final vocabularies in this ironical way than in any other. Try it on, we can hear him saying, and see whether it doesn't suit.

It is the poets, Rorty says, who invent new vocabularies. Not all poets, of course, but the ones he calls "strong poets,"† the ones that leave their mark on language, changing it by employing new metaphors and redescriptions that come to replace the old. Revolutionary scientists can perform that poetic task, too, as well as philosophers who enlarge our imagination rather than simply providing arguments. Rorty considers himself closer to the poet than to the scientist and sometimes even says he has no arguments to give (though he can hardly help himself).

> Interesting philosophy is rarely an examination of the pros and cons of a thesis. Usually it is, implicitly or explicitly, a contest between an entrenched vocabulary which has become a nuisance and a half-formed new vocabulary which vaguely promises great things. . . .
>
> The method is to redescribe lots and lots of things in new ways, until you have created a pattern of linguistic behavior which will tempt the rising generation to adopt it, thereby causing them to look for appropriate new forms of nonlinguistic behavior, for example, the adoption of new scientific equipment or new social institutions. This sort of philosophy does not work piece by piece, analyzing concept after concept, or testing thesis after thesis. Rather, it works holistically and pragmatically. It says things like "try thinking of it this way." . . . It does not pretend to have a better candidate for doing the same old things which we did when we spoke in the old way. Rather, it suggests that we might want to stop doing those things and do something else. But it does not argue for this suggestion on the basis of antecedent criteria common to the old and the new language games. For just insofar as the new language really is new, there will be no such criteria.
>
> Conforming to my own precepts, I am not going to offer arguments against the vocabulary I want to replace. Instead, I am going to try to make the vocabulary I favor look attractive by showing how it may be used to describe a variety of topics. (*CIS*, 9)

This is a rhetorical task, and by taking it upon himself in this way Rorty signals that the old quarrel between philosophy and rhetoric, between Socrates and the Sophists, is one of those binary oppositions he wants to overcome. And after all, if words are tools for coping rather than representations of reality, whatever techniques that work will do. What we want is a vocabulary that we will find satisfying; whether it is arrived at by rational argument or rhetorical persuasion is of little importance.

Liberalism and the Hope of Solidarity   Rorty calls himself not merely an ironist but also a *liberal* ironist, and we are now ready to see what that supplement to the ironical stance can add. We have been emphasizing his conviction that words, languages, and beliefs are all contingent and have their chief merit in utility; we now need to ask: What kind of utility? Useful for what? Working to what end?

As Rorty understands the term, a liberal is someone for whom "cruelty is the worst thing we

---

*It must be admitted that Rorty often writes as though this thoroughgoing contingency is something we have "discovered." But, in the light of his major theses, that cannot be right, and a more charitable interpretation is required to preserve him from inconsistency on this point.

†The term is taken from Harold Bloom.

do" (*CIS,* xv). By "cruelty" Rorty does not mean just deliberate infliction of physical pain by one person on another, but also humiliation, neglect, and the sorts of institutional and political arrangements that automatically disadvantage certain groups.

A liberal ironist, then, is someone whose final vocabulary is oriented around minimizing the amount of cruelty in the world, realizing all the while that this very conviction of hers is a purely contingent matter.* An ironist does not fight cruelty because it violates the dignity of human nature (she believes there is no human nature), nor because cruelty is something bad in itself (she can make no sense of that). No appeal to the "true nature of things" is possible for an ironist. There are no deep facts about humans, or their suffering, no absolute good or bad to appeal to, no criteria that don't beg the question. A liberal ironist admits that

> a circular justification of our practices, a justification which makes one feature of our culture look good by citing still another, or comparing our culture invidiously with others by reference to our own standards, is the only sort of justification we are going to get. (*CIS,* 57)

Neither common sense nor metaphysics can supply justifications for the ironist's values, because she realizes that "anything can be made to look good or bad by being redescribed" (*CIS,* 73). She understands that she just happens, for historical reasons, to have been produced as the sort of person who believes that being cruel is the worst thing; had she been brought up differently, she might not believe that. But for all that, her firm commitments remain firm; she sticks to her final vocabulary. She is an ironist *and* a liberal. She could say, with Rorty,

> *Our* moral view is, I firmly believe, much better than any competing view, even though there are a lot of people whom you will never be able to convert to it. It is one thing to say, falsely, that there is nothing to choose between us and the Nazis. It is another thing to say, correctly, that there is no neutral, common ground to which an experienced Nazi philosopher and I can repair in order to argue

out our differences. That Nazi and I will always strike one another as begging all the crucial questions, arguing in circles. (*PSH,* 15)

In rejecting the possibility of some neutral basis on which to argue the superiority of democratic liberalism, Rorty is trying to shift the ground on which a good society is justified. We should not try to base our argument on a foundation of antecedently existing facts which can be recognized and appealed to by all parties; as we have seen, Rorty thinks there is no such common ground and nothing of that sort to be known. Nor should we claim to see, as Marx sometimes does, the inevitable outcome of history.

> I should like to replace both religious and philosophical accounts of a suprahistorical ground or an end-of-history convergence with a historical narrative about the rise of liberal institutions and customs—the institutions and customs which were designed to diminish cruelty, make possible government by the consent of the governed, and permit as much domination-free communication as possible to take place. (*CIS,* 68)

Philosophers should get to work, Rorty says, substituting *hope* for *knowledge*—hope in the future realization of a utopian ideal for "knowledge" of already formed truths about human nature or natural right. They should busy themselves "redescribing humanity and history in terms which make democracy seem desirable," making it seem that "the ability to be a citizen of the full-fledged democracy which is yet to come . . . is what is important about being human" (*RC,* 3).

> To say that one should replace knowledge by hope is to say . . . that one should stop worrying about whether what one believes is well grounded and start worrying about whether one has been imaginative enough to think up interesting alternatives to one's present beliefs. (*PSH,* 34)

> I do not much care whether democratic politics are an expression of something deep, or whether they express nothing better than some hopes which popped from nowhere into the brains of a few remarkable people (Socrates, Christ, Jefferson, etc.) and which, for unknown reasons, became popular. (*RC,* 14)

---

*This is true for the liberal ironist's *public* vocabulary. But as we shall see, it need not hold for her *private* vocabulary.

If we ask about the content of this democratic liberalism that Rorty hopes for, he refers us to the vision expressed in J. S. Mill's little book, *On Liberty*. Here we are presented with

> a world in which nothing remains sacred save the freedom to lead your life by your own lights, and nothing is forbidden which does not interfere with the freedom of others. (*PSH,* 271)

Freedom, rather than truth, should be our principal goal.

> We ironists who are also liberals think that such freedoms require no consensus on any topic more basic than their own desirability. From our angle, all that matters for liberal politics is the widely shared conviction that . . . we shall call "true" or "good" whatever is the outcome of free discussion—that if we take care of political freedom, truth and goodness will take care of themselves.
>
> "Free discussion" here does not mean "free from ideology," but simply the sort which goes on when the press, the judiciary, the elections, and the universities are free, social mobility is frequent and rapid, literacy is universal, higher education is common, and peace and wealth have made possible the leisure necessary to listen to lots of different people and think about what they say. (*CIS,* 84)

The only limitation on freedom is the requirement that we not "interfere with the freedom of others." But this, Rorty says, demands that we make a sharp distinction between the private and the public.*

> . . . the ironist's final vocabulary can and should be split into a large private and a small public sector, sectors which have no particular relation to one another. (*CIS,* 100)

In our public role as citizens, we should be guided by the maxim to reduce the amount of cruelty in the world—cruelty being understood as interference with another person's pursuit of happiness. But we ought to refrain from imposing our version of happiness on anyone else.

> . . . there is a potential infinity of equally valuable ways to lead a human life, and . . . these ways cannot be ranked in terms of degrees of excellence, but only in terms of their contribution to the happiness of the persons who lead them and of the communities to which these persons belong. (*PSH,* 268)

In our private lives we should be free to pursue the creation of ourselves and our idiosyncratic loves in any way we find satisfactory. Since there is no such thing as a given human nature, variety and individuality should be cherished. Rorty wishes to encourage "an ever-expanding profusion of new sorts of human lives, new kinds of human beings" (*PSH,* 269). The watchword here should be *pluralism,* refusing to set any limits to the sorts of selves and communities that individuals might wish to create, save those that prevent cruelty. Those who are able to pursue Nietzschean self-overcoming should be allowed to do so; only let them not try to turn their private projects into a politics that elevates an elite few—the noble, the overmen—to a privileged place in society. "We should stop trying to combine self-creation and politics, especially if we are liberals" (*CIS,* 14). Our responsibilities to others

> constitute *only* the public side of our lives, a side which competes with our private affections and our private attempts at self-creation, and which has no *automatic* priority over such private motives. Whether it has priority in any given case is a matter for deliberation, a process which will usually not be aided by appeal to "classical first principles." Moral obligation is, in this view, to be thrown in with a lot of other considerations, rather than automatically trump them. (*CIS,* 194)*

And how is "moral obligation" understood on Rorty's view? It is obvious by now that Rorty cannot hope to ground morality in human nature (as Aristotle did), or in the degrees of goodness inherent in things (as Augustine did), or in the unconditional demands of reason (as Kant did). Morality, rather, is simply a term for what the members of a

---

*Although Rorty's pragmatic inclinations make him combat traditional "binary oppositions" (appearance/reality, knowledge/opinion, morality/prudence, absolute/relative), this is one distinction he thinks it important to insist on.

*It is not entirely clear how this view of moral obligation as just one of a number of factors fits with a liberal's view that cruelty is the "worst" thing we do.

certain community understand is "not done"—not among them, that is. We should

> cease to think of morality as the voice of the divine part of ourselves and instead think of it as the voice of ourselves as members of a community, speakers of a common language. . . . The importance of this shift is that it makes it impossible to ask the question "Is ours a moral society?" It makes it impossible to think that there is something which stands to my community as my community stands to me, some larger community called "humanity" which has an intrinsic nature. (*CIS*, 59)

Morality is a matter of

> "the sort of thing *we* don't do." An immoral action is, on this account, the sort of thing which, if done at all, is done only by animals, or by people of other families, tribes, cultures, or historical epochs. If done by one of us, or if done repeatedly by one of us, that person ceases to be one of us. She becomes an outcast, someone who doesn't speak our language, though she may once have appeared to do so. (*CIS*, 59, 60)

This parochialism about morality, Rorty thinks, is just part of the general contingency of human life. This is ironism applied to morality. But that isn't his last word on the subject, since he is, after all, a *liberal* ironist. Speaking for himself, he believes in moral progress—both that it is possible and that we have made substantial moral progress over the centuries. Progress means enlarging the "we," the people whose pain we feel as we feel our own or that of those we dearly love.

Rorty's term for this enlarged sense of our community is *solidarity*.

> The right way to take the slogan, "We have obligations to human beings simply as such," is as a means of reminding ourselves to keep trying to expand our sense of "us" as far as we can. . . . We should stay on the lookout for marginalized people—people whom we still instinctively think of as "they" rather than "us." We should try to notice our similarities with them. The right way to construe the slogan is as urging us to *create* a more expansive sense of solidarity than we presently have. The wrong way is to think of it as urging us to *recognize* such a solidarity, as something that exists antecedently to our recognition of it. (*CIS*, 196)

In my utopia, human solidarity would be seen not as a fact to be recognized by clearing away "prejudice" or burrowing down to previously hidden depths but, rather, as a goal to be achieved. It is to be achieved not by inquiry but by imagination, the imaginative ability to see strange people as fellow sufferers. Solidarity is not discovered by reflection but created. It is created by increasing our sensitivity to the particular details of the pain and humiliation of other, unfamiliar sorts of people. . . .

> This process of coming to see other human beings as "one of us" rather than as "them" is a matter of detailed description of what unfamiliar people are like and of redescription of what we ourselves are like. This is a task not for theory but for genres such as ethnography, the journalist's report, the comic book, the docudrama, and, especially, the novel. (*CIS*, xvi)

The value of increasing our sensitivity to cruelty, of enlarging the boundaries of those we count as "one of us," is not something that can be demonstrated. We cannot prove, for instance, that there is something *inhuman* in "the audiences in the Coliseum, . . . the guards at Auschwitz, and the Belgians who watched the Gestapo drag their Jewish neighbors away" (*CIS*, 189).

> We decent, liberal humanitarian types . . . are just luckier, not more insightful, than the bullies with whom we struggle. (*PSH*, 15)

> It is neither irrational nor unintelligent to draw the limits of one's moral community at a national, or racial, or gender border. But it is undesirable—morally undesirable. So it is best to think of moral progress as a matter of increasing *sensitivity*, increasing responsiveness to the needs of a larger and larger variety of people and things. (*PSH*, 81)

Why is that best? Because, Rorty believes, thinking that way is our best hope for increasing human happiness in the future.

Relativism   It should be no surprise by now to hear that Rorty is often called a *relativist*, and we will bring our consideration of his views to a close by noting his reaction to this charge. He admits that

> if "relativism" just means failure to find a use for the notion of "context-independent validity," then this charge [is] entirely justified. (*RC*, 24)

The total contingency of our vocabulary, its dependence on the history of the language and on the innovations of previous "redescribers" of things, means that everything we say is dependent on other things we say. We cannot get free of our "thrownness" (Heidegger) or our "form of life" (Wittgenstein) to see things as they are independent of that context. Whatever we say is relative to the linguistic and cultural milieu we find ourselves in.

But that said, Rorty goes on the attack.*

We so-called "relativists" refuse, predictably, to admit that we are enemies of reason and common sense. We say that we are only criticizing some antiquated, specifically philosophical dogmas. But, of course, what we call dogmas are exactly what our opponents call common sense. Adherence to these dogmas is what they call being rational. (*PSH,* xvii)

Chief among these "dogmas" is

the Greek distinction between the way things are in themselves and the relations which they have to other things, and in particular to human needs and interests. (*PSH,* xvi)

We must repudiate the vocabulary our opponents use, and not let them impose it upon us. (*PSH,* xviii)

We have seen that Rorty recommends trashing much of this vocabulary—not only the appearance/reality distinction, but also the distinctions between finding and making, discovery and invention, argument and rhetoric, objective and subjective, morality and expediency, philosophy and literature, and indeed that between absolutism and relativism itself. All of these, Rorty claims, depend on assumptions that we would be better off without. The charge of relativism, then,

should not be answered, but rather evaded. We should learn to brush aside questions like "How do you *know* that freedom is the chief goal of social organization?" in the same way as we brush aside questions like "How do you *know* that Jones is worthy of your friendship?" . . . Such choices are not made by reference to criteria. (*CIS,* 54)

Rorty believes that the liberal democracies of the West, despite their faults, are the best socie-

ties humanity has devised to date. Coming from a member of such a society, of course, this can sound awfully ethnocentric. But Rorty cheerfully admits the ethnocentrism. His defense is that *every* view is ethnocentric, since no one can escape from the social and cultural forces that formed her.

There is no *neutral,* non-circular way to defend the liberal's claim that cruelty is the worst thing we do, any more than there is a neutral way to back up Nietzsche's assertion that this claim expresses a resentful, slavish attitude. . . . We cannot look back behind the processes of socialization which convinced us twentieth-century liberals of the validity of this claim and appeal to something which is more "real" or less ephemeral than the historical contingencies which brought those processes into existence. *We* have to start from where *we* are. . . . What takes the curse off this ethnocentrism is . . . that it is the ethnocentrism of a "we" ("we liberals") which is dedicated to enlarging itself, to creating an ever larger and more varied *ethnos.* (*CIS,* 198)

Many who identify themselves as "postmoderns" share major themes with Rorty: the emphasis on contingency, doubts about truth, objectivity, and knowledge, blurring the line between rhetoric and argument. But like Nagel and Derrida too, Rorty is disturbed by some of the more extreme versions of postmodernist thinking.

Insofar as "postmodern" philosophical thinking is identified with a mindless and stupid cultural relativism—with the idea that any fool thing that calls itself culture is worthy of respect—then I have no use for such thinking. But I do not see that what I have called "philosophical pluralism" entails any such stupidity. The reason to try persuasion rather than force, to do our best to come to terms with people whose convictions are archaic and ingenerate, is simply that using force, or mockery, or insult, is likely to decrease human happiness.

We do not need to supplement this wise utilitarian counsel with the idea that every culture has some sort of intrinsic worth. We have learned the futility of trying to assign all cultures and persons places on a hierarchical scale, but this realization does not impugn the obvious fact that there are lots of cultures we would be better off without, just as there are lots of people we would be better off without. To say that there is no such scale, and that

---

*A perusal of *Rorty and His Critics* shows that many philosophers are unconvinced by Rorty's rebuttal of the charge.

we are simply clever animals trying to increase our happiness by continually reinventing ourselves, has no relativistic consequences. The difference between pragmatism and cultural relativism is the difference between pragmatically justified tolerance and mindless irresponsibility. (*PSH,* 276)

Whether this difference will hold up in the continuing human conversation is something that Rorty himself would be content to leave to the future.

1. What does Rorty mean by "de-divinizing" the world?
2. What does it mean to think of ourselves, our beliefs, and our language as completely *contingent*?
3. Why does Rorty believe we cannot take truth as a goal? What functions can the word "true" properly have?
4. What does Rorty want to substitute for the notion of "representation"?
5. What is a "final vocabulary"? What is an ironist's relationship to her final vocabulary?
6. Why are there no *essential natures* to be known?
7. What do "strong poets" do?
8. How does Rorty understand liberalism?
9. What sort of justification of her position can a liberal ironist give? What kind of justification is ruled out for her?
10. What does it mean that Rorty wants to substitute hope for knowledge?
11. Why does Rorty say that if we take care of freedom, truth will take care of itself?
12. Explain Rorty's sharp distinction between the public and the private.
13. How does Rorty understand morality? What is the goal of a liberal morality?
14. How does Rorty respond to the charge of relativism?

Physical Realism

Philosophers have often, especially since Kant, thought of their discipline as distinctively different from the sciences. As the sciences continued to triumph in one field after another, however, some began to wonder whether there was anything left for philosophers to do. As we have seen, by mid-twentieth century, many concluded that philosophy had to give up its grand aims and pretensions to knowledge. Their watchword was "analysis," their aim was clarification of thought or language, and their mode of procedure was piecemeal examination of well-defined small problems.[*] This tendency was reinforced by a growing suspicion of metaphysics, understood as a claim to access a reality beyond the reach of scientific methods.

But as the century wore on, some philosophers began once again to turn to the traditional problems centered on the nature of human beings and their place in the larger scheme of things. In the words of Karl Popper (1902–1994),

Language analysts believe that there are no genuine philosophical problems, or that the problems of philosophy, if any, are problems of linguistic usage, or of the meaning of words. I, however, believe that there is at least one philosophical problem in which all thinking men are interested. It is the problem of cosmology: *the problem of understanding the world—including ourselves, and our knowledge, as part of the world.*[3][†]

Wilfrid Sellars (1912–1989) puts it this way:

The aim of philosophy, abstractly formulated, is to understand how things in the broadest possible sense of the term hang together in the broadest possible sense of the term. Under "things in the broadest possible sense" I include such radically different items as not only "cabbages and kings," but numbers and duties, possibilities and finger snaps, aesthetic experience and death. To achieve success in philosophy would be, to use a contemporary turn of phrase, to "know one's way around" with respect to all these things, not in that unreflective way in which the centipede of the story knew its way around before it faced the question, "how do I walk?" but in that reflective way which means that no intellectual holds are barred.[4]

---

[*]See the remarks in Wittgenstein's *Tractatus* 4.111 (pp. 612–613), by the logical positivists (p. 615), and in Wittgenstein's *Philosophical Investigations* (pp. 623–626), as well as those by Ryle and Austin (pp. 620–621).

[†]Note how very different is this way of looking at philosophy from that of the early Wittgenstein, who thought that the problems of philosophy should simply vanish (p. 598), and from that of the later Wittgenstein, too, who held that philosophy "leaves everything as it is" (p. 625).

I will call the viewpoint to be discussed here "physical realism," a term used earlier in the century by Sellars' father, Roy Wood Sellars;[5] it is also called "naturalism," or sometimes "scientific realism" or simply "realism."* The central ideas of physical realism are that human beings are wholly a part of nature, and that our best account of nature is presented in the sciences.† A philosopher working in this way will try to understand "how things hang together" by making use of everything we believe that we know from whatever source—and especially from the sciences. This construction of a synoptic (seeing together) view is a job that no special science claims—not physics nor psychology nor any science in between. Philosophy, understood in this way, is integrative and holistic, though not uncritical, and in certain areas becomes part of a multifaceted interdisciplinary approach to problems.

Science, Common Sense, and Metaphysics: Willard van Orman Quine

Interestingly, this turn to a broader scope for philosophy was signaled by an attack on traditional empiricism. It may seem strange that a viewpoint taking science seriously should begin with a critique of the empiricists. Surely the methods of the sciences are decidedly empirical—tied at crucial points to observation and experiment—so how can this be?

According to Willard van Orman Quine (1908–2000), a logician of distinction and for many years a professor of philosophy at Harvard, traditional empiricists—David Hume and the logical posi-

"I see the question of truth as one to be settled within science, there being no higher tribunal."
—Willard van Orman Quine

tivists, for example—have been *dogmatic,* just the opposite of what they advertise themselves to be. Quine has a double critique of such philosophy, two objections that he says ultimately come to the same thing. Empiricists have been dogmatic (1) in believing that there is a sharp distinction between analytic and synthetic truths, and (2) in thinking that each meaningful statement is equivalent to some (perhaps very complicated) statement that refers only to immediate experience.

The first dogma allowed a neat division of labor that gave philosophers something to do. Scientists were to do the empirical work of formulating synthetic truths about the world, while philosophers could clarify notions used in science and common sense by way of definitions that were analytically true. The second dogma is expressed in Hume's advice to trace every idea back to an impression, as well as in the positivists' verifiability criterion of

---

*All such terms are imprecise, rather like signposts pointing in a certain direction. Serious thought, rigorous argument, can scarcely be carried on in terms of such "isms," which is why they occur seldom in the writings of good philosophers and have not featured prominently in this book. But they do have a use, and in this chapter I take them to point to sets of themes found in thinkers who can reasonably be grouped together but who are by no means always in agreement about everything.

†Physical realists are happy to embrace what Rorty scornfully terms "scientism."

factual meaningfulness.* Quine characterizes this second dogma as "reductionism" (*TDE,* 20), since its goal is to "reduce" talk of objects in the world (talk of pennies, say) to talk that mentions only the data of sensation.

These may seem arcane and merely technical issues, but abandoning these dogmas has far-reaching consequences. For one thing, Quine says, we will no longer have any reason to draw a sharp line distinguishing philosophy from science, or, for that matter, speculative metaphysics from natural science. These boundaries get blurred. Since eliminating metaphysical speculation had been one of the main goals of the empiricist movement from Hume to the logical positivists, this effect is quite dramatic. For another, common sense and science will be seen as alike in their basic structure. And thirdly, this critique will mark a move toward pragmatism. Let us examine these consequences.

Holism   Ever since Hume had distinguished "relations of ideas" from "matters of fact," empiricists had insisted on a sharp difference between them. Analytic truths were supposed to be true just in virtue of the meanings of their terms, telling us nothing about the world. You don't have to consult experience to know that two plus two is four or that no bachelor can be married; these are analytically true—so the story goes—and all that is required is that you understand the language. But if you want to know whether it is raining in Brooklyn now, or how fast objects fall near the surface of the earth, just understanding the sentences won't tell you. For that sort of truth you need confirmation by sensory experience. This divide was supposed to be both exclusive (no statement could be both analytic and synthetic) and exhaustive (if a statement was neither analytically true nor confirmable by sense experience, it was declared to be meaningless). That was how you got rid of metaphysics.†

The two dogmas are related in the following way. Suppose you have an ordinary factual statement about the world: "Water boils at 100° C at sea level." Call this *p* (for physical world statement). According to the early positivists, *p* was meaningful because it could be "reduced to" (or defined in terms of) a set of statements that did not talk about water or the sea at all, but only about our experiences—experiences, as we say, "of" water, thermometers, altimeters, and so on. Call this latter set of statements *e* (for statements about our experience). This reduction would yield a statement of the form "*p* if and only if *e*" that would be analytically true—true in virtue of the meanings of *p* and *e*. What *p* really means, supposedly, is *e*. Though you could confirm or disconfirm *p* empirically, no experience could either confirm or disconfirm the equivalence between *p* and *e* because that was true by definition.

But consider the correlation between the physical fact of water boiling and the relevant experiences. Given an observer in normal circumstances, when you have the one you have the other. But is that correlation a matter of *meaning?* Or is it a *fact* we discover by empirical methods? Quine argues that there is no nonarbitrary, noncircular way of determining the answer to these questions. No appeal to sameness of meaning, or to synonymy, or to definition, or to more sophisticated semantical rules will distinguish analytic from synthetic statements.* He concludes that the idea that *individual* statements of fact (*p* statements) are made meaningful by definitions reducing them to statements mentioning only immediate experience (*e* statements) cannot be sustained. To continue to think so is to accept a dogma. Our knowledge does depend on experience, but not in that atomistic sort of way.

Quine suggests, to the contrary, that

> our statements about the external world face the tribunal of sense experience not individually but only as a corporate body. . . . In taking the statement as unit we have drawn our grid too finely. The unit of empirical significance is the whole of science. (*TDE,* 41, 42)

We can see the sense in this claim if we reflect a moment on the way hypotheses are tested in sci-

*See pp. 615–616.
†See pp. 614–616 for the way positivists use this distinction for precisely this purpose.

*It is also a fact that no one ever produced an actual example of successful reduction of physical language to purely experiential language.

ence. Suppose some scientists come across an unfamiliar material. They hypothesize that its chemical composition is XYZ. How can that hypothesis be tested? Relying on theory they already are confident of, they deduce that if it is XYZ, then it will turn green when heated to 200°C. So they heat it and observe what happens.

What can they learn from this experiment? There are two cases. Suppose first that they observe it turning green. Do they now know that the substance is XYZ? No, not for certain, for there may be other reasons why this substance will turn green in the experimental circumstances. At best they have been given some reason to believe it is XYZ and other tests might confirm it further.

Now suppose that they make the experiment and it doesn't turn green? Do they know that the substance *isn't* XYZ? The perhaps surprising answer is no—though in this case they have discovered a reason for believing that it is not XYZ, and in most cases that is what they will conclude. But why can't they conclude that their hypothesis is false, period?

Here is the logical situation. The observation sentence, "This substance turns green at 200°C," does not follow from the hypothesis that this substance is XYZ alone, but only in conjunction with certain other propositions. The scientists are also relying on a law correlating XYZ with turning green and a set of sentences describing the experimental situation—e.g., that the temperature has in fact reached that level. We can represent this schematically in the following argument:

L: When XYZ is heated to 200°C, it turns green.
S: This substance is heated to 200°C.
H: This substance is XYZ.
Therefore *O:* This substance turns green.

A little reflection will convince you that the observation sentence *O* follows deductively from the *conjunction* of *L* (the law), *S* (the situation description), and *H* (the hypothesis). (Take a moment to be sure you see that it does.) Suppose now that *O* is not observed. Then we know that the conjunction of the premises (*L and S and H*) is false. Because a conjunction as a whole is true only if each of its constituent propositions is true, it must be that at

least one of the conjuncts is false, but the experiment does not tell us which one it is! In light of the failure to observe *O*, we have to retract *some* premise of the argument, but it is logically open which one it would be best to take back.

We can now see why Quine says that our statements about the world "face the tribunal of sense experience . . . only as a corporate body," and not individually. Evidence that any one of them is false will necessarily have implications for others, but it won't be determinate which others are at fault. Quine, then, endorses a version of *holism* in epistemology parallel to that favored by Peirce with respect to meaning.[*]

> The totality of our so-called knowledge or beliefs, from the most casual matters of geography and history to the profoundest laws of atomic physics or even of pure mathematics and logic, is a man-made fabric which impinges on experience only along the edges. Or, to change the figure, total science is like a field of force whose boundary conditions are experience. A conflict with experience at the periphery occasions readjustments in the interior of the field. Truth values have to be redistributed over some of our statements. Reëvaluation of some statements entails reëvaluation of others, because of their logical interconnections—the logical laws being in turn simply certain further statements of the system, certain further elements of the field. Having reëvaluated one statement we must reëvaluate some others, which may be statements logically connected with the first or may be the statements of logical connections themselves. But the total field is so underdetermined by its boundary conditions, experience, that there is much latitude of choice as to what statements to reëvaluate in the light of any single experience. No particular experiences are linked with any particular statements in the interior of the field, except indirectly through considerations of equilibrium affecting the field as a whole.
>
> If this view is right, it is misleading to speak of the empirical content of an individual statement—

---

[*] See Peirce's claim that a sign has meaning only in the context of a system of signs, p. 580. Quine's insight is also shared by the later Wittgenstein, p. 640. There is also a resemblance to Derrida's meaning of holism, though Quine does not accept that the undecidability *goes all the way down.*

especially if it is a statement at all remote from the experiential periphery of the field. Furthermore it becomes folly to seek a boundary between synthetic statements, which hold contingently on experience, and analytic statements, which hold come what may. Any statement can be held true come what may, if we make drastic enough adjustments elsewhere in the system. Even a statement very close to the periphery can be held true in the face of recalcitrant experience by pleading hallucination or by amending certain statements of the kind called logical laws. Conversely, by the same token, no statement is immune to revision. (*TDE*, 42, 43)*

To the metaphors of the "man-made fabric" and the "field of force," Quine adds yet another. Human cognition yields a *web of belief*.[6] Our beliefs, he suggests, are like the strands of a spider's web, each related to the others, none able to stand alone, and most of them anchored to the world beyond the web only indirectly. Yet there are (quite) firm attachments, as we shall see, in what he calls "observation sentences."

This picture of our intellectual life poses a problem. Consider the example again and suppose that green is not observed. How shall we decide whether to (a) reject the hypothesis, (b) revise the law, or (c) reconsider our description of the experimental situation? As Quine notes, there is even a fourth option: we could reestablish logical equilibrium by dismissing the observation report as illusory.

This is a puzzle that goes to the heart of scientific practice and it hardly seems credible that we should make such a choice randomly. Quine's solution is that we should follow "our natural tendency to disturb the total system as little as possible" (*PT*, 15), a rule he also calls "the maxim of minimal mutilation" (*PT*, 2). Applied to our example, this conservative principle would probably mean that the hypothesis (that the substance is XYZ) would be the thing to go, though that would depend on the particular case and could not be predicted in advance. We should also scrutinize the experimental situation to determine whether we have described it correctly. But to revise the law in question would mutilate the system to a much greater degree. Because a law is located nearer the center of the web of theory, changing it would force a great many other changes as well.

Yet "no statement is immune from revision," and even a law or a theory with a long history of success can be upset. That is what happens in scientific revolutions. Whatever choice is made at this point, Quine says, it should be such as to "maximize future success in prediction," as that is the test by which success in science is judged (*PT*, 2, 15). Prediction may not be our main *goal* in pursuing the game of science—we aim at understanding, he says, and control of the environment—but predictive success is "what decides the game, like runs and outs in baseball" (*PT*, 20).

We have been talking about science, but in fact Quine believes that no sharp line divides science from common sense. The same considerations that motivate the postulation of electrons are at work in positing tables and chairs as objects independent of our experience of them.

> Our acceptance of an ontology is, I think, similar in principle to our acceptance of a scientific theory, say a system of physics: we adopt, at least insofar as we are reasonable, the simplest conceptual scheme into which the disordered fragments of raw experience can be fitted and arranged.
>
> By bringing together scattered sense events and treating them as perceptions of one object, we reduce the complexity of our stream of experience to a manageable conceptual simplicity. The rule of simplicity is indeed our guiding maxim in assigning sense data to objects: we associate an earlier and a later round sensum with the same so-called penny, or with two different so-called pennies, in obedience to the demands of maximum simplicity in our total world picture. (*OWTI*, 16, 17)*

---

*Here Quine expresses agreement with Peircean fallibilism (p. 574) and joins the pragmatists in rejecting Descartes' quest for certainty based on an unquestionable foundation.

*Quine here stresses simplicity as the rule, but elsewhere he offers additional criteria for judging whether a theory does a good job: Does it conserve as much as possible of previous theories? Does it generalize? Is it refutable? Does it go too far?

Quine talks here (in this early 1948 article) of "the disordered fragments of raw experience" and of "sense data." You may be reminded of Hume's characterization of experience as "a bundle or collection of different perceptions, which succeed each other with an inconceivable rapidity, and are in a perpetual flux and movement."* Quine's idea is that common sense postulates the reality of physical objects for the same reasons that science posits atoms: to explain the course of our experience and to simplify our account of the world. Tables and chairs, then, can be thought of as "theoretical entities" posited to make sense of experience.

This notion presupposes, of course, that we can isolate and identify the elements of experience. And that in turn seems to require a language in which the course of experience can be reported and described—"play-by-play," as it were. Other philosophers have doubted that such a "private" language is really conceivable,† and in later works we find Quine characterizing the "data" that we have to work with in a much less subjective way. In *The Pursuit of Truth* (1990), for instance, he talks instead of the stimulation of our sense organs, a matter that can be characterized in as objective and public a manner as you like. He characterizes *observation sentences* as

> sentences that are directly and firmly associated with our stimulations. Each should be associated affirmatively with some range of one's stimulations and negatively with some range. The sentence should command the subject's assent or dissent outright, on the occasion of a stimulation in the appropriate range, without further investigation and independently of what he may have been engaged in at the time. A further requirement is intersubjectivity: unlike a report of a feeling, the sentence must command the same verdict from all linguistically competent witnesses of the occasion.
>
> Examples are "It's raining," "It's getting cold," "That's a rabbit." (*PT,* 3)

Although Quine admits that "observationality is vague at the edges," it is observation sentences that provide "a final checkpoint" for theory and make science objective. It is worth noting that although they are occasioned by stimulation of the sense organs, observation sentences are not *about* that stimulation; they speak of objective facts like rain, temperature, and rabbits. Observation sentences constitute "the link between language, scientific or not, and the real world that language is all about" (*PT,* 4, 5).*

Indeterminacy   Quine's commitment to observation sentences as a "final checkpoint" makes his view seem very different from that of Derrida or Rorty. But Quine is also famous for a thesis called "the indeterminacy of translation," and that makes him sound much like those postmodernists. Let us see whether we can resolve this apparent anomaly.

Imagine, as Quine himself does, a linguist trying to understand a language totally foreign to him simply by inserting himself in that culture.† He calls this task, without reliance on a dictionary or a bilingual speaker, "radical translation." Suppose he has gotten so far as to identify native indications of assent and dissent. He and one of the natives are standing in the bush when a rabbit hops by. The native says, "Gavagai." The linguist takes this, provisionally, as a one-word sentence (an observation sentence) and writes in his notebook, "'Gavagai' = 'Lo, a rabbit.'"

The linguist's aim is to pair what he is inclined to say in his language on the occasion of a certain stimulation with what the native says on that same occasion. By further questioning in similar and different circumstances, the linguist can confirm or disconfirm his hypothesis. Little by little, with many corrections, the linguist assembles a large set

---

*For Hume's description, and the consequences he derives from it, see pp. 411–412.

†Wittgenstein is a case in point. In *Philosophical Investigations* 258ff. he presents a critique of the very idea of such a "private language." Derrida's critique of *presence* in terms of language as a system of differences has the same effect; see pp. 707–710.

---

*It is the character of observation sentences that allows Quine to reject the Derridean claim that no sentence has a completely firm meaning. Note the structural similarity of this "realist" view with that of St. Thomas Aquinas, p. 287.

†Quine notes that the situation of the linguist is like that of a young child learning a language, save that the linguist has already in hand a language of his own.

of such pairings; such a set Quine calls a "translation manual."

It turns out, however, that there could be more than one translation manual correlating the native language with English, though neither one violates any convention of either language.

> A manual of Jungle-to-English translation constitutes an inductive definition of a translation relation together with a claim that it correlates sentences compatibly with the behavior of all concerned. The thesis of indeterminacy of translation is that these claims on the part of two manuals might both be true and yet the two translation relations might not be usable in alternation, from sentence to sentence, without issuing in incoherent sequences. Or, to put it another way, the English sentences prescribed as translations of a given Jungle sentence by the two manuals might not be interchangeable in English contexts. (*TI*, 5)

The meaning of the native sentence is therefore to some extent indeterminate, for all that an English speaker can say. This sounds very like Derridean undecidability and play in the language. But Quine goes on to say:

> The indeterminacy of translation is unlikely to obtrude in practice, even in radical translation. There is good reason why it should not. The linguist assumes that the natives' attitudes and ways of thinking are like his own, up to the point where there is contrary evidence. He accordingly imposes his own ontology and linguistic patterns on the native wherever compatible with the native's speech and other behavior, unless a contrary course offer striking simplifications. We could not wish it otherwise. What the indeterminacy thesis is meant to bring out is that the radical translator is bound to impose as much as he discovers. (*TI*, 5)

What makes indeterminacy a fact for Quine is that *we* construct the translation manuals. What makes indeterminacy something we can mostly ignore in practice is the linking of observation sentences to stimulations. Though no statement is in principle unrevisable, some statements are *very resistant* to revision; observation statements anchor the web of belief quite securely. Although holistic matters of overall coherence govern the formulation of our theories, they must be balanced by the tenacious hold that observation sentences have. Quine says of himself that he "does indeed combine foundationalism with coherentism, as I think it is evident that one must."[7]

It is this foundationalist aspect that both distinguishes Quine's view from that of Rorty, for whom coherence is everything, and allows him to resist the claim that science is just another ideology. Though all our theories are "underdetermined" by the evidence the world supplies, it is because experimental science is tied tightly to observation sentences that it is distinctive in the degree to which it lets the world have a say in the theories that we accept.[*] Still, it remains logically possible that we should construct two or more scientific theories of the world containing incompatible ontologies, each responsive to all the evidence available to us.

Ontological Commitment   In response to what is imprinted on our senses, then, we "project" or "posit" a more or less stable world of objects. These posits constitute our *ontology*—our view of *what there is*.[†] Every theory or systematic set of beliefs has its ontology, expresses some commitment as to what there is. The tie between these posits and experience is not to be found by defining one in terms of the other, but in the way the posits organize, simplify, and predict our experiences. There is always surplus meaning in our conception of these posits—meaning that cannot be reduced to subjective experience or sense organ stimulation—and that is true whether we posit divine beings or physical objects. That is why Quine believes that there is no

---

[*] In postmodernist terminology, Quine "privileges" science as a source of truth about the world. What might Quine say about logocentrism? Insofar as logocentrism is identified with a commitment to *presence* and immediate certainty about the truth, he would distance himself from it. No statement is immune from revision. But insofar as logocentrism means commitment to reason, logic, argument and observation, Quine would hold that logocentrism is a *good* thing.

[†] Quine prefers the term "ontology" to the similar but more historically freighted term "metaphysics," though he uses both terms.

deep gulf between science and common sense or between science and metaphysics.

> Physical objects are conceptually imported into the situation as convenient intermediaries—not by definition in terms of experience, but simply as irreducible posits comparable, epistemologically, to the gods of Homer. For my part I do, qua lay physicist, believe in physical objects and not in Homer's gods; and I consider it a scientific error to believe otherwise. But in point of epistemological footing the physical objects and the gods differ only in degree and not in kind. Both sorts of entities enter our conception only as cultural posits. The myth of physical objects is epistemologically superior to most in that it has proved more efficacious than other myths as a device for working a manageable structure into the flux of experience.
>
> Science is a continuation of common sense, and it continues the common-sense expedient of swelling ontology to simplify theory. (*TDE*, 44, 45)

Most physical realists resist talking of physical objects as a "myth," and that way of referring to them disappears in Quine's later work as well. But the idea remains that entities such as Zeus and Athena cannot be ruled out on principle as meaningless. If you think these gods are real, Quine might say, here is a challenge: Formulate a theory about them, deduce some observation sentences, and see whether this theory passes the prediction test better than its rivals. Quine bets that it won't.*

Every theory, then, commits us to an ontology, to some view about what exists. How are we to know what the sentences of a theory commit us to? Consider a sentence like, "Some dogs are white." It seems clear enough that in uttering this sentence we express commitment to the existence of dogs. But how about "white"? Are we signaling that we also believe in an additional something named *whiteness*? And for that matter, how about *doghood*? As we know, Plato thinks that in addition to the particular

sensible things we are familiar with, there is an intelligible world of Forms—eternal and unchangeable realities that sensible entities "participate" in. Only by positing the Forms, he thinks can we explain the fact that this dog and that dog are both white: Both partake of whiteness. Medieval philosophers called these items *universals*.

Quine proposes that we make use of the techniques of modern logic to clarify these matters. When we say that some dogs are white, we are actually saying that there is at least one thing that is both a dog and white: $(\exists x)$ (Dog x & White x). This sentence commits us to the existence of some x that is a dog, but it doesn't assert that there is yet another thing that exists, doghood, and still a third thing, whiteness. So we have a clear way of determining what ontology a certain sentence or theory assumes. "To be assumed as an entity is, purely and simply, to be reckoned as the value of a variable" (*OWTI*, 13).

We could, of course, assert the existence of universals like doghood, if we had a mind to. But to do that would require a sentence like this: "There is at least one thing which is doghood." But that is a very different sentence from the one we began with, and it seems clear that the original sentence does not make that commitment. Note that the criterion Quine proposes does not tell us what there *is*, but only what a certain theory or point of view or sentence says that there is.

> We look to bound variables* in connection with ontology not in order to know what there is, but in order to know what a given remark or doctrine, ours or someone else's, *says* there is; and this much is quite properly a problem involving language. But what there is is another question. (*OWTI*, 15, 16)

---

* A caution: You must be careful to make the theory refutable, unlike the typical pronouncements of astrologers that are so vague as to be "verified" by virtually anything that happens. Your theory must make specific predictions that could possibly be falsified.

---

* A bound variable is contrasted with a free variable. The formula "x is green" contains the free variable x. Such formulae have no truth value until we either specify a particular value for x (for instance, $x =$ grass) or make it a general sentence about some or all things by attaching a "quantifier." In $(\exists x)$ (Green x) the variable x is said to be "bound" by the existential quantifier that means "There exists at least one x such that. . . ." This sentence says that some things are green; it does have a truth value and is, in fact, true.

Our language does not determine what there is, but it does signal what we commit ourselves to in the way of entities. The question of whether to believe in the existence of these entities comes down to the question: Will postulating those entities make sense of our experience, simplify our story of the world, and increase predictive power? Judged that way, Quine thinks, it is right to be committed to the existence of dogs, but not to doghood—nor to most other Platonic Forms, nor to the Homeric gods. But even so, in questions of ontology Quine counsels "tolerance and an experimental spirit" (*OWTI,* 19).

Note that the question about what there is and the question about what theory of the world we should adopt become one question on this view. What is there? Our best theory will tell us (fallibly and subject to correction, of course). And how do we find the best theory? By adopting roughly scientific methods—by testing refutable theories to see which ones survive. What this means is that science becomes the criterion of what there is, the arbiter of ontology.

Natural Knowing   Suddenly that sounds revolutionary. Think back to the problem Descartes posed for himself and tried to solve in his *Meditations.* Descartes was a scientist of some distinction, but the question that worried him was this: Could all of my science be but a dream? Could it be an illusion foisted on me by a demon deceiver? How do I know that science portrays the world as it really is? In short, he felt himself faced with the formidable problem of the "external" world.

As we have seen, this problem is intimately tied to the *representational theory* of knowledge. According to this theory, we are directly acquainted only with the contents of our own minds—with patches of color in a visual field, noises in an auditory field, and so on. Do these correspond to anything external to the mind? That seems to be something that requires proof. You will recall that Descartes himself thought that our belief in an external world could be justified only by proving the existence of an infinitely good God who would never deceive us about it.

For several hundred years this problem took center stage in epistemology. Berkeley thought it could be solved by denying the independent existence of a material world—turning ideas into things. Hume despaired of solving the problem and ended in skepticism. Kant divided the question, proposing that the objective world of our experience (the world of science) was a merely phenomenal world—a world relative to us—and that reality in itself was unknowable. Hegel thought the world was truly knowable only by the World Spirit, for whom the distinction between "external" and "internal" will disappear at the end of history, though humans were in the process of developing more and more of that comprehensive view of things.

The problem survives in the twentieth century in Bertrand Russell's attempt to define physical object concepts in terms of sense data (his logical atomism), and in *phenomenalism,* the "reductive" view that we earlier saw Quine criticizing. Even the early Quine is not entirely free of entanglement with the representational theory; his talk of physical objects as a *myth,* the aim of which is to simplify and orchestrate "the disordered fragments of raw experience," fits the pattern perfectly.

In a complete reversal, Wilfrid Sellars argues that it is the representational theory that depends on a myth: the Myth of the Given.[8] According to this myth, the quest to justify our knowledge comes to rest on data that are simply *given* to us, *presented* to us.* The classical empiricists believed that what is given are sensory states—impressions of blue, warm, hard, sweet, loud, and so on. These states were thought to be basic and unanalyzable, like Hume's simple impressions or the early Wittgenstein's simple objects. They were supposedly theory-neutral and could serve as a sure and certain *foundation* for knowledge.

Sellars argues to the contrary that what is and must be basic in our conceptual scheme are objective claims like "This apple is red." It is in such terms that we learn the language. Children learn "This is a ball," "That is yellow," "Get the yellow

---

*Compare Derrida's critique of the notion of presence, pp. 707–709, and Heidegger on Being-in-the-world, pp. 649–654.

ball"; they don't learn a private sense-datum language and then infer from that foundation to something about the external world. It is a myth, Sellars says, that we are first and foremost directly acquainted with our own subjective states. Beliefs and desires are focused from the start on the so-called external world. If anything is "posited," it is raw experiential feelings, not tables and chairs.

What is crucial is appreciating the logic of "looks" talk. Coming to think that something *looks red* is a development that presupposes and builds on a claim that something *is red;* the latter, not the former, is the more primitive expression. The function of "looks" terminology is primarily to withhold assent from an objective judgment while yet suggesting a similarity with it. Looking at the ball, I am inclined to say that it is blue, but I am unsure; so I say it looks blue. In turn, "looks blue" is a step on the road that leads to believing in private subjective sensory states—and not the other way around.

In fact, Sellars says, belief that there are such states can best be understood in analogy with the postulation of theoretical entities (such as atoms) in science. Jones sometimes says, for instance, "This thing looks red," when we can clearly see that it is not. We *explain* this utterance by positing a subjective state in Jones analogous to the state he is in when he is actually observing something red. When sense datum theorists, phenomenalists, and empiricists assume that knowledge must begin with those private sensory states, they have it precisely backwards.*

This strongly suggests that epistemology, as it has been pursued throughout most of the modern period, needs a drastic overhaul. The central problem since Descartes has been how to avoid skep-

ticism about the "external" world. But now that problem looks artificial—one of those problems created by the way it is stated. If we begin with *human beings* (entities in thoroughgoing interaction with the world around them) rather than with *minds,* epistemology will look very different. And, indeed, that is what both Sellars and Quine claim. As Quine understands the epistemological problem, it concerns "the relation between the meager input and the torrential output" (*EN,* 24). That is, how does it happen that we humans produce utterances that are about the world, not about "fragments of raw experience" or surface stimulations of sense organs? What accounts for the fact that we construct both common sense and incredibly complex scientific theories, given the paucity of our evidence?

> The old epistemology aspired to contain, in a sense, natural science; it would construct it somehow from sense data. Epistemology in its new setting, conversely, is contained in natural science, as a chapter of psychology. We are studying how the human subject of our study posits bodies and projects his physics from his data, and we appreciate that our position in the world is just like his.
>
> Epistemology, or something like it, simply falls into place as a chapter of psychology and hence of natural science. It studies a natural phenomenon, viz., a physical human subject. (*EN,* 24)

Here is the situation as Quine sees it in this newly *naturalized* epistemology.* We observe Smith looking at a tree. We are cognizant (let us suppose) of the ways in which the rods and cones in her eyes are stimulated by the light reflected from the tree. We hear Smith say, "There's a tree." In normal circumstances we would say that Smith knows there is a tree before her. What we want to understand is how the stimulation of her eyes produces the knowledge expressed in Smith's utterance. Let's

---

*It may seem that Sellars' talk of positing sensory states on the basis of Jones' behavior is in direct conflict with Quine's claim that what we posit are objective entities. But not so, for two reasons: (1) to talk as Quine does of stimulation of the sense organs is already to be talking objectively of the world, and (2) although sensory states may be *causally* prior to our knowledge of the world, they are not *epistemologically* prior; that is, we do not build up our knowledge of the world on the basis of subjective foundations. Remember that the content of an observation sentence is not about subjective experience.

---

*We already used the phrase "naturalized epistemology" to describe John Dewey's theory of knowledge. A look back to this section (pp. 582–587) would provide a richer understanding of the viewpoint and indicate the ways in which Quine adapts pragmatic themes.

further suppose that psychology (perhaps combined with physiology and linguistics) can trace the processes in Smith that yield the utterance. This would give us the understanding we are seeking.

We then apply the same understanding to ourselves. If that's how Smith attains knowledge of the world around her, then that's how we do it, too. In fact, we can now say that our own perception of Smith, of the tree, and of the way Smith comes to know of the tree is *itself* a product of the very same kind of process we detected in Smith. And the epistemological question turns out to be scientifically solvable.

Note that this way of thinking about epistemology begins with observation of the world—of Smith and the tree. We could call it "third-person epistemology," or an "epistemology of the other." Only when the problem is (scientifically) solved with respect to humans or other animals generally is the solution deemed to apply also to me. I too, after all, am a human animal. Here we have a dramatic contrast with the way traditional epistemology—with its problem of the "external" world—has been conceived. Traditionally, epistemology has been thought to be a "first-person" problem.* How do I know that there is a tree before me, that I'm not deceived or dreaming? How do I know I can *trust* the processes (whatever they are) that lead me to say, "There's a tree," or "There's Smith"? How do I know that even the best psychology isn't simply an illusion? The basic problem, from this point of view, is not a factual question at all, but a normative one: Am I *justified* in believing there are things independent of my experience? Do I have a *right* to believe that?

From this point of view, there is an obvious objection to Quine's program.† Quine is simply begging the question, *assuming* we know that Smith knows about the tree, when what is at issue is whether any one of us knows anything at all. The

third-person and the first-person cases are not parallel. In the Smith case I can see both Smith and the tree—or at least I think I can. But in my own case what I have are simply my experiences (or stimulations), and I can't *compare* these items with an actually existing tree.* That my situation is just like Smith's is not something to be taken for granted; whether that is so or not is precisely the problem. The problem is not the scientific one of discovering the causal processes that lead me to my belief, but the problem of whether I am justified in trusting either my perceptions or my science—just as Descartes says.

What can a naturalized epistemologist say to this? One thing that Quine says is that this epistemological anxiety is merely a symptom of the quest for certainty, and like Peirce and Dewey, he thinks we have to give that up.† This old problem of the "external" world, trying to guarantee that our knowledge isn't deceptive, should simply be dismissed. Perhaps it will always be possible to pull back from our natural commitments and raise the skeptical worry, but we ought to go with the best knowledge we have, fallible though it may be; and our best knowledge is found in the sciences. Philosophy has no privileged place from which to judge the whole of that.

There is a second reply that can be made. The story that science tells of our history is an evolutionary one—a story of the environment selecting organisms (and hence species) that survive long enough to reproduce. Consider a deer calmly drinking from a water hole. A mountain lion approaches. Suddenly the deer tenses, raises its head, and in full alertness mode looks to the left. There must be something right about this reaction. It is not much of a stretch to say that there is something *true* in it. The deer's reaction *means* "Danger near—get ready to flee!" And what it means is correct.

---

*Remember Descartes sitting before the fire, wondering whether it is *true* that he holds a piece of paper in his hand, as he seems to.

†By Barry Stroud, for instance. See "The Significance of Naturalized Epistemology," in Kornblith, *Naturalizing Epistemology*.

---

*Here the pattern of the representational theory repeats itself. Notice that, unlike Rorty, Quine does not want to get rid of representations altogether, but to naturalize them. The aim is to account for representations in terms that do not put them outside the natural world.

†For Peirce, see p. 574; for Dewey, p. 582.

No doubt this sort of reaction is built into a deer's central nervous system. But suppose it weren't. Suppose a deer's input-output circuits were insensitive to the scent of a mountain lion. Deer reactions in the presence of a lion would then signify "All is well, continue feeding," deer would be easy prey, few would survive to reproduce their kind, and deer as a species would soon disappear. It is not much of a stretch to say that such a reaction would be in error; given a deer's innate goal of preserving its life, there would be something *false* about it. As John Dewey might say, such a reaction "will *not do*."

This suggests that a member of a species that has survived the winnowing process of evolutionary selection is *guaranteed* a certain fit with its environment. Its reactions to items that are crucial for its continued existence must be at least roughly right. Since we ourselves are such creatures, we can have some confidence that in basic matters that concern survival our expectations, our anticipations, and indeed our beliefs track the truth. Were such a capacity for truth not built into us by our genes, our ancestors would have perished long ago. As Daniel Dennett says, "Evolution has designed human beings to be rational, to believe what they ought to believe and want what they ought to want. . . . The capacity to believe would have no survival value unless it were a capacity to believe truths" (*TB*, 33; *IS*, 17). On basic matters, then, such as whether another person is nearby, we have a *right* to trust our senses. Evolutionary considerations provide a *justification* of such beliefs.

It is true that there is something circular about this justification. We begin by assuming we can know the relation between the deer and the mountain lion; we construct a theory explaining how the deer comes to know about the lion; and we then apply this theory to ourselves and think we are justified in claiming to know about the deer and the mountain lion—just what we were assuming at the start. But once we give up thinking that philosophy has some special insight, some argument that is in principle beyond the sciences, once we give up the quest for certainty and resolve to make do with what looks like our best knowledge, this circle may

not seem so forbidding. Perhaps it is only a matter of making the circle as comprehensive as possible—and resigning ourselves to fallibility as the human predicament.*

In helping itself to great gobs of the so-called external world in framing its explanations, evolutionary epistemology does not, and probably cannot, defeat traditional skepticism. Depending on your point of view, that may or may not be a problem for it. There are, however, several more specific problems that such an evolutionary epistemology faces. Let us briefly state three objections and see what might be said in reply.

First objection: It is unclear how far beyond basic needs relating directly to survival such truth-tracking extends; perhaps not very far. Some evolutionary epistemologists, however, suggest that there is an analogy between (a) an organism displaying a novel behavior in an unfamiliar situation, and (b) a scientist hypothesizing a cause for a puzzling occurrence. Both involve "guesses." Both are cases of trial and error. In the first case nature decides whether the organism's guess ("I can jump that chasm") is correct or not; if incorrect, it may be the end of the organism. In the second case, the scientist puts nature to the test to see, via observations of experimental results, whether her hypothesis ("Introducing gene X into corn DNA will make it resistant to rot") deserves to survive. Popper cleverly says that we humans have an advantage over simpler organisms because we can "make our theories, our conjectures, suffer in our stead in the struggle for the survival of the fittest."[9] Surviving species and unfalsified theories have something in common: Both have passed stringent tests of adequacy.

Second objection: False beliefs can also have survival value—as when you avoid contact with plague victims because you think they are possessed by demons. The evolutionary epistemologist must admit this. But the cure for such false beliefs is more and better science, more ingenious experi-

---

*There is a similarity at this point between naturalized epistemology and the *hermeneutic circle*. Compare Heidegger on understanding, pp. 662–663.

mentation to cull out the falsehoods. There will never be a guarantee that the hypotheses that survive are the true ones, but in eliminating one possible account after another, we can have some confidence that we are circling around and in toward the truth of the matter.

Third objection: There is evidence that we humans naturally make use of "inference rules" or heuristics that lead us astray.* Assuming that these tendencies to make mistakes have also been developed by evolutionary pressures, how can evolution be used to argue that as a rule we believe truly? In reply it must be admitted that humans are prone to make certain kinds of errors based on data available to them. But this admission shows that we have also developed to the point where we can identify these misleading short-cuts and temptations to find obvious the nonobvious. Knowing this, we can take precautions against being led down the garden path. Although there can be no certainty that we have identified all the possible slips and slides away from rationality, it is hard to see this as an objection to a naturalized, evolutionary theory of knowledge.

Physical realism, as we are understanding that term, does not necessitate naturalized epistemology, but they are harmonious, and each reinforces the other.

---

1. In what two ways does Quine believe that traditional empiricism has been dogmatic?
2. Explain why Quine thinks that our statements face the tribunal of experience "only as a corporate body."
3. What can we learn from an experiment that fails to produce a predicted observation?
4. How does Quine think of the distinction between science and metaphysics? Between science and common sense?
5. Explain "the maxim of minimal mutilation."

6. What is an *observation sentence,* and what role does such a sentence play for Quine?
7. What is an *ontology*? How do we determine what ontology we are committed to in accepting a certain belief or theory?
8. Contrast first-person epistemology with third-person epistemology.
9. How might evolutionary considerations provide a (partial) justification for our claims to know the world?
10. List three objections to the use of evolutionary considerations to justify our knowledge. List three replies.

The Matter of Minds: Daniel Dennett

It is obvious that a physical realist will need a theory of the mind. It is no less obvious that constructing such a theory will pose problems for the physical realist. He will have to give an account of mind that is consistent with science; and science seems to tell us that our minds are the wholly natural, evolutionary products of a world that is fundamentally material in character. There have been materialists in our tradition—Democritus, Epicurus, Hobbes, and Marx come to mind—but they have been a minority and their theories of the mind have not been very persuasive . The majority view, expressing what is sometimes called the "perennial philosophy," has been that mind cannot be reduced to matter but has some sort of independent status, perhaps in an immaterial soul (as in Plato, Aquinas, and Descartes), as a transcendental ego surpassing the categories of soul and body altogether (as in Kant), or as spirit (Hegel).

Intentionality   This problem for physical realists acquired a particularly sharp set of teeth in the late nineteenth century with the work of Franz Brentano (1838–1917), a German psychologist and philosopher. Brentano identifies the essential feature of mental phenomena as their Intentionality.* Each

---

*For a fascinating catalogue of such misleading procedures, see Richard Nisbett and Lee Ross, "Judgmental Heuristics and Knowledge Structures," in Nisbett and Ross, *Human Inference: Strategies and Shortcomings of Social Judgment* (Englewood Cliffs, NJ: Prentice-Hall, 1983), reprinted in Kornblith, *Naturalizing Epistemology.*

*Note that this is a technical term (deriving from medieval philosophy) and is to be distinguished from "intention" in the normal sense of the word. The latter refers to an antecedent of actions that are done for a purpose, actions that are (for that reason) intentional. Intentionality, in Brentano's sense, applies

and every mental act, he says, is Intentional, by which he means that it is *about* something, directed upon some object. You can't think without thinking *of* something, you can't hope without hoping *for* something, you can't fear without being afraid *of* something, you can't dream without dreaming *about* something, you can't remember without remembering something, and so on. There is always this "intended object" that is the focus of your mental acts. Mental acts are relational—as though there is something independent of themselves that they are aiming at.

The relation is a peculiar one, however, quite different from the relations that hold between physical objects and events. Consider the following facts. If *a* is next to *b,* it must be the case that both *a* and *b* exist. Nor could event e_1 occur before event e_2, unless both events existed. Moreover, if e_1 causes e_2, then again both must be real events. Here we have examples of relations that are spatial, temporal, and causal—arguably the fundamental characteristics of the physical world—and in each case the relation cannot hold unless both terms of the relation are existent.

But I can think about Santa Claus, dream of flying, and want a time travel machine. In each of these cases the relation holds, although one of the terms doesn't exist. There is no Santa Claus, I can't fly, and time travel machines are mere fictions. Mental acts may be directed on existing things; but they don't cease to be the acts they are, directed to the objects they are directed upon, just because those "objects" aren't there. This is very strange. It is so strange that it led Brentano to believe that mental phenomena were totally different in kind from physical phenomena.

There is an old principle usually ascribed to Leibniz that if *a* and *b* have all the same properties, then they aren't two things at all, but the same thing; "*a*" and "*b*" in this case are just two different names for that one thing. A corollary is that if *a* has a property that *b* lacks, then *a* and *b* cannot be identical; they must be two distinct things. Applied to

our case this seems to entail that mental phenomena, having the property of Intentionality, are not identical with physical phenomena that lack that property. Apparently, the mental cannot be reduced to the physical. And if that is so, then—apparently—physical realism is false. That's the problem.

Philosophers of mind in the second half of the twentieth century wrestle with this problem, many of them trying to reconcile the Brentano thesis with physicalism. Thinking about the problem has been given a boost by the advent of the computer, as well as by advances in neuroscience. These developments pose anew the old question: Can a machine think? In light of the Intentionality thesis, it might seem that the answer must be no. After all, both a computer and the brain are physical things, parts of the spatio-temporal, causal network of the natural world. But thinking is Intentional. How could a physical thing exhibit that sort of property? How could it be *about* something?

The many dimensions of this problem have led to the creation of an interdisciplinary research program known as *cognitive science.* Philosophers, linguists, psychologists, computer scientists (especially those in artificial intelligence research), and neuroscientists meet together regularly, read each other's papers, and work cooperatively, sharing results and criticisms in an attempt to solve the mysteries of the mind. This is an extremely vigorous and ongoing conversation and no brief treatment can pretend to do it justice. What we shall do here is just dip a toe into the waters at the philosophical end of this large pond, looking primarily at some work by Daniel Dennett (b. 1942).*

Intentional Systems Dennett's most famous concept is that of an Intentional System (*IS,* 3–22). He suggests that we think about a chess-playing computer. We can understand such a machine, he says,

---

to every mental act, not only to intentional actions in the usual sense of the word. When the technical term is at stake, I shall capitalize the word.

*Among the works of Dennett, you might like to look at *Brainstorms* (1978), *The Intentional Stance* (1987), *Kinds of Minds* (1997), and *Brainchildren* (1998). Other philosophers prominent in the cognitive science debates are Jerry Fodor, John Searle, Donald Davidson, Paul and Patricia Churchland, and Hilary Putnam—though there are many more.

in three fundamentally different ways. Suppose we are observing it in the middle of a game and we want to predict its next move. We can take up a *design stance* and make the prediction on the basis of its program, relying on how it is designed to operate. If we know how it is programmed, we can predict the next move on the basis of that program and the current state of play. This sort of prediction will work as long as the machine does not malfunction, in which case all bets from the design stance are off.

But even a malfunctioning computer's next move can be predicted if we adopt the *physical stance.* From this point of view we look at the actual physical constitution of the computer, the physical states the computer is in, and the causal transitions from state to state. On this basis, prediction of one state from another is possible in principle, but given the complexity of computers these days no one can make such predictions in an ongoing game.

Suppose, now, that our chess-playing computer has a program that modifies itself in the light of its wins and losses—that is, it improves with "experience"—and that we have sent it abroad for a series of games with Russian chess masters. When it comes back, no one—not even its original designers—will know its program, so prediction from the design stance will be impossible. Prediction from the physical stance remains impracticable. Is there any way, then, that we can predict its behavior? Yes. We can adopt the *Intentional stance* with respect to it.

We do this when we look at the computer as a *rational* system designed to realize certain *goals.* We are then apt to say things like this: "It wants to protect its king," and "It believes that attacking with the knight is the best way to do that." Now "wants" and "believes" are Intentional notions, of course, so in effect we are ascribing mental states to the machine. Predictions from this stance are somewhat chancy, but there isn't any better strategy available for playing such a machine. We play the computer as we would play another human being, expecting it to rationally choose the most effective move of those available in the current situation. Doing this is treating it as an Intentional System.

So does a computer have a mind? It is very natural at this point to resist, to say that these mental ascriptions are only a manner of speaking, that the computer doesn't *really* want things and believe things—not the way *we* do. It's only *useful* to speak *as if* it did. We can't take that *literally.* Surely there is nothing *in* the computer that would count as an actual desire or belief. But that reaction, of course, puts us face to face with the question: What is there in us that counts as one of these mental states? Supposing that we are physical systems "designed" by the evolutionary process—that our brain and central nervous system work on purely natural principles—how do we differ in this respect from the programmed chess-player? How can *we* be Intentional Systems? Yet we do have minds, don't we?[*]

Wilfrid Sellars calls this a clash between the "scientific" image of ourselves and the "manifest" image of ourselves. Can this conflict be resolved? A physical realist is likely to think that the key to reconciliation is the notion of *function.* The function of a thing is what it is for; the function of the heart, for instance, is to pump blood through the body. But notice that "function" is a *formal* notion, one that does not specify in detail what sort of item is suited to perform that function. Consider the idea of a fuel-delivery system for an internal combustion engine. These days most car engines are equipped with fuel injection, yet not so long ago carburetors were the norm. Carburetors and fuel-injection systems are constructed along very different lines, but they perform the same function of delivering a mix of air and fuel to the engine.

Could *belief* be a functional concept like this? That is what the physical realist claims. Ascribing a belief to a system—whether machine or human—is not attributing to the system something that is intrinsically mental, as opposed to physical; it is claiming that something in the system plays a certain *role,* performs a certain function. Exactly what that is remains unspecified from the Intentional point of view, just as one doesn't specify carburetors or fuel injection when talking about a fuel delivery system. It could be, then that believing,

---

[*]This seems a perfect example of what Wittgenstein calls the "form" of a philosophical problem: "I don't know my way about." "*This* isn't how it is!"—we say, "Yet *this* is how it has to *be!*" (See pp. 625, 626.)

desiring, hoping, fearing, and even thinking it-self—for all these concepts tell us—are just pro-cesses going on in the brain, processes that are wholly physical in nature.

Understood in this way, the lesson we should draw from Brentano's Intentionality thesis is that the mental cannot be *reduced* to the physical—just as Quine argued that talk of physical objects cannot be *defined* in terms of sense data—but that does not mean that mental talk brings with it an ontology of its own incompatible with the ontology of the phys-ical sciences. Adopting the Intentional Stance is a matter of understanding and explaining the behav-ior of a system by attributing to it internal states that are functional in nature.

On this view, for a system to believe that it is raining is for it to be in a state that is connected in various functional ways to its input and output, as well as to other functionally defined internal states. For instance, when Jones *believes* it is raining, Jones *expects to see* the streets wet, she is *inclined to reach* for the umbrella before going out, and she may *think* that she doesn't have to water the grass tonight.* Such an internal state, having multiple connections to other states—perceptual, behavioral, and men-tal—may well be a state of the central nervous sys-tem in a highly developed organism such as we are. Having such a state resident in one's brain just *is* to believe that it is raining.

Intentional ascriptions, then, constitute an over-lay, an interpretation in mentalistic terms of a sys-tem that may well be physical in nature. Many questions arise at this point and debate has been vigorous about how they should be answered. For one thing, how far down the evolutionary scale does it make sense to ascribe Intentionality? Do ants have beliefs? Do clams? Or how about a simple mechanism like a thermostat? Does the thermostat *want* to keep the temperature at a certain level? Does it now *believe* that the room is too cool and in light of that *choose* to turn on the furnace? It cer-tainly seems like we could adopt the Intentional Stance with regard to it, ascribe these properties to it, and explain its behavior in these terms. But, we

are inclined to say, it doesn't *really* have beliefs and desires—not like we do.

If we do say that, however, it seems we should specify just what is so different about us, and where the line should be drawn between those systems that are truly Intentional and those that are not. For his part, Dennett refuses to draw such a line.

> There is no magic moment in the transition from a simple thermostat to a system that *really* has an in-ternal representation of the world about it. The thermostat has a minimally demanding representa-tion of the world, fancier thermostats have more demanding representations of the world, fancier robots for helping around the house would have still more demanding representations of the world. Finally you reach us. . . .
>
> The differences are of degree, but nevertheless of such great degree that understanding the internal organization of a simple intentional system gives one very little basis for understanding the internal organization of a complex intentional system, such as a human being. (*TB,* 32, 33)

Dennett is content to let Intentional interpretation range far and wide, and simply says that it is less *use-ful* to apply it to clams and thermostats than to hu-mans and chess-playing computers. The former can be understood from the design and physical stand-points well enough. It is the complexity of the latter that makes it virtually impossible to understand, explain, and predict their behavior *except* from the Intentional point of view.

But this appeal to usefulness raises another ques-tion: Is Intentional ascription *merely* a pragmatic de-vice having no more than an instrumental use? Does it have no ontological implications whatsoever?* Although he confesses that he has written some things that suggest this, Dennett claims to be a kind of realist about belief and the other Intentional atti-tudes. Belief ascriptions, he says, trace out *real pat-terns* in the world—even though those patterns

---

*This view of belief has obvious affinities with that of Peirce. See pp. 568–570.

*Paul Churchland argues that so-called "folk psychology"—the way we naturally understand ourselves and others in Inten-tional terms—could be eliminated altogether in favor of neuro-science. Strictly speaking, he thinks, there are no such things as beliefs. See "Eliminative Materialism and the Propositional Atti-tudes," *Journal of Philosophy* 78, no. 2 (February 1981).

"I propose to see . . . what the mind looks like from the third-person, materialistic perspective of contemporary science."

—DANIEL DENNETT

won't be visible unless we use Intentional interpretation.* Dennett imagines some Martians who are super-physicists, so super that it is no trick for them to predict human behavior from the physical stance. But suppose

> that one of the Martians were to engage in a predicting contest with an Earthling. The Earthling and the Martian observe (and observe each other observing) a particular bit of local physical transaction. From the Earthling's point of view, this is what is observed. The telephone rings in Mrs. Gardner's kitchen. She answers, and this is what she says: "Oh, hello dear. You're coming home early? Within the hour? And bringing the boss to dinner? Pick up a bottle of wine on the way

home, then, and drive carefully." On the basis of this observation, our Earthling predicts that a large metallic vehicle with rubber tires will come to a stop in the drive within the hour, disgorging two human beings, one of whom will be holding a paper bag containing a bottle containing an alcoholic fluid. The prediction is a bit risky, perhaps, but a good bet on all counts. The Martian makes the same prediction, but has to avail himself of much more information about an extraordinary number of interactions of which, so far as he can tell, the Earthling is entirely ignorant. For instance, the deceleration of the vehicle at intersection A, five miles from the house, without which there would have been a collision with another vehicle—whose collision course had been laboriously calculated over some hundreds of meters by the Martian. The Earthling's performance would look like magic! How did the Earthling know that the human being who got out of the car and got the bottle in the shop would get back in? (*TB*, 26, 27)

The Earthling's knowledge is not magic, of course. But it depends absolutely on his making use of Intentional Stance concepts to interpret what is going on. Our lives are bound up in these Intentional patterns; we not only rely on them in anticipating the actions of others, we find them indispensable in understanding ourselves as both knowers and doers. "Knowing" is an Intentional notion, of course (as is "understanding") and if we regard ourselves as knowing anything we are viewing ourselves from the Intentional Stance. "Choosing to do *A*" is likewise Intentional; it involves knowing what I am aiming at, believing that doing *A* will achieve that aim, and (in the appropriate circumstances) trying to do *A*. Although for limited purposes (medical purposes, perhaps) I can regard myself purely as a physical mechanism, I cannot restrict myself to the physical stance when I act.* It is Intentionality that makes our lives *human*.

---

*Dennett compares the concept of belief to that of a center of gravity. Although it isn't an item installed at the factory or requiring periodic service, a car's center of gravity is real enough, as is proved when it rolls over in a sharp curve.

*Questions about the freedom of the will are relevant here. In *Elbow Room: The Varieties of Free Will Worth Wanting* (Oxford: Oxford University Press, 1984), Dennett makes use of the Intentional Stance to develop a quasi-Kantian, compatibilist view of human freedom, identifying increasing freedom with increasing rationality.

Granting that Intentionality is a level of interpretation beyond that of the design and physical stances, granting that it is useful—even indispensable for our form of life—and granting that it cannot be reduced to the physical, the question remains: Why does Intentional ascription work? That is, what is actually going on in complex Intentional Systems such as ourselves that allows such interpretation to succeed to the degree that it does in providing explanations and predictions.

Here a number of options are being actively pursued. Taking a cue from logic, linguistics, and computer science, some think that there must be analogues in the brain to the parts of a sentence— a kind of *language of thought.** One of the striking characteristics of thought and belief, after all, is that they can be expressed in language, and language has a grammatical and logical structure. So one can argue that distinctions between verbs and noun phrases, logical connectives, quantifiers, and grammatical transition rules must all be represented in the functioning brain if mental states are to be physically real and effective in controlling behavior. On this model, the brain is thought of as a kind of syntactic engine, a computational device operating on language-like items that in themselves are purely physical but that play functional roles that guarantee their meaningfulness.

Other philosophers find more promise in a different form of computation called *parallel distributed processing* or *connectionism.*† So-called neural nets do not operate in a linear fashion on well-defined atomistic units according to explicit rules, but can accept large amounts of data simultaneously and process it holistically. Models of the mind based on these principles are efficient in doing things that brains are very good at, such as recognizing patterns—faces, for instance. Moreover, they have

other nice features: They tolerate ambiguity well, they pick up on analogies, they can complete incomplete data sets, and they degrade slowly rather than crash all at once when some component fails. Connectionism shows much promise, but whether it will be superseded by yet another model remains to be seen.

Functionalism in one form or another sheds substantial light on the mind and its operations. But does it leave something out? Many philosophers are certain that it does. Even supposing that functionalism gives a good account of intelligent behavior and cognitive functioning, what about conscious experience, what it *feels like* to be thirsty, to love someone, to be jealous, or to remember last summer at the beach? There seems to be a subjective, first-person, qualitative, phenomenal aspect to our experience that isn't captured in objective third-person accounts of how the mind/brain functions. Is there more to mind than a computer model can capture? Or is our inclination to think so just an illusion?

David Chalmers has usefully provided a pair of terms in which to think about this. Attempting to discover how the mind works in processing information, reporting it, monitoring internal states, and controlling behavior he calls working on the "easy problems." They may be hard enough, but they have the character of "puzzles rather than mysteries." Functionalism is our best theory so far for understanding these matters. Contrasting with these problems is the "hard problem": How is it possible that our material brains should give rise to experience, to our subjectivity, in the first place? Why don't brain processes take place "in the dark," as it were? How come there is *something it is like* to be me?[10]

As you can imagine, there has been an enormous amount of argument surrounding this problem. Some, like Dennett, insist that once you have understood the structure, organization, and abilities of the mind, there is nothing further to be investigated. Others argue that there is indeed more to reality than can be captured in a third-person scientific explanation. The discussion is complex and very subtle on all sides. Let me just provide three

---

* Jerry Fodor has defended this option vigorously. See, for instance, *The Language of Thought* (New York: Thomas Y. Crowell, 1975) and "Propositional Attitudes," *Monist* 61, no. 4 (October 1978): 501–523.

† One of the most engaging treatments of the mind using these principles is Paul Churchland's book, *The Engine of Reason, the Seat of the Soul* (Cambridge, MA: MIT Press, 1995).

"intuition pumps"* that have been used to get you to see that functional, causal organization of the brain may not be all there is to the mind.

1. Thomas Nagel, in a now-classic article, asks, "What is it like to be a bat?"[11] Bats are mammals, and we assume they have experience. But what is their experience of the world like? Because bats fly in the dark, perceiving their surroundings by sonar or echolocation, their experience of the world must be very different from ours. In fact, that way of relating to one's surroundings is so alien that it is hard to imagine what the world must feel like to them. And yet, we are certain that there is *something it is like* to be a bat. What is that? Suppose we got a complete scientific theory of the bat, that we understood perfectly its physiology and behavioral psychology, its functional organization and how it works. Would we be any closer to understanding what it is like to *be* a bat? Would that help us grasp the subjective feel of bathood? It seems hard to believe it would. Even the best objective, third-person scientific account would seem to leave something out. And how bat experience is related to the bat's physical constitution—that is the hard problem.

2. Frank Jackson invites us to imagine that Mary is a brilliant scientist who has been shut up in a black-and-white room all her life, forced to investigate the world via a black-and-white television monitor.[12] She specializes in the neurophysiology of vision and has a complete understanding of the visual system of humans—of what goes on in us when we see a ripe tomato. She has a complete theory about how light affects the rods and cones in the eye, of how the optic nerve transmits signals to the visual center in the brain, and of what happens there.

Now suppose that she is released from her black-and-white environment and for the first time sees a ripe tomato. Question: Will she learn something? It seems hard to deny that she will, even though she had all the physical information about vision there could be. What will she learn? She will learn *what it is like* to see red—something that all her science couldn't tell her. She won't just *know about* seeing red; she will *experience* seeing red. And that's different. The hard problem is to explain how what she learns upon her release relates to what she knew before.

3. Could there be a creature that was physically identical to me, molecule for molecule, but differed just in this: that this creature had no mental life at all? We could call such a creature my zombie twin. This zombie would have the same functional organization that I have, would do exactly what I do, would say what I say, would even talk about its "experiences" just as I do, and so on. But inside it would be dark, empty; there would be no consciousness, no experience, nothing that it is like to be this creature.

The question is not whether zombies are likely to exist—whether, for example, my next-door neighbor might be a zombie. That is highly unlikely, given what we know empirically about the dependence of consciousness on physical states of the brain. The question is whether zombies are logically possible, conceivable. Is there any logical contradiction in the conception of a zombie? If not, then it is logically possible that I should have a zombie twin. And that is bad news for the functionalist who claims that her account can be the complete story about the mind. It does not give a complete account of the mind. It leaves something out.

Now a functionalist like Dennett is not without resources for replying to these thought experiments. With respect to the zombie story, for example, he simply denies that zombies are possible. If a creature behaves in all respects like a conscious agent, then it is a conscious agent. There is no gap between functional organization and consciousness into which one might drive a wedge. But we cannot pursue these matters further here. Suffice it to say that the consciousness issue is one of the hottest philosophical topics around these days, and is likely to remain so for many years.

---

*The term is Dennett's. An intuition pump is a little story, a thought experiment, that is designed to generate in you a certain intuition, to get you to have an "Aha!" experience in which you say, "Of course, that's how it is."

1. What property of mental acts does the term "Intentionality" refer to?

2. Why is Intentionality a problem for a physicalist account of the mind?

3. Explain the notion of an Intentional System by contrasting Dennett's three stances: design, physical, Intentional.

4. How does the notion of *function* help to reconcile Intentionality with the physical basis of mind?

5. If Intentionality cannot be "reduced" to the physical, does it follow that minds are something other than matter? Why or why not?

6. What does Dennett say about the question: Does a thermostat have a mind?

7. Is ascribing Intentional properties to things merely a matter of a useful strategy? Or do mental concepts like *belief* pick out something real? (Use the example of the Martian physicists.)

8. Contrast the "language of thought" hypothesis with the "connectionist" hypothesis.

9. What is an "intuition pump"? Describe three intuition pumps that suggest functionalism's inadequacy as a *complete* account of the mind.

For Further Thought

1. Apply the notion of postmodernism by finding examples of it in recent culture: movies, music, literature, politics, or university classes.

2. Is science our best avenue to truth about the world, as Quine and the physical realists believe? Or is it just one more tool useful for control over nature, as Rorty and the postmodernists think? Write a page or two justifying your answer.

3. Could a machine think? In light of the Intentionality of mental acts, explain your answer.

4. Is there any way to escape the complete relativism of "true-for-me" and "true-for-you"?

Notes

1. References to the following works are all to page numbers.

References to the works of Jacques Derrida are as follows:

D: "Différance" in *Margins of Philosophy* (1972), trans. Alan Bass (Chicago: University of Chicago Press, 1982).

LI: "Limited Inc a, b, c . . ." (1977), trans. Samuel Weber, in *Limited Inc* (Evanston, IL: Northwestern University Press, 1988).

PP: "Plato's Pharmacy" in *Dissemination* (1972), trans. Barbara Johnson (Chicago: University of Chicago Press, 1981).

SEC: "Signature, Event Context" (1972), trans. Samuel Weber and Jeffrey Mehlman, in *Limited Inc* (Evanston, IL: Northwestern University Press, 1988).

References to the works of Richard Rorty are as follows:

CIS: Contingency, irony, and solidarity (Cambridge: Cambridge University Press, 1989).

PMN: Philosophy and the Mirror of Nature (Princeton: Princeton University Press, 1979).

PSH: Philosophy and Social Hope (London: Penguin Books, 1999).

RC: Rorty and His Critics, ed. Robert B. Brandom (Oxford: Blackwell, 2000).

References to the works of Willard van Orman Quine are as follows:

EN: "Epistemology Naturalized," in *Naturalizing Epistemology,* ed. Hilary Kornblith (Cambridge, MA: MIT Press, 1985).

OWTI: "On What There Is," in *From a Logical Point of View* (New York: Harper Torchbooks, 1963).

TDE: "Two Dogmas of Empiricism," in *From a Logical Point of View* (New York: Harper Torchbooks, 1963).

PT: Pursuit of Truth (Cambridge, MA: Harvard University Press, 1990).

References to the works of Daniel Dennett are as follows:

IS: "Intentional Systems," in *Brainstorms: Philosophical Essays on Mind and Psychology* (n.p.: Bradford Books, 1978).

TB: "True Believers," in *The Intentional Stance* (Cambridge, MA: MIT Press, 1987).

2. Thomas Nagel, *The Last Word* (Oxford: Oxford University Press, 1997), 5, 6.

3. Karl Popper, *The Logic of Scientific Discovery* (London: Hutchinson, 1959), 15.

4. Wilfrid Sellars, "Philosophy and the Scientific Image of Man," in *Science, Perception, and Reality* (London: Routledge and Kegan Paul, 1963), 1.

5. Roy Wood Sellars, *The Philosophy of Physical Realism* (New York: Macmillan, 1932).

6. W. V. Quine and J. S. Ullian, *The Web of Belief* (New York: Random House, 1970).

7. W. V. Quine, "Comment on Haak," in *Perspectives on Quine,* ed. R. B. Barrett and R. F. Gibson (Oxford: Blackwell, 1990), 128.

8. Wilfrid Sellars, "Empiricism and the Philosophy of Mind," in *Science, Perception and Reality* (London: Routledge and Kegan Paul, 1963), 127–196.

9. Karl Popper, *Conjectures and Refutations: The Growth of Scientific Knowledge* (London: Routledge and Kegan Paul, 1963), 52.

10. David J. Chalmers, "Consciousness and Its Place in Nature," in *Philosophy of Mind: Classical and Contemporary Readings* (Oxford: Oxford University Press, 2002), 247.

11. Reprinted in Thomas Nagel, *Mortal Questions* (Cambridge: Cambridge University Press, 1979), 165–180.

12. Frank Jackson, "Epiphenomenal Qualia," in Chalmers, *Philosophy of Mind,* 273–280.

AFTERWORD

This book is a history of the Western philosophical tradition whose home is in Greece and Jerusalem, Europe, Great Britain, and America. It is also an introductory book, touching only on highlights of this Western tradition. If anything is obvious these days, it is that there are other vigorous traditions as well. This fifth edition gestures in that direction with brief profiles of the Buddha, Avicenna, Averroës, and Maimonides, but these are mere hints of riches that lie beyond the scope of the book. There is no doubt that we have much to learn from other ways of thinking about the fundamental problems, just as others have much to learn from us. But we will only be shallow partners in cross-cultural conversations if we do not understand ourselves; and the way to understand ourselves is to understand our history.

The book also gives a very inadequate hint of the lively and interesting philosophical work being done today. New problems provoke novel thinking. New technologies bring new possibilities, and these may promise good or threaten evil. Ethical problems are posed by genetic manipulation, clon-

ing, and computing. Problems of global warming, terrorism, genocide, poverty, the environment, abortion, and euthanasia call for philosophical reflection about ends and means, and about human nature. The resurgence of religion keeps the tension with reason and science alive. Reflection continues on the challenges of skepticism and the extent and character of human knowledge. We can hardly say that Kant's four questions (What can we know? What ought we to do? For what can we hope? And what is man?) have been definitively answered.

Nor has the question about relativism been settled to the satisfaction of everyone. The rise of "multiculturalism" raises questions about the extent to which every culture deserves equal respect; are there some cultures that are better than others? If so, how would one tell? Is it all just a matter of opinion, as the ancient Sophists thought? Must might make right? Though the problem sometimes seems intractable, it is impossible to avoid taking up a point of view on the question. Some are struggling to see whether there is a way to acknowledge a truth in relativism without giving up the Socratic quest altogether.*

Philosophy isn't everything. Daniel Dennett has said that if the unexamined life is not worth living

---

*For a look at recent argument about relativism, see Norman Melchert, *Who's to Say? A Dialogue on Relativism* (Indianapolis: Hackett, 1994).

(Socrates), the overexamined life is nothing to write home about either. But philosophy has the peculiar characteristic of being inescapable for us all. So we should try to think about these matters with something approaching Aristotelian "excellence," remembering what my own little old German professor once said: "Whether you will philosophize or won't philosophize, you *must* philosophize."

GLOSSARY

Here you will find brief explanations of difficult or unfamiliar terms, sometimes followed in parentheses by the name or names of philosophers with whom the term is especially—though not solely—associated.

absolute knowledge A term in HEGEL's philosophy, designating the state of consciousness when everything "other" has been brought into itself and Spirit knows itself to be all of reality.

aesthetic KIERKEGAARD's term for the style of life that aims at avoiding boredom and keeping things interesting; the pursuit of pleasurable experiences. **Aesthetics** (also spelled "esthetics") is the theory of art and of the experience of the beautiful or sublime.

alienation HEGELian term appropriated by MARX to describe the loss of oneself and control over what properly belongs to oneself in capitalist social structures. One's work and the products of one's labor, for instance, are made alien to oneself and belong to another. Existentialism stresses the general feeling of alienation among modern human beings.

ambiguity A term applied to human reality, indicating its immanence and transcendence. (SIMONE DE BEAUVOIR)

analytic A term applied to statements the denial of which is a contradiction (for example, "All bachelors are unmarried"). (KANT, **logical positivists**)

anticipatory resoluteness HEIDEGGER's term for authentically facing the fact that one is destined for death.

a posteriori A term applied primarily to statements, but also to ideas or concepts; knowledge of the a posteriori is derived from (comes *after*) experience (for example, "Trees have leaves"). (KANT)

appearance The way things present themselves to us, often contrasted with the way they really are (for example, the oar in water appears bent but is really straight). KANT holds that all we can ever come to know is how **things-in-themselves** *appear* to our senses and understanding; appearance is the realm of **phenomena** versus **noumena.** (PARMENIDES)

a priori A term applied primarily to statements, but also to ideas or concepts, that can be known *prior to* and independently of appeal to experience (for example, "Two and three are five," or "All bodies are extended"). (KANT)

argument A set of statements, some of which (the premises) function as reasons to accept another (the conclusion).

atomism From a Greek word meaning "uncuttable"; the ancient Greek view (by DEMOCRITUS and others) that all of reality is composed of tiny indivisible bits and the void (empty space). See also **logical atomism.**

attunement In HEIDEGGER's thinking, the term for a mode of disclosure that manifests itself in a mood; for example, the mood of anxiety discloses **Dasein's** not-being-at-home in the world of its ordinary concern.

authenticity Being oneself, taking responsibility for oneself in accepting the burden of having to "be here"—that is, thrown into this particular existence with just these possibilities. (HEIDEGGER)

autonomy Self-rule or giving the law to oneself, as opposed to *heteronomy,* being under the control of another. A key principle in KANT's **ethics.**

Being The fundamental concept of **metaphysics.** Doctrines of **categories** such as those of ARISTOTLE and KANT attempt to set forth the most general ways that things can *be.* The meaning of Being is the object of HEIDEGGER's quest.

Being-in-the world The most general characteristic of **Dasein,** according to HEIDEGGER; more fundamental than knowing, it is being engaged in the use of gear or equipment in a world functionally organized.

binary opposition A pair of terms, each of which lives on its opposition to the other. Examples are: appearance/reality, knowledge/opinion, one/many, speaking/writing, and good/evil. Often a target for deconstruction by postmodernists.

categorical imperative The key principle in KANT's moral theory, bidding us always to act in such a way that the maxim (principle) of our action could be universally applied.

categories Very general concepts describing the basic modes of being. ARISTOTLE distinguishes ten, including "substance," "quantity," and "quality." KANT lists twelve, the most important of which are "substance" and "causality."

causation What accounts for the occurrence or character of something. ARISTOTLE distinguishes four kinds of cause: material, formal, efficient, and final. According to most recent theories, influenced by HUME, causation is a relationship between events, where the first is regularly or lawfully related to the second.

compatibilism The view that human liberty (or freedom of the will) can coexist with determinism—the universal **causation** of all events. Classic sources are HOBBES and HUME.

contingency The opposite of necessity. RORTY, particularly, emphasizes the historical contingency of our language and point of view; neither is necessitated by the character of the world they are about.

convention The Sophists contrast what is true by nature (*physis*) with what is true by convention or agreement (*nomos*) among humans. The latter, but not the former, can also be changed by human decision.

correspondence A view of truth; a statement is said to be true, provided that it "corresponds" with what it is about—that is, it *says* that reality is such and such, and reality *is in fact* such and such. (ARISTOTLE, AQUINAS, LOCKE)

criterion A mark or standard by which something is known. The "problem of the criterion" is posed by skeptics, who ask by what criterion we can tell that we know something and, if an answer is given, by what criterion we know that this is the correct criterion. (SEXTUS EMPIRICUS, MONTAIGNE, DESCARTES, HEGEL)

Dasein HEIDEGGER's term for the way of being that is characteristic of humans. Literally meaning "being there," it designates that way to be in which one's own **Being** is a matter of concern.

determinism The view that there is a causal condition for every event, without exception, sufficient to produce that event just as it is. The philosophical relevance of determinism lies particularly in relation to human action. (DEMOCRITUS, EPICURUS, HUME, KANT)

dialectic A term of many meanings. For SOCRATES, it is a progression of questions and answers, driving toward less inadequate opinions. For PLATO, it is the sort of reasoning that moves from **Forms** to more basic Forms, and at last to the Form of the Good. For HEGEL, it is the progress of both thought and reality by the reconciliation of opposites and the generation of new opposites. MARXists apply the Hegelian doctrine to the world of material production.

différance DERRIDA's term for the destabilizing of meaning and reference by language as a system of differences; a word is what it is because it *differs* from other words, and it fails to *present* its signified meaning because it *defers* it to other interpretations.

dogmatism A term applied by philosophers to the holding of views for no adequate reason.

dualism The metaphysical view that there are two basically different kinds of things in reality; the most common dualism is that of mind and body, as in DESCARTES, for instance. (Compare **monism.**)

empiricism The view that all knowledge of facts must be derived from sense experience; a rejection of **rationalism,** the view that any knowledge of nature is innate or constructable by reasoning alone. Exemplified by HUME, LOCKE, BERKELEY, and the **logical positivists.**

enframing HEIDEGGER's term for the technological understanding of **Being** as **standing-reserve,** where everything is "set upon" to produce the maximum yield at minimum expense. Enframing is the essence or *meaning* of technology.

entelechy A goal or end residing within a thing, guiding its development from potentiality to the actuality of its **essence.** (ARISTOTLE)

epiphenomenalism The view that consciousness is an effect of physical happenings in the body but has no causal powers itself. It is just "along for the ride."

epistemology Theory of knowledge, addressing the questions of what knowledge is, whether we have any, what its objects may be, and how we can reliably get more.

essence The set of properties that makes each thing uniquely the kind of thing that it is. (ARISTOTLE, AQUINAS, DESCARTES)

ethics The study of good and evil, right and wrong, moral rules, virtues, and the good life; their status, meaning, and justification.

eudaemonia Greek term for happiness or well-being. (PLATO, ARISTOTLE, EPICURUS, the Stoics, the Skeptics)

existentialism The philosophy that focuses on what it means to exist in the way human beings do—usually stressing choice, risk, and freedom. KIERKEGAARD is a main figure, as is HEIDEGGER and DE BEAUVOIR.

facticity The way of **Being** of **Dasein.** One aspect of our facticity, for instance, is our **Being-in-the-world;** another is our **thrownness**—simply finding ourselves in existence in some particular way. (HEIDEGGER)

fallibilism The view expressed by PEIRCE, and earlier by XENOPHANES, that though we may know the truth in certain cases, perhaps in many cases, we can never be certain that we do.

falling HEIDEGGER's term for the phenomenon of being defined by others. **Dasein** inevitably *falls-in-with* what "they" say and tends strongly to *fall-away-from* itself.

family resemblance WITTGENSTEIN's term for the way many of our concepts get their meaning. There is no set of necessary and sufficient conditions for an item to be a *game,* for instance, only overlapping and criss-crossing resemblances among instances of things we call games.

Forms Those ideal realities PLATO takes to be both the objects of knowledge and the source of the derived reality of the sensible world: the Square Itself, for instance, and the Forms of Justice and the Good. Used uncapitalized for the forms of ARISTOTLE and AQUINAS, which have no being apart from the particular things that exemplify them.

free spirit A term used by certain late-nineteenth-century thinkers, such as NIETZSCHE, to symbolize their freedom from the inherited tradition—particularly the religious tradition.

Great Chain of Being The view that reality is stretched between God (or **the One**) and nothingness, with each kind of thing possessing its own degree of being and goodness. Found in PLOTINUS and AUGUSTINE; widespread for many centuries.

hedonism The view that pleasure is the sole objective of motivation (psychological hedonism) or that it is the only thing good in itself (ethical hedonism). (EPICURUS, BENTHAM, MILL)

hermeneutic circle The idea that any interpretation takes something for granted; for example, understanding part of a text presupposes an understanding of the whole, and vice versa. Every understanding lights up its objects only against a background that cannot at the same time be brought into the light. It follows that complete objectivity is impossible. (HEIDEGGER)

hubris A Greek word meaning arrogance or excessive self-confidence, particularly of mortals in relation to the gods.

hylomorphism The theory that every material object is a composite of matter (*hyle*) and form (*morphe*); matter is the potentiality of a thing, form its actuality. (ARISTOTLE, AQUINAS—with qualifications)

idealism The view that objects exist only relative to a subject that perceives or knows them. There are many forms; in HEGEL's *absolute idealism,* for instance, mind or Spirit (the Absolute) is the only ultimate reality, everything else having only a relative reality. (also BERKELEY)

inauthenticity HEIDEGGER's word for **Dasein**'s fleeing from itself into the average everyday world of what "they" say and do; not being oneself.

induction A method of reasoning that infers from a series of single cases to a new case or to a law or general principle concerning all such cases.

innate ideas Ideas that any mature individual can acquire independently of experience. Defended in different ways by PLATO and by DESCARTES, attacked by LOCKE and the empiricists.

instrumentalism DEWEY's term for his own philosophy, according to which all our intellectual constructions (concepts, laws, theories) have the status of tools for solving problems.

language-games Comparing words to pieces in a game such as chess. What defines a rook are the rules according to which it moves; what characterizes a word are the jobs it does in those activities and forms of life in which it has its "home." Language is a game we play with words. (the later WITTGENSTEIN)

light of nature DESCARTES' term for reason, in the light of which things can appear so clear and distinct that they cannot possibly be doubted.

logical atomism A view expressed by the early WITTGENSTEIN, in which language is thought of as a logical calculus built up from simple unanalyzable elements called *names*. Names stand for simple objects, which are the substance of the world.

logical positivism A twentieth-century version of **empiricism,** which stresses the **tautological** nature of logic and mathematics, together with the criterion of **verifiability** for factual statements; if they are not verifiable by sense experience, the statements are not meaningful.

logical truth Truths that are true by virtue of logic alone. WITTGENSTEIN explains logical truths as **tautologies.**

logocentrism The view DERRIDA finds dominant in our tradition, where knowledge finds a foundation in its objects being present to consciousness and reason and logic are thought to be reliable avenues to the extension of truth.

logos Greek term meaning word, utterance, rationale, argument, structure. In HERACLITUS, the ordering principle of the world; in the Gospel of John, that according to which all things were made and that became incarnate in Jesus.

materialism The view that the fundamental reality is matter, as understood by the sciences—primarily physics; mind or spirit has no independent reality. (HOBBES)

metaphysics The discipline that studies being as such, its kinds and character, often set out in a doctrine of **categories.** Also called by some "first philosophy."

monism The metaphysical view that there is only one basic kind of reality; materialism is one kind of monism, HEGELian idealism another. (Compare **dualism.**)

naturalism A view that locates human beings wholly within nature and takes the results of the natural and human sciences to be our best idea of what there is; since DARWIN, naturalists in philosophy insist that the human world is a product of the nonpurposive process of evolution.

natural law Law specifying right and wrong, which is embedded in the very nature of things; natural law is not based on custom or convention and therefore applies universally. (Stoics, AQUINAS, LOCKE)

nihilism The view that nothing really matters, that distinctions of value have no grounding in the nature of things; what threatens, according to NIETZSCHE, when God dies.

nominal essence An essence that is determined not by the true nature of things, but by the words we have for them. (LOCKE)

nomos The way things are insofar as they depend on human decision, custom, or convention. (Compare **physis.**) (Sophists)

noumena KANT's term for things as they are in themselves, quite independently of how they may appear to us; he believes they are unknowable. (Contrasted with **phenomena** or **appearance.**)

nous Greek term usually translated as "mind." In ARISTOTLE, *nous* is the active and purely formal principle that engages in thinking and contemplation; he argues that *nous* is more than just the form of a living body; it is a reality in its own right and is eternal.

objective spirit That realm in which Spirit expresses itself externally, giving rationality to institutions, law, and culture. (HEGEL)

Ockham's razor A principle stated by WILLIAM OF OCKHAM, demanding parsimony in the postulation of entities for the purpose of explanation; often formulated as "Do not multiply entities beyond necessity."

One, the 1. In PLOTINUS and Neoplatonic thought, the source from which the rest of reality emanates. 2. A translation of HEIDEGGER's term "*das Man,*" designating **Dasein** as not differentiated from the "Others," the crowd, the anonymous many who dictate how life goes and what it means.

ontic HEIDEGGER's term for the realm of ordinary and scientific facts. (Compare **ontological.**)

ontological 1. Having to do with **Being,** with what there is in the most general sense. 2. In HEIDEGGER, having to do with the deep structure of **Dasein's Being** that makes possible the **ontic** facts about average everydayness; disclosed in *fundamental ontology.*

ontological argument An argument for God's existence that proceeds solely from an idea of what God is, from his **essence.** Different versions found in ANSELM and DESCARTES; criticized by AQUINAS, HUME, and KANT.

ontological difference The radical difference in kind between any being (thing or entity) and its **Being**—that is, its sheer being-the-entity-that-it-is. (HEIDEGGER)

phenomena What appears, just as it appears. In KANT, contrasted with *noumena.* The object of study by **phenomenology.**

phenomenology The attempt to describe what appears to consciousness; a science of consciousness, its structures, contents, and objects. (In HEGEL and later in HUSSERL and HEIDEGGER.)

physis The way things are, independently of any human decision; from it, our word "physics" comes. (Compare *nomos.*) (Sophists)

pictorial form What a picture and the pictured have in common, which allows the first to picture the second. (early WITTGENSTEIN)

possible experience In KANT, a term designating the extent to which sensibility and understanding can reach, structured as they are by the **a priori** intuitions of space and time, together with the **a priori** concepts or **categories.**

possible state of affairs In early WITTGENSTEIN, the way in which objects could relate to each other to constitute a fact.

pragmatism A view developed by PEIRCE, JAMES, and DEWEY, in which all of our intellectual life is understood in relation to our practical interests. What a concept means, for instance, depends wholly on the practical effects of the object of our concept.

present-at-hand A HEIDEGGERian term for things understood as bereft of their usual functional relation to our interests and concerns; what "objective" science takes as its object. A modification of our usual relation to things as **ready-to-hand.**

primary qualities In GALILEO and other early moderns, qualities that a thing actually has—for example, size, shape, location—and that account for or explain certain effects in us (**secondary qualities**), such as

sweetness, redness, warmth. (DESCARTES, LOCKE, BERKELEY)

quiddity Latin-origin term for *what* a thing is; its essence, in contrast to its actual existence. (AQUINAS)

rationalism The philosophical stance that is distrustful of the senses, relying only on reason and rational argument to deliver the truth. (PARMENIDES and DESCARTES)

rational psychology KANT's term for the discipline that attempts to gain knowledge of the self or soul in nonempirical ways, relying on rational argument alone; KANT thinks it an illusion that rational psychology produces knowledge.

ready-to-hand HEIDEGGER's term for the mode of **Being** of the things that are most familiar to **Dasein;** gear or equipment in its functional relation to **Dasein's** concerns.

realism A term of many meanings; central is the contention that reality is both logically and causally independent of even the best human beliefs and theories.

relativism A term of many meanings; central is the view that there are no objective standards of good or bad to be discovered and that no objective knowledge of reality is possible; all standards and knowledge claims are valid only relative to times, individuals, or cultures. (Sophists)

representational theory The view that our access to reality is limited to our perceptions and ideas, which function as representations of things beyond themselves; a problem associated with this theory is how we can ever know that there are things beyond these representations. (DESCARTES, LOCKE, BERKELEY)

rhetoric The art of persuasive speaking developed and taught by the **Sophists** in ancient Greece, whose aim was to show how a persuasive *logos* could be constructed on each side of a controversial issue.

secondary qualities Those qualities, such as taste and color, produced in us by the **primary qualities** of objects—size, shape, and so on. (GALILEO, DESCARTES, LOCKE, BERKELEY)

semantics Study of word–world relationships; how words relate to what they are about. (PEIRCE)

sense-certainty What is left if we subtract from sensory experience all interpretation in terms of concepts, for example, the sheer blueness we experience when we look at a clear sky; the immediate; where HEGEL thinks philosophy must start, though it is forced to go on from there.

showing Contrasted in WITTGENSTEIN's early philosophy with *saying;* logic, for instance, shows itself in every bit of language; a proposition *shows* (displays) its sense, and it *says* that this is how things stand.

skepticism The view that for every claim to know, reason can be given to doubt it; the skeptic suspends judgment about reality (SEXTUS EMPIRICUS, MONTAIGNE). DESCARTES uses skeptical arguments to try to find something that cannot be doubted.

social contract The theory that government finds its justification in an agreement or contract among individuals. (HOBBES, LOCKE)

solipsism The view, which must be stated in the first person, that only I exist; the worry about falling into solipsism motivates DESCARTES to try to prove the existence of God.

Sophist From a Greek word meaning "wise one"; in ancient Greece, teachers who taught many things to ambitious young men but who specialized in **rhetoric.**

standing-reserve HEIDEGGER's term for the way **Being** is apprehended in a technological society—as entities ready for rational ordering, stockpiling, and use.

Stoicism The view that happiness and freedom are at hand for the asking if we but distinguish clearly what properly belongs to ourselves and what is beyond our power, limiting our desires to the former and thus keeping our wills in harmony with nature.

substance What is fundamental and can exist independently; that which has or underlies its qualities. There is disagreement about what is substantial: PLATO takes it to be the **Forms,** ARISTOTLE the individual things of our experience. Some philosophers (for example, SPINOZA) argue that there is but *one* substance: God. (also LOCKE, BERKELEY, KANT, HEGEL)

syllogism An **argument** comprising two premises and a conclusion, composed of categorical subject—predicate statements; the argument contains just three terms, each of which appears in just two of the statements. (ARISTOTLE)

synthetic A term applied to statements the denial of which is not contradictory; according to KANT, in a synthetic statement the predicate is not "contained" in the subject but adds something to it (for example, "Mount Cook is the highest mountain in New Zealand").

tautology A statement for which the truth table contains only T's. WITTGENSTEIN uses the concept to explain the nature of logical truth and the laws of logic.

teleology Purposiveness or goal-directedness; a teleological explanation for some fact is an explanation in terms of what end it serves. (ARISTOTLE, HEIDEGGER)

theodicy The justification of the ways of God to man, especially in relation to the problem of evil: What would justify an all-powerful, wise, and good God in creating a world containing so many evils? (AUGUSTINE, HEGEL)

things-in-themselves In KANT's philosophy, things as they are, quite independent of our apprehension of them, of the way they appear to us; *noumena.* Things-in-themselves are (for Kant) unknowable.

Third Man Term for a problem with PLATO's **Forms:** We seem to be forced into an infinite regress of Forms to account for the similarity of two men.

thrownness HEIDEGGER's term for **Dasein's** simply finding itself in existence under certain conditions, without ever having a choice about that.

transcendental Term for the conditions on the side of the subject that make knowing or doing possible. KANT's critical philosophy is a transcendental investigation; it asks about the **a priori** conditions for experience and action in general.

utilitarianism Moral philosophy that takes consequences as the criteria for the moral evaluation of action; of two alternative actions open to one, it is right to choose the one that will produce the best consequences for all concerned—for example, the most pleasure or happiness.

validity A term for logical goodness in deductive arguments; an **argument** is valid whenever, if the premises are true, it is not possible for the conclusion to be false. An argument can be valid, however, even if the premises are false.

verifiability principle The rule adopted by the **logical positivists** to determine meaningfulness in factual statements; if no sense experience can count in favor of the truth of a statement—can verify it at least to some degree—it is declared meaningless, since meaning is said to consist in such verifiability.

Text Credits

Extracts from Hesiod, "Theogony" in *Hesiod and Theognis,* translated by Dorothea Wender (Penguin Classics, 1973), copyright © 1973 by Dorothea Wender. Reprinted by permission of Penguin Books Ltd.

Extracts from Homer, *The Iliad,* translated by Robert Fagles, translation copyright © 1990 by Robert Fagles. Introduction and notes copyright © 1990 by Bernard Knox. Used by permission of Viking Penguin, a division of Penguin Putnam Inc.

Extracts from Homer, "Book 11: The Kingdom of the Dead" in *The Odyssey,* translated by Robert Fagles, translation copyright © 1996 by Robert Fagles. Used by permission of Viking Penguin, a division of Penguin Putnam Inc.

Extracts from John Mansley Robinson, *An Introduction to Early Greek Philosophy,* copyright © 1968 by Houghton Mifflin Company. Used with permission of the publisher.

Extracts from Aristophanes, *The Clouds,* translated by William Arrowsmith, copyright © 1962 by William Arrowsmith. Reprinted by arrangement with New American Library, a division of Penguin Books USA Inc.

Extracts from Thucydides, *The Peloponnesian War,* translated by Rex Warner (Penguin Classics, 1954), copyright © 1954 by Rex Warner. Reprinted by permission of Penguin Books Ltd.

Extracts from Euripides, *Hippolytus,* in *Euripides I,* copyright © 1955 by University of Chicago Press. Reprinted with permission of the publisher.

Extracts from Plato, *Gorgias,* translated by Robin Waterfield. Copyright © 1994 by Oxford University Press.

Extracts from Xenophon in W. K. C. Guthrie, *The Greeks and Their Gods,* copyright © 1950 by Methuen & Company. Reprinted with permission of the publisher.

Extracts from Plato, *Symposium,* translated by Robin Waterfield. Copyright © 1994 by Oxford University Press.

Extracts from Plato, *Euthyphro, Apology, Crito,* and *Phaedo* in *The Trial and Death of Socrates,* Hackett Publishing Company, 1980. Translated by G. M. A. Grube. Reprinted by permission of Hackett Publishing Company. All rights reserved.

Extracts from Plato, *Phaedo,* translated by David Gallop. Copyright © 1993 by Oxford University Press.

Extracts from Plato, *Protagoras,* translated by C. C. W. Taylor. Copyright © 1996 by Oxford University Press.

Extracts from Plato, *Meno,* translated by Robin Waterfield. Copyright © 2005 by Oxford University Press.

Extracts from Plato, *The Republic,* translated by Robin Waterfield. Copyright © 1993 by Oxford University Press.

Extracts from Renford Bambrough, *The Philosophy of Aristotle,* copyright © 1963 by Renford Bambrough. Reprinted by arrangement with New American Library, a division of Penguin Books USA Inc.

Extracts from Epicurus, *Letters, Principal Doctrines and Vatican Sayings,* translated by Russel M. Geer, copyright © 1964 by Prentice-Hall, Inc. Reprinted by permission of Prentice-Hall, Inc., Upper Saddle River, NJ.

Extracts from Lucretius, *The Way Things Are,* translated by Rolfe Humphries, copyright © 1969 by Indiana University Press. Reprinted by permission of the publisher.

Extracts from *The Handbook of Epictetus,* translated by Nicholas P. White, Hackett Publishing Company, 1983. Reprinted by permission of Hackett Publishing Company. All rights reserved.

Extracts from Sextus Empiricus, *Outlines of Pyrrhonism,* vol. I, Loeb Classical Library, vol. 273, translated by R. G. Bury, copyright © 1933 by Harvard University Press. Reprinted by permission of the publishers and the trustees of the Loeb Classical Library. The Loeb Classical Library® is a registered trademark of the President and Fellows of Harvard College.

Extracts from the *Revised Standard Version of the Bible,* copyright © 1946, 1952, 1971 by the National Council of Churches of Christ in the U.S.A. Reprinted with permission.

Extracts from Augustine, *Confessions,* translated by R. S. Pine-Coffin (Penguin Classics, 1961), copyright © 1961 by R. S. Pine-Coffin. Reprinted by permission of Penguin Books Ltd.

Extracts from Augustine, *On Free Choice of the Will,* translated by Anna S. Benjamin and L. H. Hackstaff, copyright © 1964 by Prentice-Hall, Inc. Reprinted by permission of Prentice-Hall, Inc.

Extracts from Augustine, *The City of God,* translated by Henry Bettenson (Penguin Classics, 1972), copyright © 1972 by Henry Bettenson. Reprinted by permission of Penguin Books Ltd.

Extracts from Augustine, *On Christian Doctrine,* translated by D. W. Robertson, Jr., copyright © 1958, renewed © 1986 by Prentice-Hall, Inc. Reprinted with permission of Prentice-Hall, Inc.

Extracts from *Aquinas: Selected Philosophical Writings,* translated and edited by Timothy McDermott (Oxford World's Classics, 1993), copyright © 1993 by Timothy McDermott. Reprinted by permission of Oxford University Press.

Extracts from *Basic Writings of Saint Thomas Aquinas,* Random House, 1945, copyright © 1945 by Estate of Anton C. Pegis. Used with permission of the estate.

Extracts from Aquinas, *Philosophical Texts,* translated by Thomas Gilby. Copyright © 1951 by Oxford University Press.

Extracts from *The Complete Essays of Montaigne,* translated by Donald M. Frame. Copyright © 1948, 1953, 1958 by the Board of Trustees of the Leland Stanford Jr. University, renewed 1970, 1975, 1986 by Donald Frame. All rights reserved. Used with permission of Stanford University Press.

Extracts from *The Philosophical Writings of Descartes,* vol. I, translated by John Cottingham, Robert Stoothoff, and Dugald Murdoch, copyright © 1985 by Cambridge University Press. Used with permission of the publisher.

Photography Credits

INDEX

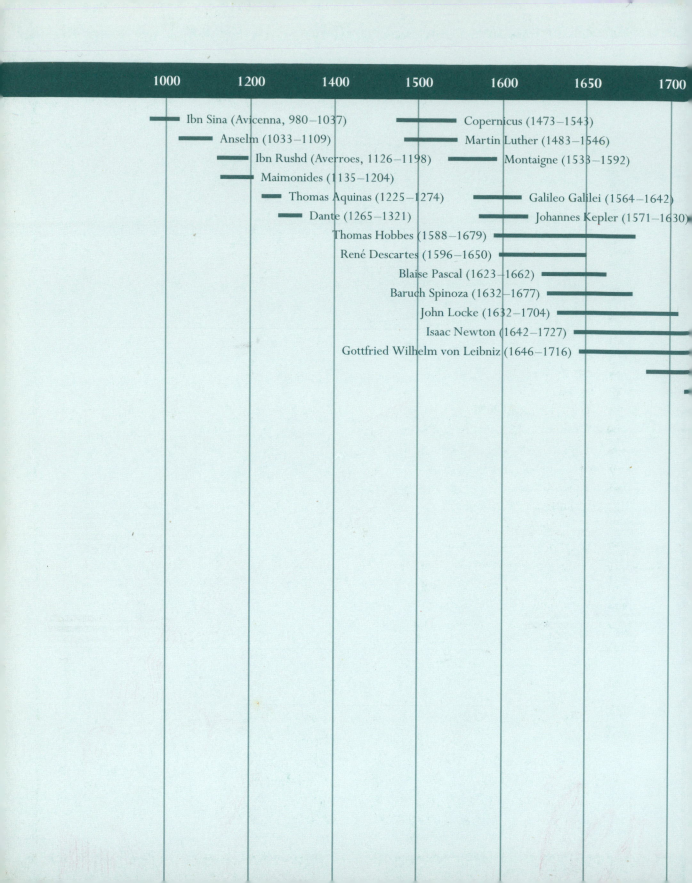

| 1000 | 1200 | 1400 | 1500 | 1600 | 1650 | 1700 |

Ibn Sina (Avicenna, 980–1037)

Anselm (1033–1109)

Ibn Rushd (Averroes, 1126–1198)

Maimonides (1135–1204)

Thomas Aquinas (1225–1274)

Dante (1265–1321)

Copernicus (1473–1543)

Martin Luther (1483–1546)

Montaigne (1533–1592)

Galileo Galilei (1564–1642)

Johannes Kepler (1571–1630)

Thomas Hobbes (1588–1679)

René Descartes (1596–1650)

Blaise Pascal (1623–1662)

Baruch Spinoza (1632–1677)

John Locke (1632–1704)

Isaac Newton (1642–1727)

Gottfried Wilhelm von Leibniz (1646–1716)